LAROUSSE
ENCYCLOPEDIA OF THE
ANIMAL WORLD

LAROUSSE
ENCYCLOPEDIA OF THE
ANIMAL WORLD

INTRODUCTION BY DESMOND MORRIS

LAROUSSE & CO., INC.
NEW YORK

THIS EDITION DISTRIBUTED BY OUTLET BOOK CO., INC.

First published in the United States by Larousse & Co., Inc.,
572 Fifth Avenue, New York, New York 10036, 1975

La Vie des Animaux, edited by P.-P. Grassé, was first
published by La Librairie Larousse in 1969

© Librairie Larousse 1969
© English translation, William Collins Sons & Co. Ltd. 1975

ISBN 0 517 231697
Library of Congress Catalog Card Number 75-7569

This edition is distributed by Outlet Book Co., Inc.
by arrangement with Larousse & Co., Inc.,

Printed in Spain by Mateu Cromo, Pinto (Madrid)

French edition

edited by
Pierre-Paul Grassé,
Member of the French Institute

contributors
Jean G. Baer
Jean Bouillon
André Brosset
Rémy Chauvin
Gustave Cherbonnier
André Franc
Roger Husson
Françoise K. Jouffroy
Noël Mayaud
Françoise Monniot
Renaud Paulian
Max Pavans de Ceccatty
Max Poll
François Rullier
Max Vachon

English edition

edited by
A. R. Waterston,
Keeper Emeritus of Natural History,
Royal Scottish Museum

contributors
Neil Ardley
David Stephen
Alwynne Wheeler

CONTENTS

CONTENTS

CONTENTS

INTRODUCTION BY DESMOND MORRIS

An encyclopedia should be a feast for the brain and an illustrated encyclopedia should be a feast for the eyes. Without question, this new work is both. It is the kind of publishing venture that converts learning from a schoolroom chore into a sensuous pleasure. Seldom have I seen such a rich and impressive collection of zoological photographs, covering the whole range of the animal kingdom, from protozoa to primates. The text, translated from the French original, and written by some of France's most eminent zoologists, is concise and clear and packed with information about each major group of animals.

I have to admit, however, that it is the brilliant colour photographs that bring me back again and again to dip into the pages of this exciting new book. They are enough to send the reader rushing out headlong to buy an expensive microscope and, with its aid, to plunge deep into the hidden world of the multitude of tiny, fascinatingly beautiful microbes; or alternatively to contemplate snatching up the nearest telephone and ordering the earliest available safari ticket to the vast open spaces where, despite all of modern man's encroachments, there still exists a breathtaking diversity of dramatic animal forms.

It is to be hoped that this encyclopedia will be as helpful to the many species it depicts as it will be to the human animals who buy it. For it would be difficult, after turning its pages, for the reader not to care about their future. All those species whose survival is threatened should be slightly less threatened after this book has been published. For it would require an unusual act of vandalism to destroy anything as appealing as the living objects depicted here.

Unicellular life

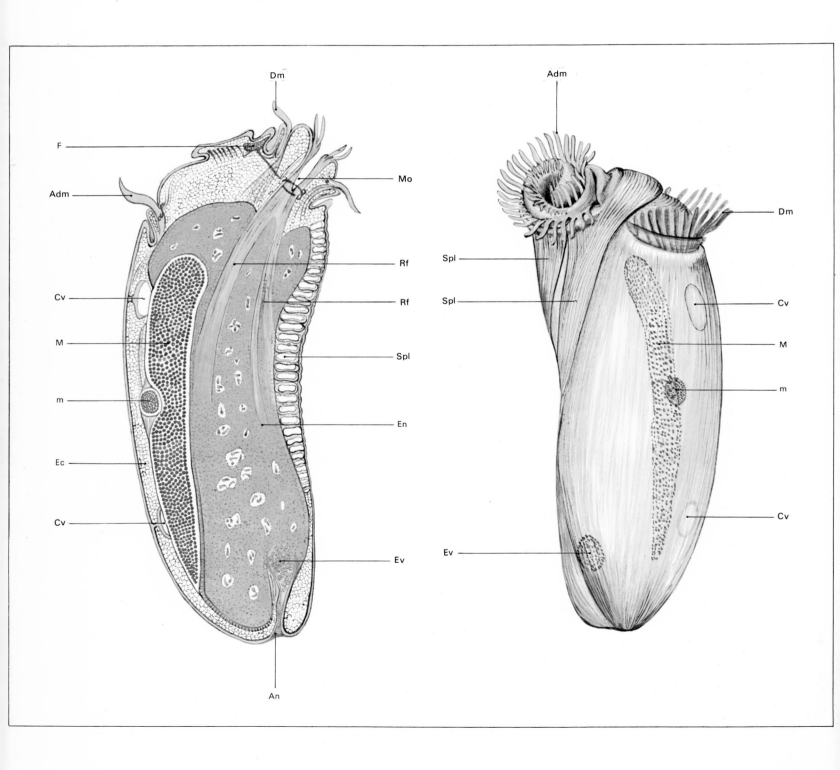

The protozoans make up the first of the great groups of creatures in the animal kingdom. Their name means 'first animals', not only because they are the first group but also because they are the simplest of all animals in structure, and therefore were the first animals to evolve upon the Earth. The protozoans consist simply of one living cell, though in a wide variety of forms. All other animals are collections of many cells working together to make up a living being. The protozoan therefore represents the basic unit of all life—the cell.

The existence of life represents the summit of order in the universe. Protons, neutrons and electrons come together to form atoms; atoms group to form molecules; certain molecules combine to form amino acids which then come together to produce proteins; from proteins, the cell is constructed, giving at first simple animals and plants, and then cells group themselves together to form the higher plants and animals. At the peak of this evolution of life, and manifesting the highest degree of order and of complexity, is man. The protozoan would seemingly be far below man, but in fact is well along the path from disorder to order—an order, however, that is soon reduced to the level of atoms after any living thing dies.

Protozoans first appeared in the sea in Precambrian times —more than 600 million years ago. These first animals were simple compared with man but, in the intervening years, many different kinds of protozoans have evolved. They inhabit a wide range of environments—from soil and decaying organic matter to fresh and salt water—and have become complicated in structure to adapt to special modes of life, even though they remain unicellular.

About 30,000 species of protozoans now exist. This may not be many compared with the million species of arthropods, but protozoans are individually far more numerous than any other animals. However, many biologists doubt that they should really be thought of as animals at all. While the phylum containing them is always called the Protozoa, it is often placed in the kingdom of the Protista—the unicellular organisms—and not the animal kingdom. The Protista contains unicellular plants as well as animals. Normally, plants and animals are totally distinct. Animals can move independently, at least for some stage of their lives, and plants cannot. Animals cannot manufacture their own food,

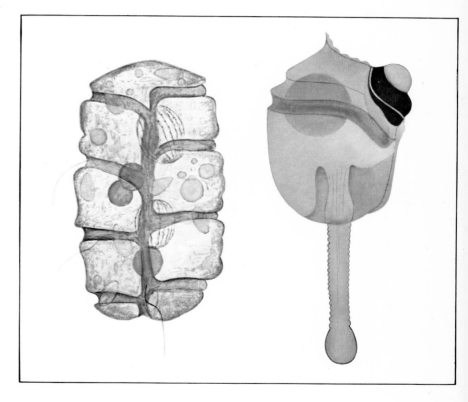

On the left, *Polykrikos kofoidi*, an individual with two nuclei, containing numerous food vacuoles. The cytoplasm seems to correspond to four fused individuals, but there are only two nuclei. The ovoid yellow bodies are poisonous organelles resembling those of medusae and starfish. *Polykrikos*, a planktonic free peridinian, without chromatophores, is a plant which has become heterotrophic, just like an animal cell (length: 200 microns). On the right, *Erythropsis pavillardi*, another peridian without chlorophyll and heterotrophic. It is highly specialized; it is part of plankton and has been caught by tow-netting in the Mediterranean and in the Pacific (length: 52—82 microns). This extremely contractile organism, has, like *Pouchetia* (other peridinians without chlorophyll), a very complex photo-sensitive organ, which deserves, at least, the name of 'ocellus'. The long appendage, or dart, borne by the flagellate, is an expansion of the longitudinal flagellar groove. It is not known how a plant acquires organelles proper to animals.

Opposite
Epidinium ecaudatum, a ciliated infusorian, lives in the paunch of ruminants; it is one of the unicellular organisms reaching the highest degree of anatomical complexity. On the left, longitudinal section passing through the mouth (cytostome) and the anus (cytopyge); on the right, in lateral view: *Adm*, peribuccal (adoral) membranelles (clusters of fused cilia); *An*, anus (cytopyge); *Cv*, contractile vacuole; *Dm*, dorsal membranelles; *Ec*, ectoplasm; *En*, endoplasm; *Ev*, excretory vacuole (caecum); *F*, fibres of neuromotor centre; *M*, macronucleus; *m,*· micronucleus; *Mo*, mouth (cytostome); *Rf*, retractile fibres (myonemes) of the mouth and pharynx; *Spl*, skeletal plates of cellulosic nature.
Epidinium demonstrates that a symbiotic organism is not bound to undergo organic degradation and on the contrary becomes highly complex. *After R. G. Sharp*

unlike most plants, and either indirectly or directly depend on plants for food. However, unicellular organisms cannot be so easily differentiated into plant and animal. For example, some protozoans can produce food by photosynthesis. In the Protista, the phylum Protozoa contains the more animal-like of the unicellular organisms.

The structure of a protozoan

A protozoan has basically the same structure as any cell in a multicellular animal. It consists essentially of a mass of protoplasm surrounded by a membrane; the protoplasm inside the cell is made up of a central body called the nucleus and a transparent viscous fluid called the cytoplasm. The

nucleus is the control centre of the cell and contains the chromosomes, which duplicate themselves when the cell reproduces itself. The chromosomes therefore bear the information that produces a new cell identical to the old, and this information is in the sequence of atoms in the strands of DNA (deoxyribonucleic acid) in the chromosomes. The cytoplasm contains various bodies: the mitochondria produce energy for the cell, the Golgi complex is involved in transporting substances in and out of the cell, the centrosomes play a part in cell division, and the endoplasmic reticulum contains the ribosomes, which is where proteins are built up from amino acids in reproduction. These bodies are known as cell organelles, because they act in the ways that organs do in higher animals. The cytoplasm also contains cavities called vacuoles.

Organelles of the protozoans

Examples of specialized organelles include contractile fibres, usually arranged in clusters and having a constant position and shape, that act like muscles. They reach a peak of development in the ciliates, which have the cell surface covered with rows of tiny cilia (hairs). In the surface, the bases of the cilia are connected by a network of fibrils, which acts to co-ordinate the beating of the cilia in what appears to be the beginnings of a nervous system. Some organelles of the exterior surface also seem to act as sensory organs.

The food vacuoles inside the cell are cavities that enclose food particles; enzymes discharge into the vacuoles, which consequently act as a stomach or even as an intestine. The contractile vacuoles are other cavities that assemble and expel waste matter from the cell, acting as a simplified kidney.

Unicellular organisms with many nuclei

There are protozoans that contain not one, but several and sometimes hundreds of nuclei. All these nuclei are similar in function and, at a given moment, the protozoan divides into as many new cells as it contains nuclei. Each of the new cells is similar in shape and function.

A group of protozoans that all derive from the same parent is called a clone; the individuals in it are identical to each other and to the parent, unless mutation occurs. In a multicellular organism, the cells cannot all divide at the same time to produce new individuals, but egg cells may divide to produce young identical to the mother by parthenogenesis, and other asexual methods of reproduction also give rise to clones of individuals.

Between two kingdoms

The Protista is made up of algae, bacteria and fungi as well as the protozoans. The more plantlike of these organisms is included in the phylum Protophyta.

This kingdom was established by the German naturalist Ernst Haeckel, but many zoologists consider that it lacks homogeneity. The bracketing of plants and animals together in a kingdom of unicellular animals is rather arbitrary. The protozoans, apart from a few exceptions, are heterotrophic—that is, they cannot make their own food supply. They are also characterized by certain modes of reproduction, for each group of protozoans has its own way of splitting the nucleus in cell division. Many unicellular plants contain

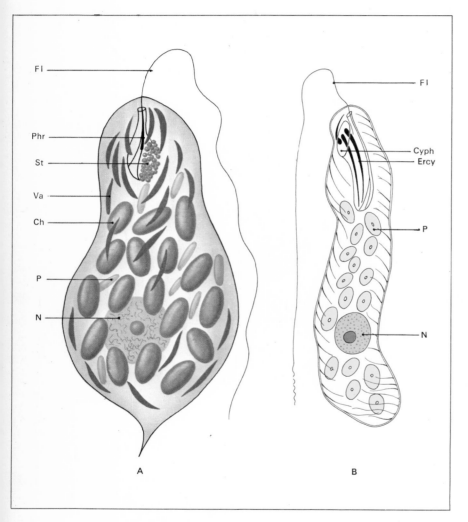

A, a typical *Euglena* provided with chlorophyll-impregnated chloroplasts (in green); nutrition is of the plant type (autotrophy). The characteristic reserve matter of *Euglena* is the starch-like paramylon in platelets or in granules (in yellow); the vacuoles have been artificially stained by brilliant cresol blue. The light-sensitive body, or stigma, is coloured orange (×500). Although provided with chlorophyll, green *Euglena* may, in certain circumstances (e.g. darkness) become heterotrophic. After P.-P. Grassé—B, a colourless flagellate, *Peranema trichophorum*, very liable to deformity in spite of the thickness of its cuticle: *Ch*, chloroplasts; *Cyph*, cytopharynx; *Ercy*, elastic skeletal rods in the cytopharynx; *Fl*, flagellum; *N*, nucleus; *P*, yellow paramylon granules; *Phr*, photoreceptor; *St*, stigma; *Va*, vacuoles.
Peranema feeds on living micro-organisms.

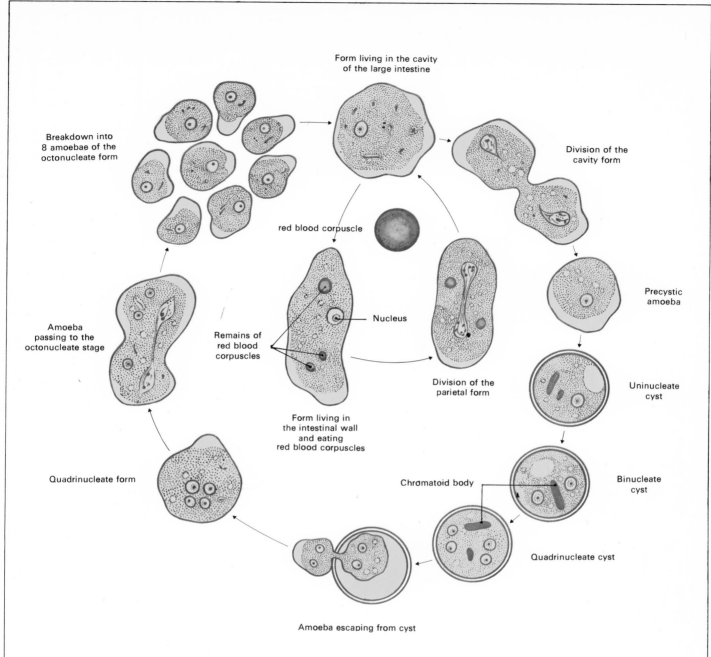

Form living in the cavity of the large intestine

Division of the cavity form

Breakdown into 8 amoebae of the octonucleate form

red blood corpuscle

Precystic amoeba

Nucleus

Amoeba passing to the octonucleate stage

Remains of red blood corpuscles

Division of the parietal form

Uninucleate cyst

Quadrinucleate form

Form living in the intestinal wall and eating red blood corpuscles

Chromatoid body

Binucleate cyst

Quadrinucleate cyst

Amoeba escaping from cyst

Cycle of the dysentery amoeba (*Entamoeba histolytica*), parasite of man.

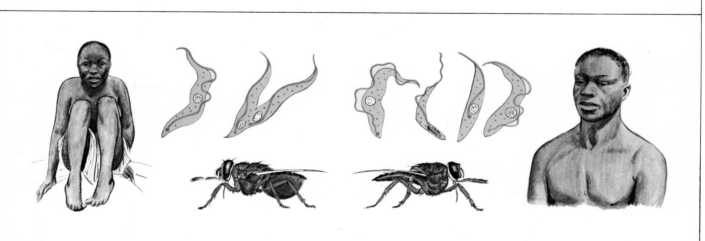

Below, cycle of the Gambian trypanosome (*Trypanosoma gambiense*); causal organism of sleeping sickness. On the left, a sufferer from sleeping sickness on whom *Glossina* becomes contaminated by absorbing blood. On the left of the sick man, trypanosomes of the blood as seen after staining; below, a tsetse fly gorged with blood. On the right, a healthy subject whom *Glossina* (bottom right, seen after digestion of blood) will infect by biting; above *Glossina*, modified trypanosomes in the fly's intestine.

chlorophyll and are able to carry out photosynthesis to make food; they are said to be autotrophic. The diatoms and dino-flagellates (minute one-celled algae) drift at the surface of the sea, making up the bulk of the plants in the plankton. They form a great pasture in the sea, constituting the basic food supply for other marine life. Small animals browse on this plankton and are then devoured by larger animals.

However, a fairly large number of protophytes exist without chlorophyll and are heterotrophic. Some are free-living, being predators, and others are parasitic on other organisms. *Polykrikos*, a dinoflagellate, may feed on the larvae of multicellular animals. *Noctiluca*, a well-known phosphor-escent dinoflagellate, is another one-celled predator of the phytoplankton. Some plant organisms are both heterotrophic and autotrophic. *Cryptomonas* possesses chlorophyll and practises photosynthesis, but it is also capable of absorbing and ingesting animal prey.

Protozoans of the order Euglenida provide another example of unicellular organisms that can exist like both plants and animals. They may be green or transparent, and are found mostly in fresh water. Some are photosynthetic and require light to live, but others are capable of surviving when kept in darkness. These heterotrophic organisms may feed directly on other organisms, but are also saprophytic—

capable of living on dead or decaying matter. At the level of the Protophyta, the separation of the plant and animal kingdoms is by no means clear-cut.

If they are not placed among the Protista, the fungi are grouped with the plants. They have many characteristics in common with plants, but by no means all. For example, fungi are not autotrophic and live as saprophytes or as parasites of plants or animals. Unicellular fungi occur, yeast being a well-known example. Such organisms must be considered as degraded plants, having multicellular ancestors.

The unicellular state is a primitive characteristic in many organisms, but may be acquired secondarily in others.

At present, no group of animals appears to provide a link between the unicellular and multicellular animals. It is not possible, therefore, to discern a common ancestor for these two groups. As the classification of an organism is to some extent a reflection of its evolution, the correct way to classify unicellular life remains an open question.

The size of protozoans

Most protozoans are so small that they are measured in microns (one micron is equal to 1/25,000 of an inch). Some

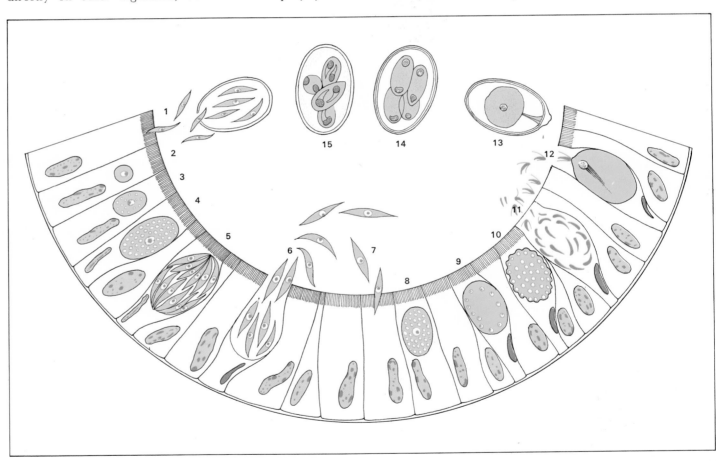

Cycle of *Eimeria perforans*, causal organism of coccidiosis in domestic rabbits: *1*, the ingested oocyst, on reaching the rabbit's intestine, bursts and liberates the sporozoites, which penetrate the cells of the intestinal epithelium; *2*, a sporozoite which has become spherical in the host cell; *3*, the coccidian grows and becomes laden with reserve material (a special starch, paraglycogen); *4*, growth continues; *5*, fission, or schizo-gony, of the parasite, as many germs as nuclei; *6*, the germs, or schizo-zoites, are liberated and proceed to infect new intestinal cells (endo-genous cycle or multiplication); *7*, penetration of a schizozoite into an epithelial cell; *8*, an element, or gamout, producing male gametes; *9*, multiplication of the nuclei of the gamout; *10*, the nuclei proceeding to the periphery of the gamout; *11*, as many male gametes as nuclei; *12*, fertilization of a large female gamete by a male gamete; *13*, the zygote (male gamete + female gamete) surrounds itself with a tough thick envelope and becomes the oocyst; *14*, in the oocyst, the contents divide and produce four binucleate elements, the sporoblasts; *15*, ripe oocyst with four spores, each containing two sporozoites. The disease caused by this coccidian is very serious: malnutrition, fairly profuse diarrhoea, congestion of the intestinal vessels, distension of the abdomen, etc. Young rabbits are least resistant to this parasite which flourishes in badly-kept hutches.

protozoans are only 2 or 3 microns in length and most species are less than 250 microns in size. Organisms of such minute dimensions can only be seen with the aid of a microscope, but several free-living protozoans are visible with the aid of a magnifying glass and a few are large enough to be seen with the unaided eye. *Spirostomum* is a ciliate that abounds in freshwater pools; it has a long slender body that reaches 1/8 of an inch in length. *Pycnothrix*, a ciliate that lives in the digestive tracts of small mammals such as coneys, reaches 1/3 of an inch in length. *Porospora gigantea*, a sporozoan, reaches twice this size. Colonies of radiolarians may grow as large as 2 inches in diameter, but the record is held by a foraminiferan, *Neusina agassizi*, which lives in the mud of cold, deep estuaries and reaches nearly 8 inches in length. Amoebas may be as small as 6 to 7 microns, but others are visible to the naked eye, *Pelomyxa* being as much as 1/8 of an inch in diameter. Some flagellates are very tiny: *Trimitus*, an intestinal parasite of fish and termites, rarely exceeds 2·5 microns in length. *Leishmania*, a parasitic flagellate that lives among the cells of mammals, is only 1·5 microns long; and *Theileria dispar*, which lives in the red blood corpuscles of cattle, is even smaller at 0·5 to 1·5 microns.

The life cycle of the protozoans

Several protozoans undergo a simple life cycle in which reproduction is asexual, by cell division or by budding. Sexual reproduction also occurs in protozoans, and it even exists among the bacteria. However, it is by no means always straightforward in nature. Many protozoans exhibit alternation of generations, in which a generation produced by sexual reproduction gives rise to a new generation by asexual reproduction. The new generation then reproduces sexually to give the next generation and so on, alternating sexual generations with asexual generations. In parasitic species, the life cycle may be very complex with the protozoans passing from one host to another at a certain stage in the cycle.

A simple asexual life cycle: the intestinal amoeba

Parasitic amoebas reproduce in their host's intestines by binary fission—cell division into two new cells—becoming more and more numerous. The amoeba that causes amoebic dysentery in man, *Entamoeba histolytica*, invades the wall of the intestine. There it feeds on blood and tissue and multiplies, causing abscesses that discharge blood and mucus into the intestine, and producing severe symptoms of dysentery. Under certain conditions unfavourable to the species, the amoebas leave the intestinal lining and each envelop themselves in a spherical membrane. Inside the sphere, which is called a cyst, the nucleus of the amoeba divides into two nuclei which then each further divide. The cysts are passed from the body, even after recovery. As they resist desiccation, they can spread the disease, and their hosts unknowingly act as carriers of it. When ingested by another human, the walls of the cyst break down and the cell containing four nuclei emerges. These nuclei further divide, and then the cell splits into eight new amoebas, each with a single nucleus. These invade the intestinal wall, thus completing the life cycle (see the diagram on page 13).

A complex asexual life cycle: the Gambian trypanosome

A flagellate protozoan is responsible for the disease of sleeping sickness. It is called the Gambian trypanosome (*Trypanosoma gambiense*), and is shaped like a twisted thong with a membrane extending along one side of its body. At one end of the body, the membrane is prolonged into a whip-like flagellum. The trypanosome is from 15 to 30 microns long and 3 to 3·5 microns broad. It swims in the blood plasma, in the lymph and in the cerebrospinal fluid.

The protozoan reproduces by division into two new daughter cells. The nucleus divides in two; the existing flagellum passes to one daughter cell, and the other daughter cell produces a new flagellum. As division is repeated, the number of trypanosomes rises in a geometric progression.

The disease is carried by tsetse flies (*Glossina palpalis* and *G. tachinoides*). When it bites a human infected with sleeping sickness, the insect takes in blood containing the trypanosomes. The protozoans remain in the insect's body, resisting its digestive action, and multiply in the midgut. Then they

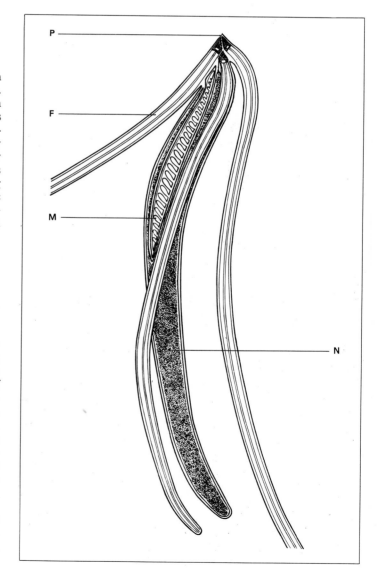

Structure of a male coccidian gamete, *Eimeria perforans*, revealed by electron microscopy: *F*, flagellum; *M*, large and only mitochondrium; *N*, nucleus; *P*, perforatorium. *After Scholtysek*

move forward and penetrate the ducts of the salivary glands, where they undergo some changes in form. When the tsetse fly then bites another human, it injects saliva containing the trypanosomes before it begins to take the blood. The trypanosomes therefore find their way back into a human host, and the disease is transmitted to another person. The disease is common throughout tropical Africa, not only in Gambia. It causes weakness and lethargy, leading to emaciation and finally death. Spraying of insecticides is helping to reduce the incidence of sleeping sickness.

In this life cycle from human to tsetse fly and back to human again, there is no sexual reproduction.

T. gambiense affects only humans, but other members of the genus *Trypanosoma* are carried by tsetse flies and affect cattle with a similar disease called 'nagana'.

Life cycles involving a sexual phase

A good example of a protozoan life cycle with a complicated sexual phase is provided by organisms of the genus *Eimeria,* which belong to subphylum Sporozoa. They produce a fatal disease called coccidiosis in domestic and wild animals. *E. propria* infects newts, *E. perforans* rabbits, and *E. tenella* fowls.

The cycle begins with a phase of asexual multiplication. In rabbits, for example, spores are ingested along with grass or other food. They break up in the small intestine under the digestive action of intestinal enzymes and release two elongated protozoans, each with a single nucleus. These are known as sporozoites. Each one enters a cell in the intestinal lining and becomes more rounded and amoeba-like. At this stage, it is known as a trophozoite, and it feeds at the expense of the cell and grows in size. As it does so, the nucleus divides several times and cytoplasm of the protozoan divides into long thin slices arranged like the segments of an orange, each bearing a single nucleus. The protozoan then splits up by a process called schizogony into several segments, each becoming a free single-celled merozoite and penetrating healthy cells in the host's intestine. The host's tissue is destroyed with consequent harm. Several generations follow each other in this way, ensuring the multiplication of the parasite within its host.

Then sexual reproduction occurs. Some merozoites become female gametes (reproductive cells) and others become male gametes. The 'female' merozoite enlarges in size and begins to resemble the egg of a higher animal; it becomes laden with

reserve foods rather like yolk. The nucleus lies to one side of the cell away from the centre. The 'male' merozoite also gets larger. Its nucleus divides many times in succession and the new nuclei proceed to the outer boundary of the cell and raise the cytoplasm around themselves into miniature knobs. Next to each nucleus are two centrioles, bodies that control three contractile flagella. Each nucleus separates itself, together with its flagella, from the parent cell and becomes a mobile male gamete, the equivalent of a sperm. The male and female gametes are strongly attracted to each other. The male penetrates the female and the nuclei of the two gametes meet and fuse, producing a fertilized egg or zygote. A tough shell forms around the zygote and it becomes an oocyst, and then the cytoplasm of the cell retracts into a spherical mass within the shell. The oocyst then drops from the intestinal wall and is passed from the body. It now remains inert until it reaches an environment containing oxygen. Then it develops further, the nucleus within the cytoplasmic mass dividing into four parts. Each part surrounds itself with a shell and becomes a spore. The nucleus and then the cytoplasm of the spore divides, so that the spore contains two long sporozoites. The cycle is complete, and a new host ingesting the spores is infected with the disease (see the diagram on page 14).

Coccidiosis can be prevented in domestic rabbits by rearing them in separate hutches, cleaning the hutches and preventing the food from becoming soiled with droppings.

Some sprozoans accomplish their asexual reproduction in one host and their sexual multiplication in another of a different species. A classic example of this is provided by the sporozoans that cause malaria: the first takes place in a man and the second in a mosquito.

A different kind of sexuality

In the previous life history, a sexuality resembling that of multicellular animals is necessary for the reproduction of the protozoan, forming an essential phase of its life cycle. In the ciliates, a kind of sexuality exists but in a very different way.

Ciliates undergo a form of reproduction called conjugation, as well as fission and other processes. Conjugation begins with two individuals coming together and adhering to each other. Inside each of these conjugants are two nuclei, one large (the macronucleus) and one small (the micronucleus). The macronucleus degenerates and disappears, whereas the micronucleus divides in the ordinary way. Then the two daughter micronuclei in each ciliate divide again, but this time a reduction division occurs and the number of chromosomes in the new micronuclei is halved.

The membrane separating the two conjugants now largely disappears. Three of the four micronuclei formed in each degenerate and disappear, and the remaining one divides again, giving two pronuclei. Each conjugant then exchanges a pronucleus with the other.

Each ciliate now has two pronuclei, one of which has come from its partner. These two fuse, producing a micronucleus rather like the nucleus of a fertilized egg. The two conjugants then separate. As each pronucleus had half the number of chromosomes, the new micronucleus has a full complement of chromosomes—a feature of sexual reproduction.

Each partner then undergoes a complex sequence of cell divisions, all of an asexual nature. The micronucleus first divides into eight new micronuclei; four of these enlarge to become macronuclei and three degenerate and disappear. Then the cell divides, each daugher cell containing two macronuclei and one micronucleus, for the one remaining

The cycle of Coccidians:

sporozoite → schizont
↓
schizozoites
|
— schizonts—schizonts . . .
↓
gametes ♀   gametes ♂
↓
fertilized egg (2*n* chromosomes)
↓
oocyst
↓

micronucleus in the parent cell divides in two. A second cell division of this kind then occurs, so that the new daughter cells each have one macronucleus and one micronucleus. These individuals now have the same nuclear state as those that began the conjugation process, and there are four new individuals for each of the conjugants. However, they are not identical to the conjugants, for nuclear material has been exchanged between the two conjugants before the new individuals were formed.

The production of new individuals bearing characteristics of both parents is of course a direct consequence of sexual reproduction, but conjugation is different from the kind of sexual reproduction found in multicellular animals. In normal sexual reproduction, two cells fuse together to form a single cell that divides to produce new individuals. In ciliates, the two cells do not completely fuse but separate after conjugation and then each proceeds to produce new individuals by fission, an asexual process.

Modes of life of the protozoans

The protozoans are confined, as indeed are all the lower animals, to water or a moist habitat of some kind.

Habitats

Amoebas, flagellates and ciliates form the great majority of freshwater protozoans and most of them are predators, capturing prey by a wide variety of means that are explained in the following pages. They are to be found in the muddy and sandy bottoms of streams and lakes, or anywhere food particles are to be captured. Some free-living protozoans—such as the ciliate *Tetrahymena*—feed solely on substances dissolved in water and can be cultivated under laboratory conditions in liquid media.

Several freshwater protozoans float or swim among the planktonic organisms that drift at the surface. These include some foraminiferans such as *Globigerina*, heliozoans, a few ciliates and many flagellates.

Moist soil shelters a great many protozoans that belong for the most part to freshwater populations. The majority feed on bacteria and for this reason have some effect on the fertility of the soil. In dry or slightly damp soils, they are present only in inert forms, such as cysts, that can resist desiccation. When rain comes, the cysts open and an active protozoan population develops in the layers of water lying between the particles of earth. The spaces between the soil particles are called interstices, and their animal populations are known as the interstitial fauna.

Marine protozoans

Radiolarians and ciliates float among the plankton in countless numbers, and ciliates insinuate themselves into the spaces between grains of sand on the seabed. Foraminiferans are also planktonic, and rest on the seabed as well. All marine protozoans feed on living prey.

Phoresy and parasitism

Phoresy is the phenomenon by which one animal is trans-

ported about by another. Various flagellates and ciliates fix themselves to mobile animals and remain there for their entire existence. A great many protozoans indulge themselves in this way, and it is a practice that sometimes ends in parasitism.

Entire groups of protozoans are parasites, and many parts of an organism may be invaded by them. The intestine may become a home for amoebas, flagellates, sporozoans and ciliates; the kidneys may contain sporozoans; ciliates and sporozoans are parasites of the body cavity; the blood plasma may act as host to trypanosomes; and *Plasmodium* causes malaria by parasitizing red blood cells. The effect on the host varies from one parasite to another. Sometimes it is benign,

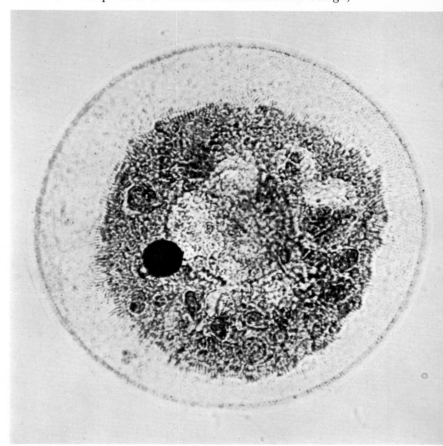

Type of Thecamoeban: *Arcella*, view of lower surface. Thecamoebans are found mainly in acid waters; they abound in peat bogs. *Phot. Aldo Margiocco*

but sometimes it is so harmful as to cause death. Death of the host of course brings about death of the parasite too, showing a great lack of adaptation on the part of the parasite.

Symbiosis

There are several known cases of symbiosis between protozoans and multicellular animals. This kind of union is one that benefits both partners. Flagellates live in the gut of termites, and ciliates live in the belly of ruminants and caecum of horses. These protozoans play an important, even essential, part in the digestion of cellulose, which is the staple food of their hosts. Multicellular animals, with a few exceptions, do not produce the necessary enzymes to break down cellulose and rely on protozoans to provide them. In return

Trichonympha agilis, which lives, as a symbiont, in the alimentary canal of lucifugous termites. *Above*, the animalcule, seen in its entirety, engulfing (by phagocytosis) a fragment of wood, which it is about to digest. (×1000). *After O. Swezy*

Below, A, anterior end seen in almost axial longitudinal section passing through the centrosome, just above the small tube formed by the bases of the flagella and of the circular fibrils. The longitudinal sections of the flagella show the basal granule which has the structure of a centrosome and the starting point of the flagella. (×30,000). *B*, a para-axial section of the *Trichonympha*'s flagellate region. The flagella can be seen, *C, opposite page*, in transverse sections (9 pairs of longitudinal peripheral fibrils, one axial pair of longitudinal fibrils, 9 triple sets of longitudinal fibrils, no axial fibrils), arranged in rows, and the transverse sections of the basal bodies (×30,000); transverse sections of more highly-magnified flagella (×45,000). The *Trichonympha* have among other peculiarities that of being anaerobic; the slightest trace of oxygen kills them. Their mitochondria have no respiratory enzymes, as have aerobic protozoans; the function of DNA, in which they are very rich, has not been discovered. *Phot. P.-P. Grassé*

for this beneficial action, the protozoans receive food and shelter from their hosts.

Geographical distribution

Whether it is located at the equator or in the temperate zones, a pond always harbours much the same kind of protozoan life. However, this does not imply that protozoans are infinitely adaptable and do not require special ecological conditions. A thecamoeban protozoan can be found living in the mountains of Kivu, and is also encountered in the sphagnum moss among the peat bogs of the mountains of the Auvergne in central France. This is because the protozoan is very selective in its habitats, requiring water of a certain acidity and temperature. Although widely differing in location, the two habitats are virtually identical, consisting of water of the same acidity and almost the same temperature.

Parasitic species accompany their hosts throughout almost the whole of the latter's geographical range; they have followed their hosts in the course of migrations and have evolved along with them. No matter what their location, the rectal ampullae of common and edible frogs harbour exactly the same genera of amoebas, flagellates, opalines and ciliates. The same can be said of the ciliates that are parasitic in ruminants and horses. The flagellates of termites are less attached to specific hosts, but those of *Cryptocercus,* a large wood-eating cockroach of the Rocky Mountains, and of *Mastotermes darwiniensis,* Darwin's termite, are strictly specific.

The protozoans that cause malaria in humans—*Plasmodium vivax, P. malariae* and *P. falciparum*—are closely confined to our species.

Although some gregarines are found in only a single host species, others live as parasites in dozens of different species.

A parasite that is strictly specific in its choice of host has adapted itself to the precise set of conditions to be found only in that particular host and no other. Such overspecialization

A   B

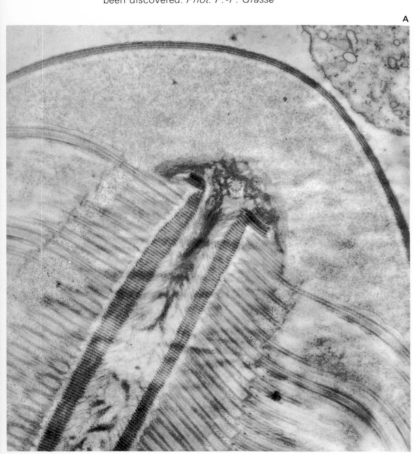
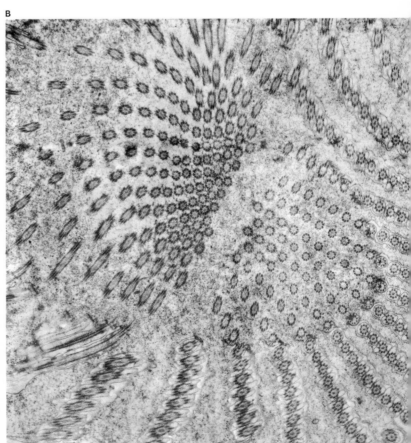

is dangerous for a species, for it will not be able to survive in the absence of its host.

The main groups of Protozoans

The classification of the protozoans is complex, and uncertainties exist about the division of the phylum as they do about the position of the protozoans themselves. However, most zoologists now recognize that the phylum Protozoa is made up of four subphyla further divided into nine classes. The subphylum Sarcomastigophora comprises three classes: the Mastigophora or Flagellata (flagellates), the Opalinata (opalines), and the Sarcodina or Rhizopoda. The subphylum Sporozoa (sporozoans) contains three classes: the Telospora, the Toxoplasmea and the Haplosporea. The third subphylum is the Ciliophora (ciliates), which contains one class, the Ciliata. The final subphylum is the Cnidospora, comprising two classes: the Myxosporidea and the Microsporidea.

The subphylum Sarcomastigophora

The class Mastigophora (Flagellata)

The flagellates are grouped together in a single class because they all possess one or more whip-like flagella as a means of locomotion. There are some flagellates that are animal-like and others that are plant-like, but as this work is concerned only with animal life, only the former—the zooflagellates—will be examined.

In the zooflagellates, we find several evolutionary lines grouped together, though the precise relationship between them is difficult to determine.

The flagellum is a long filament that arises from a body called the blepharoplast, which is similar to the centriole of the cell of a metazoan (multicellular animal). It is surrounded by a delicate membrane, and nine pairs of fibrils arranged on its periphery run along its entire length. A tenth pair lie along the axis. The blepharoplast has a slightly different structure, possessing only peripheral fibrils in nine groups of three. From each group, two fibrils are continued into the flagellum.

The flagellum can beat with a wave-like motion, the wave progressing from the base to the free end. The rhythm of the beating of the flagellum is often characteristic of a group or even of a single species of flagellate. Some flagellates swim through the water by moving the flagellum in a spiral rather like the screw of a ship; others make jerky swimming movements, interrupted by leaps; some with several flagella bunch them together and sweep the bunch up and down rather like the strokes of a paddle.

The movements of the flagellum seem to stem from a mechanism similar to that of muscle fibres, for various parts of the flagellum contract to bend it. The long molecules of protein in the fibrils telescope, those in one row of molecules sliding between those of a preceding row. The action is not unlike the way the bristles of a pair of brushes intermesh when they are pushed together.

The order Protomonadida

The first group of zooflagellates to be considered is made up of small species, some of them free-living but most parasitic. Among the protomonadine flagellates are some redoubtable pathogens (organisms which cause disease). The film surrounding their bodies is lined internally with a continuous layer of fibrils arranged side by side and parallel to each other; the fibrils are so fine that only the great power of the electron microscope can reveal them. These flagellates have one or two flagella.

Next to the blepharoplast is an organelle called the kineto-

The trypanosome of sleeping sickness. *Trypanosoma gambiense,* seen in a blood-smear after staining. *Phot. Aldo Margiocco*

c

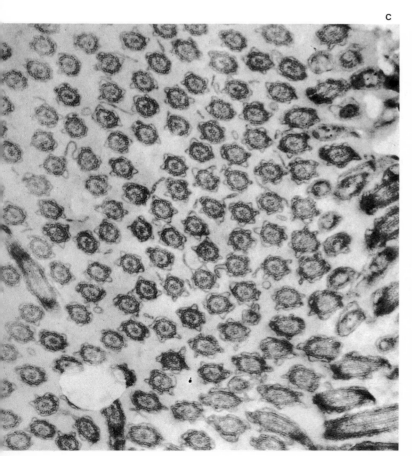

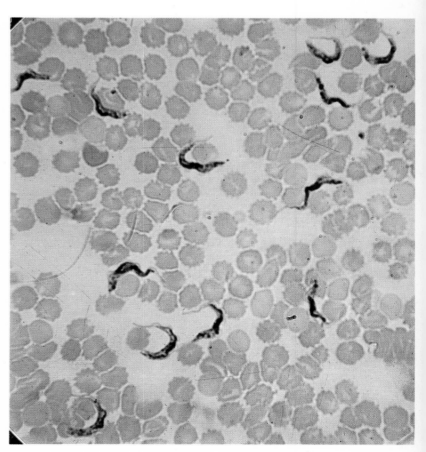

plast. It has the structure of a mitochondrion but is much bulkier, and it contains a substantial amount of DNA. When the flagellate divides, this organelle is drawn out, and becomes shaped like a dumb-bell before it breaks in two.

The order Protomonadida contains *Trypanosoma* and related genera. In appearance, these flagellates are ribbon-like with pointed ends, and often twisted into helical shapes. The blepharoplast lies at the posterior (hind) end of the body

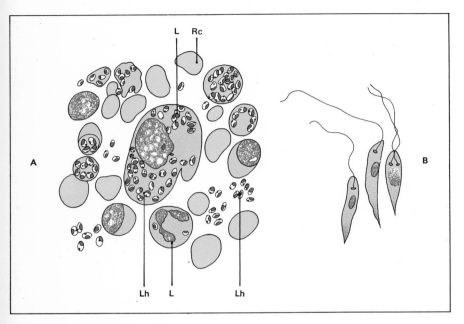

A, *Leishmania donovani*, causal agent of infantile splenomegaly (hypertrophy of the spleen) and of kala-azar, in a smear from spleen pulp. Some *Leishmania* (*Lh*) are free, out of the cells, others are contained in the white corpuscles (*L*); *Rc*, red corpuscles (× 1,500).—B, *Leishmania tropica*, causal agent of oriental sore, arising from a culture made on blood agar. *After E. Brumpt*

behind the nucleus. The flagellum rises from the blepharoplast and runs along the top of the body towards the anterior (front) end. It does not fuse with the body, but a film of cytoplasm is connected to it to form an undulating membrane running along the body.

Sexual reproduction is unknown in *Trypanosoma* and related genera.

All of the trypanosome family of protozoans are parasitic. At first they were parasites of insects, inhabiting the digestive tract. Then, in various ways, they spread to other animals. The transmission of the protozoans would have passed through plants, for infected insects eating plants would have injected the protozoans into the plant juices. But the protozoans are also transmitted in cysts expelled by the insect in its droppings, and these cysts would have been placed on plants. Either way, an animal later eating the plants would become infected with the protozoans. The flagellates would then have become adapted to specific animal hosts, and various life cycles would have become established.

The case of trypanosome parasites of aquatic vertebrates is more complex in its development; here, the original host would have been a leech and the protozoans would have been passed from leeches into fishes, amphibians and reptiles.

The life cycle of *Trypanosoma gambiense,* which causes the dreadful disease of trypanosomiasis or sleeping sickness in tropical Africa, has been thoroughly investigated. The symptoms of the disease are loss of weight, congestion of the lymph glands, and oedema (swelling in the body's connective tissue). An early period of fever and over-excitement is followed by a long period of increasing lethargy and eventually prostration; nervous lesions occur, affecting the membranes enveloping the brain and spinal cord. If untreated, the disease results in death a year and a half to three years after infection. The treatment is by injection of various drugs, the best of which is pentamidine as it acts selectively against *T. gambiense.* It can also be used as a preventive measure, for an injection of the correct proportions will produce resistance to infection for about six months. Another kind of sleeping sickness is caused in Africa by the protozoan *Trypanosoma rhodesiense.* It is spread by the tsetse fly *Glossina morsitans,* whereas *T. gambiense* is transmitted by *Glossina palpalis.* This second form of the disease, known as Rhodesian sleeping sickness, is treated with the drug suramin.

Many other trypanosomes are parasitic on wild and domestic animals. *Trypanosoma brucei* is carried by several species of *Glossina,* including *G. palpalis,* and it produces the disease called nagana, especially in horses. The disease is characterized by serious emaciation, a copious nasal discharge, subcutaneous haemorrhages and considerable swelling of the body. Death follows two to three months after infection. Cattle and antelopes are also liable to infection, but are less susceptible to it than are horses.

Trypanosoma congolense attacks oxen, pigs, and horses, making it impossible to raise these animals in certain parts of tropical Africa. Antelopes and elephants can resist its effects; the trypanosome exists in their blood but does not multiply to a great degree. However, they do act as carriers and contaminate tsetse flies.

Other pathogenic trypanosomes have different life cycles. For example, *Trypanosoma evansi* occurs throughout the tropics (except in Australia) and attacks many animals, being particularly lethal to mammals of the horse and camel families. It has caused immense damage in India and northern Africa, causing a disease called surra in horses and debab in dromedary camels. The trypanosome is carried by biting flies such as horseflies (*Tabanus*), and does not undergo any transformation in this intermediate host. Immediately after biting an infected animal, the insect retains a little blood containing a few trypanosomes on its mouthparts; these subsequently inject the protozoans into the insect's next victim. It has been claimed, no doubt correctly, that *T. evansi* is only an older form of *T. brucei* that has become introduced into regions where the tsetse fly is absent and transmitted by other means.

Trypanosoma equiperdum was once widespread in western Europe; it now exists from the borders of the Mediterranean and southern Russia through Asia as far as Java. It causes a disease called dourine in horses and mules, and is transmitted directly during copulation. The infective trypanosomes swim in secretions from lesions produced on the genital organs of both male and female partners, and pass into the bloodstream of the animals. It has been found possible to infect horses by placing the trypanosomes on the conjunctiva of the eye, showing that the protozoans are well able to cross membranes and enter the bloodstream. Horses and mules suffering from dourine become emaciated, their backs start to cave in, the genital organs swell, and paralysis eventually results, followed by death fourteen to sixteen months after infection. Not all members of the horse family succumb to the disease. The ass enjoys a strong immunity to *Trypanosoma equiperdum,* although the trypanosome does multiply in its blood to some extent.

Chagas' disease, which is rife in Central and South America, is caused by a special kind of trypanosome known as *Trypanosoma cruzi* or *Schizotrypanus cruzi,* The transmitting animals are large bloodsucking assassin bugs that live in thatched roofs and among vegetable matter in garbage. The trypanosome multiplies in the intestine and is eventually excreted from the insect. In this way the trypanosomes are deposited on human skin during sleep, and they make their way through the moist mucous membranes of the eyes, nose and mouth, and genital and anal passages into the bloodstream. Abrasions of the skin and wounds are an open door to the parasites. They penetrate to the cells of the muscles and the brain, and of the reticuloendothelial system, a system of highly specialized cells scattered throughout the body which ingest red blood cells and other bodies. The trypanosomes lose their flagella and multiply inside the cells by binary fission. The new organisms emerge from the cells, grow new flagella and migrate into the blood of their host. Chagas' disease produces facial oedema similar to myxoedema and can cause serious heart trouble, although more often than not it clears up of its own accord after a fortnight to a month. Chronic cases are very serious, and may result in myocarditis leading to death.

Trypanocide drugs which are effective against other kinds of trypanosomiasis have little effect on this American variety of the disease. Destruction of the carrier bugs (*Triatoma, Rhodnius* and others) has produced excellent results in the campaign against Chagas' disease.

The Leishmania

Leishmania is another genus within the order Protomonadida. It is closely related to *Trypanosoma*, and also attacks humans. It lives in the cells of its host and has lost the outer portion of its flagellum. *Leishmania* are very small, two to six microns

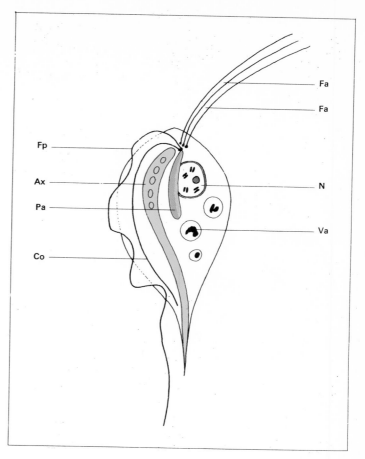

Organizational plan of *Trichomonas* with 3 anterior flagella: *Ax*, skeletal axis or axostyle; *Co*, chromatic rod; *Fa*, anterior flagella; *Fp*, posterior flagellum with an undulating membrane; *N*, nucleus with 8 paired chromosomes and a nucleolus; *Pa*, parabasal body or dictyosome; *Va*, vacuoles containing phagocytozed bacteria (×2,500).

in length, and therefore may invade a cell in great numbers. In certain conditions, they will acquire a complete flagellum.

These flagellates attack various parts of the body. *Leishmania donovani* lives in the cells of the liver, spleen, bone marrow and the lymph glands, while *L. tropica* proliferates in the white corpuscles just below the skin. The former species causes a disease known as kala-azar, dum-dum fever or black fever in man, and is known mainly in India, northern China, Manchuria and the Upper Nile. The main symptoms are fever and enlargement of the spleen and liver. The liver undergoes cirrhosis, and in the final stages of the disease, the mucous membranes of the alimentary canal become ulcerated and bleed, while the number of white corpuscles decreases. The death rate of those infected is very high unless treatment is forthcoming. Intravenous injections of antimony compounds such as tartar emetic, or better still of amidines such as pentamidine, result in a high proportion of cures—as many as ninety per cent of cases. Dogs act as reservoirs of *Leishmania donovani*, for they are more or less immune to the protozoans. The disease is transmitted by sand flies (tiny biting flies of the genus *Phlebotomus*) either from infected humans or from carrier dogs. A few cases of kala-azar have been reported from the Mediterranean.

A skin disease known by a variety of exotic names, such as Oriental sore, Delhi boil and Aleppo evil, is caused by *Leishmania tropica*. It occurs in the Mediterranean and also in Asia and South America. The disease produces ulcers on the

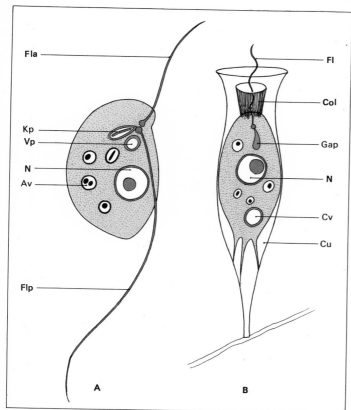

A, the jumping bodo (*Bodo saltans*)—B, a choanoflagellate (*Salpingoeca gracilis*): *Av*, food vacuole; *Col*, collar; *Cu*, cuticle; *Cv*, contractile vacuole; *Fl*, flagellum; *Fla* and *Flp*, anterior and posterior flagella; *Gap*, Golgi (or parabasal) apparatus; *Kp*, kinetoplast; *N*, nucleus. Both live in wet hay and in pools.

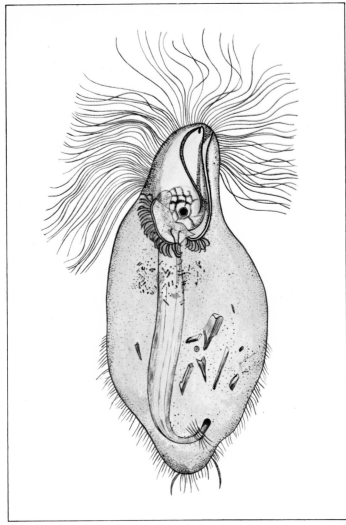

Joenia annectens, wood-eating symbiont of the yellow-necked termite (*Calotermes flavicollis*).

Below, *Giardia intestinalis* of man seen in intestinal mucus.

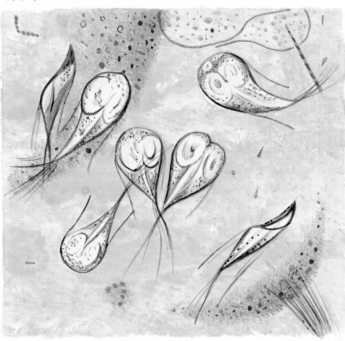

skin that begin with a small pimple and spread out before slowly healing, leaving a bad scar. Treatment as for kala-azar is often successful, though some ulcers get better without medical care. The trypanosomes are transmitted by *Phlebotomus*, usually in the autumn.

The order Protomonadida contains some free-living flagellates. Those of the family Bodonidae, of which a few species are parasitic, have two flagella, one pointing forward and the other trailing behind. They live in stagnant water. The Choanoflagellata have a single flagellum surrounded at the base by a collar. To swim, the flagellum is used in the way that a boatman sculls with a single oar. This protozoan may become fixed to a support, where it often secretes a thin and transparent cuticle (covering) around itself.

The orders Trichomonadida and Hypermastigida

These two orders are closely related orders of flagellates and include a great variety of species, usually of complex structure. Nearly all live as parasites or as symbionts (symbiotic organisms) within the alimentary canal and other body cavities, particularly the urinary bladder, vagina and urethra.

The best-known genus of the Trichomonadida is *Trichomonas*, which parasitizes a very large number of species, including leeches, molluscs, insects and vertebrates including man. These flagellates are pear-shaped and vary in size from six to thirty microns in length and three to fifteen microns in breadth. They possess four or five flagella; three or four point forwards and one backwards. This latter flagellum is housed in a groove in the body at its free end. Species of *Trichomonas* take in food particles from their host's intestine and also microbes to be found there, interfering with digestion. They may occupy specific hosts; *Trichomonas batrachorum* parasitizes frogs and *T. lacertae* lizards, for example. Man harbours three trichomonads. *Trichomonas elongata* can be found in the mouth, *Pentatrichomonas hominis* in the large intestine, and *Trichomonas vaginalis* in the vagina and, more rarely, the male urethra. Only this latter species can become really harmful; it then produces irritation of the mucous membranes and causes discharges to occur.

The order Hypermastigida contains species with many flagella, sometimes several thousands. They abound in the gut of some insects, particularly cockroaches and termites. Most are not parasites but exist in symbiosis with their hosts. These insects feed on wood, but many of them are unable to digest the cellulose it contains. The flagellates ingest the fragments of wood in the insect's gut and produce enzymes that digest the cellulose, forming various products of food value to the insect as well as themselves. The presence of the flagellates is essential to their hosts, for if the flagellates in a termite are killed (which can be done by exposing the termite to a temperature of 31°C (88°F) or more, or to an atmosphere of oxygen at three to four times atmosphere's pressure), then the termite subsequently dies of starvation, even if it is fed with wood.

The order Diplomonadida

This order is the last of the class Mastigophora to be discussed, though the class contains nineteen orders altogether. The prefix *diplo* means double, and refers to the doubling of all the organelles in the cell; there are two nuclei and two sets of four flagella, for example. These flagellates are either free-living in stagnant water rich in organic matter, or they are parasitic. *Giardia intestinalis* is common in man, and lives in the lining of the duodenum. It is transmitted via cysts passed in the faeces, and causes mild intestinal disorders.

The class Opalina

These protozoans have long puzzled biologists when it comes to classification. They are now regarded as being closely related to the flagellates but having special characteristics of their own, thus placing them alongside the flagellates as a separate class. They live as commensals in amphibians and, more rarely, fish and reptiles. Commensals are animals that live in close association with one another, doing each other neither harm (unlike parasites) nor good (unlike symbionts). Opalines are mostly to be found living in the rectal ampulla (a swelling in the rectum) of frogs and toads. They have from two to hundreds of nuclei, and are covered with rows of hair-like cilia. They have neither mouth nor appendages, and absorb nutrients dissolved in the fluids that surround them.

Opalines reproduce sexually. In fact they enter into a sexual phase at the same time as their hosts enter their own

they remain until the amphibians have bred, and tadpoles have hatches from their eggs. The tadpoles ingest the cysts, and the protozoan's life cycle can now continue. The cysts hatch out on reaching the tadpole's intestine, producing male and female gametes (sex cells) each with a single nucleus. The female gametes are large organisms and the male gametes are small. They move about in the intestinal cavity and meet and fuse together. The resulting zygote (fertilized egg) increases in size and its nuclei multiply as it assumes the structure of an adult opaline. When the tadpole metamorphoses into an adult amphibian, the opalines migrate to the rectal ampulla.

The class Sarcodina (Rhizopoda)

Protozoans of the preceding classes move with the aid of flagella or cilia. The protozoans classified in this group have the ability to put out extensions of their body called pseudopodia (false feet) to move themselves along, and to take in food. Pseudopodia are projections of the cytoplasm of the cell. They take on the most varied appearances: swellings, warts, filaments, etc.

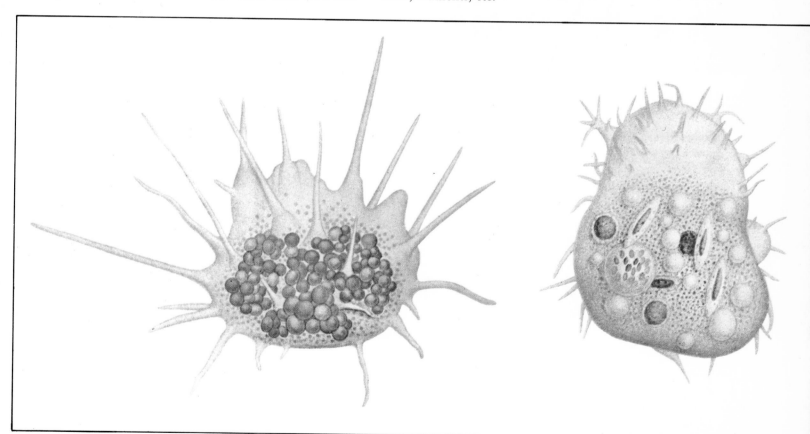

Two large free amoebae: left, *Dactylosphaerium*; right, *Dinamoeba*. After Scheffer

breeding season; presumably, the hosts' sex hormones act on the protozoans. During the spring in temperate climates, when the amphibian is about to breed, the opalines divide into small individuals, each with only a few nuclei. These individuals then become encased in cysts. When the amphibian enters the water to breed, the cysts are passed out with the faeces and fall to the bottom of the water. There

The amoeba (order Amoebida)

Amoeba is the name of a genus of the Sarcodina and a member of the first order of the class, the Amoebida. The amoeba is perhaps the best-known of all protozoans, famed because it is the simplest possible animal that can exist. It consists of little more than a mass of cytoplasm containing a nucleus and

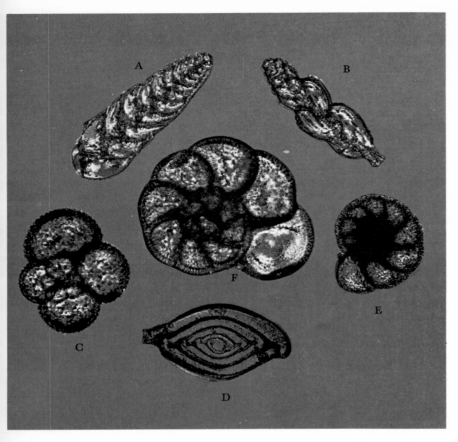

Some tests of fossil Foraminifera found in sand: *A, Bolivina; B, Uvigerina; C, Globigerina; D, Spiroloculina; E, Rotaliforme; F, Cibicides* (×25). *Phot. Aldo Margiocco*

An acantharian, *Diploconus fasces*: *My*, contractile filaments, or myonemes; *Psr*, reticulated pseudopodia; *Psf*, filiform pseudopodia; *Sp*, spicules; *Zo*, zooxanthellae. It is by contracting its myonemes inserted on the spicules, as well as in the cytoplasm, that the acantharian increases in volume and rises towards the surface; relaxation leads to a decrease in volume and the downward sinking of the animalcule. All acantharians contain zooxanthellae (Cryptomonadina), of unknown nutritive value. *After Schewiakoff*

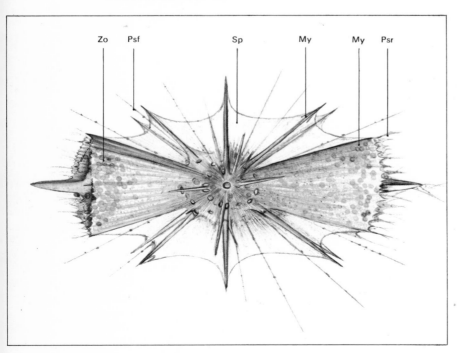

various vacuoles (cavities), for it has no permanent organelles. Yet it is obviously not a simple organism, for it performs all the essential activities of an animal. It moves by extending a pseudopod at any place on its body, and then the rest of the body flows into the pseudopod. It feeds by capturing other micro-organisms, extending pseudopodia around the prey and then engulfing its victim. The food is then digested in the food vacuole. An amoeba can also rid itself of waste matter, respire, reproduce and respond to changes in its environment. The amoeba is a truly remarkable animal, for it has virtually no special organs for carrying out all these functions.

Protozoans of other groups may become amoeboid at some stage of their lives. A flagellate may lose its flagella and begin to move by forming pseudopodia. It has even been suggested that all amoebae are a temporary phase in the life cycles of flagellates. This opinion is most likely an over-statement, for many protozoans appear to exist permanently in the amoeboid state. There is difficulty in distinguishing one kind of amoeba from another.

The amoebae vary in size, but many are among the larger protozoans. *Chaos*, which lives in stagnant water and in damp earth and feeds on microbes, reaches a length of 1/5 of an inch. *Amoeba proteus*, the common amoeba of fresh water, is about 1/40 of an inch long. Many species are parasitic. Three species at least live in the large intestine of man: the intestinal amoeba (*Entamoeba coli*), the dysentery amoeba (*Entamoeba histolytica*), and *Endolimax nana*. The life cycle of the second of these protozoans, which is the only one of them to have serious pathogenic effects, is described on page 15.

The cysts formed by *Entamoeba histolytica* are evacuated from the body with the faeces. In this way, the species is disseminated, although it must reach another host for the protozoan to complete its life cycle. Hygiene puts a stop to amoebic dysentery simply by preventing transmission of the cysts and completion of the life cycle.

The symptoms of the disease are unpleasant. It manifests itself by the frequent passing of blood-stained stools, ulceration of the intestine and, in some cases, abscesses of the liver and even of the brain (for the amoebas may be carried there in the bloodstream). Left untreated, the condition is likely to become chronic and is often fatal. The most effective treatment is with the drug emetine, an alkaloid extracted from ipecacuanha. It may be supplemented with antibiotics such as tetracyclines.

In another order of the Sarcodina called the Testacea are the thecamoebas. These protozoans have bodies enclosed in cases that are siliceous (composed of silica) or calcareous (calcium carbonate). The short pseudopodia appear through openings in these 'shells'. The thecamoebas prefer acidic water, and so are found in abundance in peat bogs.

The order Foraminifera

The order Foraminifera comprises some 18,000 species, both living and fossil, within the class Sarcodina. Nearly all live in the sea, some being tolerant of brackish water whereas others form colonies in the open sea.

The body of a foraminiferan is enclosed with a calcareous or horny shell, but very rarely a siliceous one. There are one or more apertures in the shell, through which the thread-like pseudopodia protrude. The shells of foraminiferans come in a wide variety of shapes and sizes. They may consist of a single chamber or of several successive chambers arranged in a straight line or in a spiral. The smallest are as little as 1/2500 of an inch across, whereas the largest is nearly eight inches in diameter. This latter size is exceptional for a foraminiferan, and 1/5 of an inch is more usual as a maximum size.

The life cycle of a foraminiferan comprises a sexual phase alternating with an asexual phase.

The asexual phase begins with a small amoeba-like protozoan containing a single nucleus; around the cytoplasm of the cell is deposited a thin calcareous shell perforated with small holes. Successive chambers are then added to this first chamber in a spiral formation. During this phase, the foraminiferan increases its size and the number of nuclei increases. When it has completed its growth, the nuclei pass out of the chambers and, surrounded by cytoplasm, form a delicate network of nuclei. This network divides into several individual protozoans, each containing a single nucleus. Multiplication of the original organism in this way is called schizogony.

The sexual phase now commences. Around each of the amoeba-like protozoans resulting from schizogony, a calcareous shell larger than that formed in the asexual phase grows. Several other chambers may be added to this first chamber. The nucleus divides, producing thousands of new nuclei. These nuclei grow and then leave from chambers at the outer surface of the organism. Each nucleus is surrounded by a sphere of cytoplasm and the resulting cell possesses two flagella. Each of these cells is a male or female gamete (sex cell), although both kinds are identical in form. Pairs of gametes fuse together, lose their flagella, and produce a zygote. This zygote develops into the amoeba-like organism that begins the asexual phase, and the life cycle is complete.

In some species, the asexual phase may comprise several generations before the sexual phase occurs.

Foraminiferans are all able to move freely at some stage of their lives, but many settle to the sea bottom or fix themselves to aquatic plants or to hydroids. Some are pelagic, floating at or near the surface of the open sea and forming part of the plankton. When these foraminiferans die, their remains gradually settle to the sea bottom, forming an ooze covering the sea floor. About a third of the ocean bottom is covered with foraminiferan ooze, notably of species of *Globigerina*.

Deposits of foraminiferans over millions of years built up deep layers of ooze on the seabed. In the course of time, these layers hardened into rock and the seabed has been forced above the water to form the land in many places. Such rocks are called sedimentary rocks, and much chalk, limestone and marble is composed of the remains of foraminiferans that lived in the sea long ago.

The Actinopoda

The Actinopoda comprises a subclass within the class Sarcodina. The pseudopodia of these protozoans are delicate and radiate out from the body, each having a central filament. Most have skeletons formed of spicules made of minerals. Actinopods are mostly marine and constitute an important part of the marine plankton. They are found at various depths, depending on the species. Those of the order Heliozoa are found mostly in fresh water.

The order Acantharia

This order within the Actinopoda comprises only marine protozoans. They are characterized by a skeleton composed of twenty radial spicules that project from the centre of the body in precise directions.

There is disagreement as to the chemical composition of these spicules. According to some authorities, they consist of strontium sulphate, which is known as celestite or celestine to mineralogists. However, others consider the spicules to be made of a double silicate of aluminium and calcium. The outer layer of the cell's cytoplasm (the ectoplasm) is gelatinous, whereas the inner layers of the cytoplasm (the endoplasm) is pigmented yellow, brown, red or blue in many cases.

Some of the Acantharia reproduce by binary fission, but they resort mainly to sexual reproduction. They produce small gametes, spherical in shape and possessing two

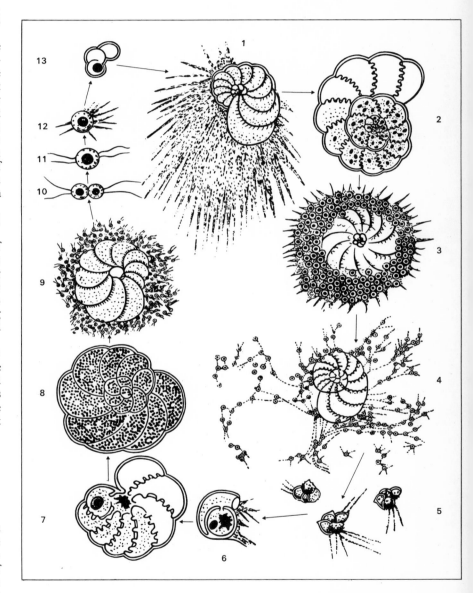

The cycle of a polystomella (*Elphidium crispum*): *1*, vegetative individual with long reticulated pseudopodia; *2*, multiplication of nuclei (the cytoplasm, situated outside the shell, is not shown); *3*, emergence of the nuclei; *4*, breakdown into small uninucleate amoebae; *5*, each amoeba becomes an individual which will produce gametes; *6*, the first chamber in the shell is comparatively large; *7*, more advanced stage; *8*, chambers with single nuclei (exterior cytoplasm not shown); *9*, emergence of nuclei and cutting of cytoplasm into gametes with two flagella; *10*, ferilization (union) of two similar gametes; *11*, zygote or fertilized egg; *12*, transformation into ameoba; *13*, formation of the shell, the first chamber of which is small. Polystomellas live on the most varied sea bottoms. Their flat-spiralled shell is finely perforated.

flagella. Only gametes originating from different individuals fuse to produce a zygote. As it grows, the protozoan acquires a skeleton and other organelles. This breeding takes place in deep water below fifty fathoms.

Acantharians are planktonic organisms that float at different levels according to the time of day. They do this by changing their volume and therefore their density. The spicules bear contractile filaments that act like small muscles. These contract and draw the outer layer of the cytoplasm away from the centre. The acantharian's volume increases and its density decreases, so that it rises towards the surface. When the filaments relax, the cytoplasm shrinks and the animal becomes denser and sinks.

Acantharians feed on unicellular plants, such as diatoms, ciliates and other micro-organisms, which they catch in their pseudopodia.

The order Radiolaria

The radiolarians are easily distinguished from the acantharians. The skeleton is either composed of silica or is absent; where it is present, it is never made of radial spicules. A central horny capsule of variable shape separates the endoplasm and ectoplasm.

All radiolarians live in the sea, drifting with the current. There is an immense variety in the form of the skeleton. Sometimes it is made up of many separate pieces of silica and sometimes of just one piece deposited in the cytoplasm. The shapes are often beautiful; spiny spheres, stars, or globes perforated with intriguing patterns of holes are often to be seen.

Radiolarians breed either asexually by binary fission, or sexually by fusion of gametes.

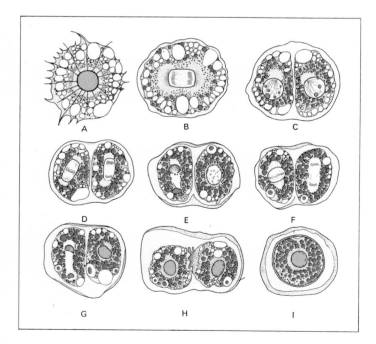

Cycle of *Actinophrys sol* with autogamy: *A*, stage preparatory to gametogenesis; *B*, end of the first division; *C*, the two gametocytes; *D*, first maturation division; *E*, end of the first maturation division (a polar body in each gamete); *F*, second maturation division; *G*, end of the second maturation division (two polar bodies extruded in each gamete); *H*, fusion of two gametes (male gamete on the right); *I*, zygote surrounded by cyst membrane (×760). *Actinophrys* uses pseudopodia and axopodia to capture its prey. *After K. Belar*

Several species of radiolarians live as colonies. These are either spherical or sausage-shaped and may reach an inch in diameter. The numerous members of the colony live together beneath a common envelope of jelly, linked together by their ectoplasm.

Radiolarians live and feed like acantharians. There are many instances where members of both orders have entered into symbiosis with pigmented flagellates belonging to the order Cryptomonadida; the flagellates that are confined to the ectoplasm of the radiolarians lose their flagella and assume a spherical shape. These flagellates are known generally as zooxanthellae. It is believed that they contribute to the feeding of their hosts, synthesizing carbohydrates for them by photosynthesis. Zooxanthellae are also symbionts of multicellular animals, particularly the giant clam (see page 118).

The order Heliozoa

Members of the third order of actinopods live mostly in fresh water. They are spherical with many fine radiating pseudopodia, giving them the appearance of a sunburst from which their name, which is Greek for sun animals, derives. At the centre of the body is a corpuscle, called the centroplast, from which radial filaments and axopodia, which are like rigid flagella, arise. The skeleton is made up of isolated spicules embedded within a gelatinous layer. Some genera have no skeleton at all.

Free-living heliozoans float in the water. They feed on various micro-organisms, capturing them with the axopodia. Several heliozoans may join forces to capture a large organism, becoming closely joined together as they digest it. They resume separate lives as soon as the meal is over. A few heliozoans live fixed by a stalk to a support, and these sessile (fixed) species are mostly marine.

Heliozoans usually multiply by binary fission, but they also resort to a special kind of sexual reproduction called autogamy. *Actinophrys*, for example, draws in its axopodia and pseudopodia and becomes completely spherical. Then it surrounds itself with a fairly thick membrane and undergoes binary fission. The two new individuals then undergo nuclear divisions, giving four nuclei per individual. Only one of these is functional and the others degenerate. The number of chromosomes in the nucleus halves during the division process. The individuals become gametes; one assumes a male role and sends out a pseudopodium towards the other to capture it. The two fuse and the two nuclei come together to establish a nucleus with the full number of chromosomes. The resulting cell is equivalent to a fertilized egg, though it becomes cyst-like and remains dormant for a long time before developing. When conditions are favourable, the cyst hatches and gives rise to an *Actinophrys* individual that acquires pseudopodia and axopodia, and leads an active life.

The subphylum Sporozoa

The sporozoans make up the second subphylum of the Protozoa. Virtually all of them are internal parasites and they have no organs of locomotion, though some are able to move by changing the shape of the cell body. The body is simple in form and possesses one nucleus. Sporozoans absorb food directly from their hosts, and respire and excrete waste matter by diffusion through the cell wall. They are called sporozoans because the life cycle, which may be as complex as the animal is simple, commences with a sporozoite, of which there are usually several enclosed in a tough case called a spore. Protected within the spores, the protozoans can safely transfer from one host to another, often an essential feature of their life cycle.

The sporozoan's life cycle consists of an asexual phase and a sexual phase, and usually involves penetration of the host's cells at some stage. Sporozoans are haploid throughout most of the cycle; that is, the nucleus contains unpaired chromosomes as occurs in gametes (sex cells). They become diploid, gaining twice the haploid number of chromosomes in pairs, only at the very brief stage of zygote formation before subsequent division.

The subphylum is made up of three classes: the Telosporea, which have elongated sporozoites; the Toxoplasmea, which undergo asexual reproduction only and do not form spores; and the Haplosporea, which have small spores. A closely related subphylum, the Cnidospora, comprises similar parasitic protozoans (see page 34). They also possess spores, but differ from the Sporozoa in the structure of the spores.

The two main orders of the Telosporea will be considered: the Coccidia or coccidians, and the Gregarinida or gregarines. The life cycle of the coccidians has already been discussed in the section describing the life cycle of the genus *Eimeria* (see page 16). The asexual phase consists of several generations, in which reproduction occurs by schizogony, many merozoites being formed. In typical gregarines, the asexual phase is limited to the growth of the individuals; the individuals change imperceptibly and directly into gamonts, individuals that generate gametes. Union of the sexes takes place at the gamont stage, before the gametes separate from them. Fertilization occurs after separation of the gametes, being effected by gametes from different parent cells. The resulting zygote forms spores in a similar way to the life cycle of coccidians.

Sporozoans produce a characteristic carbohydrate called paraglycogen, which is similar to glycogen (animal starch) but more highly polymerized.

The order Coccidia

The protozoans of this order form a homogeneous group with a strong identity. The schizonts, the stages that undergo schizogony, are immobile and rich in paraglycogen. The male gametes, comma-shaped and bearing three flagella, differ greatly in appearance from the female gametes, and also from the gametes of the Gregarinida.

The Coccidia are divided into two groups according to their sexual behaviour: the Adeleida and the Eimerida. In the first, gamonts of opposite sexes pair, the male producing a small number of gametes. In the second group, the gamonts develop separately and no pairing occurs before gamete formation. The male gives rise to many triflagellate gametes, which actively seek out and fertilize the female gametes.

The Adeleida, by pairing of the gamonts, are similar in behaviour to the gregarines. These sporozoans become parasites of insects, occupying the fatty tissue, intestine and Malpighian tubules (which have an excretory function); of myriapods (intestine, testes and Malpighian tubules); of gastropod molluscs (kidney); of earthworms (body cavity); and of leeches (testes).

Many Adeleida are parasites of the blood corpuscles of vertebrates (back-boned animals), especially fishes. The parasites are transmitted from one vertebrate host to another by a blood-sucking invertebrate. In mammals, only one adeleid is known—*Hepatozoon muris* in the mouse. *Haemogregarina* parasitizes fishes, frogs and turtles, the details of its life cycle remaining obscure.

The Eimerida include hundreds of species, several of which are pathogenic (disease producing). Most undergo their life cycle in the same host, but some require two hosts.

The single-host cycle will serve as an example for a brief explanation of the pattern of reproduction to be found

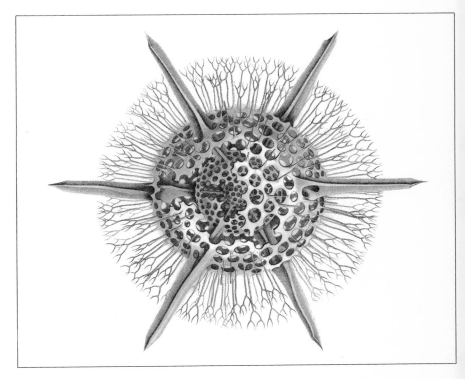

Siliceous skeleton of *Haliomma echinaster*, a spheroid radiolarian, opened to show the latticed inner shells. The diametrical axes pass through the shells without being deflected. *After E. Haeckel*

among this group. The zygote secretes a membrane around itself, producing an oocyst. Within the oocyst, the nucleus divides twice in succession and the cytoplasm divides into four; each resulting quadrant becomes surrounded by a shell and then undergoes a division into spores. The number of spores varies from one genus to another. From the spores, the long sporozoites emerge. These undergo schizogony into many merozoites, which separately form gametes of different sexes. The gametes unite to form a zygote, completing the life cycle.

The eimeridan coccidians are very widespread and occur in many vertebrates, including man. Among them are to be encountered some redoubtable parasites that produce a disease called coccidiosis in animals. The disease may be fatal, and is liable to affect domestic animals such as rabbits, chickens, pheasants and cattle. Oocysts of coccidians belonging to the genus *Diplospora* have been found in humans, but multiplication of the protozoan has not been observed in human tissue.

Among the eimeridan coccidians that occupy two hosts is the genus *Aggregata*, which carries out schizogony in the intestinal walls of crabs and reproduction by gametes in the intestines of cephalopod molluscs (cuttlefishes and octopuses). The crab is contaminated with protozoans by ingesting spores liberated by cephalopods in their wastes; the cephalopod then takes over as the second host by eating infected crabs.

Plasmodium—the malarial parasite

A group of sporozoans that parasitize the blood cells and tissues of vertebrates make up the sub-order Haemosporidia in the order Coccidia. They differ from other coccidians in that the zygote is mobile. Schizogony occurs within blood cells and the blood systems of vertebrates, and the life cycle is completed by spore formation in blood-sucking arthropods as intermediate hosts. The spores are not resistant to external conditions and so transmission between the hosts occurs in both directions when the arthropod bites the vertebrate.

The best-known parasites of this sub-order are those of the genus *Plasmodium*, which causes malaria. The spindle-shaped sporozoites, ten microns long by one in breadth, are injected into the human body by the bite of an infected mosquito of the genus *Anopheles*, being contained in its saliva. They are conveyed in the bloodstream to the reticuloendothelial system, a system of cells scattered around the body that are involved in resisting infection. The sporozoites also penetrate to the liver. They invade cells, developing into bulky schizonts up to sixty microns in diameter. These multiply their nuclei and then break up by schizogony into

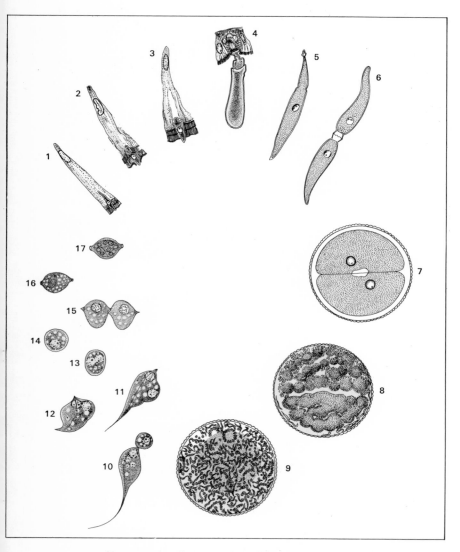

Above, cycle of a gregarine (*Stylocephalus longicollis*) which lives fixed, in the vegetative state, to the cells of the mid-gut of *Blaps*, a cellar beetle; *1*, fixation of the sporozoite to an intestinal cell; *2, 3* and *4*, growth stages; *5*, mature individual which has become detached from the intestinal wall and slips freely into the intestinal cavity; *6*, union by confrontation of two individuals of opposite sex (after loss of their anterior segments); *7*, the gametocyst is formed by secretion around the partners of a spherical mucous envelope (it is expelled with the faeces); *8*, formation of reproductive elements or gametes; *9*, sexual mêlée; *10*, fertilization; *11–14*, fusion of two gametes; *15*, two zygotes, each surrounded by a shell, have become spores; *16* and *17* (eight sporozoites are formed by repeated divisions in the spore). The spore swallowed by a *Blaps* bursts in the mid-gut due to the action of digestive enzymes. The liberated sporozoites fix themselves to the intestinal wall and a new cycle begins. The adult individual measures up to 600 microns. The sexes of the gamonts are recognized by some differences in the organelles (mitochrondria, Golgi apparatus) and in the abundance and size of the grains of paraglycogen. *After L. Léger*

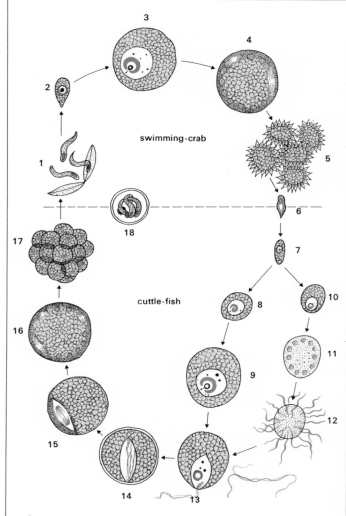

Above, cycle of *Aggregata eberthi*, a coccidian which carries out its schizogony (asexual multiplication) in the intestine of a swimming-crab (*Portunus depurator*) and its gamogamy (sexual reproduction) in the spinal caecum of the intestine of the cuttlefish (*Sepia officinalis*): *1*, the spore, ingested by the crab along with the cuttlefish's faeces, hatches in the intestine; the liberated sporozoites pass through the mucous membrane of the intestine, penetrate into the intestinal connective tissue and are there transformed into a bulky schizont (*2* and *3*), which multiplies its nuclei (*4*), divides its cytoplasm, from which are detached small schizozoites (*5*); if the cycle is to continue, the swimming-crab has to be eaten by a cuttlefish. When the schizozoites (*6* and *7*) reach the intestine, they pass through its epithelium and lodge in the sub-mucous membrane. They become producers of male gametes (*10, 11, 12*) and female (*8, 9*). The fertilized egg (*13*) undergoes nuclear division many times (*14, 15, 16*). Each nucleus is isolated, surrounded by a spherical mass of cytoplasm, becomes a spore (*17*), in which 3 sporozoites (*18*) are formed. The mature spores are passed out in the faeces. Every aged cuttlefish is parasitized by *Aggregata*. *After Dobell*

merozoites containing a single nucleus. The merozoites either contaminate new cells or pass into the blood and enter the red corpuscles. Schizonts are again formed in either case, and schizogony again occurs, liberating more merozoites. This cycle is repeated several times. After about ten days, the parasites become so numerous that the sudden bursting of many cells by schizogony causes a chill and the sudden release of toxins by the resulting avalanche of merozoites produces a fever. Cycles of chill and fever then recur, either regularly every two or three days or irregularly.

After several generations, gamonts are produced instead of schizonts, but they cannot develop further in a human host. The life cycle of the protozoans can only continue in a mosquito.

A female mosquito biting an infected person draws a little blood into its stomach. The gamonts in the blood are not digested. In the mosquito's intestine, the female gamont hardly changes but the male gamont divides its nucleus three or four times. The new nuclei move to the periphery of the cell and several filaments of cytoplasm, each containing one nucleus, grow from the cell. The filaments are twelve to fifteen microns in length and separate from the gamont to become free male gametes. These move to meet the female gametes that have formed with little change from the female gamonts, and fertilization occurs producing a zygote. The zygote moves in an amoeba-like way into the lining of the intestine, in which it becomes surrounded by a thin flexible membrane, forming an oocyst. The nuclei inside increase greatly in number, and the cell splits up into a number of long spindle-shaped cells, each containing a single nucleus. This is the equivalent of spore formation in other sporozoans. The oocyst then bursts, liberating the spindle-shaped sporozoites, which migrate to the salivary glands and accumulate in their ducts. When the mosquito now bites a human, it injects the sporozoites into the body and the life cycle is completed. It takes from one to three weeks for the mosquito's section of the cycle to be effected.

Three species of *Plasmodium* infect man and all are transmitted by *Anopheles* females. The three species are:

Plasmodium falciparum, which undergoes schizogony at irregular intervals or may lack a cycle altogether. It produces aestivo-autumnal malaria or malignant tertian fever, and is particularly common in the tropics. The form of malaria is the most dangerous kind, producing frequent and irregular attacks of fever or persistent fever.

Plasmodium vivax, which undergoes schizogony every 48 hours. It produces a benign tertian fever with attacks on alternate days. This kind of malaria may recur after the first bout has subsided, but it is not as serious as malignant tertian malaria, which does not recur. Benign tertian fever was once common in temperate regions as far north as Finland.

Plasmodium malariae, which undergoes schizogony every 72 hours, causing the attacks of fever to occur every three days. This form of malaria is known as quartan fever. It is common in sub-tropical countries, but attacks may recur long after a person has left a malarial region.

Malaria is one of the most serious endemic diseases known to man. For centuries it has rendered uninhabitable marshy regions, where mosquitoes breed, and it still hinders development of such regions in many places.

Malaria manifests itself by a number of symptoms, which are not very characteristic of the disease if each is taken in isolation. The attack of fever gives the patient the impression of a severe chill for it begins with violent shivering; however, it ends with heavy sweating. Anaemia occurs as the red corpuscles are destroyed by schizogony of the parasites, increasing in extent with every cycle of the disease. Hyper-

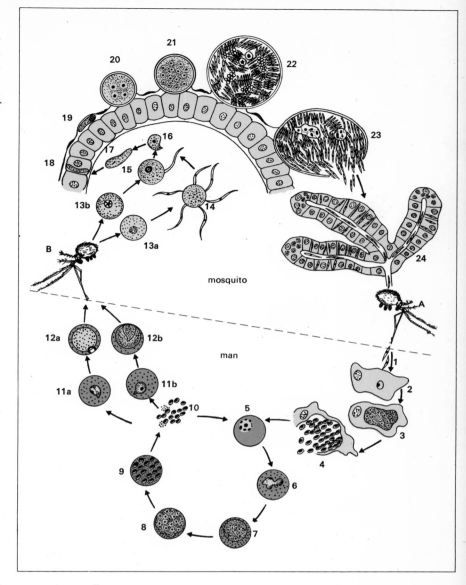

Life cycle of *Plasmodium vivax*, agent of benign tertian malaria, transmitted to man by an anopheline mosquito: *1*, sporozoites inoculated into man with the saliva injected by the anopheline at the beginning of its blood-sucking; *2*, liver cell, penetrated by sporozoite; *3*, sporozoite in the same cell at the term of its growth and having become multinucleate; *4*, the liver cell bursts, liberating the small uninucleate elements, or schizozoites, resulting from the cutting up of the multinucleate sporozoite, or schizont; *5*, red blood corpuscle, after penetration by a schizozoite; *6–9*, growth and nuclear multiplication of the schizont in the red blood corpuscle; *10*, bursting of the red blood corpuscle, liberation of the schizozoites and of the cytoplasmic remains of the corpuscle, synchronous with the attack of fever (this multiplication in the host's blood is repeated every three days, at intervals of 48 hours, by infestation of the corpuscles by the liberated schizozoites); *11b, 12b*, future female gamete; *11a, 12a*, gamont or mother element of male gametes; *13b*, female gamete; *13a*, producer of male gametes; *14*, male gametes freeing themselves from the large cytoplasmic residue of the element which has engendered them; *15*, fertilization; *16–17*, mobile zygote (amoepoid); *18*, zygote passing through the wall of the mosquito's intestine; *19*, zygote stopped in the peri-intestinal tissue; *20–22*, growth of the zygote, then nuclear multiplication and formation of the sporozoites; *23*, bursting of the enlarged zygote: liberation of the sporozoites, which migrate into the cavity of the salivary glands and are inoculated into the human victim at the beginning of biting. *A*, head of the anopheline injecting the saliva; *B*, head of the anopheline after having taken its meal of blood. In man (liver then blood) stages 1 to 12; in the mosquito (intestinal cavity, peri-intestinal tissue, cavity of the salivary glands), stages 13 to 24. *Plasmodium vivax* is the commonest species of the genus on earth—from latitude 60° N to latitude 30° S. *P. falciparum*, which in order to develop in its anopheline host requires a temperature of 20–21° C, is scarcely found outside tropical regions. *After classical data*

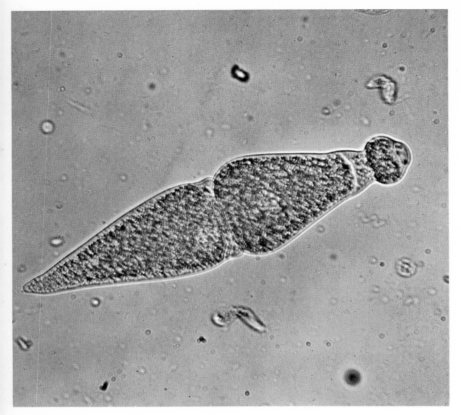

A gregarine (*Gregarina ausoniae*), parasite of the lucifugous termite (*Reticulitermes lucifugus*) associating in syzygy. The rear individual or satellite has its protomerite segment crushed against the posterior part of the primite which precedes it (×500). *Phot. Aldo Margiocco*

Below left, portrait of *Paramecium*: *Cv*, contractile vacuole; *Dc*, cuticle in relief with point of insertion of cilia; *Fv*, food vacuole; *O*, oral groove or cytostome; *T*, trichocyst.

Below right, diagrammatic representation of the male gamete of *Stylocephalus longicollis*: *C*, centriole; *Erg*, ergastoplasm (only three of the peripheral membranelles have been shown); *F*, flagellum; *G*, Golgi apparatus; *L*, lipid inclusion; *M*, mitochondria; *Mi*, microtubules; *Ms*, membranous structure; *N*, nucleus.

trophy of the liver and spleen occurs, accompanied by loss of muscular strength. This is the main pattern of symptoms that occur in a malaria victim. Complications may occur, particularly invasion of the brain cells to produce cerebral malaria, which is a significant factor in infant mortality in tropical regions.

If malaria is untreated, most patients recover after a series of attacks of fever. An attack does not give immunity from the disease, and it may recur spontaneously without reinfection by mosquitoes. However, repeated attacks often become less and less severe. Even so, malaria can kill. Death is often due to anaemia, but the exhaustion produced by the attacks of fever reduces resistance to other diseases so that patients may die of complications, even trivial ones.

The war against malaria is being waged on several fronts. One is to destroy the sporozoans within the human body with the aid of drugs. Quinine is the traditional remedy, but it is now seldom used because of its toxic effects. Newer drugs can prevent the disease occurring, stop an attack and cure a victim, though the parasites may become resistant to certain drugs after prolonged use so that new ones must be sought. Destruction of the mosquitoes is another way to prevent the disease. Draining of marshes and spraying with insecticides has eradicated malaria from many places. It is not necessary to rid a region completely of mosquitoes, for once the disease has been prevented in humans, mosquitoes will be unable to transmit it from person to person.

Europe (apart from some parts of the Danube basin), the United States, Cuba, most of Brazil, Uruguay and a few tropical countries have freed themselves from malaria.

Monkeys, a few rodents and some bats also harbour species of *Plasmodium*. The primate parasites are similar to those of man, but there are sufficient differences to prevent their developing in man. Many birds, some lizards and a few snakes are also hosts to other *Plasmodium* species.

The order Gregarinida

The sporozoans of the order Gregarinida are parasites only of invertebrates and lower chordates. They live in the intestine or other visceral cavity, or in the body cavity.

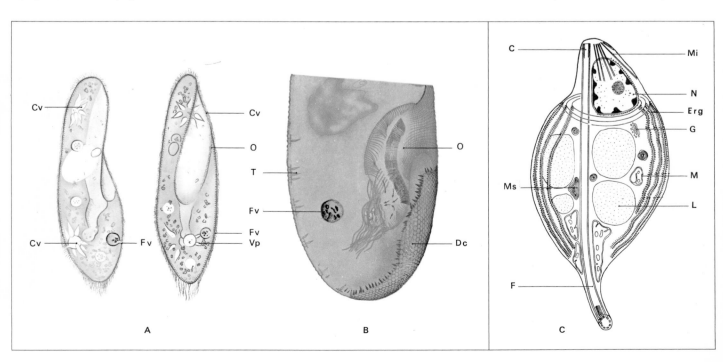

Gregarines may grow to a comparatively large size, and many are visible to the unaided eye. In most species, the long body is divided by two transverse partitions into three segments, of which only one possesses a nucleus.

The mode of reproduction is unusual. The gregarines are either male or female, although no external characteristic indicates the sex. They form pairs that become surrounded by a case called the gametocyst. Within this case, many gametes of both sexes form by division of the partners. A zygote forms as a pair of gametes unite, and a hard case is produced around it. Inside this case or oocyst, the zygote divides to form eight worm-like sporozoites. The gametocyst is cast out from the host, and then bursts to liberate the oocyst. The oocyst is ingested by a new host and dissolves to set free the sporozoites inside, each of which then becomes a gregarine. This life cycle is remarkable for the lack of schizogony, although a few gregarines have retained or reacquired this feature.

The subphylum Ciliophora

The third subphylum of the Protozoa is made up of a single class—the Ciliata. Both subphylum and class get their name because these protozoans bear cilia. The ciliates are also known as infusorians, a former, less precise name.

Ciliates are the most complex of the Protozoa. Although they vary widely as a result of the evolution of many separate lines, they have not lost their fundamental characteristics, which are three in number. All ciliates have two kinds of nuclei, the macronucleus and micronucleus. The former, which is the larger, is involved in feeding and the latter is concerned with reproduction. The second characteristic is the possession of vibrating cilia, which are similar in structure to flagella. The distribution of the cilia is used as the basis of classification within the class. Reproduction involving conjugation (as described on page 16) is another feature of the ciliates.

Ciliates have become adapted to all aquatic habitats, and examination of any drop of water—fresh, brackish or salt—will reveal them. They are also parasites of both vertebrates and invertebrates, being found mostly in the intestine. Some species live as commensals in the digestive tract of herbivorous mammals, feeding on substances in the host's food without doing them any harm.

The best-known ciliate is *Paramecium*, which lives in stagnant fresh water. *Paramecium caudatum* is about 1/100 of an inch in length, and serves as a good example of the class. The body is cigar-shaped and covered with rows of whiskery cilia. It swims vigorously, propelled by the beating of the cilia. A shallow groove, known as the oral groove, extends along the lower surface of the animal, making it asymmetrical. The asymmetry causes the protozoan to swim with a corkscrew motion, turning anticlockwise as it moves forward. The outer surface is covered with an elastic membrane called the pellicle. Rows of cilia of uniform length are arranged lengthwise along the body. The front end of the body is rounded and the back end pointed. From the front end, the oral groove runs diagonally back about halfway across the body and ends in a mouth called the cytostome, from which a tube (the cytopharynx) extends into the body.

The outer layer of cytoplasm, the ectoplasm, contains many spindle-shaped trychocysts, which can protrude from the surface between the cilia and probably aid in defence. The inner layer, the endoplasm, is more fluid than the

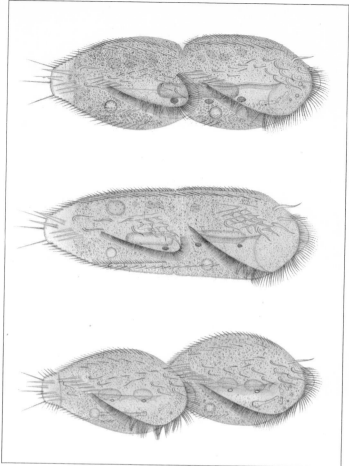

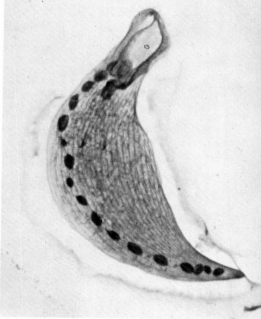

End of the division of the spirostome, *Spirostomum ambiguum*. A long cytoplasmic cord still joins the two brother organisms and the macronucleus. *After Stein*

Three illustrations of the transverse division of a ciliated hypotrich, *Stylonychia mytilus*. Note the cirri, a tuft of closely agglomerated cilia. used for walking. The regeneration of the missing parts in the brother organisms is well under way. *After Stein*

Left, a vorticella in a drop of water. *Right,* a fragment of the buccal region, of a *Blepharisma*, impregnated with silver. *Phot. Margiocco and Truffau*

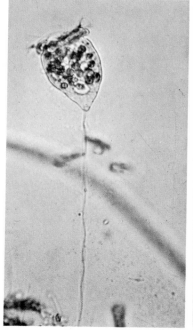

ectoplasm and contains the usual cell structures—mitochondria, Golgi apparatus, food vacuoles, and so on. There are two contractile vacuoles, one at the front of the body and one near the back. Each consists of a cavity from which canals radiate outwards. The canals collect liquid from the cytoplasm and discharge it into the vacuole, which then contracts and empties the liquid through a pore to the exterior. The two contractile vacuoles work alternately; as one vacuole contracts, the other expands.

Paramecium feed on bacteria. It is estimated that *Paramecium caudatum* consumes between two and five million bacteria in 24 hours. They will also eat yeast, for *Paramecium* can be raised on sterile media containing juices extracted from yeasts. Small protozoans are also accepted.

The cilia along the oral groove beat in waves to sweep water towards the mouth. Unwanted particles in the water are rejected at the mouth, but particles of food value are passed along the cytopharynx. At the bottom of the cytopharynx, a food vacuole containing the food particles forms. The vacuole becomes detached from the cytopharynx and circulates through the body, first moving towards the back and then frontwards and finally back towards the oral groove. As it moves, enzymes pass into the food vacuole from the endoplasm, and the food particles are digested. The vacuole gets smaller as digestion continues. It eventually arrives at the cell anus, a pore through which undigested wastes are evacuated to the exterior.

Paramecium reproduce by binary fission for most of the time. The macronucleus becomes drawn out into a dumbbell shape and divides into two equal nuclei. The micronucleus divides into two new nuclei that move to opposite ends of the cell, and the cell divides into two across the middle. Any parts lacking from each new cell are rapidly regenerated. On occasion, two individuals will come together and reproduce by conjugation, which involves an exchange of nuclei between them before division. Only individuals of two different types or 'sexes' will undergo conjugation together.

Conjugation enables hereditary factors to be passed on so that new generations of ciliates will not be identical to their parents. When it occurs a reciprocal exchange of nuclei happens and, in certain 'sexual' types, it is also accompanied by the formation of a bridge of cytoplasm between the two partners. When the bridge breaks after conjugation, each partner retains half of it and it is by means of these bridges that certain properties are transmitted. This can be shown by experiments with rabbits. Two races of *Paramecium* possessing different antigenic properties are brought together. They each produce different antibodies in rabbits and so can be identified. If two conjugants, one from each race, do not unite by means of a cytoplasmic bridge, then their descendants retain the antigenic properties of both races. However, if a bridge is established in conjugation, the descendants will possess antigenic properties of only one of the parents and not the other.

Other forms of reproduction exist that involve reorganization of nuclei. Autogamy, which occurs in *Paramecium*

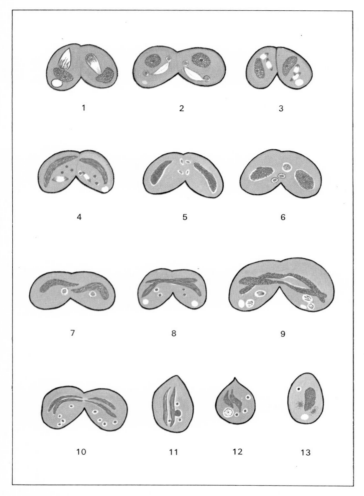

Conjugation of the parasitic infusorian, *Collinia branchiarum*, which lives in the blood of freshwater shrimps (*Gammarus*): *1*, the partners have become partly fused and the small nuclei (micronuclei) carry out their first division (each contains six chromosomes); *2*, end of this division; *3*, end of the second division: only three chromosomes can now be seen at each pole of the achromatic figure of division—the reduction in the number of chromosomes (meiosis) has taken place; *4*, each conjugant contains then four small nuclei, three of which degenerate. The fourth is in course of division; *5*, the nuclei of this division, or pronuclei, have the value of sexual elements (gametes), one from each couple passing into the other conjugant; this is the phenomenon of the exchange of pronuclei; *6*, in each conjugant, the pronuclei fuse and thus form a nucleus with six chromosomes; *7*, the large nuclei (macronuclei) lengthen; *8*, the nucleus of fertilization has undergone its first division; *9*, the daughter nuclei divide in their turn; *10*, the couple, with four small nuclei in each conjugant; *11*, the couple becomes dissociated: one of the ex-conjugants with four small nuclei, one of which enlarges to become the macronucleus, and two fragments of the macronuclei of the conjugants destined to disappear; *12*, the macronucleus has greatly increased in size; *13*, the reconstituted *Collinia*, with its macronucleus and its micronucleus. The two small supplementary nuclei disappear. The inconstant part of conjugation concerns the reconstitution of the nuclear apparatus after a variable number of nuclear then cytoplasmic divisions. But these variations do not change the final result. *After Bernard Collin*

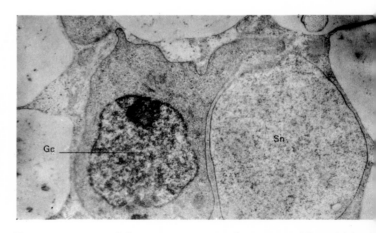

Transverse section of *Sphaeromyxa sabrazesi*, a myxosporidian which lives as a parasite in the gall bladder in the seahorse, seen under the electron microscope: *Gc*, germinal cells; *Sn*, somatic nuclei (×15,000). *Phot. P.-P. Grassé*

aurelia, may interrupt continued binary fission. This ciliate contains one macronucleus and two micronuclei. The two micronuclei divide twice to give eight new micronuclei, and the macronucleus degenerates. Two move towards the cell mouth and the remaining six then disintegrate. The two nuclei fuse like gametes to produce a zygote-like structure that then divides twice to produce four micronuclei. Two become macronuclei and two divide further as the cell itself divides in two, forming two new cells each with one macronucleus and two micronuclei. Binary fission then begins again. Hereditary changes can occur during autogamy.

When the environment becomes unfavourable, all ciliates can encase themselves in cysts and resist desiccation, cold and starvation. When a pool or any other body of water dries up, the mud of the bottom dries out and the wind scatters dust about. Mixed with the dust are ciliate cysts, and the protozoans will reappear as soon as the cysts find water. Populations are therefore quickly established in puddles and temporary pools, and infusions made by boiling dried plants in water will contain ciliates (hence their other name of infusorians).

The Ciliata comprises a large number of genera and species. Modern classification of these is very complex and a matter for the specialist; only some of the major groups will be discussed here. Classification is based on the arrangement of the cilia and also on some other features such as the shape of the mouth.

The class Ciliata is subdivided into four subclasses, each made up of a varying number of orders. The first subclass, the Holotricha, comprises protozoans in which the cilia are distributed in various patterns over the body, but the cilia are always simple; for example, the cilia next to the mouth are not modified for feeding or are only slightly modified. These ciliates include some very common ones. *Chilodon* has a flattened body and is ciliated only on its under-surface and around the mouth; the mouth cilia form a funnel that functions like a trap to capture food. *Paramecium* and *Colpoda* are kidney-shaped, with their mouths situated in depressions on the under-surface. *Colpoda* multiply in cysts, but cyst formation in *Paramecium* has not been completely confirmed. The Holotricha includes many parasitic protozoans: *Collinia* live in the blood of the gills of small freshwater shrimps (*Gammarus*), and *Anoplophrya* lives in the intestines of marine worms and lobsters, and in the seminal vesicles (sacs) of earthworms.

The second subclass, the Suctoria, bear cilia only in the free-living young stages. The adults are not free-living, but are attached by a stalk to a support in marine or fresh waters. Suctorians also attach themselves to aquatic animals and they are also parasitic. They bear delicate tentacles, which capture prey and empty the soft contents of their bodies. There is no mouth. *Acineta* is a common, free-living suctorian; *Sphaerophrya* is parasitic in other ciliates such as *Paramecium* and *Stentor*.

The third subclass is the Peritricha. These ciliates have a disk of cilia around the mouth but few cilia elsewhere. At the opposite end of the cell to the mouth, the ciliate may become temporarily or permanently attached to a support in the water. The body is often bell-shaped. Many ciliates of this subclass form colonies; *Vorticella* is a common solitary species.

The fourth and final subclass of the Ciliata is the Spirotricha. These ciliates have their cilia arranged into vibrating organelles, groups of cilia being fused into tentacle-like cirri or fin-like membranelles. Among them is *Stentor*, a trumpet-shaped ciliate and, at 1/10 of an inch, one of the largest protozoans. Around the bell of the trumpet, which acts as the mouth, are rings of membranelles. Normally *Stentor* swims

freely in fresh and salt waters. To feed, it attaches its lower, small end to a water plant or similar object and vibrates the membranelles to set up a water current and sweep microorganisms into the mouth. *Stentor* can contract its body and assume a globular or even spherical shape when it is swimming. The colour varies greatly, but it is often greenish due to the presence of symbiotic algae within the cytoplasm.

Other members of the Spirotricha include the order Hypotrichida, which have rows of cirri along the lower surface that may act like legs. *Euplotes* and *Stylonychia* are the most common. The order Entodiniomorphida contains some of the

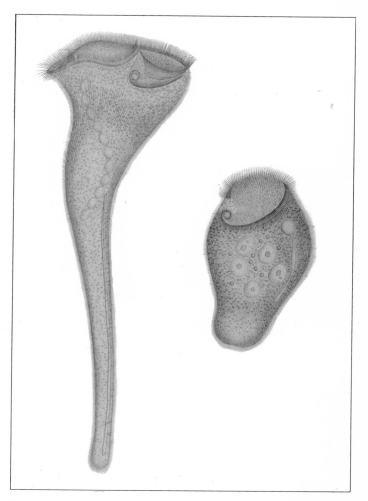

The polymorphous stentor (*Stentor polymorphus*) lives in small pools containing dead leaves. When relaxed, it has the shape of a megaphone (hence its name); when it contracts, it becomes globular. The large nucleus (macronucleus) is shaped like a string of beads (×400). *After Stein*

Roach (*Leuciscus rutilus* L.), bearing subcutaneous cysts of *Myxobolus*. *After R. Poisson*

most complex protozoans. Among other characteristics, it possesses an outer 'skeleton' of small plates composed of polysaccharides; this feature is analogous to the chitinous exoskeleton of arthropods. These ciliates live as commensals in the digestive tracts of ruminants. Ciliates of the order Tintinnida are characterized by feathery membranelles. They also secrete around their bodies a bell-shaped case composed of polysaccharides. The marine plankton contains very large numbers of these ciliates.

The subphylum Cnidospora

The cnidosporans are the last of the four subphyla of the Protozoa to be discussed. Spore formation places it in close proximity to the Sporozoa, but the spores are sufficiently different in structure to place these protozoans in a separate

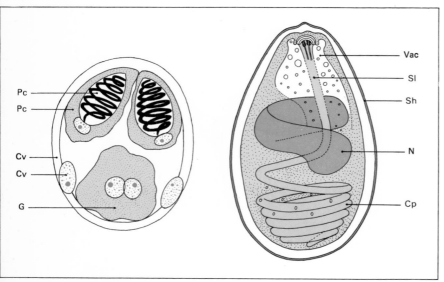

Spore of myxosporidian in diagrammatic form: *Cv*, valve cell; *G*, germ or zygote with two nuclei; *Pc*, polar capsule with its coiled filament (× 3,000). Spore of microsporidian in diagrammatic form: *Cpf*, coiled polar filament; *N*, nucleus; *Sh*, shell; *Sl*, sleeve of filament; *Vac*, vacuole.

subphylum. They are parasitic, the spores possessing filaments that attach them to their hosts. There are two classes: the Microsporidea and the Myxosporidea.

The Microsporidea, as their name indicates, possess small spores, each having one or two filaments. They are parasites of the cells of arthropods and fishes. The classic example of a microsporid is *Nosema bombycis*, the cause of pebrine diseases in silkworms. The spore is egg-shaped and only two to three microns long. Having been ingested by the silkworm, it liberates an amoeboid stage that forms cells with many nuclei. These cells invade the eggs of their host as they are in the process of formation. When the silkmoth later breeds, the disease is transmitted and affects the larvae (the silkworms). The disease is of economic importance, and can be prevented by destroying the eggs of infected moths. A related species, *Nosema apis*, causes disease in honey bees.

The class Myxosporidea

The electron microscope has revealed that this group of protozoans possess undeniable multicellular characteristics. There are three orders, of which the best-known is the Myxosporidia. These ciliates live as parasites in the tissues and visceral cavities of fishes; a few species attack amphibians

and reptiles. Infections cause severe losses in fish stocks.

In the inactive state, individual myxosporidians are spherical, lens-shaped or leaf-like. More often than not, they are large enough to be visible to the naked eye. Each individual is a syncytium, which consists of a mass of cytoplasm enclosed within a membrane and containing many nuclei not separated from each other by cell membranes. It also contains several amoeba-like cells that move about within the syncytium. The nuclei and the cytoplasm around them are perishable, but the mobile cells are in fact spores and they are capable of survival should the syncytium break up. These cells are germ cells. The system is rather like a multicellular organism, consisting of a perishable body and germ cells that are capable of surviving indefinitely outside the body. However, the method of reproduction in the Myxosporidia differs radically from that of multicelled animals. Even so, the similarity is sufficient to consider that these protozoans may be descended from metazoans (multicellular animals) or from multicellular organisms that have not progressed beyond the separation of the germ cells from the body.

The myxosporidian spore consists of two valves (half shells), an amoeba-like germ cell with a single nucleus, and two polar capsules with coiled filaments. A polar capsule is a cell containing a single nucleus, occupying a large vacuole in the cytoplasm; the filaments are coiled spirally within the cell but are capable of being stretched out.

An example of a myxosporidian is *Myxobolus pfeifferi*, which lives in the gills, muscles and connective tissue of barbels. It causes large tumours up to nearly three inches in diameter to form on these fishes. In the infected organs, the syncytia multiply by breaking up into spheres measuring 1/18 to 1/12 of an inch across. The tumours burst, liberating the spores into the water. These are then swallowed by the barbels, and new syncytia form in their bodies.

The Myxosporidia attack various organs of fishes. The gall bladder attracts *Sphaeromyxa* in seahorses, *Ceratomyxa* in anglerfishes and flatfishes, and *Chloromyxum truttae* in trout (producing jaundice in the last). Muscles are also attacked, *Chloromyxum histolyticum* causing degeneration of the muscles in mackerel. Connective tissue and cartilage may be affected, *Myxosoma cerebralis* living in the cranial cartilages of young salmon and affecting their movements. The body cavity may harbour myxosporidians, as may the urinary bladder. Reptiles and amphibians are also affected, and the gall bladders of toads and frogs may be infected with *Myxidium*.

Two more orders complete the class Myxosporidea. The Actinomyxidia are parasites of aquatic annelids, and the Helicosporidia are found in arthropods.

Life cycle of *Opalina ranarum*, parasite of frogs (*Rana temporaria* and *R. esculenta*): *1*, multinucleate adult form living in the frog's rectum, two nuclei divide; *2a* and *2b*, two modes of fission of the cytoplasm; *3*, cytoplasmic division preceding encystment, producing individuals with a small number of nuclei; *4*, precystic individual with four nuclei; *5*, cyst as it is expelled into the water by the frog at breeding time; *6*, cyst ingested by a young tadpole; *7*, the individual having just left the cyst; *8a*, producer of female gametes (reproductive individuals); *8b*, last division of the individual producing male gametes; *9*, male gamete; *10*, pairing of a male gamete with a female gamete (the larger one); *11*, the fused couple (zygote); *12*, first nuclear division of the zygote; *13*, zygote with ten nuclei; *14*, some zygotes, with small numbers of nuclei, are encysted—these cysts when evacuated are ingested by other tadpoles, in which they form gametes which behave like those originating from the primary cysts. The individual of figure 13 becomes the individual of figure 1 by passing from the tadpole's intestine to the frog's rectum in the course of metamorphosis. *A*, adult frog about to breed; it contains stages 1, 2, 3, 4 and the cysts 5; *B*, very young tadpole ingesting stage 5, stages 6 and 7 take place in its intestine; *C*, older tadpole; *D*, almost wholly metamorphosed frog (it is in the intestine of frogs that stages 8 to 14 take place). The life cycle of *Opalina* is closely adapted to that of its host and is regulated by the amphibian's sex hormones.

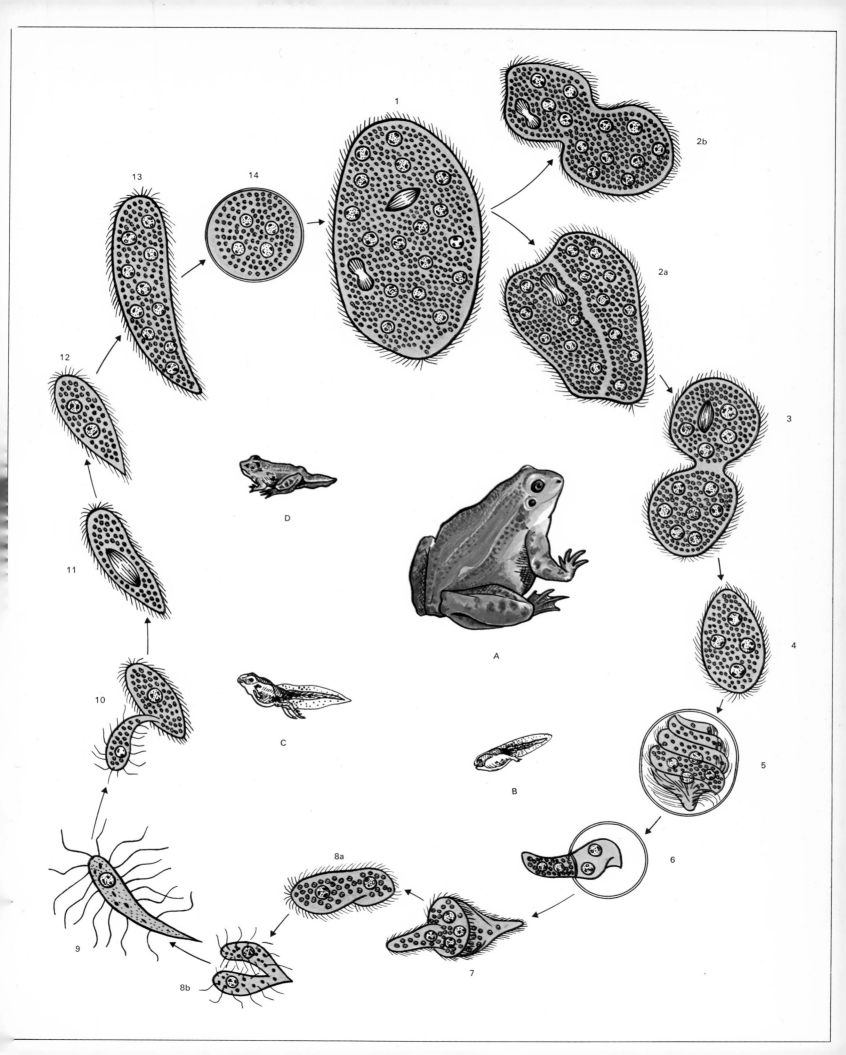

Sponges

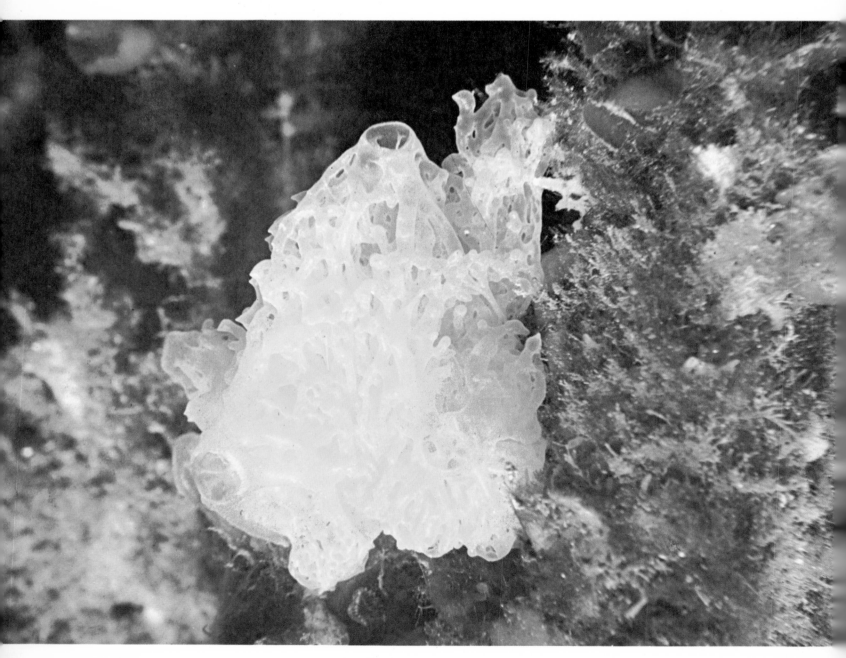

Clathrina clathrus is a calcareous sponge with an entire cavity (homo-coel), remarkable for the wide scope of its polymorphism; it has an encrusting, sheathing, cone-like, or compact appearance (the individual represented here has the cone-like shape, with several large openings or oscula). Port-Vendres, Pyrénées-Orientales: photograph taken at a depth of 9 fathoms. *Photo J. Théodor*

Sponges look like plants, for almost all of them live a fixed life and are unable to move, and they do not have any organs or any movable parts or limbs. Yet they are genuine animals, even if they are very simple ones. The cells that constitute a sponge make up layers of tissue, grouping the sponges with the multicellular animals. Their many differences from other animals indicate that sponges are an offshoot from the main-stream of evolution.

Sponges have been known from the beginnings of recorded history, but it was not until 1765 that naturalists realized that they are animals and not plants. It then took nearly another century for the sponges to be assigned their correct place in the animal kingdom.

The animal kingdom is now generally divided into two sub-kingdoms: the Protozoa or single-celled animals and the Metazoa or many-celled animals. Within the Metazoa there are three branches. The great majority of animals belong to the Enterozoa, meaning they are animals with a digestive tract. Sponges have no digestive tract and the individual cells ingest food; they make up the branch Parazoa (from the Greek *para*, meaning beside). The other branch is the Mesozoa (middle animals), which consists of simple worm-like creatures that have an external layer of digestive cells.

The sponges also make up a single phylum within the Parazoa. This phylum is called the Porifera, meaning pore bearers, as the surface of a sponge is covered with many pores.

A skeleton in the bathroom

'I will do anything ere I will be married to a sponge' exclaims Portia in *The Merchant of Venice*, referring slightingly to the drinking habits of one of her suitors. Anything that soaks up liquid tends to be called a sponge, but this para-doxically is not a property of the animals that originated the term. The bathroom sponge is in fact the skeleton of a sponge from which all the flesh has been stripped. The skeleton is made up of a network of fibres of an elastic material, and water is easily sucked up into the spaces between the fibres and squeezed out again. Nowadays, most of the sponges used for cleaning are made of artificial materials.

The fibres of the skeleton of a natural sponge are com-posed of a protein called spongin. The fibres grow in the living tissue of the sponge just as a vertebrate animal grows bone or horn. About 5000 species of sponges are known. Almost all are marine animals, and they are found in all of the world's oceans. One family of about 150 species

inhabits fresh waters around the world. A study of sponges soon shows that the supple and smooth network of spongin that makes up the bathroom sponge is not the most common skeletal formation in sponges. Usually, a sponge has a rigid skeleton composed of mineral substances; used in the bath-room it would tear the skin to shreds. It consists basically of spicules (needles) of silica or calcium carbonate built into a lattice. In the siliceous sponges of the class Hexactinellida—the glass sponges—the skeleton often consists of a delicate basketwork of glassy threads. These sponges are collected from the deeps of the Indian Ocean.

Classification

The subphylum Porifera is divided into four classes on the basis of the chemical nature of the skeleton.

1. Class Calcarea. The skeleton is composed of spicules of calcium carbonate. The surface is often bristly. *Clathrina, Leucosolenia, Sycon.*
2. Class Demospongiae. The skeleton is composed of silic-eous spicules, or of fibres of spongin, or of both. The spicules are not six-rayed as in glass sponges. *Oscarella, Reniera, Sub-erites, Cliona, Spongilla, Ephydatia, Euspongia* and *Hippospongia* (bath sponges).
3. Class Hexactinellida. The skeleton is composed of siliceous spicules, usually six-rayed (consisting of six branches). The spicules are separate or make up a framework. *Euplectella, Farrea.*
4. Class Sclerospongiae. This is a recently-discovered class of coral-like sponges living in shallow tropical waters. The skeleton is huge—as much as a yard in diameter—and com-posed of crystals of calcium carbonate laid on a base of organic fibres. A thin layer of tissue containing siliceous spicules covers the skeleton. *Ceratoporella, Merlia.*

Because they contain solid spicules or tough, horny fibres, the skeletons of sponges can be found long after the animals themselves have died. The remains of sponges are found as fossils in rocks dating back to Precambrian times—more than 600 million years ago.

Fossil sponges, apart from a few exceptions, differ little from present-day species. The Archaeocyatha of the Cam-brian period (500 to 600 million years ago) were shaped like a whorl of leaves with walls made of two membranes joined by radial partitions; according to a few zoologists, these

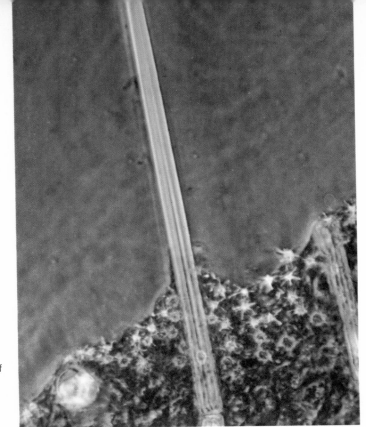

Section of the periphery of the sponge *Tethya lyncurium*: a large axial spicule pierces the siliceous 'skin' made up of a layer of small star-shaped spicules. *Phot. Pavans de Ceccatty*

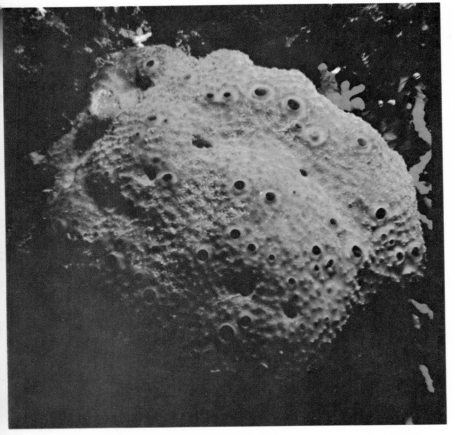

The bath sponge, *Hippospongia equina*, when alive has a skin bristling with the fibres of its horny skeleton, and large openings (oscula) bordered by iris-like membranes. It lives in tropical seas, as well as the Mediterranean. *Phot. P. Coulet*

Natural habitat of some Mediterranean sponges, such as Halichondrinae, proteiform and orange or red, which live in association with algae, corals, sometimes with their polyps expanded, Neptune's lace, and Bryozoa; molluscs leave their gelatinous eggs on them. *Phot. P. Coulet*

animals may represent an intermediate stage in an evolution from protozoans to sponges.

Domestic use

Of the several thousand species of sponges, only a few can be used in the home. Two species, *Euspongia officinalis* and *Hippospongia equina*, are the basis of commercial sponge fishing, which is mainly carried out in only two areas—the warm shallow waters of the Mediterranean Sea and the Gulf of Mexico. The sponges are prised from rocks on the bottom by divers or by dredging them up in various ways. The flesh is killed by treading the sponges, and then removed after it has decayed by beating and washing. The resulting domestic sponges are often cleaned and bleached before being sold. With the advent of the artificial sponge, sponge fishing has declined. The natural supply has decreased in any case, and many natural sponges are now raised in artificial conditions. It takes several years for a sponge to grow to a useful size.

Zoophytes—animals with a plant-like appearance

It took a long time and a great deal of research before the true nature of sponges was realized. Observations carried out by Ellis as long ago as 1765 indicated that sponges are animals and not plants. In 1801, Lamarck listed them as animals to be classified among the polyps, which included the coelenterates, bryozoans and a few other aquatic animals.

Superficial observation would lead one to call sponges plants. Although the sponge's bare skeleton may look like the skeleton of an animal, often being hard and brownish, a sponge has a totally different appearance when alive. Many sponges are coloured as brightly as flowers, and those with branched skeletons look like exotic plants growing in the seabed. Sponges may also encrust themselves over rocks, rather as mosses do, and they may appear spherical or cup-shaped, not unlike fungi. However, despite all these resemblances to plants, sponges cannot perform the vital auto-trophic processes of plants; that is, they cannot produce their own food from the substances that surround them. Some green sponges may appear to be able to carry out photosynthesis, but these sponges owe their colour to the presence of microscopic plants in their tissues, such as the green algae found in some freshwater species. Unlike chlorophyll, the pigments that sponges themselves contain lack the power of photosynthesis. Sponges are therefore true animals, unable to manufacture their food supply and able to build their tissues only by consuming organic substances existing in other organisms. They are microphagous, feeding on bacteria and food particles suspended in the water.

Finding a place in the animal kingdom

Observations of how sponges obtain their food supply established that they are animals, but there still remained the problem of how to classify them within the animal kingdom. Could they be protozoans? That would mean that they were unicellular animals living in vast colonies of thousands of individuals, but capable of acting in a more or less co-ordinated way and of building a single skeleton in each colony. This suggestion was believed for some time. Then it was proposed that sponges are in fact metazoans. They appear to resemble multicellular animals in that each cell specializes to some extent in one or more particular functions and con-

The green cliona, *Cliona viridis*, is a siliceous sponge, the gaping oscula of which can be seen in the photograph. It fixes itself to varied supports, e.g. shell and calcareous rock: it perforates these, burying itself in the thickness of them, leaving only its oscula outside. As it grows, it develops outside the support, extends itself over it (covering form) or envelops it entirely (solid form). Size and shape are extremely variable; some individuals from the South Seas weigh, when fresh, nearly 4 cwts. *Under-sea photo. Théodor*

tributes to the well-being of the complete animal and is dependent on it. We know this is so today, although it took a long time to establish this fact because sponges have so many features that are unlike other multicellular animals. This is recognized in the placing of the sponges in a separate branch of the Metazoa—the Parazoa. Indeed, some experts separate the Parazoa from the Metazoa completely.

The temptation to separate the two groups is great. If a sponge feeds like an animal, it is more in the physiology of cell nutrition than in its anatomical adaptations for feeding and feeding behaviour. Sponges are sessile creatures, living fixed to a rock or to the shell of another animal, either alive or dead. The sponge can move only if transported by another animal, and therefore depends on the mercy of the current or its host to bring food its way. In order to feed and grow, the sponge filters the surrounding water, drawing it into the depths of its tissues through a multitude of small pores covering the surface of its body. Each of these orifices admits the water to a canal system running throughout the body of the sponge. The canal system may be simple, but is usually complex; it can be likened to the blood vessels that run throughout the tissues of higher animals. The water is pumped through the pores by the action of whip-like flagella. These flagella grow from the cells that make up the inner lining of the body wall of the sponge, and line some or all of the canals in the sponge. The cells are called choanocytes. The base of each flagellum is housed in a collar extending

from the cell body. Such a cellular organization is by no means unique to the sponges, for the choanocytes resemble protozoans of the flagellate order Choanoflagellida. The resemblance raises the question as to whether the two groups are related in any way.

The beating of the flagella of the choanocytes draws water deep into the sponge's internal cavities. The same mechanism pumps the water along the canals, and out through an opening called the osculum. In a simple sponge, the pores open into a large central cavity called the spongocoel and the osculum is at the top of this cavity. Most sponges are more complex, and have narrow radial canals leading from the pores to the spongocoel, which may consist of a whole series of canals connecting to the exterior through several openings lying among the pores. The body surface may also be constructed so that it contains small incurrent canals that lead to the pores.

The surface of the sponge is therefore pierced by a large number of orifices—by pores and incurrent canals leading water into the sponge, and by one or more oscula expelling water. The name Porifera, which summarizes this unique feature, was given to the sponges in 1836. The flow of water through the body of a sponge can be truly phenomenal. The large sponges of the Bahamas have been recorded as filtering water at the rate of about half a gallon per minute, or more than 600 imperial gallons per day.

A sponge, therefore, is a fairly compact fleshy animal,

with a body that consists anatomically of a water vascular system made up of flagellated canals and external openings. The skeleton varies greatly in nature, but is always deployed throughout the canal system to support the tissues surrounding the canals. It maintains the outline of the sponge, though its structure is unlike that of the skeleton of any other metazoan.

The internal circulation system is used to provide the sponge with food. The cells exposed to the water, especially the choanocytes, extract plant debris, micro-organisms and any other food particles suspended in the water. Like many protozoans and many cells of metazoans, such as the white blood corpuscles of vertebrates, the cells of sponges extend a short projection of the cytoplasm around their prey and then draw it back into the cell, which engulfs it. This process of ingesting micro-organisms is known as phagocytosis. The Russian bacteriologist Ilya Metchnikov studied this phenomenon in sponges before discovering that it occurred throughout the animal kingdom; it operates as a means of nutrition and also as a way of defending an organism against bacteria. The discovery gained Metchnikov the Nobel Prize for physiology and medicine in 1908.

Recent research

Sponges may have a unique anatomy, but when it comes to their individual cells, it may seem that they hardly differ from other animals. In fact, it is the detailed study of the cells and tissues of these animals that yields the most meaningful observations about them.

The animal nature of the sponge and its metazoan character has been confirmed by an impressive body of recent research.

On the Tunisian Sea, rich in commercial sponges, a specialized fishing fleet still operates. After having been dredged up, the sponges are pulled out of the water, leaving their genital products and larvae behind. They are then strung out on a rope to dry. *Phot. Pavans de Ceccatty*

Cross-fertilization

Under the influence of factors that are still not completely understood, and among which ecological changes and conditions certainly play an important role, sponges begin sexual activity and produce gametes (sex cells) in their tissues. In certain species, it is believed that the male and female sexes exist as separate individuals (although they cannot be distinguished from one another); other species, much more common, are hermaphrodite. In the hermaphrodite species, a delay occurs in the production of gametes of different sexes. Sperms are not produced at the same time as eggs, so that fertilization can occur only when the gametes of two separate individuals meet; this is cross-fertilization.

The various mechanisms of fertilization operate in very set ways. The sperms, which are like the sperms of metazoan animals in structure, are formed in spermatic cysts, which are small chambers disseminated throughout the canal systems or sometimes concentrated at their very heart. Each cyst acts as a testis, and is crammed with sperms. In this way, the sponge shelters a large number of testes scattered throughout its body or concentrated into particular areas. The cysts liberate the sperms into the water circulating through the canals, and they are swept rapidly to the exterior by the exhalant currents. The sperms are free-swimming, being able to move with the aid of a flagellum, and eventually reach other sponges. They are sucked in through the pores of a sponge and circulate through its canal system.

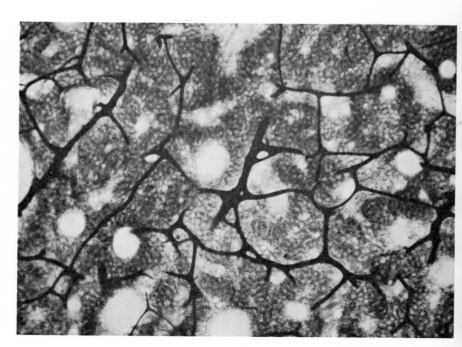

In all the spaces of the horny network of the bath sponge, the living tissues trace canals, vast lacunae and tiny hollow spheres, in which the water circulates continuously. *Phot. Pavans de Ceccatty*

If cross-fertilization is to occur, the new sponge will have entered the stage at which it is producing female gametes or eggs. These are formed in the flagellated chambers lining the canals and move to positions under the choanocytes. The eggs are numerous, being scattered throughout the tissue of the sponge. The presence of the eggs beneath the choano-cytes seems to influence the sperms and guide them towards the flagella lining the canals. There the sperms are captured by the choanocytes by the process of phagocytosis, but they are not digested. Instead they are transported by the choanocytes to the eggs, thus effecting fertilization (see the diagram on page 45).

The extraordinary properties of the sponge's cells

The choanocyte therefore has a dual function within the sponge. It is primarily built to aid nutrition, for the choanocytes capture food particles and digest them in their food vacuoles as well as using their flagella to produce water currents that bring the food particles to them. Then, as mentioned above, choanocytes are also involved in sexual reproduction. This multiplicity of functions within one particular cell is not a metazoan characteristic at all, for the multicelled animals normally assign one particular function to each group of cells within their bodies.

In some sponges, the choanocytes can take on yet another job. In the case of the males of the bath sponge *Hippospongia equina*, the testes develop in the flagellated chambers themselves, and it is the direct transformation of choanocytes into sperms that produces the gametes. In the females, however, the processes of egg formation are the same as those described above: the eggs form independently of the choanocytes, which later function in bringing the sperms and eggs together to effect fertilization. One of the first consequences of this observation was a querying of August Weismann's biological theory, which states the formation of germ cells or sex cells is always distinct and independent of the other groups of cells in the body. It was in the sponges that confirmation was found for counter arguments to this theory, which was also called into question by evidence culled from the Coelenterata and the Bryozoa phyla.

Be that as it may, the particular way in which sponges undergo sexual reproduction leads to a proliferation of countless embryos within the lining of the canal wall of the female parent or of the hermaphrodite parent that is in its female phase. The embryos develop flagella on one surface, and then separate from the parent and are swept out through its osculum to become free-swimming larvae. In the months of May and June, Mediterranean sponge fishermen find that bath sponges emit, at the least pressure, a thick whitish fluid containing millions of gametes and larvae. The fishermen have discovered that this embryonic fluid is beneficial in healing wounds.

The development of the embryos of sponges also gives rise to difficulties when it comes to relating sponges to the Metazoa.

The fertilized egg divides three times to produce eight cells arranged in a circle like slices of a cake. The next division produces eight more cells as an upper layer above the first eight cells. The first layer will become the epidermis (outer surface) of the sponge and the second layer will become the choaonocytes. This second layer is called the blastula and, as it develops, each cell acquires a flagellum on its inner surface. The embryo becomes a hollow sphere with internal flagella. In calcareous sponges, the embryo then turns itself inside-out so that the flagella point outwards. This stage is called an amphiblastula, and it is at this point that the embryo detaches itself from its parent and becomes a larva, swimming with the aid of the flagellated cells. The larva eventually settles and fixes itself to a support, and grows into a

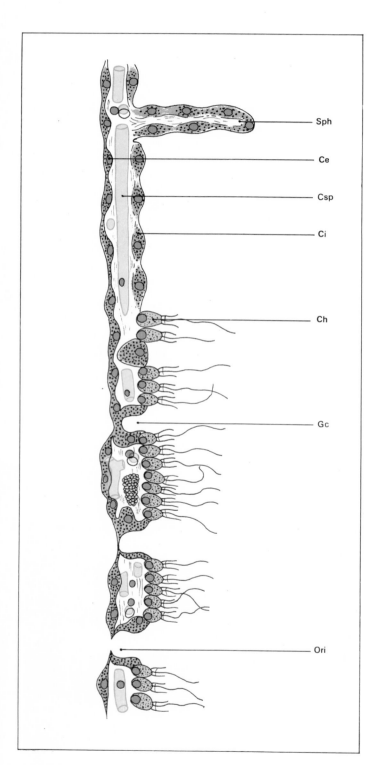

Longitudinal section of the wall of the oscular tube of a calcareous sponge, *Clathrina coriacea: Ce*, cells of the outer covering; *Ch*, flagellated collar cell; *Ci*, cells of the inner covering; *Csp*, calcareous spicule; *Gc*, gastral cavity; *Ori*, inhalant orifice; *Sph*, circular sphincter for closing the osculum; *After E. A. Minchin*

young sponge. The outward turning in its embryonic development is similar to a stage in the development of colonies of the protozoan flagellate *Volvox*.

Development is somewhat different in siliceous sponges. The larval stage takes the form of a ciliated ball, similar to certain coelenterate larvae. However, its evolution into the adult state and the development of its cell layers are peculiar to sponges.

Although the embryonic development of calcareous and siliceous sponges has similarities with the protozoans in one case and coelenterates in the other, it nevertheless leads to a common type of animal. This type is found in two phyla—the Porifera and the Coelenterata—and it is characterized by the possession of two fundamental layers of tissue. The external or peripheral layer is the ectodermal layer, and the internal layer is the endodermal layer. Such animals are known as diploblastic, and they differ from all other metazoans, which are triploblastic and develop their organs from three layers of tissue.

It is possible to relate the diploblastic animals to the triploblastic animals by considering that their development stops at the two-layer stage, whereas the more highly evolved triploblastic animals temporarily assume this form in the course of their development towards a more complex architecture. This illustrates the fundamental biogenetic law or theory of recapitulation, put forward by the German zoologist Ernst Haeckel, which states that animals repeat, in the course of their development, the forms that their ancestors underwent in the course of evolution. Thus, the embryonic stage (the gastrula) of highly evolved metazoans corresponds to the diploblastic forms of primitive metazoans.

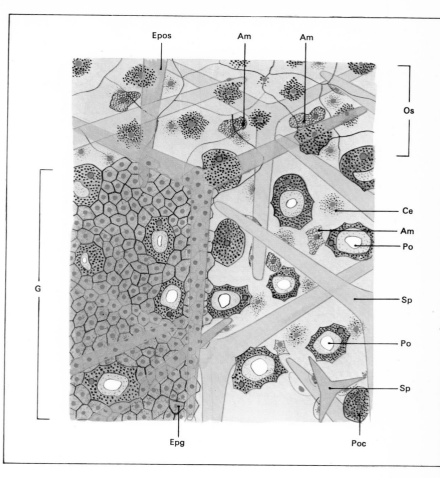

Portion of the wall of a calcareous sponge, *Clathrina coriacea*, seen from within (gastric surface). The gastric epithelium is represented only at the level of the bracket *G*. Elsewhere, it has been removed, except in the upper part of the diagram (bracket *Os*), which corresponds to the osculum and in which the gastric epithelium is replaced by an epithelium with large granulose cells. *Am*, granulose amoeboid cells; *Ce*, cell of the outer epithelium; *Epg*, epithelium of the gastric cavity; *Epos*, cells of the oscular epithelium; *Po*, cells of an inhalant pore or porocytes; *Poc*, porocyte contracted; *Sp*, calcareous spicules. This representation is a diagrammatic reconstruction which does not account for the extreme contractility of the cells constituting the wall of the sponge. *After E. A. Minchin*

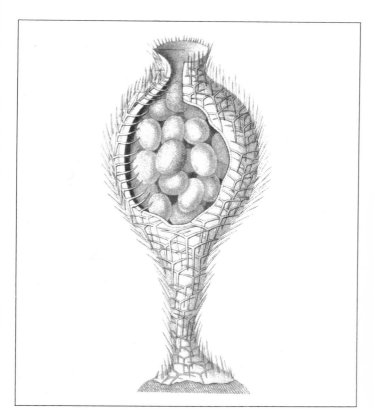

The sycon is the prototype of the calcareous sponges; it is a sac lined internally with flagellated collar cells (homocoel sponge). It lives in most seas. This specimen has its gastral cavity wide open to show the developing eggs that fill it. In the course of their development, many sponges pass through a sycon stage. *After E. Haeckel*

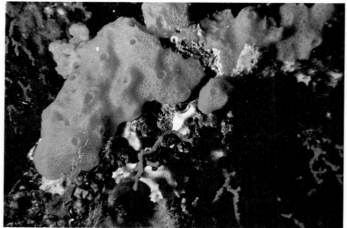

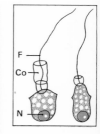

Flagellated collar cells or isolated choanocytes: *Co*, collarette; *F*, flagellum; *N*, nucleus.

On the demosponge, *Hymeniacidon sanguinea*, one can distinguish very clearly the different openings of the system of internal canals. The inhalant pores are much smaller and more numerous than the exhalant oscula. This fine species is found in exceptional abundance on some Mediterranean sea bottoms. *Phot. P. Coulet*

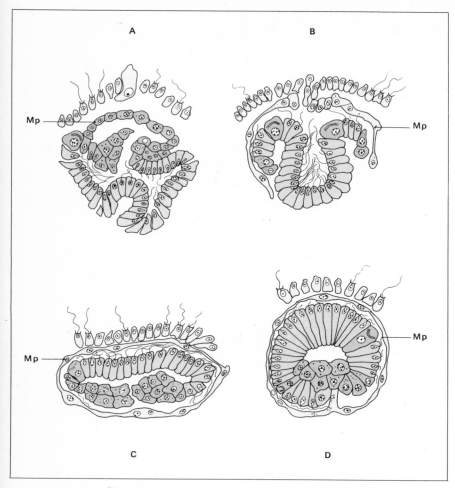

Phases of the embryonic development of the calcareous sponge *Sycon raphanus* showing the turning inside out of the embryo at the blastula larva (stomoblastula) stage: *A*, the blastula seen in section at the beginning of extraversion; *B*, the larva has opened out and the lips of the opening are inverted, i.e. their outer surfaces become inner, and vice versa; *C*, extraversion is completed. (*Mp*, membrane described as placental, is formed by the larva but separated from it, and serves to feed the larva developing in its mother's body.) A similar turning inside out of the walls is observed in the volvocale genus *Volvox*. After O. Duboscq and O. Tuzet

Raising sponges from cuttings

So far, we have dealt with the sexual reproduction of sponges, but sponges are also capable of asexual reproduction. The mechanics of this form of reproduction furnish us with more proof that these animals are far from simple, however primitive they may be in relation to the Metazoa in general. The somewhat haphazard method of sexual reproduction is here abandoned for a far more certain mode of propagation.

The freshwater sponge *Spongilla lacustris*, which is commonly found in sunlit running water, provides a good example of asexual reproduction. At the onset of unfavourable climatic conditions, small spherical buds with tough walls reinforced with spicules form inside the sponge. These buds are known as gemmules. As the sponge dies and its body disintegrates, the gemmules are shed into the water. Their tough coverings resist external conditions until these again become favourable, for example in the spring. Then the mass of cells inside the gemmule leaves its covering, and begins to grow into a new sponge.

This method of reproduction is found in all freshwater sponges and in some marine species. In the latter, the gemmules often develop into free-swimming larvae. Many other sponges increase by budding. Buds develop on a sponge and either separate and grow into new individual sponges, or remain on the parent sponge and increase its bulk.

Sponges have extraordinary powers of regeneration. Some sponges can be pushed through the mesh of a piece of fine silk so that they are broken up into a mass of separate cells. These cells will then move towards each other in an amoeba-like fashion, and congregate together to form a small new sponge identical in form to the old sponge. It is therefore possible to cut a sponge up into small pieces and, given suitable conditions, each piece will grow into a new sponge —rather like growing plants from cuttings. Raising sponges in this way could be more profitable than fishing for sponges; when the natural supply of sponges declined, experiments in commercial sponge culture began. Trials succeeded in India and British Honduras just before the Second World War but were subsequently abandoned. Sponges are now raised commercially in Florida and Italy. Pieces of sponge about three inches across are fixed to a support of concrete or a similar material in clean running water. The sponges grow

More or less encrusted on the rock, *Chondrosia reniformis* of the Tetractinellida (blue-brown), is side by side with *Hymeniacidon sanguinea* (spicules with single axis, red); the latter's water-bearing canals converge towards the gaping osculum and are remarkably swollen. *Phot. P. Coulet*

slowly, and it takes several years for them to reach a marketable size.

Sponge culture is also taking place in laboratories, though on species highly unsuitable for domestic use. Biologists are examining all the various modes of asexual reproduction of which sponges are capable, reopening old lines of inquiry with the aid of the latest developments in chemistry and tissue culture and, of course, the electron microscope.

Complexity is unnecessary

A study of the anatomy of a sponge shows a system of canals varying in complexity and a skeleton, and very little else. However, this simple structure should not lead one to suppose that sponges are incapable of carrying out every fundamental animal function. Respiration, digestion and excretion all take place in the individual cells, as they do in protozoans. There is no need for the special organs—stomachs, intestines, blood vessels, etc.—that make up the anatomy of more complex creatures. Another group of organs that the sponge does not require are organs of de-

threaten oyster beds, for the sponges are liable to eat the plankton that the oysters need to grow.

The paradox of sponges

There are several features of sponges that do not always make sense. Sponges seem to be able to get away with certain details of structure that could not possibly occur in other animals and are therefore difficult to explain.

It is possible to make grafts between two different genera of Mediterranean sponges, and natural hybrids of two different species are to be found in Antarctic waters. That two animals classified as entirely separate species can come together and produce a living hybrid challenges the validity of the general principles that establish the biochemical personalities of groups of animals. Normally, substances called antigens in the invading tissue stimulate antibody production in the host tissue, and the two react to reject the foreign tissue. This mechanism fights infection. One would imagine, therefore, that antigen-antibody systems do not form in sponges, as hybrids can be made between different

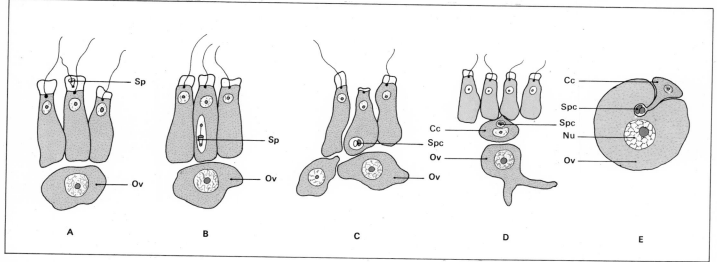

Indirect fertilization of the calcareous sponge, *Sycon raphanus*: *A*, penetration of the spermatozoid *Sp* into the collarette of a choanocyte (flagellated collar cell); *B*, the spermatozoid has penetrated into the choanocyte; *C*, in the choanocyte, the spermatozoid is surrounded by a vacuole with a thick membrane. It becomes the spermiocyst (*Spc*), and loses its flagellum and its collar; *D*, the choanocyte leaves its place, moves like an amoeba and carries the spermiocyst; it is named, then, 'carrying cell' *Cc*; under this cell is an oocyte; *E*, shown in greater magnification, the carrying cell *Cc* inoculates the spermiocyst into the egg. *Nu*, nucleus; *Ov*, oocyte or egg. Before being fertilized, the oocytes fall into the cavity of a flagellated chamber, then resume their places again under the choanocyte. *After O. Duboscq and O. Tuzet*

fence, for sponges seldom fall prey to other animals. Their skeletons and the unappetizing secretions that they produce effectively deter almost all other creatures from trying to eat them, though some molluscs and insect larvae feed on sponges. The sponges themselves shelter all kinds of small aquatic creatures within their canals—crustaceans, molluscs, worms and even fishes. Some crabs take advantage of the regenerative powers of sponges to defend themselves. They tear off pieces from a sponge and then apply the pieces to their shells. The sponges regenerate themselves and come to cover the crab's shell; as few predators will attack sponges, the crab is safe beneath one. Some hermit crabs actually live inside a cavity in a sponge. Sponges will also grow naturally on marine animals, especially molluscs. They may

species. However, the existence of such systems has been reported in these animals.

Ciliated cells of the larvae of *Mycale contarenii* normally give rise to the choanocytes of the adult sponge, but in some cases this evolution does not occur and the choanocytes form from other cells. Such observations contravene many theories of embryo formation.

The pores and oscula of sponges can close and open and one would therefore expect to find contractile cells. Such cells normally contain the muscle proteins actin and myosin, but these proteins have not been detected in sponges.

Cells that resemble the nerve cells of higher animals have been found in sponges, but experimenters have been unable to detect any impulses travelling through these cells.

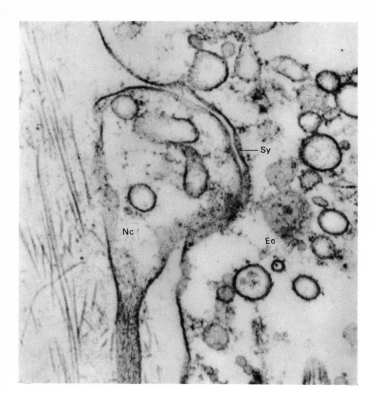

Polarized contact or synapse (*Sy*) between the fine prolongation of a cell of nervous type (*Nc*) and the body of an epithelial cell (*Ec*), in *Tethya lyncurium* (electron microscopy). *Phot. Pavans de Ceccatty*

'Budding' polarized junction, of similar morphology to that of a synapse, between two cells of nervous type in *Hippospongia equina*. The fine prolongation (*Nc*) of a cell is articulated with the periphery of the other's body (*Bo*). Cellular differentiation in sponges goes further than was thought, but remains far from that observed in the Triploblastica (electron microscopy). *Phot. Pavans de Ceccatty*

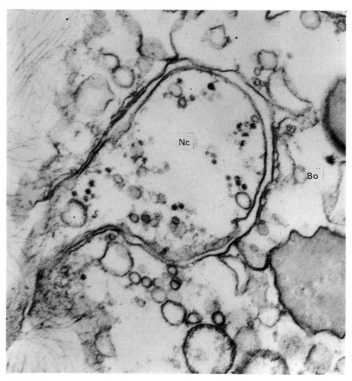

A republic of cells

In spite of all the paradoxes that come to light when sponges are studied, these animals should not be thought of as a group totally apart from other animals. They are a group to be placed beside the others—the Parazoa—but within rather than outside the Metazoa, for there are too many resemblances between the sponges and the other metazoans for a link not to be forged between them. Examples of similarities can be found in the structure and formation of the gametes, in the chromosomes, and in nuclear division. To take just one example of a common factor that seems to link the two groups firmly together, chemical analysis and electron microscopy have revealed that fibres of spongin are composed of the fibrous protein collagen, which is common to all metazoans but is unknown in protozoans as well as plants.

...and a society of workers

Sponges should therefore be thought of as multicellular beings. Their mode of existence follows the same basic pattern as that of the all other metazoans, which is a pattern in which various activities are integrated into a co-ordinated whole. The pattern is very simple in the sponge, there being an outer layer of cells that forms a protective epidermis and an inner layer of cells that individually perform the essential functions of respiration, digestion and reproduction. Like the higher animals, the sponge is a coherent organism in which groups of cells take on different tasks, rather as workers are organized into different groups on a production line. The strict compartmentalization and narrow specialization of the cells of higher animals does not occur, but the basic pattern is the same.

Sponges do not possess organs as higher animals do, but their cells are gathered into different kinds of tissues. The tissue is an intermediate stage between the fundamental cell and the organ, for organs are made of tissues which are made of cells. In turn, the higher animals are assemblages of organs. We can consider the sponge as the primitive tissue, a mode of life reflecting the basis on which all higher animals —and ultimately ourselves—are built.

Such reflections on the basic nature of sponges and their implications regarding the remainder of the animal kingdom have not been a preoccupation of man for very long, even though sponges have been known to mankind for many centuries. Rather, mankind has been more concerned with the practical uses of sponges. Sponges have never ceased to be familiar to us as features of everyday life, since the time when the women of ancient Greece soothed their babies by giving them a piece of sponge soaked in honey to suck, since the 13th century when doctors in Europe used burnt sponge to treat scrofula, and since the 16th century when the same remedy was recommended for goitre (not without success, for the sponge contained iodine which is essential in the treatment of goitre). Nowadays a natural sponge is a possession of some value, for whereas an artificial sponge might be good enough for washing the car, there is no substitute for a real sponge at bathtime. As supply declines, so value rises, and no modern well-appointed bathroom should be without a natural sponge or two. Next time you luxuriously lather yourself with one, spare a thought for the lowly creature that provides you with such comfort.

Above
On a bottom rich in red coral, the siliceous sponge *Petrosia dura*, with oscula wide open, is browsed on by a spotted nudibranch mollusc, *Peltodoris atromaculata. Phot. P. Coulet*

Below
Verongia aerophoba is a hexactinellid sponge which lives in shallow water. Under-sea photograph taken at five fathoms, at Cape Creus, between Cadaques and Puerto de la Selva. *Phot. Théodor*

Coelenterates

The coelenterates include some of the most beautiful animals in the sea: the plant-like sea anemones, the stony corals, the spreading sea fans and the quill-like sea pens, all of which live on the seabed; and the shimmering jellyfishes, which drift or swim serenely through the sea. For all their beauty, they are animals to be treated with caution, for they inflict painful stings on an unwary predator.

The coelenterates make up the phylum Coelenterata. The name means 'hollow intestine' in Greek and refers to the animals' digestive tract, which is like a sac and has only one opening. Food is taken in and waste eliminated through this single orifice. The name Cnidaria is also commonly used for this phylum. It comes from the Greek word for nettle, and refers to the stinging tentacles that these animals use to capture their prey and to defend themselves. Some authorities prefer the term Cnidaria, because the phylum Coelenterata once included the ctenophores (comb jellies) as well as the coelenterates. The two groups are now distinct, and the ctenophores make up their own phylum. The ctenophores do not possess nematocysts (stinging cells), and so the name Cnidaria accurately distinguishes the sea anemones, corals and their allies from the comb jellies. However, the name coelenterate is in popular use for them, and their phylum will therefore be referred to as the Coelenterata. It reflects the fact that these animals are the most primitive of the Enterozoa—the great group of multicellular animals that possess a digestive tract. Their most primitive characteristic is the formation of tissues from two embryonic layers of cells, the endoderm and ectoderm. They share this feature with the sponges. All other animals of the Metazoa—the multi-celled animals—build their tissues from three layers of cells.

The coelenterates assume two forms. They may exist as a polyp, which is a larva-like creature with a tube-shaped body; one end is closed and attached to a support, and the other end is open, forming a mouth surrounded by tentacles. Alternatively, a coelenterate may be found as a medusa, an umbrella-shaped animal composed of jelly-like tissues armed with tentacles surrounding a mouth on the under-surface.

Many coelenterates assume both forms during their life cycle. Reproduction is usually asexual in the polyp stage and always sexual in the medusa stage.

Coelenterates are mostly marine creatures, although a few are to be found in brackish water and fresh water. They are world-wide in distribution, and occur in an immense variety of forms and colours. There are about 10,000 species. The smallest are microscopic, but the largest jellyfish weighs almost a ton and has tentacles over 100 feet long. Coelenterates often form large colonies, but many live singly.

The phylum Coelenterata is divided into three classes: the Hydrozoa or hydroids; the Scyphozoa or jellyfishes; and the Anthozoa or corals and sea anemones.

The Acropora or Madrepora are madrepore corals known in the fossil state since the Tertiary era. They are represented in the fauna of the reefs by numerous wonderfully-coloured species (*left*).

Under-seascape in a New Caledonia coral reef. Sponges, madrepores, sea anemones and gorgonians are exposed in all their magnificence, strangeness of shapes and explosion of colours, in perfectly transparent tepid water. *Phot. Théodor*

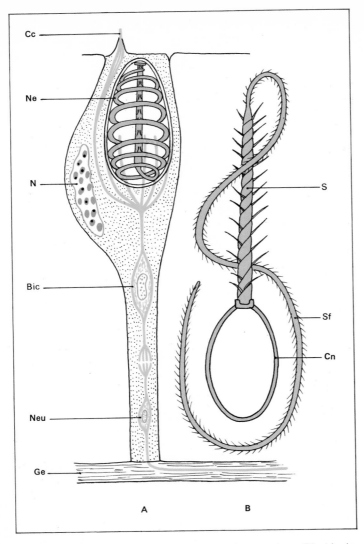

A, diagram of the stinging cell of an acephalous medusa: *Bic*, bipolar nerve cell which sends out fibres around the nematocyst *Ne*, a stinging device, full of poison; *Cc*, cnidocil or sensitive process, the excitation of which triggers off the evagination of the nematocyst; *Ge*, mesogloea; *N*, nucleus of the stinging cell; *Neu*, neurone playing the role of association cell. *B*, diagram of the evaginated nematocyst: *Cn*, capsule of the nematocyst; *S*, shaft of the filament; *Sf*, stinging filament.

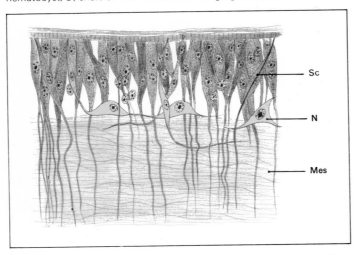

Transverse section of the ectoderm of a coelenterate polyp. In yellow, neurones *N*, against the mesogloea and the sensory cells *Sc*. This nervous system displays indisputable progress over that of the sponges. *After Bozler*

The class Hydrozoa

In the coelenterates of this class, the mouth opens directly into the digestive cavity, there being no pharynx. Also, the gastric cavity is not divided by partitions (septa), as is the case in the other classes.

The orders within this class are the Hydroida, in which the polyp stage is well developed; the Trachylina, in which the medusa stage is most developed; the Milleporina and Stylasterina, which have polyps surrounded by calcareous external skeletons; the Siphonophora, which live in large colonies that swim or float in the open sea; and the Actinulida, which are small, ciliated, solitary hydrozoans.

The orders Hydroida and Trachylina

These are the simplest of the coelenterates in structure, and their features serve to describe the basic characteristics of the Coelenterata. Most exist as polyps and medusae, the fixed polyps producing free-living medusae by budding and the medusae uniting to breed polyps. However, the Hydroida have well-developed polyps and small medusae; some, such as *Hydra* of fresh waters, undergo no medusa stage. In the Trachylina, the polyp stage is reduced and may be absent, and the medusae are of some size.

Polyps

Polyps generally form colonies by budding off new members and only rarely are they solitary. *Hydra* is a solitary polyp that has been much studied.

A hydroid polyp consists fundamentally of a hollow tube surmounted by a dome (the hypostome) at the top of which is the mouth; the mouth is surrounded, in most cases, by a crown of tentacles. The dome or hypostome and the tentacles play an essential role in capturing prey. The mouth leads directly to the gastric cavity, which takes up the interior of the tube. More tentacles may line the outside wall of the gastric cavity. On the walls appear protuberances that become free-living medusae or gonads that remain fixed to the polyp and produce eggs or sperms. The gastric cavity is closed towards the base of the polyp, which in colonial polyps is occupied by a region called the stolon that is concerned with the support of the colony.

Between the gastric cavity and the stolon is a muscular sphincter that prevents bulky fragments of prey passing from the gastric cavity into the stolon. The stolon consists of a tubular network of body cells, and is enveloped in a sheath composed mainly of chitin and called the perisarc. The stolon is the most important and durable structure in hydroid colonies. The stolons of some of the members serve to fix the colony to a support and give it its shape, but they also preserve the means of renewal of the colony. In many species, the medusae and gonads develop in the stolon region. Furthermore, when external conditions become severe, as in winter, the whole of the colony may die and disintegrate, leaving only the protected stolons. When conditions improve, a new colony will grow from the stolons.

The stolons of a colony may grow outwards, forming a colony that spreads out over a support. Alternatively, they may grow upwards and then branch outwards, forming bushy or feather-like growths. New polyps are formed as the existing members of a colony bud, and they communicate with each other by means of a common digestive cavity. Some polyps do not form colonies but live a solitary existence. These polyps do not possess a stolon, and they fasten themselves to a support by means of an adhesive disc, as in *Hydra*, or by an anchoring device, as in *Branchiocerianthus*.

Different kinds of tentacles are to be found in hydroids, depending on the distribution of the nematocysts. In the most primitive species, the tentacles are similar in structure and are haphazardly arranged around the mouth and the gastric cavity. In more specialized forms, the tentacles are arranged in several circles; in some, these take the form of two crowns of tentacles, one around the mouth and the other around the gastric cavity. Other species may have only one ring of tentacles around the mouth, and this ring may be incomplete. Finally, there are some species, such as *Protohydra* and *Limnocnida*, which are always devoid of tentacles.

In the suborder Anthomedusae of the order Hydroida (the

cerned with sexual reproduction, and still others that play a defensive role in the colony, being armed with stinging cells or with chitinous spines. These various types of polyps are particularly to be found in colonies of *Hydractinia echinata*, which is an athecate hydroid (a hydroid not protected by a theca or shield) that lives on mollusc shells inhabited by hermit crabs.

The body wall of a polyp is made up of two layers of cells. One, the epidermis or ectoderm, is external and has a protective role and the other, the gastrodermis or endoderm, is internal and is concerned with digestion. These two layers are separated by a thin non-cellular sheet called the mesoglea, which is secreted by both the surrounding layers and serves to support the body. The epidermis forms the outer covering of the animal's body; it is made up mainly of epitheliomuscular cells that contain fibrils attached to the mesoglea. The fibrils contract to shorten the body and tentacles of the hydroid. Other kinds of cells are to be found

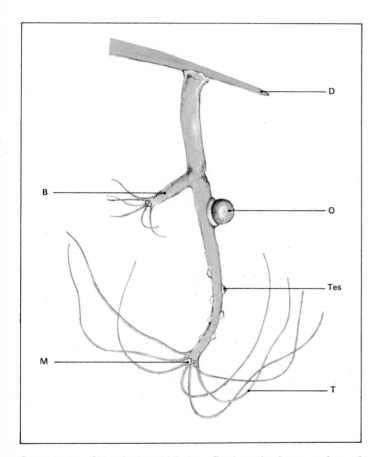

Green hydra, *Chlorohydra viridissima*, fixed to the lower surface of duckweed, *Lemna*, showing both a tentacled bud and genital organs of both sexes: *B*, bud; *D*, duckweed; *M*, mouth; *O*, ovary; *T*, tentacles; *Tes*, testes.

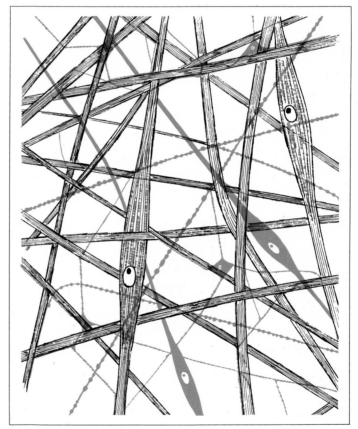

Under the ectoderm of medusae, there extends a network (or plexus) of true nerve cells, or neurones (coloured red), which transmit the stimuli received by the sense organs, as well as the impulses controlling the movements. *After Bozler*

gymnoblast hydroids), the horny perisarc that envelops the stolon region stops at the level of the sphincter. In the Leptomedusae (the calyptoblast hydroids), the perisarc continues beyond the stem to form protective cup-like shields around the base of the tentacles and around the medusa buds. These shields are known as the hydrotheca and gonotheca respectively. The tentacles can be withdrawn into the hydrotheca for protection.

In colonies of hydroids, the component individuals often occur in several different forms and have different functions. There are some polyps concerned with nutrition, others con-

between the epitheliomuscular cells. They include nematocysts (stinging cells), interstitial cells concerned with regeneration, nerve cells, sensory cells and glandular cells.

The nematocyst is characteristic of the Coelenterata. It is not in fact a complete cell, but a structure within a modified interstitial cell known as a cnidoblast. The nematocyst is a capsule containing a coiled thread tube. The tube may be uniform in diameter or may consist of a dilated shaft and a tapered filament; each of these parts may be smooth or armed on the inside with spines of varying size and appearance. The arrangement and combination of these various elements makes it possible to distinguish about twenty types of nematocyst structure, on which the classification and identification of hydroids depends. The capsule of the nematocyst also contains a fluid that is usually capable of paralysing the prey. The bottom part of the cnidoblast below the capsule contains the nucleus of the cell and a group of fibres that connect the cell to the mesoglea. The top of the cell bears a lid for the capsule and a bristle called the cnidocil. The nematocyst works in rather the same way as a harpoon. The cnidocil may act rather like a mechanical trigger and 'fire' the stinging cell, but other factors such as the mere presence of prey in the water also cause it to discharge. The capsule opens and the thread tube is ejected and sinks like a harpoon into the prey, which consists of larvae, small crustaceans and worms. As it leaves the cell, the tube is turned inside-out (like the finger of a glove being turned inside-out), and the spines that were formerly on the inside now stick out from the tube and inject the paralysing fluid into the prey. The thread tube cannot be withdrawn to strike again, and both it and the cnidoblast are digested by the hydroid and replaced by a new cell.

The kind of nematocyst described above is only one of several kinds. Some thread tubes produce a sticky secretion and attach themselves to the prey rather than penetrate the body of the prey. Others coil themselves around part of the prey. The discharge of the thread tube from the cnidoblast is probably caused by a combination of chemical and mechanical stimuli, and the cnidocil is believed to play an important role in the perception and transmission of these stimuli.

Organisms living commensally with coelenterates, such as hermit crabs occupying mollusc shells covered with hydroids and sea anemones, are immune to the toxins produced by their defenders' stinging cells. The serum of animals that have such an immunity will confer immunity on other animals injected with it. However, immunity to the toxins of coelenterates is exceptional for these toxins are in most cases anaphylactic; that is, the first injection of the toxin makes a wounded organism highly sensitive to the toxin so that if the first injection does not kill, a second weaker injection will do so. The first demonstration of the phenomenon of anaphylaxis was made by injecting coelenterate toxin into a dog.

Interstitial cells that remain in an undeveloped state are often inserted between the epitheliomuscular cells. They are concerned with the replacement of cnidoblasts and other kinds of cells, and also with asexual reproduction by budding and sexual reproduction by the formation of gametes. However, recent experiments have shown that these cells are not indispensable to the survival of a mutilated hydroid, for the animal may regenerate its tissues from ordinary epithelial cells.

The gastrodermis, or internal layer of the hydroid's body, is composed mainly of epitheliodigestive cells. They absorb and digest food particles that result from the breaking-up of ingested prey, acting as phagocytes to take in the particles. Between these cells are found various kinds of glandular cells, the enzyme secretions of which play a part in the disintegration of the prey and its digestion within the gastric cavity. The gastrodermis also contains nerve cells like the epidermis, forming a nerve network connecting the contractile fibrils and sensory cells.

Hydroid polyps are voracious, feeding on small crustaceans, worms and larvae. The prey, stung and paralysed by the nematocysts on the tentacles, is conveyed by the tentacles to the gaping mouth. It then slowly travels down the gastric cavity, breaking up more and more as it progresses.

Hydroids are found mostly in coastal waters, fixed to rocks or seaweed or to other animals such as molluscs,

crustaceans and tunicates. They also live within other organisms; for example, *Tubularia ceratogyne* and *Dipurena halterata* are found in sponges and *Eugymnanthea* in mussels.

These species may also be found at greater depths if suitable support is at hand. *Tubularia* and *Stylactis* and certain plumularians, which are feather-like in appearance, occur at depths of more than 500 fathoms. At the greatest depths can be found a few species living fixed to loose material on the bottom. These include *Branchiocerianthus imperator* at 2700 fathoms and *Aglaophenia galatheae* at 3800 fathoms.

Most colonies of hydroids are small in size, being from 1/10 of an inch up to 8 inches in height. However, some plumularians and *Branchiocerianthus imperator* may reach 7 feet in length. Very rarely, hydroid colonies are pelagic and are found in the open sea. Examples include *Pelagohydra mirabilis* and *Margelopsis*.

Some hydroids are commensal with other animals; *Hydrichthyes* lives on fishes, for example, and *Eugymnanthea* (mentioned above) lives on the mantle and palps of mussels. Others become parasites, such as *Polypodium hydriforme*, which lives freely for one part of its existence and then becomes a parasite of sturgeons' eggs.

Medusae

The medusa stage of the orders Hydroida and Trachylina is totally different in appearance from the polyps, and they are in fact often known as jellyfishes, as are other medusae of the Hydrozoa as well as the Scyphozoa. The medusa is fundamentally radial in symmetry. The body or 'umbrella' usually takes the shape of a bell, a mushroom, or a disc. The convex upper surface is known as the exumbrella, and the lower concave surface is the subumbrella. The edge of the exumbrella is provided with sense organs such as ocelli (eye-spots), statocysts (balance organs) and cordyles (modified tentacles). It may also be armed with stinging cells.

In the centre of the subumbrella, hanging like the clapper of a bell, is the manubrium, which is the equivalent of the hypostome in a polyp. It is like a cylindrical or four-sided tube and is often surrounded by tentacles. The opening of the manubrium is the mouth of the medusa. The undersurface of the umbrella is partially closed with a horizontal ring of muscular tissue called the velum. The presence of a velum distinguishes most medusae of the Hydrozoa from the Scyphozoa, the true jellyfishes, in which it is lacking and leaves the underside of the umbrella open. The greater part of the body of the medusa is occupied by a gelatinous mass corresponding to the mesoglea; the outer layer of tissue on both external surfaces is the ectoderm, and the endoderm lines the gastric cavity inside the medusa, which opens to the exterior via the mouth. Although they look very different, the fundamental similarities of polyp and medusa can easily be seen if one realizes that the medusa is upside-down in relation to the polyp.

The gastric cavity is fairly complex in structure. The manubrium connects to the stomach in the middle of the bell of the medusa, and from the stomach radial canals, usually four in number, lead to a ring canal that extends all the way around the edge of the umbrella. From this ring canal, smaller canalculi may extend into the tentacles hanging from the edge of the umbrella. The tentacles may also be in groups of four, emphasizing the radial symmetry of medusae.

The medusae have a two-layered structure, just as the polyps do. The exumbrella, the subumbrella, the velum and the manubrium are all bounded on their external surfaces by an ectodermal layer of cells. The whole of the gastric cavity, including the various canals, is lined with an endodermal layer. Between the two layers is situated the mesoglea, but this is modified into a gelatinous mass in the medusae instead of a thin sheet as in the polyps.

The various groups of medusae in the orders Hydroida and Trachylina are distinguished mainly by the structure of the sense organs.

The suborder Anthomedusae of the Hydroida is distinguished in the polyp stage by the absence of a theca; they are athecate hydroids. The medusa stage possesses ocelli that consist of cups containing pigment and nerve cells surrounding a crystalline formation. The ocelli are situated above the ring of stinging cells around the edge of the umbrella. The Anthomedusae possess tall, bell-shaped umbrellas and the division of the radial symmetry into four parts or sectors is well-marked, there being four radial canals and four groups of tentacles.

The coelenterates of the suborder Leptomedusae are thecate in the polyp stage. The medusae are flattened compared with the tall umbrellas of the Anthomedusae, and usually have more than four radial canals and numerous tentacles. These medusae also possess statocysts (balance organs) but no ocelli, thus orientating themselves in a different way from the Anthomedusae. The statocysts are situated in the velum and are ectodermal in origin, as are the ocelli of the Anthomedusae. The statocysts consist of hollow chambers containing special cells called lithocysts. The walls of the chambers are lined with nerve cells provided with long, sensory hairs. Depending on the position of the medusa, the lithocysts press against one particular part of the chamber wall, and signals are transmitted from the nerve cells there to the nervous system, informing the medusa of its position.

The Limnomedusae, a third suborder of the Hydroida, and the Trachymedusae and Narcomedusae, both suborders within the Trachylina, also possess statocysts. The latter two suborders have tentaculocysts, which consist of minute club-like tentacles that issue from the ring canal. Unlike the statocysts, these organs derive from the endoderm and not the ectoderm.

The tentaculocysts are also balance organs. At their ends they contain one or two endodermic cells containing granules. Each little tentacle is pulled down by gravity and at its base are ciliated sensory cells that press against the walls of the pocket containing the tentaculocyst. Depending on the angle of the tentaculocyst in relation to the body of the medusa, different signals will go to the nervous system and inform the medusa of its orientation in the water.

Unlike polyps, medusae have a nervous system consisting of two nerve rings, both situated at the base of the velum but separated from each other.

The great majority of medusae of the Hydroida and Trachylina lead a pelagic existence and are to be found in the marine plankton. They are capable of some independent movement. The umbrella and velum can be contracted against the elastic mesoglea, which acts like a spring. The body of the medusa flexes to and fro, drawing in and expelling water to drive the animal through the water. The power produced by the medusa is feeble and serves to prevent it sinking, so that it remains at the surface of the sea, or to enable it to rise through the water towards the surface. Medusae do move horizontally through the water, but only when they are borne by the currents or blown by the wind. Some medusae are to be found at great depths, *Solmissus* achieving 2700 fathoms. Several medusae do not live a free existence at all, but remain fixed to a support for most of their lives. These sessile medusae include *Eleutheria*, *Cladonema* and *Gonionemus*.

The medusae of the Hydroida and Trachylina are usually small in size and rarely measure more than 1/5 of an inch across. A few reach 2 inches and the largest, *Aequorea*, may be as big as 8 inches in diameter.

Like polyps, these medusae are essentially carnivorous. They feed on small planktonic crustaceans, on arrow worms, and on planktonic larvae of many kinds.

Sexual reproduction

The gonads, which produce the gametes or sex cells, are usually of ectodermal origin and the sexes are separate, except in a few hermaphrodite forms such as *Eleutheria* and some species of *Hydra*. Most medusae shed their sperms and eggs directly into the sea, where they meet by chance. A few species possess incubatory chambers, including *Eleutheria*. The fertilized egg divides into two basic layers of cells, giving rise to a ciliated larva known as a planula. After a short period of free life, the planula settles on a support and develops into a new colony of polyps. Some species pass through an intermediate larval stage called the actinula: *Tubularia* is an example.

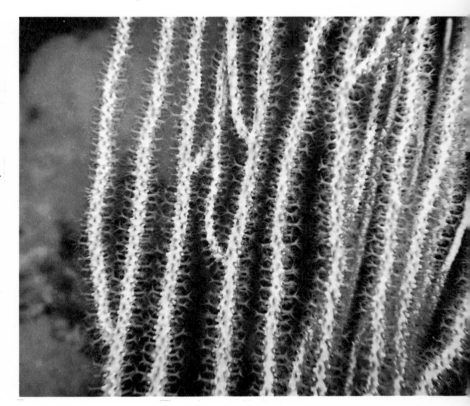

Enlarged fragment of a bushy gorgonian, *Eunicella stricta*, showing the secretory polyps of the axial skeleton supporting the polypary. Basically, gorgonian colonies branch into a single plane, forming a fan with rays often fused to each other. *Phot. Théodor*

In many colonies, the medusae do not develop to the extent of separating from the colony and beginning a free existence. They remain fixed to the colony, and the larvae emerge from them.

The Hydroida complete a life cycle with an alternation of generations, the medusae reproducing sexually and the polyps reproducing asexually. But such an alternation of generations is not mandatory throughout the Hydrozoa. The suborders Trachymedusae and Narcomedusae within the Trachylina, and the Actinulida, another order of the

Hydrozoa, do not go through a polyp stage at all. Their larvae grow up into organisms identical to themselves.

The polyps of hydroids may produce various types of buds. These are:

(a) growth buds, which give rise to new polyps, either solitary or colonial;

(b) medusa buds, which produce either free-swimming or sessile medusae;

(c) propagatory buds, which are of various types that ensure direct dissemination of the species;

(d) resistance buds, which are capable of surviving unfavourable environmental conditions.

Some medusae multiply asexually, producing medusa buds. They include *Limnocnida* and *Eleutheria*.

The buds always originate from a projection of the body wall of the parent hydroid. In *Hydra*, the bud consists of an extension of the gastric cavity, so that it contains both ectodermal and endodermal layers and mesoglea. Medusa budding is characterized by the formation of a special ectodermal growth, the medusan nodule, which seems to originate from a single cell in certain cases.

As a new individual need not always form from both fundamental layers of tissue, these coelenterates—both polyps and medusae—have great powers of regeneration. Polyps can be cut into small pieces that will each grow into a new individual. A polyp split across the mouth will grow into a two-headed individual if the sections are kept apart. Sections that are too small to regenerate alone will join with each other and then regenerate; in this way, a polyp can be shredded by passing it through a piece of silk and then the fragments will join to form new individuals—rather as sponges do.

The orders Milleporina and Stylasterina

The millepores and stylasters differ from the other orders of hydrozoans in having a covering of calcium carbonate forming a shell-like outer skeleton.

In the course of development of a colony of these hydrozoans, the individual members die but their calcarous skeletons act as supports on which new individuals grow. As generation succeeds generation, the colony grows in size but only the outer surface contains the living polyps. The remainder is made up of the remains of former individuals, rather as coral masses form.

The surface of the calcareous mass is covered with large and small cup-like chambers in which the polyps are situated. A colony is made up of different kinds of polyps with different functions. The large chambers of gastropores contain polyps called gastrozooids, which are concerned with obtaining food. The smaller chambers, or dactylopores, house the dactylozooids, which are concerned with defending the colony. All the polyps in the colony are joined to each other by a common gastric cavity, which consists of many branches extending throughout the colony within the skeletons.

The millepores get their name because the openings of the chambers in a colony look like a thousand pores in its surface. The stylasters are named after the style, a central outgrowth at the bottom of the polyp chambers. However, there are many more differences between the two orders than their names alone indicate.

The gastrozooid polyps of stylasters have stumpy tentacles and the dactylozooids have no tentacles at all. This is in direct contrast to the millepores, in which the gastrozooids are

knob-shaped and armed with nematocysts and the dactylozooids have tentacles. The millepore polyps are therefore able to inflict a powerful sting on any unwary predator, and this characteristic gives them their common name of fire corals.

In primitive species, the dactylozooids are scattered haphazardly among the gastrozooids. In more specialized forms, the dactylozooids tend to be grouped around the gastrozooids in the form of a circle or a star. The colonies possess individuals of both sexes, and small medusae are formed within the skeletons. These are liberated but die a short distance from the colonies in which they originated, having first shed their gametes.

Millepores and stylasters live mainly in tropical seas, where they are to be found among coral reefs. Millepores are usually white or yellow in colour, and form massive blocks. Stylasters are often highly coloured, usually red or violet, and form in tree-like shapes. A few species exist in temperate seas.

The order Siphonphora

The siphonophores are hydrozoans which form colonies that float or swim in the open sea, mainly in tropical waters. They are often known as jellyfishes, and include the redoubtable Portuguese man-of-war (genus *Physalia*).

A siphonophore colony is made up of both polyps and medusae. It is highly polymorphous; that is, the individual members of the colony are divided into several groups that each have a special function, and the individuals are modified accordingly. There are three basic kinds of polyps: gastrozooids and dactylozooids, which are concerned with feeding and defence respectively, and gonozooids, which are reproductive polyps. Medusan individuals function as swimming organs or floats, protective shields and gonophores, which are concerned with reproduction.

A siphonophore either swims by means of a swimming bell, a modified medusa that pulsates to propel the colony through the water, or floats by means of an air-filled sac consisting of a highly modified medusa or polyp. Some siphonophores possess both organs. Beneath hang groups of individuals, called cormidia, attached to each other. A cormidium is typically composed of a gastrozooid polyp without tentacles but with a mouth; a dactylozooid armed with a stinging tentacle; two gonozooids, one male and one female; one or

Siphonophores, *Diphyes sieboldi* (×5), from plankton in the Bay of Naples; these occur in warm seas between latitudes 48° N and 40° S. *Phot. Aldo Margiocco*

several cytozooids that are excretory polyps; and an aspidozooid, a protecting shield-like body.

These groups of individuals bear filaments that hang below the float or swimming bell. They may be several yards long and inflict a powerful sting, as in *Physalia*. The filaments form a kind of net that both traps and paralyses the prey, and then transports it to the gastrozooids for digestion. The products of digestion are then shared by the other individuals in the colony.

A remarkable example of commensalism exists between *Physalia* and fishes of the genus *Komeus*. The fish swims with impunity between the filaments of the jellyfish, perhaps finding shelter there.

Human swimmers are not as lucky as *Komeus*, and anyone accidentally swept by the trailing filaments gets a vicious sting. Though rarely fatal, the injury should receive medical attention as soon as possible. The siphonophore is easily identified by its float, which looks like an upturned plastic bag delicately coloured pink or blue. It is dangerous to approach closely, for the stinging filaments may extend six feet beneath the siphonophore. Accidents may occur because siphonophores cannot always be seen, for they can contract the float and sink beneath the surface.

Siphonophores are extraordinary examples of colonial organisms. However, they have carried specialization of individuals to such lengths that they are unable to regenerate missing parts.

Several other hydrozoans resemble siphonophores in being polymorphous colonies that float freely in the open sea by means of a gas-filled float. They consist entirely of colonies of modified polyps and contain no medusae, and for this reason they are no longer classified in the order Siphonophora, but make up the suborder Chondrophora within the order Hydroida. They include *Velella*, called the 'by-the-wind sailor' because its float is shaped like a sail and catches the wind, and also *Porpita*, which has a disc-shaped float.

The Chondrophora look superficially somewhat like medusae, but are completely different internally. In *Velella*, an outer ring of tentacle-like dactylozooids hangs beneath the float, surrounding inner rings of gonozooids. At the centre of the underside is a large gastrozooid, consisting principally of a large mouth. The float that makes up the top surface of the colony has a large sail rising like a ridge across it. The rest of the float is made up of several chambers that, like the sail, are filled with air. Tracheae (air tubes) lead from the chambers into the interior of the body, which is also traversed by a network of cavities connecting the polyps. For the first time, we see a rough outline of aerial respiration appearing in animals whose mode of life is essentially aquatic.

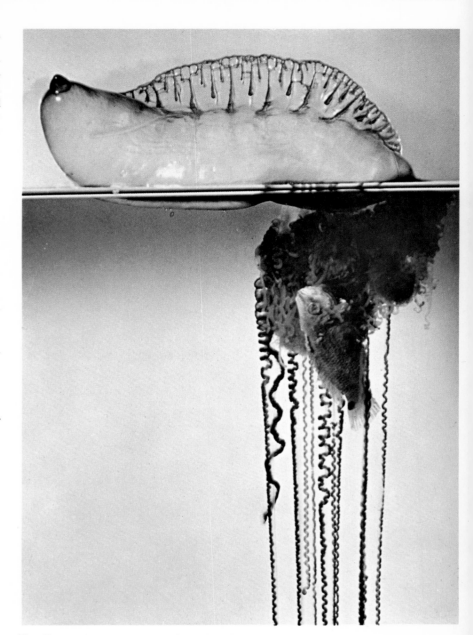

The Portuguese man-of-war, *Physalia physalis*, has an enormous pneumatophore which serves as a float and harbours the colony of polyps under it. In the fishing filaments (up to 25 yards long), a fish has been caught which, poisoned by the stinging cells (cnidoblasts), is attacked by the nutritive polyps or gastrozooids. (Sea nettle was the name formerly given to the physalias). *Phot. Wilson*

The class Scyphozoa

The class Scyphozoa consists of the true jellyfishes. What we call a jellyfish is the medusa stage of these coelenterates; the polyp stage is minute or does not occur at all.

Jellyfishes can often be seen floating at the surface of the sea, often in large groups that form brightly-coloured patches on the water. They swim by rhythmic movements of the umbrella. The two hundred species are all marine, being found in both tropical and temperate waters around the world. After a storm, large numbers of them are sometimes washed up on a beach. On land, they become helpless masses of jelly, unable to move, and they soon dry out and die.

Scyphozoans are animals with tetrameral symmetry; that is, they are divided into four identical sectors around an axis. The polyp lives a sessile existence, fixed to the seabed.

It is shaped like a minute trumpet and varies in size from about 1/4 of an inch to an inch. The body is made up of three regions: an upper oral region comprising a mouth surrounded by tentacles; a central column-shaped gastric cavity; and a lower stalk-like region that ends in a disc with which the polyp attaches itself to its support. The disc secretes a layer of chitin that may extend to envelop the whole polyp in a protective shield or scyphotheca. In colonial forms, such as *Stephanoscyphus*, the covering is well developed and surrounds the stalks of the polyps, forming a support for the colony. The mouth opens immediately into the gastric cavity, as in hydrozoan polyps, and there is no pharynx. However, the gastric cavity is no longer a simple hollow chamber within the body; it is crossed by four partitions, septa, which divide the cavity into separate chambers. The ectoderm (outer layer) of the oral region grows inwards,

55

forming four or more gastric pouches. The number of gastric pouches and the number of tentacles connected to them may vary from one species to another.

These scyphopolyps have no sense organs. They reproduce by processes very different to those of the Hydrozoa. At some point, the polyp undergoes strobilation or transverse fission; constrictions develop around the body and deepen so that the polyp begins to resemble a pile of saucers rather than a trumpet. The edges of the saucers consist of several lobes. The polyp then splits into the saucer-shaped pieces, which are small individual medusae called ephyrae. Alternatively, the ephyrae may form one by one from the polyp.

At other times, the scyphopolyp may undergo another form of asexual reproduction and produce new polyps by budding. This phase may last for many years (under laboratory conditions, more than ten years). The polyps

important differences between the two classes. The body is umbrella-shaped, but there is no velum around the margin of the underside. At the edge of the umbrella, there is a fringe of closely-spaced delicate tentacles. Among the tentacles are regularly spaced notches containing the sense organs. These are more highly developed than those of hydrozoan medusae, and contain an eye-spot or ocellus; a hollow statocyst containing calcareous granules, which acts as a balance organ; and two sense pits to help with food recognition. In the centre of the under-surface is a manubrium containing the mouth, as in hydrozoan medusae, but it is usually surrounded by four tentacle-like arms bearing stinging cells.

The mouth connects through the manubrium to a small gastric cavity from which four gastric pouches lead off. Another difference is evident here, for the pouches contain

Above: acephalous medusae of the genus *Cotylophora* live in the waters of the Mediterranean, the Red Sea and the western Atlantic.
Above right: Chrysaora (*C. hyoscella* in this instance) belongs to the same family as *Pelagia* and, like them, lives in all the oceans. The species

shown is male in its youth and female after it has become mature.
Opposite page: Pelagia, and probably *P. noctiluca*, live in the open sea in all the oceans, between 60° N and 50° S. *Phot. Aldo Margiocco and J. Six*

multiply actively, producing buds on the walls of the gastric column or the stalk region; the buds develop into new polyps. Resting buds, capable of delaying their development, may also form; they are covered with a protective layer of chitin.

The ephyra produced as the polyp undergoes fission swims from its parent, inverts itself and grows into a scyphomedusa or adult jellyfish. Compared with the hydrozoan medusae, a scyphomedusa is a large organism. Most range in size from a few inches to more than a foot in diameter, but a few are enormous. A stranded specimen of *Cyanea arctica*, the giant jellyfish, found over a century ago had a bell $7\frac{1}{2}$ feet in diameter and tentacles 120 feet long. The length of the tentacles alone make it the world's longest animal; with the tentacles spread out, it would cover some 245 feet!

Scyphomedusae look superficially like hydrozoan medusae, even though they are so much larger, but there are some

gastric filaments that bear stinging cells. These filaments are able to kill any prey that might still be alive after entering the mouth. Canals lead off the gastric pouches and connect to a ring canal around the edge of the umbrella. The division into four gastric pouches parallels the similar division of the gastric cavity in scyphopolyps. In *Semaeostoma* and *Rhizostoma*, the septa bounding the pouches degenerate as the medusa grows. The manubrium has lips of varying shape. In *Rhizostoma*, the lips are fused together, sealing off the central mouth, and there are no arms. In their place, there are many small pores in lobes on the underside.

The basic organization of the scyphozoan medusa is similar to that of the hydrozoan medusa. The mesoglea, which is the gelatinous jelly of the jellyfish, contains the gastric cavity, pouches and canals. These internal organs are lined by gastrodermis and the outer surfaces by epidermis,

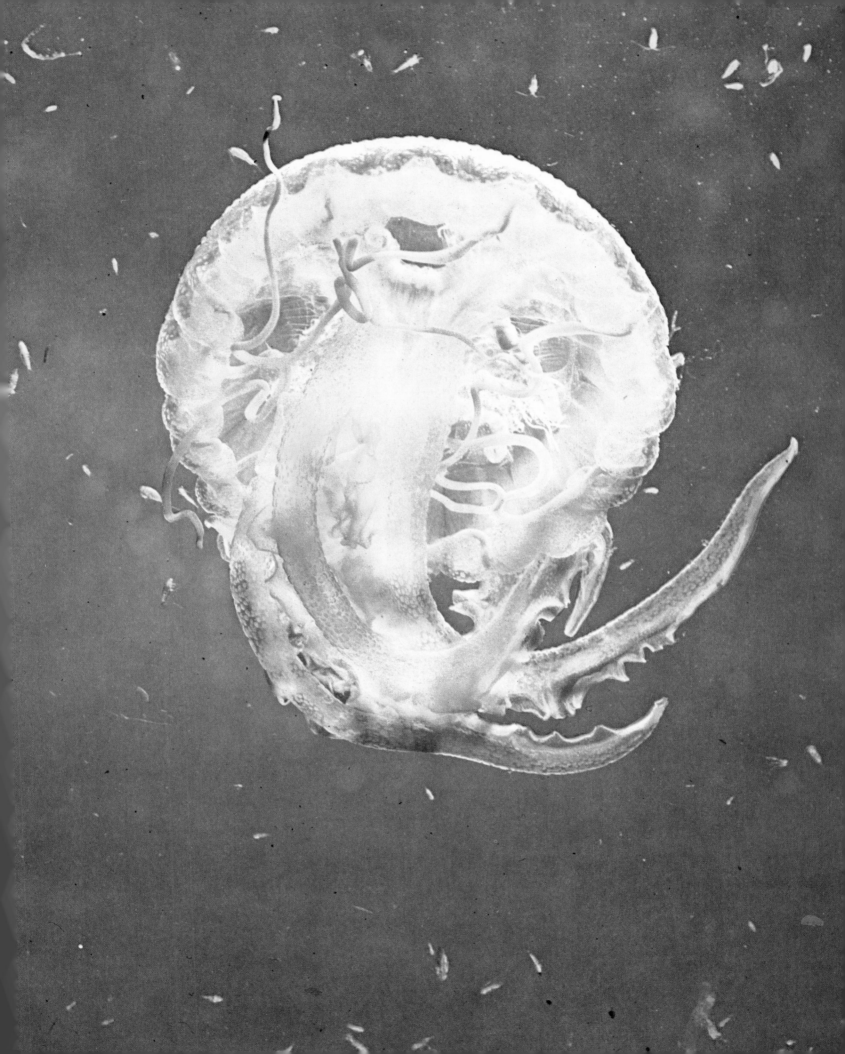

as in hydrozoans. The mesoglea differs, however, in that it contains cells whereas the hydrozoan mesoglea is noncellular.

The nervous system is not made up of nerve rings as in hydrozoan medusae, but there is a nerve net that is most developed at the edge of the umbrella. It serves to co-ordinate the contractions of the umbrella for movement and also feeding actions.

In the scyphomedusae, the sexes are usually separate. The gonads are situated inside the gastric pouches and are therefore of endodermal origin, which is unusual in the hydrozoans. Exceptions include *Chrysaora*, which is her-maphrodite, and *Stygiomedusa fabulosa*, which undergoes asexual reproduction. The latter species is also remarkable in that it is found at depths of more than 1500 fathoms.

Most scyphozoans undergo an alternation of generations in their life cycle. The medusae produce sperms or eggs that unite in the gastric cavity of the female jellyfish. The fertilized egg or zygote emerges from the female's mouth and settles on the arms surrounding it, where it develops into a planula larva. This larva escapes and swims freely before settling on the sea floor, where it develops into a polyp. The polyp eventually reproduces asexually to give medusae as described above, completing the life cycle.

Some scyphozoans do not go through all these stages. The jellyfish *Pelagia* does not pass through a polyp stage, and the animals of the order Stauromedusae, which includes *Lucernaria* and *Haliclystus*, live a fixed life and never enter the medusa phase. Jellyfishes that live only as medusae are usually found in the open sea, whereas jellyfishes that undergo the complete life cycle remain close to the coast.

Scyphomedusae possess fairly strong powers of regenera-tion and are capable of growing various missing parts, such as the arms that surround the mouth.

The medusae swim by means of rhythmic pulsations of the umbrella, which force out water from the underside of the jellyfish and propel it through the water with the upperside foremost. Jellyfishes are highly voracious animals, feeding on various other planktonic animals that drift at the surface of the sea. *Chrysaora* displays a preference for other medusae, especially those of the hydrozoans. *Rhizostoma* has pores instead of a mouth, and therefore feeds on small particles of food to be found in the water. Like many other planktonic animals, jellyfishes live some distance below the surface during the day, and come to the surface at night. Some descend below 3200 fathoms.

A few cases are known, like that of *Physalia* and *Komeus*, where fishes and crustaceans live safely among the tentacles of jellyfish or even within the shelter of the umbrella. This is curious, as the scyphozoan jellyfishes are the most dangerous of the coelenterates. The most venomous are *Chiropsalmus*, whose sting may prove fatal to human victims.

A few jellyfishes are of commercial importance, especially *Rhopilema esculentum*, a member of the order Rhizostomae occurring in the waters of eastern Asia, which is edible and highly valued by the Chinese and Japanese.

The class Anthozoa

The name Anthozoa comes from Greek words meaning flower animals. It is a highly appropriate name, for these coelenterates are like flowers both in appearance and in their mode of life, as they live fixed to a support beneath the water and cannot move. Most people know them better as sea

anemones and corals. There are about 6000 species and they are all marine. They occur only as polyps, either solitary or colonial. Medusae are never formed.

Anthozoans are particularly beautiful animals. They are often brightly coloured and occur in a great variety of forms, from the delicate tracery of sea fans and corals to the squat bodies of sea anemones with their elegant crowns of tentacles. They are found throughout all the world's oceans and at all depths, but they abound in warm shallow waters, where they fix themselves to the sand or gravel or the sea floor as well as to rocks.

Whatever their external appearance, the anthozoans have polyps that are basically similar to each other and which resemble the polyps of other coelenterates in many ways. They are basically tube-shaped, with a mouth at the top surrounded by tentacles; the tube is closed at the bottom and fixed to a support in some way. The mouth does not open directly into the gastric cavity, for there is a gullet between them. Along the gullet are one or several grooves called siphonoglyphs. The polyp can contract to protect itself, closing its gullet, but water can still reach the gastric cavity through the grooves. The gastric cavity itself is partially divided by radial septa (partitions). The septa continue above the gastric cavity, and divide the interior of the body between the gullet and outer wall into compartments. Holes in the septa allow water to pass from one compartment to another. The crown of tentacles is usually arranged into one or more circles around the mouth, although *Limnactinia* has none. The interior of the body is lined with an endodermal layer and the exterior surface is ectodermal; between them comes the mesoglea, which contains cellular elements. Anthozoans are usually of separate sexes, and their sexual cells are of endodermal origin.

Some of these characteristics have much in common with the Hydrozoa, others resemble the Scyphozoa, and a few differ from both classes. It is therefore appropriate to confine the anthozoans to their own class within the Coelenterata. The class is divided into two subclasses: the Alcyonaria or Octocorallia and the Zoantharia or Hexacorallia. The anthozoans of the former class are characterized by eight pinnate tentacles; that is, they have branches arranged like the barbs of a feather. In addition, the interior of the body is divided by eight septa, and there is a skeleton (usually in-ternal) of separate calcareous spicules, a horny material or amorphous calcareous matter, or a combination of these constituents. The polyps are small.

The Zoantharia differ from the Alcyonaria in that the polyps are strong, are equipped with a varying number of tentacles (but never eight), and typically have six or a multiple of six septa. The skeleton, when present, may either be horny or of solid calcareous matter without spicules.

The subclass Alcyonaria

The anthozoans of this subclass are virtually all colonial animals. They prefer tropical waters and mostly live a fixed life. They are often covered with other fixed animals, such as sponges, hydrozoans and bryozoans.

A colony consists of many individuals joined by tubes called solenia that connect the gastric cavities. Water con-taining food and oxygen circulates through the tubes to all the individuals. New individuals arise by budding from various parts of the colony. The solenia are surrounded by a common mesoglea in which the skeleton forms. The outer covering of the mesoglea, the ectoderm, may form a common layer of tissue over the skeleton.

Two types of solitary Anthozoa: *below*, an *Actinia*, or sea anemone, living in deep water in the coral reefs: *above*, large Cerianthi, letting off the 'fireworks' of their numerous tentacles and sharing the habitat. *Aquarium at Noumea. Phot. R. Catala*

Gorgonians are probably the most 'zoophytic' of the Cnidaria, the hydroid and medusoid phases alternating between generations. These *Melitoda*, living on the coasts of the New Hebrides, prove it. In under-seascapes, they look like shrubs or bushes. *Phot. Théodor*

In the primitive species, such as *Cornularia*, the skeleton is simply a chitinous covering. In others, it is formed of calcareous spicules that are separate or fused together, either by a horny substance or a calcareous cement, or it is made up of a network of horny fibres or is a solid calcareous mass.

The form of the skeleton varies greatly, and it is possible to distinguish many different types of corals. One of the best-known is *Corallium rubrum*, the red coral in jewellery. The coral is fished for in the Mediterranean Sea, the Red Sea and in Japanese waters; it is found on rocky bottoms at depths from 15 to 150 fathoms. It has stiff branches and stands erect in the water; from the branches, the dazzling white polyps protrude in calm water. If disturbed, the polyps contract and withdraw back into the skeleton for protection.

One of the most attractive of the alcyonarian corals or octocorals is the sea fan (*Gorgonia*), which belongs to the same order as the red coral. It has a delicate fan-like skeleton formed of calcareous spicules sheathed in a horny substance. The fans may be very large, and reach two or three yards in size.

Organ-pipe coral is another well-known coral, named for the appearance of its skeleton, which is made up of blood-red, thin tubes grouped together like the pipes of an organ. The polyps project from the ends of the tubes. Its appearance is also reflected in its Latin name, *Tubipora*, one species even being named *Tubipora musica*.

Dead-man's fingers (*Alcyonium*) is another coral with an exotic common name. It is common in tropical and temperate waters. It is a soft coral; that is, the polyps are rather indistinct and housed in a fleshy mesoglea containing scattered spicules for stiffening. The colony takes the shape of several finger-like pink-white lobes, hence its name.

The sea pens get their name from the way they resemble quills stuck into the seabed. The colony is made up of a long central polyp forming the shaft of the quill, and secondary polyps that bud off the central shaft to form the vane of the quill. The secondary polyps are of two kinds: autozooids, which feed and reproduce, and siphonozooids, which maintain the circulation of water throughout the colony. The division of functions between different groups of polyps recalls the organization of a siphonophore colony. The central polyp is profoundly modified, consisting of a long stalk, the peduncle, which is sunk into the seabed; and the rachis, on which the other polyps are borne. The skeleton contains isolated calcareous spicules. Species occupying the same order as the sea pen (*Pennatula*) include *Veretillum* and *Pteroides*, which are both illustrated, and *Renilla*, the sea pansy. They all have the same basic form, but in *Veretillum* the rachis is like a column, and in *Renilla* it is broad and disc-shaped, producing a 'flower' of polyps around the central stalk.

Another beautiful octocoral is the blue coral, *Heliopora*, often mistaken for one of the true corals described below because its skeleton is compact and massive. It is composed of crystalline fibres of aragonite associated with iron salts.

The subclass Zoantharia

The coelenterates of this group are often known as the hexacorals, because the polyps usually bear six tentacles or a multiple of six (*Limnactinia*, which has none, being an obvious exception). The number of septa dividing the body cavity into a series of chambers is also six or a multiple of six. However, the name is not a very good one, because the

Detail of the polyps

Veretilla, *Veretillum cynomorium*, shows clearly the organization of that of the Pennatulaceae (sea pens). On the founder polyp, forming the column of the colony, the secondary polyps are arranged with 8 tentacles (octocorals) (Banyuls-sur-Mer, Pyrénées Orientales). *Opposite page:* enlarged detail of this photograph. *Phot. J. Six*

Diagram of a sea anemone seen in radial section: *Ac*, acontia; *Bm*, basal muscle; *Cm*, circular muscle; *M*, mesentery; *Ml*, longitudinal muscle of a mesentery; *Ov*, ovary; *Ph*, pharynx; *T*, tentacle. *After Delage and Hérouard*

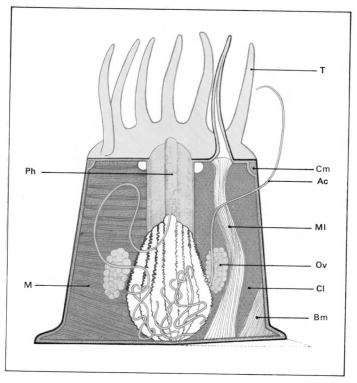

A sea pen, *Pteroides griseum*, common in the littoral waters of western Europe, seen in position on the sea-bottom. The colony consists of a rolled stem with the base sunk in the sand, and into which are inserted symmetrically two series of leaf-like expansions bearing the polyps. *Phot. J. Six*

This alcyonarian (*Alcyonium acaule*) forms beautiful colonies on the rocky slopes of the western Mediterranean, on bottoms between 5 and 16 fathoms deep (Port Vendres). The fleshy coenosarc, with dense mesogloea containing few spicules, is traversed by tubes through which the polyps communicate with each other. *Phot. Théodor*

subclass contains the sea anemones as well as corals.

Most of the polyps that make up the Zoantharia are fixed to a support by a glandular pedal disc at the base of the body. However, a few can creep with the aid of muscles around the disc, and some can swim a little by movements of the gastric column and tentacles. *Minyas* and some others secrete a chitinous porous mucus from the base; this mucus serves as a float and enables them to rise to the surface of the water.

The subclass Zoantharia is made up of five orders. The Actiniaria contains the 1000 species of sea anemones, which are solitary polyps without a skeleton. They usually have a pedal disc. The Madreporaria contains the 2500 species of stony corals. These anthozoans are mostly colonial and

possess compact calcareous skeletons in which the polyps occupy cups; they include the famous reef-building corals of tropical seas. The order Ceriantharia resembles the sea anemones, but a pedal disc is not present. The Zoanthidae also have no skeleton or pedal disc, but are mostly colonial. The fifth order is the Antipatharia, or black corals, which have plant-like horny skeletons.

The polyps that possess no skeleton usually develop powerful muscles, making it possible for them to contract. The animal brings its tentacles over its mouth, and then shuts, rather like a purse being closed. The polyps with skeletons are more protected and are characterized by weak muscles, mostly being unable to contract the tentacles.

The order Actinaria (sea anemones)

A sea anemone is the most typical of anthozoans; it is solitary, powerful, devoid of a skeleton, and has gastric partitions always arranged in pairs.

Sea anemones abound in shallow inshore waters, where they are to be found fixed to rocks or buried in the sand or mud. Some live in deep water; *Galantheanthemum hadale*, for example, hails from the Philippine Trench, where the greatest depth is 5570 fathoms. They are voracious animals, usually carnivorous, and are capable of consuming prey such as crabs and fishes that are their own size or even bigger than themselves. They are formidable adversaries, for the stinging cells on the tentacles are very powerful. Some species also have long stinging filaments attached to the edges of the partitions in the gastric cavity. These filaments are called acontia, and they are extruded from the mouth and through holes in the body wall called cinclides if the sea anemone is disturbed. They therefore seem to play a protective role as well as aid in digestion of the prey.

Some sea anemones can reach a large size. Many measure from 12 to 16 inches in diameter, and *Stoichactis kenti* of Malaysian waters has a diameter of more than 3 feet. Sea anemones are also capable of living for many years; a captive

specimen of *Cereus pendunculatus* is reported to have achieved the age of 65!

Most sea anemones are ovoviviparous. The ciliated larva develops inside the mother and is born through the mouth. The larva then swims freely for some time before becoming fixed nearby. Other sea anemones practise external fertilization, the eggs and sperms being shed into the sea. Although they are not colonial, close groups of anemones do form. Asexual reproduction also occurs, the anemone splitting into new individuals by fission, and these animals have great powers of regeneration.

Some sea anemones live in mutually beneficial partnerships with other animals, notably on mollusc shells inhabited by hermit crabs. The strawberry cloaklet anemone, *Adamsia palliata*, is always found on a shell inhabited by the hermit crab *Pagurus prideauxi*. The anemone stretches its body and mouth so that it completely surrounds the shell, and positions itself in such a way that the mouth and tentacles are beneath the mouth of the hermit crab. In this way, it shares the food taken by its host. The hermit crab benefits from the protection given by the sea anemone, and it no longer finds it necessary to change shells as it grows, for the sea anemone can enlarge the crab's home by secreting an extension to the shell. The two partners are highly dependent on one another; if the crab does leave the shell, the sea anemone will die unless it can find another host. Another example of symbiosis involving sea anemones and crabs is to be found with *Bunodeopsis prehensa*, which lives attached to the pincers of the crab *Lybia tessellata* of the Indian Ocean. At the slightest provocation, the crab waves its anemone-infested pincers at its enemy and thus gains a formidable reputation.

Sea anemones of the genus *Stoichactis* usually shelter small fishes of the family Pomacentridae between their tentacles. Whereas other fishes are stunned by the stings of the tentacles, the Pomacentridae take cover among them at the least disturbance. Each anemone has a pair of fish, which seem to feed it. If separated from their hosts, they do not survive for long but fall prey to swifter predators. But they can adapt to another anemone, as aquarium studies have shown, provided they find one in time. They will even transfer to a different species if need be.

The order Madreporaria (stony corals)

The stony corals or true corals are mostly colonial polyps, forming skeletons that either encrust their supports or grow from them in branching tree-like formations. A few species, however, are solitary; they include *Fungia*, *Caryophyllia* and *Balanophyllia*.

The most individual characteristic of the madreporarian corals is their ability to build a solid calcarous exoskeleton; that is, a skeleton that lies outside the polyp's body rather than a skeleton occurring within the polyp as in the octocorals. Each coral polyp in a colony is connected to the others by flat extensions of the body wall. The skeleton is secreted by these extensions so that each polyp sits in a cup-like depression called a theca. Ridges rise from the base of the cup, and the polyp folds itself around the ridges. The structure of the body is very similar to that of a sea anemone. Only the surface layer of colony contains live polyps. New polyps are formed by building from older polyps or from the body wall extensions connecting the polyps. As they grow, they cover the older polyps, which then die. In this way, the

Sagartia parasitica detached from a gasteropod shell, formerly the home of a hermit crab. It adapts itself to diverse species of these crustaceans. The association is neither constant nor compulsory; the associates, when separated, live normally. *Phot. J. Six*

The snakelocks anemone, *Anemonia sulcata*, is the most common sea anemone on western Atlantic coasts, forming vast settlements on the rocky bottoms. The cells of the ectoderm of this actinian are full of zooxanthellae, unicellular algae belonging to the peridinian class. *Phot. Théodor*

Two solitary madrepore corals. *Above: Cynarina lacrymalis*, which lives on bottoms about 16 fathoms deep in the fringing reefs of New Caledonia. The partitions of the inner calcareous skeleton are visible. *Below: Plerogyra sinuosa*, in the act of eating a fish (*Apogon*); the prey has been seized and killed by the tentacles and introduced by them into the gastric cavity, where it will be digested. In the two corals, the tentacles are retracted. *Aquarium at Noumea. Phot. R. Catala*

colony continually increases in size and this is how coral reefs build up.

Coral colonies assume a great variety of form. The polyps are often closely packed, their cups forming rows or ridges in whorls and other patterns. Brain coral gets its name because it is covered in a maze of ridges that resemble the convolutions on the surface of the human brain. Differences in the structure of the colonies are used to classify corals. They may be arborescent or tree-like (*Lophohelia*); ramified or branching (*Poecilopora, Dendrophyllia, Acropora*); solid and massive (*Meandrina, Siderastraea*); or lamellar or plate-like (*Euphyllia*).

Most true corals require warm water to live, and so they are only found near the surface in tropical seas. The polyps contract and withdraw into their cups during the day, for they feed only at night when their main food, the small organisms of the plankton, rises towards the surface. Polyps with long tentacles feed like sea anemones. Small polyps or polyps with reduced tentacles make more use of their cilia and mucuous secretions to catch prey and bring them to the mouth. There are many cases of commensalism between corals and other animals, notably the crabs of the genus *Cryptochirus* that live among the formations of the solid corals of the Fayiidae.

Coral reefs and atolls

A coral reef is composed of several kinds of madrepore anthozoans. Other anthozoan corals and hydrozoan corals live alongside them, together with fragments of shells, all fused together with calcareous algae. The sight of a coral reef is one of the most beautiful and fascinating spectacles that the natural world has to offer. To any zoologist it is a paradise, for so many different kinds of animals live among the formations—sponges, worms, molluscs, bryozoans, echinoderms, tunicates and fishes of the most brilliant and varied colours.

Coral reefs are very special places, for the coral polyps can survive only within a narrow range of environmental conditions. They require water that is perfectly clear, for any trace of mud is fatal to the polyps. The water must be well aerated, and the reefs grow more quickly on the side that faces the open sea, for there the water is rougher and richer in oxygen.

Temperature requirements are very precise. Coral reefs do not grow at temperatures below 18°C (64°F) and they usually flourish only above 22°C (72°F). The presence of coral reefs is a useful way of defining the tropics, but there are certain tropical regions where they do not occur. True corals live mainly in two regions: the Caribbean Sea and adjacent waters, such as the coast of Florida, Bermuda, the Bahamas, etc.; and the Indo–Pacific region—from the east coast of Africa and Madagascar across the Indian Ocean and Pacific Ocean as far as the Hawaiian islands, the northeast coast of Australia and the Philippines. They are absent from the western coasts of Africa and America because of cold currents that flow north from the Antarctic Ocean. Furthermore, coral reefs will only grow where the sea floor is rocky and not below a depth of forty fathoms.

However, there are some exceptions to these rules, and coral reefs do exist in the cold depths of the North Sea, built by the arborescent coral *Lophohelia* at 100 to 300 fathoms. Many other corals are found in deep cold waters, but they are species that do not build reefs. Some occur as deep as 4400 fathoms, where the temperature varies from 1°C (34°F) to 5°C (41°F) and the darkness is total.

Even in the most favourable of habitats, the growth of a coral reef is slow; it is estimated to increase at a rate of from 1/5 of an inch to 8 inches per year. A reef 100 feet thick would therefore be at least 150 years old but may have taken as long as 6000 years to build up. This figure may not represent the age of the reef, for once a reef reaches the surface, it stops growing upwards and will only grow outwards. In fact, all the coral reefs known at present probably began life between 10,000 and 30,000 years ago.

Coral reefs are of several kinds, and three general classes are distinguished: fringing reefs, barrier reefs, and coral islands or atolls.

Fringing reefs are situated along the edge of a coast and are joined to the shore. They extend no more than a quarter of a mile from the shore. They are not broad but may be very long, as in the reefs of Pernambuco, Brazil.

Barrier reefs lie parallel to a coast but are situated several miles offshore with a lagoon between the reef and the shore. The best-known of all coral reefs is the famous Great Barrier Reef along the northeast coast of Australia. Lying as much as 90 miles off shore, it is about 1200 miles long. This reef, and other coral reefs in adjacent areas, are in danger from the depredations of the crown-of-thorns starfish, which is eating the coral polyps there (see page 263).

Coral islands or atolls are common in the Pacific Ocean. They are ring-shaped islands that enclose a central lagoon and are usually a few miles across. The largest is an atoll in the Marshall Islands that is 176 miles long. Breaks in the reef connect the lagoon to the ocean, and the passages are always situated to the leeward of the island.

A coral island simply consists of a low layer of sandy soil lying on top of the reef where it breaks the surface. Atolls possess neither rivers nor springs; the only source of fresh water is the rain. The flora and fauna of a coral island is therefore rather scanty and very special.

A single stretch of coast may sometimes provide examples of all three kinds of coral reefs. Coral reefs may attain a considerable thickness, and often extend several hundred yards below the surface. We know that reefs will not form at depths below forty fathoms, and so the formation of such deep reefs requires explanation. Several theories of reef formation have been advanced.

Darwin's theory, or the theory of subsidence, proposes that all coral reefs first form as fringing reefs along a coast. The reef grows from the land that slopes down beneath the sea from the coast. Then the land slowly subsides, carrying the reef with it. But the coral continues to grow, always building the reef up to the surface of the water. If the land in question is a large piece of land, then the coastline will recede from the reef, forming a barrier reef some distance offshore with a stretch of water in between. However, if the land is an island, it will disappear completely beneath the waves. The reef will build up over the top of the submerged island, forming a coral island. This theory will only be correct if the rate of subsidence is the same as or slower than the rate of formation of the coral.

The Semper–Murray theory proposes that coral reefs do not always form from fringing reefs, but may form on the top of

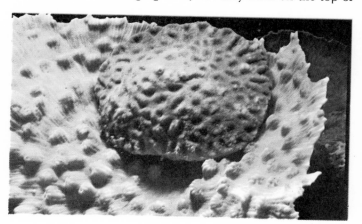

'Starred corals' constitute a group of Madreporaria which naturalists have not yet completely distinguished from each other. The favias, *Favia speciosa* (below), and *Favites* (above) are part of them. The specimen above rests on another madrepore (*Mycedium*). The *Favia* is luminous when seen under ultraviolet rays. *Aquarium at Noumea. Phot. R. Catala*

undersea volcanic mountains (seamounts) when deposits of sediment raise their summits to the level where corals can begin to grow.

Agassiz' theory suggests that wave action eroded rocks so that they became submerged and corals could begin to grow on them.

Daly's theory proposes that reef formation may be linked to the last ice age. The freezing of water into large ice caps lowered sea level by about 40 fathoms below the present level. Erosion would then have lowered islands to this level, and when the ice caps melted and sea level rose, reefs formed as they became submerged. The rise in temperature that took place at the end of the ice age would also have favoured coral formation then.

Borings have been carried out on coral islands to test these theories, and they do not support any one particular theory but suggest that different kinds of formation took place in different places. Boring to a depth of more than 1000 feet on Funafuti revealed the existence of 28 genera of reef-building corals, 22 of which are still to be found at the present day living above 33 fathoms. These results suggest that Darwin's theory is correct for deep corals. Confirmation came with deeper borings on Bikini and Eniwetok. The Bikini investigation brought up sand from a depth of 2500 feet, and deeper borings on Eniwetok came to hard rock,

both suggesting that subsidence had occurred there. This does not mean that all atolls are formed as a rocky island subsides, and boring tests have supported aspects of Daly's theory in places.

The Zoanthidae

Finally, these are anthozoans which are colonial and rarely solitary. The polyps are small and many live attached to other animals. The associations are often specific, *Epizoanthus* confining itself to hermit crabs, for example. In colonial forms, the polyps are attached to each other in a similar way to the Alcyonaria but they differ from them internally.

The order Antipatharia (black corals)

The black corals are so named because the colonies possess black, spiny skeletons. They consist of several horny stems, some of which may be branched to give a plant-like appearance. Some colonies form in long spiral shapes, like coiled springs. The polyps are slender and cannot be contracted. Black corals live in tropical seas, sometimes at great depths.

The order Ceriantharia

These anthozoans are like burrowing sea anemones. They have no pedal disc, but do not need one as they do not have to attach themselves to a support. They hide beneath rocks or stones; bury themselves in the mud, sand or gravel of the sea floor; or occupy holes in rocks or empty shells. The mouth and tentacles extend from the burrow or shelter to obtain food. If disturbed, the polyp may contract and retreat below the surface or into its home. The bodies of these anthozoans are often enveloped in a gelatinous sheath encrusted with grains of sand and various debris.

Left
The dendrophyllias (*Dendrophyllia*) are madrepores which form branched colonies, each being made up of comparatively few individuals. By day, their tentacles are retracted, by night, they are spread out. The dendrophyllias live at a fairly considerable depth, 15–30 fathoms. *Aquarium at Noumea. Phot. R. Catala*

Opposite
Protolobophyllia is a solitary madrepore, from the reef zones of New Caledonia, found on bottoms below 20 fathoms. *Above*, seen in natural light; *below*, in ultraviolet light; luminous Madreporaria offer more iridescent colours in the latter than in natural light. *Phot. R. Catala*

Ctenophores

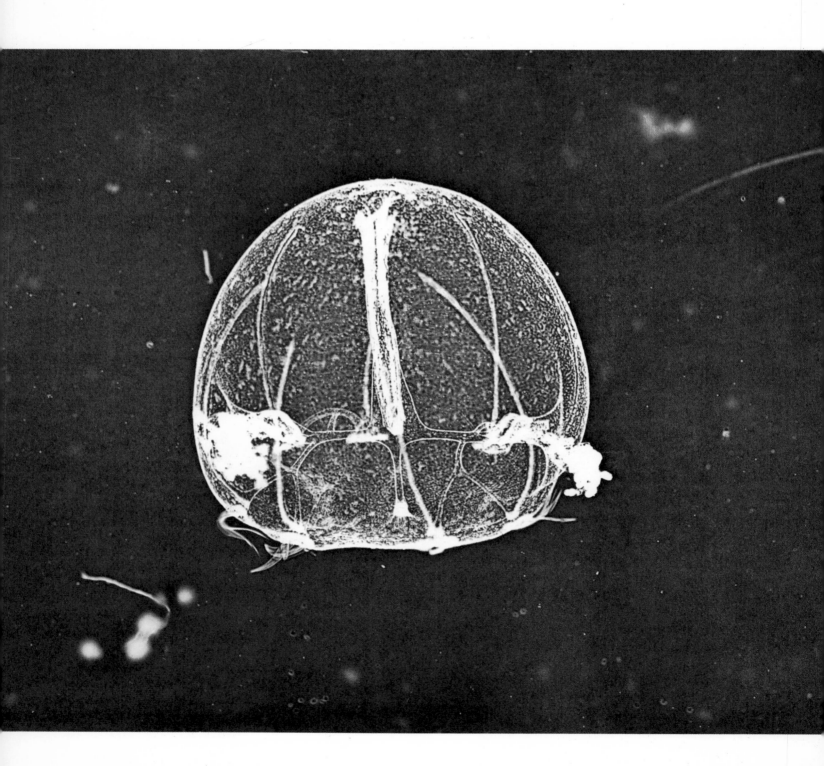

The ctenophores drift and swim among the plankton, their transparent jelly-like bodies gleaming with iridescence. They float easily, as their bodies contain 97 per cent water. Ctenophores look somewhat like jellyfishes, and were once classified with them, but they are in fact very different animals. They could represent a major step in evolution, for their tissues originate in the same way as those of all higher animals.

Unless you have the good fortune to be at the seashore when coastal waters are invaded by ctenophores, you may never appreciate their delicate beauty. They get their common name of comb jellies from the rows of comb-like plates that beat to propel the animal through the water. The action causes the crystal-like body to gleam with flashes of iridescent colour. Comb jellies vary in shape. *Pleurobrachia* is with justification commonly called the sea gooseberry, for it looks just like a gooseberry with two long trailing tentacles. *Cestus* has the romantic name of Venus' girdle, for it resembles a long crystal ribbon.

In common with other planktonic animals, ctenophores do not swim so strongly that they can overcome the force of the currents and tides, which carry them considerable distances. The currents and tides may also cause vast numbers of ctenophores to assemble in a small area of water. As they are voracious animals, and consume their planktonic neighbours with gusto, they can have serious economic effects in places. Invasions of comb jellies may seriously deplete stocks of shell-fish such as oysters and crustaceans, and food fishes such as herring, cod and sardines, by destruction of their eggs and larvae. They may keep their own numbers down by consuming each other, and ctenophores also fall prey to larger predators such as adult fishes. Although they may sometimes be so numerous as to be considered pests, the comb jellies generally play an essential role in the maintenance of the food chains in the sea.

The structure of ctenophores

There are about eighty species of ctenophores and they make up the phylum Ctenophora, which is Greek for 'comb-bearers', referring to the organs of locomotion possessed by these animals. They all swim freely in the sea and are mostly to be found near the surface, although some species live in

Larva of Venus' girdle, *Cestus veneris*, seen in profile. It has the characteristic features of the Ctenophora: slit-shaped mouth, flattened pharynx, lateral tentacles still contracted, network of gastric caniculi—an architecture which is found in many ctenophores. Venus' girdle lives at medium depths. *Phot. Hernandez-Nicaise*

deep water. As a group, ctenophores occur in all the world's oceans, and two species, *Pleurobrachia pileus* (the sea gooseberry) and *Beroe cucumis*, which lacks tentacles, are individually world-wide in distribution.

The ctenophores resemble the coelenterates in several ways. They consist principally of a gelatinous mass separating an external ectodermal layer of tissue and an internal endodermal layer. In addition, the internal organs consist

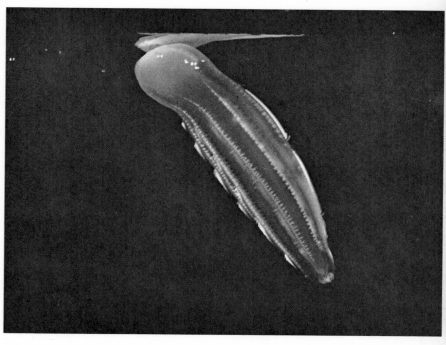

Beroe forskali swims on the surface, its progress being governed by the rhythmical beating of its comb plates, the lower row of which, seen here, moves more quickly than the others. *Phot. P. Coulet*

solely of a gastric cavity with side branches. Symmetry is also similar. Coelenterates possess radial symmetry; that is, they are symmetrical about a central axis. Ctenophores possess this feature too, but in ctenophores and some coelenterates it is overlaid with bilateral symmetry, the kind of symmetry in which one half of the body is a mirror image of the other half. This combination is known as biradial symmetry, and is seldom encountered outside the Coelenterata and Ctenophora.

But there are several fundamental differences between the two phyla. Locomotion is different, ctenophores swimming by beating the rows of combs along their bodies, whereas medusae force water out of their bells to move through the sea. The muscles originate neither from ectodermal nor endodermal tissue, but a third kind of tissue—mesodermal tissue. This kind of tissue is not found in coelenterates. The organization of the digestive cavity is also different. In coelenterates, food enters and waste leaves the cavity via the mouth. In ctenophores, there are canals that pass from the stomach and open to the exterior through pores at the opposite end of the body to the mouth. Waste can be eliminated through these pores, as well as through the mouth. All the features show that ctenophores are somewhat more highly evolved than the coelenterates. Another great difference is that very few ctenophores capture their prey with stinging cells like those of coelenterates. Instead their tentacles are armed with adhesive cells of a kind found nowhere else in the animal kingdom.

The sea gooseberry, *Pleurobrachia*, will serve as an example of the Ctenophora to explain the body structure in detail. It is shaped like a gooseberry, but is somewhat larger, about the size of a plum. At one end, called the oral pole, is situated the mouth. This is shaped like a slit, and through it runs a bilateral plane of symmetry that divides one side of the animal from the other. From the centre of each side extends a long retractile tentacle. The bases of the tentacles form a second plane of symmetry—one that separates the back of the animal from the front. At the opposite end to the mouth, the aboral pole, is a sense organ that enables the ctenophore to detect its orientation in the water. When the animal swims, it does so with the oral pole to the fore.

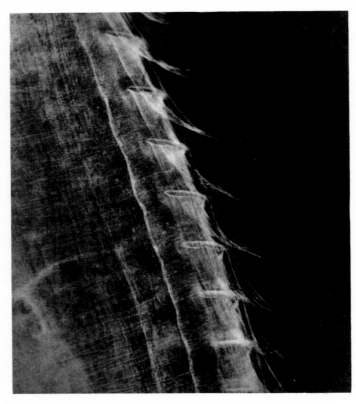

Each comb plate, is constituted by lines of agglomerated vibratile cilia which beat in harmony. *Phot. Hernandez-Nicaise*

The surface of the body is lined with eight rows of comb plates, each consisting of a group of cilia. The rows stretch from the aboral pole towards the oral pole, and the comb-plates beat in perfect co-ordination to propel the ctenophore through the water. As they beat, a constant play of iridescent colours is produced.

Internally, the mouth connects via a long pharynx to the central stomach, from which small digestive canals radiate outwards, once again showing the radial symmetry that exists in these animals.

The phylum is divided into two classes, simply named the Tentaculata, which possess tentacles, and the Nuda, which do not. The Tentaculata comprises four orders, which may be distinguished by a consideration of their symmetry. The Nuda contains only one order.

In the first tentaculate order, the Cydippida, the three planes of symmetry are all well marked. These ctenophores are roughly spherical or ovoid, and they include *Pleurobrachia* described above. In the second order, the Lobata, the tentacular plane of bilateral symmetry is reduced so that the body is compressed between the tentacles. On either side of the mouth are two large lobes bearing comb rows, as in *Mnemiopsis*. In the order Cestida, this compression is carried so far that the body is drawn out into a ribbon along the oral plane (the plane of the mouth). This order contains the elegant Venus' girdle (*Cestus veneris*), which is two inches wide by more than a yard long. The comb rows and tentacles are situated along the edges of the ribbon.

In the fourth order of the Tentaculata, the Platycnenea, the compression is on the oral-aboral axis, so that the body is flattened. These ctenophores crawl over the sea floor or float with the mouth downwards. The order includes *Ctenoplana* and *Coeloplana*. In *Tjalfiella tristoma*, which is a parasite or commensal of colonial polyps, the body structure is so modified that it can only be identified as a ctenophore from its larvae. Before they metamorphose into the grossly misshapen adult, the larvae bear a close resemblance to those of the Cydippida. The single order Beroidea within the Nuda comprises thimble-shaped animals, with a wide mouth and large pharynx.

Analysis of the development of ctenophores is not always as easy as in the case of *Tjalfiella*. Ctenophores reproduce sexually and are hermaphrodite, the gonads releasing sperms and eggs into the gastric canals. Fertilization and growth of the larvae usually take place externally in the sea. The unusual development of *Tjalfiella* was noticed because it keeps its larvae in incubatory pouches, which is not a frequent practice among the ctenophores.

Embryology has made it possible to clear up one of the most controversial points in the classification of the Cteno-phora. In the past, these animals have been placed with the sponges and coelenterates as being diploblastic; that is, made up only of ectodermal and endodermal tissues. The external surface, the mouth, the pharynx and the tentacles are ectodermal, and the gastric cavity and its canals are endodermal. Between these two layers and making up most of the body is a gelatinous substance that was previously thought to be similar to the mesoglea of coelenterates. Recent detailed study of the formation of connective tissue and muscle cells in the 'mesoglea' has revealed that they originate independently of the ectoderm and endoderm. They constitute a true third layer—the mesoderm—and ctenophores may therefore be classified with all the higher animals as being triploblastic—having all their tissues originate from three basic layers of tissue in the embryo.

The triploblastic nature of the ctenophores distinguishes them most fundamentally from the coelenterates, and their method of capturing prey is equally different from that of their neighbours. In place of stinging cells, almost all cteno-phores possess special unique cells called colloblasts or glue cells. These cells cover the surface of the tentacles, and their outer surface is covered with a hemisphere of sticky granules. The underlying part of the cell is anchored in the tentacle by a straight filament, and by a coiled spiral filament that acts

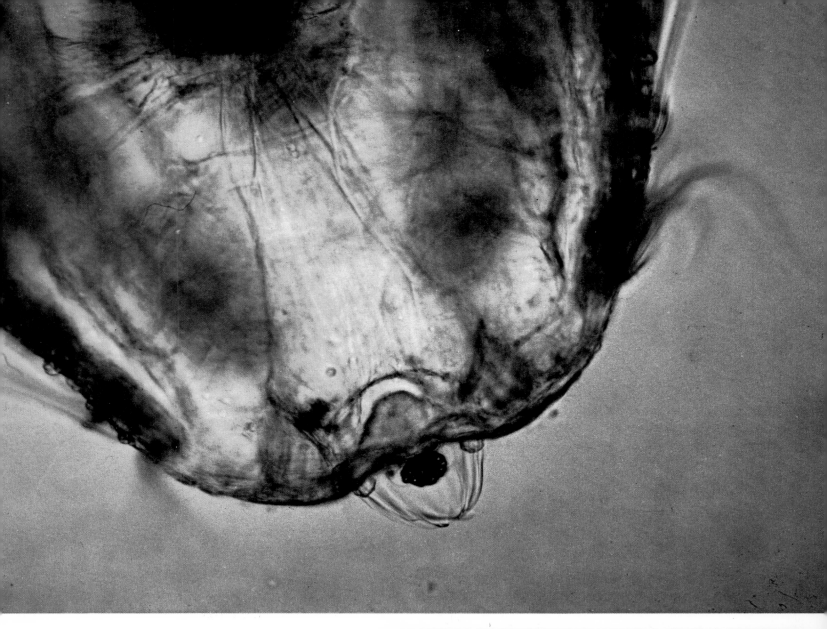

At the opposite pole to that of the buccal slit is the balancing organ, or statocyst. The weight of a small spherical mass, clearly visible, is brought to bear on delicate springs making the animal sensitive to the least change in position. Thus, the Ctenophora have 'refined' evolution, by developing an extremely sensitive balancing organ. *Phot. Pavans de Ceccatty*

like a spring to help pull in the captured prey. The tentacles are then wiped over the mouth to transfer the prey to the pharynx.

The sense organ of ctenophores is an extraordinary structure. It consists basically of a set of tufts of cilia supporting a calcareous mass beneath a bell-shaped cover. The angle at which the mass presses down informs the ctenophore of its orientation. Nerves connect to the comb rows to co-ordinate the beating of the comb plates and maintain equilibrium. The system is fairly sophisticated, for the animal takes up a different position depending on whether it is swimming or floating.

The place of the ctenophores and the coelenterates in evolution is very unclear. It is possible that they are the most primitive of the true metazoans, and that higher animals developed from them. But it could also be true that they are a degenerate regression from flatworms. Most authorities tend towards the former view, believing that the mesoderm and nerve network continuously develop through evolution rather than deteriorate.

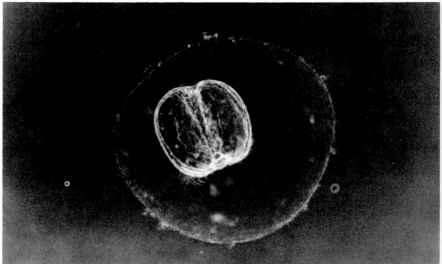

The *Beroe* lay eggs surrounded by a transparent mucous matrix, in which they develop. Before hatching, the embryo, which has vibratile comb plates, turns round while still within the shell; it has already assumed the characteristic shape of a ctenophore. The egg of a ctenophore readily lends itself to experimentation and has been the object of elaborate research. *Phot. Hernandez-Nicaise*

Platyhelminths and nemathelminths

In the mind of the layman, the word 'worm' (or helminth, to the zoologist) conjures up an image of a moving mass of ill-formed unclean creatures, crawling in mud or putrid matter. In fact, they are living beings like any others, variously organized and difficult to place in a coherent system of classification. They are divided into parasitic species (which are the best known and most numerous), and free-living species, found in all humid waters and soils.

The free-living platyhelminths (class Turbellaria)

Free-living platyhelminths occur in fresh, brackish or salt water. They are flat ribbony worms, usually small, with flexible bodies that move in a gliding motion with the help of the vibratile cilia with which they are covered.

The body cavity is full of star-shaped cells (parenchyma), joined to each other by long fine cytoplasmic expansions. In the meshes of this network of tissue, amoeboid blood cells circulate. The worm's integument is made up of very brightly coloured rods, the rhabdites, formed by cells from the parenchyma, composed, apparently, of reserve matter.

The alimentary canal has one opening, usually in the middle of the ventral surface, which serves as mouth and anus. The pharynx is muscular and leads to the gut. The latter may be a simple blind tube or have three or more branches.

Digestion is intracellular, as in the Cnidaria, each cell engulfing food particles by its pseudopodia and passing un-digested waste matter into the intestinal cavity. When the alimentary canal is full of debris, the worm swallows water which it then expels violently through the mouth. There is therefore no defecation, but rather intestinal washing.

The excretory apparatus consists of small tubes (tubules) distributed all over the animal and capped at their inner ends by one or several cells called flame cells. These bear flagella which beat in the lumen (cavity) of the tubule. The excretory tubules open into two longitudinal collecting ducts situated on each side of the body.

The nervous system comprises an anterior pair of cerebral ganglia, the brain, from which run, towards the rear, two longitudinal cords linked by a network of nerve cells. These animals have, therefore, no true central nervous system.

The Turbellaria are hermaphrodite (see diagram opposite).

Those which have only three intestinal caeca, the Tri-cladida, possess extraordinary powers of regeneration; one

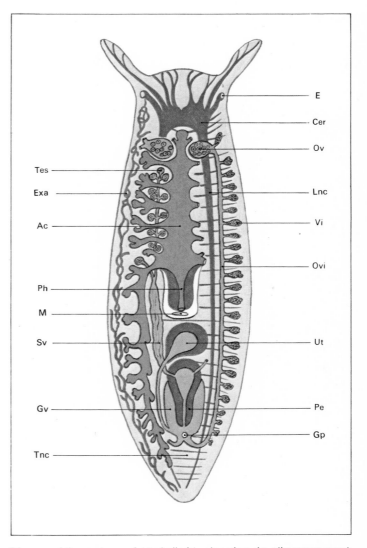

Diagram of the anatomy of a turbellarian planarian: *Ac*, alimentary canal; *Cer*, cerebral ganglia; *E*, eye; *Exa*, excretory canals; *Gp*, genital pore; *Gv*, genital vestibule; *Lnc*, lateral nerve cord; *M*, mouth; *Ov*, ovary; *Ovi*, oviduct; *Pe*, penis; *Ph*, pharynx; *Sv*, seminal vesicle; *Tes*, testes; *Tnc*, transverse nerve commissure; *Ut*, uterus; *Vi*, vitellarium. The true egg is produced by the ovary, but it receives its nutritive materials from a special gland, the vitellarium.

In humid tropical forests and especially in those of southeast Asia, terrestrial Turbellaria—planarians—are much in evidence. The planarian represented here, an undetermined *Bipalium*, was found gliding over a wet leaf in a forest near Singapore. Size, about 1½ inches. Some species are much larger. *Phot. Ivan Polunin*

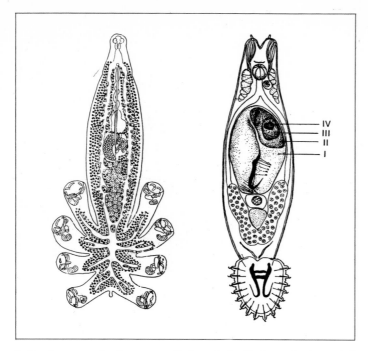

Left, a fine example of monogenetic trematode, *Cyclocotyla chrysophrii*, which lives as a parasite on the gills of the common sea bream, *Pagellus centrodontus*, of the North Atlantic. *After Llewellyn—Right, Gyrodactylus elegans*, an external parasite of cyprinid fishes; this trematode is viviparous. The fertilized egg develops in the maternal uterus and produces, by fragmentation (polyembryony) four embryos at once (I, II, III, IV), one of which contains the other three; these develop much more slowly than their enveloping brother and pass into its uterus (hermaphrodite). The latter, when it becomes adult, lays the most advanced of its brothers. *After Fuhrmann*

Diagram of an oncomiracidium, a ciliated and armed larva, typical of the monogenians: sucker or haptor with its hooks, buccal sucker, covering of vibratile cilia. (Actual size: 300 to 500 microns).

The diplozoons, e.g. *Diplozoon paradoxum*, constitute normal 'Siamese brothers'. Sexual maturity occurs only when two individuals have been able to fuse. They live fixed to the gills of freshwater fish. *After D. G. Baer*

fragment of the body can recreate the whole organism.

The sense organs consist of rudimentary eyes and, here and there, sensory cells of indeterminate function.

Turbellaria are very numerous, and they are classified in several orders: Polycladida, Tricladida, Rhabdocoela, Alloiocoela and Acoela.

The Polycladida are almost all marine, fairly large (from less than one inch to more than four inches), with at least three branched digestive caeca. Some complete their embryonic development as larvae swimming freely among the marine plankton; they are flesh-eating, and occur in the most varied habitats, including algae, rocks and coral.

The Tricladida, or planarians, inhabit all waters and some species are terrestrial. Their habits are more or less the same as those of the Polycladida. The terrestrial species live in damp places (in humus, under bark, cavities in trees, under stones). They have extensive powers of regeneration. They have very frequent asexual reproduction by scission of the body followed by regeneration of the missing parts.

Other orders of lesser importance complete these two large groups; among the Acoela, there is the strange Convoluta (about $\frac{1}{4}$ of an inch), which lives on the French Atlantic coast in the tidal zone, on algae and in sand. The bodies of some species of Convoluta is full of intracellular algae (Chlorella), which live as symbionts. Another peculiarity is that these Convoluta in their daily routine follow the rhythm of the tides, exposing themselves to allow for photosynthesis when the tide ebbs, and sinking into the sand when the tide flows. When placed in an aquarium this rhythm is maintained for a few days only.

The obscure world of the parasitic worms: platyhelminths and nemathelminths

Every living being occupies a habitat which is peculiar to it, and which is limited by the organism's ability to adapt to conditions which are sometimes extreme. This is particularly striking in parasitic worms, the adults of which inhabit the natural cavities of their hosts. Intestine, liver, lungs, heart, kidneys and bladder all constitute habitats or distinct ecological niches, each one of which may harbour a special fauna of helminths. The success of this hidden existence is proved by the occurrence of parasitic helminths in all groups of vertebrates.

Under normal conditions, the parasite never seriously threatens its host's life, even if it is present in large numbers. Moreover, to destroy its host would amount, for a parasite, to suicide. But if the host loses all or part of its natural resistance (and this frequently applies to animals kept in captivity) it becomes adversely affected by the toxins produced by the parasites.

The parasitic worms include all the species of helminths which have adopted this strange existence. From the morphological and biological point of view, however, two broad but unrelated phyla are recognized: the platyhelminths or flat worms, and the nemathelminths, or round worms.

The platyhelminths include both a very important group of free-living species, the aforementioned Turbellaria, and three classes of parasites: the Monogenea, the Cestoda and the Trematoda. Plathyhelminths are, as a general rule, hermaphrodite. They are parasites of vertebrates and invertebrates and, in most cases, have complicated life cycles.

The class Monogenea

The Monogenea live as ectoparasites on the gills or body surface of marine and freshwater fishes. They stick to the host by means of an adhesive apparatus, the sucker, at the rear end of the body. Often, this is a complicated device consisting of sclerous parts, shaped like hooks or anchors. In some groups, it is made up of several fixing organs, each of which has the structure of a claw, with a fixed part on which a mobile part rests. Thus there are two types of sucker, some having on their surface mobile hooks of different sizes, and others having symmetrically arranged claws. Secondarily, however, the arrangement of the claws on the suckers may become asymmetrical, depending on whether the worm is fixed on the right or the left gills.

The development of the Monogenea is direct, but often includes metamorphoses. A larva, or oncomiracidium, develops in the egg, which hatches spontaneously; it is usually ciliated, with a larval sucker.

The eggs frequently have polar prolongations, often very long, but are not attached to the host when laid. They either sink to the bottom or remain suspended in mid-water, their filaments intermingling; then, grouped in clusters, they are raised in the backwash created by the movement of a fish and sucked in by its respiratory movements; they then become attached to the gills, where they hatch.

Comparatively little is known about the cycles of the Monogenea of marine fishes, but, as several of their larval forms are known, it can be stated that they are accomplished through the metamorphoses of the larval suckers. Similar cycles are observed in several species which parasitize freshwater fish.

The cycles of some Monogenea have become aberrant as a result of biological specialization or of the adaptation of the parasites to vertebrates which are terrestrial, but spend part of their existence in water.

A polyembryonic cycle

Gyrodactylus lives on several kinds of freshwater fish and does not lay eggs, but is viviparous. In the course of development, the embryonic cells split up into four groups, each of which develops separately. This can be referred to as polyembryony, but it differs from other known types because the four larvae are encased in each other, so that the larva which is laid contains the three others; these, in turn will be laid separately afterwards. It is understandable, therefore, that in the confined space of an aquarium or a pond almost all the fish will become infested in a comparatively short time. When parasites accumulate on the gills, the fish die of asphyxiation.

Diplozoon, two beings in one, and its cycle

On the gills of some cyprinoids is found a very curious member of the Monogenea, peculiar in that it consists, more or less, of two fused individuals. This species, *Diplozoon paradoxum*, lays eggs with a coiled filament, from which hatch ciliated larvae (oncomiracidia), equipped with a larval sucker with which they fix themselves to the host's gills. There they undergo a metamorphosis, involving the appearance of a sucker on the ventral surface and of a rounded protuberance on the dorsal surface. Having reached this stage, called diporpa, the further development of the larvae ceases, unless two of them manage to seize each other, using

their suckers, by the dorsal protuberance. Once this has been effected, the two individuals fuse, the suckers as well as the dorsal protuberances being reabsorbed. There is also fusion of the two intestines, so that food absorbed by one also benefits the other. From this stage onwards, the Siamese twins pursue their development simultaneously and their suckers grow to the adult size. Because the two individuals are joined together in the shape of a cross, there is reciprocal fusion of the male and female genital ducts, and, therefore, permanent cross-fertilization. Well named, *Diplozoon* (double animal) represents a unique case in the animal kingdom, since the species is formed by two fused individuals, the egg of which produces only one larva.

Polystomum

The cycle of the freshwater Monogenea has favoured the adaptation of worms to vertebrates, other than fish, living in water permanently or during part of their existence. Amphibians are subject to parasitism by *Polystomum* found in

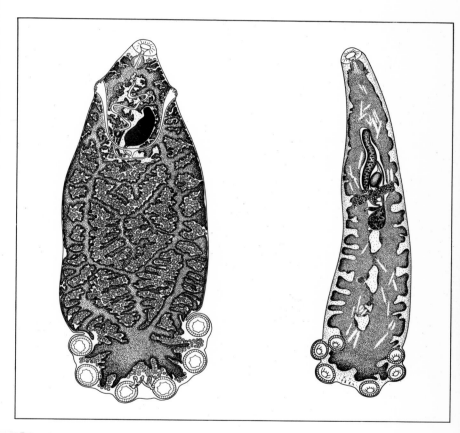

Cycle of *Polystomum integerrimum*, parasite of the common frog (*Rana temporaria*); it lives in the urinary bladder or on the gills of tadpoles. On the left, an adult taken from the urinary bladder; on the right, a larva which has lost its covering of locomotory cilia having just fixed itself to a tadpole's gill, where it grows. When the outer gills are reabsorbed, and the monogenean larva shifts to the inner gills. When the operculum, through which the forelimb will emerge, opens, the larvae of *Polystomum* escape from the branchial cavity, move along the surface of the young frog's body and, via the cloacal opening, penetrate into the urinary bladder, in which the worm becomes adult ($\frac{1}{4}$ of an inch). It is only fit for breeding when the young frog becomes sexually mature and goes to the water to mate. The eggs of *Polystomum* are passed out in the urine and, on reaching the water, liberate the larva (an oncomiracidium). If the temperature is high and the tadpole is at an advanced stage, the *Polystomum* larva becomes fit for breeding before reaching the perfect adult form; it is then described as neotenic. It lays from the age of 25 days. Its size does not exceed $\frac{1}{8}$ of an inch.

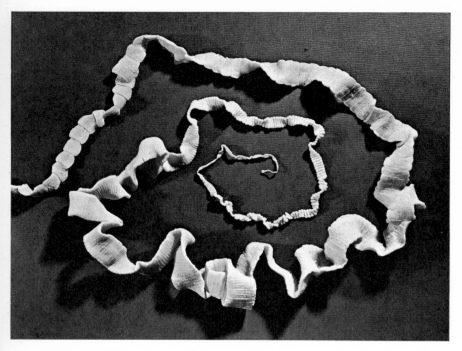

Fore part of the beet tapeworm (*Taenia saginata*), which lives in the small intestine of man. Its larva develops in the inter-fascicular tissue of the muscles of Bovidae. The adult may reach nearly 40 feet in length. This species has no hooks on the head-like scolex. *Phot. Margiocco*

Organizational plan of one ring of an adult tapeworm (*Calliobothrium verticillatum*), parasite of the sea dog (*Mustelus canis*)—a Selacian fish; *Go*, genital opening; *Ov*, ovary; *Sg*, shell gland; *Tes*, testes; *Ud*, uterine duct; *Ut*, uterus; *Va*, vagina; *Vd*, vas deferens or deferent duct; *Yd*, yolk duct; *Ygl*, yolk gland. *After J. G. Baer*

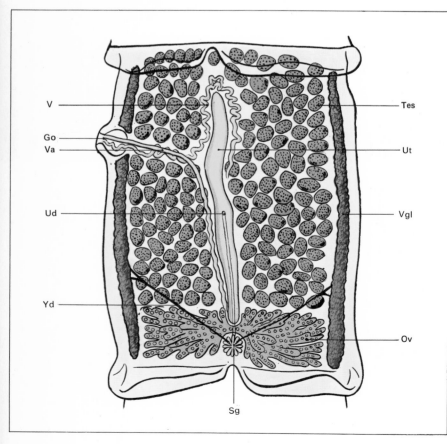

the urinary bladder. The eggs are passed with the urine when frogs go into the water to spawn, and give rise to a ciliated oncomiracidium provided with a larval sucker. These larvae hatch, usually at the same time as the tadpoles, and, fixing themselves to the gills of the latter, they become sexually mature before reaching the perfect form of the species; this is the phenomenon of neoteny. When, at metamorphosis, the tadpole's gills are reabsorbed, the *Polystomum* larvae escape through the operculum which opens in the gill cavity to allow the emergence of the young frog's forelimb. Travelling along the host's body, these larvae penetrate the cloaca to reach the urinary bladder. The interest of this cycle lies in the selective synchronization of the *Polystomum*'s cycle with that of its host, the common European frog, a process which excludes, for instance, the edible frog or the toad. The host's hormones seem to act on the *Polystomum*, and hence the synchronization of the cycles.

The class Cestoda (tapeworms)

Sometimes called solitary worms, cestodes can occasionally reach a length of several yards.

Organic degradation and germ production

Cestodes are characterized by the absence of an intestine. However, the integument is made up of a tissue in which the cells are fused (syncytium); and the structure of this, as revealed by the electron microscope, is analogous to intestinal cells. In other words, cestodes have their absorptive tissues on the outside of the body, a characteristic not only unique but also admirably adapted to an existence in their host's alimentary canal, as well as favouring a high rate of growth. New segments are continually being formed in the anterior region; they reach sexual maturity towards the middle region, and the last ones, full of eggs, are detached continuously.

The tapeworm is fixed to its host's intestine by the head, or scolex, an anchoring apparatus which is provided with foliated or rounded muscular suckers. The scolex often bears a retractile muscular rostrum, armed with hooks, imbedded in the intestinal wall.

Each segment contains a hermaphrodite reproductive apparatus, and self-fertilization is usually the rule. The production of eggs is, therefore, enormous and may continue without interruption for several years. The daily laying of the broad tapeworm of man, *Bothriocephalus latus*, is estimated to be about a million eggs; and as its lifespan may exceed twenty years, the production of eggs exceeds seven thousand million. However, losses are heavy, because of the complicated life cycle.

The tapeworm cycle

The egg contains an onchosphere larva, which is equipped with three pairs of tiny hooks and can develop only in a favourable host which has swallowed the egg. This intermediate host, either an invertebrate or a vertebrate, will thus harbour the infective larval form. As a rule, it does not belong to the same species as the final host in which the worm becomes adult; nevertheless, it must be eaten by the latter, and therefore the intermediate and final hosts live in the same habitat, the first being an element in the second's food chain.

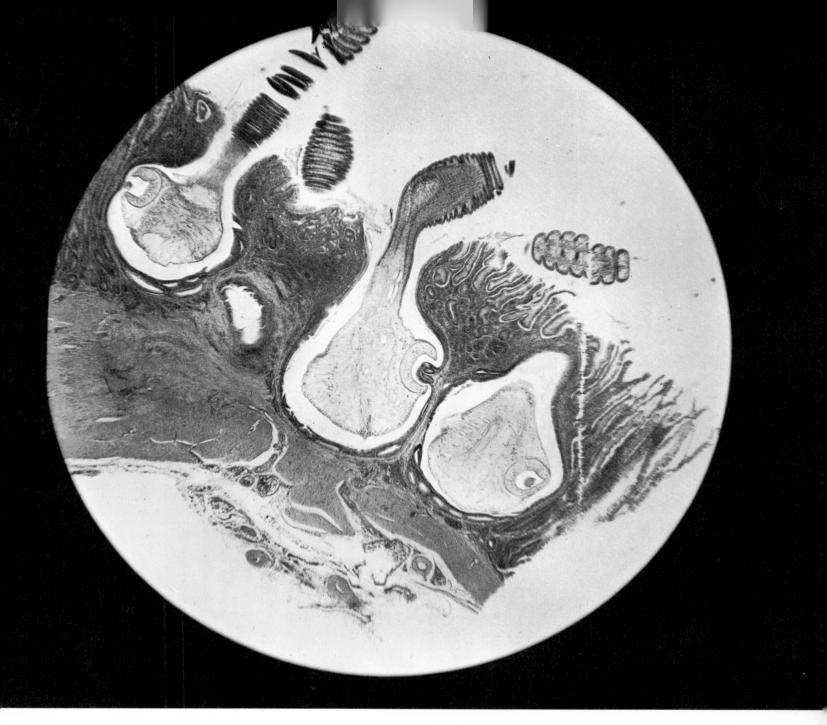

Section of the intestinal wall of a guillemot, *Uria*, with three cestodes (*Anomotaenia meinterzhageni*) fixed in position. The intestinal wall can be clearly seen to be 'sucked up' by one of the suckers of the middle individual (× about 100). *Phot. J. G. Baer*

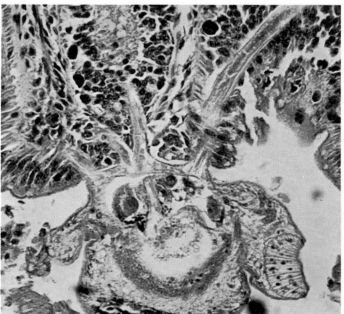

Section showing the scolex with 'tentacles' of *Parataenia medusae*, buried in a ray's intestinal mucous membrane. The prolongations of the scolex have a fixative and not an absorbent role. (×150). *Phot. J. G. Baer*

Infesting larvae are characterized by a completely constituted scolex. There are, however, considerable differences in the structure of the larval feeding organs with which nourishment is obtained from the intermediate host. In some forms budding occurs and a single larva will produce a large number of infective scoleces by this means. In *Taenia echinococcus*, for instance, the cysticercus larva or bladder worm becomes a sac containing hundreds of scoleces (a hydatid cyst), thus illustrating the connection which exists between the number of eggs produced and the risks of failure involved in the evolutionary cycle. In fact, *Taenia echino-*

coccus, which lives in the dog, has only four or five proglottides (reproductive segments) about half an inch long and therefore produces a small number of eggs; this is made up for by the presence of a large number of adult worms resulting from the absorption by the dog of a single infective larva or cysticercus.

As a rule, the development from the onchosphere to the larva takes place entirely in a single intermediate host, but there are a few groups of cestodes; among these is found the broad tapeworm of man, the cycle of which requires two successive intermediate hosts, the first always being an

Cysticercus larva of a tapeworm: *Sc*, invaginated scolex.

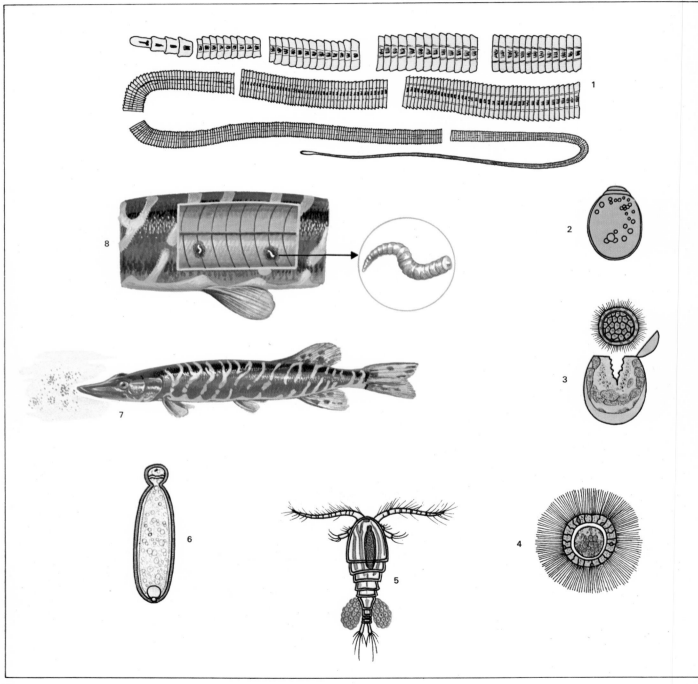

Cycle of the broad tapeworm (*Diphyllobothrium latum*), parasite of the small intestine of man. When adult, this tapeworm may measure 6–26 feet in length. *1*, fragments of the adult tapeworm; *2*, egg; *3*, hatching of the egg enveloped in its embryophore; *4*, hexacanth larva swimming in water with the help of its embryophore covered with flagella; *5*, *Cyclops* which is infected by swallowing the embryo; *6*, procercoid larval stage which has developed in the small crustacean; *7*, the pike which is infected in its turn by eating the copepod; *8*, the plerocercoid larva, lodged in the fish's flesh, infects the man who will ingest it. The broad tapeworm is most frequent in lacustrine fishes, especially in Switzerland, the Baltic, the delta of the Danube, Siberia and Japan.

invertebrate. This cycle is carried out almost invariably in an aquatic environment, and the larval development is effected in two stages, interrupted by a change of intermediate host, the first one being eaten by the second.

Some typical cycles

It is possible to distinguish, from the biological point of view, two kinds of cycles, depending on whether the infective larvae are in an aquatic or terrestrial intermediate host.

Cycles of aquatic species

In spite of the large number of cestodes of marine animals, including some which are highly specialized (e.g. the parasites of dog fish), in no case has the developmental cycle been successfully analysed—notwithstanding the presence of infective larval forms in cephalopod molluscs, Cnidaria and even marine mammals (whales). It is probable that these cycles call for two successive intermediate hosts.

Several cycles taking place in the freshwater type are perfectly known. Among them the three following types may be distinguished.

Cycles with two obligatory intermediate hosts
The first host is a copepod (suborder Copepoda) crustacean which swallows the onchosphere, the second a fish in the musculature of which the infective plerocercoid larvae (the second stage) develop. The final host of the larva is a predatory fish, such as the pike. This cycle is observed in *Triaenophorus crassus*.

Cycles of two obligatory intermediate hosts with an optional waiting host
The beginning of the cycle proceeds as above, and the infective larva develops in the fish, i.e. the second host. However, although the second intermediate host may be eaten by a predatory fish, a pike or a large trout, finishing the cycle does not depend on this action. The plerocercoid larvae are not digested in the predatory fish, but are re-encapsulated in the wall of the intestine or of the peritoneal cavity, at the same time remaining infective and without developing. In this way a large fish may accumulate hundreds of larvae in the course of its existence. This optional third host, the 'waiting host', therefore increases the chances of propagation of the adult worm. Such is the cycle in the case of *Diphyllobothrium latum*, the broad tapeworm of man and of fish-eating mammals, e.g. the dog, fox, cat, and bear.

Cycle with a single obligatory intermediate host
In *Ichthyotaenia*, a parasite of fishes, the infective plerocercoid larva is formed in the first intermediate host, also a copepod, which is then eaten by a fish, the final host. However, there is again the possibility of an extra intermediate host, a fish, in which the plerocercoid larvae accumulate. This waiting host has become almost indispensable in the cycle of the neighbouring genus, *Ophiotaenia*, for the chances of a snake (the final host for this species) catching a small fish are greater than those of its swallowing copepods.

Many species of cestodes of birds and mammals also have aquatic cycles with a single intermediate host, an insect, crustacean or mollusc, in which the infective cysticercoid larva develops.

From the biological point of view, such cycles are interesting because they do not necessarily imply that the final

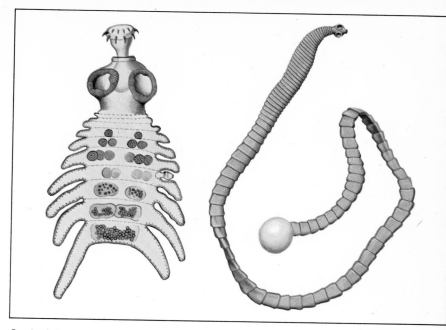

On the left, an aberrant tapeworm, *Tatria biremis*, parasite of the black-necked grebe (*Podiceps nigricollis*). Its segments bear lateral prolongations. The last segments are full of eggs. The scolex shows its circular suckers and a retractile bulb armed with hooks. On the right, *Taenia taeniaeformis*, an advanced larva taken from a rat's liver. Its last segment ends in a vesicle representing a non-proliferating part of the cysticercus. *After J. G. Baer*

Cycle of *Dipylidium caninum*, tapeworm of the small intestine of the dog (6–16 inches in length): *A*, scolex with its retractile rostrum almost entirely invaginated; *B*, segment (proglottid) full of eggs showing its two lateral genital openings; *C*, eggs grouped in a capsule; *D*, larva of flea which is infected by eating the capsules evacuated by the dog with its faeces, and which have remained in the dust and debris of the kennel; *E*, the adult flea, which, when eaten by the dog, infects it through the cysticercoid larvae (*F*) it contains.

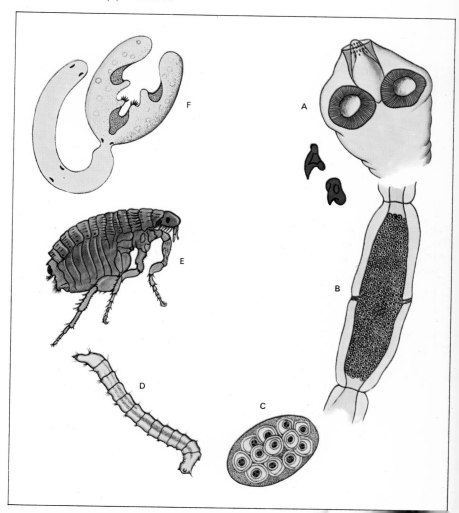

hosts are exclusively aquatic (e.g. ducks), but that, living on land, they feed in water (waders, some small mammals). By analogy with the trematodes, it is probable that the cestodes of bats also evolve in an aquatic environment in the larvae of aerial insects, thus ensuring the transportation out of the water of the infective larvae.

Cycles of terrestrial species

With very few exceptions, all the terrestrial cycles develop in the presence of a single intermediate host, which is either an

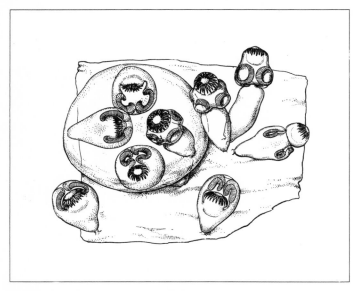

Echinococcid tapeworm (*Echinococcus granulosus*), fragment of a hydatic cyst or sac, showing the multiple formation of cysticerci larval stages by the generative membrane of the cyst. *After Fuhrmann*

Cycle of the beef tapeworm, *Taenia saginata*: *1*, anterior region of the adult in the small intestine of man; *2*, a reproductive segment or proglottis, when mature (ramified uterus, full of eggs); *3*, the hexacanth embryo within its egg; *4*, dirt containing the eggs is found in meadows and cattle become contaminated by swallowing these eggs; *5*, the cysticercus; *6*, the cysticercus ingested by man devaginates its scolex, the proglottides already having developed behind it.

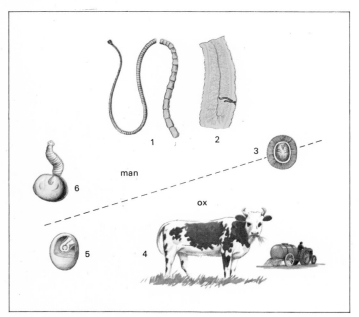

invertebrate (insect, mollusc, etc.) or a vertebrate (rodent, insectivore, herbivore, etc.). In *Hymenolepis fraterna* of the mouse and the rat, the intermediate host has become optional, because the cycle is telescoped; the cysticercoid, instead of being formed in an insect's body cavity, develops in the lining of the intestine of the final host which has ingested the eggs. However, once the larva has been constituted, it frees itself from the lining and fixes itself to the surface of the intestinal mucous membrane, where it is transformed into an adult worm.

The class Trematoda (flukes)

The Trematoda are unsegmented flatworms, each being provided with a mouth and a blind intestine (without an anus). The mouth is surrounded by a sucker followed by a muscular pharynx, which functions like a suction pump. In spite of the presence of a functional digestive system, the integument also plays a part in the absorption of food. However, the ultra-structure of the trematodes is less complicated than that of the cestodes. The main fixation apparatus is a ventral sucker. The reproductive system is hermaphrodite. Exceptionally, in *Schistosoma*, the sexes are separate and there is sexual dimorphism. The adult worms are found in the intestine, the liver and gall bladder, and the pancreatic ducts, as well as in the lungs, and, exceptionally, in the blood vessels. Whatever the location of the fluke, the eggs must be conveyed to the external environment via the natural passages.

The development of the cercaria stage (final larval stage), starting from the miracidium larva (which is formed in the egg), takes place in the first intermediate host. It is characterized by an intense multiplication of larvae.

The first intermediate host is an aquatic or terrestrial mollusc. The miracidium larva is usually ciliated and swims in search of the intermediate host, but it sheds its covering of cilia as soon as it penetrates a mollusc's tissues, penetration being facilitated by the enzymes secreted by cells in its anterior end. When the egg does not hatch spontaneously, it is eaten by the mollusc and the larva is released in its stomach by the action of the digestive juices. The multiplication of the larval germs takes place at the expense of the embryonic cells contained in the miracidium. They multiply very rapidly and form elongate and sometimes ramified larvae, or 'sporocysts', which invade the mollusc's hepatopancreas.

The sporocyst's evolution may take place in either of two directions, depending on whether it produces within itself a second generation of sporocysts, called 'daughter sporocysts', or whether larval forms—which have a mouth, pharynx and rudimentary intestinal diverticulum (tubular sacs), and are called 'redia'—are formed. Moreover, between these two second generation larval forms there are all the morphological intermediates; they are therefore considered as equivalent developments.

Within these second generation larvae arise the cercariae, the larval forms which will escape from the mollusc to lead short-lived independent lives in the surrounding environment —where they will meet the second intermediate host. The number of cercariae produced is high and production continues as long as the mollusc remains alive. An often quoted example is that of a winkle, isolated in order to prevent any secondary infestation, which produced, in five years, 5,000,000 cercariae. After seven years, daily production was still 1600,

The common liver fluke, *Fasciola hepatica*, parasite of cattle; it can be up to 1¼ inches in length. *Phot. Aldo Margiocco*

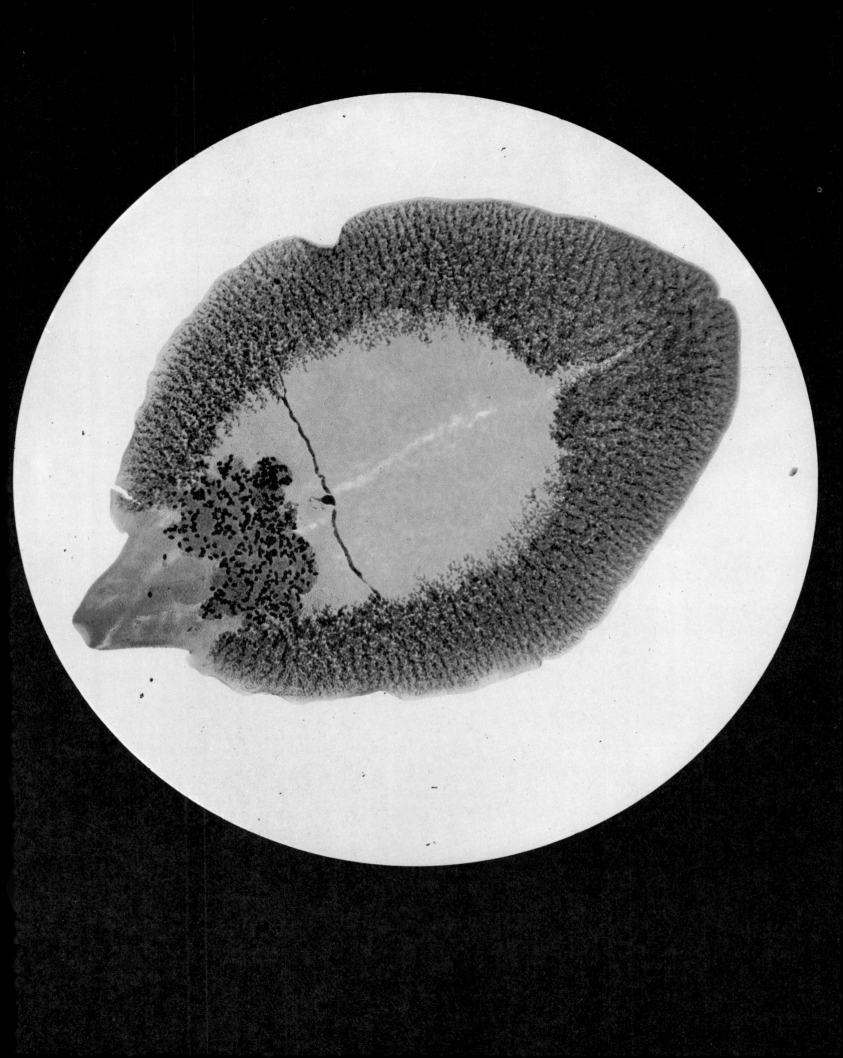

and only the accidental destruction of the mollusc interrupted the experiment.

There exists a large number of different types of cercariae, distinguished mainly by the shape and size of the tail, a locomotory organ adapted to the environment and shed at the time of penetrating the second intermediate host. The cercaria's body resembles a tiny trematode with its suckers and its bifid intestine. There is also a considerable development of glandular cells opening in the neighbourhood of the oral sucker. The latter often has a spiny covering or a very hard stylet, at the base of which open the excretory ducts of the glands. This penetrating apparatus enables the cercaria to pass through the integument of the second intermediate host. In cases where the cycle does not include a second intermediate host and where the cercaria becomes encysted in the outside environment, one finds many small unicellular glands opening on the surface of the body; the secretion of these glands forms the wall of the cyst.

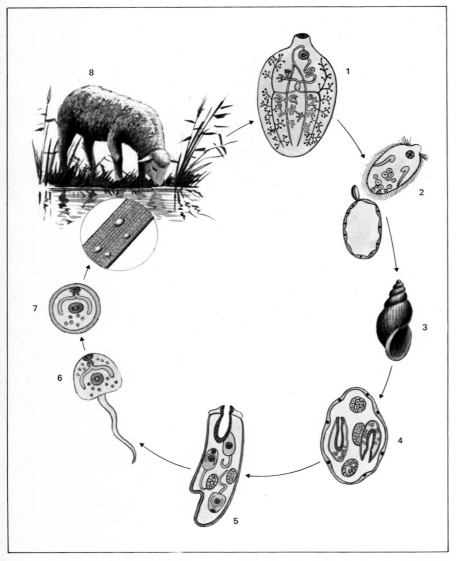

Life cycle of the common liver fluke *Fasciola hepatica*: *1*, adult fluke living in the biliary ducts of the sheep; *2*, egg hatching and releasing the miracidium larva (130 microns long); *3*, the dwarf pond snail, *Limnaea trunculata*, which in Europe is the intermediate host of the common liver fluke; *4*, sporocyst with cellular masses and rediae; *5*, redia with cercariae and cellular masses; *6*, cercaria (300 microns, excluding tail); *7*, metacercaria; *8*, metacercariae on an aquatic leaf which, when eaten by the sheep, will infest it. The common liver fluke is a dangerous parasite which causes degeneration of the hepatic tissue around the bile ducts.

In the second intermediate host, the cercaria is transformed into an infective larva or metacercaria, which is usually encysted. Within the cyst, the structure of the future worm, and especially the advanced rough outline of the sexual organs, are already apparent.

Some typical cycles

Although aquatic evolutionary cycles are by far the most frequent and most varied, it is nevertheless possible to recognize a small number of exclusively terrestrial cycles, which present adaptations inherent to these conditions.

Aquatic cycles

There is no need to list here the very numerous known aquatic cycles, but only those which present a special interest from the biological point of view, at the same time underlining the variations and the possibilities of passages from aquatic intermediate hosts to final terrestrial hosts.

In *Plagiorchis*, cercariae are produced in the sporocysts of a freshwater mollusc. They are equipped with a perforatory stylet as well as a bulky glandular apparatus, with which they penetrate into the second intermediate host, an arthropod, which in turn is eaten by a bird or a mammal. The fact, for the cercaria, of being encysted in a winged insect's larva opens to it new environments in which it may meet final hosts. Such, for example, is the cycle of *Plagiorchis micracanthos*, a parasite of bats. But it happens that the cercaria becomes encysted in the mollusc itself, which affords the parasite a chance of passing into the intestine of a final mollusc-eating host.

In *Opisthorchis*, a parasite of the biliary and pancreatic passages of birds and mammals, the cercariae, produced in rediae (intestinal sacs), encyst under the skin of freshwater fishes. It follows that the final hosts are piscivores. In some parasites of frogs, *Gorgodera* of the urinary bladder and *Halipegus* of the sublingual (under the tongue) cavity, the cercariae are eaten by the second intermediate host, a mollusc or a crustacean, in which they are encysted. Finally, in *Glyphthelmius*, the metacercariae are encysted in the skin of the final host, again a frog, and are cast off and eaten when strips of epidermis are detached at the time of moulting. In *Ptychogonimus*, a parasite of the shark, the cercariae do not emerge from the sporocyst, and the latter is expelled from the first intermediate host to be eaten by a crab, in which the cercariae become encysted.

In several species, including *Fasciola hepatica*, the common liver fluke of sheep and cattle, the cercariae become encysted on vegetation near to or floating on water.

It can even happen that the second intermediate host is suppressed and that some cercariae are encysted in the sporocyst, which by then contains only metacercariae. This is the case in *Diphterostomum brusinae*, harboured by a marine fish, which becomes infested by eating molluscs containing parasites. On the other hand, in *Plagioporus sinitsini*, a parasite of the gall bladders of freshwater fish, the sporocysts, coloured yellow or red and containing the metacercariae, are expelled from the mollusc by the anus. They may survive at least 24 hours in water and are swallowed by the final host. It is probable that the two cycles are secondarily shortened, with loss of the second intermediate host, the latter having become superfluous as a result of the formation of metacercariae in the sporocyst.

The metacercaria stage no longer exists in the cycle of trematodes, such as *Schistosoma* (the cause of human bilharziasus), which live in the adult state in the blood vessels. Instead, the cercariae directly penetrate the skin of the final host to reach the blood vessels, in which they are transformed into adult worms.

In some very specialized forms, such as the Strigeidae, which are harboured by reptiles, birds and mammals, the penetration of the cercaria into the second intermediate host is followed by a metamorphosis of the infective larva. In this same group, one sometimes observes a larval stage between the cercaria and the metacercaria, called the 'mesocercaria', which is formed in the second intermediate host. However, this additional host is optional, as it may be replaced by a migration into the organism of the second intermediate host.

Terrestrial cycles

In *Brachylaemus*, species of which infest birds and mammals, the eggs are eaten by a mollusc and hatch in its intestine. There are two generations of ramified sporocysts, the second of which produces cercariae with a very short tail. When several molluscs are agglomerated, the cercariae leave the intermediate host and penetrate by the renal opening into the kidney and the pericardial cavity. The metacercaria is not encysted and moves about freely within the organ in which it finds itself. Consequently, the cycle involves two successive hosts (terrestrial molluscs), or a single host, the organs of which are parasitized successively.

A lesser liver fluke
In the lesser liver fluke, *Dicrocoelium dendriticum*, which lives in the bile ducts of herbivorous mammals, the egg hatches after having been eaten by the mollusc, a land snail. The second generation of sporocysts produces cercariae with long tails, buccal stylets and bulky glandular apparatus. These cercariae pass into the snail's pulmonary cavity, in which they become encysted, but without losing their tails. The cysts are gradually enveloped by mucus secreted by the mollusc and are expelled by way of the respiratory orifice when the intermediate host climbs on to vegetation in damp weather. There, covered in mucus, they adhere to the plants and are eaten by ants. In the intestine of the second intermediate host, the cercariae are liberated from their cysts and pass through the wall of the intestine to become encysted in the ant's body cavity, in which they become metacercariae. Strangely enough, one of the cercariae usually penetrates into the ant's sub-oesophageal ganglion, with the result that the latter keeps hanging on to the grass by its mandibles; this naturally favours its absorption by the final host.

A highly-coloured parasite
The adaptation of the cycle of *Leucochloridium*, a parasite of birds, to terrestrial life is very marked. The first intermediate host, *Succinea*, is a mollusc which lives in damp places, but does not enter the water. The eggs are swallowed by the *Succinea*, and develop into ramified sporocysts, producing

Opposite left: diagram of a Trematode: *Eb,* excretory bladder; *Ec,* excretory canal; *Ep,* excretory pore; *Ib,* intestinal branch; *Lc,* Laurer's canal; *Lec,* lateral excretory canal; *Os,* oral sucker; *Ov,* ovary; *Pe,* penis; *Ph,* pharynx; *Pnr,* pharyngeal nerve ring; *Sg,* shell gland; *Sv,* seminal vesicle; *Tes,* testes; *Ut,* uterus; *Vd,* vas deferens; *Vs,* ventral sucker; *Yd,* yolk duct; *Yg,* yolk glands.

Opposite, right, free ciliated larva or miracidium of *Parorchis acanthus,* from the Fabrician pouch of the herring gull, *Larus argentatus,* showing its internal organism: nervous system, glandular cells, excretory cells, and an already formed redia; in the redia can be seen cellular spheres which will produce the other stages of the cycle. The duration of free life of the miracidia does not seem to exceed 24 hours. *After Rees*

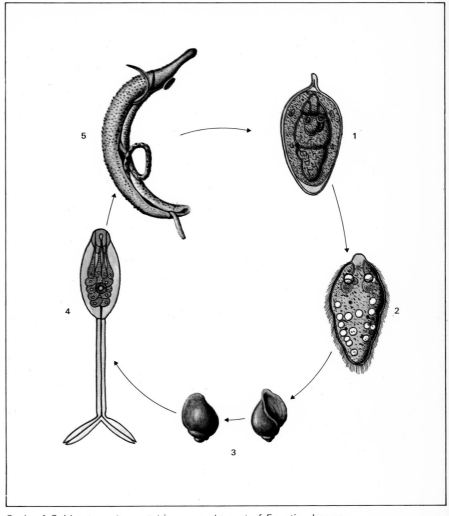

Cycle of *Schistosoma haematobium*, causal agent of Egyptian haematuria or bilharzia: *1,* egg fallen into the water and swollen; *2,* miracidium larva; *3,* intermediate host, an aquatic pulmonate mollusc, a bullin (*Bullinus*); *4,* the furcocercaria which emerges from the bullin, swims and passes through the wet skin of the man who is bathing; *5,* the adult couple in the human blood vessels. In order to lay, the worms enter the capillary vessels of the bladder, which they tear with spurs attached to their eggs.

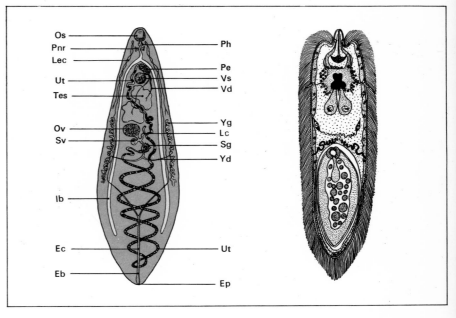

tailless cercariae, which are encysted in a thick mucous envelope and accumulate in the diverticula of the sporocyst. These tiny diverticula are coloured by brownish-red or green and red rings of pigment, and end up by penetrating the inside of the mollusc's tentacles, which they dilate to such an extent that the coloured bands shine through transparently. At the least touch, the dilated tentacle breaks, freeing the diverticulum, which then becomes completely detached from the sporocyst, and climbs, with rhythmical pulsating movements, to the surface of the leaves. Full of metacercariae and resembling small caterpillars, the coloured diverticula attract birds, which become infested by eating them.

Accelerated development in trematodes

In trematodes, the phenomenon of progenesis, i.e. the maturation of the gonads and their activity as early as the metacercaria stage, occurs fairly often. Theoretically, progenesis suppresses the final host, or rather the latter is placed upon the second intermediate host. However, it is optional and its appearance seems to depend, above all, on the nutritional conditions encountered by the metacercariae in the second intermediate host. However, in the case of *Ratzia parva*, the final host has never been identified; the progenetic metacercaria produces eggs within cutaneous cysts on a toad, and the eggs are liberated after the shedding of the skin.

Further migrations in the final host

In trematodes which live in the intestine, the swallowed metacercariae hatch and become fixed straight away to the intestinal mucous membrane. In cases where other organs are parasitized, a migration of metacercariae occurs. It takes place directly from the intestine towards the biliary or pancreatic ducts in the Dicrocoeliidae and the Opisthorichiidae; in *Fasciola*, the metacercariae pass through the intestinal wall and, from the peritoneal cavity, reach the biliary passages by penetrating the surface of the liver. The same initial path is followed by the metacercariae of *Paragonimus*, but, from the peritoneal cavity, they pass through the diaphragm to penetrate the lungs and lodge in the bronchi. In trematodes which are parasites of blood vessels, however, the eggs laid in the capillary vessels migrate passively in the blood stream to the urinary bladder or the intestine (in birds and mammals), or the gill filaments (in fish).

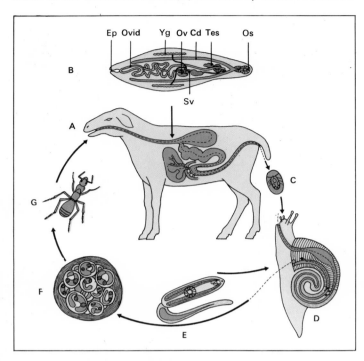

Cycle of the lesser liver fluke of sheep, *Dicrocoelium dendriticum*; *A*, the sheep, final host, infested by swallowing the ant; *B*, the adult fluke (*Cd*, intestinal caecum; *Ep*, excretory pore; *Os*, oral sucker; *Ov*, ovary; *Ovid*, oviduct; *Sv*, seminal vesicle; *Tes*, testes; *Yg*, yolk gland); *C*, egg embryonated and ingested by the snail; *D*, snail, first intermediate host; *E*, isolated cercaria; *F*, cercariae covered in mucus as they emerge via the pneumostome (snail's respiratory opening); *G*, ant, second intermediate host which has ingested the cercariae (the metacercariae are formed in the ant). The lesser liver fluke of sheep does less harm than the common liver fluke.

Head of a *Succinea*, with tentacles dilated and coloured by the diverticula of the sporocyst of *Leucochloridium*. This alteration is considered to be an admirable adaptation of the parasite to its means of transmission.

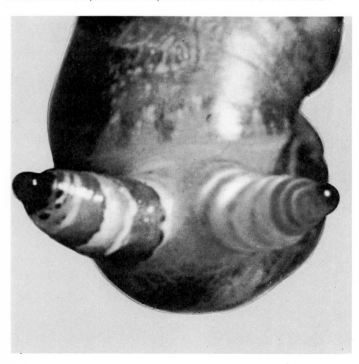

The class Nematoda (roundworms)

The Nematoda contain almost as many free-living species in the soil or water as species which are parasites of almost all the groups of vertebrates, as well as many invertebrates, especially insects. They are round-sectioned worms, usually filiform and between 1/10 and 1/16 of an inch long, but capable of reaching more than three feet in exceptional cases.

The body wall is formed by an elastic cuticulo-muscular sheath, which marks the limits of a cavity containing the intestine and the reproductive organs. The lips around the mouth are often mobile, and equipped with sensory endings. An interesting modification of the buccal (cheek) cavity is observed in some strongyles, especially in *Ancylostoma*, a parasite of man. The cavity, or bursa, is kept wide open as a result of the presence of hardened parts—curved teeth or equally hardened sharp blades, which sink into the intestinal mucous membrane. At the bottom of the bursa, there open glands, the secretion of which digests the host's tissues. The worm fixes itself by sucking up the intestinal mucous membrane, which is then liquefied within the bursa before being sucked up by the pharynx. The sub-mucous blood capillaries are injured and, consequently, the blood flows into the bursa and passes into the worm's intestine, where it is digested.

When a large number of worms is present, the resulting numerous micro-haemorrhages produce anaemia in the host (ancylostomiasis, or miners' anaemia).

The pharynx is a muscular pumping organ which, with peristaltic contractions, conveys liquid food rapidly into the intestine. Towards the middle level of the pharynx is the nerve ring, the main centre from which the nerves run. The intestine, rectilinear in shape, leads to a short rectum and the anus is on the ventral surface, at the posterior end of the body.

The sexes are usually separate and dissimilar in appearance. In the females, the genital opening is on the ventral surface, but its position varies according to species; it opens into a short tube with a muscular wall, the vagina, leading into the uterus.

In the male, the genital duct always opens at the posterior end, in the upper part of the rectum, the distal portion of which is therefore a cloaca. In most males, there are two chitinous copulatory spicules, capable of protruding into the cloaca. The role of these spicules is to keep the partners together during mating. In some groups the males have, in addition, lateral expansions of the tail end, which grip the female round the body forming a copulatory pouch. There have been cases of copulation becoming permanent—the two partners become fixed at the level of the female genital pore (*Syngamus*), the worms between them forming a Y. It also happens that sexual dimorphism is so pronounced that the male (or sometimes several males) lodge within the female's actual genital passages, e.g. *Trichosomoides*, a parasite of the brown rat's urinary bladder.

Nematodes are divided into two large subclasses: the Phasmidia and the Aphasmidia. These are distinguishable by the presence, in the former, of a pair of small sensory organs, the amphids, extremely varied in shape; they are situated in the roof of the buccal cavity behind the lips.

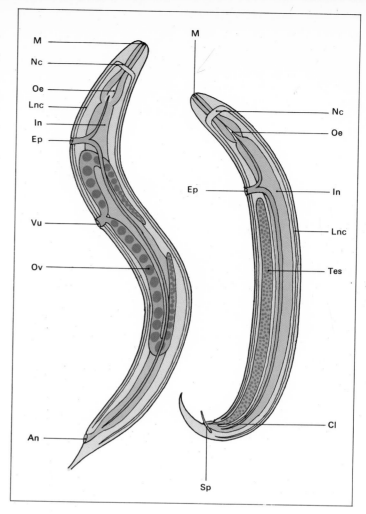

Diagram of the anatomy of a nematode, on the left female, on the right male: *An*, anus; *Cl*, cloaca; *Ep*, excretory pore; *In*, intestine; *Lnc*, longitudinal nerve cord; *M*, mouth; *Nc*, nerve collar; *Oe*, oesophagus; *Ov*, ovary; *Sp*, spicule; *Tes*, testis; *Vu*, vulva.

Left, ascaris of the horse (*Parascaris equorum*): the two individuals on the right are females, the individual on the left, a male (end twisted in a crook). *Phot. Aldo Margiocco*

Post-embryonic development

In all nematodes, whether free or parasitic, post-embryonic development is characterized by five larval stages, separated by four moults, the last stage ending in the adult worm. In the Aphasmidia, the first larval stage may be infective for a new host; in the Phasmidia (the majority of the parasitic nematodes), it is always the third larval stage which is infective. It happens that the larva moults once or twice in the egg and, consequently, that it hatches at the second or third stage.

Evolutionary cycles of aphasmidian nematodes

Single host cycles

In the Trichocephalus of rodents (*Trichuris muris*), and no doubt also in that of man (*Tr. trichiura*), the swallowed egg hatches in the intestine. Here the four successive moults occur and the worm becomes adult.

Cannabalism exists in many cycles

In *Capillaria*, there is a tendency for adult worms to leave the intestine and to establish themselves in other organs. In the common shrew, for instance, one finds *C. exigua* in the gastric mucous membrane, *C. incrassata* in the mucous membrane of the bladder, *C. soricicola* in the liver, and *C. splenicea* in the spleen. These four species are found simultaneously in the same shrew and, each having its micro-environment, its ecological niche, they do not compete with each other. Yet, although the eggs of the species living in the mucous membrane of the alimentary canal or of the bladder are evacuated to the exterior, the same does not apply to those eggs accumulated in the liver and in the spleen. However, as the lifespan of a shrew scarcely exceeds eighteen months, these eggs are liberated during the course of post-mortem decomposition. One can also envisage transmission by cannibalism; however, as it is necessary for the egg to spend a certain amount of time in the exterior (in a humid environment or even in a dried-up state) before the cycle can resume, cannibalism is not considered to represent a normal phase of the cycle.

On the other hand, cannibalism is indispensable to complete the life cycle of *Trichina*. This parasite is viviparous, burying itself deep in its host's intestinal mucous membrane, and its larvae reach the striated musculature by way of the circulatory system. Trichinosis may be transmitted to a very large number of hosts, essentially mammals, among whom man represents an occasional host, infestation usually arising from the meat of a pig which has itself eaten a rat or a mouse. It is, in fact, rodents with cannibal habits which constitute the habitual hosts of *Trichina*.

The lesser roundworm of man (*Strongyloides stercoralis*)— female; actual size 1/25 of an inch. *After Looss*

Cycles with an intermediate host

In *Capillaria contorta*, a parasite of crows, the intermediate host, a small earthworm, is again optional, since infestation is produced also when the bird ingests the eggs directly. On the other hand, in *C. plica*, an inhabitant of the urinary passages of ducks, the intermediate host, a small aquatic oligochaete, has become indispensable.

Dioctophyma renale, or the giant strongyle, may reach over three feet in length and lives coiled within the kidney of a dog or of other mammals, among which man may be accidentally included. Its cycle involves two intermediate hosts, the second of which may be optional. In fact, if infestation succeeds when the dog swallows the first host, a freshwater oligochaete, it has more chance of being effected by means of the second, optional host—a fish. The chances of a dog eating a fish harbouring the larval form are greater than those of its swallowing a tiny aquatic oligochaete.

Evolutionary cycles of phasmidian nematodes

In view of the fact that it is always the third larval stage which is infective, the cycle will be characterized from the biological viewpoint by the way in which the infective larval stage penetrates or transfers to the final host. One will thus have cycles called monoxenous, involving only one host, the final host, and cycles called heteroxenous, with at least one intermediate host, both of which may be complicated by migrations of larvae into the organism of the final host.

Single host cycles

Primitive type

In *Strongyloides stercoralis*, a parasite of man, the females, all parthenogenetic, live deeply buried in the intestinal mucous membrane and lay eggs which hatch on the spot, so that the larvae are found in the stools. The cycle may be accomplished in two ways: either the larvae of the third stage, cast out into the exterior environment, penetrate directly through the skin to reach the intestine via the circulatory and pulmonary passages; or the larvae, although remaining in the intestine, rapidly become males or females and feed on the intestinal content.

The fertilized females lay; their larvae, eel-shaped, are cast out into the exterior, and behave like larvae of parthenogenetic origin. The existence of these two kinds of cycles seems based on their nutirtional nature.

Non-migratory type

One of the simplest cycles is that of the *Oxyuris* parasites of insects, in which the eggs contain a larva on the point of moulting for the second time, so that each egg is already infective after a few days. On the other hand, in *Oxyuris equi* of the horse and *Enterobius vermicularis* of man, the female worms emerge from the rectum by the anus to lay their eggs in the anal region. The whole mass of the eggs laid at one time is at the same stage of development and becomes infective after six hours, making possible an intense infestation of the host by transport to the mouth. In most of the Trichostrongylidae, intestinal parasites of ruminants, the eggs hatch on the ground and the infective larvae are found on grass.

Trans-pulmonary migrations

This type of cycle is observed, among others, in the ancylostomes, among which are the intestinal parasites of man. The third larval stage is found in the ground, and the larvae penetrate the host by the surface of the skin, from which they are drawn into the lungs by the circulation of the blood. However, when infestation is produced accidentally by way of the mouth, migration via the lungs does not occur.

In the ascarids of man (*Ascaris lumbricoides*), of the pig (*Ascaris suum*), of the horse (*Parascaris equorum*), and of the calf, the larva moults within the egg. When the latter is swallowed by the final host, the larva hatches and, passing through the intestinal mucous membrane, migrates by way of the bloodstream into the lungs, where the third larval stage is formed; this larva then migrates into the bronchi, then into the trachea. The swallowed infective larva fixes itself to the intestinal mucous membrane and is transformed into an adult worm. By studying the cycle of other species of ascarids, one is led to interpret the trans-pulmonary cycle as a telescoped two-host cycle, in which the migration of the larva presumably replaces the intermediate host.

Syngamus

On the other hand, in *Syngamus trachea*, which lives in the respiratory passages of birds (particularly farmyard birds), migration of ingested larvae takes place from the intestine into the lungs. However, this cycle may also involve an optional intermediate host, an earthworm, which ingests the eggs and contains the infective larva. This alternative presumably possesses a selective advantage for the infestation of birds eating earthworms and is probably thus in the process of becoming a heteroecious cycle, i.e. having different stages on different hosts.

Uncinaria lucasi

This unique type is found in *Uncinaria lucasi*, an anclyostome parasite of the fur seal of the Pribilof Islands. The eggs hatch in the ground, in which the infective larvae are found. The latter penetrate the skin of the fins and belly and take up their abode in the layer of fat and, in the females, the mammary glands. The infective larvae, inhabiting the ducts of the mammary glands, infect young seals through their mother's milk. The worms are adult after a fortnight. However, one of the peculiarities of this cycle is that, towards the age of six months, the young get rid of their worms spontaneously and do not again become infested. It follows therefore that only very young seals are capable of transmitting the infestation, as the adult seals never harbour adult worms. On the other hand, as infestation can take place only on the seals' annual return to land for breeding, the eggs and infective larvae survive in the ground during the winter.

Trans-placental migrations

Trans-placental migration of the larvae proceeding from the maternal organism is the most frequent mode of infestation in the ascarid of the dog. It is also observed, as an alternative, in the ascarid of the calf.

Heteroecious cycles

Parasites of the intestine

In *Porrocaecum ensicaudatum*, a parasite of birds, larvae moult once in the egg, which is eaten by and then hatches in the intestines of an earthworm. The larvae pass into the circulatory system, where the infective larvae become lodged. After ingestion by the final host, having reached the gizzard, the larvae bury themselves under the horny layer, moult there, grow and then pass into the intestine, where they become adult.

The eggs of *Ascaris columnaris*, a parasite of carnivores, already contain larvae at the second stage. They are eaten by

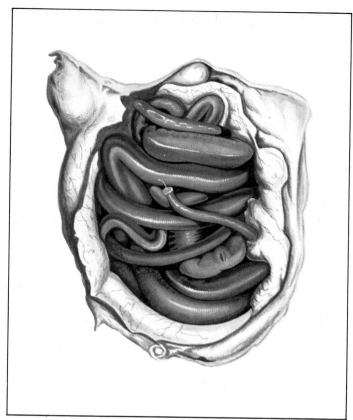

The giant strongyle, *Dictyophyma renale* (female 8–40 inches, male 6–16 inches), seen in position in a dog's kidney. This strongyle is the largest of the nematodes. The final host (otter, dog, etc.) is infected by eating raw fish.

Evolutionary cycle of the fowl whipworm, *Capillaria contorta* (female ½–1 inch by 50–70 microns, male 1¼–2 inches by 100–120 microns). This nematode (A) lives in the oesophagus and crop of fowls (E) and usually buries itself in the wall of these organs. The eggs (B) are passed out with the faeces. They develop in the earth, then are ingested by an earthworm, such as *Eisenia, Allolobophora* (C), in which they hatch; the larvae have their growth stopped in the worm's tissues. The hen is infected by eating earthworms (D). This *Capillaria* communicates very serious and often mortal disease to fowls.

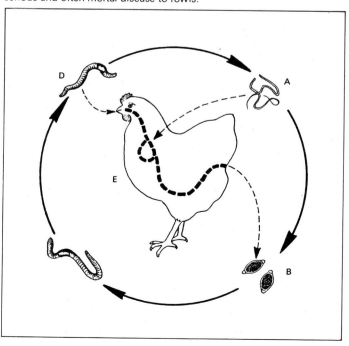

mice, the larvae migrating into the organism; infective larvae are found in most of the organs and, especially, in the brain.

Extra-intestinal parasites

The *Metastrongylinae*, inhabitants of the lungs, are represented in the pig by *Metastrongylus elongatus*, whose eggs are eaten by an earthworm, the infective larvae being found in its vascular system. Having reached the pig's intestine, after ingestion of the worm by the latter, the infective larvae pass through the intestinal mucous membrane and enter the lymphatic vessels, to be drawn finally into the lungs.

In related species, parasites of ruminants (*Protostrongylus*), the eggs hatch in the external environment, and the larvae penetrate into the foot of terrestrial molluscs, where the infective larvae finally accumulate.

Adult worms in blood vessels

Angiostrongylus vasorum is a parasite of the right side of the

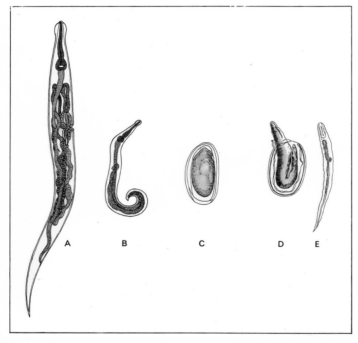

The oxyuris of man, *Enterobius vermicularis*: A, female ($\frac{1}{4}$–$\frac{1}{2}$ inch) B, male (1/12–$\frac{1}{6}$ inch); C, egg (50–60 microns); D, hatching of the egg; E, larva. The eating of raw vegetables which have been manured with human faeces contributes to the spread of this very common parasite.

heart and of the pulmonary artery of the dog. The eggs hatch in the lungs, from which the larvae are got rid of by way of the intestine, without undergoing any moult. They thus arrive in the external environment and penetrate slugs, in which the infective stages are found. Having reached the dog's intestine by ingestion of slugs, the infective larvae penetrate into the capillary vessels to reach the right side of the heart and the pulmonary artery, where they reach adulthood.

A. cantonensis also lives in the pulmonary vessels, but in those of the rat in the Far East and the Pacific. The inter-

mediate host again is a slug or other gasteropod. When the infesting larvae are swallowed by the rat, they migrate by way of the bloodstream to the brain; there they remain until the adult stage, when they make their way later into the pulmonary vessels. This cycle also involves a series of optional intermediate hosts—both invertebrates and mammals—thus favouring a vast dispersion of the infective larvae. The worm has been observed in the cerebrospinal fluid of man; it used to cause meningeal troubles. (Many cases of meningitis with eosinophil white globules have been reported, sometimes even in an endemic form; for instance in Thailand, where the inhabitants eat raw molluscs).

Pneumostrongylus tenuis, a parasite of deer in Canada, has an analogous developmental cycle, also with a mollusc as the intermediate host; but the adult worms remain in the meninges. The larvae pass by way of the blood from the intestine into the meninges and thence to the marrow of the spine at the dorsal roots level. After forty days, they pass—without causing serious lesions—into the subdural space, in which they become adult. The adult worms accumulate in the cranial region and especially in the rear part of the sphenoid cavity at the base of the skull. The eggs, non-embryonic, are laid in the capillaries and then transported to the lungs, where the larvae hatch. Although the host does not seem to display nervous symptoms, pulmonary lesions, clots of blood, and necrosis are caused by the eggs. On the other hand, in the moose and the sheep, also hosts of this parasite, nervous troubles and paraplegia sometimes occur, emanating from lesions of the spinal cord due to the larvae.

Adult worms in connective tissue

The filariae, some of which produce diseases in man in tropical regions, are viviparous; the larvae, or microfilaria, are found in the circulating blood or close to where the worms are located under the skin (*Onchocerca*).

The larvae reach the infective stage after being sucked up by blood-sucking insects; these larvae then accumulate in the sheath of the mouthparts. When the insect sinks its stylets into a favourable host, the sheath, now swollen with larvae, breaks and liberates the larvae at the surface of the skin, which they penetrate.

The equatorial filaria (*Loa loa*) is transmitted to man by two species of clegs (genus *Chrysops*). The causal organism of onchocerciasis (*Onchocerca volvulus*) is transmitted by the black *Simulium*.

The Medina or Guinea worm (*Dracunculus medinensis*), on the other hand, pierces the skin at the bottom of an ulceration and liberates its larvae when it touches water. It lives under the skin, chiefly in the lower limb of man and some other mammals. This worm may reach a length of more than three feet. It is in the blood cavity of the intermediate host, a copepod crustacean (*Cyclops* and other general), that the infective larva is found. The final host becomes infected by drinking unfiltered water.

The choice of host

The hazards encountered by the parasite at its various larval stages are many, what with adapting both to the intermediate host and to its terrestrial or aquatic habitat. It follows that the chances of a cycle being completed would be extremely slim, practically nil in terms of probabilities, if there did not exist regulatory processes acting at all stages and governed at one and the same time by internal causes peculiar to parasites and to their hosts, and by external causes.

The rate of reproduction

Among the processes that are genetic in origin one of the most striking is the often impressive increase in the number of larvae. There exist, for instance, in the cestodes, adaptive mechanisms of this kind, of which the best known is the continuous formation of reproductive segments. The last segments, as they mature, become small sacs full of eggs which are detached from the worm one by one or in groups. They are expelled along with the faeces of the host. The production of new segments is ensured by a zone of intense proliferation situated at the rear of the scolex (anterior hood-like extension).

A second mechanism manifests itself in the form of budding larvae, producing hundreds and even thousands of infective larvae. Thus, in trematodes, the number of eggs produced is much smaller, but each egg contains a miracidium (larva) which will produce in the first intermediate host thousands of larval forms, each potentially infective. Female nematodes lay eggs and larvae without a break; it has been calculated that a female ascarid may lay, in all, 20 million eggs, at a rate of 2000 a day. The number of microfilaria circulating in the blood of a filariasis case is also very high; in regions where secondary hosts of the order Diptera (two-winged flies) are highly endemic, i.e. are in their specified habitat, they are infested in nature. The polyembryony (formation of more than one embryo in a seed) and viviparity of *Gyrodactylus* also represent a mode of multiplication of larva in the Monogenea.

The need of specific hosts

The distribution of the successive stages of a cycle in the parasite's different hosts can be either closely or loosely related. The relationship between hosts and parasites is called 'parasitic specificity', and its analysis is complicated, involving simultaneously several sciences, such as biochemistry, ethology, and ecology.

The parasite distribution/host ecology relationship

Not all the species of fish in a given lake are parasitized by the same worms. Moreover, the aquatic fauna is not uniformly distributed throughout water. There are identifiable ecological niches. The cyprinids, carps, tenches, etc., will frequent the muddy bottoms, rich in aquatic plants, among which they find food; the plankton feeders such as perch,

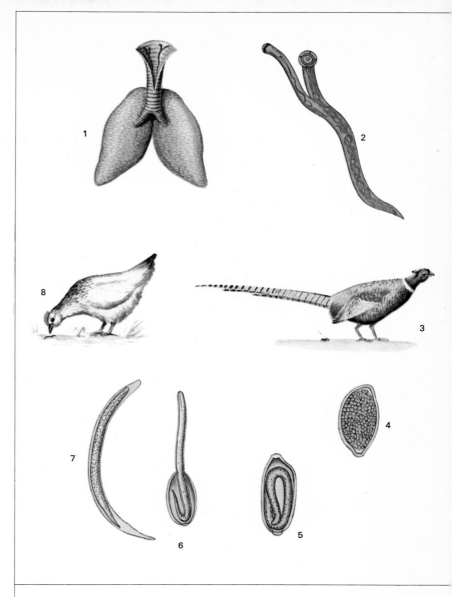

Evolutionary cycle of the tracheal syngamus, *Syngamus trachea*: *1*, worms in position in the bird's trachea; *2*, the couple enlarged; *3*, the host (here a game pheasant), the droppings of which contain the eggs of *Syngamus*; *4*, unsegmented egg; *5*, embryonated egg; *6*, larva emerging from the egg; *7*, underground infective larva; *8*, the new host, a hen, is infected by pecking at the infective larva. Infestations result in heavy losses among fowls living on fouled hen-runs.

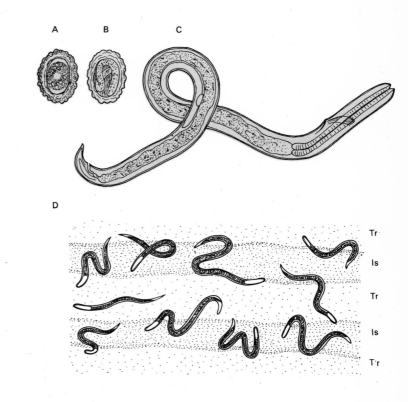

Some stages in the cycle of the *Ascaris* of man: *A*, undivided egg; *B*, infective embryonated egg; *C*, migratory larva; *D*, migratory larva in the trachea of a rat, infected experimentally. From the trachea, these larvae go to the pharynx, then are swallowed by the host; the larvae become adults in the small intestine of man. (*Is*, inter-annular space; *Tr*, tracheal ring.)

trout and other salmonids, seek out mainly clear, deep, cool water, and the mouths of rivers. The pike, a carnivorous fish, will move about in all directions in pursuit of its victims, foremost of which are cyprinids because they are easy to catch. In each ecological niche, one can distinguish the micro-habitats of the benthic invertebrates (non-plankton feeders), such as molluscs, annelids, gammarids and larvae or adult insects.

Leaving the aquatic milieu for the marshes, ecological conditions again change as one gets further from the humid zone and as the vegetation changes from reeds to shrubs, then to trees and forest. The marsh-dwelling fauna, of amphibians, reptiles, birds and mammals, is more varied, but also more specialized. It thus offers many possibilities to parasites, for the invertebrates, potential intermediate hosts in it, are plentiful and extremely varied.

Finally, the terrestrial fauna is distributed between the northerly arctic region, the high alpine and the burning tropical desert, passing through all the intermediate zones. Each large geographical unit has a characteristic fauna, adapted to its climate.

The parasitical specificity involving migratory birds has not yet been clarified in a satisfactory manner, but it would seem that it is in the north, in the nesting places, that the young become infected or are infected by their parents with food. On the other hand, it is believed that they do not contract infestation while wintering in tropical or sub-tropical countries with the larvae of local parasites. The European cuckoo may be an exception as it never carries helminths from its adoptive parents.

Rejection by the host

It should not be thought that the distribution of helminths in their hosts is governed exclusively by the latter's ecology and ethology. There are also biochemical and genetic adaptive mechanisms, which can deter or favour penetration of larval forms and, therefore, further development. These intrinsic mechanisms are of great importance in localizing and expanding helminths.

Several kinds of Monogenea live on the gills of the Cyprinidae, but the same species can be found on two or more hosts only if the latter form hybrids between them. Experiments carried out in aquaria have shown that intense infestations by Monogenea confer an immunity on fish which protects them against over-infestation. As the larvae of Monogenea are inhibited or even killed by contact with the mucus secreted by the gills of immunized fish, it could be that the composition of the branchial mucus constitutes the selective factor in this case.

In the same way, it has been shown that the larvae of trematodes do not develop indifferently in any mollusc, but that there apparently exists a close relationship between one species of mollusc and a specific miracidium (larva), and specific sporocyst, in which hatch specific rediae. For instance, the cercariae of *Schistosoma haematobium* always emerge from *Bullinus*, whilst those of the neighbouring species, *S. mansoni*, are invariably formed in Planorbidae. The chromatographic study of the composition of the mucus secreted by various species of freshwater molluscs highlights not only qualitative and quantitative biological differences between two species of the same genus, but also between geographical races of the same species. Some of these components being soluble in water, it seems logical to admit that there is formed around the mollusc, a zone which attracts the miracidia or, on the other hand, repels them. Certainly,

in the cases in which the mollusc eats the egg, it is another biological process which comes into play—even if the egg hatches in the mollusc's stomach, it is still necessary for the miracidium to penetrate the wall of the organ in order to develop in the hepatopancreas (liver). In the cycle of the broad tapeworm in man, it is possible to infest several copepods experimentally; however the species of *Diaptomus* are infested more easily than those of *Cyclops*, and, among the species of the first, some are more favourable hosts than others.

The degree of larval development is influential

The degree of individual development of infective larvae seems also to play an important role. The metacercariae of trematodes already possess adult constitutions, but lack functional gonads. It follows that the worms sometimes produce eggs only a few days after arrival in the final host's intestine, and fairly often even, in laboratory experiments, in hosts having no close zoological affinities with the natural final hosts. Metacercariae of the trematodes of birds are, for instance, capable of becoming adult in white mice. This helps explain the exceptional presence in man of trematodes that normally live in rodents. One therefore understands why, in nature, similar fauna of trematodes are sometimes found in very different hosts, but live in the same ecological conditions. Conversely, the more a final host or group of final hosts are ecologically specialized, the more their trematodes will be specific.

The infective larvae of cestodes are formed essentially by a scolex surrounded by protective envelopes; the latter also have a trophic (nutritional) function. Even if the larva manages to fix itself at the scolex to the intestinal mucous membrane, it is still necessary for environmental conditions to facilitate its metamorphosis, as well as the growth of its strobilus and the maturation of the reproductive organs. The biochemical conditions favouring this transformation are apparently very specialized, judging by the high degree of dependence of the adult worms on their hosts. This pronounced specificity observable in the cestodes is independent of ecological conditions, but is related to the zoological position of the host, and is probably fixed hereditarily. For instance, ducks, rails, herons, grebes and small waders, although they inhabit similar if not identical habitats, each possess an individual fauna of cestodes. In mammals, this specificity is observed at the level of families and, in the selachians, at the level of the large groups of rays and sharks.

In nematodes, ecological specialization of the hosts also entails that of their parasites; there exists, moreover, a biochemical barrier, at least for the species inhabiting the intestine. It is known, for instance, that the infective larvae of *Ascaris* of the pig may also form in the human lungs, but are incapable of becoming adult when they reach the intestines, as do the larvae of *Ascaris* of humans.

Pathogenic action of helminths on their hosts

It is probable that all the parasitic helminths exercise pathogenic (disease-producing) action on their hosts, but that, in normal circumstances, the latter surmount its effects by establishing a physiological equilibrium. For example, animals living in unfavourable conditions and weakened by inadequate food, as often happens in zoos, succumb to the pathogenic action of their worms. In nature, on the contrary, animals often are literally crammed with parasites, for instance the okapi or certain bustards; these exhibit no sign of enfeeblement or of physiological troubles, but decline rapidly in captivity, unless rid of the parasites.

Depending on the localization of parasites in the host, the pathogenic effects will be more or less pronounced. When they are numerous or large in size intestinal parasites extract, for their metabolism, substances equally essential to their host. As a general rule, competition for food works out to the host's advantage, as it usually absorbs more than it actually uses for its economy. However, the serious pernicious anaemia which is sometimes observed in a human carrier of the broad tapeworm of man is due to lack of vitamin B, the greater part of which has been absorbed by the cestode.

The reactions caused by intestinal worms are usually discrete, being confined to the place where they are fixed. A cestode's scolex, though often deeply imbedded in the intestinal mucous membrane, hardly gives rise to marked lesions of the tissues. Even a scolex like that of *Polypocephalus*, with tentacles deeply sunk in the intestinal villi, leaves the tissues intact. It is mainly the nematode, equipped with a buccal capsule, that makes microlesions and causes localized haemorrhages; the seriousness of the haemorrhage is naturally in proportion to the intensity of the infestation.

Trematodes in large numbers sometimes completely block the pancreatic ducts of birds and mammals, but without causing apparent histological lesions other than a marked dilation of the wall of the ducts. In the biliary ducts, on the other hand, trematodes, and sometimes also cestodes, always cause lesions, with destruction of the epithelium of the mucous membrane and neoplasm as well as sclerosis of the biliary ducts and eventual cirrhosis of the liver.

Helminths living in the host's various tissues always set up local reactions and the formation of antibodies in the blood; the presence of these antibodies often facilitates diagnosis in human or veterinary medicine. Once helminths have been present for some time in the tissues, usually the local reaction is that of the host organism towards a foreign body; this it seeks to isolate by the formation of a reactive envelope of connective tissue. The larvae of nematodes, which spend only a short time at the level of the lungs, have an antigenic power, as do the larvae of *Ascaris* of humans; their antibodies persist even after all the larvae have migrated into the intestine (see p. 90). It follows that the larvae will stage, at the level of the lungs, at the time of a subsequent infestation, a strong localized reaction, resulting in eosinophilia (increase in the number of white corpuscles with eosinophil granules), infiltration of the tissues and sometimes oedema (Loffler's syndrome). However, the larvae of *Ascaris* of humans and those of *Ascaris* of the pig possess common antigens, so that in both cases modification of the organism occurs. However, in the pig, if Loffler's syndrome is initiated, no adult larvae will be found in its intestine.

When the larval forms of cestodes are localized in the brain or in the spinal cord, their presence is usually indicated by compression phenomena of the nerve centres. Among the cysticercal larvae responsible for such lesions, one of the best known is that of *Taenia multiceps*, which lives in the adult state in the dog's intestine and in the larval state in the sheep's brain, causing the disease known as gid or staggers.

One cannot mention all the cases or all the types of lesion, but it emerges from their comparative study that lesions are, usually, independent of the nature of the worm which has produced them. In fact, the way in which the host organism reacts towards the parasites is much more important than the nature of the parasite itself.

Section of muscle of pork containing encysted larvae of trichina, *Trichinella spiralis*. The adult male measures about $\frac{1}{16}$ inch by 40 microns, the female about $\frac{1}{6}$ inch by 60 microns. *Phot. J. G. Baer*

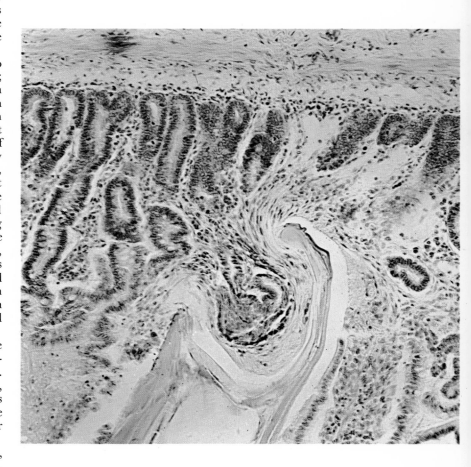

Ancylostoma of the dog, *Ancylostomum caninum*, fixed to the intestinal mucous membrane. In its ample buccal cavity, it sucks up a villus. Ancylostoma causes haemorrhages by its bites through its anti-coagulant buccal secretions (×110). *After a preparation by Golvan; Phot. J. G. Baer*

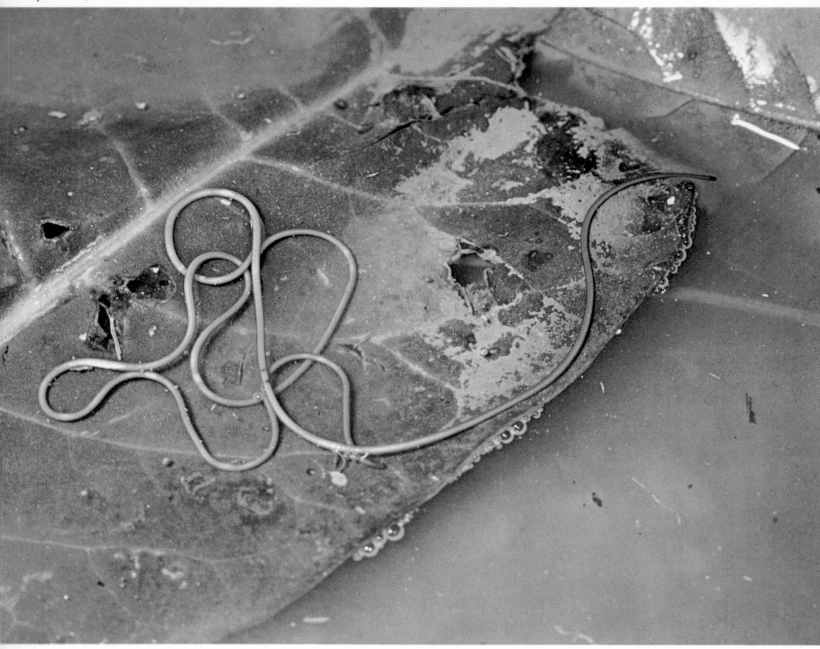

The gordids (here *Gordius aquaticus*) are roundworms (nemathelminths), filiform in the adult state, and coiled round themselves in an intricate manner (their name alludes to this characteristic: Gordian knot). Development is carried out in the visceral cavity of an insect, myriapod or spider, whence the adult actively emerges when the host is within close reach of fresh water. After mating, the female lays. From the egg emerges a larva, called echinoderoid, which leads a free life. If conditions are unfavourable, the host is contaminated by swallowing the larva, which passes through the intestinal wall and falls into the visceral cavity, where it develops. Natural size. *Phot. Aldo Margiocco*

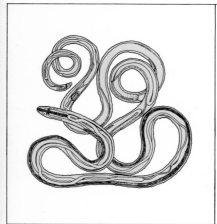

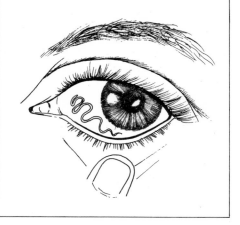

Loa loa worm, among the most common in equatorial Africa. The individual represented here is a female measuring just over 2 inches in length. *Loa loa* lives by preference in and moves about in the subcutaneous tissue. It causes 'ambulant' oedemas. It produces very small larvae (microfilaria), which pass into the blood. They are found in daytime in the peripheral blood. Not very dangerous in small numbers, these microfilaria cause very serious troubles when in abundance. *Right, Loa loa* worm moving about under the ocular conjunctiva. This filaria, very mobile, moves about in the sub-cutaneous or articular connective tissue, causing fleeting oedemas. *After Füleborn*

The nemerteans

This group includes worm-like (vermiform), thread-like (filiform) and ribbon-like animals which have characters relating to the genuine platyhelminths.

They are covered with vibratile cilia, and have a proboscis, sheathed at the anterior end of the body. The alimentary canal is straight and includes both mouth and anus. The circulatory system, entirely closed, consists of a dorsal vessel and of two lateral vessels, all joined at the front. In some species of nemerteans, corpuscles contain haemoglobin. The excretory apparatus is like that of the planarian worms: flame-cells communicating with the exterior by canaliculi (protonephridian type).

The nervous system consists of two anterior ganglia situated above the alimentary canal and joined to each other by two bands which form a ring that circles the proboscis.

The sexes are separate: the gonads are repeated along the body, and the fertilized eggs produce free-swimming larvae of varied types—the pilidium (of the heteronemerteans) is shaped like a Roman helmet. These larvae are part of coastal plankton.

The regenerative power of nemerteans is in some species very considerable; a fragment of *Lineus socialis*, delimited by two transverse sections, regenerates a whole individual, with head and tail; a violent excitation, mechanical or chemical, causes the spontaneous transverse cutting-up of the nemertean into several stumps capable of regenerating complete individuals.

Nemerteans subjected to fasting do not die. They follow an extraordinary involution. Their cells devour each other. Dawydoff managed to obtain some *Lineus lacteus* measuring one hundred microns and made up of about ten cells, although the adult can reach more than three feet in length!

The size of nemerteans varies from less than $\frac{1}{4}$ of an inch to more than sixty feet. They live for the most part in the sea, either free, or in the gills of ascidians or in mantle cavities of molluscs. They feed on live prey captured with the help of the exsertile proboscis. Some nemerteans live in fresh water and a few species are terrestrial.

The *Lineus* are the best known nemerteans; very long, some of them reach well over 60 feet in length. The species represented here is *Lineus geniculatus*, which lives on the coasts of western Europe. Actual size, 8–12 inches. *Phot. J. Six*

Annelids

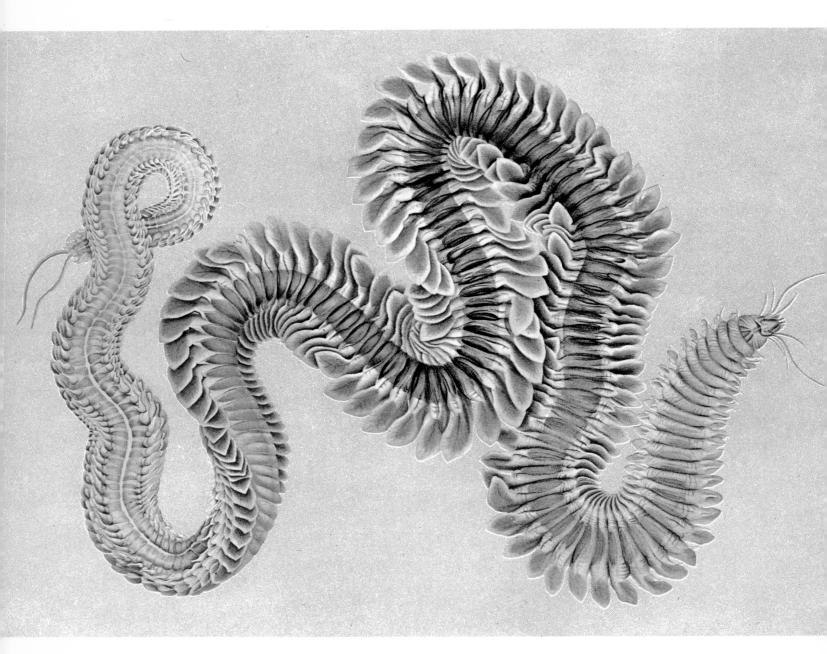

The king ragworm, *Nereis virens*, one of the finest annelids of the Atlantic fauna (England, Norway, western Europe, Atlantic coast of North America, and the Pacific); up to 20 inches long. Thousands of species of polychaete annelids are found in marine waters: from the cylinder-shaped *Nereis* and *Nephthys* to the flattened *Aphrodite*, from the wanderers to the settled lugworm, *Arenicola*. After W. C. McIntosh

In the Annelida, more clearly than in the Arthropoda, the segmented structure of the body consists of a long suite of compartments all containing the same organs and through which a linear alimentary canal passes from end to end. These identical elements in no way upset the individual's unity, for control of the whole is ensured by a brain housed in the first fused segments which constitute the head.

The annelids are worms with bodies formed of successive segments, all fairly similar to each other.

The nervous system consists of a dorsal brain, from which runs a perioesophageal collar. This is prolonged throughout the animal's length by a ventral chain and possesses, typically, one pair of ganglia per segment. The circulatory system is closed. The alimentary canal extends from one end of the body to the other, and excretion is through nephridia found usually in pairs in each segment—segmentary organs. Annelids have a bilateral symmetry, retained incidentally by all the animals more perfected than they are.

Annelids are divided into three classes: Polychaeta (with which are associated Archiannelida), equipped with numerous cutaneous bristles; Oligochaeta, with few bristles; and Hirudinea, with none.

The class Polychaeta

These annelids, of which there are about 6000 species throughout the world, are aquatic animals, and almost all are marine.

Shape

The body, made of multiple segments, is usually vermiform, and each of its segments bears lateral expansions, the parapodia; the latter are imbedded with clusters of bristles (chaetae). These bristles are used as supports for movement, whether in swimming, or in crawling on or within the marine sand, or in progressing within their tube.

The size of polychaetes is extremely variable, since it ranges from less than 1/200 of an inch to several feet. However, the most common length is a few inches.

The structure of some polychaetes

It is difficult to describe briefly what a polychaete worm is, for, despite a remarkable uniformity in general plan, there is

an astonishing range of variation in this group, depending on families. Between the latter, moreover, no clearly marked evolutionary lines have been established, as happens in other groups, and it is very difficult to identify the relationships which may exist between them. Also, most writers avoid speaking about different orders within the Polychaeta and are content to juxtapose the various families.

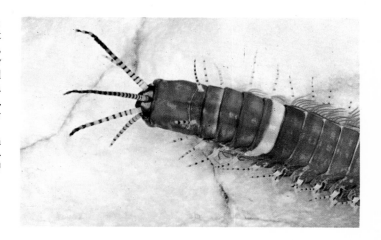

Anterior region of *Eunice torquata* (length, 4 inches). On the head rise five appendages or antennae (not similar to those of arthropods); the lower one on the right is hidden by the upper one on the same side. Two cirri (appendages) on the second segment behind the head are clearly visible. On the sides are parapodia with thread-like gills. Eunices are found on littoral bottoms in most seas. *Phot. J. Six*

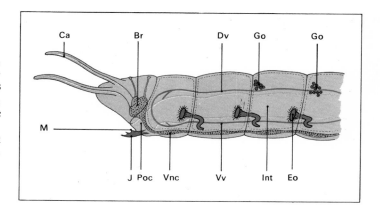

Organizational plan of a polychaete annelid, longitudinal view; *A*, antenna or head appendage; *Br*, brain; *Dv*, dorsal vessel; *Eo*, excretory organ (nephridium); *Go*, gonads; *Int*, intestine; *J*, jaw; *M*, mouth; *Poc*, perioesophageal collar; *Vnc*, ventral nerve chain; *Vv*, ventral vessel.

A fairly accurate idea of the polychaete class can be obtained by describing three known and representative species: *Perinereis cultrifera*, *Arenicola marina* and *Mercierella enigmatica*.

A nereid (ragworm)

Perinereis cultrifera is a very common nereid (or ragworm) on all European coasts and, moreover, is found in most seas throughout the world. It is a worm about four inches long, which is found under the pebbles of beaches, in fissures in rocks or in eel grass. Its back is greenish, and along it there runs, from one end to the other, a beautiful red median vessel. It is a vigorous animal and its firmness on the hook makes it very popular for sea-fishing. The head is trapezoid in shape, with four large black eyes, two small tentacles in front, and two large palps more or less inclined towards the ventral surface. On the buccal ring behind the head are four pairs of tentacular cirri. A muscular proboscis may jut out towards the front and show two sharp horny jaws, which the animal uses to seize fragments of algae. There are numerous horny denticles (paragnaths) on the proboscis: their shape and arrangement characterize this species. Each segment is provided with muscular parapodia, well-irrigated with red blood and bears many compound chaetae (bristles), and they too are well-defined in shape. The animal tapers noticeably towards the rear and ends in two long cirri. Although provided with powerful muscles to move about by undulating rapidly, the nereid is inclined to stay at home,

Type of polychaete annelid, the lugworm (*Arenicola marina*) lives buried in the sand; tufts of filaments are its respiratory organs or gills. The head is merely a small spherical mass situated at the animal's front end; bristles can be seen on the rear segments (left). *Phot. J. Six*

leaving its shelter only to seek its food, and during breeding time.

The fisherman's lugworm

Arenicola marina is quite different in appearance. It is a large soft sausage-shaped worm which lives buried in the muddy sand of beaches. Its presence there is betrayed by a crater an inch or two deep hollowed out in the sand and by a cone of castings about four inches from the crater. The animal lives in a U-shaped tube, the ends of which lead respectively to these two points. The usual length of the lugworm is between four and eight inches, and its diameter is about half an inch.

It is reddish or greenish in colour, leaving on the hand which grips it a liquid which stains the skin yellow. From the anterior end a large soft pinkish proboscis (peristomium) shoots out from time to time, seizing sand and swallowing it continuously, whilst at the other end the anus expels sand which has passed through the intestine. It is in this way that the crater is formed.

The lugworm's anterior region includes six segments equipped only with tufts of bristles, then come thirteen segments bearing both bristles and tufts of red arborescent gills, and finally a fairly large number of other segments devoid of any appendage. The lugworm's bristles are of two kinds: large and small slender chaetae, and sturdier hooks which enable the animal to insinuate itself into the sand. Some muddy beaches, especially near low water mark, are densely dotted with lugworm casts.

The lugworm is sought after as a bait for flatfish, and to a lesser degree as bait for whiting.

Mercierella enigmatica

Mercierella enigmatica is yet another different form. Its small slender body, about an inch and a half in length, is entirely covered by a calcareous tube which the animal has secreted. Hanging on to the walls of its tube, the animal can thrust out its anterior part which ends in an indistinct head, and from which emerge two delicately slashed gill lobes, surrounded by a large collarette extending over seven segments and forming the animal's thorax. A slightly concave operculum with blackish chitinous spines is borne by the end of a gill filament. After the thorax, which is embellished with seven pairs of tufts of long slender chaetae and six double rows of small short bristles or uncini, is the abdomen, which is much longer and salmon-pink, contrasting with the yellowish green of the first segments; it too bears long chaetae and uncini.

The living tube is cylindrical, with an opening characteristically like a trumpet. Often the openings which have succeeded each other in time form prominent interlocking collarettes.

Mercierella live in large colonies: their tubes are joined to each other, and form very large masses which sometimes block sluice-gates or sink small boats to which they have attached themselves.

Bristles, organs of locomotion

The bristles are cuticular projections, grouped in fairly thick clusters, which emerge from the parapodia. Under the action of muscles inserted on the periphery of the cluster, the bristles may effect movements in any direction, all together or only a few of them, according to the animal's needs. Their shape is variable. Some are simple, i.e. formed of one piece, strong and needle-shaped like the aciculum, which, contained within the parapodium, gives it a certain rigidity; others are hair-like capillary bristles, or limbed bristles, which are flattened and more or less leaf-like; yet others have denticulations concentrated either at the tip, or more usually, strung out over the whole length of the bristle. Among the simple bristles, some, which are very short, take on the shape of an indented plate: they are the uncini, which are bunched together in large numbers, on a fairly long line, in the integuments of sedentary polychaetes. The whole, seen from above, looks like a zip fastener.

Above: *Serpula vermicularis* is almost part of the rock so solidly is it fused with it. *Serpula* can withdraw to the bottom of its tube, using a conical operculum to block the opening. Most of the time, it displays an elegant tuft of gills striped transversely with iridescent colours, bright red, pink or white. *Serpula* is found in all the world's seas. It measures 2–3 inches in length. *Phot. J. Six*

Bottom left: in some places, serpulids build reefs, often of imposing dimensions, with their conjoined tubes. Such reefs have been fossilized, and some have been known to form large banks (Cretaceous of Brunswick, of Dresden, etc.) *Phot. F. Rullier*

Bottom right: Protula tubularia, like Serpula, lives in a white calcareous tube, encrusted strongly on the rock. It is seen here on a bottom of calcareous algae, its tuft of rosy white gills, with red and orange zones, spreading outwards. It is found in all seas. It barely exceeds $2\frac{1}{2}$ inches in length. *Phot. Aldo Margiocco*

Other bristles are compound. They consist of a shaft, whose base is sunk in the integument, and of a mobile part, taking the shape of a straight or curved fish-bone, a bill-hook, or a broadened oar-shaped blade. All these bristles are microscopic and, even when greatly enlarged, still appear very sharp, at least in their most delicate intricacies.

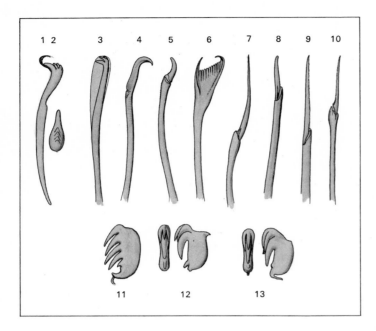

Polychaete bristles: *1*, ventral hook of *Clymene*, seen in profile; *2*, ventral hook of *Clymene*, seen from above; *3*, simple bristle of a spionid; *4*, simple bristle of *Paraonis*; *5*, compound bristle of a syllid; *6*, simple bristle of *Diopatra*; *7*, compound bristle of *Eteone*; *8* and *9*, compound bristles of *Phyllodoce*; *10*, compound bristle of *Eteone*; *11*, uncinus (hook-like bristle) of *Terebella*; *12*, uncinus of *Polymnia*; *13*, uncinus of *Polymnia*.

Living tubes

Many polychaetes wander across the sand, insinuating themselves into gravel, slipping into fissures in rocks or swimming in mid-water, without being protected by any external covering: these are the ones usually called errant polychaetes, e.g. *Perinereis cultrifera*. Others, including the lugworm, which is classed as sedentary, have rows of uncini, but live almost in the same fashion: at the very most they line the walls of the burrows that they dig in the sand with mucus. Others, like *Myxicola*, secrete a tube of mucus which is transparent and nearly half an inch thick; finally some, the true sedentaries, secrete, with the help of their epidermal glands, a tube in which they live hidden. These tubes are very varied. Some are like greyish or reddish rubber pipes, sticking out of the mud, and have a slight elasticity: the tubes of the peacock worms *Sabella* and *Spirodrapha* are of this sort, as well as most of the tubes of the other fan worms. They may be more or less covered with minute fragments of sand, shells, sea-urchins' spines, spicules of sponges and Foraminifera. Other tubes are made of agglutinated sand, like those of the *Leiochone*, or of a thin layer of hardened mucus on which grains of sand are thickly glued together, e.g. *Hermella*, whose juxtaposed tubes form solid masses which have been blamed for the silting-up of Mont-Saint-Michel Bay. *Pectinaria* build themselves an elegant tube with

a base of siliceous cement which joins together grains of sand juxtaposed flat, like the elements of a mosaic. The Serpulidae (*Serpula, Protula* etc.) secrete a calcareous tube, sometimes very solid, whilst the *Chaetopterus* weave thin, flexible parchment-like tubes nearly a foot in length. Hanging on to the inside of its tube by its uncini, a sedentary polychaete may either emerge completely, leaving the tube behind, or else merely thrust the tuft of its gills or cephalic filaments outside the tube.

Food

Many polychaetes equipped with strong proboses and sharp jaws are predatory and feed on small crustaceans, molluscs or other worms. This applies particularly to *Eunice, Aphrodite*, and *Polyodontes*, which are often caught by line-fishing; many syllids stick their mouth to a small prey, perforating its integument with their pharyngeal tooth and sucking up its contents in less than a second. Many others, like most of the Nereidae, feed on algae. The deposit-feeders, like the lugworms or *Pectinaria*, ingest the sand and digest the organic particles it contains. Microphagous worms, e.g. the serpulids and sabellids, spread out their branchial crowns to the fullest extent and allow the densely ciliated feathery filaments to create currents of water, which bring fine planktonic organisms to their mouths.

Pectinaria koreni, pale pink and capped with gold, lives planted in the sand with its head down. Its conical tube, formed from a fine mosaic of grains of sand, shelters it completely; only its golden comb of sztae emerges and turns over the sand just like two small forks. It is found in the Mediterranean, the Black Sea, the Atlantic, the English Channel and the northern seas of Europe. It reaches 2 inches in length and its tube reaches $3\frac{1}{2}$ inches. *Phot. F. Rullier*

Terebellids act a little differently, stretching their long gill filaments out as far as possible; each one brings what it has managed to contact to the animal's mouth. One of these worms, measuring about two inches in length, may thus extend a fan of filaments around it that stretches for about eight inches.

Sexual reproduction and trochophore larva

The immense majority of the polychaetes have the sexes separate, although their gonads are not generally differentiated. Eggs and sperm are usually liberated into the sea, although some species incubate their eggs either internally or in a cocoon. The result is a swimming larva, the trochophore, which moves about actively by spiralling through the water with its many cilia, and which is also sometimes carried by currents for very long distances. This happens mainly with species whose larvae remain pelagic for several weeks, and this obviously favours the widespread dispersal of these species.

Many polychaetes do not change their appearance in any way at breeding time, while others undergo a few slight modifications of their chaetae—*Nephthys*, for instance, or the Amphinomidae: but some are completely transformed in a few weeks or even in a few days and assume the 'epitokous', or reproductive, form. This transformation is complete in several eunicids, and especially in several dozen species of Nereidae.

While the genital products which fill the body cavity ripen, the eyes become enormous, and the congested palps curve inwards like the feelers towards the ventral surface. The segments of one or several parts of the body are squeezed together and become broader as they shorten, the parapodia are modified, becoming embellished with foliated lamellae, and all the bristles fall and are replaced by two large clusters of swimming bristles bearing a blade-shaped joint. The body wall loses most of its longitudinal muscles and the alimentary canal is partly liquefied. The worm now finds itself at the epitokous stage, and is called a heteronereis. Now ready to breed, it is shorter and more coloured than the atokous, or non-sexual, form from which it is derived.

The nuptial dance

The nuptial dance takes place in an unexpected and spectacular manner. It is carried out at the same time by many individuals belonging to the same species, and may involve several neighbouring species.

When the time comes, these worms, which habitually remain hidden in the algae, rush out from their lairs and begin to dance in the middle of the water. At Roscoff in France, this happens to *Platynereis dumerilii*, *Leptonereis glauca* and various others from June to September, at the first and last quarters of the moon.

The first worms appear a little after ten o'clock in the evening. To see and catch them, one must go by boat to where they live above the rocks covered with sea-wrack and sea-tangle. They can be attracted by lowering a brilliantly lit lantern to the sea bottom, then gently pulling it towards the surface. Suddenly, rising from the shadows and quickly traversing the lighted zone, the first worms appear. They are males. Like arrows, they come into the light and dive again, then return again. Soon, the fireworks really start, like a galaxy of shooting stars with several hundreds, sometimes thousands of worms interlacing at top speed. Then a more

The alciopes (here *Alciopa contrainii*) are annelids which swim in mid water and are part of pelagic fauna; the body is transparent, except for the large eyes which are coloured red. Found in Strait of Messina. (Natural size × 2.) *Phot. Aldo Margiocco*

Trochophore larva of an annelid of the genus *Nephthys*. It is part of plankton and swims with the help of its girdles of vibratile cilia. *Phot. Wilson*

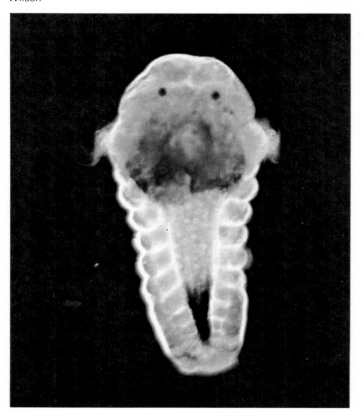

bulky form appears—a female. The males rush to meet her, until there is a living ball of several hundred males moving frantically around the female. This is the nuptial dance.

The female expels her eggs in large spurts, whilst the males all ejaculate into the sea together; the water is covered with animals almost completely emptied of their substance and the mass of eggs and sperm turns the water milky-white. If a new female arrives, the whole performance is re-enacted. It may last for one or two hours, and an astonishing number of worms may take part in these gambols. Towards midnight, everything quietens down and will not be resumed until a fortnight later, when the moon will again be favourable. The lunar rhythm is strictly observed and it is quite useless to try to go and watch the rising of the *Nereis* on either the night before or after the fateful day. This explosion of life, these millions of small beings whose existence is determined in a few minutes make this nuptial dance one of the most beautiful natural spectacles it is possible to witness.

Laboratory experiments have shown that the female's ova emit a substance which induces emission of the sperm by the male.

The fertilized eggs develop rapidly, without passing through the stage of the trochophore larva, so habitual in polychaetes.

Other species belonging to the Eunicidae also have roughly similar nuptial dances, except that only the posterior part of

Chloeia flava, a beautiful salmon-coloured polychaete, here represented resting on its ventral surface. Notable are its very large bristles and the varied patterns covering its dorsal wall. It is found on sandy bottoms, in all warm seas, especially in the tropics. It ranges from 2 to 5 inches in length. *Phot. Aldo Margiocco*

the worms, crammed with gametes, rises to the surface. The natives of the Samoan islands are highly appreciative of this palolo, as they call it, which is linked to the lunar cycle. There is widespread rejoicing when they gather and eat it.

Asexual reproduction

The facility with which many polychaetes regenerate parts

of their bodies explains the fact that many of them may also breed either by scissiparity or by budding. The most typical example of the first mode is found in *Dodecaceria*, a small species living in a calcareous alga, *Lithothamnion*. The worm sheds successive segments one by one; each of them regenerates a head and a trunk, and multiplies its segments; and these, in their turn, separate from each other and recommence the preceding process.

True budding does not need previous cutting of the worm. Some part of the body, variable according to species, directly buds a new animal, which may remain joined to the stock for a long time or become detached from it fairly rapidly. The syllids are very remarkable in this connection. *Autolytus*, for example, buds a linear chain of stolons, few in number and of fairly similar size; *Myrianida* may also have about thirty successive stolons hanging on to the stock: the whole moves with a single wriggling movement. The stolons nearest the stock, on which they have just been formed, are very small and their size increases with age, as they get further away from the stock.

These stolons are filled with gametes and all those belonging to a single chain are of the same sex. The male chains are made up of small individuals provided with multiple sensory appendages and with large swimming bristles. They had been named polybostrichus long before they were seen attached to their stock, because they were thought to represent an unknown species. The chains of female individuals are made up of sacs called sacconereis, which are very rounded by the mass of ovules they contain and poorly equipped with sensory apparatus. At maturity, polybostrichus and sacconereis separate from their stocks and swim actively to meet each other.

The emission of the gametes takes place in the sea, as does fertilization.

These few examples give only a very sketchy idea of the various modes of reproduction which exist in polychaetes, for they are countless.

Distribution of the Polychaeta

Living in all the seas, polychaetes are cosmopolitan. The same species are often found from the pole to the equator. There are, however, a certain number of forms confined to the polar seas, and others which are found only in the tropics. Most of them live in pure sea water, being unable to accept desalination; a certain number pass into brackish water and are found mainly in estuaries, coastal ponds and canals with access to the sea; and a few manage to live in fresh water, such as the species of the rice-fields in Japan (*Ceratocephala osawai*), the sabellids of Lake Baikal, and especially the serpulid *Marifugia cavatica*, which has been found solely in the fresh water of the deep caves of Moravia.

Another serpulid, *Mercierella enigmatica*, very close to *Marifugia*, has shown during these last few years its tremendous power of expansion. In less than fifty years, it has spread all over the world. After the First World War, it suddenly appeared in the canal from Caen to the sea in extreme abundance. About the same time it was found in the London docks; in 1924 it turned up in Spain, then in the Lake of Tunis. From 1924 onwards it was reported in an increasing number of places. Towards the years 1950–55 it rapidly invaded the whole periphery of the Mediterranean, to such an extent that a recent survey revealed twelve new *Mercierella* stations in coastal ponds.

This species, probably native to India, must have been brought to Europe by ships plying between India, England

and the port of Caen, especially during the 1914–18 war. Presumably during a stop in India, *Mercierella* tubes became fixed to the hull of a ship which brought the worms to Europe and, during a spell in port, the larvae became fixed to banks and to the hulls of other ships, and thus their dissemination began. It was mainly in estuaries, coastal ponds, and canals flowing into the sea, i.e. in brackish water, that *Mercierella* was first discovered. In these protective environments, without the violent battering of the waves, their fairly fragile tubes would not be broken and it was possible for colonies to thrive. It was noted in 1952 that in less than 3 months, the banks of the Rance were covered with a continuous layer 8 inches thick of *Mercierella* tubes, which represents a weight of about 29 pounds of limestone to the square yard. *Mercierella* also thrives very well in pure sea water or even in water where the salt content is exceptionally high: in the Lake of Tunis, in which the salinity of the water in summer is almost double that of normal sea water, one finds flourishing colonies of these worms, piled up in enormous heaps, which are a hazard to small ships.

Classification

Archiamelida

Small forms totally, or almost totally, devoid of bristles, but very like polychaetes by their morphology and their way of life: *Protodrilus, Polygordius, Nerilla.*

Order Polychaeta errantia

Polychaetes usually devoid of a tube and leading a free life. They have well-developed heads bearing eyes, many sense organs and a prehensile proboscis, often with jaws. The segments of the body are all similar and bear well-developed parapodia.

The chief forms are *Aphrodite, Hermione, Harmothoe, Phyllodoce, Nereis, Nephthys, Eunice, Syllis, Autolytus, Myrianida.* They are predatory animals.

Order Polychaeta sedentaria

Polychaetes which either secrete a tube or live buried in the sea bottom. The head is often indistinct and poor in sense organs, the proboscis is soft, when it exists, and has no jaws. The parapodiae are reduced, and the anterior region is usually somewhat different from the posterior region.

Polychaeta include the genera *Aricia, Chaetopterus, Arenicola, Sabellaria* (Hermelles), *Sabella, Spirographis, Terebella, Serpula, Mercierella.* Many are filter-feeding microphagous forms; others have mud-eating habits.

The class Oligochaeta

The oligochaetes are worms with bilateral symmetry, composed of a series of segments very similar to each other, each bearing a small number of bristles.

Most are terrestrial and burrowing (the earthworms); others are mud-dwellers and live in fresh water; and some are marine.

The smallest ones, such as *Chaetogaster*, are less than 1/25 of an inch in length; many earthworms are from 2 to 8 inches long, and the giants of the group, which are found in tropical countries, may exceed 10 feet in length (e.g. *Megascolides australis*).

Most have a rather pale red body, the colour being due either to the pigments they contain, or as a result of the transparency of their integument revealing their blood, which is red due to the respiratory pigment erythrocruorin.

Like polychaetes, the bodies of oligochaetes are divided

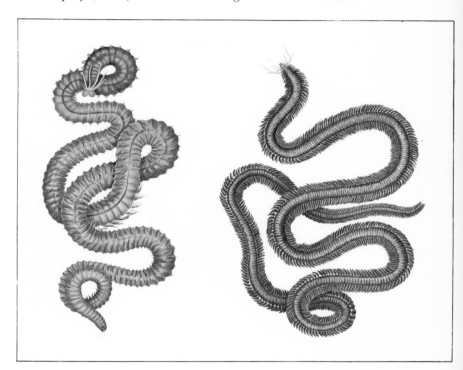

Left, a beautiful polychaete annelid, the red rock worm *Marphysa sanguinea,* which lives in clefts in rocks, where it secretes large quantities of mucus in which it moves about; it is also found under large stones, between tide-marks. Secure in its galleries filled with water, it can survive being left stranded. North to south Atlantic, Mediterranean. (Slightly enlarged.) *After W. C. McIntosh*
Right, a paddle worm, *Phyllodoce lamelligera,* of north Atlantic. It lives in the laminaria (large brown algae) zone, and is found mainly under stones (×1.5). *After W. C. McIntosh*

into three parts: the prostomium, a small cone situated in front of the mouth; the soma, which constitutes the whole length of the body; and the pygidium, or tail end.

The chaetae are usually distributed in four clusters for each segment. They are not borne by parapodia, but are buried in the integument itself. They are always simple, shaped like a spear, but they enable the animal to get a grip on the ground and, by the opposed play of the body's circular and longitudinal muscles, enable it to crawl.

Oligochaetes usually breathe through their skins, which are very well irrigated; several have intestinal breathing and some possess gills, either all along the body (*Branchiodrilus*), or confined to the posterior part (*Dero, Branchiura*).

Oligochaetes are hermaphrodite and have very complicated genital organs. During mating, each of the pair plays in turn the roles of male and female for the other partner. Laying usually takes place in a cocoon.

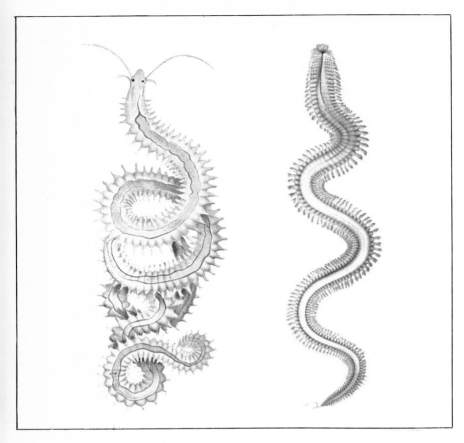

Examples of parthenogenesis (*Eiseniella*) and of self-fertilization (*Limnodrilus*) are also known. In other ways, the power of regeneration is great in oligochaetes. This does not mean, as one often hears said, that by merely putting a spade through an earthworm two genuinely live worms can be obtained. Experiments have shown that many simultaneous conditions have to be satisfied: place of cutting, asepsis, etc.

Most oligochaetes living in the soil feed on the organic matter it contains. Marine species either keep to the constantly submerged zone, or else a little higher, and then undergo twice daily immersion from the tides.

Others are tree-dwelling and lodge under the bark or in the axils of leaves, where organic matter collects. Some are found even in glaciers and feed on small algae. Some again are commensals of other worms; several are predators and some are parasites, living, for example, on the gills of crayfishes and resembling tiny leeches.

The role of the earth-dwelling oligochaetes

The role of worms in the formation of vegetable mould has been known for a long time, both for physical and particularly chemical modifications. For modifications of the first kind, one thinks chiefly of aeration, mixing of the soil, and

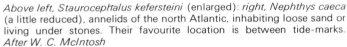

Above left, Staurocephalus kefersteini (enlarged): *right, Nephthys caeca* (a little reduced), annelids of the north Atlantic, inhabiting loose sand or living under stones. Their favourite location is between tide-marks. *After W. C. McIntosh*

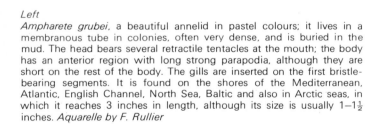

Left

Ampharete grubei, a beautiful annelid in pastel colours; it lives in a membranous tube in colonies, often very dense, and is buried in the mud. The head bears several retractile tentacles at the mouth; the body has an anterior region with long strong parapodia, although they are short on the rest of the body. The gills are inserted on the first bristle-bearing segments. It is found on the shores of the Mediterranean, Atlantic, English Channel, North Sea, Baltic and also in Arctic seas, in which it reaches 3 inches in length, although its size is usually $1–1\frac{1}{2}$ inches. *Aquarelle by F. Rullier*

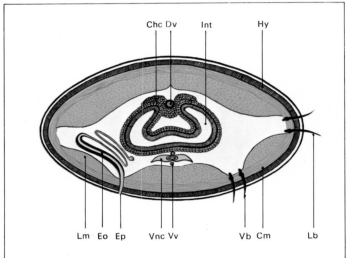

Above

Diagram of a transverse section of an earthworm: *Chc*, chloragogen cells; *Cm*, circular muscles; *Dv*, dorsal vessel; *Eo*, excretory organ or nephridium; *Ep*, excretory pore; *Hy*, hypodermis; *Int*, intestine; *Lb*, lateral bristle; *Lm*, longitudinal muscles; *Vb*, ventral bristle; *Vnc*, ventral nerve cord; *Vv*, ventral vessel.

Left

Earthworms are hermaphrodite—when they mate, they function both as male and female. The two partners place themselves ventral surface against ventral surface. Each ejects sperm which is transported into the other's seminal receptacle. In the earthworm the male pores are separated from each other by about fifteen segments; the sperm follows a groove running from one pore to the other (two symmetrical and parallel grooves in each individual). The eggs are laid in clusters, in a cocoon made of hardened mucus, secreted by the glands of the clitellum. *Phot. Ch. Martin*

the increase and stabilization of porosity. Modifications of the second kind refer to the transformation of plant debris into humic derivatives and their mixing with the soil's mineral constituents. This leads to the manufacture of colloidal complexes which constitute the chief characteristic of a mulch, greatly facilitating the action of the various bacteria which preside over the different cycles of transformation, especially that of nitrogen.

In cultivated land, the number of earthworms is always high; it may be nearly $1\frac{1}{4}$ millions per acre in meadows and well over $1\frac{1}{2}$ millions in gardens. In these conditions, each year about 40 tons of earth are worked by earthworms in an acre. The fertility of the soil is considerably increased thereby. As a result of these findings, the wholesale rearing of earthworms has been envisaged and actually carried out. The U.S. and Germany have earthworm farms producing up to 500,000 worms per day. At the time of the collapse of the Dutch dikes in 1953, sea water destroyed all the earthworms, so that it was necessary to re-introduce them.

Classification

The 3000 species of Oligochaeta are divided into a dozen large well-defined families, but it is difficult to group them into systematic unity on a broad scale. We will confine ourselves to pointing out the two following orders.

Order Terricolae—the earthworms

Large species living in the soil: *Lumbricus*, *Allolobophora*, the typical worms living in our countryside, *Eisenia*, the brandling found in dung-heaps, *Megascolides*, the giant earthworm, *Pheretima musica*, a large species from Java which makes a clearly audible squeaking noise, by rubbing its bristles against stones.

Order Limicolae—the aquatic Oligachaetes

These are found in the mud of ponds and streams: *Tubifex*, *Nais*, *Chaetogaster*, or living as parasites on the gills of crayfishes: *Branchiobdella*.

The class Hirudinea (leeches)

Leeches are annelids whose bodies, flattened or cylindrical and devoid of bristles, comprise 33 segments, these superficially divided into smaller rings. The anterior and posterior extremities each bear a sucker. The anterior sucker surrounds the mouth, which has either jaws or a proboscis; the posterior sucker is blind and is used for fixation. The body cavity is almost entirely taken up with connective tissue.

Leeches are free or external parasites, occurring in the sea, fresh water, or on land.

They are hermaphrodite and have a very complex reproductive system, which frequently presents anomalies.

Mud worms, or *Tubifex*, are oligochaete annelids which live in fouled waters, poor in oxygen; they can even exist without this gas for 48 hours, obtaining their energy from anaerobic decomposition of their glycogen. If the oxygen content falls, the worms thresh about, thus renewing the water with which they are in contact. They live stuck in the mud, inside a mucous tube, standing vertically with their head down and feed on mud; $1-1\frac{3}{4}$ inches in length. *Phot. Aldo Margiocco*

Bottom right, the brandling (*Eisenia foetida*) is a typical earthworm which lives in almost all regions of the world, as much at home in the rigours of the sub-Arctic as in tropical heat. It lives in manure heaps and feeds very readily on dead leaves and other vegetable debris. It is used for experiments in many laboratories. *Phot. J. Six*
Bottom left, the medicinal leech (*Hirudo medicinalis*), a blood-sucking species, was formerly much used in medicine. It feeds by the actual sucking of blood, but also by the saliva it injects which contains substance, hirudin, which has an anti-coagulant effect on the blood. The medicinal leech lives in ponds and swamps in Europe and Asia. Up to 4 inches in length. *Phot. J. Six*

They range in size from half an inch (*Glossiphonia hetero-clita*), up to about eight inches for *Pontobdella* and the medicinal leech.

Leeches usually move slowly by alternate fixation of their two suckers after the manner of looper caterpillars, but most of them can also swim quickly, by undulating like small eels.

Leeches have inconspicuous sense organs: microscopic sensory buds, photoreceptor cells, ocelli, Bayer's organs and cyathiform organs. These organs, however, enable them to

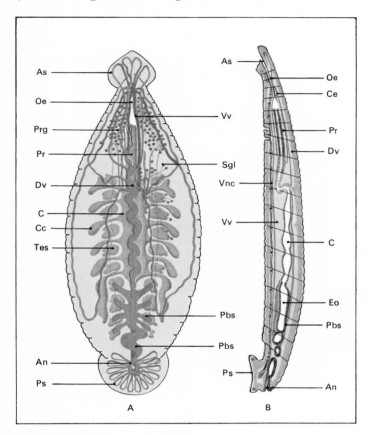

Organizational plan of a typical leech (*Glossiphonia complanata*)— (A): *An*, anus; *As*, anterior sucker; *C*, crop; *Cc*, crop caecum; *Dv*, dorsal vessel; *Oe*, oesophagus; *Pbs*, peri-intestinal blood sinus; *Prg*, prostomial glands; *Ps*, posterior sucker; *Sgl*, salivary glands; *Tes*, testes (10 pairs); *Vv*, ventral blood vessel; (B): *An*, anus; *As*, anterior sucker; *C*, crop; *Cer*, cerebral ganglion; *Dv*, dorsal vessel; *Eo*, excretory organ; *Oe*, oesophagus; *Pbv*, peri-intestinal blood vessel; *Pr*, proboscis; *Ps*, posterior sucker; *Vnc*, ventral nerve cord; *Vv*, ventral vessel. This leech is very common in stagnant freshwater. It reaches 1–1¼ inches in length.

perceive and locate certain stimuli very quickly, for example the taste or smell of blood. During a fishing expedition for medicinal leeches, several persons who had gone into the water wearing boots had seen nothing for a whole hour, when

a fisherman whose boots were spattered with a conger's blood arrived on the scene. In less than ten minutes more than fifty leeches had fixed themselves to his boots, although none of the fishers around him had attracted a single one.

The medicinal leech was for a long time used in therapy, in the days when bleeding was a remedy for all ills; it has now been almost totally replaced by cupping.

Hirudin is a secretion which is emitted by the worm as it sucks. The absorbed blood is preserved for several months in the animal's alimentary canal, in an untainted, liquid state.

Classification

The class Hirudinea comprises 300 species divided into 4 families.

Family Acanthobdellidae

Acanthobdella peledina is the only species; it is a parasite of salmonid fishes.

Family Rhynchobdellidae

Leeches with a protrusible proboscis and no jaws, parasites either of freshwater fish (*Piscicola*, *Glossiphonia*) or of marine fish—*Pontobdella* on rays, each of which may carry a dozen, *Branchellion* on rays and torpedo-fish, *Ozobranchus*, which lodges in the mouth of crocodiles, freshwater turtles and pelicans.

Family Gnathobdellidae

Having the pharynx equipped with three jaws. *Hirudo medicinalis*, or medicinal leech, *Haemopis sanguisuga*, inexactly described as horse leech, *Limnatis* or true horse leech, *Haemadipsa*, terrestrial arboreal leech of tropical Asia, which drops on passers-by and inflicts on them very painful bites which take a long time to cure.

Family Pharyngobdellidae

Not very muscular pharynx, no jaws. *Erpobdella*, small dark-coloured freshwater leeches, which feed on molluscs and planarians.

Spirographis spallanzanii lives on the sea bottom, emerging like a living flower from its elastic tube. Fixed to a wall of rock or to a pebble sunk in the sand, it sways gently in its branchial crown striped in white, violet, and yellow to brown. Its body consists of a thoracic region, with few segments, and a long abdomen. It is found on all the coasts of Europe, and as far afield as the Indian Ocean. The animal reaches 8–12 inches, its tube up to 30 inches, and its tuft when spread out may be 2–10 inches across. It lives easily in marine aquaria. *Phot. J. Six*

Lophophorates and Rotifera

The lamp-shell (*Terebratula vitrea*) is an example of the Brachiopoda group. This species lives in shallow water and is related directly to a long line of fossil forms. *Phot. Aldo Margiocco*

When zoologists are unable to recognize the affinities of certain animals, or to assign them to an exact place in the animal kingdom, they create new systematic units or even subphyla. This applies to the lophophorates, which include disparate groups whose relationship is not obvious, but which have in common the facts that they bear a crown of tentacles (lophophore) covered with vibratile cilia which convey planktonic micro-organisms to their mouths, and that their eggs develop by spiral cleavage.

Lophophorates

This term designates a group of multicellular coelomate animals whose affinities are difficult to define, in spite of the very detailed knowledge we have of them. They have in common the fact that they bear on the anterior region (a more or less pronounced head) a crown of tentacles (lophophore) covered with vibratile cilia and arranged either in a circle or in a horseshoe converging towards the mouth.

All, or almost all, are fixed to a substratum and feed on micro-organisms (bacteria, unicellular algae, Protozoa, microscopic larvae, etc.) which are held in suspension in the water; for this reason they are described as microphagous.

Lophophorates all have small eggs, deficient in yolk, which develop by spiral cleavage. At the eighth stage of cell division, the cells form two layers of four superimposed and alternating with the bottom ones. This arrangement results from the fact that in the course of the cell divisions the mitotic spindles (where the cells divide) are not vertical, but inclined at an angle which is constant for a given species.

The larvae of the lophophorates, although very diverse, are related to the free-swimming larvae of the polychaete annelids and molluscs.

Among them are classified the Phoronidea, the Endo-procta, the true Bryozoa or Ectoprocta, and the Brachio-poda. The vast majority live in the sea. A few species are tolerant of brackish water and a small number of others have become adapted to fresh water.

In the first three classes, asexual reproduction, by way of budding, is important.

The Phoronidea

These animals live in vermiform tubes, products of their integumentary secretion. Their lophophores are horseshoe-

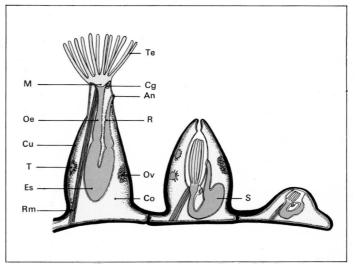

Diagram of the organization of a colony of Bryozoa, fragment of a file of individuals. On the left, completely developed individual; in the middle bud which has almost reached the term of its formation; on the right, young bud. *An*, anus; *Cg*, cerebral ganglion; *Co*, general body cavity (coelom); *Cu*, cuticle; *M*, mouth; *Oe*, oesophagus; *Ov*, ovary; *R*, rectum; *Rm*, retractor muscle; *S*, stomach; *T*, testis; *Te*, crown of tentacles.

shaped. The alimentary canal is bent like a U; mouth and anus, which are close together, are on the ventral surface, towards the centre, and there is also a vesicular system with haemoglobin and two excretory organs.

Reproduction is normally sexual, but when cut transversely, the two portions will regenerate the missing parts.

The only well-defined genus is *Phoronis*, which lives in almost all the seas but is found only on parts of the bottom where special conditions obtain. *Phoronis* species are from one to two inches long; the tufts of their lophophores project from their twisted chitinoid tubes.

The Ectoprocta (true Bryozoa)

Almost all of these are fixed to a support and are colonial. The anus opens outside the lophophore, whose tentacles may be retracted into a sheath. They have neither excretory nor circulatory systems. Asexual reproduction by budding gives rise to colonies, which are sometimes very large. Each individual (zooid) lives in a chamber, or zooecium, the walls of which are very often calcified.

Some zooids undergo profound anatomical modifications and become specialized: some are assigned to defence, others to cleaning up, and so on.

Colonies contain both male and female zooids. Budding is carried out from a stolon. Sexual reproduction manifests itself with various peculiarities—for instance the egg penetrates into an incubatory cavity (a rudimentary chamber) in which development takes place.

When bad weather creates conditions unfavourable to brackish and freshwater species, they produce dormant buds (hibernacula), which are isolated from the colonial body.

Some freshwater species (e.g. *Cristatella*), whilst remaining colonial, are mobile. The zooids are in parallel rows on a common plantar sole which creeps on the substratum.

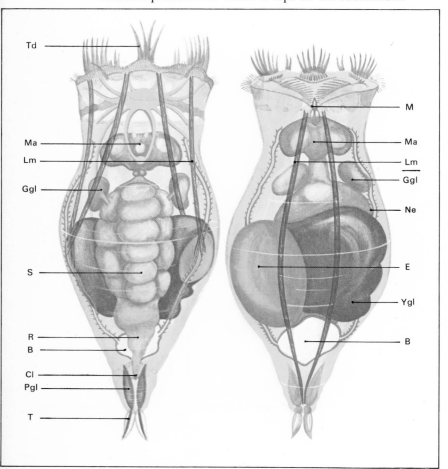

Organizational plan of a swimming rotifer, able to fix itself by its 'toes': *B*, bladder; *Cl*, cloaca; *E*, egg in the ovary; *Ggl*, gastric gland; *K*, kidney or nephridium; *Lm*, longitudinal muscles; *M*, mouth; *Ma*, crushing stomach or mastax; *Pgl*, pedal gland; *R*, rectum; *S*, stomach; *T*, toe; *Td*, trochal disc with strong cilia; *Ygl*, yolk gland.

The Endoprocta

These are small, and may be solitary or colonial. The mouth and anus are situated inside the lophophore.

Colonial species of individuals from buds on a creeping stolon are, except for one freshwater genus, all marine.

The Brachiopoda

In this class the body is contained in a bivalve shell, fixed to a support either directly or by means of a stalk. Unlike bivalve molluscs, the shell consists of two valves which are not symmetrical with regard to each other. One is dorsal and the other ventral, and the animal lies inside the shell on its back as if in a cradle fitted with a lid. The lophophore is made up of two ciliated arms, supported by an internal calcareous skeleton (brachial apparatus), and coiled like a spiral, on either side of the mouth. The body envelope secretes the shell, which is porous, and furrowed with canaliculi.

Brachiopods reached their peak in the Secondary era. Since the Tertiary era, they have declined, and at present they comprise 260 recent species, as against 2500 fossils.

The Rotifera

This is a group of minute aquatic animals most of which are only a few hundred microns in length; the largest do not exceed 1/25 of an inch. The majority live in fresh water.

Although they do not have an individualized head, the mouth is situated ventrally in an anterior region which is crowned by a strong band of vibratile cilia: the lophophore. The rest of the body is covered with a cuticle which may become thickened so as to form a shield. Often, the body tapers towards the rear and ends in an adhesive organ.

The alimentary canal consists of a pharynx, containing a grinding apparatus made up of several hard and complicated jaws (the mastax), an oesophageal tube, a dilation, or stomach, and an intestine; the anus is at the posterior end. The nervous system is made up of a small cellular mass, the cerebral ganglia, situated at the height of the pharynx and dorsally to it; from this ganglia run pairs of nerves connected to the various organs. The excretory system consists of two tubular organs (the protonephridia). At their distal ends are closed ampullae, or flame cells, in whose cavities beat a cluster of lashing cilia. The waste products in the blood which fills the body cavity pass through the wall of the ampullae. The ovary has two parts: the germarium or true ovary, which produces the eggs, and the vitellarium or yolk gland. The male, usually smaller than the female, has a simpler organization.

Most of the tissues forming the organs of rotifers are syncytia, made of a mass of cytoplasm in which the nuclei are not separated by membranes.

Rotifers usually feed on micro-organisms which, carried by the whirling current created by the beating of the ciliated lophophore, are conveyed directly into the mouth. Some are suctorial and suck up the content of algae or micro-organisms.

Breeding shows very remarkable peculiarities. The females extrude eggs with a thin shell, which develop without having been fertilized (natural parthenogenesis) and produce females; at a given moment they produce eggs giving rise to males, which are small and have no alimentary canal, although the other organs are functional. Fertilized eggs have a thick shell, are resistant to desiccation and cold, and develop only after a diapause.

Certain species of rotifers have the curious faculty of losing their water and becoming dehydrated, without dying. They then fall into a state of very reduced animation, or anhydrobiosis. If they are rehydrated, they again become active.

Some rotifers swim in the water, becoming plankton. Others live on the bottom, on which they move about like leeches or 'looper' caterpillars. Yet other species are sessile, and are carried by other animals.

A branched colony of marine Bryozoa. *Under-sea photo J. Théodor*

Molluscs

No group of animals is more diverse than that of the molluscs. What could be more different in appearance than a mussel, an octopus, a slug and a transparent *Clio*? Yet all are closely related animals descended from a single ancestor. Highly adaptable, molluscs have conquered all environments, from the depths of the sea to the greatest mountain ranges, and are at home in fresh as well as salt water and in air.

A diverse group

If a supreme being presided over the creation of the animals, a mood of levity must have possessed him when he came to the molluscs. For these are odd creatures, varying in length from 1/25 of an inch to more than 50 feet and often twisted into unusual shapes such as spirals. Their name, which simply means 'soft-bodied', gives no hint of their great diversity of form. Some have arms, others eyes, some have both and others neither. Many are protected by shells, but others are naked. The feature linking all 50,000 species together in a single phylum of the animal kingdom are apparent only to one who has studied them intimately. And not only is the structure of molluscs unusual. Their behaviour, their relations with other animals and their ways of breeding —these are also strange and individual.

The function of the shell

A walk along any seashore will reveal mollusc shells of great beauty—delicate, long razor shells, fan-like scallops, coiled whelk shells or flat oyster shells, coated inside with an iridescent sheen of nacre or mother-of-pearl. The outsides of the shells are often patterned in striking colours but, however magnificent their appearance, their main function is to act as a shelter and protect the soft bodies of their owners from predators. Not all molluscs possess such shelters; in squids, for example, the shell is hidden inside the body. However, such unprotected creatures have other methods of defence and can move rapidly to escape their enemies.

Several molluscs—oysters, scallops, snails, octopuses and squids—are gastronomic delicacies, but others have a poor

Murex brandaris and its eggs. Frequent on the rocky coasts of the Mediterranean, this *Murex* is characterized by a long siphon and the long spikes adorning its shell. It possesses a 'purple gland' and, for this reason, was exploited in antiquity, like other closely-related *Murex*, for the colouring properties of its purple. This substance, greenish initially, changes colour under the influence of light. *Phot. Aldo Margiocco*

Theoretical plan of a mollusc: *Am*, adductor muscle; *An*, anus; *Dg*, digestive gland; *E*, eye; *Exp*, expansions of foot; *F*, foot; *G*, gill; *Go*, gonad; *H*, heart; *M*, mantle; *Mo*, mouth; *Ns*, nervous system; *Pc*, pallial cavity; *Pe*, pericardium; *R*, rectum; *Ra*, radula; *S*, stomach; *Sh*, shell; *St*, statocyst; *T*, tentacle.

reputation and are considered harmful. Molluscs can devastate plantations, pierce the hulls of boats, destroy piers and wharves. Even edible molluscs must be treated with caution for they can transmit virulent diseases if they have grown in polluted waters.

On another plane—that of the zoologist—molluscs have a very different reputation, and a very high one. Anatomical research of the nineteenth and early twentieth centuries did not give much idea of the complexity and efficiency of the various ways in which these animals are adapted to their environments. These adaptations, especially the co-ordination of ciliary actions, can only be described as perfect. Respiration, the taking of food particles and body cleansing often depend on ciliary mechanisms of great precision.

Parasitical molluscs

Several molluscs are internal parasites of echinoderms and have undergone such a marked simplification of their internal structure that they can be recognized as molluscs only by observing their larvae. The larvae possess features, such as a coiled shell, that definitely identify them as molluscs.

The main types of molluscs

It is probable that molluscs evolved from annelid worms, losing the segmentation of these animals and gaining their own very individual characteristics in the process. If this is

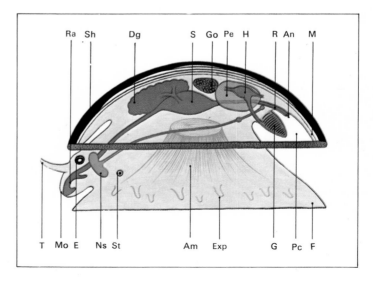

in fact the case, this process of evolution would have taken seven different routes to arrive at the seven different classes of molluscs designated by zoologists today. These classes are the Monoplacophora, Aplacophora, Polyplacophora, Lamellibranchiata, Gastropoda, Scaphopoda and Cephalopoda.

Of all these classes, which are each diversified to a lesser or greater degree, the monoplacophorans give the clearest evidence of the affinity of molluscs to annelids, for molluscs of this class have several sets of organs. The aplacophorans have no shell, but hard needle-like spicules toughen the outer surface. The polyplacophorans or chitons possess a shield of eight hard, overlapping, plates. The gastropods, or snails, slugs and limpets, have a single shell, often coiled into a spiral shape, but the shell may be internal or lacking altogether. Scaphopods or tusk shells also have single shells, but always in the shape of a long, thin, slightly curved cone. The lamellibranchs are also known as bivalves, and possess a double shell strongly hinged together at one end. The cephalopods—the squids, cuttlefishes and octopuses—have either an external spiral shell as in the nautilus, or an internal shell in which vestiges of the spiral shape still exist.

The structure of the mollusc

All molluscs are basically made up of a head, a foot, and a visceral mass, which contains the stomach and most of the other organs. A lining called the mantle covers the visceral mass, and the external shell grows from the outer surface of the mantle. These parts may be highly modified from one class of mollusc to another. The head no longer exists in the

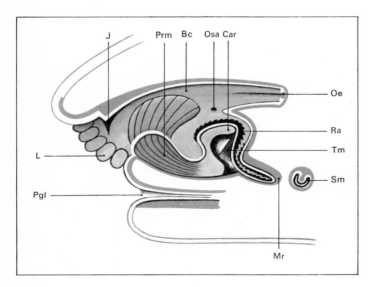

Diagram of the buccal mass of gastropods in sagittal section: *Bc*, buccal cavity; *Car*, radular cartilage; *J*, jaw; *L*, lip; *Mr*, matrix of the radula; *Oe*, oesophagus; *Osa*, orifice of salivary glands; *Pgl*, pedal gland; *Prm*, protractor muscle of radula; *Ra*, radula; *Sm*, section of matrix; *Tm*, tensor muscle of radula.

lamellibranchs, for example, and the foot, which is usually below the mollusc, is transformed in the cephalopods into a crown of powerful arms that surround the head and bear numerous suckers. In gastropods, the visceral mass is twisted horizontally through 180°, causing the nervous system to deform into a figure-of-eight shape and producing a degeneration of organs on one side of the body. The twisting or torsion, as it is called, is not present in the gastropod larva, and occurs when the mollusc becomes adult. There is

no equivalent to this strange deformation process elsewhere in the animal kingdom and it is unique to gastropods. A possible explanation of this biological mystery might be the appearance in the past of a successful mutation possessing asymmetry of the larval shell muscles. This hypothesis was put forward by Garstang who composed a famous ballad on the subject in 1928 and is strongly supported by the embryological researches of Dr Doris Crofts in 1955; however it still remains a hypothesis only.

The asymmetry resulting from torsion of the visceral mass has a profound influence on the organization of gastropods, although in some cases it is reduced to such an extent that the torsion is not visible, at least in outward appearance.

The importance of the mollusc

Extraordinary powers of adaptation to different environments have enabled gastropods to leave the ocean, where they originated, to live in estuaries and then in fresh water, and finally to proliferate on land. Such wandering has required a series of major physiological changes.

Almost all habitats harbour molluscs of some kind or other. Many crawl on the rocks and seaweed of the shore, and on coral reefs. Others bury themselves in mud or sand and circulate water through their bodies to gain plankton to eat and oxygen to breathe. *Janthina*, with its fine violet shell, drifts at the surface of the sea, and a vast number of delicately coloured or almost transparent molluscs swim actively in the waters of the oceans.

In fresh water, whether still or running, live *Limnaea*, *Planorbis* and *Physa*, all equipped with a 'lung' to breathe the air of an air bubble they carry with them. They periodically return to the surface to renew the air bubble. Hiding in the sandy or muddy bottoms of rivers or lakes may be found bivalves of the Unionidae, their shells coated inside with pink, white or bluish mother-of-pearl.

On land, a wide range of molluscs adapted to breathing air have evolved.

The mantle and mantle cavity

The most unusual feature of molluscs is undoubtedly the mantle cavity. The mantle is a fold of tissue that covers the top of the visceral mass and extends out on either side of it; the space between the sides of the visceral mass and the mantle, or between the mantle and the foot, is the mantle cavity. The cavity is wide open in primitive molluscs and in aquatic species, it tends to enclose the gills. But the surface of the mantle cavity can also take up oxygen as well as the gills, and in air-breathing species, the cavity acts as a lung and the gills are lost. The cavity is then no longer open to the environment, except for a narrow orifice. This controls the movement of air in and out of the lung, and cuts water loss to a minimum, making life possible for molluscs in arid climates.

Dorid and eolid nudibranchs. The back of the dorids forms a fold, or notum, which more or less overlaps the foot, as is shown by the roof in ventral view of *Platydoris speciosus*; whereas the eolids are characterized by the presence of long regularly arranged papillae. The egg-mass of the former takes the shape of a long ribbon coiled around itself; that of the latter is like a very long string. A, *Spurilla neapolitana* and its eggs; B, *Ceratosoma sp.*, New Caledonia; C, *Ceratosoma francoisi*, New Caledonia; D, *Platydoris speciosus* (Pacific), ventral surface, New Caledonia; E, *Aeolis sp.*, Mediterranean; F, *Glossodoris* on a sponge, New Caledonia. *Phot. R. Catala, J.-M. Baufle and Jean Tardy*

A

B

C

D

E

F

The gills and cilia

The gills are made up of broad, flat plates covered with hair-like projections called cilia. The plates are numerous and very close to each other, forming a large respiratory surface. Blood reaches the gills from the heart, is replenished with oxygen in the gills, and then returns to the heart, travelling throughout the body on its passage between heart and gills. To function perfectly, the gills not only need a constant renewal of water but they must also be kept in a state of absolute cleanliness. The problem is complicated by the fact that bivalves and gastropods often live in water containing large amounts of suspended particles. Many of them also pass all the waste products of digestion from the kidneys and anus into the mantle cavity.

The solution to these problems of hygiene is a model of elegance. Water currents are set up by the beating of the cilia lining the gills or the walls of the mantle cavity. Water is driven into and out of the cavity by the action of cilia and possibly also by muscular action. But the gill cilia strain the particles from the water, so that only clean water bathes the gill plates. The trapped particles are then expelled together with the mollusc's waste products when water is driven out of the mantle cavity.

Although mainly concerned with breathing, the mantle cavity also has a food-collecting function in bivalves and some gastropods. Many of the particles in the water are food particles and are of use to the mollusc. It may be necessary to sort one kind of particle from another and, in bivalves, zones of specialized cilia direct particles of food value towards the mouth while other zones of cilia channel undesirable particles to the part of the mantle cavity where water is expelled.

The mantle cavity has yet another function in the cephalopods. These molluscs can contract the mantle cavity so violently that water is forced out of the body in a jet, propelling the cephalopod rapidly backwards through the water. In this way, the mollusc can escape its predators.

Eating

From microscopic plankton to deep sea divers

The kind of food eaten, and also the functioning of the digestive system, varies appreciably from one kind of mollusc to another. Some take minute plankton particles from the water, whereas others eat comparatively large creatures. Molluscs of the former class include sedentary molluscs such as *Vermetus*, which spread out long nets of thin filaments to catch food particles. The molluscs then absorb the nets together with the micro-organisms that they have captured. Bivalves take food particles from the water with the aid of beating cilia. Other molluscs that exist on microscopic food particles include some that suck the blood of organisms by piercing their flesh with fine bristle-like structures. At the other end of the scale are the cephalopods, armed with tightly gripping tentacles and powerful jaws. Although deep-sea divers have little to fear from giant squids or octopuses, cephalopods are able to capture and tear apart such well-protected creatures as crabs and lobsters.

However, bivalves and cephalopods apart, most molluscs eat by rasping their food with a file-like tongue called a radula. Both plants and animals serve as food. The radula itself is only a flexible strip armed with rows of tiny sharp teeth, sometimes tens of thousands in number. What is remarkable is the way in which it functions. The radula is supported by a complex set of muscles called the odontophore. This normally lies inside a chamber beyond the mouth, but it may be raised to the mouth or even protrude from the mouth. The radula is folded into a groove when not in use, but it spreads out as it is raised so that the teeth are brought into action. The odontophore moves to and fro, applying the radula to a plant or animal so that fragments of tissue are scraped away and drawn down into the oesophagus behind the radula. From there, the food is taken to the stomach.

The radula may undergo several modifications. The teeth of *Philine* act like claws and can transport entire small animals into the gizzard, where they are crushed. In *Conus*, the teeth are few in number and needle sharp, and borne on a long proboscis. Just one of these teeth, sunk into a small fish or an annelid, injects sufficient poison to paralyse the victim instantaneously. The prey is then carried to the mouth on the proboscis and swallowed whole.

The stomach of a mollusc attains a very high degree of specialization, especially where micro-organisms make up the diet. Currents in the stomach fluid are set up by the beating of different groups of cilia. Particles of nutritive value are carried towards the digestive gland and subjected to the action of enzymes, but waste particles are directed to the intestine. Digestion of the particles is aided by the crystalline style, a gelatinous rod that projects into the stomach. The rod rotates and rubs against the stomach wall, wearing away and liberating enzymes. The stomach of carnivorous molluscs is much simpler.

Reproduction

Molluscs have as great a variety of methods of ensuring reproduction as they have of respiration and of obtaining food.

Molluscs have strange mating habits

Several classes of molluscs—the aplacophorans, polyplacophorans, bivalves and lower gastropods—are archaic in their breeding and practise external fertilization, which takes place in the sea. In these creatures, the gonads, which may be of either or both sexes, expel sperms or eggs through a short duct

Mating of slugs (*Arion*). After long and strange preliminaries, mating is effected by the complete extrusion of the genital organs of both partners, which form a bulky mass and are retracted after the transfer of a spermatophore from one individual to another. *Phot. Graf*

or through the kidney into the mantle cavity from which the sperms or eggs are shed in the sea. The first improvement on this haphazard method of breeding is found in higher gastropods. The genital passages, instead of opening into the mantle cavity, continue to the exterior of the body. A penis has developed at the end of the sperm duct, and fertilization has become completely modified to take place internally.

Such a development has enabled the gastropods to conquer the land, where external fertilization is impossible.

These higher gastropods are found among the three main groups of gastropods—the prosobranchs, which are mostly marine and have separate sexes, and the pulmonates and opisthobranchs, which are almost all hermaphrodite. The penis has a wide and extraordinary variety of shapes in these molluscs, and may be decorated with all kinds of accessories —teeth, scales, spines and hooks. It is large in size, and constitutes a considerable part of the mollusc's body. In the hermaphrodites, the penis is usually placed in front of the female orifice. The sexual apparatus of the Viviparidae, which are freshwater prosobranchs, is somewhat unusual as the sperm duct is prolonged to the end of the right tentacle, beyond the eye. The tentacle, appreciably enlarged, serves as the penis. *Sapha amicorum*, a Red Sea opisthobranch, is even more aberrant, for this organ protrudes from its mouth. The female organs may also vary, though within more modest limits.

Many hermaphrodite gastropods do not fertilize themselves but, like the unisexual gastropods, have to mate in order to breed. The placing of the genital organs dictates that, after various preliminaries, the molluscs confront each other head to foot. Mating may be reciprocal, with each creature fertilizing the other, or only one-sided. Sometimes, as in the case of the edible snail, it is preceded by a strange ritual in which each of the animals sinks several sharp chalky 'darts' into its partner's body.

Less violently, some slugs become entwined on the branch of a shrub or tree. Mucus secreted by the slugs secures them to the branch if they should fall off it, and becomes drawn out into a filament as the union progresses. Eventually mating ends as one of the partners falls to the ground. The other climbs back to the branch and swallows the thread of mucus.

In the sea, the sea hare (*Aplysia*), *Akera* and some pleuro-branchs (Notospidea) mate in chains of three or more individuals. The animal at the beginning of the chain behaves only as a female, and the others act as males for those that precede them in the chain and as females for those behind.

Self-fertilization

Some aquatic pulmonates are hermaphrodite but do not possess a penis. However, in the absence of such an organ they are able to fertilize themselves. Sperms and eggs meet in the individual's own genital passages, and there the eggs are fertilized. The very rare phenomenon of self-copulation has also been reported in this group, for some of the molluscs do have a penis and are able to use it to fertilize themselves.

Copulation of the cephalopods

Modes of copulation are different again in the cephalopods, in which the function of the penis is carried out by one of the arms or tentacles. With the help of this arm, called a hecto-cotylus, small packets of sperms can be transferred into the female's mantle cavity. In the argonaut, the hectocotylus even becomes detached from the male's body in order to reach the female. Before its true function was realized, it was thought to be a parasitic worm!

Changes of sex

Bivalves such as oysters and shipworms may undergo unusual changes of sex during their lifetimes. Although within a single population there may exist true males and true females, there are also individuals in which an alternation of sex occurs, usually with a transitional hermaphrodite stage. Some of these molluscs are male for a year or less, then become female, then change back to male, and so on. It is no exaggeration to say that all aspects of hermaphroditism may be observed in bivalves and gastropods. The cause for such changes of sex may be environmental and brought about by the presence of certain secretions in the water.

The young mollusc, similar to the trocophore of the annelids, betrays the ancestral origins of molluscs.

Eggs fertilized in the sea often become free-swimming larvae encircled with bands of cilia and known as trocophores. Annelids have similar trocophore larvae, showing that molluscs may once have evolved from annelids. As

Egg-mass of the nudibranch mollusc, *Doris*. The *Doris*, lay their egg-mass, a long irregularly shaped ribbon, on the sea bottom fixed by one edge. The eggs, very small and numerous and arranged in lines, are coated by a mass of gelatinous mucus. *Phot. J. M. Baufle*

growth proceeds, the band of cilia enlarges into a ciliated lobe, the adult organs begin to grow, and the embryo becomes a larva. This lobe is called a velum, from its veil-like appearance, and the larva is known as a veliger larva. Only molluscs have veliger larvae. The cilia of the velum wave to propel the larva and to wash food into its mouth. In bivalves, the free-swimming larvae develop similar ciliated lobes and the rest of the body becomes enclosed in two minute valves. Gastropods lay their eggs in fairly hard shells, ribbons or gelatinous strings, which may reach over sixty feet in length in the case of *Aplysia*. The eggs hatch into free-swimming larvae.

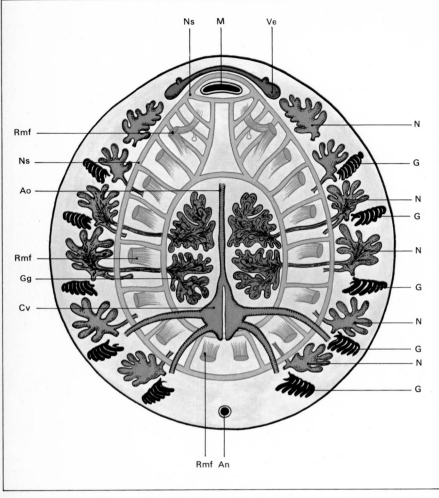

The velum of these larvae is particularly beautiful, being transparent or dotted with purple, brown, yellow or orange spots. In action, it curves and sways in a delicate flowing movement like the hem of a ballerina's robe caught in the dream-like slow motion of a never-ending underwater ballet. But the veliger's ballet soon comes to an end, for the velum disappears as it grows; it ends its free-swimming existence and falls to the sea bed to live as an adult mollusc among rocks or seaweed.

Not all mollusc larvae enjoy a free-swimming phase. The terrestial pulmonates are an example. On the other hand, cephalopod larvae are exceptionally good swimmers and are sometimes capable of carrying out fairly long migrations.

The classes of molluscs

Monoplacophora

On 6th May 1952, an event of great scientific importance took place. On that day, the grappling hook of the *Galathea*, a Danish oceanographic vessel operating west of Costa Rica, brought up from a depth of about 2000 fathoms ten specimens of an unknown mollusc which, after study, was named *Neopilina galatheae*.

The announcement of this discovery caused a sensation in the zoological world, for this mollusc is a veritable living fossil. It was far more primitive than any mollusc then known and had affinities with annelids as well as molluscs. Simple external examination revealed five or six pairs of gills lying in a groove between the foot and the mantle on each side of the body. Dissection showed similar sets of organs inside the body; there were eight pairs of muscles, and several excretory organs, nervous systems and reproductory organs.

This replication of organs is not only a feature of modern annelids, but also of fossil molluscs. Fossil mollusc shells have been found with indications that six pairs of muscles had been attached to them. But these archaic forms were thought to have been extinct since Devonian times—that is, for 345 million years. The startling discovery of 1952 was confirmed six years later when another research ship, the *Vema*, captured four specimens of a closely related mollusc from a depth of about 3000 fathoms off the coast of Peru. It was named *Neopilina (Vema) ewingi*.

Between these molluscs and polyplacophorans or chitons there are similarities in detail but also appreciable differences: *Neopilina* has a conical shell, almost limpet-like, whereas chitons have shells of separate plates that overlap like tiles on a roof. Moreover, metamerism (the division of the body into segments each containing a set of organs) is much more marked in *Neopilina* than in the chitons. *Neopilina* is the only living survivor of the class of monoplacophorans. Its distant ancestor may also have the other molluscs and the arthropods as descendants.

Diagram showing the organizational plan of the monoplacophoran *Neopilina: An,* anus; *Ao,* aorta; *Cv,* cardiac ventricle; *G,* gills; *Gg,* gonads; *M,* mouth; *N,* nephridia (kidneys); *Ns,* nervous system; *Rmf,* retractor muscles of the foot; *Ve,* prebuccal velum. The nephridia, gills and retractor muscles of the foot, as well as the gonads are repeated as in a segmented animal.

Chitons on a rock face. Like other molluscs of the Polyplacophora, these chitons (*Acanthochitona*) hang on very tenaciously to walls of rock, but, if detached from them, they roll themselves up into a ball, like wood-lice. They are covered on the back with complex calcareous plates articulated with each other. *Phot. J. Vasserot*

Aplacophora

At first sight, the aplacophorans or solenogasters hardly give one the impression of being molluscs at all. They have no shell and are long, worm-like animals. But some have a reduced foot and in others two gills emerge from a posterior anal cavity. The outer surface of the body is often covered with a hard cuticle containing calcareous spicules of various shapes. In the Crystallophrissonidae, there is a hard plate devoid of spicules in the neighbourhood of the mouth.

Several small aplacophorans burrow in mud, in which they feed on micro-organisms, but others crawl over hydroids, eating their tissues with the aid of a multi-toothed radula. Aplacophorans are world-wide in distribution, and have been found from the Arctic to the Antartic at depths down to 2000 fathoms.

Polyplacophora

The polyplacophorans or chitons cannot be confused with any other class of molluscs, for they look so different. The shell is made up of eight separate plates overlapping each other and arranged in a series running from head to rear. All other shelled molluscs have one-piece shells or, in the case of the bivalves, two halves that hinge together. Chitons live on rocks at the seashore, and are perfectly adapted to such an environment for the broad oval foot clamps them tightly in position so that they are not washed away by the waves. It often requires a chisel to break them loose, so tenaciously do they cling. The plates of the shell fit together to form an oval shield. The way in which the plates are arranged in a series recalls the articulated bodies of some arthropods, for when a chiton does become detached from its rock, it rolls up and arches its back like a wood-louse.

Along the whole of its circumference, the shield of plates is overlapped by a fleshy girdle containing hard spicules and forming a tough outer edge to the shell. The plates are protected by a horny outer layer called the periostracum, and running through them are very fine grooves carrying nerve branches that end at the surface in unpigmented eyes, or in small pigmented eyes that are sometimes well developed.

Chitons are herbivorous, and have a long alimentary canal that is folded several times. *Acanthochitona fascicularis* is common at many places on European coasts. Its plates are very conspicuous, unlike those of the large *Cryptoplax*, which is confined mostly to the North Pacific.

Bivalvia

This class of molluscs is also known by two former names—Lamellibranchiata and Pelecypoda. They are generally known as bivalves because they are enclosed within two half-shells or valves that hinge together. The valves remain half open in the absence of danger, but snap tightly together whenever a predator threatens. Bivalves are very strange animals in that they do not have heads. But what would be a matter of serious consequence to most other animals has little effect upon a bivalve for the functions normally associated with the head are redistributed elsewhere in the body.

A gastropod can use the eyes and tentacles on its head to make a deliberate and active search for prey, but the bivalve must necessarily undertake a passive existence. It is sedentary, straining from the water food particles that are wafted towards its mouth by the beating of its cilia.

However, a bivalve is able to sense its environment. The sensory faculties of the gastropod's tentacles are transferred in a bivalve to the edge of the mantle, which frequently bears long sensitive projections or sometimes even rows of simple or complex eyes.

The mantle presses against the inner surface of the valves and thickens them by secreting successive layers of shell on them. An inner layer of nacre or mother-of-pearl builds up in thickness as the bivalve grows older.

At one end, the two valves are held together by an elastic ligament, which acts to hold the valves half open. One or two powerful adductor muscles also connect the two valves and close them against the action of the ligament whenever necessary. The two valves fit tightly together, any corrugations along the edges exactly meshing with one another.

With the well-known exception of the edible oyster, which is dull and unprepossessing in appearance, the shells of bivalves are remarkable for their beauty. They are gracefully and symmetrically curved, patterned with radial or concentric markings in a wide variety of colours. Marine bivalves are particularly colourful. The species of *Tellina*, for example, are a delicate pink, sometimes all over and sometimes mixed with light-coloured streaks or patches.

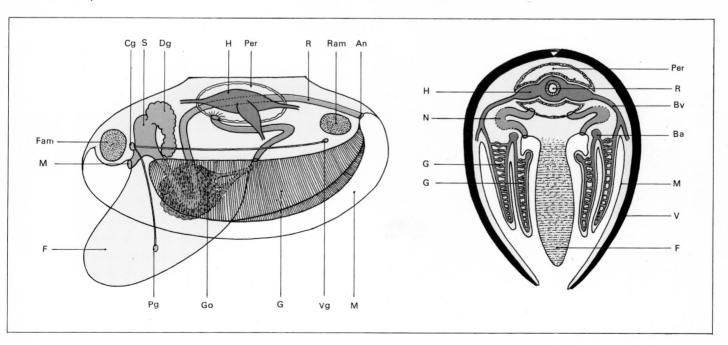

Diagrams of the organization of a bivalve mollusc. *On the left*, view of the left side; *on the right*, view in transverse section; *Aam*, anterior adductor muscle; *An*, anus; *Ba*, branchial artery; *Bv*, branchial vein; *Cg*, cerebral ganglia; *Dg*, digestive gland; *F*, foot; *G*, gill; *Go*, gonad; *H*, heart; *M*, mouth; *N*, nephridium (kidney); *Pam*, posterior adductor muscle; *Per*, pericardium; *Pg*, pedal ganglia; *R*, rectum; *S*, stomach.

Yellow, orange, blue, violet and green are other colours found in marine bivalves. Many are spotted, or dotted with dark triangles on a light background, or embellished with delicate designs. Freshwater bivalves are less striking, as green, blue and light brown colours predominate.

Some bivalves, such as mussels, attach themselves firmly to wave-worn rocks or piers by the byssus, a bundle of tough filaments ending in adhesive discs. The byssus is secreted by glands in the foot of the mollusc. However, most bivalves live buried in mud or sand, in places where the water is often turbid or muddy. The lives of these creatures are governed by two conflicting necessities. On one hand, they must take in large amounts of water to strain from it sufficient micro-organisms to live, yet this water must not contain so many suspended particles that they clog the gills and prevent the bivalves from breathing. The water is therefore filtered before it reaches the gills. This occurs at the entrance to the mantle cavity, either between the edges of the mantle or at the entry to the inhalant siphon. The siphon consists of two tubes that are extensions of the mantle. They are long enough to rise to the surface of the mud or sand if the bivalve is buried. Water is drawn in through the inhalant siphon, and waste products are discharged through the exhalant siphon.

Biological or physiological peculiarities

The symbiosis of Tridacna and the zooxanthellae

The first explorers to land in some of the islands of Australasia were surprised to discover that the inhabitants obtained fresh water by placing huge bowl-like shells under trees with large, broad leaves. Water dripped from the trees during tropical downpours and filled the shells. These shells, which were as much as five feet across, were valves of the giant clam (*Tridacna*).

Lima hians, seen from the right side. The edge of the mantle of this bivalve bears many highly developed tentacles, which lengthen when at rest, but may suddenly contract and even be spontaneously severed towards their tips. Their function seems to be a tactile one. *Phot. J. Vasserot*

Giant clams live among coral reefs in shallow water. When undisturbed, the huge valves open and the mantle protrudes, a delicate green, violet, blue or purple in colour. The colour results from the presence in the mantle tissue of countless zooxanthellae, minute single-celled algae that are not parasites but live in symbiosis or partnership with the clam. Being plants, the zooxanthellae make carbohydrates by photosynthesis for the benefit of their host, which in turn provides them with shelter and with inorganic minerals. Several parts of the mantle even contain transparent lens-like organs that serve to concentrate light rays on the zoo-xanthellae and promote photosynthesis.

Pearls

Pearls, the most natural of jewels, are produced by four species of *Pinctada*. These are the pearl oysters of tropical seas —the Red Sea, Indian Ocean, Pacific Ocean and (to a lesser degree) the Atlantic Ocean.

When a foreign body, living or inanimate, penetrates the mantle of a pearl oyster, it is surrounded by a sac formed by the growth of epithelium (mantle lining) around it. The mantle secretes thin, concentric layers of nacre or mother-of-pearl around the body, and a pearl slowly builds up in the mantle.

Pearl formation is the pearl oyster's way of rendering foreign bodies harmless. Most pearls in fact form by the entry of larvae of trematodes and cestodes into the mantle. Pearls are not found in every pearl oyster and diving for pearls is a very hit-and-miss affair.

In the early years of this century, a Japanese research worker named Mikimoto developed a way of deliberately 'seeding' pearl oysters so that pearls would grow inside them. He raised pearl oysters under conditions very similar to those found in the ocean, and inserted in the body of each oyster a small bead of mother-of-pearl partly covered with a small strip of epithelium from the mantle. The 'cultured' pearls produced by this method are almost indistinguishable from natural pearls.

Several other bivalves apart from oysters also produce pearls, although they do not attain the perfection of oyster pearls. Those of *Pinna*, which are reddish, of *Tridacna*, and of *Mya*, which are whitish, and the lustreless leaden pearls of mussels are mere curiosities of little value. But in earlier times, the pearls of freshwater pearl mussels such as *Unio* (*Margaritifera*), with their vermilion or pink sheen, were in demand.

Boring molluscs

Some bivalve molluscs—*Lithophagus*, *Saxicava* and *Pholodacea* —are able to drill holes in rocks. Little is known about this astonishing ability, though it seems that the valves, the foot and perhaps acid secretions may be involved. The shipworm (*Teredo*) is able to bore long, thin tunnels in submerged wood and eventually destroys old wrecks and wooden piles, especially in salty seas. The molluscs bore with the aid of their narrow, roughly-surfaced shells, which rasp through the wood. Boring molluscs are a serious menace, for they render wooden jetties and piers unsafe after a period of time.

The main groups of bivalves

For classification purposes, the bivalves are divided into three subclasses that differ in the structure of the gills. The degree of complexity of the gills is a reflection of the progress of evolution of the bivalves. In the primitive subclass Protobranchia, the gills consist of rows of short, flat filaments, whereas in the large subclass Lamellibranchia, they are enlarged and folded into a W shape, bearing ciliary connections between the filaments (the filibranchs) or fleshy connections (eulamellibranchs). The third subclass is the Septibranchia, in which the gill is reduced to a muscular partition perforated by a few slits and dividing the mantle cavity.

The protobranchs

There are two orders in this subclass made up of bivalves with or without siphons. They include *Nucula*, *Yoldia* and *Solenomya*.

The lamellibranchs/filibranchs

The species of this group of bivalves are numerous and diverse. They include such well-known molluscs as mussels, oysters and scallops of temperate seas, as well as the pearl oysters of tropical oceans. The hinges of filibranchs may be straight and very long, as in arkshells (*Arca*), or short, or even reduced.

Mussels are popular as food in many countries, and they can be gathered from rocks and piers, where they cluster in their thousands. Mussels can be 'farmed' by sinking large wooden stakes or branches into the water so that mussel larvae carried by the currents will settle and grow.

European oysters belong to two species. The flat oyster (*Ostrea edulis*) thrives mainly to the north of the Loire estuary in France whereas the Portuguese oyster (*Crassostrea angulata*), which has a more concave and less regular shell, is normally found to the south of this river.

Once there were natural beds of flat oysters, especially at estuaries, but such natural beds are no longer exploitable and oysters must be cultivated. Oyster farmers collect the larvae or spat, often using curved roofing tiles coated with lime. The oysters are then settled in the oyster beds a few months later. In parts of France, oysters are raised in beds having clay bottoms rich in micro-organisms. The oysters from these beds have a greenish tinge because they absorb in their gills a green pigment shed by *Navicula*, a blue diatom, into the water.

Great scallops (*Pecten*) are very unusual bivalves because they are able to move rapidly. Normally they rest on the bottom lying on their rounded valves. But if danger threatens, they can suddenly clap the valves together, producing a jet of water that shoots them away from a predator. Scallops use this technique particularly to escape from starfish, which are able to prise them open. They are highly valued as food and the smaller and more colourful queen scallops (*Chlamys*) are also considered delicacies. They attach themselves to rocks by a tough byssus, as do mussels.

Lithophaga, or the sea date, has long, narrow valves and hollows out cavities in rocks, in which it lives. *Vulsella* has fairly thin valves and lives in sponges. Fan mussels (*Pinna* and *Atrina*), which lie with the slender tips of their shells buried in the sand or mud, often grow very large. Thorny oysters (*Spondylus*) have thick valves often armed with sharp spines.

Limpet (*Patella*), ventral view. The broad foot acts as a very effective sucker, enabling the limpet to stand up to the buffeting of the waves. Around it, the gill extends in a thin circular lamina. The limpet moves about within restricted limits on the rocks, browsing on their covering of algae; it always seems to return faithfully to its lair. *Phot. Aldo Margiocco*

The razor shell (*Solen marginatus*) is well known and sought after on beaches. This 'razor', with gleaming shell, is hidden at some depth with the help of its very dilatable foot, which digs the sand and anchors itself in it at the same time drawing the rest of the animal after it. When disturbed, *Solen* contracts its foot and shuts its valves very suddenly. *Phot. J. Six*

The lamellibranchs/eulamellibranchs

These bivalves have specialized hinges and are grouped into many diverse families of which one of the best known is the Unionidae, the freshwater mussels or freshwater clams. Found in rivers throughout the world, the Unionidae have an unusual life history, which has been best studied in the American species. The eggs are not left to the mercy of the river current, but are incubated in the gills of the parent. There they develop into larvae called glochidia, and are expelled from the parent. Each glochidium bears a tiny bivalve shell which may bear hooks and trails behind it a long, sticky filament. If the hooks or filament happen to touch a fish, it sticks fast. The hookless larvae make their way to the gills of the fish. The larva stays with its host for two or three months before growing into an adult mollusc. Then it drops away and begins an independent life. Glochidia that do not find a fish die within a few days.

In tropical regions, some unionids may have to face long periods of drought. They survive by burying themselves in the mud of a pond or lake before it dries up, and closing their valves so that they are airtight and watertight. They then live a sluggish existence embedded in the dry mud for six to eight months, becoming active again at the first sign of rain.

Eulamellibranchs abound on the seashore. They include the common cockle (*Cerastoderma edule*) and other cockles; the venus shells (*Venus*), carpet shells (*Venerupis*) and other members of the family Veneridae. There are also the peppery furrow shell (*Scrobicularia piperata*) with its peppery taste,

Radiographs of gastropod shells seen in profile; they are intended to show the helicoidal coiling around an axis, the columella. (The shells belong to the genera *Pirula* and *Dolium*.) *Phot. Dr Gerard*

Ovula ovum, the poached egg snail, is a beautiful marine prosobranch gastropod, the foot of which bears contractile expansions that fold over the shell. *On the left* is one with a shell covered only to a limited extent; *on the right*, the shell is completely hidden by the expansions of the foot. *The Aquarium at Noumea. Phot. R. Catala*

wedge shells (*Donax*), and the flat, delicately-coloured tellins (*Tellina*). Razor shells (*Ensis*) with their shells shaped like cut-throat razors, burrow very rapidly and are difficult to catch alive. Gapers (*Mya*) have long, sturdy siphons, enabling them to live more than a foot beneath the surface.

The septibranchs

This order comprises only a few genera of molluscs found in all seas. It includes *Verticordia*, *Poromya* and *Cuspidaria*.

Scaphopoda

At low tide on many sand and mud beaches, it is possible to spot little, narrow shells shaped like miniature elephant's

tusks. These are scaphopods, commonly known as tusk shells or tooth shells. When the sea returns, the mollusc buries itself in the sand or mud with the aid of its active powerful foot, leaving the tip of the shell above the surface and poking out into the water. Water enters and leaves the shell through a small hole in the tip of the shell, enabling the scaphopod to breathe.

Next to the mouth, which is situated behind the foot, are situated a large number of filaments. These filaments stretch out through the sand or mud. They probably capture and convey foraminifera to the mouth, but it is also possible that the cilia of the filaments direct much smaller organisms and fine sediment to the mouth.

Species of *Dentalium* are to be found on beaches, but this scaphopod also inhabits deep waters as well as inshore waters, being found to a depth of 2000 fathoms.

Gastropoda

The ancestor of the gastropod molluscs must have had a coiled but symmetrical shell, and was closely related to *Bellerophon* of the Palaeozoic era. However, it seems that a mutation occurred in this ancestor by which its body became twisted, as happens when the gastropod larva becomes adult. Three subclasses now exist: the Prosobranchia, which are mostly marine and breathe with gills; the Pulmonata, in which the gills are replaced by a lung and which, after becoming adapted to freshwater life, became common in all continents; and the Opisthobranchia, which are mostly marine molluscs and do not always possess a shell.

The molluscs of all three orders have a head with eyes at the ends of long stalks, and most have a radula with which they scrape their food. This long rasp may bear from a few to several thousand teeth of extraordinarily varied shapes. The shell is typically coiled in a spiral, for the torsion of the visceral mass also causes twisting of the mantle; as the mantle secretes the shell material, a convoluted shell results. However, in some species the shell is reduced and internal or disappears altogether. If the shell is lost, the visceral mass may be untwisted as well. But such molluscs would have evolved as a twisted gastropod became untwisted, for their larvae first become twisted and then untwist as they develop.

The prosobranchs

In these gastropods, the effect of torsion is to bring the gill or gills in front of the heart, and to twist the nervous system of the visceral mass into a figure-of-eight. The animal crawls on its foot, which is flattened out like a broad sucker beneath the molluscs. If danger threatens, it can often retreat into its shell and close the opening; as the foot withdraws into the shell, it pulls into place behind it a chitinoid plate known as the operculum.

The abalone or ormer (*Haliotis*) is well-known as a gastronomic delicacy, especially in the western United States and Japan, and it also possesses a beautiful nacreous shell. The shells can often be seen lying empty on the sea bed. They are easily recognized by the line of holes along one edge, the last of which serve as an exit for the current of water that circulates through the mantle cavity. Keyhole limpets (*Diodora*) have conical shells with a hole at the top, which has the same function. This distinguishes it from the limpet (*Patella*) which has a similar conical shell but no hole. Small top shells are numerous in temperate waters. In tropical seas, they grow large and are exploited for their mother-of-pearl. *Angaria*, a fairly close relative of the Indo–Pacific region, has strange curved and branching appendages to its shell, and *Turbo* has a curious convex and heavy operculum, which may be smooth or embellished with rounded projections.

Two groups of prosobranchs exhibit unusual behaviour for an order that is predominantly marine. Some of the nerite molluscs (*Nerita*) can spend hours stranded on rocks clear of the water without coming to harm; others are to be found only in brackish water or even in fresh water. Even more aberrant (for this subclass) are the gastropods of the family Helicinidae, which have abandoned the water and live on bushes and trees.

Also unusual is the viviparous river snail (*Viviparus*) of European rivers, which has its right tentacle transformed into a penis. In the tropics, the Pilidae, such as the freshwater *Ampullaria*, are very strange in being amphibious, for their mantle cavity contains gills but also functions as a lung.

The periwinkles (*Littorina*), which include the molluscs known as winkles, are mainly prosobranchs of sea coasts, but some of them are to be found in mangrove swamps living on trunks a few yards above the water.

The shells of *Rostellaria*, *Strombus* and *Pterocera* are different in shape from those of the other gastropods, for the opening is irregular in shape and may be surrounded by curved spikes. Such shells, common in the tropics, are known as scorpion shells.

More regular in shape, cowrie shells (*Cypraea*) are embellished with spots of many colours in various designs and colours. So attractive are they that these shells were once used as money in some primitive communities. The mantle normally covers the shell when the mollusc is alive, and is similarly dotted with spots of pigment. The shells of *Trivia*, close relatives, and *Simnia* are covered with a richly coloured mantle.

Necklace shells (*Natica*) burrow in sand and bore into bivalves to obtain food. *Janthina* and *Recluzia* float in the open sea on a raft of air bubbles and tow their egg-bearing capsules behind them. In the same environment live the beautiful *Atlanta*, a glassy rose or brown, and the crystal-like *Pterotrachea*.

The higher prosobranchs include the helmet shell (*Dolium*) with its poisonous saliva; *Murex*, whose shell often bristles with sharp spikes and which produced a purple dye esteemed by the Romans; the agile *Nassa*, which feeds on carrion that it can scent from a distance; the elegant Turridae; and the awl shells (*Tereba*), bottom-living molluscs with very elongated shells. Among the finest in appearance are the cone shells, though they must be treated with caution as some possess a poisonous barb. Fortunately not all cone shells are harmful, and several are eagerly sought after for their rich but delicately embellished designs. *Conus gloriamaris*, the most prized, is known only from a few specimens, and for a long time it was thought to have become extinct. Recent discoveries indicate that it is still living, but it would seem that it can only be found at greater depths than was previously thought.

Triton nodifer, the largest marine gastropod in Europe. Closely related, exotic species are used as 'trumpets' and, in fact, the natives of various countries use such shells, after having broken off the tip of the spire, as horns. *Phot. J. Six*

The European viviparous river snail (*Viviparus*), fairly common, is a good example of a prosobranch adapted to life in fresh water. Its shell is very often encrusted. The figure *on the left* shows, in profile, the inhalant siphon at the front of the shell; *on the right*, seen from the front and open, the exhalant siphon is shown, via which the water which has bathed the mantle cavity is expelled. *Phot. R. H. Noailles*

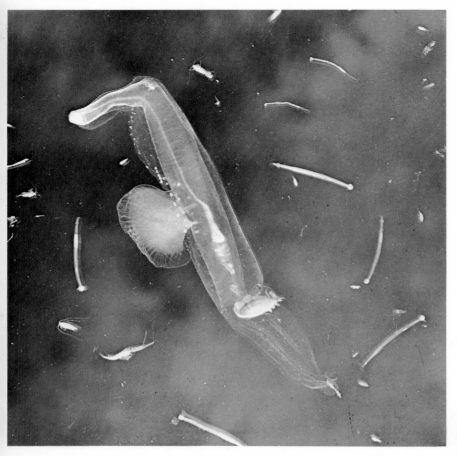

The pulmonates

The subclass Pulmonata contains an immense number of species, of which representatives are to be found in all continents. Most pulmonates are either adapted to life in fresh water or never leave the land; only a few are marine species. The subclass comprises two orders.

The order Basommatophora have eyes at the base of their tentacles. The best-known aquatic members of this group are *Limnaea*, *Physa*, *Planorbis* and *Ancylus*, which has a limpet-like shell.

In the order Stylommatophora, the eyes are situated at the ends of the tentacles. On land, besides familiar molluscs like slugs and snails, there is a great variety of pulmonates of modest dimensions and little-known habits. *Testacella* has a reduced shell confined to the rear of the body. Many slugs have no external shell; they avoid desiccation by secreting mucus in large quantities.

In South America live the large molluscs of the Strophoceilidae, which lay eggs more than an inch long. *Achatina fulica*, indigenous to Africa, is also known for its considerable size as well as for the damage it does to crops, especially in India and Sri Lanka where it has been introduced.

The Helicidae are the most developed of the pulmonates. There are many European species, but only the edible or Roman snail (*Helix pomatia*) and the smaller garden snail (*Helix aspersa*) are of economic importance.

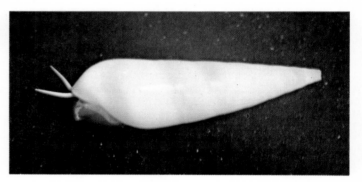

The opisthobranchs

These molluscs are marine animals, highly diverse in their structure as well as their behaviour. Some zoologists classify them with the pulmonates in a group called Euthyneura.

The shell can vary enormously in shape from one genus to another. The most primitive opisthobranchs, such as *Acteon* and *Bulla*, have a spiral shell into which they can withdraw. The shell is a low cone in *Umbraculum* and *Tylodina*, which breathe by means of a long feather-like gill on the right side of the body. In pelagic species, the shell may become very unusual. *Creseis* has a tapered shell, rather like a hollow needle, and the shell of *Diacria* narrows from its opening to a flat plate. *Cymbula* has a slender, elegant boat of transparent cartilaginous material for protection. But shells are the exception in the opisthobranchs; the shell tends to become internal in this group, and in most of its members the shell disappears. Molluscs showing no trace of a shell nor of a mantle cavity are called nudibranchs.

Gills are well developed in the more primitive families, but in others they often disappear and are replaced by respiratory papillae or by accessory gills. The basic shape of the gastropod body is modified sufficiently to produce perfect

Pterotrachea mutica, a pelagic heteropod mollusc, of crystal clear transparency, shows remarkable adaptation to a swimming life. Its dorsal fin, shaped like the head of a hatchet, results from a partial transformation of the foot, the other part being relegated to the caudal portion; a very long and unexplained fragile filament runs from the caudal region. The shell exists only in the larval stages; the visceral mass, reduced, can be seen behind the fin. *Phot. Aldo Margiocco*

Balcis alba are small molluscs with gleaming shells which live as ectoparasites on echinoderms. Adapting to this mode of life, their sucking proboscis has lengthened considerably and become specialized. However, they do not appreciably injure the organisms at whose expense they live (*Right*). *Phot. J. Vasserot*

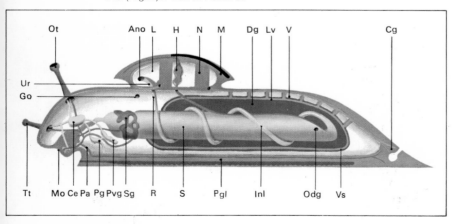

Organization plan of the slug (*Arion*): *Ano*, ano-urinary orifice; *Ce*, cerebral ganglia; *Cg*, caudal gland; *Dg*, digestive gland; *Go*, genital orifice; *H*, heart; *Inl*, intestinal loop coiled round the stomach; *L*, lung; *Lv*, lateral vein; *M*, mantle; *Mo*, mouth; *N*, nephridium (organ of Bojanus or kidney); *Odg*, orifice of digestive gland; *Ot*, ocular tentacle; *Pa*, pedal artery; *Pg*, pedal ganglia; *Pgl*, pedal gland; *Pvg*, pleuro-visceral ganglia; *R*, rectum; *S*, stomach; *Sg*, salivary gland; *Tt*, tactile tentacle; *Ur*, urethra; *V*, veins; *Vs*, ventral venous sinus.

The notoriety of the achatinas (in this case *Achatina balteata*), is based mainly on the fact that the agate snail *Achatina fulica*, introduced into Asia, has devastated many plantations (tea, cocoa, etc.). In Africa itself, they do not cause serious damage. These bulky pulmonates' shells sometimes exceed 6 inches in height. *Phot. J. Six*

Below, mode of penetration of the parasitic mollusc *Entocolax* into its host, a holothurian (echinoderm). *Entocolax*, in the visceral cavity, is hanging on to the wall of its host; it has the shape of a pear, the large end being the one which is fixed, while at the free end—or the pear's long pedicle (mollusc's snout)—is the mouth; the alimentary canal is limited to an oesophagus. The ovary occupies the base of the pear and projects into a cavity, the incubation cavity, which is in fact the dilated oviduct. All the individuals of this type are females. *1–4*, stage of penetration; *5–6*, stages of development; *7–8*, swollen part of an adult female. The pygmy males (*M*), in an almost larval state, live in the incubatory cavity of the female. *Co*, cocoons filled with eggs; *Ic*, incubatory cavity; *Oe*, oesphagus; *Ov*, ovary; *S*, shell; *W*, wall of the host. *After the data of several authors*

Below left, the pygmy male of *Entocolax ludwigi*: *Dd*, deferent duct; *T*, testis. This tiny male has a spherical shape and is made up for the most part of a testis. When the latter has been emptied of its sperm, the male dies and disintegrates. *After Heding and Mandahl-Barth*

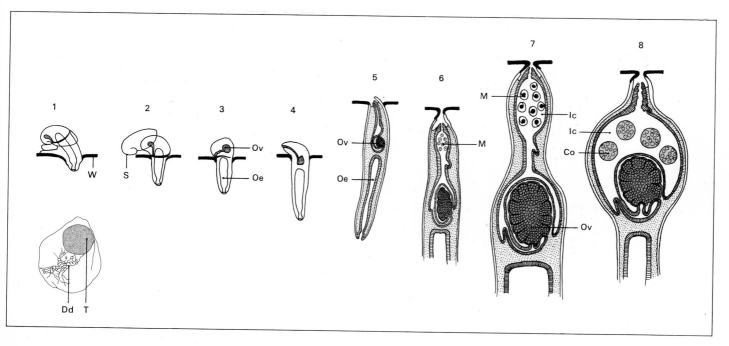

bilateral symmetry, so that the right side is an exact mirror image of the left, at least so far as external shape is concerned.

The order Saccoglossa, for a long time allied with the nudibranchs, have a special kind of radula. Instead of falling from the body, the worn teeth accumulate in a pouch. Outwardly symmetrical, some have gills or respiratory papillae, but others breathe through the skin. Others have no heart, and their circulation is produced by rhythmic contractions of projections in the outer surface.

Spurilla neapolitana devouring a sea anemone. Like the other eolid nudibranchs, *Spurilla neapolitana* has its back covered with papillae (cirri), arranged in transverse rows. *Phot. Jean Tardy*

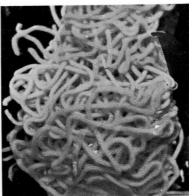

The sea hare, *Aplysia*, and its egg-mass. It moves as a result of the co-ordinated beating of its two broad lateral lobes, the parapodia. When alarmed, the sea hare expels a purple liquid. It lays on algae-covered littoral bottoms at the beginning of spring, an ovigerous string, made up of large numbers of very small eggs; this string may reach to more than 60 feet in length. *Phot. R. H. Noailles and J. M. Baufle*

Opisthobranchs of the order Anaspidea possess extended flaps of the mantle that are used for swimming and also cover the vestigial shell. *Akera* lives on sandy or muddy bottoms, but the herbivorous sea hare (*Aplysia*) congregates at rocks covered with algae.

Many opisthobranchs live on sponges, on which they browse, or on coelenterates. This applies to the order Nudibranchia. Although they have no shell, nudibranchs vary enormously in appearance; they may be smooth, warty, or covered with papillae (projections) of all sizes arranged into regular patterns of many designs. Some are dull in colour but well camouflaged, for they match the background of rocks and algae over which they crawl. Others are brightly-coloured—carmine, orange, violet, ultramarine, or lemon yellow, for example. The same animal may be able to change colour and display a wide variety of hues.

The most common nudibranchs are small or medium in size. However *Hexabranchus*, with its flat, oval body covered with raspberry red patches on a creamy background, reaches twelve inches in length. It swims by undulating its whole body and, like many of the most beautiful nudibranchs, it is found in tropical seas.

Pelagic nudibranchs are comparatively few in number. *Phylliroe* is one of the most unusual. It has a narrow (laterally compressed) transparent body, and on its reduced foot it bears a small organism that for a long time was thought to be a parasitic jellyfish. This was disproved in 1963, when the truth about the strange life of *Phylliroe* came to light. At the veliger stage, the *Phylliroe* larva penetrates the umbrella of the jellyfish *Zancled* and lives as a parasite on the jellyfish. There it develops into an adult and outgrows its host.

Like several other nudibranchs, *Phylliroe* is luminous and shines brightly in the darkness. *Plocamopherus* gives off very brief flashes of light at the least touch. Little is yet known about the nature of this phenomenon.

Cephalopoda

The cephalopods are all marine animals and not the most diverse of molluscs, although fewer species exist now than in the Palaeozoic and Mesozoic eras, but they are unquestionably the most developed molluscs for they are the most intelligent of all invertebrates. Brains do not go with beauty, however, for they are monstrous to look at.

The octopus, with its beady eyes and sharp beak encircled by a crown of waving tentacles laden with powerful suckers, looks as spine-chilling as any deep-sea monster could. In fact, divers often refer to them as almost lovable creatures, not at all harmful. Most sea monster stories, if they have any basis in fact, probably arose from a sighting of the giant squid. Weighing as much as two tons and measuring more then fifty feet in length, the giant squid is the most massive of all invertebrates. It is rarely seen, for it is a denizen of the deep and does not normally come to the surface. It would make a formidable adversary if it were more common for, far below the surface, it regularly does battle with the great sperm whale.

In all cephalopods, the foot is transformed into a set of tentacles armed with suckers and growing from the head. The name of this order of molluscs reflects this anatomical peculiarity, for cephalopod means 'head-foot'. Some cephalopods have two extra tentacles, longer than the others and bearing suckers at the tip. In the centre of the crown of tentacles is the mouth, from which emerges a beak made of two sharp pointed jaws. The suckers are fixed directly to the

tentacles or grow on stalks and may be equipped with claws. They are circular in shape and have highly sensitive edges. As a sucker touches an object, muscles move the back of the sucker to create a sucking effect and the object is gripped tightly. Cephalopods capture their prey and also cling to rocks in this way.

The body varies in shape from one kind of cephalopod to another. Octopuses are globular, squids are shaped like long cones, and cuttlefishes are broad and flattened. The mantle cavity opens near the head, admitting water to the gills for respiration. Water does not leave the mantle cavity by the same opening, but instead is expelled through the funnel, an opening near the tentacles, by contraction of the mantle. The mantle is very muscular and can contract powerfully and suddenly, producing a strong jet of water from the funnel. This action drives the cephalopod backwards, a mode of locomotion comparable with that of the jellyfish. As an extra means of defence, ink from an ink sac opening into the funnel may be squirted into the jet, producing a cloud of ink in the water. The dark cloud may hide

Two beautiful eolid nudibranchs: *above, Berghia caerulescens; below, Coryphella pedata.* The eolids no longer have gills, and their breathing is effected through the skin, especially through the dorsal papillae (very numerous in *Berghia*, less so in *Coryphella*). Eolids feed on Cnidaria (hydroids, corals, etc.), on which they literally browse; the cnidocysts of their prey accumulate in the intestinal diverticula. Eolids are among the most richly-coloured molluscs. *Phot. J. Tardy and F. Salvat*

the cephalopod like a smoke screen, or it may distract the predator from the chase.

Fins may also aid movement, though they are not the principal means of motion. The cuttlefish has fins along the side of its body. In the squid they are at the other end of the body to the tentacles.

Cephalopods may undergo very rapid changes in colour. The cuttlefish normally lies half-buried in the mud or sand on the bottom, blending its colour with its surroundings.

Octopuses are difficult to spot for the same reason. However, if the cuttlefish is disturbed, it loses its pale colour and suddenly develops black strips on a light background. This phenomenon is a reflex action involving the chromatophores, cells full of dark pigment in the cephalopod's skin. When the cells dilate, they show up dark brown. The reflex is triggered off by a visual stimulus, for covering one of the eyes prevents colour changes occurring on that side of the body. Many cephalopods exploit this faculty to the full; cuttlefish have

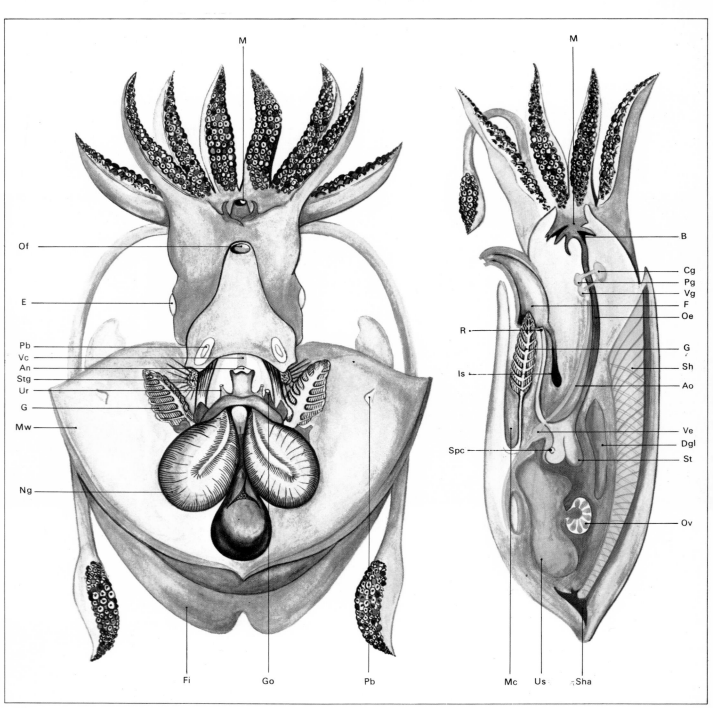

Female cuttlefish (*Sepia*). On the left, the mantle cavity has been opened, the two flaps of the mantle are folded down on each side of the body. On the right, very diagrammatic longitudinal section: *An*, anus; *Ao*, aorta; *B*, parrot-like beak (jaws); *Cg*, cerebral ganglia; *Dgl*, digestive gland; *E*, eye; *F*, funnel; *Fi*, fin; *G*, gill (ctenidium); *Go*, female genital orifice; *Is*, ink sac; *M*, mouth; *Mc*, mantle cavity; *Mw*, mantle wall; *Ng*, nida- mental gland; *Oe*, oesophagus; *Of*, external opening of funnel; *Ov*, ovary; *Pb*, press button fixing funnel to mantle; *Pg*, pedal ganglia; *R*, rectum; *Sh*, shell; *Sha*, shell apex; *Spc*, spiral caecum; *St*, stomach; *Stg*, stellate ganglion; *Ur*, ureter; *Us*, excretory sac or kidney; *Vc*, vena cava; *Ve*, ventricle; *Vg*, visceral ganglia.

been observed to capture small fish by lying motionless in wait near seaweed whose colour they have assumed.

The skin of many deep-water cephalopods contains light-producing organs as well as chromatophores. These may be distributed throughout the body or confined to certain regions of the skin. Captured alive, these animals produce a light show of extraordinary beauty. The body of *Thaumato-lampas diadema* was described by its discoverer, Professor Chun, as being adorned with a diadem of brilliant gems glittering in a myriad of different colours—ruby red, ultra-marine blue, snow white and sky blue.

Bioluminescence may be produced by luminous bacteria, a luminous secretion, or by special light-producing organs known as photophores. As well as luminescent cells, the photophores contain reflectors and lenses to intensify the light. A few species, including *Toxeuma* and *Bathothauma*, carry their photophores on long eye-stalks. It is possible that these cephalopods produce light to illuminate the dark places in which they live and move.

The method of reproduction is known in only a few species of cephalopods. However, it seems that in most the sperm is transferred from the male to the female by one of the arms,

detached from the male in order to reach the female. However, males have been found within the shells of the females and it is possible that they may live in symbiosis with them. Such a partnership would ensure the survival of these cephalopods, which would otherwise be left very much to chance.

Octopuses lay eggs, fixing them to rocks or sea plants. Larvae hatch from the eggs and may live among the plankton before becoming adapted to life on the bottom.

The principal cephalopods

Unlike the other existing cephalopods, the pearly nautilus (*Nautilus*) is a veritable relic of the Palaeozoic era. It is distinguished from the other cephalopods by possessing four gills, whereas all the others have two gills. Another primitive feature is the very simple eye, for the eyes of other cephalopods are well developed and like vertebrate eyes in structure.

Nautilus has an external shell divided by internal partitions into several compartments. The shell and the number

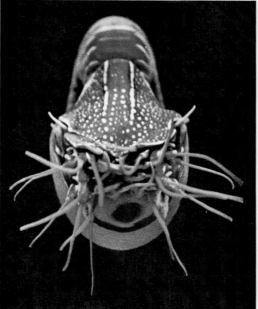

The pearly nautilus (*Nautilus*) of the once numerous Nautiloida group, which now includes only six living species. These cephalopods have four gills. The head bears numerous small arms, provided with suckers and which can be retracted into sheaths. They have neither ink sac nor chromotophores. The eye, which is very simple, has no crystalline lens;

light reaches the retina through a very small opening. In normal position, the shell is oriented in such a way that the last chamber and the animal it shelters are turned downward. *The Aquarium at Noumea. Phot. R. Catala and Aldo Margiocco*

specially modified for this purpose and known as the hectocotylus. In the common octopus, the male extends the hectocotylus and caresses the female from a distance, introducing the tip of the arm into her mantle cavity and there discharging his spermatophores (small packets of sperm).

Vampyroteuthis has no hectocotylus, but spermatophores have been found in two receptacles placed in front of the female's eyes, presumably deposited there by the funnel of the male.

The mode of fertilization in *Argonauta* is more of a mystery. The female is massive compared with the tiny male, being twenty times his size. The male has a hectocotylus arm that is at first enclosed within a sac. This may somehow become

of compartments grow as the cephalopod grows, and it lives in the outermost and most recent compartment. Through the centre of each partition runs a siphuncle, a tube connected to the rear of the body. The entire shell is filled with gas at a pressure that seems to be controlled through the siphuncle. As a result, *Nautilus* floats at the surface, even after death. At the front end, *Nautilus* bears two crowns of tentacles, one external and the other internal, but the arms have no suckers. Creatures similar to *Nautilus* were very common in prehistoric times, but nowadays they are to be found only in the Indo–Pacific region.

The other present-day cephalopods are divided into three orders—the Decapoda, Vampyromorpha, and Octopoda.

The decapods

Decapods get their name because they possess ten arms. The most familiar is the squid (*Loligo*), the flesh of which is considered a delicacy in many countries. It belongs to the most varied group of decapods, the Teuthoidae; which contains many other excellent swimmers, such as *Chiroteuthis*, slender-bodied and crowned with very long tentacles. Several genera—*Abralia, Onychoteuthis* and *Galiteuthis*—possess suckers that are armed with claws. *Ommatostrephes* and *Illex* hunt mackerel, which they kill with a single bite at the nape of the neck. But of all these various animals, it is the giant squid (*Architeuthis*) that inevitably is the most famous. One can well understand the trepidation of those Newfoundland fishermen who, on 2nd November 1887, approached a vast animal that had become stranded on the shore. It measured 55 feet in

Egg-mass of the common cuttlefish (*Sepia officinalis*). As can often be seen on the coast at low tide, the eggs, or sea grapes, are attached in groups to seaweed. A small window cut in the elastic envelope makes it possible to see embryos at different stages of their development. *Phot. Aldo Margiocco*

length, the head and body making up 20 feet of the total and the tentacles stretching another 35 feet. The weight was estimated at 2 tons. Another specimen, 2 feet longer overall, was washed up in New Zealand 9 years later; the tentacles accounted for 49 feet of its length, so that the Newfoundland squid kept its record as the biggest invertebrate ever found, a record still unbroken today.

Formidable though they are, giant squids are not absolute

masters of the ocean depths. Sperm whales have been found with sucker marks scarring their sides and with huge tentacles in their stomachs, indicating that giant squids fall prey to the whales. Whales breathe air and have to surface periodically to breathe. It is possible that mariners in earlier times may have seen a sperm whale surface while locked in combat with a giant squid. This would have made a fisherman's story to end them all and could soon have become transformed into a terrifying tale of sea monsters.

The vampyromorphs

This order of cephalopods—the vampire squids—comprises a small number of genera. It includes *Melanoteuthis lucens*, a strange-looking creature with enormous eyes and luminous organs, reminiscent of a grinning mask. Another vampyromorph of similar appearance, *Vampyroteuthis infernalis,* has only tiny tentacles that retract into pouches.

The octopods

Octopods possess eight arms, lacking the two extra-long tentacles of squids and other decapods. They are almost as diverse a group as the decapods. The bottom-living octopods, for example, are very different from the common octopuses of temperate coastal waters. The former are often described as having extremely soft and sometimes transparent bodies—*Alloposus mollis* is among them. The common octopus (*Octopus*) lives in burrows that it takes great pains to build. It hunts crabs and molluscs, whose remains pile up near the entrance to the burrow. Lesser octupuses (*Eledone*) live farther from the shore than do common octopuses. Both these two octopods have webs of skin connecting the lower parts of the tentacles, forming a structure like an umbrella that enables them to grip their victims more firmly. Their suckers differ, *Eledone* having a single row on each arm and *Octopus* a double row.

Ocythoe displays sexual dimorphism (a difference between the sexes) of an unusual kind. The female is comparatively large, weighing several pounds, whereas the male is so small that it lives in the gill cavity of a salp (a free-swimming ascidian). The female lives in clefts in rocks. At breeding time, the male leaves its host to find the female.

A similar disproportion in size occurs in the argonaut or paper nautilus (*Argonauta*), which is a very different creature to the pearly nautilus (*Nautilus*). Unlike *Nautilus* but like the other cephalopods, *Argonauta* has no true shell. However, as if to rival its namesake, the female builds an elegant curved 'shell' of a translucent paper-like substance. The shell is made from a secretion produced by two of the arms. It does not adhere firmly to the female's body, but she does not survive if she is permanently separated from the shell. The eggs are incubated in the shell.

Two views of the octopus (*Octopus vulgaris*), the compact body of which contrasts with the great development of the eight arms with suckers; the arms prolong the head and are joined to each other at their base by a broad membrane used to envelop prey. Many chromotophores are scattered over the skin, the colour of which harmonizes more or less with that of the octopus' rocky habitat. The lairs of octopuses can be recognized by the carapaces of crustaceans and the shells of molluscs abandoned near their entrances. *Phot. Fronval and J. Six*

Allies and ancestors of the arthropods

The distribution area of *Peripatus* corresponds, broadly, to the fragments of Gondwana land as geologists conceive it: Australia, India as far as the Himalayas, Madagascar, southern Africa, the Congo, and South and Central America, including the West Indies. Whatever the value of the hypothesis of Gondwana, broken up at the end of the Primary era, the fact remains that the discontinuous distribution of *Peripatus* bears witness to an extremely ancient origin.

Peripatus live in damp places, within close reach of water; forest galleries suit them very well. They penetrate into rotten wood or slip beneath the carpet of dead leaves or into fissures in the ground. But some put up strong resistance to drought (central Australia). Some species are gregarious and others solitary. The feeding habits of *Peripatus* are mixed. They are carnivorous and attack varied prey: small molluscs, worms, insects, etc. They attack their victims by projecting a stream of glue, secreted by two glands (glue glands) which open at the top of two strong papillae situated on either side of the mouth. Some feed on termites. The immobilized prey, held fast by the glue, is killed and eaten by *Peripatus*. Phot. Dr Ralph Buchsbaum

Some present-day animals appear to be direct descendants either of the ancestors of the arthropods or of animals that evolved from these ancestors independently of the arthropods. These animals are the minute tardigrades, which have the common though inappropriate name of water bears, and the onychophores, which are aptly known as walking worms. They are important because, as 'living fossils', they are most likely to enlighten us on the origin of the arthropods.

The onychophores

The onychophores, commonly known as velvet worms or walking worms, look like long, thin slugs that walk on two rows of small, stumpy legs ending in short claws. They range from half an inch to six inches in length, and are found hiding in dark moist places—under logs and stones—in the tropics and temperate regions of the Southern Hemisphere.

Peripatus capensis, of southern Africa, is representative of the onychophores. The head has a pair of antenna-like appendages, at the base of which are two small eyes. The eyes are structured like those of the annelids. From the mouth emerge two small horny jaws. Behind the head stretches the body, the only external signs of segmentation being the pairs of legs, from 14 to 44 in number. The body can be retracted to a high degree, the skin being covered with a flexible chitinous cuticle that undergoes moulting. Like terrestrial arthropods, *Peripatus* breathes by means of tracheae (delicate ingrowths of the body wall). This is an insect-like feature, and the heart is also built like that of an insect.

Each segment of the body contains a pair of small excretory organs resembling the nephridia of annelids. They open at the inner base of each leg. The muscle is not striated, like arthropod muscle, but smooth like annelid muscle.

The onychophores therefore combine both annelid and arthropod features. This duplicity causes problems in classification, for some zoologists place these animals in a phylum of their own—the Onychophora—whereas others consider them to make up a subphylum or even a class of the phylum Arthropoda. They are ancient animals, for Cambrian fossils resemble today's species. While unlikely to be the ancestor of the arthropods, they do suggest that arthropods are descended from annelid stock. The onychophores were probably one offshoot of this stock, and the arthropods evolved from another offshoot. They indicate the considerable variations that take place in evolution. The onychophores achieved a stable form early on in the development of the animal kingdom and have retained this form ever since. The arthropods, by contrast, have since progressed in a wide variety of directions.

The tardigrades

Tiny animals less than a millimetre (1/25 of an inch) long, the tardigrades or water bears show no segmentation and their heads are poorly defined. They progress slowly (hence their scientific name) on four pairs of stumpy legs ending in short claws. Although there is no chitin in the cuticle, water bears moult every month. Apart from the lack of segmentation, the general body plan is similar to that of an arthropod. Like the latter, tardigrades have no cilia. However, the muscle is smooth, like onychophore muscle. There is no circulatory system; perhaps the animal's size makes it unnecessary.

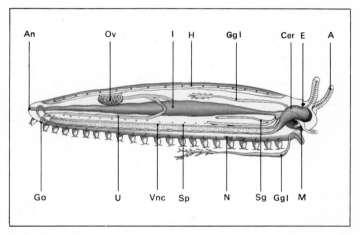

Organizational plan of *Peripatus: A,* antenna; *An,* anus; *Cer,* cerebral ganglia; *E,* eye; *Ggl,* glue gland; *Go,* genital opening; *H,* tubular heart; *I,* intestine; *M,* mouth; *N,* nephridium (kidney); *Ov,* ovary; *Sg,* salivary gland; *Sp,* spiracle or respiratory opening; *U,* uterus; *Vnc,* ventral nerve cord. Some species of *Peripatus* do not lay, but incubate their eggs in the dilated oviducts; they are viviparous.

Tardigrades need to live in water. They are found in the sea (from which they probably spread to the land), in fresh water, in damp moss and lichens, and in moist soil. If their environment dries up, tardigrades contract in size and sink into a state of suspended animation, which may last for many years without any damage to the organism. Their resistance to their surroundings in this state is truly phenomenal; they can spend eight hours in liquid helium and still survive! Yet as soon as the apparently lifeless animal is placed in water, it becomes rehydrated and resumes activity.

The water bears occupy a phylum of their own—the Tardigrada—in the animal kingdom. Like the onychophores, they represent an offshoot from the main line of evolution that led to the arthropods.

Arthropods

Preliminaries to the mating of *Araneus diadematus*. The male approaches the much larger female; the pedipalps (jaw-like appendages) can be seen in front of the head, between the first and second left legs. *Phot. John Markham*

The arthropods occupy an eminent position in the animal kingdom. With a million different species, they number more than all the other groups of animals put together. The arthropods have evolved in a myriad of ways to adapt to all possible habitats on the land, in the sea and the air, from the depths of the oceans to the summits of the highest mountains, from the poles to the equator.

The Arthropoda, the largest phylum of the animal kingdom, is of the greatest antiquity. There is every reason to believe that it formed some time before the Cambrian era (that is, more than about 600 million years ago), because fossils from this time are already clearly pointing in the arthropod direction. Arthropods are highly adaptable and in the course of time have lost none of their vigour. The phylum shows no sign of weakening and, along with man, arthropods are probably the most characteristic of present-day terrestrial fauna.

Arthropods possess bilateral symmetry (the right side is a mirror image of the left side in external appearance), and the body is divided into a number of segments. They get their name, which means 'jointed foot', from the articulated appendages that are borne in pairs, usually one pair to each segment of the body. The body is covered with a tough covering called a cuticle, which is composed basically of protein and chitin. It functions as an exoskeleton to protect internal organs as well as support the muscles. The muscle is striated, and vibrating cilia are always lacking.

The classification of the arthropods is subject to debate, but two sub-phyla of living species are generally recognized: the Chelicerata (scorpions and spiders) and the Mandibulata (crustaceans, insects, centipedes and millipedes). To these may be added the Onychophora.

The Chelicerata

This large group is composed of three very unequal classes: the Arachnida, Pycnogonida and Merostomata. The first class is great and varied, whereas the second is made up of the comparatively small number (500 species) of sea spiders and the third is composed largely of fossil species. Arthropods of the Chelicerata may be distinguished from those of other sub-phyla in that they lack true antennae and jaws.

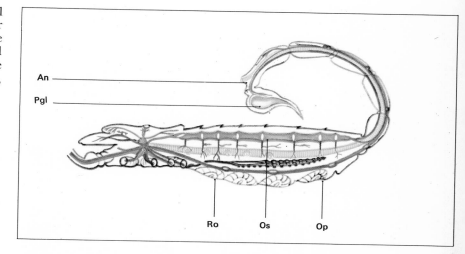

Diagram of the partial organization of a scorpion. In red, circulatory system, heart and vessels; in blue, the nervous system; in yellow, the alimentary canal; in green, the poison gland *Pgl*; in violet, the female genital system. *An*, anus; *Os*, ostioles or opening of the heart tube; *Ro*, stigma, respiratory opening. Ambulatory legs and buccal appendages are not represented.

Organizational plan of a spider: *Abn*, abdominal nerve; *Ch*, chelicerae; *Chgl*, cheliceral glands; *Clo*, cloaca; *E*, eyes; *Go*, genital opening; *H*, heart; *I*, intestine; *L*, lungs; *Ldc*, lateral digestive caeca; *Mst*, dilator muscles of stomach; *Mt*, Malpighian tubules; *Ost*, ostiole; *Ov*, ovaries; *Pp*, pedipalp; *S*, spinnerets; *Sgl*, silk glands; *Soe*, Sub-oesophageal ganglionic mass; *Sst*, suctorial stomach; *Tr*, tracheae.

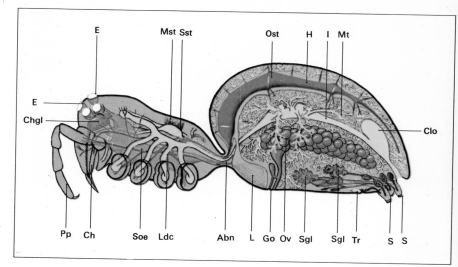

The arachnids

The class Arachnida consists of nine orders of living animals. Most are known since the Carboniferous period (about 300 million years ago). They are the Scorpionida (scorpions; 600 living species); Pedipalpi (whip scorpions; 150 species); Palpigrada (micro-whip scorpions; 50 species); Araneae (spiders; 30,000 species); Solpugida (sun spiders; 570 species); Pseudoscorpionida (false scorpions; 1000 species); Podogona (ricinuleids; 20 species); Phalangida (harvestmen; 2200 species); and Acarina (mites and ticks; 20,000 species).

The basic structure of an arachnid

Arachnids consist of two body sections jointed together. These are the cephalothorax (head and chest) and the abdomen. Arachnids are easily distinguished from all other arthropods by the six pairs of appendages. These are borne on the cephalothorax, and consist of two pairs of mouth parts (one pair of short fang-like cheliceras and one pair of leg-like pedipalps) and four pairs of walking legs. Apart from these

The European black widow spider, *Latrodectus tredecimguttatus*, is by far the most poisonous of the Eurasiatic spiders; its bite causes general discomfort, severe pains and a lowering of the body temperature. Female on its web, near its cocoons filled with eggs. After mating, she devours her much smaller partner. *Phot. Aldo Margiocco*

common features, the various orders differ appreciably in appearance and are easy to tell apart.

A few appendages may also exist on the second section—the abdomen—but they are profoundly modified. Examples are the comb-like tactile organs of scorpions and the thread-producing spinnerets of spiders. In the Acarina, the cephalothorax and abdomen are fused together.

The life of arachnids

The arachnid's life is divided into two main periods. In the first, the young arachnid remains immobile, building its body by consuming the yolk contained in the egg or supplied by the mother. This period is made up of several stages, the embryo becoming a pre-larva and then a larva. The second period commences as the young arachnid becomes mobile, and can feed itself by capturing prey. It moults several times, passing through various nymphal stages and finally emerging as an adult that is able to breed.

Embryonic life and moulting

The embryo grows within the egg. In oviparous orders (spiders, harvestmen and sun spiders), the egg contains sufficient yolk to enable the embryo to complete its development there. In other orders, there is not always enough yolk and the embryo must receive extra nourishment to complete its development. In ovoviviparous arachnids (false scorpions), the embryos develop in an external incubatory chamber whereas in viviparous forms (scorpions), they remain within the mother.

Some scorpions, however, have eggs rich in yolk that could perhaps be laid, but instead they remain in the oviducts and there develop into larvae. Other scorpions have eggs that are poor in yolk. These latter arachnids develop functional mouth parts at an early stage so that they can obtain nourishment within the mother, but the former do not develop special organs. Nevertheless, both kinds of larvae later become identical kinds of nymphs.

This difference in members of the same order is difficult to explain. How, too, can one explain the reproduction of *Lychas*? This scorpion produces eggs that have no yolk, but after the follicles have shed their eggs, hormones are secreted that inhibit the development of further eggs. Such a suspension of egg-laying is rare among the arachnids. In this case, it allows the female to give birth every 40 or 42 days to new generations of larvae. Yet, however they begin life, the scorpion larvae become free and independent nymphs that are alike in both appearance and behaviour.

In some arachnids—the scorpions and false scorpions—there is a genuine mother-embryo relationship comparable to that found in gestating mammals. How such things come about by the chance mutations of evolutionary change perplexes zoologists.

Hatching does not always mean the end of an immobile life. In spiders, for example, there are several more stages of development in which the animal builds its muscular, digestive, circulatory and nervous systems. Each stage is called an instar. In arachnids, there is at least one larval instar, and often two or three. The larvae remain in the mother, in the nest or, in the case of some spiders (*Lycosa*) and scorpions, take refuge on the mother's back. Then they moult and become free-living nymphs, capable of capturing prey and feeding themselves. The only thing left incomplete is the formation of the reproductive organs. This is achieved after more moults at the last instar, and the nymph becomes an adult arachnid.

The larvae of mites and ticks (Acarina) have only three pairs of legs, as do insects. However, counting the number of legs is a convenient way of distinguishing adult insects from adult arachnids, should the general difference in appearance not be sufficient to tell them apart. Insects have three pairs of legs and arachnids four pairs.

The banded argiope (*Argiope bruennichi*). *Above*, female watching over its egg cocoon; *bottom left*, close-up of the cocoon, partly open; *bottom right*, the same after opening; the cluster of eggs is exposed. *Phot. Aldo Margiocco and Michel Boulard*

Nymphal life and moulting

The number of instars (development stages) that take place while the animal is in the nymphal phase of its life varies greatly among the various orders of arachnids. Each new instar is preceded by a moult, and so the number of moults indicates the number of instars. It is always the same only among the false scorpions and certain mites. In these, there is always a first (proto-), second (deuto-) and third (trito-) nymphal instar before the adult phase is attained. The number of instars varies among other groups, but it is in the sun spiders that the variations are most important. In the course of its nymphal life, it is possible to distinguish two general periods. The first 'juvenile' period comprises three instars. Then comes a 'finishing' period from the fourth instar onwards. This may be the adult stage, but it may also be the beginning of new nymphal instars. Thus, certain individuals belonging to the same species are, as in the false

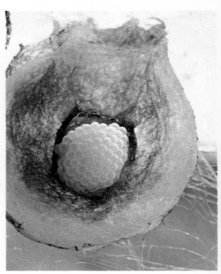

The banded argiope (*Argiope bruennichi*) capturing a grasshopper.
Phot. J. Six

A crab-spider (*Misumena vatia*), capturing a fly on a grass panicle. It has
the ability to take on the colour of its surroundings (homochromy).
Phot. Edouard Cauvin

scorpions and some mites, adult from the fourth instar onwards, whereas others are not adult until the fifth, sixth,
seventh, eighth or even the ninth instar. This variability in
the number of instars and therefore of moults is much more
pronounced in the sun spiders than it is in the spiders,
harvestmen and scorpions.

Moulting of the cuticle is necessary to pass from one instar
to the next. This always takes place in the same way. The
cuticle ruptures along the front of the cephalothorax, producing an opening through which the animal can squeeze,
albeit sometimes with difficulty. The chitin in the new skin
of the animal is sufficiently flexible and soft to enable it to
emerge. Muscular activity and blood circulation are at a
peak during moulting.

For the arachnid, as for any other arthropod, moulting is a
critical period during which it is defenceless. But its behaviour
at this time varies greatly from one species to another. The
scorpion, for example, is able to walk as soon as it has left its
old cuticle; indeed, it only stops moving during the few
hours when it is casting off its old skin. Certain spiders, on the
other hand, make special preparations for moulting. The
animal refuses food, withdraws into a shelter and the blood
circulation stops. The composition of the blood changes and
the rate of cell division rapidly increases. The false scorpion
prepares for moulting by eating a large amount and then
fasting. The animal builds a retreat in which it shuts itself
away for a fortnight, assuming an embryo-like position and
falling into a state of torpor during which it becomes translucent.

The internal changes which must take place when these
arachnids moult have not been closely studied. More is
known about the physiological changes that occur when sun
spiders moult. In *Othoes saharae*, active life, in the course of
which it feeds avidly, never lasts more than two or three days.
Preparation for moulting and the casting of the old skin then
take the next month or more. The sun spider first becomes
sluggish and refuses all food and then, after twenty days,
becomes paralyzed. Its legs and mouth parts fold back and
the cephalothorax is raised. The posture, which is characteristic of moulting, persists for about ten days. The old
cuticle is then shed, taking a few hours. It then takes the sun
spider from eight to ten days to recover and resume normal
activity.

These extraordinary phenomena, of total inertia and
apparent death, indicate that a profound internal transformation is taking place, in which tissues are being broken down
and subsequently reconstructed. The animal's behaviour at
this time enables a close study to be made of it, and the
activities of the various special cells and glands that produce
the changes are now well understood.

In the Acarina, which exhibit a wide variety of moulting
behaviour, there are many examples of easy moults. But
moulting also occurs that is preceded or accompanied by the
destruction of tissue (histolysis) and therefore by paralysis.
It is important to note that, in the other arachnids, moulting
always produces a similar though physiologically more
advanced creature, however violent an upheaval it may
cause in the animal's life. But in many acarids, on the other
hand, the internal changes result in a very different animal
to the one that preceded it and one emerges that has re-
gressed in comparison. A good example is provided by the
extraordinary development of *Balaustium florale*. The first
stage is a prelarva without legs or mouth, followed by an
active larva possessing organs and appendages. Succeeding
moults give rise to an inert protonymph, an active deuto-
nymph, an inert tritonymph and finally an active adult. In
each state, the acarid has a different life and structure, the
inert states being regressions from the preceding active states.

Feeding

Arachnids are essentially carnivorous creatures, except for some acarids that feed on plants (*Tetranychus*—the infamous red spider mite, *Bryobia*, Eupodidae, Oribatei, Eriophyidae) or on inert substances such as decaying matter (Sarcoptidae). The prey, seized in the mouth parts or trapped in a web, is brought to the mouth, which is situated between the bases of the pedipalps and the first legs. Connected to the mouth is a muscular pharynx or sucking stomach that is adapted for sucking up liquids from the prey. The prey must therefore be treated, both mechanically and chemically, to render it suitable for sucking. The normal sequence of events is

so engorged with blood that they swell up to several times their original size), and the vegetarian acarids that take their food from the tissues of plants. Harvest mites or chiggers, the larvae of certain acarids, cause severe itching by their method of feeding. They prey on vertebrates, puncturing the skin and discharging a saliva that destroys the red blood cells of the host's tissues around the puncture. The liquefied tissues are then sucked up by the mite. However, it is in the false scorpions that the phenomenon of external digestion becomes most complex. The buccal cavity immediately behind the mouth is transformed into a filter. The prey is held by the cheliceras and entirely dissolved by injection of salivary or digestive juices or juices produced by the glands in the cheliceras. A nutritious paste is formed that is sucked up continuously by the mouth. Waste matter is rejected by the

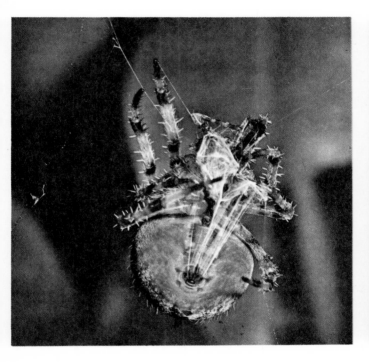

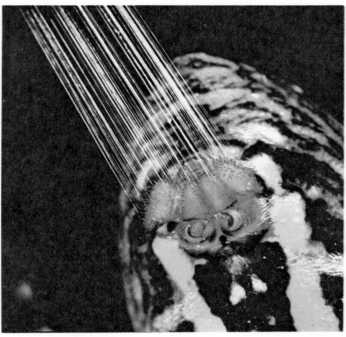

Garden spider (*Araneus diadematus*) and *Argiope bruennichi*, females seen from below, in the act of weaving their web. The spinnerets are short abdominal appendages borne by the 10th and 11th segments of the body, into which open the canaliculi of the silk glands. The spider's thread is made up of numerous strands issuing from the different canali-

culi (*right*); the posterior pair of spinnerets participates in the fotmation of this thread. Not all the threads forming the web have the same composition. Some, smeared with glue strung out in small drops, are used to capture prey which stumble into the web and stick to them tenaciously. *Phot. John Markham and Aldo Margiocco*

illustrated by scorpions, sun spiders, harvestmen and most spiders. The prey is gripped in the cheliceras and crushed by the pedipalps, being partly dissolved by saliva or regurgitated digestive juices. In some acarids (Oribatei), hairs on the cheliceras act as rasps and tear the prey into tiny fragments that can easily be swallowed.

This preparation of the prey is a kind of external digestion. Bristles around the mouth and on the pedipalps and cheliceras sort digestible from non-digestible matter. The food passes from the mouth to the pharynx and then along the oesophagus to the midgut or intestine, into which the liver opens. Here digestion is continued, the digestive organs almost completely filling the abdomen. Waste matter passes out along the short hindgut.

This nutrition process is simplified in some arachnids, the prey being punctured and its contents sucked up without it being crushed first. This method is used by certain spiders, parasitic ticks that feed on the blood of their hosts (becoming

filtering action inside the mouth, and expelled periodically from the mouth with the aid of bristles on the cheliceras.

Hunting

The arachnids have so far shown themselves to possess some astounding features—the nymphal development of acarids, the feeding methods of false scorpions, the larval life of scorpions and the moulting behaviour of sun spiders. But the methods by which arachnids capture their prey surpass even these achievements, for they show by their ingenuity the high degree of mental evolution achieved by these animals. The most varied and remarkable hunting methods are exhibited by yet another order of arachnids—the spiders.

Spiders use the delicate threads produced by their spinnerets for many purposes. They construct shelters and refuges, and they spin cocoons to house their eggs. But their most extraordinary constructions are their webs. Glittering with beads of dew on a sunny morning, the fine tracery of a spider's web is one of the marvels of nature. Spun in patterns that vary from one species to another, the webs usually act as passive traps for unwary insects. Some spiders make active traps, *Menneus* spinning an elastic net between its legs and sweeping it through the air to catch a passing insect, and *Cladomelea* dangling a sphere of sticky silk at the end of a long thread from one leg and using it like a sling to seize its prey. The trapdoor spiders (Ctenizidae) dig a burrow closed by a little silken door; when an insect ventures near, the spider darts from its hiding place to capture its imprudent victim.

The hunting methods of spiders are extremely efficient. Having trapped their prey, they can use poison fangs in the chelicerae to kill them. Bird-eating spiders are known to consume lizards, snakes and mice as well as small birds. Some spiders are even venomous to humans. But even though the great majority of spiders are harmless to man, this does not prevent many people from fearing them, however irrationally. Also feared are the scorpions, which paralyze their prey by stinging them with the sharp sting at the base of the abdomen. The victim is then seized in the pincer-like pedipalps and torn apart by the chelicerae. The false scorpions, although they look rather like small scorpions, lack a sting and capture their prey with their pincers.

Defence mechanisms

When an arachnid is attacked, its most common reaction is to flee or sometimes to simulate death. In spiders and harvestmen, the appendage that is seized by the assailant comes

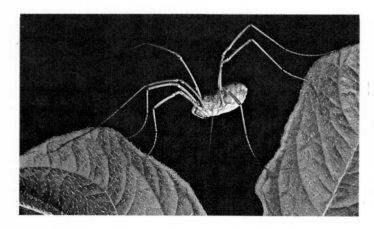

A harvest spider, or opilionid (*Phalangium opilio*), running from one leaf to another. Length of the body: ⅓ inch. The head and the abdomen are in one piece. The legs are shed as soon as they are gripped or pinched (autotomy), and for a few minutes carry out jerky movements like those of a man reaping a meadow. *Phot. J. Six*

away from the body, enabling its owner to escape. The loss is only temporary, for the lost part grows again at the next moult. Some arachnids produce sounds when attacked, to scare off an attacker. Wolf spiders and scorpions may drum on the ground or on dry leaves with the abdomen or feet, and other arachnids stridulate by rubbing two regions of the body against each other, such as the cephalothorax and abdomen, or both chelicerae or two legs. Then there are the harvestmen, which anaesthetize their attacker with a substance secreted by the stink glands of the cephalothorax and distributed over the body by grooves in the surface.

Phoresy, parasitism, and biological peculiarities

A strange phenomenon is sometimes encountered in the arachnids; this is phoresy, which means the transport of one animal by another. It is not rare to find fertilized female false scorpions clinging to the legs of flies. In this case, the phenomenon may be caused by the decomposition of material in the false scorpions' surroundings. This rotting matter attracts flies, and the females cling to them. Being at the height of their period of gestation and therefore of intense appetite, it would seem that the false scorpions become phoretic to feed from their hosts. But phoresy is more likely undertaken as a means of distributing the young. Spreading of the species also seems to be the reason for phoresy in certain mites. *Parasitus* attaches itself to an insect host—usually a bee or beetle—as either a nymph or an adult. In spite of its name, it is not parasitic and does not attack its host.

Phoresy is not a permanent way of life for arachnids. For the most part, they live freely. However some arachnids, especially acarids, are truly parasitic. Ticks live only as parasites, feeding on birds and mammals. They attack poultry, domestic animals and even man, causing anaemia in small animals when numerous. Ticks are dangerous because they may transmit diseases to their hosts. Fevers of various kinds may result from tick bite, particularly spotted fever in man. The mortality rate was high until effective vaccines were developed.

Arachnids are not only dangerous because some are parasitic on man, but also because some are venomous. Scorpions present a real danger in North Africa, Mexico and southern Africa, and the bite of a few spiders, particularly the black widow (*Latrodectus*) of the tropics, can be fatal. Sera and antivenins exist to counteract their effects.

A few biological peculiarities of arachnids may now be mentioned. Arachnids are essentially solitary animals from the nymph stage onwards, though societies of adult spiders, both temporary and permanent, are known. The great majority of arachnids are terrestrial, but aquatic spiders do exist. The best-known is the water spider (*Argyroneta*), which lives underwater by spinning a diving-bell for its home and filling it with air bubbles. Some spiders produce threads of gossamer that catch the wind and carry them through the air; they are sometimes found floating at altitudes of several thousand feet. The cuticles of sun spiders and especially of scorpions become fluorescent when exposed to ultraviolet rays. Certain desert species of scorpions are extremely resistant to gamma rays, the reason for which is still unknown.

Sexual life and reproduction

The sexual life of arachnids is so remarkably varied that only a sketch of it can be given here. Very few arachnids really mate in such a way that insemination is actively carried out by the male, although the harvestmen and some acarids possess a penis. In many arachnids, the sperm is introduced into the female genital passage by a modified appendage of the male—certain feet in freshwater mites, the pedipalps in spiders and water mites, and the chelicerae in sun spiders. In others—scorpions, false scorpions and certain mites—an object called a spermatophore is used to transfer the sperm from male to female. The male *Chelifer*, a common false scorpion, deposits sperm onto a stalk stuck to the ground and then leads the female on to the stalk.

Whether fertilization is direct or indirect—that is, whether the two sexes actively come into contact with each other to mate or not—sexual behaviour varies enormously between different families, genera or even species of arachnids. The many variations created by evolution to ensure that reproduction occurs may be so ingenious as to disguise the fundamental character of their sexual behaviour.

One of the most common features of mating behaviour is a preliminary ritual to ensure the submission and fertilization of the female. This may be violent in character, as in the sun spiders; the male sun spider grasps the female between his pedipalps and presses her abdomen against the cephalothorax. In false scorpions and spiders, the male or both partners perform a succession of dances or they may simply touch each other. Species that do not actively mate employ a wide variety of techniques to persuade the female to mount the spermatophore. The male false scorpion, like some acarids, dances in front of the female, places his genital region on the ground, raises the spermatophore and fills it with sperm. Then he retreats and quivers to signal to his partner that she should come and bestride it. In scorpions, the male helps the female to carry out this act and dances with her, holding her by the pedipalps. The male *Phrynichus* turns his back on the female as he constructs the spermatophore and fills it with sperm. Then he turns around, retreats and goes into a trance. As he does so, he touches the female with his long legs in an invitation to her to mount the spermatophore. *Schizomus* is different again. The female places herself behind the male and seizes the appendage at the end of her partner's abdomen with her cheliceras. Thus stimulated, the male deposits a spermatophore and moves forward, so as to fertilize the female.

There are many differences in the structure of the spermatophores of different species. Those described above are merely passive objects on which the sperm is deposited, and which the female then encloses within her genital passage. In scorpionid scorpions, the spermatophore bends in two under the female's weight; this pressure causes a sperm chamber situated at the bend to open. In buthid scorpions, a kind of piston is housed at the base of the spermatophore and injects sperm into the female.

The best-known characteristic of the mating of arachnids is the inclination of the female spider to devour the male after the act has taken place. In fact, such behaviour is not usual and the male normally survives. Some spiders, like certain acarids and scorpions, avoid any such risk by undergoing parthenogenesis and reproducing without the aid of the male. This may be only occasional or it may take place in cycles.

The Acarina, extremely numerous in species and yet imperfectly known, form a world in which the strangest anatomies and the most unexpected habits are encountered. The species represented here, the feathery-footed erythrea (*Erythraeus plumipes*), although a wanderer, is capable of weaving a silken web. *Phot. J. Six*

A tick, *Ixodes*, common in the woods of Europe. It fixes itself on and then sucks the blood of mammals. After spending a certain time on its host, the tick falls to the ground and moults there. The male fertilizes the females while fixed to the host; a few days later, they fall to the ground, where they lay. The ripe female is *2 inch in length.* The tick transmits to cattle a protozoan, *Microbabesia bovis*, which parasitizes the red corpuscles of the blood, causing a serious disease accompanied by haematuria. *Phot. Aldo Margiocco*

Argyroneta on its bell (*bottom left*). The water spider, *Argyroneta aquatica*, is the only one of its order capable of moving freely under water. It comes to the surface periodically to expel the vitiated air from its lungs and to take in a new supply of fresh air. It weaves under the water a pouch of silk fixed to aquatic plants and fills it with air in the following manner: it rises to the surface, thrusting most of its abdomen and its hind legs out; when it draws it abdomen back into the water, the spider has created, because of its hairy coat, a layer or cushion of air, which it stores in the silken pouch it has woven. It utilizes the air from its pouch or bell, in which it spends a good part of its life hibernating (*bottom right*). *Phot. R. H. Noailles*

The *Galeodes*, or wind spider (here *Galeodes arabs*), belongs to the order of Solifuga. It lives exclusively in hot countries, and has the outward appearance of a spider. Notice its powerful chelicerae, ending in strong claws, and the extreme length of its pedipalps (jaw-like appendages) which have tactile functions. *Galeodes* feeds on live prey captured on the run. *Phot. Aldo Margiocco*

The *Thelyphoni* (*Thelyphonus caudatus*), all'Indo-Oceanians, belong to the order of Uropyga. They have a post-abdomen resembling a many-jointed whip. The first pair of legs, which are very long, are used as exploratory tactile appendages. They feed on live prey, insects, small molluscs, etc., which they capture at night. *Phot. Aldo Margiocco*

Buthus occitanus in an attacking posture; the raised abdomen will strike the enemy like a dart and inject poison into it. *Phot. E. Sochurek*

Classification of arachnids

The arthropods of the class Arachnida may be defined as having the body divided into two parts, the cephalothorax bearing six pairs of appendages and the abdomen bearing no true appendages (in the order Acarina, the two parts are fused together). The cephalothorax, the front part, never bears antennae. It bears the eyes, which are always simple. The first pair of appendages, the fang-like cheliceras, are situated in front of the mouth and possess at most four joints (sections). The second pair of appendages, the pedipalps, are situated beside the mouth and often end in pincers. The remaining four pairs of appendages are walking legs. There are no mandibles, and the alimentary system possesses a sucking pharynx to extract liquids from prey or plants. The cephalothorax is unsegmented (except in the order Solpugida), but segmentation of the abdomen varies. The respiratory system, with some exceptions, is made up of tracheae opening into the abdomen; gills are never present. The back of the abdomen contains the heart. The sexes are separate, the genital organs opening into the abdomen. Arachnids are mostly oviparous, their development being divided into two main periods; the first is characterized by the existence of larvae sometimes possessing embryonic feeding organs, the second by nymphal stages separated by moults. They are mostly terrestrial animals.

There are nine separate orders in the class; none of them are sufficiently alike to form sub-classes.

Order 1: Scorpionida (Scorpions)

Scorpions are long arachnids, the cephalothorax being broadly joined to the abdomen without any obvious waist between the two parts. The cheliceras are small but the pedipalps are large with formidable pincers. The abdomen has twelve segments, on the second of which are a pair of comblike tactile organs. The last six segments form a narrow tail with a sharp poison sting at the end. There are four pairs of book lungs, which are made up of several leaflike plates and are unique to arachnids. Scorpions are viviparous. They range in length from half an inch to eight inches. *Isometrus maculatus*, worldwide tropics; *Pandinus imperator*, tropical Africa; *Buthus occitanus*, southern Europe.

Order 2: Pedipalpi (Whip Scorpions)

The whip scorpions have flat abdomens of twelve segments narrowly joined to a thinner cephalothorax with eight eyes. The cheliceras are two-jointed and very small, while the pedipalps are large with pincers. The first leg on each side of the body is elongated into a feeler. There are two sub-orders. The Uropygi give the order its name of whip scorpions because the abdomen ends in a long whip-like flagellum; there is no sting. They also have odoriferous glands. The size ranges from three-quarters of an inch to three inches. *Telyphonus* (India); *Mastigoproctus* (America). The second sub-order is called the Amblypygi. Although classified with the whip scorpions because of their general anatomy, these arachnids possess no whips at the ends of the abdomen. They also differ from the Uropygi in not having odoriferous organs. They are tropical arachnids not exceeding two inches in length. *Phrynichus, Charon* (cave-dwelling).

Order 3: Palpigrada (Micro-whip Scorpions)
The micro-whip scorpions are very small, not exceeding 1/10 of an inch in length. The cheliceras are three-jointed and the pedipalps like walking legs with claws. They are blind, there being no eyes. The abdomen has eleven segments with a slender whip-like 'tail' of fifteen segments. *Koenenia mirabilis*, Mediterranean basin.

Order 4: Araneae (Spiders)
The cephalothorax and the globular abdomen are both unsegmented in the spiders, and joined by a narrow waist. The cheliceras are small and two-jointed, being armed with a poison duct. The pedipalps are short, the bases being enlarged to form 'maxillae' used in chewing the food and the number of eyes varies from none to eight. Respiration is by two to four book lungs, some with tracheae. Spinnerets on the abdomen extrude silk. Spiders are oviparous, usually laying their eggs in cocoons. There are two sub-orders: the Orthognatha with horizontal cheliceras, and the Labidognatha with vertical cheliceras. Included in the former sub-order are the Ctenizidae, the family of trap-door spiders, and the Theraphosidae, which includes the tarantulas. The latter sub-order includes the Theridiidae, in which family is the dreaded black widow (*Latrodectus*); Agelenidae, which includes *Tegenaria*, a house spider; Lycosidae, the hunting spiders; Argiopidae, the orb weavers with geometric webs; Thomisidae, the crab spiders; and Salticidae, the jumping spiders. Spiders range in length from 1/25 of an inch up to nearly four inches.

Order 5: Solpugida (Sun Spiders)
The cephalothorax has six segments and bears large two-jointed cheliceras ending in pincers.

The pedipalps are leg-like. There is no waist, and the abdomen has ten segments. There are no spinnerets. Sun spiders are found in warm, dry regions and range in size from 3/4 of an inch to three inches. *Galeodes,* the 'tarantula' of Egypt; *Solpuga*.

Order 6: Pseudoscorpionida (False Scorpions)
The false scorpions are easily distinguished from the scorpions. They are much smaller, not exceeding 1/3 of an inch in length, and have a rounded abdomen without a 'tail' or sting. The cephalothorax is broadly joined to the abdomen, which has eleven segments. The cheliceras are small and two-jointed, and the pedipalps are large and bear pincers, like those of scorpions. There are none, one or two pairs of eyes. Glands near the cheliceras produce silk for spinning nests. *Chelifer cancroideas*, the house or book scorpion.

Order 7: Podogona (Ricinuleids)
These arachnids are small, not exceeding 2/5 of an inch in length. There is a small hood covering the cheliceras and there are no eyes. The first and second of the abdomen's six segments form a waist. The ricinuleids are tropical and rare. *Ricinoides* (Africa); *Cryptocellus* (America).

Order 8: Phalangida (Harvestmen)
The harvestmen are often known simply as 'daddy long-legs', the four pairs of legs being very thin and extremely long. The body is round and small, the cephalothorax being broadly joined to the abdomen, which is faintly segmented. The cheliceras are three-jointed and the pedipalps possess no claws. The cephalothorax bears stink glands. *Phalangium*.

Order 9: Acarina (Mites and Ticks)
The cephalothorax and abdomen are fused together and there is no segmentation. The cheliceras and pedipalps vary, but are very small compared to the legs. The acarids are small to microscopic in size. The order is made up of five sub-orders, distinguished from each other by the differences in the stigmata, openings of the tracheae. These sub-orders are: the Onychopalpida, free-living acarids with a radula-like organ to rasp food; the Mesostigmata, free-living and commensal forms including *Parasitus*; the Ixodides or ticks, which are parasitic; the Trombidiformes, which include red spider mites (*Tetranychus*), harvest mites or chiggers (*Trombicula*), and water mites; and the Sarcoptiformes, which includes itch and mange mites such as *Sarcoptes*.

The Crustaceans

The class of crustaceans, along with the classes of insects, centipedes and millipedes, make up the sub-phylum of arthropods with mandibles. The best-known crustaceans are crabs, shrimps, prawns, lobsters, crayfish, woodlice and barnacles. Most can be broadly distinguished from other arthropods by their aquatic way of life. Specifically, crustaceans have two pairs of antennae, whereas arachnids have none and all other arthropods one pair. A typical crustacean feature is the presence of biramous appendages—that is, appendages that are forked (though the two branches of the appendage may not always resemble each other).

Classification

It was only in 1800 that Cuvier, referring to them in his *Lessons on Comparative Anatomy*, made the crustaceans a class apart. The name had previously been attributed for a long time to animals with a hard but flexible outer covering as opposed to the hard but brittle shells of molluscs; it derived from the Latin word *crusta*, meaning a hard shell. The term crustacean now signifies an animal having other, more specific features, for some other arthropods as well as crustaceans possess such a tough outer covering. This exoskeleton is composed of flexible chitin, hardened in many cases by the presence of calcium carbonate. The composition can easily be demonstrated. If a piece of the carapace of a crab or lobster is placed in hydrochloric acid, an effervescence will occur as the calcium carbonate in the material dissolves in the acid. All that remains is a flexible membrane of chitin similar to that covering insects. If another piece of carapace is burned, the chitin disappears and a white powder is left that can be identified as calcium carbonate.

All arthropods have a rigid covering and so must moult as they grow, casting off the old skin and growing a new, larger one. The new skin of some crustaceans, such as crabs and lobsters, takes some time to harden, and these animals are soft-bodied after the moult. They are grouped together in the subclass Malacostraca (from the Greek words *malacos*, soft, and *ostracon*, shell). The small aquatic crustaceans, such as water fleas, do not accumulate sufficient calcium carbonate to harden the skin. They therefore resemble insects, and are grouped informally under the name Entomostraca (Greek *entomon*, insect).

Habitat

Most crustaceans are marine creatures and are found near the shore, in the open sea among the plankton, and on the sea bed at all depths. Undersea exploration—including the pioneering expedition carried out by the British *Challenger* at the end of the last century and more recent expeditions by specially equipped oceanographic vessels, such as the Danish *Galathea*, the Russian *Vitaz* and the French *Calypso*—has revealed the existence of strange crustaceans at depths of thousands of fathoms.

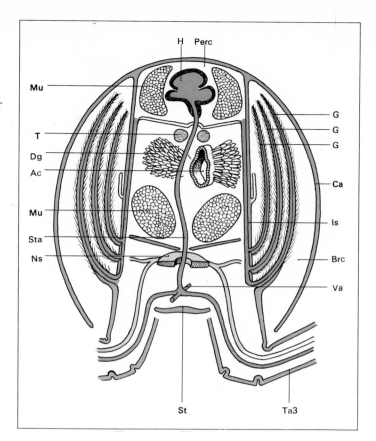

Section of a crayfish, passing through the 12th segment: *Ac*, alimentary canal; *Brc*, branchial cavity; *Ca*, calcified carapace; *Dg*, digestive gland; *G*, gills; *H*, heart, with two visible openings; *Is*, internal skeleton (duplication of the dorsal carapace); *Mu*, muscle; *Ns*, nervous system, ganglion of the ventral cord; *Perc*, pericardiac cavity; *St*, sternum; *Sta*, sternal artery; *T*, testis; *Ta3*, 3rd pair of thoracic appendages; *Va*, ventral artery.

The hermit crab, *Paguristes oculatus*, lodges its abdomen in an empty gasteropod shell on which, invariably, is fixed a sponge, *Suberites domuncula*, which often reaches the volume of a large apple and which may be associated with other species of hermit-crab. The sponge seems to be unable to live without its walking support. *Phot. Aldo Margiocco*

These shrimps (*Hymenocerca elegans*), which live in the lagoons of South Sea atolls, are extremely eccentric: their antennae, instead of being whip-like, are leaf-shaped; their carapaces are camouflaged and expand into broad lobes on the sides. Unlike most shrimps, the *Hymenocerca* do more walking than swimming. *Phot. R. Catala*

Not all crustaceans live in the sea. Some have left the oceans, their original home, and colonized freshwater habitats, taking up their abode in the clearest running water as well as the most stagnant pools. Some live in the water filling cracks and fissures in the ground, as well as in underground deposits of water. Other crustaceans have left water altogether, and have evolved to live on land. They are to be found living among mosses, under stones, bark or dead leaves, or simply buried in the ground. The most familiar terrestrial crustacean is the woodlouse. Among the strangest are those, such as the coconut-palm crab, that climb trees to eat fruit.

Finally, there are some crustaceans that, in their adult form, do not look like crustaceans or even arthropods at all.

The best-known are the barnacles, which look superficially so much like molluscs that they were once classified as molluscs. These crustaceans may only be identifiable as arthropods by examining their larvae, which are always typically arthropod in character. They live as parasites on fish, mammals, worms, or even on other crustaceans, or they are sessile, living fixed to rocks, seaweed or flotsam.

Adaptation to water

The most obvious adaptation to life in water is the presence of gills. Most crustaceans bear gills comparable to those of

---

Classification of the crustacea

Crustaceans may be defined as arthropods in which there are usually two main body parts, the cephalothorax and abdomen. The head of the cephalothorax consists of five segments fused together, and bears two pairs of antennae, a pair of jaws, and two pairs of maxillae (food-handling appendages). The segments of the thorax may be distinct or fused, but the abdominal segments are usually distinct. A carapace often covers the cephalothorax, and the abdomen ends in a telson (a distinct final part). Respiration is by gills or, rarely, through the body surface. The sexes are mostly separate. The class is made up of about 26,000 species divided into eight subclasses.

Subclass 1: Cephalocarida
The most primitive crustaceans. Small and slender, no eyes or carapace, nine pairs of appendages behind the head. Marine. *Hutchinsoniella*.

Subclass 2: Branchiopoda
Second maxillae reduced or absent, leaf-like appendages, at least four pairs of legs on thorax, carapace in form of dorsal or bivalve shield. Mostly freshwater. *Triops*, *Daphnia* (water flea).

Subclass 3: Ostracoda
Minute. Carapace bivalved, two pairs of thoracic appendages. Freshwater and marine. *Cypris*.

Subclass 4: Mystacocarida
Microscopic and elongated. Antennae prominent, thorax of four segments. Found among damp sand grains. *Derocheilocaris*.

Subclass 5: Copepoda
Small. No carpace, typically six pairs of thoracic appendages, no abdominal appendages. Sea, brackish and fresh water. Free-living and parasitic. *Cyclops*, *Calanus*, *Lernaea*.

Subclass 6: Branchiura
(Fish lice) Flat body, large carapace, compound eyes. Sessile in sea and fresh water. *Argulus*.

Subclass 7: Cirrepedia
(Barnacles) Adult sessile, the carapace forming a mantle enveloping the body, usually with plates containing calcium carbonate. Attached by first antennae. Six pairs of appendages used to gather food. Abdomen vestigial. Larva free-swimming. Marine. *Balanus*, *Anatifera*, *Sacculina*.

Subclass 8: Malacostraca
(Lobsters, crabs, crayfish) These crustaceans typically consist of nineteen segments (five head, eight thorax, six abdomen) with the head fused to one or more of the thoracic segments. A carapace is usually present and the abdomen has appendages. There are two series: the Leptostraca with an abdomen of seven segments and comprising a single order, Nebaliacea, of marine crustaceans with a bivalve carapace; and the Eumalacostraca, which have an abdomen of six segments. Within this latter series are four divisions.

Division 1: Syncarida. No carapace. One order, Anaspidacea. *Anaspides*, fresh waters of Australia.
Division 2: Peracarida Carapace, if present, is not fused over last four or more thoracic segments; females have brood pouch in thorax where young develop. Five orders. Mysidacea: the carapace covers most of the thorax; *Mysis*. Cumacea: carapace covers only three or four segments; *Diastylis*. Tanaidacea: small carapace covering only two thoracic segments; *Apseudes*, *Tanais*. Isopoda: no carapace, body flattened dorso-ventrally (horizontally); *Ligia*, *Armadillium*, *Oniscus* (woodlouse), *Idotea*. Amphipoda (sand hoppers): no carapace, body flattened laterally (vertically); *Gammarus*, *Caprella*, *Phronima*.
Division 3: Hoplocardia Carapace fused with first three thoracic segments, second thoracic appendage enormously developed for capturing prey. One order, Stomatopoda (mantis shrimps). *Squilla*.
Division 4: Eucarida Carapace large and fused to all segments of thorax and covering thorax. Eyes stalked. Two orders. Euphausiacea: thoracic appendages all biramous; *Euphausia*, krill. Decapoda: thoracic appendages mostly uniramous (undivided), five pairs of walking legs; *Crangon*, shrimp; *Palinurus*, spiny lobster; *Homarus*, lobster; *Astacus*, crayfish; *Pagurus*, hermit crab; *Cancer*, edible crab.

fish. They are even present in the woodlice and crabs that lead a terrestrial existence.

Another aquatic feature is the presence in many crustaceans of swimmerets, appendages that aid in swimming and in water circulation for respiration. The total number of appendages varies enormously, there being one pair per segment or less. However, the number of appendages can help to identify a crustacean, for there are always more than four pairs (except in sessile and parasitic species). Insects always have three pairs of legs and arachnids four pairs. The two pairs of antennae on the head is another distinguishing feature, all other arthropods having one pair or none.

Sessile and parasitic crustaceans can only be classified by study of their larvae, which possess typical crustacean features. In the adults, the features undergo modifications that may lead to their atrophy or even complete disappearance. Their development is characterized by complete transformations in form, recalling the metamorphoses that take place among the insects.

The ghost shrimp (*Caprella*) has such a characteristic appearance that it cannot be confused with any other crustacean. It is classed among the Amphipoda. Long and slender, with its body 'broken' towards the rear and all its raptoral legs ready to pounce, it vaguely recalls a praying mantis. These shrimps live among the algae or branched zoophytes, moving about like tree-dwellers in a forest. The gills can be seen at the base of their legs. *Phot. R. H. Noailles*

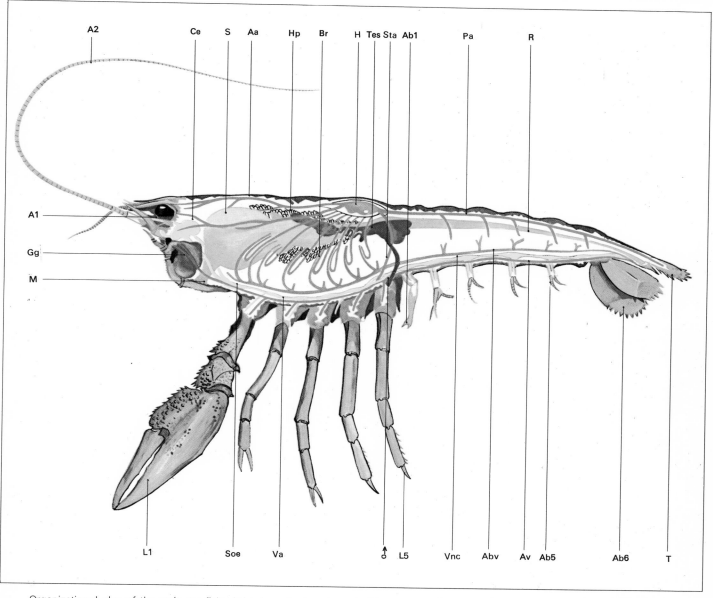

Organizational plan of the male crayfish: *Aa*, antennal artery (aorta); *A1*, antennule; *A2*, antenna; *Ab1* to *Ab5* and *Ab6*, abdominal appendages; *Abv*, abdominal vein; *Br*, efferent branchial artery; *Ce*, cerebral ganglia; *Ggl*, green gland or excretory organ; *H*, heart; *Hp*, hepatopancreas or digestive gland; *L1* to *L5*, walking legs; *M*, mouth; *Pa*, posterior aorta; *R*, rectum; *S*, stomach containing the gastric mill; *Soe*, sub-oesophageal ganglia; *Sta*, sternal artery; *T*, telson; *Tes*, testes; *Va*, ventral artery; *Vnc*, ventral nerve cord; ♂, male orifice.

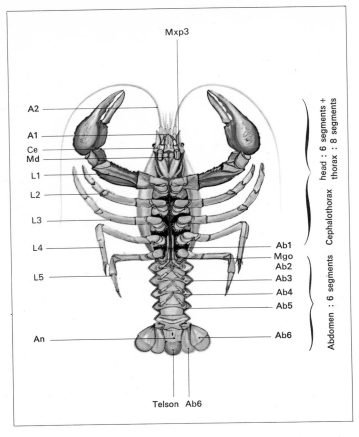

Ventral surface of the male crayfish (*Astacus astacus* = *A. fluviatilis*): *A1*, antennule; *A2*, antenna; *Ab1* to *Ab6*, abdominal appendages (*Ab1* and *Ab2* transformed into copulatory appendages, *Ab6* combines with the telson to form the tail fin); *An*, anus; *Ce*, stalked compound eye; *L1* to *L5*, the 5 pairs of thoracic walking legs; *Md*, mandibles; *Mgo*, male genital orifice; *Mxp3*, 3rd pair of maxillipeds which hide the maxillules, the maxillae and the first two pairs of maxillipeds.

This photograph shows clearly the very long antennae of the spiny lobster (*Palinurus*), which act as tactile organs. *Phot. Fronval*

The structure of crustaceans

Crustaceans were formerly classified either as Annulosa, because their exoskeleton is composed of a series of rings or ringed segments that may either move independently or are fused to each other, or as Articulata because each segment bears on its ventral (underneath) surface a pair of appendages each made up of a series of joints. (Joints in this sense refer to the different sections of the limb and not the connections between them.)

While crustaceans are classified now on the basis of other features, these observations remain true. It is therefore usually easy, by counting the number of pairs of appendages, to find out whether any segments have fused together in a particular animal.

Fusion of the first five segments to form the head is present in almost all crustaceans, though some authorities maintain that there may be a sixth fused segment bearing no appendage and preceding the other segments. It is also common to find the head fused—either to some of the first segments of the thorax, as in the Cumacea, or to the whole of the thorax, as in the Decapoda—to form a cephalothorax. However, in the division Hoplocarida of the Malocostraca, the first two segments of the head can be moved independently. The first segment bears the eyes, and the second segments bears the first pair of antennae. The third segment carries the second pair of antennae and its upper surface is fused to the carapace, which covers the succeeding segments.

It is often possible to distinguish a head, thorax and abdomen, even where fusion links the first two parts together, as each part is composed of very different segments. Segmentation may disappear in the adults of parasitic species, and in some free-living species having a bivalve shell of two hinged halves, as in the ostracods and water fleas.

Compound eyes and ocelli

The eyes are borne on stalks in the higher crustaceans of the division Eucarida, such as crabs and crayfish. These stalks may reach an extraordinary length in some crabs, and are made up of two or three joints, the last one bearing the cornea. A large number of crustaceans have no eye stalks, the eyes being fixed on the head and immovable. This applies to the sand hoppers (Amphipoda), to the woodlouse and other crustaceans of the Isopoda whether terrestrial or aquatic, and to *Triops* and other members of the order Notostraca of the subclass Branchiopoda, commonly known as tadpole shrimps.

The crustacean eye sometimes has a smooth cornea, or the cornea may be divided into facets. These facets may be square, as in crayfishes and prawns, or hexagonal, as in crabs and squillas. But whether it is smooth or faceted, the eyes are compound and made up of many simple eyes grouped together. Compound eyes are unique to crustaceans and insects. Other crustaceans such as *Triops* have simple eyes called ocelli. There are usually three ocelli; they may be separate but are more often grouped together to form a median eye, as in the single eye of *Cyclops*.

Ocelli are to be found in crustacean larvae, and they may persist unchanged into the adult forms.

There are some blind, eyeless species of crustaceans. The best-known are the underground water shrimps and crayfish, such as *Orconectes pellucidus* and *Palaemonias ganteri*, found in Mammoth Cave in Kentucky. *Niphargus*, a shrimp ranging from $\frac{1}{5}$ of an inch to nearly 2 inches in length, and *Asellus cavaticus*, an isopod, haunt the dark underground waters of Europe. To this list must be added the deep-sea shrimps and other crustaceans discovered in the course of recent oceanographic expeditions. All these blind creatures show no trace of eyes, the skin at the places where the eyes should be appearing no different from that elsewhere on the head.

Antennae

Crustaceans possess two pairs of antennae. These normally take the form of slender feelers comprized of a variable number of joints rising from some fewer, thicker joints at the bases of the antennae. The antennae are usually biramous—that is, divided into two parts. They may be made up of a pair of feelers, or there may be one feeler and a thin blade instead. This pattern of bifurcation into two like or unlike parts is also found in the other appendages. On the antennae are many hairs that act as organs of touch and taste or smell, and the antennae also play a role in establishing the crustacean's balance. How they function in these ways is not always exactly known.

The antennae vary a great deal in shape from one group of crustaceans to another. They may be transformed into organs of locomotion, or they may be used for grasping and gripping. In the larvae of *Triops*, and many ostracods and water fleas, modified antennae serve as oars for swimming; in males of the Branchiopoda (*Branchippus*, *Chirocephalus*, *Artemia*) and some free-living copepods (especially the order Harpacticoida), the antennae are prehensile and can grip objects; in some parasitic copepods (*Caligus*) and the barnacles, the antennae serve to anchor their owners.

Mouthparts

The crustacean's mouth lies on the lower surface of the head behind the first pair of antennae, the antennules. It is surrounded by jointed appendages that grip the food and chew it. Behind the upper lip, and independent of it, lies the first pair of mouthparts, the mandibles. These are always stout and powerful and, unlike the jaws of insects, are each

In the coral reefs, all is colour and strange shapes. The crustaceans do not escape this rule, e.g. this squill (*Squilla maculata*) in a hunting attitude in front of a magnificent solitary polypary of *Funcia*. Native to New Caledonia. *Phot. R. Catala*

provided with a two or three-jointed projection called the mandibular palp. Handling of the food is the job of the next two pairs of mouthparts, the first and second maxillae. The second maxillae, although quite separate from the mouth, correspond to the lower lip of insects.

These are the basic components of the mouthparts to be found in crustaceans. As with the other appendages, modification is to be found in several groups. In the copepods (*Cyclops*), amphipods (*Gammarus*) and isopods (woodlice), the appendages of the first segment of the thorax, which is usually fused to the head, also function as mouthparts. They are described as gnathopods or maxillipeds. In the Cumacea, such as *Diastylis*, the appendages of the first two thoracic segments function as two pairs of maxillipeds and are involved in touch, taste and food handling. In the decapods, such as crabs, shrimps and lobsters, the maxillipeds number

Left

The water-louse (*Asellus aquaticus*) is the most common, fresh-water isopod in the palaerctic region. It is fond of cool slow-flowing waters. It does not swim, but walks with agility on the bottom, or on plants. The underside of the females' thorax has plate-like expansions (oostegites), which make a pouch (marsupium) in which the eggs are retained until hatching. *Phot. R. H. Noailles*

Right

Wood-lice or terrestrial isopods live in humid places, their gills being moistened by the secretion of tegumentary glands. In some species, the bases of the abdominal legs are followed out into small more or less tubular cavities (pseudotracheae), which function as do the tracheae of insects. *On the left*, a *Porcellio*; on *the right*, a beach wood-louse or sow-bug. *Tylos armadillo*, which can roll itself into a ball. *Phot. J. Six and R. H. Naoilles*

The barnacles, including *Elminius modestus* represented here, are intimately fixed to their support; only the larvae are free. They stick to rocks and often to those which are left uncovered between tides. When this happens they close their operculi and become so many small hermetically-sealed boxes. They feed on micro-organisms caught in the water which filters through the bristles of their cirri. *Phot. J. Six*

Diagram of the plates of a barnacle (ventral view): *C*, carina (keel); *Clp*, carinolateral plate; *R*, rostrum; *Rlp*, rostrolateral plate; *Sc*, scutum; *Tg*, tergum.

thorax, hiding their segmentation. However, examination of the under-surface of the creature and a count of its appendages makes it possible to confirm the number of segments composing the thorax.

In some decapods, including crayfish and shrimps, the carapace extends in front of the head to form a canopy called a rostrum. The rostrum is comparatively much larger in the larva than the adult decapod.

The existence of a hard carapace reinforced with calcium carbonate deposits gives the crustacean a solid support for its muscles as well as a shield for the nervous system. At the junctions of the thoracic segments, the membranes lining the interior of the segments join to form chitinous blades. In crayfish and lobsters, these blades make up a series of vaults that form an internal canal in which the nervous system is safely housed.

In some lower crustaceans, the carapace extends to cover virtually the whole body. In *Triops*, it forms a large shield over the body with only the tip of the abdomen extending from one end. The ostracods such as *Cypris* go one stage further, for in these animals the carapace is divided into two halves that hinge together like the bivalve shells of some molluscs. The shell can enclose the whole crustacean, though normally the antennae and a pair of legs protrude.

In the Cirrepedia or barnacles, the free-swimming larva eventually settles and fixes itself to a support, there to remain for the rest of its life. The dorsal (back or top) part of the cuticle develops to form a mantle that grows to surround the body. The mantle may stay soft, but usually several hard, calcareous plates (plates of calcium carbonate) develop in the mantle. The number and arrangement of these plates varies from one species to another. In the goose barnacles (*Lepas*, *Pollicipes*), elegant shield-shaped plates enclose most of the

three pairs. In the Stomatopoda (squillas), the appendages of the fourth and fifth segments of the thorax also serve as maxillipeds, making a total of five pairs.

The maxillipeds are in fact modified legs, a fact that becomes obvious in the development of crabs. In the first stages of active life, all the crab's legs are used for locomotion. But after a few moults, they lose their first shape and function and become transformed into auxiliary mouthparts.

Finally in parasitic species, the mouthparts often become highly modified. The isopod *Aega* has mouthparts that are adapted to penetrate and suck blood from their hosts. The copepod *Lernaea* attaches itself to its host by the second maxillae, the adult creature being so modified that it resembles a worm. In the fish louse *Argulus*, the second maxillae are transformed into sucking discs.

The thorax

The first five segments of the crustacean's body—the head— are followed by the thorax which, in the higher crustaceans, consists of eight segments. In the freshwater shrimp (*Gammarus*) and woodlouse, the first segment of the thorax is fused with the head and it is easy to make out the other seven segments. But in many of the higher crustaceans, the thoracic segments are more or less masked by the carapace. In squillas, the carapace covers only the first five segments, leaving the other three free to move, and in the hermit crabs and squat lobsters (*Galathea*), only the last thoracic segment remains independent. In the majority of the Decapoda, the thoracic segments are all fused to the carapace, which extends over the whole of the thorax and the head, welding them together to form a complete cephalothorax. The carapace extends over the top and the sides of the head and

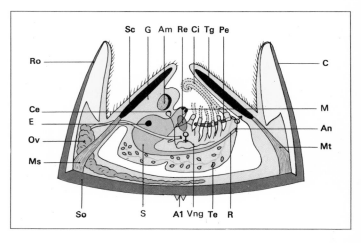

Organizational plan of a barnacle (cirripede crustacean): *Al*, vestiges of antennules; *Am*, adductor muscle; *An*, anus; *C*, carina (calcareous plate); *Ce*, cerebral ganglia; *Ci*, cirri; *E*, eye; *G*, section of the gill; *M*, mouth; *Ms*, muscle of scutum; *Mt*, muscle of tergum; *Ov*, ovary; *Pe*, penis; *R*, rectum; *Re*, excretory organ; *Ro*, rostrum; *S*, stomach; *Sc*, scutum; *So*, calcareous sole, *Te*, testes; *Tg*, tergum; *Vng*, ventral nerve ganglia; ♂, male orifice; ♀, female orifice. The first larva of cirripedes is a nauplius which, although leading a free life, undergoes a moult and becomes the cypris larva, enclosed in a carapace of two valves, which are inserted on the mid-dorsal line. The cypris fixes itself to a solid support by its antennules; its ventral surface then takes on a preponderant growth and the larva thus changes in orientation; while this change is taking place, the region situated in front of the mouth lengthens and forms a short peduncle, whilst the calcareous plates develop in the thickness of the integument. The swimming legs are transformed into permanent appendages, the cirri, covered with long hairs. The eyes, antennae and abdomen regress and the crustacean appearance is lost. Indeed, Baron Georges Cuvier himself, the founder of comparative anatomy, placed cirripedes among the molluscs.

body, a stalk extending from the shells to fix the crustacean in position. In the acorn barnacles (*Balanus*), the plates form a rigid cone around the whole of the body. The plates are able to open and allow the long, delicate thoracic appendages to fan out through the water to gather food particles. But if danger threatens or if the barnacle is left high and dry by the retreating tide, the plates close tightly and isolate the animal from the outer world, enabling it to survive.

In parasitic forms, the thorax undergoes even greater modification. *Lernaea* females, for example, lose all trace of segmentation and develop a worm-like body in which there is no distinct thoracic region.

The appendages of the thorax assume the most diverse forms and perform the most varied functions among the crustaceans. In the Branchiopoda, such as *Triops*, the thoracic appendages are leaf-like organs. They aid in respiration by fanning water to the gills. In the Copepoda, the appendages constitute powerful swimming organs. The thoracic appendages of the sessile barnacles are completely different, being transformed into feathery tentacles that sweep through the water like a net, trapping any food particles and conveying them to the barnacle's mouth. Different again are the appendages of some parasitic amphipods, which end in hooks so that they can cling tightly to their hosts. In this way, *Cyamus* is a parasite of whales and *Caprella* of seaweeds.

In the Stomatopoda, such as *Squilla*, the second pair of maxillipeds take the form of long, thin claws armed with spiny claspers for grabbing prey. The appendages look so much like the forelegs of a praying mantis that the crustaceans of this order are known as mantis shrimps.

In the Decapoda, the first three pairs of thoracic appendages are maxillipeds and used in feeding. The remaining five pairs are known as walking legs, and order gets its name from these ten legs. However, they are capable of modification away from their general purpose of locomotion. In crabs and crayfish, the first pair of walking legs is transformed in a pair of sturdy claws with strong pincers used for both offence and defence. In the male fiddler crab (*Uca*), there is a marked asymmetry of the pincers, one being several times the size of the other.

The second and third pair of walking legs may end in tiny prehensile pincers, as in crayfish. In the prawn (*Palaemon*), the pincer on the second pair of legs is more developed than that on the first pair. In some other decapods, the third, fourth and fifth pairs of legs end in pincers, as can be seen in *Anchylomera*, for example.

The two claws of the pincer at the end of the thoracic appendage each consists of separate pointed joints. The penultimate joint is fixed and the final joint opens and closes under the action of powerful muscles. Fishermen and fishmongers can render live lobsters harmless by slipping a small piece of wood into the gap between the joints, thus preventing the muscle from opening the pincer.

There are many variations in the structure and use of the walking legs. In the Raninidae, the four hind pairs are broadened into swimming oars whereas, in portunid crabs, only the fifth pair is modified for swimming. In *Dromia*, the last two pairs are prehensile and used for hanging on to objects and in this way, these crustaceans become covered by sponges. In the hermit crabs, which have soft bodies and make their homes in discarded shells, the last two pairs of walking legs, being of no use, are almost completely atrophied.

Exploration of the ocean depths has revealed the existence of some remarkable shrimps (*Benthecisymus*), whose last pair of thoracic appendages have lost their usual shape. Instead of looking like legs, they are elongated and slender, function-

ing as delicate antennae with very highly developed organs of touch. However, in spite of their different appearance and use, the basic structure of a crustacean appendage can still be recognized in them.

The thoracic appendages, and the other crustacean appendages too, consist of three basic parts, however modified they may be. These parts are called by the names given them at the beginning of the twentieth century by the French zoologist Milne-Edwards. Nearest the body is the protopodite. From the middle of this section springs the endopodite and to the side is the expodite. In this way, the biramous appendage branches into the endopodite and exopodite. Each of the three parts may be of one or several joints.

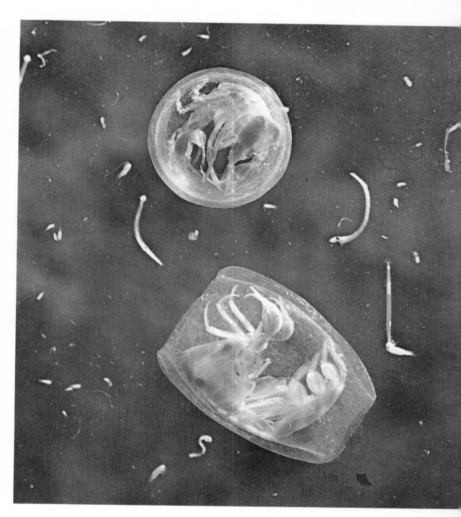

The female phronima (*Phronima sedentaria*), an amphipod, lives in pelagic tunicates, having eaten the bodies and left only the tunic. The female rears its young in its 'cask'; the male leads a free life in deep waters. *Phot. Aldo Margiocco*

In the Decapoda, the thoracic appendages are mostly uniramous and consist of the endopodite growing from the protopodite. But in the other order of the Eucarida, which includes krill (*Euphausia*), all the thoracic appendages are biramous. In the females of the Peracarida, such as isopods and amphipods, the exopodites of the thoracic appendages are shaped like plates and form an incubatory chamber or brood pouch where the embryos develop.

A fourth section called the epipodite is present in the maxillipeds and walking legs of decapods. It is simply a flap that separates the gills, which lie at the bases of most of the thoracic appendages. The rows of gills are situated in a gill

Prawn of the coral reefs, many-coloured, elegant and an excellent swimmer, such is the *Rhynchonicetes. Phot. R. Catala*

chamber covered by the sides of the carapace. The chamber opens beneath the body, at the sides of the legs. Water is drawn into the gill chamber by the fanning action of the second maxilla.

The abdomen

The last part of the body is the abdomen, sometimes and incorrectly called the tail of the crustacean. Differences in structure of the abdomen distinguish three tribes in the order Decapoda. In the first tribe, the Macrura (lobsters, shrimps, prawns, crayfish), the abdomen is well-developed and can be bent forward under the body rapidly and powerfully. By quick movements of the abdomen, the crustacean can dart backwards to escape danger. The abdomen is the part of a lobster or crayfish that is so esteemed by gourmets.

In the tribe Anomura (hermit crabs), the soft abdomen is hidden away inside the empty shell of a gastropod mollusc. It therefore takes up the shape of the mollusc shell, becoming asymmetrical, and plays no part in locomotion.

The third tribe, the Brachyura (true crabs), have abdomens that are reduced and plate-like in shape and bent forward under the cephalothorax. The abdomen is narrow and triangular in the males but broader in the females.

There are six abdominal segments in all decapods, plus the

telson at the end. The telson is rudimentary and bears no appendages, making up the centre of the tailfin in crayfish and lobsters and containing the anus.

The thoracic and abdominal segments are so similar in amphipods and isopods that it is sometimes difficult to distinguish them. The abdomen must originally have been composed of seven segments, for a seventh segment is distinct in the embryo. However it becomes rudimentary in the adult and frequently disappears completely—this can be observed in *Idotea*. Fusion of the abdominal segments may also occur, either partially or completely. In *Asellus*, the abdomen is reduced to a single unsegmented part, and in the parasitic *Cyamus* it becomes vestigial and only a minute trace of the abdomen remains.

Each of the six segments of the abdomen typically bears one pair of appendages. As happens in the case of the thoracic appendages, they undergo considerable modification and become adapted to the most varied uses. Squillas use their abdominal appendages for swimming; hermit crabs use them to hook on to a shell; crayfish and spiny lobsters use them to carry eggs, and isopods use them in copulation.

The sixth pair of appendages may become broad and fin-like, making a tailfin with the telson, as in crayfish.

In the males of some Macrura, such as the deep-sea shrimp *Sergestes*, the first pair of abdominal appendages are prehensile. In the hermit crabs, on the other hand, the first segments do not develop legs and legs are found only on the left-hand side of the following segments.

In isopods, the abdominal appendages are highly modified into membranous gill-like breathing organs, which can obtain oxygen from damp surroundings on land.

In spite of this great diversity in appearance and function, a basic plan or organization exists as with the thoracic appendages, and it is possible to distinguish a protopodite, endopodite and exopodite in most cases.

Locomotion

Apart from woodlice, sea slaters (*Ligia*), sandhoppers (*Orchestia*), and a few terrestrial crabs, most crustaceans live in water and their most usual mode of locomotion is swimming. They can move easily in the water, for their solid carapaces do not weigh them down. Apart from swimming, many crustaceans are also able to run or walk along the bottom. Crabs will flee swiftly from danger, scuttling sideways on their walking legs. Lobsters and spiny lobsters are hindered in running by their long abdomens and prefer to walk. However, if danger suddenly threatens, they can flick the abdomen and tailfin and dart backwards in a flash to escape from their attacker.

Edible prawns (*Leander*) live in shoals along rocky coasts and prefer swimming. Others, the penaeid prawns, live in the open sea and are excellent swimmers.

Finally, there are countless small planktonic crustaceans that simply drift in the water. They are usually accompanied by the larvae of other crustaceans that move to the sea floor on becoming adult.

In addition to the swimmers and walkers, a few crustaceans are climbers. Some decapods are able to emerge from the water and climb up rocks, clinging to ridges and projections in the surface of the rock. Others can hoist themselves onto mangrove trees, and there are even some crabs that can climb coconut palms. They then knock down the coconuts from the trees and descend to eat them on the ground. This habit is reflected in the coconut crab's scientific name, *Birgus latro*, for *latro* means robber.

Crustaceans have, in fact, tremendous muscular power for their size. If we measure the amount of effort expended by a crab in closing a pincer in relation to its body weight, and then measure the same ratio for a man squeezing a hand, we find that the crab's pincer is more than thirty times as powerful as the human hand!

Sexual dimorphism

Apart from the Cirripedia (barnacles), Cymothoidae, and a few shrimps—which are hermaphrodite—all crustaceans have separate sexes. Obvious external differences distinguish the two sexes.

In the decapods, the positions of the genital passages is characteristic of the sexes. That of the male is usually placed in the first joint of the last pair of thoracic legs, or sometimes on the ventral surface of the last segment of the thorax. The female opening is placed further forward, being situated on the ventral surface between the third pair of thoracic legs in the Brachyura, or at the first joint of these legs in the Macrura and Anomura. In the Brachyura, the shape of the abdomen also distinguishes the sexes. In the male it is narrow and triangular, and in the female it is very broad.

In some crustaceans, the differences between the sexes are so great that early authors thought that they belonged to

different species. This is especially true of the isopods of the Aranizidae, which are parasites of various marine fishes in the early stages of their lives. The males, which develop to swim freely and have a broad head with very strong mandibles, were called maxillary anceae. The females, on the other hand, remain fixed to the fish and have a small head with little mouthparts; they were called blueish praniza.

Another parasitic isopod is *Bopyrus*, which is to be found in shrimps and prawns. The *Bopyrus* larva settles in the gill chamber of its host and develops into a female. Subsequent larvae that settle alongside become males. The two sexes are very distinct from each other. The females are blind and disc-shaped, looking like coloured swellings, whereas the males have eyes and an elongated body divided into distinct segments. The parasites moult at the same time as their host, and also destroy their reproductive organs.

Another kind of sexual dimorphism, very pronounced, is exhibited by the isopods *Entonisci*, which are parasites of crabs and hermit crabs. The female lives enveloped in a membranous sac inside the crab's body. It is so modified that, without knowledge of its life cycle, one would be hard put to recognize it as a crustacean at all. It has no visible segments, but fleshy irregular lobes. The male is lost among the lobes of the female and the eggs. It retains the appearance of a crustacean from its early life, and it is always accompanied by several male larvae whose testes are already full of sperm. These larvae probably serve as complementary males and ensure reproduction.

In the isopods mentioned above and some copepods that are parasites of fish, one can find the kind of sexual dimorphism in which the male is many times smaller than the female. This is not uncommon in the animal kingdom and also occurs in some arachnids, for example. In *Lernaea*, which is a parasite on the gills of fish, the females are comparatively big and worm-shaped and blind. The males, which hang from the females, are tiny in comparison; they also have segmented bodies with sturdy maxillipeds and a simple eye.

The shape of the antennae may also differentiate the two sexes. In *Phronima*, which are amphipods, the females have short antennules whereas those of the males are very long. Different antennae distinguish the sexes in the Cumacea.

Mating

In crabs, shrimps and crayfish, short preliminary rituals usually precede mating, which occurs either immediately after the female moults or outside a moulting period. However, terrestrial crabs of tropical regions, which dig burrows in beaches, indulge in long nuptial displays. Males and females each possess their own burrow and each individual lives within a specific territory, which it defends against its neighbours. When the male becomes sexually mature, he displays colours of bright orange, green, blue and purple and one pincer grows much larger than the others. To attract a female, the male makes unusual postures and strange, intricate dances—rather like the courtship displays of birds. Like birds too, rival male crabs may fight each other in a dispute over territory or a mate. Once a female has chosen her partner, mating takes place on the beach or at the bottom of a burrow, depending on the species. These

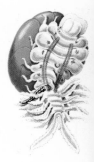

The bopyrids are isopods which parasitize decapod crustaceans. The pygmy males retain a crustacean appearance, whereas the females, swollen with eggs and relatively enormous, lose their isopod appearances. *After Giard and Bonnier*

crabs are popularly called hailing crabs, callers or fiddler crabs, from the way the pincers move about. They belong to the genus *Uca* and others.

The legs also play an important role in bringing the sexes of many species together. The male clasps the female with his second pair of legs, and carries her with him whether he is walking or swimming. If he should lose his grip on his mate, he soon catches her again. This mating behaviour is true of most amphipods, such as *Gammarus*, and isopods such as *Idotea* and *Asellus*, in which the male and female may move about for hours clasped tightly together. Usually the partnerships do not last very long and male and female part after mating. However, permanent pairs do form, especially in the various parasitic isopods that have dwarf males, such as *Bopyrus*. One well-known example of permanent pair formation is to be found in the shrimps of the Pontoniidae, which live commensally with molluscs or sponges. There is a popular tradition in Japan of offering newly-weds a *Euplectella* (glassy sponge) containing a couple of *Pontonia* as a symbol of fidelity.

In the majority of decapods, as in the isopods, the first two pairs of abdominal legs are used as copulatory organs. In the ostracods and branchiopods, the antennae of the male are prehensile and are used to hold the female during copulation.

Care of the eggs

Crustaceans usually produce a considerable number of eggs, the number being apparently related to the extent of the protection that the mother offers them. Amphipods and isopods harbour their eggs in a brood pouch and rarely lay

more than 100 eggs. Shrimps produce 200 or 300, crabs and lobsters 20,000–25,000, and the spiny lobster between 120,000–150,000.

In the higher crustaceans, the female's abdominal legs are used to carry the eggs. The eggs cluster round the legs in bulky masses. Crabs carrying eggs raise their abdomens to keep them clear of the sea floor. These crabs are somehow able to recognize when the eggs are ready to hatch, and they then choose a suitable place and lay the eggs in the sea. The shrimp takes extreme care of its eggs, as it lays comparatively few. It is a long task, for the eggs do not hatch until approximately six months after laying.

Copepods usually carry their eggs in one or two long tube-shaped sacs. Many ostracods carry their eggs with them inside the valves of the carapace until they hatch. The water fleas (Cladocera) give their eggs total protection, housing them in an incubatory chamber situated beneath the dorsal surface of the shell. The amphipods and isopods have similar brood pouches for the eggs formed by branches of the thoracic appendages. The eggs hatch inside these chambers or pouches.

There are also crustaceans that do not carry their eggs about in their wanderings. Among the ostracods, *Cypris* simply lays its eggs on aquatic plants. Most of the branchiopods lay their eggs at the bottom of ponds or any support they happen to come across. The females take no further interest in their eggs, leaving them to the mercy of predators and other dangers. But the eggs are not totally helpless; if the pond should dry up, the eggs are capable of surviving prolonged desiccation. They hatch as soon as the water returns, which explains why ponds become restocked with these animals so soon after refilling with water. The embryonic development of these crustaceans is fully realized only if the eggs have undergone desiccation. The long resistance to

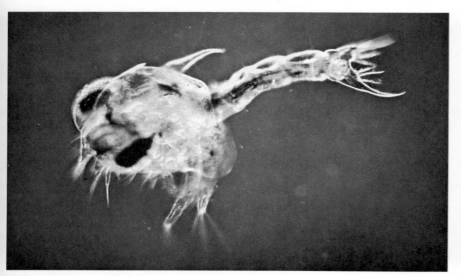

Planktonic larvae of decapod crustaceans: *top left*, zoaea larva of a crab; its abdomen is normally developed compared with the bulky cephalothorax; *above*, megalopa larva of the same; the abdomen has decreased in size, whilst the cephalothorax and the eyes have become preponderant; *bottom left*, the metazoaean larva of *Porcellana longicornis*, the two long spines of which are considered as flotation organs but disappear in later stages of development. *Phot. R. H. Noailles and Takemura*

desiccation by *Artemia* eggs makes them useful to aquarists, for they provide a fish food that can readily be stored.

Parthenogenesis

Some species of crustaceans are able to reproduce by parthenogenesis; the eggs laid by the female hatch without being fertilized by the male. In the water fleas, such as *Daphnia* and *Leptodora*, the females breed throughout most of the year by parthenogenesis, producing more females so that males are absent. But when the conditions of the surroundings become unfavourable, as when winter approaches or when ponds begin to dry up, the parthenogenetic females give birth to individuals of both sexes. After mating, the females lay in their incubatory chambers special large eggs known as winter eggs. These eggs have a hard shell and will be able to withstand the approaching cold or desiccation. The wall of the incubatory chamber hardens and separates itself from the body at the following moult, forming an egg case, an *ephippium*, that falls to the bottom of the pond. When conditions get better, as spring arrives or the pond refills, the eggs hatch, always giving birth to females that breed only parthenogenetically.

There is, therefore, an alternation of parthenogenetic and sexual generations, as in plantlice. The breeding of branchiopods in some regions—for example, various races of *Artemia* and *Trichoniscus*—is effected by a kind of parthenogenesis called geographic parthenogenesis which is generally

Common shore crab (*Carcinus maenas*), with a parasitic barnacle (*Sacculina*) attached (ventral view). The abdomen appears as an apron resting against the parasite. *Phot. J. Vasserot*

Daphniae or water-fleas (*Daphnia*), breeding by parthenogenesis. The eggs, situated between the body and the carapace, develop directly without the help of a spermatozoid. Notice the single eye, made up of a small number of visual unities, each one of which has its own little lens. These small crustaceans are very common in fresh water throughout the world. *Phot. R. H. Noailles*

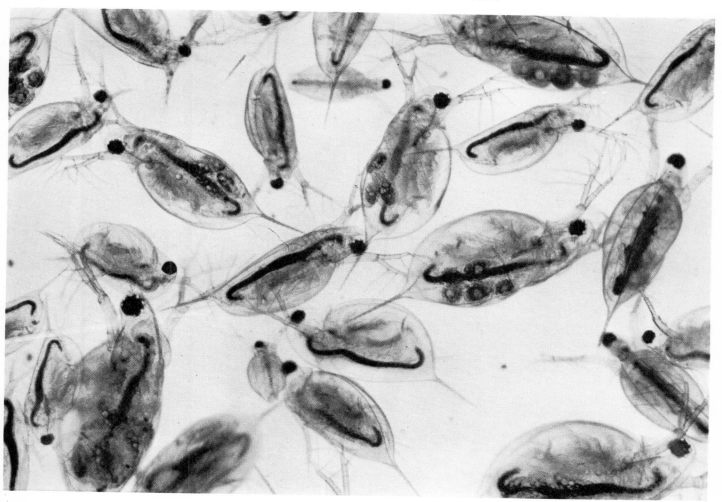

accompanied by polyploidy, a doubling of the normal number of chromosomes.

The nauplius larva

Although the larvae of crustaceans display a diversity of appearance which matches that of the adults, they can nevertheless be classified into a small number of types.

From the egg there usually emerges a certain kind of larva called a nauplius larva. It has an ovoid body without any visible segmentation; on its dorsal surface there is a simple

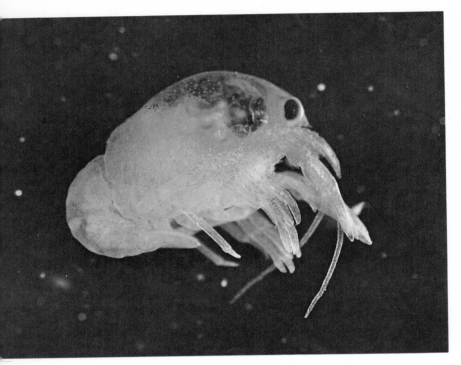

The new-born larva of the white-footed crayfish (*Astacus pallipes*) possesses all the adult's parts; the nauplius stage is simply sketched in the course of development of the egg itself. The larva, richly provided with yolk, lives on its own reserves, fixed to the hairs of its mother's abdominal appendages. *Phot. R. H. Noailles*

median eye and on the lower surface three pairs of appendages. The first pair, made up of two joints, act as antennae and are sensitive to touch. The second and third pairs, which are forked, are organs of locomotion, acting like oars to propel the larva through the water. These appendages also waft food particles in the water towards the mouth.

The first pair of appendages eventually become the antennules in the adult crustacean. The second pair produce the antennae and the third pair the mandibles. After the first moult, the rudiments of new appendages and a forked tail appear behind the three pairs of primitive appendages; the larva has reached the metanauplius stage. Then comes the protozoaea stage, characterized by the appearance of a cephalothoracic shield, a thoracic region and an abdominal region. This protozoaea then changes into a zoaea, characterized by an arched rostrum at the front of the shield and a long spine along the thorax. The zoaea is succeeded by the mysis, so-called because it resembles the opossum shrimp

Mysis. After further moulting, the adult stage is attained.

It should be noted that not all crustaceans pass through this complete series of stages; there are many that skip some of them. However, many crustaceans are born in the nauplius state and gradually reach the adult form after a series of moults; this is true of the branchiopods and the copepods. Others, such as the ostracod *Cypris*, hatch in the nauplius form but are already enveloped in a bivalve shell like that of their parents. The ostracod *Cypridina* and *Daphnia*, a branchiopod, emerge from the egg looking very much like adults; this is also true of the majority of the amphipods and isopods.

The great majority of the decapods hatch in the zoaea stage, varying in appearance from one genus to another. However the marine shrimp *Penaeus* hatches in the nauplius stage and proceeds through all the stages outlined above to the adult form, whereas the eggs of crayfish hatch to give larva looking like miniature adult crayfish.

The development of fixed forms, such as the barnacles, whether they are attached to an inanimate object or are parasitic on another animal, begins with a nauplius stage. The larvae are free-swimming, and serve to distribute these crustaceans before they become fixed.

Moulting

Whereas insects moult only when they are larvae, crustaceans moult throughout their lives. This means that they continue to grow larger as they grow older without reaching a final, definite size. However, growth becomes slower and slower with age, so that the final size of a particular species will be within a small range of lengths. The male is usually bigger than the female.

The largest crustacean is the giant spider crab (*Macrocheira kaempferi*) found off Japan, which measures as much as twelve feet from the tip of one leg to another. The largest lobster (*Homarus americanus*) ever found measured four feet from the tailfin to the tip of its pincer. At the other end of the scale, the smallest crustacean is *Alonella*, a water flea, which is only a hundredth of an inch long.

Colour changes

Crustaceans vary greatly in colour, their skins containing pigments of red, orange, yellow, violet, green, blue, black and many other hues. The pigments are situated in special pigment-containing cells called chromatophores in the surface layer of the cuticle. They usually belong to the carotenoid group of pigments, which are mostly yellow to red in colour, and the melanins, which are dark pigments, are absent. Other pigments that may be present include ommatins (reds, browns, blacks), guanin (white) and cyanocrystallin (blue). It is the latter pigment that gives the lobster its blue colouring; it is changed into red zooerythrin by heat, which is why cooked lobsters appear to be red.

However, cooking is not the only way to make a crustacean change its colour. Some decapods also have the ability to vary the hue of their skins to match their surroundings. The aesop prawn (*Hippolyte varians*) lives among seaweeds, but is almost impossible to spot because it takes on the exact shade of the seaweed, whatever colour it may happen to be. This was first observed in the weed-infested Sargasso Sea. It is caused by a flow of several pigments among the chromatophores.

The process is controlled by hormones; this discovery was made in 1928 and it was the first time that any evidence of hormone action was uncovered in the invertebrates.

Crustaceans that live in dark underground waters are devoid of pigments, and it might seem that deep-sea species should also be colourless for they too live in total darkness. However, this is not so. A few deep-sea crustaceans are only slightly coloured; *Elasmonotus* is greyish white and *Polycheles* is so transparent that its internal organs can be seen through its rosy-white cuticle. Most exhibit beautiful tints of red to violet, and some are boldly patterned, *Nephropsis agassizi* having a red body with a handsome orange back. These species have been found as deep as 3000 fathoms, and the depth makes no difference to the colours.

Light-producing crustaceans

Some ostracods such as *Cypridina*, and certain copepods (*Saphirina*, *Pleuromma*) and shrimps (*Heterocarpus*, *Aristeus*), emit trails of phosphorescence that form into a luminous cloud around the creatures, concealing them from view. The phosphorescence is produced by the secretion of glands that surround the mouth and the bases of the legs. The fanning action of the legs, which normally acts to create currents of water for respiration, whirls the luminous trails from the glands into a cloud. The production of light is in this case a defensive action, similar to the smoke-screens of ink produced by octopuses.

Deep-sea crustaceans also emit light, but in a different way. They do not emit a luminous substance but bear luminous cells called photophores. These cells are situated in various parts of the body. Many crustaceans of the Euphausiacea bear photophores on the eye stalks, at the bases of the thoracic legs, and along the ventral surface of the abdomen, making a pattern of light on the underside. In some of the

Copepods (here *Pseudocalanus elongatus*) make up a very substantial part of marine animal zooplankton. In a cubic mile, their mass is, overall, greater than that of fishes. They feed on unicellular organisms (diatoms, peridians, coccolithophorids, etc.). *Phot. Wilson*

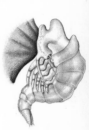

Right
Parasitism reaches an extreme degree in diverse crustaceans: barnacles, copepods, isopods. It is very often accompanied by profound anatomical degradation which reaches its peak in the Rhizocephala, relatives of the barnacles, which retain nothing of the crustacean except their nauplius and cypris larvae. Represented here is a parasitic barnacle, *Laura gerardiae*, which lives fixed to a Mediterranean black coral, *Gerardia lamarcki. After Giard and Bonnier*

luminescent decapod prawns, such as *Sergestes*, the photophores also lie in lines along the sides of the body. They are complex cells, containing pigment layers, reflecting layers and lenses to colour and concentrate the light produced in the cells.

The production of light must be advantageous to the crustacean in some way. Perhaps the patterns of photophores attract prey, or act as a recognition signal to other members of the same species. The light is produced in the same way as in other luminous animals. It results from the oxidation of a substance called luciferin produced in the tissues and blood. An enzyme called luciferase acts as a catalyst. The reaction is almost entirely cold, producing light with virtually no heat.

Hermit crabs

The most interesting group of crustaceans probably consists of the hermit crabs. They begin their lives as free-swimming larvae, but as they grow, the abdomen remains soft. When a hermit crab reaches adult age, it makes up for its lack of a hard covering by seeking out a gastropod mollusc shell of suitable size and placing its abdomen inside the shell. The head and pincers of the crab extend from the opening of the shell to find food. The shell is a temporary home, for the hermit crab continues to grow and must find a larger shell from time to time. The shelter does not remain bare but becomes covered with sea anemones, hydroids and sponges. The crab and its companions may benefit each other by their association. The animals on the shell get scraps of food from the crab's meals and in return, the crab's normally conspicuous shell is effectively camouflaged. If sea anemones should cover the shell, the crab gets an extra form of defence for they can sting any predator that ventures near.

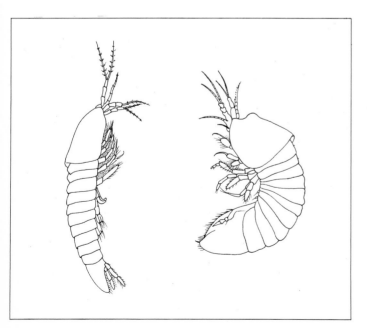

Thermosbaena mirabilis, a small crustacean living in littoral underground waters. It was found for the first time in the warm springs at Gabes (Tunisia). *After T. L. Monod*

Crustaceans form a vital food link

Crustaceans constitute a vital link in the great food chains of the sea. They make up an important part of the plankton, the mass of minute organisms, both plant and animal, that drift in the surface layers of the sea. Small crustaceans and crustacean larvae eat the phytoplankton—the plants of the plankton—and in turn provide food for the larger marine animals that cannot eat the phytoplankton. Such animals include all kinds of fishes and sharks, and even whales, such as the great blue whale, that strain their food from the water rather than hunt it. Herring shoals follow clouds of *Anomalocera* copepods, which swim in such numbers that they whip up the surface of the sea as if it were raining heavily. Krill, which consists of countless multitudes of the shrimp *Euphausia superba*, is a basic food of Antarctic waters. Fishermen look for crustaceans, for where they mass, fishes are sure to follow and the best catches are likely to be made.

Crustaceans and man

Most people know crustaceans as delicacies for the table. Prawns, shrimps, lobsters and crabs are fished commercially

This large crab, *Paromola cuvieri*, with legs as slender as stilts and short antennae, resembles the sea spiders (*Maia*), but is quite different from them. It lives at medium depth. *Phot. Fronval*

Left
The mystacocarid, *Derocheilocaris remanei*, of Mediterranean littoral underground waters. *After Cl. Delamare*

on a large scale from the sea, and freshwater crayfish are eagerly sought after in lakes. We eat only decapod crustaceans, but other crustaceans are of indirect value to man, for they form a vital element of the food chains that support the marine fish we eat. Attempts at rearing crustaceans, centred mainly on the crayfish, have not yet proved successful.

Crustaceans do provide us with food, either directly or indirectly, but they are otherwise rather harmful animals. Some are involved in the transmission of diseases to man, playing the part of an intermediate host for parasitic worms.

A species of *Cyclops* in India, Arabia and Africa transmits the human Guinea worm (*Dranunculus medinensis*) to people drinking water. *Diaptomus* and *Cyclops* are carriers of larvae of the fish tapeworm *Dibothriocephalus latus*, which grows in humans eating raw fish that have fed on the copepods. Freshwater crabs and crayfish transmit lung flukes (*Paragonimus*) to people that eat them in the Far East, India and Africa.

Some barnacles such as *Balanus* attach themselves to the hulls of boats, producing an unsightly crust and reducing speed because they increase the drag of the boat. Cleaning off barnacles in dry dock is an expensive business.

Other crustaceans attack the wooden piles of jetties and quays, riddling them with their burrows. The best known are the boring amphipod *Chelura* and the isopod *Limnoria*, commonly known as the gribble. These crustaceans bore into the wood to make nests for themselves in the outer layers. Succeeding generations burrow down into the wood to make their own nests, and eventually the whole wooden pile is riddled with holes. The waves gradually begin to break away the outer surface of the pile, and it slowly decreases in diameter and finally collapses.

Another harmful crustacean is the Chinese mitten crab (*Eriocheir sinensis*), which is found in profusion in the Yangtze and also in increasing numbers in the fresh waters of Europe. This crustacean is a menace, for it undermines the banks of canals and dykes, causing serious damage. The flooding that occurred in the Netherlands in 1953 was catastrophic because the Chinese crabs had weakened the dykes with their burrows, and the dykes could not withstand the great pressure of water placed on them. International conferences have been held in recent years to find a way of combating this pest.

Recent discoveries

The vast and varied class of the Crustacea is far from being entirely known. Discoveries made in recent years have brought to light four new groups of crustaceans, for example.

The first two groups are now considered to be sub-classes of the Crustacea. The Mystacocarida are microscopic animals that live among damp intertidal sand on sea coasts. They were first discovered in 1943, and several other species have since been found. They are all grouped in the single genus *Derocheilocarus*. The other sub-class is the Cephalocarida, which live in mud at the bottom of bays along the Atlantic and Pacific coasts of the United States. There is a single genus, *Hutchinsoniella*, containing two species. These crustaceans were first found in 1955.

The other two groups are orders. The Thermosbaenacea comprises two genera, *Thermosbaena* and *Monodella*. The former was first discovered in a hot spring in Tunisia in 1924 and is unknown elsewhere; the latter first came to light in the Mediterranean in 1949 and was also found in Texas in 1965. The Speleogriphacea consists of only a single species. It was discovered in 1957 and lives only in the underground waters of a cave in Table Mountain, near the Cape of Good Hope.

The hermit-crab *Eupagarus bernhardus*, lodges its abdomen in a gasteropod's shell (often a whelk); a bulky sea-anemone, *Sagartia parasitica*, instals itself on the whelk, masking almost entirely the shell with the sole of its foot. *Below*, the animal, taken from its shelter, shows its abdomen twisted in a right hand spiral (like the gasteropod) and bearing at its extremity two attachment hooks. *Phot. J. Six*

This millipede (*Polydesmus collaris*), or diplopod is common in woods in western Europe; it feeds on decomposing vegetable matter. (×2.5.) *Phot. Aldo Margiocco*

The iulid millipedes are common in woods and forests in temperate and tropical regions. Represented here is an *iulus* from Kenya, closely related to the European *Schizophyllum*, climbing on a tree-trunk. *Phot. Aldo Margiocco*

The Myriapods

The centipedes make up the class Chilopoda and the millipedes the class Diplopoda within the sub-phylum Mandibulata. Apart from the crustaceans and insects, two small classes complete this sub-phylum: the Pauropoda, which resemble tiny millipedes, and the Symphyla, which are commonly known as garden centipedes but may be directly descended from distant ancestors of the insects. The four classes are collectively known as the myriapods.

The myriapods are animals of widely differing appearance. Their only common feature is the possession of many short legs that are borne on distinct segments, making them symmetrical creatures. The differences between them are sufficient to group them in 4 classes, which have been separate evolutionary lines for a very long time. The first fossil millipedes date from the Silurian period (about 400 million years ago). Some fragments of centipedes are reported in Carboniferous rocks (about 300 million years old), but the class is well represented in the Cretaceous period (about 100 million years ago).

Ventral surface of a *Iulus*, a myriapod of the order Diplopoda, showing the two pairs of locomotory legs per segment. The legs are activated by a wave which travels from front to rear.

However, recent study has shown that the structure of the segments of these animals is less radically different from class to class than had previously been thought. There is therefore some scientific justification in grouping them together as myriapods, a name that simply means 'many feet'. There are about 12,000 species altogether: 3000 centipedes, 8000 millipedes, 300 pauropods and several symphyles. They are all terrestrial animals, often hiding away in dark places to avoid the light.

Anatomical characteristics

It is easy to tell a millipede from a centipede, for the former has two pairs of legs on each body segment and the latter has only one pair per segment. The bodies are made up of numerous distinct segments, there being as many as 100 or more in millipedes and up to nearly 200 in centipedes. Pauropods are minute millipede-like animals of a few segments they never exceed 1/10 of an inch in length. Symphyles have twelve pairs of legs and look like small centipedes; they are white in colour and never grow more than $\frac{1}{3}$ of an inch in length.

However, there are many other distinguishing features to be found among the myriapods. Centipedes have flattened bodies and the head bears a pair of long, jointed antennae, a pair of mandibles (jaws) and 2 pairs of maxillae (mouthparts). There is no division into head, thorax and abdomen, and the head is followed by 15 to 181 body segments. The first body segment bears a pair of poison claws, and all the remaining segments except the last two each bear a pair of walking legs. Millipedes are very different from centipedes. Their bodies are cylindrical and protected by a hard layer of chitin containing calcareous deposits. There is a head, thorax and abdomen, as in most other arthropods. The head bears a pair of short antennae and one pair of mandibles. There is one pair of maxillae, often fused together to form a platelike structure called the gnathochilarium. A short thorax of 4 segments follows the head, all but the first segment each carrying one pair of legs. Then comes the abdomen of 9 to over 100 segments, each with two pairs of walking legs.

Pauropods resemble millipedes, but have no eyes. The body consists of only eleven or twelve segments and there are nine or ten pairs of legs. Symphyles look like small centipedes, but they have no eyes and always bear twelve pairs of legs.

There are several other basic differences between centipedes and millipedes. The sexual organs are placed at the rear of the body in centipedes, but in millipedes the genital opening is near the front of the body behind the second pair of legs. The sexes are separate. The nervous system comprises a cerebral ganglion (brain) and a long ventral nervous chain, there being two ganglia to each segment in millipedes and only one in centipedes. In both animals, the eyes (when present) are simple ocelli, except in *Scutigera*, which has faceted eyes. *Scutigera* is the long-legged centipede that is sometimes a domestic pest in Europe, North Africa and North America.

Myriapods breathe by means of tracheae, and the heart is always situated dorsally (along the back).

The life of myriapods

Embryonic and larval life

Myriapods are mostly oviparous. They produce eggs that are rich in yolk, enabling the embryo to develop without requiring food from its mother. However, the parent protects the eggs in various ways. Symphyles defend their brood against predators and keep the eggs free of mildew. *Geophilus* and *Scolopendra*, which are both centipedes, also combat mildew and coil themselves around the eggs to protect them. The females of the centipede *Lithobius* and the millipede *Glomeris* house their eggs in egg-cases that they cover with soil. *Polydesmus*, another millipede, lays its eggs in bell-shaped shelters containing air-holes, the material being cemented together with a secretion from the anal glands.

The larva that emerges from the egg has only eight segments and three pairs of legs (like an insect), except in centipedes, whose larvae have seven complete segments with seven pairs of legs, and a terminal segment bearing a pair of buds where feet will later grow. In several cases, the young myriapod emerges in a pre-larval state called a pupoid: it is rather like a pupa, being enveloped in an unsegmented membrane bearing only the tooth used in hatching.

Post-larval life

The perfecting of a myriapod from its larval state to the adult state progresses in two main ways. In the majority of millipedes, the number of segments (and of legs) increases at each moult. This anamorphous development, as it is called, also occurs in the order Lithobiomorpha of the Chilopoda. In other myriapods, the larva is born with a full complement of segments and then simply grows in size. This kind of development is known as epimorphous and it occurs in the orders Scolopendromorpha and Geophilomorpha of the Chilopoda. Both kinds of development may take place in one species. The centipede *Lithobius*, for example, increases its number of segments in a first development period and then grows to its full size without acquiring any more segments in a second development period.

Moulting is induced by the secretion of hormones. In millipedes, it is accompanied by such profound internal

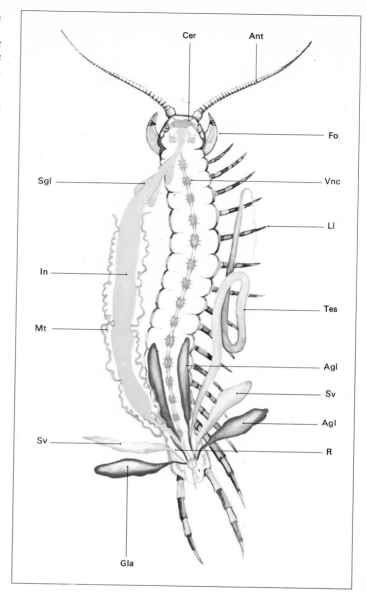

Dissection of a male centipede (*Lithobius*) of the order Chilopoda: *Agl*, accessory gland; *Ant*, antenna; *Cer*, cerebral ganglia; *Fo*, forcipule or poison claw with its poison gland; *In*, intestine; *Ll*, locomotory leg; *Mt*, Malpighian tubules; *R*, rectum; *Sgl*, salivary glands; *Sv*, seminal vesicle; *Tes*, testes; *Vnc*, ventral nerve cord.

Diagram of the organization of a myriapod of the order Diplopoda: *An*, anus; *Cer*, cerebral ganglia; *Ct*, cardiac tube (heart); *Go*, male genital pore; *Ia, Im*, anterior and middle intestines; *M*, mouth; *Mt*, Malpighian tubules; *R*, rectum; *Rgl*, rectal glands; *Sgl*, salivary glands; *Tes*, testes.

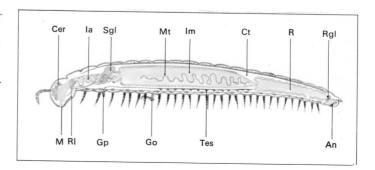

changes that the animal is immobilized and it must first take shelter. The new cuticle hardens as it becomes enriched with calcareous salts. In centipedes, the moult occurs after a very short period of immobility. A strange process of growth called periodomorphosis takes place in some millipedes. After the adult has bred, it becomes immobile and moults; the external genitalia then once more atrophy and the animal must moult again before it can breed once more. This phenomenon of suspension of sexual functions may be repeated several times.

Feeding and other biological activities

Millipedes are rather slow-moving animals; the legs move with a kind of wave-motion to carry the animal over the ground and they are so many that rapid movement is impossible. Millipedes are therefore unable to hunt animals and mostly eat dead plant matter. They sometimes cause serious damage to crops, especially strawberries, potatoes and cotton, but they are also useful for some millipedes destroy insect pests and mildew and cleanse the soil with their

Centipede, *Scolopendra cingulata*, devouring a scorpion (*Buthus occitanus*). *Phot. J. Vasserot*

excrement just as earthworms do.

Centipedes are much better adapted for hunting and killing animal prey. They are agile creatures and have poison claws situated near the mouth, making them redoubtable carnivores. Some centipedes are even capable of causing painful bites to man. The prey is swallowed whole after it has been killed. The food is then sorted in the gizzard and digested in the midgut.

Some species of *Geophilus*, a centipede, are phosphorescent and leave luminous stinging trails in their wake; these are produced by a liquid secreted by glands beneath the body. Some millipedes have a strange defence reaction; certain segmentary glands secrete a strong poison based on hydrocyanic acid and quinone which becomes active only as the substances are emitted.

Some species of *Schizophylum*, a millipede, occasionally travel in very large numbers, forming long marching columns containing thousands of individual millipedes. These migrations may be so large that they interfere with rail traffic. Their cause is unknown.

Scutigera and *Lithobius*, both centipedes, are able to shed their appendages as a defence reaction; the lost limbs are subsequently regenerated. Sometimes these legs are used to produce sounds that repel enemies. Some centipedes, such as *Alipes*, produce sounds by rubbing the outer joints of their hind legs together. Stridulatory organs also exist in some millipedes and are located in the hind region of the body.

Some myriapods infest man. Millipedes are occasionally found in human intestines, although they are not permanent parasites. Centipedes have been known to make their way into the nasal cavities during sleep; they may even penetrate into the sinuses.

Sexual life and reproduction

Fertilization is effected in myriapods in several different ways. In some millipedes, the sperm is placed directly into the genital opening of the female by the male, using walking legs especially modified for this purpose. This is an active form of copulation. In others, fertilization is less direct. A spermatophore (sperm packet) is produced and deposited at the female's genital opening. In the pauropods, the male weaves a silken web and places the spermatophore on it; the female is then guided to the web.

Centipedes never copulate and employ spermatophores instead. The spermatophore is produced after a series of movements or dances executed by the two partners. In *Scutigera*, the male lies beneath the female and produces a spermatophore that sticks to the ground; he then leads the female to it so that she will be fertilized. The tiny symphyles begin in the same way, but the female takes up the spermatophore from the ground in her mouth and the sperm is stored in two small reservoirs situated inside the mouth cavity. When she lays an egg, it is transported to the mouth and then placed on a support—such as a blade of grass—chosen in advance. As the egg leaves the mouth, it is covered with sperm from the reservoirs, producing a kind of external fertilization. It is difficult to imagine the various evolutionary circumstances that have brought about such a strange method of reproduction.

Mating of two millipedes (*Graphidostreptus tumuliporus*), natives of Chad. *Phot. J. A. Demange*

The ventral view of the anterior end of a centipede a *Scolopendra* from Guinea. Notice the single pair of legs per segment and the two strong poison fangs (forcipules) which flank the mouth. *Phot. Aldo Margiocco*

Insects

Structure and physiology

Insects, as a class, comprise innumerable species. However, despite a most astonishing variety of structures, they have common characters making it possible to recognize them at a glance. They all have six legs, and their bodies are divided into three clearly separated regions: head, thorax and abdomen.

The head has the parts of the mouth, as well as a pair of antennae; the thorax governs the three pairs of legs and sometimes one or two pairs of wings. The abdomen, either more or less bulky, is terminated by the genital parts, which, according to species, are very variable in shape and construction. Finally, the relative development of these three parts of the body also varies, depending on the order to which the insect belongs.

One of the essential characteristics of insects is their small size. Giants do exist, such as the Hercules beetle (more than six inches long), and the Goliath beetle *Goliathus* (four inches), and some stick insects (more than one foot). But most insects are well below these dimensions, and a large number are extremely small, like *Alaptus magnanimus* of the Mymaridae. This animal lays its eggs inside the eggs of other insects. There is plenty of room for this, since the insect does

Nocturnal moths find their way about mainly by an acutely sensitive sense of smell (males perceive a female's presence at a distance of several kilometres); it is the antennae which bear the thousands of olfactory receptors. This is a male gypsy moth (*Lymantria dispar*) with its antennae widely spread. *Phot. J. Six*

not exceed $\frac{1}{100}$ of an inch in length. It seems that, in a remote past, the first insects reached greater sizes, for instance the giant dragon-fly (*Meganeura moyni*) of the Carboniferous, the wing-span of which exceeded two feet. However, the insect may be considered very generally as an animal with reduced body dimensions; this characteristic has many important biological consequences.

The first is the possibility that the breathing processes may be based largely on the diffusion of oxygen, which, as a result, has only a short distance to go in order to penetrate all the tissues. The air tubes, called tracheae, which branch out into all the organs, perform the breathing function in almost all cases.

Reduction in size implies another consequence which is not immediately apparent. The relative increase in body surface in relation to weight leads to a considerable increase in water loss in the greatly preponderant terrestrial insects. It is therefore necessary for the outer covering, known as the integument in insects, to be strengthened with waterproof materials.

Unfortunately, this measure alone cannot ensure survival in all cases because, ironically also because of their small size, insects inhabit micro-climates very different from the climate in which humans operate. When a tiny ground-beetle, for instance, crosses a road heated by the summer sun, the temperature at that level is much greater than that experienced by a man at head height: temperatures of 50° C are by no means rare close to the surface of the ground. Generally, therefore, the insect will be exposed to extreme conditions, from which it will often not be able to escape because its field of movement is so circumscribed. It is for this reason that insects have developed astonishing resistance to the hardest environmental conditions.

Some inhabitants of very dry commodities, like meal, can dispense with drinking by keeping all their water within the body and living on the metabolic water manufactured by their organic machines. Others, for unexplained physiological reasons, have modified their functions to such an extent that they develop only in conditions suitable to lower organisms such as bacteria and some algae. Extreme examples of this are *Grylloblatta*, fairly bulky insects which live in the snow of glaciers, and are so much at home in it that they die if they are reared at ordinary temperatures; or the larvae of certain Diptera which swim quite comfortably in the water of hot springs, whose temperature may exceed 50° C. Larvae of the fly *Psilope petrolei* live in pools of petroleum, the paraffin of which they attack with the help of various organisms which live in symbiosis in its intestine.

If conditions become harder still, the insect may stop its life cycle completely, only resuming when the environment becomes more favourable. Quite simply, it allows itself to freeze in the water of northern lakes, although, in fact, while its outward appearance is like an icicle, it has recently been discovered that it is not really frozen. Physiologists have discovered, in fact, that the bodies of hibernating species contain a very large quantity of glycerine, sometimes as much as 20 per cent; the result is that this anti-freeze preserves them as it protects the water in the radiators of our cars. (The reality is less simple, as some insects can live at a temperature of −47° C, but at this low temperature, no anti-freeze or glycerine remains effective.)

Insects have a universe different from ours; their habitats with special micro-climates are not accessible to us; nor are the sensory messages they receive all of the same nature as those which inform us.

Vision is exercised by means of compound eyes, made up of multiple elements (ommatidia), the small images they provide being combined into one, which is of poor quality—insects are generally very myopic and decidedly astigmatic. However, they are much more sensitive than we are to the movements of objects, and their visible spectrum is different from ours: for the most part, they do not see red, distinguish ultra-violet as a colour, and do not confuse polarized light with normal light.

As for hearing, some insects seem not to possess the sense at all; but others are very well provided with the sound-producing, or stridulating, organs and with tympani. Their sound spectrum is also different from ours, for many perceive ultra-sounds up to very high frequencies.

Finally, the insect's sense of smell poses problems which physiologists and physicists find very difficult to solve: the sensitivity of some night butterflies to the female's odour is so great that biologists have been led to imagine a new theory for them, based on the possibility of perception of the infra-red spectrum of individual molecules.

An African cerambycid, *Ceroplesis adusta*, well known for the beauty and the freshness of its colours; it will lay its eggs in the shrub it is sitting on. *Phot. Michel Boulard*

Integument and glands

Chemical composition

First of all, it is necessary to dispose of the popular fallacy that the insect's outer covering, or integument, is essentially formed of chitin. It was shown a long time ago that this is not so. A certain proportion is always present, but it may be quite small. This substance may be compared roughly to the cellulose in plants. It results from the union of numerous molecules of a nitrogenous sugar, glucosamine; whereas cellulose, which is simpler, is only formed from an association of molecules of sugar. Both are fibrous and flexible substances; but, in many cases, the insect's covering is very hard and thick. This is because it contains in abundance a quite different substance, sclerotin, which is almost literally tanned leather. It is a protein material, which is impregnated by a phenolic (carbolic) substance and then hardens to a considerable degree; just how hard this is is shown by the fact that the points of the mandibles (see Digestive System, p. 166) of wood-gnawing insects can also perforate lead, silver, copper and zinc, i.e. they are harder than those metals. Sclerotin forms the essential basis of all the body walls

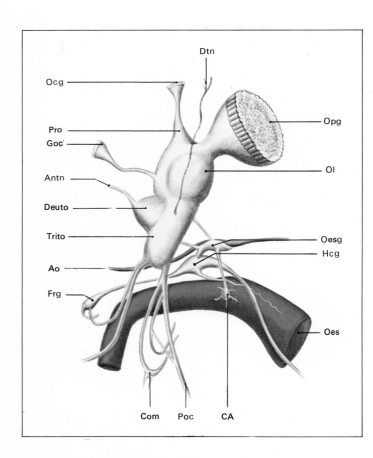

Lateral view of a locust's central nervous system: *Antn*, antennal nerve; *Ao*, aorta; *Ca*, corpora allata; *Com*, sub-oesophageal; *Deuto*, deuto-cerebron; *Dtn*, dorsal tegumentary nerve; *Frg*, frontal ganglion; *Hcg*, hypocerebral ganglion; *Ocg*, ocellar ganglion; *Oes*, oesophagus; *Oesg*, oesophageal ganglion; *Ol*, optical lobe; *Opg*, optical ganglion; *Poc*, peri-oesophageal commissure; *Pro*, protocerebron; *Trito*, tritocerebron.

and appendages which need special reinforcement, for instance the nerve arrangement (venation) of the wings, the stylets of the ovipositor in the female, or the mouth parts used for biting or piercing.

But chitin and sclerotin mixed in the cuticle are not able to fulfil one important physiological function, namely the retention of water. This is the business of a special extremely thin outer layer, the epicuticle, deposited on the surface of the integument. Often it is less than one micron in thickness, but as it is composed of impermeable waxes, it is an effective barrier against loss of water. The epicuticle is extremely fragile, so a very effective insecticide may be a simple abrasive powder, for instance magnesium or aluminium which quickly kills the insect by eroding the epicuticle. If a caterpillar is allowed to crawl over a sheet of paper lightly sprinkled with an abrasive, it dies quickly, for the particles are trapped between the intersegmental membranes. It is also because of the sudden disappearance of this film of wax that many insects' resistance to heat breaks down suddenly at a certain temperature.

It is not known exactly how these waxes, some of which have a high melting point, reach the surface of the cuticle; in some insects they seem to be dissolved in a volatile solvent, which enables them to pass through the cuticle's microscopic pores.

We can now more usefully examine the microscopic structure of this outer covering, the integument. From the exterior, the first layer is the epicuticle, its variable texture being caused by folds or excrescences of the layer beneath, the exocuticle. This is much thicker than the epicuticle, and is very often impregnated with pigments, the most frequent of which is melanin (black). Below this, the endocuticle, made up of the superimposition of lamellar layers, is very thick and sclerotized and is often differentiated into small columns of very varied shape and thickness. Running through the exo- and endocuticles are microscopic channels, the pore canals, which open under the epicuticle. Finally, below the endocuticle is a layer of hypodermic cells, arranged on a single foundation, varying in thickness according to the portion of the integument considered, and whose protoplasm contains many embedded pigment particles.

Hairs and their functions

The surface of the integument, as has been said, is far from being flat. The hypodermic cells very often give rise to long hairs, extremely variable in size and shape, or to flattened scales, as in lepidoptera. Towards the interior, the integument sends forth highly developed closed tubes (diverticula), the apodemes, which will be discussed in connection with the internal skeleton.

Insulators

The hairs of insects, when they are thick (as in bees and many nocturnal moths), have an important function. In fact, although insects are animals with a variable temperature, their vital processes are not carried out without giving off heat; it cannot, however, function below a certain thermal limit. Many diurnal insects, therefore, obtain this minimal quantity of calories by heating themselves in the sun, and their integuments are usually bare. Crepuscular and nocturnal insects use another technique, which consists of beating their wings or making the large alar muscles of the thorax vibrate. This raises the temperature of the thorax, so that in the large nocturnal hawk moth, *Sphinx ligustri*, it may be 17° C above the temperature of the outer air. But if the hairs of its thorax are shaved, the temperature of the thorax itself hardly rises to 8° C above that of the surrounding atmosphere.

Sensory hairs

Most important of all, a large number of insect hairs have a sensory role. Every true hair is connected to a nerve ending or associated with a sensory cell. It can even be said that, in insects, a large number of different senses are assumed by hair organs. The sense of touch is perhaps the most important: any bending or deformation of the hair causes the excitation of the nerve cells situated at its base. Hairs are also the basis of those curious organs which replace the balancing organs of other animals, informing the central nervous system as to the relative positions of the different segments of the body.

Hairs are also the organs of two senses, taste and smell, which tend to be separated in vertebrates. It is not possible to say exactly, in insects, where the first begins and the second ends. Finally, a certain number of hairs are sensitive also to vibrations and sounds; again, it is not possible to separate clearly in insects the sense of hearing and of vibration. It seems that the transition from one to the other is imperceptible.

The colours of insects

Naturally, it is in the integument that the pigments which give an insect its particular colour are localized, except in some species with transparent integuments, in which the internal milieu and the body fats may play a certain role in coloration. The colours of insects are extremely varied and of a very diverse chemical nature. Some pigments come quite simply from food and constitute, as it were, the waste matter which the animal is unable to eliminate. This applies to many red pigments—the carotenoids of the carrot and of leaves. Other colours have no chemical basis, for instance in the scales of some butterflies: they are simply peculiarities in the structure of the scale, made of thin layers, which diffract light or reflect it in a special manner, thus giving rise to interference colours, often very brilliant and metallic (those of the blue wings of the Amazonian *Morpho*, for instance).

Integumentary glands

The integument is also the site of extremely varied odoriferous glands, which are repugnant to predators or attractive within the species (like the bee's Nassonoff glands), wax glands which, in a number of four-winged insects, produce the wax used for the building of the nest. There are also glands secreting the moulting liquid, which are dealt with later in the section.

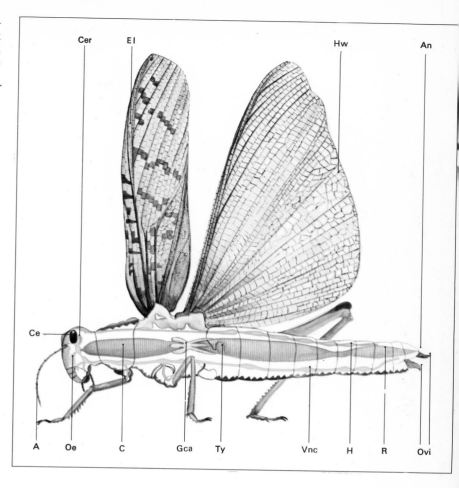

Diagram of the organization of a locust, *Locusta* here taken as a generalized insect. Partial dissection: *A*, antenna; *An*, anus; *C*, crop; *Ce*, compound eye; *Cer*, cerebral ganglia; *El*, elytron; *Gca*, gastric caecum; *H*, heart; *Hw*, membranous hind wing; *Oe*, oesophagus; *Ovi*, valves of the ovipositor; *R*, rectum; *Ty*, tympanum; *Vnc*, ventral nerve cord.

The Odonata—insects in which vision takes precedence over all the other senses—have enormous compound eyes, as can be seen from the much enlarged head of the blue Aeshna (*Aeshna cyanea*). *Phot. J. Six*

Morpho butterflies pride of the Amazonian fauna, owe their magnificent metallic colours to one phenomenon of interference of light falling on the numerous thin superimposed layers in the scales which cover their wings. *Left,* males; *right,* females. *Phot. Luiz Soledad Otero*

The internal skeleton

The internal skeleton is infinitely varied, although it is always composed of tubes, folds or ingrowths, which issue from the integument and to which the muscles are attached. It will suffice to consider the extent to which the musculature of a caterpillar and of a ground-beetle may differ, given the pecularities of their shapes and of their modes of locomotion, to understand the differences of their internal skeletons and their complexity.

It is within the head that this skeleton is most interesting and most complicated; the internal structure of the head is often given the name of tentorium. It develops from paired segmental rudiments which fuse at a later stage, with the result that they can hardly be recognized as distinct in the perfect insect. Usually it is possible to distinguish the body and arms of the tentorium which, overall, has an X shape. The body of the tentorium extends to the internal and central portion of the occipital cavity and on it rests the anterior part of the gut. The cerebral ganglia and the muscles of the mandibles have complex connections with the tentorium.

The internal skeleton of the thorax is hardly less complicated, especially in the portions verging on the base of the wings and of the legs. There is no anatomical zone in the insect which has more exercised the ingenuity of anatomists than the sclerites at the base of the wing. They have recently been under fresh scrutiny in bumble-bees, the special problem being to establish how many wing-beats (up to 1000

per second in Diptera of the genus *Forcipomyia*) can be transmitted by the muscles at the base of the wing. There is a complicated system of buffers and mobile parts which not only transmits the fundamental motor impulse but also makes it possible, by the action of small accessory muscles, to modify the angle of the edge of the wing; and all this at the formidable rhythm of several hundred vibrations per second at least. The vibrations must certainly be largely spontaneous, for it is inconceivable that a muscle could contract and expand such a large number of times per second.

The digestive system

The mouth parts of insects are as different as are their modes of life. There are three pairs, of which the first two, mandibles (or true jaws) and maxillae, are situated on the sides of the mouth. The third (maxillules) is underneath, fused into a single piece to form the lower jaw (labium). This bears a complex formation, the hypopharynx, into which the salivary ducts open.

Biting mouthparts (as in Odonata, Orthoptera, Coleoptera, etc.) seem to be the most primitive. Each mandible is a strong, very hard tooth, articulated with the head by two projections from its base; the maxillae, or accessory jaws, are composed of several parts, including a spined or toothed blade and a jointed palp. The labium is flanked by two palps.

The ant-lion larva has its mouth closed by coalescence of the lips; it can take only liquid food, which it sucks through the hollowed-out fangs of a capillary tube (formed by the apposition of the mandible and the jaw, or maxilla). The insect which has just seized its prey begins by injecting into it, through its jaws, digestive juice which liquefies the muscles and other organs; the enzymes having acted, the ant-lion sucks up the liquid which fills the prey. The strange larva represented here is that of the North African ant-lion, *Necrophylus troglophilus*, which has an inordinately long neck (in reality the prothorax). The body is buried in the sand, and the head, at the end of its 'handle', describes arcs of a circle and captures any insect which passes within its reach. *Phot. J. Carayon*

In licking insects, the mouth parts are modified profoundly. In bees and other Hymenoptera, the mandibles scarcely differ and the very elongate maxillae retain most of their parts, but the labium becomes a long tongue covered with hairs, along which runs a capillary duct leading to the digestive tube; this is the lapping-sucking apparatus, making it possible for the insect to extract nectar. In Lepidoptera, the tongue, which is sometimes enormously long (almost as long as the body in the humming bird hawk moth, *Macroglossa*), is formed only from the maxillae. Each one is a half-tube which engages tightly with its counterpart at the edges; the maxillae thus form a tight capillary tube. The extension and coiling of this long tube into a regular spiral are not easy to understand. When the tongue is coiled, a whole series of small muscles are in a relaxed state and the upper surface of the lingual tube is flat; but if the small muscles contract, then the upper surface becomes concave, which causes uncoiling. The mandibles have disappeared.

In piercing and sucking insects, such as Hemiptera or Diptera, the mouth parts become fairly strong sharp stylets. The apparatus differs according to orders; in the Hemiptera, it is made up of a very elongate tubular labium, within which fine needles move. These are in fact modified mandibles and maxillae.

It is difficult to understand the mechanism which makes it possible for extremely finely bristled stylets, like those of greenflies for instance, to sink into comparatively hard bodies. The stylets slide along each other and sink for a tiny fraction of an inch into the milieu one after the other. It can be shown by means of mechanical models that cables formed of four elements, mobile in relation to each other, may be made to progress rapidly.

In some Diptera (e.g. the house-fly), the mouth parts disappear, or nearly so, and their place is taken by a fleshy proboscis used for sucking.

Some devices of the mouth parts, consisting mainly of long fine hairs, make it possible for small aquatic insects to filter water through a screen of very fine bristles similar to the baleen of a whale; they can then retain Protozoa, microscopic algae and even colloidal particles.

The varied diet

The diets of insects have been the object of special study in recent years, because of their important economic repercussions.

There are fairly numerous cases of external digestion. Either the mandibles, with a fine duct running through them, or the mandibles and the very long maxillae pressed against each other to form a capillary tube, make it possible to inject digestive juices into the prey and then to re-absorb the nutritive liquid when the juices have done their work. This is how the predatory larvae of ground-beetles, tiger-beetles, ant-lions and the diving beetles, *Dytiscus*, operate; in the last case, external digestion takes place with lightning-like speed, and in a few minutes the inside of the prey may be completely liquified.

A large number of insects are phytophagous, i.e. they consume plants, but not like a cow browsing on grass. Insects attack plants in many different ways. The browsers (crickets, caterpillars, etc.) attack leaves at the edge or in the middle of the stalk. Beside them is placed the huge tribe of leaf miners, composed of tiny larvae which spend their life between the leaf's upper and lower epidermis; moreover, they gnaw at only one of them, usually the upper one, because it is richer in nutritive materials.

Scarcely less numerous are the piercing insects. They do not penetrate the leaf, but are content with sinking their fairly long stylets into it, as do bugs and green-flies. These stylets are not used haphazardly, but seek out the phloem ducts in which the elaborated sap circulates; it is only when the stylet plunges into these ducts that the food pump begins to function. In fact, capillarity alone suffices to make the liquid rise into the insect's oesophagus, as has been demonstrated by botanists who study sap: one of the best means of obtaining it pure is, in fact, to cut the rostrum of a green-fly near the head, and to watch a bead of pure sap forming at the

Cynips tozae (a gall-wasp) causes, by its bites on the black oak, the formation of spherical oak apple galls, each with a crown of tuberosities towards the upper pole. *Phot. Aldo Margiocco*

end of it. The main defect of this liquid is that it is not very concentrated, being poor in nitrogen and in various vitamins; but numerous and varied creatures which live in symbiosis lodged in the insect's mouth parts are able to provide it with what it lacks.

Then come the gall makers, the study of which constitutes a branch of entomology, cecidology. A special substance injected in the saliva of the females produces a tumour on the leaf. This tumour, which can be enormous, and frequently has a complex but constant structure, may be bristling with hairs, or, as in the case of the elm green-fly, contain a large central cavity. Inside are the insects, covered with a silvery coating which also surrounds a large drop of water within the cavity. It is clear that the temperature, humidity and probably also the composition of the atmosphere of these chambers are very far removed from outer conditions and that the elm green-fly lives in them in a world of its own.

The flower is exploited in a different way by innumerable insects. In it they particularly seek out the sugary secretion of the nectar-bearing glands. An idea of the number of interested

The black ant (*Dendrolasius fuliginosus*) is partial to the honeydew excreted by plant-lice which suck the elaborated sap of plants. *Phot. J. Six*

species can be obtained by observing the large umbels of the marsh hog-weed in the middle of summer. A great number of Hymenoptera, Diptera and Lepidoptera visit flowers in the adult stage; they take from them not only sugars, but also

a very concentrated nitrogenous food, pollen. By transporting the pollen from flower to flower, insects render to agriculture the inestimable service of cross-pollination. Of course the insect which has been studied mostly from this point of view is the bee, which can transport considerable quantities of nectar to the hive. At the height of the honey season, hives increase daily in weight by five pounds and sometimes more. A hive in fact needs several dozen pounds of nectar per year in order to subsist, and at least 26 pounds of pollen. These products are stored in the hive, and undergo a special elaboration before being distributed to the larvae. The nectar loses its water and the nature of its sugars is modified. Pollen undergoes intense lactic fermentation; in this case one can speak of pre-digestion.

Another source of sugary matter which is exploited by various insects is constituted by a secretion or honey-dew of arboreal plant-lice, in which ants and bees are especially interested. The red ants of the woods collect about 200 pounds of it per ant-hill per year. The honey of some country districts may rise to thousands of tons, and comes largely from honey-dew secreted by aphids.

Wood, living or dead, also attracts ravagers. If it is living, its composition becomes increasingly similar to that of leaves, but if it is dead, other food problems arise and quite different insects attack it. Dead wood contains little more than cellulose, a few other glucocides or sugars, a complex body, lignin, and a small proportion of proteins and mineral salts. This does not prevent some insects, like *Hylotrupes* (the domestic longhorn beetle), from feeding on it; but they only do so as a last resort, for it takes several years for the larva of *Hylotrupes* to develop into a perfect insect, unless the milieu is enriched with nitrogen (in which case it may complete its full growth in a few months).

The most closely studied wood-eating insect is the termite, of which there are many species, all presenting a common physiological character: they contain in their rectal paunches either a rich fauna of very special flagellates, or a bacterial flora, capable of digesting the cellulose in the wood assimilated by the insect. The termite itself is quite incapable of doing so: if it is plunged into oxygen, it suffers no direct ill effects, but its fauna of flagellates is destroyed and the insect dies of hunger, although continuing to eat. Some termites use another method of attacking wood: one finds in their termitaries very strange objects, fungus gardens which are like small wooden sponges that have been chewed and soaked in saliva. On these compost beds, the termites sow a special fungus (*Termitomyces*). It was formerly thought that they browsed on its fructifications, like the leaf-cutter ants (*Atta*), which also grow fungi, but this is not so. It has recently been established that it is neither the upper part of the compost bed nor the sporangia (small spheres of spores formed by the fungus) which are eaten, but its lower part. The fungus only partly attacks the cellulose, but by liberating a substantial amount of cellulose, it hydrolyses the lignin, therefore making the wood almost completely suitable for the termite. This is a unique arrangement in the world of insects. But this is not all: the cellulose is broken down by bacteria which live as symbionts in the insect's hind gut, anaerobically (i.e. without oxygen) producing fatty acids used as nourishment by the termites.

Termites are not the only insects with a digestion aided by various micro-organisms. In the case of the petroleum fly, symbiotic bacteria hydrolyse the paraffin, and in the hive-attacking wax moth, *Galleria mellonella*, a quite analogous case is found. Wax, like paraffin, is an extremely stable substance, but it cannot resist an intestinal bacterium of *Galleria*, which manages to hydrolyse it. Another very stable substance, keratin (which forms hairs, feathers and horns), is attacked by the caterpillars of various moths and by the larvae of small beetles, such as *Anthrenus*; but, in this case, the help of a symbiont is unnecessary, for these insects themselves produce enzymes which break down the sulphuretted bridges of the molecules of keratin and transform them into assimilable material.

Food metabolism repairs the losses in body substances and maintains energy exchanges. From this point of view, the reserves of insects are essentially constituted by sugars, glycogen and fat. A large quantity of these is needed (which perhaps accounts for the ravenous appetite of many insects), for loss of energy in insects is very high. A migratory locust in flight burns its reserve fat and loses 8 per cent of its body weight in an hour's flying; but it is capable of flying for many hours. This is nothing in comparison with insects which burn not fat but carbohydrates: for the same lapse of time, for instance, a bluebottle loses between 27 and 35 per cent of its weight. By way of comparison, a jet fighter, in the same time, loses only 12 per cent. On the other hand, the muscles of man and the higher animals, similar in muscular metabolism to insects, consume almost as much.

The circulatory apparatus

It must be clearly understood first of all that the circulatory apparatus and the circulation do not play the same role and have not the same importance in insects as they do in vertebrates. The blood has no respiratory role and does not carry any pigment which transports oxygen. It is the tracheae (air tubes) which bring the oxygen into the organism. An insect can therefore be bled white without seeming to be particularly affected: in fact, for the insect this merely amounts to momentary suspension of life, since its blood is used only for transporting food materials and the products of excretion. The heart—which may be removed without immediate apparent effect—is also much less important than that of vertebrates, and functions with much less precision.

The circulatory apparatus is roughly similar in all insects. It consists first of all of the heart, or dorsal vessel, extending along the dorsal side of the abdomen and sometimes prolonged towards the front into a long aorta. It is divided into a variable number of contractile chambers, which empty into each other, from back to front, following a fairly regular rhythm. The heart is enclosed in a zone limited towards the bottom by a membrane (the dorsal diaphragm), which is provided with special wing-shaped muscles extending from the neighbourhood of the heart to the periphery of the body. Around the heart are large cells. These are richly provided with tracheae and full of bulky pigment grains, which are products of excretion. On the lower part of the abdomen above the nerve chain, there is frequently another diaphragm, the ventral. It seems that, in many insects, the blood follows an opposite direction in each of the chambers delimited by these diaphragms: from back to front in the dorsal one, from front to back in the ventral one. There are, over and above these organs, numerous accessory hearts or pulsating organs which help to propel the blood into the narrowest and least accessible parts of the body, for instance the prothorax in the bee, near the large wing veins, to the base of the antennae, and so on.

The quantity of blood varies a good deal according to species, according to different stages in the same species and, for a single individual, according to many other diverse factors. Its colour varies, but its pigments have no respiratory role, except in a few cases, such as that of the larvae of chironomids; their red colour is due to haemoglobin, a rare exception in the insects. This pigment differs from that of mammals; it seems that it constitutes only an adjunct and not an essential factor in breathing. The blood contains a variety of leucocytes (white blood cells); and there is little agreement among experts on the classification of these. It may be that there is only a very small number of basic types, varying in form and general appearance according to circumstances. They undoubtedly have a role analogous to that of white corpuscles; they ingest waste cellular debris and foreign bodies accidentally introduced into the blood. They appear to play a certain part in the forming of scars from wounds.

It is usual to consider as annexes to the circulatory system cells full of fats and waxes which are found in all insects and which are usually referred to by the name of adipose bodies. They store various reserves, not only fats, but also protein, as in the winter bee for instance. Among this cellular complex or near it are other cells, the oenocytes, which are often full of a pale yellow pigment. Their role is disputed. It seems that they present a series of modifications connected with moulting.

The respiratory apparatus

The tracheal tubes bring oxygen to the organs of insects. The tracheal system is very complex and varies from species to species. One of its pecularities, found in the most active insects, is the contraction in many places of the tracheal tubes to form very bulky and numerous sacs (in the bee and the cockchafer, for instance). It is not known whether or not this system is as effective for the oxygenation of the tissues as that of vertebrates, in which the blood receives its oxygen supply in a very specific part of the body, then carries it towards the tissues. Moreover, there are arthropods, such as some forms of spiders, which possess both tracheae and lungs. Insects can survive conditions which would quickly cause the death of a vertebrate, especially asphyxia. The vacuum obtained by the water air-pump does not kill certain insects; and the air can be re-introduced suddenly without upsetting them either. What is more, it was noticed a long time ago by entomologists that certain very common butterflies, the burnet moths (*Zygaena* and neighbouring genera) are not killed in the entomologist's cyanide bottle: this is because they possess a system of respiratory transporters which is not inhibited by cyanide. Finally, another paradox, which would baffle many physiologists working on vertebrates alone: one cannot, in insects, draw a complete parallel between the production of bodily heat and the consumption of oxygen, nor pass indifferently from one to the other as a measure of metabolism. In fact, if one places a bee in an atmosphere of nitrogen, it does not die, unlike any mammal, and the calorimeter shows that it continues to produce a little heat; it has recourse to anaerobic respiration—it survives without oxygen.

Ventilation by continual respiratory movements by no means takes place in all insects. Even very active forms like cockroaches carry out ventilation movements only at irregular intervals. These normally consist of regular lowering and raising of the ventral part of the abdomen in relation to the dorsal part, but it is also possible to find telescopic move-

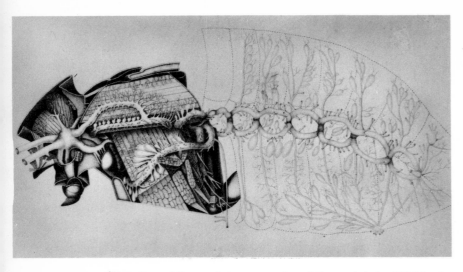

Dissection of the respiratory apparatus of the cockchafer (*Melolontha melolontha*) showing the main tracheal trunks and the aerial sacs which depend on it. *After H. Strauss-Durkheim*

are used also as physical gills: the oxygen is progressively absorbed by the insect and replaced by carbon dioxide gas, so that the oxygen dissolved in the water reaches a higher tension than that of the plastron and passes from the water into it. But the film of air gradually disappears and the insect has to rise to the surface to replenish its air supply.

The excretory apparatus

The excretory organ of insects differs from its counterparts in annelids (the nephridia) and in vertebrates (the kidney): it consists of long tubes called the Malpighian tubes, the size and number of which vary according to species. They originate at the junction of the midgut with the hind gut, continue in a forward direction, and, when they are very long, as is often the case, are folded several times in the visceral cavity.

The tubules are composed of large cubic cells arranged in a single layer, and present a variable appearance; their most usual colour is pale yellow. Their functions are studied by the injection of a colouring agent into the visceral cavity. It can then be seen that the Malpighian tubules, when they are very numerous (as in the bee and many other insects), by no means have equivalent properties: in fact, after the injection of several colouring agents together, the tubules can be seen to be coloured (i.e. they absorb and reject the colouring agents) in extremely varied ways. Moreover, it is not rare for a colouring agent to be expelled only by the distal or proximal extremity of one of the tubules, which means that they do not have the same properties throughout their length.

The Malpighian tubules excrete urea, uric acid, salts of sodium, potassium, ammonium, and other substances. Water taken from the blood is used to flush out waste matter, but most is reabsorbed by the wall of the hind gut and returned to the blood, which limits water loss and explains the production of fairly dry faeces. In the larvae, the products of excretion may have unexpected uses: they may be used, for instance, to reinforce the walls of the cocoon. Sometimes also, as in some Coleoptera (*Lebia*) or in some ant-lion larvae (*Myrmeleon*), the Malpighian tubules secrete silk which will be used to make the cocoon.

We have seen that the residues of the absorption of elaborated sap, which form the copious excretions of green-flies, are used by bees and ants as sugared food; the same often applies to other insects, e.g., scale insects, an interesting species of which, *Trabutina mannipara*, lives on tamarisks in the deserts of the Middle East. In this case the excreta dry quickly and drop to the ground in the form of shining scales which may be carried by the wind; nomads feed on them and it was perhaps this manna which made it possible for the Hebrews to subsist in the Sinai desert.

Insects elaborate many other substances which may be considered as products of excretion, but which do not necessarily come from the Malpighian tubules. They include, for instance, the very numerous poisons, of which the

ments, the different segments of the body fitting rhythmically into each other. To this are added openings and closings, regular or not, of the valves of the external openings or spiracles (stigmata). It has been observed in some insects that, on inspiration, the thoracic stigmata open, whereas those of the abdomen are closed; on expiration, the reverse takes place. This probably produces an air current directed and circulating from front to rear (from thorax to abdomen), but this is not general. Hibernating chrysalises often present phenomena very difficult to explain, such as the sudden expulsion of puffs of carbon dioxide.

Aquatic insects present adaptations to immersion which vary from one group to another, and from one species to another. Several have no gills and continue to inhale air in its natural state: some portions of their ventral integument are covered with fine, close-set water-repellent hairs, which tenaciously retain a layer of air at the time of diving. The stigmata open into this air plastron, and the insect periodically rises to the surface to renew the supply. These plastrons

Moulting is a complicated and important act in the insect's life; it is accompanied by profound physiological changes and upsets the animal's whole economy. Two phases of the moult of the desert locust, *Schistocerca gregaria*, are shown here. *On the left*, larval moult; *on the right*, final moult, the one from which the perfect insect emerges. *Phot. J. Six and Atesa—Atlas-Photo*

best known are those of bees and wasps, but there are many others. The bee's poison has been particularly well studied and its chemical composition has been almost completely elucidated; the fact is that it has undoubted therapeutic action on various rheumatic ailments, as is shown by statistics recording that bee-keepers are clearly less prone to this type of disease than others.

The products of excretion may gradually poison the environment in which the insect lives, as in several species of meal worms, which secrete caustic carbolic substances. These substances, applied to the organs of the adult or the larva, cause various kinds of deterioration or malformation.

Wax, on the other hand, which is produced by a considerable number of insects (scale insects and other Hemiptera), and not only by the bee, has no harmful effect and may, on the contrary, protect them against bad weather, as well as against their enemies. Some scale insects produce wax in such large quantities that its commercial exploitation may rival that of beeswax.

The endocrine glands

The discovery of internal secretion glands, or endocrine glands, and of hormones in insects was made only forty years ago. The hormonal mechanism of moulting was the first to be discovered, and was elucidated by the English biologist Sir Vincent Wigglesworth.

The water scorpion (*Nepa rubra*), is common in pools and ponds; with flattened body and wings held close to its dorsal surface by a push-button system of attachment, it moves comparatively slowly. It rises rhythmically to the surface to breathe and bears at its hind end a tube, or breathing siphon—at the base of which open the breathing orifices (stigmata). The water scorpion is carnivorous, feeding on live prey. It does not swim much and walks on the bottom or climbs amongst submerged plants. *Phot. J. Six*

Moulting

Moulting, or shedding of the integumentary cuticle and of the internal lining of the fore and hind gut, is a commonplace phenomenon, which is effected in different ways. The new cuticle, soft after the casting off of the old, hardens and, being more ample than the one it replaces, makes it possible for the insect to grow.

The process in itself is very complicated: the initial impulse comes from a special group of neuro-secretory cells, situated in the zone of the brain called the *pars intercerebralis*. There then occurs in the integument a series of changes which we shall study further on. These lead to the shedding of the old cuticle, which usually splits on the mid-dorsal line of the thorax and from which emerges the insect of the following stage. But, at least in insects with complete metamorphoses (known as Holometabola), there emerges from the larval skin a completely different insect at the final moult. The new insect is often equipped with wings and genital organs which are more or less developed. What then has happened between the last larval stage and the adult stage?

Everything depends on the presence behind the brain of a pair of tiny glands (*corpora allata*), which are at the height of their secretory activity during the larval stages; and as long as they function and secrete the juvenile hormone, a new cuticle similar to the old one will form under the the one the larva has just shed. Physiologists believe that the brain, at a specific moment, suppresses the *corpora allata*, but just how is not known. All that is known is that, in a very wide range of insects, the juvenile hormone is present in the larva and absent in the adult. These remarkable conclusions are the result of essentially very simple experiments which were carried out on *Rhodnius prolixus*: this insect has a very elongate head on which one can readily perform ablation and ligature operations. The removal of the *corpora allata* from a larva leads to immediate metamorphosis, even in larvae which are still very young, which results in the production of pygmy adults. But if *corpora allata* of young larvae are implanted in the body of a larva ready to carry out its last moult and to be transformed into an adult, it carries out an extra moult and is transformed into a giant larva. German chemists have recently managed to isolate the juvenile hormone, or at least a substance which has most of its properties: this is farnesol, a compound which is encountered in the course of the synthesis of certain fats or waxes in many animals and plants; this is why it is widely distributed in nature. It seems that farnesol or related compounds stimulate the genes which maintain the larval form. Moreover, the hormone can be applied to this or that part of the body, and this leads to changes which are limited to the part in question, which may remain larval while the rest of the integument passes to the adult state. In nature, this hardly ever occurs, unless adverse conditions hinder or upset the normal equilibrium between the hormones and the organism; this may happen, for instance, to mealworm larvae (*Tenebrio*), reared at too low a temperature, which are transformed into monsters mid-way between larvae and nymphs or between nymphs and adults. This transformation under adverse conditions is called prothetely or metathetely.

In other insects, especially in the stick insect, *Carausius morosus*, the juvenile hormone appears to exercise its action for an abnormally long time, for the female reaches maturity and begins to lay without showing the least trace of wings and while many parts of her body present indisputable juvenile characters. It is to a variant of these phenomena that the name neoteny, i.e. the development of adult characters in an individual which remains larval in general appearance, is given. It is sometimes possible, moreover, in removing the *corpora allata*, to note the existence of hidden neoteny. In the cockroach, for instance, adults operated on in this way moult anew and are transformed into ultra- or super-adults. The prolonged influence of the juvenile hormone previously prevented them from doing so.

The mechanism of moulting has not been totally explained by the most recent experiments, since these deal with only the hindering rather than the triggering factors. In *Rhodnius*, it seems that one of the triggering factors is the distension of the integument caused by the blood which this insect sucks until it is considerably swollen. The excitation of certain nerves brought about by this distension stimulates cells of the *pars intercerebralis* in the brain which activate a special gland, the prothoracic gland, situated, as its name indicates, in the

connected with the genital apparatus depend on the hormone of the *corpora allata*. Removal of the ovaries induces the abnormal enlargement (hypertrophy) of the *corpora allata*; the implantation of these glands restores the ovaries to their normal size; and they therefore exercise a reciprocal influence on each other. However, some butterflies, the *corpora allata* of which have been removed in a larval stage, may acquire functional ovaries and even lay fertile eggs. Here, too, a regulatory hormone emitted by the brain controls the functioning of the *corpora allata*; and a hormone originating from the prothoracic gland controls the development of the ovaries and of the testes, as well as the maturation of the gonads. In this case, too, the hormones of the *corpora allata* probably play a role inhibiting the development of the gonads—that is, fundamentally still the role of juvenile

In gregarious locusts, the group acts on the individual and modifies its colour. For instance, the larvae represented above are of the desert locust, *Schistocerca gregaria*; one, on the left, has been subjected to the effect of the group; the other has developed in isolation. *Phot. J. Six*

prothorax. (The prothorax is situated nearest to the front of the insect.) This gland's function is to secrete the moulting hormone, or ecdysone (recently isolated in a chemically pure state). If the neuro-secretory cells of the brain have not suppressed the *corpora allata*, a larval moult occurs; otherwise, the larva is transformed into an adult.

This, then is the hormonal mechanism of the moulting of insects; it undergoes considerable variations in different cases. In a large butterfly, the hormonal regulation of which has been carefully studied, everything starts off in this way, until the prothoracic gland induces its transformation stage from larval stage to maturation (pupation), the *corpora allata* being excluded. Then development stops and the chrysalis (pupa) enters a resting stage, or diapause, under the influence of a special hormone produced by the sub-oesophageal ganglion. The neuro-secretory activity of the cerebral cells then stops for many months, i.e. the winter. A period of cold followed by a rise in temperature then reactivates the cells of the *pars intercerebralis*, which are excited anew the prothoracic glands, and metamorphosis is completed.

Hormones and breeding

The maturation of the ovaries and possibly that of the glands

hormones—whereas the prothoracic glands probably have an accelerating effect. But, at least in some flies, the existence of a third hormone is suspected. This is in the neurosecretory cells of the brain and in the *corpora allata*, and probably acts directly on ovarian function.

Hormones and changes of colour

A large number of insects are sensitive to the coloration of the environment and probably adapt themselves to it by a nervous or neuro-hormonal mechanism based on the eyes. One case is especially remarkable, namely that of the stick insect, *Carausius morosus*. Over and above the changes in colour which depend on the nature of the substratum, it displays other regular changes depending on the daily passage from light to darkness. These changes are not produced by the extension and retraction of pigmentary cells, the chromatophores, which are present in many invertebrates, for insects do not possess cells of this type. One observes only the migration, concentration or dispersion of brown and red granules contained in the hypodermic cells. These movements are controlled by a hormone found in the brain, and also, though in a smaller quantity, in the ventral and sub-oesophagian ganglia and in the *corpora allata*.

Migratory locusts and certain crickets undergo changes in coloration brought about by grouping or isolation. In these phenomena there are also hormonal interactions, in which the *corpora allata* are involved. The changes in hue of the pigment cells of *Corethra* (culicid Diptera) also depend on hormonal action, but there is less information available about the action of hormones on the pigment of insects than on those of, say, crustaceans.

The moulting process

Having some idea of the causes which trigger moulting, we must return to the complex unfolding of the phenomena in the course of this crisis in the insect's life; there is little doubt that each part in it depends on an equilibrium of the hormonal factors or on a special hormone.

Under the action of the moulting hormone, the cuticle is separated from the underlying epidermis and between them there appears a special liquid—the exuvial liquid or moulting fluid. At the same time, the epidermis grows and its cells actively multiply and secrete the rudimentary forms of the new cuticle. Immediately, enzymes appear in the exuvial fluid which digest the old cuticle; finally, the liquid, with all the products of digestion, is re-absorbed through the new cuticle and is brought back into the general economy of the organism. Thus, the space between the old and the new cuticle becomes almost dry. But Wigglesworth rightly points out that it is only the chitin, comparatively soft as it is, which can be digested in this way. What about sclerotin, this extremely tough and hard protein which was mentioned earlier? Thin lines of rupture appear in this, usually along the dorsal part of the body. They exist in the insect outwith moulting times, corresponding to linear zones composed only of chitin and unsclerified. Therefore, the moulting fluid can completely digest the cuticle along these lines, and the least pressure is enough to break the thin layer of epicuticle which is all that covers the line of rupture. Immediately, the insect, strongly contracting its abdominal muscles, greatly increases the pressure (in some species, by up to $3\frac{3}{4}$ inches of mercury) in its thorax and sometimes even swallows air to increase it still more. It escapes from its old skin by the line of rupture of the thorax, hangs on to a branch and spreads its wings, still under the influence of the thrust of the blood. A hormone determines moulting by causing the hardening and the coloration of the cuticle, which take place simultaneously throughout the body.

The genital glands

The plan of the external genital organs of insects is extremely complicated and variable, but, on the other hand, the internal anatomy of the genital glands is fairly simple and uniform. The females possess a series of tubes (oviaroles), in which the eggs ripen progressively, descending slowly towards the oviducts and receiving, on the way, their supply of yolk. They escape at the end into a common tube (oviduct). The male organs present a somewhat similar arrangement. The system of accessory glands is complicated and varies from one species to another; its physiological role has not been determined.

Female genital apparatus of the cockchafer: *Acgl*, accessory gland; *Od*, oviducts; *Ov*, complete ovary; *Ov'*, ovary without the distal parts of the ovarioles; *Sv*, seminal vesicle; *Vu*, vulva. Although the genital organs of the various orders of insects are based on the same plan, they differ a good deal in detail.
After H. Strauss-Durkheim

The Membracidae are bugs of the order Homoptera which can be recognized by the extraordinary development of the pronotum (roof of the first thoracic segment) which is prolonged above the abdomen by a fairly elongate point. This pronotum, according to species, is most varied in appearance. Compared with the insect's body, it is huge and quite disproportionate. This unexplained hypertrophy seems to be more of a hindrance than an advantage for the species.
Here are just a few examples of African and American Membracidae: *top left*, female *Oxyrachis pendata* mounting 'guard' over her eggs, arranged chevron-fashion, on the bark of a tree; *top right*, mating of *Monocentrotus hyalipennis* (Africa); *middle left*, the mother with her larvae (Africa); *middle right*, two adults—male just after moulting and the female on the left with tricorn pronotum (tropical Africa); *bottom left*, female and male *Hamma rectum* with ultra-hypertelic pronotum (Africa); *bottom right*, *Ceresa bubalus* sucking the sap of a plant (temperate North America, introduced into Europe a little before 1930). *Phot. Michel Boulard and Edouard Cauvin.*

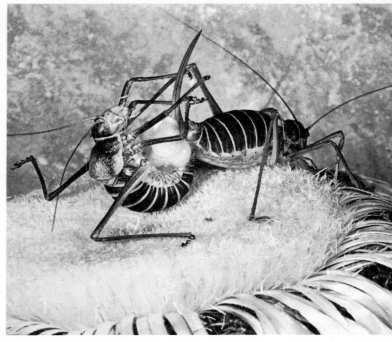

The mating of the short-winged katydid.

Top left, the couple: the male has sent out its call and the female has answered it. In insects, 'musical' emissions make recognition possible and facilitate the coming together of individuals of opposite sex. They set off compulsory and oriented movements (phonotaxy).

Top right, the mating; the male places its bulky spermatophore at the entrance to his companion's genital passages. *Bottom left:* on completion of the act, the female moves away, paying no more attention to the male while carrying the spermatophore like some trophy. *Bottom right:* a little later, she bends over herself and eats the part of the spermatophore which does not contain sperm. The couple belongs to the species *Ephippiger terrestris*. Both sexes of these katydids have very abbreviated wings; the elytra (forewings) present a musical organ (mirror) in both the female and the male. Ephippigers are very characteristic of Mediterranean fauna; a single species, *Ephippiger ephippiger*, has taken a northerly course and reached the Rhine; it has penetrated into central Europe coming from the East. The western and eastern routes both start from the southern shores of the Mediterranean. Laying takes place on land, the ovipositor firmly sunk in the ground. *Ephippiger terrestris* lives only in southern France and northern Italy. (Actual size: 1–1½ inches). *Phot. J. Six*

Pair of burnet moths (*Zygaena sarpedon*) under an inflorescence. Copulation in this species lasts for several hours. *Phot. J. Six*

The eggs

The formation of the eggs calls for a considerable quantity of proteins, sugar and fats, especially as, in some species, they are very numerous: although the cabbage white butterfly lays only 600, *Drosophila* lays 3000. One of the chief characteristics of social insects is the enormous number of eggs laid by a single fertile individual, or queen; a queen bee may lay up to 20,000 eggs per day or one egg every 4½ seconds, and that during more than 100 days of annual activity. The queens of the polygynous ant *Formica polyctena* are not very fertile and probably do not lay more than about twenty eggs per day; but there may be more than 5000 queens in one nest, which amounts to 100,000 eggs per day. It is true that a good number of these eggs are used to feed larvae—if this were not the case, the ground of our forests would long ago have been covered with a thick blanket of ants. Finally, the monstrous queens of some termites (*Bellicositermes, Macrotermes* and *Amitermes*), which are as big as sausages—whereas the workers surrounding them are not much bigger than our ants—lay an egg every 2 seconds and may live to an age of 50 years or even longer! This means that their progeny amount to many millions.

The weight of the eggs of a *Drosophila* far exceeds that of the mother, which is a good indication of the alimentary metabolism of the female during ovogenesis. However, some butterflies absorb no food in the adult stage and depend entirely for the production of eggs on larval reserves. In these cases, the eggs are already completely developed in the nymph (chrysalis) of mature age. They are laid shortly after emergence from the chrysalis and the female does not survive long after laying.

Mating

The union of the sexes in insects occurs in diverse ways which involve an almost unimaginable variety of structures and behaviour. Setting aside the simplest cases in which the penis is simply inserted into the female's vagina, one passes immediately to insects such as bugs of the genus *Anthocoris*, in which the penis bursts the wall of the female's genital tracts and liberates the sperm into the body cavity. In some cases, the existing female genital tracts are not used and the sperm is injected by the male laterally or dorsally through the body wall. Even in the young female, which has not yet mated, a special spot appears on the dorsal cuticle which is the very place through which the male will later thrust his penis. The sperm then spreads all through the body cavity, and subsequently accumulates rapidly near the ovaries, in which it is united with the oocytes.

In many insects, the sperm is contained in a fairly complex gelatinous capsule, the spermatophore. This may be implanted at the entrance to the female's vagina, into which it empties progressively; but sometimes nature adopts the oddest and most improbable ways to ensure the transfer. In the springtails (*Collembola*), for instance, the male possesses a spermatophore equipped with a kind of pedestal, which he fixes to the ground. He then goes in search of the female, and lifts her by the mandibles, in such a way that her external genital opening caps the sperm mass and engulfs it. Then the spermatophore empties into the female genital tracts.

Development of a hemimetabolic insect: *Sehirus dubius*, the thesium shield-bug (Hemiptera of the Heteroptera sub-order). *On the left*, the

Acoustic and chemical stimuli . . .

Often, males and females are some distance apart from each other, but various stimuli make it possible for them to be brought close together. These stimuli may be acoustic, as in

eggs and the newly hatched young; *top right*, a larva before the last moult; *bottom right*, the adult or perfect insect. *Phot. J. Six*

most of the grasshoppers: their stridulation has several roles. First of all, it warns possible rivals not to approach; but it also calls the females, who could not be located visually in the thickness of the meadow grass.

Often, location is of a chemical nature. The classic example is that of the females of the large nocturnal hawk moths, Sphingidae, and silk moths, Bombycidae, which have at the apex of the abdomen a tiny scent gland whose secretion attracts the male at a distance of almost six miles! Obviously, this poses extremely difficult problems, for it can be calculated that in a radius of six miles, there could not be at the periphery more than one molecule per cubic yard! Under these conditions, the sense of smell as we know it can no longer even assume a directing role. So various authors have presented a theory which seems strange at first, but which is gradually gaining acceptance: male moths are probably sensitive not so much to smell, but to the vibrations of the molecule in the infra-red. To simplify the theory a good deal, it is probably not a nose that the males possess, but rather an infra-red spectrometer. In any case, it is certain that the attraction does call for the emission of particles of matter, for if the female is kept in an air-tight glass bell-jar, she no longer attracts males. Similarly, a female deprived of her scent glands is no longer attractive; and finally, if one places side by side a female who has undergone such an operation, and the glands which have just been removed from her, the male will disregard the female and try to mate with the tiny glands beside her. This was demonstrated, almost a century ago, by the French biologist Edward Balbiani.

. . . and nuptial displays

In other cases, attraction does not operate over such long distances, but the male must, as it were, win over the female, whose first reflex seems to be to avoid his advances. The most remarkable devices ensure the success of this delicate phase. In cockroaches, for instance, the male raises his wing-cases and thus exposes certain glands placed at their base. The female approaches and sucks up their contents. The male takes advantage of this to attach his spermatophore. In some species of crickets, the male extends his hind legs towards the female who approaches them and breaks in them certain spines from which flow a substance of which she is apparently excessively fond, and the male takes advantage of this to mate and deposit his bulky spermatophore.

Other still more complex procedures may be used, and, strangely enough, they can only be compared with the behaviour of birds. The very common small flies of the genus *Empis* indulge, like some birds, in a nuptial offering. The male is accepted only if he offers the female prey wrapped up in silk; the female does not eat this but rolls it between her legs. In other *Empis* species, the silk ball is empty, but this symbolic present is nevertheless indispensable to mating. One finds in birds similar symbolic presents of a yet uneaten prey, twig or branch with blossom. It does not follow, however, that

The vapourer moth, *Orgyia antiqua*, of the family Lymantriidae is remarkable for its sexual dimorphism. The male is an ordinary looking moth; the female has no wings, and mates and lays on her cocoon (*above*). If the female is not fertilized, she still lays and the eggs develop normally—a good example of optional parthenogenesis. The caterpillar (*below*), which lives on oak, hornbeam, pine, spruce, larch, etc., is characterized by the tufts of hairs if bears on each segment and by clusters of much longer bristles. *Phot. J. Six*

the still unknown mechanism of these acts is the same in birds as in insects.

The grayling butterfly *Hipparchia semele* performs a complicated nuptial dance, which has been very closely studied by the zoo-psychologists of the objectivist school. The male waits for the female on certain sites, which are always the same, and rushes towards her, then circles her, carrying out a special gliding flight; after a short time, the female alights on the ground, and the male then describes around her a series of semi-circles before coming up to face her. If the female accepts mating, she slips her antennae between the male's slightly parted forewings, in which scent scales are situated. The male then copulates.

One of the most astonishing cases is connected with the social Hymenoptera, bumble-bees and hive bees. Male bumble-bees always follow the same route in the woods, marking the branches bordering their path with the secretion from their mandibulary glands; the secretion gives off a special odour. This defines a rounded track in which the females seeking copulation will be grouped. In hive bees, the males, which are never seen gathering honey because their probosces are too short, fly off only to assemble, sometimes in considerable numbers, in certain fixed places, where they set up such a commotion as to give the impression of a swarm. These assembly places incidentally have been known from time immemorial by apiculturists, who call them bee balls. Some are known to have been held in the same place for more than sixty years! The queens make their way to these assembly places, in which the males accept mating, which they refuse elsewhere. Even a queen held in the experimenter's hand may be accosted by the males. But in any other place, the males do not even approach them. This apparently explains the failure of countless attempts to obtain the mating of female bees with specially-chosen males under artificial conditions: no doubt the desired site was missing. It is not known by what criteria the males choose these sites.

Laying

Laying brings into play behavioural mechanisms just as astonishing as mating. Some insects spare their progeny part of the hazards of existence by giving birth to them in an advanced stage of development (viviparity); not only does the larva hatch in the mother's uterus, but also, at least in *Glossina*, it no longer depends wholly on the reserves of the egg. Special lactiferous glands open into kinds of papillae just at the level of the larva's mouth. The larva breathes by pushing its spiracles clear of the mother's vaginal orifice. Following what evolution, and in accordance with what laws, does nature create such closely related devices in lineages as far apart as mammals and insects?

Other insects operate a short circuit of another kind, developing parthogenetically, as in plant-lice. This means that the unfertilized ovum develops into a genetically exact adult. In some cases, not only is reproduction viviparous, but also, while the young are still in the mother's oviduct, embryos are already developing in their own genital tracts.

If the young are laid at the egg stage, the mother will build

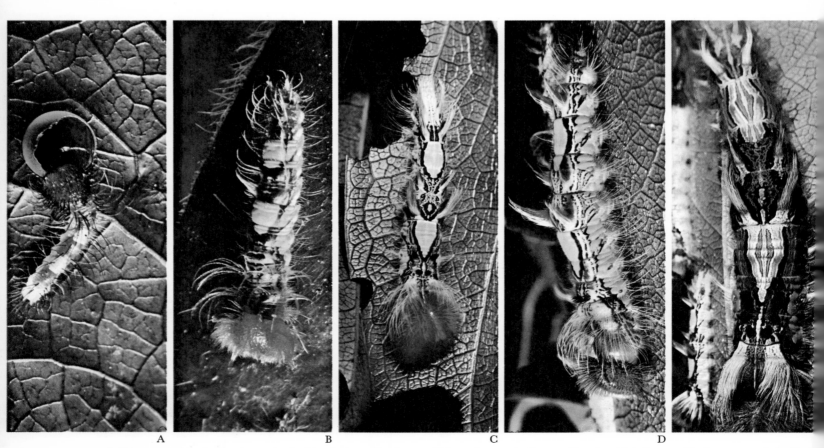

A   B   C   D

Different stages in the development of a *Morpho* butterfly: *A*, caterpillar emerging from the egg, shell of which can be seen; *B*, caterpillar after first moult; *C*, caterpillar after third; *D*, caterpillar in process of moulting *E*, caterpillar after fourth. *Opposite page: F*, caterpillar preparing for

them a shelter composed either of a leaf rolled and cut artistically, as with many leaf rolling weevils (*Rhynchites*), or of the ovary of a sterile flower, which she will contrive to fertilize. This is the case in the small moth *Pronuba yuccasella*, which makes a ball of pollen and transports it on the pistil of the yucca flower, situated so far from the stamens that its fertilization is impossible without intervention. Finally, sometimes, as in mole-crickets or earwigs, the mother remains next to the eggs and tends them until they hatch. However, apart from the social insects, maternal care is very rare in insects.

Cycles of metamorphosis in insects

For some time, entomologists have noticed that metamorphosis follows very different paths in the various orders.

The Greek word metabole, meaning change, has been the basis of best describing them. At the foot of the insect family tree there are primitive small forms, some of which are very old and go back at least as far as the Devonian period: Collembola, Protura and Thysanura. Like all arthropods, they are characterized by moulting, they have no wings and their external appearance undergoes little change: for this reason, they are called Ametabola.

The Prometabola are the first insects in which wings appeared, and their origin is also very ancient, for they are held to have been related to the Paleodictyoptera of the Permo-Carboniferous. Their great speciality is what one might call double metamorphosis, for the last larval stage (sub-imago) possesses functional wings, but it undergoes another moult to produce the final imago, which is also winged. This case is unique in insects, but it does seem that, in the Paleodictyoptera, the last larval stages had wings.

We pass from there to the Hemimetabola or insects with incomplete metamorphosis. These include Odonata, Plecoptera, Orthoptera, Isoptera, Dermaptera, Embioptera, Zoraptera, Mallophaga, Thysanoptera and Hemiptera. In these, metamorphosis occurs between the last nymphal stage and the adult stage; there is no sub-imago. The nymphs do have alar (wing) buds, but they are not functional. Then come the Holometabola, which have a complete metamorphosis. These insects (Hymenoptera, Coleoptera, Lepidoptera and Diptera) have a rest stage between the larva and the adult: this is the nymph (chrysalis or pupa). In the course of a nymphal stage, the wings start to develop, but remain enclosed in sacs, from which they emerge at the imaginal stage. The nymphal cuticle immediately splits, the wings emerge from the nymph's alar sheaths and are extended until they reach their final size in the imago.

Here, metamorphosis occurs only between two stages, as in the Prometabola and the Hemimetabola, but two qualitative changes are observed. The first is between the last larva and the nymph, the second between the nymph and the adult. The larvae differ from those of the Hemimetabola

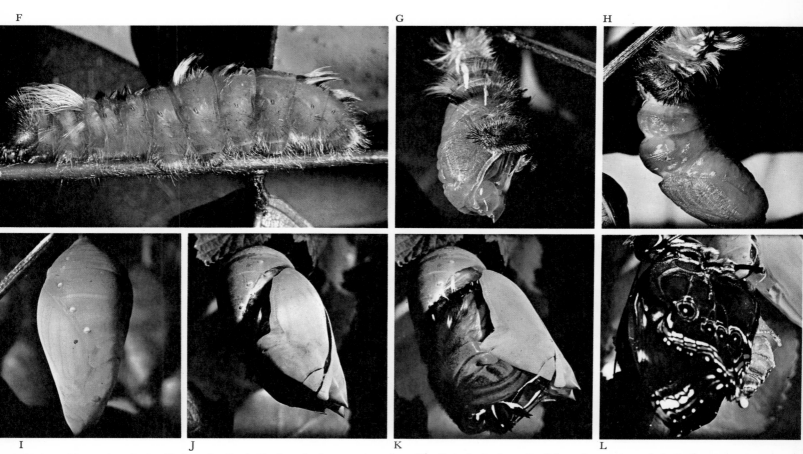

nymphosis and becoming shorter (3 days duration); *G*, chrysalis frees itself from larval skin; *H*, more advanced stage; *I*, complete chrysalis; *J*, chrysalis splits; *K*, butterfly frees itself from its envelope; *L*, butterfly emerged, wings not yet extended completely. *Phot Soledad-Otero*

because they have no alar buds; their morphology is varied. They may have legs and pro-legs like caterpillars; or, on the contrary, they may be completely without them (maggots of flies). Usually, larvae which have legs and lead an active life are found rather in the primitive groups, like rove-beetles and ground-beetles; the legs disappear in the most evolved groups, like the weevils (Curculionidae). The same applies to the Hymenoptera; the lower forms (saw-flies) have larvae which are like caterpillars, but, again, their appendages are suppressed (apodous) in the most evolved parasites and in the social species.

How should metamorphosis be interpreted?

One obviously wonders about the meaning and biological utility of metamorphosis. Some authors, who adhere to the explanations of neo-Darwinism, think that the larvae, being devoid of wings, may devote all their energy not to movement, but to obtaining food and building up reserves; and, leading a somewhat inactive life, they would not risk damaging their wings, which are always quite fragile. Wings would therefore be reserved for the only phase of life during which it will be advisable to distribute their eggs most advantageously and to choose the best possible environment for the development of offspring.

Only one point is plausible in this opinion, namely that the flight of an insect is in fact very wasteful of energy, and consumes a good deal of fat or glucosides, as the case may be. As for the rest, we have no knowledge of how to measure the biological advantage produced by a mechanism as complicated as that of metamorphosis. Moreover, the countless species of insects in which the larvae are very active, and the equally numerous ones in which the adult has no wings, do not seem to be less successful in life than the others.

As the tendency towards complete metamorphosis progresses, the larvae appear to hatch at more and more precocious stages of development. In the Neuroptera, Mecoptera, Trichoptera and Lepidoptera and in the lower Coleoptera and the lower Hymenoptera, the larvae have legs; but, in these last two orders at least, the larvae of the higher forms apparently hatch before the legs are developed, and remain thus during the whole of their larval development. In the Diptera, all the larvae are born without legs.

Another theory has it that larval evolution has developed independently from the evolution of the adult. In the higher forms, the larva is often immersed in a superabundant nutritive environment and has nothing to do but assimilate, so that all the useless organs, like those of locomotion, may degenerate without disadvantage. This would be, fundamentally, a form of parasitic degeneration. This applies, above all, to the larvae of the social insects and to those of the parasitic Hymenoptera and Diptera, weevils, and wood-eating insects.

In support of the second theory, of larval evolution independent from that of the adult, various facts can be quoted, as, for example, the development in the larvae of organs quite different from those of the adult and which will completely disappear at metamorphosis. Instances of this are the tracheal gills of the aquatic larvae of Odonata, Ephemeroptera and Plecoptera, which, in these three cases, have developed on different regions of the body and have not evolved in the same way. Again, countless silk-producing glands which no longer exist in the adult, are constituted by salivary glands in Lepidoptera and Hymenoptera, and become tarsal (pertaining to the terminal part of the leg) in the Embioptera, and also a special zone of Malpighian tubules emitted by the anus in the Neuroptera and some Coleoptera.

It seems also that metamorphosis radically separating the period of growth (larva) from that of differentiation (nymph) and of reproduction (adult) leads to a considerable acceleration of development, perhaps because it suppresses the interferences and the delays which would occur if each process was not independent of the two others. The primitive forms with incomplete metamorphosis or without metamorphosis may thus pass through twenty to forty stages, which develop over a period of several months or even years. In contrast, the most evolved species have only five or six larval stages. In the higher Diptera, a generation may develop entirely in a few days, or in a few weeks in the higher Hymenoptera like the bee. This enables insects to take full advantage of food resources when they are plentiful, but of short duration. Moreover, the success of the Holometabola is greater than that of the Ametabola, as is shown by the following table:

Homometabola	..	..	..	..	537,960 species
Hemimetabola	..	..	..	..	83,650 species
Peurometabola	..	..	..	..	1420 species
Ametabola	..	..	..	..	1270 species

Hermaphroditism

The life cycle of insects presents itself under infinitely varied aspects. This is due to hermaphroditism (fairly rarely), but more often to parthenogenesis, combined with the existence of several different larval forms. Hermaphroditism, with the presence in the same individual of testes and ovaries, although sometimes in different degrees of development, is found in rudimentary form in the stone fly *Perla marginata*: this possesses between the two testes a non-functional mass of ovarioles. On the other hand, hermaphroditism is completely functional in the scale insect *Icerya purchàsi*, which can even fertilize itself. Finally, in one dipteran which lives among termites, *Termitoxenia*, hermaphroditism is again complete and includes even the presence of separate genital orifices. The testes mature first, then the body undergoes profound morphological alterations, the abdomen becomes very bulky (physogastric), and the ovaries develop in their turn. In this case, the insect may fertilize itself, and may also pair reciprocally with another individual.

Parthenogenesis and alternation of generations

Parthenogenesis is very frequent in insects, and manifests itself in countless ways. It has developed, in the course of evolution, in the most diverse groups. There is arrhenotoky, when the unfertilized eggs produce males and the fertilized ones females, as in the hive bee; thelytoky, when the unfertilized eggs almost always produce females; and amphitoky, when both sexes may come from virgin eggs.

Parthenogenesis may be compulsory or optional. Optional parthenogenesis is found in insects in which the eggs may be, although not always, fertilized. The classic example of this is the hive bee; here, the queen—if she so wishes—fertilizes her eggs, which then produce females; if they are unfertilized, they produce parthenogenetic males. The latter is a case of optional arrhenotoky, which is found also in many aculeate (prickly) and tenthredinid Hymenoptera, in the Thysanoptera (*Anthothrips*), the American race of the white-fly (*Trialeurodes vaporariorum*), and others. Optional thelytoky is rarer; it exists, for instance in one race of the scale insect *Lecanium hesperidum*, and in many phasmids. Optional amphitoky occurs in many moths (Psychidae, *Orgyia*, etc.).

In cases of compulsory parthenogenesis, the eggs produced during a specific period remain virgin. It may be constant in some species of phasmid (*Caurasius morosus, Bacillus rossii*), in which males appear only rarely (and which usually are sterile intersexes) or not at all (some Psychidae, Coleoptera such as *Otiorrhynchus*, and the Thysanoptera).

Optional parthenogenesis has developed in plant-lice (aphids) and gall-wasps (cynipids), among others. It may depend on the climate or on diverse variations of the nutritional environment.

For plant-lice, a typical cycle is as follows. A fertilized egg, produced in autumn by the only sexual generation of the year, hibernates. From this egg is born the female founder of the wingless, viviparous, parthenogenetic generations which will live on the plant in which the winter egg was laid. Several such generations are produced, but as the season advances, some finally acquire wings. These winged emigrants may fly away to a plant of another species, but they are still virgin and viviparous. If they have changed plant, they are called exiles, and their appearance may differ radically from that of individuals which have remained on the mother plant. The exiles will produce exclusively virgin and wingless individuals; those which have remained on the mother plant will give birth to either wingless or winged generations. Finally, when winter is about to start, there appear, in the colonies of the two species of plants, winged, virgin and viviparous individuals, called sexuparous, since these produce the sexual generation. These sexuparous insects always return to the primitive host plant, and the sexual generation which they produce on it generally shows pronounced sexual dimorphism, the male usually being winged and the female without (apterous). The females, this time, are oviparous, and it is they who, after fertilization, lay the winter egg.

In some plant-lice, migration is effected from one organ of the plant to another, for instance from the leaves to the roots, as happens in the course of the cycle of the phylloxera of the vine (*Dactylosphaera vitifolii=Phylloxera vastatrix*). The sexuparous females are of two kinds: some produce only males, others only females (a larger egg). These sexuparous females lay their eggs on the vine's aerial portion, i.e. the leaves. The true sexual generation, which arise from these eggs, are wingless, small, and have atrophied mouth parts and intestines. After mating, each female lays only a single egg, which will survive the winter, and produces a female founder. It is known that various species of American vines, such as *Vitis riparia, Vitis rupestris* and *Vitis berlandieri*, are scarcely troubled by the attacks of the root-dwelling insects which kill the European vine (*Vitis vinifera*). Some eighty years ago, the European wine region was saved by grafting local vine-plants on to these species with resistant roots.

In Europe, in some cold climates, neither the winged nor the true sexed generations are formed. Instead, the species maintains itself through the indefinitely parthenogenetic root-dwelling females and the insect goes from one vine-stock to another by passing through cracks in the ground—*Phylloxera* does not breed in sand.

Parthenogenesis may be complicated by a strange phenomenon, paedogenesis, or precocious parthenogenetic reproduction of the young, no longer within an adult, but within a larva. This type of cycle is found in some gnats, the Cecidomyidae, such as *Miastor* and *Oligarces paradoxus*. In *Oligarces*, winged females of the sexual generation lay eggs which develop normally into larvae, but within each larva there rapidly develop a large number of other larvae, which emerge by perforating the skin of their progenitor. Some of these second generation larvae also produce larvae by paedogenetic means. But some will produce larvae, still by paedogenesis, which, passing through an extra stage, will cease to show the same process (characterized by a considerable increase in size), and will soon become pupae. From them will emerge male and female sexed insects, which will re-start the cycle after having mated. One can imagine the number of descendants produced by a single pair of sexed insects which breed in this way. It is put at several thousand larvae.

Oviparity and viviparity

Although a very large number of insects breed by laying eggs, there are some which are ovoviviparous, i.e. the first embryonic stages take place in the maternal oviduct. This is the case in many scale insects, in the bed-bug, *Cimex lectularius*, and in certain flies. This may go so far that the new-born larva is already able to crawl. There is thus a transition towards true viviparity, in which the larva develops completely in the maternal oviduct and is active from the moment of its expulsion (larviparity); sometimes, it is so advanced that it is transformed into a pupa at the time of its emergence (pupiparity). Larviparity is found in many mayflies, e.g. *Cloeon dipterum*; in aphids, in *Hemimerus talpoides*, a kind of earwig living in the fur of the Gambian rat (*Cricetomys gambianus*); in the Polyctenidae, Hemiptera living in the fur of sloths (*Cholaepus*); in many chrysomelid beetles; in the Strepsiptera, some psocids and Diptera, especially the Cyclorrhapha. It is in the last-named that pupiparity reaches its summit, especially in tse-tse flies or glossinas: the larva develops in the mother's dilated oviduct or uterus, feeds on the glandular secretions of the wall, and is not expelled until it is about to metamorphose.

Apart from the extraordinary case of the uterus of the glossinas, there are other ways of helping the larva to develop in the maternal milieu. In the mayfly *Cloeon*, each ovariole produces only one egg, and the rest of the organ degenerates and becomes the food on which the young larva feeds, the latter developing *in situ*, as soon as the egg has reached the oviduct. In other insects, the egg, with no shell and little or no yolk, develops in the basal part of the ovariole. Its nutrition is ensured either by the follicular cells (some Chrysomelidae and aphids), or more rarely by localized expansions of the neighbouring tissues, which act as a placenta, e.g. *Archipsocus* and *Hemimerus*.

Different forms of one and the same species: the phases

In one and the same species, under the action of environmental factors, considerable modifications in colour, size, shape and rate of development may occur. The rate of development varies in enormous proportions, according to temperature and quantity of food at the insect's disposal.

Thus, the predatory hemipteran *Perillus bioculatus* shows, under the influence of temperature, a considerable darkening, which may almost obliterate its red, white and yellow pattern. The same applies to *Pyrrhocoris*. It seems that, as a general rule, cold darkens the integument. Sometimes, two forms alternate with the seasons; this applies to the map butterfly (*Araschnia levana*), which has a spring *levana* form, golden fawn with black spots, and a summer *prorsa* form, bigger, with white stripes on a brown background. Many tropical butterflies also have two forms—a wet season form and a dry season form—which differ strikingly from each other in shape as well as colour markings.

Among the geographical variations, some are connected with external factors and are not transmitted by heredity, and others are genetically established.

The phases of locusts and of some moths constitute a quite different phenomenon. In these cases, it is not the physical external factors which come into play, but population density. Grouping alone produces in the larvae considerable modifications in pigmentation and morphology, with the result that for a long time it was thought that two different species were involved.

Some connections between insects and man

The class Insecta includes four-fifths of the animal species.

The variety of its forms provides entomologists, amateur or professional, with an inexhaustible field of inquiry. There is never a year that passes in which, even in Europe, at least a few dozen new species are not described and the figures for tropical regions are of course much higher. Also, the beauty of their colours and the strangeness of their forms make insects incomparable as 'raw material' to be exploited by decorators and designers.

However, the interest of insects is not limited to these particular usages: the fact is that, of all the classes of the animal kingdom, none, including even mammals and man, has shown more striking success.

Insects owe their success to their anatomical organization, to their functions, to their powers of adaptation and their fertility. This combination of qualities has enabled them to occupy, apart from most of the marine environments, the whole of the biosphere. Even in the polar regions well above the eternal snow-line, in the deepest caves and grottoes, in the thickness of the ground, in the most diverse liquid environments—Californian oil wells, super-salty pools of the deserts or on maritime cliffs—insects, and very often insects alone, are found.

This universal success of insects poses many and varied problems for man. On the plane of philosophy, man tends to judge the whole animal evolution in human terms. He is in the habit of judging biological success according to whether the solutions adopted are similar to the ones he himself has reached.

Now, it can be said that the solutions adopted by the insects are always different—even in their essence—from human solutions. Man's greatest rival obeys none of the rules which he himself follows.

One may explain this divergence partly by invoking the action of physical or chemical laws which cannot be exercised in the large animals. Thus, the relations of many aquatic insects are controlled by surface tension. For reasons of size, these forces play only a minimal role at the level of man. The diffusion of respiratory gas by tubes to the cells appears to be inapplicable to mammals; the gaseous exchanges resulting from it are too slow and too incomplete to be able to satisfy the very active metabolism of animals which, in general, are at least of medium size. The dimensions and the weight of the external skeleton limit the size each species can attain, more surely than does the internal skeleton.

These examples could easily be multiplied. They detract nothing from the interest of the success obtained, even if no teaching applicable directly to the higher vertebrates can be drawn from them. In fact, the insects show clearly that, confronted with problems of adaptation necessary for survival, the animal kingdom proposes several different but equally efficacious answers.

The problem, far from being purely theoretical, assumes considerable practical importance at a time when the need for increased food resources calls for a stepping-up of agricultural production and the maximum return from all tilled land. As disease-carriers and destroyers of crops, livestock, buildings or the goods of man, insects are amongst the most redoubtable enemies of humanity.

What is more, in the course of the last few decades, they have managed to bring new defensive measures to bear, and to become comparatively immune to most insecticides. The arsenal patiently assembled by entomologists in the past needs complete renewal. In the struggle between insect and man, a struggle on which the survival of human society partly depends, it will be a long time before the last resources of chemistry have been called into action. Thus, knowledge of insects is of exceptional interest, an interest unique in the whole animal kingdom; it can be said without exaggeration that man's knowledge of insects, and of the means to counter their encroachments, has become part of the need to understand the environment in his fight for survival.

This knowledge is opposed to the concept that evolution concerns only the human species, the other lineages being merely unsuccessful attempts pursuing their adaptation, without participating directly in real evolution.

The world of insects— the broad sub-divisions

The classification of insects has been founded successively on the presence or absence of wings, the characters of the mouth parts, the mode of post-embryonic development, and on anatomical characters presented by the Malpighian tubules, the reproductive apparatus, etc.

Recently, as a result of the work of palaeontologists, it has been possible to propose a new classification which takes into account all the known characters and the probable affiliation of the groups.

Insects are divided into two broad groups (sub-classes): the Apterygota (or Ametabola), characterized by the basic absence of wings. This primitive absence of wings is accompanied by progressive and direct development, without metamorphosis; and the Pterygota (or Metabola), normally winged, in which the absence of wings is a secondary character. Their development may comprise a true metamorphosis or progressive transformation, always passing through a critical phase at the moment of acquiring functional wings.

The Apterygota

A fauna of more than 400 millions years ago

This sub-class is fairly heterogeneous.

Its first three orders, grouped in the super-order Entotropha, are characterized by their mouth parts, which are hidden in the head.

The order Protura

The Protura consist of tiny insects, seldom exceeding 1/12 of an inch in length, living in soil, in leaves and mosses, or under stones. Their bodies are very elongated, with an abdomen of 12 segments. Alone of all the insects, they are devoid of antennae and never have compound eyes. Alone also, among the insects, they hatch with a number of abdominal segments less than the adults, and their development is progressive.

The order Collembola (springtails)

The Collembola are small insects, seldom exceeding 1/5 of an inch in length, sometimes brightly coloured and covered with scales. The abdomen never has more than 6 segments, but bears special ventral appendages: a ventral tube on the first abdominal sternite, a retinaculum on the third segment, and a furcula or springing organ situated on the hind margin of the fourth abdominal sternite. This consists of an unpaired base, articulated and provided with special muscles, the manubria, prolonged into 2 apendages, which engage with the retinaculum before a leap is made.

Like the Protura, the Collembola have no Malpighian tubules or tracheae.

By these diverse characters, they are so far removed from the insects that it has sometimes been proposed to separate them from insects completely; however, they are grouped with the Protura and the Diplura, in the super-order Entotropha, in which the mouth parts are hidden in the head by a tegumentary fold which covers mandibles and jaws. And, while the great majority of zoologists consider them primitive, they are thus indisputably insects.

In spite of their small size, the Collembola are very important. The oldest insect fossil known, *Rhyniella praecursor*, discovered in the old red sandstone of the middle Devonian, is a collembolan.

Several species are injurious to man: a species of *Hypogastrura* sometimes devastates cultivated mushrooms, and species of *Sminthurus* multiply to the extent of being harmful to the lucerne plant in Australia and to sugar cane in Louisiana.

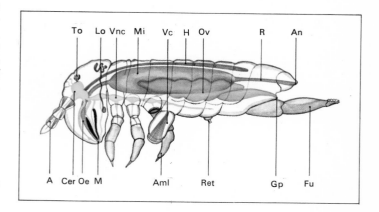

Organizational plan of a colembolan. *A*, antenna; *An*, anus; *Aml*, ambulatory leg; *Cer*, cerebral ganglia; *Fu*, furcula (leaping apparatus); *Gp*, genital pore; *H*, heart; *Lo*, labial excretory organ; *M*, mouth; *Mi*, midgut; *Oe*, oesophagus; *Ov*, ovary; *R*, rectum; *Ret*, retinaculum; *To*, Tomosvary's organ (possible auditory function); *Vnc*, ventral nerve cord; *Vt*, ventral tube.

Other species including the Cyphoderinae of ant-hills and termitaries, and especially species of the genus *Calobatinus*, which move about on the queens of certain termites, e.g. *Bellicositermes*, are inquilines (parasites) of social insects.

The order Diplura

The Diplura include Japyx and the campodeids. Their species are sometimes large (*Heterojapyx* of Australia, Madagascar and the Pamir area reach up to two inches in length). They have very elongated bodies, ending in long, many jointed appendages (cerci), e.g. Campodeidae; short multi-articulated and glandular cerci, e.g. Projapygidae; or brown, sclerified uni-articulated claw-shaped cerci, similar to those of earwigs (Japygidae).

The Diplura, always blind, with Malpighian tubules absent or atrophied, live in humus, under stones, mosses or leaves, or sometimes in caves. Some campodeids have bodies covered with coloured scales which are liable to fall.

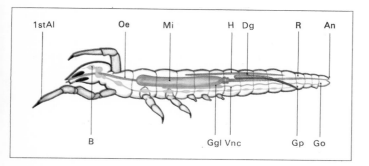

Diagram of the organization of a proturan. *Al*, first ambulatory leg simulating an antenna; *An*, anus; *Cer*, cerebral ganglia; *Dg*, dorsal gland; *Ggl*, gonad; *Go*, genital opening; *Gp*, glandular pore; *H*, heart; *Mi*, midgut; *Oe*, oesophagus; *R*, rectum; *Vnc*, ventral nerve cord.

The order Thysanura (bristle-tails)

The counterparts of the Entrotropha are the Ectotropha, or Thysanura, in which the mouth parts are visible externally.

Their species are of small to medium size, about an inch long at most. The body is often covered with scales which easily rub off. The abdomen ends in three many jointed processes: one pair of cerci and an unpaired median filament.

The order comprises two sub-orders, distinguishable through numerous characters.

The Archaeognatha (or Machilis)

These have cylindrical or laterally compressed bodies: the antennae are close together at their base. They have compound eyes and 3 ocelli (simple eyes); 7-jointed maxillary palps; and, sometimes, styles on the thoracic legs. Archaeognatha live in mosses and dead leaves, sometimes (*Petrobius*) amongst boulders and in rock crevices at the high tide mark, on shrubs and trees in the tropics, and may be found at altitudes of 13,000 feet or more.

The Zygentoma (or Lepisma)

These insects have comparatively broad and flattened bodies; the antennae are normally wide apart at their base. They have grouped ocelli or none; five-jointed maxillary palps; and no styles on the thoracic legs. In temperate regions, they are rare and domestic in habits.

The common household silver-fish, *Lepisma saccharina*, is well known for the damage it causes to books. Its counterparts in the tropics are larger species, which are also destructive.

In tropical regions, they are also found under stones (they are very abundant in the Sahara), as burrowers in sand-dunes (in the Namib Desert) or as inquilines, especially harvesting ants, of termitaries and ant-hills, where they are fed by their hosts, often collecting morsels of food which fall between two ants in the course of normal food exchange.

The Pterygota and the conquest of the air

This sub-class embraces normally winged forms as well as wingless forms, especially among the parasites; the wingless state is secondary. Their development is always epimorphous. The abdomen never bears articulated appendages—except in the terminal region—but it sometimes shows fleshy tiro-legs and, in larvae, articulated tracheal gills.

The classification of the Pterygota, which include more than ninety per cent of the known species of insects, has been revolutionized by recent research on fossil insects. They can be divided into four sections.

Section 1—The Paleoptera

These are primitive forms, in which the wings cannot be folded backwards and have only two axillary articulations. Their development is progressive, but, the larvae being aquatic and the adults aerial, the last or penultimate moult is marked by significant transformation (hemimetabolism): development of the wings, opening of the stigmata (spiracles) of the tracheal network, and loss of the lateral or posterior tracheal gills and of the rectal gills, among others.

To them are joined an entirely fossil super-order, the Palaeodictyoptera (larval characters only very imperfectly known), and two super-orders comprising present-day forms.

The colourless *Japyx* are generally blind, and live under buried stones or in fissures in the ground. Very archaic, they are the survivors of the primitive insects, their evolution having been stationary for thousands of years. (Actual size: about ¼ inch). *Phot. Graf*

Mating of dragonflies (*Pyrrhosoma*). The male is at the front of the tandem; with the forceps at the end of his abdomen, he has seized the female by the neck; she thrusts her abdomen forward and proceeds to place her genital opening under her partner's second abdominal segment. Under this segment is a complex copulatory organ which the male, before mating, has filled with sperm, his genital pore opening under the ninth abdominal segment. The female collects the sperm from the small reservoir; when the operation has been completed, the couple separate. The female will be able to lay shortly afterwards. *Phot. Edouard Cauvin*

The order Ephemeroptera (mayflies)

These insects have an abdomen ending in a pair of articulated filiform cerci, and a median paracercus; wings with simple venation in a fairly dense network, with at the outer edge short, intervening veinlets between each pair of normal veins; hind wings often reduced in size, and sometimes minute or non-existent.

Present-day Ephemeroptera are also called Plectoptera. They present a characteristic which is unique in insects, that of moulting again after having acquired functional wings. The

The larvae of the large dragonflies such as Aeshna live at the bottom pf still and more or less muddy water. They feed on live prey—insects, crustaceans, small tadpoles—seizing them with the two claws at the tip of their mask (a modification of the labium) folded under the head; the claws are released suddenly like a spring. This larva of a blue *Aeshna cyanea* is devouring a tadpole which, seized by the mask, is brought within range of the mouth parts which tear it. *Phot. J. Six*

adult stage is thus preceded by a winged stage called subimago, which flies about before undergoing the final moult.

The larvae frequent mainly stagnant or slow-flowing water; some live in mid-water and swim. Others walk on the bottom, or else, by burrowing, dig galleries in the mud of the bottom; their abdominal tracheal gills, instead of being arranged on their sides, are then relegated to their back and are sometimes covered by the first pair, which acts as a protective cover. Some genera are adapted to fast-flowing water, e.g. *Heptagenia* and *Ecdyonurus*. Their bodies are flattened, with broad heads and usually broadened legs, the femur being flattened and provided with long hairs. These adaptations enable them to adhere closely to the substratum and avoid being carried away by the current.

Finally, the small group of *Prosopistoma* includes some species known throughout the Old World. Its larvae, discovered in 1746 in France, were for a long time regarded as crustaceans. They have the latter's short body, enveloped in a large oval shield, beyond which projects the tip of the abdomen, which ends in three hairy appendages. It was not until a century after they were discovered that these strange larvae were classed with the Ephemeroptera, and the adult

became known only in 1954. *Prosopistoma* live in running water, and sometimes in torrents.

The larvae of may-flies eat algae, small organic particles and, sometimes, carrion. The adults, which are unable to take food as their mouth parts are atrophied, have a very short life; from this pecularity, the name of the order has been taken.

In the males, adult life is limited to a nuptial dance, in which numerous individuals take part. After mating, the female has time only to lay her eggs in or on the water, in one or several clusters, before dying. The eggs often have filaments which unfold in the water and anchor them to plants.

In some running-water species, mass emergence of the adults takes place and the river banks may then be covered with a thick layer of 'manna' made up of their bodies. On the banks of the Saône in France, one species, *Polymitarcys virgo*, has in some years provided up to 100 tons of manna.

Mayflies are important in the diet of gush-water fishes and are the models for a number of artificial 'flies' used by anglers.

The order Odonatoptera

The Odonatoptera have abdomens ending in two relatively short, thick cerci. The venation forms a dense network with numerous transverse veins. The super-order comprises the fossil Meganisoptera and the present-day Odonata, or dragon fly, in which the wing has a sclerified area (the pterostigma) on the leading edge near the wing-tip, and complex venation.

The larvae are of two quite distinct types. Some (those of the Anisoptera) have spindle-shaped bodies, and abdomens ending in three small pointed processes forming a pyramid covering the opening to a capacious rectum. This plays a double role. Because of its strong musculature, it can contract violently and project the larva forward, pumping out the water which normally fills it. Thus the larvae of Anisoptera, which move at a slow pace when walking, are equipped with jet propulsion for swift movement. The wall of the rectum also shows a very dense covering of tracheae, and is the seat of active respiratory exchange. Many larvae of Anisoptera, e.g. the Gomphidae, have bodies covered with compound hairs, to which are fixed particles of mud ensuring effective camouflage.

Others (those of the Zygoptera) have narrow, elongated bodies ending in three elongate-oval filaments near the back which are tracheal gills. Progression is by walking, or by swimming with undulating body movements.

In both types, the larvae are carnivorous and actively predatory, seizing their prey with their lower lips, which are transformed into articulated 'masks' and capable of being extended in front of the head. The highly developed compound eyes of these larvae provide them with excellent vision, and enable them to capture prey with great precision.

The adults are as actively predatory as the larvae. Constantly in flight, usually very swift, they are mainly diurnal; however, in the tropics, and at certain times of the year at least, several species of *Gynacantha* are crepuscular.

The Anisoptera, or dragon flies, become very large, and their bodies are usually robust; they often fly very high, are capable of covering considerable distances, and have been found some distance out to sea. Some species carry out substantial migrations, without returning to their starting point. When at rest, the Anisoptera have their wings spread out and often slightly drooping.

The Zygoptera, or damsel-flies, are slender and elongate in shape, with stalk-like wings sometimes with very bright coloration (especially in the Far East), a fact which explains the name of the genus *Calopteryx* (having beautiful wings). They can only fly for short distances and spend most of their time at rest, on outstanding plants at the water's edge with their wings folded back vertically above the abdomen. Some species have torrent-dwelling larvae with flattened and broadened bodies, which adhere firmly to the bottom.

Mating is remarkable and one often sees couples of dragon flies flying near water. The male's copulatory apparatus, oddly enough, is on the ventral surface of the second and third abdominal segments, and he fills this apparatus, which is often very complicated, with sperm. To achieve this, he arches his abdomen until its tip comes into contact with the copulatory apparatus. Then he grasps the female by the neck with the help of the appendages at the tip of his abdomen, which are equivalent to the copulatory parts of other insects. The couple flies thus, in tandem, for a while, then the female arches her abdomen and puts her genital opening in contact with the male's copulatory apparatus and receives the sperm.

In the Anisoptera, usually one egg only is laid at a time. The female lets this fall into the water, or detaches it by striking the water with the tip of her abdomen.

In the Zygoptera, the eggs are inserted into the tissues of plants at the water's edge, and the small larva passes through a primary phase, without appendages, in the course of which it frees itself from the plant and reaches the water.

Blue Aeshna (*Aeshna cyanea*). *Phot. J. Six*

Calopteryx splendens, the most beautiful of the European dragonflies, flutters on the banks of streams, alighting on rushes and other plants swayed by the current. *Phot. Merlet—Atlas-Photo*

Section 2—The Polyneoptera

In these, as in the Oligoneoptera, the wings, provided with three axillary articulation sclerites at the base, fold backwards on the body when at rest.

In the Polyneoptera, the area between the hind wings has many longitudinal veins. There is no device making it possible to join the two wings on the same side. The Malpighian tubules are numerous.

The ootheca or egg-case of *Empusa pennata* is remarkable for the long erect stem which rises from its hind end (× 2). *Phot. Edouard Cauvin*

Development is progressive in the forms in which larvae and adults are either aerial—with development at each moult of the elements of wings and of the abdominal appendages (paurometabolism)—or show an appreciable change at the imaginal moulting separating the aquatic larvae from the aerial adults, as in the Plecoptera or stone-flies. There are never more than two cerci, the median filament being absent.

Polyneoptera are divided into three super-orders.

The super-order Blattopteroidea

This super-order includes the Dictyoptera, the Isoptera and the Zoraptera.

The order Dictyoptera

The Dictyoptera comprise cockroaches and mantids. Very different in habits and appearance, these two sub-orders have in common a number of primitive characters: biting mouth parts; five-jointed tarsi (terminal parts) on all legs; an abdomen with ten segments, the last one having articulated cerci, and the sub-genital plate in the males bearing styles; forewings somewhat chitinized, but with visible venation, the hind wings, membranous, folding fan-like when at rest. Mantids are characterized by their front legs being raptorial (prehensile).

The eggs are laid in an ootheca, an envelope with a characteristic texture (a tough chitinous case in cockroaches, foamy and with the consistency of parchment in mantids). In some cockroaches, the oothecae are not liberated, the membrane remains thin and the animal is viviparous. In mantids, the new-born larva is enveloped in an embryonic membrane, the amnion, in which its appendages are wrapped; it frees itself from the ootheca, then moults and emerges as a normal larva, which looks like a miniature adult.

Among the cockroaches, three species (*Blatta orientalis*, *Periplaneta americana* and *Blatella germanica*), are very frequently commensals of man and cause serious damage. Apart from what they destroy or taint by their unpleasant smell, they may also be carriers of a dangerous hepatitis virus. The large black Hymenoptera, *Evania*, parasitize the oothecae, and accompany domestic cockroaches into houses, especially in the tropics.

A fair number of cockroaches are cave-dwellers, being fond of the guano accumulated in them by bats or swallows, and they are equally at home in dry or damp caves. In Africa and in Madagascar, they may occur in such swarms that the whole mass of guano seems to be in perpetual motion.

Some wood-eating cockroaches harbour a very rich intestinal fauna of flagellates, in particular *Cryptocercus* of the Rocky Mountains, in a dilation of the hind gut. All cockroaches have in their fatty tissue cells laden with symbiotic bacteria, without which the eggs do not develop normally since they elaborate vitamins. These bacteria are hereditary, passing from the fatty tissue to the eggs contained in the ovary.

Mantids, which reach about four inches in length, are predators which lie in wait for prey; the very flexible

An ootheca of the large cockroach, *Polyphaga aegyptiaca*, much enlarged. Cockroaches lay their eggs in thick tough cases with chitinous walls (the oothecae). *Phot. J. Six*

articulation of their neck makes it possible for them to follow prey with their eyes until it comes within reach.

Many Mantidae have foliated expansions on their body and legs which enable them to blend with their surroundings. Some Asiatic mantids are astonishingly like flowers, especially bright-coloured orchids; and one species from Indo-China mimics a tiger beetle.

Mating in mantids is generally prolonged and may continue even if the male is beheaded or partly eaten by his mate.

The oothecae of mantids, to a greater extent than those of cockroaches, are attacked by parasites and specialized predators, such as dermestid beetles, chloropid flies, and chalcid wasps; among the latter, the *Rielia* are found normally in the adult state under the wings of mantids, and when the time comes for the ootheca to be prepared they crawl down along the host's abdomen to lay in the eggs as they are laid.

The order Isoptera (termites)

The order Isoptera, termites or white ants, groups together insects primitive in their morphology, but remarkable for the degree to which polymorphism exists. They have strictly defined castes, and their social life is probably the most highly-developed in the insect world.

Three species are known in Europe: the yellow-necked termite (*Calotermes flavicollis*), from the Mediterranean region and common in tree-stumps; the lucifugous termite (*Reticulitermes lucifugus*) and the Saintonge termite (*R. santonensis*), which are dangerous destroyers of houses and of archives in southern Europe. Colonies of these insects have managed to become established and to survive for some time, even as far north as Paris. Other species cause similar damage in Asia, America and the Indo-Pacific Ocean.

A much larger number of species live in the tropics and are known there mainly for their constructions: the mushroom termitaries with one or more superimposed hoods of *Cubitermes*, the cathedral termitaries of the African *Bellicositermes*, the ball-shaped nests in trees of the *Nasutitermes*, the large flattened north-south orientated nests of the Australian compass termite (*Amitermes meridionalis*), and the tumuli of varied shapes, e.g. *Syntermes* of South America.

Although normally averse to light and fond of humidity, as a result of which a few species move about in the open air only at night and use for preference networks of covered galleries, some genera, such as *Hodotermes*, organize veritable expeditions which take place in the open and in full daylight. The marching of these columns in the African forest undergrowth can be heard a long way off, for it is accompanied by a constant noise due to the undersides of the insects' heads striking the ground or dead leaves.

The order Zoraptera

The Zoraptera number only about twenty tropical species of very small size. They are flesh-eating, and live in the ground or under bark. There is remarkable sexual dimorphism in the adults: there are winged individuals, which are coloured and have eyes or ocelli, and wingless individuals, which are white and blind.

Two winged yellow-necked termites (*Calotermes flavicollis*), together with advanced larvae. *Phot. Aldo Margiocco*

A white soldier, which will become a perfect soldier and a small worker of the termite of Natal (*Bellicositermes natalensis*). *Phot. Aldo Margiocco*

Top left: once she has been fertilized and after having killed and devoured her unfortunate spouse, the praying mantis, *Mantis religiosa*, lays on the most varied surfaces, (branches, stones, walls). As she lays, the mantis emits a foamy mucus in which the eggs are held fast; as it dries, the mucus hardens and forms the ootheca. A year later, the young mantids hatch and, shortly afterwards, set about hunting prey in proportion to their small size. They present a fairly strong homochromy of colours ranging from bright green to pale brown. *Phot. J. Six*

Top right: larva of Empusa (*Empusa pennata*), which cocks its back over its abdomen flanked with foliated appendages and which, when it moults, assumes the colour of its surroundings. *Opposite page:* adult male Empusa with green elytra. This beautiful species lives in southern Europe and north Africa. *Phot. Edouard Cauvin*

Mantis religiosa (*left*) in the terrifying attitude it assumes when faced with danger, e.g. in the presence of a lizard. *Phot. Edouard Cauvin*

The male cricket (*above left*), as it rubs its elytrons one against the other, transmits its love song—answered, in turn, by a female (*Gryllus bimaculatus*). *Phot. J. Six*

Left, green grasshopper. *Tettigonia viridissima*, in laying posture; she introduces her ovipositor into the ground, where she will lay her eggs. *Phot. Aldo Margiocco*

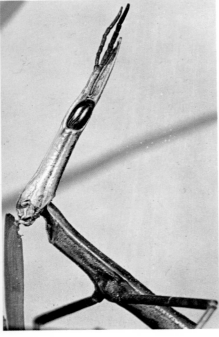

The super-order Orthopteroidea

This super-order consists of a group of comparatively primitive forms, as follows.

The order Plecoptera (stone-flies)

Plecoptera, which have aquatic larvae, are found throughout the world. Among the most ancient known insects, they can be traced as far back as the lower Permian. The adult has its wings, with fairly simple venation, folded flat on its back. The wings are sometimes atrophied in the males of mountain-dwelling species. The abdomen ends in two long cerci and often shows marked secondary sexual characters, which may extend to the abdominal segments as a whole.

The larva's body ends in two long articulated cerci; it breathes through its skin or through clusters of tracheal gills situated at the articulations of the thorax and the apex of the abdomen. These larvae have a predilection for pure, cold running water.

The adults never move far from the water's edge and fly mainly in the evening.

Larval development is remarkably slow, as it may take up to three years and be spread over about forty moults. Rudimentary hermaphoroditism (both male and female reproductive organs in one individual) has been noted in some species of *Perla*. In the mountain-dwelling species, *Nemura* and *Leuctra*, two forms of males may occur, differing in the development of their wings.

The order Notoptera

This order comprises a few wingless medium-sized species, in which the abdomen ends in two cerci. The females have an egg-laying organ, the ovipositor. The Notoptera have a restricted distribution in the mountainous regions of North America and Japan; the species of *Grylloblatta* are at home only in temperatures in the region of $0°$ C and live in contact with the snow.

The order Cheleutoptera (stick- and leaf-insects)

The Cheleutoptera, or Phasmida, hardly represented in Europe, are very rich in tropical species, some of which reach more than a foot in length. They are usually shaped like twigs of trees, with walking legs, short cerci and rudimentary ovipositors. There may or may not be wings, the first pair (elytro) in some cases being reduced to small scales or absent. Brown, green or grey in colour, the body often

The *Proscopus* are the strangest of the grasshoppers which inhabit South America. Those represented here come from Uruguay. Very slender and exceedingly long, the head is extremely drawn out to the front. As shown in the mating (*far left*), the male is much smaller than the female. The close-up (*left*) represents a female eating a plant. These insects live in grassy places. *Phot. J. Six*

bears spines or excrescences which help to camouflage the insect in vegetation when it is motionless, a pose which it frequently adopts. The eggs, stuck to plants or scattered abroad singly, are very hard, with an ornamented outer coat, and are often provided with a breakable flap for the moment of hatching.

The leaf-insects have flattened leaf-shaped bodies (hence the name), and the venation of the elytra is arranged like the veins of a leaf.

Some phasmids are first-rate laboratory material, especially *Carausius morosus* and *Sipyloidea sipylus*, of Javanese origin but acclimatized in Madagascar and more recently in France.

The mole-cricket, *Gryllotalpa gryllotalpa: on the right,* the adult; *on the left,* the foreleg transformed into a digging tool. *Phot. J. Six and Aldo Margiocco*

The eggs are laid singly and are often inserted into the tissues of plants.

The Ensifera include many families, vegetarian or carnivorous, the main ones being the Tettigoniidae or long-horned grasshoppers, the tropical Gryllacridae and the Gryllidae or crickets. A fair number of Ensifera of the two latter families are cave-dwelling. Some crickets live in ant-hills.

Finally, there are the leaf-like katydids (*Pterochroza*), the camouflage of which reaches an amazing perfection.

In the Ensifera, the sperms are transmitted to the female by means of a spermatophore, a fairly complex gelatinous vesicle which envelops the sperms.

Ensifera may cause damage to crops. This is the case with *Ephippigera* and *Barbitistes* in Europe; mole-crickets are particularly harmful because of the underground galleries they excavate in flower-beds, thus severing the roots of young plants. Burrowing is facilitated by the front legs, which are

The order Orthoptera (grasshoppers and locusts)

The Orthoptera are characterized by hind legs, each with a strongly developed femur, almost always capable of jumping, and by an ovipositor of variable length.

They are divided into Ensifera and Caelifera.

The Ensifera have very long antennae, tarsi with three or four joints, a very long ovipositor which is often curved like a sword blade and is formed by projections from the eighth and ninth abdominal plates; the elytra of the male each have a stridulatory organ formed by a particularly strong vein, which has a series of teeth. This stridulatory vein, or bow, rubs against the thinned-down edge of the other elytron and makes it resonate. This sound-producing apparatus has a corresponding auditory apparatus in the shape of a cavity in the tibias of the forelegs, which have a tympanic membrane connected with sensory cells. This tibial ear is very sensitive and can pick up high frequency sounds, which are involved in the recognition of species, in the coming together of the sexes and in the delimitation of territories.

very short and strong, with the front tibia very dilated, and by the general shape of the body, which is almost cylindrical.

A giant African cricket, *Brachytrypes membranaceus*, causes a great deal of damage, as well, appearing at the beginning of the rainy season and cutting plants at ground level. In some parts of Africa these large crickets are also regarded as a delicacy.

The Caelifera

The Caelifera are species with cylindrical or laterally-flattened bodies, short antennae and ovipositors formed of four short valves. They include the Acrididae, or true grasshoppers and locusts, and the Tridactylidae, or pygmy mole crickets, as well as the extraordinary burrowing *Cylindrachaeta* of Australia and South America. In desert regions, in high mountains, and, for some tropical groups (Eumastacidae), in many other environments there are wingless forms. Among the desert-dwelling grasshoppers, especially in southeast Africa, there are also forms with

The stinking cricket, *Zonocercus variegatus*, is found throughout tropical Africa. Prolific, sometimes, without ever carrying out migration, it can be destructive to crops. *Phot. J. Six*

flattened, humped bodies which merge readily with the colours of the boulders which surround them.

Stridulation, which is very common, is produced by rubbing a row of small pegs, borne by the inner surface of the hind femur, against a hardened vein of the elytron, which then vibrates. The receiving organ is situated at the base of the abdomen, which has a tympanum on each side.

The Califera present to a very high degree of perfection the phenomenon of gregarious and solitary phases.

They include species which are amongst the most destructive of all insects, including:

—the desert locust *Schistocera gregaria*, from northern Africa to eastern Pakistan;

—the migratory locust *Locusta migratoria*, which covers almost the whole of Africa, including Madagascar and southern Asia, and which forms fairly numerous local races;

—the red locust *Nomadacris septemfasciata*, from southern tropical Africa and Madagascar;

—the brown locust *Locustana pardalina* of southern Africa;

—the South American locust, *Schistocerca paranensis*, which is found throughout the American tropical area;

—the Moroccan locust *Dociostaurus maroccanus*, in northern Africa;

—various species of swarming grasshoppers (*Melanoplus*) in North America and *Chortoicetes* in Australia.

To these species, which are regularly destructive and have marked phases, there must be added species which occasionally show a tendency to gregariousness and may cause appreciable damage, like the stinking grasshopper, *Zonocercus variegatus*, in tropical Africa.

The order Embioptera

Embioptera are small insects, with elongated bodies, living under stones and bark, especially in tropical regions. The males are usually winged and the females wingless. The forelegs are hypertrophied and the first joint of the tarsus, which is greatly enlarged, contains silk-producing glands; these glands possess fine threads, emitted by large hollow bristles, which are used for weaving the loose silken tunnels in which these insects live. In these burrows *Embia* can move either forwards or backwards with ease.

The order is represented in Europe by only two wingless genera, *Haploembia* and *Monotylota*.

The super-order Dermapteroidea

This is an extremely isolated super-order which includes medium to small-sized species, recognizable by their elongated bodies, which end in two strong claw-like cerci, by their forewings modified into short elytra and by their broadly developed fan-shaped hind wings, with a sclerified part over-lapping the elytron. Many species are wingless or two-winged. The order Dermaptera (or earwigs) are remarkable, among insects, by the possession of a double penis.

Most species live under leaves or bark, or sometimes caves or ant-hills; they are omnivorous, but often primarily vegetarian.

Two very specialized parasitic forms are included with them: *Hemimerus*, which is viviparous and lives on the Gambian rat, *Cricetomys gambianus*, in tropical Africa; and *Arixenia*, which has a short broad body and well-developed legs, and is found on Indo-Malaysian bats.

Section 3—The Oligoneoptera

The Oligoneoptera can be distinguished by the fact that the veined section of each wing has only a single longitudinal vein (which is simple), that there is a fixed number of Malpighian tubules in the various families, and that it is always low, except in the Hymenoptera. All the representatives of this section have complete metamorphoses: this means that between the wingless larva, without compound eyes, and with tarsi formed of a single claw joint, and the adult, usually winged, with compound eyes and multi-articulated tarsi, there always exists a resting form (pupa, nymph or chrysalis), the outward appearance of which differs from the adult's and which is the seat of considerable anatomical and histological modifications.

The Oligoneoptera group includes the higher insects and

Rambur's embiid, *Embia ramburi*, lives in small groups under stones, where it weaves silken tubes in which it moves about. The silk-bearing glands are contained in the swollen joint of the tarsi of the forelegs. In this photograph, at the bottom, a brown adult; on its right, two larvae. *Embia* owes its name to the fact that it walks with equal facility backwards or forwards. It is numerous in the stony and dry Mediterranean regions. *Phot. Aldo Margiocco*

Procrustes coriaceus, a ground beetle common in western Europe and the Mediterranean, attacking a snail (*Helix aspersa*) on which it feeds. It lives in meadows, gardens, etc. Length: up to 1½ inches. *Phot. Aldo Margiocco*

Earwigs live under stones, bark or in damaged fruit. Shown here is *Forficula auricularia* (length: ½–¾ inch), the most common of the earwigs. *Phot. J. Six*

the four numerically largest orders, which are probably also those best known: Coleoptera, Lepidoptera, Diptera and Hymenoptera.

In the group five super-orders can be distinguished, one of which includes only very deformed parasitic forms.

The tiger beetles are pre-eminently predators: they hunt the prey on which to feed on the run. On the *opposite page*, notice the mouth parts, which are redoubtable offensive weapons. The larvae lie in wait in the vertical pits they dig in the ground. Bent in the shape of an S, they hang on to the wall by strong hooks borne on the dorsal surface of the third abdominal segment. *Above*, the species represented is *Cicindela silvatica*, which inhabits the pre-Alps of Dauphine and Savoie, and the Jura. It is found in central Europe as far as the Balkan Peninsula. Length: just over ½ inch. *Phot. J. Six*

The super-order Coleopteroidea (beetles)

This super-order consists of the single order Coleoptera. (Fossil forms have been grouped in the extinct order of Protocoleoptera, in which the elytra still show traces of complex venation.)

Beetles are characterized by: their forewings, which are transformed into horny elytra more or less enveloping the body; by veins replaced by simple parallel striae; and by their mouth parts, normally of the biting type.

The Coleoptera range from very small insects, the Trichopterigidae, or ptilliids, some of which do not exceed 1/100 of an inch in length, to the giant longhorns such as *Macrocinus*, with legs more than 8 inches long, dynastids like *Dynastes hercules* of the West Indies, more than 6 inches long, and the South American *Megasoma*, with an enormous body 4½ inches long.

Because of their often brilliant coloration, their strange forms, the solidity of their external skeleton, the ease with which they can be kept and the considerable number of species (more than 300,000 known up to the present), the Coleoptera are the most studied and the best known of all the insects, apart from the Lepidoptera.

Although it contains no enemies of man as deadly as mosquitoes and other biting flies, or like the hungry hordes of locusts, the order Coleoptera nevertheless exerts considerable influence on the human economy and, to a lesser degree, on public health.

The species of the Bostrichidae, Lyctidae, Scolytidae and Cerambicidae families attack timber. *Hylotrupes bajulus*, the small domestic longhorn, is responsible for the destruction of framework, made of coniferous wood, and sometimes of inner walls in many parts of northern Europe. Some Scarabaeidae, and especially cockchafers (*Melolontha*), are known for their mass emergences in 'cockchafer years'—and for the damage done by their grubs' teeth to the roots of a great variety of crops. Many Chrysomelidae (the Colorado beetle of the potato, the turnip flea-beetle of crucifers, the vine flea-beetle and many weevils), Curculionidae (*Cosmopolites* of the banana plant), and Bruchidae (in leguminous seeds) cause substantial damage to a great variety of crops. Even in groups which are usually flesh-eating, such as the carabid

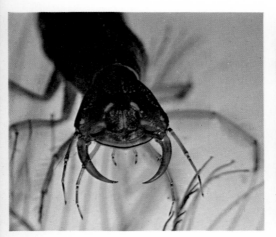

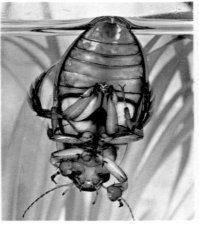

The brown diving beetle, *Dytiscus marginalis*, is one of the finest aquatic Coleoptera in Europe. Its larva keeps its mouth closed, but its mandibles are traversed by a duct which opens at their tip. It sinks its mandibles into the prey (insect, snail, tadpole), injects digestive juice into it, and once the latter has acted on the prey's tissues it sucks up the liquid. (Length: 1½ inches). *In the middle*, a male breathing, ventral view; notice the suckers borne by the forelegs; *on the right*, dorsal view of female; notice the fluted elytra (forewing). *Phot. R. H. Noailles and J. Six*

ground-beetles, certain vegetarian species may become pests: *Calathus* and *Ophonus* attack crops in market-gardens, and *Abax* fields of cereals.

Enemies of crops and man

Many species with omnivorous tendencies may multiply and reach pest proportions in the special conditions created by the development of crops: Elateridae (click-beetles), such as *Agriotes*, and Tenebrionidae, such as *Gonocephalum*, are in this category.

Finally, stored foodstuffs are devastated by the Tenebrionidae (especially *Tribolium*, the flour beetle, and *Tenebrio*, the meal worm), the Curculionidae (the rice and grain weevils *Sitophilus*), the Cucujidae, and certain bostrychids and scolytids, to name only the principal culprits.

A certain number of Coleoptera are harmful to man and

mainly tropical, and remarkable for the reticulation of the elytra and for the structure of the male genitalia. Their larvae resemble caterpillars.

The Adephaga
These have the first three segments of the abdomen (the foremost one having disappeared in the Coleoptera) fused in a single arc; all the tarsi are five-jointed. Their larvae have six-jointed legs. The Adephaga include forms which are usually carnivorous. They may be terrestrial, as with Rhyzodidae, Carabidae, or aquatic, e.g. Dytiscidae, Gyrinidae. Some of these forms show astonishing larval or adult adaptatations.

Among the underground, wingless, blind and unpigmented forms, such as *Aphaenops* which is strictly confined to caves, there are some which lay only one very large egg, producing a larva which neither feeds nor grows and metamorphoses very quickly. This is a shortening of development found in some cave-dwelling Bathysciinae (*Speonomus*).

The larvae of Ozaenidae have abdomens ending in sclerosed discs, formed by several abdominal segments, which

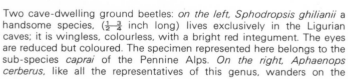

Two cave-dwelling ground beetles: *on the left, Sphodropsis ghilianii* a handsome species, ($\frac{1}{2}$–$\frac{3}{4}$ inch long) lives exclusively in the Ligurian caves; it is wingless, colourless, with a bright red integument. The eyes are reduced but coloured. The specimen represented here belongs to the sub-species *caprai* of the Pennine Alps. *On the right, Aphaenops cerberus*, like all the representatives of this genus, wanders on the

stalagmitic walls of caves. Legs and antennae are very long; the eyes are lacking and the tegument is pale. The genus *Aphaenops* is distributed in the caves of the French Pyrenees, from the valley of the Ariège to that of the Nive. It only penetrates into Spain at the level of the Basses Pyrenees. *Aphaenops cerberus* is particularly common in the Moulis cave (underground laboratory of French scientific research). *Phot. Margiocco*

livestock. Several staphylinids of the genus *Paederus* emit acrid substances causing serious vesicular dermatitis and capable of causing eye trouble and a fair number of species serve as hosts, obligatory or accidental, to nematodes and tapeworms which are parasites of vertebrates.

The classification of Coleoptera is still not settled; four suborders are generally recognized.

The Archostomata
Very primitive, known since the Permian, these are represented now by a very small number of species of Cupedidae,

block the galleries they hollow out in wood. These discs, which are glandular, are also found in the Paussidae—symbionts of ants and termites in that they enjoy a mutually-beneficial partnership. The larvae of the tiger beetles, Cicindelidae, which dig themselves burrows of variable shape, stop up the openings to them with their flattened, rounded and hardened heads. When they are at rest, their eyes are at surface level and the larva thus watches prey moving about on the ground. In most of these larvae, the bodies of which are broad and fleshy, movement within the burrow and fixation to the walls are made possible by com-

plex, articulated hooks, and placed in the middle of the abdomen. The larvae of Gyrinidae bear tracheal gills on the sides of the abdomen.

Among the carabids, some species are parasites of other insects; *Androya* develop in Madagascar at the expense of the larvae of *Cetonia* while they are in the process of becoming nymphs, and an American ground beetle of the genus *Brachinus* parasitizes the nymphs of whirligig-beetles and a *Lebia*, the larvae of *Galerucella luteola*, the elm-leaf beetle.

The Paussidae, which are symbionts of ants or termites, usually have tufts of yellow secretory hairs (or trichomes), which their hosts lick. They have very complex clubbed antennae in which the joints are often fused.

The water beetles (Gyrinidae, Dytiscidae, Noteridae, Haliplidae and Hygrobiidae) have adapted to aquatic life in varying degrees. The whirligig-beetles (Gyrinidae), some of which are confined to running water, are the most extensively adapted. These insects, which normally live on the surface of the water, come together in groups where there is sunshine. The body of the whirligig beetle is very flattened, with sharp-edged elytra which are often prolonged rearward into a double tip, framing the apex of the abdomen and forming a balancing device. The legs are very short, with the joints of the tarsi closely set together to form a very effective oar. The highly developed eyes are divided into two separate halves, one dorsal and one ventral, giving both aerial and aquatic vision.

Thus equipped, whirligig-beetles seize small insects that fall on to the water and are kept on top of it by surface tension, as well as those which rise from the depths towards the surface.

The Haplogastra

In these insects, the second abdominal plate is visible on the sides of the body, but reduced in the middle. The larvae have only five joints on their legs. This order includes a series of very large superfamilies. The Staphylinoidae are one of the most numerous of these superfamilies, with a long series of cave-dwelling and parasitic species belonging to several families. The hosts are termites or ants.

The first family, the Silphidae, include the burying beetles *Necrophorus*, and *Silpha*, certain species of which are plant-eating and attack beetroot. Other species, which specialize on a diet of snails or caterpillars, are classified in the sub-family of the Bathysciinea—ground- and especially cave-dwellers. This sub-family includes unpigmented species, with swollen rear bodies, and a fairly large chamber between the elytra and the back of the abdomen. The Staphylinidae have elongated bodies, with short truncated elytra, leaving most of the abdomen exposed. They include predatory forms,

eaters of decaying organic matter and many species normally associated with animal hosts. Many are symbionts of ants and some (e.g. *Dorylophilus*), closely mimic their hosts. Some have smooth, short hard bodies (*Pygostenus*), and some secretory hairs (*Lomechusa*). The species which are symbionts of termites often have bladder-like (physogastric) stomachs, with the abdomen hypertrophied, folded over the body, fleshy, and sometimes provided with glandular protuberances. Some physogastric staphylinids assume various body shapes, and several degrees of physogastry may occur. It is not understood whether these stages succeed one another in the development of the individual or whether they represent separate fixed individual types.

The Pselaphidae includes very small species (from 1/100 of an inch to 1/5 of an inch long). These are remarkable for their clublike antennae, their hypertrophied maxillary palps with the last joint developed, their thoraxes, which often have deep cavities, and their abdomen apexes which are not covered by the elytra. The Pselaphidae feed on live prey or on organic debris, and are found under stones, leaves, or bark. Some species are cave-dwellers; many which live buried deep in the ground are blind, wingless, and have

The devil's coachhorse, *Staphylinus olens*, is recognized by its large size ($\frac{3}{4}$ inch), its short truncated elytra (forewing), and its black erect abdomen. Its larva is very agile and carnivorous. It is found throughout western Europe. *Phot. J. Six*

elongated appendages. Finally, many species are symbionts of ants. The Clavigerinae is constantly associated with ants, which feed them and at times carry them about. This subfamily have tufts of secretory hairs, and an antennal club made up of a single joint.

The Scydaenidae are as small as the Pselaphidae, and their elytra are almost always developed and cover the abdomen. Their antennae end in an interrupted club. They live in humus, or deep down in the ground.

The Leptinidae have only a small number of very small species; these live in the fur of beavers (*Platypsyllus*), desmans (*Silphopsyllus*) or, intermittently on rodents and insectivores (*Leptinus*). The larvae of *Platypsyllus* are external parasites like the adults; those of *Leptinus* are free-living.

The Ptiliidae, or Trichopterygidae, include the smallest of all the Coleoptera (from about 1/100 of an inch to about 1/12 of an inch long). These are remarkable for their wings, the membrane of which is more or less reduced, and replaced, as a support surface, by a dense fringe of long hairs.

They are found in the soil, under bark or in dead leaves. The Histeridae are characterized by their extra hard exoskeletons, their abdomens, which are visible at the apex, their clubbed antennae and their heads, which are sometimes retractile and hidden beneath a projection of the prosternum. Many Histeridae are symbionts of ants and show hypertrophy of the elytral and thoracic area, while others have tufts of secretory hairs. Some Histeridae which live under the bark of trees have an extremely flattened and foliated body.

The aquatic or at least the damp-loving Hydrophilidae are not as well adapted to swimming as the other water beetles; the large species (*Hydrous, Hydrophilus*) nevertheless have a hydrodynamic body shape. The mandibles of many larvae of Hydrophilidae have a duct by means of which the digestive saliva is injected into live prey or the plants on which they feed. The eggs of Hydrophilidae are laid in a nacelle-like cocoon attached to the mother's abdomen and carried about by her sometimes even until the birth of the young larvae. The Sphaeridiinae are attracted to very fresh cow-dung, in which they literally swim. Some Hydrophilidae, living in very damp earth, cause serious damage to turnip crops (*Helophorus*).

The Scarabeoidae are characterized by an antennal club, developed only on one side of the axis, and lamellae. They live in flowers (Cetoniidae), eat leaves (Melolonthinae), or dung (Geotrupidae, Scarabaeidae). Their larvae develop in decomposing organic matter: vegetable-mould, carrion, dung or sometimes mushrooms. Many genera are symbionts of ants or termites, and some have atrophied mouth parts and tufts of secretory hairs. The females are often sedentary and sometimes wingless (Pachypodinae, Pleocominae), and the males take part in nuptial flights in large numbers. In many Scarabeoidae, the males have a hypertrophied antennal club, whose great development is probably due to a multiplication of the sensory endings, especially the olfactory receptors.

Several families can be distinguished. In the Passalidae and Lucanidae the clubs of the antennae are made up of fixed comb-shaped lamellae (Pectinicornes). Their larvae live in wood or under bark, except for a few species which are found in the ground with the adults, attacking buried wood. Most of the male Lucanidae have hypertrophied mandibles, to which they owe their popular name of stag-beetles.

The Acanthoceridae can roll themselves into a ball: the articulations of the head, thorax and elytra are very loose, the very flattened legs rest closely against the abdomen and, when they are rolled up, the head rests on the tip of the abdomen. They eat moulds and are sometimes symbionts of termites.

The Trogidae have rough textured bodies formed of rows of complex tubercles. They are very numerous in dry regions, and are often associated with the burrows of mammals and with birds' nests; they feed on decomposed organic matter.

The Geotrupidae, or dor-beetles, comprise numerous dung and fungus feeding species. The Scarabaeidae, including the scarabs, are the most numerous family, some genera having more than 1500 species.

The Heterogastra

This is the most heterogeneous sub-order. The second abdominal sternite of the Heterogastra is either whole or totally involuted. Among the 200 or so families recognized, several comprise only a few tropical species. The Lampyridae (glow-worms and fire-flies) and the Drilidae eat snails, which they paralyze by an injection of saliva which gradually digests the snail's tissues. The females are wingless, and in some Malaysian species (*Duliticola*) are completely larviform and of giant proportions. The Cantharididae are small flower-dwelling species which, in some genera, show extraordinary differentiation of the male's copulatory organ. Their sexual behaviour is sometimes elaborate, the male caressing tufts of hairs on the protuberances on the fore part of the female's body during the preliminaries to mating. The Tenebrionidae, an immense family, mainly tropical, are made up of black species, often wingless. Their elytral form is sometimes very complicated, as in *Pimelia*, *Blaps*, and *Tentyria*, which colonize dry zones (e.g. beaches, deserts) and forms with brilliant coloration native to forests, and especially tropical forests.

In the deserts of Africa and Arabia, the Tenebrionidae show a very extensive range of adaptations. Some species have a white covering on top, formed either by a chalky secretion, or by a layer of fine scales or hairs. Others are unpigmented and nocturnal. Several are burrowers with reduced tarsi or claws and hypertrophied legs, with the tibiae dilated into toothed blades. Some genera (*Cardisoma*, *Lepidochora*) are flattened into sharp-edged discs; they literally swim about in the yielding sand of the dunes. A series of very small genera is made up of blind wingless species, living in the soil.

The Mordellidae have laterally compressed bodies with a triangular transverse section; their larvae live in the stalks of plants.

The Meloidae contain species remarkable for their morphology; their antennae, especially those of the males, are very complex, with lobes and teeth. In the oil beetles (*Meloe*), the hind part of the abdomen is not covered by the elytra, and in the female it becomes greatly distended by the eggs. The life history of Meloidae is very complicated, for in the larval state they are all parasites of insects. The hosts are usually Hymenoptera, but sometimes Orthoptera, and the development of the larvae includes hypermetamorphoses, that is to say several larval types succeeding each other.

In the European oil beetles, the young larvae reach the nourishing cell of their host (in which they will live first at the

The cellar beetle, *Blaps* (up to 1½ inches in length), are large uniformly black beetles and are characteristic of the countless Tenebrionidae group. The adults, like their larvae, feed on debris of all kinds. Shown here is a Morroccan species. *Phot. J. L. S. Dubois*

expense of the larva of the hymenopteron, then of its provisions) by three different methods.

The eggs may be laid by the female at the entrance to the nest of a specific hymenopteron. On hatching in the autumn, the larvae remain lumped together at the entrance to the nest and take no food throughout the winter. In the spring, they attach themselves to the male hymenopteron, which are the first to hatch; they then pass to the females at the moment of

The various states of the rose-chafer, *Cetonia cupraea* (length: ¾–1 inch). *Top left*, the adult eating pollen in a cyclamen flower; *right*, the larva, a white worm, which has the curious habit of crawling on its back. *Bottom left*, the white worm, shortened, is seen in its cocoon made of excrement and of agglutinated particles of earth; it is on the point of metamorphosis; *on the right*, the nymph freed from the larval skin. The whole of larval life takes place in leafmould or humus. *Phot. Aldo Margiocco*

mating and from there drop on to the egg when the bearer visits a cell.

In a second group, the young larvae climb on to plants, become established in the flowers and fix themselves to insects which come to collect honey. Those which are lucky enough to find a suitable host in this way continue their development; the others, having become unsuitably attached—to the butterflies or flies, for instance—die of starvation.

Finally, the young larvae themselves may seek out a host's cell, and manage to pass through some crack in the ground or in the nest to reach the egg.

These young larvae, known as triungulins because of the trifid terminal claws on their tarsi, bear in the first two groups a tuft of frontal hairs which help to ensure fixation on their host.

Among the Meloidae is placed the large group of mylabrids. *Zonabris* has an elongated body covered with transverse black and yellow stripes, and *Lytta*, the blister beetle,

The female oil beetle, *Meloe proscarabaeus* (length: up to 1¼ inches) is wingless (abbreviated elytra only) and has a relatively large abdomen, occupied almost entirely by hypertrophied ovaries. The adults collect nectar from flowers. The fertilized female, after a fairly complicated nuptial ceremony, lays at random on the ground. The larvae, or triungulins, are very agile, living on flowers and hanging on to solitary bees which come to collect pollen and nectar. *Phot. J. Six*

Click beetles or Elateridae (here *Ampedus cinnabarinus*) are characterized by their flattened shapes, oblong contours, and their ability to jump by sudden release of the lamina which runs from their prosternum into a cavity in the mesosternum; the insect, projected into the air, turns on itself and tends to fall on its feet. The larva, or wire-worm, is like that of the mealworm, but is more slender and has a very hard integument. *Phot. J. Six*

has a brilliant metallic green body, from which is extracted cantharidin, a vesicatory powder formerly much used pharmaceutically and constituting a dangerous poison.'

The Rhipiphoridae have only a very small number of species, always rare and still not very well known, which are parasites of Orthopteroidea and undergo hypermetamorphoses like the Meloidae.

The Elateridae, or click-beetles, are made up of large species. Their bodies are always elongated, the legs and antennae being accommodated in grooves underneath the body. Many species have a special jumping apparatus which uses the thoracic muscles and a pointed posterior protuberance on the prosternum, which fits into a cavity in the mesosternum. The click-beetle uses this jumping mechanism to turn itself over from its resting position on its back; its short legs, on the ventral surface, would not be much help for this purpose.

The adults are found on the ground, under stones or bark; their larvae, or wire-worms, are very like meal-worms. Diet is usually vegetarian or humus-based, but the larvae of many species, at the end of their cycle, need a meal of flesh and are constantly associated in their host tree with another insect, usually a cerambycid, whose larvae they consume.

The Buprestidae often have elongated bodies, similar to those of the Elasteridae, but they usually have very conspicuous metallic colours and integuments which are often sculptured, whereas the Elateridae are brown, reddish, grey or black and have hairy integuments with simple sculpture. Legs and antennae are accommodated in special cavities on the lower surface of the body. The adults are often flower-dwelling.

The larva has a soft elongate body, flattened and broadened at the level of the thorax, in which the head is set (hammer-headed). They bore flat galleries in dead wood and their metamorphosis into nymphs takes place in a special chamber. *Trachys* have larvae which burrow in leaves. The tropical species are often of large size, those of the temperate zones being smaller.

The Dermestidae are small beetles whose bodies are covered with close-set hairs or coloured scales. Their larvae have complex compound hairs. They develop, as a general rule, at the expense of desiccated organic matter of animal origin, and can feed on wax, chitin, wool, and so on. The larvae are sometimes commensals of birds' nests or of caterpillars' and spiders' webs, and they may even develop into external parasites of young birds. One genus lives in the oothecae of mantids. The adults are found either in animal organic matter such as hides, dried meat, or smoked fish, in burrows or nests, or on flowers (*Anthrenus, Attagena*). The Dermestidae cause considerable damage and are among the most serious enemies of entomological collections. Their adaptation to human productions and provisions has greatly facilitated their dispersion, so much so that many species are at the present time cosmopolitan and it is even difficult sometimes to determine their place of origin.

The Ptinidae are small, down-covered species. The front part of the body is usually narrow and the elytra very swollen. Ptinidae develop in dried-up organic matter, mainly of vegetable origin, and they cause serious damage to food stocks. Some adults are found on flowers.

The Anobiidae comprise species with elongated downy bodies, heads hooded by an extension of the cuticle covering the first segment of the thorax (pronotum), short legs and toothed antennae ending in a club with elongate joints. Known as death-watch beetles, Anobiidae live in dry wood, and especially in furniture and structural timber, to which they cause serious damage. The larvae have a thick fleshy body, slightly hook-shaped.

The alder buprestid, *Dicerca alni* (length: ¾ inch), lives in the larval state in sapwood and on the decaying or fallen trunks of the alder (*Alnus glutinosa*). It appears from April to August and is distributed from Portugal to the Caucasus and in northern Africa. *Phot. J. Six*

The vast Clavicornia group is made up of insects, usually small, living in organic matter. Some species destroy stocks of stored foodstuffs, others live at the expense of these destroyers. Among them may be mentioned the Corylophidae, not more than ⅛ of an inch long; the head of the Corylophida is hidden by the pronotum. Some species have mandibles shaped like long articulated hooks, which can reach out to seize prey.

The Bostrychidae and the Lyctidae include only wood-eating species, which often attack structural timber, furniture and bamboo (a fact which has considerable importance in the far East and tropical Africa). The former have cylindrical bodies whose elytra often end in a kind of toothed crest, delimiting a fairly deep cupule, an apparatus which ensures the airtight closure of galleries and is used in movements involving the disposal of sawdust to the rear. The latter, which include the powder post beetles, have very flattened bodies. They are sometimes associated with the former; they are found on the floors of galleries, and are constantly in motion, except when, placed under the body and between the legs of a *Bostrichus*, they settle down and rest. The larvae of the two families are very similar, the bodies being soft, thick and arched, and somewhat swollen on the front part and on the head.

Ladybirds of the genus *Adalia* (length ⅕ inch) are among the worst enemies of aphids, on which they feed exclusively as seen here. *Phot. J. Six*

The ladybird, *Halyzia 14—guttata* (length: ⅛ inch approx.), feeds exclusively on fungi growing on leaves. *Phot. John Markham*

The Coccinellidae, well-known as lady-birds, are divided into three groups; eaters of green-flies, eaters of mildew, and herbivores. The seven spotted lady-bird, *Coccinella septempunctata*, eats green-flies. Among its cousins, *Rodalia* were introduced as a counter-measure against certain scale insects of the genus *Icerya* in countries into which the scale had been introduced by man, but in which there were no ladybird beetles specializing in attacking this prey. This introduction, which was one of the first and greatest successes in the biological struggle, has given the coccinellids a special place among the useful insects.

The plant-eating coccinellids or Epilachninae are covered with very fine, dense hairs. Some species are very destructive, especially in the tropics. In Europe, *Epilachna chrysomelina* attacks the Cucurbitaceae (gourds, melons, etc.).

The tortoise beetle, *Cassida* (length: ⅓ inch), in the heart of a daisy. The *Cassida* have flattened bodies so that they resemble tiny tortoises. Their metallic colours—green to golden yellow—are very beautiful. The larvae feed on plants and cover their bodies with excrement which is held in position by their forked tails. *Phot. J. Six*

The Coccinellidae are known for their propensity for forming dense groups, made up of thousands of individuals, under stones, on trees or in houses, at the beginning of winter. Some trees are used year after year, although there is apparently nothing to distinguish them from the others. Other Coccinellidae, among the green-fly eaters, carry out considerable migrations, connected with the seasonal swarming of the greenfly on which they rely for food.

The Chrysomeloidea form a very substantial group which includes many families, as a rule all plant-eating. The Crioceridae includes the asparagus beetle which in Europe attacks Liliaceae, and the lily beetle, *Lilioceris merdigera*, which lives on the leaves of cultivated lilies, and covers itself with a protective sheath made from its excreta. The adult of the Cassididae has a circular extremely flattened body, with the head hidden under the pronotum. Many tropical cassidas have brilliant, metallic colours, or transparent spots, which disappear or fade after death. The eggs are laid in a mass enveloped in a protective secretion, or ootheca. The young larvae have at the end of the abdomen a lengthy forked protuberance on which successive moults accumulate to form a protective sheath. These larvae live exposed on the leaves, the stalk of which they eat. The Cryptocephalidae consist of many small metallic-coloured species, in which gold and red are dominant. The close-set articulations of the body give them the shape of seeds. The eggs are laid one at a time, each egg being held between the female's hind tibiae after laying, and covered with a protective layer of caked excrement.

The Clythridae protect their eggs in the same way, and the larvae increase the size of the protective shell moult after moult, successively. The very hard head, with its flattened brow, fits perfectly into the opening in the shell. Many Clythridae are symbionts of ants. The Sagridae comprise very large tropical species with exceptionally well developed hind femora. The largest number of species is found among the Chrysomelidae and the Galerucinae, which have at their disposal toxic secretions emitted by special glands (*Melasoma populi*), or, on the occasion of a reflex emission of blood, haematuria. The Halticidae have swollen hind femora and

The Colorado beetle, *Leptinotarsa decemlineata* (length ⅜ inch), feeds on plants of the Solanaceae family and has a predilection for the leaves of the potato plant. *Left*, advanced larva eating a potato leaf; *middle*, a newly-emerged female nibbling at a leaf; *right*, female just after laying about 30 eggs. Starting from central US, the Colorado beetle has invaded almost all potato-growing regions. *Phot. Noailles and Six*

are strong jumpers. Some species develop as burrowers inside leaves.

The Bruchidae, close relatives of the Chrysomelidae, live in seeds. The Anthribidae, which are mainly tropical, sometimes grow large, and live under the bark of trees, in forests; some species attack scale insects.

The longhorn beetles include the Prionidae, characterized by their dark hues, their highly developed mandibles and their toothed antennae. They include the largest species of European longhorns (*Ergates faber*), and various exotic varieties (*Titanus giganteus*, from Amazonia). They live in dead, partly decomposed wood; adult females and larvae are attracted by escapes of carbon dioxide, which concentrates them in regions in which wood is in the process of decomposition.

The Cerambycidae, also longhorns, include species of variable size, often with metallic or bright colours, and with slender antennae which are much longer in the males than in the females. The larvae with their elongate fleshy bodies, heads set in the pronotum, which is slightly sclerified, and very short legs, live in stalks or in wood. The larvae of some species frequent roots: *Vesperus*, which attacks vines in the Roussillon district of France, has a larva with a very short broad body, which is not at all like the usual larval type. This larva moves about freely under the ground from one plant to another, as do certain larvae of Saharan Cerambycidae. The change of the Cerambycidae into the nymph stage takes place in an ovoid shell, rich in calcium salts, lining the inside of a cavity hollowed-out just under the bark. Adults of the Cerambycidae are usually diurnal and are found on flowers or fruit in the sun (*Cerambyx*). In the mountains of Europe, species of *Leptura* are very common on the flower heads of Umbelliferae. The adult *Prionus* is nocturnal, and *Lamia* occurs on foliage, branches or piles of wood.

The Brenthidae comprise species which are sometimes large, with very narrow elongated bodies. They live in wood or under bark, and some species are symbionts of ants. These beetles are remarkable for the modifications of their antennae and legs, which are toothed or lobate. Essentially tropical, the Brenthidae have only one European species, a symbiont of ants, but they are often found, in ports, under the bark of imported timber.

The weevils, Curculionidae, constitute perhaps the most important family of Coleoptera from the economic viewpoint. They have in common the possession of a head prolonged forwards into a rostrum which is sometimes longer than the body (*Balaninus*). The antennae are bent after the first segment of the antenna (scape), which is very large, and the club is formed by three closely linked joints, sometimes fused into a single one, gleaming and smooth (Calandrinae). *Braehyrhyncha*, whose rostrum is relatively short and broad, has a larva which is usually free, living in the earth at the base of plants. Stenorhyncha has a very long slender rostrum. Its larva normally lives within vegetable tissues, sometimes as a burrower in leaves, often in the gall which results from its attack. Many species (*Apion*, for instance) live in the pods of leguminous plants. Others bore galleries in the base of plants (Ceuthorhynchinae). The Cossoninae group exploits dead wood and numerous species utilize driftwood cast up on the beach. Some species are symbionts of ants or termites. The species of *Ciona* have larvae which live on leaves and are covered with their excreta like the larvae of *Criocera*.

The Cryptorhynchinae group is remarkable for the high degree of specialization of its adult form: the rostrum engages in a groove on the ventral surface of the body, which sometimes runs from the prosternum to the abdomen; the legs are accommodated in grooves on the sides of the body; finally,

the front part of the body rests very closely on the back part and the whole forms a single one-piece mass, without fissures.

Although they are plant-eating, some Curculionidae are found in deserts. They then have, usually, a very coarse sculpture, like *Brachycerus*.

The biological cycle of the Curculionidae is often based on that of the host plants. In the case of *Derelominus*, which develops in the flowering-periods of palms, and especially of

The hazelnut weevil, *Balaninus nucum* (length: about $\frac{1}{4}$ inch), inserts an egg into a hazelnut, and its larva directly devours the kernel or causes a gall to appear within the shell and here it develops. *Phot. J. Six*

oil palms, this imposes on the larva a very rapid development, which cannot exceed a few days.

To the Curculionidae are attached two families which are not clearly distinguished from them by either larval or imaginal characters; they have in common a relatively short body, a very short rostrum, short strongly clubbed antennae, and mouth parts adapted to the consumption of soft organic substances. They are the Scolytidae and the Platypodidae, which live in wood or seeds. The female bores galleries in which the eggs are laid and the young larvae of the wood-eating species establish a network of radiating individual galleries. Several species feed not on wood but on special fungi (*Monilia candida*, for instance), designated by the general term ambrosia. The larvae do not bore individual galleries, but live in short cul-de-sacs floored with this fungus, on which they feed. The spores of the fungus are transported in special organs in the female and sown in the new galleries.

The hind extremity of the elytra of the Scolytidae and of the Platypodidae bears a row of tubercles, teeth or spines, delimiting a declivity which is often rough or spiny, and sometimes very concave. The forward edge of the pronotum projects and is covered with dense granules.

Female of the elephant weevil, *Balaninus elephas*, on an acorn; here it will hollow out, with the help of its immense rostrum, a small cavity to deposit an egg. The larva eats the cotyledons of the acorn and then undergoes its metamorphosis. Adult is about $\frac{1}{3}$ inch. *Phot. Margiocco*

Longicorns often combine beauty of colouring with elegance of shape. *Bottom left* shows *Chlorophorus trifasciatus; middle,* larva of a *Cerambyx* in its gallery; *right,* nymph of the same. *Phot. Aldo Margiocco, R. H. Noailles and J. Six*

The super-order Neuropteroidea

Known since the Permian, this super-order is made up of fairly dissimilar forms grouped into three orders.

The order Megaloptera

Adult Megaloptera have two pairs of wings with very similar venation and numerous veins, but without a pterostigma (a hardened area on the front edge). The larvae are aquatic, and have on the sides of the abdomen jointed appendages, the tracheal gills. They are actively carnivorous in the larval state. The Sialidae, which is cosmopolitan, contains small forms. The large Corydalidae, the males of which often have enormous mandibles, are mainly in the Southern Hemisphere and are not found in Europe.

(*Above*), mating of weevils (*Bryochaeta quadrimaculata*). (Natural size × 10). *Phot. Michel Boulard*

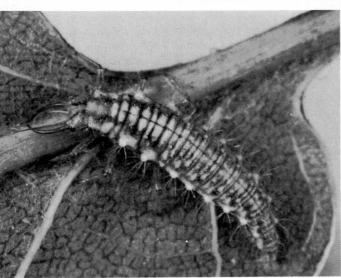

An adult green lacewing, *Chrysopa vulgaris* (length: ¾ inch), its eggs fixed to a leaf by long delicate peduncles, and its fully grown larva after having got rid of the skins of the covering plant-lice. *Phot. J. Six*

The larva of the alderfly *Sialis lutaria*, lives in the mud of rivers; it is carnivorous and attacks all the small animals that pass within its reach. On completing its growth, it emerges from the water and digs itself a shelter in the soil where it completes its metamorphosis. The adult lays on leaves or branches or a stone situated above the water. The new-born larvae make their own way to the aquatic habitat. *Phot. R. H. Noailles*

(*Right*), Scolytids are Rhynchophora—(weevils in the broad sense)—which in the larval state live in wood. *Hylurgus ligniperda* shown opposite, live exclusively on pines; the newly bored hole will lead to the gallery where the female will deposit her eggs. Scolytids are amongst the worst enemies of forest trees. They live in temperate regions of Europe; length: $\frac{1}{8}$ inch. *Phot. J. Six*

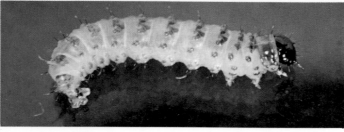

The scorpion fly, *Panorpa communis* (length: $\frac{1}{2}$ inch); its larva lives in the ground and looks like a caterpillar. Note the absence of pro-legs, and the presence at the hind end of the body, of a fixation apparatus (pygopod), which is in fact the extroverted rectum bearing four suckers provided with hooks; this complex acts both as a sucker and as an anchor. *Phot. J. Six and E. Cauvin*

The order Rhaphidioptera

The Rhaphidioptera is composed of comparatively few small species, which have two pairs of very similar wings, with a pterostigma. They have very long narrow prothoraxes, and the female has a long ovipositor.

Carnivorous, they live on tree-trunks and in bark; the nymph or pupal stage, like that of some Planipennia, is active, and moves about before hatching.

The Planipennia (ant-lions)

The Planipennia, a large heterogeneous order, is made up of very small species (certain Coniopterygidae) and Ascalaphidae more than four inches in length. The two pairs of wing

are very similar, with close-set venation rich in transverse veins. The larvae are predatory, and have mouth parts forming a hollow duct which they use to inject prey with toxic saliva.

They include: ant-lions, or Myrmeleonidae, which have short clubbed antennae—in some species the larvae dig a pit in the sand and seize insects which venture over the edge, hastening their fall to the bottom of the trap by throwing sand at them; Ascalaphidae, with long antennae and sometimes brilliantly coloured wings, whose larvae often live on the bark of trees; Nemopteridae, whose hind wings are reduced to a thin very elongate strip, broadened like oars at the tip; Chrysopidae, each of whose eggs is borne on a slender stalk adhering to twigs or leaves, and the adults of which have transparent wings and very bright metallic eyes; Osmylidae, whose larvae, which are aquatic, sometimes live in freshwater sponges; and finally Mantispidae, whose forelegs are prehensile like those of mantids, and whose larvae develop at the expense of spiders' eggs.

The super-order Mecopteroidea

The orders Mecoptera and Trichoptera

This super-order is made up of the Mecoptera, or scorpion flies, remarkable for their larvae which look like caterpillars and have abdominal false legs, and three more recent and

much larger orders. Adult scorpion-flies are carnivorous and seize their prey with their forelegs. Mating is preceded by a nuptial display, in the course of which the male offers a small drop of saliva or a prey which the female consumes. The best-known genus is *Panorpa*, found throughout the Northern Hemisphere. One European genus appears where snow is lying (*Boreus hyemalis*).

The Trichoptera or caddis flies have hairy wings without scales; the larvae are provided with tracheal gills. The adults, crepuscular or nocturnal, do not seem to feed. Their eggs are laid in clusters, in a characteristic shape for the various species, on aquatic plants. With rare exceptions, the larvae are aquatic, but some species live on the ground under fallen leaves in forests.

One whole group possesses walking larvae, which are bare, usually carnivorous, with elongate, narrow and very mobile bodies; they are campodeiform and are similar to the larvae of ground-beetles. Others are eruciform, resembling caterpillars; the body is soft and short, but without abdominal pro-legs and with highly developed attachment hooks at the tip of the abdomen. The larvae have silk glands, opening into the mouth, in the middle of the labium. The silk is used for the building of mobile cases or of fixed nets.

The mobile cases are covered with all kinds of debris; twigs of wood or blades of grass arranged either along the major axis, or perpendicular to it; fragments of leaves; small shells, and grains of sand. In running water, the cases often have lateral expansions to increase their surface of adhesion to the bottom, and the materials are usually grains of sand.

Ant-lions live in sandy places in which their larvae hollow out their craters, buried at the bottom of which they await the passing of prey. *Above*, adult *Creoleon lugdunense*; *below*, craters at the bottom of which the ant-lion larvae lie in wait for their victims. *Phot. J. Six and Aldo Margiocco*

One genus (*Heliocopsyche*) constructs a spirally coiled case similar to a snail's shell.

The nets take the form of sheets stretched vertically across the current between aquatic plants, or pockets arranged in a more or less pentagonal pattern along the rocks over which the water flows, or on the face of waterfalls. The larvae move about on these nets and feed on the microscopic algae and small animals which get entangled in them.

The order Lepidoptera (butterflies and moths)

Lepidoptera, which have scale-bearing wings, normally have their mouth parts transformed into a proboscis, which can be rolled up and is sometimes very long. The wings on one side can usually be yoked to each other by a coupling device. The caterpillars have abdominal pro-legs, and nymphs or chrysalises are always surrounded by a hard smooth skin, with a few exceptions.

Lepidoptera are divided into Homoneura, which are

An adult caddis fly, *Phryganea* (length: ½ inch), and its larval case made of shreds of plants held together by silken threads (*right*). *Phot. J. Six and R. H. Noailles*

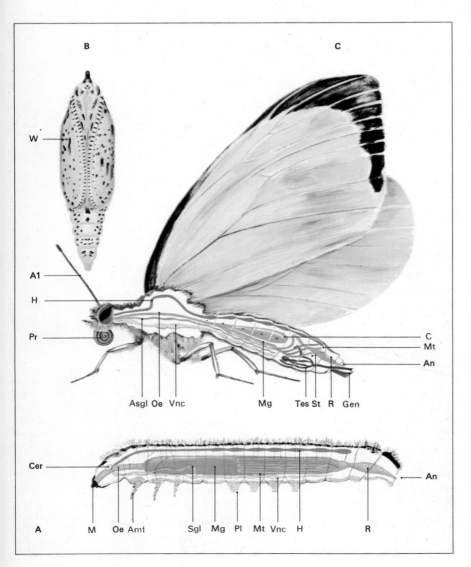

The three stages of the large white cabbage butterfly (*Pieris brassicae*): A, the caterpillar; B, the chrysalis; C, the butterfly. *Al*, antenna; *Aml*, walking leg; *An*, anus; *Asgl*, atrophied silk gland; *C*, suctorial crop, *Cer*, cerebral ganglia; *Gen*, genitalia; *H*, heart; *M*, mouth; *Mg*, midgut; *Mt*, Malphigian tubules; *Oe*, oesophagus; *Pl*, pro-legs; *Pr*, coiled proboscis; *R*, rectum; *Sgl*, silk gland; *St*, respiratory openings, spiracles or stigmata; *Tes*, testis; *Vnc*, ventral nerve cord; *Ws*, wing sheaths.

The caterpillars of moths of the family Psychidae live in cases made of twigs of wood stuck together with silk. The caterpillar fixes its case to a branch or to a petiole by a silken cable. *Below*, the caterpillar is seen nibbling a bramble leaf, as well as the thread which keeps the case suspended. In several species of Psychidae, the sexually mature female retains a larval appearance and never leaves its case. *Phot. Edouard Cauvin*

primitive, and Heteroneura, which are more highly evolved.

Homoneura have similar or almost similar venation in the four wings, with numerous veins. They include the small Micropterygidae, whose larvae have eleven pairs of legs, and the Hepialidae or ghost moths, some of which become very large. The hepialid caterpillars bore galleries in the tissues of plants or live in the ground. Depending on species, hepialids may be nocturnal or diurnal; there are species in which the male attracts the female by the emission of scent.

The Heteroneura include the majority of the Lepidoptera.

Many families, grouped under the general but unsuitable name Microlepidoptera, are normally nocturnal and have caterpillars which develop into burrowers in leaves, fruit, galls, nests, organic debris, ant-hills, termitaries and the fur of mammals.

The biology of these species is very varied. Some are aquatic, and others are strictly confined to particular plants. The American *Tegeticula alba* is found only in yuccas. The adult female yucca moth has a special appendage on her maxillary palp which is used for accumulating balls of yucca pollen, which she subsequently deposits on the pistil before laying her eggs in the fertilized flower. The caterpillars feed on the seeds of the host plant.

Many caterpillars are protected by a case, either of vegetable origin, or of silk.

The Psychidae are known by their sexual dimorphism and

Parasitic lepidoptera are very rare. The Epipyropidae are an exception to this rule: the caterpillars parasitize Hemiptera of the families Jassidae and Fulgoridae. Here an *Epiprops* caterpillar (length: ¼ inch), covered with white powdery wax, is fixed to the side of a fulgorid (*Ricania cervina*), sucking its sugary secretions and eating its wax. Found in Congo-Brazzaville. *Phot. Michel Boulard*

slender feathery tongues. The wings usually have five separate lobes on each side.

The Geometridae or carpet moths are variable in size; their wings often have a jagged and always fairly angular outline. Their caterpillars, slenderly built, and with atrophied abdominal pro-legs in front, fix themselves by the rear part, or by the two extremities of the body. Caterpillars and adults are very often camouflaged, and may change colour to blend with their surroundings.

Near the Geometridae are placed the Uraniidae. One of these, the *Chrysiridia madagascariensis* or *Urania ripheus*, has been commemorated by a postage-stamp. Easily recognized by its brilliant metallic colours, this butterfly carries out migratory movements of considerable scope on the edge of the forest

Two Microlepidoptera. *Left,* the clothes moth, *Tineola biselliella* (½ inch), *right,* the white plume moth, *Pterophorus pentadactyla* (1 inch).

by the curious cases in which the larvae and wingless females live. Made from vegetable, animal or mineral debris, and arranged regularly on a woof of silk, they are to be found hanging on plants and are often easily visible; some reach seven inches in length. Depending on sub-families, the female, which is comparatively mobile, may either emerge from her case at mating time, or, on the contrary, never leave it.

The Aegeriidae or clearwing moths consist of species which have a wasp-like appearance, transparent wings almost without scales, and a body variegated with alternate white or yellow and dark transverse bands.

The Tortricidae, which have broad wings lying almost flat when the insect is at rest, have numerous species. The caterpillars often join leaves together by a network of silk, or twist them into a cluster, hence their name.

The Pterophoridae, or plume moths, which often make their way into houses, have their wings deeply divided into

zone of the Malagasy table-land. Beautiful species also live in Amazonia.

The Lymantriidae are fairly heavy species, with hairy wings and bodies. The caterpillars are also hairy and provided with brushes or tufts of highly coloured hairs, which often have stinging properties. Sexual dimorphism in the Lymantriidae is very marked, and in the genus *Orgyia* the female, small-winged or wingless, may not leave the cocoon even for mating.

The Noctuidae are made up of very numerous sub-families, some large species being notorious for the damage they cause to crops.

The Arctiidae have hairy caterpillars, often called woolly bears.

The Bombycidae are the silk moths, with heavy hairy bodies, pronounced sexual dimorphism and no proboscis; the bombycid of the mulberry-tree, whose caterpillar is the silkworm of commerce, is included among the Bombycidae.

The Attacidae or Atlas moths are the biggest and heaviest night flying moths. Their brightly coloured caterpillars have regular projections or spines. The adults, which exhibit pronounced sexual dimorphism (in the antennae, shape of the body, and size), often have transparent scaleless windows on their wings, for which reason they are sometimes called peacocks. Some species—and especially the moon-moth of Madagascar—have long tails on their hind wings.

The extraordinary long-range power of attraction of the female of many Attacidae and Bombycidae is well known; it is felt by males over distances of several miles.

Although all the moths just discussed are habitually nocturnal, the Sphingidae or hawk moths are usually crepuscular. There is however a diurnal group which has transparent wings (*Macroglossa*, the humming bird hawk moths). Adults have slender wings, the hind ones being smaller. The caterpillars have a horn sticking out of the eighth abdominal segment, and they are brightly coloured. Chrysalises have a proboscis which is arched and well clear of the body.

Having a span of up to eight inches, the Sphingidae are very swift in flight. The species collects nectar from flowers by unrolling a proboscis which sometimes reaches one foot in length. The death's head hawk moth attacks hives. Many Sphingidae carry out long migratory flights.

These nocturnal or crepuscular moths, grouped under the general term Heterocera, have as their counterpart the Rhodalocera or diurnal butterflies. These have antennae which are simple and swollen towards the tip, and no coupling device in the wings. Normally, when at rest, they have their wings erect and close together. More visible and better known than the Heterocera, the Rhopalocera have far fewer species. Many make themselves conspicuous by their nuptial displays and dances, and by their development of mimicry.

The Papilionidae comprise the swallow tail butterflies whose species are often very large (more than ten inches), with very brilliant colours, and hind wings usually with long tails. They are widely distributed in the tropics but only the occasional species is found in Europe. The caterpillars, which are highly coloured and often spiky, have on their necks a reversible forked glandular protuberance, the osmetrium, which has an excretory function.

The Pieridae, the typical form of which is the cabbage white butterfly, are medium-sized species, their coloration often being variegated with yellow, brown and black on a white background.

The Lycaenidae boast a large number of species, especially in the tropics. They are usually small, often being brown or blue, but sometimes a very bright metallic colour. The caterpillars usually look like small slugs and are frequently associated with ants.

The Nymphalidae, which are often large, are widely distributed in the tropics, and remarkable for their brilliant colours; for example, the South American Morpho, the males of which are metallic blue. They are also remarkable for their ability to alter colour to suit their environment (mimetism). This is often striking in forest species, which take on, underneath, the appearance of dead leaves.

With them are associated the medium-sized Satyridae, whose wings are usually rounded and have black, blue or white eye-like spots on a brown background. Their caterpillars often live on monocotyledons.

Although the biology of adult Lepidoptera is remarkably homogeneous, the same cannot be said of their larvae. The caterpillars are normally plant-eating and are often restricted to a small number of plants or even to one alone. Some (especially among the Microlepidoptera) are burrowers, and cause gall-formation. Others bore galleries in the trunks of trees or in the flowering stems of the Amaryllidaceae (Cossidae, Aegeriidae, Thyridiidae, some large Hesperiidae). However, some have behaviour patterns which are aberrant for the group.

There are aquatic caterpillars, breathing through their skin or by means of tracheal gills, and sometimes also by means of an air-bubble held in the mop of hairs. These tracheal gills are similar to those of the Trichoptera.

The caterpillars of *Nymphula* live in a case formed by a rolled-up piece of water-lily leaf cut by the insect out of the

The lappet moth, *Gastropacha quercifolia* (Span: male 2¼–2¾ inches, female 3–3½ inches), when at rest spreads its hind wings out horizontally, while keeping its forewings raised like a pointed roof. It belongs to the family Lasiocampidae which is related to the silk moths, Bombycoidae. *Phot. Edouard Cauvin*

Looper caterpillar of Geometridae or carpet moths. The direction of movement is from right to left. *Phot. J. Six*

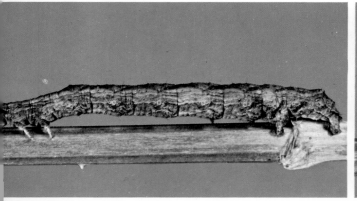

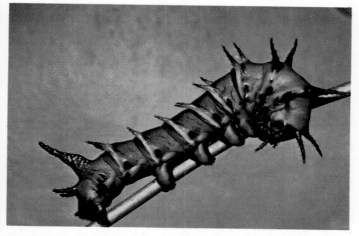

Some caterpillars from equatorial Africa. *Top left* is *Dactylocercus*, which bears two slender ringed horns on each of its segments: *right*, another very spiny caterpillar. *Bottom left*, flattened, very stinging caterpillar living on the cocoa tree; *right*, caterpillar of an undetermined species of cochlidiid. Several caterpillars belonging to this family have a retractile head and stinging hairs. The thoracic legs are very short and the abdominal legs are replaced by suckers; thus the caterpillar gives the impression of being stuck to the leaf which supports it. *Phot. Pujol and Boulard*

lower surface of the leaf. Others live in the pitchers of insectivorous plants (*Sarracenia* and *Nepenthes*); they become adapted to the highly digestive liquid contained in these pitchers and feed on insects which have fallen in.

A number of Tineidae and Phycitidae are linked not to plants, but to dry organic matter used by man (horn, leather, hairs, wool, silk, meal, dried fruits) or accumulated by insects (*Galleria mellonella* consumes the wax in the honeycombs of bees). With them may be associated the Tineidae, eaters of guano, which are common in caves in the tropical region. Finally many caterpillars are linked to the most diverse animals. Thus, the caterpillars of some pyralids live in the fur of sloths and it is believed that they eat the algae which grow on the hairs of their host. Others live in the burrows of mammals or in the nests of birds, such as African weaver-birds or Australian parakeets which nest underground. Their cycle is then based on that of their host.

Several species, in the south of Africa and in India, live in association with *Stegodyphus*, social spiders; they keep the nest and its environs clean, clearing up the remains of prey and the bodies of spiders, without themselves being caught in the web.

Many are linked to other insects. Some are commensals, consuming the wax of bees' honeycombs (*Galleria* and *Achroia grisella*), or moving about on wasps' nests (*Polistes* or *Vespula*). The transition between commensals and parasites is provided by some Epipyropidae which fix themselves to the back of fulgorid bugs after the first moult. Some eat the wax emitted by their host, others feed on the host itself. Others again eat lac insects (*Tachardia lacca*) in India or the wax of the gumlac insect, *Gascardia madagascariensis*, in Madagascar. They appear to consume the waxy secretions of their victims as much as they do the latter themselves.

The Lepidoptera themselves are not immune to attacks by other caterpillars. The collective nests of *Coenostegia* (Thaumatopoeidae) regularly shelter, in Madagascar, several foreign species which consume the chrysalises without attacking the caterpillars. In another thaumatopoeid, *Anaphe*, from South Africa, the caterpillars are devoured by the pyralid *Zophodiopsis hyaenella*. Finally the large larvae of Attacidae are attacked by the pyralid *Sthenauge parasitus* (South America).

Lepidoptera have close and complicated links with ants and termites. In parts of southern Asia and in Africa, Tineidae live in termitaries, usually as rubbish-eaters; on hatching, the young larvae are no different from the ordinary forms of their group, but as they grow there appear and develop on the sides of their body articulated protuberances, the dactylonemes, which are probably secretory. These appendages are very long in *Plastopolypus* of the Congo.

In the ant-hill, some caterpillars find only shelter and food scraps in the nest; sometimes they eat the eggs, but are still not attacked by the ants, which confine themselves to licking

The large cabbage white butterfly, *Pieris brassicae*, lays on crucifers as well as on the large nasturtium (*Tropaelum*); the eggs have their micropyle opening (through which the spermatozoids penetrate) opposite their point of attachment. *Phot. Aldo Margiocco*

Top, the spurge hawk-moth, *Celerio euphorbiae* (span: 2½–2¾ inches). *Bottom*, caterpillar of the death's-head hawk-moth feeds on solanaceous leaves (here tomato). *Phot. Aldo Margiocco—J. Six*

The common swallowtail, *Papilio machaon* (span 2¾–3½ inches); of the family Papilionidae is one of the ornaments of the European fauna. Its caterpillar (2 to 2½ inches) lives on Umbelliferae and on the strawberry plant. When it is alarmed, it shoots out a forked process (the osmestrium) like two red horns from behind its head. The osmeterium emits a strong smell like that of carrots; it is regarded by some biologists as a defensive organ. *Phot. J. Six*

The Apollo butterfly, *Parnassius apollo* (span: 2¾–3¾ inches), of the family Papilionidae, flies in June–July on the flowery slopes of the Alps, Pyrenees, Jura, etc. its caterpillar feeds on stonecrops and saxifrages. *Phot. J. Six*

Two Lycaenidae: *left*, the chalkhill blue, *Lysandra corydon* (span: 1–1¼ inches); its caterpillar lives on clover; *right*, the common blue butterfly, *Polyommatus icarus* (span: 1–1½ inches); its caterpillar lives on broom, the strawberry-plant, etc. *Phot. J. Six*

them. These caterpillars are often wrapped in a silken case, and those of *Hypophrictoides dolichoderella* accumulate in it nymphs of *Dolichoderus* on which they feed. Some Lycaenidae are even more closely associated with ants; their caterpillars have, on the back of the seventh abdominal segment, a special gland, the myrmecophilous organ, which produces a sugary secretion actively licked by the ants. The ants seek out the young caterpillars of Lycaenidae, which, at this stage, look rather like small slugs and eat foliage or fruit. They carry the caterpillars off to their ant-hill in which they feed them on regurgitated secretions and on their eggs, in exchange for

A chironomid and its larva, the blood worm; the red colour is due to haemoglobin dissolved in the blood. *Phot. J. Six and Edouard Cauvin*

the product elaborated by the myrmecophilous organ. For some species at least, such as *Maculinea arion*, this diet is absolutely indispensable for normal development.

Finally the caterpillars of *Cyclotornidae*, after having begun life as ectoparasites of Jassidae (leaf-hoppers), are carried into the ant-hills with their host, and complete their development at the expense of the ants' eggs.

The order Diptera (flies)

The Diptera have only one pair of wings, the forewings, the hindwings being replaced by a pair of clubs with slender stalks, the halteres or balancers. The adult's mouth parts are of the sucking, or piercing type. The larvae are apodous and, usually, the head is indistinct.

Their biology is very varied, with externally parasitic species in the adult state and many others with parasitic larvae. There are two sub-orders.

The Nematocera

These have long antennae, with multiple joints arranged behind each other. Their palps are pendent and their larvae always have a well individualized head (the larvae are called eucephalous). The sub-order includes both terrestrial and aquatic forms. The Cecidomyidae usually cause the production of galls on plants. Among the Cecidomyidae, as has already been mentioned; parthenogenesis associated with paedogenesis considerably multiplies the number of descendants of a single individual.

The larvae of the Mycetophilidae and of the Bibionidae develop in fungi or humus. The Bibionidae may hibernate in the larval state, and the larvae sometimes form substantial accumulations. The Tipulidae, crane-flies or daddy-long-legs, are large insects with elongated bodies, striped with brown and yellow, with very long fragile legs which easily break off. Tipulidae sometimes dance in the light of lamps or in a beam of sunlight in the forest. Many of their larvae live in sodden ground, in marine clay or in water. A number of species of *Tipula* are wingless or two-winged. In spite of their size and their resemblance to mosquitoes, they are mostly harmless. The tiny owl midges Psychodidae, whose larvae live in damp soil, earth or organic debris, comprise on the one hand forms with scaly wings, roof-shaped when at rest, which are often seen on walls in humid places, and which are harmless, and on the other hand harmful species, tiny in size, some of which attack man, the sand flies. Sand flies (*Phlebotomus*) are carriers of diseases such as leighmaniasis. Some African species are cave-dwellers.

The midges, Ceratopogonidae, whose larvae live in sand or earth, are always minute. They are harmful and, in the tropics, transmit virus fevers. Many bite other insects, especially Lepidoptera and Odonata. There are two other families of Nematocera, whose larvae are normally aquatic. The larvae of the Chironomidae, or gnats, live in fresh water or in the sea. Some species, with wingless females, may develop at a fairly considerable depth in tropical seas. Some Chironomidae, however, live out their cycle in damp ground or terrestrial vegetable debris.

The Blepharoceridae look like mosquitoes, but their larvae, which are torrent-dwelling, possess suckers used for fixation.

The other families are harmful. They are the Simuliidae, or blackflies, which have small, short hump-backed bodies, dark in colour, with short but multi-articulated antennae. Their larvae usually live in running water and are equipped with apparatus for fixation to the substratum. The change to the nymphal stage takes place in the water, under cover of a silken case, and the nymph or pupa has two large respiratory thoracic plumes. The African species of Simulium may be carriers of onchocerciasis and, in Central Europe, attacks by black flies cause great concern to farmers, for they drive cattle beserk. In regions where they abound, for instance on the high treeless plateaux of Madagascar, their attacks are sometimes literally unbearable, but fortunately they cease at sundown, and usually as soon as one gets under trees. Some African species lay their eggs on freshwater crabs.

The Culicidae embrace all the mosquitoes and biting gnats. They vary in size from 1/12 of an inch to ¾ of an inch and their wings often have a pattern of scales. The males, which have broad feathery antennae, do not bite, but the females, with rare exceptions, require at least one and sometimes several meals of blood to ripen their ovaries for laying.

The larvae are aquatic and include the Culicinae, which have a long repiratory siphon at the end of the abdomen, and which hold themselves obliquely or perpendicularly to the surface; and the Anophelinae, with no siphon, which lie horizontally under the surface. Both are found in fresh water, whether still or running, and sometimes in brackish water; some *Aedes* and a special form of *Anopheles gambiae* breed in onshore waters, with variable salinity. Many species colonize the small puddles of water resulting from the activity of man or domestic animals (footprints of oxen in clay, empty tins, tanks, and so on) or those which gather in fruit or fallen leaves. Some develop in the water which tropical plants accumulate at their leafbases as well as in pools in the forks of trees. The inhabitants of the reservoirs formed by the ensheathing leaves of the traveller's tree, or *Ravenala*, of Madagascar, have immense nymphal respiratory trumpets often several times as long as the body. These larvae normally feed on algae and on micro-organisms, but some species, like *Megarhinus*, are carnivorous and eat other mosquito larvae.

The adults are sometimes quite indifferent to the species

Crane flies, with their very long legs, flutter above the grass or walk very awkwardly. Usually, they hang indiscriminately by one pair of legs. They lay in the soil, where their larvae live by feeding on the roots of plants. *Phot. J. Six*

Mobile larvae and nymphs of *Culex*, including some coming to the surface to breathe, each using its terminal siphon. *Phot. R. H. Noailles*

Simuliid from Brazil (length: 1/10 inch) biting the back of the hand; its intestine is already full of the blood it has just sucked. This tiny dipteron— its larva lives in running water—is a pest in some tropical countries; thousands may attack man and domestic animals at a time. In South America, the bite of *Simulium amazonicum* is much feared, because it causes severe pain and bruises several inches in diameter which last for weeks. Simuliids transmit filariasis and arbor-viruses (virus transmitted by arthropods) to man and other animals. *Phot. E. S. Ross*

of their victim; they fly and bite at precise hours which are characteristic of the various species, and, in tropical forest areas, they are to be found, depending on the time of day, at well-defined levels above the ground. Their movements are governed by temperature, humidity and light.

In Africa, several species of *Anopheles* are cave-dwellers, and their biology is upset by the constant climate of their habitat.

Finally, the *Harpagomyia*, instead of biting, inserts its proboscis into the mouth parts of ants of the genus *Cremastogaster* and feeds on the matter which the ant regurgitates.

The Culicidae, carriers of malaria and filariasis, were among the first insects to be attacked with D.D.T. Technicians who had thought it possible to eliminate them entirely were surprised by the appearance of resistant forms which thwarted their efforts. The most that is hoped for now is to reach a precarious and uncertain equilibrium.

Mosquito, *Culex molestus* (length: ¼ inch), biting a man on the hand—at the beginning of the bite and at the end of it. The blood absorbed is seen through the transparent abdominal wall. *Phot. Edouard Cauvin*

Female horsefly *Tabanus bovinus* (1 inch). The horsefly is one of the largest Diptera in the European fauna; its short but powerful proboscis inflicts a cruel bite. Only the female feeds on blood; the smaller male has reduced mouth parts and does not bite. *Phot. J. Six*

The Brachycera

Brachycera have short antennae with few joints, erect palps, and bodies which are usually shorter and thicker than that of the Nematocera. The larvae, eucephalous (i.e. with a well-defined head) in the primitive Brachycera, are acephalous (i.e. with a reduced head) in the rest. In the front part of the body there are two curved toothed hooks, representing what is left of the mouth parts; the stigmata are also relegated to the rear end of the body.

On the basis of the mode of hatching of the nymphs, Brachycera are divided into Orthorrapha, the nymph of which is mobile, and Cyclorrapha, the nymph of which is enclosed in the last larval skin, transformed into a small hardened case or puparium.

The Asilidae and the Mydaidae are fairly large, growing to two inches in length, often with a hairy body. They have hard, strong, fairly short proboses. Active predators, they catch their insect prey on the wing, and are often selective in their choice. Their larvae are also predatory. Some tropical Asilidae, such as *Hyperechia*, have very thick hairy bodies like carpenter bees (*Xylocopa*). Others have an inordinately elongated slender abdomen.

The Tabinidae, horse flies or clegs, also usually have strong piercing proboses, and feed, in the adult state, on the blood of their hosts, usually vertebrates. Some African species feed on the sap of plants. Many Tabinidae are, at least in a mechanical sense, carriers of bacteria and protozoa of the blood (trypanosomes).

The Bombylidae or bee-flies, which are often similar in outward appearance to bumble-bees because of their dense covering of brown, black or tawny hairs, have stiff, often very long, proboses which are sometimes longer than their bodies. These are not used for piercing; the adults collect nectar from flowers without landing, just like the Sphingidae. Some larvae of Bombylidae develop in the oothecae of grass-hoppers and locusts.

These three families have exceptionally powerful flight and changes of direction take place at lightning speed.

The Dolichopodidae are slender-bodied flies with bright, often metallic colours. They may be seen resting on foliage, especially in humid regions.

Among the Cyclorrhapha are the Syriphidae, hover-flies. The shapes of their bodies, and their systems of coloration (bright and dark transverse bands) recall the Vespidae. Their flight is extremely rapid. Some of the larvae feed on aphids and look like small elongated slugs, crawling on branches or leaves, covered with the skin of their prey.

The Trypetidae, or fruit flies, whose wings have contrasting patterns, often cause the appearance of galls, especially in the flower heads of Compositae.

The Phoridae are generally very small flies, and the females are often wingless, although this sometimes applies to both sexes. They live in decomposing organic matter, in fruit, or on the bodies of other insects, especially the wings of butterflies. Many wingless species, which have misshapen broadened bodies, are associated with termites. There are some which parasitize these same insects. One species of the genus *Wandolleckia* lives in colonies on the foot of the large African snails of the genus *Achatina*.

The minute flies of the *Termitoxeniidae* are wingless symbionts of termites, whose bodies are deformed and herm-aphrodite, a very rare occurrence in insects.

The Drosophilidae, or lesser fruit flies include the flies attracted to fermenting organic matter, the vinegar or wing flies, *Drosophila*. These are basic material for the study of genetics, and one of the most used laboratory animals. Among the Drosophilidae, there are some whose larvae live as commensals in the frothy liquid produced by certain Malagasy Homoptera, others which are leafminers, and still others which live as parasites.

The Agromyzidae are small short flies, usually black, characterized by their wing venation. Their larvae develop within leaves, in which they make passages with characteristic shapes. The Pupipara are parasites and are confined to vertebrates. They are bloodsuckers, usually with a strongly chitinized body, and with wings which may be atrophied. A single egg is incubated in the genital passages and laid either as an adult larva or a pupa. The *Hippoboscus* of the horse provides a good example. The Nycteribiidae, external parasites of bats, are pupiparous and wingless, with flattened bodies, hypertrophied legs with strong claws, and erect heads. The Streblidae, to which bats are also hosts, are still more degenerate and develop as subcutaneous parasites.

The Muscidae include the majority of common flies and are made up of medium to large species whose bodies are covered with strong bristles set well apart. The larvae feed on vegetable matter or carrion, but may develop in live animals by utilizing pre-existing wounds. The sheep introduced into Australia are thus attacked by the larvae of a blow fly which has also been imported. Toads are often killed by a blow-fly (*Lucilia bufonivora*) which lays its eggs on their skin; its larvae penetrate the natural orifices and cause serious damage to the nasal cavities, eyes, etc. The larvae of *Tachinus* are parasites of other insects. Their eggs are laid either in the host's body, or on the host, or on plants. In the first case, the young larva after hatching very often remains within the shell of the egg, which remains in communication with the exterior and keeps the larva in contact with the air.

The tse-tse flies, Glossina, lay a single egg which is incubated in the female genital passages and shed as a fullgrown

America, the human warble-fly *Dermatobia hominis*, entrusts its eggs to other insects (flies and mosquitoes); on contact with man, the young larvae leave the egg and bury themselves under the skin. These 'macaque worms' create small purulent tumours. The lesions inflicted on humans are, usually, limited, but cases are quoted of individuals literally eaten alive by macaque worms in South America.

The Oestridae, warble or bot flies, consist of flies which are parasites of vertebrates, usually with a specific host, and whose larvae may migrate in the host's body. Those whose development is simplest produce cutaneous lesions from which the full-grown larva breaks free; others are localized in one organ, e.g. *Cuterebra emasculator* of the scrotum of North

Bluebottles, *Calliphera* (up to $\frac{1}{2}$ inch), have roughly the same biology as the greenbottles, *Lucilia*. Their larvae develop in decomposing animal matter; however, some parasitize living animals, molluscs, land snails and slugs. *On the right*, a pupa which has been formed for 24 hours; *in the middle*, the maggot; *on the left*, a larva in the process of contracting to become a pupa. *Phot. J. Six*

Female—recognizable by its non-contiguous compound eyes—greenbottle of meat. *Lucilia sericata* (about $\frac{1}{2}$ inch). Its larvae, or maggots, develop in meat, which they liquidize by their saliva—rich in proteolytic enzymes. These larvae feed only on fluids. *Phot. J. Six*

larva which pupates in soil. Tse-tse flies are notorious as carriers of trypanosomes and are responsible for spreading sleeping sickness and cattle diseases.

Other Calliphoridae have larvae which attack humans and other mammals. In Africa, the larva of *Auchmeromyia luteola*, the Congo floor maggot, lives on the floors of huts, and bites at night. *Cordylobia anthropophaga*, the Tumbu fly of Africa, has very active larvae which penetrate beneath the skin of man and of some of his commensals (rat and dogs); a small boil then forms around the larva, or Cayor worm. In South

Hoverflies or syrphids are Diptera which change diets according to the stage in their life cycle. The larva feeds aridly on aphids, consuming dozens per hour. The adults—here that of the girdled hoverfly, *Syrphus balteatus* (about $\frac{1}{2}$ inch)—feed at flowers. *Phot. J. Six*

Among the worst enemies of the caterpillar of the large cabbage white butterfly (*Pieris brassicae*) is the ichneumon, *Apanteles glomeratus*; the latter's larvae originate from one laying, becoming full grown at the same time. They emerge simultaneously from the host's body and spin themselves individual cocoons made of yellow silk. The caterpillar, pierced all over, dies on the spot. *Phot. Aldo Margiocco*

American squirrels or *Neocuterebra* of the soles of elephants' feet. Others are confined to the natural cavities of sheep and antelopes, especially the frontal sinuses. In the ox warble fly *Hypoderma bovis*, which damages its host's skin by its exit holes, migration is complex. The egg, ingested by the ox as it licks its legs, hatches into a larva which penetrate the suboesophageal mucous membrane in which it grows until the following spring, when it migrates to the lumbar region, and finally reaches the skin in which the maggot, having become

a warble, forms a purulent tumour. At maturity the larva escapes from the tumour and pupates in the ground producing an adult fly which resumes the cycle by laying its eggs on the animal's limbs.

The super-order Siphonaptera (fleas)

This super-order comprises only fleas, named also Aphaniptera. Wingless external parasites given to biting, fleas are usually mobile, passing easily from one host to another. Some species remain permanently fixed to their host, and others are finally buried in its skin and take on the appearance of an internal parasite (chigoe fleas). The larvae are similar to those of the lower Diptera; they are apodous, with a differentiated head. The antennae of fleas are short and have a broad club. Many species have on the thorax rigid combs, or ctenidia, which are found in other externally parasitic groups.

Although linked, for their food, to vertebrate hosts of given species, fleas are governed in their distribution by precise conditions of temperature and humidity. It is these conditions which define, for instance, the distribution area of *Xenopsylla cheopis*, the rat flea, transmitter of bubonic plague.

The super-order Hymenopteroidea

The super-order comprises essentially the order of Hymenoptera, characterized by two pairs of membranous wings, sometimes absent or reduced, or the hind pair alone atrophied or non-existent. The two wings on one side are joined by a coupling device. The mouth parts are of the biting type or take the form of a proboscis. The abdomen ends in a complex ovipositor, capable of becoming a very long borer or sting. The Malpighian tubules are very numerous. The larvae are apodous, with slightly curved bodies, heads not well differentiated and weak mouth parts. Parthenogenesis is very common.

The Hymenoptera are divided into two sub-orders.

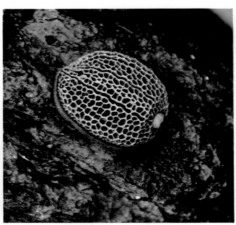

Left, a tse-tse fly, *Glossina palpalis* (about ½ inch); the piercing proboscis, used to penetrate human skin. *Phot. E. S. Ross*
Centre, the *Microdon* (⅓ inch) are Diptera of the family Syrphidae the larvae of which live as commensals in ant-hills. The larva has a slug-like appearance, its body being dorsally convex and covered with a hard integument, flat ventrally and soft—like a slug's foot. *Phot. Aldo Margiocco*

Right, the forest fly, *Hippobosca equina* (¼ inch), belongs to the group of pupiparous flies; it develops entirely in the maternal genital passages and the female lays fully developed larvae which pupate immediately. The adult runs about in it's host's coat, feeding exclusively on blood. Its yellowish colour and its long legs have led to it being called 'spider fly'. *Phot. Aldo Margiocco*

The sub-order Symphyta

The Symphyta, or saw-flies, are usually characterized by the possession, in the females, of a toothed saw at the apex of the abdomen, sometimes replaced by a piercing ovipositor, and by the absence of any narrowing between the thorax and the abdomen. They are always plant-eating in the larval state. From the biological point of view they are divided into two groups. The leaf eaters live without cover on leaves, and their caterpillar-like larvae have abdominal pro-legs, and are sometimes covered with protective secretions. The endophytes comprise both species developing in plant tissues or galls, and species living in wood (Siricidae), in which they bore galleries.

The sub-order Apocrita

In these insects the body is always narrowed between the abdomen and the thorax, the female has a piercing ovipositor or sting, but never a saw, and the larvae are apodous, with poorly differentiated head and mouth parts. They are divided into two series.

Terebrantia have many-jointed antennae and reduced wing venation. The female has a borer or sting and the larvae are parasitical.

Aculeata have antennae with a maximum of thirteen joints and total wing venation. The females have a sting and the larvae normally consume food provided by the mother or by workers.

Among the 4 super-families of Terebrantia, should be mentioned the Cynipidae, whose size varies between 1/25 and 1/5 of an inch. The abdomen is compressed laterally and the female has an extrusible ovipositor. Cynipidae develop in plant galls, of which the gall of the oak—formerly used by man in dyeing and tanning, and known as an oak apple—is the best known. The shape of the gall is specific. Many Cynipidae show an alternation of generations: a bisexual generation is followed by an agamous parthenogenetic generation of females. Each generation may use a different plant, or different parts of the plant, for instance the roots for the sexual generation and the leaves for the agamous generation. This applies to *Cynips calicis*, whose bisexual generation exploits *Quercus cerris*, while the agamous generation uses the pedunculated oak. Furthermore, the females may be wingless in one generation, and winged in the other.

Beside the gall-dwelling Cynipidae are ranged several families of parasitic insects.

The Ichneumonidae consists of species which may attain large proportions. Their bodies are usually elongated and slender, their stings often very long, and their antennae straight. They usually lay their eggs in their host's body after paralysing it with a sting. The host is located by smell, but the laying itself depends on chemical sensations perceived at the level of the sting. The eggs may also be laid on the body of the victim (temporarily paralysed) or close by; in this case, the larva, which may be externally parasitic, moves freely about. Finally, in species which are parasites of bees, the ichneumonid larva consumes its host's provisions after having eaten its larva.

Some ichneumonids, like many representatives of the following families, lay in parasites and not in the primary host; they are called hyperparasites.

The adults are flower-dwellers; but they may also absorb the organic liquids issuing from wounds made in prey intended for their larvae.

The Braconidae, which are very close to the Ichneumonidae, have similar habits; their adult larvae weave cocoons, and these are sometimes so numerous (more than 1000 in a death's-head hawk moth caterpillar) that the skin of a host is completely covered with them.

The Chalcididae have elbowed antennae, reduced wing venation, fairly compact bodies and metallic colouring. They are small, ranging from about 1/50 to 1/4 of an inch in length. The females sometimes feed on liquids exuded by wounds caused by the ovipositor. Most species parasitize the larvae, nymphs or even the eggs of their hosts, while others attack adult scale insects. Some species develop in seeds, and a whole group lives in figs, which they fertilize.

The phenomenon of polyembryony, which is found in the Braconidae and Ichneumonidae also occurs in the Chaleididay. The egg (*Ageniaspis, Trichogramma, Encyrtus*), laid in the eggs of insects or their larvae, undergoes in the course of its development a division into multiple clusters of cells, some of which will produce sterile larvae and others larvae completing their development. From one egg there may emerge up to 2000 adult wasps. This is, however, only one of the processes ensuring considerable fertility for chalcids. The rapid succession of normal generations leads, in the case of certain non-polyembryonic species, to a single female producing as many as five million descendants in twelve generations, in a single year.

(*Below right*), Ooencyrtus is a chalcid wasp of the family Encyrtidae (about 1/4 inch); here it is laying in the string of eggs of a trepanid moth, *Epicampoptera strandi*. Phot. M. Boulard

Enicospilus ramidulus (on the left) is a beautiful ichneumon which parasitizes caterpillars of moths. (Up to 1 inch in length). *Phot. J. Six*

Mating of the hedgehog flea, *Archaeopsylla erinacei* (1/10 inch). *Phot. J. Six*

Ants, in spite of their small size, are very heavily armed. Their mandibles are shears, the edges of which bristle with pointed sharp denticles. *Left*, worker corpse-ant, *Paltothyreus tarsatus* (1–1¼ inches), which in Africa sends its pillaging columns to raid termitaries (the name corpse-ant comes from the putrid smell given off by these insects). *Right*, the head of a large-headed worker, or soldier of an *Atta* (¼ inch), a South American leaf-cutting ant which cultivates mushrooms—its basic food. *Phot. Aldo Margiocco and J. Six*

The Serphidae, or Proctotrypidae, are similar in size to the Chalcids, but their antennae are only rarely elbowed and are usually slender. The cuticle is not metallic, but is often roughly sculptured. The Serphidae are parasitic insects. Some cases of polyembryony and of parthenogenesis are known. The hatching of the egg buried in the host's tissues may occur, as in the chalcids, at a very precocious stage in development. The tiny larva, whose form is very complicated and quite unlike that of the full-grown larva, but which is practically unorganized, bathes in the host's organic fluids and feeds by osmosis.

The Bethylidae, which are mainly tropical, often form collective cocoons for all larvae emerging from a single host. Mating then takes place within the cocoon before the adults emerge.

The Chrysididae, or cuckoo-wasps, medium to large in size, with very hard strongly sculptured cuticles, brilliantly adorned with often contrasting metallic colours, live at the expense of the larvae of solitary Hymenoptera. The egg is laid in the stocked cell, but the chrysid larva develops only when its host's larva has finished its food supply. It then sucks its blood.

The Dryinidae, whose larvae are external parasites of leaf hopper bugs (Jassidae), are remarkable for the transformation of the female's forelegs into pincers; these pincers are constituted by the last joint of the tarsus and by the claw, whereas in mantids and mantispids clutching is made possible by the bending of the tibia over the femur, the tarsus playing no active role.

The Scoliidae, which are about 1½ inches long, have thick hairy bodies and strong digging legs. The females paralyse the larvae of scarabeids (*Cetonia*, cockchafers, and rhinoceros beetles), on which they lay an egg; the larva develops on the spot at the expense of this live prey.

The small or medium-sized Mutillidae, usually variegated in brown, red and yellow, have winged males and wingless females. The female surveys the ground, mainly in dry zones; when she finds a bee's nest, she pierces its wall and introduces an egg. The larva develops as a parasite of its host's larva. Two Malagasy species of *Mutilla* parasitize chrysalises of limacodid moths and some African species attack the pupae of the tsetse fly *Glossina*.

The Formicidae or ants are remarkable for their highly organized social life and complex polymorphism. Males and females (queens) are normally winged and workers are wingless. In tropical species a wingless soldier caste is developed to protect the nests. Their nests display a remarkable variety of architecture and their colonies vary from a few individuals to over 500,000. They feed on both animals and plants, and some species feed on fungi which are grown in special fungus gardens. Their colonial existence has led to the acquisition of many specialized inquilines (living as a 'guest' with another

insect) or myrmecophiles (other insects living as 'guests' with ants). Some of these (lycaenid larvae, beetles, aphids and other bugs) have developed symbiotic relationships with ants: others, however, are mere hangers-on, and a few chalcid wasps and flies are even parasites. Some ants have developed slavemaking habits, raiding the nests of other species for workers. A few are parasitic, laying in the nests of unrelated species. There are over 3500 species of ants and they are the dominant insects of the tropics.

The Pompilidae, some American species of which reach two inches in length and four inches in wing-span, are recognized among the paralysing Hymenoptera by their antennae, which are curved into a crook at the tip. Tropical forms often have brilliant metallic colours. They hunt spiders, digging their burrows only after they have captured prey, and using only one victim to feed each of their larvae. This leads them to hunt large-sized species; thus the brilliantly-coloured South American pepsis attack the enormous bird-eating spiders (*Mygale*).

The Ceropalidae are bracketed with the Pompilidae, and indeed steal their prey. They use this for their larvae, because they can no longer hunt on their own account.

The Vespidae, or true wasps, are easily recognizable by their striped black and yellow livery on the abdomen. Their social structure includes males, queens and workers, and they construct large paper nests to protect the broad combs.

The Eumenidae, which are often quite large, have a stalk connecting the thorax to the abdomen, which then swells into an almost globular shape. Eumenidae are widely represented in the tropics. Solitary insects, they build their nests in earth or in leaves, or dig burrows with straight

The black ant, *Lasius niger* ($\frac{1}{8}$–$\frac{1}{5}$ inch), has an underground nest with numerous chambers and galleries, where the cocoons and advanced larvae occupy the upper regions. Here, *above*, three workers transport cocoons (nymphs, surrounded by a silken shell). *Below*, the queen surrounded by numerous workers, three of which are licking her vigorously; in the foreground, cocoons. *Phot. J. Six*

This beautiful insect with metallic colours is a ruby-tailed wasp, *Chrysis* (½ inch), the larva of which lives as an external parasite of other Hymenoptera, either a solitary bee or wasp. The perfect insect feeds on nectar and pollen. *Phot. Edouard Cauvin*

The female pompilid or ringed spider-hunting wasp, *Crytochilus annulatus* (¾–1¼ inches), attacks wolf spiders (*Lycosa*) and other large spiders. (This one was photographed while on the hunt for prey). It is the largest of the French pompilids (*below, left*). *Phot. J. Six*

The potter wasps (here *Eumenes mediterraneus*) are solitary wasps, very closely related anatomically to social wasps. Their habits are those of the sphegids; they paralyse their prey and transport them, according to species, into nests prepared in advance and which are in fact cells either isolated or arranged in a row. These cells are hollowed out of the ground or masoned with clay-like soil, or set up in a row in reeds or hollow stems. As in so many Hymenoptera, the fertilized eggs produce females; the virgin eggs males. *Phot. Aldo Margiocco*

chimneys sometimes finely cut like lace; sometimes they nest in hollow stems. They paralyze insect larvae and provision their brood cells with one or more larvae of Coleoptera, Lepidoptera or sawflies for each egg laid.

The Masaridae, closely related to the Vespidae, provide their larvae with honey, in burrows hollowed out of the ground and ending in a single cell, or in small cells built on the ground.

The large Sphecidae are variegated in brown and black. The abdomen is on a lengthy stalk, and they hunt prey which is characteristic of each species: caterpillars, locusts and grasshoppers are hunted by *Sphex*, and Coleoptera, Diptera, Hemiptera, Collembola, or spiders are the prey of *Sceliphron*. The nest is normally prepared in advance, whether it consists of a burrow made up of one or several cells, or of a gallery bored in a leaf-stem, or of a masoned earth construction. After capture, the prey is dragged along the ground (*Ammophila* thus transporting caterpillars, *Liris* bringing home crickets) or carried through the air. It is placed in the nest, which receives an egg and is then closed. Sometimes the egg is laid before the cell has been provisioned. Genera such as *Larra*, parasites of mole-crickets, imitate *Scolia* and confine themselves to temporarily paralyzing their victim and fixing the egg on its body, without building a nest. The mole-crickets recover from their paralysis after a short time, but carry their parasite about with them from then on.

The Apidae, a main group of Aculeata, are bees of various sizes, with short, broad hairy bodies. Their legs are not adapted to burrowing, but they have hairy brushes on their legs or bodies, used for carrying pollen, and elongated tongues capable of reaching the nectar of flowers. They may be either solitary (most species) or social, and they stock their nests with plant products such as pollen and nectar. Social life is highly developed in bumble-bees and the domesticated hive bee *Apis mellifica*, which have a caste system consisting of males (drones), females (queens) and workers.

The order Strepsiptera

With the Hymenoptera is associated the order Strepsiptera, consisting of externally parasitic forms. The males are winged, but have only hind wings, with the membrane folding fan-wise; the forewings are replaced by a pair of balancers. The females, which are wingless, do not leave their host's body and are fertilized on the spot.

The Strepsiptera parasitize species of solitary bees, ants, leafhopper bugs, certain plant bugs and stick insects. In the Hymenoptera they cause parasitic castration which is marked by the disappearance of the secondary sexual characters in the females. This is known as stylopization. from the best known genus, *Stylops*.

Section 4—Paraneoptera

This section consists of hemimetabolous species, with the exception of some scale insects and of Aleurodes, (white flies), whose metamorphoses, which are very complex, do not fit into the usual pattern. It is characterized by the vein of the jugal field, which, although single, is branched in its distal region.

The section is divided into three super-orders.

The super-order Psocopteroidea

The order Psocoptera

These are small species, with biting mouth parts and wings arranged roof-wise when at rest. Often the wings are reduced or non-existent. They live on plants, under stones or dead leaves and in houses (book lice), and eat organic debris, algae and fungi. Genera *Psocus*, *Trogium*, etc.

The Mallophaga (biting lice)

Small species, and always wingless, Mallophaga are flat-bodied external parasites of birds and certain mammals. The mouth parts are of the biting type and the legs, which are very strong, act as a fixing apparatus.

The Anoplura (sucking lice)

These are also small species, always wingless, very flattened and externally parasitic. They suck the blood of mammals, except marsupials.

The mouth parts are of the sucking-biting type; the legs, especially the front ones, are very strong and act as clamps, the tarsus folding over a process on the tibia.

Firmly linked to their hosts, Anoplura are very sensitive to variations in temperature. They leave their hosts as soon as the host dies and has cooled. The genera include *Pediculus* (lice), *Pthirius* (crab-lice) and others.

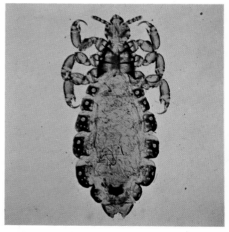 

Above left: the human louse, *Pediculus humanus* (length: male 1/12 inch, female 1/10 inch), has two sub-species or varieties; one lives on the head, the other on the body; here a female *P. humanus corporis*, or body-louse, is the transmitter of exanthematic typhus and of the *Rickettsia* which causes five-day fever. *Phot. Aldo Margiocco*

Above right: the crab louse or pubic louse *Phthirus pubis* ($\frac{1}{16}$ inch), is recognized by its bulky shape and its head connected to the thorax, as well as by its powerful claws formed by the tarsi of the second and third pair of legs; it can move on to the other hairs of the body, especially the armpits and sometimes even the eyebrows. The eggs are fixed to hairs. To date, no pathogenic germ has been discovered as being transmitted by crab lice. *Phot. Aldo Margiocco*

The super-order Thysanoptera (thrips)

Thrips are small species, rarely exceeding 1/12 of an inch in length, with elongated bodies. Colours range from yellow to black, and the mouth parts are of the biting type. The wings are very narrow with reduced venation and fringed with long hairs (setae).

The abdomen of the female ends in a toothed ovipositor or in a tube, depending on group.

With the exception of the Aelothripsidae, which prey on aphids, the Thysanoptera are plant-eaters. Some species cause damage to crops.

The metamorphosis of *Thrips* is very curious. The larvae, on hatching, have all the characters of adults (except for the development of the wings), but the last two pre-imaginal stages are immobile and undergo profound internal modifications: the mouth parts and antennae atrophy, whilst the muscles of the wings develop. Although there is no morphologically recognizable nymphal phase, there is nevertheless destruction and reconstruction of organs, characteristic of complete metamorphosis.

The super-order Hemipteroidea

These insects have mouth parts of a highly modified biting type. There are two pairs of wings, of which the forewings are

Shield bugs (Pentatomidae) are mostly vegetarian and suck the sap of the plants. The stinking eurydema, *Eurydema oleracea* ($\frac{1}{6}$ inch), attacks crucifers; their punctures cause yellowing of the leaves which die when heavily attacked. *Phot. Edouard Cauvin*

The Reduviidae are strong and bellicose predators which attack a wide variety of prey, insects, vertebrates; several feed on blood, e.g. the *Triatoma* (1¼ inches) and their allies, which abound in South and Central America. The bite of these predatory bugs is usually very painful, whereas that of the blood-sucking species is quite painless. *Above left,* the irascible reduvius, *Rhinocoris iracundus* ($\frac{1}{2}-\frac{3}{4}$ inch), which has just hatched and is still on the egg-cluster consisting of eggs fixed to a leaf; this species is predatory. *Above right,* another predatory species from tropical Africa, attacking a membracid and sucking its blood. *Phot. M. Boulard and J. Six*

usually sclerified, with only the outside portion membranous (hemielytra), in the order Hemiptera. In certain Homoptera the wings are uniformly sclerified, like the forewings of grasshoppers. In greenflies they are entirely membranous like the hind wings. The hind wings may be reduced in male scale insects.

The Hemipteroidea are all either vegetarians or predators except for one family, the Cimicidae, which consists of externally parasitic bloodsucking species.

There are two orders: Hemiptera, which have well differentiated hemielytra (formerly called Heteroptera); and Homoptera, with either identical pairs of wings or the forewings more rigid than the hindwings.

The order Heteroptera

The Heteroptera figure among the largest insects, with some water boatmen (*Belostoma*) exceeding four inches. They comprise terrestrial species, species living on the surface of the water and aquatic species.

Heteroptera very often shelter symbiotic bacteria. These may be intracellular (blood cells and special cells, the mycetocytes of the fat bodies) as in Reduviidae and Cimicidae, or they may form crypts around the intestine, in liaison

The water boatman, *Notonecta* ($\frac{1}{2}$ inch), swim rapidly, always on their backs. They are active predators, common in fresh water throughout the northern hemisphere. They hibernate in mud or debris on the bottom. *Phot. R. H. Noailles*

with it or isolated, as in Pentatomidae. Sometimes they constitute isolated organs, called mycetomes, as in Lygaeidae. These symbionts characterize the species with specialized diets, vegetarian or predatory, but their role is still not understood; probably they provide growth factors. The modes of transmission of the mycetomes are interesting and varied. The symbionts may pass into the egg in the process of maturation, or be deposited on the egg at the moment of laying, or, in the Plataspidae, be deposited by the female beside the eggs, in a drop sheltered by a protective envelope. The young larvae come to this drop and absorb the symbionts as soon as they hatch.

Terrestrial forms comprise several families, including Pentatomidae, or shield bugs. These bugs have very large sclerified dorsal shields (scutellum), separating completely, at the rear, the horny part from the hemielytra. The best known type is the green woodland bug (*Nezara viridula*), but there are larger tropical forms with brighter colouring. Some, like *Eurygaster* of the Middle East, cause serious damage to cereals. With the Pentatomidae are bracketed the tropical Plataspidae, in which the scutellum covers almost the entire hind part of the body, the insect taking on an appearance rather like a scale insect. The Plataspidae often remain together in groups originating from one laying; the eggs are in fact joined together in an ootheca deposited on a tree-trunk. The

Some shieldbugs (Pentatomidae) are flesh-eating and live on caterpillars, the blood of which they suck. The example below is *Aspavia acuminata* ($\frac{1}{3}$ inch), from equatorial Africa, which is sinking its rostrum—the bite is probably painless if not anaesthetizing—into a stinging caterpillar. *Phot. Michel Boulard*

The pond skater—here *Gerris gibbifer* (about ½ inch)—glide on the water like skaters on ice. The tips of their legs are coated with a fatty substance which is not wetted by water; the weight of these insects being slight, the surface of the water is for them a carpet over which to glide. They mount the current, then let themselves be carried down by it in interminable comings and goings which have earned them the name of weavers or tailors. *Gerris* live in groups, hunting other insects. *Phot. J. Six*

The bed-bug, *Cimex lectularius* (¼ inch), attacks man, sucking his blood while he sleeps. Extremely resistant, it can endure fasting for several months. Up till the present, no microbial disease is known to be transmitted by it. *Phot. J. Six*

young remain in contact after hatching, and slowly ascend the trunk, feeding as they go.

The Coreidae, which are small and often have elongated bodies in Europe, are sometimes giants, with flattened bodies and hypertrophied hind femora, in the tropics. They are vegetarian species.

The Reduviidae are recognized by their very short sturdy curved rostra, and by their legs, which are often used to capture prey. Predatory and agile, some move about, without getting caught, on the webs of spiders, whose eggs they eat and from which they steal their prey. The Emesinae group, with very slim bodies and elongated appendages, consists of cave-dwelling species which can be seen walking slowly on the walls and the roofs of tropical caves (*Bagauda*). *Ptilocercus* are ant-eaters; the ants, attracted by the odorous secretion of a sternal gland, pass within reach of the hunter, which catches and sucks them dry.

Among the Reduviidae, *Triatoma* and neighbouring genera of South America present a double interest: carriers of a deadly trypansome causing Chagas's disease, which they inject into the humans whose blood they suck, they have also served as a basis for the discovery of hormones in insects.

The Tingidae, which are plant-eating and hardly more than a ¼ of an inch in length, often have partly transparent reticulated cuticles. The cover of a first thoracic segment (prototum) is very often pitted with deep cavities, and has raised edges. Several species cause galls.

The Cimicidae groups together a series of small species around the ordinary bed-bug (*Cimex lectularius*). They are also wingless, and suck the blood of vertebrates. Birds and bats shelter special and highly original genera. Breeding in the Cimicidae is remarkable in that the male's copulatory organ engages not in the female genital passage, but in a special organ, Ribaga's organ, whence the spermatozoids make their way via the tissues to the ovary.

In the small family Anthococidae, the male's penis passes through the female's abdominal wall at any point, not one fixed beforehand.

Closely allied to them are the Polyctenidae, very specialized external parasites of bats.

Aradidae, which have black, foliated, very flattened bodies, often wingless, live under bark and feed on fungi.

Several Heteroptera living at the water's edge, rarely passing on to the water, such as the Saldidae, which hop about on the banks, provide a natural biological transition to those which live on the surface of the water, moving about by gliding without sinking under the surface. They include the Gerridae or water skaters, with very elongate narrow bodies and long legs, the Hydrometridae (water measurers), smaller in size, with shorter legs and slower movements, the Veliidae (water crickets), and the Hebridae, which are tiny and have triangular bodies covered with a very dense layer of fine short close-set hairs. A neighbouring family, the Haloveliidae, lives on the surface of the sea, gliding on the water and feeding on Cnidaria and pelagic molluscs.

Walking Heteroptera, such as the water-scorpion *Nepa* are found in stagnant water. *Nepa* has a flattened body prolonged into a long respiratory siphon, and *Ranatra* has a rod-shaped body. There are swimming species ranging from the giant *Belostoma*, which carry on their back eggs laid by a female of the same species, to the tiny *Plea*, about 1/10 of an inch long. The water boatmen, *Notonecta*, have bodies like the hulls of boats and hind legs adapted for swimming. They swim on their backs. Most of the aquatic Hemiptera are predators and have forelegs adapted for capturing prey. The large *Belostoma* capture fish and the tadpoles of batrachians.

The order Homoptera

The Homoptera comprise seven main groups:

Cicadas have two pairs of wings, both membranous. Large insects, they are recognizable by the stridulatory apparatus which is discussed below. They are diurnal insects, especially active in sunlight. The larva is of the burrowing type, provided with greatly enlarged toothed and spiky forelegs. It develops by sucking the roots of plants. Its life cycle is very long, possibly lasting, in some species, more than ten years, although the adults have a comparatively short life.

The Cicadellidae family includes numerous small leaf-hoppers with sclerified forewings, with many destroyers of crops and species as commonplace as *Aphrophora*, whose larvae secrete a froth called cuckoo's spittle. This is the viscous liquid emerging from the anus and flowing over the insect, which always has its head turned downwards. The air coming from the stigmata makes bubbles in the liquid.

Fulgoridae are essentially tropical and often large (several inches long). Their heads are very often prolonged into almost horizontal beaks, sometimes like a miniature crocodile's head, or curved upwards at the tip like horns.

The Psyllidae is made up of small species whose two pairs of wings are membranous. Their larvae are often flattened, closely attached to plants and fringed with wax. Many psyllids cause galls.

The Aleurodidae are always small (less than 1/5 of an inch) and show very marked sexual dimorphism. The adult males have two pairs of roof-shaped wings, with very reduced venation, usually covered with a thin powdering coating. The female deposits eggs which are isolated and stick to the leaf in a circle around her. The small larva is active, degenerating at the first moult when its appendages and eyes are reduced.

The transformation of the larvae of *Aleurodes* into adults is very interesting; although hemimetabolous, the insect undergoes profound modifications of the tissues, similar to that of insects with complete metamorphosis. Aleurodes are among the very few animals whose cells have only half the full number of chromosomes, all of which are n chromosomes. Several are harmful to crops.

The larvae of the frog hoppers (⅓ inch) of the family Cercopidae live in an accumulation of air bubbles caught in a viscous liquid. The sap is sucked in such abundance that it re-emerges copiously through the anus; it is mixed with a viscous substance which makes it possible for the bubbles, formed by the air coming out of the respiratory openings (spiracles), to remain in being without bursting. The larva emerges periodically from its frothy shelter to take fresh air. These strange masses are known as cuckoo spits. *Phot. Aldo Margiocco*

Aphidae or green-flies, include among the group many other enemies of crops. They have fleshy bodies about 1/10 of an inch long, and the abdomen bears on the sides, towards the rear, two erect glandular tubes or small horns. The wings are membranous and usually dark-coloured. Green-flies are polymorphous, with not only winged sexual forms but others which are wingless and parthenogenetic. Polymorphism accompanies a complex reproductive cycle described at the beginning of this chapter.

The hosts of *Chermes* are conifers. Its cycle is complicated. In autumn the fertilized female lays a single egg on a spruce tree. From this a hibernating larva emerges. This lays in the following spring, and from its eggs emerge larvae which develop in a leafy gall; the winged adults which emerge from it reach a pine, fir or larch and lay in it; the small larvae pass through the winter and in spring produce both winged and wingless forms; the winged ones of both sexes return to the spruce and lay a fertilized egg; and the wingless ones pursue their cycle by parthenogenesis on the secondary host. The complete cycle therefore takes two years, although one of the two phases may disappear in some species.

The case of the *Phylloxera* of the vine, which is an aphid, has already been discussed (p. 183).

Scale insects have a sexual dimorphism similar to that of *Aleurodes*. The males have one pair of wings, the forewings,

Scale insects, always or almost always small in size, are deadly parasites of plants, which they poison by the saliva that they inoculate. *Right*, a mussel-scale (*Mytilaspis*) on an orange; *left*, scale insects on the stem and pods of a cocoa tree. *Phot. Aldo. Margiocco and R. Pujol*

with the hind wings reduced to stumps. The antennae are hypertrophied, very long and hairy. The females are wingless, and usually immobile (except certain *Orthezia* and *Ortheziola*), hanging on to plants and usually covered by a wax shell. Many species lay their eggs in sacs carried by the mother. Scale insects may be found on flowering or non-flowering plants which have a system of ducts used to transport nutritive material. Some young or adults live on the roots of plants, with or without ants, and the nectar regurgitated by many scale insects is utilized by the ants.

Scale insects are among the deadliest enemies of fruit crops (e.g. the San José scale, *Aspidiotus perniciosus*), and the damage they cause is aggravated by the fact that their waxy coating protects them against most insecticides. Their saliva is very toxic to plants.

A few species are useful to man, for instance the nopal scale insect, in Mexico, which produces a red dye, carmine, the *Tachardina*, a scale insect which secretes lacquer, in India, and the gum-lac insect, *Gascardia*, secreting what the inhabitants of Madagascar call ant-wax (lokombitsika). Some

species have also been used successfully in the struggle against prickly pears in Australia and Madagascar.

Care of the young

In quite a number of insects, the female remains in the neighbourhood of the young and affords them a certain measure of protection. In the simplest case, this protection is purely physical. Thus, the females of psychid moths, wingless and slow, lay in the bottom of the cases which they build and which shelter them. The eggs are covered by the mother's body until hatching, after which the young larvae disperse.

In the earwig, *Forficula*, the mother actively looks after her eggs, removes anything that soils them, moves them about within the nest, and repels any insect which approaches, even the male. This care seems to be necessary, for, in her absence, the eggs are attacked by mildew and perish.

A certain number of tortoise-beetles, *Cassida*, (Chrysomelidae), cover their eggs with their bodies, and they too remain with them until the young larvae have completed their first moult.

At a higher level, the mother prepares food for the young. This preparation may take place without the female ever being in close contact with the young, the measures she takes being limited to the building and stocking of a shelter. Thus, many longhorn beetles, Cerambycidae, lay in the branches of trees, after having detached from the base of the bough a ring of bark and fibrous material. The treated branch withers, which permits the growth of the larva.

Some weevils, Curculionidae, scoop out the pulp of certain fruits and deposit their egg in contact with the stone.

The leaf roller weevils (*Rhynchites*, *Attelabus* and *Apoderus*) cut out a fragment in the leaf-stalk, which remains attached to the leaf only by a slender thread. Then they roll this withered fragment into a cylinder, closed at both ends, which receives the egg and affords shelter and food to the larva. The outline of the section of the limb is closely connected with the position of the veins and the normal edge of the leaf; the relation between the two is so precise that it can be mathematically expressed. Perhaps less gifted, some *Rhynchites* borrow the 'cigars' prepared by kindred species and lay their eggs in them.

It is interesting to recall that moths of the genus *Syllepta* roll cylinders out of *Dombeya* leaves identical to those of *Rhynchites*; but the caterpillar of *Syllepta* makes its own shelter instead of using one prepared by its mother.

The dung beetles

A certain number of Scarabeidae (*Onthophagus* and *Scarabaeus*), all dung- or carrion-eating, and also various Dynastidae, deposit a store of rotten leaves, dung or decomposed carrion in a subterranean cavity. Burial may take place on the spot, but often the female transports the provisions intended for the larvae over some distance, in the form of a fairly regular ball (sacred beetle, *Scarabaeus sacer*). Among these transporters, some push the ball in front of them, like the minotaur beetle (*Typhaeus typhaeus*); some roll it between their elongated hind legs, which sometimes have curved tibiae, as if they were getting a better grip on their burden (*Sisyphus*); others load the ball of dung on to their elytra and

A lantern bug, *Fulgora lampetis* (about 2½ inches), Central America. The enormous prolongation of the head is not luminous, as believed formerly. *Phot. C. M. Hladik*

Dictyophara europaea belongs to a family closely related to the Fulgoridae. It flies and jumps with remarkable ease. Its only peculiarity is its sugar loaf head; compared with the tropical Fulgoridae it is of very modest size (½ inch long). *Phot. Edouard Cauvin*

The Aleurodes or whitefly (½ inch) of the coffee tree appears like a tiny white star attached to the lower surface of leaves. It secretes a wax which, in this case forms divergent rays from the insect's body. Only the larva is mobile; after having become fixed, it moults and its legs and antennae are then reduced to vestiges. After a third moult, the insect undergoes further metamorphosis; it passes through a special state (puparium), of strange and varied shape, and emerges in the winged adult state. *Phot. R. Pujol*

hold it in position with their hind tibiae (*Eurysternus* of South America). The nutritive mass, more or less spherical, thoroughly softened by the mother's mouth parts, is uniformly sown in micro-organisms and perhaps partly predigested. It may entirely fill chambers arranged along an axis or be enveloped in a sheath of earth occupying only a part of the nest cavity. The egg is almost always isolated from the mass which has thus been prepared; it is sometimes laid before the nest is stocked (dor beetles, *Geotrupes*), sometimes placed in a small depression with very smooth walls at the top of the mass, and often separated from the outside by a stopper porous enough to allow air to pass.

In the scarab genus *Gymnopleurus*, and the true scarabs, the two sexes are believed to collaborate to the extent of specializing their tasks. The size of the burrow varies with species. Some African *Sisyphus* do not even dig a burrow, but fix their ball of dung to a blade of grass. Many beetles fit up a small chamber only a few inches deep, at the back of a ridge of sand; but the minotaur beetle bores tunnels more than three feet deep, sometimes in the hard ground of forest paths. In the burrows of *Heliocopris* there is room for four fist-sized balls of dung.

In *Copris*, the female instals masses of dung in a large underground chamber, and lays an egg in each mass. She then remains in the burrow and keeps a constant watch on these unusual cradles, keeping them clear of the mildew which might form on them.

The burial of dung matter by the scarabaeids takes on considerable importance in the tropics, ensuring both the clearing-up of the surface and the enrichment of the soil. Hingston, in India, goes so far as to state that it is thanks to their efforts that the human species is able to survive without being smothered in its own excrement.

Mason wasps and solitary bees

Many solitary Hymenoptera, Apidae and Vespidae build nests made up of cells more or less side by side, stocked with honey, pollen, or prey which is either dead or paralyzed. Paralysis ensures the prolonged survival of the prey and guarantees fresh food for the larva. The cells may be simple cavities scooped out in the ground (Ammophila), but they are often considerable edifices.

Potter wasps, *Eumenes* for instance, build cells in loose earth, hemispherical and opening to the outside by a wide neck. Each cell receives a ration of paralyzed caterpillars or spiders, an egg is fixed to the upper part of the cell, and it is then closed. Often arranged in small groups, these cells are contained in a mass of loose earth and the nest as a whole takes on the appearance of a pie with roughly oval contours.

Others, especially leaf-cutter bees, (*Megachile*) and mason wasps, (*Odynerus*), make use of natural cavities: empty snail shells, hollow pieces of bamboo or reed, etc. Each shelter houses a series of cells built of earth or resin, or sometimes of fragments of leaf neatly cut out of plants with broad stalks. Each cell in turn is stocked and receives an egg before being closed. This mode of building cells one next to the other, in such a way that the first one to be prepared has all the others on top of it, poses a very special problem. At the moment when the adult hatches, it has to free itself quickly, otherwise it dies of suffocation. In many species of Apidae, the development of the male, which is smaller, is more rapid than that of the female, with the result that the males appear first. In order that the males will be in a position to free themselves on hatching without destroying the brood by forcing their way through cells still occupied by nymphs, it is necessary for the eggs in the first cells to produce females and for those in the last cells, which are nearest the exit, to produce males. Laying is therefore precisely regulated, the female eggs in each series of cells being laid before the male ones. The sex of the egg seems therefore to be a matter for the mother to decide.

When the paralyzed prey is introduced into a shelter prepared by the mother, the building of the shelter may precede the hunting, and in this case it sometimes even receives an egg before the prey has been captured. When the ration necessary for a larva is only one victim, it often happens that the burrow is prepared only after hunting, near the spot where the prey was captured.

One cannot, however, speak of family structure in the paralyzing Hymenoptera, for the mother does not enter into contact with her progeny. A simple family structure (the mother and her young) appears in some predatory Hymenoptera, such as *Bembex*, which keep their larvae supplied with flies and renew the food ration throughout the whole of larval life.

Among the bees, *Allodape*, from the south of Africa, feed their larvae, lodged in cells bored in the pith of dead stalks, with a mixture of pollen and nectar, which they prepare in advance and distribute as required; they are aided in their nursemaid duties by the first daughters to hatch.

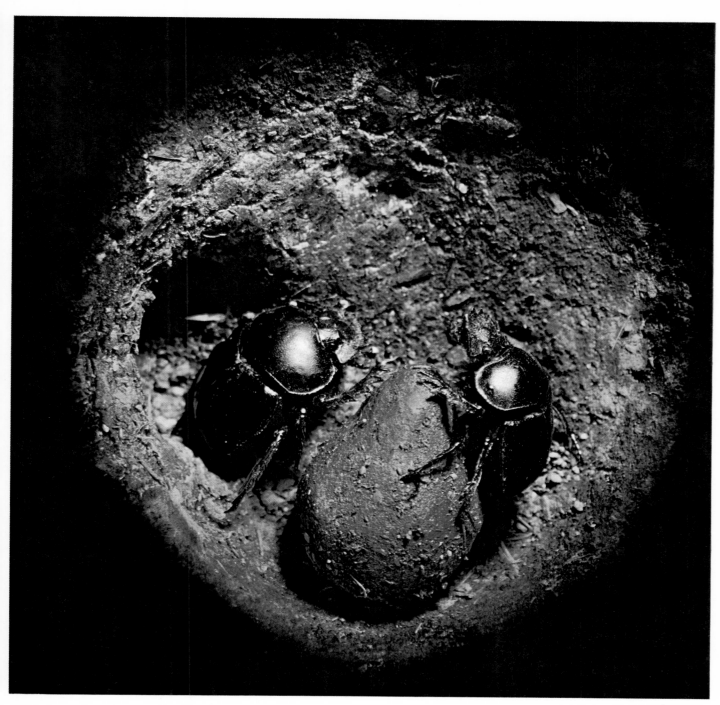

The sacred scarab, *Scarabaeus sacer* (1¼ inches), in spite of the homage paid to it by the Egyptians, is just a common dung beetle. It makes up balls out of herbivores dung and then buries and lays its eggs on it; the larvae feed on dung. *Opposite, left,* the scarab rolls its ball backwards; *right,* two individuals busy themselves with the same ball. Transportation by two insects is not rare; the rollers are of identical or different sex.

Above, the ball, transported under the ground, has been moulded into the shape of a pear: on it the scarab lays; the underground chamber into which the ball of dung will be introduced can be seen on the left. The sacred scarab lives in the Mediterranean basisn, and, eastwards as far as Afghanistan. *Phot. Aldo Margiocco and J. Six*

A rudimentary family society

In some, notably the fungus-eating Scolytidae, the family is of the polygamous type, the male moving about within a network of a few communicating galleries, each of which is the domain of a female and its larvae.

In other Scolytidae, known as ambrosia beetles, the female, sometimes helped by the male, digs a gallery which has lateral chambers arranged in a regular series. Special fungae develop along the galleries starting from spores transported by the females, which literally cultivate them, whilst eliminating other species. These fungae feed the larvae. The facts remain somewhat obscure, and symbiosis of this type has been unsuccessfully sought in the African passalid beetles.

235

The sub-social Necrophon (sexton beetles)

As far as the species of *Necrophorus* are concerned, it has been noted that groups of females bury the corpses of vertebrates, and fashion from these corpses balls of flesh arranged along a gallery. The females feed young larvae by regurgitating the product of predigestion of these corpses: advanced larvae feed directly on the balls of food material put at their disposal.

A last example of loose family community is provided by the Staphylinidae of the genus *Bledius*. Living in large colonies in humid clay or seashore sands, *Bledius* hollows out a network of galleries. The laying galleries are accompanied by series of cells intended for the reception of the eggs, and their walls are covered with algae which are eaten by the young larvae.

In favourable sites, some solitary bees, Apidae, also form very populous colonies, in which, however, each individual operates on its own account, without being influenced by its neighbours.

Sexual dimorphism

The two sexes in insects often differ very profoundly.

The sexual characters comprise primary sexual characters (copulatory and laying organs, sting, ovopositor, etc.), and secondary sexual characters, unrelated to fertilization or laying. These secondary sexual characters are often apparently completely useless: dilation of the head, tubercles or horns on the fore part of the body, spines on the legs, fusing of the abdominal sternites, terminal spurs on the tibiae, coloration, and so on. However, a closer examination shows that these characters may facilitate copulation (e.g. stria on the elytra of female *Dytiscus*, adhesive suckers on the tarsi of the males in the same insects, long forelegs of the Clythridae, etc.). Another function may be the discovery of females (e.g. hypertrophied antennae in certain Lepidoptera and Scarabeidae. In some of these the club of the antenna, which bears sensory endings, may be longer than the rest of the organ, as in the glaphyriine moths of Yunnan).

So far, except in the Lampyridae, it has not been possible to demonstrate the existence, in insects, of hormonal secretions affecting the determination of the secondary sexual characters. It is probably that their action is exercised at a very early stage, even during the embryo's formation, hence the difficulty involved in showing how they operate.

Among the commonest secondary sexual characters must be mentioned the wingless nature of females. In the simplest cases (e.g. in the pleocomine scarab beetles of North America) the female is bigger, bulkier, and wingless, but with normal elytra and legs. Very often the wings and elytra disappear, or are reduced to small scales, as in cockroaches, grasshoppers, certain African Mantidae, and *Pachypus* among beetles. The body is then often, but not always, unpigmented and comparatively soft, but the antennae and the legs are normal. Although the female tends to remain on the ground, or sometimes in its burrow, it still leads a free life.

In the Drilidae and Lampyridae, the female is usually larviform; much larger than the male, with soft skin, she no longer shows any trace of wings or elytra, and her simplified appendages, too, are of a larval type.

A fair number of Lepidoptera have short-winged or wing-

less females; this applies to the higher Psychidae, certain Megalopygidae, vapourer moths (*Orgyia*) well known in orchards, mountain-dwelling species of ghost moths, (Hepialidae), and many others. Winglessness reaches its peak in the Psychidae, in which the female is reduced to a sac with very short appendages, enclosed in a case. Exceptionally, in the pyralid with an aquatic caterpillar, *Acentropus niveus*, there are two forms of female, one winged and aerial like the male, the other short-winged and aquatic.

Two sub-orders of Homoptera, white-flies, *Aleurodes*, and scale insects, are constantly wingless and larviform in the female, whilst the male is winged.

Among the parasitic insects, some have wingless females, while the males are winged; this applies to the *Silphopsyllus desmanae*, an external parasite of the desman (*Desmana*) of Transcaucasia, and to *Thaumatoglossa*, a dermestid beetle developing in the eggs of Mantidae.

The limit of dimorphism is reached in the Strepsiptera, internal parasites of various insects (stick insects, leaf hopper bugs and solitary bees). The normal male leaves its host's body and flies away, whilst the female, except in the *Mengeidae*, remains fixed in it, is fertilized on the spot and never emerges. She is reduced to a bag of atrophied appendages. In the Mengeidae, the female is a little less degenerate and has functional appendages.

Dimorphism of the wings must not, however, be considered as a properly sexual character, for in many species of insects (some pond skaters *Gerris*; weevils, *Sitona*; ground beetles such as *Carabus* and *Calathus*; Diptera, and Psocoptera), it may characterize certain lineages and be manifested in unequal degrees. Various individuals of the species may then show normal wings, short non-functional wings, or no wings at all. The skeleton and the musculature of the thorax undergo transformations parallel to those of the wings, but not always concomitant.

On the other hand, quite numerous species—especially in the Plecoptera, some Trichoptera and Tipulidae—there are populations with short and, usually, non-functional wings at high altitudes; in other Trichoptera, the summer populations have females with normal wings and the winter populations females with atrophied wings.

Finally, in the Chalcid of figs, or *Agaonidae*, the wingless condition is reversed: it is the females which, possessing wings, move about from one flowering plant to another, while the males, devoid of wings, remain constantly shut up in the hypertrophied receptacle.

Sexual characters whose development is linked to the size of individuals are never directly connected with reproduction: lengthening of the antennae or the legs, dilation of the head, hypertrophy of the mandibles and development of horns or other protuberances from the head or thorax.

In a very general way, these characters grow faster than the overall size of the animal, the divergence in rate of growth sometimes being considerable. But it is always possible to establish a precise relationship between the size of the sexual variant and that of the body. Moreover, at least in the scarabs and stag beetles, several forms may exist within one species, differing in the rate of growth of indi-

vidual parts of the body. It is as if they were emergent species, distinguished at the beginning only by a special mode of development of the sexual variants.

Communication—non-social insects

Whether they belong to a social complex, or are solitary, insects have to be capable of finding and making contact with a partner to ensure the reproduction of the species; for this purpose they have various means of communication at their disposal.

In their dances, which are displays of conventional movements, bees communicate information about the size, distance from the hive and location of a source of food supplies. In termites and ants, scent trails are used to direct the movements of armies.

Luminous insects

One means of communication used by insects, especially glow-worms (*Lampyris*), and fire-flies (*Pyrophorus*) is the discontinuous emission of light signals. Their photogenic organs emit light, varying usually from green to red, the spectrum of each species being characteristic. It may be emitted continuously (even the eggs of some Lampyridae

are luminous) or intermittently, in which case the rhythm of light flashes is also characteristic of species and sex.

The luminous organs are definitely for signalling, since males and females are known to communicate by these means. Luminous emissions of one respond to those of the other, and enable males to head in the direction of females and join them for mating. Signals normally start at sunset, when the intensity of the sunlight falls below a certain level.

The light emitted is called 'cold' and has been closely studied. The photogenic organ is complex. A lower layer of cells laden with crystals of urates and xanthine forms a reflector, and an upper mass of cells with numerous granular inclusions, very strongly innervated and provided with a dense network of tracheae, provides the light.

The emission of light depends on a neurosecretory control system in which adrenaline is involved. It is produced by an enzymatic reaction. The enzyme luciferase, sensitive to heat and destroyed at a high temperature, makes possible the oxidation at moderate temperatures of a substance which is normally stable up to high temperatures, luciferin, to oxyluciferin, with emission of light. This reaction, like all enzymatic reactions, maintains an equilibrium between the substances, and the colour of the light, a function of the speed of oxidation, depends on the specific luciferase.

It is less well known that other insects may be luminous. In some the luminescence is due to an association with luminous bacteria which is temporary and usually lethal. Many larvae of Diptera present luminescence of this generalized type. However, the larva of a cave-dwelling New Zealand mycetophilid fly, *Arachnocampa luminosa*, also possesses a true photogenic organ. The ends of the four Malpighian tubules are swollen and fixed against the rectum on a reflecting layer formed by the cells protecting the tracheae.

It is not possible to place the remarkable South American lantern bugs, *Fulgora*, in this series since their alleged luminescence has not been observed again since it was first reported.

Odorous insects

The emission of odours by insects is common. The musky odour of *Aromia moschata*, the metallic green longhorn beetle

Syromastus marginatus (½ inch) is one of the commonest coreid bugs in western Europe; it belongs to a sub-family which includes more than 1500 species. It spreads a very penetrating acrid smell. *Phot. J. Six*

which develops in the wood of old willows, is well known. *Osmoderma eremicola*, a large chafer beetle living in the leaf-mould of hollow trees, has an odour like Cordovan leather; and many bugs, especially shield bugs, give off a most unpleasant and persistent odour if they are touched. Other insects, rare or little known, have even stronger odours, such as a tiny ground beetle which can make a whole room smell.

The emission of odours may play two different roles.

Many species emit repugnant odours, often accompanied by the explusion of distasteful acrid substances, either through special glandular orifices, or through membranes at the joints, often accompanied by the exudation of a drop of blood. This is called autohaemorrhaea (voluntary haemorrhage), and is very well known in Coleoptera (coccinellids, tenebrionids, etc.) Habitual predators, especially lizards, mammals and birds, are acquainted with these odours and avoid attacking the insects which produce them. Batrachians, and especially toads, seem to be less knowledgeable in this respect, although they too reject evil-smelling prey after seizing it.

On the other hand, odour may have the power to attract. This power is exercised within one species (e.g. male termite following the female termite) and may be perceptible over a considerable distance. Thus females of Saturniidae and of Bombycidae, heavy and lacking in mobility, attract the males of their species from several miles around. The same attraction helps the males of *Pachypus* (Scarabeidae), whose females never leave their burrows, and those of the North American *Pleocoma* (Scarabeidae), whose females are immobile, to find their partners, but indicates only a general direction. Having reached the neighbourhood of the female, the males begin to mill around confusedly, and the meeting of the sexes may become a matter of chance.

It seems probable that the winged males of the Strepsiptera also find their females by sense of smell.

Odours also play an attractory role between different species. It is the essential factor in the positive relations between myrmecophiles and ants and is involved in the choice of prey by parasites.

Musical insects

Many insects emit sound signals, either audible to man or as ultrasounds. In some cases, for instance in *Lilioceris* (Chrysomelidae) and in the Orthoptera, it has been possible to establish that signals emitted by the males are perceived by the females. The role played by singing in the social life of crickets is well known. It ensures both the bringing together of the sexes and the delimitation of the territory claimed by individuals. In mosquitoes, the sound emitted by the females attracts the males and some thought has been given to the possibility of making use of this fact in anti-mosquito measures.

In termites, the sound emitted by the soldiers possibly constitutes an alarm signal.

However, much has yet to be discovered about the real significance of the sounds emitted by numerous species. Specific sounds have yet to be recorded and classified.

The devices used for the emission of sound signals are extremely varied.

The simplest is the striking, repeated more or less rhtymically, of a sclerified part of the body, head, pronotum or abdomen against the substratum, ground, or wood. This produces a tapping sound, like that of the death-watch beetle. More often, the sound is made by rubbing a vibrant part against a fixed part of the body: ridges or crests on the

Insects of special interest

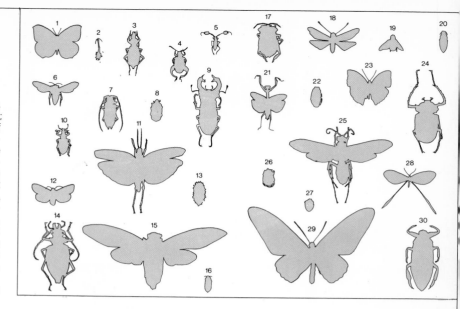

(following pages)
1. *Gonepteryx cleopatra* (Lepidoptera; Reridae), the Cleopatra butterfly, inhabits the whole of Europe. 2. *Trachelophorus giraffa* (Coleoptera; Attelabidae), is a Malagasy weevil with exaggerated development of some of its organs. Its head and its prothorax, lengthened to an extraordinary degree, make it from the anatomical point of view one of the most unbalanced insects in existence. Its structure borders on monstrosity. 3. *Coptolabrus marginithorax* (Coleoptera; Carabidae), from China. It would be quite commonplace if its lively colours did not lend it some originality. 4. *Sagra buqueti* (Coleoptera; Chrysomelidae, Sagrinae), from Java. Its larva gives rise to the galls in which it develops. The hypertrophy of its rear femora would seem to suggest an aptitude for jumping, but it has not manifested this ability. 5. *Cosmisoma diana* (Coleoptera; Cerambycidae), is a beautiful longicorn beetle from Colombia. 6. *Aglae caerula* (Hymenoptera; Apidae), from tropical America, is a bee with solitary habits. 7. *Anaplophora horsfieldi* (Coleoptera; Cerambicidae, Lamiinae), from China. 8. *Heterorrhina imperatrix* (Coleoptera; Cetoniidae), a chafer from Japan. 9. *Lucanus cervus*, a male stag beetle. It is part of the European fauna. The very pronounced sexual dimorphism shown takes the form of hypertrophy of the mandibles in the male. 10. *Cyphus augustus* (Coleoptera; Curculionidae), a beautiful weevil from Brazil. 11. *Phymateus saxosus* (Orthoptera; Pyrgomorphidae), is a grasshopper from Madagascar. The *Phymateus* are the most richly-coloured grasshoppers. 12. *Eudaphaenura catali* (Lepidoptera; Noctuidae), from Madagascar. 13. *Julodis hirsuta* (Coleoptera; Buprestidae), from Madagascar. 14. *Psalidognathus friendi* (Coleoptera; Cerambycidae), a female longicorn from tropical America, remarkable for the power of its mandibles. 15. *Tosena fasciata* (Hemiptera; Cicadidae), from southeast Asia. It is a cicada with very bright colours. 16. *Buprestis (Yamina) sanguinea* (Coleoptera; Buprestidae), a small species from Spain and Morocco. 17. *Oncomeris chrysopterus* (Hemiptera; Pentatomidae), from the Moluccas. 18. *Ascalaphus libelluloides* (Neuroptera; Ascalaphidae), from the Mediterranean basin. This ant-lion has wandering carnivorous larvae, which run on sandy soils and do not dig crater traps. 19. *Rutilia fulgida* (Diptera; Tachinidae), from Australia. Like all the tachinids, its larvae live as parasites of other insects. 20. *Metatenia clotidae* (Coleoptera; Buprestidae), from the island of Bougainville (Solomon Islands), remarkable for the beauty of its colours. 21. *Iris oratoria* Dictyoptera; Mantidae), from the Mediterranean basin. This very beautiful mantid has similar habits as the praying mantis, but it has much prettier colours. 22. *Plusiotis resplendens* (Coleoptera; Scarabeidae, Rutilinae), the golden scarab, is a native of Costa Rica. This is the one referred to by Edgar Allan Poe in his story *The Golden Scarab*. 23. *Cymothoe coccinata* (Lepidoptera; Nymphalidae), from equatorial Africa. 24. *Cheirotomus parryi* (Coleoptera; Euchiridae), male with outsize forelegs, from northern India. 25. *Pepsis heros* (Hymenoptera; Pompilidae), from tropical America; is the largest of the wasps. It is a hunter of mygales (the largest spiders). 26. *Phaneus auricollis* (Coleoptera; Copridae), from Venezuela and Colombia. It is a male dung-eater of commonplace appearance and insignificant size, but very prettily coloured. 27. *Lamprocon's spiniger* (Hemiptera; Pentatomidae), a small shield bug from Bhutan at the edge of the Himalayas. 28. *Nemophera sinuata* (Neuroptera; Nemopteridae), an oar-winged ant lion from the Mediterranean basin. Its hind wings are reduced to a narrow oar-like organ. Its larva has an exceptionally long prothorax. 29. *Troides brookiana* (Lepidophera; Papilionidae), a male birdwing butterfly from Indo-Malasia and Borneo. 30. *Belostoma indicum* (Hemiptera; Belostomatidae), from Asia. The pan-tropical genus *Belostoma* contains the largest aquatic bugs ($1\frac{1}{2}$–$4\frac{1}{4}$ inches in length).

Collections of the Laboratory of Entomology of the French National Museum of Natural History. (Reduction by 85 per cent). *Presentation R. Bernard*

fixed part set in motion teeth on the mobile part.

This method is used by the Hemiptera and is particularly well-developed in the Coleoptera. It utilizes the most diverse organs:

back of the head and front edge of the pronotum (Hydrophilidae, Erotylidae, Languridae and Tenebrionidae);

hind margin of the pronotum and mesonotum (Cerambycidae);

second last dorsal segment of the abdomen against the hind margin of the elytra (Dynastidae);

first leg joints on cavities where the legs join the body (some **Scarabaeidae** and *Ranatra*);

base of the hind femora against the edge of the pronotum (Cerambycidae);

wings against the eleytra (Trogidae);

wings against the back of the abdomen (Pentatomidae);

rostrum against the groove of the prosternum which shelters it (Reduviidae);

tibia against the abdomen (**Nabidae** and **Scutellerinae**).

One individual may possess several sound apparatuses. This applies to the male *Notonecta*, which presents a couple formed by the inner end of the fore femora and the surface, and a couple between the inner surface of the fore femora and a spur of the forelimbs.

In a small number of species, the sound apparatus is found not only in the adults, but also in the larvae. This applies especially to the Scarabaeidae, whose larval stridulatory apparatus is borne on the mandible (a striated area) and the base of the maxilla (a row of teeth), and to the Geotrupidae, the Lucanidae and the Passalidae, in which the apparatus is situated in the middle and hind pairs of legs. In the Geotrupidae, the hind pair is reduced by atrophy of the tibia and fusing of the second segment of the leg and the femur into a comb. In the Passalidae, the reduction goes further still, and the hind leg consists of a simple knobbly and unarticulated blade.

A certain number of Lepidoptera have similar sound-producing apparatuses such as that of the *Parnassius mnemosyne*, which, in the female, rubs the hind legs against the under-side of the hind wings. A series of African and Malagasy Agaristidae have an apparatus in which the base of the forewing presents a striated fold which is rubbed against by transverse ridges on the end of the tibia and tarsus of the intermediate legs. In this device a rudimentary form of sound-box (which characterizes the sound apparatus of cicadas) appears in the nymphalid genus *Ageronia*. In these South American butterflies, two pairs of protuberances, situated on the inner surface of the base of the forewings, rub, during flight, against two thoracic protuberances. They are preceded by a membranous sac.

In many insects, the sound is caused by emitted air. The

squeak of the Sphingidae is produced by the sudden expulsion of air in the alimentary canal which makes the sclerified parts of the roof of the mouth vibrate. The variable sound made by mosquitoes is believed to be caused by the vibration of a membrane in the thoracic tracheae, which are highly developed.

The very rapid beating of the wings of Hymenoptera and Diptera produces sound signals, as does the very rapid vibration of the antennae of certain Hemiptera.

In cicadas, the sound-producing organ is much more complicated. It consists of a cavity in the hind segment of the thorax, communicating with the exterior by means of the spiracles, and separated from two deep cavities situated at the base of the abdomen by a membrane reinforced with chitinous ridges and controlled by a powerful muscle. This membrane is called the timbal. The abdominal cavities communicate with the exterior by an opening which may be uncovered by the action of raising the abdomen. Between the two abdominal cavities, a third cavity in the centre is closed by two fine membranes, the mirrors. The sound, which may probably be modified by movements by the flap closing the orifice of the abdominal cavities, is produced by the movement of the timbals. They are pulled by their muscle, then suddenly released; it is amplified by the mirrors, and the cavities act as a sound box.

In the Orthoptera, both the emission and reception organs are known, and their complexity clearly demonstrates the biological importance of sound messages.

In locusts and grasshoppers, stridulation is obtained by rubbing a line of small pegs on the inner surface of the hind femora against a vein on each elytron. The arrangement of the tubercles gives the sounds their specific characters, the insect being able to vary their rhythm. The auditory organ consists of a paired cavity at the base of the abdomen, covered by a tympanum and containing ganglionic nerve cells which a nerve fibre joins to rounded sensory cells receiving the excitations.

In the Ensifera, the stridulatory organ is borne on one of the two elytra (long-horned grasshoppers), or on both (crickets), in the form of a thickened stridulatory vein or bow, normally rubbing against the thinned-down inner edge of the other elytron. The auditory organ is situated in the fore tibiae, in which a slit, sometimes masked, communicates with a cavity closed by a tympanum masking the receptors.

Singing seems to be a monopoly of the males; the females emit only weak sound signals. The female, attracted by the male's singing, approaches him. The rhythm of the singing varies with the distance between the courting couple. The acoustic analysis of the singing of Orthoptera has been carried to considerable lengths, and it has been possible to demonstrate a whole range of expressions corresponding to particular situations.

Means of defence

Insects have at their disposal for defence purposes a wide range of weapons: chemical (acrid or malodorous secretions, projection over a distance of caustic gases, for instance in *Brachinus*), mechanical (mandibles, spines, claws), combinations of chemical and mechanical (stings, wounding probosces, and detachable stinging hairs of some adult lymantriid moths).

They also have passive methods of protection: cases made from excreta, coverings made from larval skins or the skins of prey, cases made of silk and covered with various debris, and shelters made by folding leaves, boring wood or burying themselves.

Mimicry

Insects also use a special camouflage, derived from their specific shapes or coloration; this camouflage, very often incorrectly described under the umbrella term of mimicry, deserves to be dealt with at some length.

Camouflage in fact takes various forms, and insects provide particularly striking examples of homochromy (where the general colour of the environment is assumed), of homotypy (protective resemblance to an object) and of mimicry (protective resemblance to another animal). It is probably in these forms of camouflage that the most highly perfected devices in this field are to be seen.

It has been known for a long time that the colour of some insects changes with that of the environment. Praying mantids, phasmids and leaf insects are green or brown, and when a green mantid larva is reared on a brown background, it turns brown in the course of successive moults. In this case no sudden change is involved. Sudden changes are known, in insects, among the Cassidae, and appear to be unconnected

Cicadas (1–3 inches), musical insects which are the largest of the Homoptera have a very long underground larval life, feeding on sa

242

with the coloration of the environment, although related to diet. Others, in the Cassidae, the Cicindelidae and the desert Tenebrionidae, are due to sudden excitation or to a change in humidity, but are of very short duration.

Precise experiments, carried out especially on aquatic Hemiptera, have shown that homochromous insects are less easily captured by predators than individuals of the same species whose coloration contrasts with that of the background. Some grasshoppers living on scorched soils take on a black coloration.

Homochromy reaches its peak in the genus *Pterochroza* or leaf-like katydids of South America. The general shape of the wings, when folded over the body, is similar to that of a leaf; the resemblance is rendered more striking by notches imitating attacks by caterpillars, and by the distribution of spots similar to those on the dried-up parts of leaves, or caused by fungus or leaf-miners. Certain butterflies, especially some Nymphalidae, show a similar homotypy: the hind wing is lengthened and imitates the stalk of a leaf, and one line, starting from the stalk and running across the lower surface of the two wings, is amazingly like the midrib of the leaf.

Leaf insects imitate the contour and the colour of leaves in a surprising way.

The elongate stick insects resemble dead twigs; the folding of the legs along the body, the acquisition of spines and the lack of movement reinforce the illusion.

Finally, desert grasshoppers, especially in southwest Africa (*Eremocharis insignis*), present the appearance and coloration of the small irregular pebbles which are strewn over arid soils.

Although it is impossible to give a satisfactory explanation of these amazing copies, the striking thing is that the insect's posture heightens the effect of the imitation. Thus in the Nymphalidae, the angle the body makes with the substratum is the same as that of the fallen leaf, so that the position of the leaf-butterfly appears natural. The insect's immobility increases its resemblance to the objects surrounding it. It is again this immobility which causes many insects, especially Lepidoptera, to disappear from the sight of man (but not necessarily from that of predators). Their colorations embody all the subterfuges of camouflage: irregular but softened contours, spots, the existence of contrasting spots which break up the object's normal contour, and patterns whose orientation or centre are not the same as those of the insect itself. The Nymphalidae of tropical forests are among the finest examples of cryptic (camouflaging) colouring; even in temperate climates, butterflies such as the Catocalinae are hard to spot as soon as they alight on bark. Often the surface coloration or that of the hind wings is very conspicuous; the disappearance of these brilliant colours at the moment when

which they suck from roots (*left*): having become full-grown the nymph—larva with rudimentary wings—(*middle*) emerges from the ground, climbs on to a stem and stays, turning into a beautiful adult (*right*). The species here is *Munsa clypealis* from tropical Africa. *Phot. Boulard*

the insect alights and folds its wings allows it to become unobtrusive and merge with its surroundings.

The term mimicry means the imitation by the insect of another animal—usually another arthropod (arachnid or insect).

Mimicry may occur in species which are also protected by acrid secretions, a repellent odour or a hurtful sting. This mimicry, which is common only in the tropics, has been called Müllerian, after the Brazilian biologist F. Müller who was the first to describe it. The species naturally protected very often have bright and violently contrasting colours: they are said to have aposematic or warning coloration. Frequently several species, which are all inedible and belong to various groups, have the same aposematic coloration. Attempts have been made to explain this by pointing out that if possible predators learned more easily to recognize inedible species—and the fewer different types there are the easier such learning becomes—the animals endowed with warning or aposematic colours would be specially protected.

Very often, however, although the model is protected by its secretions or its weapons, the mimic has no other protection available. One speaks then of Batesian mimicry, from the name of the naturalist H. W. Bates who discovered it during his extensive travels in Amazonia.

Ants, lycid Coleoptera and especially a long series of

A strange grasshopper, Acridian (1–1¼ inches), from equatorial Africa. It is an apterous form, the colours of which blend with the ground—covered with small patches of moss or greenish lycopods; by contrast, its compound eyes, globular and rosy, shine like two lanterns. *Phot. Michel Boulard*

Hymenoptera (wasps and Sphegidae) and Lepidoptera (Danaidae, Acraeinae, Castniidae, and Arctiidae) serve as models. Imitation is based on colour and pattern, but also on shape. Quite frequently spots of bright colour, interrupting the contour of the body, modify the animal's appearance without actually modifying its shape. Among the insects and spiders imitating ants (they are called myrmecomorphs) some show a lengthening of the body, or a narrowing

simulating the loose articulation of the head and of the abdomen with the thorax in ants, while others have bright spots on the sides.

The relations existing between mimics and models are variable. Sometimes the mimic develops in close association with its model. Certain large asilid flies with compact bodies covered by a thick mop of tawny or black erect hairs (e.g. *Hyperechia*), are amazingly similar to *Xylocopa*, large carpenter bees lodging in dead wood, and develop at their expense.

More often, mimic and model live in the same region, sometimes forming mixed groups, but have no direct relations.

Finally, it happens, for instance with a Malagasy tabanid with a wasp-like appearance, that the relations between mimic and model are totally unknown. As Shelford established in Borneo and Bates observed in Amazonia, a model may be mimicked by a considerable number of species, belonging to different groups. When this is the case it is not clear if all the mimics stick to the central model, or if direct copies are produced between the various species thus brought together.

The mimic may occur within a family, even within an order. Thus, many clerid beetles mimic chrysomelids and tenebrionids, and chrysomelids mimic lady-birds.

More often, the model belongs to another order. Among the Coleoptera, cases are known of eastern chafer beetles (*Cetonia*) mimicking bumble-bees, of cerambycids mimicking sphegids, of clerids resembling *Mutilla*, and of Lampyridae copying cockroaches.

Interpreted as a decisive argument in favour of Darwinism, mimicry has been intensively studied, especially among the Lepidoptera.

Several categories are recognized. Thus certain families or sub-families appear to imitate, en bloc, other families or orders. The clearwing moths (*Sesia*) are mimics of Hymenoptera, as also are a group of South American Syntomidae; the African Lycaenidae of the Lipteninae sub-family mimic the Acraeinae to such an extent that it is necessary to study the morphological characters in detail in order to distinguish between the representatives of two sub-families so far removed from each other.

In general, mimicry affects certain species of a genus and not the others. One of the best examples of this is afforded by the large black and white African papilionid *Papilio dardanus*. The male occurs as a normal swallow-tail butterfly, with tailed hind wings; it is quite recognizable everywhere. But in continental Africa the female of the species is extremely polymorphous and—except for one Ethiopian race—not at all like the male. In each of the regions of continental Africa where it has been possible to observe and rear them, it has been noted that these females, normally with rounded hind wings, and tailless, were so like protected species (and especially Danainae) as to be readily taken for them. Each female form of *P. dardanus* has a corresponding different species of Danainae. In Madagascar and in the Comoro Islands, on the other hand, where the species is represented by two different races, males and females appear to be identical. The 'primitive' type seems to be that of the protected females and not that of the 'male-shaped' females. Mimicry has probably therefore not acted in this case as a stimulant to evolution, but has possibly ensured the conservation of primitive forms.

Finally, it is possible that, in at least a part of the area of a species, models do not exist, whilst the mimic continues to

The Indian stick insect, *Clitummus extradentatus* (6 inches and more) mimics to perfection a dry branch.

Opposite page: two leaf-like katydids (1½–2¼ inches) of the African equatorial forest belt. *Phot. R. Pujol*

imitate them; this is what happens in Madagascar with the forms of *Hypolimnas* copying the Danainae *Danaus chrysippus* and *D. plexippus.*

The intepretation of mimicry is difficult. It is obviously necessary to distinguish between the factors determining the appearance of special forms or colorations, and those which make possible the survival of these forms.

In a general, but not absolute, way, the characters of mimicking species are found in ordinary species, perhaps less obvious, or isolated and not grouped, but still such as to be quite recognizable. This applies to the mimetic females of *Papilio dardanus* already mentioned. Mimicry does not therefore give rise to new characters.

Its utility and effectiveness as a protection have been much discussed.

It is certain that in the case of the Lepidoptera of the Amazon which participate in flights grouping numerous species, the imitation of a protected species by an unprotected species is effective, in so far as the first is much more abundant than the second. This proportion does not always seem to be maintained and if it is reversed, mimicry jeopardizes the survival of the protected species itself. In many other cases, the comparative rareness of the mimic, or its habits, do not give imitation a chance to tell in its favour. On the other hand, the analysis of mimicry has often been pushed to ridiculous lengths, with great efforts being made to interpret the least detail as an example of protective imitation. This has been carried to the extent of seeing, in the shape of the head of the lantern bug, *Fulgora*, an imitation of the alligator's head.

The study of mimicry and its astonishing 'successes' must be restored to a more serious footing, remembering that protection, if there is protection, is directed not against man, but against predators and parasites. The deadliest enemies of insects are parasites which lay in the eggs or in the larvae of their hosts, without ever meeting them. This does not mean that the protection given to adults cannot be useful, but it is necessary to demonstrate it experimentally in each particular case, and, at present, this condition is only rarely fulfilled.

Right: a complex case of mimicry; bumble-bees, cuckoo bees: and syrphid flies. *Above*, the terrestrial bumble-bee (*Bombus terrestris*), a worker collecting honey from a daisy; *middle*, belonging to the same family as bumble-bees, *Psithyrus vestalis*, lives, however, as a parasite of their societies; *below*, a variety, *Volucella bombylans*, the larvae of which live as parasites on the eggs, larvae and nymphs of bumble-bees. *Volucella bombylans* has its varieties coloured to match the different species of bumble-bees it parasitizes. *Phot. J. Six*

Echinoderms

The echinoderms make up a varied collection of some of the most beautiful and some of the ugliest marine animals. They include the lovely flower-like feather stars and the elegant brittle stars, as well as the spiky sea urchins and the leathery sausage-shaped sea cucumbers. Yet all possess a radial symmetry—at its most obvious in the identical arms of the starfish. Echinoderms are often considered to be among the most highly evolved of the invertebrates, possessing some features that anticipate the vertebrate animals.

Echinoderms constitute one of the best defined phyla in the animal kingdom. The phylum Echinodermata is divided into two sub-phyla: the Pelmatozoa, mostly living a fixed life, and the Eleutherozoa, free to move but usually sedentary in habits. The Pelmatozoa contains one class of living echinoderms, the Crinoidea or sea lilies and feather stars, and five classes of fossil representatives. The Eleutherozoa, on the other hand, contains only one fossil class and four living classes. These four are the Holothuroidea or sea cucumbers, the Echinoidea or sea urchins, the Asteroidea or starfishes, and the Ophiuroidea or brittle stars.

There are about 5500 living species of echinoderms and they are all marine creatures. They are of moderate size, the largest starfish spreading to nearly 3 feet across and one sea cucumber reaching a length of 6 feet. These creatures are small in comparison to some fossil echinoderms. One fossil crinoid had a stem 70 feet long.

Although the various classes are very different in appearance, they all follow a broadly similar plan of organization. This has three essential features. Echinoderms possess radial symmetry, usually with five identical units surrounding the centre of the body, though bilateral symmetry may be superimposed over the radial symmetry and almost mask it completely; they also possess an external skeleton made up of calcerous (calcium carbonate) plates fixed rigidly together or articulated—though the plates are very small and contained in a leathery outer skin in the sea cucumbers; and, finally, they have a kind of internal hydraulic network called the water vascular system which exists in no other group of animals.

The radial symmetry is defined by grooves that start at the central mouth and radiate outwards. They divide the body into ten sectors: five radii, such as the arms of starfishes, brittle stars and feather stars and the bands of tube feet (little tentacle-like projections) of sea urchins and sea cucumbers; and five inter-radii, the regions between the five radii.

Except in sea cucumbers, the outer covering consists of a delicate epidermis overlying a skeleton of calcareous plates, often furnished with spines. In sea cucumbers the plates take the form of minute spicules embedded in a leathery skin. They are composed of aragonite, a particular mineral form of calcium carbonate. In all the other echinoderms, the plates are of calcite, another form of calcium carbonate. In most of the sea urchins, the plates interlock tightly together, giving the impression of being fused into a solid shell. In starfishes, brittle stars and feather stars, the plates are articulated so that the skeleton is flexible, making movement of the arms possible.

The water vascular system consists of a network of canals connected to the outside by pores usually situated on a special plate of the skeleton called the madreporite. Water enters the canals through these pores. The canals lie in a ring around the mouth, from which they extend along the radii; there, they connect with the tube feet. Water is forced into the tube feet and the increased pressure makes them extend from the radii, serving to fix the echinoderm in one position or to move it about, and to capture and handle food.

Sea urchins

The echinoderm that best lends itself to an account of the essential organs of the class Echinoidea is a common sea urchin of European coasts, *Paracentrotus lividus*. These sea urchins are often to be seen clinging to rocks just below the surface. They look like flattened hemispheres two to three inches across and are covered with sharp spines. The shells of dead urchins, devoid of spines, may be found on the bottom. The soft body is edible and sea urchins may often be purchased. The spines can be removed by brisk brushing and immersing the animal in bleaching fluid.

The lower surface of the echinoderm is flat and rests on a rock. The mouth is situated at the centre of the undersurface and the anus is at the centre of the top of the urchin. It occupies a tiny hole in a central plate that is surrounded by five hexagonal plates each containing a genital pore through which eggs or sperm are discharged into the sea. One of these plates contains the madreporite, and is riddled with holes

The starfish *Astropecten aurantiacus* may reach 2 feet in diameter. Its arms, which are very long, are fringed by highly developed marginal and ventral plates, the former covered with fine granules and small spines, the latter with long lateral spines, which, taken as a whole, are like the teeth of a comb. The long yellow podia or tube feet, with white suckers, are so numerous that it is hard to believe that they are arranged in only two rows along the ventral surface of the arms. With the help of its tube feet, the starfish can move on vertical rock walls or on the vault of undersea caves as easily as in the horizontal position. *Phot. J. Six*

through which sea water enters the water vascular system. These six plates together form the periproct.

From the periproct twenty rows of hexagonal plates extend around the body to the mouth, making up the shell, or test, as it is more strictly called. Ten of these rows are perforated with a line of holes through which the tube feet protrude, and they are grouped together in pairs to form five radial bands known as ambulacra. Between them come the other ten rows of plates, also grouped together in pairs to form five inter-radial bands or inter-ambulacra, which are broader than the radial bands. All the plates have small swellings called tubercles on which the spines are situated. The spines are articulated on the tubercles, and muscles at their bases can swivel the spines around. Among the spines

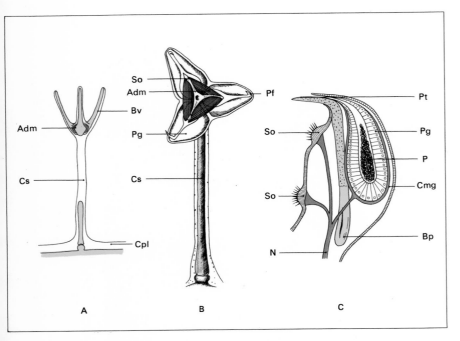

Pedicellariae. A and B, tridactyl pedicellaria with three valves, ×100; C, glandular pedicellaria, seen in partial section, ×300. Adm, adductor muscle of the valves; Bp, bony part; Bv, bony valve; Cmg, compressor muscle of poison gland; Cpl, calcareous plate; Cs, calcareous stem; N, nerve; P, poison; Pf, poison fang; Pg, poison gland; Pt, poison tooth; So, sense organ.

are some curious organs called pedicellariae that serve to defend the sea urchin and may help to capture prey; they also keep the body clean of debris or small organisms. They consist of a set of jaws at the end of a long flexible stalk. The jaws are normally kept open but if a foreign body should touch the pedicellariae, the jaws immediately close. They grip so strongly that the pedicellariae will be torn off rather than release their hold. Some urchins possess pedicellariae with poison glands connected to the tips of the jaws. The poison may be very toxic. In man, the bites of poisonous urchins cause severe pain, especially the tropical species *Toxopneustes pileolus*. Slackening of the muscles and narcosis may occur, and death may ensue by asphyxia.

Organizational plan of a regular sea-urchin. Al, Aristotle's lantern or chewing apparatus; Amp, ampullae or vesicles of tube feet; An, anus; Anr, apical nerve ring; Cinpl, calcareous inter-radial plate with spine; Dgl, digestive gland; Impl, interradial plates; Is, intestinal siphon; M, mouth; Mp, madreporite plate; O or T, ovary or testis; Oe, oesophagus; Or, oral water vascular ring; P, podium or tube foot; R, rectum; Rc, radial water vascular canal; Rnc, radial nerve cord; Rpl, radial plate; Stc, stone canal (leads to madreporite); To, tooth of Aristotle's lantern.

On each of the ambulacra near the mouth are situated small transparent club-shaped organs called sphaeridia. These are sensory balance organs that inform the urchin of its position in the sea.

Aristotle's lantern and other internal organs

The internal organs of a sea urchin are bathed in the fluid filling the body cavity. The gonads, which produce sperm or eggs, hang down beneath the periproct at the centre of the urchin's top-side. They are firmly attached by membranes called mesenteries to the interior of the shell, as is the digestive tract, which coils around inside the body cavity between the mouth and anus. The tract commences, behind the mouth, with a complicated structure called Aristotle's lantern because it resembles an ancient Greek lantern in shape. This connects to a short oesophagus that leads to the stomach and then the intestine, which describes two complete circles inside the shell before connecting to the rectum and anus.

The food of a sea urchin is often plant matter, which requires prolonged digestion, hence the elongated digestive tract. It also requires elaborate preparation before digestion

Aristotle's lantern crushes the food taken in through the mouth, and is the most complicated crushing organ to be found in animals. It is shaped like a five-sided prism, and is made up of forty closely-articulated calcareous structures operated by muscles. The prism consists of five triangular jaws each with a white calcareous tooth. These masticate the food in a series of very complex actions. The lantern also serves to pump the fluid in the body into the gills, which surround the mouth, and so it is also important in respiration.

The gonads consist of five lobed glands and fill a good part of the body cavity. They are yellowish-white in males and orange in females, and develop considerably in size at breeding time. They are connected to the genital pores in the periproct by fine ducts.

The nervous system of a sea urchin consists of a ring of

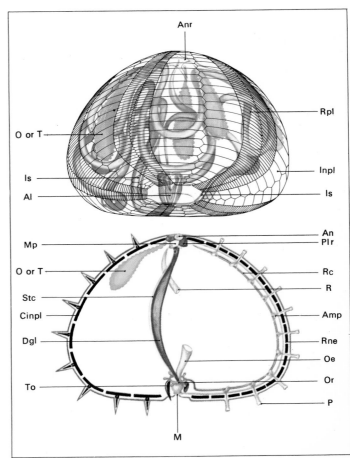

nerves circling the oesophagus from which nerve branches extend out along the five radii to the tube feet and to the internal organs. There is also a superficial nervous network that connects with the skin, the spines and the pedicellariae. There is no definite respiratory system or circulatory system as such, but instead a haemal system. A fluid rich in protein and laden with free amoebocytes (which are present in the blood in other animals) circulates through the body cavity, driven by the action of cilia, and bathes the internal organs. The fluid passes through the gills that surround the mouth, gaining oxygen and losing carbon dioxide as it does so.

The water vascular system, which is unique to echinoderms, consists of a ring canal situated around the mouth, from which five radial canals branch off to connect with the tube feet. Behind each tube foot is a bulb-shaped ampulla, which contracts to force water into the tube foot and so extend it. Each sea urchin contains five double rows of ampullae, which lie along the inside of the shell. Here a direct resemblance to the starfishes can be noted, for the ampullae look like five arms curled up inside the urchin's shell. The ring canal around the mouth is connected to the exterior by the stone canal, which is a tube with calcified walls, leading through the centre of the body cavity to the madreporite at the top of the shell. Joined to the stone canal over the greater part of its length is the brown gland, which probably has an excretory function. The liquid in the water vascular system is sea water with traces of urea and ammonia. It moves very slowly from the madreporite to the canals, driven by the action of cilia on the pores of the madreporite and in the stone canal.

The sea urchin's beauty—its bright colours and elegant spines

Sea urchins number about 900 living species and vary enormously in appearance. Several, particularly those of tropical seas, are often strikingly coloured. The order Cidaroida, such as *Cidaris cidaris* of European coastal waters, possess shells of remarkable beauty; the ambulacra are clearly defined with rows of large tubercles each surrounded at the base by a crown of fine projections. Other exotic sea urchins of this order have enormous spines like triangular rods projecting from a mass of overlapping spatula-shaped spines surrounding the shell. Urchins of the order Diadematoida, which are common throughout the Indo-Pacific region, have long slender hollow spines that may reach one foot in length. They are armed with fine teeth that can inflict painful wounds. Some other sea urchins have soft, flexible leathery shells in which the plates are not joined edge to edge but are loosely embedded in the skin.

All the sea urchins mentioned so far are 'regular' sea urchins; that is, the mouth and anus are at opposite ends of the body. Several sea urchins have the digestive tract arranged in a different way, and the anus is displaced from the top of the shell to a point nearer the mouth, either to the side or underneath the shell. Such urchins are called 'irregular'. If the anus is found at the side, the shell in this region of the body is truncated or flattened slightly.

Many irregular sea urchins do not live on rocks or the sea bed, but bury themselves in the sand or mud of the sea floor. One of the commonest of these urchins is *Echinocardium cordatum*, often known as the sand urchin or the sea potato. Like other burrowing urchins, it is highly modified to adapt to its unusual environment. The spines do not project stiffly from the shell, but are long and silky and lie over it. The shell itself is heart-shaped and made up of thin plates adorned with numerous granules of various sizes. Such an arrangement of spines aids in burrowing, and the shell need not be strong as

the urchin is unlikely to be attacked by predators. The posterior (back) side is truncated and bears the anus, and the anterior (front) side has a deep groove that runs up and over the shell. Not being needed for locomotion, the tube feet assume other roles. Some are involved in respiration and feeding, and others construct a funnel from the urchin to the surface. Some tube feet dig a soakaway, or pit, beneath the posterior side to take waste products away from the body. Around the shell are three bands of ciliated spines known as fascioles, which pump strong currents of water through the burrow and over the shell. These fascioles vary in number and arrangement from one genus to another. *Spatangus*, the purple heart urchin, has a single fasciole just below the anus, which is on the posterior side; *Brissopsis lyrifera*, the lyre

Perched on the rock, the regular sea-urchin *Cidaris cidaris* erects its long pointed spines, each one articulated on a large tubercle and surrounded at the base by a collar of small flattened spines. It manages to get about by the combined movement of its long tube feet and the short spines on its oral surface. Its greyish denuded test is magnificently sculptured.
Phot. Aldo Margiocco

urchin, gets its odd name because the fasciole on the top surface of the shell is shaped like the frame of a lyre. The lyre is not easily seen unless the spines are removed.

The radii are profoundly modified in these irregular sea urchins. In *Echinocardium*, the ambulacra are petal-shaped and they are not all equal in size. They are arranged in a ring around the apex of the shell. The posterior plates in irregular urchins are broad but the anterior plates are reduced in size and surround the mouth, which is placed towards the front of the animal. In some genera, broad pores pierce the anterior radii and from them emerge tube feet that are modified into food-tasting organs. The mouth takes the form of an arched slit across the lower surface towards the front of the shell; it has a lower spoon-shaped lip which is used when burrowing in sand or mud. The masticatory apparatus of the regular sea urchins totally disappears in most of the irregular sea urchins. However, a very reduced lantern exists in the Clypeasteroida or sand dollars, the mouth of which remains central.

Variations in the shape and ornamentation of the shells of irregular sea urchins are numerous, and range from very

In spite of its fair size, its enormous triangular rod-like spines and its pedicellariae, the sea-urchin *Heterocentrotus mammillatus* has just been attacked and emptied of its viscera by this star-fish, harmless though the latter may look. Already, some of its large spines are lying about on the sea-floor which is strewn with lumps of *Porites* and elegant branched corals. Splendid reef fishes pass by indifferently.

Starfishes of the family Oriasteridae (*left*) live mainly in reefs of the Indo-Pacific region. They are remarkable for their large brightly coloured spines, distributed as in this species of *Protoreaster*, on the dorsal and lateral surfaces of the disc and the arms. Other members of this family, the *Culcita*, are pentagonal, very thick, and covered with large granules. All are brilliantly coloured with a mixture of red, green and yellow. To facilitate egg laying, the animal raises itself on the tip of its arms at the same time curving its body sharply inwards. *Noumea Aquarium. Phot. Catala.*

Bottom, left and right: a large sun star (*Solaster*) wedging a sea-urchin (*Psammechinus*) against the glass wall of an aquarium as it swallows it. *Phot. Jean Vasserot.*

flattened pentagons to raised globes. Most noteworthy are the sea urchins of the genus *Pourtalesia*: their very fragile shells may look like elongated ovals, triangles or pyramids. Unfortunately, these sea urchins live only in deep water and are difficult to obtain intact.

Starfishes

The common starfish may appear very different from the regular sea urchin, but in fact it is basically very similar. There are still five radii but they are separated from the inter-radii and spread out into five arms. The digestive tract still occupies the centre of the body with the mouth below and the anus above, but it is compressed into a central disc surrounded by the arms. This is the basic plan of *Asterias rubens*, the common starfish of Europe, and this starfish will serve as a good example to explain the features of these animals in more detail.

The starfish and its thousand feet
The starfish crawls on its under-surface, in the centre of which is the mouth. From the mouth, five ambulacral grooves extend out along the undersides of the arms. Each groove possesses four rows of tube feet equipped with suckers, similar to those of the sea urchin. The sea urchin can move about by a certain amount by extending and retracting its tube feet and so too can the starfish, though with more facility than the sea urchin for it can bend its arms. Each arm ends with a modified tube foot called a tentacle, a tactile organ that explores objects as the starfish advances. In this way, the starfish feels its way forward, but it can also to some extent see what lies ahead. As it moves, the end of the advancing arm is raised so that an eye spot under the tentacle is exposed. This eye spot is bright red in colour and made up of nearly two hundred pigmented hollows filled with a colourless jelly, over which lies a kind of crystalline lens and a membrane. It is no more than a very imperfect eye, for the starfish does not seem to be able to perceive either shapes or movements of objects, but merely differences in illumination.

Apart from the grooves along the arms, the whole surface of the starfish is covered with a skin concealing polygonal plates fitting together to form an external skeleton, as in the sea urchin. The inside of each ambulacral groove is paved with plates perforated with pores for the passage of the tube feet. The plates on each side of the grooves bear small cylindrical spines that can bend over the tube feet to protect them. The plates at the edges of the arms are equipped with longer and more solid spines, their bases being surrounded by a collar of pedicellariae, which function in the same way as in sea urchins. The upper surface of the arms is covered with more spines and pedicellariae.

Breathing through its skin
The spines and pedicellariae guard the skin-gills, which are little finger-like projections of the body cavity through holes in the skeleton. The fluid in the body passes into and out of the skin-gills in ceaseless motion. Respiration takes place there, but the skin-gills also have an excretory function. Some of the waste products enter the skin-gills in the form of coloured grains; they concentrate at the tip of the skin-gill, which constricts below the grains, isolating them in a little packet that is soon detached from the rest of the skin-gill.

The anus lies in the centre of the top of the central disc, forming a minute hole there. At the edge of the disc is the madreporite, which admits water to the water vascular system. It is made up of about twenty thin plates arranged like the spokes of a wheel, and is pierced with microscopic holes. The starfish is divided into two equal halves by a plane passing through the madreporite and the arm opposite it, so that it possesses bilateral symmetry as well as radial symmetry.

The internal organs
The mouth of the starfish is completely devoid of any organs for chewing the food; there is no trace of an organ similar to the sea urchin's lantern. It is simply surrounded by spines; their role is to protect the mouth and probably to help push food into the mouth. From the mouth, a broad short oesophagus leads to the comparatively vast stomach. The stomach is five-sided in shape and fills almost all the interior of the disc, but without being coiled into spirals, just as in the sea urchin's stomach and intestine. A very short rectum connects the stomach to the tiny anus. The starfish passes to its stomach very little food that is not digestible, so it has no need for a long intestine. The digestive function of the intestine is taken over by ten branch-like caeca or digestive glands, two of which lie in the upper half of each arm. Solid food ingested by the starfish does not penetrate to the caeca, but the fluid products of digestion pass to them through tubes from the stomach, carried by a current set up by the highly ciliated wall of the stomach.

Useful substances from digestion pass from the caeca into the body fluid. The caeca are rich in amino acids, which are

Arm of a starfish of the genus *Protoreaster*, showing the large marginal spines and the tube feet with broad suckers which are arranged in two rows in the ambulacral groove. *The Aquarium at Noumea. Phot. R. Catala*

kept in reserve for the formation of sperm or eggs in the gonads. The ten gonads are housed in the arms below the caeca, again two to each arm. At breeding time the gonads enlarge and the caeca become reduced as the amino acids are used up. The gonads resemble bunches of grapes and open to the outside by canals situated at the base of the arms.

The nervous system is roughly similar to that of the sea urchin, there being a nerve ring around the mouth and nerve branches extending from it into the arms. The branches possess two nerve cords, one inside the lower surface and one along the upper surface of the arm. The water vascular system has two interesting pecularities; the ring canal has five sacs called Polian vesicles that regulate the system, and ten small projections called Tiedemann bodies, which produce the free amoebocytes in the fluid filling the system.

The four orders of starfishes

The shapes of starfishes, the ornamentation and the distribution of the plates that constitute the skeleton, and the arrangement of the tube feet, skin-gills and pedicellariae have led to

Very spiny starfish, of the genus *Acanthaster*, an inhabitant of the coral reefs. It crawls over the coral, browsing on the polyps, leaving behind it a wake of inanimate coral. *Phot. J. Théodor*

This cushion star (*Porania sp.*), of the family Poraniidae has a thick, squat pentagonal body, with very short arms. The edges of the body, which are slender, bear tufts of small spines arranged on the dorsal marginal plates. *Phot. Jean Vasserot*

the classification of the 1600 living species of starfishes (class Asteroidea) into 4 orders. These are further grouped into 2 sub-classes. The first sub-class, the Somasteroidea, consists of starfishes in which there is no skeletal ring framing the mouth. There is only one order, the Platyasterida, and it includes *Platasterias*, which is a living fossil found off the west coast of Mexico. All its close relatives have been extinct for 400 million years. The order also includes the earliest known starfish, the fossil *Villebrunaster*.

The second sub-class, the Euasteroidea, comprises starfishes having a skeletal ring around the mouth. It is made up of three orders: the Phanerozona, Spinulosa and Forcipulata. The last order contains the best-known starfishes, and includes *Asterias rubens*, the common European starfish described above. It is characterized by a disc of medium size with almost cylindrical arms, and the marginal plates along the edges of the arms are hidden by the skin; in addition, the upper surface is covered with small regularly-arranged spines surrounded at the base by a collar of pedicellariae with crossed jaws rather like scissors. The skin-gills are distributed throughout the body, and each arm usually has four rows of tube feet ending in suckers. As well as *Asterias*, the Forcipulata includes *Marthasterias glacialis*, the spiny starfish, which has fewer but larger spines on its upper surface than *Asterias* and which, in deep-water specimens, reaches a span of over three feet. There is also the small *Coscinasterias tenuispina* which is closely related to *Marthasterias*, although it possesses six to nine arms instead of its relative's five. Division of the radii increases the number of arms.

Also possessing crossed pedicellariae, but having the tube feet in two rows, is *Brisingella coronata*. This is a beautiful European starfish; it has a bright red upper surface and its underside is almost white. The disc is small, just over one inch in diameter, but the arms often exceed twenty inches in length. These starfishes are very fragile and usually live at fairly considerable depths; it is rare to be able to capture them intact.

Starfishes of the order Phanerozona have flattened bodies and the arms possess two rows of conspicuous marginal plates forming a clear-cut border to each side of the arm. The skeleton is composed either of plates adorned with granules, or of plates that are bare or covered by the skin. The skin-gills are all on the upper surface, and the pedicellariae are never crossed but take other forms. The tube feet are in double rows, ending either in suckers or in points. To this order belong the Astropectinidae, which have long arms with comb-like sets of spines, and *Luidia*, in which only the lower marginal plates can be seen. *Luidia* possesses varying numbers of arms, *L. sarsi* having five and *L. ciliaris* having seven. The large *Oreaster* starfishes of tropical seas are splendid to see; they are blue to grey in colour, and have a very thick disc and arms surmounted by enormous bright red conical tubercles often arranged in one or several central crowns. They can raise themselves up on their arms, rather as a camera is supported on a tripod. *Culcita* are basically pentagonal starfishes, but they are so swollen that they can easily be mistaken for large, brilliantly coloured sea urchins.

The last order, the Spinulosa, contains species covered with small spines borne by plates which are usually arranged in an irregular network and concealed under the skin. The marginal plates are small and hard to make out—if they can

The *Luidia* starfish has a small disc bearing long narrow fragile arms. Its dorsal surface is covered with groups of plates in which the spines are arranged in circles. *Luidia* live in all the seas and are often red with bright and dark spots. The one shown here, from the coasts of New Caledonia, raised on its arms in an egg-laying posture, is showing its long conical tube feet which have no suckers. *The Aquarium at Noumea. Phot. R. Catala*

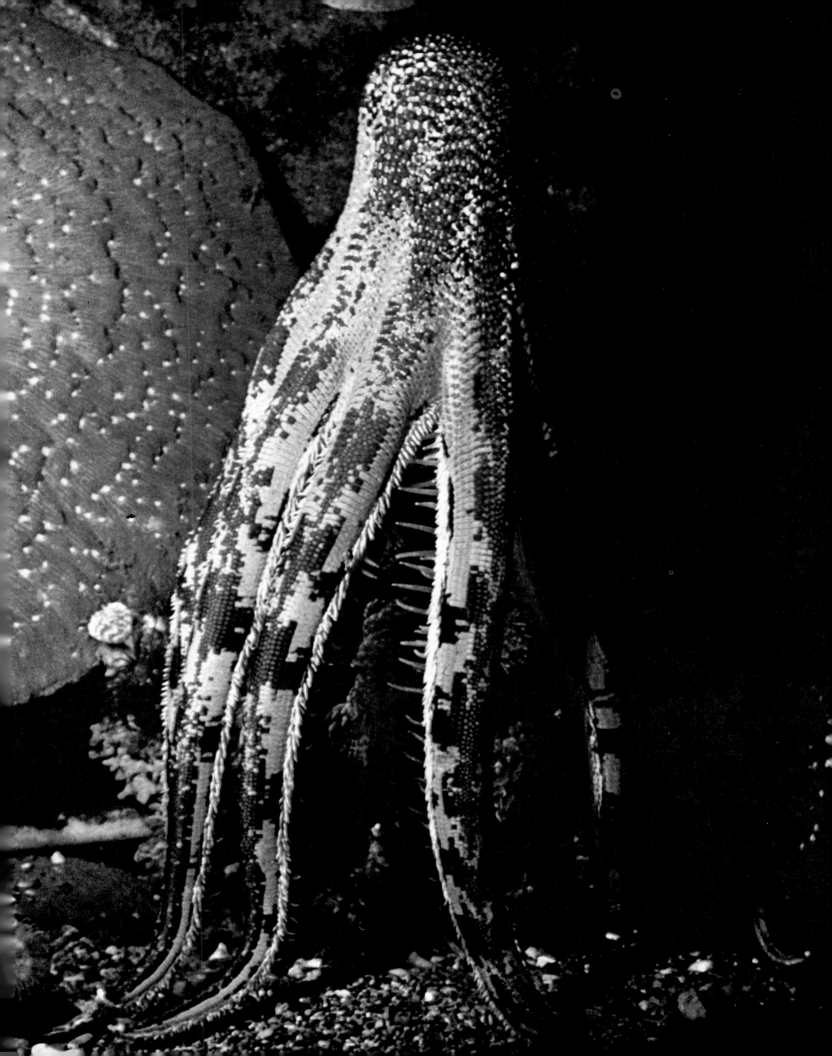

be seen at all. Pedicellariae are usually lacking and are very simple in design if present. The tube feet are in double rows and each end in a sucker. Representative species include *Echinaster sepositus*, which is orange-red, has rounded arms, and bears skin-gills only on the upper surface. It is very abundant in the Mediterranean Sea. Very similar in appearance but rare is *Henricia sanguilolenta*, which bears skin-gills on both surfaces. The small *Asterina gibbosa* has very blunt arms making it almost pentagonal in shape; it is often found in beds of seaweed or under stones. Of similar shape is *Anserpoda membranacea*, which is paper-thin at the margins; it is scarlet above and light yellow below, edged with red. *Acanthaster planci* is known throughout the Indo-Pacific region under the evocative name of 'mother-in-law's cushion', for it is covered with a forest of long strong sharp spines. Among the most spectacular of the Spinulosa is *Solaster papposus*, the sunstar. It has a large reddish-purple disc surrounded by up to thirteen short, lighter-coloured arms, all covered with small spines. It is an arctic species, and the English Channel marks its southernmost limit.

Brittle stars

Brittle stars now make up the class Ophiuroidea, but for a long time they were placed in the same class as the starfishes. This is not surprising, because the two groups of animals are superficially very alike. Brittle stars differ from starfishes in that their arms, which are five in number and always long and slender, continue as far as the mouth and are not fused to the edge of the central disc as in starfishes. Moreover, these arms are solid and made up of successive joints, and are not hollow and unjointed as in starfishes. It follows that the disc must contain all the essential organs of a brittle star. The mouth opens into a short oesophagus, which is followed by the sac-like stomach, which has pockets housed between ten bursae (pouches) in the lower wall of the disc. The bursae

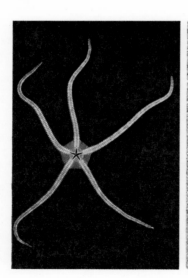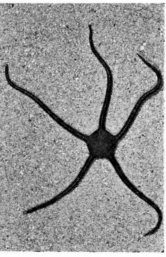

This ophiuroid or brittle star (*Ophioderma longicauda*) is very common on the coasts of Europe, both Atlantic and Mediterranean. It is a large species with a blackish brown disc, adorned with very fine granules. This disc bears 5 long and very flexible cylindrical arms, which may reach 8 inches in length. The ophiuroid lives in shallow water, on rocks or in clefts in stones, sometimes among seaweed. It is a very voracious creature, and can be captured on a hook with animal bait. *Right*, dorsal surface; *left*, ventral surface. *Phot. J. Six*

have a respiratory function. The gonads are in numerous small ovoid sacs implanted in the walls of the bursae, with which they communicate by a tiny orifice that becomes functional only at breeding time. The bursae open to the exterior by pairs of slits situated at the base of the underside of each arm. Sperms and eggs are passed out through the slits into the sea, as is waste matter, for brittle stars have no anus.

The brittle star's arms
The arms of a brittle star are plainly different to the arms of a starfish. There are always five, whereas a starfish may have up to fifty arms. They are also much more slender. But the main differences are internal. Except for a single species, no brittle star has its digestive or reproductive organs situated in its arms. The arms are made up of a large number of solid joints that articulate with each other by means of a complex ball-and-socket mechanism; in this way, the joints are rather like vertebrae. The arms are powered by muscles between the joints. The outer surface of the arm consists of an external skeleton made up of one upper plate, two side plates bearing spines and one lower plate. On the lower surface of each arm are two rows of tube feet transformed into palps (often called tentacles) that emerge from two pores situated between the lower plate and the side plates. The palps are not involved in the starfish's locomotion, carried out by movements of the arms and the spines, but rather in respiration and in sensing the environment. They also participate in carrying food towards the mouth.

The upper surface of the disc is covered with joined or overlapping plates; these may be clearly visible or hidden beneath the skin. The plates are bare or adorned with spines or other projections. Towards the arms, a pair of plates called the radial shields are inserted among the other upper plates. They are sometimes well developed. In the centre of the disc's upper surface is a rosette formed of six large plates.

The undersurface of a brittle star is bare or covered with overlapping plates. In the centre is a star-shaped mouth, the points of the star extending to the bases of the arms. In between the points are the five inter-radial regions. From the edge of the disc towards the centre of the mouth, each of the inter-radii is made up of a buccal plate, one of which contains the madreporite, and two elongated plates followed by two oral plates. Rows of spines on the edges of the inter-radii act as teeth. All these plates are actuated by muscles to open and shut the mouth, and so function as jaws.

The two orders of brittle stars

Present-day brittle stars number about 2000 species. They make up the class Ophiuroidea, which is divided into 2 orders: the Euryalae and the Ophiurae.

The Euryalae are characterized by having the disc and arms covered with thick skin, which may contain a mosaic of granules, but not with a layer of plates. The arms may split into a considerable number of branches, and their joints are articulated so that they can twist through all planes. To this order belongs the magnificent basket star (*Gorgonocephalus*), which get its scientific name because the branches of the arms envelop the disc just as snakes surround the heads of the gorgons in Greek legend.

The Ophiurae have their discs and arms covered with plates that may be hidden by the skin or by granules. The arms can move only horizontally in the majority of these brittle stars. There are several families, differentiated by the ornamentation of the disc and, especially, by the shape and arrangement of the mouthparts. Among the species found on European coasts is *Ophiothrix fragilis*, with its long ringed spiny arms of varied colours. Large numbers of these brittle stars are to be found in large beds lying two or three deep on the sea floor. *Ophiura texturata*, another European species, buries itself just below the sand when the tide is out, leaving a mark like a gull's footprint on the beach. It can be lifted but must be treated gently for, as the name suggests, brittle stars break their arms or split their discs easily. *Ophiura* is orange to reddish in colour and has long, semi-rigid arms extending from a disc with clearly marked plates.

Feather stars and sea lilies

The feather stars and sea lilies make up the class Crinoidea. They occur in two forms. Sea lilies attach themselves permanently to the sea floor by a stalk, but feather stars are free-swimming creatures. However, the basic plan of organization is similar, and the feather star *Antedon bifida* of European coasts will serve as an example of the class.

The feather star's flower-like appearance
The main organs of the feather star are situated in a small central body protected by calcareous plates. From this body, the long slender feather-like arms extend. The body is cup-shaped and its shell consists of two circles of inner plates, five

Comatulids or feather-stars are brilliantly coloured. They are found on European coasts, often in shallow water, on rocks or among algae; but they flourish most in tropical seas and coral reefs. Hanging on to the substratum by the cirri of their calyx, they spread out their long feathery arms in an admirable multicoloured fan. Most of the species have 10 arms, in rare cases 5, but some have from 60 to 200 around their disc; they wave them about ceaselessly, thus setting up a current which is respiratory as well as helping in the capture of micro-organisms, which they convey to their mouth by the movements of their small tube feet and by coiling up their arms. When they are on the move, their undulating style of swimming is most attractive. *The Aquarium at Noumea. Phot. R. Catala.*

This tangled complex is in fact an ophiuroid of the family Gorgono-cephalidae. The small central disc, bearing the mouth and the anus, sends out long arms which ramify several times and become entangled in all directions to produce the characteristic Medusa's head appearance, hence the name 'Gorgon' given to some of these animals. *The Aquarium at Noumea. Phot. R. Catala*

radial and five inter-radial, grouped around a central plate, though only the central plate is apparent. This central plate corresponds to the top of the skeleton in starfishes and sea urchins. It bears about thirty cirri, which are short slender and flexible tentacles made up of articulated joints; the last joint is hook-shaped, enabling the feather star to use its cirri to grip on to the various objects it encounters.

From the radial plates of the central body there extend ten very long arms made of joints similar to those of brittle stars. The joints are joined by powerful muscles, giving the arms great flexibility; however, like brittle stars, the arms break easily. Each joint bears a pinnule, a pointed branch of the joint growing to one side of it. As each arm consists of many small joints, the succession of pinnules along the arms gives them a feather-like appearance. Along one surface of the arm, corresponding to the lower surface of the arm of a starfish, runs an ambulacral groove lined with cilia and containing the tube feet modified into palps. As in brittle stars, these projections are not used for locomotion, but are concerned with respiration, sensing the environment and passing food towards the mouth.

Radial symmetry about the central axial gland

The essential organs of the feather star are contained in a soft disc the size of a pea that is housed in the central body. Near the centre of the disc is the mouth, which is simply a pentagonal orifice that never closes. As in starfishes, the mouth is on the same side of the body as the arms, but this surface is now the upper surface because the feather star (and the sea lily) orientate themselves upside-down compared with starfishes. To avoid confusion, the surface containing the mouth is called the oral surface and the opposite surface (lower in

crinoids, upper in starfishes) is called the aboral surface.

From the mouth run five grooves, each of which immediately divides into two branches. The resulting ten grooves then extend along the arms to become the ambulacral grooves. The anus is also on the oral surface of the feather star, and is usually situated at the top of a bulky conical protuberance called the anal tube that rises from the disc. Behind the mouth is a short vertical oesophagus, followed by a wide stomach that turns anti-clockwise along the walls of the internal disc and leads to the anus via an intestine and short rectum. In this way, the digestive tract is wound around a central cavity in the disc, and this space houses a bulky axial gland joined to the walls by straps of tissue. It is called an axial gland because it is at the axis of symmetry of the feather star. It probably produces hormones.

The mouth is surrounded by a ring canal from which five radial canals extend and divide into two before penetrating the hollow axes of the arms. The gonads also lie along the arms and extend into the pinnules. At breeding time, the gonads swell with sperm or eggs, bursting their walls and releasing their products. The rest of the feather star's internal cavity is partly filled with a large number of connecting plates, virtually transforming it into a sponge. The body wall is lined with small vibrating mechanisms that keep the body fluid in motion but also gather brownish granules of waste matter. These then become detached and are engulfed by the amoebocytes in the body fluid. The nervous system consists of an aboral system comprising a central ring and a nerve branch to each arm, and also an oral system connecting to the cirri.

The prehistorically abundant class

There are about 600 living species in the class Crinoidea. Most of these are feather stars and only about 80 are sea lilies. However, these animals were abundant in earlier times, and thick beds of limestone often consist of fossil crinoids. There are about 5000 fossil species.

Feather stars are not very numerous on European coasts, where they are represented only by some twenty species found from the shoreline down to more than a thousand fathoms. *Antedon bifida*, the common European feather star, ranges in colour from red to bright violet, and *Leptometra phalangium* is bright green with very long cirri. Found off Scandinavian coasts in beds of thousands of individuals is *Hathrometra sarsi*. Feather stars are most common in tropical seas, where their extraordinary shapes and brilliant colours make them worthy companions of the splendid animals of the coral reefs.

Feather stars swim most elegantly, slowly beating alternate arms in gentle waves. But only the adults are able to swim freely, for the larvae are fixed to the bottom by a stalk. In the larva, all the body plates are clearly visible, the central plate being prolonged to form the stalk. The young feather star acquires certain organs such as the cirri during several weeks of settled life, and then it detaches itself from the stalk and begins its free life.

The sea lilies resemble the larval feather star in general, but their skeletons are modified in various ways from one species to another. The arms and central body with its anal tube are much the same as those of the adult feather star, but the cirri are to be found at the end of a long stalk extending from the central body and at intervals along the stalk. The cirri at

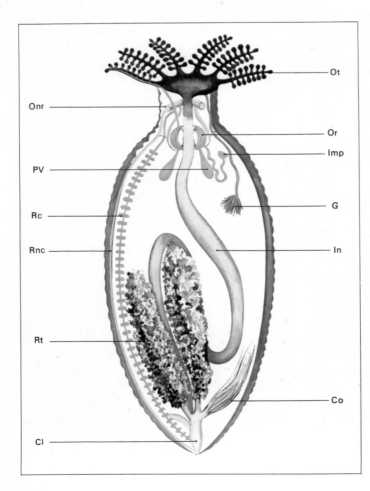

Organizational plan of a holothurian or sea cucumber. *Cl*, cloaca; *Co*, Cuvier's organ; *G*, gonad; *Imp*, internal madreporite plate; *In*, intestine; *Or*, oral water vascular ring or ring canal; *Onr*, oral nerve ring; *Ot*, oral tentacles; *Pv*, Polian vesicle; *Rad*, radial ambulacral canal; *Rnc*, radial nerve cord; *Rt*, respiratory tree ('lung').

the end of the stalk act like roots in anchoring the stalk to the seabed. Sea lilies look like long-stalked flowers growing from the sea floor, their crown of feather-like arms gently wafting in the current. They are mostly tropical creatures. *Bathycrinus wyvillethomsoni* is a beautiful dark green species of warmer European waters. It grows to a foot in height, and forms immense flowery meadows on the floor of the Bay of Biscay.

Sea cucumbers

None of the echinoderms so far described—sea urchins, starfishes and brittle stars, feather stars and sea lilies—look much alike in spite of their basic similarities, and the sea

Ocellated holothurian of the order Aspidochirotae living in the coral reefs and capable of reaching, when fully extended, more than 2 feet in length. The animal, which has just been disturbed, projects through its anus, in a defensive reflex, long sticky threads from its organs of Cuvier. These extend in a broad fan in which the would-be predator is eventually caught. *Phot. J. Théodor*

cucumbers look different again. Some of the most common species look like large black puddings or cucumbers, while those from the deepest parts of the ocean take on extraordinary shapes. They live buried in mud or sand at the sea bottom or hide away in holes in rocks, among corals and sometimes in sponges; they also lie or crawl about in the seaweed on the bottom. Sea cucumbers are to be found anywhere from the seashore to the greatest depths. A few species live in the open sea and are free-swimming.

Apart from their individual appearance, sea cucumbers can be distinguished from all other echinoderms by the lack of a

The mouth of a sea cucumber has a simple projecting circular lip, and is totally devoid of any apparatus for chewing the food. It is followed by a large pharynx surrounded by a crown of calcareous plates consisting of five radial parts and five to fifteen inter-radial parts. The plates are joined flexibly together, giving a certain degree of elasticity. Five large muscles that may travel the whole length of the body are connected to the radial plates. The pharynx is connected by a short oesophagus to a small muscular stomach, after which comes a long intestine that coils and loops throughout the body cavity before it ends at a cloaca and anus, usually opposite the mouth. The intestine makes a complete spiral turn in a clockwise direction and is attached to the body wall by inter-radial mesenteries (membranes).

The nervous system and the haemal system (the primitive circulatory system) are similar to those of other echinoderms. The water vascular system is somewhat different; it consists of a ring canal behind the mouth, from which five radial canals extend to the tube feet and fine branches connect to long ampullae, or expansions, that control the movement of the tentacles. One or more Polian vesicles shaped like small sacs are attached by slender stalks to the ring canal, as well as a stone canal ending in a small madreporite like those in other echinoderms (except crinoids, which have none). But, unlike that of other classes, the madreporite of sea cucumbers usually floats freely within the body cavity, taking in body fluid instead of sea water. Only exceptionally is the madreporite fixed in the body wall, putting the water vascular system in communication with the external environment.

From the cloaca behind the anus, a large canal extends and divides into two tree-like branched tubes that reach far inside the body cavity. These are the respiratory trees. Sea water is pumped in and out of the trees by the muscular action of the cloaca, and oxygen in the water passes into the body fluid through the trees. The trees also act to remove carbon dioxide and other waste products, thereby serving an excretory as well as a respiratory role. Some water undoubtedly passes into the body fluid via the respiratory trees.

Two more internal organs connect to the external environment. A cluster of white tubes called Cuvierian organs are attached to the trunk of the respiratory trees or to the wall of the cloaca in the Aspidochirota. When the sea cucumber is attacked, white sticky threads are ejected to entangle the predator. The remaining organs are the gonads, which consist of one or two bunches of tendrils connected to a single duct that opens between or near the tentacles.

The holothurian of the order Dendrochirotae, *Ludwigia planci*, is one of the most common on French coasts; it is found from the littoral zone up to more than 55 fathoms in depth, crawling on the mud, imbedded in cracks in rocks or holding tenaciously on to the bottom. Light brown in colour, with a broad black tentacular tuft spotted with white, its prismatic shape, accentuated by the distribution, on its 5 radii, of semirigid tube feet, has earned it the name of 'sea cucumber'. *Phot. J. Six*

skeleton made up of calcareous plates fixed together. Instead, the soft skin is reinforced with microscopic plates and spicules, giving it a leathery texture.

The sea cucumbers number about 900 living species and make up the class Holothuroidea. This class is divided into five orders. Three of them possess tube feet, but in the others tube feet are absent.

Radial symmetry typical of an echinoderm

Sea cucumbers with tube feet are typically shaped like cylinders. The cylinders have five bands of radial tube feet running from one end to the other separated by five inter-radial bands which are bare or contain small tube feet. The mouth is at one end of the cylinder and the anus at the other. To this extent, sea cucumbers are rather like sea urchins that have become stretched from globes into cylinders. The tube feet end in points or suckers that may be supported by a calcareous disc. The mouth is surrounded by a tuft of ten to thirty tentacles, the shape and arrangement of which distinguish the three orders of footed sea cucumbers from each other. The order Dendrochirota have tentacles with tree-like branches, whereas the other two orders, the Aspidochirota and Elasipoda are peltate—that is, branch only at the tops of the tentacles, where they form discs or shields. In the Aspidochirota, there are from fifteen to thirty tentacles and usually twenty; in the Elasipoda, the tentacles vary from ten to twenty in number. The number of tube feet also distinguish these two latter orders, for the Aspidochirota have many and the Elasipoda few.

The five orders of sea cucumbers

As we have seen above, the footed sea cucumbers are classified into three orders, partly on the basis of the number and kind of tentacles they possess. But several other features distinguish one order from another. As well as possessing peltate tentacles, the Aspidochirota have a solid calcareous crown around the pharynx to which the body muscles are attached, they have respiratory trees and they possess many tube feet. Among the species of this order that inhabit European waters is *Holothuria forskali*, commonly known as the cotton spinner, which lies on the bottom in shallow water. Its common name refers to its ability to expel sticky white threads when attacked; the genus name *Holothuria* (and the class name Holothuroidea) also refers to the habit sea cucumbers have of expelling threads or even internal organs as a means of defence, for it is derived from Greek words meaning 'forceful expulsion'. Another species is *Stichopus regalis*, which has a flattened body with large conical formations on its thin edges.

The Elasipoda have peltate tentacles like the sea cucumbers of the previous order, but their tube feet are few and respiratory trees are absent. They are unusual in that some of them are pelagic species, being found at the surface and at great depths. Their appearance may be extraordinary—some species of *Psychropotes* look like leeches, and *Pelagothuria natatrix*, a well-known pelagic species, looks like a jellyfish.

The third order, the Dendrochirota, have branched tentacles, though their tube feet are many and they possess respiratory trees like the Aspidochirota. However, the calcareous crown is different, for it is made up of many parts assembled into a mosaic and, in addition, there are no Cuvierian organs. The family Cucumariidae are like cucumbers in shape; their tube feet emerge from the radii and interradii. In *Cucumaria lefevrei*, the tube feet end in suckers, giving the animal a good all-round grip. The Thyonidae are covered with fine tube feet all over the body, giving them a hairy appearance. The Psolidae are very strange; they resemble certain sea squirts, for the soft undersurface is flattened, and bears two or three rows of tube feet on which the animal crawls. The upper surface is covered with strong overlapping plates from which emerge two funnels, one bearing the mouth and the other the anus. The Rhopalodi-

nae are like swollen bottles with long narrow necks. The skins of the sea cucumbers of this order vary enormously in appearance, for the spicules take various shapes: knobs, turrets, curved ridges, even delicate basket shapes. These features are used to distinguish different species.

The two remaining orders of sea cucumbers do not possess tube feet. In the Molpadida, they are modified into small anal projections. These sea cucumbers are sausage-shaped and often have short tails. There are usually 15 (rarely 10) finger-like tentacles, and respiratory trees are present. The skin is often coloured red or violet. *Molpadia musculus*, is an abundant Mediterranean species; it lives on muddy bottoms between 30 and 110 fathoms deep.

In the final order, the Apoda, tube feet are entirely absent, as are respiratory trees (respiration taking place across the body wall). There are from ten to twenty simple tentacles, finger-like or feathery in appearance. The Apoda are worm-like, and have smooth, rugged or warty skins. In *Synapta*, tiny anchor-shaped projections attached to the spicules protrude from the skin and grip the surroundings; these sea cucumbers even cling to the fingers if picked up. The Apoda of European waters burrow mostly in mud or sand. Some such as *Leptosynapta minuta*, barely reach half an inch in length whereas *Leptosynapta inhaerens*, which is somewhat

The black sea cucumber, *Holothuria forskali*, when it lives in shallow water, is a beautiful dark green, almost black, colour, which contrasts sharply with the white tip of its dorsal papillae. This colour becomes lighter with depth, and, towards 200 fathoms, the holothurian becomes a very light greenish yellow. When disturbed, the animal projects, through its anus, a mass of long whitish sticky threads secreted by the Cuvier organs; it is these in which it entangles its enemies. *Phot. Jean Vasserot*

transparent, exceeds a foot in size. But these sea cucumbers are dwarfed by some of the brilliantly coloured *Synapta* of tropical seas, which may reach more than five feet in length and two inches in diameter.

In the Far East, about forty species of sea cucumbers are caught for food. The body walls are boiled and then dried in the sun to produce trepang, which is used to make soup. Some 10,000 tons are exported every year.

Modes of life

Habitats

Echinoderms are to be found in all the oceans, living from the shoreline down to the bottoms of the deepest trenches in the sea floor. Small apod sea cucumbers (*Myriotrochus*), about 1½ inches long, live in the deeps of the Atlantic, Indian and Pacific Oceans at depths of 5500 fathoms and more. Sea urchins, brittle stars and starfishes do not seem to occur deeper than about 3000 fathoms. Sea lilies are most numerous between 500 and 1100 fathoms. Feather stars inhabit inshore waters and are numerous in coral reefs, especially in the area bounded by the Philippines, Indonesia and New

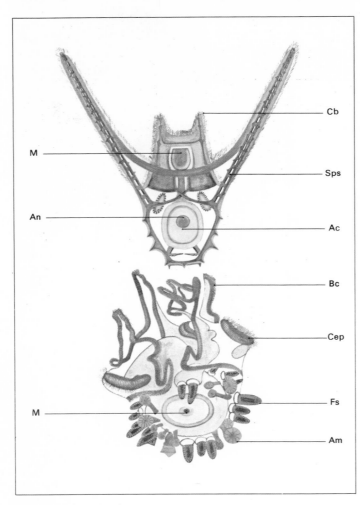

Above, diagram of a pluteus larva of a sea-urchin; *below*, pluteus in course of metamorphosis; the young sea-urchin in process of formation can clearly be seen. *Ac*, alimentary canal; *Am*, first tube feet of the ambulacra; *An*, anus; *Cb*, ciliated band; *Cep*, ciliated epaulette; *Fs*, first spine; *M*, mouth; *Sps*, spicular skeleton.

Guinea. However, they also occur in great numbers in Arctic and Antarctic waters. *Hathrometra sarsi* is often found in populations of thousands in the seas around the North Pole.

Many brittle stars live solitary, isolated lives—hiding under stones or among seaweed or coral, or buried in mud or sand—but they are also to be found in immense beds on muddy bottoms in the Atlantic Ocean, Mediterranean Sea and English Channel. Fishermen often bring up their nets to find them festooned with the common brittle star *Ophiothrix fragilis*, which is a beautiful species, being adorned with a bright mixture of yellows, reds, greens and maroons. *Acrocnida brachiata* lives buried in sand, two or three of its arms poking out from its burrow. It is so plentiful on some English Channel beaches that several dozen of these brownish creatures may be uncovered with a turn of the spade.

Ordinary sea urchins are as much at home among seaweed as on muddy or stony bottoms, rocks or coral reefs. *Paracentrotus lividus* can use its teeth and its spines to bore a hole into solid rock and there make it its home. This sea urchin continues to grow and may get too large to be able to leave its burrow. Sea urchins of the order Diadematoida of warm seas huddle together in cavities carved out of blocks of dead coral; only their barbed spines emerge from the cavities, perpetually whirling in readiness to inflict a very painful wound on any predator or imprudent swimmer. Irregular sea urchins are usually to be found buried in sand, mud or gravel on the sea bed. *Echinocardium cordatum*, the sand urchin or sea potato, is a common irregular sea urchin of European beaches, where it can be found at low tide level. It digs itself a hole some eight inches below the surface, scooping out the burrow with some spoon-shaped spines on its undersurfaces, which, like small shovels, dig and throw back the sand. A thin tube connects the cavity housing the sea urchin to the surface. The walls of the tube are cemented with mucus and along it some highly-specialized tube feet with sensory tips extend to the surface.

Starfishes live on the sea floor over which they can move with some agility. Most sea cucumbers occupy the same habitat, and can crawl about slowly. The tube feet end in suckers, so that sea cucumbers can attach themselves solidly to rocks by their feet, or lodge themselves in clefts in rocks and even inside large sponges. The apod sea cucumbers such as *Synapata*, which do not have tube feet, live buried in mud or sand with only their crowns of tentacles showing. Finally, there are the sea cucumbers that live in the open sea. *Pelagothuria* floats by extending its long tentacles, which are rather like the tentacles of an octopus; and the common *Stichopus regalis* can actively swim even by undulating its body after the manner of the cuttlefish.

Postures adopted by echinoderms
Echinoderms orientate themselves in several different ways. Starfish, brittle stars and sea urchins position themselves so that their mouths are placed against the surface to which they cling; that is, the mouth is on the lower surface of the animal. Feather stars and sea lilies both assume the opposite position, for the mouth is always on the upper surface. The majority of sea cucumbers crawl on their lower surface, which possesses three rows of tube feet, and the mouth is situated at the front of the body.

Obtaining food

Except for brittle stars, echinoderms are slow-moving animals and find their food without straying very far from

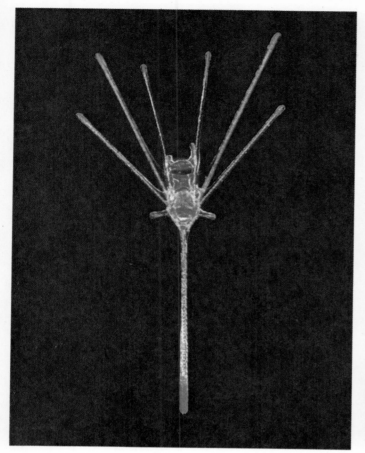

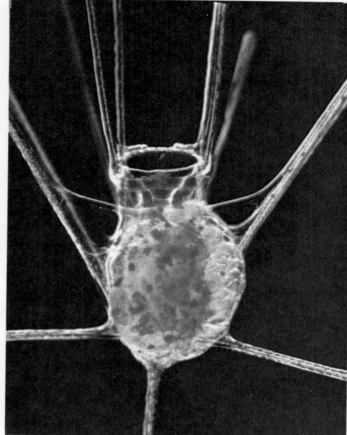

Echinopluteus larva of the irregular sea-urchin *Echinocardium cordatum*. The body, compressed laterally, is provided with 5-pairs of very mobile erect arms, surrounding the oral lobe and the regions close to it, and with a pair of postero-lateral arms directed laterally; its apex is prolonged into a very long process. All these formations are supported by calcareous rods which fit into a complicated embryonic skeleton. *Echinocardium cordatum* is common in the sand of the coasts of Western Europe. Its test, which is heart-shaped, is covered with long fine greyish spines. It may be collected in large numbers on beaches, somewhat like potatoes, by digging in the sand. *Phot. Wilson*

their homes. Crinoids capture plankton organisms drifting in the water with the palps that lie along the grooves in the arms. The prey is immobilized and then covered with a thick coating of mucus, after which the palps transport the piece of food by rapid and co-ordinated movements towards the mouth, where it is engulfed. Some brittle stars also feed on plankton in the same way as crinoids, but most of them are carnivorous and voracious creatures and will capture and eat worms, crustaceans, small sea urchins—virtually anything that comes their way. Usual·y, the prey is pushed by the palps along the undersurface to the mouth, but some brittle stars seize their victims by grasping them in their arms. Brittle stars that live buried in the sand let the ends of the long arms protrude from their burrows and rake them over the bottom to find food. *Astropartus mediterraneus*, a handsome greyish animal with a diameter of at least twenty inches, has long arms with numerous branches that form a trap rather like a spider's web for everything that comes near. After trapping the prey, the arms coil up into a ball and push the food into the wide-open mouth.

Starfishes are also voracious predators, and are adapted for consuming relatively bulky prey, such as mussels, oysters and scallops, large gastropods and even small fish. *Asterias rubens*, the common European starfish, invades mussel and oyster beds in thousands and ravages them completely in a few weeks. The starfish is such a successful predator because it has the strength and patience to open the shells. It grips the mollusc in its arms and fastens its sucker-ended tube feet over the two valves. It then applies sufficient force for a long enough time to force the valves apart gradually. Then, the starfish makes its stomach protrude from its body and pushes it into the soft flesh of the mollusc. The victim is paralyzed by the stomach's gastric juices and then completely digested, leaving the shell totally empty. Even sea urchins are not immune to attack by starfish. They put up a frantic defence with their spines and pedicellariae, but the starfish finally turns them over and pushes its stomach in through their mouths to clean out the flesh inside. Species of starfishes that do not possess suckers on their tube feet are able to open their mouths so much that they can swallow their prey whole. In this way, *Luidia ciliaris* of European coasts consumes molluscs more than $2\frac{1}{2}$ inches long. Sometimes the prey is so bulky that the skin of the upper surface of the starfish ruptures.

The depredations of the crown-of-thorns starfish, *Acanthaster planci*, have placed the Great Barrier Reef along the northeast coast of Australia in danger. These starfish prey on the living coral animals in reefs and although the coral formations do not immediately disappear, they lose their magnificent colours as the coral animals are eaten. A population explosion of the starfish occurred in the 1960s and, by 1974, 2/3 of the Great Barrier Reef had been attacked and reefs in the eastern Pacific were in danger. The possible causes were pollution by insecticides and fungicides washed from the shore, and the elimination of the starfish's natural predators.

Sea cucumbers capture food with their crowns of tentacles.

The tentacles sense the seaweed, rocks, sand or mud around the animal and, being coated with sticky substances secreted by their mucous glands, capture any food particles they happen to touch. The tentacle, encrusted with food particles, is placed in the mouth and then sucked clean just as a child may smear his or her finger with jam and then lick off the jam. As soon as it has finished sucking a tentacle, the sea cucumber pops another one into its mouth. This process takes place without interruption, the sea cucumber continuously sampling its environment. It is not rare to see a tentacle removed from the mouth and then used to prevent the food inside from falling out.

Sea urchins are carnivorous, herbivorous or omnivorous. Carnivorous species feed mainly on fixed or stationary animals such as hydroids, bryozoans, sponges, tube-dwelling annelids and small ascidians, but they can also deal with crustaceans, molluscs and even dead fishes, which they crush with the teeth of their Aristotle's lantern. The herbivorous species browse on algae. Irregular sea urchins eat sand or mud to extract food particles from it, and also detritus and micro-organisms brought to the mouth by the combined action of the spines and pedicellariae.

Breeding

Planktonic larvae and metamorphoses
In most echinoderms, the sexes are separate and they practise external fertilization, shedding their sperms or eggs directly into the sea. Subsequent fertilization occurs purely by the chance meeting of sperm and egg. The fertilized egg develops into a planktonic larva that drifts in the water as it continues to grow. After a few weeks it settles on the bottom before undergoing a metamorphosis into a miniature adult. The free-swimming larvae of echinoderms have various names: pluteus in sea urchins and brittle stars, bipinnaria in starfish, and auricularia in sea cucumbers and the crinoids.

A few echinoderms are hermaphrodite, possessing both male and female gonads; however, the two sets of gonads do not mature at the same time and self-fertilization does not occur. In *Asterina gibbosa* there are separate sexes, but all the young adults are males that are subsequently and permanently transformed into females at a later stage.

Another method of reproduction may occur accidentally if a starfish or brittle star is cut in two. The two halves regenerate their lost parts, becoming two complete animals. A new individual may even be reconstituted from as little as one arm.

The action of the sperm
Breeding is not always as hit and miss as shedding sperms and eggs at random into the sea. At breeding time, some sea cucumbers assemble in groups of several hundred individuals. The presence of the males' sperms in the water induces the females to produce eggs. Sea urchins and brittle stars are similarly gregarious. Going a stage further, genuine copulation sometimes occurs. In the starfish *Archaster typicus* of the Philippines, the male lies on top of the female with his lower surface pressed against her upper surface. *A. angulatus* of Mauritius congregates in dense groups before mating in a similar way.

Arctic and Antarctic species
Sea urchins of the orders Cidaroida and Spatangoida (heart urchins) retain their eggs at the surface of the body, where they can develop without risk of predators. The eggs are

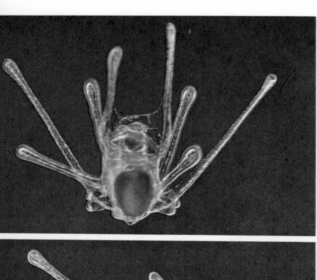
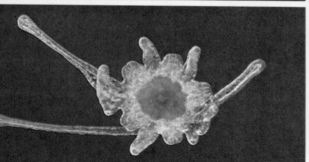

The ophiopluteus larva of the brittle-star *Ophiocomina nigra*, shaped like a compressed cone, has 4 pairs of symmetrical arms, of unequal length, and is fringed by a regular ciliated band enabling it to swim. (1) Metamorphosis occurs at the swimming larva stage; the rough outline of the young ophiuroid is formed on the oral surface and in the larva's median posterior part (2); the arms are re-absorbed, the larva falls to the bottom, the young ophiuroid becomes detached (3) and begins its free life. *Phot. Wilson*

placed around the mouth or the periproct, or in the grooves of the shell, which are protected by spines and serve as incubatory pouches. *Eucidaris nutrix*, a sub-Antarctic species, shelters its eggs in a kind of tent formed by spatula-shaped spines around the mouth.

Some starfishes can arch their bodies so that they form a kind of vault within the arms in which the eggs accumulate and develop; others carry their young on their backs among their spines. In *Leptasterias groenlandica*, a species of circumpolar Arctic waters, the young develop within stomach pouches. The Pterasteridae have a chamber below the upper surface in which the eggs are laid; water currents pass through the chamber to bring oxygen to the eggs. The Brisingidae, a deep-sea family, shelter their young within a kind of basket formed in the angle of the long slender arms by their spines. Some brittle stars are also incubatory, and at least four species exhibit a curious difference between the sexes. *Amphicyclus androphorus* from the Mozambique coast and *Astrochlamys bruneus* of Antarctic waters both have dwarf males that for much of the time are attached to the mouth of the large female or perch on top of her. Many cold-water brittle stars are viviparous (give birth to live young). The eggs are brooded in the slit of the genital bursae and sometimes the young develop in the ovaries. In *Amphipholis squamata*, a cosmopolitan species common on European coasts, the embryos seem to eat the walls of the genital bursae.

Most sea cucumbers of cold waters incubate their young. *Cladodactyla crocea* shelters its young between the feet on its upper surface. *Psolus*, a sea cucumber of the order Dendrochirota, has large overlapping plates along its back. The young shelter within a chamber having a roof of plates supported by pillars. Other sea cucumbers have from one to five ventral sacs that open near the mouth and contain up to several dozen embryos. The eggs may also adhere to the body surface by means of a sticky secretion until the larvae hatch. The female of an abyssal species, *Bathyplotes tizardi*, sticks its eggs to the male's tentacles, where they continue their development. *Leptosynapta minuta*, an apod sea cucumber only $\frac{1}{3}$ of an inch long found in European waters, incubates its eggs in the body cavity; the embryos are usually two in number and arranged head-to-tail. They are 'born' by the mother's body bursting near the anus.

Regeneration

As we have seen, echinoderms are able to grow again or regenerate parts of their bodies that have been shed as a defence mechanism or have been torn away by a predator. The starfish shows the greatest powers of regeneration, and it is not unusual to find a starfish in the process of growing a new arm. *Linckia*, for example, sheds one or more of its arms at the level of the disc. New arms then grow out of the disc from the stumps of the old ones. Meanwhile, the severed limb also acts as if it has lost the other arms, and develops several buds that grow into new arms. As they grow, the outline of a disc takes shape. The developing starfish then has a comet shape, for the original arm suggests the tail of a comet and the regenerating disc and arms the head of a comet. Regeneration is usually complete within six months, a new starfish identical with the old being formed.

Brittle stars shed and regenerate their arms even more quickly and easily than starfishes. Some divide into halves down the middle of the disc, the division avoiding the mouthparts, which are left unaffected. The young of *Ophiactus*

virens, a small green brittle star of the Mediterranean Sea, regenerate themselves in this way.

Sea urchins are able to regenerate all the organs that adorn the shell: the tube feet, the spines, the pedicellariae and the sphaeridia (the sensory organs near the mouth).

Feather stars break their arms at certain points if they are physically disturbed and even if they are bathed in bright

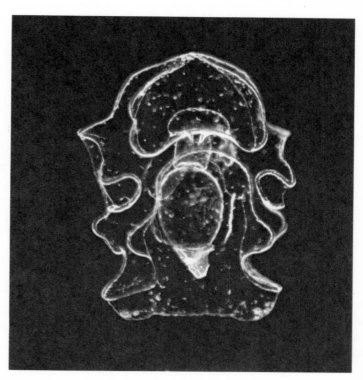

Auricularia larva of apod holothurian, *Labidoplax digitata*. As a result of the incomplete segmentation of the coelom, the embryo, unlike those of other classes of echinoderms, has become asymmetrical; 2 of the coelomic cavities exist only on the left side. *Phot. Wilson*

light. The central body may regenerate into a new feather star, provided that the nervous centre has remained intact.

Sea cucumbers have no arms to lose in self-defence, but the internal organs may be ejected through the anus or by rupture of the body wall and then grown again. *Synapta* even fragment into several pieces by a series of strong muscular contractions; however only the forward part, which contains the essential organs, is capable of regenerating into a complete new animal.

Defence mechanisms

Sea urchins appear to be the best defended of echinoderms. They are armed with fearsome spines which, in some species, have fine barbs and are covered with a glandular tissue that secretes a poisonous substance. Such spines are capable of inflicting severe, often fatal, wounds on would-be predators. The pedicellariae, nestling among the spines, form a second line of defence. Those provided with poison glands are particularly dangerous, the tropical *Toxopneustes pileolus* causing severe paralysis of the facial and respiratory muscles that may even prove fatal. Such effective means of defence lead crustaceans and small fishes to seek shelter among the long spines of the magnificent *Diadema* of tropical seas. However, the sea urchin's defences are not completely invincible, for they cannot protect urchins from attack by large crustaceans, certain starfishes, reef fishes and seabirds.

Starfishes are much less well armed than sea urchins. Apart from the few species that have pedicellariae at the base of their spines or scattered over the body surface, or a toxic mucus that sometimes covers the skin, starfishes have no means of defence. Their stomachs do emit a paralyzing substance, but this is used to deal with prey rather than with predators.

Brittle stars also seem to be defenceless, but it must be remembered that both brittle stars and starfishes are able to regenerate missing arms and even parts of the central disc, so defence is much less necessary in these animals than in the sea urchins, which have less ability to regenerate.

Feather stars and sea lilies have very solid arms and great powers of regeneration; the only vulnerable part seems to be

Asterias rubens, a starfish very common on the coasts of Europe, often orange coloured, sometimes bright red or purplish-blue, has its dorsal surface covered with small spines on which are planted straight pedicellarae. This deadly predator attacks beds of oysters and mussels, ravaging them in a matter of weeks. The tube feet are firmly attached to the mollusc's two valves; the starfish then exercises continuous traction which results in the shell being forced half-open; it then introduces its everted stomach and digests the soft parts of the oyster or the mussel. To get rid of this undesirable intruder, oyster-breeders have no option but to capture it; in fact, when it is cut and thrown back into the sea, it regenerates as many perfectly constituted starfish as there are fragments. *Phot. J. Six*

the soft central disc. Although well protected by calcareous plates, some small gastropod molluscs bore into crinoids to eat out the soft parts. Feather stars of coral reefs are often victims of the voracious parrot fish.

Such slow and soft creatures as the sea cucumbers would appear to be very easy prey. However, the skin is often noxious and each species seems to possess a special poison; would-be predators get to know this and avoid sea cucumbers. Sea cucumbers with Cuvierian organs are capable of active defence, for they eject sticky threads through the anus that adhere to any predator and immobilize the attacker. The sea cucumber then separates itself from the threads, which break off at their bases.

The larva of this starfish (*Luidia sarsi*) is a bipinnaria with a highly developed pre-oral lobe and with very long mid-dorsal arms (*top left*). The larva swims actively and gives rise to a small starfish (*right*), which,

Parasitism and commensalism

All these means of defence do not prevent a very large number of organisms from attaching themselves as parasites to echinoderms. Ciliated protozoans live in the skin of starfishes, in the intestines of sea urchins, in the body fluid or on the tentacles of apod sea cucumbers, and in the respiratory trees of footed sea cucumbers. Two nematodes, one of which may exceed three feet in length (*Ichthyonema grayi* and *Oncholaimus echini*) and the planarian *Syndesmis echinorum* are found in the body of the common sea urchin, *Echinus esculentus*. Trematodes are parasites of the digestive tract of sea urchins and brittle stars. The mesozoan parasite *Rhopalura ophiocomae* occupies the incubatory pouches of *Amphiura squamata*, a brittle star, and destroys its reproductive organs. Several crustaceans are parasites of echinoderms, but are extraordinarily modified as a result. The barnacle *Dendrogaster* inhabits the body cavity of sea urchins, starfishes and brittle stars, but the adult form is reduced to a lobed mass and its crustacean nature is apparent only in the larval form. Many copepods take refuge in the oesophagus and body cavity of sea cucumbers, or cause galls to protrude from the body surface and shelter in them. The small crab inhabits the rectum of the sea urchin, causing a deformation of the periproct. *Antedon bifida*, the rosy feather star, is parasitized by *Myzostoma cirriferum*, a small polychaete worm that anchors itself to its host by hooked parapodia (leg-like organs). Other species of *Myzostoma* bury themselves in the skins of crinoids, in which they cause gall formation.

But the most remarkable parasites of echinoderms are molluscs. The bivalve *Entovalva perrieri* lives in the intestine of the sea cucumber *Synapta*. Another bivalve, *Devonia semperi*, fixes itself to apod sea cucumbers of the genus *Protankyra* by its foot, which is transformed into a sucker. Small gastropods of the family Melanellidae often attach themselves to the anal tube of feather stars, burying themselves in the skin and taking in the internal fluid of the tube. These parasites are often difficult to spot, for they are accompanied by crustaceans that have the same colour as the feather star and thereby disguise the parasites. *Parenteroxenos dogieli* is so modified by its parasitism that it has no shell nor any internal organs except the gonads. It takes the shape of a thin and highly coiled worm. Its host is the sea cucumber *Cucumaria japonica* which reaches about four inches; yet the parasite, when uncoiled, may extend for more than three feet. A gastropod of the same genus parasitizes another sea cucumber, *Stichopus tremulus*. (See also Molluscs.)

Commensalism, in which the host is not harmed by the presence of other animals, is common in echinoderms. Infusoria are found in large numbers on the skin of starfishes and apod sea cucumbers. The polychaete *Acholae squamosa* shelters in the ambulacral grooves of the starfishes *Astropecten* and *Luidia*. Many copepods, hydroids, bryozoans and sponges live on the skin of brittle stars, and on the shell or spines of sea urchins. The amphipod *Urothoe marina* lives on *Echinocardium cordatum*, the latter's spine bearing bivalves of the genus *Montacuta*. In European and Indo-Pacific waters, *Fierasfer* or *Carapus*, a narrow flattened fish about 6 inches long, inhabits the cloaca and dilated intestine of the sea cucumbers *Stichopus* and *Holothuria*, occasionally emerging to feed. *Nannophiura*, a tiny brittle star barely 1/25 of an inch in diameter, lives permanently perched on the spines of irregular sea urchins of the genus *Laganum*.

as soon as its first tube feet are formed, (*bottom left*), falls to the bottom, becomes detached from its larval tissues, and begins its free life (*right*). *Phot. Wilson*

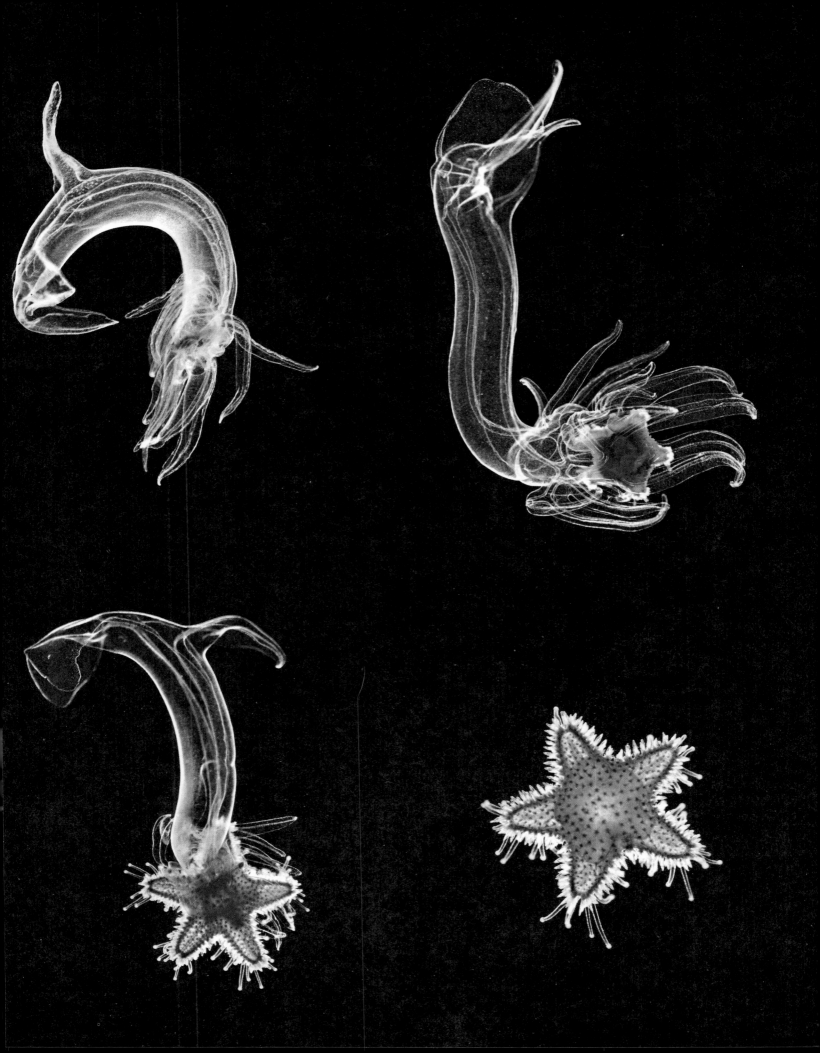

Forerunners of
Vertebrates

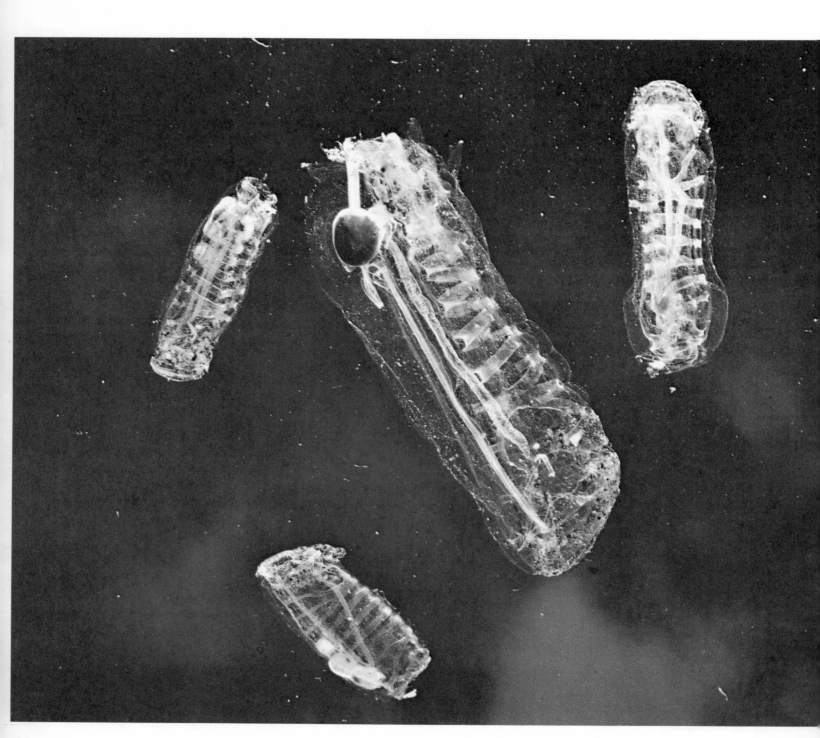

The preceding chapters of this book have been devoted to the invertebrates—the animals without backbones—and the chapter following this one will cover the animals with backbones—the vertebrates. In between these two great groups of the animal kingdom come a few animals that possess structures having some features of a backbone. While they may be forerunners of the vertebrates only in that they precede the vertebrates in classification, it is not unreasonable to see the fish-like lancelet or amphioxus as a prototype of the vertebrates.

The vertebrates—lampreys, sharks and rays, bony fishes, amphibians, reptiles, birds and mammals—are distinguished from the invertebrates by the presence of a stiff backbone that runs the length of the body and acts as its principal support. These animals make up a group of the phylum Chordata. The group is called the Craniata, which signifies the presence of a skull or cranium. The phylum is usually completed by another group called the Acrania because its members possess no cranium. It comprises two sub-phyla: the Cephalochordata (lancelets or amphioxus) and Tunicata (tunicates). These animals are usually placed in the same phylum as the vertebrates because they possess a notochord, which is a flexible rod running most of the length of the body and supporting it. It has the same function as the vertebral column (backbone) of a vertebrate, though it is present only in the larvae of tunicates and not in the adults. The vertebrates also possess a notochord in the early stages of their lives, and it is later replaced by a vertebral column. It is this possession of a notochord either throughout life or at some stage of life that distinguishes the chordates (animals of the phylum Chordata) from other animals.

The discovery of the fish-like lancelets and of the tunicates, the larvae of which look like tadpoles, was greeted with great enthusiasm among zoologists about a century ago. These creatures seemed to indicate a link between the vertebrates and invertebrates, and zoologists speculated (and still do) that the fishes and, ultimately, man evolved from invertebrates via the lower chordates. Other groups of animals came under scrutiny for such evidence, and two more phyla are associated with the lower chordates. These are the Hemichordata (tongue worms and acorn worms) and the Pogonophora (beard worms). The hemichordates have a projection from the mouth cavity that was at first interpreted as being a notochord. However, embryological studies have shown that it is made of a different kind of tissue to the notochords of chordates and is not an equivalent structure. Resemblances do exist between the two phyla in the structure of the gills and nervous system.

The pogonophorans have resemblances to the hemichordates, and it seems certain that some connections exist between them and the tunicates, lancelets and vertebrates. All the groups are very old, as fossils prove, but this does not mean that a common ancestor may be attributed to all of them. Probably they derive from parent stocks that are closely related, and have since evolved in different directions. Similarities between their larvae and the larvae of starfish lead many zoologists to propose that the vertebrates may have evolved from echinoderms via hemichordates and the lower chordates. But others favour a theory in which the chordates are descended from annelids.

The hemichordates

Despite the name, hemichordates are not closely related to chordates. They are so named because of their similarities to the chordates. The pharynx is perforated with slits and transformed into an organ of respiration resembling the gills of fishes. Another chordate-like feature is the structure of the dorsal nerve cord. The projection of the mouth cavity that was once thought to be a notochord is called the buccal pouch. Two less important features of hemichordates are the presence of bilateral symmetry, and the division of the body into three successive regions: proboscis, collar and trunk.

The phylum is divided into three classes that are so different in appearance that only detailed study shows them to be closely related.

The class Enteropneusta

Hemichordates resembling annelid worms

These hemichordates are popularly called tongue worms or acorn worms. They are wormlike creatures with a proboscis and collar that together look like an acorn. Acorn worms are all marine creatures and are found throughout the world. There are about seventy species. They bury themselves in mud and sand, and also are to be found among coral reefs and at the bottom of beds of seaweed. They vary in length from an inch up to eight feet.

Acorn worms can be found burrowing in the sand of the lower shore. They dig a U-shaped tube with two openings in the sand and are difficult to extract from their burrows, for the body is soft and breaks easily. Although an acorn worm may at first sight appear to be an annelid worm, it is in fact very different. The proboscis at the front of the body has a rounded point, and is used to burrow through the mud or sand. The proboscis is believed to fill with water through pores on its dorsal (upper) surface, and burrowing is also aided by muscular movements of the trunk. Behind the proboscis, the body narrows to a short 'waist' and then broadens into the collar. The mouth is situated like an ever-open funnel in the collar. The acorn worm feeds by swallowing water and mud or sand and extracting any food particles and micro-organisms, excreting the used sand or mud through the anus at the rear end of the body. The excreted material forms a coiled cast at the rear opening of the burrow. The dorsal nerve cord broadens out in the collar in a way comparable to the nervous systems of chordates.

The trunk lies behind the collar and is by far the longest part of the body. It broadens at the level of the pharynx, immediately behind the collar. The pharynx is wide and contains U-shaped gill slits on either side that connect to the exterior. The gonads are situated in the wall of the pharynx and open between the gill slits. The eggs or sperms are released directly into the sea and fertilization occurs by chance. Behind the pharynx, the ducts of the hepatic caeca (liver sacs) open into the digestive tract and aid digestion. The hepatic caeca can often be seen as two rows of prominent ridges lying midway along the trunk. The intestine runs the whole length of the body, connecting with the anus at the rear end of the trunk.

The nervous system lies in the body surface, and is concentrated into the two nerve cords that are sunk in grooves running along the upper and lower surfaces of the entire trunk.

It might seem strange that the acorn worms have no sense organs. The nerve endings are distributed all over the skin, and it is thought that those of the proboscis and collar are sensitive to touch, but there are no particular sensory organs. However, the acorn worm leads a very sedentary life and is in no need of eyes or such organs. Having hollowed out a burrow, it simply strains water and mud or sand through its body. Acorn worms do leave their burrows from time to time, but it is not known whether they are capable of finding their way back or simply dig a new burrow after each sortie.

Acorn worms possess a circulatory system. There are two blood vessels, one upper and one lower and each lying beneath a nerve cord. The two vessels are joined above the buccal pouch, and there are branches of the vessels near the gill slits. Circulation is probably effected by contractions of the vessel walls.

Acorn worms are capable of regeneration. If they are cut in two across the body, the rear portion will grow a new front part, but the front portion will not regenerate the missing rear part. Regeneration occurs even if the rear portion is very small.

The class Pterobranchia

Hemichordates resembling moss animals

The pterobranchs are small marine animals which live mostly in colonies. They bear virtually no external resemblance to the acorn worms and in fact look rather like bryozoans or moss animals. The members of the colony live in chitinous tubes that join together to form a branching structure. The colony spreads out over a rock or the sea bed, or stands on its own. The individual pterobranchs are never more than $\frac{1}{4}$ of an inch long, but the colonies may reach several inches in size.

The individual pterobranch bears little more resemblance to an acorn worm than does a colony. Compared with an acorn worm, the body is highly compressed. The collar region bears one or more pairs of feathery arms called lophophores which are involved in respiration and collecting food. Beneath the collar there is a muscular disc containing glands that secrete a material from which the tube forms. This disc corresponds to the proboscis of the acorn worm. Gill slits are usually absent, and the digestive tract is coiled so that the anus opens behind the collar. At the end of the short trunk is a stalk connecting one individual of a colony to the next. Reproduction is often by budding, and the bud arises on the stalk. The tube is perforated at this point and the bud secretes a new tube around itself as it grows and develops into a new individual. However, some pterobranchs reproduce sexually, and some are free-living and do not form colonies.

There are only about twenty species of pterobranchs. They live in both shallow and deep waters and are found mostly in the southern hemisphere. In Europe, they are located mainly in the Norwegian fiords.

The third class of hemichordates is called the Plancto-sphaeroidea and they are known only from their larvae, which are transparent and pelagic.

The pogonophorans

The only independent multi-cellular animals with no digestive cavity

It would be difficult to imagine animals stranger than the phylum Pogonophora. They were discovered in Indonesian waters in 1900 and given their name, which means beard-bearers in Greek, because of the long beard-like tentacles that stream from the head. Their common name, beard worms, also reflects their strange appearance. Since 1900, some 80 species have been dredged from the depths of the oceans in most parts of the world. Pogonophorans can best be compared in appearance to very fragile pieces of sewing thread varying in length from 2 to 12 inches and in diameter from 1/50 to 1/10 of an inch. These threads are usually colourless but sometimes tinged with red, and are contained in transparent chitinous tubes that presumably stand in the ooze on the seabed. The tubes may be as much as 5 feet long.

The body, like that of a hemichordate, is divided into three regions. The first, the protosome, bears the long tentacles, which are hollow and covered with pinnules and rows of cilia on the outer surface. Each pinnule is made up of a single cell and plays an important role in respiration. Two capillary blood vessels run along the inside of each tentacle and are linked to the general circulatory system.

Pogonophorans have no trace of a mouth, an anus or a digestive tract. Several theories have been advanced to explain how they feed but none are conclusive. As these animals were discovered fairly recently and live in a highly inaccessible habitat, little is known of their biology. Presumably, they move up and down their tubes and spread out the tentacles to trap food particles in the water. Some authors have suggested that the nutritive substances are then absorbed through the skin, but the whole animal is covered with an uninterrupted cuticle that would seem to prevent absorption. However, the cuticle is thinner on the pinnules of the tentacles and absorption might take place there. If this is so, there should first be external digestion of the food

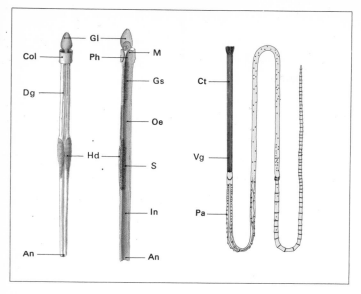

Left, diagram of a *Balanoglossus*: View of dorsal surface (*left*) in a saggital section (*right*). *An*, anus; *Col*, collar; *Dg*, dorsal groove; *Gl*, gland; *Gs*, gill slits; *Hd*, hepatic diverticula; *In*, intestine; *M*, mouth; *Oe*, oesophagus; *Ph*, pharynx; *S*, stomach. *After Y. Delage*

up a separate group called the Acrania. This classification is based on the features that the lower chordates have in common with the other chordates. But there are several important features that they do not have in common with the other chordates. For example, the lower chordates have no skull and therefore no brain or any sensory organs that would be connected to a brain. They also lack jaws, vertebrae, and paired limbs. For some zoologists, this is sufficient to place them in a separate phylum, the Protochordata, comprising the same two sub-phyla of tunicates and lancelets, while the Chordata is made up only of the vertebrates. Such a classification implies to some degree a consideration that the lower chordates are a side-branch of the mainstream of evolution towards the vertebrates.

However, many authorities feel that the common features

particles and therefore special digestive glands should be present in the cuticle; however, such glands have not been found. Another possibility is that bacteria in the mud around the pogonophoran may be able to liberate nutritive substances that would spread into the sea water and be directly absorbed by the animal. But no really satisfactory explanation of the feeding of pogonophorans has yet been made.

The mesosome, the second region of the body, is short but the third region, the metasome, is very long. It bears adhesive papillae (small projections) and rings of papillae that are used to anchor and to move the pogonophore inside its tube.

The nervous system runs throughout the cuticle and there are no sensory organs. The circulatory system is simple, consisting of one dorsal blood vessel and one ventral vessel. The blood flows forward in the ventral vessel and backwards in the dorsal vessel, as in chordates. The blood contains haemoglobin and the heart contains dense muscular fibres.

Pogonophorans live in groups in the mud of the seabed. They have separate sexes, fertilization taking place in the female's tube and being effected by transfer of a spermatophore (sperm packet). The eggs develop in the upper part of the female's tube and completely block it. This gives rise to another pogonophoran mystery, for how can the female continue to breathe and feed?

In addition to their chordate features, pogonophorans have some unique but very primitive characteristics. The phylum is a very ancient one, for fossil representatives have been found.

The lower chordates

Ancestors of the vertebrates

Zoologists are not agreed on the classification of the lower chordates, just as they cannot agree on the probable evolution of the vertebrates. Many place the tunicates and lancelets as sub-phyla within the phylum Chordata, making

A beach on the Island of Nossi-Bé at low tide with burrows of Balanoglossi, whose anal end is in line with the top of the hillock-like castings. *Phot. G. Termier*

of lower chordates and vertebrates are sufficiently important to place both groups within the same phylum. These features are the presence of a notochord at some stage of life; the presence of a dorsal nerve chord that forms in the embryo by a folding of the layer of tissue called the ectoderm; and the presence at some stage of gill slits in the pharynx (present only in embryonic development in reptiles, birds and mammals, including man). Such common features could well indicate that a lower chordate is the ancestor of the vertebrates.

All the lower chordates are marine animals.

The tunicates

The sub-phylum Tunicata is made up of three classes of animals of widely-differing appearance. They are all called tunicates because they are encased in a hard covering called a tunic. The first class, the Ascidiacea or ascidians or sea squirts, live fixed to the bottom as adults; the second class, the Thaliacea or chain tunicates, are free-swimming animals with cask-shaped bodies that sometimes live in long chains of individuals; the third class, the Larvacea, are tadpole-like creatures that swim at the surface of the sea. There are about 2000 species of tunicates, and they are found in all seas at all depths.

The ascidians (sea squirts)

Aristotle, who was an observant naturalist as well as philosopher, described a simple ascidian, giving it the name tethyum—perhaps after Tethys, a sea nymph in Greek mythology. Our modern common name is somewhat more prosaic, 'sea squirt' referring to the ascidian's habit of squirting water from its body openings when touched.

Ascidians are common marine animals, living on rocks, loose sediments, seaweeds and on animals. They live solitarily or colonially, varying in size from 1/25 of an inch to 20 inches. They are mostly fixed animals, but some live freely in mud or sand and deep-sea ascidians seem to be capable of movement. Ascidians are cylindrical or globular in shape. The shell or tunic is a tough sac pierced by 2 orifices at the top. The animal feeds by filtering food particles from the water, which enters through the incurrent siphon—the orifice at the centre of the top of the ascidian. The water leaves by the other orifice, the excurrent siphon, which is situated to one side of the incurrent siphon. When disturbed, the ascidian contracts its body violently to squirt out water as a defence mechanism.

The incoming water passes from the incurrent siphon to a basket-shaped branchial sac within the body. This sac is pierced with many openings called stigmata and lined with vibrating cilia. The cilia beat to set up a current of water through the openings of the branchial sac. Respiration takes place at the stigmata, so that they act as gill slits.

Along the wall of the branchial sac is the endostyle, a vertical groove bearing mucous cells. Food particles are trapped by the mucus and then moved down the groove to the bottom of the branchial sac, where they enter the oesophagus. The oesophagus connects to the stomach, which is situated beneath the branchial sac, and here the food particles are digested. The stomach leads to the intestine, where the nutritive products of digestion are absorbed. Waste matter passes along the intestine to an anus situated near the excurrent siphon, where it mixes with the water that has passed through the gill slits and is on its way out of the body.

The nervous system is extremely reduced. It consists of a single cerebral ganglion from which nerves run to all the organs. This ganglion controls simple reflex actions, such as the opening and closing of the siphons and muscular movements of the mantle (the tunic's inner lining). The circulatory system contains a heart situated near the stomach, and large blood vessels lead from each end of the heart, distributing blood throughout the body tissues and to the gill slits. The flow of blood may reverse direction for short periods—a feature unique to tunicates—for there are no valves in the heart or blood vessels.

The gonads are also situated alongside the stomach. Ascidians are hermaphrodite, and possess both ovaries and testes. Ducts from each lead to the excurrent siphon, where both sperms and eggs are discharged. Some ascidians reproduce by budding.

Ascidians display great variety of colour. The colonies are often magnificent sights, for they look like brightly-coloured masses covered with stars or flowers. In fact, the stars or

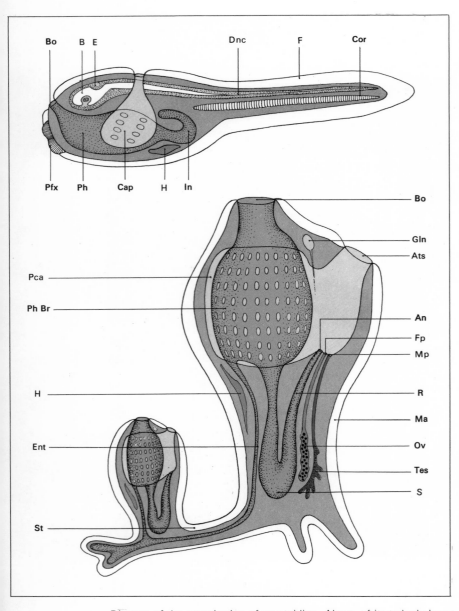

Diagram of the organization of an ascidian. *Above*, of its tadpole larva; *below*, of the fixed adult. *An*, anus; *Ats*, opening of atrial or exhalent siphon; *B*, brain; *Bo*, branchial opening or mouth; *Dnc*, dorsal nerve cord; *E*, eye; *Ent*, endodermal (epicardial) tube forming new individuals; *F*, fin; *Fp*, female pore; *Gln*, ganglion; *H*, heart; *In*, intestine; *Ma*, mantle or tunic; *Mp*, male pore; *Not*, notochord; *Ov*, ovary; *Pca*, peribranchial (atrial) cavity; *Pfx*, papilla of fixation; *Ph*, pharynx; *PhBr*, pharynx acting as a gill; *R*, rectum; *S*, stomach; *St*, stolon; *Tes*, testis.

flowers are simply groups of individual ascidians sharing a single common excurrent siphon.

Ascidians filter enormous amounts of water, passing as much as 20,000 times their own volume of water through their bodies in a day. It is not therefore surprising that they can build up high concentrations of rare metals that occur as traces in sea water. *Phallusia*, for example, may contain 6 parts per 1000 of vanadium (calculated on its dry weights), whereas sea water contains only 2 parts of vanadium in 1000 million parts of water.

Reproduction

In most ascidians, the fertilized egg develops into a larva inside the body. The larva then emerges and grows quickly.

In others, the egg develops in the sea. The ascidian larva looks like a tadpole, with a head containing a rough approximation of the adult organs and a tail supported by a notochord. The larva enjoys a few hours or days of free-swimming life, and then attaches itself to a rock or some other support by adhesive glands at the front of the head. In a short time the tail is then partly absorbed into the body and partly cast off. The adult organs rapidly form, and a tunic grows around them to produce a small adult ascidian.

A colony of ascidians extends itself by budding. This occurs quickly in several ways which differ considerably from one family to another. The differences in budding and in gill structures serve as a basis for the classification of the ascidians.

A bunch of clavellinas (*Clavellina lepadiformis*) fixed to a gorgonian coral. *Port-Vendres region. Phot. J. Théodor*

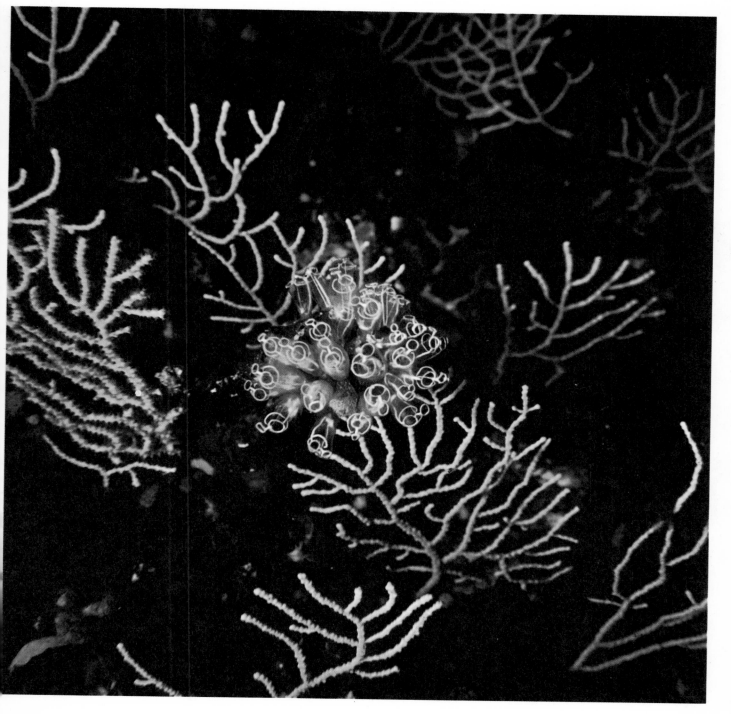

273

Classification of the ascidians

The Aplousobrancha

The sub-phylum comprises four orders divided into several families. These ascidians possess a simple branchial sac. The sac wall, which is flat, is perforated by transverse rows of ciliated stigmata separated by blood vessels called transverse sinuses.

All the members of this order are of the compound type, forming colonies in which individuals share a common tunic. The shape of the colonies depends on the mode of budding, but the individuals are joined to each other, inside the common tunic.

1. The Clavelinidae are small and not brightly coloured. The individuals, or zooids, stand up like small clubs from the colony. They are fixed to their supports by hair-like structures called rhizoids, some of which thicken and bud to form new individuals arranged in clusters.

2. The Polycitoridae live mainly in tropical seas. They are smaller, being no more than 1/5 of an inch long. A projection becomes detached from the body at the base of the gill, and extends along the side and divides into buds that produce new ascidians. The individuals remain very close to one another and are protected by a common tunic. The colony takes the form of a cushion or of finger-like lobes. It is often difficult to make out the individual ascidians in the colony, for they are

open into a common orifice called a cloaca. The post-abdomen develops buds that grow into new individuals beside the parent.

The colonies of this family, like those of the Polycitoridae, may be brilliantly coloured. A particularly striking example is *Fragarium*, known as the sea strawberry.

4. The Didemnidae are as common as the ascidians of the preceding families. Their colonies do not form in compact masses but in encrusting growths. The individuals are very small, being only about 1/25 of an inch in length. Budding is complicated. The parent zooid develops 2 buds, an anterior (front) one on the oesophagus and a posterior (hind) one on the rectum. The anterior bud grows into the posterior portion of a new zooid, which joins with the anterior portion of the parent to complete the new individual. Meanwhile, the posterior bud develops into the anterior portion of a new zooid and joins with the posterior part of the parent to form another new individual. In this way, the parent divides into 2 new zooids. The zooids remain in contact and the colony extends over its support. In some species, the tunic contains many star-shaped calcareous spicules and is opaque.

The Didemnidae grow over a great variety of surfaces. They are found on rocks, on seaweed (especially *Laminaria*), on other ascidians, and on the shells of crabs and bivalve molluscs.

The Phlebobrancha

The branchial sac of the phlebobranch is complicated by the

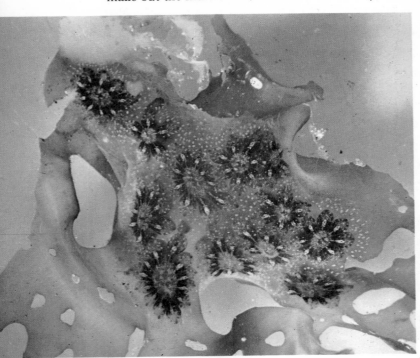
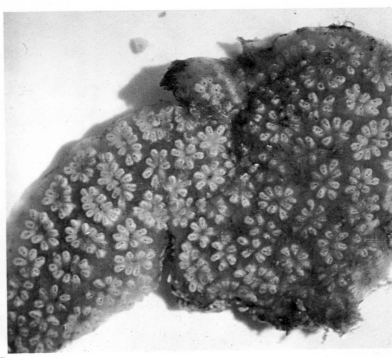

Two views of *Botryllus schlosseri*. The botrylli, compound ascidians, are polymorphic. *Phot. F. Monniot*

hidden by the very dark skin of the tunic and by the grains of sand that accumulate on it.

3. The Polyclinidae are like the Polycitoridae in appearance. The body is elongated and divided into three regions: the thorax containing the gills, the abdomen containing the digestive tract, and the post-abdomen containing the gonads. Each zooid is from $\frac{1}{2}$ an inch to 2 inches in length and $\frac{1}{5}$ of an inch in diameter, and they cluster together in definite patterns. The excurrent siphons of the zooids in a cluster all

papillae that lie on its inner surface. These small protuberances arise from the transverse sinuses, and form regular longitudinal lines. They often split into three at their tips. The papillae lengthen and meet above the gill wall to form bars parallel to the endostyle and perpendicular to the transverse sinuses with which they communicate, making a kind of inner grille within the branchial sac.

This order is divided into four main families.

1. The Cionidae are very common ascidians, and are often

found in the dirty waters of ports, encrusting the sides of the quays and fouling the hulls of ships. Some of the species are simple; that is, each individual has its own separate tunic. They are a transparent bright yellow and reach several inches in length, and the body can be contracted to a high degree. The compound species, such as *Diazona*, are green or violet and very fragile; they break apart as soon as they leave the water.

2. The Corellidae are all solitary animals. They possess a digestive tract that is situated to the right of the branchial sac, unlike all other ascidians, and the stigmata are arranged in spirals.

3. The Ascidiidae, the commonest phlebobranchs, comprise simple species. They are fixed to a rock by the left surface of the cartilaginous tunic, and are often bright pink in colour. They are moderately large, reaching four inches or more.

4. The Perophoridae form transparent colonies. The individual zooids are small—about 1/10 of an inch long. They are linked to each other by a fine stalk containing a blood vessel, and give rise to new individuals by budding. The colony is made up of a loose network of zooids, and the internal organs can be clearly seen through the transparent tunic. Careful observation has revealed that the hearts of the membranes of a colony all beat in perfect synchronization.

The Stolidobrancha

The gill formation is more complex in these ascidians than in those of the previous orders. Many blood sinuses are formed by joining together of the gill papillae and they come together in longitudinal folds of the branchial walls, thus increasing its surface area.

1. The Styelidae have four gill folds, and comprise several hundred species. Some are simple ascidians, such as *Styela* and *Polycarpa*, and others, for example *Botryllus* and the Polystyelinae, are compound. The Polystyelinae form buds that separate from the parent; the resulting zooids grow against one another but each retains its own tunic. *Botryllus*, a common sea squirt of shallow waters, forms colonies containing rosette-shaped groups. Each group contains from three to twelve individuals clustered around a common cloacal siphon. The rosettes stand out in bright colours against the dull background of the jelly-like mass in which they live.

2. The Pyuridae are always solitary. Their gills are extremely complicated, forming prominent folds within the body cavity. The folds contain rows of pyramidal funnels called infundibula that are pierced by elongated stigmata. Among them are some edible ascidians; *Microcosmus sabatieri*, known in France as 'le violet' or 'biju', is eaten on the Mediterranean coast.

The ascidians of the Pyuridae have a very thick, rugged tunic, on which seaweeds and invertebrates fix themselves and camouflage the tunicates against the rocks on which they settle. Some species fix themselves to small supports, such as shells and small pebbles. They grow much larger than their supports and develop a bushy covering of fauna on their tunics. This in turn serves as a shelter for smaller animals. This habit is reflected in the name *Microcosmos*, which is Greek for small world, for the ascidian surrounds itself with a small world of sea creatures that serve as food for bottom-living fish.

3. The Molgulidae are solitary and usually live in loose mud and sand on the seabed. They have soft tunics and may bury themselves so that only the siphons show above the sand; fishermen call them 'sand eggs'. The gills are folded but differ from those of the other families in possessing stigmata that are arranged in two overlapping spirals.

The Molgulidae have a well-defined annual cycle. Several species breed in the summer, which is not unusual for ascidians of temperate seas. But after laying their eggs, the adults die. The development of the young sea squirt stops just after metamorphosis from larva to adult, and the animal remains very small throughout its first winter. Growth resumes when spring arrives and is rapid. This phenomenon also occurs in other ascidian families, especially in compound ascidians.

This large ascidian, common on the Mediterranean littoral, is *Phallusia mammillata*, whose very thick tunic has the consistency of cartilage. *Phot. J. Six*

The Aspiraculata

These ascidians form an order that is not based on gill structure for the simple reason that they do not possess a branchial sac. They live on the seabed at great depths and are covered with Foraminifera, to which they adhere by fine rhizoids. These animals do not eat microscopic food particles like the other ascidians, but feed on small crustaceans; in fact, they are the only lower chordates that feed in this way.

The chain tunicates

The chain tunicates make up the class Thaliacea within the sub-phylum Tunicata. Their general structure is similar to that of the ascidians: the larvae possess a notochord and tail that is lacking in the adults, and they are also filter feeders. But their habitat and method of reproduction is different. Chain tunicates are free-swimming animals of the open sea, and may be colonial or solitary. They swim by taking water into their cask-shaped bodies and then forcing it out in a jet by contracting the rings of muscles around the body. An alternation of generations occurs in reproduction; in general, fertilized eggs give rise to individuals that then reproduce asexually by budding to form new individuals that produce eggs and sperm, and so on. The asexual generation may consist of chains of individuals joined or linked together, hence the common name for this class.

There are three orders: Pyrosomida, Doliolida and Salpida. They are all marine animals and enveloped in permanent tunics formed from cellulose.

The Pyrosomida
This order contains only one genus—*Pyrosoma*. The name is Greek for 'body of fire', for these are phosphorescent animals. They live in tropical seas and make up floating colonies that range from a few inches to twelve feet in length. The colony is made up of a vast number of small individual tunicates, all ranged side-by-side in a long tube-shaped tunic.

Each individual of the colony has two siphons, one at each end of the body. The incurrent siphon, or mouth siphon, of each individual opens towards the centre of the tube. The mouth siphon leads into a branchial sac perforated by transverse gill slits. Beneath is a cavity containing the digestive tract, the heart and the gonads. It opens to the exterior via an excurrent cloacal siphon.

The colony is transparent and often colourless, but each

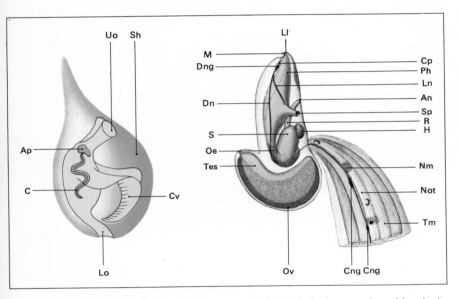

On the left, diagram of an Appendicularia in natural position in its gelatinous shell. *Ap*, the Appendicularia; *C*, central cavity of the shell; *Cv*, lateral chambers; *Lo*, lower opening; *Sh*, shell; *Uo*, upper openings. *After Y. Delage*

On the right, organizational plan of an Appendicularia, looking at the right side. *An*, anus; *Cng*, caudal nerve ganglion; *Cp*, ciliated pit; *Dn*, dorsal nerve; *Dng*, dorsal nerve ganglion; *Eo*, exhalent opening; *H*, heart; *Ll*, lower lip; *Ln*, lateral nerve; *M*, mouth; *Nm*, nucleus of muscle cell; *Not*, notochord; *Oe*, oesophagus; *Ov*, ovary; *Ph*, pharynx; *R*, rectum; *S*, stomach; *Tes*, testis; *Tm*, tail muscles. *After Y. Delage*

individual has two luminous organs situated close to the mouth siphon and sometimes brightly coloured. They are made up of cells full of luminescent bacteria, and produce an intense blue-green light. At night, pyrosomas may mark the wake of a boat through tropical seas with a trail of fire.

Pyrosomas are hermaphrodite. Each individual in a colony produces a fertilized egg, and the embryo that develops on its surface forms the asexual generation. By budding, the embryo produces a stem that coils around the egg and divides into four parts. These four parts become four new

individuals joined together in a little colony. The central yolk of the egg is gradually absorbed, producing a cavity that becomes the cavity at the centre of the new colony. Each individual buds, building the colony into a replica of the original colony.

The Doliolida
In the pyrosomas, the stage normally found in nature is the sexual generation or blastozooid. In the class Doliolida, the asexual generation or oozooid is more usual. In *Doliolum*, this is a solitary transparent barrel-shaped tunicate reaching as much as two inches in length. Each end of the barrel possesses a siphon through which water enters and leaves the body. The body is ringed by bands of muscle equally spaced apart and forming opaque bands under the thin transparent tunic. The muscles contract to force water from the body in a jet, thus moving the animal through the water. The body is divided into two cavities, the pharyngeal cavity occupying the front two-thirds of the body and the cloacal cavity in the rear third. The partition between the two cavities is perforated by gill slits through which the incoming water passes. Behind the pharynx are situated the digestive tube and the heart. There are sensory cells on the edges of the siphons and all over the body.

Beside the heart is a small closed tube called the stolon. In reproduction this lengthens and develops a number of small buds. Each bud then moves, carried by special mobile cells surrounding it, to an appendage that is attached to the rear top end of the animal. The appendage grows into a long tail bearing many buds. The buds are nourished by the rest of the body, which is known as the 'nurse'. They eventually develop into barrel-shaped individuals and break free from the nurse. These individuals then undergo a similar process of bud formation as the nurse, but their buds develop into the sexual generation, producing hermaphrodite barrel-shaped individuals with male and female gonads. These individuals, the blastozooids, then produce fertilized eggs, from which a tadpole-like larva complete with a notochord in its tail develops. The larva then metamorphoses into the adult nurse stage, the oozooid, completing the life cycle.

This very complex development occurs in the genus *Doliolum*. It is different in other genera, but an alternation of generations is always involved in reproduction.

The Salpida
The Salpida, or salps, occur in two forms, one as solitary individuals and the other as groups of individuals. The solitary form is the asexual generation and the group form is the sexual.

The solitary form is cylindrical or prismatic in shape, and surrounded by a transparent but tough tunic. The upper surface bears a pigmented eye, and the body wall contains either complete or incomplete circular bands of muscle. There are two cavities—the pharyngeal and the cloacal—separated by an oblique partition perforated by only two gill slits. The digestive tube, heart and stolon are grouped together in a small mass, called the nucleus, at the base of the endostyle, which is situated in the lower side of the body.

The salp's eye immediately distinguishes it from the other chain tunicates. It is made up of pigmented cells, retinal cells and intermediate cells. A network of nerve fibres joins the retinal cells to a cerebral ganglion, which is also in the upper surface of the body. Salps also have tactile cells distributed throughout the body and especially around the mouth. Finally, the nucleus contains luminous cells.

The life cycle of a salp is as complicated as that of *Doliolum*. In the solitary form, the stolon increases in size and a tail

Amphioxus in its natural environment on a sandy bottom. The individual, vertically aligned in the sand, its head stretching upwards, has taken up the animal's normal position. In the foreground are 2 individuals, one swimming by transverse undulations of the body, the other burying itself in the sand by its hind end. *Phot. J. Six*

forms and trails behind the salp, rather as in *Doliolum*. Buds form and develop on the tail into separate individuals; however, instead of breaking away, they remain attached to the solitary adult, forming a chain of new individuals. The chain may contain several hundred salps. It does not form in a straight line, for the buds are staggered in position, finally becoming arranged side-by-side in two rows. Each individual leads its own life and is not dependent on the parent. Eventually, fragments of the chain—either individuals or short chains—break away and begin a separate existence. These animals are the sexual generation, and possess ovaries and testes instead of stolons. They reproduce while still connected to one another but may become totally separated first. Although hermaphrodite, the gonads of either sex develop at different times, so that eggs from one individual are always fertilized by sperm from another. The fertilized eggs develop within the adult's body, being connected to the parent via a placenta-like structure—a feature of the higher vertebrates. The young that hatch from the eggs are the asexual solitary salps, and no larvae form during the life cycle.

Salps may be so numerous that they produce dense solid masses in the sea. They occur in coastal and deep waters to a depth of 750 fathoms.

The Larvacea

Also known as appendicularians, tunicates of this class are distinguished from other classes by three important features. They do not have a cellulose tunic; they do not reproduce by means of alternation of generations; and they have a permanent swimming tail which contains a notochord. Their structure is much the same as that of an ascidian tadpole, and some authorities claim that the appendicularians are derived from ascidians by neotony (a form of life in which an animal retains larval characteristics throughout its life).

Appendicularians are small animals and do not grow to more than $\frac{1}{5}$ of an inch in length. Some are transparent but others are brilliant shades of orange or violet. Although it does not possess a cellulose tunic, the appendicularian secretes a mucus that forms into a transparent gelatinous chamber around the tiny animal. The chamber does not adhere to the body, and so is completely different from the tunics of the other tunicates. The chamber has two openings through which water enters. The water first passes through a screen of crossed threads to strain out large particles, and then is filtered through fine nets of mucus filaments to trap micro-organisms for food. The chamber also contains a special escape tunnel and hatch by means of which the

the appendicularian can leave the chamber immediately if disturbed. It then secretes a new chamber a little later.

There is still little biological information on the appendicularians. They do, however, constitute a substantial part of the plankton at the surface of the sea. A common genus of European waters is *Oikopleura*.

Amphioxus (The lancelets)

The lancelets, commonly known as the amphioxus, make up the sub-phylum Cephalochordata of the phylum Chordata or Protochordata. They are small and slender fish-like animals, a translucent white in colour. The body is highly flattened, being from 2 to 3 inches long but only $\frac{1}{5}$ of an inch in width. There are about 30 species, and they live in coastal waters in tropical and temperate regions. There are only two genera: *Branchiostoma* (also known as *Amphioxus*) and *Asymmetron*. The former has pairs of gonads whereas the latter, as its name implies, has unpaired gonads.

Discovered in 1774, the lancelet was at first placed among the molluscs. In the following century, it began to be considered the ancestor of the vertebrates because it has several vertebrate features—the vertical position of the digestive tract, the notochord and the nerve cord; the presence of gill slits in the pharynx; and the arrangement of muscles along the animal. However, there are also invertebrate features, for some organs are repeated in the way that they are in segmented animals—there are about 100 pairs of nephridia (excretory organs) and about 25 pairs of gonads. Lancelets have therefore long excited zoologists for their apparent position in the animal kingdom as a link between the vertebrates and invertebrates. Their anatomy has been the subject of numerous studies and their biology still poses problems. However, it is certainly likely that lancelets resemble some ancient ancestor of the vertebrates.

Lancelets are world-wide in distribution. They are to be found on all the European coasts from Scandinavia, through the North Sea, English Channel and Atlantic coasts to the Mediterranean Sea. However, they are only to be found where the bottom is made up of loose gravel or coarse sand, where the water is shallow and clean and where a fairly strong current is flowing. Where these requirements are well satisfied, lancelets may live in such abundance that they are cast up and stranded on beaches in rough weather.

Lancelets breed in the spring. The sexes are separate and fertilization is external, the eggs developing rapidly into small, planktonic, asymmetrical larvae. They grow quickly, reaching an inch in length by the beginning of the summer. Then they move to the bottom and complete their metamorphosis into adult lancelets. They then grow another two inches, taking a couple of years to do so.

Lancelets feed by straining suspended food particles from the water. There is a double barrier consisting of a row of comb-like buccal cirri in front of the mouth and a circle of fine tentacles around the mouth, to prevent grains of sand or gravel entering the body. The mouth is simply a circular opening in a membrane called the velum situated beneath the head. The barrier around the mouth is very necessary, as the lancelet burrows in sand or gravel by undulating its body. After travelling for a short distance beneath the surface, it thrusts its head above the surface, the rest of the body remaining buried. The end of the tail may also emerge. There it stays, filtering its food from the water. If disturbed, the lancelet will swim away, but its movements are rapid and brief, for it tires quickly. It can swim both forwards and backwards.

Although known to science for only two centuries, the lancelet has been known to man for much longer. For many centuries, lancelets have been fished for food in southern China. The catch amounts to as much as a ton every day, and the animals are eaten fresh or dried. In Europe, they are not plentiful enough to be of any use as food.

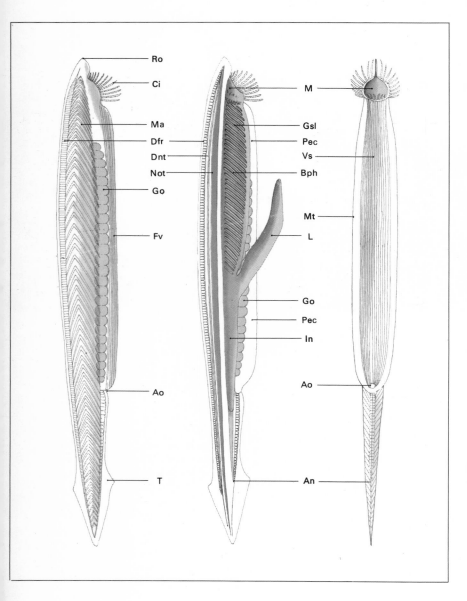

Diagram of the organization of Amphioxus. *On the left*, external view of right side; the gonads are seen by transparency; *in the middle*, the animal open; *on the right*, in ventral view. *An*, anus; *Ao*, atriopore or opening by which water escapes from the peribranchial cavity to the exterior; *Bph*, branchial pharynx; *Ci*, cirri (around mouth); *Dfr*, dorsal fin rays; *Dnt*, dorsal nerve tube; *Go*, gonads; *Gsl*, gill slits; *In*, intestine; *L*, liver; *M*, mouth; *Ms*, muscle segments; *Mt*, lateral fold or metapleure; *Not*, notochord; *Pec*, peribranchial cavity (atrium); *Ro*, rostrum; *Tf*, tail fin; *Vs*, ventral surface with longitudinal folds.

Opposite
A group of solitary ascidians: *Halocyntnia papillosa*. Phot. Fronval

Lampreys and fishes

The lampreys and fishes are in reality two distinct zoological groups. The former lack a lower jaw and its skeleton, and have many fundamental differences from the present-day fishes, but the fact that they live in water and have a fish-like appearance makes it convenient to group them together, and refer to them generally as fishes.

Both are superclasses. Technically the Agnatha (the jawless fishes) and the Gnathostomata (the fishes with jaws), are primitive vertebrates, not because their earliest fossils appear as far back as the Silurian Period, but because their organization is primitive. In general, they are aquatic, breathe by means of gills, and have fins which are supported by an inner skeleton of cartilage or bone. All have a vertebral column to which the close-packed muscles of the body are attached, which in turn provide the main locomotive power, while the fins which are variously developed serve as rudders, stabilizers, wings, propellers, and even limbs. All fishes have a brain which is connected to various sensory organs—taste buds, barbels, nasal organs, the lateral line system, the eyes and ears.

The greater part of the world's surface is covered by water. The oceans offer an enormous variety of habitat from their inter-tidal region to the sea floor in the deepest trenches, as well as at the surface and at all levels between. Freshwater habitats, although less vast, are nevertheless as complex and range from torrential mountain streams to near polar lakes, and warm lowland streams, lakes and swamps. Practically every sizeable body of water, marine or freshwater, has fishes inhabiting it, the only exceptions being a few naturally uninhabitable areas such as the Dead Sea and the bottom of the Black Sea, and areas where man by his activities has polluted the environment so severely that fishes can no longer live. These apart, fishes are found in practically every accessible aquatic habitat throughout the world. In adapting to these varied habitats it is not surprising that a very large number of species have evolved. A generally accepted estimate of the number of known species is 20,000 (which is at least equal to the total number of all other vertebrate animals) and new species are being described each year.

With such a large number of living animals and the very many more which have existed in the past (only a few of which have been recovered as fossils), it is not surprising that many differing views exist concerning the alignments and relationships of the major classification of fishes. The system basically adopted here has gained a measure of acceptance since its proposal in 1966; its higher categories are set out below; details of lower groupings, where important, are given in the text.

Jawless fishes (Superclass Agnatha)—Lampreys and hag-fishes

Jawed fishes (Superclass Gnathostomata)
  Cartilaginous fishes (Class Elasmobranchiomorphi)
    Sharks and rays (Infraclass Elasmobranchii)
    Ratfishes or chimaeras (Infraclass Holocephali)
  Bony fishes (Class Teleostomi)
    Lungfishes (Infraclass Dipnoi)
    Coelacanth (Infraclass Crossopterygii)
    Other fishes (Infraclass Actinopterygii)
      Bichirs and sturgeons (Division Chondrostei)
      Bowfin and garpikes (Division Holostei)
      All other fishes (Division Teleostei)

The jawless fishes (agnathans)

The jawless fishes which form the superclass Agnatha were for many years regarded as being primitive fishes. They are today grouped in a distinct superclass, parallel to the jawed fishes (superclass Gnathostomata) which includes all other living fishes. The agnathans are mostly known as fossil fishes, notable for the heavy bony skeleton—particularly developed as an armour—which enclosed the head in a shell and protected the body with large scale-like bones. The group as a whole reached a peak of development in the Upper Silurian and Lower Devonian, filling ecological niches which in our time have been exploited to the full by the jawed fishes.

In contrast to the heavily-armoured fossil agnathans the living species are completely unprotected by armour. They share with the fossil species the character which gives them their name—they have no jaws, and thus no mouth except for a suctorial disc. The living species also have only a cartilaginous skeleton which has resulted in their leaving few traces in the fossil record. The only known fossil lamprey is the Upper Carboniferous *Mayomyzon*, which seems to have

The very long fins and brilliant coloration of the Siamese fighting fish (*Betta splendens*) are a result of selective breeding for these qualities. The males are very aggressive to other males. Freshwaters of southern Asia. *Phot. Aldo Margiocco*

Top of page: a lampern (*Lampetra* sp.) attached by its oral sucker to the glass of an aquarium, showing its lack of true jaws and horny teeth. *Researchers—Russ Kinne*

This photography of a lamprey shows very clearly the seven gill openings and suctorial mouth. *Steinhart aquarium, San Francisco. Phot. Researchers—Russ Kinne*

are found in Europe and Asia, and the North American *Ichthyomyzon* and *Entosphenus*. In the southern hemisphere the group is represented by two genera, *Geotria* and *Mordacia*. Members of both genera are anadromous, breeding and spending a larval life in freshwater and then migrating to the sea, where they live as parasites on other fishes. Several species in the northern hemisphere have a similar life style, but there are also entirely freshwater-dwelling, non-parasitic species.

All members of the family have elongate, eel-like, scaleless bodies, a broad sucking disc for a mouth, a single nostril set in the mid-line of the head, and a series of rounded gill openings along the anterior side. In addition, the skeleton is wholly cartilaginous, the only fins developed being folds along the back and mid-line of the tail; there are no pectoral or pelvic skeletons or fins. Internally, their organization is simple: they have only two semi-circular canals in the inner ear, the pineal organ is well developed, but the spleen is absent.

Lampreys have a relatively complicated life cycle. The species which are parasitic as adults usually migrate to the sea, or in some large drainage basins to a large lake, for the feeding and maturing cycle of their lives. They enter rivers, often making very long migrations up-river to spawning beds where the eggs are shed amongst stones and pebbles in a roughly hollowed nest. The young lampreys, usually known as prides or ammocoetes, spend an extensive larval life buried in mud in the river, feeding by filtering minute organisms from the surrounding mud. Only when they are well developed, and sometimes five years of age, do they migrate to the sea and begin their parasitic life. Other lampreys are not parasitic when adult, but in these species the greater part of the animal's life is spent as a larva and it does not feed once mature, but spawns once and dies.

Possibly the best-known of all the lampreys is the sea lamprey (*Petromyzon marinus*) found on both the North American and European coasts of the North Atlantic, and widely in the freshwaters of these continents. It is a large species growing to 35 inches; dark grey on the back with yellowish blotches on the sides and belly. A parasitic form, it feeds on a wide variety of marine and freshwater fishes, attaching itself by its powerful sucking disc and rasping away their skin and flesh with its sharp teeth at the centre of the disc, sucking its victim's blood whilst doing so. This lamprey penetrated through the man-made Welland Canal in eastern North America, gained access to the Great Lakes and established a virtually landlocked population spawning in the rivers and migrating to the lakes to feed. The consequences of this invasion were catastrophic for many of the larger native fishes of the Great Lakes, and the fishing industry on the lakes declined severely. Because of the serious losses an intensive programme of research and experiment in control of the lamprey was initiated especially in the United States with considerable success.

The genus *Lampetra*, which is represented in North America, Europe and North Asia, contains both migratory parasitic species, such as the lampern (*Lampetra fluviatilis*) of Europe,

been very similar to the lampreys of the genus *Lampetra*.

Some forty species of living agnathan fish are recognized today. They are divided between the lampreys of the subclass Hyperoartii. which are mainly freshwater animals, and the hagfishes, subclass Hyperotreti, a group of marine fish.

The lampreys (Petromyzonidae)

Lampreys are widely distributed in the waters of the temperate regions of the world both in the northern and southern hemispheres, but they are not found in the tropics. In the northern temperate regions several genera occur, such as *Petromyzon* and *Lampetra*, lampreys found in eastern North America and Eurasia, *Eudontomyzon* and *Caspiomyzon* which

Left, the hagfish, *Myxine glutinosa*, showing the eight barbels surrounding the mouth, the eel-like shape, and the lack of eyes. From a water-colour in Cuvier's *Animal Kingdom* (French edition). *Phot. Lauros Right*, sea lamprey (*Petromyzon marinus*) showing the general body

form of the lampreys. This shows the freshwater juvenile stage of the species, the adult is much darker. Found in the North Atlantic and in freshwater in Europe and North America. From a water-colour in Cuvier's *Animal Kingdom. Phot. Lauros*

and the river lamprey (*L. ayresi*) of the Pacific coast of America, and non-parasitic forms like the brook lamprey (*L. planeri*) of Europe. They are all relatively small, the largest growing up to 24 inches, but the non-parasitic species rarely attain 12 inches. Many of them are, or have been at some time, locally favoured as food, but their chief value wherever they occur is as bait for commercial or sport fishermen.

In New Zealand the native migratory lamprey (*Geotria australis*) was also considered to be an especial delicacy. In this species, which grows to about twenty inches, the adult male develops a fleshy pouch under the head. Its life history is essentially the same as the North Atlantic *Petromyzon*. *Geotria*, and the pouchless *Mordacia*, both occur in the rivers and neighbouring oceans of temperate South America, Australia, and New Zealand.

The migratory species of lampreys throughout the world have generally declined because of the building of dams and weirs in rivers, and also because of the pollution of estuaries in the developed countries.

The hagfishes (Myxinidae)

There are some fifteen species of hagfishes which all live in temperate seas, except for one species in deep, and thus cool water, off Panama. Various members of the family occur in the North Atlantic, North Pacific, and off New Zealand, Chile, Patagonia, and South Africa. In contrast to the lampreys, they live their entire life in the sea.

Hagfishes are elongate and scaleless, and their fins are poorly developed, only a low fleshy fold of skin running along the rear end of the body in the mid-line. The mouth is small, with rather thick lips (but no true jaws), and a pair of stout barbels either side. The single nostril lies at the extreme tip of the head and has a pair of barbels, one either side. The nostril leads indirectly into the pharynx. Gill openings vary in number with species from a pair (*Myxine*) to as many as fifteen pairs (*Eptatretus*). The eyes are small, covered with skin and evidently non-functional, but this virtual blindness is compensated for by the well developed nostrils. The most notable feature of all hagfish species is the copious mucus secreted by mucous pores along the sides.

The only hagfish occurring in the North Atlantic is *Myxine glutinosa* which is found from the Arctic southwards to Biscay and to North Carolina on the American coast. Its distribution is patchy, however, and it seems to be confined to areas where the sea bed is soft mud in depths of 55–165 fathoms. The hagfish grows to a length of 24 inches, and varies in colour from brown-grey to pale pink. In sheltered waters (as for instance in the Norwegian fiords) it burrows into the bottom, living in a small mound within a crater. It is known to feed on bottom-living worms and crustaceans, but also attacks fish trapped in nets or hooked on long lines, boring into the body cavity, usually starting at the gills or the vent, and consuming the viscera and muscles until only skin and bone are left. The extent of its attacks on fish free to swim away is not known but they probably rarely fall victims; the hagfish should be regarded as a scavenger rather than a predator or a parasite. However, where the hagfish is common fishermen find it undesirable to fish using static methods.

Several of the North Pacific hagfishes are also well-known for their habit of attacking trapped fish and amongst them the Pacific hagfish (*Eptatretus stouti*) is a serious nuisance. Off Monterey, California, losses of up to 41 per cent of lingcod caught in trammel nets, and up to 28 per cent of captured salmon are reported. This species is found from southern California to British Columbia. It grows to 25 inches, and is dark brownish-red often tinted with purple or blue. It lives on fine mud or clay bottoms in depths of around 20 fathoms.

In *Eptatretus* the sexes are separate, but *Myxine* is hermaphrodite (in any one individual, only one element of the single sex organ matures). Members of both genera lay eggs enclosed in transparent horny capsules about one inch long and 0.4 of an inch wide. The capsule has short hooked spines at the ends which serve to anchor it to other egg cases, and to the substrata. The shell is honeycombed with minute pores through which the male's sperm enters to fertilize the egg. The end of the capsule is raised like a lid to enable the young hagfish to escape when developed. Unlike lampreys they do not pass through a free-living larval stage, but adopt the scavenging life style of the adults soon after hatching.

Fishes

The major group of living fishes are those equipped with jaws (the superclass Gnathostomata), to which all present-day fish including the sharks and bony fishes belong. The group is subdivided according to differences in structure, but all have the basic similarity of a series of bony or cartilaginous arches which form the jaws (mandibulary arch), the hyoid arch, and the gill arches, which bear the respiratory gills. Some more primitive groups possess a spiracle between the mandibular and hyoid arches which assists in respiration. The gills either discharge water directly through a series of gill slits (as in the sharks), or into a common chamber covered by the gill cover.

In contrast to the jawless fishes, the gnathostomes have three semi-circular canals in the inner ear, and at least one pair of nostrils either side of the snout. Their bodies are usually covered with scales. In addition to the vertical fins (one or more dorsals, a tail fin, and anal fin or fins), they have paired fins associated with the internal pectoral girdle and pelvic bones. In most living fishes the fins are supported by bony skeletal elements.

Present-day fishes with jaws are classed into two major divisions, the cartilaginous fishes (class Elasmobranchiomorphi) and the bony fishes or teleosts (class Teleostomi). Both are subdivided. Within the class of cartilaginous fishes there are two major divisions—the sharks and rays (infraclass Elasmobranchii—formerly Selachii) and the ratfishes or chimaeras (infraclass Holocephali). The teleosts form a more complex assemblage, including some very diverse groups, but today dominate the waters of the Earth. According to the most recent classifications they are composed of five major categories: sturgeons (Chondrostei), bowfins and garpikes (Holostei), bony fishes (Teleostei), the coelacanth (Crossopterygii), and lungfishes (Dipnoi).

Sharks and rays (Elasmobranchii)

A well-known group of mainly marine fishes which have cartilaginous skeletons, although often the vertebrae are calcified and appear to be bony. They all possess a series of separate gill slits on the sides of the anterior body, or beneath the body. Many also have a spiracle or opening behind the eye, most obviously developed in the bottom-living rays. Characteristically they also show a heterocercal (unevenly divided) tail, the vertebral column continuing along the upper lobe of the tail; this is best demonstrated in the sharks.

All the sharks and most of the rays have one or two dorsal fins, but the anal fin is not often present and then only in some sharks in which it is small. Pectoral and pelvic fins are well developed, the former being extremely expanded in the rays in which they form the large 'wings' which make up the greater part of the body area. The body is usually covered with small placoid scales, which are like minute teeth embedded in the skin, leaving the free, often pointed, edge towards the tail. These scales, which are known as dermal denticles ('skin teeth'), give sharks and many of the rays their characteristic rough skin. They are similar in form to the teeth in the jaws, which in most sharks and rays are pointed, lying in several rows and continuously replaced from the inside as they wear or are damaged; some elasmobranchs, particularly those which feed on hard-shelled animals, have ranks of flattened crushing teeth in their jaws.

Fertilization is internal in all sharks and rays. Males have paired copulatory organs on the inner side of the pelvic fins with which sperm is transferred to the female's genital aperture. Some elasmobranchs give birth to living young, most being ovoviviparous (i.e. the young develops within the mother, but nourished by yolk from the egg, not by a maternal connection). Others produce horny, hard covered egg cases which enclose the eggs singly while they develop on the sea-bed. In comparison with bony fishes the elasmobranchs pro-

The jaws of a male shark (*Isurus oxyrhinchus*), a predatory, fish-eating species. The teeth are large and sharp, and lie in the jaws in several rows; only the outer row or two are functional, the inner rows are composed of replacement teeth which will move forwards as the outer teeth wear or fall out. *Phot. Aldo Margiocco*

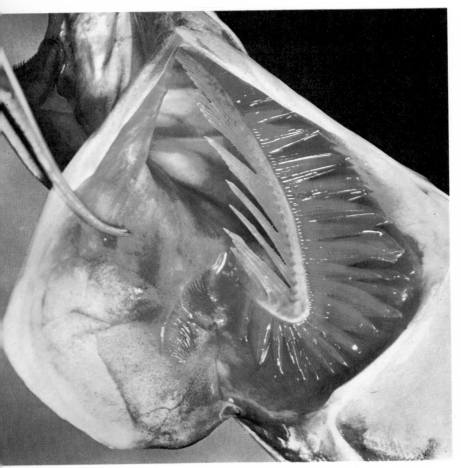

The gills of a mackerel (*Scomber scombrus*). Each gill arch supports the red, blood-rich gill filaments which take up oxygen from the water, while the paler gillrakers form a sieve which catches planktonic food organisms in the water. *Phot. Aldo Margiocco*

duce few eggs or young during their lives, which is testimony to the efficiency of internal fertilization as a means of reproducing.

Some twenty-one families of sharks and fifteen families of rays are recognized currently; there are between five and six hundred species contained in both groups.

Horn sharks (Heterodontiformes)

Horn sharks (family Heterodontidae) are the only living representatives of this order of sharks which has existed since the Devonian. They live today only in the shallow water of the Indian and Pacific Oceans. Their dentition is distinctive with pointed sharp teeth in the centre of the jaws and broad, rounded teeth at the sides; their diet consists principally of hard-shelled invertebrates.

The Australian Port Jackson shark (*Heterodontus philippi*) grows to around five feet in length, while the species common on the Californian coast, the horn shark (*H. francisci*) is smaller at four feet. Both lay eggs which are protected by a characteristic horny dark brown case with a spiral edge.

Six-gilled and seven-gilled sharks (Hexanchiformes) are members of an order which show many primitive features, including the persistent nature of the notochord and the incompletely segmented vertebral column. They are characterized by their number of gill slits, six or seven according to species. All have a single dorsal fin placed far back along the body and long, rather broad tail fins. Two families are represented: the Chlamydoselachidae, of which there is only one species, the frilled shark (*Chlamydoselachus anguineus*); and the Hexanchidae or combtoothed sharks, of which there are several species.

The frilled shark has been found in the North Atlantic, the North Pacific and off South Africa. It is slender-bodied, almost snake-like in appearance and grows to 6½ feet. The first gill slit extends to below the throat and has a frilled edge. The combtooth sharks, so called because the teeth have parallel rows of comb-like cusps, are also found world-wide in the temperate and tropical oceans. The six-gilled shark (*Hexanchus griseus*) is well known from both the North Atlantic and the Mediterranean, and grows to a length of 16 feet. Both it and the smaller seven-gilled shark (*Heptranchias perlo*), are world-wide in their distribution but are rarely encountered as they are mainly inhabitants of deep water.

The true sharks (Lamniformes)

This order includes all the remaining families of living sharks and is the largest single group. There are three main divisions, the true sharks, the dogfishes, and the spiny finned sharks. Their general features include two dorsal fins, an anal fin (with the exception of the spiny-finned sharks), and five gill slits. In most the body is slender and torpedo shaped, and the jaws are equipped with numerous pointed teeth, each having a triangular, often large, central cusp. Up to seventeen families are recognized in this order, and they are represented in all tropical and temperate seas, from the surface to the deep sea.

Sand sharks (Odontaspididae)
The sand sharks are represented in tropical and warm temperate seas by several species, some of which grow to a moderately large size, for example the Australian grey nurse (*Odontaspis arenarius*) which reaches fifteen feet. In general they are shallow water, coastal species, heavily built with long sharp teeth. Most eat fishes, but off South Africa and Australia they are feared as man-eaters. One species (*O. ferox*) lives in the Mediterranean and tropical Atlantic.

Mackerel sharks (Isuridae)
A small family of large pelagic sharks which all have an elegantly streamlined body and a high, curved tail fin. They are active, powerful swimmers, probably the fastest of the sharks, the tail fin being designed for speed. Some of the members of this family have a body temperature higher than the surrounding water—an unusual feature in fishes. The best known member of the family is the dreaded white shark or man-eater (*Carcharodon carcharias*), a huge species which attains a proven 21 feet, the most aggressive and dangerous of all sharks. Like its relatives it is a fish of the open sea, but on occasions it comes into shallow water. It is found world-wide in tropical and warm temperate seas; in the Atlantic it has been found as far north as northern Spain and Nova Scotia, and it also occurs in the Mediterranean. Its teeth are broad and triangular with serrated edges. Its normal food consists of virtually any smaller fishes it encounters, but the remains of seals, dolphins, and sea birds have been found in its stomach. Attacks on swimmers have many times involved this shark, and a large specimen is capable of engulfing the greater part of a well grown man. It has also been reliably reported to attack small fishing boats. Attacks on man are mainly confined to the warmer regions of its range.

The porbeagle shark (*Lamna nasus*) and the mako (*Isurus oxyrhinchus*) belong to the same family and have generally similar features. Both are large, active predators living at the surface of the ocean and feeding on fishes. In the North Atlantic both are widespread, although the mako is more southerly in its distribution, entering British waters only in summer and then staying offshore. A relative of the porbeagle, the salmon shark (*L. ditropis*) occurs in the North Pacific. All the members of the family are ovoviviparous, but the number of young in a litter is low, usually a single pup or two.

Thresher sharks (Alopiidae)
The thresher or fox sharks comprise a small family which are all characterized by an extremely long upper lobe to the tail fin, often more than half the length of the body. The family is widely distributed in all tropical and temperate seas. In the North Atlantic the thresher (*Alopias vulpinus*) is found both in the open sea and in coastal waters, but in the latter chiefly in summer and autumn. It feeds on a wide range of pelagic fishes, herding them, it is believed, into a compact shoal by repeated blows of its long tail. It grows to a length of twenty feet.

Basking shark (Cetorhinidae)
A huge shark, the second largest living species of fish, which appears to be distributed in the temperate seas of both northern and southern hemispheres. In the North Atlantic the basking shark (*Cetorhinus maximus*) is fairly common off the open ocean coasts of the British Isles and eastern America. Its habit of cruising slowly at the surface has given it the name of basking shark (or on the west coast of Ireland sunfish). It was at one time fished for locally, mainly by harpooning, but also by stretching strong nets across the mouth of a bay. Its greatest value lay in the oil stored in the huge liver, but such fisheries have ceased to operate within recent years.

The basking shark grows to a length of at least 34 feet, and may weigh up to six tons. Its most distinctive features, beside its size, are the vast gill slits which extend from high up on the back almost to the mid-line ventrally, the long bristle-like rakers on the inner face of each gill arch, and the minute

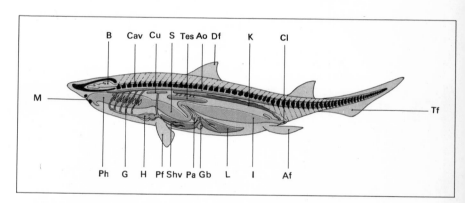

The anatomy of a male shark. *Ao*, aorta; *B*, brain; *Cav*, cartilaginous vertebrae; *Cl*, cloaca; *Cv*, anterior cardinal vein; *Df*, dorsal fin; *G*, gills; *Gb*, gall bladder; *H*, heart, *I*, intestine; *K*, kidney; *L*, liver; *M*, mouth; *Pa*, pancreas; *Pf*, pectoral fin; *Ph*, pharynx; *S*, stomach; *Shv*, sub-hepatic vein; *Tes*, testis; *Tf*, tail fin; *Vf*, ventral or pelvic fin.

teeth, single pointed and in four to seven rows. Its mouth is extraordinarily wide. The basking shark feeds on planktonic organisms, small crustaceans, invertebrate larvae, and fish eggs and larvae, quite indiscriminately, swimming gently in the plankton-rich surface zone with its mouth wide open, filtering the water through its gill rakers which retain the food. In some parts of its range it seems that the basking shark sheds its gill rakers and hibernates during winter when the plankton is sparse; occasional specimens have been caught in which the gill rakers are small and newly grown.

Whale shark (Rhincodontidae)
The whale shark is the largest living species of fish. Although precise measurements are few, there is little doubt that it grows to a length of fifty feet and possibly more on occasions. Weights are even less reliably recorded, but it probably attains a maximum of twenty tons. Like the basking shark it

is a plankton feeder, possessing gill rakers which filter the small crustaceans and fishes on which it feeds. However, it occasionally eats larger fishes, and one was observed capturing small

The nurse hound or greater spotted dogfish (*Scyliorhinus stellaris*), swimming. It usually keeps near the bottom where it finds its food, chiefly crustaceans and molluscs. This individual is a male; the claspers forming part of the pelvic fins can be clearly seen. Very common in European seas. *Phot. J. Six*

Egg-case of the nurse hound (*Scyliorhinus stellaris*). The young fish is newly hatched. These cases are usually concealed amongst algae in shallow water. *Phot. R. H. Noailles*

tuna which were feeding on smaller fishes. Despite its size it is completely harmless, its teeth being minute and curved.

It is quite distinctive on account of its size, its wide flattened snout and its broad mouth. The head and back have broad ridges running along their length, and the back is deep blue with rounded white blotches. Ventrally, it is white.

Although this species and the basking shark are so large, little is known about their biology. The breeding habits of the basking shark are unknown and all that is known of the whale shark's is that specimens around $14\frac{1}{2}$ inches long have been found occasionally in large egg-cases. The discovery that the whale shark was oviparous was in itself surprising as its closest relatives are live-bearers.

Requiem sharks (Carcharinidae)

The largest family of sharks with numerous species found world-wide in tropical and temperate oceans. They are typical sharks, slender-bodied, with two dorsal fins and five gill slits. All are active predatory species and some grow to a large size, being dangerous to bathers and underwater swimmers. Amongst the dangerous species is the tiger shark (*Galeocerdo cuvier*) which is found throughout tropical and sub-tropical seas, wandering into temperate waters rarely during warm seasons. Next to the great white shark it is probably the most aggressive and dangerous of the sharks. It grows to a length of about eighteen feet. Its broad head and, when young, tiger-like stripes on the back are distinctive.

The blue shark (*Prionace glauca*) grows to $12\frac{1}{2}$ feet, but its slender shape prevents it from attaining a very great weight. Distinguished by its shape, its extremely long pectoral fins, its brilliant indigo blue back and snow white belly, it is world-wide in its distribution, being found at the surface of the open sea in all tropical and sub-tropical regions. In summer

it migrates into temperate waters, as off the British Isles and New England, but it usually stays offshore. Its food consists of a wide range of schooling, pelagic fishes and squids.

The members of the genus *Carcharinus* are world-wide in tropical and warm seas and are represented by numerous species. Some, such as the white tip shark (*C. longimanus*) and the dusky shark (*C. obscurus*) are pelagic open-sea fish; others, such as the bull shark (*C. leucas*) are found inshore. The bull shark is an Atlantic species, sluggish in habit and rather stout-bodied. It eats a wide range of fishes and squids, is well-known as a scavenger, grows to twelve feet and because of its inshore habitat, occasionally attacks swimmers. It is this species which enters, and is common in, the fresh-water Lake Nicaragua, where it has frequently been known to attack man. Closely related Indian Ocean species (*C. zambezensis* and *C. gangeticus*) also occur in large rivers even in freshwater. These sharks are viviparous, the yolk sac of the embryo forming a placental attachment to the maternal oviduct by which for a while the young shark is nourished.

A small, shallow-water relative of these sharks, found in European waters, is the tope (*Galeorhinus galeus*). It grows only to 6½ feet in length, and feeds extensively on bottom-living fishes such as flatfish. Its chief value is as a sport fish for anglers, although its flesh is quite edible, and a Pacific relative, the soupfin shark (*G. zyopterus*) which ranges from British Columbia to California is widely used for shark-fin soup by the American Chinese.

Hammerhead sharks (Sphyrnidae)

This is a family of tropical and warm temperate sharks which are all distinguished by a flattened head with wide lobes forming the hammer. There are relatively few species, which differ from one another in the shape of the head, but all have their eyes at the extreme edge of the lobes and nostrils well spaced apart on the front of the head.

The smooth hammerhead (*Sphyrna zygaena*) is a tropical species which in the eastern Atlantic occurs regularly north-wards to Portugal, and very rarely as far north as Britain. It grows to fourteen feet. It is considered to be dangerous to man, as is the rather larger great hammerhead (*S. mokarran*) which is likewise found in all tropical seas. These are strong-swimming active sharks frequently seen in inshore waters at the surface, and even in estuaries. Their food, however, seems to be mainly bottom-living fishes, especially sting rays whose tail fin spines have been found embedded in the hammerhead's mouth and stomach.

Dogfishes (Scyliorhinidae)

This large family of small, chiefly bottom-dwelling sharks includes some sixty species. The family is widely distributed in warm and temperate seas, and its members are found in shallow coastal water as well as in the deep sea. One of the most abundant species in British waters is the sandy or lesser spotted dogfish (*Scyliorhinus canicula*), found mainly on sandy or gravelly bottoms in depths of one to sixty fathoms. It feeds chiefly on crustaceans, fishes and some molluscs, and grows to thirty inches. A second rather larger species is the nurse hound or larger spotted dogfish (*S. stellaris*) which attains five feet. It too is found in European waters, and like all members of the family lays its eggs in distinctive egg-cases with long tendrils at the corners by which they are fastened to seaweed. A deeper water species, the blackmouthed dogfish (*Galeus melastomus*) which grows to thirty inches, is found off the west coast of Britain in 100 to 400 fathoms, while another species of dogfish (*Apristurus laurussonii*) is found still deeper in 275 to 825 fathoms. The egg-cases of both species lack tendrils at their corners.

The streamlined shape of a shark helps in their mastery of the seas. The powerful tail provides the propelling power, and the pectoral fins are held rigid to counteract the tendency to nose-dive. A photograph taken in the clear water of the Touamotou Islands. *Phot. J. Théodor*

Carpet sharks (Orectolobidae)

The carpet sharks or nurse sharks are related to the dogfishes and like them are relatively small, shallow-water, bottom-living sharks. The nurse shark (*Ginglymostoma cirratum*) is the only Atlantic species, but is mainly confined to the tropical regions. It grows to fourteen feet, and is frequently seen lying on the sea bed close to reefs. It is ovoviviparous. The carpet sharks are widely distributed and well represented in the Indo-Pacific, all of them having a distinct often fringed barbel on each side of the mouth, and most are boldly patterned and even brightly coloured.

Smooth hounds (Triakidae)

A rather small family of slender-bodied sharks found in shallow water in tropical and temperate seas. All bear living young, most simply retaining the eggs within the mother's body until the young are fully formed, although some are viviparous. They all have flattened teeth which form a pave-ment-like dentition suitable for crushing the hard shelled crustaceans and molluscs on which they feed. The most common European species is the starry smooth hound (*Mustelus asterias*) which is grey with white spots and grows to four feet. The well-known northeastern Pacific leopard shark (*Triakis semifasciata*), which is boldly marked with black blotches on a light background, is commonly seen in aquaria.

Spiny dogfishes (Squalidae)

This group of sharks is rather distinctive and, in the past, has been elevated to the rank of an order, the Squaliformes. Its members are distinguished by having two dorsal fins, each of which has a sharp spine in the front. The tail fin is relatively small, and the anal fin is totally lacking. They are world-wide in distribution except for extreme polar seas, and are found in shallow inshore water, as pelagic open ocean fishes, and in the deep sea.

A number of closely similar species are found in temperate oceans. Of these the best known is the North Atlantic spurdog (*Squalus acanthias*), a shark growing to four feet, which is pale grey on the back densely covered with white spots. It is an abundant fish between Norway and the Mediterranean, and occurs widely along the North American east coast; it is probably identical with the spurdog in the North Pacific. It gives birth to living young (being ovoviviparous) in litters of four to eleven, but only after a gestation period of from eighteen to twenty-two months. As sexual maturity is not attained until eleven years (male) and nineteen to twenty years (females) this shark is very vulnerable to large scale fisheries. In British waters it is fished for commercially, the flesh being marketed as 'flake' with other dogfishes. The dorsal spines are long and sharp, and the tissue lining the groove in the posterior edge contains toxins which make a deep wound very painful and inflamed.

Numerous members of this family are found in deeper water. Amongst them is the velvet belly (*Etmopterus spinax*), a very common small shark growing to 21 inches, found in mid-water over the continental shelf to 120 to 380 fathoms. Its underside has numerous small pores which secrete a luminous mucus; light production of any kind is rare in sharks. The

A juvenile leopard-shark (*Stegostoma tigrinum*) seen on the bottom of the Aquarium at Noumea. Above it is the egg-case from which it may have emerged. The adults are spotted rather than striped. *Phot. R. Catala*

shovelnosed shark (*Deania calceus*) is so called because of its very long, flattened snout. It grows to a length of 46 inches, is a dull grey in colour and probably hunts in mid-water in depths of 330–780 fathoms. This, and the Portuguese shark, (*Centroscymnus coelolepis*), are both common to the west of Britain, but the latter is found in deeper water still. Both are ovoviviparous, the Portuguese shark producing litters of up to eighteen at a time.

Dwarf sharks and Greenland shark (Dalatiidae)

This is a small family of world-wide distribution related to the Squalidae, and like them lacking an anal fin, but they also lack spines in the dorsal fins. One of the larger members of the family, the 'darkie Charlie' (*Dalatias licha*), is relatively common along the continental slope of the British Isles in 200 to 350 fathoms. Several small pelagic sharks also belong to this family. One such is *Isistius brasiliensis*, which grows to twenty inches long, is of world-wide range in tropical oceans, and has a brilliantly luminous underside, the light emanating from minute pores. The smallest known shark, the dwarf shark (*Squaliolus laticaudus*) which grows to nine inches, is found both in the tropical Pacific and Atlantic Oceans. The Greenland shark (*Somniosus microcephalus*) by contrast is a veritable giant, growing to 21 feet. It is heavy-bodied, with rather small fins except for the tail, and is found only in the cooler parts of the North Atlantic including Arctic waters. It feeds on a wide range of fishes, seals, porpoises, and sea birds, and is well known as a scavenger at fish-processing factories and whaling stations. It is found from the surface to depths of 330 fathoms. With a reputation for being sluggish, it is often known as the sleeper shark, but its diet suggests that it can be an active predator. It was formerly of economic value to the Eskimos and Greenlanders who captured it for its liver oil as well as its flesh.

Bramble shark (Echinorhinidae)

A family containing possibly only one species is the bramble shark (*Echinorhinus brucus*), which lives in temperate and tropical waters of the oceans. It is a heavy-bodied shark found rarely on the British coast but more commonly to the south. It is usually caught in 220 to 500 fathoms and is reported to feed on crabs, fishes, and spurdogs, although details of its life history are little known. It is dark brown in colour, and can easily be recognized by the large thorny plates which are buried in the skin. It grows to ten feet.

Sawsharks (Pristiophoridae)

The sawsharks are found in the Indo-Pacific, and are highly distinctive in that they have long, rather pointed snouts which are bordered on each side with large, sharp and uneven teeth. In this they resemble the sawfishes (Pristidae) which are more closely related to the rays. The sawsharks, however, have long barbels on the underside of the snout, two large dorsal fins, and no anal fin. Two genera are included in the family: *Pristiophorus* which has six gill slits and *Pliotrema* which has five. Members of both genera are sluggish fish which root around in the sand and weed on which they live, detecting food with their sensitive barbels. They rarely grow longer than four feet.

Angel sharks (Squatinidae)

In many respects the angel sharks or monk fishes appear to be intermediate between the sharks and the rays. They are flattened from above, but the pectoral fins are not attached to the head and the gill slits are lateral. Their shark-like features include a terminal mouth, well-developed dorsal fins and a broad tail. They have complex barbels above the mouth. They swim by swinging the tail from side to side, not by undulating the pectorals as the rays do. The family is distributed in all warm temperate seas and is represented by numerous rather similar species.

The only representative in British waters is the monkfish (*Squatina squatina*), which ranges all along the south and west coasts and occurs occasionally in the North Sea. It becomes distinctly more abundant in summer, probably as a result of a northerly migration. It grows to six feet and may weigh up to seventy pounds. It lives mainly on the sea bed feeding chiefly on flatfishes and rays, but also eating crustaceans and molluscs. It is a live-bearing shark which produces litters of between nine and sixteen young in the summertime.

The rays and their allies (Rajiformes)

Although the essentials of their anatomy are similar to the sharks, the rays must be seen to be a distinct evolutionary line. Externally they differ from sharks by having ventral gill slits and by having the pectoral fins fused to the head; associated with these features the spiracle is usually well developed and the eyes are dorsally placed. In many species the dorsal fins and even the tail fin are reduced in size, or absent. Most members of the family are adapted to life on the sea bed, but a few species are found in fresh water.

Electric rays (Torpedinidae)

The electric rays or torpedos are well known for their electrical abilities. The kidney-shaped electric organs occupy most of the rather thick pectoral fins, and are made up of a series of hexagonal columns each comprising many electroplates. The electric rays can produce a series of discharges—although of decreasing strength—but the maximum voltage produced is around 220 volts in the large *Torpedo nobiliana*. In general, the larger the fish, the greater number of electroplates its organs contain and the higher the voltage. Their electrical ability is mainly offensive, for they secure comparatively large prey by stunning it with an electric discharge, but it clearly has a defensive function as well.

Members of the family are found in all tropical and temper-

The electric ray or torpedo (*Torpedo marmorata*) lives and feeds on the bottom. It partially conceals itself in sand. The electric organs occupy the major part of each 'wing' between the mid-line and edge of the disc. Maximum length: 24 inches. *Phot. Aldo Margiocco*

(Left) This enormous shovel-nosed sand shark *Rhynchobatus djeddensis*) lives in the tropical Indian and Pacific Oceans. It grows to a length of 10 feet, and feeds on echinoderms, crustaceans, and molluscs. Its flattened body suggests that it is a bottom-living species, the mouth is rather small, but the series of gill slits are well developed. *Phot. R. Catala, the Aquarium at Noumea*

A guitarfish (*Rhinobatus* sp.) caught off the Atlantic coast of the Sahara; note the ray-like anterior body and the shark-like tail. *Phot. J. L. S. Dubois*

ate seas, living mostly in shallow water inshore, although some species are found in the deep sea at depths of 580 fathoms. In general, they are rather thick-bodied with soft, scaleless skins, small eyes and rather small mouths. Most have a large tail fin (which is used in swimming) and two dorsal fins, although some have only a single dorsal fin (for example the South African *Narke capensis*), or none at all, as in *Temera hardwickii* of the Indo-Australian archipelago.

Three torpedos occur in European waters. Of these the electric ray (*T. nobiliana*) is the most common, and also the largest member of the family growing to a length of 6 feet and a weight of 110 lbs. Its colouring is plain, brown to black on the back, white ventrally, and the spiracles are smooth edged (a distinguishing feature). It occurs northwards to Scotland, and in the western Atlantic from North Carolina to Nova Scotia, as well as in the Mediterranean. The marbled electric ray (*T. marmorata*) is found in the Mediterranean and northwards to English waters, but is in general rare to the north. It is considerably smaller, and can be distinguished by its brown marbled back and by having a series of papillae around the spiracle edge. Like all electric rays these two species are ovoviviparous.

Sawfishes (Pristidae)

Sawfishes are the most shark-like relatives of the rays in that the body is only slightly flattened, and the tail is long and rounded in cross-section with a well-developed tail fin. Their most conspicuous feature, however, is the very long, flattened snout which bears on its sides formidable pointed teeth—the familiar 'saw' of curio shops and dockside taverns. Their ray-like features include ventral gill openings and horizontally enlarged pectoral fins.

Sawfishes are common in all tropical oceans in shallow water, and especially in river mouths such as the Congo and Amazon estuaries. The small-toothed sawfish (*Pristis microdon*) is found in fresh water, as in Lake Nicaragua and the River Zambezi. Sawfish use the saw to dig in the bottom mud, uncovering invertebrates and fishes which are then eaten; incidentally they damage submarine cables which have often been recovered with their teeth embedded in the insulation. Although not dangerous to man they have been known to inflict severe injuries when enmeshed in fishermen's nets.

This *Potamotrygon* is a stingray which lives in freshwater. The group is found both in Africa and South America. It is viviparous; the egg develops in the maternal oviduct whose walls secrete a liquid, or uterine milk, which nourishes the embryos. *Phot. Postel*

The largest species is the greater sawfish (*P. pectinatus*) which grows to a measured 25 feet, although it reputedly attains 35 feet. It is worldwide in distribution in tropical oceans, and in the western Atlantic ranges as far north as New York. A smaller species (*P. pristis*), which grows to 15 feet, is found in the Mediterranean and the eastern Atlantic northwards to Portugal. Like the other sawfishes it is ovoviviparous, the eggs being retained within the mother's body until the young are fully developed. At birth the saw teeth are soft, flexible and covered with gristly tissue.

Guitarfishes (Rhinobatidae)

This family of rays possesses certain shark-like features. All have enlarged and laterally developed pectoral fins, and ventral gill slits, but they have rounded shark-like tails with a well developed tail fin. The guitarfishes or fiddle-sharks are found in shallow water in tropical and warm temperate oceans. They are bottom-living fishes feeding on crustaceans and molluscs, rooting with the long angular snout in the sand and mud in search of prey. In the western Atlantic from the Gulf of Mexico to North Carolina, the spotted guitarfish (*Rhinobatus lentiginosus*) is relatively common and can be found foraging in the breakers so that its dorsal fins are exposed at the surface. The slightly larger *R. rhinobatus*, which grows to 39 inches, is found in the eastern Atlantic as far north as Biscay and in the Mediterranean.

Members of the related family Rhynchobatidae are veritable giants by comparison. The shovel-nose sandshark (*Rhynchobatus djeddensis*) of the tropical Indo-Pacific, grows to ten feet and a weight of at least 500 lbs. It is occasionally caught by anglers.

Rays and skates (Rajidae)

The rays are a large family of bottom-living fishes widely distributed in shallow water in temperate and cool seas, and found in tropical waters also, usually in deeper water. They are totally adapted for life on the sea bed, being flattened with huge pectoral fins which are connected to the head, and with a thin tail with very small dorsal fins. They swim by undulating the edges of the pectoral fins, moving gracefully over the sea bed, but most of the time they lie partially buried by sand or gravel. Many rays feed on bottom-living crustaceans, worms, and molluscs, but a few species eat actively-swimming fish. These rays have long teeth and are frequently coloured on the underside as well (whereas most rays are white ventrally and have backs coloured to blend with their surroundings).

Rays have a pair of electric organs in the tail but they are neither large nor powerful. It is probable that their main function is for communication and recognition of their own species, and possibly the opposite sex. Rays are oviparous, the egg being laid in an oblong, dark, horny capsule with slender points (presumably anchoring devices) at the four corners and small slits to allow oxygen to penetrate.

There is no biological difference between rays and skates, the latter name usually being applied to the larger species which were commercially exploited although of recent years almost all ray species have been marketed in Britain as 'skate'. Some fifteen species are found commonly around the coasts of the British Isles, while others are found in deep water. The most common inshore species is the roker or thornback ray (*Raja clavata*) which grows to 34 inches in length. It is found on mud, sand or shingle in depths of 1–33 fathoms. The newly hatched young are usually found in the shallowest water, but the mature female comes inshore to lay her eggs. This species is immediately distinguished by the large-based thorns which are embedded in the skin both on the back and underside. The Europe skate (*R. batis*) is a large fish, growing to eight feet in length, which occurs from the Arctic Ocean to Madeira and the Mediterranean. It is a deep water species, usually found in 55 to 330 fathoms, and for this reason is more common off the western coasts of Britain. A similar species attaining approximately the same size is the big skate (*R. binoculata*) which ranges from southern California to Alaska.

The stingray (*Dasyatis pastinaca*) usually lives close to the sea bed, often partly buried. This series of photographs shows the swimming movements when the fish is active; the enlarged pectoral fins beat regularly like wings, but their edges 'ripple' to allow more precise orientation. Notice the long spine on the top of the tail which makes the stingray a danger to bathers and fishermen. *Phot. Fronval*

Deep water rays (Anacanthobatidae)

This is a small family of deep sea rays which are probably world-wide in their distribution in tropical seas but are known only from very few specimens caught in the Gulf of Mexico, off South Africa, and off New Zealand. *Springeria folirostris*, which has been found in the Gulf of Mexico in depths of 165 to 280 fathoms, has a sharply pointed snout with leaf-like flaps either side. Mature males have branched and spiny tips to their claspers.

Stingrays (Dasyatidae)

The stingrays are distinguished by their almost rectangular body shape and by their long whip-like tails which have neither dorsal nor tail fins, but have one or more long, serrated-edged spines on the top side. Like other rays they are well adapted for life on the sea bed. Their gill openings are ventral, and the large spiracle behind each eye is used to draw in water to the gills. This is then exhaled through the gill openings.

Stingrays are mainly found in shallow warm water, although some species penetrate cooler, temperate waters in warm seasons. One such is the European stingray (*Dasyatis pastinaca*) which occurs regularly on the Channel coast and in the southern North and Irish Seas each summer following a northward migration. This species grows to eight feet in length and feeds mostly on bottom-living organisms, chiefly molluscs and crabs. Like its relatives it is ovoviviparous, but embryos in a late stage of development are nourished by secretions from the mother's uterine tissues.

Freshwater stingrays (Potamotrygonidae)

This family of stingrays is found only in the rivers and lakes of central and northern South America and tropical West Africa. Members of the family are distinguished by their disc-shaped bodies, with moderately long, thickset tails which are flattened towards the end. They all have one or two long, sharp, serrated-edged spines on the tail, grooved along their length with venom-packed tissue on the underside. Wounds from these spines are very painful and produce severe injury. Most river stingrays are small, the Paraguayan species *Potamotrygon motoro* growing to twelve inches in width.

Butterfly rays (Gymnuridae)

These small rays differ from the stingrays in that they have very wide pectoral fins and an extremely short tail. Some have spines in their tails while others have a small dorsal fin. They are of world-wide distribution in tropical and warm temperate coastal waters. The tropical Atlantic species, *Gymnura altavela*, has a 'wing span' of six feet and is one of the largest members of the family.

Eagle rays (Myliobatidae)

The eagle rays are widespread in tropical and warm temperate oceans of the world. Most are moderately large fish, some of the larger species growing to eight feet in width. They are more active than the long-tailed stingrays, swimming freely in mid-water and at the surface with graceful strokes of their powerful wings. The development of the pectoral fins into long pointed wings, which begin behind the eyes, and the long tail, are distinguishing features.

The eagle ray (*Myliobatis aquila*) of the eastern Atlantic is a summertime visitor to the coasts of Britain, but is found off Africa and in the Mediterranean at all seasons. Like other members of the family it feeds exclusively on hard-shelled molluscs and crustaceans, and where, for example, oysters are cultivated it can prove to be a pest. The spotted duck-billed ray (*Aetobatus narinari*), which is of circumtropical distribution, is often seen in vast shoals, and is a more serious predator on valuable shellfish. Like its relatives it has broad, flattened teeth which form a mosaic 'pavement' in the jaws, ideally suited for eating hard-shelled animals.

Devil rays or mantas (Mobulidae)

While the eagle rays have partially adopted a pelagic mode of life, the members of the family Mobulidae are wholly surface-living. Their body plan has changed since they abandoned their bottom-living lifestyle. The pectoral fins have become elongate and more wing-like, the front edge of the pectoral fin is separated to form a small highly mobile funnel, the tail is small and in some species has a small dorsal fin, in others a short serrated spine. The mouth is broad and set across the end of the head, although the jaw teeth are small and in several rows.

Devil rays are usually very large indeed. The European species *Mobula mobular*, which is found in the Mediterranean and from West Africa to Spain and Portugal, attains a span of 17 feet. The tropical Atlantic specids *Manta birostris* (which is probably identical to the mantas of the Indo-Pacific) is even larger and grows to 22 feet in width. Despite their size they are harmless to man for they feed entirely on the small planktonic crustaceans and young fish which they filter from the sea water through a dense mesh of gill rakers in the pharynx. As they swim forward the head fins twist to form a scoop which channels the water into the mouth and thus on to the gill rakers. It is an interesting example of convergence that the largest sharks (whale shark, basking shark), rays (*Manta*), and whales (blue whale) are all plankton feeders filtering their food from the water by means of similar sieves.

Mantas have occasionally been observed to leap clear of the water, landing with a loud report. It has been conjectured that this is done to rid themselves of parasites, but this is not likely to be a successful means of doing so. In the absence of other evidence it can only be suggested that they leap for the pleasure derived from doing so. The force required to raise a 3000 lb. fish out of the water is clearly considerable and although they are usually seen swimming slowly at the surface, they are capable of great bursts of speed. Devil rays are frequently seen with the sucker fishes *Echeneis* attached to their fins, and related species are found in the mouth of the larger fish attached by means of their sucker-disc.

Ratfishes or chimaeras (Holocephali)

The chimaeroids, which are usually known as ratfishes, ghost sharks, or elephant fishes form a group which superficially appears to be intermediate between the sharks and the bony fishes. It is, however, generally agreed that they are more closely related to the sharks and represent an early offshoot from the basic shark line. The skeleton is wholly cartilaginous. They lay eggs protected by a thin outer casing, and the male has pelvic claspers which are used in copulation. The claspers are more complex than those of sharks, being basically double on each side, the anterior limb having a spiny surface; male chimaeroids also have an appendage on the front of the head, the tip of which is spiny. In this group there are four gill slits covered by a gill cover, and the spiracle is absent. The teeth are set in the jaws but are permanent, growing continuously to make up for wear, and not being replaced as are those of sharks and rays. The most striking feature, however, is that the upper jaw bone is fused to the cranium and does not lie loose as it does in sharks.

Three living families are recognized, all marine and mostly occurring in the moderately deep to deep sea.

Ratfishes (Chimaeridae)

These are the most numerous of the chimaeroids. Members of the family are distributed in the cooler regions of Atlantic, Indian, and Pacific Oceans, but the number of species is probably fewer than thirty. The ratfish (*Chimaera monstrosa*) is very common in the northeast Atlantic from the Azores northwards to Norway. It is a deep water species common in 165–275 fathoms and only rarely found in shallower water. Off the west coast of the British Isles it is caught in great numbers by trawlers fishing on the deeper grounds, but it is not landed, for the flesh has a bitter taste. It grows to a length of five feet. In deeper water another ratfish (*Hydrolagus affinis*) is captured. Its depth range is from about 300–1290 fathoms and it is found on both sides of the North Atlantic. Unlike the shallow water ratfish, which is a light brown in colour, *Hydrolagus* is a deep sepia above and below, with blue-grey teeth. It is relatively small, attaining only 49 inches. A related species (*H. colliei*) occurs in shallow water along the North Pacific coast of America.

Long-snouted ratfishes (Rhinochimaeridae)

This small family contains probably only four species, found in deep water in the North Atlantic, North Pacific, and off South Africa. All have extremely long pointed snouts and this alone distinguishes them from all other ratfishes. *Harriotta raleighana* is probably widespread in the North Atlantic at depths of 500–1425 fathoms, and grows to about 39 inches in length. A similar species, *Rhinochimaera atlantica*, which grows slightly longer, is found in rather shallower water along the lower continental shelf. Both have been caught in deep water to the west of Britain.

Ghost sharks (Callorhinchidae)

These ratfishes are found only in cool-temperate and cold regions of the southern hemisphere, off southern America, New Zealand, Australia, and South Africa. They are distinguished by having a very elaborate, ploughshare-shaped tip to the snout. One of the best known is the Australian and New Zealand *Callorhinchus milii*, a silvery fish with a brown back which is found in very shallow water. It grows to 39 inches and is said to be well flavoured.

Lungfishes (Dipnoi)

The lungfishes are in everyday terms living fossils. The majority of the recognized groups are known only as fossils dating from the Devonian, Carboniferous, and Permian periods, but six species still live, all in freshwater and widely distributed. Four species live in Africa (Protopteridae), one species in South America (Lepidosirenidae), and one in Australia (Ceratodontidae). Of these the Australian lungfish shows the most primitive features. They have several features in common, including a heterocercal tail. The body is covered with heavy, shiny cosmoid scales which are similar to those on the head, the nostrils open internally to the roof of the mouth, and the teeth (which are internal and do not lie

The spotted duck-billed ray (*Aetobatus narinari*) feeds on bivalve molluscs, especially oysters, whose hard shells its flattened teeth crush. It is frequently seen at the surface, often in huge shoals, and may jump out of the water. In this photograph a shark sucker (*Remora*) is attached to the ray's back, an uncharacteristic position as they usually fasten to the underside. *Phot. Russ Kinne—Photo Researchers*

The roker or thornback ray (*Raja clavata*) is common in shallow water in the seas of western Europe. Its colour is very variable but is always a good match with the seabed. It is often caught in trawls and by anglers. *Phot. J. M. Baufle*

Lepidosiren paradoxa, the South American lungfish, a relative of the African Protopterus. More elongate than Protopterus, it also possesses a double lung with which it breathes air; its gills are very small, but young fish have large external gills which supply oxygen until they are large enough to swim to the surface. Phot. Russ Kinne—Photo Researchers

Below, drawing of the main skeletal parts of the coelacanth. Adf, anterior dorsal fin; Af, anal fin; Not, notochord; Pdf, poster:or dorsal fin; Pf, pectoral fin; Tf, tail fin; Vc, vertebral column; Vf, ventral or pelvic fin. After J. Millot and J. Anthony

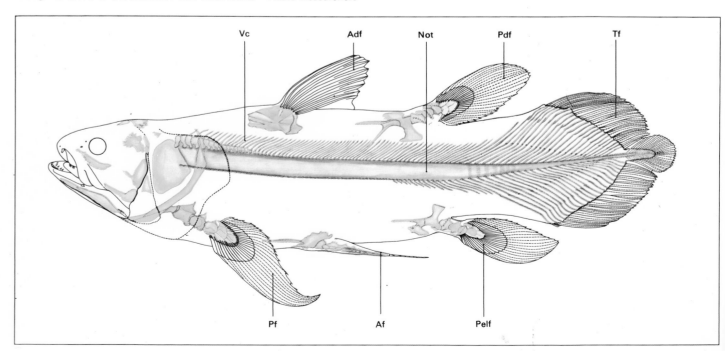

on the jaw edges) are formed by paired and complex tooth plates of characteristic appearance.

Australian lungfish (Ceratodontidae)

The Australian lungfish is the sole living representative of one of the branches of the Dipnoi which is basically very similar to fossil fishes from the Triassic. The body is rounded at the front but compressed towards the tail, which has one single continuous fin; the scales are very large and rounded, and the pectoral and pelvic paired fins are paddle-like. The large lung lies above the gut in the mid-line of the body.

The lungfish (*Neoceratodus forsteri*), sometimes called the barramunda or Burnett salmon, grows to 57 inches in length, and is native to the Burnett and Mary rivers in southeastern Queensland, although it has been introduced to other Australian rivers. It lives in slow-flowing parts of the rivers which in times of drought may become stagnant. In such emergencies it breathes using its lung, which is plentifully supplied with alveoli (air cells). At other times it obtains its oxygen from the water by means of its four pairs of gills. The Australian lungfish does not aestivate in dried up surroundings as do the other lungfish.

The Australian lungfish is a carnivorous species which eats a wide range of animal life and a little plant material. It spawns in pairs during the period August to October, shedding its eggs over the vegetation to which they stick. Unfortunately, this lungfish has become much rarer in its native rivers and it is now strictly protected, but its introduction into other Australian rivers and lakes is seen as a form of insurance against total extinction. Its survival to the present day is probably due to the scarcity of competitors and predators in its isolated environment.

South American lungfish (Lepidosirenidae)

This lungfish *Lepidosiren paradoxa* lives mainly in the swamps and densely-weeded waters of the Parana and Amazon river systems in South America. These shallow waters are flooded seasonally then dry up in the dry season, and the lungfish is uniquely equipped to survive in this relatively harsh environment. It possesses a pair of lungs which communicate with the oesophagus through a ventral connection, and using these it breathes air. Its gills are small, and air-breathing is a regular way of life, the lungfish coming to the surface to gulp air every few minutes. In times of drought it aestivates, driving a burrow downwards at an angle. As the water-level drops, the fish plugs the entrance with mud to lie with its tail curled over its head within a mucous covering. When the rains come it emerges to become active.

The lungfish breeds during the early part of the rainy season in a burrow made by the male who guards the eggs and later the young. The pelvic fins of the male at this period have much branched, highly vascularized projections along their length. Their function is not known but it has been suggested that they may supply oxygen to the eggs which are in the oxygen deficient burrow. The young have four pairs of external feathery gills, and an adhesive gland on the underside by which they hang on to vegetation; both are lost after a short period and at a length of 1½ inches the young can breathe air. The adult lungfish grows to a length of 50 inches.

African lungfishes (Protopteridae)

Four species of *Protopterus* are currently recognized from the freshwaters of central tropical Africa, all rather similar in general appearance, with an elongated body, broad head, and long pectoral and pelvic fins. They are well-known as air breathing fishes and for their ability to form a cocoon in the dry season within which they can survive for months, and

even years if necessary. As the water level falls in the lake or swamp, the lungfish makes a burrow deep into the mud with a hollowed chamber at one end; within this the fish curls up with its tail over its head, secreting thick mucus which forms a shell around it leaving only a small opening at the mouth. Motionless, and with its body functions reduced to a minimum, the lungfish regularly survives through a normal dry season, and will tolerate drought of up to two years (in artificial conditions they have lived up to four years).

One species (*P. aethiopicus*), which lives in eastern and central Africa, mainly in the larger lakes and rivers, is rarely required to aestivate in this manner. It is as dependent on atmospheric oxygen as the other species, and on a calm day can be seen in the lakes, coming to the surface to gulp air, then diving again with a splash of the tail. It grows to be large (at least seven feet in length) and is the largest of the African lungfishes.

The reproductive habits of the group are similar to those of *Lepidosiren*. The eggs are laid in a shallow nest scooped out of the swamp (*P. annecteus* and *P. aethiopicus*) or in a channel in the bank (as in *P. dolloi*) the end of which has a ventilation shaft to the air. The eggs and young are guarded by the male,

Right, the brain of the coelacanth is small in proportion to the size of the cranial cavity and is hidden within a fat-filled cavity. The optic lobes are relatively small, but the olfactory region of the brain is well developed, which suggests that *Latimeria* depends more on smell than sight in finding prey. *Phot. J. Millot and J. Anthony*

Below, the coelacanth (*Latimeria chalumnae*) caught off the Comoro Islands in the Indian Ocean. A female over 4½ feet in length, weighing some 88 pounds in the collection of the National Museum of Natural History in Paris. *Phot. J. M. Baufle*

the latter for up to five weeks, and large males of *P. aethiopicus* have been known to attack fishermen intruding into the nest area (but native fishermen often search out the nest and harpoon the parent fish). The young lungfish has three pairs of well-developed external gills, and an adhesive gland on the thorax by which it attaches itself to vegetation. The internal gills are poorly developed and the lungs are used throughout their life (the external gills being lost when the fish is around six inches in length).

Crossopterygii

The crossopterygians are well-known as fossil fishes, but only one species, the coelacanth (*Latimeria chalumnae*), has survived to recent times. This, like the fossil fishes, has two dorsal fins and a symmetrical tail, and the pectoral and pelvic fins are borne upon short limbs. The body is covered with heavy scales, the skull is hinged in the middle, the notochord persists and bony vertebrae are present.

The bichir (*Polypterus senegalus senegalus*) inhabits certain rivers in West Africa—Gambia, Upper Volta and Niger—living in the swampy margins and breathing air. It is a living representative of a group which is known from Cretaceous fossil remains.

The crossopterygians form an infraclass divided into two groups, the rhipidistians, now known only as fossils, and the actinistians, to which group the coelacanth belongs. The rhipidistians were large and voracious fishes which existed from the Middle Devonian to the Lower Permian. They were distinguished by the arrangement and number of the dermal bones in the head, and especially by having nostrils opening into the roof of the mouth. The pectoral fin was set upon a limb which resembles the tetrapod forelimb, and it is from this group that the terrestrial tetrapod vertebrates of today (amphibians, reptiles, birds, and mammals) are descended.

The second group (Actinistia) is a rather specialized group found as fossils from the Middle Devonian and surviving through to the present day, but changing very little during that period. They have only two external nostrils and none internally. The second dorsal fin and the anal fin, as well as the pectoral and pelvic fins are set on short limbs. The head jaw bones are simplified in comparison with the rhipidistians.

The coelacanth (Latimeriidae)

The chance capture of a coelacanth in December 1938 by a South African trawler fishing off the mouth of the Chalumna River, off East London, was the first indication that this important group of fishes still survived. Although it was impossible to preserve the entire body and eventually only the skin was saved, the late Professor J. L. B. Smith of Rhodes University, Grahamstown, recognized the remains and from 1939 onwards wrote a series of important articles on the appearance and survival of this 'living fossil'. The importance of *Latimeria chalumnae* as a remarkable zoological relic of a group close to the ancestors of the tetrapod vertebrates was quickly recognized.

Professor Smith was inspired by this first capture to devote much energy and time to obtaining further specimens, but it was not until December 1952 that a second specimen was caught, this time off the island of Anjouan, in the Comoro archipelago, northwest of Madagascar. Since then nearly a hundred specimens have been caught off the Comoros, all by native fishermen, and many museums around the world now possess specimens. The anatomy of the coelacanth has been subject to detailed study by the French scientists Professor J. Millot and Dr J. Anthony, who published their observations in two admirable publications.

The coelacanth is dark brown to blue with odd scales light in colour. It attains a length of six feet and weight of up to 200 lbs. It is a heavy-bodied fish with a large head, two gular plates on the throat, and heavy scales. The tail has a characteristic small central lobe within the broad fin, and the dorsal, anal, pelvic, and pectoral fins all have short peduncles— exactly as do the fossil coelacanths. Live specimens are exceptionally slimy, and the whole body contains copious quantities of oil; even the swim bladder is oil-filled.

The coelacanth lives in depths of 80–130 fathoms in the much creviced, nearly vertical coral and rock-faced slope around the Comoro islands. Native fishermen catch them on baited hooks, and no other method is successful due to the terrain. When alive, the coelacanth makes gentle sculling movements with its lobed fins; the pectoral fins are especially mobile and they can twist on their axis through 180°. The appearance of the massive tail suggests that if necessary it can swim powerfully by sweeps of the tail; the delicate manoeuvring described above is probably mainly used in keeping station or in feeding.

The discovery in January 1972 of a large female coelacanth with large eggs, 3½ inches in diameter, in the right ovary, was the first evidence on the breeding of the species. Only nineteen yolky eggs were present, each rather bigger than a tennis ball. As there was no sign of a shell it has been suggested that they are probably laid in this condition.

Latimeria has been one of the most important zoological discoveries in the vertebrate field in this century. It has provided a stimulating opportunity to substantiate evolutionary theories, and to compare knowledge gained from fossil material with a living animal. It also demonstrates how much is still to be discovered about the fauna of the sea.

Chondrostian fishes (Chondrostei)
Bichirs (Polypteriformes)

This is a small group of freshwater fishes found today only in Africa. Their relationships with the bony fishes have been disputed and variously interpreted, but they are presumed to be the relics of an early group of fishes, the palaeonisids, which ranged in time from the Lower Devonian to the Cretaceous.

The living forms have elongated bodies, encased in heavy enamel-like scales which are arranged in diagonal rows. The dorsal fin is composed of a series of free, spine-like finlets, and the pectoral fins are lobed and supported on a muscular, scale-covered base. The head is covered with a number of plates, the arrangement of which distinguishes them from all other bony fishes. They also have a two-lobed swim bladder, the one on the right side being the larger; both are cellular and used for air breathing. The young fish have a pair of long, feathery external gills, one above each pectoral fin.

Bichirs and reedfish (Polypteridae)

The bichirs are confined to the fresh waters of tropical Africa from the southern Sahara (including the Nile) to the extreme south of the Congo basin.

All the bichirs are secretive, normally lying under aquatic plants by day and active only at night. They are usually found in turbid water, often in the densely vegetated river banks and lake margins. They are predatory, eating small fishes and amphibians. Spawning usually takes place during the rainy season. In the aquarium the fish has been seen to make a nest in the centre of a clump of aquatic plants in which the very small, numerous eggs are laid. The newly hatched larva has a special gland under each eye, which secretes an adhesive mucus by which the larva hangs from the vegetation. The Nile bichir (*Polypterus bichir*), which is found in the Nile and lakes Rudolf and Chad, is a relatively large fish attaining a length of 28 inches. The bichir (*P. senegalus*), which is divided into subspecies, ranges from the central African lakes to the Senegal, Gambia, and Niger river systems.

The reedfish (*Calamoichthys calabaricus*) is the only other member of this family. Its body is extremely elongated, with a small head, the dorsal finlets are well separated, and the pelvic fins are absent; it is a beautiful lime green, yellowish on the belly. It lives in slow-flowing streams and still waters of West Africa, especially the Niger Delta and the Cameroons. Like the bichirs it can use its lung-like swimbladder to breathe air when the water in which it lives becomes too low in dissolved oxygen. The reedfish usually lives in dense submerged vegetation, often in swampy regions.

Sturgeons (Acipenseriformes)

The sturgeons are a group of bony fishes presenting a number of rather primitive features, in particular a heterocercal tail, which makes them unique amongst the bony fishes. Certain features of bones on the skull are distinctive. Recent classifications have suggested that they should be grouped with the bichirs (Polypteriformes), and that both groups are relics of the palaeoniscid fishes. The Palaeonisciformes, a very well represented order amongst fossil fishes, and a number of other fossil orders, together with the bichirs and sturgeons make up the Chondrostei.

The sturgeon is a long, thin fish with a pointed head and a toothless mouth on the underside of the snout. Two pairs of barbels are present round the mouth, which has remarkably protrusible jaws. Only two families are recognized: the Acipenseridae and Polyodontidae.

Sturgeons (Acipenseridae)

The family is represented only in the northern hemisphere. There are some 25 species recognized, of which the greatest number live in central Eurasia. Some are confined to freshwater, but the majority are migratory, feeding in the sea and breeding in freshwater. The best known is the Atlantic sturgeon (*Acipenser sturio*) the natural range of which extends from Norway and the Baltic Sea along the Atlantic and Mediterranean coasts of Europe to the Black Sea. It is a large fish, attaining a length of nearly 10 feet and a weight of 470 lbs. It is a migratory species which enters large rivers to spawn in freshwater. Unfortunately the sturgeon is now a very rare fish through most of its former range. The only river basins in which it is known to breed on the Atlantic coast are the Garonne in France, and the Guadalquivir in southern Spain. A few are found in the Russian Baltic Lake Ladoga, and in the Mediterranean. The decline of this magnificent fish is probably due to pollution of the lower reaches of most large rivers in Europe, to insurmountable barriers in the rivers, and to the incredibly wasteful slaughter of mature females for the sake of their unshed eggs for caviare.

Two species of sturgeon, the Russian sturgeon (*A. gueldenstaedti*) and the sevruga (*A. stellatus*) are heavily exploited for caviare and meat in the Black Sea and Caspian Sea basins, but the fishery is now controlled and conservation measures have succeeded in maintaining viable populations. Several species are also found in North America, of which the white sturgeon (*A. transmontanus*) is found in Pacific coast rivers. This is a very large fish, growing to at least 15 feet in length and 1800 lbs. in weight. Although the white sturgeon migrates within the river it is not often captured in the sea. The young fish feed on bottom-living invertebrates but adults eat considerable amounts of fish. Another North American species, the lake sturgeon (*A. fulvescens*) is found only in freshwater, in rivers and lakes in eastern Canada and the United States.

The beluga (*Huso huso*) is a migratory sturgeon found in the Black and Caspian seas and the Adriatic, and differs from the other sturgeons in that it has a very wide mouth. Unlike

Left, the European sturgeon (*Acipenser sturio*) a fish which has become scarce through overfishing and pollution. *Right,* sterlets in a rearing pond in Iran. *Phot. R. Fruchon and J. Cooke—Photo Researchers*

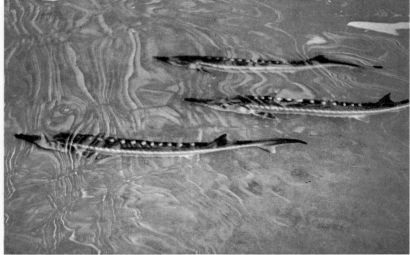

The paddlefish *Polyodon spathula*, is a freshwater sturgeon which lives in the Mississippi River system, but now much restricted in its range. It feeds on planktonic organisms which are swept into the mouth as it swims along. *Phot. Russ Kinne—Photo Researchers*

most of its relatives it feeds extensively on fish. It is a huge fish, growing to at least 15 feet and a weight of 1½ tons, but even so it is smaller than the kaluga (*H. dauricus*), its relative in the River Amur basin in Siberia. Both species have been fished for in the past and are now less common than they were at one time.

Paddlefishes (Polyodontidae)

Although related to the sturgeons the paddlefishes do not much resemble them, except in size. The skin lacks the rows of heavy scutes which typify the sturgeons, the snout is very elongate and paddle-like, and there are no barbels round the mouth. Only two species are known: the paddlefish or spoon-bill (*Polyodon spathula*) which lives in the whole of the Mississippi system, and the Chinese paddlefish (*Psephurus gladius*), a native of the Yangtze River, which attains a length of 22 feet. The biology of the latter is very little known, but the North American paddlefish is a plankton eater which lives in the larger rivers. It breeds in the most turbulent regions of the river on stony bottoms in spring. The young fish has at most a small bump at the end of its snout, but as it grows it attains a proportionally greater length until, when mature, the snout is a third of the length of the body.

Both members of the family are captured for the sake of their flesh and eggs; *Polyodon* in particular has become much rarer, probably due to fishing and also the development of rivers as well as pollution.

Holostean fishes (Holostei)

This small group of fishes shows a number of primitive features. In some classifications they are regarded as close to the sturgeons, but in others they are grouped with the teleosts (to which they are more closely related) to form the Neopterygii. They are represented by no more than ten living species, all found in the New World. All have very solid, shiny, enamel-like scales, and rather asymmetrical tail fins. They also have a lung-like swimbladder which opens into the top side of the foregut, and can be used for breathing air. None of them are prime food or sporting fishes, and all are known to destroy substantial amounts of more prized fishes.

Bowfin (Amiidae)

The single representative of this family, the bowfin (*Amia calva*) is confined to the freshwaters of eastern North America. It lives in backwaters and stillwaters in densely overgrown and often poorly oxygenated waters, and breeds in spring in a shallow nest on the bottom. The male guards the eggs (which may number up to 70,000), and the young fish until they reach a length of about four inches. The bowfin is dull green or brown in colour. The body is densely covered with thick scales, and the head with bony plates. The dorsal fin is long and low, the anal fin short, and the tail fin rounded with the body axis turning upwards into the upper part of the fin. It grows to a length of 36 inches.

Garpikes (Lepisosteidae)

Garpikes are distinguished by their long, thin shape; the snout is long, with elongate well-toothed jaws, and the body is long although rounded. The scales covering the body are diamond shaped, shiny enamel-like scales. The dorsal fin is small, opposite the anal, and both are close to the tail. The tail fin is rounded and heterocercal.

They are all found in freshwater in North America, and in brackish water as far south as the Gulf of Mexico and Cuba. Some nine species are recognized. The alligator gar (*Lepisosteus spatula*), is one of the largest species, growing up to 9½ feet in length. It is frequently found in salt or brackish water around Florida and the Gulf of Mexico, and in freshwater in the Mississippi system. It is a voracious predator eating large quantities of fishes and even ducks from the surface of the swamps in which it lives. The longnose gar (*L. osseus*) ranges from Quebec to northern Mexico. It is distinguished by a very long snout, olive-brown back and white belly, although the young are more brightly coloured. Like other gars, its habit is to hang still in the water, hidden by vegetation, waiting for prey to come close. Then, with a sudden thrust, it snatches its prey—almost always a smaller fish—crosswise in its jaws. It spawns in freshwater in late spring in the shallows, the eggs

The shortnose gar (*Lepisosteus platostomus*). From a water-colour in Cuvier's *Animal Kingdom*. Phot. Lauros

being sticky and adhering to vegetation or the stones of the river bed. Newly hatched young have an adhesive sucker on the snout by which they cling to vegetation at first. The shortnose gar (*L. platostomus*) is distinguished by its broad snout, and clear, unspotted sides. It is a rather small species, growing to 30 inches, which lives in clear, if silty water in the larger rivers of the Mississippi system.

Bony fishes (Teleostei)

The bony fishes are the group to which the great majority of the twenty thousand or so fishes belong. They have diversified to occupy all the major living spaces of the sea and freshwater. They differ from such groups as the garpikes in the lack of ganoin in the dermal bones and scales, and in having a symmetrical tail fin (homocercal) the rays fanning out from flattened bones, the hypurals, at the end of the vertebral column. The arrangement of the bones of the head is simplified, the tooth-bearing bones of the upper jaw are attached only at the anterior end of the head, and the lower jaw is simplified.

The classification of the teleosts is complicated, and in many areas still unsettled. A recently proposed and in some ways radical reclassification, which was published in 1966, listed eight super-orders, thirty orders, and 413 families. Some of the earlier classifications had many more of each grouping. The selection made here will attempt to include the most important and largest of the families.

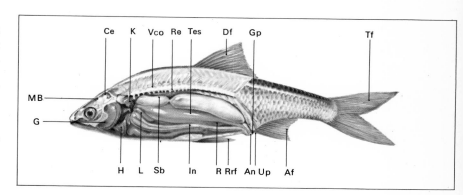

Male roach (*Rutilus rutilus*), dissected, viewed from left. *Af*, anal fin; *An*, anus; *Ce*, cerebellum; *Df*, dorsal fin; *G*, gills; *Gp*, genital pore; *H*, heart; *In*, intestine; *K*, kidney; *L*, liver; *Mb*, midbrain; *Pvf*, pelvic fin; *R*, rectum; *Sb*, swimbladder; *Tes*, testis; *Tf*, tail fin; *Up*, urinary pore; *Vco*, vertebral column.

Tarpons and their allies (Elopiformes)

The most primitive of all the teleosts, this order is distinguished from the others by the possession of one or more bony plates (gular plates) beneath the throat, a lateral line across the snout, very numerous branchiostegal rays supporting the gill cover, and numerous but undifferentiated teeth on both jaws and palate. Their scales are large and cycloid. Only three families are represented by living fishes. They all have a transparent 'leptocephalus' larva at an early stage of development.

Tarpons (Megalopidae)

Superficially the tarpons resemble giant herrings, with which they were at one time grouped, but they have a complete lateral line system and a rounded belly. The two species are both found in tropical seas. The better-known species is the tarpon (*Tarpon atlanticus*), a famous game fish of Florida and West Indian seas. It ranges from Nova Scotia to Brazil, and on the tropical African coast, and although often taken offshore is most usually captured in coastal waters, even in brackish estuaries or freshwater. The tarpon breeds well out to sea and is incredibly prolific, each female producing twelve million or more eggs. The larvae are transparent, long and narrow, and float at the surface of the sea, although the young fish are found in inshore waters often in swamps and inland pools. These are frequently poorly oxygenated, but the young tarpon gulps air at the surface, passing it from the gullet to the swimbladder which serves as a lung. Few other fishes can survive in such conditions and the tarpon benefits by the lack of predators and competitors.

The Atlantic tarpon grows to eight feet in length and a

weight of 350 lbs., considerably larger than the ox-eye tarpon (*Megalops cyprinoides*), which ranges from the East African coast to the central Pacific. Its biology and habits are similar to those of the tarpon, and it is popular with anglers. In Java the larvae are collected and reared in enclosed freshwater pools, but the flesh is relatively poor.

Ten-pounder and bonefish (Elopidae and Albulidae)

The ten-pounder (*Elops saurus*) is a pelagic fish found in all tropical seas and highly regarded by anglers for the way it leaps and fights. Adults are common inshore even in the surf, and the young live in estuaries and coastal swamps; spawning, however, takes place far out to sea and the larvae drift inshore. It feeds on fishes and crustaceans and grows to a length of four feet.

Albula vulpes, the bonefish, is also world-wide in tropical seas, and is—like its relatives—an angler's species although growing only to a length of three feet. Its snout projects in a distinctive way and the mouth is ventral; when feeding, shoals of bonefish work their way over the bottom in a distinctive head-down attitude, their tails breaking the surface. It eats bottom-living invertebrates.

The tarpon (*Tarpon atlanticus*), a large primitive bony fish. It lives in the tropical Atlantic, usually well offshore but the young fish inhabit salt-marshes, swamps and estuaries. Fishing for the tarpon is a popular sport. *Phot. Karl Maslowski—Photo Researchers*

The herring and its relatives (Clupeiformes)

This order is probably the most important group to the fisheries of the world. Its members range through all tropical and temperate seas, and even penetrate into the cool near-polar seas; everywhere they are captured by man, many larger fishes, sea birds, and cetaceans. The order includes several well-known fishes, for example the herrings, pilchards, shads, and anchovies. All are rather elongated, usually with a compressed body, silvery scales, finely toothed jaws, and fins composed entirely of branched rays. The swimbladder has two anterior lobes which connect to the inner ear, and an opening near the anus, by means of which the pressure in the swimbladder can be decreased on rising in the water.

Herrings (Clupeidae)

This very large family includes the herrings, pilchards, and shads. The Atlantic herring (*Clupea harengus*), is well-known and widely distributed from Norway to Portugal and from Labrador southwards to Cape Hatteras. It lives in the open sea as well as in coastal waters, and will tolerate brackish conditions (as in the Baltic Sea). Throughout this range the herring is divided into a number of races, distinguished partly by the number of vertebrae they possess but also by biological differences such as growth rate, migrations, and time of spawning. Migrations take place throughout the year in different places but most are relatively local.

Some races of herring spawn in the spring—usually those on coastal banks; but others spawn in the autumn offshore, even as deep as 110 fathoms. The eggs are shed in quite discreet spawning grounds and form a carpet over the sea bed, often many layers deep. The larvae, however, are planktonic, while the young fish form large shoals at the surface close inshore. Throughout life the herring feeds on planktonic organisms, especially small crustaceans, although other invertebrates and small fishes are also eaten. In its turn it is eaten by many sea birds and other fishes, although man is its principal predator.

Herring-fisheries have existed now for many centuries and at times have played a major role in the rise to prosperity of European nations. The traditional fisheries were in the Baltic, in the North Sea, and along the Norwegian coast, and ships from many countries exploited the seemingly limitless stocks. In recent years, however, it has become clear that the stocks can be overexploited, for the North Sea fishery (which was the mainstay of many Scottish and English ports) has virtually ceased.

According to many authorities the herring found in the North Pacific is only superficially distinct from the Atlantic herring, and is known as *Clupea harengus pallasi*. This sub-species ranges from the coast of northern Baja California to Alaska, and on the Asian coast southwards to Japan and Korea. Like its Atlantic relative it is an important commercial fish especially to the fishing industries of Japan, Korea, and the U.S.S.R. Its biology is closely similar; spawning takes place mostly in shallow water, from tide level to six fathoms, the sticky eggs adhering to algae, rocks, pilings, or the gravel sea bed. The newly hatched larvae are about ¼ of an inch long and tend to stay close to the sea bed at first; their diet includes copepods, diatoms and invertebrate, eggs but enlarges after a month or so to include invertebrate larvae and young fish, although copepods remain the most important element as they are when the herring is adult. At all stages of its life the herring is the prey of other fishes, and sea birds, sea lions, and cetaceans feed heavily on the adults.

On the European coast young herring are frequently found in mixed shoals with the related sprat (*Sprattus sprattus*). This is a small fish growing at most to eight inches in length, which is distinguished from the herring by having a sharper, saw-toothed edge to its belly. Its dorsal fin is placed behind the level of the pelvic fins, and its back is a pale green colour. It is found from the Norwegian coast southwards to the Mediterranean and the Black Sea, but is typically an inshore shallow water species which forms enormous shoals. Unlike those of the herring, the eggs of the sprat are pelagic, floating at the surface, or just below, until they hatch. The young fish are particularly numerous close inshore and in estuaries. The sprat is important economically; the first year young are caught and marketed as whitebait (often mixed with young herring), and substantial quantities of adult fish are caught, most being used for fish meal.

The sardine or pilchard (*Sardina pilchardus*) is another important member of the family, distinguished by grooved gill-covers, large but fragile scales, and a rounded body. It attains the northward limit of its range in British waters, rarely being found north of the English Channel and the southern coast of Ireland. It is common in the Mediterranean, and off the Portuguese and French Atlantic coasts. It is a pelagic schooling fish found near the surface at night and down to a depth of about thirty fathoms by day. The young fish live inshore in their first year, but the adults usually live rather more offshore. The sardine is an important food fish, but because of its oily flesh it does not keep well in the fresh state, so it is usually canned or salted; the small fish in oil are well-known as canned sardines.

Elsewhere in the world pilchards are economically very important, two of the best known being the Californian pilchard (*Sardinops caeruleus*) and the South African pilchard (*S. ocellata*). Both these species have been heavily exploited for food, but the Californian pilchard (which ranges from Alaska to Baja California) was over-fished and catches declined dramatically in the 1940s. Other species of *Sardinops* are found off Australia and South America and are potentially important food resources.

The shads form a rather distinct group of herring-like fishes with deep bodies, the ventral edges of which have sharp scales. Most shads are migratory, living part of their lives in the sea but spawning in freshwater in rivers or estuaries. There are two European species, the allis shad (*Alosa alosa*) and the twaite shad (*A. fallax*). Both are now much reduced in numbers due to pollution of river mouths and dams, and weirs in rivers; the allis shad in particular is a relatively rare fish these days. The twaite shad still occurs in numbers in many rivers, especially the River Severn in springtime; it spawns at night on gravelly shallows with much splashing and leaping. It is often known as the May-fish because of its occurrence in rivers in this month.

Several species of shad occur on the Atlantic coast of North America, but most, like the European species, are now much rarer than they were. The American shad (*A. sapidissima*) is native to the Atlantic from the Newfoundland coast to Florida, but between 1871 and 1886 it was introduced to the Pacific coast, established itself and is now found between Alaska and Baja California. It is a large fish, growing to 30 inches in length, which enters river mouths in spring and migrates in huge schools 200–300 miles upstream to sand and pebble beds to spawn. In colonial days the vast shoals of shad made important fisheries but their numbers have declined since then, although it is by no means an uncommon fish. The alewife (*A. pseudoharengus*) is another well-known shad which ranges from Nova Scotia to North Carolina, and which the early colonists also found incredibly abundant. Like other shads it feeds primarily on plankton, principally on copepods and other crustaceans, but it also eats young fishes; it spawns in quiet backwaters and in slow-flowing stretches of rivers, and the adults move downstream after spawning. The eggs stick to stones, brushwood, or any other solid matter, and hatch in about a week; the young alewife begins to follow the adults downstream at about a month, reaching the sea at a length of about four inches.

Anchovies (Engraulidae)

The anchovies are related to the herrings but differ from them most obviously in the shape of the head, the snout being prominent and the jaws very large. This gives the mouth great flexibility and the gape is enormous. Anchovies are distributed around the world in tropical and warm temperate seas; the greatest number of species is found in the Indo-Pacific. They are mostly small fish, forming huge shoals and living at the surface of the sea where they feed on plankton. They are preyed upon by many of the larger, valuable fishes, such as tunas, and are directly exploited by man in important fisheries around the world.

The European anchovy (*Engraulis encrasicolus*) grows to a length of about eight inches and is distributed from northern Scotland (where it is uncommon) to North Africa, and in the

After the metamorphosis of the leptocephalus eel larva the young elver is quite transparent. Later they become normally pigmented. They are extremely abundant in river mouths in springtime. *Phot. Aldo Margiocco*

Mediterranean and Black Seas. In the south of this range it is heavily fished, often with shore seine nets and purse seines to which the fish are attracted by lights. They are not usually marketed fresh, but are normally packed in barrels with salt or canned with oil to form a highly flavoured delicacy.

A small anchovy, the anchovetta (*E. ringens*) which grows to a length of seven inches, has made Peru the world's leading fishing nation with catches of ten million tons a year. The waters off Peru are enriched by upwelling of nitrate and phosphate-rich water from the deep sea, which leads to heavy growth of plant plankton. Millions of anchovies congregate to feed on the plankton. The immense deposits of guano on the coastline here are a result of the great flocks of sea birds

which have been drawn here to feed on the anchovies over past centuries, but within recent years the fish have been directly exploited by Peruvian fishermen. In 1972 and 1973, however, the El Niño current brought warm water down from equatorial regions and no upwelling took place. As a consequence plant plankton was sparse and the anchovetta failed to appear. The total catch dropped by more than half, with serious consequences to the fishery and repercussions around the world, for the anchovies are converted into fish meal for animal feed.

Wolf herring (Chirocentridae)

This family contains a single species, the wolf herring (*Chirocentrus dorab*), an Indo-Pacific fish of wide distribution. It is very like a huge herring, growing to a length of twelve feet, but has large fang-like teeth in both jaws. Its food consists of fishes and squids, and it lives in the surface waters of coastal areas. Despite its size it is not valued as a food fish; its flesh is full of small bones. It leaps and struggles actively when captured, and its teeth are capable of inflicting severe wounds.

Spiny eels and halosaurs (Notacanthiformes)

This order is composed of deep sea fishes, all rather eel-like in form. There are two major families, the spiny eels (Notacanthidae), and the halosaurs (Halosauridae). The spiny eels have a series of sharp spines along the back and in the anterior part of the anal fin; their jaws are ventral with small teeth, and they are believed to browse on bottom-living animals in a head-down attitude. One North Atlantic species, *Notacanthus chemnitzii*, which grows to 48 inches in length, appears to feed entirely on large pink actinarian sea anemones. The halosaurs are more slender, with a single dorsal fin and no spines. They are found in all deep oceans, living close to the bottom. Although little is known of their biology, halosaurs are known to go through a larval stage remarkably similar to the leptocephalus larva of the eels.

Eels (Anguilliformes)

Most of the eels are marine fishes, and those which live in freshwater (members of the family Anguillidae) breed in the sea. Eels are all elongate fishes, lacking pelvic fins and in many cases pectoral fins as well. The vertical fins are reduced in size and are confluent with the tail fin. The opercular bones are reduced in size and the gill openings are small; eels can respire by pumping water in and out of the gill opening, and do not need to 'gulp' with their mouths. Eels swim by a sinuous motion of the body: a wave motion passes down the body and the dorsal and anal fins impart the forward thrust. The lifestyle of eels is usually sedentary. Most species haunt crevices in rocks and coral or live in wrecks, and some burrow in sand or mud; but they all perform vast migrations half-way across the ocean basins to spawn. Young eels are thin, transparent, elongate larvae, known as Leptocephalus larvae, pelagic for their early stages but assuming a bottom-living mode of life on metamorphosis.

Several hundred species of eels are recognized, divided into twenty or so families.

Freshwater eels (Anguillidae)

This is probably the best-known family of eels for they are found in freshwaters of most temperate and subtropical areas of the world, and at some time in their lives in all seas except the eastern Pacific and polar seas. All breed in the sea, the larvae migrating towards land and entering river mouths as elvers. Here they commence a period of feeding and growth lasting for several years before the onset of sexual maturity causes the adult eel to migrate to the sea. Fishes with this lifestyle are known as catadromous species.

The European eel (*Anguilla anguilla*) is widely distributed on the coastline of Europe from the Arctic Circle to the Black Sea, and along the North African coast. It is a large fish, attaining a length of five feet, although only females attain this size (males rarely reach thirty inches). As adolescent fish eels live in lakes, ponds and rivers, often tolerating rather poor conditions; substantial numbers live in river mouths and in coastal waters. In freshwater they feed mainly on crustaceans, insect larvae, and young fish; large specimens are reputed to eat ducklings and water voles. On attaining

Leptocephalus larva of moray at an early stage of metamorphosis. *Phot. Aldo Margiocco*

The moray (*Muraena helena*) is a typical eel; it has no paired fins; its laterally compressed snake-like body has on its back a well-developed fin. The moray swims with an undulating motion, but usually lies hidden in rock crevices. An aggressive carnivorous fish, it can inflict a cruel bite if molested. *Phot. Fronval*

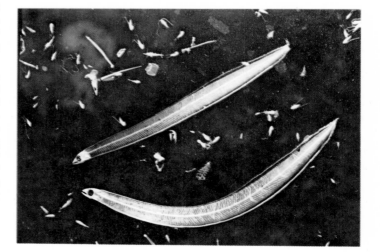

sexual maturity the eels move downstream, enter the sea, and virtually disappear, for no breeding eel has even been captured. However, the smallest larval stages are found in the vicinity of the Sargasso Sea and it is assumed that it is in this region that eel spawns. As leptocephalus larvae they drift eastwards with ocean currents until after a period of nearly three years they reach the European shore line. The closely related American eel (*A. rostrata*) spawns in an area just to the west of the European eels' spawning ground. The larvae of this species, however, complete their migration to the coast in just one year. Although the American eel is edible it is not much exploited as a food-fish. The European species in contrast forms valuable fisheries in many parts of its range. Other members of the genus *Anguilla* are found in Japan and eastern Asia, southern Africa, New Zealand and South Australia; all spawn in the ocean and it is believed make extensive migrations to reach their spawning grounds.

Moray eels (Muraenidae)

The morays are the most widely distributed and most numerous of eel families. They are found in tropical and warm temperate regions of all the oceans. They lack both

Above, the conger (*Conger conger*) a common marine eel on European coasts. It grows to a large size, and may weigh 100 pounds. It migrates to distinct breeding areas, one in the Antarctic, another in the Mediterranean. The larva is of typical leptocephalus type. Notice on this young specimen the lateral line pores. *Phot. J. Six*

pectoral and pelvic fins, have the gill openings greatly reduced in size, and most have numerous sharply pointed teeth in the jaws. Most moray species grow to a length of about three feet, but some attain ten feet in length and can be aggressive and dangerous to approach.

One species is found in European seas, the moray (*Muraena helena*), which attains a length of 3½ feet, and lives in the Mediterranean and eastern Atlantic northwards to Biscay. Its habit of lurking in crevices in rocky areas with only its head protruding is typical of the family. Its food consists mostly of fishes but it eats crustaceans and squids occasionally; it is most active at night-time.

Conger eels (Congridae)

Congers are rather heavy-bodied eels with pectoral fins, and the upper jaw longer than the lower; they all lack scales. The family is widely distributed in the temperate and tropical Atlantic, Pacific, and Indian oceans, mostly in shallow inshore water; but a few species occur in the deep sea.

The European conger (*Conger conger*) is large, attaining seven feet in length and a weight of 150 lbs. It lives in inshore waters (small ones even live in tide pools) down to a depth of 50 fathoms, but most of the larger fish occur in wrecks or on rocky reefs. It feeds on a wide range of fishes, but also eats crabs and lobsters, as well as cephalopods like the cuttlefish and octopus. A similar species (*C. oceanica*), is found on the Atlantic coast of North America from Cape Cod southwards. It is slightly smaller, growing to only five feet, but its biology and general appearance are similar to the European species. Both these congers spawn in deep water off the continental shelf in relatively localized spawning areas. The larvae are typical eel leptocephalus larvae which drift shorewards close to the surface.

The garden eels of the genus *Heteroconger* are rather specialized in that their fins are reduced. They form burrows in sandy sea beds from which the first third of the eel protrudes, swaying in the current and feeding on small planktonic animals swept past by the current. They live in colonies, each eel in a separate burrow down which it retreats at the first sign of danger.

Deep sea eels (Simenchelyidae, Nemichthyidae, Cyemidae)

The slime eel (*Simenchelys parasiticus*) has possibly the most specialized lifestyle of all eels as it is largely parasitic in habit. Its short snout and flattened teeth enable it to burrow into the body tissues of larger fishes while its skin secretes copious quantities of mucus (all features of the hagfishes which have similar habits). The slime eel has been captured in deep water (380 to 760 fathoms) off the east coast of North America (Long Island to Newfoundland), off the Azores, southern Africa, and Japan.

Snipe eels belonging to the family Nemichthyidae are mid-water open ocean eels found in all but the polar seas. The snipe eel *Nemichthys scolopax*, is found in mid-water in the north Atlantic in depths of 200 to 1000 fathoms. It is an elongate fish, growing to 48 inches, but at this length only about one inch deep in the body. Its jaws are long and beak-like, and it is dark chocolate brown overall. Its biology is

Right, the arawana (*Osteoglossum bicirrhosum*) is found in the freshwaters of tropical South America, living in shallow, weedy lakes and backwaters usually at the surface. Its closest relative is the gigantic *Arapaima,* found in the same area. *Phot. J. Six*

virtually unknown, although the very elongate leptocephalus larvae are moderately common.

The bob-tailed snipe eel (*Cyema atrum*) is the single representative of the family. World-wide in its distribution in the deep tropical oceans, *Cyema* is a bathypelagic eel living in depths of 550 to 2850 fathoms. The adult is jet black in colour. Its general appearance is like a dart: the jaws are long and beak-like, the eyes are minute, and the body is elongated and flattened with well developed dorsal and anal fins which end abruptly as if the tail end had been chopped off. It grows to a length of about six inches. The semi-transparent, deep-bodied, leaf-like leptocephalus larvae have been captured in shallower water than the adult; metamorphosis takes place at a length of about four inches.

Gulper eels (Saccopharyngiformes)

The gulper eels are a highly distinctive group of fishes with huge jaws, a minute head, and a very elongated body and tail. The general impression is of an eel with an immense mouth. Their systematic placement has for long been a matter of doubt: some features, notably their general shape, their cranial osteology and the fact that they pass through a leptocephalus larval stage suggest that they are related to the eels, but their anatomy is so different from the eels that they have often been placed in a separate order. They are represented by three families, the Saccopharyngidae, the Eurypharyngidae, and the enigmatic Monognathidae.

The whip-tail gulper eel (*Saccopharynx ampullaceus*) is one of the largest species known, growing to 54 inches in length. It has been found only in the north Atlantic, in isolated areas near Portugal, Madeira, the Azores, and off Greenland. Most of the known captures have been made near the surface but it may live at depths of about 1000 fathoms. Other species occur in deep water in the Indian and Pacific Oceans.

The gulper eel *Eurypharynx pelecanoides* is the only species contained in the family Eurypharyngidae. It occurs in the tropical Indian, Pacific, and Atlantic oceans, although the greatest number captured have been taken in the Atlantic. It is a bathypelagic species, found mostly in depths of between 770 and 1,530 fathoms. This gulper eel (which grows to 24 inches in length) is the most extremely developed of the whole order: its jaws are enormous and the eyes are set high up and right forward on the snout; it also has a luminous tip to its tail. Although details of its biology are not well known, a number of small fish have been found in the stomach of captured specimens. Because its body structure is not that of an active predator it is deduced that the gulper eel swims with its vast jaws swung open, fishing constantly for food items in the sunless sea. It has also been suggested that the luminous tail tip might act as a lure to smaller fishes.

Bony tongues (Osteoglossoidei)

These are tropical freshwater fishes represented by relatively few but distinctive species in South America, Africa and Asia. In general they are rather elongated large fishes, with large scales and bony heads. All have well developed cellular swimbladders which are used to breathe air.

Bony tongues (Osteoglossidae)

This is a small family containing only four genera. The tropical freshwaters of South America contain two of these:

one, the arapaima or pirarucu (*Arapaima gigas*), at fifteen feet in length, is often claimed to be the largest living freshwater fish. It is widely distributed in the Amazon basin northwards to Guyana. It gulps air at the surface of the water with a considerable noise. The arapaima feeds on other fishes, and is itself a valuable food-fish to the natives of South America. It breeds in April to May in a hollow in a sandy bottom in which the eggs are laid and protected by the adult fish. The other South American species is the arawana (*Osteoglossum bicirrhosum*) which is found in the same area but grows to only 39 inches in length. This is distinguished by the long chin barbels, rather deep compressed body and long anal fin. It lives in large schools, swimming at the surface in shallow reeded backwaters and lakes, often just breaking the surface with its snout.

The Asiatic members of the family belong to the genus *Scleropages*. The barramundi (*S. leichardti*) is found in the Fitzroy River of eastern Australia, while the closely related northern barramundi (*S. jardini*) occurs in northern Australian rivers, New Guinea and Papua. *S. formosus* is found in Borneo, Sumatra, Malaysia, and Thailand. All have large scales, bony heads, strongly angled jaws, and a pair of barbels on the lower jaw. They are predatory, feeding on insects when

A featherback (*Notopterus chitala*), which is found in rivers and swamps of India, Malaya, Thailand, and Java. It gulps air at the surface, absorbing it in its complex swimbladder. *Phot. Thys van den Audenaerde*

young, and crustaceans, fishes, and amphibians as they grow larger. The eggs and young larvae are carried by the female in a pouch in the mouth. The barramundis grow to a length of about 35 inches.

The African representative of the family is *Heterotis niloticus*, a widespread fish in the Upper Nile, and the rivers of Chad, Niger, Senegal and Gambia. It grows to a length of thirty inches, and has an interesting modification to the fourth gill arch which is of spiral form and produces copious mucus in which microscopic food organisms are trapped. It excavates a nest, some four feet in diameter with high walls of mud and vegetation, within which the eggs are laid and guarded by the parents. Newly hatched larvae have external gills, but adults regularly breathe air at the surface.

Butterfly fish (Pantodontidae)

The African butterfly fish (*Pantodon buchholzi*) is the only member of this family. It attains a maximum length of four inches, and is found in the still, often stagnant backwaters of rivers, ditches, and ponds in the Niger and Congo basins. It

Mormyrids are exclusively African freshwater fishes; many of them have distinctive trunk-like snouts. They are equipped with an electric organ on the sides of the body which enables them to detect prey, predators or obstacles in the water. The mormyrid illustrated is *Gnathonemus brevicaudatus*: members of the genus *Gnathonemus* have a long, finger-like and sensitive chin-barbel. *Phot. Brichart*

Another mormyrid: *Campylomormyrus cassaicus* a young specimen showing the downward pointing tube-shaped snout, whose length increases with age but is characteristic of the species. *Phot. Brichart*

lies motionless just below the surface of the water, snapping at any insect which alights on, or falls into, the water, and can leap out of the water and glide for a short distance in pursuit of prey. Its very long pelvic and tail fin rays allow it to stand on the bottom in shallow water. Its eggs and young larvae float at the surface.

Mormyrids (Mormyriformes)

The mormyrids inhabit the freshwaters of tropical Africa and include two families of which the Mormyridae have numerous genera and species. They vary in size from a few inches to more than six feet in length. Most of them share a number of features: the body is elongated and compressed, the tail fin is rather small, and the dorsal and anal fins are far back and opposite one another. Many species have a tube-like snout, with the tip of the lower jaw bearing a thick barbel. The swimbladder is complex and in contact with the inner ear, which suggests that it functions well as a sound receiver. Mormyrids also have a muscular electric organ in the tail, which produces continuous pulses of electricity serving as a warning sense to locate predators and obstructions in the water, and for keeping in contact with other members of the shoal.

Elephant-snout fishes (Mormyridae)

The numerous genera comprising this family are differentiated by their teeth, the development of the snout, and the position of the mouth and nostrils. Some, like *Stomatorhinus*, are confined to a single river basin (in this case the Congo), but others such as *Mormyrus* are found in several river systems. The development of the snout varies greatly. One species, *Gnathonemus ibis*, a fish of twenty inches length found in the Congo system, has an extremely long snout almost as long as its body. However, members of the genus *Petrocephalus* have a smoothly rounded forehead and underslung mouth.

One of the larger species, the Cornish-jack, *Mormyrops deliciosus*, grows to sixty inches and a weight of forty pounds; it lives in the Zambezi system and the Congo basin. Its snout is scarcely elongated and it feeds on small fishes, insects and crustaceans. It is a valuable food-fish locally. The elephant-snout fish *Mormyrus kannume* lives in the River Nile and many of the African Great Lakes including Lake Victoria, where it haunts the weeded shallows feeding on bottom-living insects—especially midge larvae. Its electrical abilities are well developed and it produces a constant stream of impulses most numerous when the fish is active, but continuing at low level when at rest. By surrounding itself with an electrical field it can detect predators and obstacles in its near vicinity in the rather murky water it inhabits. Like other mormyrids its hind brain is well developed, associated with the co-ordination of sensory impulses of this kind. Most mormyrids build nests in submerged vegetation in shallow water, in which the eggs and young are guarded.

Gymnarchidae

The sole representative of this family is *Gymnarchus niloticus*, a species of wide distribution in tropical Africa from the Upper Nile through western Africa (but not in the Congo basin). Its body form is long and eel-like: the pelvic, tail, and anal fins are absent and the pectorals are small, but the dorsal fin is long, originating just behind the head and running far along the back. *Gymnarchus* swims by undulating its long dorsal fin, moving equally well backwards or forwards. It lives mostly in swamps, ox-bow lakes, and in slow-flowing rivers, all

Salmon are migratory. Ascending the river from the sea, the adult fish have to reach the headwaters to find suitable spawning beds. Natural torrents are rarely an obstacle, but some high weirs and artificial dams do prevent their migration. *Phot. Lane Thompson-Rapho*

turbid water conditions in which well-developed electrical detection powers are required. Adults feed mostly on fishes, the young on insects and young fish. *Gymnarchus* breeds by building a spherical nest of grass about forty inches in diameter in the flooded swamp, in the centre of which the eggs are laid and guarded by the parents. The newly hatched young have external gills and an enormous yolk sac. *Gymnarchus* is a highly prized food fish, its rich oily flesh often being reserved for ceremonial occasions in western Africa.

Feather-backs and moon-eyes (Notopteroidei)

This suborder contains two divergent groups of fishes which are grouped together on account of structural similarities.

The feather-backs (family Notopteridae) are freshwater fishes found in tropical Africa and southeast Asia. They have rather elongated compressed bodies with an extremely long anal fin, originating on the belly and running the whole length of the fish; most species have a small feather-like dorsal fin. They swim by gentle wave motion along the anal fin, moving backwards or forwards with equal ease. By day they lie quietly near the surface under vegetation, but they become active at night. Several species are known to breathe air by means of the swimbladder, amongst them the Asiatic *Notopterus chitala* and the African *Papyrocranus afer*.

The moon-eyes (family Hiodontidae) are found in North American freshwaters. They are superficially herring-like, with a silvery, rather deep body, a blunt snout, and a long anal fin. The moon-eye (*Hiodon tergisus*) grows to about seventeen inches in length and is usually found in clear lakes and streams. The gold-eye (*H. alosoides*) is slightly larger and found in the Great Plains and the Mississippi basin from Lousiana northwards in turbid waters, especially fast flowing rivers. It is a well-flavoured food fish and has some reputation as a sporting species.

Salmon and their relatives (Salmoniformes)

This large order of fishes is found in both freshwater, mainly in the northern hemisphere, and in the sea world-wide. Although the best known are the salmonids, the salmons and their close relatives the trouts and charrs, there are very

307

many, often small and little-known deep sea relatives. Many have a rayless adipose dorsal fin, the pelvic fins are placed on the belly and even just below the pectoral fins, and the tail fin has a strengthened skeleton by fusion with the hypural bones.

The order is divided into a number of suborders, some of which contain numerous families.

Salmon and trout (Salmonidae)

This important family of well-known sporting and food fishes is distributed in the temperate and polar regions of the northern hemisphere. Many are migratory species which spawn in freshwater but spend a major part of their lives in the sea; others are purely freshwater. Many of the sporting species, such as the trout and rainbow trout, have been widely redistributed by man, and they are now found in Africa, South America, New Zealand, Australia, and elsewhere.

The Atlantic salmon (*Salmo salar*) is confined to the northern parts of that ocean, in the west from Labrador and Greenland southwards to the Connecticut River, and on the European coast from the Russian Arctic coast to northern Spain. Its range has shrunk in the past centuries, and although it is still far from rare it is much less abundant than it was at one time. Pollution of the lower courses of rivers, weirs and obstructions, destruction of spawning beds and overfishing have all affected the salmon adversely.

The salmon is an anadromous migrant, returning from the sea to the river of its birth to spawn in redds in the headwaters of the river. The adults ascend some large rivers as far as 200 to 300 miles to spawn in mid-winter. The female excavates a redd in the gravel bed of the river in which the large eggs are laid and fertilized by the male. They become covered by gravel moved in later redd building and stay buried until the spring, when they hatch. Even then the alevins, each of which carries the remnant of the yolk in a bulging yolk sac, remain in the crevices of the gravel and only emerge once the yolk has been used up, in about six weeks. Once it becomes active the fry feeds on small crustaceans and their larvae and quickly grows. At a later stage of its infancy it is known as a parr, and the sides are boldly patterned with rounded black blotches—the parr marks. Sometime between the second and sixth year of life the parr marks are overlaid with dense silvery pigment and the young salmon, now known as a smolt, begins to move towards the sea, usually during April to June. In the estuary the smolt acclimatizes itself to the sea water, feeding heavily on marine crustaceans and fishes, and then moves out along the coast to the open sea. Many salmon leaving the European coast migrate across the Atlantic to feeding areas off west Greenland. Others move into the Norwegian Sea. They return to the natal stream after from one to four years to spawn; although most salmon die after spawning, a small proportion return to spawn a second and third time. The sea-going phase is essentially a feeding and fattening period—the mature fish do not feed in the river and following spawning are emaciated and exhausted. Known as kelts, these fish often fall prey to fungal and bacterial disease as well as to predators.

In the North Pacific there are six species of salmon belonging to the genus *Oncorhinchus*, which differ from the Atlantic salmon mainly in having more fin rays in the anal fin. They are exceedingly important commercial fish to the countries bordering the North Pacific. Basically their biology is the same as that of *Salmo salar*, but each species breeds in different parts of the river, some close to the mouth, others 1000 miles upstream. The chinook or king salmon (*O. tshawytscha*), a large fish which may weigh up to 100 pounds, and reaches a length of five feet, has been captured over 1250 miles up the Yukon River. It is a valuable food fish throughout its range,

which extends from California to Alaska, and Japan to the Siberian coast. The most valuable of the Pacific salmon is the sockeye (*O. nerka*) which is found in the same area. This species is also found as a non-migratory species in lakes, when it is known as the kokanee, a fish which rarely grows longer than sixteen inches. The humpback salmon or pink salmon (*O. gorbuscha*) rarely migrates upstream further than 70 to 80 miles to spawn. It is of considerable value as a food fish especially on the Asian coast, although it is modest in weight (average about six pounds), but because of its food value it was introduced to the North Atlantic in the Newfoundland area and in the White Sea, an introduction which appears to have been successful as specimens have been caught off Norway, Iceland, and the British Isles.

The trout (*Salmo trutta*) is a European fish, typically an inhabitant of clean, cold, well-oxygenated water. Its natural range extends from Iceland and northern Norway, to the British Isles and Spain, but it also occurs as far east as the Black Sea as a freshwater fish. It is a very variable species, which exists in three forms: the brown trout (*S. trutta fario*) the small, densely spotted inhabitant of rivers and small lakes; the lake trout (*S.t. lacustris*), a larger, clear blue-silvery fish with small black spots, found in the larger lakes of Europe; and the sea trout (*S.t. trutta*) a migratory silvery fish which spends a feeding period in the sea. (The use of sub-specific names for these forms is a matter of convenience, not a recognition of genetical differences.) The sea trout, which grows to an average weight of about ten to twelve pounds, is found only in the northern parts of the range of the species.

On account of its popularity as a game fish the trout has been introduced to many parts of the world including North America. It is not so well suited to intensive culture as the rainbow trout (*S. gairdneri*) which is native to the Pacific slopes of North America from northwest Mexico to Alaska, but is now almost world-wide in range due to introduction and cultivation. It is more tolerant of warm water than the brown trout and can be reared in quite small ponds. In recent years its intensive culture in fish farms has attained the status of an industry in Europe, as it has been in North America for a long time. In some farms the fish are kept in small ponds at high densities and fed on concentrated dried food so that they attain a marketable size in a year or eight months. In others the object is to raise larger fish which will be released into lakes and rivers for anglers to catch. Although rainbow trout have been introduced to British rivers regularly for nearly fifty years, very few naturally reproducing populations have been established.

Another North American salmonid which has been introduced to Europe as a game fish is the brook charr, often known as the brook trout (*Salvelinus fontinalis*). Its original distribution was from Hudson Bay and Labrador, southwards to the upper Mississippi system, but it is found now in many parts of North America outside this range. It is distinguished by the smallness of its scales, the light leading edges to its ventral fins, and the clear but delicate dark mottling on the sides. A native European relative, the Arctic charr (*Salvelinus alpinus*), is a migratory, anadromous fish along the Norwegian and Icelandic coasts, entering rivers to spawn; to the south it is found in many lakes, particularly those in mountainous areas. The populations in these lakes do not migrate to the sea but are the descendants of charr which migrated during the immediately post-glacial period when the land was depressed by the weight of ice and these lakes and their rivers were accessible from the sea. Most of these lacustrine charr populations have been isolated for from 10,000 to 15,000 years. The charr also occurs in the arctic regions of North America.

The whitefishes of the genus *Coregonus* are similarly

regarded as early post-glacial invaders of the rivers and certain lakes of northern Europe and America. Most are silvery fish, with small jaws which are equipped with minute teeth. In Arctic regions they are common as migratory fishes entering rivers to spawn, and although one species, the houting (*Coregonus oxyrhinchus*), is found in the Baltic and estuarine areas of the North Sea, most of the European whitefishes are found in lakes. Northern and western regions of the British Isles have several populations, notably the gwyniad of Llyn Tegid (Lake Bala) in north Wales, the vendaces and schellies of the English Lake District, the powan of Loch Lomond and other Scottish lochs, and the pollans of Ireland. These all stem from two parent species which were found in the ice lakes which covered most of northern Europe after the last ice age.

The graylings are similarly distributed. One species, the Arctic grayling (*Thymallus arcticus*), occurs from the central regions of the U.S.S.R. to western North America, while the

the smelt (*Osmerus eperlanus*), which is found in the sea, in estuaries, and as a freshwater fish landlocked in lakes in both Europe and North America. The capelin is extremely abundant and forms an important source of food for many other species of fish, especially the cod, as well as sea birds, whales, and dolphins.

Some systematists regard the whitefishes, graylings, capelin and smelt as representatives of three separate families, the Coregonidae, Thymallidae, and Osmeridae.

Argentines (Argentinidae)

This is a group of marine salmon relatives, mostly rather small and found world-wide in tropical and temperate oceans, often close to the bottom in depths of up to 500 fathoms, although some species live in mid-water. They all have large eyes, large shiny scales, and small mouths, and most have an adipose fin. All the known species are pale yellowish green above, silvery on the sides. One of the most

The rainbow trout (*Salmo gairdneri*) is native to the Pacific slopes of North America but has proved so suitable for artificial rearing that it is now distributed almost world-wide in temperate areas. *Phot. J. Six*

grayling (*T. thymallus*), ranges across Europe to the Volga river. Both are recognizable by their high and many-rayed dorsal fins and small adipose dorsal fins. They are confined to cool, clear, and unpolluted rivers in which they feed on insects and insect larvae, crustaceans and molluscs. Both species breed in springtime.

The smallest of the salmonid fishes are the marine capelin (*Mallotus villosus*), an inhabitant of the northern North Pacific and North Atlantic from the Faroes northwards, and

familiar is the Atlantic argentine (*Argentina silus*), which occurs on the European coast from Norway to Ireland, and off North America from the Gulf of Maine to Labrador, on the edge of the continental shelf from 50 to 500 fathoms deep.

Bristle-mouths and hatchet fishes (Gonostomiatidae and Sternoptychidae)

These two families contain many of the abundant bathy-pelagic fishes which live in the dark or twilight zones of the deep sea. Many of them have arrays of luminous organs on the head and undersurface, although their background colour may be black, brown, or wholly silver. The luminous organs, or photophores, help to ensure that the shoal keeps together, help to baffle predators, and also make the individual fish more difficult to distinguish in silhouette against the light from the surface. Most photophores have a glandular structure, the light being produced by the action of the enzyme luciferase on an organic compound called luciferin.

Bristle-mouths are widely distributed in the deep sea but are probably least common in polar seas. Most are small (rarely more than 3 inches in length) slender and fragile. Their mouths are large with long jaws equipped with many thin, sharp teeth. Some species are extremely abundant, especially those of the genus *Cyclothone* which are of great

Lantern fishes are representative of the fauna in the twilight zone between the well lighted surface of the sea and its completely dark deep layers. These fish have rows of light organs which can be seen in the living animals for *Myctophum* approaches the surface during the night. *Phot. Aldo Margiocco*

importance in the economy of the deep sea as predators on smaller animals and prey for larger fishes. One of the few bristle-mouths to be found regularly in shallow water on open ocean coasts is the pearlsides (*Maurolicus muelleri*), a 2½ inch long fish with gleaming pale blue light organs on the underside. World-wide in its distribution, it is often caught by being attracted to the surface by lights, and is occasionally found stranded on the shore.

The marine hatchet fishes are very distinctive in shape; the head and body are compressed, deep, and very thin with a sharp edge to the belly and a thin, narrow tail (forming the handle to the body's hatchet blade). Numerous species exist,

and the group is world-wide in the open sea from the surface to a depth of about 1000 fathoms. Like the bristle-mouths and most of the animals dwelling in the twilight zone, they migrate vertically, rising towards the surface at night. Hatchet fishes are all intensely silvery in colour on the flanks and belly, only the back being pigmented; they have rows of elongated photophores on the belly. Their eyes are large, and in the genus *Argyropelecus* are turned upward.

Dragon fishes (Stomiatidae and Melanostomiatidae)

These two families of elongate deep-sea fishes have dorsal and anal fins placed far down the body close to the tail and small pectoral fins close behind the head. They have large jaws, many large teeth, and a long chin barbel. They are always taken in the open ocean, often in depths of around 500 fathoms, but the maximum depth appears to be 1000 fathoms. They are active, fast-swimming fishes with rows of luminous organs on the underside and often a large photophore beside the eye. The tip of the barbel is also luminous and is believed to be used as a lure to attract prey. In some dragon fishes the barbel is long and whip-like, in others it is shorter, with a complex tip. The Stomiatidae have scales covering their whole bodies, but the Melanostomiatidae are scaleless, and are usually more slender and toothy.

Viper fishes (Chauliodontidae)

Viper fishes form small family of deep-sea fish found in all the major oceans and also large seas such as the Mediterranean. Only six species are known, all with huge fangs in their jaws, elongate bodies, and regular hexagonal patterned scales. Their internal anatomy is adapted to put their large teeth to good use; the first neck vertebra is very long and acts as a shock absorber against the impact and struggle of the prey, and the head is very mobile and swings upwards while the lower jaw drops open to form a wide gape. Although viperfishes rarely exceed twelve inches in length, they can swallow comparatively large prey.

Smooth-heads (Alepocephalidae)

Deep-water fishes of world-wide distribution, the smooth-heads are mostly small, characterized by a small mouth and weak dentition. Most have large, rather fragile scales on the body, but the head is scaleless and covered with smooth, black skin. Some, such as *Zenodermichthys socialis*, a 6-inch long Atlantic species, are completely scaleless. A larger smooth-head, *Alepocephalus bairdi*, is common at 300 to 500 fathoms in the North Atlantic; it attains a length of 36 inches and feeds extensively on deep-sea jellyfishes. Despite its size and abundance locally it is not used for food; its flesh is soft and insipid.

Pikes (Esocidae)

The Esocidae form a small family containing a single genus and five closely similar species distributed in freshwater across the northern hemisphere. They are all elongated fishes, with a pointed head, large rather flattened snout, a wide mouth with numerous teeth, and dorsal and anal fins opposite one another and close to the tail. All five species are predators, living for preference in weeded conditions and lying in wait for prey, at which they hurl themselves.

The pike (*Esox lucius*), is widespread throughout Europe and eastwards through the U.S.S.R., Alaska, and northern North America (where it is known as the northern pike). It is typically a fish of shallow lakes, quiet rivers, and backwaters. It spawns in early spring, often in flooded areas such as watermeadows and on shallow weed beds; the female is larger than the males which accompany her while she sheds her eggs over the vegetation. The young fish (known as jacks in England) live in densely weeded marginal vegetation feeding on insect larvae and crustaceans, but as they grow they begin to eat small fish. Adult pike eat mostly fish, but large ones will take waterfowl and aquatic mammals on occasions. This species grows to a length of five feet and a weight of sixty pounds, but only the largest waters will hold fish in excess of thirty pounds.

The muskellunge (*E. masquinongy*), which is restricted to the American Great Lakes and rivers between the St Lawrence River and the Ohio, is much larger, growing to seventy pounds in weight, although at one time fish of 100 pounds were caught occasionally. Like the other pikes it is a highly-favoured angling fish, and edible, factors which have contributed to its comparative scarcity today. The Amur pike (*E. reicherti*), which lives in the Amur River in the eastern

Mud-minnows are best represented in North America where three species live, one of them the Alaska blackfish (*Dallia pectoralis*), which lives in rivers and marshes in Alaska and Siberia. Its ability to survive through the Arctic winter is remarkable; not only is the water temperature near zero for a long period, but the level of dissolved oxygen is very low. The mud-minnow *Umbra krameri* lives in the basins of the Danube and Dniester rivers, and is the only native species in Europe, although the eastern mud-minnow (*U. pygmaea*) has been introduced to the rivers of northern France and Belgium. Its natural range is along the east coast of the U.S. from Florida to New York. It grows to a length of three inches.

Galaxiids (Galaxiidae)

All of the salmoniform freshwater species are confined to the northern hemisphere with the exception of the galaxiids, a group of rather small fishes found in the southern tip of

The pike (*Esox lucius*) is the most carnivorous of all the European freshwater fishes. It lies in wait, hurling itself on prey (almost always other fish) passing within its reach. It reaches well over 30 pounds in weight. *Phot. J. Six*

U.S.S.R., is also a locally important food fish. The other pikes are the North American pickerels (*E. americanus* and *E. niger*), both relatively small species.

Mud-minnows (Umbridae)

Mud-minnows are the closest living relatives of the pikes, but in contrast they are small fishes, rarely growing to eight inches. They are rather stout-bodied fishes with dorsal and anal fins opposite and placed close to the tail fin; their bodies are covered with large scales. They live in the muddy bottoms of stagnant, shallow pools, swamps, and the back-waters of rivers, burrowing in the bottom in drought conditions and surviving by breathing air, gulping at the surface and filling the highly vascularized swimbladder.

Grasseichthys gabonensis, discovered recently in the rivers of Gabon, is the smallest African fish (about ¾ inch). *Phot. Dr. Gery, Gabon Biological Mission*

Africa, South America, southern Australia, Tasmania, and New Zealand. Most species are migratory, spawning in freshwater but spending part of their lives in the sea. Some are rather slender fishes, but the majority are thickset with a large head; all have dorsal and anal fins opposite and close to the tail. The largest member of the family is the New Zealand giant kokopu (*Galaxias argenteus*), which is reputed to grow to 28 inches, although now rarely found longer than 10 inches. Formerly a common fish, it has become much rarer throughout both islands, possibly as a consequence of the introduction of brown trout into many New Zealand rivers. Another New Zealand species, the brown mudfish (*Neochanna apoda*), which grows to 5 inches in length, lives in muddy creeks, ditches, and ponds. In drought conditions it can survive buried in the mud, breathing air by means of a lung-like swimbladder.

Lantern fishes and their allies (Myctophiformes)

This order is composed entirely of deep-sea fishes, some inhabiting the upper layers of the sea while others live on the sea floor. It includes a number of families which have been associated with the salmoniform fishes although recent classifications suggest that they are not so closely related.

Lantern fishes (Myctophidae)

Probably the best known and most abundant of all families of deep-sea fish, the lantern-fishes are distinguished by the many photophores clustered along the sides and belly and on the head. Their arrangement is constant from species to species. Most myctophids are small, usually less than six inches long, and live in the upper layers of the sea at 350 to 500 fathoms depth by day time. At night they come up near the surface. In one common species in the North Atlantic (*Myctophum punctatum*), males and females have different patterns of light organs, which suggests that their main function is for species and sexual recognition in the half-light in which they live.

Tripod fishes (Bathypteroidae)

Related to the lantern fishes, but differing greatly in lifestyle, the tripod fishes are bottom-living fishes found in all tropical and temperate oceans usually on soft, muddy bottoms in depths of 260 to 2000 fathoms. They have slender bodies, flattened heads and minute eyes, but their most characteristic features are the very long upper pectoral, pelvic and tail fin rays. Observations made in the Mediterranean from a bathyscaphe have shown that *Bathypterois* rests on the sea bed on the long fin rays, with its body well clear of the mud. A related family, the Ipnopidae, which are rather similar in general appearance but do not have long rays, are also blind. The tropical Atlantic species, *Ipnops murrayi*, which lives on the bottom in 800 to 1900 fathoms, has pale yellow lens-less eyes which can still detect light falling on the retina, but in other members of the family the eyes are completely concealed by thick skin.

The beaked salmon and its relatives (Gonorhynchiformes)

The beaked salmon or mousefish (*Gonorhynchus gonorhynchus*) of the family Gonorhynchidae, is widely distributed in the Indo-Pacific in temperate areas. It lives on sandy bottoms, burrowing into the sand and feeding on small invertebrates,

and grows to a length of about eighteen inches. It is an elongate fish with a rounded body completely covered with rough-edged scales. The snout is pointed, the mouth ventral and it has a barbel mid-way between snout tip and mouth.

Recent classifications of the bony fishes have suggested that the closest relatives of this species are found in the African freshwater fishes of the families Kneriidae and Phractolaemidae (and that they are all included within the superorder Ostariophysi). *Phractolaemus ansorgei* is a drab-coloured fish, about six inches in length, which lives in the muddy, heavily weeded waters of the lower basins of the Niger and Congo Rivers. It feeds on small bottom-living invertebrates which it sucks up from the mud with its tubular mouth. The swimbladder is well supplied with blood vessels and is connected to the oesophagus; it acts as an air-breathing lung.

Several species of the family Kneriidae are known in two genera *Kneria* and *Parakneria*, members of both of which live in the fresh, fast-flowing waters of African mountainous regions. They have rather slender, but ventrally flattened bodies, with broad pectoral fins which clearly serve as suction devices for clinging to stones in the swift current. In the species of the genus *Kneria* males have a cup-shaped disc on the gill covers by means of which they keep closely attached to the female during spawning. Most kneriids are small: the Rhodesian and Transvaal species *K. auriculata* grows to only three inches, but despite that occurs in hill streams at altitudes of nearly 4000 feet and is sometimes seen wriggling up the damp dam walls and over rock faces to attain a higher pool.

Related to these fishes are the minute, dainty, and quite transparent African fishes *Cromeria nilotica* and *Grasseichthys gabonensis*, a species living in great numbers in the Ogowe basin in West Africa, which reach sexual maturity when only $\frac{3}{4}$ of an inch in length.

The Ostariophysans (Ostariophysi-Otophysi)

Except for certain marine catfishes the ostariophysans are all freshwater fishes. They are overwhelmingly the dominant group of fishes in freshwater and are widely distributed in the Americas, Europe, Africa and Asia, but are represented in Australia by a few catfishes, and are absent throughout the oceanic islands of the world. They all possess the important feature of a swim-bladder connected to the inner ear by a chain of small bones (ossicles), the Weberian apparatus, which is derived from the four anterior vertebrae. This feature acts as a hydrophone and gives these fish very sensitive hearing.

The broad outlines of the classification of the ostariophysans is simple. There are two orders, the Cypriniformes and the Siluriformes. The first is composed of three divergent groups: the characins, the gymnotids, and the carp fishes. The second order contains numerous (around thirty) families of catfishes, the affinities of many of which have not been resolved. There are possibly six thousand species.

Characins and carp fishes (Cypriniformes)
Characoid fishes (Characoidea)

The characins are confined to the waters of tropical Africa and South and Central America. They have non-protractile mouths bounded by the maxillary and premaxillary bones in

A

The tetras are among the most beautiful aquarium fishes. They are natives of South America; *A, Paracheirodon innesi*, the neon tetra; *B*, the cardinal tetra (*Cheirodon axelrodi*); *C*, the Serpa tetra *Hyphessobrycon serpae. Phut. A. L. I. and J. M. Baufle*

B

C

The marbled hatchetfish (*Carnegiella strigata*) lives in small forest pools in tropical South American freshwaters. This small fish and some of its relatives are really flying fish; they are capable of flying for several metres over the surface of the water. The family (Gasteropelecidae) is very closely related to the Characidae. *Phot. Visage Albert*

The silver-dollar fishes (*Metynnis* sp.), resemble the piranhas, but are entirely herbivorous. They live in large shoals in the densely weeded backwaters of the Amazon basin. *Atlas-Photo—Lauros*

the upper jaw and well developed specialized teeth. They have fully scaled bodies and most species have two dorsal fins, the second being a small adipose, rayless fin. They vary in length from an inch or so to six feet and have occupied most of the ecological niches in the freshwaters of these areas. There are numerous species and the number of families represented is still uncertain.

True characins (Characidae)

Widely distributed in both tropical Africa and America the characins are a divergent family containing the beautiful aquarium tetras and some of the largest and most voracious predators known. They are all carnivorous.

The African tiger fishes of the genus *Hydrocyon* are well-known as predatory game fish, elongate-bodied, with huge fang-like interlocking teeth. The largest species, *H. goliath*, is known only from the Congo basin and Lake Tanganyika, and grows to a length of 6 feet and a weight of 125 pounds (although estimates of fishes of 150 pounds have been made). Another, rather smaller species, *H. vittatus*, is widely distributed in the Nile, Niger, Volta and Zambezi basins, as well as several of the larger lakes. Both species feed exclusively on other fishes.

Amongst the many beautifully coloured and lively aquarium fishes belonging to this family are both African and American species. Of the former, *Phenacogrammus interruptus* is a magnificent pearly-blue fish, about four inches in length with long thread-like fins. In the Congo, to which river it is indigenous, its long fins are rarely seen because another characin, *Belonophago*, lives by trimming the fins of other fish with its shear-like jaws. When young, members of the genus *Alestes* are often kept as aquarium fishes. One of the most widely distributed species, *Alestes nurse*, ranges from the Nile to the Niger, as well as Lakes Albert, Rudolf, and Chad. Its body is yellowish-brown with a brassy iridescence, and the tips of its fins are vermilion. It grows to about sixteen inches in length and is locally a valuable food fish. The tetras are all American species. One of the best known, and for long a favourite aquarium fish is the neon tetra (*Paracheirodon innesi*), which was discovered in 1936 in the River Amazon, near the Brazilian–Peruvian borders. Its brilliant, but delicate, coloration and lively behaviour make it a perfect aquarium fish. More recently discovered relatives, notably the cardinal tetra (*Cheirodon axelrodi*) are as colourful and popular. The cardinal tetra lives in forest pools in the Upper Rio Negro and the tributaries of the Orinoco. Practically the whole of the sides and belly are a deep cardinal red. The rivers and forest pools of tropical South America are inhabited by many species of the genera *Hyphessobrycon* and *Hemigrammus* which are imported to Europe and North America as aquarium fishes; amongst them are the red tetra (*Hyphessobrycon flammeus*), which lives in the area of Rio de Janeiro, and the jewel tetra (*H. callistius*), from the middle Amazon and northern Paraguay which is closely related to the Serpa tetra (*H. serpae*). Unfortunately, although many of these fishes are well known in the aquarium, their biology has not been studied in the wild and in some cases it is not known for certain whence they came.

Piranhas (Serrasalmidae)

The several members of the piranha family have a considerable reputation for ferocity. Many travellers' tales are told of horses and even men attacked by a school of piranhas while crossing a river and reduced to bones, saddle and harness within minutes. Piranhas are found in the Amazon and northeastern South America; all are deep-bodied with small scales, an adipose dorsal fin, and sharp cutting teeth in rather short strong jaws. The largest species is *Pygocentrus piraya*, which grows to 24 inches in length and is widely distributed in the lower Amazon basin. Like the other species it feeds mainly on fishes and lives in schools, which quickly gather when a large animal is attacked. Large specimens are formidable fish to handle, snapping their jaws and struggling to bite the whole time. This notwithstanding, small piranhas are often kept as pet fish in aquaria.

In many classifications the piranhas are included within the family Characidae.

Hatchet fishes (Gasteropelecidae)

This small family of tropical South American fishes, distributed from Panama to La Plata, are often kept as aquarium fish. They are extremely deep-bodied, the back being almost straight while the belly curves down deeply in a 'keel'. The pectoral fins are long and set high on the sides. These fish live close to the surface of the water feeding on surface-living insects, insect larvae, and crustaceans. When disturbed they break through the surface and fly for short distances, their pectoral fins moving with great rapidity and making a buzzing sound. Several species are known, probably the best-known, and certainly the earliest described, being *Gaster-

A piranha (*Serrasalmus* sp.). Piranhas are carnivorous characins, whose teeth have two or three sharp points. They live in shoals and will attack large-sized prey, sometimes even man. Piranhas live in streams and rivers of tropical South America. *Phot. J. Six*

opelecus sternicla, from Surinam and Guyana. It attains a length of only 2½ inches.

Other characoid families (Erythrinidae and Citharinidae)

Amongst the numerous other families of characoid fishes are the Erythrinidae, South American fishes with rather elongated closely scaled bodies, scaleless heads, and large mouths with conical curved teeth. *Erythrinus erythrinus* lives in the often temporary pools in river beds, feeding on insect larvae and young fishes. The water in which it lives is often poorly oxygenated and it can breathe air by means of its specialized swimbladder. The family Citharinidae is African, and is composed mainly of very deep-bodied fishes which grow to a length of up to thirty inches. Some, such as *Citharinus citharinus*, which ranges through the Nile, Niger, Senegal and other rivers, are important commercial fishes. Several members of the family eat vegetable matter, some specializing in eating weed, like *Distichodus* which has a deep body and very small teeth.

Cyprinoid fishes (Cyprinoidei)

This suborder of ostarophysan fishes have no teeth in the jaws, although they have powerful and elaborate teeth in the back of the throat (the pharyngeal teeth) borne on the last, modified gill arches. The mouth is protractile and often equipped with sensory barbels around the lips. They have a single dorsal fin which often bears an ossified ray in front; there is no adipose fin. The group is widely distributed in North America, Europe, Asia and Africa, inhabiting freshwater. There are probably about two thousand species which have filled most of the ecological niches available to the group.

The carp (*Cyprinus carpio*), is intensively cultured both as a food fish in its natural form, and as an ornamental species. The Koi or Hi-Goi carp from Japan are famous for the variety of their colours, ranging from canary yellow to bright red and including golden brown. They are the ornament of pools in Japanese gardens. *Phot. J. M. Baufle*

The carp family (Cyprinidae)

Carp form a large and diverse family which includes most of the fishes found in British lakes and rivers, and has many representatives in North America. The family is also well distributed throughout Asia and Africa. Many of the species included are valued food-fishes, and others are well known to anglers and aquarists.

The carp (*Cyprinus carpio*) was originally distributed in the basins of the Black and Aegean Seas, notably in the River Danube, but has been introduced across Europe and North America, and into parts of South America, Asia, Africa, Australia, and New Zealand. Its present wide distribution is due to its edibility and also to its tenacity of life, for carp can endure long exposure to air, high temperatures and conditions of poor oxygenation. Unfortunately, in many parts of the world it has proved to be destructive of the native fishes, and as in parts of the United States it is necessary to control its numbers. The carp thrives in slow-flowing rivers, lakes and ponds, preferring warm conditions and densely weeded areas. It spawns in summer when the water temperature reaches 23–24° C, shedding the eggs on vegetation in shallow water with much splashing and rolling. Young carp eat small bottom-living crustaceans and insect larvae. The larger fish eat larger prey animals and in summer eat quantities of vegetation also.

In favourable conditions carp grow to a large size quite quickly. Carp farmers (who can offer quick growing varieties ideal conditions) can market reasonable fish for the table in two years. A twelve year old carp may well weigh 33 pounds

and measure 30 inches in length. In the wild they may live for as long as 20 years, but few do. In captivity they certainly survive for 40 to 50 years, but the existence of centenarian carp is purely legendary.

Because of its long history of domestication and artificial breeding, numerous varieties of carp exist. The wild, or king carp is a fully scaled, rather slender-bodied fish. Mirror carp are deep-bodied and have scales only along the lateral line and the bases of the fins, while leather-carp are quite scaleless. Ornamental varieties are also popular as pet fish, especially the golden varieties such as the Hi-goi and Koi carps.

The goldfish (*Carassius auratus*) is another popular ornamental fish which, as a result of selective breeding, is now seen in numerous forms. Most goldfish are rather deep-bodied, with a long dorsal fin which has a serrated spine in the front (as does the shorter anal fin); when young they are a deep greeny-bronze but as they grow they develop a golden sheen. Ornamental varieties exist which have doubled and lengthened fin rays (veil-tails), protruding eyes (telescope-eyed), thick-set and elliptical bodies (egg fish), scaleless, particoloured bodies (Shubunkin), and wart covered heads (lion fish), few of which are as attractive as the plain-coloured natural fish. Goldfish are ideally suited for life in small ponds and aquaria as they tolerate extremes of heat and low dissolved oxygen levels very well. They rarely breed, however, unless the water temperature exceeds 25° C (77° F).

The closely related crucian carp (*Carassius carassius*) shares many of the qualities of the goldfish in that it will thrive in shallow pools, often low in oxygen and high in temperature. Its native range appears to be from the U.S.S.R. through Europe to eastern England. Both the goldfish and the crucian carp lack barbels on the lips.

Other familiar European cyprinid fishes are the bream (*Abramis brama*) and the silver bream (*Blicca bjoerkna*), deep-bodied fishes with long-based anal fins. Neither has barbels, but the bream, which is the larger fish (growing to 24 inches in length) has a very mobile mouth which protrudes as a

The veil-tail is a well-known mutation of the goldfish, *Carassius auratus*, characterized by the elongate and double tail fin. Goldfish are ideal fish for a domestic aquarium, as they are very tolerant of variations in temperature. *Phot. Z. F. A.*

tube, an adaptation for feeding on the bottom. A differing lifestyle is adopted by the bleak (*Alburnus alburnus*), a slender-bodied, silvery fish, which has a steeply angled mouth and feeds on surface-living insects and planktonic crustaceans.

Some cyprinid genera contain numerous species. The genus *Barbus* is one such and comprises several hundred species. Some of these, like the tiger barb (*B. pentazona*), is a native of the Malayan peninsula, Sumatra, and Borneo, are small and beautiful aquarium fishes, rarely growing longer than two inches. Others, like the European barbel (*B. barbus*) are moderately large, growing to forty inches, while the huge mahseer (*B. putitora*), which is found all along the Himalayas from Kashmir to China, grows to nine feet in length. It is one of the most famous of India's sporting fishes. Another remarkable barbel is the blind species from the caves of Thysville, Congo (*Caecobarbus geertsi*), an unpigmented and abundant inhabitant in these totally lightless caves. As with some other cave fishes the newly hatched young have eyes, but in the course of growth they degenerate and become covered by skin. Other sightless cyprinid fishes are known, amongst them *Iranocypris* from Iran and *Phreactichthys* from Somaliland. The latter lives in underground water-courses and is only captured accidentally in water drawn from wells.

Suckers (Catostomidae)

The suckers are best represented in North American freshwaters although some species live in northern Asia. They are similar in external appearance to the carp-like fishes except that they have thick, bristle-covered lips, and very protrusible mouths. They also have a single row of very numerous pharyngeal teeth. One well-known species is the white sucker (*Catostomus commersoni*) a 25 inch long inhabitant of large streams and lakes between Labrador and Nova Scotia, southwards to Georgia and New Mexico, and westwards to the upper Fraser River. It is a bottom-living fish feeding entirely on benthic organisms; its flesh was an important food resource for the aboriginal Indians and the early fur trading Europeans.

Hillstream loaches (Homalopteridae)

This is a small family of highly adapted freshwater fishes found in streams in southeastern Asia. All are relatively small with the anterior part of the body flattened and the pectoral and pelvic fins laterally expanded to form a virtual sucking disc. These fish live in torrential hillstreams, the sucker-like body enabling them to cling to rocks in the rushing water. They inhale water through slits at the side of the mouth (so as not to break the additional suction pressure of the lips) and the gill openings are often held shut for short periods, both adaptations to their special lifestyle.

Loaches (Cobitidae)

Loaches make up a family of mostly small, slender-bodied fishes, widely distributed in Europe, Asia and the northeast of Africa. They attain their greatest abundance in southeast Asia. Loaches are bottom-living fishes, often laterally compressed and with a flattened belly, with several barbels around their mouths. Some species have the swimbladder housed in a bony capsule. They are found in widely differing habitats from swiftly-flowing hillstreams to slow-flowing rivers and even stagnant ponds. The pond loach (*Misgurnus fossilis*), a widespread species in Europe, is able to survive conditions of low oxygenation by gulping air at the surface. Oxygen is removed in an intestinal pouch and waste gases pass out through the anus. The spined loach (*Cobitis taenia*) has a double spine beneath each eye, and lives buried in mud or filamentous algal mats in slow-flowing rivers. The stone

loach (*Noemacheilus barbatulus*) grows to five inches in length, lives mostly under stones in fast streams, but lacks the spines. Both are found in Europe and Britain, but the spined loach is confined to eastern England.

Three freshwater fish living in British and European rivers *A*, the chub (*Leuciscus cephalus*), widely distributed in large and small rivers, an omnivore very fond of insects. *B*, the silver bream (*Blicca bjoerkna*) which lives in slow-flowing rivers and lakes, principally in eastern England. *C*, the bleak (*Alburnus alburnus*), an abundant surface-living fish, which feeds on insects. *Phot. J. Six*

Knife fishes and electric eels
(Gymnotidea)

The gymnotids form the third major group of the cypriniform fishes. They are eel-like South American freshwater fishes with an extremely long and well developed anal fin but no dorsal or tail fins, except in the members of the family Apteronotidae, in which they are rudimentary. The long anal fin is the chief propulsive organ, moving the fish forward by wave-like rippling of the fin, although if provoked the fish can swim actively like an eel. Recent revisions suggest that four families should be recognized: Gymnotidae, Apteronotidae, Rhamphichthyidae, and Electrophoridae.

Electric eels (Electrophoridae)

The electric eel is native to the creeks, pools and streams of northeastern South America, including the Guyanas and the Orinoco and lower Amazon basins. It can grow to a length of eight feet, and its electrical abilities are legendary. The electric organs run along the greater part of its body, derived from the musculature of the sides. There are three parts to each organ: along the centre is the principal lateral organ capable of powerful discharges of up to 550 volts and of killing most small animals which come within range, and above and below this are low-powered organs. The latter are used for the detection of prey and for the location of solid objects in the rather sedimented water in which the electric eel lives.

The major electric organs are composed of columns of wafer-thin electric plates grouped in numerous rows. The electroplates are mostly connected in series and although the charge produced by each is small, collectively they build up to the most powerful produced in the animal kingdom.

Knife fishes (Gymnotidae)

Knife fishes are more compressed from side to side than the electric eel and the anal fin is very long, with the anus under the throat and the body cavity highly modified. They live in rather turbid water and are most active at night or in light of low intensity. They possess weak electric organs which they evidently use for navigating. The banded knife fish (*Gymnotus carapo*) is widely distributed between Guatemala and the Rio de la Plata in Argentina, in shaded creeks and drainage channels in the lowlands. When small it feeds on small crustaceans and insect larvae, but when full grown it eats shrimps and fishes. It is often kept in aquaria, but in its natural habitat it is fished for and eaten. It grows to about 24 inches in length.

Catfishes (Siluriformes)

The catfishes have long barbels around the mouth, usually four pairs, and it is these whisker-like barbels which give their name to the group. Many catfishes live in rather turbid waters, and most live on the bottom, so their barbels bear taste buds with which they can detect food and assess its quality. Most species have relatively small eyes. The Weberian apparatus is very highly developed, and the small bones which form it are fused into a single unit. The swim-bladder in some species is housed in a bony capsule, and in many others it is reduced to a single, anterior chamber, which may be divided into left and right chambers. This modification of Weberian ossicles and swimbladder results in

a highly efficient acoustic system, capable of receiving sounds as well as producing audible noises—a singularly useful ability in water in which vision is poor.

Most catfishes have completely scaleless skins, although some such as the South American callichthyids and loricariids have a solid body armour, more plate-like than scaly. Several families have an adipose fin on the back between the rayed dorsal fin and the tail, and these and others have strong spines in the dorsal and pectoral fins.

The great majority of catfishes are freshwater fishes. Probably rather more than half live in the freshwaters of South America, but they are also well represented in North America, Africa and Asia; relatively few species occur in Europe and Australia. Two families are found in tropical seas.

Marine catfishes (Ariidae and Plotosidae)

The ariid catfishes are world-wide in tropical and sub-tropical seas, being found especially in estuaries. They are active fishes, often swimming in schools near the surface. Some attain a moderate size and are used locally for food, although their capture is hazardous as they have sharp pectoral spines which can inflict painful wounds. The gafftopsail catfish (*Bagre marinus*) is found on the Atlantic coast of North America from Cape Cod to Panama. Its dorsal fin has a long thin filament (the gafftopsail of its name) and it grows to 24 inches in length. Males of this species, and other members of the family, carry the eggs in their mouth until shortly after they hatch. These catfishes are also well-known sound producers.

The plotosid catfishes are confined to the basin of the tropical Indo-Pacific. They have a short first dorsal fin with a sharp spine at its front, and a long second dorsal fin joined to the tail and anal fin. The pectoral fins each have a strong spine. One species, the barber eel (*Plotosus lineatus*) is frequently seen in harbours, shore pools, and estuaries along the Indian Ocean coastline. When young it has a characteristic habit of forming tight-packed schools often looking like a huge ball moving in the water.

Silurid catfishes (Siluridae)

This family contains the only indigenous European catfishes, and it is confined to the freshwaters of Eurasia. As a group they are distinguished by the lack of a spine in the dorsal fin which is itself very small, and sometimes even absent, and by the very long anal fin.

The best known European catfish is the wels (*Silurus glanis*) which is also the largest wholly freshwater fish in Europe. It lives in large rivers and lakes and is widely distributed in central and eastern Europe, and less abundantly in the Rhine and western Europe. It has been introduced to England but is confined to a few isolated lakes, where it grows to a length of 10 feet (there is a report of one in the River Dnieper of 16 feet and a weight of 675 pounds). Like many catfishes it is active at night and in the half-light, lying close to the bottom under river banks or in hollows during daylight. When young it feeds on aquatic insects, but as it grows it feeds increasingly on fishes and when full-grown there are few aquatic animals it will not eat. In eastern Europe it is an important commercial fish, and is raised in fish farms. A second European catfish, *Silurus aristotelis*, lives in the River Achelous in Greece; its biology is little known.

Some silurids, such as the glass catfish (*Kryptopterus bicirrhis*), are popular aquarium fish. This species lives in the Malayan-Indonesian region, and forms small schools which are active in daylight, usually to be seen in mid-water in a tail-down posture. Unlike most catfishes it has abandoned the dull concealing coloration of a bottom-living fish, and is virtually translucent, only the eye and body cavity being pigmented and visible. It grows to about four inches.

North American catfishes (Ictaluridae)

These catfishes live in freshwater in North America between Canada and Guatemala, but have been introduced by man to other parts of the world. In most respects they are typical catfishes with long whisker-like barbels round the mouth, a large adipose dorsal fin, a short rayed dorsal fin with a strong spine and strongly spined pectoral fins.

The madtoms of the genus *Noturus* are small (rarely growing longer than eight inches) and represented by numerous species. They have venom glands at the base of the pectoral fin spines and wounds from these can be very painful. The rather larger catfishes and bullheads (genus *Ictalurus*) are also widely distributed. Some like the blue catfish (*I. furcatus*) which grows to five feet and a weight of eighty pounds are valuable food and sporting fishes. Two smaller species, the black bullhead (*I. melas*), and the brown bullhead (*I. nebulosus*), have been introduced to Europe, and the latter

The electric eel *Electrophorus electricus*, is the most powerful electric fish. Its electric organs occupy 4/5 of the body, and when discharged will kill other fishes, and give severe shock to man. They can produce brief bursts of power, at first as large as 500 volts, but declining slowly. *Photo Researchers—Paul Crum*

The electric eel lives in deeply shaded creeks and backwaters of rivers in tropical South America. Living usually in very turbid water it relies heavily on its electrical abilities to navigate as well as detect predators or prey. *Atlas-Photo—Lauros*

Plotosus lineatus, a marine catfish abundant in the Indian Ocean and west Pacific, especially among coral reefs and in harbours. The dorsal and pectoral spines have venom glands and inflict painful dangerous wounds. *Photo Researchers—Russe Kinne*

also to New Zealand, in no case with beneficial effects on the native fish fauna.

Bagrid catfishes (Bagridae)

Widely distributed in tropical Africa and Asia, as far east as Japan, the bagrids are scaleless, rather slender-bodied fishes, with small eyes and a large adipose fin. The dorsal and anal fins have a stout spine. They are bottom-living, mainly nocturnal or crepuscular in activity, and several species make quite loud noises. Many of them are moderately large and are locally valuable food fishes. Amongst these are the numerous members of the African genus *Chrysichthys*; one specimen from the Congo, probably *C. cranchi*, weighted 275 pounds. *Bagrus docmac*, which probably grows to a maximum weight of 75 pounds, lives in the rivers of Nigeria, Ghana, the Nile basin, and the Great Lakes of Africa. These and the other species in Africa and Asia are all predatory fishes.

Air-breathing catfishes (Clariidae and Heteropneustidae)

The clariids are a large family of African and southern Asian freshwater catfishes containing numerous species. Many are rather eel-like in body form with a broad head and four pairs of long barbels round the mouth. The dorsal fin lacks a spine and some species have an adipose dorsal fin. They are

Auchenoglanis occidentalis, a large catfish, widely distributed in tropical African rivers and lakes. The young fish are found in shallow water, the adults are particularly common in swamps. *Phot. Max Poll*

The young glass catfish (*Ompok bimaculatus*) is almost completely transparent. The viscera form the dark mass situated behind the head. It lives in southeastern Asia. *Phot. J. M. Baufle*

distinguished by the presence of an accessory air-breathing organ either extending behind the gill chamber or developed as arborescent organs in the back of the gill cavity. This supplementary means of obtaining oxygen enables them to live in deoxygenated water such as swamps and to survive in times of drought.

Clarias lazera lives in lakes and swamps from Syria and Israel and throughout the Nile, Congo, and Niger basins. It grows to a length of 55 inches and is an important food fish locally. A more restricted distribution is shown by the blind and unpigmented Somaliland species, *Uegitglanis zammaranoi*, which lives in underground water courses but can be caught at the bottom of artesian wells. Another species, *Gymnallabes tihoni*, lives in swiftly flowing streams and in this well oxygenated habitat the suprabranchial arborescent breathing organ is not developed.

The two members of the family Heteropneustidae are both found in Asia. They are closely related to the clariids and, like them, have accessory breathing organs, although they take the form of two long, hollow cylinders in the muscles of the back but connected to the gill cavity. *Heteropneustes fossilis* is found from India and Sri Lanka to Vietnam and Thailand in ponds, ditches, swamps and muddy rivers. It grows to a length of 27 inches.

Glass catfishes (Schilbeidae)

A relatively small family of Asian and African catfishes which

have a flattened compressed body, a very long anal fin, a short dorsal fin (and in some species an adipose fin also). Most are relatively small fishes, and although some are large enough to be of commercial value, others are kept in aquaria. A number of members of the family have abandoned the typical catfish bottom-living life style and are surface-living fishes of open waters, often seen in schools near the surface at rest at an angle to the surface. Many of them are translucent.

The members of the African genus *Eutropius* are moderately large and are locally valuable as food fishes. One species (*E. niloticus*) occurs throughout northern and central Africa, in the southeast being replaced by the butter barbel (*E. depressirostris*) of South Africa, which is highly thought of as an angling species. The African glass catfish (*Physailia pellucida*) is found in the upper Nile basin, and has the habit of resting in a tail-down position near the bottom; it has an adipose dorsal fin but no rayed fin on the back.

Tadpole catfish (Chacidae)

A single species, *Chaca chaca*, represents this family. It lives in freshwater in India, Burma, Sumatra, and Borneo. Its head is greatly flattened and the mouth is broad with fleshy flaps attractive to little fishes which are snapped up as they approach. It is entirely bottom-living, lying in near-perfect concealment in streams and pools in the lowland regions. Its broad head and slender tail are tadpole-like.

Other African catfishes (Malapteruridae and Mochokidae)

The electric catfish (*Malapterurus electricus*) is immediately distinguished by its heavy build, by the well-developed adipose fin (the only dorsal fin), and general greyish-brown coloration with rounded black blotches. It is widely distributed in tropical Africa living in swamps and reed-beds bordering slow-flowing rivers. It is well known for its powerful electrical abilities which originate in the muscle layers immediately beneath the skin, and produce discharges of up to 450 volts, sufficient to kill other fishes and stun a man if in close contact. It uses its electrical power to obtain food in the form of small fish, but it is also clearly defensive in function. Throughout its range it is regarded with special esteem: its image appears in many ancient Egyptian pictographs and its organs are used in Africa as veritable panaceas for ill health.

Members of the family Mochokidae are the most abundant African catfishes. Most have a rather high, thickset body, with rayed dorsal fin and a large adipose fin. Both dorsal and pectoral fins have a heavy spine. The mouth is equipped with short, branched barbels, and the lower jaw has fine teeth which act as a rasp as the fish glides over rocks or plant leaves, scraping off the algae which grow there. In the species of the genus *Euchilichthys*, which live in hill streams, the mouth is developed as a broad adhesive sucker.

The members of the genus *Synodontis* are less specialized. Numerous species are recognized, many of them small, but others, like *S. schall*, grow to sixteen inches in length and a weight of over two pounds. It is found from the Nile to Senegal and Nigeria, as well as in Lakes Chad, Albert, and Rudolf. It feeds mainly on invertebrate animals, at least when well grown. The upside-down catfish (*S. nigriventris*) lives in streams in central Zaire, its strange name being due to its habit of swimming on its back, the normal obliterative coloration being reversed so that the belly is darker than the back. Its habit is associated with its diet of algae browsed from the underside of leaves of water plants. Many of the *Synodontis* catfishes swim indiscriminately on their backs or normally.

South American catfishes (Callichthyidae, Loricariidae and Aspredinidae)

The members of the family Callichthyidae are immediately distinguished by the heavy bony shields which enclose the body like armour plate. Numerous species in the genera *Callichthys*, *Corydoras*, and *Hoplosternum* are known, many well-known aquarium fishes. They are usually deep-bodied, the mouth small and ventral and with several well developed barbels. The dorsal fin is high and they have an adipose fin with a spine on its front edge. All are bottom-living fishes and some live in swamps which become deoxygenated. In this situation they gulp air at the surface, absorbing the oxygen in the hindgut. The cascarudo (*Callichthys callichthys*), which is widely distributed in northern South America, grows to a length of seven inches, and deposits its eggs in a bubble nest made by both parents at the surface amongst water plant leaves.

The loricariids inhabit the rivers of northern and central South America. They are heavily armoured, their heads and bodies being enclosed in bony scales, although in one group the belly is scaleless. Most species are bottom-living, with ventral mouths and broad, fringed lips with which they nibble at the algae growing on rocks or plants. This family is unique amongst fishes in having a small peg-shaped process on the upper iris which partially covers the pupil. This iris-lobe expands in bright light to almost cover the pupil and thus has the same function as the iris muscles of the higher vertebrates.

The banjo catfishes (Aspredinidae), so called because of the wide flattened head and slender tail, live in the rivers and inner estuaries of northern South America. In *Aspredinichthys tibicen*, which grows to five inches in length, the eggs are incubated by the female which carries them on the underside of her body attached to short, spongy papillae.

Parasitic catfishes (Trichomycteridae)

This family of small rather slender-bodied and loach-like catfishes is found in tropical, northeastern South America. Most of the species whose habits are known are crepuscular or nocturnal and lie buried in daylight in sand or amongst leaf-litter on the river bed. Some appear to be non-parasitic, but others are known to eat the scales or to live in the gill-chambers of other fishes. *Stegophilus insidiosus* is a frequent parasite of the gills of other catfishes, sucking blood and eating gill tissue. The very small candiru (*Vandellia cirrhosa*), a three inch long native of the Amazon and its tributaries, has similar habits but is infamous from the occasions when it has penetrated the urethra of humans urinating in the water, attracted to the stream of urine as they are to water exhaled from a larger fish's gill opening. The consequences both to fish and human are frequently fatal. It is thought that its normal lifestyle is to engorge itself with blood from a fish's gills and then to lie buried in the river bed for a while before attaching itself to another host.

Flying-fishes, toothcarps and sandsmelts (Atheriniformes)

This order, which contains several divergent groups, was for many years separated as three distinct orders. It includes the mainly marine suborder Exocoetoidei which is composed of the flying-fishes, garfishes and sauries, the mainly fresh-water toothcarps or killifishes (suborder Cyprinodontoidei) of which the mollies, platies, and rivulines are examples, and the sand-smelts or silversides (suborder Atherinoidei) which are found in both salt and fresh water. Most of these fishes are surface-living, with pelvic fins placed on the belly, the fins without spines and cycloid scales.

Flying-fishes and half-beaks (Exocoetidae)

The members of this family are distributed world-wide in tropical seas with seasonal migrations into temperate oceans. Flying-fishes do not actually fly, they glide, propelled by active swimming below the surface. Some species have both pectoral and pelvic fins enlarged, and in these the lower lobe of the tail fin is longer than the upper lobe. They use this lobe to increase their speed at take-off by sculling along the water. These double-winged species are capable of more sustained and controlled glides than the species which have only the pectoral fins enlarged. All species use their gliding ability to escape from predators, especially the dolphin-fishes (*Coryphaena* sp.).

Exocoetus volitans is an open ocean species found in all tropical seas; it grows to a length of twelve inches and is one of the two-winged species. The Atlantic flying-fish (*Cypselurus heterurus*) is found in the Mediterranean and in the eastern Atlantic between Angola and Portugal (very rarely occurring in British waters). On the American coast it ranges from southern Canada to southeastern Brazil. It usually lives in

Synodontis contractus is a small but squat African catfish. Among other peculiarities, it has branched barbels, emits sounds by rubbing the base of its pectoral spines in their sockets, and swims on its back, which results in its pigmentation being extended to the whole of its ventral surface. *Phot. Brichard*

the coastal zone, not far out to sea. Like most flying-fishes its eggs are large and equipped with long adhesive filaments by which they attach to floating algae or flotsam.

In the half-beaks the lower jaw is elongated into a sharp beak but the upper jaw remains short. In general appearance they are similar to flying-fishes but the pectoral fins are not greatly enlarged. They are all surface-living, schooling fishes which feed on the absolute surface plankton, including young fishes. A common inshore species on the American Atlantic coast is the ballyhoo (*Hemiramphus brasiliensis*), a fifteen inch long, greenish-blue fish, silvery below. Another very in-

teresting half-beak is *Dermogenys pusillus*, a three inch long inhabitant of the fresh and brackish water of Thailand, Malaysia and the Sunda Islands. This fish gives birth to living young, the male possessing a modified anal fin which acts as a gonopodium.

Garfishes and sauries (Belonidae and Scomberesocidae)

The garfishes are mainly marine tropical and warm temperate fishes which live in surface waters. They have very elongate bodies and long jaws equipped with sharp teeth. Their body form suggests their alternative names needlefishes or long-toms. They are found both inshore and in the open sea and frequently jump clear of the water. The European garfish (*Belone belone*) grows to three feet in length and is widely distributed between Scotland and the Black Sea. Like other species its eggs are spherical and covered with fine filaments which both serve to keep the egg afloat and tangle in floating weed. Its bones are bright green in colour.

The sauries or skippers are also surface-living fishes found in the open sea and most common in tropical and warm temperate regions. The Atlantic saury (*Scomberesox saurus*) grows to eighteen inches in length, is widely distributed and is an important source of food for many commercially valuable fishes such as tunas and billfishes. The sauries are long-bodied with elongate jaws but possess a series of finlets behind the dorsal and anal fins.

Toothcarps (Cyprinodontidae)

The toothcarps are a very large family of mainly freshwater fishes found in tropical and warm-temperate regions throughout the world except for the Australian region. They have a rather flattened head, projecting lower jaw, fully scaled body and fine teeth in the jaws. They are all egg-laying species and some African species are so-called annual fishes, laying their eggs during the brief tropical wet season then dying as the water dries up while the eggs survive buried in mud until the next rains. They are all adaptable little fishes, able to survive in extremes of heat, salinity and drought that would be fatal to most fishes.

In Spain two native species occur, *Valencia hispanica* and *Aphanius iberus*, both restricted to swamps and marshes on the Mediterranean coastline and now much restricted in numbers by drainage of their habitats and the introduction of the American mosquito fish *Gambusia affinis*. This species has been introduced to many parts of the world where the temperature does not fall below 20° C, as a predator on the anopheline mosquito which carries malaria. Many of the native toothcarps are equally capable of destroying mosquitoes and have found *Gambusia* an active competitor.

Africa contains a great wealth of indigenous toothcarps, many of striking beauty and popular aquarium fishes. The genera *Aphyosemion* and *Epiplatys* are found mainly in forest areas, and the males are brilliantly coloured and have enlarged dorsal and tail fins. The females lay their eggs on plants or even buried in the bottom. In the genera *Aphyosemion* and the savannah inhabiting genus *Nothobranchius* several species are known to produce drought-resisting eggs. One such is *N. taeniopygus* which is widely distributed in eastern Africa, in Uganda, Tanzania, and Zambia, living in swamps and temporary streams. It breeds during the rainy season, the eggs being deposited in the mud in which they lie throughout the dry season. With the rains the eggs complete their development and hatch, and within six to eight weeks the fish become mature. This life cycle is finely adapted to the seasonal variation in climate.

In South America other toothcarps have evolved a similar lifestyle. The Argentine pearlfish or pavito (*Cynolebias belotti*) is found in ephemeral pools, often small and shallow, in the flood plain of rivers in La Plata basin in Argentina. These pools frequently have a very high temperature and dry up in the dry season. This fish grows to a length of three inches and is often kept in aquaria. In eastern California and southwestern Nevada, in the arid Death Valley system, another toothcarp lives in even harsher conditions. This is *Cyprinodon milleri* which attains a length of only 1¾ inches and lives in salt lakes 250 feet below sea level at extremely high temperatures, where in summer salt is crystallizing out around the edges of the pools. Other species of *Cyprinodon* are found elsewhere in North America. The sheepshead minnow (*C. variegatus*) is found in salt marshes, estuaries, harbours and shallow bays from Cape Cod to Mexico. Other toothcarps inhabit lakes such as Lake Titicaca (numerous species of *Orestias*) and the African lakes. Among the latter is *Lamprichthys tanganyicanus*, which lives in Lake Tanganyika and grows to a length of six inches. The slender shape of its body and lines of pearly blue spots make it one of the most beautiful of a brightly coloured family.

Live-bearing toothcarps (Poecilidae)

This large family of small fishes occurs naturally in the Americas, from the southern United States to Argentina, but is now found in many parts of the world as the result of introduction. They occupy a great diversity of habitats from saline coastal marshes to forest and mountain streams and pools. Many feed on aquatic algae and plants, and several species are well known as destroyers of mosquito larvae and have been deliberately spread to tropical parts of the world in attempts to control malaria (especially *Gambusia affinis*).

All the members of this family give birth to live young. The males have either the anterior several rays of the anal fin, or the whole fin, modified to form a gonopodium, a movable elongate tube by which the sperm, contained in a spermatophore, is transferred to the cloaca of the female. Liberation of sperm is slow and the one mating can result in several litters of young being produced. The eggs develop within the ovarian cavity, and the young fish is still enveloped within the membrane at birth, although it bursts immediately after. The poeciliids are thus ovoviviparous. Associated with their individual mating habits the sexes are different in appearance, males usually being brilliantly coloured often with large fins, and displaying actively before the rather larger female.

On account of their bright colours, active behaviour, and their tenacity of life, the poeciliids are popular aquarium fishes. One of the most popular is the guppy or millions fish (*Poecilia reticulata*), originally found in northern Brazil, the Guianas, Venezuela, Barbados, and Trinidad, but now found in many parts of the world due to the liberation of unwanted pet fish (colonies have been established even in Britain, living in warm water discharged to rivers). The male grows to only 1¼ inches in length, half the length of the female, and is greenish brown above with two dark spots and metallic tints of green and blue on the sides. Intensive selection in aquarium-bred fish has resulted in many elaborately coloured and huge-finned fish being produced.

The mollies are also popular aquarium fish. They are larger, the sailfin molly (*P. latipinna*) growing to a length of nearly five inches. It lives in fresh and brackish water in the southeastern parts of North America from Carolina to Yucatan, Mexico. The dorsal fin is long based, and in the male very high. In wild fish the coloration is olive brown with a pearly iridescence and lengthwise rows of red and blue spots. Black mollies are melanistic forms especially

cultivated for the aquarium. Another common molly, also frequently seen as a melanistic form, is *Poecilia sphenops*, a species with a rather smaller dorsal fin. The platy (*Xiphophorus maculatus*) is an extremely variable fish both in the wild and in the aquarium. Its natural range is along the Atlantic slopes of Central America where it lives in coastal pools, ponds, and slow-flowing streams. The swordtails are closely related; the best known is the swordtail (*X. helleri*) which originates in the streams, swamps and coastal marshes of

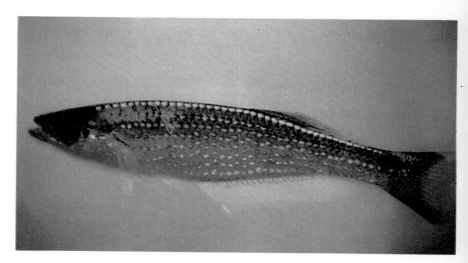

The mosquito fish (*Gambusia affinis*) feeds for preference on insect larvae (especially mosquitoes) swimming on the surface by snapping at them from below. It is native to the eastern and southern states of North America, but has been introduced in many parts of the world to control mosquitoes. The large individual is female; the small ones, males x 2.5. *Phot.* J. Six

Lamprichthys tanganyicanus (family Cyprinodontidae), the largest of the African toothcarps, is an endemic species of Lake Tanganyika. It lives at the surface eating plankton. *Phot.* Brichard

Mexico and Guatemala. Male swordtails have characteristically elongate lower rays to the tail fin (forming a 'sword') usually red or orange in colour. This is a very variable species, and several subspecies have been described. A popular aquarium fish, usually seen as a uniformly red variation, the swordtail not infrequently changes sex. Older females sometimes develop male characters, growing a tail sword and developing a gonopodium.

Four-eyed fishes (Anablepidae)

This is a remarkable family of toothcarps which contains only three species found in rivers and coastal areas of Central and northern South America. They are ovoviviparous, the males having a copulatory organ formed from the anal fin. *Anableps anableps* is widely distributed in shallow coastal waters living at the surface or partially covered by water on a muddy bank, and watching for aerial or aquatic prey or predators simultaneously. Its eyes protrude above the outline of the head, each being divided across its centre by a band of opaque tissue which effectively separates it into upper and lower halves. Each half eye has a separate retina and the lenses are differently shaped so that the fish has as acute vision in air as it has in water. None of the known species grows longer than twelve inches.

Sand-smelts and silversides (Atherinidae)

This family of mostly small fishes lives in schools in shallow water in tropical and temperate seas, with a few members in freshwaters. Most are rather slender-bodied fish with two dorsal fins, the first composed of slender unbranched rays. They have protrusible, finely-toothed mouths, fully-scaled bodies, and often have a conspicuous silvery line along the sides. Numerous species are known, and some are fished for commercially; but most form important links in the food chains of other fishes and sea birds.

The sand-smelt (*Atherina presbyter*) is widely distributed in the eastern Atlantic from Denmark and Scotland to the North African coast, and in the Mediterranean. It is found close inshore in sandy bays and estuaries in large schools and spawns in high shore pools in midsummer, the eggs having long filaments which tangle in the algae or with one another. It grows to about six inches in length. The hardhead silverside (*Atherinomorus stipes*), is a common species in the Caribbean, although it ranges from Florida to Brazil. In daylight it is almost transparent, with only the narrow silvery line showing, but at night it becomes darker and the silver stripe is obscured.

One of the most remarkable of the silversides is the Californian grunion (*Leuresthes tenuis*), a seven inch long fish found from Monterey Bay to San Juanico Bay, Baja California. It spawns throughout the summer, spawning coinciding with the spring tides when the grunion strand themselves near high tide mark, the female burying into the sand to deposit her eggs while the male sheds sperm into the sand by her head. The male is swept out to sea by the next high wave, the female following on succeeding waves. The eggs lie buried in the sand for two weeks when the next high tides will cover them with water and they hatch, but they will stay viable for up to a month if the intermediate tides are not sufficiently high.

Freshwater atherinids (Melanotaeniidae and Phallostethidae)

Members of the family Melanotaeniidae are freshwater fishes found in Australia, New Guinea, and Madagascar. They are similar to the silversides but are deeper in the body and often more colourful. The crimson-spotted rainbow-fish (*Melanotaenia fluviatilis*), which grows to $3\frac{1}{2}$ inches in length, is a widely-distributed fish in eastern Australia, and is occasionally kept in aquaria. Its eggs bear fine threads by which they are attached to water plants.

The phallostethids are small fishes found in fresh and brackish water of the Philippine Islands, Malaysia and Thailand. They are slender-bodied, fully scaled fishes, with two dorsal fins, the first of which is a single short spine. In the male the pelvic bones, part of the shoulder girdle, and two ribs are adapted to form a long copulatory organ. Despite this they are not live-bearers for the eggs are laid on the bottom in an advanced state of development. The Thailand species *Phenacostethus smithi* grows to only $\frac{3}{4}$ of an inch in length, and lives in freshwater pools, ditches and canals in turbid water. It forms small schools near the surface, feeding on micro-organisms; it is almost completely transparent.

Cod-like fishes and cusk-eels (Gadiformes)

The bony fishes of this order have only soft rays in their fins and have the pelvic fins placed close behind or below the head. The pectoral fins are narrow-based and lateral in position. This order includes the cod-fishes and hakes, the rat-tails, and according to some classifications the brotulids and cusk-eels. The eel-pouts should also be included within it. With or without these additional families most of the gadiform fishes are marine and the order has a world-wide distribution.

Cod-fishes (Gadidae)

The members of the cod family are amongst the most important food fishes of the northern hemisphere. They are widely distributed in the cool temperate and even polar regions of both the North Atlantic and North Pacific, although a few species are also found in the cool temperate southern hemisphere. One wide-ranging species, the burbot (*Lota lota*) is found in freshwater in Europe, northern Asia, and North America.

All members of the cod family have a very characteristic tail fin. It has two equal lobes with all the rays symmetrically placed around the basal bones—the tail fin thus always resembles a partially opened fan. Some members of the family have three dorsal and two anal fins, others have only one or two dorsal fins and a single anal fin. Many cod-fishes have a distinct barbel on the chin, and others have well developed barbels on the lips and snout; these barbels, as well as the lips, and often the rather elongated pelvic fin rays, are richly supplied with sensory organs which help the fishes' constant search for bottom-living food organisms. The bottom-living forms, such as cod and haddock, are well known as sound producers, members of the school keeping in touch with one another by a series of distinctive grunts and groans.

The cod fishes produce very large numbers of eggs, sometimes amounting to millions. These, and the larvae, are pelagic, floating at the sea's surface and often being widely distributed by ocean currents. Not surprisingly, many of the species are widely distributed in their ocean basins. Young gadids play a very large part in the food web of the northern seas, preying on planktonic animals, and themselves forming the food of larger fishes, marine mammals and birds.

The Atlantic cod (*Gadus morhua*) is found in coastal waters of the whole North Atlantic and ranges from Biscay to the Barents Sea, around Iceland, southern Greenland and from Hudson Bay to North Carolina. The Baltic Sea population is distinguished as *G. morhua callarias*, but differs little from the Atlantic subspecies.

The cod fisheries of the Newfoundland and Icelandic banks are particularly well known, but those of the Barents Sea and the Norwegian coast are hardly less valuable. The cod forms a number of local races which perform quite lengthy migrations for feeding and breeding, although they

Male rivuline toothcarps of the genus *Aphyosemion* are among the most brilliantly coloured fish. Here are two which prove it: *Above, Aphyosemion christyi*, Congo; *Below, Aphyosemion nigerianum*, Nigeria. *Phot. J.-J. Scheel*

stay separate from one another. This tendency, which is also seen in the herring and other fishes, is of importance to the fisheries because local overfishing could result in greatly reduced stocks.

The cod is most abundant in water of 90 to 160 fathoms, although it ranges down to 230 fathoms and can also be found close inshore. Schools of cod are generally to be located from 9 to 15 fathoms above the sea bed, although they also forage on the bottom eating bottom-living crabs, molluscs and worms. Fish is their principal food and a wide variety of species are eaten including sprat, herring, capelin and sand-eels.

Other important members of the family are found widely in the North Atlantic. Of these the haddock (*Melanogrammus aeglefinus*) is probably the best known. Dark in colour above, it has a conspicuous black lateral line and a rounded sooty blotch on each shoulder. The haddock is found in coastal waters from the North Sea northwards to the Barents Sea, around Iceland, and from Newfoundland to Cape Cod. It is more closely confined to the sea bed than the cod and feeds principally on bottom-living animals such as worms, brittle stars and molluscs, and occasionally sponges which tend to taint the flesh unpleasantly.

The coalfish or saithe (*Pollachius virens*) has a similar distribution, but on the American Atlantic coast it is known as pollack. It too is an important commercial fish, although its flesh is not of the quality of either cod or haddock, being darker and rather coarse. The saithe grows to a large size (up to 48 inches) and is an active predator on fishes, mainly capelin, sand-eels, codling, and herring, as well as crustaceans. The related European pollack (*Pollachius pollachius*), which is found from Norway to Portugal and in the Mediterranean, is very similar in build and habits. It differs in having the lateral line sharply curved over the pectoral fin. It is not an important food fish but is popular with anglers fishing in coastal waters.

The whiting (*Merlangius merlangus*) is caught both by commercial fishermen and anglers. As its name suggests it is light coloured, pale olive-yellow above and silvery on the sides and belly. It is a mid-water fish feeding on smaller fishes as well as crustaceans such as shrimps. It is particularly common in inshore waters, and small whiting can be caught in sandy bays in only a few feet of water. The eggs and larvae are planktonic. The young fish are often found living amongst the trailing tentacles or under the bodies of jellyfishes, a habit they share with young haddock, although different species of medusa are involved.

Other well-known members of the cod-fish family are the long-bodied lings, of which three species are found in European waters: the common ling (*Molva molva*), the blue ling (*M. dypterygia*), which is found in deep water to the north of the British Isles, and the Spanish ling (*M. macrophthalma*), which is smaller and more southerly in its distribution. All the lings are fished for commercially; they have two dorsal fins, the second of which is very long, as is the anal fin, and a long chin barbel. They are large fish, the common and the blue ling both exceeding five feet in length. The rocklings on the other hand are small, and have barbels (from two to four) on the snout, as well as a chin barbel. Several of the better-known species live amongst rocks, and both the five-bearded rockling (*Ciliata mustela*), and the shore rockling (*Gaidropsarus mediterraneus*), can be found commonly on rocky shores in pools and under boulders on the British coast. All the rocklings have a low fringe of fine rays on the back which vibrate constantly, and are thought to have a sensory function.

Other relatives of the cod include the blue whiting (*Micromesistius poutassou*), an open ocean species living in the surface waters of the North Atlantic (with a close relative *M. australis* in near-Antarctic seas), and the walleye pollock (*Theragra chalcogramma*), of the North Pacific. Both northern species are fished for to provide fish meal and to a lesser extent food.

Hakes (Merlucciidae)

Although closely related to the cod-fishes the hakes are sufficiently distinct to be recognized as a family. There are probably as many as ten species but they are all closely similar in general appearance. All are rather long-bodied, with two dorsal fins and a single anal fin. The lower jaw projects, and the jaws and roof of the mouth are well provided with long, sharp teeth.

Hake are widely distributed in the temperate and subtropical waters of both Atlantic and Pacific Oceans. Along the North American Pacific coast *Merluccius productus* is found; on the Atlantic coast the hake is *M. bilinearis*; European waters are inhabited by *M. merluccius*; and New Zealand seas by *M. australis*. All are valuable food fish living on the lower continental shelf in moderately deep water.

The European hake is a very fine food fish which has unfortunately been overfished until it is now relatively uncommon. The hake lives in depths of 100 to 300 fathoms usually just above the sea bed, and migrating towards the surface at night. It eats a wide range of fishes, squids and crustaceans. Silvery grey in colour overall, it can be distinguished by its body form, and the jet black skin inside its mouth and gill covers.

Rat-tails or grenadiers (Macrouridae)

Rat-tails are found in the deep sea in all the oceans but are least common near the poles. Close relatives of the cod-fishes and hakes, they are distinguished by the large broad head, a very short trunk, and an extremely long tail which gives the group its popular name. There is usually a short dorsal fin above the trunk, sometimes a long, low second dorsal fin, and always a very long, but low anal fin.

Products of fishing carried out at a depth of over 250 fathoms on the bottom of the South Atlantic: *Chaunax pictus* (Chaunacidae), a small red globular angler-fish; *Dibranchus atlanticus*, another small angler with a very short, broad body, brownish in colour; *Hymenocephalus italicus* (Macruridae), a rat-tail, a group abundant in the deep sea. *Phot. Max Poll*

The cod (*Gadus morhua*), shows the several dorsal and anal fins, and the chin barbel, which are features of the family Gadidae. *Phot. Wilson*

Many rat-tails are bottom-living fishes and their general build is such that their natural swimming posture is at a head-down angle to the sea-bed. With their sensory chin barbel and underslung jaws they are well equipped for this life-style. Others are found in mid-water, and have large terminal jaws, well endowed with teeth. Some of these species have light organs on the belly close to the anus, sometimes equipped with a lens to concentrate the light. In addition, the rat-tails have a well developed lateral line system along the sides, which is elaborated around the head region with large sensitive cells. Sound reception is acute, for the inner ear is highly developed. Almost all species have a swimbladder but in most species only the males have drumming muscles attached; female rat-tails must live a life of silence.

Rat-tails are the dominant group of fishes on the lower continental shelf down to very great depths where they are replaced by the brotulids, although some do occur in abyssal depths. Most of the shelf and upper continental slope species have large eyes, but the size of the eye progressively decreases in species inhabiting greater depths, and the bathypelagic species *Echinomacrurus mollis*, which is found at around 2750 fathoms, is virtually blind.

Despite their abundance rat-tails have not been commercially exploited until recently, when Russian fishing vessels began to catch the widespread North Atlantic species *Coryphaenoides repestris*, which grows to a length of nearly three feet. A related species is caught in quantity by the Japanese fleet in the North Pacific. Recent experimental trawling by British ships has shown that the former species is abundant to the west of Britain and yields flesh of good quality. Rat-tails may eventually prove to be a valuable food resource which can be exploited as other fish stocks diminish.

Brotulids and cusk-eels (Ophidiidae)

This is a varied and successful family of mainly marine fishes best represented in tropical and warm temperate seas where they range from the bottom of the deepest ocean trench to the shallow inter-tidal zone. A few interesting species live in freshwater, many of them in subterranean waters. In general, they are slender-bodied, with a rather broad head, and soft-rayed fins. Brotulids have slender, two-rayed pelvic fins just behind the head; in the cusk-eels the fins are similar but placed on the throat. The cusk-eels are mainly small, an average length being about twelve inches, although some grow much larger; most burrow in sand or turtle-grass beds.

In the deep sea the number of brotulids is very great. Two deep-living species are *Grimaldichthys profundissimus* and *Bassogigas crassus*. Both have been captured in the Atlantic Ocean, the former at a depth of 2760 fathoms, the latter at 1950 fathoms, although an unidentified *Bassogigas* has been caught at 3800 fathoms. A number of the deep-sea brotulids

have very degenerate eyes or are even totally blind.

The brotulids have also invaded freshwaters in a number of regions, most notably underground streams and caves. In Cuba two species (*Lucifuga subterraneus* and *Stygicola dentatus*) are found in underground streams, while in the Bahamas *Lucifuga spelaeotes* lives in a small limestone sink near Nassau. The Cuban *Lucifuga* is ovoviviparous, giving birth to living young, as do a number of marine brotulids. Other similar species are *Typhlias pearsi*, which lives in the Balaam Canche cave in Yucatan (Mexico), and *Caecogilbia galapagosensis* which inhabits freshwater streams within the volcanic rock of the Galapagos Islands. Most of these species are unpigmented and are either blind or have the eyes greatly reduced. Their closest relatives all appear to be the littoral, crevice-dwelling, marine species found in these regions, species similar to the Caribbean black widow (*Stygnobrotula latebricola*), a three inch long inhabitant of the hollows and crevices of coral heads and submarine caves in which it keeps close to the sides and roof.

Pearlfishes (Carapidae)

The pearlfishes are related to the brotulids and are included within the gadiform fishes in some classifications. They are world-wide in tropical and temperate seas—slender fishes with long-based anal fins, large pectorals, and no pelvic fins; the anus is placed on the throat. They are secretive, and once past their larval stages live a near parasitic life within the body cavity of sea cucumbers, sea urchins, starfishes, tunicates, and clams. One species at least lives inside pearl shells and it is occasionally found trapped within a layer of nacre embedded in the shell. A European pearlfish (*Carapus acus*) grows to eight inches and is found in the Mediterranean and Adriatic. Adults are usually found within the body cavity of the holothurians *Stichopus regalis* and *Holothuria tubulosa*. To some extent they feed on the internal organs of these sea cucumbers.

Angler-fishes (Lophiiformes)

In the angler-fishes the first ray of the dorsal fin is highly modified and equipped with a fleshy tip which serves as a bait to lure prey close to the mouth. The pelvic fins, when present, are placed on the throat; and the pectorals have few but enlarged supporting bones which in bottom-living forms result in limb-like fins which can be used for crawling over the sea bed. The skull is simplified and the mouth is large, usually with strong teeth.

Three main groups are recognized: the angler-fishes, the frogfishes and batfishes, and the deep-sea anglers. The last contains the greatest number of families and species.

Angler-fishes (Lophiidae)

This is a relatively small family of bottom-living fishes in the Atlantic, Pacific, and Indian Oceans. All have flattened broad heads, with wide, large-toothed jaws. The first ray of the dorsal fin, placed just behind the eye, is long, and has a fleshy tip which acts as a lure to small fishes. Fish are enticed close to the head, and then the opening of the mouth sweeps the prey in with the inrushing water. Angler-fishes always match the sea bed perfectly in colour and have small fleshy flaps around their body which help to break up their outline.

One of the two species found in European waters is the angler-fish *Lophius piscatorius*. This fish occurs from the Barents Sea to North Africa, and in the Mediterranean and Black Seas. It lives in shallow inshore water down to a depth of 550 fathoms, usually on muddy, sandy, or shingle grounds. It feeds on a wide range of fishes and has occasionally been

reported to capture sea birds, particularly diving birds. Although only the tail contains sufficient flesh to market it forms a moderately important commercial fish. The flesh is white and fibrous, faintly reminiscent of scampi. The second European angler-fish (*L. budegassa*) occurs in the Mediterranean and on the Atlantic coast as far north as Scotland. It is smaller, growing to twenty inches in length (*L. piscatorius* grows to five feet). The North American goosefish (*L. americanus*), which ranges from Newfoundland to North Carolina, is similar to *L. piscatorius*.

Frogfishes (Antennariidae)

Frogfishes are more rounded in body shape. The skin is loose and covered with small fleshy flaps, and the limb-like pectoral fins make the fish extraordinarily mobile, crawling rather than swimming. The frogfishes have exchanged swimming ability for extraordinary camouflage and subtle feeding techniques. They are found only in tropical seas.

One well-known species is the sargassum-fish (*Histrio histrio*), a pelagic species found in the floating *Sargassum* weed at the surface. It crawls through the weed clumps, a near-perfect match for its surroundings, feeding on planktonic creatures, including those living amongst the weed. It grows to eight inches in length. Another species, the longlure frog-fish (*Antennarius multiocellatus*), is the most common bottom-living Caribbean species. It glides over the sea bed with its two dorsal spines spread either side apparently in deliberate mimicry of a gastropod mollusc.

Batfishes and their relatives
(Ogcocephalidae and Chaunacidae)

Batfishes are the most bizarre-looking of the bizarre lophii-form fishes. They are relatively small in size, distributed world-wide in tropical seas (where they live in shallow water), and also in the deep sea. The body is flattened, almost triangular, but circular in some species, with a short tail. The mouth is small, and above it, but beneath the snout, is a short lure. Batfishes crawl over the sea bed on their limb-like pectoral fins, feeding on an assortment of small fishes, molluscs, crustaceans and worms. The long-nosed batfish (*Ogocephalus vespertillo*) is found in shallow water between Brazil and Florida, and very rarely northwards to New York. The only European batfish is the deepwater Atlantic species *Dibranchus atlanticus*.

Chaunax pictus is a small (up to 18 inches long) angler-fish found in all oceans at depths of 100 to 300 fathoms. It appears to live only on muddy bottoms, in which it may burrow. A very distinctive round-bodied fish with a loose, prickly skin, and a small dorsal ray and lure, it is the only representative of the family Chaunacidae.

Deep-sea anglers (Ceratioidei)

This suborder, the largest and most diverse of all the groups of angler-fishes, contains at least ten families. Although some are well known, others are represented by at most a few specimens and our knowledge of their biology is minimal. As a group they inhabit the middle waters of the deep sea, living close to the surface when young but going deeper as they mature. They differ from other angler-fishes in that they lack pelvic fins. Most species are rather round-bodied, with large heads, wide mouths and numerous long teeth. Males are generally much smaller than the females and in several families become parasitic on the female once they are adolescent. In these groups the male attaches itself to the female by its jaws. In time its lips fuse with the female's skin, the circulatory systems link up, and all the male's organs (except for its gonads) degenerate, the male becoming wholly dependent on the female for life support. This is the extreme example of a number of basic differences between the sexes, for males lack the fishing lure which in females is well developed and often luminous, and males have well developed nostrils by comparison with the females.

The largest deep-sea angler is *Ceratias holboelli* (family Ceratiidae) which grows to 47 inches in length, although the parasitic males are at most 2½ inches long. The female is heavy-bodied and flabby, with the skin covered with large conical spikes. The adults appear to live in 100 to 550 fathoms in mid-water, but the round-bodied young live at the surface. Occasional specimens are captured in the North Atlantic by commercial fishing vessels, but from the relatively few records of occurrence of adults they must be sparsely distributed.

Some of these ceratioid fishes have extremely well developed fishing lures. *Gigantactis macronema* (family Gigantactidae) has been found both in the Atlantic and the eastern Pacific. The adult female has an enormously long 'fishing rod' (illicium)—up to three times the body length. Males in this family are not parasitic and have notably well developed nostrils. *Linophryne arborifera* (family Linophrynidae) is remarkable for the very long, much-branched chin barbel, while the illicium on the snout has a swollen, luminous lure with a branched tip. This species has been captured in the Atlantic, Pacific and Indian Oceans at depths of 55 to 1650 fathoms. Although a number of larval males have been caught adult males have not; they are believed to be parasitic. *Eridolychnus schmidti* belongs to this family and is distinguished by its lack of skin pigment as well as by the rounded lure set on the snout without a long ray supporting it. It grows to 3¼ inches in length, and one female of this length has been found to have three parasitic males attached to her body.

Most of the deep-sea anglers have very large teeth (*Erido-*

chnus being an exception), but the extreme development is shown in *Lasiognathus saccostoma* (family Oneirodidae) which has the long teeth on the upper jaw pointing outwards. The jaw can be swung downwards so that the teeth form a trap. This fish is wholly black in colour, and the fishing rod is very long with a small, unevenly branched lure at its tip. Only one specimen has been captured, a female fish, three inches long, taken at 1143 fathoms in the Caribbean Sea.

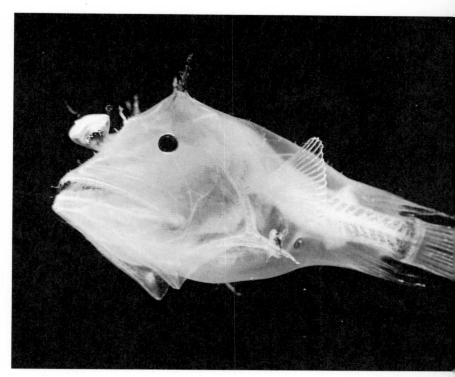

Eridolychnus schmidti, a deep-sea ceratioid angler-fish belonging to the fauna of the dark abysses. One of the most remarkable peculiarities of these anglers is the presence of pigmy males which, after a short free existence, fix themselves to the female (here on the head), and become parasitic upon the female. *Photo Researchers—Peter David*

Toadfishes (Batrachoidiformes)

This order of mainly bottom-dwelling inshore marine fishes is found in tropical and warm temperate seas. A single family (Batrachoididae) is recognized. They are usually stout thickset fishes with a broad head, dorsally placed eyes and a large mouth. Some, like the Atlantic midshipman (*Porichthys porosissimus*), which ranges from Virginia to Argentina, and grows to twelve inches in length, have rows of small light organs in a distinct pattern on the underside. This fish also makes loud choruses of growls, grunts and whistles, especially in the breeding season. The oyster toadfish (*Opsanus tau*) which is common from Cape Cod to Cuba in shallow water on muddy bottoms or in eel-grass beds, is another well-known vocal fish. In the seas of Central America and northern South America there are several species of venomous toadfish (*Thalassophryne* sp.) which have venom glands attached to the hollow gill-cover spines. If trodden upon or handled carelessly they can inflict a very painful wound.

This antennariid frogfish can blend perfectly with its background thanks to the numerous fleshy flaps on the body and fins. *Photo Researchers—Jane Burton*

Clingfishes (Gobiesociformes)

The clingfishes form a group of mainly small fishes distinguished by their flattened shape and the powerful sucker on the belly formed by modification of the pelvic fins. Most are found in shallow inshore waters, some even in intertidal areas, but a few species are found in freshwater in Central America and the Galapagos Islands. A common European species, the shore clingfish (*Lepadogaster lepadogaster*) is found on rocky shores in Britain spawning in summer under rocks. It grows to 2½ inches in length.

Ribbon-fishes and moon fish (Lampridiformes)

This family contains perhaps twenty species of marine fish of very differing appearance. In most the maxillary bones forming the upper jaw are protrusible (not the premaxillae as in other fishes), the fins are without spines and the pelvic fins, when present, are set near the pectorals and bear up to seventeen rays. These fish are inhabitants of the upper layers of the open sea; one species, *Stylophorus chordatus*, lives in the twilight zone in deeper water and has tubular eyes.

The fifteen-spined stickleback (*Spinachia spinachia*) is widely distributed in European seas. The male builds a nest amongst seaweed in shallow water and guards the eggs in it. *Phot. J. M. Baufle*

Ribbon-fishes (Trachipteridae and Regalecidae)

As their name suggests these fish are very elongate with deep, laterally-compressed bodies. The dorsal fin is long, beginning just behind the head and running to the tail fin which is composed of several upward-pointing rays. In the North Atlantic the deal-fish (*Trachipterus arcticus*), is widely distributed, occurring from the African coast to beyond the Arctic Circle and to west Greenland. It grows to a length of 8½ feet, and is bright silver with several dusky spots on the sides. It lives at depths of 100 to 500 fathoms and is occasionally seen at the surface. Most of the known specimens have been found cast ashore after storms.

The oar-fish (*Regalecus glesne*) is an even larger ribbon-fish, for it grows to 23 feet in length. It is found world-wide in tropical and temperate seas, and is believed to live at depths of 160 to 330 fathoms. Again few specimens (other than young ones) have ever been caught, most of the known occurrences being due to stranding after storms. The first section of the dorsal fin is composed of very long fin rays each with a fleshy flap at its tip. Sightings of this huge fish with an apparent crest on its head could account for some sea-serpent reports.

Moon fish (Lampridae)

The moon fish or opah (*Lampris guttatus*) is world-wide in its range, being especially abundant in tropical and warm-temperate oceans at depths of 65 to 220 fathoms. It is a mid-water fish, and an active predator on squids and other fish such as the blue whiting (*Micromesistius poutassou*), and the silvery pout (*Gadiculus argenteus*). Very little is known about its biology. It is a relatively large fish, growing to five feet in length, and to a weight of 160 pounds. Its body is deep, forming a smooth oval, and it is rather thickset, with a high dorsal fin and large pectoral and pelvic fins. The back is deep blue, the sides and fins red, and the fish is covered overall in white spots.

Squirrelfishes and their relatives (Beryciformes)

This order of spiny-finned fishes shows many primitive features in the skeletal structure. They typically have spines in both dorsal and anal fins, and a spine and from three to

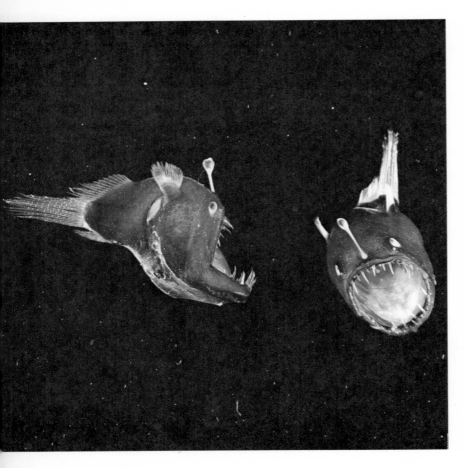

Two deep-sea angler-fishes (*Melanocetus* sp.). The large, dagger-teeth show them to be females, which live mainly in depths of 500–1000 fathoms. The conspicuous 'club' between the eyes, is a movable, luminous lure with which prey is enticed to within snapping range. *Photo Researchers—Peter David*

thirteen rays in the pelvic fins. Members of this group are entirely marine, and include several deep-sea families, as well as the shallow-water tropical squirrelfishes.

Squirrelfishes (Holocentridae)

These fishes are abundant on rocky or coral reef areas in tropical and warm-temperate seas. Many are bright red in colour, but striped patterns are numerous. In general they are rather deep-bodied fishes with large eyes, spiny fins, and rough-edged scales; one genus (*Holocentrus*) has a large spine at the corner of the gill cover. Most are nocturnal, hiding in caves or crevices in coral during daylight and becoming active at night. They are all able to make audible sounds, clicking, grunting and croaking to communicate with other members of the school. A common species in the western Atlantic is the longjaw squirrelfish (*Holocentrus ascensionis*), which occurs between Bermuda (and exceptionally off New York) and southeastern Brazil. It grows to two feet in length, inhabits rocky or coral areas from the shore-line to a depth of fifty feet, and feeds mostly on crustaceans.

Other beryciform fishes (Berycidae, Anomalopidae)

Most of the members of the family Berycidae are rose-red in colour and live bathypelagically in the open sea at depths where red is invisible due to the filtering of the sun's light. *Beryx splendens* is a typical member found in depths of 100 to 400 fathoms, probably world-wide. It has been captured on a number of occasions in the eastern North Atlantic off the British coast, and is commercially exploited off Japan. The related family Anomalopidae is represented in the East Indies and the Caribbean. *Anomalops kaptoptron*, a 12 inch long inhabitant of the seas of the East Indies in depths of 13 to 16 feet, is active at night swimming in schools just off the reef. It has an oval light organ below each eye which contains luminous bacteria. As light-giving bacteria cannot simply be turned off by the fish, the light is masked by the rotation of the whole organ inwards so that the black lining is external. In life the fish blinks its light rapidly.

Dories (Zeiformes)

The dories and their allies are rather more specialized than the berycomorphs. They have spines at the front of the dorsal and anal fins, fewer pelvic rays, but still a single spine in each pelvic fin, and fewer rays in the tail fin. This is a relatively small order containing six families, mostly little-known deep-sea fish. Two families which are well represented in shallow seas are the Caproidae and Zeidae. The boarfish (*Capros aper*) lives in the Mediterranean and eastern North Atlantic from Senegal to Ireland, and, rarely, to Norway. It is brick red with orange stripes, grows to about $6\frac{1}{2}$ inches in length and lives at depths of 55 to 220 fathoms amongst rocks and in crevices.

The John dory (*Zeus faber*) has a similar range but is found in shallower water (from the surface to 100 fathoms). Its remarkably deep and compressed body, large eyes and huge mouth are very distinctive. Although it is not of athletic build it is a very efficient predator, stalking small fishes head on until it is close enough to jerk its very protrusible jaws forward to catch its prey.

Dunckerocampus caulleryi, a marine pipe-fish from New Caledonia, is remarkable for its coloration. In nature it lives on the lower sides of overhanging coral heads. *Phot. R. Catala, the Aquarium at Noumea*

Pipe-fishes are closely related to the sea-horses and like them their gills are in tufts, and their bodies covered with bony plates. *Syngnathus pelagicus* of the Sargasso Sea is said to mimic the Sargassum weed among which it lives. The male incubates the eggs in a groove on the ventral surface of its tail. (×3.) *Phot. Aldo Margiocco*

Sticklebacks and pipe-fishes (Gasterostiformes)

This is an order which includes two divergent groups, the sticklebacks and the pipe-fishes and their allies, which have at times been separated as distinct orders. The mouth opens at the end of a tubular snout, and the gills are reduced in size or tufted. Many fishes have a bony armour on the body, and the pelvic fins (when present) are placed well along the body.

Sticklebacks (Gasterosteidae)

Sticklebacks are widely distributed in both freshwater and the sea in the northern hemisphere. Some species inhabit wholly marine habitats, others are confined to freshwater, but most can adapt to either and are thus euryhaline fishes. Most sticklebacks are small, with torpedo-shaped bodies, and are scaleless (except that some have bony plates along the sides). They are distinguished by a series of sharp spines along the back, variable in number and size.

The three-spined stickleback (*Gasterosteus aculeatus*) is one of the most familiar fishes in Europe and North America. It is distributed from Ireland eastwards across Europe and northern Asia, and through the northern United States of America and Canada. In the south of its range it is mainly a freshwater fish, to the north it lives in the sea, and it is occasionally encountered far out to sea. In freshwater it lives in large rivers (mainly at the banks), small streams, ditches and ponds. It is usually confined to well-weeded areas. It breeds in spring, the male becoming brightly coloured, most notably red on the throat and belly, and building a nest of plant fibres on the bed in which the eggs are laid by one or more females. The male guards the eggs and the newly-hatched young. Another common stickleback is the nine-spined stickleback (*Pungitius pungitius*) which is also found throughout the northern hemisphere. As its name suggests, it usually has nine rather short spines on the back (although it may have up to thirteen spines). It lives in heavily weeded, sometimes almost swampy conditions, usually in small streams and ponds, and can tolerate conditions of low oxygenation better than *Gasterosteus*. The breeding biology of the two species is similar, but *Pungitius* builds its nest in vegetation above the bottom. In the eastern coastal region of North America from Newfoundland to Virginia the four-spined stickleback occurs (*Apeltes quadracus*); it is occasionally found in freshwater but is primarily a sea fish. The only marine stickleback in European waters is the sea stickleback (*Spinachia spinachia*), a species growing to eight inches in length and very elongate, with fifteen spines on the back. It lives in inshore waters, in sheltered bays where there is sufficient growth of fine algae and eel-grass. The sea stickleback builds a nest, about the size of a man's fist, amongst algae in spring, in which the eggs are laid.

Shrimp-fishes and snipe-fishes (Centriscidae and Macroramphosidae)

The shrimp-fishes are confined to the tropical Indo-Pacific. They are elongate and compressed, their bodies are covered with bony plates, and their snouts are long. The body ends in a stout spine; the tail fin is displaced below the body. It is the habit of shrimp-fishes or razor-fish (as they are sometimes called) to swim in a vertical position, with either the head or the tail uppermost. This is very well illustrated in the *Aeoliscus strigatus*, which mimics the long black spines of sea urchins. The body is marked with lengthwise black stripes on the back and sides, and is so compressed as to resemble the spines exactly. These fish have also been reported to swim in small schools on the roof and sides of caves.

The snipe-fishes (Macroramphosidae) are world-wide in their distribution, being found most abundantly in tropical and warm temperate seas. All have a similar body shape, with a long snout and a large dorsal spine placed far along the back. They are mid-water fishes. The slender snipe-fish (*Macroramphosus gracilis*) is found in the Mediterranean and in the Atlantic from off Portugal to South Africa. Occasionally it is stranded on the shore after strong winds. The young fish are pelagic and have been found with and within the by-the-wind-sailor (*Velella*), a pelagic siphonophore.

Flute-mouths and trumpet-fishes (Fistulariidae and Aulostomatidae)

These two families could be thought of as transition stages between sticklebacks and pipe-fishes. The trumpet-fishes (Aulostomatidae) are found in tropical oceans, only three species being recognized. They have a series of spines on the back, the body is covered in scales, and a network of fine bones forms a sub-dermal armour. Flute-mouths or cornet-fishes (Fistulariidae) are also found in tropical seas but they lack scales and fin spines. Members of both families are

The eyes of a sea-horse (*Hippocampus* sp.) are protuberant and can swivel in all directions giving it all-round vision; they are adept hunters of small crustaceans. *Phot. J. Six*

The red scorpion-fish (*Scorpaena scrofa*), a Mediterranean and warm temperate Atlantic inhabitant of stony offshore grounds. *Phot. Fronval*

Sea fan with sea-horses (*Hippocampus ramulosus*); in deeper water the red would be indistinguishable from black, and the sea horse would be concealed. *Phot. Fronval*

A sea perch, *Anthias anthias*, an abundant fish on rocky areas in the Mediterranean and Atlantic, north to Portugal. It lives in shoals in the entrances of caves. *Phot. F. Guiter*

Portugal and throughout the Mediterranean, living on sandy and muddy grounds at depths of ten to fifty feet. It feeds almost exclusively on small crustaceans, but will eat young fishes as well. A smaller species, Nilsson's pipe-fish (*S. rostellatus*), is probably more common on the British coast and lives in water only one to ten feet deep. The sargassum pipe-fish (*S. pelagicus*) is found only in tropical and warm temperate oceans and lives amongst the fronds of the floating Sargassum weed. The worm pipe-fish (*Nerophis lumbriciformis*) is a dark-coloured species found on rocky shores on the British coast. It is one of the species in which the eggs are attached to a groove on the belly.

Many species of sea-horse are known, and they are world-wide in their range although most common in tropical waters. The most common European species is *Hippocampus ramulosus*, which grows to 6½ inches in length, and ranges from the Mediterranean to the southwestern coasts of Britain. It lives in shallow water amongst eel-grass and *Posidonia* beds, clinging to the vegetation by its tail. In the western Atlantic the dwarf sea-horse (*H. zosterae*), occupies a similar habitat but grows to a maximum length of only 1½ inches. It ranges from Bermuda and Florida to the Gulf of Mexico and Cuba.

Scorpion-fishes and their allies (Scorpaeniformes)

This order of spiny-finned fishes is particularly characterized by a heavy bony ridge running across the cheek. As a rule members of the order have numerous, often large spines on the head, and the body is fully scaled; but some groups, such

The red snapper (*Lutjanus sebae*) lives on reefs and rocky bottoms between 10 and 15 fathoms deep and is a valuable food-fish; large specimens may weigh as much as 48 pounds. It is widely distributed in the Indo-Pacific region. The fish on the left has a young grouper attached *Phot. R. Catala, the Aquarium at Noumea*

as the sea-snails, are soft-bodied and scaleless. In several groups, most notably the scorpion-fishes and stone-fishes venom glands are associated with the fin spines. The order is very diverse in choice of habitat: many species live in the shallow sea, others are found in the deepest ocean depths and some families live in freshwater.

Scorpion-fishes (Scorpaenidae)

This family of marine fishes is found in all tropical and temperate seas. Most have spiny dorsal and anal fins and large spiny heads, and all are scaly. In temperate regions the

elongate with very long snouts, which are flattened in the trumpet-fish and rounded in the flute-mouths. Trumpet-fishes haunt coral and rocky shallow waters generally floating gently and approaching their prey stealthily; flute-mouths are more active, darting in small shoals around shallow reefs and turtle-grass beds. They grow to a length of six feet.

Pipe-fishes and sea-horses (Syngnathidae)

The syngnathids are mainly inhabitants of shallow inshore waters, but a few species are found as planktonic open ocean inhabitants, while rather more have colonized freshwater, especially in tropical areas. They all have segmented bodies formed by skeletal rings beneath the skin, and all have dorsal fins (which form the chief organ of propulsion). Some species have pectoral, tail, and small anal fins, in others these fins are absent. The pipe-fishes are generally elongated and thin bodied, but sea-horses are more robust and have prehensile tails. All have long tubular snouts.

The male fish broods the eggs and developing young, either attached to a shallow hollow on the lower side of the abdomen, or protected by a fleshy fold on the anterior tail region. In the sea-horses this pouch is especially well developed.

In European waters there are thirteen species of pipe-fish and two sea-horses, most being confined to the Mediterranean and Black Sea. In British waters the most frequently found species is the great pipe-fish (*Syngnathus acus*) which grows to twelve inches in length. It ranges from Norway to

The red firefish or turkey fish (*Pterois volitans*), has immense pectoral fins, which look like wings when fully extended. It is widely distributed in the tropical Indo-Pacific, often found on reefs. The long spines have venomous tissue and wounds from them are very painful. *Phot. Fronval*

are important food fishes. Many of the tropical species have venom-laden spines.

In the North Atlantic there are two species of red-fish, sometimes called Norway haddock (*Sebastes marinus* and *S. viviparus*). Both are fished for commercially by vessels from Europe and North America. *S. marinus* grows to a length of 32 inches and a weight of about 30 pounds. It lives in water 60 to 350 fathoms deep on the edges of offshore banks and the continental shelf, at night rising into mid-water to feed on fishes, shrimps and other crustaceans. In addition to man it is preyed upon by Greenland halibut, cod, and sperm whales. The North Pacific has a very large number of members of the genus *Sebastes* (52 species in Californian waters alone); often known as rose-fishes, many are valuable food.

The Mediterranean species belonging to the genus *Scorpaena* are camouflaged fishes, usually living amongst algae well concealed by their coloration and the fleshy lappets of

are broad-headed fishes, with warty skins, and strong sharp spines in the dorsal fin. At the base of each spine is a venom gland which can eject poison through the hollow spine. The habit of the stone-fish is to lie amongst coral and rock in shallow-water areas, perfectly concealed by its craggy outline and 'camouflage' coloration. If a fisherman or bather steps upon the fish, the dorsal spines puncture the skin and the resulting wound is severe and very painful. Loss of the affected limb is not infrequent and deaths have been alleged to occur.

Gurnards (Triglidae and Dactylopteridae)

The gurnards or sea-robins (family Triglidae) are world-wide in tropical and temperate seas. Most are small, but some attain a length of 24 inches. They are relatively elongated with broad bony heads, and the lower rays of the pectoral fins separate to form long finger-like feelers. These are used to

The giant Mediterranean grouper (*Epinephelus guaza*) a fish which haunts the coastal zone, in rocky areas. It has become extremely rare in places due to the activities of under-water sportsmen who find them easy prey. *Phot. Guiter*

This highly coloured tropical grouper has to a large extent the same habits as the one found on Mediterranean coasts. It usually inhabits rocky places with numerous caves and crevices. Some groupers are real heavy weights of over 300 pounds. *Atlas-Photo—Lauros*

skin on the head and body. Their flesh is edible and is the basis for the famous bouillabaisse of the French coast. Many of the tropical members of this genus have venom spines in their fins. They share this feature with the fire-fishes or turkey-fishes (*Pterois* sp.), an Indo-Pacific genus, the members of which all have very long slender spines in the dorsal fin. Wounds from these spines can be very painful because they are venomous. *Pterois volitans* is a typical representative. It is red and black in bands with white margins, living close to reefs but often seen swimming over open ground. It can be identified by its coloration and very long fin rays, which act as warnings for its dangerous spines.

Stone-fishes (Synanceiidae)

The stone-fishes are close relatives of the scorpion-fishes and are, like them, confined to the tropical Indo-Pacific. They

probe the sea bed for food organisms as the fish creeps slowly over the bottom. Gurnards are well-known sound producers, making audible grunts and groans by vibrating the very large swimbladder by means of special muscles.

One of the most abundant and largest gurnards of British seas is the tub gurnard (*Trigla lucerna*). This grows to 24 inches in length and may weigh up to 11 pounds; it ranges from the Norwegian coast southwards to North Africa and the Mediterranean, living in shallow water at 10 to 80 fathoms. The very large pectoral fins are a brilliant peacock blue, with green and black spots.

The so-called flying gurnards (Dactylopteridae) are related to the sea-robins but can be distinguished by the enormous development of the pectoral fins and by the heavy, spiny head. They are tropical and warm temperate sea fishes. *Dactylopterus volitans* lives in the Atlantic, from Massachusetts to Argentina, in the Mediterranean, and from Portugal to West Africa. It lives on the sea bed, 'walking' over the sand on its short pelvic fins while searching for food with the short, anterior pectoral rays. When alarmed it spreads its huge, brightly-coloured pectoral fins in warning. Despite its name it does not leave the water to fly.

Bullheads or sculpins (Cottidae, Comephoridae and Cottocomephoridae)

The bullheads (usually known as sculpins in North America) are a very numerous group of marine and freshwater fishes in the northern hemisphere, particularly well represented in the North Pacific. The freshwater bullhead or miller's thumb (*Cottus gobio*) is a common inhabitant of rivers through England and parts of Wales. Usually found under stones or in dense weed beds it becomes more active at dusk. Other bullheads are found on the coasts of Europe, the sea scorpion (*Taurulus bubalis*), a large-headed long-spined species growing to about 5 inches in length, being particularly common on rocky shores in the British Isles. In North America several sculpins are found in freshwater, one of the most widely distributed being the slimy sculpin (*Cottus cognatus*) which is found from Virginia and the Great Lakes to eastern Siberia. It grows to $4\frac{1}{2}$ inches in length, and lives mostly in cool, running water on sandy and rocky bottoms in rivers and less often in lakes.

In Lake Baikal, in central U.S.S.R., a whole group of sculpins have evolved during the long isolation of the lake, and numerous species are known each of which appears to have occupied a different ecological niche. The live-bearing sculpins (sometimes called Baikal cod) of the family Comephoridae, are almost translucent, slender-bodied fishes which live bathypelagically during daylight and come to the surface at night. Both the known species are viviparous.

The members of the family Cottocomephoridae are more numerous in the lake. They differ by having teeth in the roof of the mouth and by certain skeletal features. The longwing sculpin (*Cottocomephorus comephoroides*) is a pelagic species living in schools at depths of 80 to 550 fathoms, but coming into shallower water in winter. It spawns in shallow water near the shore in early spring, the males guarding the eggs in nest holes under stones. Most of the numerous members of this family are bottom-living species, some found in shallow water, others in deep water in this very deep lake.

A small Mediterranean sea bream (*Diplodus vulgaris*), which has two cross-bands on the sides of its body. It is a very common fish amongst algae-covered rocks in shallow water. The fish in the centre, with numerous cross-bands is the raver *Diplodus cervinus*. Phot. Fronval

A sea bream (*Dentex filosus*), from the west coast of Africa; it reaches a length of 3 feet and weighs up to 26 pounds. Species of the genus *Dentex* are fished for commercially on a large scale off the coasts of Morocco and Angola. Phot. Max Poll

Lumpsuckers and sea snails (Cyclopteridae)

This is a rather distinctive family of marine fishes found in inshore waters and the shallow sea in cool temperate and polar seas, and in the deep sea elsewhere. They are rather plump heavy-bodied fishes, usually with a conspicuous and powerful sucker disc on the underside. The skin is scaleless or covered with bony plates or prickles. The great majority of species are bottom-living, but some are bathypelagic in the open sea. These either have a small sucker disc or none at all.

The lumpsucker (*Cyclopterus lumpus*) is widely distributed in the North Atlantic, in the east from the English Channel to the Arctic, around Iceland and Greenland, and in the western Atlantic southwards to New Jersey. It grows to a length of 24 inches (it is the largest member of the family) and is essentially a bottom-living fish found from intertidal regions to 165 fathoms, although it also lives in mid-water in the deep sea especially to the north of its range. It spawns in early spring in rocky areas, occasionally on the shore, the eggs being laid in large clumps in crevices guarded and aerated by the male. The newly-hatched larvae are pelagic but later come inshore and are found attached to sea weeds. In northern Europe and the U.S.S.R. the lumpsucker is exploited as a food fish. It is also eaten by the sperm whale, seals and the Greenland shark.

Sea snails look remarkably like tadpoles. The head is broad and rounded, the tail thin, and the skin soft and scaleless. Some species, like the British Montagu's sea snail (*Liparis montagui*), are found on rocky shores between tidemarks. Others such as the sea snail (*L. liparis*) are found sub-littorally down to 100 fathoms. This species grows to 7 inches and ranges from the English Channel to the Arctic Circle. A closely similar species, *L. inquilinus*, occurs on the North American Atlantic coast where it lives in association with bivalve molluscs.

Perch-like fishes (Perciformes)

The members of this order are very numerous and differ from one another in many ways, although all possess certain features in common. All have some spiny rays in the fins, typically a first dorsal fin with several sharp spines. The pelvic fins are close to the pectoral fins and are composed of an outer solid spine and five soft rays. The tail fin has only seventeen principal rays, and the mouth is flanked only by protrusible premaxillary bones. Most perch-like fishes have scaly bodies, the free edge of the scale being toothed.

The perciform fishes have evolved into the most abundant, even dominant, shallow-water fish group in the sea, although numerous species are found in freshwater, especially in the northern hemisphere, Africa, and Asia. About 150 families are recognized: of these the following are necessarily a very sparse sample.

Sea perches (Serranidae)

Sea perches make up a family of mainly tropical sea fishes, although some live in temperate waters and others in fresh-water. In general they are heavy-headed, rather stout fish, with a spiny anterior dorsal fin and toothed scales. Predatory, and usually living in shallow water, many grow to a large size—the largest, the tropical sea perches, exceed 1000 pounds in weight. Several serranids have been shown to be hermaphrodite, eggs and sperm being found in the same fish in some species, as in the belted sand-fish (*Serranus subligarius*) which is found off Florida.

The bass (*Dicentrarchus labrax*), an inshore and estuarine fish found from the British coast to the Mediterranean, is a popular game fish, as is the striped bass (*Roccus saxatilis*) of the North American Atlantic coast. The jewfish (*Epinephelus itajara*) is found on both the Atlantic and Pacific coasts of America. It is also a fine sporting fish, living amongst wrecks, under coral ledges, and in caves, and feeding on a wide range of marine life. It grows to a weight of 700 pounds. Other large *Epinephelus* species are found in the Indo-Pacific.

Sea breams or porgies (Sparidae)

The sea breams are marine fishes found around the world in tropical, warm temperate, and seasonally in temperate seas. They are most abundant in the tropical Atlantic and Indian Oceans. Dentition in this family is well adjusted to diet. Many sea breams feed on hard-shelled animals and have flat crushing teeth in the sides of the jaws. Others are predators on fishes and have large sharp teeth, while a third group

graze on fine algae and possess sharp-edged incisors in the jaws.

Many sea breams are reddish in colour, especially those which live at moderate depths on the continental shelf. The European red sea bream (*Pagellus bogaraveo*), which is found from the Canary Islands and the Mediterranean northwards to Scottish waters, is an example. Bright pink on the sides, the fins are deep red. As an adult it lives at depths of 80 to 160 fathoms, although smaller fish are found inshore. It feeds extensively on crustaceans and is a valued food fish in southern Europe. The dog-toothed breams of the genus *Dentex* are also extensively fished for in shelf water off the west coast of tropical Africa, especially in the Gulf of Guinea and off Angola. Many of these are large, heavy fish with fine flavoured flesh; the only species which enters British waters, and then only rarely, is *Dentex dentex*, which grows to 39 inches in length.

The saupe (*Sarpa salpa*), an 18 inch long sea bream which ranges from the Mediterranean (where it is very abundant) southwards to South Africa, has compressed teeth and feeds on algae scraped off the rocks and sea weeds. It is always seen in closely packed schools. One of the well-known North American sea breams is the jolthead porgy (*Calamus bajonado*), which occurs between New England, Bermuda and the West Indies. It usually lives in clear water around reefs in depths down to 25 fathoms. It is an excellent food fish.

Croakers or drums (Sciaenidae)

This is a large family of mainly marine fishes found in all tropical and temperate oceans, especially in estuaries. One species lives in freshwater in North America. They are particularly distinguished by their ability to make sounds by means of muscles attached to the very large swim bladder which acts as a resonating chamber. Many species live in turbid waters and their ability to make and hear sounds contributes to their success.

The freshwater drum (*Aplodinotus grunniens*) is widely distributed in North America, ranging from Ontario to the Gulf of Mexico. It grows to about four feet in length and fifty pounds in weight. This fish lives in deep pools in the main channels of rivers, lakes and reservoirs, feeding on bottom-living invertebrates—mainly crustaceans and molluscs. Like all its relatives, its otoliths (earstones) are relatively large and are often kept as curios.

The meagre or maigre (*Argyrosomus regius*) is a large croaker found in the Mediterranean and eastern Atlantic occasionally reaching British coasts. Its long, rather slender body with a long second dorsal fin and short anal fin are typical of the family. It attains a length of six feet, and where it is common it is a very valuable food fish. It is very probable that the South African kabeljou or kob, and the Australian mulloway, both valued food and game fishes, are but sub-species of this fish. Throughout tropical waters croakers form a large part of the catch of trawlers and fishermen working on sandy or muddy sea beds; their economic value is very great.

Jacks, dolphin fishes and remoras (Carangidae, Coryphaenidae and Echeneidae)

The jacks, scads and pompanos (Carangidae) are an important group of marine fishes of numerous species and very divergent shapes. Some are slender, streamlined fishes, others are deep-bodied, and the most extreme are almost plate-like. Many have a line of heavy plates along the tail.

The scad or horse mackerel (*Trachurus trachurus*) is a common European fish which ranges as far to the south as South Africa. It is a schooling fish, found in shallow water when

Coris angulata a tropical Indo-Pacific wrasse which changes colour with age; this one is in process of becoming darker, as is shown by its rear half. *Phot. R. Catala, the Aquarium at Noumea*

The butterfly-fish (*Forcipiger longirostris*), which is wide ranging in the tropical Indo-Pacific, is an inhabitant of coral reefs. Its extremely long snout and small, sharp-toothed mouth are adaptations for extracting small animals amongst the crevices of the coral. *Phot. Fronval*

The beaked coral-fish (*Chelmon rostratus*), is one of many beautiful reef-dwelling butterfly-fishes from the tropical Indo-Pacific. *Phot. Fronval*

young, but larger specimens tend to live offshore. The very young fish frequently live amongst the trailing tentacles of certain large jellyfishes. A similar association has been observed between jellyfishes and the young of the pilot fish (*Naucrates ductor*), but this fish, which grows to a length of 24 inches, is best known for its habit of 'piloting' larger fishes, sharks, turtles, and sailing ships, keeping in close proximity to the larger body. It is said to benefit by picking up scraps from the shark's meals, but it seems more probable that the pilot fish uses the association for protection and as a 'stalking-horse' to come close to prey.

The dolphin fishes (Coryphaenidae) are world-wide in their distribution in tropical seas. The dolphin fish or dorado (*Coryphaena hippurus*) is well known as a schooling fish of the open sea, although the schools often keep company with rafts of algae or flotsam at the surface. Juveniles are boldly barred and live amongst floating algae, but the adults are brilliant turquoise blue or green, silvery below, with yellowish ventral fins. Dolphin fishes are active predators, chasing flying fishes especially. They may grow to five feet in length and a weight of ninety pounds.

Remoras or shark suckers belong to the family Echeneidae. They are usually small fishes with a highly distinctive oval sucker disc on the top of the head, formed by modified dorsal fin rays in the form of slats either side of the mid-line. The remora uses this disc to attach itself to sharks, large fishes, certain whales and turtles, with which it travels. It derives some protection from this association and is said to release its hold and feed on scraps left over from the hosts feeding, but as one species at least acts as a parasite-cleaner the association is probably more complex than this suggests. The only shark sucker to occur in British seas, and that rarely, is *Remora remora* which accompanies the blue sharks (*Prionace glauca*) that invade the western English Channel each summer. The largest species is the shark sucker (*Echeneis naucrates*), which grows to 38 inches in length, and is associated with a large number of hosts. It is often observed free-swimming. One of the least-known is the whale sucker (*Remilegia australis*), a stout-bodied species which has been found on whales and dolphins.

Butterfly-fishes and damsel-fishes (Chaetodontidae and Pomacentridae)

These two families are not closely related, but members of both are abundant fishes on coral reefs and they are particularly brightly coloured, so it is convenient to treat them together.

Butterfly-fishes and angel-fishes (Chaetodontidae) are inhabitants of all tropical and warm temperate seas, especially where there are coral reefs. They are deep-bodied, laterally compressed fishes, usually with protuberant snouts and fine teeth (Chaetodon literally means 'bristle teeth'). The development of the snout, most extreme in *Forcipiger longirostris*, a widespread Indo-Pacific species, is an adaptation to differing feeding habits. *Forcipiger* feeds exclusively on the small crustaceans and worms which inhabit crevices in the coral; some members of the genus *Chaetodon* feed on the coral polyps themselves, neatly nipping off the emergent 'head'. The spotfin butterfly-fish (*C. ocellatus*) occurs from New England southwards to Brazil, and is one of several species known to have a night-time coloration very different from its brilliant daylight colouring. At night it becomes much darker and hides in a crevice.

A major group within the Chaetodontidae are the angel-fishes, which have a heavy spine on the lower edge of the gill cover. Some systematists regard them as belonging to a separate family, the Pomacanthidae. The angel-fishes are also brightly coloured, many of them having very different colour patterns when young. One of the best known is the emperor angel-fish (*Pomacanthus imperator*), a brilliantly coloured and boldly marked Indo-Pacific species, which is abundant on coral reefs and around rocks, and in which juvenile and adult are differently marked.

The damsel-fishes (Pomacentridae) are abundant fish in tropical seas and also occur in temperate waters. They are deep-bodied rather plump little fish with blunt snouts. The lateral line is in two sections and they have only a single nostril. The family includes the castagnole (*Chromis chromis*) of the Mediterranean and eastern Atlantic from Portugal to the Cape Verde Islands. The anemone-fishes (genus *Amphiprion*) are well-known fishes which live in association with large sea anemones. Sometimes called clown-fish because their colour pattern of alternating dark and light bands suggests a clown's clothing, they are Indo-Pacific fishes. *A. percula* of the west Pacific is a common fish in coral areas, sheltering within the large *Stoichactis* anemone. It even spawns on the coral or rock close beside its invertebrate host. The adults live in pairs with the anemone as the centre of a territory which is fiercely defended.

Left, the damsel-fish (*Chromis chromis*), common in the Mediterranean and tropical eastern Atlantic, belongs to the family (*Pomacentridae*) rich in reef-dwelling species. *Atlas-Photo—Lauros. Right,* the zebra angel-fish (*Pomacanthus semicirculatus*) lives on the tropical Indo-

Pacific coral reefs. This magnificent fish changes its colour with age. Here are two nearly adult individuals; the two posterior white lines will disappear with age. *Phot. R. Catala, the Aquarium at Noumea*

Above, clown-fishes (*Amphiprion ephippium*), with their associated sea anemone (Indo-Pacific). *Phot. Fronval.*

Wrasses and parrot-fishes (Labridae and Scaridae)

The wrasses are marine fishes found in tropical, sub-tropical and temperate seas, although in numbers they attain their greatest variety in the tropical Indo-Pacific. As a group they are particularly colourful, juveniles and females frequently differing markedly from adult males in coloration. They are shallow-water fishes, with conical or canine teeth in the jaws as well as flattened crushing teeth in the pharynx. Most species are relatively small, usually less than twelve inches long, but the Indo-Pacific giant wrasse (*Cheilinus undulatus*) grows to seven feet in length and a weight of 420 pounds.

In British seas the largest species is the ballan wrasse (*Labrus bergylta*), which grows to twenty inches in length. It is found from Scottish waters to the Canary Islands and in the Mediterranean, usually on rocky shores and offshore reefs in one to five fathoms depth. The cuckoo wrasse (*L. mixtus*) is found over the same area, but in deeper water (twenty to a hundred fathoms); in this species males are conspicuously coloured blue and orange, while the females are dull orange with three brown blotches across the back. The smaller cork-wing wrasse (*Crenilabrus melops*) is frequently found on rocky shores in the British Isles. In this species, as in some other wrasses, the adults construct a nest in the seaweed in which the eggs are laid and guarded. The larvae, however, are pelagic and may be found far out to sea.

Numerous species of wrasse are known for their parasite-picking habits, including at least one European species, the small-mouthed wrasse (*Centrolabrus exoletus*). This lifestyle is perfected in the cleaner-fish (*Labroides dimidiatus*), a four inch long Indo-Pacific species found on coral reefs. This brightly coloured fish adopts a territory usually close to some landmark like a coral head and beside which it displays in characteristic fashion. Larger fish come to this territory and allow the cleaner-fish to remove parasites from the skin and fins, and will even open their jaws and gill-covers to allow access to the mouth and gills. The wrasse is not harmed by the larger fish. Observations made on this species show that some of them change sex from female to male with age. The bluehead (*Thalassoma bifasciatum*), which lives in the western Atlantic between Bermuda and the West Indies, has similar cleaning habits when young.

Parrot-fishes are found in tropical and warm temperate seas, and are distinguished from the wrasses by having teeth in the jaws fused into a massive parrot beak, while the pharyngeal teeth are arranged in rows. Their teeth are adapted for feeding on hard substances and their normal diet consists of algae and coral browsed off the coral reef and crushed by the pharyngeal teeth to form a sandy paste. They are very important animals in the wearing away of reefs and the formation of coral sand. Most parrot-fishes are active by day and retire to a crevice or cave at night to sleep. Several species, such as the blue parrot-fish (*Scarus coeruleus*), found between the Carolinas and the Caribbean, secrete a mucous envelope around themselves while in their crevice, the sleeping bag forming an outer protection against nocturnal predators. Almost all parrot-fishes are brightly coloured, males and females of the same species usually having different colours or colour patterns.

Surgeon-fishes and cardinal-fishes
(Acanthuridae and Apogonidae)

The surgeon-fishes are so called because most of them have a sharply pointed, blade-like, erectile spine each side of the tail, reminiscent of a surgeon's scalpel. The spines can be erected so that they point forwards and make a fearsome weapon when the tail is lashed from side to side.

Surgeon-fishes (which are also known as tangs) are numerous in species and are particularly abundant in the tropical Indo-Pacific, although a few species live in the tropical Atlantic. Mostly they are colourful, deep-bodied fishes with rounded foreheads and only slightly protuberant snouts. Their teeth are specialized, chisel-like, and adapted for rasping algae off coral and rock faces. Several species have gizzard-like stomachs as a result of their diet of algae and coral sand. One remarkable-looking species, the unicorn-fish (*Naso brevirostris*) has a well-developed 'horn' on the forehead when adult; its use is unknown.

Many cardinal-fishes are red in colour, which has resulted in their common name. They are widely distributed in shallow tropical and sub-tropical seas, especially on coral reefs where they are often very abundant. Many are nocturnal fishes, hiding under rocks or in caves during daylight. In several species the males are known to mouth-brood the eggs (males often having deeper, wider heads than females); in another species the male picks up the egg-clump in its mouth if danger threatens.

Perches, North American basses and cichlids
(Percidae, Centrarchidae and Cichlidae)

The family Percidae is a group of freshwater fishes found originally only in the temperate regions of the northern hemisphere, although introduced in modern times to other areas such as Australia, New Zealand, and South Africa. Members of the family have a sharply spiny dorsal fin, the anal fin has two spines and the operculum is spiny. In Europe the perch (*Perca fluviatilis*) is widely distributed, especially in lakes and slow-flowing rivers. Its bold colouring, greenish

A   B

C   D

Four beautiful Indo-Pacific coral-reef fishes. *A,* a rabbit-fish, *Lo vulpinus. B,* an emperor fish, *Pomacanthus imperator. C,* the surgeon-fish, *Paracanthus hepatus. D,* an angel-fish, *Apolemichthys xanthotis. Phot. R. Catala, the Aquarium at Noumea and Fronval*

brown on the back with five to seven dark cross bars, and bright red fins, make it an unmistakable fish. It spawns in spring, the eggs being laid in strings wound around vegetation. A smaller relative, the ruffe (*Gymnocephalus cernua*), is less widely distributed, in England being found mainly in the eastern counties. The largest members of the family are the pikeperches (*Stizostedion* sp.) which are elongate predators growing to 36 inches in length. In Europe, the zander (*S. lucioperca*) is widespread and has been introduced to England. In North America the genus is represented by the walleye (*S. vitreum*), an inhabitant of large clear lakes and rivers. The yellow perch (*Perca flavescens*) is the North American representative of the European perch; the two are so similar that they may be no more than subspecies.

The North American basses (Centrarchidae) are one of the characteristic groups of the fauna of that region. It includes the sunfishes and black basses which are so popular as anglers' fishes. They are generally deep-bodied, with spiny dorsal fins and finely-toothed scales. The smallmouth bass (*Micropterus dolomieui*) has been introduced to Europe (and unsuccessfully to England) and is now well established in France where it competes directly with brown trout and preys on other fish. This, and the larger largemouth bass (*M. salmoides*), which grows to 32 inches in length, are both popular sporting fishes. Many of the smaller centrarchids are very colourful fishes, for example the pumpkinseed (*Lepomis gibbosus*) which is often kept in cold-water aquaria, and has

The teeth in the jaws of a parrot-fish are fused into a sharp-edged beak. They are typical inhabitants of coral reefs, and graze on the coral to obtain the plant and animal-life it contains. *Phot. R. Catala, the Aquarium at Noumea*

The golden-lined soap fish (*Grammistes sex-lineatus*) a widely distributed Indo-Pacific reef fish. Its skin secretes a toxic mucus which is distasteful to predators. *Phot. Fronval*

The European red mullet (*Mullus surmuletus*), prefers well oxygenated shallow water; it feeds on varied prey. They are seen here feeling the sand with their long barbels which are rich in taste buds and serve to find food. Red mullets are often known as goatfishes. Above the mullets swims a (female) rainbow wrasse, *Coris julis*. The males of this species are brightly coloured, mainly blue and orange; some females change sex as they become older and are coloured and behave like the males. *Phot. Théodor*

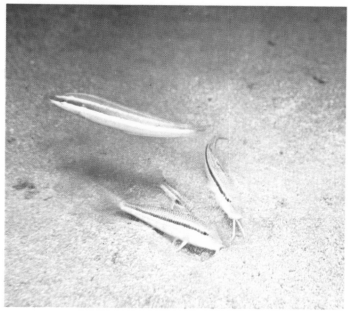

also been introduced to Europe. The centrarchids spawn in shallow nests hollowed out in the river or lake bed, the eggs and young being jealously guarded by the male fish.

The cichlids (Cichlidae) are a large family of freshwater fishes found in Africa, Asia Minor, Madagascar, India and Ceylon and America except for the cool temperate south and north of Texas. As a family it is remarkably successful, having evolved into a multiplicity of species filling most, if not all, available niches, and showing a bewildering variety of body forms and lifestyles. They are differentiated by having a single nostril each side of the snout, by having anterior spines in the dorsal and anal fins, and by the presence of lower pharyngeal bones usually joined together.

Some South American cichlids are popular aquarium fishes, notably the angel-fish (*Pterophyllum scalare*) which is strongly compressed and has long dorsal and anal fin rays and barred coloration. Although apparently eye-catching in the aquarium, its extreme thinness and subtle colouring conceal it perfectly in the densely weeded streams in which it lives. Even more spectacularly coloured is the pompadour or discus (*Symphysodon discus*) which lives in similar habitats in the

Amazon region. In this species the newly hatched young are nourished on the mucus of the adult's skin. Numerous other South American cichlids are known.

In Africa the fish fauna of the Great Lakes especially is dominated by cichlids. Some species of *Tilapia* such as *T. mossambica* and *T. heudelotii* are tolerant of brackish water and are found in coastal regions, the former on the east coast and the latter on the west coast. In lakes such as Tanganyika which have a relatively high salt content cichlids are completely dominant, about 150 species occurring there in many endemic genera. Here *Boulengerochromis micropelis* is a pelagic predator reaching a length of 3 feet and feeding on other cichlids. There are herbivorous shallow-water species (*Tilapia* sp., *Simochromis sp.*), insectivorous species (*Lamprologus*), which grow to lengths of between 1 and 20 inches, and even deep-water species (*Trematocara* sp.), which have been found as deep as 82 fathoms.

In Lake Malawi also there is a complex fauna of cichlids which includes *Haplochromis compressiceps*, which, as its name suggests, has a highly compressed, laterally flattened head and body. It obtains much of its food as a general predator, eating invertebrates and small fishes which it stalks by keeping head-on to its prey, but this is supplemented by its habit of attacking other fish from the side and biting out an eye with its sharp cutting lower teeth.

The breeding habits of many cichlids also exhibit many specializations. Many species are territorial, laying their eggs in a nest cleared out of the lake or river bed by the parents, who also guard the eggs. Others, such as some *Tilapia*, brood their eggs, and later the young fish, in their mouths which are distended considerably during egg-carrying. Mouth brooders usually have fewer, larger eggs than nest builders.

The ruffe (*Gymnocephalus*), is a widely distributed European freshwater fish, which occurs in the rivers of England. It feeds on live prey of small size. *Phot. J. Six*

Archer-fish and climbing perch (Toxotidae and Anabantidae)

The family Toxotidae contains several species of archer-fishes, all living in fresh and estuarine water in the coastal regions of Asia, between the Philippines and Australia, and westwards to Burma and India. The best known is the archer-fish (*Toxotes jaculator*), which grows to nine inches in length, and like its relatives catches its prey by knocking insects, spiders or caterpillars from overhanging foliage by spitting a jet of water. It can hit an insect-sized target at ten feet distance with accuracy.

The climbing perch family (Anabantidae) is distributed in both Africa, where there are numerous species, and in Asia (a single species). The last is the climbing perch (*Anabas testudineus*), which is found from southern China and the Philippines throughout Indo-Malaysia to India and Sri Lanka. It grows to ten inches in length, and is very abundant in canals, ditches and lakes, capable of living in anaerobic water by breathing air through supplementary respiratory organs housed in the gill cavity above the gills. It travels overland by flexing its tail against the ground while remaining propped up on its pectoral fins and gill covers, and can travel far from water in this way. It is able to climb the lower trunk of the rough barked *Palmyra* palm, and perhaps other trees, but does not do so as a way of life.

Marine burrowing percomorphs (Trachinidae, Uranoscopidae, Ammodytidae)

The weevers (family Trachinidae) are found on the coasts of Europe and as far south as West Africa. They are mostly small fishes. The largest species, the greater weever (*Trachinus draco*) grows to only 16 inches in length, and occurs from Norway to Morocco, and throughout the Mediterranean at depths of 16 to 55 fathoms. The lesser weever (*T. vipera*) is common in shallow water from mid-tide level to 15 feet, and is confined to sandy bottoms. In all species the spiny first dorsal fin and the head spines are equipped with venom glands and are capable of inflicting a severe and very painful wound. As weevers lie buried with only the top of the head showing it is not uncommon for bathers or paddlers to step on the dorsal spines and receive a painful wound. Weevers are also always a hazard to shrimp-fishermen.

The stargazer family (Uranoscopidae) are marine fishes of all tropical and warm temperate seas. They too burrow in sandy or muddy bottoms with only the eyes and tip of the mouth exposed, and also have a large spine on the gill cover with a venom gland at its base. The sole European species is *Uranoscopus scaber*, which is common in the Mediterranean and eastern Atlantic northwards to Portugal. Stargazers have a flap of skin on the lower jaw which they protrude from the mouth and vibrate to lure smaller fishes within reach. They also have well developed electrical organs behind the eyes which by setting up an electric field around the fish, warn of approaching prey. It may also deter predators.

The Ammodytidae are sand-eels or sand-lances, a small group of marine fish found especially in the North Atlantic but also occurring in the North Pacific. They are very elongated, with pointed heads. The lower jaw is the longer, and they burrow very ably in sandy sea beds. Several species occur in British waters, of which the eight inch long inshore sand-eel (*Ammodytes tobianus*) is most likely to be seen. The greater sand-eel (*Hyperoplus lanceolatus*) lives offshore and grows to a length of about fourteen inches. All sand-eels are important prey for other marine fishes as well as sea birds. A relatively recent fishery in the North Sea has exploited them extensively for reduction to fish meal. They are themselves edible if suitably prepared.

Antarctic cod (Nototheniidae)

This family is confined to the waters of the Antarctic and near polar seas. They are in no way related to the cod family but play a similarly important role in the ecology of high latitudes in the south as the cods do in the north. Most are bottom-living, rather sedentary fishes feeding on invertebrates and algae. One species is pelagic (as are juveniles of all species), and another (*Harpagifer bispinis*) is found on rocky shores in the subantarctic region. Members of the family have very varied body forms.

The discus or pompadour (*Symphysodon discus*) is a cichlid living in fresh water in tropical South America. The newly hatched young are nourishes on the mucus produced by the skin of their parents. *Phot. J. Six*

The archer-fish (*Toxotes jaculator*) lives in fresh and brackish water from the Philippines and northern Australia to Burma and eastern India. It spits a stream of water at an insect on an overhanging plant, knocking it into the water, where it is snapped up. It can hit accurately at 10 feet range, and as well as being able to see and judge the distance accurately, its aim must allow for the difference in refraction between water and air. *Photo Researchers—Burton*

The pearl gorami (*Trichogaster leeri*), well known to aquarium enthusiasts, lives in the densely weeded swamps of southeast Asia. It has a modified gill cavity making aerial respiration possible for a time, and breeds by building a large bubble nest at the surface in which the eggs develop, guarded by the male. *Phot. J. Six*

Squirrel fish, (*Holocentrus rutus*), emerging from a cave at Pennekamp State Park, in Florida. This species occurs widely in the Caribbean, and north to Bermuda. *Photo Researchers—Ron Church*

The sharp-nosed climbing perch (*Ctenopoma oxyrhynchus*). Like its relatives, this African species has a special organ in the gill cavity which allows it to breathe air. It lives in swamps. *Phot. Max Poll*

Freshwater spiny-eels (Mastacembelidae)

A small family of freshwater fishes which are found in tropical Africa, the Euphrates basin, and south and southeast Asia. They are scaly fish with long eel-like bodies, compressed tails, and a row of sharp spines along the back; they have a fleshy snout with well-developed tubular nostrils. Most spiny-eels live in heavily overgrown lakes, canals and rivers, usually hidden amongst the vegetation. Some species live in low-salinity estuarine areas. Probably the most specialized is *Caecomastacembelus brichardi*, which lives under the flat boulders and rocky crevices of rapids in the River Congo; it has become blind and devoid of pigmentation. In Asia especially the spiny-eels are used as food. *Mastacembelus armatus*, which occurs from India to Thailand, Java and Borneo, grows to 29 inches in length and is a locally important food fish, although its slippery skin and powerful body make it hard to hold once caught, and its dorsal spines can inflict painful wounds.

Blennies and gobies (Blenniidae and Gobiidae)

The blennies are mostly small fishes found world-wide in tropical and temperate seas. A few species are found in freshwater but the great majority are found in the shallow water, even between tidemarks, and close to the bottom. They are scaleless, rather elongated, with characteristic two-

A blenny; note the broad pectoral fin—the pelvic fins are small and placed well forward. *Photograph taken at the Steinhart Aquarium. Photo Researchers—Russ Kinne*

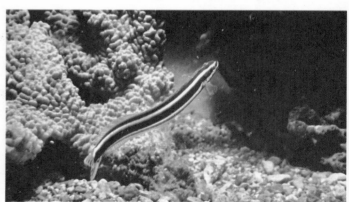

This blenny (*Runula albolinea*) from the reefs of New Caledonia mimics the wrasse, *Labroides dimidiatus*. The wrasse is a cleaner-fish which picks parasites from larger fishes and is usually not molested. The blenny-mimic relies on this to approach other fishes and bites their fins and bodies. *Phot. R. Catala—the Aquarium at Noumea*

rayed pelvic fins beneath the pectoral fins. Many have elaborate tentacles above the eye and elsewhere on the head.

The most abundant blenny on the European coast is the shanny (*Blennius pholis*), which lives, mainly between tidemarks, from Orkney to southern Portugal and Madeira. It is common under rocks and in tide pools on rocky shores, but quickly colonizes sandy pools provided they contain algae or pilings which offer shelter. It breeds, as do most blennies, in a crevice, the eggs being fastened to the underside of a rock and guarded by the male. Another European species is Montagu's blenny (*Coryphoblennius galerita*), which reaches the northernmost limit of its range in western Ireland. It is distinguished by possessing a transverse flap of skin across the head between the eyes. It grows to four inches in length. A third European species, *B. fluviatilis*, is found in freshwater and estuaries along the Mediterranean coastline.

Blennies have evolved many fascinating life styles, some of them involving mimicry. One of the best known is the four inch long *Aspidodontus taeniatus*, a widespread species in the tropical Indo-Pacific, which mimics in colouring and behaviour the cleaner wrasse *Labroides dimidiatus* (see p. 341). The blenny uses this resemblance to approach closely to other fishes before attacking them and nipping off pieces of skin, scales, or fin with its large curved teeth.

Judged by the numbers of species, and often the number of individuals, the gobies, and their relatives the sleepers, are amongst the most successful of fishes in inshore waters. They abound in most shallow water, tidal pools, estuaries, and even fresh water in tropical and temperate regions. The gobies are distinguished by having joined pelvic fins making a cuplike sucker; in the sleepers the fins are separate. Most species are small and live in crevices or in contact with the sea bed, although some are pelagic.

Several species live in British seas, amongst them the giant goby (*Gobius cobitis*), which grows to 8 inches in length, and the rock goby (*G. paganellus*) which is smaller; both live on rocky shores only. Sandy seashores are inhabited by the sand goby (*Pomatoschistus minutus*), estuarine and intertidal sand pools by the common goby (*P. microps*), while in sea beds of pebble and shell lives the painted goby (*P. pictus*); all three species grow to between $1\frac{1}{2}$ and 3 inches.

A blind goby (*Luciogobius pallidus*) has been found in artesian wells in Japan, and on the Californian coast the blind goby (*Typhlogobius californiensis*) lives in crevices on rocky shores down to depths of 25 feet; it is uniformly pink and blind. Many other gobies which burrow have much reduced eyes.

The mud skippers of the genera *Periopthalmus* and *Boleophthalmus* are gobies which live in the mud in mangrove swamps. They regularly live above water level, either on the mud or by climbing mangrove roots, feeding on insects and avidly defending their territories from one another. They breathe air but need to retain water in the gill cavity to effect respiration: from time to time they return to the water. With the exception of a West African species, they are found only in the Indo-Pacific.

Mackerels and tunas (Scombridae)

These fishes are perhaps the best adapted of all for life near the surface of the offshore seas. The body is perfectly streamlined; the snout is pointed, the anterior fins contract into a narrow slot, and the dorsal and anal fins end as a series of finlets (which greatly aids the fish's swimming ability). The tail is widely-spread. These fishes are the great swimmers of the ocean, the vertebrae interlocked and solid to provide firm anchorage for the mighty tail muscles. In the large tunas even the body temperature is up to 10° higher than ambient, which must aid the efficiency of the muscles, which are also particularly well supplied with blood vessels.

Mud hoppers (*Boleophthalmus* sp.), differ from mud skippers by the greater height of the first dorsal fin and by the elongate tail. The adults are very aggressive and frequently fight each other. These gobies occur widely on the coasts of southern Asia. *Phot. Ivan Polunin*

The mackerel (*Scomber scombrus*) is a small species, rarely growing to a length of 22 inches, which inhabits the North Atlantic. In the west it ranges from North Carolina to Labrador, and it is found in the Mediterranean and Black Sea. The mackerel lives in huge schools near the surface, often close inshore. It feeds on plankton and fishes, especially young clupeoids and sand-eels, and is in turn eaten by larger tuna, sharks and big fishes. The chub mackerel or Spanish mackerel (*Scomber japonicus*) is a rather smaller species, world-wide in its range in tropical and warm-temperate seas which occasionally occurs on the British coast. Both are valuable food fishes, the latter especially off the Californian and Japanese coasts.

The tunny or blue-fin tuna (*Thunnus thynnus*) is possibly the world's largest bony fish, specimens up to 14 feet long and 2000 pounds weight having been reported. It is widely distributed throughout the Atlantic Ocean, most abundantly in tropical and warm seas, migrating seasonally into the temperate zones. Related species occur in the Indo-Pacific (*T. maccoyii* in the south, *T. orientalis* in the north Pacific). It is a predatory species feeding on a wide range of smaller fishes, squids, and crustaceans. It migrates over vast distances, the tuna found in summer off the Norwegian coast having mainly come from the Mediterranean, although some large specimens are known to cross the Atlantic.

Probably more than any other tunny the Atlantic blue-fin shows the effects of over-fishing. Where once large fish were common in the autumn in the North Sea they are now never seen, and the Norwegian fishery begun in the late 1950s mainly for young fish increased to substantial proportions during the 1960s only to crash suddenly.

A smaller tuna, the albacore or long-finned tunny (*T. alalunga*), which grows to 51 inches in length, is also extensively exploited throughout the world in warm seas. A large fishery in the Bay of Biscay is operated by French vessels, and a more important area is off the Californian coast. The albacore is also a fine sporting fish which grows to a weight of 50 pounds. It is distinguished from other tunas in British waters (where, however, it is rare) by the extreme length of the pectoral fins. Another important tuna is the yellow-fin or Allison tuna (*T. albacares*) which is a cosmopolitan tropical species with bright yellow finlets. Despite its large size (it grows to 80 inches in length) it is often found in inshore waters. Many other tunas also range the oceans, amongst them the bonito or skipjack (*Sarda sarda*), the oceanic bonito (*Katsuwonus pelamis*), the false albacore or little tuna (*Euthynnus alletteratus*), and the long-bodied Spanish mackerels, kingfish, cero and barracuda (*Scombermorus* spp.).

Sword-fishes or bill-fishes (Ziphiidae and Istiophoridae)

These fish are relatives of the tunnies, and, like them, fast-swimming oceanic fishes of wide distribution. Many of the bill-fishes are renowned as sporting fish in tropical seas, but several are also important food fishes. All have a pronounced beak-like snout, that of the sword-fish being flattened above and below, while in the Istiophoridae it is round in cross-section.

The sword-fish (*Xiphias gladius*) is the sole representative of its family, and is distributed world-wide in tropical and warm seas; it occasionally occurs in British waters. It lives in surface waters of the ocean, although it has been found as deep as 330 fathoms. It grows to a length of about 16 feet, but despite its size and widespread distribution its biology is little known.

Ten or so species are included in the bill-fish family Istiophoridae, most of which are open sea fish of tropical regions. The family includes the sail-fishes (*Istiophorus* spp.) which have high, sail-like dorsal fins, and the marlins (*Tetrapturus* spp. and *Makaira* spp.). All are predators growing to a large size and most of them are favoured as sporting fishes.

Flatfishes (Pleuronectiformes)

There are probably about 500 different kinds of flatfish, divided into three suborders. The majority are coastal, inshore fishes always living close to the sea bed, but a few species are found in freshwater and some in deep water. All flatfishes, except the two members of the family Psettodidae, lack spines in the fins, but the most obvious feature of the whole group is their asymmetry. When newly hatched the larva is like a normal fish larva with one eye each side of the head, but with growth the skull bones become distorted and one eye migrates to the other side of the head until it lies beside the other. Other changes of some complexity ensue. In some families the pectoral and pelvic fins or the jaws become unequally developed. The eyed side is always coloured, the blind side unpigmented. In the great majority of flatfishes it is one side or the other which invariably bears the eyes, but in some species reversed specimens are more or less common (in British waters reversed flounders are frequent, but soles extremely rare).

Psettids (Psettodidae)

This is the most primitive family of flatfishes. Its members have spiny rays in both dorsal and anal fins, the teeth are large, and the migrating eye reaches only as far as the top of the head. It seems to be a matter of chance whether it is the left or right side which is pigmented. Two species only are recognized, the West African (*Psettodes belcheri*) and the Indo-Pacific Queensland halibut (*P. erumei*). Both live in water about 25 fathoms deep and both are fished for commercially.

Left-eye flounders and turbots (Bothidae and Scophthalmidae)

The bothids are a large group of mostly small flatfishes which have both eyes on the left side of the head, pelvic fin bases unequal and the dorsal fin origin close to the tip of the snout.

The white marlin (*Tetrapturus albidus*), which lives off the American Atlantic coast from Nova Scotia to Brazil, is believed to reach a weight of 150 pounds. It has a great reputation as a sporting fish, especially in the West Indies. *Photo Researchers—A. J. McClane*

A plaice (*Pleuronectes platessa*), swimming clear of the bottom; the whole fish undulates, with its fins spread out. *Phot. J. Six*
Bottom left, head of a flounder (*Platichthys flesus*), much enlarged to show the asymmetrical mouth and that the two eyes are on the same side of the body. The newly hatched flounder is symmetrical; during its development as a planktonic larva the eye on the left side moves over the head to finish close to the right eye. Profound changes occur to the nerve arrangement and skeleton of the head during this metamorphosis, but once completed the young flounders live on the sea bed. The flounder usually has both eyes on the right side. *Phot. J. Six*
Bottom right, the mackerel (*Scomber scombrus*) lives in shoals; it is an active swimmer, feeding on planktonic fish and crustaceans. It makes seasonal, but local, migrations following the warm currents which, from spring onwards, approach the coasts of Europe. *Phot. Aldo Margiocco*

Puffer-fishes (*above, Tetraodon* sp.; *below, T. stellatus* of the Indo-Pacific) have teeth fused into a beak. They store water or air in a sac attached to the stomach and can blow themselves into a balloon shape. Their flesh contains a toxic substance, which paralyses the respiratory muscles, and can be fatal if eaten. *Phot. Fronval*

Most species are found in tropical and temperate seas, particularly in shallow water. The peacock flounder (*Bothus lunatus*), which grows to eighteen inches in length and is found from Bermuda to Brazil, has its eyes spaced widely apart (more distant in males than females). The only common northern European members of the family are the scaldfishes (*Arnoglossus* spp.) which are small and usually live offshore in fifteen to sixty fathoms' depth.

The family Scophthalmidae includes a number of large flatfish with both eyes on the left and pelvic fins with equally broad bases. This group includes the turbot (*Scophthalmus maximus*) which ranges from Scotland to North Africa and throughout the Mediterranean. It is a large flatfish, growing to 39 inches in length, and found mostly at depths of between

20 and 40 fathoms. An extremely valuable food fish, although not caught in large quantities, it commands a high price. On the Atlantic coast of North America a closely similar, but smaller species occurs, the window-pane (*S. aquosus*).

The brill (*S. rhombus*) is another common European species found close inshore, usually on sandy bottoms, and young brill can be found in sandy tide pools on the British coast. It can be distinguished by the scales on its body; the turbot is scaleless but has bony tubercles. In water of 27 to 165 fathoms between Iceland and Morocco the megrim (*Lepidorhombus whiffiagonis*) is common; it is distinguished by its large mouth and eyes.

Right-eye flounders (Pleuronectidae)

The most obvious difference between the members of this family and the preceding one is that normally they have both eyes on the right side of the head. The family includes many well-known and important food fishes, and is represented in the Atlantic, Indian, and Pacific Oceans. The plaice (*Pleuronectes platessa*) is the most important flatfish in the fisheries of Europe, and ranges from the Barents Sea to North Africa and the Mediterranean. It is most common between 15 and 40 fathoms, and feeds on bottom-living invertebrates, especially molluscs, crustaceans, and worms. Its warm brown colouring with bright orange spots is very distinctive. Very similar in shape, but duller in colour, the flounder (*Platichthys flesus*) is found over much the same range, but is more common in estuaries and inshore waters. It is the only European flatfish to penetrate into freshwater. It is also frequently found reversed (i.e. its eyes on the left). The dab (*Limanda limanda*), the lemon sole (*Microstomus kitt*) and the halibut (*Hippoglossus hippoglossus*) are all common or important food fish in the eastern North Atlantic. The latter is a huge fish, specimens of eight feet length and 700 pounds weight having been caught in deep water. It is also found off the North American Atlantic coast. A related species (*H. stenolepis*) occurs in the North Pacific.

Soles (Soleidae)

The soles are of world-wide distribution in tropical and temperate seas. They have both eyes on the right of the head, the preoperculum is covered by skin, and the dorsal fin begins well forward by the mouth. Most bury in sandy or muddy bottoms in shallow coastal waters, but a few are found in the deep sea and some live in freshwater in tropical regions. *Typhlachirus caecus*, a sole found in the Malacca Strait, has only vestigial eyes; it is the only known blind sole. In Europe the most familiar species is the sole (*Solea solea*) which ranges from Norway and Faeroe to North Africa and the Mediterranean. Young specimens can often be caught close inshore but the large fish live in depths of ten to forty fathoms. It is a valuable commercial fish, and its flesh is greatly esteemed (usually as Dover sole). Most of the North American 'soles' are in fact members of the preceding families.

Tongue soles (Cynoglossidae)

Members of this family are tropical marine fishes. Both eyes are on the left side of the head, they have very elongate narrow bodies, the dorsal and anal fins are united with the tail, and they lack pectoral fins. Especially in the Indo-Pacific the tongue soles are locally important food fishes. Occasionally they are imported frozen into the United Kingdom, mostly the rather large *Cynoglossus senegalensis*, a West African species. Its flesh is of high quality.

The plectognaths (Tetraodontiformes)

This order of curiously shaped fishes is mostly found in shallow seas in tropical and warm temperate regions, although some are oceanic in habit, and others live in freshwater. All have small mouths, usually with well-developed incisor teeth, sometimes forming a sharp beak; the gill opening is reduced in size. There are around two hundred species belonging to eight families.

Triple-spines and trigger-fishes (Triacanthidae and Balistidae)

The triple-spines are so called because they have a strong spine in each pelvic fin and one large spine and several smaller ones in the first dorsal. They are best represented in the Indo-Pacific in shallow water, but several deep-water species have been found in the Atlantic as well as the Indo-Pacific—for example *Atrophacanthus danae*, found in the Celebes Sea at about 1000 fathoms. *Triacanthus brevirostris*, a ten inch long inhabitant of the seas from the Persian Gulf to Japan, is particularly common in heavily silted, low salinity estuaries.

The trigger-fishes and file-fishes (Balistidae) are mainly tropical and are well-known members of coral reef communities. Many are conspicuously coloured. They are compressed, deep-bodied fishes with rat-like teeth in the jaws, and a long first dorsal fin spine. This spine is locked into place by the second and cannot be depressed until the second (trigger) spine is released. The pelvic fins are reduced to a single thick spine on the belly. Many of the reef-dwelling trigger-fishes wedge themselves into crevices by the erection of the dorsal and pelvic spines if threatened; others merely erect the spine, thus presenting a difficult mouthful to a predator.

The black-barred trigger-fish (*Rhinecanthus aculeatus*), widely distributed in the Indo-Pacific, is typical of the brightly coloured species. The only species living in European seas is the trigger-fish (*Balistes carolinensis*, sometimes known as *B. capriscus*) which is mainly oceanic in habit and occurs throughout the tropical Atlantic. In warm summers it occurs in some numbers off the western coasts of Britain.

Puffer-fishes and porcupine-fishes (Tetraodontidae and Diodontidae)

In the puffer-fishes the teeth are fused into a beak formed of two plates above and below. The skin is often covered with small prickles which are erected when the body is inflated with air or water. Most are shallow-water inshore fishes, especially common in tropical and warm temperate zones. Some live in freshwater, for example *Tetraodon mbu*, which lives in the Middle and Lower Congo, and grows to 29 inches in length, and the rather smaller *T. lineatus* which is found in the Nile and other African rivers. Other puffer-fishes are oceanic in their life style, amongst them the members of the genus *Lagocephalus*. The puffer-fish (*L. lagocephalus*) is a rather long-bodied species, deep blue on the back and white ventrally, which ranges through the tropical Atlantic and Mediterranean. Very rarely it is captured on the oceanic coasts of the British Isles. Its Indo-Pacific relative (*L. scleratus*), which closely resembles it, is known to be virulently poisonous if the liver, gonads or blood are eaten. Many other puffer-fishes are also poisonous, including the fugu fishes of Japan (*Sphoeroides* sp.) which have to be expertly prepared by trained cooks to make highly esteemed, but non-toxic, dishes.

The porcupine-fishes or burr-fishes (Diodontidae) are a small family of tropical marine fishes which have long spines all over the body. Like the puffer-fishes they inflate themselves with air or water to erect the spines.

Box-fishes (Ostraciontidae)

The names box-fish, trunk-fish, and coffer-fish are all used for these fishes because of the hard, shell-like covering which envelops the whole body, with spaces only for the mouth, eyes, gill openings, vent, and fins to protrude. Several species have cow-like horns on the front of the head. Swimming is effected by sculling movements of the tail, dorsal and anal fins, but the typical progression is rather slow and stately.

A

B

, two trigger-fishes, and *B*, the black-barred trigger-fish (*Rhinecanthus aculeatus*). In these fishes the teeth are sharp and rat-like, especially suited to browse algae and encrusting animals off rocks and coral. All have a depressible, heavy dorsal spine. *Phot. J. M. Baufle—J. Six*

351

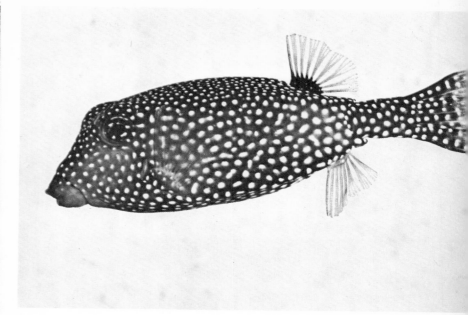

A box-fish (*Ostracion lentiginosum*), of wide distribution in the Indo-Pacific. It lives in shallow water around reef-edges. It eats various invertebrates and also browses on corals. It produces a toxic mucus and is for this reason rarely molested by predators. *Phot. J. Six*

Porcupine fish (*Diodon hystrix*) an inhabitant of tropical seas. *Phot. Fronval*

Some box-fishes secrete a toxic substance, clearly a deterrent to predators, when they are alarmed.

Box-fishes normally live quietly, close to the sea bed. They are world-wide in tropical seas and in some areas are relatively common. The blue-spotted box-fish (*Ostracion tuberculatus*) is a wide ranging Indo-Pacific species which grows to eighteen inches in length; it is one of the largest members of the family. The smooth trunk-fish (*Lactophrys triqueter*) is a common shallow-water inhabitant of the western Atlantic from Massachusetts and Bermuda to Brazil.

Ocean sunfishes (Molidae)

The members of this family are in many respects the most specialized of all plectognath fishes. They are all oceanic, most of them large to very large, and all have highly modified tails. The fish becomes wholly head and trunk, with short-based but high dorsal and anal fins. The pectoral fins are small, the pelvics absent, and the teeth are fused into a single unit in each jaw to form a sharp beak. The body is very deep.

The sunfish (*Mola mola*) is found in all temperate and tropical seas. It is not common anywhere, but the majority of specimens seem to have been caught in warm temperate regions. Sunfish are often seen floating helplessly at the surface of the ocean, but these are probably sick or dying fish, and the normal habitat is in the upper 100 to 300 fathoms of the sea. The sunfish feeds extensively on jellyfishes, sea gooseberries, planktonic fishes and crustaceans. It grows to a length of about thirteen feet and a weight of over a ton, but most of the specimens captured in British waters are only about three feet in length.

Despite its size the biology of *Mola mola* is little known, and still less is known of its relatives *Masturus lanceolatus* and *Ranzania laevis*. The former has been found world-wide in tropical oceans and its biology is probably similar to that of the sunfish; few adult specimens have ever been examined (it is at least as large as *Mola*) but the planktonic young stages are well known. The slender sunfish (*Ranzania laevis*) is rather longer than deep, but has a knife-like edge to the abdomen. It is relatively small, growing to 31 inches in length, but is brightly coloured, deep blue on the back, light on the sides, with brilliant silvery black-edged stripes curving across the head and sides.

The trigger-fish or file-fish (*Balistes carolinensis*) lives in the open Atlantic in tropical and sub-tropical seas, and in the Mediterranean. In warm seasons it may occur as far north as the English Channel and the Irish Sea. *Phot. Fronval*

Amphibians

The amphibians, also known as batrachians, are mainly water and wetland animals. Their skins are always moist and often sticky. They have evolved very little since remote times—about the end of the Palaeozoic era—when they were beginning to leave the water and come ashore to breathe the atmosphere. The giants among them disappeared long ago, and those which still exist today are of small or medium size.

Amphibians are a class of the vertebrates, and have special characters. They have four limbs adapted for walking or leaping, their temperature is variable, and their skins are bare and moist. Only fully developed amphibians breathe atmospheric air. They have three-chambered hearts, giving them a double, but imperfect, blood circulation. Almost all go through a tadpole stage in their metamorphosis to adulthood.

There are about 2500 species in the class Amphibia. These species are divided into three orders: Apoda or Gymnophiona (75 species), Urodela (300 species), and Anura (2100 species).

The origins of amphibians

Evolution from fishes to amphibians apparently took place in the Devonian period, about 400 million years ago, most likely in marshes that were subject to seasonal dry-out. In other words, their fish ancestors would be regularly submitted to muddy or dry land conditions.

What we know about these Devonian fish and their sole present-day survivor, the coelacanth, suggests that some of them, equipped with both gills and lungs, were able to come ashore as the first amphibians. They could breathe either oxygen dissolved in water or atmospheric oxygen. How the fin developed into a walking limb is as yet unknown.

The Ichthyostega

The remains of the *Ichthyostega*, obviously amphibian, are found in the old red sandstone of Greenland—a rock formed in lagoons during the Devonian period. The biggest of these fossils is three feet in overall length, the head being about a fifth of the total. The skeleton closely resembles that of the crossopterygian fishes (Osteolepiformes). These amphibians had powerful teeth of varying shape and size, and the four limbs characteristic of all land vertebrates including man. *Ichthyostega* looked like a very large salamander.

The clawed toad (*Xenopus laevis*), is a native of tropical Africa. It has been used for some time to provide early warning of pregnancy: if a female toad is injected with urine from a pregnant woman, the gonadotropic hormone it contains induces a dramatic development of the ovary of the toad. *Phot. Aldo Margiocco*

The labyrinthodonts

The great breakthrough of the amphibians took place probably between the end of the Palaeozoic era and the beginning of the Mesozoic era, with the appearance and proliferation of the types known as labyrinthodonts. The name has been given to them because of the internal structure of their teeth, which resembles that of their fish ancestors—the crossopterygians.

The labyrinthodonts appeared about 275 million years ago (Mississipian period), and were apparently directly derived from *Ichthyostega* or their immediate relations. The original forms had weak limbs and lived near water: they are known as the embolomeres. By the Permian period they had evolved into large robust amphibians known as rachitomes, which were much more closely associated with land and were able to walk. Some of these types were carnivores.

By the Triassic period, labyrinthodonts were beginning to follow a new evolutionary path. One might say they began to evolve backwards, because they returned to the water to

The spectacle salamander (*Salamadrina terdigitata*) lives only in Italy, in mountainous or wooded sites in Liguria and the Apennines. It haunts cool places, near springs and streams, but enters the water only for the purpose of mating and laying. Here, three females in the act of sticking their eggs to a branch. Total length 3 to 4½ inches. *Phot. Aldo Margiocco*

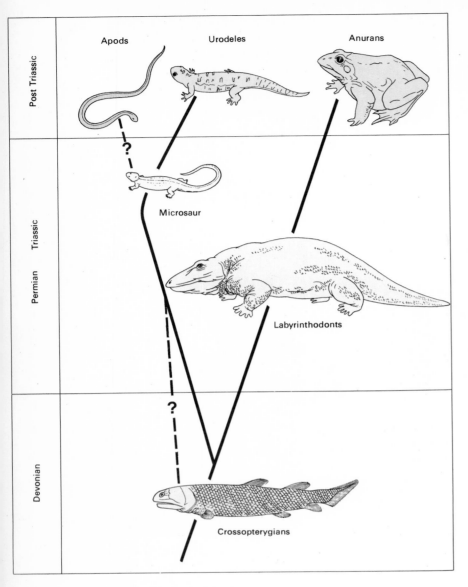

Diagram of the evolution of the Amphibia, whose parent stock (simple or double according to theories) is found among the crossopterygian fishes. *After E. H. Colbert*
Ichthyostega, the oldest known tetrapod, whose remains were discovered in the old red sandstone (Upper Devonian) of Greenland. It is a composite being, half crossopterygian fish (osteolepiform)—half-amphibian. *After E. Jarvik*

become the stereospondyls. The last labyrinthodonts died out at the end of the Triassic period.

The modern amphibians

There are many valid reasons, for assuming that the labyrinthodonts were the ancestors of present-day toads and frogs. Fossils, such as *Protobatrachus* from Madagascar's Triassic period, indicate the feasibility of the labyrinthodonts evolving into jumping amphibians.

Scientific opinion is divided as to the origin of the tailed amphibians which some palaeontologists and anatomists consider to be directly derived from the crossopterygians.

They quite rightly point out that the Urodela (tailed amphibians) have retained more ancient characters than the Anura (jumping amphibians). In Urodela, the skull and the roof of the mouth are very like those of the crossopterygians; but no fossils have been found to establish a link between them and the crossopterygians.

Some palaeontologists consider Urodela as the archaic form that made the reverse trip from the land back to water or swamp. They claim to be able to see in the skeleton of Urodela indications of this backward step (regressive evolution). They believe that the ancestor of Urodela was one of the leptospondyls (labyrinthodonts) of the Lower Permian period, and attribute the same origin to the Gymnophiona or Caecilians. But the fossil record is so scant that, in this field, the imagination has a clear run.

Types of amphibians

Amphibians are simply classified because there are only three orders, which differ in a number of important ways. The orders are: the Anura, the Urodela, and the Gymnophiona. Some zoologists consider that these three large orders of amphibians are really subclasses.

The anurans

The Anura, or jumping amphibians, are represented by frogs, toads and tree frogs, all of which begin their lives as tadpoles. With a few exceptions, they pass through a complex metamorphosis to reach the fully developed form. After metamorphosis, they shed their tails. All of them have hind legs well adapted for jumping.

The oldest anurans are the Leiopelmidae. The genera are *Leiopelma* from New Zealand and *Ascaphus* from the Pacific northwest of the U.S. Both genera have biconcave vertebrae. The *Aglossa* (tongueless frogs) comprise the Surinam toad (*Pipa*) of South America, and the clawed toads (*Xenopus*) from Africa, whose tadpoles have long barbels (protruberances round their mouths), and which feed on micro organisms. The adult does not leave the water.

The Discoglossidae of Europe include the painted frog (*Discoglossus*), the fire-bellied toad (*Bombina*), with bright yellow body and bluish black spots, and the midwife toad (*Alytes*). *Discoglossus* also inhabit North Africa and the family extends into Asia and the Philippines.

In Europe, the family Pelobatidae is represented by the mud-diver (*Pelodytes*), which has a vertical pupil, and the shade-foot toads (*Pelobates*), which burrow by day and come out only at night.

The toad family (Bufonidae) is cosmopolitan and includes a large number of genera and species. The true toads (*Bufo*) are found in Europe, Asia and America, while the *Nectophryne* and *Nectophrynoides* are found in tropical Africa.

Closely related to the toads is the Leptodactylidae family which is widely distributed in South America and Australia. A few species of this family are found in North America, including the well known bull-frogs, with their powerful croak.

The tree-frogs, or Hylidae, are found mostly in trees, as their name indicates. They have suction pads on the tips of their fingers and toes, so are able to anchor themselves firmly to the smoothest surfaces.

The anuran family with the largest number of species is that of the true frogs, or Ranidae. The great genus is *Rana*, which is found almost everywhere.

The urodelans

Although they all resemble salamanders in one way or another, urodelans show greater diversification than the anurans. With the exception of one species, they are found only in the northern hemisphere.

The Hynobiidae are an Asiatic family, and mostly ground dwellers. They have underdeveloped nasal vomerine bones and in some species the lungs are rudimentary. The genus *Hynobius* is found from the Ural Mountains to Japan.

The giant salamanders (Cryptobranchidae) which still live in water, have retained a number of larval characteristics. The hellbender (*Cryptobranchus alleghaniensis*), from North America, is typical in this way, retaining its gill-openings as an adult. The giant salamander of Japan (*Megalobatrachus japonicus*) is the largest of all amphibians.

The mole salamanders (Ambystomidae) are a North American family, notable for their biconcave vertebrae. There are two main genera: *Ambystoma*, including the famous axolotl, the neotonic form (see p. 377) of the tiger salamander, and *Dicamptodon*, the Rocky Mountain salamander, in both of which the eggs are fertilized internally.

The Salamandridae (the true salamanders and newts) are found over the whole of the northern hemisphere: *Salamandra* (Eurasia), *Pleurodeles* (Spain and Morocco), *Triturus* (Eurasia, North Africa), *Diemictylus* (North America), *Euproctus* (Pyrenees, Corsica, Sardinia), *Chioglossa* (Iberian Peninsula) and *Salamandrina* (Italy).

The Plethodontidae, which have no lungs, are all North American, except for one European species. The genera are *Pseudotriton*; *Hydromantes* (with the species *H. genei* which has a discontinuous distribution in northern Italy, in southeast France, Corsica and California); *Typhlotriton* and *Typhlomolge* which live in caves; and *Bolitoglossa altamazonica* which extends its range a little south of the Equator, and is fairly common in the Amazon region. It is the only Urodelan found in the southern hemisphere.

Mud-puppies (Proteidae) retain many of their larval characters when adult—for example, external gills and underdeveloped legs. There are two genera: one is the European *Proteus* or *Olm* which is eel-like and found only in caves. The other is the North American mud-puppy (*Necturus*) which lives in surface water.

The family Sirenidae is North American, with two genera, *Siren* and *Pseudobranchus*. They, too, retain certain larval characters—gills, lidless eyes and the absence of hind legs.

The green tree frog (*Hyla hyla*), common in southern Europe. *Phot. J. Six*

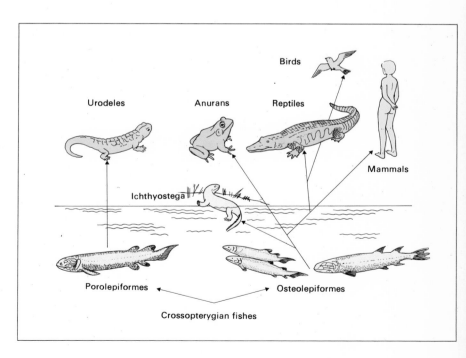

Diagram of the origin of the tetrapod vertebrates, starting from the crossopterygian fishes. *From the data of contemporary palaeontologists*

The great siren, *Siren lacertina* (about 2 feet long), the lesser siren, *Siren intermedia*, and the mud siren, *Pseudobranchus striatus*, are all native to the United States. Sirens are perennibranchiate, their hind limbs and girdle have been lost and they lead a cryptic life in fresh waters from Maryland to southern Florida. *Phot. J. Joly*

Batrachoseps attenuatus, the worm salamander, belongs to the family Plethodontidae, all save one of which are American. They are salamanders without lungs breathing exclusively through their skin. The animal is very long and crawls by undulations of the body, which presses sometimes on the front, and sometimes on the rear of the support. *Phot. A. Margiocco*

The species *Eurycea* are members of the family Plethodontidae. They live in places which are damp and dark; some species are found only in caves. The long-tailed salamander, *Eurycea longicauda*, shown here, is a species which spends most of its time on land, under stones or trunks of trees in damp places; it lays in water, like European newts. It can grow to inches. *Phot. A. Margiocco*

The gymnophions (caecilians)

These are blind, limbless amphibians, whose atrophied eyes are hidden under the skin. They have neither shoulder nor pelvic girdles. They have elongated worm-like bodies, and ringed skins which, in many species, are dotted with tiny internal scales. Between the eye and the mouth there is a slit with a protruding tentacle which is highly sensitive to touch (tactile). Great increase in body length, making these amphibians more and more snake-like, resulted in the development of a number of other snake-like characters: for example, a great increase in the number of ribs—up to 200—and atrophy of the left lung. This similarity of characters is known as 'convergent evolution'. Another example of convergent evolution is the similar appearance of the swift and swallow, two unrelated species.

The length of the caecilians varies from four inches to four and a half feet. The giant of the order is *Caecilia thompsoni* which is found in Colombia. Males have a copulatory organ which enables them to fertilize the females internally. In several species, among them *Typhlonectes*, the young develop in much the same way as mammals, that is, in a womb. Others lay eggs—the American *Rhinatrema* is one of them—and their young, which have external gills, probably develop in water, like frog tadpoles.

No fossils have ever been found of the amphibians in this group. The species alive today are found in South America, tropical Africa, the Seychelles and other islands of the Indian Ocean. None is found in Madagascar. This distribution suggests that the group is a very old one.

Caecilians live in moist earth, burrowing like the earthworms which are their main food. As they are difficult to observe, little is known of their habits. *Ichthyophis*, from India, has eyes that are just visible under the skin and *Typhlonectes*, from South America, lives in the water.

Typhlonectes compressicauda was recently found in the lower course of the Amazon; it lives in water and is nocturnal. This species has an electricity generating apparatus which scientists have not yet been able to investigate. It is able to emit electrical impulses in a regular pattern, and these are probably used for direction finding or to detect prey in the way that bats use echolocation. Besides hunting live prey, this amphibian also eats carrion.

Habitats

The term 'amphibian' is descriptive of a way of life. By definition, it means that, as a class, amphibians spend part of their lives in the water and part ashore. In fact, some of them spend all their lives in the water; many spend part of their lives there; and some are able to live out of it altogether.

Those amphibians that spend their lives away from the water are, as one would expect, species that can give birth to fully developed young (viviparous). They include the black salamander and the brown cave salamander (*Hydromantes genei*) of Europe; the Guinea mountain toad (*Nectophryroides occidentalis*); and several North American lungless salamanders.

Amphibians that never leave the water include *Proteus* and *Necturus* (urodelans) and *Xenopus* and *Pipa* (anurans). In the third group—those that spend part of their lives in the water and part ashore—birth and metamorphosis take place in water. After that, they live ashore to a greater or lesser extent. The toad returns to the water only to mate and spawn. The edible frog, on the other hand, does not stray far from its native pond except to catch prey or to bask in the sun. At the first sign of danger, it dives into the water. All the amphibians have to guard against the drying up of their skin, which causes it to harden and upsets respiration through it.

A very large number of the Anuran amphibians, perhaps 50 per cent of them, live in trees. Tropical rain forest provides tree frogs with the ideal environment, and that is where most of them are found. They are well adapted to a forest life. On their fingers and toes they have tubular glands with a sticky secretion. Equipped with such adhesive pads, frogs can climb the smoothest trunks and cling to the glossiest leaves. They have an additional bonus in that their colouring blends with their surroundings and changes with the background.

A few amphibians are able to breed in brackish water—the smooth newt (*Triturus vulgaris*), the palmate newt (*Triturus helveticus*) and the green toad (*Bufo viridis*). The Philippines has a species that takes over crabs' burrows in the tidal zone.

Tadpoles of the yellow-bellied toad (*Bombina variegata*) have been found in the outflow from the Berchtesgaden salt-marshes; those of the green toad (*Bufo viridis*) in the muddy, briny waters of the Zicksee in Austria; and those of the natter-

The dermophis (*Dermophis thomensis*), from the Island of San Thomé, West Africa, is a viviparous limbless amphibian; its young when newly-born have external gills. *Phot. Aldo Margiocco*

jack toad (*Bufo calamita*) in the pools of Saintes-Maries-de-la-Mer in the French Camargue. The natterjacks of the Friesian Islands spawn in water with a high salt content. Other species spawn in the du Plan marshes of the Giens isthmus in south-east France, but breeding in such places is not always successful. When spring rains are heavy, the tadpoles develop without hindrance because salinity is kept low. On the other hand, if the rainfall is slight, salinity remains too high, and all the tadpoles die. The critical salinity level is four milligrammes per litre; the tadpoles begin to die when it exceeds this.

Tadpoles of the painted frog (*Discoglossus pictus*) and of *Discoglossus sardus* can also survive and grow up in brackish water. They have been seen in the salt lakes of Tunisia, in the swamps of the Gulf of Gabes, and at the mouth of the Bayorie —a small river near Banyuls-sur-Mer. Research has revealed that the tadpoles of *Discoglossus sardus* die when the salinity exceeds five milligrammes per litre. Nevertheless, it appears that low salinity speeds up the tadpoles' development.

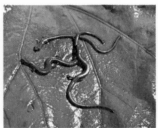

The Pacific worm salamander (*Batrachoseps pacificus*) is a North American plethodontid which has entirely terrestrial habits. It lays on land, and watches over its eggs until they hatch. *Phot. E. Sochurek*

The *Mantella* are small frogs of variable size (up to two inches in length), which inhabit tropical regions; they are remarkable for their very bright colours. *Above*, the multicoloured mantella (*Mantella cowani*). *Below*, the golden mantella (*Mantella aurantiaca*). *Phot. J. Six*

The natterjack toad (*Bufo calamita*) is remarkable for the shortness of its hind legs, consequently it is a poor jumper. It is found throughout Western Europe, including Great Britain. It lives mainly in sandy places. Its tadpole is very small, reaching about 1 inch. The adult measures 2½ to 3 inches from the tip of the snout to the cloaca. *Phot. Aldo Margiocco*

The marbled newt (*Triturus marmoratus*), whose very handsome coat is variegated with green and pink, goes to the water to breed. When the mating season is over, it returns to the land, adopts a lair, under a tree-trunk or a stone in a damp and dark place, emerging at night to look for insects, earthworms etc. Maximum size: 6¼ inches. *Phot. J. Six*

The hind legs of the spade-foot toad (*Pelobates cultripes*) have two horny black spurs which enable the animal to burrow in sand. It is quite at home in the dunes of the Atlantic and Mediterranean coastal regions. Size from snout to cloaca: ♂ 3 inches ♀ 3½ inches. Its tadpoles reach a very large size. *Phot. E. Sochurek*

High altitude species

It is well known that many amphibians can live at high altitudes—up to five thousand feet. Above that height, they become less common.

The black salamander (*Salamandra atra*) of the Alps is found between 2600 feet and 9800 feet, so is a real mountain species; but it cannot compare with *Batrachuperus pinchoni*, found in northern China, which has been recorded at 13,000 feet. Tadpoles of the midwife toad (*Alytes*) are not uncommon at altitudes up to 6500 feet.

Palmate newts breed in many Pyrenean lakes at altitudes between 5500 and 6500 feet. In the Pyrenees and Corsica, salamanders of the genus *Euproctus* are found up to 9800 feet. They like very cold water. The Spanish frog (*Rana iberica*) is another mountaineer, found in forested areas of the Pyrenees between 3200 and 4900 feet.

Adjustments of temperature variations

Amphibians are cold blooded. Unlike birds and mammals, they have no control mechanism, so their body temperature varies with their surroundings. Like all other animals, they

The giant South American or marine toad (*Bufo marinus*) reaches 10 inches in length. Its parotid poison glands behind the eye are very bulky and full of pores. The glandular warts on the sides and the legs also have glandular pores. *Phot. J. Six*

live in habitats where the prevailing temperature suits them, but they are well adapted to considerable variation. The temperature that suits the green toad best during its daily resting period is 72° to 74° F, but amphibians, as a class, can put up with variations in internal temperature of up to 104° F. They are not, however, as good as warm blooded animals at withstanding extreme differences in the temperature of their surroundings. When the temperature falls too low, they go into hibernation; if it becomes too high, they aestivate.

Research has shown that there is some sort of relationship between soil-type and the distribution of species. For example, *Hyla andersoni* is found only in ponds containing sphagnum, which means it needs acid water.

Unexpected habitats

Some species are found in underground water, for example the *Proteus* of the Caves of Carniola (Yugoslavia), the Texas blind salamander (*Typhlomolge*), and the grotto salamander (*Typhlotriton*) of North America.

Other species burrow into loose soil. The spade-foot toad (*Pelobates*) is well adapted to this. In a way, it is like the mole, having horny spade-like growths to assist it in digging. The pig-nosed frog (*Hemisus*), and some other species, have wedge-shaped snouts that help them to burrow.

The anatomy of amphibians

Skin and poison glands

Besides being moist, the skin of the amphibians is supple and free, being loosely attached to the underlying muscles. This is especially true of the anurans which have areas of lymph between the skin and the viscera over which it glides. The skin is kept moist by secretions from its own numerous glands. In some species, these glands become very prominent and produce poison or repellent fluid. Toads produce such a secretion from their parotid glands (in front of the ear); salamanders and the *Alytes* from a gland situated behind the eye. Hylidae (tree-frogs) have small poison glands distributed over the whole body surface.

Amphibian poisons have not been as widely or closely studied as snake venom. The poison of toads and salamanders contains alkaloids that have a paralysing effect on the heart and thorax muscles. Two poisons have been identified in the toad—bufotenine and buftalin, the latter being derived from bufotoxine which is related to digitalin. This explains its effect on the heart.

Some Indians in Colombia use the poison of the little *Dendrobates* frogs for their arrows. They obtain it by heating the bodies of the frogs over a fire. The poison oozes out and is gathered in a dish where it is allowed to ferment. The arrowheads are then dipped in the liquid. When dry, the poison remaining on the arrowhead is powerful enough to kill small animals, like birds and monkeys, but does not affect large mammals or man. The active principle of this poison is batracine (alkaloid).

Amphibians have no fangs or other inoculatory apparatus for injecting poison and are, therefore, virtually harmless. Their poison acts by contact and can cause severe irritation of the mucous membranes. A dog that has worried a toad will foam at the mouth for some time afterwards. Animals that swallow toad poison suffer nausea, a slowing down of the pulse, and some degree of paralysis. The main function of these skin poisons seems to be protective, but certain water birds, snakes and lizards, are not put off any more than owls are put off by the musk glands of shrews. It is now thought that the alkaloids secreted by amphibians vary from one species to another.

The tissue underlying the skin of amphibians contains numerous irregular star-shaped cells, known as chromatophores. Species with contractile chromatophores can literally change colour according to the contracted or expanded state of the cells. In most species, this is controlled by the intermediate lobe of the pituitary gland. The hormone that dilates the cells is called intermedin.

The secretions of some amphibians have characteristic smells. The common toad and the spotted salamander smell of vanilla. The spotted mud frog (*Pelodytes*) and the spade frog

(*Pelobates*) smell of onion, the fire-bellied toad of garlic.

Like snakes, the amphibians periodically cast, or slough, the outer layer of their skin. The frequency of sloughing varies from one species to another, the record being held by the green tree frog of Florida (*Hyla cinerea*) which sloughs every day of its active life. Toads slough at intervals of from three to ten days. As a general rule, the skin comes away in one piece and the animal then usually eats it.

Sloughing is not the result of the animal becoming too big for its skin: it has various causes, connected with endocrine secretions. A newt ceases to slough if its thyroid gland is removed. Frogs and salamanders do not slough after removal of their pituitary glands. It is obvious, therefore, that the thyroid and pituitary glands play an important part in sloughing. Sloughing is also influenced by feeding and by atmospheric conditions, especially temperature.

The skeleton

Amphibians have fewer skull bones than fish. The jaw bone is articulated to the skull by the scaly part of the squamosal (temporal) bone. The nostrils and eye sockets have wide orifices.

The structure of the limbs is fundamentally the same as in all land vertebrates, including man. Articulation of the legs is the same as in mammals—the fore limbs by the solid shoulder or pectoral girdle, and the hind limbs by the pelvic girdle. In anurans, the hind legs are specially developed for jumping.

Fore and hind legs have three segments, as in mammals. The foreleg has the upper arm (humerus), the forearm (radius and ulna), and the hand and fingers (equivalent of the mammalian carpals, metacarpals and phalanges). The hind legs have a thigh bone (femur) and calf (tibia and fibula), and the ankles and bones of the foot (equivalent of the mammalian tarsus, metatarsus and phalanges).

The skull is joined to the spinal column by means of the two articulating surfaces, or condyles, at its base (occipital condyles). There are no ribs. The pelvic girdle is articulated to a single sacral vertebra. In the anurans, the number of vertebrae is very small.

Modification of the hind limbs, by the considerable lengthening of the thigh, leg and tarsal bones, gives the anurans great jumping powers. The long foot and ankle give extra thrust when the animal is swimming or hopping. Mammals like hares and jerboas also have disproportionately long hind limbs, and are also great leapers.

The digestive system

Whether they have teeth or not, amphibians swallow their prey without chewing it. The tongue has become a device for capturing prey. It flicks outward, catches the prey and curls back into the mouth. In frogs, the tongue is attached to the floor of the mouth with its tip pointing backwards.

The circulatory system

Whereas mammals have a true four chambered heart—two auricles and two ventricles with left and right sides sealed off from each other—amphibians have two auricles and an imperfectly divided ventricle. Mammals and birds have a true double circulation. Oxygenated blood is carried to the left

Skeleton of the sp[...] ted salamander. *P[...]* *Aldo Margiocco*

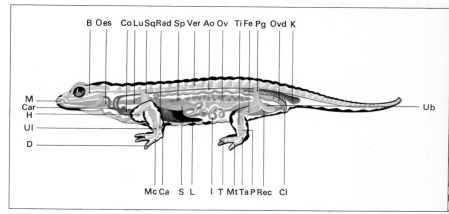

Diagram of the anatomy of the female salamander: *Ao*, aorta; *B*, brain; *Ca*, carpus; *Car*, carotid artery; *Cl*, cloaca; *D*, digits; *F*, fibula; *Fe*, femur; *H*, heart; *Hu*, humerus; *I*, intestine; *K*, kidney; *L*, liver; *Lu*, lung; *M*, mouth; *Mc*, metacarpals; *Mt*, metatarsals; *Oes*, oesophagus; *Ov*, ovary; *Ovd*, oviduct; *Pg*, pelvic girdle; *Rad*, radius; *Rec*, rectum; *S*, stomach; *Sg*, pectoral girdle; *Sp*, spleen; *T*, toes; *Ti*, tibia; *Ub*, urinary badder; *Ul*, ulna; *Ver*, vertebra.

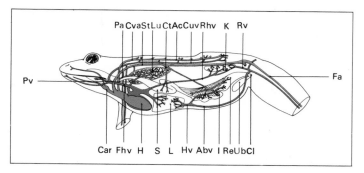

Circulatory, respiratory and digestive systems of the frog (*Rana*). In red, the heart and arteries, in blue, the veins.
Abv, abdominal vein; *Avc*, anterior vena cava; *Car*, carotid artery; *Cl*, cloaca; *Ct*, coeliac trunk; *Cua*, cutaneous artery; *Cuv*, cutaneous vein; *Fa*, femoral artery; *H*, heart; *Hv*, hepatic portal vein; *I*, intestine; *K*, kidney; *L*, liver; *Lu*, lung; *Pa*, pulmonary; *Pv*, pulmonary vein; *Pvc*, posterior vena cava; *Re*, rectum; *Rv*, renal vein; *S*, stomach; *St*, systematic trunk; *Ub*, urinary bladder.

auricle by the pulmonary veins, passed to the left ventricle and distributed to the body via the aorta. The de-oxygenated or venous blood from the body is returned to the right auricle by way of the great caval veins. It passes to the right ventricle and then via the pulmonary artery to the lungs where oxygenation takes place.

In amphibians, on the other hand, because of the incomplete division of the ventricle, there is some mixing of arterial and venous blood, although the mixing is not as great as was once thought. What really happens is that the great artery leaving the heart pumps first some venous blood, followed by some mixed blood, and then pure arterial blood. In amphibians, oxygenation of the blood also takes place through the skin, and there is a two-way system between heart and skin as between heart and lungs.

The respiratory system

In amphibians, the skin plays a greater part in respiration than the lungs. Even when out of the water, they have to breathe through their skins. Lung breathing alone is not sufficient to maintain life. When frogs are hibernating under water, they have to breathe entirely through their skins.

Having neither diaphragm nor intercostal muscles, amphibians cannot expand their chests to take in air in the way birds and mammals do. They draw the air in through their nostrils with the mouth closed; then the nostrils close and air is forced into the lungs by the rhythmic lowering and contraction of the throat muscles. Throat pulsations in the common frog can be as high as one hundred and forty per minute. As the skin of amphibians takes in more oxygen than the lungs, it is not surprising that it releases more carbon dioxide.

The nervous system and sense organs

The nervous system of amphibians is better developed than that of fishes, especially on the forepart of the body. The eye of the frog has a retina with specialized photoreceptors. Hearing is moderately developed, only a few amphibians lacking a middle ear. Frog tadpoles, anuran tadpoles, and purely aquatic urodelans, have sensory pores on their bodies, known as lateral line organs, which function by responding to vibrations in the water. Some of the sensory cells in this line are thought to be sensitive to air currents and variations in temperature. These cells are not found in fishes.

The reproductive organs

Male amphibians—except in a few cases like the tailed frog—have no external reproductive organs. The supposed tail of the tailed frog is really a protruding cloaca, enabling the male to penetrate the female and introduce his sperm. In all other cases fertilization of the eggs takes place in the water.

Reproduction and the sexual cycle

In cold or temperate regions, the breeding season of amphibians follows on quickly after the end of hibernation, although in some species it is later and spread over a much longer period.

The sexual cycle

Amphibians, in the course of the year, undergo a series of sexual changes, controlled by the release of hormones into the blood from several sources, including the ovaries and testes. When the animals emerge from hibernation, the testes are full of ripe spermatozoa and the ovaries contain hundreds, perhaps thousands, of eggs almost ready to be laid. Soon after mating—within a few days in fact—testes and ovaries have been emptied. They quickly shrink in size. Over the next few months, their cells build up again, ripening for the next breeding season.

During the breeding season amphibians do not eat; later the search for food becomes their main preoccupation. By late summer, testes and ovaries have regained their spring size.

Secondary and permanent sexual characteristics

Permanent differences between the sexes are few and not always obvious. In some frogs, the ear-drum is bigger in the male than in the female. Colour differences are rare, one exception being the Yosemite toad (*Bufo canorus*) in which the male is uniformly olive green, while the female has black spots edged with white on her reddish or yellowish body. In *Leptodactylus*, the arms of the males are much stronger than those of the females.

Seasonal sexual characteristics
These are much more common and more easily recognized. In the urodelans, brighter colours in the breeding season are common. Male marbled newts and alpine newts become flushed with red, blue and green on their flanks and bellies. The male crested newt grows a pronounced notched crest along his back. At mating time, the tail of the male palmate newt elongates into a slender thread. The skin of the male Californian newt becomes smooth, and dark dots appear at the base of his thighs. In females, the lips of the cloaca swell greatly.

Males of the Plethodontidae have cutaneous glands along their backs. These become active in the mating season and their secretions attract the females.

In the breeding season, toads and frogs develop horny thickenings on thumbs, hands and forearms, according to species. The growths on the fingers, generally known as nuptial pads, have a cluster of black or brown spines. Although they help the males to hold on to the females at the time of amplexus (sexual embrace), this may not be their only function. It has been suggested that they might be used by males during fighting. The pads are shed after the breeding season, quickly in frogs, much more slowly in toads.

The development of secondary sexual characteristics in males follows the release of the hormone testosterone by the testes. After the breeding season, the testosterone level falls and the testes shrink back, then ripen again in the next breeding season. No sexual characteristics develop in castrated amphibians.

Glandular secretions control the development and activity of the reproductive organs, and the pituitary plays a large part in this, although changes in temperature and climatic conditions probably play a part. The sequence of events is probably along the following lines: climatic factors—action on the hypothalamus—action on the pituitary (hypophysis)—action on the reproductive organs—appearance of secondary sexual characteristics and sexual behaviour.

Mating of the common European toad (*Bufo bufo*). Phot. E. Sochurek

Breeding places

Amphibians have their preferred breeding places and, after hibernation, they make their way there. Frogs, which hibernate in the mud of ponds, usually have to travel short distances, but they will travel hundreds of yards, or up to a mile, if they have to. Many toads make long journeys to their spawning grounds.

It has long been known that frogs and toads return each year to spawn in the same pond. It has been suggested that frogs find their way to their own pond by smell, in which case wind direction is important to them. Toads, on the other hand, do not appear to be guided by scent because they will return to a pond that has been filled in or drained. It still is not known how they find their way, because experiments have made it clear that they are not guided by sunlight or landmarks.

Many years ago, one researcher moved a number of toads from their spawning pond to another that seemed to him equally suitable. Most of the toads quickly returned to the pond of their own choice. He then released a number of toads between their own pond and another where frogs were spawning. Every one of the toads made its way back to its own pond.

In a homing experiment, 444 small Carolina toads were caught near their breeding pond and liberated at varying distances from it. Of those liberated at 300 yards from their pond, 60 per cent returned. Two toads released at 350 and

The red salamander (*Pseudotriton ruber*) is a plethodontid from the eastern United States. It lives hidden under stones and moss, but sometimes remains permanently in the water. Up to 7 inches in length. *Phot. E. Sochurek*

850 yards were back at the pond in 24 hours, but only eight were recovered from 43 released a mile away. Newts also return to their own ponds to spawn, but they do not usually have to travel far.

Breeding season
This varies from one species to another. The common frog of Europe (*Rana temporaria*) breeds early, in the period February/March; the colder the climate, the later it spawns. The edible frog (*Rana esculenta*) and the common toad (*Bufo bufo*) breed later, and their breeding season is more extended. The midwife toad (*Alytes*) spawns throughout the summer. The natterjack toad mates and spawns several times between March and September.

The arrow poison frogs (here *Dendrobates tinctorius*) are small frogs of the South American tropical forests, remarkable for the vigour of their colouring. The males put the young on their back and carry them to the water. *Phot. J. Six*

The following spawning timetable has been drawn up for North American amphibians:
January–July: the slender axolotl (*Ambystoma gracile*)
February–May: the red-spotted newt (*Diemictylus viridescens*)
March–April: the Jefferson salamander (*Ambystoma jeffersonianum*)
April: the lesser Siren (*Siren intermedia*)
April–August: the spring salamander (*Gyrinophilus porphyritious*)
May–June: the olympic salamander (*Rhyacotriton olympicus*) and the mud-puppy (*Necturus maculosus*)
May–October: the three-toed amphiuma (*Amphiuma means tridactylum*)
June–July: the red-backed salamander (*Plethodon cinereus*)
July–September: the four-toed salamander (*Hemidactylium scutatum*) and the tree salamander (*Aneides lugubris*)
August–September: the hell-bender (*Cryptobranchus alleghaniensis*)
September–December: the marbled salamander (*Ambystoma opacum*)
September–May: the California newt (*Taricha torosa*)
This timetable highlights two important factors—the influence of climate, combined with the physiological characteristics of each species.

In tropical areas, the reproductive rhythm is usually geared to the rainy season. Biologists who have reared painted frogs (*Discoglossus pictus*) have discovered that it is possible, at certain times of the year, to induce mating and spawning simply by heating the aquarium in which they live.

Breeding
The great majority of amphibians mate in the water and, except in a few cases, fertilization of the eggs take place there. The male fertilizes the eggs after the female has extruded them.

The mating of anurans
The male anurans are the first to arrive at these spawning grounds. During the day, they bask in the sun and, at nightfall, they utter their mating calls. Male toads and frogs swim after the females. Other species lie in wait until a female swims near them, taking action only when one appears in the immediate vicinity. Mating anurans take up the position known as amplexus. The male frog or toad climbs on to the back of the female and locks her in an embrace with his forearms behind and under hers. This is known as axillary mating. The midwife toad mates on land, as do many tropical species which lay their eggs in tree nests or carry them on their bodies.

The grip of the male, during amplexus, is strong and not easily broken. In the eighteenth century, an Italian priest, called Spallanzani, proved this in a brutal way. Working with male common toads and Italian frogs, he demonstrated that wounding them, burning them or mutilating them would not force them to release their grip on the female.

It seems clear that the male releases his spermatozoa in response to the muscular rhythm of the female—a reflex action. The spermatozoa released in the water fertilize the eggs—one sperm to one egg.

The female *Dendrobates auratus*, a small South American frog, lays her eggs on the ground and the male covers them with his sperm. In this species, there is no amplexus, but for several hours before the eggs are laid, male and female go through a ritual of jumping on to each other or against each other.

The mating of urodelans
Urodelans leave their hibernation quarters when the outside temperature and humidity have risen to a critical point. It is now known that emergence is triggered off by the release of a hormone from the hypophysis. This hormone, prolactin, is the same one that stimulates the secretion of milk in female mammals when their young are born.

The migration of urodelans to their spawning grounds has been closely studied, the western red-bellied newt (*Taricha rivularis*) from the San Francisco region being one example. Research demonstrated that this species always returns to the same part of a stream and will persist in trying to return there even when forcibly diverted from its route. Blinded specimens return to their starting point in the same way as those with all their faculties. But newts whose nostrils have been sealed with vaseline had great difficulty in finding their way—an indication that the sense of smell is important.

Males become greatly excited at the scent of a female, even when no female is present. If a male is put into a basin in which females had spent some time, it goes into a sort of trance and begins searching for them. The same response can be induced by offering the male a stick that has been in contact with the cloaca of a spawning female.

But more than the sense of smell is involved. In the mating season, the male can be excited if waves are stirred up in the basin by means of a glass rod. Eyesight also plays a part, and a male will become greatly excited at the presence of a female separated from him by a sheet of glass.

Crested newts (*Triturus cristatus*) in nuptial livery. The female is coming to the surface to breathe, the male is swimming. Up to 6½ inches in length. *Phot. John Markham*

Mating in the urodelans can be very simple or complex. In the case of the hell-bender, the mere presence of eggs laid near him by a female will stimulate the male to release spermatozoa without bodily contact or amplexus.

In many urodelans, the males have skin glands, usually on the cheeks and back, whose secretions attract and excite females at mating time. These glands are known as Hedonic or voluptuary glands. Smell, therefore, plays an important part in the behaviour of both sexes.

The display of the crested newt (*Triturus cristatus*) has been closely studied. When a male crested newt sights a female, he circles her, sniffing her all over. Then he takes up a position in front of her and strikes his ritual attitude. With his fore limbs firmly anchored to the ground or vegetation, he spreads his fingers wide, arches his back and fans his tail. The female's response to this display is to stand tall on all four legs, as though on stilts, and freeze. Presently, the male begins to move round her, striking her head with his flank or tail. If the female shows no interest, and moves away, he follows her. If she remains unresponsive, he stops parading.

The display may last for some time, with the male parading in front and the female moving up and down and from side to side. Eventually, he expels a spermatophore from his cloaca. In the spermatophore, which is produced by the glands of the cloaca, spermatozoa are stored. The male drops one or more of these capsules on the bottom of the pond. The female swims down to them and grips them, one at a time, in her swollen cloaca. Some species manage this without the use of their legs. In others, the legs are used to assist insertion.

The rough-skinned newt (*Taricha granulosa*), which lives in North America, has much the same habits as the European marbled newt. *Phot. Aldo Margiocco*

The sexual display of *Taricha* (North America Salamandridae) comprises a long phase when the male straddles the female, holding her in double amplexus. The species seen here is the rough-skinned newt *Taricha granulosa*; at mating time, the male's skin becomes granulose. After his straddling bout, the male deposits his spermatophores on the bottom of the pool or of the aquarium, and the female comes and picks them up with the lips of her swollen cloaca. *Phot. Jean Joly*

Egg-mass of a common European toad (*Bufo bufo*): it consists of a long string of transparent mucus in which the eggs, like small black pearls, are arranged in two rows. *Phot. Aldo Margiocco*

The walls of the spermatophore dissolve in the female's body, freeing the spermatozoa, which remain there until she is ready to lay her eggs. The spermatozoa are released as she lays, over a period of up to ten days. This method of fertilization means that spawning is independent of mating. The female lays about a hundred eggs, perhaps more, placing them, one at a time, on aquatic plants where their mucous walls become swollen with water. Once the spawning season is over, the urodelans usually leave the water, but they still live in wet places.

Most urodelans stick their eggs singly to plants or submerged stones. Hell-benders, on the other hand, lay them in strings. The Hynobiidae produce large quantities of mucus at spawning time. The eggs are caught up in this, in a sac which is then fixed to some solid support. Some of the land-based urodelans lay their eggs in damp spots—in holes in the ground or in trees. The red-backed salamander (*Plethodon cinereus*) lays her eggs in a cluster and fixes them to the roof of some small cavity, usually under a tree stump. The dusky salamander *(Desmognathus fuscus)* retreats underground at this time, with her eggs coiled round her body in a string.

The spawning of anurans

Frogs lay their eggs in gelatinous clusters which become masses of jelly by the absorption of water. These float on the surface— clear masses of jelly, polka-dotted with black. Toads lay their eggs in long strands which they wind round water plants. In frogs, each egg has an adhesive mucous matrix that joins it to its neighbour in the cluster. Toad eggs have a common mucous matrix.

Ascaphus truei of North America spawns in running water, attaching its strings of 28 to 50 eggs to the undersides of stones.

At spawning time, some of the anurans produce a mucous fluid which they beat into foam with their hind legs. This mass then floats to the surface. The American and the Australian *Leptodactylus* spawn in this way. The Mexican frog *(Leptodactylus labialis)*, which spawns on the banks of swamps or rivers, also produces foam. The frothy mass containing the eggs is hidden in small holes in the banks.

Frogs lay from a few hundred to several thousand eggs. *Rana catesbeiana*, the bull frog of the U.S., lays from 10,000 to 20,000, and Woodhouse's toad (*Bufo woodhousei*) from 25,000 to 26,000, arranged in pairs, like the common toad's.

The midwife toad

In the case of the midwife toad (*Alytes obstetricans*), the male looks after the eggs. This species, which lives among heaps of stones—in banks, quarries and gardens—is a truly land animal; much more so than any other European species. It mates on land at night. In amplexus, the male squats well forward, grasping the female at the neck, rubbing her cloaca with his toes. This action, which lasts for about twenty minutes, probably triggers off egg-laying. The male fertilizes the eggs as they are extruded and collects them between his hind legs, which are crossed over the female's cloaca.

The female lays more than a hundred eggs, wrapped in sticky strands of mucus from two to nearly three feet in length. The male twists the strands round his hind legs; then the pair separates. The male carries off the spawn and spends the next three weeks with the strands wrapped round his hind legs. From time to time during this incubation period, he refreshes the spawn by plunging into a pool or puddle for a short period. It is during such a plunge that the tadpoles hatch out and fall into the water, where they remain until they have completed their metamorphosis.

Nest-building anurans

Nest builders are found mainly among the frogs and tree frogs. The flying frog of Java (*Rhacophorus reinwardti*) builds its nest in a bush near water. At laying time, the female produces large amounts of mucus, which is beaten into foam by the male covering her. The foam froths among the leaves of the bush to form the nest. The outside of the nest quickly hardens, while the foam inside becomes fluid. The tadpoles hatch in the fluid. Then the rain dissolves the outer covering and they fall into the water.

The Japanese gliding frog (*Rhacophorus schlegeli*) makes its

The giant salamander of Japan (*Megalobatrachus japonicus*), some specimens of which reach about 5 feet and weigh 22 pounds, is very long-lived: individuals, caught in the adult stage, have lived for more than 50 years in captivity. The giant salamander of China (*M. davidianus*) is smaller (about 3 feet) and was made known to European naturalists by the celebrated Père David. *Phot. Kasusuke Mori*

Male midwife toad (*Alytes obstetricans*) carrying an egg mass which it will keep for the whole period of incubation (about 3 weeks). *Phot. Chaumeton-Jacana*

369

nest on the ground. While in amplexus, the pair dig a hole, a little above water level, on the bank of a pool or rice-swamp. When this has been completed, the female produces mucus which she beats vigorously with her hind legs until it becomes foam. In this foam she lays her eggs. As soon as they appear, the male fertilizes them with his sperm. Now male and female start digging a passage from the nesting hollow to the water. The passage opens under the surface and, along it, the tadpoles swim to reach the water, where they complete their development. The liquefied mucus from the foam helps to make their descent to the water easier.

The nests of some species are made simply of leaves packed close together without foam. Such nests often overhang a pool into which the tadpoles fall as they hatch. The Makis tree-frog (*Phyllomedusa*) and the *Agalychnis* from South and Central America make nests like this.

The blacksmith tree-frog (*Hyla faber*) of Brazil makes small pools, like basins, for the tadpoles to grow up in. In still river shallows, or other still water, the male constructs a circular basin of earth with smooth parapets about a foot in breadth. Mating, spawning and the development of the tadpoles takes place in these small pools.

Mating of midwife toad: the female is laying whilst the male is covering the eggs with sperm. *Phot. Jean Joly*

Oviparity and viviparity in amphibians

Animals are born either inside or outside the mother's body, and each species can be described according to how it gives birth to its young. There are three types—*oviparous, viviparous* and *ovoviviparous*.

Oviparity

The great majority of amphibians are oviparous, which means that they lay eggs—eggs rich enough in content to permit complete development of the young, at least to the tadpole stage, independent of the mother. Yolk is the controlling factor. Eggs with moderate yolk—like those of *Bufo, Rana* and *Triturus*—produce tadpoles which, after a long metamorphosis, become like their parents.

Big eggs, with abundant yolk, produce young that are identical with their parents, except in size. The tree salamander

(*Aneides lugubris*) of the United States is a good example of this. It lays from ten to twenty eggs in a hole in the ground or in a hollow tree, often as high as thirty feet from the ground. The female remains with the eggs, which are a quarter of an inch in diameter, during the incubation period. Each egg capsule has a stalk which anchors it to the 'nest'. All stalks converge so that the spawn looks like a small bouquet. The tadpole has external gills whose function is still not understood. It grows up in the egg and, when it finally emerges, it is an inch-long replica of its parents, capable of leading an independent life within a few days. After hatching, it absorbs the remains of its external gills.

Other anurans complete their development within the egg, so that the emerging young look like small adults. The eggs of such species have a high yolk content and are laid out of the water in humid places. In this category are the Madiana tree-frog (*Hylodes martinicensis*), a Mexican tree-frog (*Hylella platycephala*) and one from the Solomon Islands (*Rana opisthodon*).

The pipas

The pipas of South America have a unique method of reproduction. At the time of mating, the pair hold a territory of up to five square feet, which they defend against others of their kind by uttering warning cries. When ready to spawn, the female leads the male to the surface. There she lays her eggs, which the male immediately fertilizes. The eggs develop on the female's back, and it used to be believed that she put them there by means of an 'egg-placer' which, in fact, does not exist. What really happens is that, after spawning, male and female return to the bottom and wait for the eggs to rain down. They settle on to the female's back and become fixed there. Her skin grows over them, enclosing each one in a little pocket covered by a flap and, in this strange habitat, the eggs develop. The pipa tadpole has a broad tail which seems to act as an absorbent. When the young pipas eventually hatch, they are almost identical to the adults, so, in this case, metamorphosis outside the egg is practically eliminated.

Darwin's toad

Darwin's toad (*Rhinoderma darwini*) is a mouth breeder. The eggs float on the surface of the water in spawn clusters of twenty to thirty. Throughout the mating period, the males mount guard near the clusters; then, when the tadpoles are about to hatch, they swallow them. With the aid of his tongue, each male pushes the near-hatching egg clusters into his greatly extended vocal pouch. The elastic walls of the pouch have a dense network of blood vessels, and secrete a mucus that probably helps to nourish the tadpoles, which complete their development out of all contact with the water. When the young have reached a certain size—big enough to fit them for an independent existence—the male nurse ejects them from the pouch, literally vomiting them, an expulsion made possible by vigorous contractions of his abdominal muscles. All the members of this group are small, about an inch in length, and are found in the beech forests of south Chile and Argentina.

The male of *Sooglossus sechellensis*, a frog from the Seychelles, also looks after its young. In this case, the female deposits her spawn on the ground. The male stays close by until the tadpoles hatch. Then they take up position on his back, held there by suction, and grow on until they become small frogs. Very little is yet known about this phenomenon.

Males of the small tropical American frogs, *Phyllobates* and *Dendrobates*, carry the newly hatched tadpoles on their backs to pools where they complete their development.

The maruspial tree-frogs

The South American tree-frogs are worthy of special mention because they reveal a variety of relationships between embryos and the mother. These frogs lay few, but very large, eggs. The female of one species, *Cryptobatrachus evansi*, carries the spawn on her back. Protruding folds of skin along her flanks act as a gutter which prevents the eggs from slipping. In another species (*Flectonotus goeldi*), the folds of skin are more developed, forming a cup which holds the eggs securely. In the marsupial tree-frog (*Gastrotheca*), the skin folds are fused in front, forming a horse-shoe shaped pouch which opens backwards. In *G. ovifera*, the pouch has a wide mouth; in *G. marsupialis*, it is narrow. After fertilization, the male frog pushes the eggs into the pouch with his hind legs, helped by the female who raises the rear end of her body while he is doing so. In the pouch, the eggs are bathed in secretions of mucus and, according to species, complete all or part of this development there.

Gastrotheca marsupialis gives birth to tadpoles that finish their growth in the water; *G. pygmaea* and a few other marsupial tree-frogs give birth to small, completely developed little frogs. The female of *G. marsupialis* opens the slit of her pouch with one of her toes when the young are ready to emerge.

Oviparity with metamorphosis

The common fire salamander

The common fire salamander (*Salamandra salamandra*) is found in temperate regions of Europe, part of Asia Minor, Syria, and North Africa. It ranges high through the contours, being found up to 3200 feet in the Massif Central, to 3900 feet in the Alps and to 6500 feet in the Pyrenees. This salamander enters the water only to give birth to its young. Family size varies from ten to seventy, and the young are about an inch long at birth. The eggs leaving the ovaries are held in the oviduct—formerly called uterus because of their function—and it is here that development takes place.

Inside the eggs, the sole nourishment of the young is yolk. This has been tested experimentally with eggs taken from a female salamander and immersed in pure water. The larvae that hatched out were normal and viable. In this species, there is some uterine cannibalism. It is now known that the first tadpoles to free themselves from the membrane of the egg eat undeveloped eggs and dead embryos, and it is thought that the biggest larvae are capable of eating the smallest ones.

Salamanders are stay-at-homes, and will spend many successive years in the same small area, leaving it only to breed. A salamander's territory averages about 80 square yards. Animals removed a distance of 325 yards from their own territorial boundaries find their way back quite easily.

Prey consists of insects, molluscs and earthworms. Hunting begins at dusk—outside humidity has to be right before the animal will emerge—but it is not strictly nocturnal. After a summer rain storm, hundreds of salamanders may be seen on the move where the light is poor.

Although amphibians, salamanders are poor swimmers, and it is even said that they can be drowned while giving birth to their young in the water. They reach breeding condition at the age of four years, by which time they are about six inches long.

Mating, which takes place on land, is preceded by a courtship display. The male rubs himself against the female, passes beneath her, then seizes her in one arm with his tail coiled round her. In this position, the two cloaca are directly opposite, so it is easy for the male to insert a spermatophore into the female cloaca. This remains in the oviduct, stuck to its wall, ready to fertilize the eggs as they are produced. The spermatophore remains active for up to two years.

The fire salamander (6 to 8 inches) exists all over Europe; it has several geographical sub-species. This one belongs to the sub-species *Salamandra salamandra salamandra*, found mainly in central Europe. *Phot. Aldo Margiocco*

The tree salamander (*Aneides lugubris*) inhabits North America and has a predilection for laying in hollows in trees full of leaf-mould; it is sometimes content to lay in a cavity situated beneath a rotten tree-trunk. Length about 5 inches. *Phot. Aldo Margiocco*

Viviparity

Common enough in fishes, this is rare in amphibians. Two viviparous species are the black or alpine salamander (*Salamandra atra*), a urodelan, and the Guinea mountain toad (*Nectophrynoides occidentalis*), an anuran.

The black salamander

The black salamander (*Salamandra atra*) is an alpine species, found between 2600 and 9800 feet. In general habits, it closely resembles its relative, the common fire salamander, which is a lowland as well as a mountain species.

In the black salamander, the ovaries function normally, each producing about thirty eggs; but although all the eggs pass into the oviduct and are all fertilized, only one from each oviduct develops. The first one to reach the oviduct is the privileged one. It is the only one with a normal capsule; all the other eggs have an imperfect matrix. The privileged egg develops normally, but slowly; all the others in the oviduct degenerate into pulp.

The gestation period is from three to four years, and can be longer. There are three distinct phases in the development of the tadpole in the uterus. During the first stage, the privileged egg develops in the normal way; from it the tadpole emerges at term and eats the yolk that fills the oviduct-uterus. A year later, the larva reaches $\frac{3}{4}$ of an inch in length. By the end of the second year, it has used up the uterine yolk and acquired external gills. These are used, not for breathing, but for absorption of nutriments secreted by the uterine wall.

The young, at birth, are about two inches long; they look like small adults and behave like adults. Metamorphosis is cut out altogether. The lengthy gestation period is related to the rigours of the alpine environment, and, each year, development of embryo and tadpoles stops for about seven months.

Nectophrynoides occidentalis is completely viviparous. The ovary sheds three or four eggs at a time into each oviduct (uterus). They are about 1/100 of an inch in diameter, which is very small for amphibians, and do not contain yolk for the complete development of the young. Instead, they feed on nourishment secreted by the uterus. Each egg produces a tadpole about 1/5 of an inch in length, which develops in the uterus until it is about four times as long, including its hind legs. By then, it is a miniature toad, and is expelled from the uterus.

Gestation in this toad lasts for nine months, which is the same as in man. There is no tissue connecting the mother to her young, as there is in mammals. It is now believed that, from the beginning, the tadpole absorbs the uterine liquid in which it is immersed.

The development of the tadpole in the uterus depends on the hormones produced by the corpora lutea. The corpora lutea found in the ovaries of pregnant females (wherever a ripe egg has been produced) secrete hormones that prevent the ripening of further eggs there, and induce and maintain the secretions of the uterine glands. The corpora lutea disappear immediately after birth of the young toads.

Post-embryonic development

The eggs, which are always spherical, vary in size from 1/25 to 1/6 of an inch in diameter, according to species and yolk content. Each egg is contained in a mucus envelope that swells quickly in water. The eggs look like large cooked particles of tapioca with a small opaque mass in the centre.

A   B   C

Mating of the common fire salamander. *A*, the male straddles the female; *B*, the male passes under the female. *C*, the male bears the female on his back before depositing his spermatophore. *Phot. Jean Joly*

The ovaries of pregnant females contain yellow bodies called 'corpora lutea' (found in all mammals) corresponding to the number of eggs that have been laid. Corpora lutea last throughout the gestation period, stimulating uterine secretions that feed the larvae and inhibiting ovarian activity.

If larvae with external gills are removed from the uterus and put in water, they re-absorb their gills and grow breathing gills, very like those of the common fire salamander. This, of course, doesn't happen in nature, but it establishes that viviparity in the black salamander has not deprived its young of the ability to develop independently of the mother.

The brown cave salamander (*Hydromantes genei*) is also viviparous, but very little is known of its breeding biology.

The Guinea mountain toad

This small toad is found on the Nimba mountain grasslands of Upper Guinea. During the dry season, it withdraws into deep fissures, where it finds the humidity necessary for its survival.

The tadpole

Inside the egg, the embryo develops to the larval stage, when it becomes a mobile tadpole. At this point, it breaks from the egg by its own efforts. The egg shell is very thin and weakened by secretions from glands situated on the embryo's head. In a few species internal pressure causes it to burst—the green tree-frog (*Eleutherodactylus ricordi*) of Florida, for example. The tadpole has an egg tooth like that found in chicks, with which it tear

Opposite, African frogs of the genus *Chiromantis* (here, *Chiromantis xerampolina* from Mozambique) are entirely terrestrial. In the dry season, they keep to humid sites; in the rainy season, they venture anywhere. The couple shown here are about to lay. The female ejects from her cloaca a large amount of mucus, which she beats with her rear legs as if it was the white of an egg; she lays in this frothy mass the surface of which hardens and forms a crust. The mass of eggs is placed on top of a pool of water; the tadpoles emerge after 3 to 4 days. During incubation, the mother keeps her body pressed against the eggs. Length of *Chiromantis*: 3 inches. *Phot. Aldo Margiocco*

The brown cave salamander (*Hydromantes genei*) is the only plethodontid living outside America. It is found in north Italy and in France
(Alpes-Maritimes, Vaucluse). This urodelan has no lung. The end of its
tongue is shaped like a mushroom; it can be thrust up to 2 inches out of
the mouth and capture insects caught in the saliva. Total length: about 4
inches. *Phot. Aldo Margiocco*

Egg-mass of the European tree-frog (*Hyla hyla*). The eggs, although each
one is isolated in its matrix, are grouped in a mass and stuck to aquatic
plants. Notice, on the left, an egg surrounded with a halo which is made
from albuminous fluid. The egg, oriented under the influence of weight,
has its ventral pole uppermost. *Phot. Aldo Margiocco*

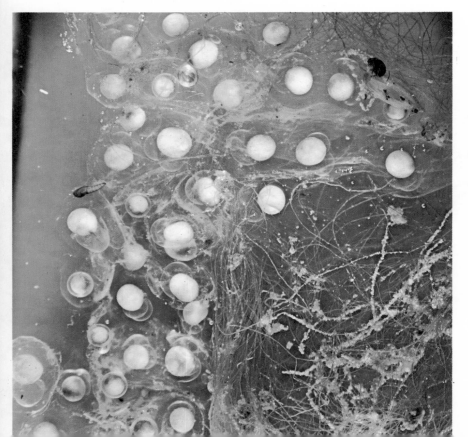

open the envelope of the egg. The egg tooth is shed soon after
the tadpole breaks out.

There is no marked difference between the tadpoles of
urodelans and anurans. At birth, both have external gills but
no legs. In other respects, they are quite different.

In urodelans, the anterior and posterior regions are equally
developed, and their external anatomy differs only very
slightly from that of adults. Anuran tadpoles, on the other
hand—frogs and toads—have a globular anterior region and a
long flattened swimming tail. The anterior region, popularly
called the head, is, in fact, the whole body.

The habitat in which the anuran tadpoles are hatched varies
with the requirements and anatomical peculiarities of each
species. Most commonly, tadpoles live in water which is rich in
vegetation (*Rana, Bufo*). Tadpoles hatched in running water
have flattened bodies and a sucker on their undersides, which
allows them to hold on and prevents them from being washed
away by the current (*Ascaphus*). Tadpoles that feed on tiny
food particles (microphagous tadpoles) are found in stagnant
water. They have broad lobed mouths and, when feeding, they
swim on their backs to nibble at the bacterial surface film for
the protozoa living there (*Xenopus*). Tadpoles that swim have a
well developed tail fin. The tadpoles of tree-frogs, on the other
hand, have hardly any fin. Carnivorous tadpoles have a
moderately developed fin and horny teeth (*Scaphiopus*).

When anuran tadpoles reach a certain size, they change
rapidly in form and anatomy: this is metamorphosis. All their
bodily functions become greatly modified—digestion, respiration, circulation and excretion. Their way of life and their
behaviour also change markedly.

Metamorphosis

Metamorphosis in anurans

Growth of hind legs; growth of fore limbs and the emergence
of these limbs from their membrane; transformation of the
skin which becomes wrinkled and develops glands and
pigmentation spots; disappearance of the tail.

Anatomical or biochemical changes

Transformation of the alimentary canal, which becomes
shorter and changes from the vegetarian to the carnivorous
type; development of the lungs, previously little more than
non-functional pouches; modification of the blood circulation
making lung breathing possible; transformation of the excretions.

Metamorphosis in urodelans

This is much simpler and more progressive than in the anurans.
The limbs appear early in life, and the external gills are
present for a long time. The respiratory system is modified and
the lungs develop earlier. The skin changes noticeably in
thickness and the tail loses its fin partially or totally.

The mechanism of metamorphosis

The tissues and the organs which will disappear become
degenerate and are attacked by white blood corpuscles. New
organs are formed from the basic outlines which were stopped
in the course of embryo-genesis, or from undifferentiated cells.

Development and metamorphosis of the frog: 1, 2, 3, 5, 7, 8, *Rana
temporaria*; 4, 6, 9, 10, *Rana esculenta. Phot. G. Termier and J. Six*

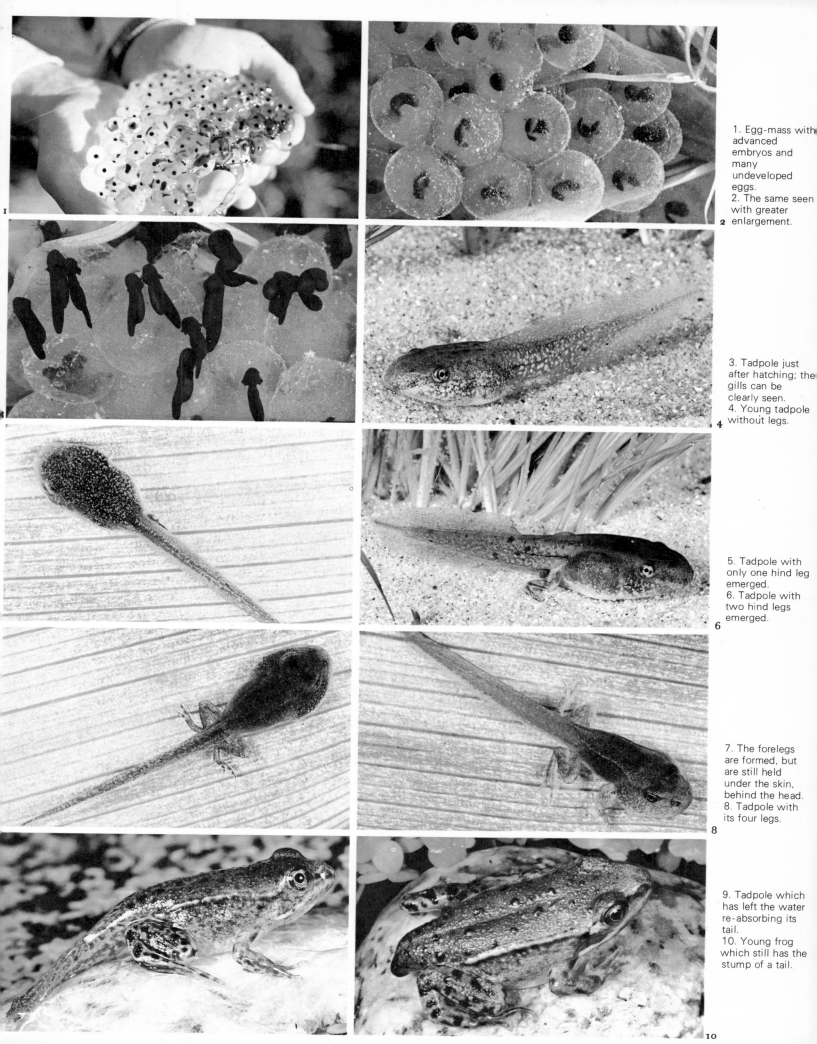

1. Egg-mass with advanced embryos and many undeveloped eggs.
2. The same seen with greater enlargement.

3. Tadpole just after hatching; the gills can be clearly seen.
4. Young tadpole without legs.

5. Tadpole with only one hind leg emerged.
6. Tadpole with two hind legs emerged.

7. The forelegs are formed, but are still held under the skin, behind the head.
8. Tadpole with its four legs.

9. Tadpole which has left the water re-absorbing its tail.
10. Young frog which still has the stump of a tail.

Larva of marbled newt (*Triturus marmoratus*) preparing to snap up a gnat (bloodworm) larva, then ingesting it after capture. Notice the height of the tail fin and the external gills. *Phot. J. Six*

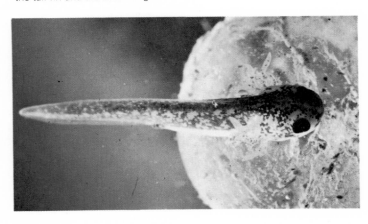

Tadpole of spectacle salamander (*Salamandrina terdigitata*) just after hatching; the gills are external and the animal has no limbs. *Phot. Aldo Margiocco*

Internal causes of metamorphosis

In 1912, a biologist called Gudernatsch carried out some experiments with tadpoles. Working with the tadpoles of *Rana esculenta* and *Rana temporaria*, he fed them liver, spleen, thymus, suprarenal and thyroid, and soon noticed that tadpoles fed on thyroid developed rapidly and far in advance of the timetable for their species. From this he deduced that normal metamorphosis in these species was controlled by secretions of the tadpole's thyroid gland. He then went on to confirm this experimentally, by removing the thyroid gland from tadpoles about a fifth of an inch long. At this stage in its development, most of the rudimentary outlines of the tadpole's organs are already present, but not all in their place. Thus, the rudimentary outline of the thyroid gland is there, but still near the surface of the body. This makes its removal easier.

It soon became clear that, when the operator removed only the thyroid region without touching the mouth zone, the tadpoles continued to develop almost as though they had not been operated on. But when the time came for metamorphosis, they remained tadpoles, whereas tadpoles of the same age that had not been operated on changed into small frogs. But those operated on continued to grow fast to twice the normal size, and some were kept for more than three years without showing any sign of metamorphosis. Their sexual organs, however, developed as they would have done had metamorphosis taken place.

The thyroid gland, however, is not the only one that plays a part. Tadpoles whose hypophysis has been removed do not grow, or metamorphose, or acquire functional sex organs.

The function of the hypophysis is controlled by a region at the base of the brain, known as the hypothalamus, which functions like an endocrine gland. The connecting link between hypophysis and hypothalamus is established some time in the embryo stage. If tadpoles are given an implant of hypophysis that has not been so linked with the hypothalamus, they metamorphose slowly in the early stages, and metamorphosis stops before the appearance of the fore limbs. A hypophysis that has not been activated by the hypothalamus cannot, therefore, carry out all its functions. If the hypothalamus region is removed from a tadpole, metamorphosis ceases.

From this, it is concluded that the hypophysis can control thyroid activity only in association with a functioning hypothalamus. The nature of the substances that act thus on the hypophysis is not known. But the substances are recognizable, for they can be seen as coloured globules travelling along the nerve fibres forming the stem that links the brain with the hypophysis, and passing into the venous capillaries that enter the gland.

External causes of metamorphosis

The activity of the hypothalamus is a seasonal rhythm, but the causes remain unknown. They are not entirely internal factors because it has been established that the activity of the rhythm of hypothalamus/hypophysis/thyroid varies according to the food eaten by the tadpole, the temperature and the daylight. Here are some facts to demonstrate the effect of the environment on metamorphosis.

In France, the midwife toad (*Alytes obstetricans*) spawns in May and June, and over-wintering of the tadpole is the general rule. Metamorphosis begins when the days are lengthening but the weather is still cold. Experiments have shown that a rise in temperature speeds up metamorphosis. Thus tadpoles subjected to a temperature of 78° F develop quickly. Extreme cold, on the other hand, holds up metamorphosis. Tadpoles of the midwife toad subjected to a temperature of 39° F will remain tadpoles for up to two years. This is also true of tadpoles living at high altitude and, in the Pyrenees, metamorphosis is spread over several years.

Neoteny

The term 'neoteny' came into use with the discovery of the axolotl. More than a century ago, the French General, Forey, brought the first specimens from Mexico to the Paris Museum of Natural History. The amphibians were of a hitherto unknown species which the Indians called axolotls. A close study of them revealed that they were larvae, and it was assumed that they would metamorphose in the usual way. They didn't. Contrary to expectations, and against all previous experience, the female axolotl spawned in 1865. This posed the question: could the axolotl still be considered a larva in view of the fact that larvae do not spawn?

The next surprise was when some of the tadpoles from this spawning metamorphosed in the usual way. It was now clear that the axolotl, under certain conditions, spawns while a tadpole, whereas under other conditions, it metamorphoses. Later research came up with the answer to this phenomenon. Removal of a tadpole's thyroid glands results in a giant capable of developing mature sex organs while remaining a tadpole. The same result is obtained by removing the thyroid gland from anuran tadpoles, but they do not become completely sexed, and this is the great difference.

In the axolotl, as in all urodelans, the development of evacuatory ducts is independent of metamorphosis. In urodelans, arrested development of the tadpole does not result in arrested development of the sex organs. In the anuran tadpole, although the gonads develop in the absence of thyroid, the evacuatory ducts do not. This explains why the axolotl can breed while it is a retarded tadpole.

It is now known that neoteny in the axolotl is due to thyroid gland deficiency. If it is given gland material, or the extract thyroxine which is its active principle, metamorphosis quickly begins. Development of the reproductive organs, on the other hand, does not depend on thyroid: it depends on the hypophysis which is, in turn, controlled by the hypothalamus. Neoteny, therefore, is the name given to a tadpole that is able to spawn.

In several species of newts, particularly the smooth newt (*Triturus vulgaris*), neoteny occurs accidentally. It occurs also in varying degree among American salamanders and other urodelans. In *Ambystoma punctatum* and *A. maculatum* neoteny occurs only occasionally. On the other hand, in *A. tigrinum* it is common in the coldest areas of the Rocky Mountains, whereas on the eastern plains, metamorphosis is the rule. Under laboratory conditions, metamorphosis can be triggered off in neotenic individuals simply by giving them thyroid.

Permanent neoteny

Two American salamanders, *Eurycea tyrenensis* and *E. neotenes* have never been observed under natural conditions in other than neotenic form. Nevertheless, metamorphosis can be induced by thyroid treatment. In these species, therefore, neoteny is not totally stable.

But there are species in which neoteny appears to be permanent, and no-one has yet succeeded in changing this by administering thyroid.

Proteus, from the caves of Carniola, retains a larval skin and external gills throughout its life. The American *Necturus* is the same. It is thought that, in the past, these species underwent complete metamorphosis in the usual way, but have lost the ability to do so.

If the skin of an axolotl is grafted on to a *Proteus* which has been given an injection of thyroxine (the active agent of the thyroid secretions) the axolotl's skin metamorphoses on the *Proteus* which otherwise remains unchanged. On the other hand, if *Proteus* skin is grafted on to salamanders during their metamorphosis, it undergoes changes, the same as in the

urodelans themselves at this time. The skin becomes loose and thin, and loses the special cells (Leydig cells) characteristic of urodelan larvae. It would seem that the skin of *Proteus* does possess the latent ability to metamorphose, but cannot do so on *Proteus* itself. There seems no doubt that, one day, scientists will be able to induce metamorphosis in *Proteus*, organ by organ, by transplanting them in axolotl or other urodelans.

The spotted salamander (*Ambystoma maculatum*) is widely distributed in North America, from the Saint Lawrence to Florida and, westwards, as far as Texas, Oklahoma. The individual shown *above* is an adult which has metamorphosed normally. In the mucous matrix of the spotted salamander's eggs algae develop. The association is favourable to both: the infected eggs develop quicker than those which are not, their mortality is lower, and the algae have an accelerated growth in the matrix enveloping an embryo. *Phot. E. Sochurek*

The frog (*Rana*) captures flies by thrusting out its tongue which is fixed to the floor of the front of the mouth. The tongue is large, fleshy, pointed and coated with viscous saliva.

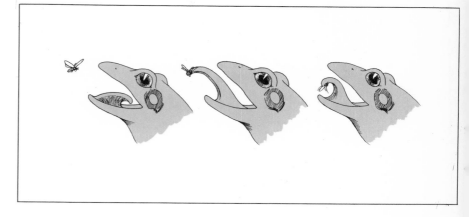

After metamorphosis

Not all amphibians that complete their metamorphosis survive afterwards. All of them lose weight, and many of them die in the following months. To get some idea of the extent of the death rate we have only to consider the number of eggs laid in relation to the number of individuals that reach maturity. In the course of her life, a female amphibian will lay thousands, perhaps tens of thousands, of eggs. And there will be males to fertilize them all. Yet the number of amphibians in the world does not increase. In other words, one breeding pair produces only another breeding pair. All other offspring die before reaching breeding age.

Sometimes the entire population of metamorphosed amphibians will leave the breeding pool at the same time—as in the case of Hunter's spade-foot toad (*Scaphiopus hunteri*).

Growth and longevity

Young amphibians, according to species, mature in two to four years. The Sardinian painted frog, at the end of its first year, reaches about an inch in length and weighs less than three hundredths of an ounce. At the end of the second year, it weighs more than a quarter of an ounce; at the end of the third year, it weighs an ounce. Most species reach sexual maturity at three to four years of age when they mate and spawn for the first time.

The longevity of amphibians is great:	
Painted frog	(*Discoglossus pictus*): 29 years;
Bronzed frog	(*Rana clamitans*): 10 years;
Bull frog	(*Rana catesbeiana*): 16 years;
Common European toad	(*Bufo bufo*): 36 years;
Marine toad	(*Bufo marinus*): 15 years;
American toad	(*Bufo terrestris americanus*): 31 years;
Yellow-bellied toad	(*Bombina variegata*): 30 years and more;
European tree frog	(*Hyla hyla*): 10–22 years;
Waltl newt	(*Pleurodeles waltl*): 20 years and more;
Axolotl	(*Ambystoma tigrinum*) larva: 25 years;
Spotted salamander	(*Ambystoma maculatum*): 25 years;
Fire-bellied newt	(*Triturus pyrrhogaster*): 25 years;
Californian newt	(*Taricha torosus*): 21 years;
Amphiuma or blind eel	(*Amphiuma means*): 27 years;
The great siren	(*Siren lacertina*): 25 years;
Hell-bender	(*Cryptobranchus alleghaniensis*): 29 years;
Giant salamander	(*Megalobatracus japonicus*): 52 years.

Daily life

The activity of adult amphibians is regulated by the seasons—governed mainly by temperature, humidity and the state of the gonads. In West European and North American species the annual cycle can be summarized in three phases: reproduction, aestivation and hibernation.

Some species are active by day; others only at night. But time of day is not the only factor involved in their activity cycle. Temperature and humidity exert their influence, and these are variable. It has also been suggested that atmospheric electricity affects the activity of salamanders.

A few species are adversely affected by light. *Amphiuma*, for instance, shuns light completely, and it has been shown that ultra-violet rays very quickly damage its skin. Most toads come out at dusk and hunt in the early part of the night.

Amphibians cannot tolerate a dry atmosphere for long. They have always to be near water. In a dry atmosphere, their skin moisture evaporates rapidly and hardens. An amphibian with dried-up skin dies quickly.

The olm or blind cave salamander (*Proteus anguinus*) is strictly confined to subterranean streams in caves in Dalmatia. When exposed to light, this perennibranch becomes pigmented, but its eyes remain undeveloped. *Phot. J. Six*

Food and hunting

Anuran tadpoles

Most anuran tadpoles are vegetarians, but they are sometimes carnivores. It is as easy to rear frog or toad tadpoles on cooked salad as on meaty bones. With the tiny teeth of their horny beaks the tadpoles can scrape off the smallest particles of flesh from a bone. Like ants, they can clean bones completely, so are ideal preparers of skeletons for study purposes.

Many species of tadpoles are omnivorous, feeding on algae, diatoms, small crustaceans and worms. The African clawed

The painted frog (*Discoglossus pictus*) North Africa, Spain, and the south of France. *Phot. J. L. S. Dubois*

The bull frog (*Rana catesbeiana*), which is very voracious, feeds on fish, insects, frogs, molluscs, and even small birds. It lives in North America, to the east of the Rocky Mountains. Introduced into the regions bordering the Pacific and into Japan, it has become thoroughly acclimatized there. It has a very strong voice. *Phot. Aldo Margiocco*

frog (*Xenopus*), which feeds on micro-organisms, has no horny beak. But it has real teeth, well adapted for scraping. It is a remarkable fact that tadpoles, despite their variable size, are bigger than the perfect amphibians they grow into. Completion of metamorphosis is accompanied by a marked reduction in size. The young of the midwife toad are much smaller than the tadpoles. The extreme case is that of the paradoxical frog (*Pseudis paradoxa*) of South America. In this species, the tadpole

Snakes are the greatest enemies of amphibians. Here is a grass snake (*Natrix maura*), from southern and eastern Europe, engulfing a natterjack toad (*Bufo calamita*). *Phot. Aldo Margiocco*

may reach the gigantic size of ten inches, whereas the young frog it turns into is only two and a half to three inches long.

Urodelan tadpoles

Urodelan tadpoles are light and agile, and feed exclusively on live prey—the larvae of insects and small planktonic crustaceans. The prey is seized in the mouth and swallowed. Urodelan tadpoles have numerous teeth in the roof of the mouth but these are used only for catching and holding.

Adult amphibians are carnivorous and predatory: they do not eat carrion. They recognize prey only when it moves, and movement triggers off the predatory behaviour pattern.

The table opposite shows the diet of various amphibians.

In a few rare urodelans, vegetable matter has been found in the intestines—up to eighteen per cent in the American mud-puppy.

The behaviour of the hunting toad is conditioned by two factors—hunger and the movement of the prey. Motionless bodies provoke no reaction in a toad, even when they are newly dead. But if you drag a body along by a thread, the toad will pursue, capture and swallow it. The toad will even follow and

snap up a piece of paper dragged along in the same way. But it is immediately rejected. It is clear, therefore, that it is the movement of the prey that initiates the predatory response.

When the toad catches up with a prey, it stands tall on its legs and towers above it, sometimes remaining motionless for several seconds. But before the toad snaps it up, the prey has to move again. Movement is closely linked with the final act of predation. Insects that remain motionless are safe from the toad because they do not trigger the snapping reflex. In other words, sitting still is a better defence than running away.

Similar behaviour can be observed when an adder chases a mouse: the adder gives up if the mouse freezes. Obviously, sight is important in such a predator/prey relationship.

Each eye sees an object independently. When a prey is sighted, the animal moves its head until it can see it with both eyes. One-eyed toads will stalk on to their prey in an arc. Being less able to judge distance, they attack the prey several times and compensate for their handicap by great liveliness. It has been shown, experimentally, that a lure, three to four inches long, will attract the attention of a toad up to ten feet away.

From this, it seems clear that, in nature, toads can see prey clearly at a distance of a few yards. Toads hunt mainly at twilight or during the night, and their eyes are well adapted to such conditions, the retina being richer in rods than in cones.

During the breeding period, the toad (*Bufo*) does not hunt or eat, although it will sometimes seize prey coming within its reach. This, however, is a simple reflex.

Outside the breeding period, *Bufo bufo* haunts gardens and such places. When it goes out to hunt at dusk, its stomach is empty. Toads captured at about 10 p.m. in summer usually have plenty of food in their stomach and intestine—worms, molluscs, beetles and ants, and often, bees, to which toads are partial.

Rana temporaria prefers to hunt insects, but also takes molluscs, worms, spiders and wood-lice. Some amphibians are extremely voracious. Field mice, frogs, snakes and shrimps have been found in stomachs of the American bull frog (*Rana catesbeiana*).

Rana crassipes, the frog from Gabon, is found in streams of clear acid water, with beds of mixed sand, clay and vegetable debris. These frogs are nocturnal and, at nightfall, build pyramids of sand where the water is about two and a half inches deep. The tops of the pyramids reach surface level. The frogs burrow into these pyramids and lie in ambush there, with only their eyes and nostrils showing. Any prey passing within reach is snapped up; then the frogs kick up a cloud of sand and bury themselves again. By morning, all the pyramids have disappeared as the result of the action of the current and the

American green frog (*Rana clamitans*):	
Insects, 72%	Crustaceans, 2%
Spiders, 7%	Myriapods, 2%
Young amphibians, 3%	Earthworms, 2%
Molluscs, 3%	Various and unidentified, 5%
American toad (*Bufo americanus*):	
Insects, 77%	Wood-lice, 2%
Spiders, 2%	Myriapods, 10%
Molluscs, 1%	Vegetable matter, 1%
Earthworms, 1%	Various and unidentified animal remains, 6%
Amphiuma or blind eel (*Amphiuma means*):	
Insects, 34%	Molluscs, 3%
Crayfish, 13%	Spiders, 1%
Reptiles, 12%	Fish, 17%
Amphibians, 20%	
Two-banded salamander (*Eurycea bislineata*):	
Insects, 62%	Spiders, 14%
Annelidae, 10%	Wood-lice, 14%

frogs' own movements. If a frog is taken from its pyramid and put down in bare sand, it will bury itself in less than three seconds. It digs itself in by circular movements of its legs, like the Spanish spade-foot toad (*Pelobates cultripes*).

Balls of twigs, and leaf debris mixed with mosquitoes, moss, earthworms and snails have been found in the stomachs of *Discoglossa*. The biggest recorded haul from a single stomach weighed 1/5 of an ounce and was made up of 247 organisms!

Urodelans feed on mobile aquatic vertebrates, but some adults will accept vegetable matter. The North American siren, which lives among aquatic vegetation, is carnivorous, but its stomach usually contains a proportion of vegetable debris.

The axolotl is an active predator on small anuran tadpoles. Cannibalism occurs among newts kept in aquaria. The large Japanese salamander will attack fish, amphibians and the smallest of its own kind. The hell-bender (*Cryptobranchus alleghaniensis*) kills large numbers of fish and shrimps. Pebbles as big as nuts, no doubt eaten along with the prey, have also been found in its stomach.

Amphibians can do without food for long periods. A burrowing toad from Ceylon lived for 390 days without food. A *Proteus* has been known to exist for eight years without eating. Six *Discoglossus pictus*, experimentally subjected to fasting, had lost sixty per cent of their weight after a year, but were still actively alive.

The yellow-bellied toad *Bombina variegata*; *above*, view of smooth and brightly coloured ventral surface, *below*, dorsal view. Dorsal warts contain glands whose secretion gives off a smell of garlic. *Phot. Vasserot*.

Enemies and parasites

Amphibians are subject to attack by many enemies; but mortality is compensated for by high fertility. They are preyed upon by mammals like foxes and hedgehogs; birds like storks, herons and ducks; and certain aquatic snakes. In Africa and America, the large *Mygale* spiders are capable of killing small specimens.

Discoglossus is eaten by shrews, genets, mongooses, storks and herons. Snakes prey on tadpoles and, on the island of Levant, can decimate the population. *Dytiscus* larvae catch tadpoles and suck out their body fluids.

A variety of commensal parasites is found in the rectum of most amphibians, the main ones being protozoans like opalines, trichomonads, and many others. The intestines, lungs and blood contain nematodes, trematodes and trypanosomes.

Competition between tadpoles

There is some competition between species. Newts, for example, are fond of the eggs and small tadpoles of *Discoglossus*.

The edible frog (*Rana esculenta*) the laughing frog (*Rana ridibunda*) and the *Discoglossus* are found in similar habitats. But frogs prefer big pools and avoid brackish water, whereas *Discoglossus* is found in streams or pools even where there is some salinity. The two genera are rarely found together, but

Male of edible frog (*Rana esculenta*) croaking, its two vocal sacs fully distended. The colour of this species varies from bright green to fairly light brown, including shades of grey and black. *Phot. J.-P. Varin-Jacana*

Discoglossus quickly disappears from a stream if *Rana esculenta* or *Rana ridibunda* is introduced.

Man is the amphibian's most serious competitor and predator. By draining marshes, he deprives many species of a breeding place. He hunts the edible species for food. In his war against the malarial mosquito, he destroys eggs and tadpoles.

Defence

Frogs living beside water dive immediately at the first sign of danger: that is their defence against enemies. Burrowing is a defence reflex. Some species hide in dens. Some toads, when confronted by an enemy, puff up their bodies and open their mouths: others freeze, simulating death. *Bufo superciliaris* of Africa lies on its back, folds its legs together and remains perfectly still. Body colour is another means of protection. The green of some tree-dwelling species blends with the foliage; in others, their colour matches the tree trunks. A few exotic species, which live among grass, have longitudinal stripes on their bodies.

Poisonous skin secretions are also a method of defence. There is a record of a frog that died after swallowing a salamander. If a salamander is offered to a captive hedgehog, the hedgehog will bite at it eagerly, but it quickly releases its hold and withdraws to root about in the ground in obvious discomfort.

Populations

Very little is known about the social behaviour of amphibians. By marking individuals, it has been shown that some species display the rudiments of territorial behaviour, but there is nothing definite to suggest the existence of true social life, although, in some species, there may be a form of social grouping.

In Sardinia, a census of *Discoglossus* was carried out in small streams during darkness. In these streams, which irrigate a valley of 1400 acres, 3599 *Discoglossus* were counted. If we assume that 25 per cent escaped the census, the total population must have been in the region of 5000 adults—that is, just over three frogs per acre. In fact, populations of *Discoglossus* are usually more dense than that, for they remain in the immediate vicinity of streams, leaving them only when it is raining. In a natural population of 500, it was found that 296 were at least a year old, 147 were two years old, and 57 (including seven females) were of greater age. On the basis of censuses carried out in April 1958 and 1959, it has been calculated that only 15 per cent of a metamorphosed population reaches maturity.

In the Forest of Berce (Maine-et-Loire) repeated sampling of 2½ acres produced 119 common fire salamanders—about one per 100 square yards. In the park of La Flèche, the count was 158 salamanders per 2½ acres or approximately one per 76 square yards.

Calls and their meanings

Urodelans are almost completely silent, but the same cannot be said of the anurans whose calls can be heard in all latitudes during the early hours of the night. Their calls vary from the fluting of *Alytes* to the deafening concert of *Rana*, the hammering of the blacksmith tree-frogs (*Hyla faber*), and the bellowing of the bull frogs (*Rana catesbeiana*)—from organized choirs to free-for-all cacophonies. The organ that produces these sounds is the larynx, situated, as in other animals, at the entrance to the windpipe (trachea). Air expelled from the lungs sets up vibrations of the vocal cords, and the sound they produce is often amplified by the vocal sacs. These vocal sacs are tubular extensions of the floor of the mouth, with simple slit openings.

The edible frog (*Rana esculenta*) is sometimes green, sometimes brown. Its eyes are spangled with gold. The tympanum can be seen behind the eye.
Phot. J. Six

They are thin-walled but muscular, and their position varies from species to species. Natterjack toads and tree-frogs have a single sac under the throat. In the Italian frog, there are two sacs, clearly divided and partly internal. In edible frogs, there are two lateral sacs behind the mouth.

When a frog calls, it inflates its sac or sacs, which distends the skin. Sacs described as internal are those placed where the skin is not elastic and not easily distended. In such species, there is less distension than in others.

A few species can croak while submerged, with nostrils and mouth closed. This produces a sort of ventriloquial effect. Only species with partial internal vocal sacs can do this, the fire-bellied toad (*Bombina variegata*) being an example. Species with no vocal sacs are not necessarily mute. The common toad

Tree-frog (*Hyla*) calling, the distended vocal sac in the throat acts as a sound-box, amplifying the croak. *Phot. Michel Boulard*

(*Bufo bufo*), the agile frog (*Rana dalmatina*), and many others can call, but their calls are not so loud.

Different calls have different meanings, and may be divided as follows: sexual calls; distress calls; the territorial call uttered by males to advertise their presence and inhibit

intrusion; the rain song of tree-frogs which coincides, it is said, with a sudden rise in atmospheric humidity.

Some frogs, toads and tree-frogs sing in chorus. In the case of *Rana esculenta*, the chorus is said to be led by the calling of a trio, with others joining in until the whole population is in full voice. The biological significance of choruses is unknown.

Almost the only sounds uttered by urodelans are cries of distress when they are seized or attacked. The giant salamander of Japan is said to utter piercing cries in such circumstances.

Hibernation and aestivation

Amphibians react quickly to fluctuations in temperature and humidity. Being cold-blooded, they can be paralysed by a fall in temperature. Similarly, they have no defence against a fall in humidity, which is usually linked to a rise in temperature. They react to both in the same way—by seeking a hide-out where the microclimate suits them. There, they remain in a state of torpor until climatic conditions are favourable again.

In cold or temperate regions amphibians go into hibernation when the autumn temperature falls below a certain level. Some species hibernate in the mud of ponds; others in trees. At Port-Cross, the painted frogs hide in caverns formed by the roots of green oaks growing among rocks, or under dead leaves and pine-needles. Dozens of them may be found huddled together in such a den—sometimes in the company of natterjacks, spotted mud-frogs and wall lizards; but they do not become completely torpid and, if dislodged, become active immediately. Apparently they even feed a little in winter, probably by snapping up passing prey. Frogs taken from ponds that are being cleaned quickly become active.

There is a great variation in the duration of hibernation. It is thought that frogs in the high Alps emerge from hibernation in June and retire again in September, which means that they are inactive for eight months of the year. On the other hand, frogs in the south of England and Ireland occasionally spawn in December, after only two months' hibernation.

The physiology of hibernation in amphibians, and the factors influencing it, are still not clearly understood. It is thought that a cool period is necessary for the ripening of the eggs in species inhabiting cold or temperate countries. During hibernation, frogs use up fats and not carbohydrates as food reserves. The supply of air in the lungs is not renewed, and breathing activity is minimal. When frogs come out of hibernation, they migrate at once to ponds where they can mate and spawn.

The term *aestivation* refers only to amphibians that inhabit regions with a pronounced summer-winter variation. When the temperature is high, and humidity low, newts and salamanders hide in holes in the ground or under fallen trees, where they can keep cool and moist. There, they remain inactive, waiting for rain, which brings them out again.

In tropical regions, where drought and rainy seasons alternate, amphibians become torpid as soon as the atmosphere becomes too dry. This is aestivation.

The axolotl, a larval (and albino) form of *Ambystoma tigrinum*, has the peculiarity of not metamorphosing and yet being able to breed. This ability to breed under a form which is not the adult state is called neoteny. *Phot. John Markham*

Reptiles

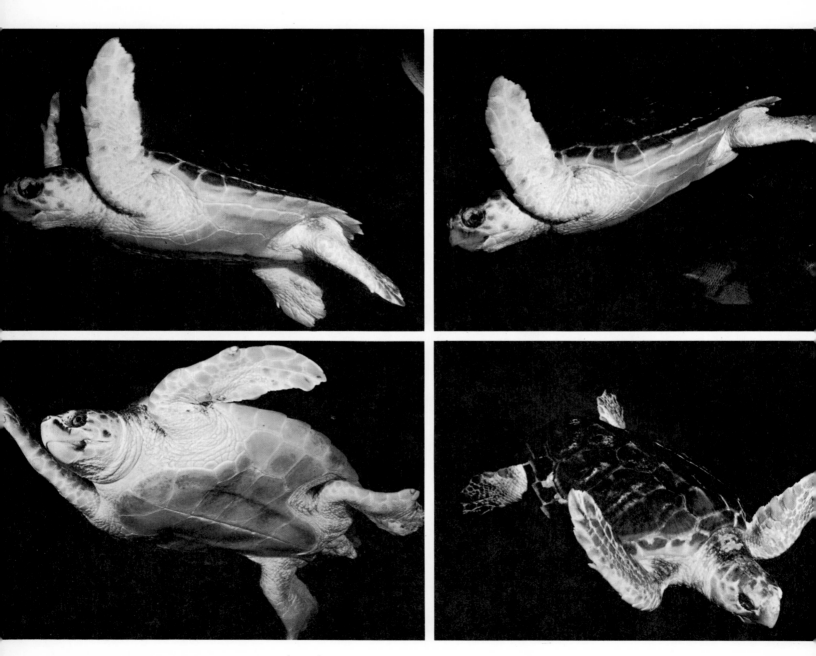

The loggerhead turtle (*Caretta caretta*) is perfectly adapted to living in the open sea. This plate represents four of its attitudes during swimming. It is found in all the tropical seas. It is occasionally caught on the coasts of Europe, carried there by ocean currents. Its diet is excluvively carnivorous. Its flesh, which is not of good quality, has no commercial value. The loggerhead lays in the sand of tropical beaches, above the level reached by the highest tides. It uses its hind legs to dig a hollow 18 inches to 2 feet deep, in which it lays from 150 to 160 eggs. According to the temperature, incubation lasts from 30 to 60 days. *Phot. Lauros-Atlas Photo and J. Six*

The great reptiles that once ruled the world—on land, in the air and on the water—have all disappeared. Their present-day descendants are mostly small and hardly noticed. People, on the whole, are not attracted to reptiles, considering them ugly, even dangerous. Yet many of them are notable for their elegance of form and their variety of coloration.

Reptiles are vertebrates, but they do not all conform to a pattern. There is a striking difference, for example, between a tortoise and a snake. Yet they have many characteristics in common that put them in the same class.

The reptilian skin is dry, never slimy or wet. It is always covered by a thick, sometimes a very thick, horny coat, without glands. In this respect alone reptiles are fundamentally different from fishes and amphibians. Under their skins, reptiles have flat, bony plates. The combination of these with the skin makes up the familiar scales.

There are more bones in the reptilian skull than in that of mammals. In all of them, the skull is articulated to the backbone by a single knob or condyle.

The reptilian mandible is different from that of mammals. It is made up of several bones and articulated with the skull in a different way.

As in amphibians, the heart has a single ventricle, partly divided by a septum, and there is a double aorta, the arches of which meet at the back of the heart. Separation of arterial and venous blood is not complete, as it is in mammals, so there is a slight mixed circulation. The crocodile is an exception to the general rule: its heart has two ventricles.

The upper bone of the fore and hind legs (humerus and femur) are horizontal; the middle bones (radius/ulna; tibia/fibula) are vertical. The terminal bones are horizontal and turn outwards. No part of the reptilian reproduction cycle takes place in water. There is no tadpole stage. The embryo develops membranes—amnion and allantois—which, within the egg shell, enclose cavities full of liquid. In this fluid environment, the young reptile develops.

Reptiles were the first vertebrates to sever all ties with the water, although some present-day species still live in rivers or swamps. This, however, is no more than clinging to the original habitat. Eggs are not laid in water; nor do embryos develop there. Structure and function are more advanced than in amphibians. Reptiles, for example, have a neck similar to that of birds and mammals. This gives the head a varying degree of mobility—sometimes a considerable degree, as in tortoises.

In amphibians, the roof of the mouth is made up mainly of the underside of the skull. By contrast, reptiles have developed a bony plate which divides the mouth into upper and lower compartments and serves as a false palate. The nostrils open into the upper compartment which provides for breathing and

sense of smell. This compartment, in turn, opens into the pharynx at the level of the gullet and windpipe (oesophagus and trachea). The crocodile is the only reptile in which the palate becomes a continuous lamina separating the nasal and buccal cavities.

The rib cage is closed ventrally, as in mammals, by a breast bone (the sternum) with which the tops of the ribs are articulated or fused (except in snakes).

The reptilian brain is more developed than that of amphibians. Its anterior roof, or pallium, is thicker and richer in neurons (which have a sensory function). The developed kidney of the adult reptile is an advance on the embryonic kidney of the amphibians.

The very beautiful dark green snake (*Coluber viridiflavus*) of Europe is highly aggressive. It feeds on a variety of animals including, as this photograph shows, fledglings (here a European blackbird, *Turdus merula*). It sometimes exceeds 6 feet in length. It is sometimes nicknamed the whip because of its long slim tail. *Phot. A. Margiocco*

A history of reptiles

The gradual development from amphibian to reptile was completed about 250 million years ago. The oldest known reptiles are the cotylosaurs, which closely resemble the group of amphibians known as seymouriamorphs. For a long time, palaeontologists included the seymouriamorphs among the reptiles. But they had to be separated after the discovery of a lateral line system on their skulls, which is characteristic of fishes and amphibians. The cotylosaurs appeared towards the

the skull and towards the base of the mandible.

In the cotylosaurs, there is a sub-group with great evolutionary potential: the captorhinomorphs, e.g. *Captorhinus* and *Labidosaurus*. In these, the structure of the inner ear is very primitive, and they have no temporal openings. Some palaeontologists consider that the tortoises, the plesiosaur and the lepidosaur (Rhynchocephalia, saurians and ophidians) were derived from these reptiles.

From the upper Carboniferous period onwards, the pelýcosaur made its appearance. Its representatives are very closely related to the captorhinomorphs. All were lizard-like, the biggest exceeding three feet in length. Some of them (*Varanotis*, *Sphenacodon*) were carnivorous; others (*Edaphosaurus*) were vegetarians.

According to recent research, the pelycosaur gave rise to two flourishing offshoots. One of these, the theropsids, persisted into the age of mammals. The other, the archosaurs, evolving through groups that soon became extinct, resulted in forms very different from each other—birds and crocodiles, dinosaurs and pterodactyls.

At one time, diadectomorphs were thought to have played an important role in the origin of reptiles. Later research, however, has shown such close affinities between this group and the seymouriamorphs (stegophalian amphibians) that some researchers now classify them among the amphibians. In the present state of knowledge, it seems wise to attribute the same ancestors to the captorhinomorphs and to the pelycosaurs. As now classified, these reptiles show a unity of composition which was lacking in the earlier theory.

This new theory of reptilian evolution attaches little importance to certain skull characteristics once thought important—the temporal openings. Cotylosaurs had a continuous skull roof: no other reptiles except tortoises have this feature. Temporal openings lie between the bones covering the cheeks, and appear to be concerned with the extension of certain muscles or the development of new ones. Formerly, reptiles were classified according to the position, and number, of temporal openings and, on this basis, present-day reptiles were thought to be derived from fossil diapsids which had two temporal openings, one high and one low.

Many palaeontologists now reject this theory. According to their theory the diapsid state arose from two different lines. One of these was derived from the synapsid crocodiles—crocodiles and birds (one low temporal opening on each side of the skull). The other line was derived from the anapsids, with no temporal openings—the lepidosaurs (Rhynchocephalia, lizards and snakes). These palaeontologists hold that the diapsid state, in itself, had no precise evolutionary significance.

Thus, the division of reptiles into two clear-cut evolutionary lines—the Sauropsida and Theropsida—seems to have been invalid. The facts, as now known, suggest that there was no such clear-cut division and that reptiles, as a class, are probably more homogeneous than they were once thought to be.

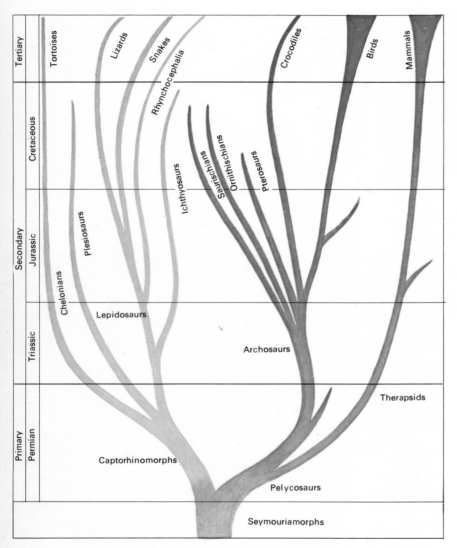

Genealogical tree of the reptiles, showing also the origin of birds and mammals.

end of the Carboniferous period and flourished during the whole of the Permian period.

The skull wall of the cotylosaurs is a mosaic of dermal bones. As their name suggests, they are formed by, and in, the tissues underlying the skin (sub-cutaneous tissue). The mosaic is broken only by the eye sockets, the nostrils and the auditory orifices. The masticatory muscles are inserted within the top of

Tortoises

Tortoises, whose skulls have no temporal openings, may have evolved from the captorhinomorph cotylosaur, but there is no proof of this. The oldest chelonian (tortoise) fossils date from the Permian period, and have bony carapaces with a tortoiseshell covering. Fossil tortoises were not very different from those of the present day: for example, a giant marine turtle, which flourished during the upper Cretaceous period, had flippers over seven feet in length and a fenestrated or compartmented-looking carapace.

A case of convergence:
The ichthyosaur, resembling the dolphin

The ichthyosaur became adapted to life in the open sea. Its remains have been very well preserved in compact limestones, so its anatomy has been fairly well established. It was dolphin-shaped, with limbs that had become transformed into paddles. In the earliest species, fore and hind-paddles were of the same size. In later forms, the hind-paddles were smaller. The pelvis of ichthyosaur was not directly connected with its backbone. Its matching conical teeth were like those of the dolphin. In Jurassic times, the ichthyosaur lived like the dolphin of today. Dolphins and ichthyosaurs are a good example of *convergent evolution*.

It is known that ichthyosaurs fed on cephalopod molluscs, as remains of these have been found in their stomachs. The ichthyosaur was ovoviviparous: fossil females have been discovered containing advanced embryos.

The plesiosaur—skilful hunter

The plesiosaurs also lived in the open sea. The plesiosaur has been aptly described as a 'snake strung through the body of a turtle'. Plesiosaurs had broad bulky bodies and two pairs of swimming paddles, long thin, flexible necks, which made them skilful hunters, and long tails. They appeared in the Triassic period and, although derived from small types, they reached giant size in the Cretaceous period: for example, the elasmosaurs, which were about forty feet long. Although their bodies were not very suitably adapted for rapid swimming, there seems no doubt that they lived in the open sea, where they preyed upon fish.

The dinosaur gave rise to the largest land animals, both herbivore and carnivore

Dinosaurs were derived from primitive archosaurs, and one of their ancestors could have been *Euparkeria* (middle Triassic), which had two temporal openings separated by the squamosal and postorbital bones.

Dinosaurs have been classified in two orders. The first group had a hip bone structure like that of birds. This type belongs to the group known as ornithischian (bird hips). The second group had a hip bone structure like that of present-day reptiles, and is known as saurischian (reptile hips).

The saurischians

Many of the saurischian dinosaurs had long, well-developed hindlegs and short forelegs. One of these, *Struthiomimus*, stood about eight feet tall. The skeleton of *Struthiomimus* resembles an ostrich with a long dragging tail. Although originally carnivores, many saurischians became plant-eaters that walked on all four feet. Among these were *Diplodocus*, *Brontosaurus*, and *Camarasaurus*, reaching from 75 to 87 feet in length. These were the largest land animals of all time.

Saurischians had small heads and large bodies. Their brains were disproportionately small. Despite an apparent lack of adaptability, these dinosaurs lived for millions of years and, if abundance of fossils is any guide, were extremely numerous.

Theropods were also saurischian dinosaurs. They walked on their hind legs and, although they retained a number of archaic characters, were a powerful branch. Almost all of them were carnivorous. The fossil record reveals many remarkable forms. The *Ornitholestes* of the Jurassic period were scarcely more than seven feet in length. They had powerful tails and stood upright. Light and agile, their bird-like appearance was accentuated by their strong hind legs. Their fore limbs, which were short and clawed, must have been

Ichthyosaurus, a fossil of the Jurassic.

Diplodocus, a dinosaur of the American Cretaceous.

used for seizing prey, which they would then tear apart with their strong teeth.

Allosaurus of the Jurassic period, although similar in appearance, was a giant type up to 36 feet long. It must have been a formidable carnivore. All the available fossil evidence suggests that it habitually attacked large prey, probably vegetarian dinosaurs. *Tyrannosaurus*, which lived in the Cretaceous, was the most powerful carnivore of them all. Its total length was nearly fifty feet and, when it reared on its hind legs, its head was sixteen to twenty feet above the ground.

The ornithischians

The ornithischians are the other great branch of the order of dinosaurs. This order included several types, the most primitive of which were the ornithopods, iguanodonts and the duck-billed dinosaurs. Some walked on two legs, others on four. Watercourses and lakes were their usual habitats.

The iguanodonts flourished about 140 million years ago and were the first dinosaurs to be described entirely from fossil remains. Fossilized bones were found in England in 1822, but the great finds came from Belgium, and these made accurate reconstruction possible. Iguanodonts had long narrow snouts flattened like a duck's bill and they probably guttered in mud, as ducks do. During the same period, the Cretaceous, iguanodonts with horns and crests inhabited North America.

The stegosaurs of the Jurassic were mailed dinosaurs. On their backs, they had alternated rows of erect bony plates. Their tails were tipped with four enormous spikes like bulls' horns. *Stegosaurus* had a small pointed head and a very tiny brain weighing no more than a few ounces. Like all the armoured dinosaurs, it was a plant eater and walked on four legs.

Horned dinosaurs, the third important group of ornithischians, were the last to appear on the scene. The earliest fossils of these animals were discovered in the sedimentary rocks of the lower Cretaceous period. In geological terms, therefore, they had a short existence, having disappeared by the end of the Cretaceous.

Psittacosaurus, from the Mongolian lower Cretaceous period, was a small dinosaur. Its skull was thick and narrow, and its squat limbs foreshadowed those of *Triceratops* and later types.

Protoceratops, from Mongolia, was 5 to 7½ feet long and walked on four legs. Its upper jaw was curved downward like a parrot's beak. Its fossilized eggs have been found in Mongolia, sometimes grouped together, indicating that they had been laid in a nest. Eggs have also been found containing embryos, the embryo lacking the bony frill behind the skull which was characteristic of adults.

Triceratops was the end of the line of this group of prehistoric monsters. The skull of this adult giant had a great bony frill rising in front of the neck, and two large sharp forward-pointing horns. On its nose, it had a single horn like a rhinoceros. *Triceratops* was the biggest of the horned dinosaurs, more than 30 feet long, and the only animal capable of resisting attack by *Tyrannosaurus*. It had a powerful neck, and leg muscles attached to the bony armoured plating of the head and neck. The head was really a weapon in itself, offensive and defensive.

Flying reptiles

Also descended from the archosaurs were the flying reptiles, or pterosaurs, which were the first vertebrates capable of sustained flight. They made their entry in the Jurassic period. Their fore limbs had become wings. Their body weight was reduced and their nerve centres more highly developed.

The skulls of these flying reptiles had two temporal openings with well-fused bones. The number of their vertebrae had decreased. The bones of their limbs were hollow (pneumatic) like those of present-day birds. With the development of the fore limbs into flying wings, the hind legs became weaker. The pterosaur, in fact, was a poor walker. Its structure was adapted to its new mode of life—the attachment of the shoulder girdle to the vertebral column being strong and narrow, while the breast bone had broadened out to provide anchorage for the powerful wing muscles. The fourth finger of the hand was extremely long and formed the leading edge of the wing. The other fingers remained short and claw-like and were probably used for grasping and for hanging at roost.

These reptiles, in one form or another, existed for 120 to 150 million years. In the beginning, they were of medium size—for example, *Ramphorhynchus* of the Jurassic period. But, by the Cretaceous period, they had become giants like *Pteranodon*, with a wing span of 27 feet: more than twice that of the biggest present-day condor. Their bodies were small in relation to wing span, and it is reasonable to suppose that they were gliders as well as true flyers. Despite their flying abilities, they were not as perfectly formed as the birds, or even the bats, of today.

It is generally accepted that the pterosaurs were warm-blooded. Weight has been lent to this theory by the discovery of hair and gland traces on a fossilized fragment of wing membrane belonging to *Ramphorhynchus*. No scales have been found even on the best preserved pterosaur fossils from the finest lithographic limestones.

Crocodiles, Archeopteryx and birds

Among other descendants of the archosaurs are crocodiles (see page 433), *Archeopteryx* and birds. In the evolution of reptiles and birds, *Archeopteryx* stands at the crossroads. Its remains, perfectly fossilized in the lithographic Jurassic limestones of Selenhofen, in Bavaria, are obviously half-reptile, half-bird. Its structure will be described in detail in the chapter on birds.

The end of the giant reptiles

The day of the giant reptiles was long; but it had its night. At the end of the Mesozoic era, all the giants—aquatic, terrestrial, aerial, vegetarian and carnivorous—disappeared. This total collapse and extinction of a group at the height of its ascendancy is one of the unexplained facts of the history of life on our planet. Many theories have been put forward. But why should so many lines, differentiated by antiquity, origin and way of life, have been blotted out almost simultaneously?

It has been said that over-adaptation to their environment rendered the dinosaurs unable to adapt to new climatic conditions. The facts are mostly against this, for many lines disappeared before the end of the Mesozoic era—that is before there was any great climatic change. The suggestion that they died of epidemic disease is plausible, but not based on any known facts. There was, however, a considerable rise in sea level at the end of the Mesozoic era, which could possibly have brought about a change in climate and, therefore, in habitats, thus making life impossible for the majority of reptiles.

The catastrophe did not take place overnight; it was spread over many centuries. The survivors are our present-day reptiles—Rhynchocephalia, crocodiles, tortoises, lizards and snakes. They are a small remnant, but they are all thriving and likely to survive unless destroyed by man.

The anatomy of reptiles

Tegument and scales

There is no such animal as a slimy snake. The skin of a reptile, unlike that of an amphibian, is always dry and impermeable, because of its horny surface and the almost total absence of tegumentary glands. As a result, reptiles are able to colonize, and survive in, the most arid areas, such as deserts and steppes.

Under the reptilian skin (sub-cutaneous tissue or *dermis*) there are numerous cells containing pigments (coloured particles). These cells are the chromatophores, variously named according to the colour of the pigment. From them the reptiles derive their body colour and, in some cases, such as the chameleons and the *Anolis*, cell activity enables the individual to change colour to match that of its background. Reptiles in this group are discussed later.

In the sub-cutaneous tissue or *dermis*, there are bones involved in the formation of the scales. Reptilian scales are, therefore, half-dermic, half-epidermic. Body scales reach their maximum development in tortoises and crocodiles.

Sloughing

Snakes and lizards periodically cast their skin. In almost all lizards, the skin comes away in strips, but in snakes it comes off in one piece. It splits along the whole length of the body, probably triggered by enzyme action; but this is not clearly understood. The *Anolis*, and probably some geckos, swallow the cast skin immediately they are out of it.

As a general rule, young reptiles slough more frequently than fully developed adults; but the relationship between growth and sloughing is not yet clearly understood. Some experiments indicate that sloughing is dependent, at least partially, on the activity of hormones secreted by the pituitary and thyroid glands. It is known that a reptile will slough more frequently if its metabolism is speeded up by a prolonged rise in the temperature of the environment. Most snakes slough two or three times a year. Some do so more frequently.

The skeleton

The reptilian skeleton is complex and its study is outwith the scope of this book. The beginnings of a palate appear in lizards and snakes, but this is almost complete only in tortoises and crocodiles. In crocodiles, the nasal cavities do not open directly into the buccal cavity. The skull of the tortoise has no openings other than the eye-sockets, the ears and the occipital opening. In other reptiles, the skull vault has two pairs of temporal cavities, some of them capable of fusion. The skull is jointed to the spine by a single knob or condyle. The lower jaw is made up of six bones, the principal ones being the dental, articular and angular.

Although limb structure is quite ordinary, the position of the limbs in relation to the body is transverse (see above). As a result, the reptilian body hardly clears the ground: in other words, reptiles crawl.

The digestive and respiratory systems

There are few special features about the reptilian digestive system, and any such features will be pointed out in context.

Reptiles, having no muscular diaphragm, have to swallow air. Otherwise, their respiratory system is quite ordinary.

The circulatory system

The circulation of the blood in reptiles is different from that of birds and mammals, and there is considerable variation between one reptilian order and another.

All reptiles have a three-chambered heart, located near the rear of the thorax. The heart has two auricles—the right being

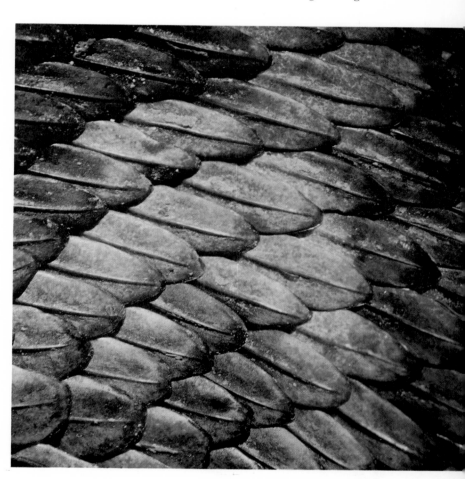

The dorsal scales of vipers (here, the asp, *Vipera aspis*) are keeled. *Phot. Aldo Margiocco*

larger than the left—and a single ventricle, associated with an arterial bulb which is the source of the large arterial trunks. Although the ventricle is single, it is partially split into right and left cavities by incomplete fleshy partitions. The aortae, right and left, come from the left cavity, and the pulmonary artery from the right.

As in the amphibians, the structure of the reptilian ventricle means that there is incomplete separation of arterial and venous blood. But the total mixing of arterial and venous blood is prevented, to some extent, by various devices. The tortoise is a case in point. In this case, the ventricle is partially divided into a dorsal compartment and a pulmonary compartment. The partition is a muscular crest on the cardiac muscle. When the heart contracts, this muscular crest separates the two compartments. The valves of both auricles open into the dorsal compartment. Oxygenated blood from the lungs passes from the left auricle into the dorsal compartment to supply the two aortae. Most of the blood from the right auricle enters the pulmonary compartment to supply the pulmonary artery. Analysis of blood gases has shown that ninety per cent of blood from the right ventricle passes into the pulmonary artery, while the left auricle supplies blood in equal quantity to the two aortae.

In crocodiles, there is complete partition of the ventricle but the two aortae are united near their base by an opening called the foramen of Panizza. The persistence of two aortic arches and the foramen suggests the mixing of arterial and venous bloods. In practice, there is no mixing, which is prevented by valvules situated at the opening of the left aorta.

The nervous system

The nervous system of the reptiles is more advanced than that of the amphibians. The cerebral hemispheres are well developed. The neurones, located near the surface, are so organized that each group is concerned with different kinds of sensory messages, and control of the appropriate responses.

Montpellier snake (*Malpolon monspessulanus*) just after moulting.
Phot. J. L. S. Dubois

The sense organs

The senses of touch and smell are acute in reptiles, but have no particular distinguishing features.

Vision

Vision is generally good, eye structure being related to way of life—nocturnal, diurnal or crepuscular.

Nocturnal species have a narrow vertical pupil, a retina with a single category of photoreceptors and crystalline hyaline rods. Diurnal species have a round pupil (vipers are exceptions): the crystalline is yellow and all the photoreceptors are cones. Crepuscular species have a round pupil, slightly coloured crystalline, and cones passing through the rods. Crocodiles and tortoises do not appear to have any special under-water adaptation.

Crocodiles have three eyelids—one transparent and two ordinary. Many lizards have similar eyelids. In the burrowing lizards and all the snakes, the transparent horizontal eyelids have become fused to form the 'spectacle' which is shed along with the rest of the skin at sloughing time. Hence the opaque eye of the snake when it is changing its skin.

The pineal eye

It is well known that many lizards have an eye on top of their heads. At least, it is an eye-like structure, located beneath an opening in the parietal bone. In most modern reptiles it is vestigial; but it is well developed in a few—for example, the common slow-worm, monitors, skinks and others. Although the pineal eye looks like an organ for seeing, its actual function is still a mystery. No research has yet been able to explain its significance. In the most ancient reptiles, there were two such eyes, probably functional. The upper wall of the pineal eye has a rudimentary lens; its lower wall has a retina with photoreceptor cells. Behind and beneath the pineal eye lies the epiphysis which resembles a gland and is connected by a stalk to the roof of the diencephalon (the part of the fore-brain situated between the cerebral hemispheres and the optic lobes).

The ear and hearing

Contrary to popular belief, not all reptiles are deaf. They have an ear provided with a spiral (cochlea) not found in fishes or amphibians.

In the crocodile, the cochlea is uncoiled; nevertheless, crocodiles are thought to have good hearing. In reptiles, as in birds, a single bone, known as the stapes, conducts vibrations from the eardrum to the inner ear. In most reptiles, this is shaped like a rod or column and is known as the columella. Snakes have no eardrums or middle ear cavity, but the columella persists. They are deaf, or nearly so, although they react quickly to ground vibrations.

Tortoises appear to have fairly good hearing. It is known that terrapins can register sounds of a frequency from 80 to 5000 cycles per second. Some lizards respond to sounds between 80 and 10,000 cycles per second.

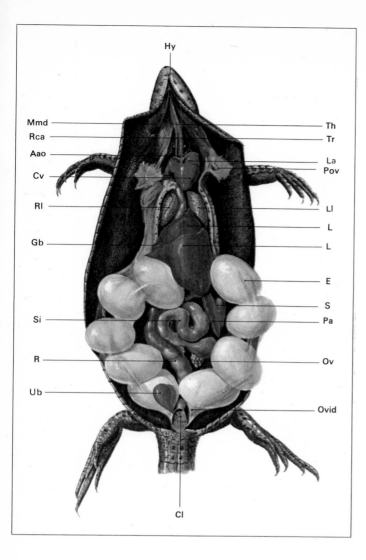

The sand lizard, *Lacerta agilis*, after dissection, ventral view. *Aao*, left aortic arch; *Cl*, cloaca; *Cv*, cardiac ventricle; *E*, eggs; *Gb*, gall bladder; *Hy*, hyoid bone; *L*, liver; *La*, left auricle; *Ll*, left lung; *Mmd*, mandible muscles; *Ov*, ovary; *Ovid*, oviduct; *Pa*, pancreas; *Pov*, peritoneal opening of oviduct; *R*, rectum; *Rca*, right carotid artery; *Rl*, right lung; *S*, stomach; *Si*, small intestine; *Th*, thyroid; *Tr*, trachea; *Ub*, urinary bladder.

Senses of smell and taste

Snakes and lizards have long, slim, active and deeply forked tongues. Constant flickering of the tongue is characteristic of snakes, but not so much of lizards. Among the lizards that act in this way are the slow-worm and the monitors. When withdrawn, the tongue is housed on a sheath lying below the glottis and opening in front of it. Snakes have a notch in the upper jaw to allow the tongue free movement out and in. Lizards do not have this notch. When a snake bites or feeds, its tongue is withdrawn.

What is the function of this forked tongue? In some cases, a sense of taste has been attributed to it. For example, *Dasypeltis*—an egg-eating snake—is said to be able to distinguish between real birds' eggs and dummies presented to it by an experimenter.

The gecko's tongue is fleshy and covered with fine hairs at its extremities. The tongue is used to catch tiny insects which are then snapped up in the jaws.

Snakes, in addition to their nasal organs, have a pair of special structures known as Jacobson's organs. It is now known that the snake's tongue is used to pick up scent particles which are then passed to Jacobson's organs for identification. These organs are found in some mammals and amphibians, but they reach their greatest development in snakes and lizards. They are deeply pigmented and situated below the nasal organs of which they are outgrowths, although they have no connection with the nose. A duct from each opens on to the palate. The cavities of Jacobson's organs are highly sensitive. It is now established that Jacobson's organs pick up the scent particles passed by the tongue to the palate. They are, therefore, the 'clearing house' for scent impressions. Snakes find each other, and their way, by gathering scent particles. When an adder or other poisonous snake loses a prey after striking, it finds it again by tracking with its tongue.

Sensory pits

Crotaline snakes—rattlesnakes, copperheads and bushmasters—have a conspicuous sensory pit on each side of the snout, between the eye and the nostril. Each pit is partly enclosed by a hollow of the jaw-bone, and a membrane divides it into an inner and an outer chamber. Recent research has shown that these organs are highly sensitive to the slightest variation in the surrounding temperature. Boas, for example, can distinguish temperature differences of .2 degrees centigrade or less. Blindfolded crotalines can distinguish between warm and hot electric light bulbs moved in front of them at a distance of twenty centimetres.

The pits are also sensitive to infra-red radiation from the bodies of prey. Blind rattlesnakes can recognize warm objects in this way. Boas and pythons have numerous pits above and along the upper lip. These seem to function in the same way as the facial pits, and they are also thermoreceptors.

Reproduction

Secondary sexual characteristics and sexual dimorphism

With a few exceptions, sexual dimorphism in reptiles is not strikingly obvious.

In tortoises, the differences are slight. The tail of the female American wood turtle (*Clemmys insculpta*) is slender compared with the male's, and there is some difference in the angle of the plates of the shell. The eyes of the male eastern boxturtle (*Terrapene carolina*) are red; the female's are brown or dark grey. Male red-eared terrapins (*Pseudemys scripta*) blacken with age, whereas females remain multi-coloured. In this species, males develop fore-claws only when sexually mature, and it is thought that these claws are used for holding the female.

The males of certain lizards become more brightly coloured in the breeding season. The sand lizard (*Lacerta aquilis*) becomes green on the head and flanks, while the throat of the Margovillat lizard (*Agama colonorum*) becomes bright orange-yellow.

Generally speaking, male lizards are bigger than females, but this is not an absolute rule. Male lacertid lizards have special glandular organs—femoral, anal and abdominal.

These organs secrete a yellow waxy matter, and are under the direct control of the hypophysis, but their function is unknown.

The males of several iguanidae have wattles, dorsal crests and other erectile parts which are always brightly multi-coloured.

The head of the male chameleon is horned and has brightly coloured protuberances. The male basilisk (*Basiliscus*) has a helmet or bonnet, not found in the female.

Sexual dimorphism in snakes is never obvious, so it is almost impossible to tell the sexes apart without close examination of the sex organs. Generally, however, female snakes are longer and heavier than males, sometimes strikingly so. In adders,

The South American rattlesnake, *Crotalus durissus*, sub-species *terrificus*, is widely distributed in South America. It is a very dangerous species, with very strongly neurotoxic poison. *Phot. A. Margiocco*

males are usually more contrastingly marked than females. Male grass snakes rarely exceed 4 feet in length, whereas females reach a length of $5\frac{1}{2}$ feet. In the Madagascan rear-fanged snake (*Langaha*), the tip of the snout is prolonged in both sexes, but foliated only in the female.

Contrary to the general rule, male crocodiles are usually bigger than females. Examination of two nine-year old Mississippi alligators showed the male at more than 8 feet in length and the female at 7 feet.

Nuptial displays

Despite their ungainliness, tortoises carry out nuptial displays before mating. The males of *Pseudemys* and *Chrysemis* (aquatic

genera) have long claws on the third and fourth digits of their forefeet. They use these claws for stroking the side of the female's face. This display takes place in water, the male facing the female and caressing her while swimming backwards.

Males of some land tortoises elbow the female and bite her neck and carapace. Some aquatic species behave in the same way. During copulation, the male mounts the female, hanging on to the edge of her carapace by his claws.

Land tortoises mate on land; aquatic ones in the water. During the breeding season, the males of many species fight furiously among themselves. They bite each other on the neck and each tries to turn the other on its back.

When copulating, male crocodiles seize the female's neck in their jaws, then mount her back or flank, immobilizing her tail with a hind leg. Fertilization of the eggs takes place in the oviduct, as in birds.

The nuptial display of lizards is often accompanied by fighting, the male biting and jostling the female. Males of diurnal lizards recognize the female, at least partly, by her colour (visual information); but it is by no means certain that the sense of smell is not involved to some extent. In nocturnal species, the sense of smell is certainly important.

Male Asiatic geckos, at mating time, hold a territory which they defend against all other males of their own species. When fighting, geckos utter cries that sound like hand-clapping.

The most complex nuptial displays are performed by the Iguanidae. American chameleons (*Anolis*), which have the ability to change colour, are more or less social lizards, with a hierarchical system. On the breeding ground, each male takes up a position in accordance with his status in the social hierarchy.

The iguana (*Sceloporus undulatus*) recognizes the female of his species by her colour. He approaches her with a jerky, stiff-legged gait. Every now and again he stops, and sways from side to side, as though greeting her. The female's first reaction is to move away, leaping about with her back arched. Once they come together, the male bites her neck or shoulders and holds on so long as she continues to struggle. Once her resistance ceases, mating takes place.

The nuptial display of snakes can be complicated and puzzling. The behaviour pattern of some species has been studied, but none of them in great detail. It is probable that males identify females mainly by chemical messages. It is known that Dekay's snake (*Storeria dekayi*) from North

Green lizard (*Lacerta viridis*) in ventral view showing the line of the femoral pores and the transverse cloacal slit. *Phot. R. H. Noailles*

The male Jackson's chameleon (*Chamaeleo jacksoni*) is easily recognized by the three strong horns pointing to the front, on top of its snout.

In the female, the development of the horns is much less noticeable. This chameleon lives in tropical and equatorial Africa. *Phot. Aldo Margiocco*

America, and *Thamnophis sirtalis* do so by skin odours and information transmitted to Jacobson's organs. But visual recognition cannot be ruled out. It has been observed that male pine snakes (*Pituophis melanoleucas*) do not display to females about to slough.

Male boas and pythons have spurs alongside the cloaca (paracloacal spurs) which they vibrate and rub against the back and side of the females at mating time. Once the snakes are entwined, the male carries on with this stimulation until the female presents her cloaca to allow the insertion of one of his two hemipenes (copulatory glands).

The male adder crawls beside the female, tapping her back with his chin and flicking his tongue against her body. The play of the male's tongue upon the female's body is a prelude to copulation.

The so-called dance of the adders, once looked upon as a form of courtship, is, in fact, performed by males in territorial rivalry. The snakes face each other with the fore part of their bodies erect. They sway and entwine, each trying to push the other to the ground. In the end, one breaks off the struggle and glides off, pursued by the victor. In the adder dance, there is no biting. In some species that behave in this way, biting does occur. Combats of this kind occur in spring and autumn.

Fertilization

In all reptiles, fertilization is internal, and is brought about by a male copulatory organ. Lizards and snakes have two of these,

395

but only one penetrates the female. The sperm retain their vitality and power of fertilization for long periods. Reptilian eggs vary in shape from species to species, ranging from the spherical to the almost perfect elliptical. Egg size varies with the size of the species—from a few millimetres in small species to ten centimetres in the case of some crocodiles. The shell texture of the eggs of snakes and lizards is often like parchment or leather. The shell contains very little calcium. The eggs of tortoises and crocodiles, on the other hand, contain much more calcium and are more like birds' eggs. They are, therefore, more fragile.

Inside their shells, the eggs of reptiles and birds are very similar. The white of snake and lizard eggs is a thin layer surrounding the yolk. In tortoise and crocodile eggs, there is a much greater proportion of white. Usually the white of the reptilian egg is not very fluid and tends to keep its shape when the egg is shelled. The white of tortoise eggs does not coagulate when boiled. Tortoise and crocodile eggs are edible.

Egg-laying

Tortoises and crocodiles are, without exception, oviparous. The eggs are laid in sand or, in the case of some crocodiles, in

Adder (*Vipera berus*) having exserted its two hemipenes. *Phot. R. H. Noailles*

nests prepared by the female. In snakes and lizards, a high number of species is ovoviviparous, but oviparous species are in the majority. The number of eggs laid in a breeding season varies widely between species.

Chelonia mydas lays from 70 to 150 eggs (and even 200, it is said)	*Rhineura floridana* (Amphisbenida), 2
Chelydra serpentina, 8 to 80	*Elaphe longissima*, 5 to 8
Dermochelys coriacea, 90 to 130	*Natrix natrix*, 11 to 53
Gopherus agassizi, 2 to 6	*Coluber viridiflavus*, 5 to 15
Testudo hermanni, 4 to 12	*Heterodon platyrhinos*, 8 to 61
Lacerta viridis, 6 to 21	*Micrurus fulvius* (coral
Lacerta muralis, 3 to 9	snake) 2 to 4
Phrynosoma coronatum, 13 to 37	*Alligator mississippiensis*, 15 to 88

Incubation

Tortoises and turtles

Tortoises bury their eggs in sand (marine turtles come ashore on sandy beaches to lay) or hide them in a cavity under a stone or in a hollow tree. Some tortoises take the greatest care in hiding their eggs. It is claimed that the tortoise of the Bahamas (*Pseydemys malonai*) hollows out the ground above its eggs a few days before they are due to hatch, but the eggs are normally abandoned completely. Depending on the species, and the surrounding temperature, the eggs take from four to twenty weeks to hatch.

Snakes

Snakes lay their eggs underground—in hollow trees, under tree roots, under stones, under tree-stumps and in dung heaps. Being very poor diggers, they almost invariably use ready-made nesting sites. Most species take no interest in their eggs or young, but there are a few exceptions. One of the exceptions is the female python. She incubates her eggs by coiling her body round them. The young, however, are abandoned within a few days of hatching.

Indian cobras (*Naja naja*) remain together after mating. About a month after mating, the couple dig a hole in which the female lays her eggs. During the incubation period, these are guarded by the male and female in turn. The female mud snake (*Farancia abacura*) of the western United States, lays her eggs in a cavity in the ground and remains coiled round them until hatching time. The American rat snake (*Elaphe obsoleta*) stays near her eggs. From time to time, after having basked in the sun, she makes contact with them, warming them with the heat she has stored up.

Lizards

Lizards, having claw-like feet, are able to dig their own nesting cavity, and do so as often as not. Lizards' eggs vary from hard to soft, but gecko eggs are hard and oval shaped (clutch is one or two). Eggs of *Lacerta* are moderately hard (eight to twenty, or more, are laid). The eggs are laid on the ground, on sand, under stones or in hollows. Lizards of the genera *Eumeces* and *Ophisaurus* dig the cavities in which they lay their eggs. The females remain in the nest and turn the eggs over periodically, as birds do. From time to time they help incubation by heating their bodies in the sun. They are said to help the young from the shells but contact goes no further than this.

Crocodiles

Crocodiles lay big, elongated eggs with a white, bird-like shell. The Mississippi alligator prepares a large nest of mud and vegetable debris, in which she lays her eggs some time between May and July. The female, who carried the nesting materials, packs them by crawling over them. The completed nest is a yard in height and two yards in diameter. The female

The Indian cobra, sometimes called the hooded cobra (*Naja naja*), carries out pre-nuptial dances similar to those of the vipers. What they signify is not known exactly, for the individuals which display often belong to the same (male) sex. Whatever the explanation, these contests or ritual posturings take place during the mating season and seem to be connected with breeding. As long as the various phases of this are not exactly known, doubt must remain as to the place occupied by the dances in sexual behaviour. *Phot. Zuber-Rapho*

Mating of the viperine snake, *Natrix viperinus*: *top*, couple seen from above; *above*, the two genital regions seen from below, one only of the hemipenes effecting intromission. *Phot. R. H. Noailles*

Embryonic development

The development of reptiles is like that of birds, and takes place entirely out of water. The embryo has an umbilical vesicle, amnion and allantois. Its membranes, and the liquid they contain (amniotic liquid), effectively protect it against all danger of drying out.

Hatching

Like birds, the young reptile has an egg tooth at hatching time. The egg tooth (*ruptor ovi*) is situated at the tip of the snout, and is used to open the shell. The tooth is very hard and can break the shell by tapping. Young snakes lose the egg tooth in two or three days. In lizards and turtles, it can persist for up to a fortnight. Young geckos are exceptional in having two egg openers for breaking out.

Ovoviviparity and viviparity

In many species of lizards and snakes, the fertilized eggs remain in the oviduct and complete their development there. This is ovoviviparity. But development is not the same in all the groups under this heading.

In some groups the egg retains its shell, but it becomes very thin and there are some exchanges between embryo and mother through it. These exchanges are mainly respiratory and only to a small degree nutritive. The egg itself contains almost everything necessary to produce a normal viable embryo. The viviparous lizard (*Lacerta vivipara*) belongs to this group. The eggs of the slow-worm (*Anguis fragilis*) have very thin shells which are torn by the young when the mother expels them. The same thing happens in vipers and rattlesnakes.

There is one group in which the relations between mother

mounts guard beside the nest, urinating on it regularly to keep it moist and perhaps to help fermentation of the vegetable debris. The temperature in the egg chamber remains more or less constant, and over two degrees centigrade higher than that of the surrounding atmosphere.

Incubation lasts from nine to ten weeks. When the young emerge, they grunt to attract the female. If the nesting material is too tightly packed to allow them to emerge, the female loosens it up to free them. The mother keeps close watch on the young from the moment they leave the nest and continues to look after them for a period varying from one to three years. Near the edge of the swamp, she hollows out a lair for them— from nine to twenty feet in diameter—where they grow up, still under her protection, and she will attack any predator in their defence.

But the Mississippi alligator is exceptional. Other crocodilians (*Crocodylus, Caiman*) do little or nothing more than construct a nest, built like that of the alligator's.

A female green lizard (*Lacerta viridis*) has just laid two eggs in a hollow under a stone. The eggs are about ¾ inch long. Incubation lasts from two to three weeks. *Phot. Aldo Margiocco*

and embryo are much more intimate. This is the viviparous group. Most come from Australia (*Tiliqua* and *Lygosoma*) but the cylindrical skink (*Chalcides*) of Europe and Africa and the mabuyas (*Mabuya*), found throughout the tropics, are similar. In these groups, the egg membrane disappears. The wall of the oviduct then develops folds rich in glands. Here the wall of the umbilical vesicle of the allantois develops and the maternal tissues are linked with the foetal membrane. In this way, these reptiles resemble the placental mammals.

The foetal membrane absorbs everything it needs for growth from the glands of the oviduct. In some cases, the fully developed young are born still wrapped in their foetal membranes; in others, they are born unenclosed, having shed the membranes in the oviduct. The Australian snake (*Denisonia*) is also viviparous.

Parthenogenesis ('virgin birth')

Parthenogenesis is extremely rare in vertebrates. Until recent time, its occurrence was doubted. It was first reported in two genera of two viviparous fishes (*Poecilia Mollienisia*, and *Poeciliopsis*).

The discovery of parthenogenesis in lizards dates from 1958, the species concerned being *Lacerta saxicola*, found in the Caucasus. The most reliable data have been provided by American biologists and refer to various species of *Cnemidopherus*—found from the southern states of the United States to the Amazon. Several races of these species are exclusively parthenogenetic—being represented entirely by females. Parthenogenetic females produce only females.

Some of the races with 2N of 38 chromosomes (*Cnemidophorus neomexicanus* and *C. tesselatus*) are diploid (that is, they have paired chromosomes). Hybridization of a diploid parthenogenetic female with a male of a bisexual species gives triploid females (3N of 57) capable of reproducing again by parthenogenesis.

Growth and longevity

Reptiles grow quickly. The Mississippi alligator, which is about eight inches long at birth, reaches two feet two inches at a year old, three feet six inches at two years, four feet eight inches at three years, six feet five inches at six years, and about nine feet at nine years. These figures are for males. Females are smaller. Growth slows down markedly after puberty, but still remains appreciable. Individuals of exceptional size are always very old. The following table shows the potential life span of some reptiles:

> *Alligator mississipiensis*: 56 years
> *Crocodylus acutus*: 13 years
> *Crocodylus nilotious*: 50 years and upwards
> *Testudo gigantea*: more than 152 years
> *Testudo sumeirii*: 150 years (?)
> *Terrapene carolina*: 138 years
> *Emys orbicularis*: more than 100 years
> *Sphenodon*: 28 years
> *Heloderma suspectum*: 20 years
> *Anguis fragilis*: 33 years
> Various snakes: from 3 to 30 years
> Lizards: 20 years at the most

It would seem that species that hibernate live longer than those that are continuously active.

Locomotory movements

Because of the structure and position of their limbs, reptiles almost invariably move with their bodies close to or touching

Hatching of the green lizard (*Lacerta viridis*); the eggs are up to ¾ inch in length by ½ inch in diameter. The ones shown here were found in a hole dug by their mother by using her hind legs. The young lizard hatches without receiving any help; to open the shell, which has the consistency of parchment, it uses the sharp hatching tooth at the tip of its snout. The new-born lizard measures about 3 inches. *Phot. Aldo Margiocco*

the ground. But some species can move at great speed. For example, the acanthodactyls and the tropidosaurs of the deserts can run so fast in hot sun that it is almost impossible to catch them.

Being cold blooded, reptiles react to extremes of hot and cold, their body temperature varying with that of the atmosphere. Their nervous and muscular activities are affected by temperature. Cold slows down their movements progressively, and movement ceases at around 32° F.

Crawling

Four-legged reptiles have two speeds: walking and running. Some of them—the basilisk (*Basiliscus*), the flying dragons, the collared lizard (*Creptaphytus*), and the desert iguana (*Dipsosaurus*) run very quickly on their hind legs, which have great muscular power. At full speed, the basilisk can cross small streams almost without touching the water. A snake travelling on land moves in much the same way as one swimming in water—by lateral undulations of its body. This is serpentine motion. Snakes moving in this way take advantage of every small irregularity on the ground and, since ground is rarely absolutely smooth, they can move without difficulty. On a smooth surface they are in difficulties. In the serpentine movement the scales on the underside—the ventral shields—play no special part. The body moves as a whole by muscular action, the tail following the line of the head and neck.

Boas and pythons move in a different way. They can travel in a straight line and, in this movement, only the ventral shields are used. Their style of travel is known as the *caterpillar* movement. In this case, the ventral shields take a grip by their free edges and become, literally, linear feet.

Another type of movement is known as side-winding, used for travelling on loose surfaces. The snake travels obliquely in a series of double loops.

Climbing

Snakes that live in trees, able to climb vertical trunks and glide along branches, are specially adapted (*Dendreaspis* and *Elaphe*). The most highly developed species have prehensile tails. In the most advanced climbing snakes there is a ridge or keel along each side of the body where the ventral and dorsal scales meet. The tops of the ribs fit into this ridge (snakes have no breast-bone). During climbing, these keels take hold of the smallest projections or irregularities. This explains how some snakes, *Elaphe* for instance, can climb trunks with rough surfaces. The oriental *Chrysophelia ornata* can climb vertical walls and tree trunks by anchoring its shields on the minutest projections.

Some lizards are specially adapted for climbing. Geckos and some *Anolis* have adhesive pads on their hands and feet, while others, like the chameleons, have clawed hands and feet, forming pincers.

Swimming

Some reptiles, especially marine species, are excellent swimmers. Turtles are as at home in the water as fish. Their limbs have evolved into swimming paddles, and this is the outstanding feature of their adaptation to aquatic life. Tortoises use their limbs as oars. Crocodiles, when swimming, hold their limbs against their bodies and lash their powerfully muscled tails from side to side. Lizards swim in much the same way, although in some species the whole body undulates. Snakes swim in the same way. Species that spend most of their lives in water, sea snakes for example (*Hydrophis*), have vertically flattened tails.

The hatching of the European grass snake *Natrix natrix. Phot. R. H. Noailles*

The vital domain: territoriality among reptiles

With the exception of turtles, the great majority of reptiles live a settled life—sedentary. There should be no misunderstanding about the term *sedentary* because it applies to a great many species that travel widely without being migratory. These wide-ranging species are hunters, found mainly in semi-desert zones, where they have to travel great distances to find prey. Good examples are the vipers of the Sahara that range widely to find the rodents on which they prey.

Most reptiles remain in a well defined territory for long periods (*Lacerta viridis* and *Vipera aspis*, 3 years; *Crotalus viridis* 10 years). Size of territory varies from species to species. It has been shown that the plains garter snake (*Thamnophis radix*) holds from 120 to 360 square yards; the prairie rattlesnake (*Crotalus viridis*) 25 acres; the asp (*Vipera aspis*) up to 108 square yards; the desert monitor (*Varanus griseus*) from 500 to 1200 acres (desert); the gopher tortoise (*Gopherus agassizi*) 10 to 100 acres (desert); the eastern box turtle (*Terrapene carolina*) 2½ acres (tropical environment).

Some male lizards defend their territory, and in some *Anolis* there is a social hierarchy based on male dominance. The

The aesculapian snake *Elaphe longissimus* is extremely agile and voracious. This one has climbed a vine-plant in which a woodchat shrike (*Lanius senator*) has its nest, and is making a mere single mouthful of the still living fledgling. *Phot. Aldo Margiocco*

biological value of concentration—as in the congregations of male iguanas on the Galapagos beaches—is unknown.

Classification

The order Chelonia: tortoises and turtles

There are few zoological groups whose members so closely resemble each other as tortoises and turtles. Yet, even here, where the close relationship is indisputable, there are enough differences to suggest separate evolutionary lines. Diversification is, however, not wide, and consists, as it were, of variations on a single basic theme.

The tortoise is not the only animal cased in armour as a defence against its enemies: the *Glyptodon*, which once roamed the pampas of the Argentine, was also heavily armoured with bony plates.

Despite apparent drawbacks, the tortoise has been a biological success. Yet it is no more than an armoured shell with five holes—four to accommodate its slow-moving stumps of legs and one for its small head on its longish neck. Paradoxically, it is a most healthy, robust animal with tremendous resistance to disease and adverse conditions.

The chelonian form first emerged in the Triassic, when there were already many thriving reptile species. Since then, tortoises have persisted and prospered. Their exact origin is not known. No link has yet been discovered between the Triassic tortoises, already equipped with a carapace, and other reptiles. So, in the world of reptiles, the evolutionary isolation of chelonians is still a mystery.

The main types of tortoises

Chelonians may be described as reptiles with a relatively small skull without temporal cavities, and toothless jaws sheathed in horn to form a sharp-edged beak. The body is contained in a shell consisting of a flat ventral plastron, fused to the arched dorsal buckler or carapace. The ribs, which are inserted between the vertebrae, fit under the plates of the carapace to which they are fused. The leathery turtle (*Dermochelys corialla*) is an exception to this last rule.

Tortoises fall into two main groups, classified according to the way they withdraw their necks into the carapace. In Cryptodira, withdrawal is by bending of the neck on the median vertical plane, and, in Pleuredira, by lateral bending. Because this peculiarity appears to be associated with other fairly constant characteristics, it is used as the criterion for classifying chelonians. It should be noted that the pelvis of Cryptodira is attached to the carapace by ligaments, while that of Pleuredira is attached by bone.

Two turtles are difficult to classify. One is the luth or leathery turtle, whose skeleton is unattached to the carapace. The others are the soft-shelled turtles (*Trionyx*). Although they are genuine cryptodires, they are classified separately because of the lack of a horny covering on the carapace.

Cryptodira

The Chelydridae (snapping turtles)

The Chelydridae, or snapping turtles, are found in North American swamps and rivers. Snapping turtles cannot withdraw their broad mobile heads completely under the carapace. They have long tails with spiny crests. The most widespread species, *Chelydra serpentina*, is a predator and carrion eater, finding prey and carrion on the bottom of streams and ponds. It is used by some Indians to find the bodies of people who have been drowned. For this purpose the Indians choose a specimen measuring up to three feet in length. The turtle is roped and released into the water from a small boat, then handled like a dog. The turtle finds the body by its sense of smell.

Another species in this group is the alligator snapping turtle (*Macrochelis temmincki*) which reaches a great size and weighs up to 220 pounds. This species is found in the Mississippi and its tributaries. Its hunting style is to lie in ambush on the bottom, remaining motionless with its mouth wide open. It is well camouflaged by its colour and its crested carapace resembles a mass of algae. From its mouth there then appears a pink, worm-like appendage of the tongue, which is controlled by muscular action. The worm-like appendage, wriggling like a worm, attracts fish which are snapped up by the turtle. In the southeastern United States, the flesh of the alligator turtle is considered a delicacy.

The soft-shelled turtles (*Trionyx*) are of ancient origin, their first known remains dating from the upper Jurassic period. They reached the height of their development towards the end of the Cretaceous. Today they are still found in large numbers in tropical watercourses and swamps. A single American species (*Trionyx spinifera*) is found as far north as Canada (St. Lawrence, Lake Champlain).

These turtles have flattened skulls. The bones of the carapace are encased in thick, tough tissue instead of horny armour. The marginal bony plates are more or less replaced by cartilage. The lips are fleshy, which is unusual, and very different from the beak of other turtles. The tip of the snout is prolonged into a kind of proboscis which serves as a breathing tube, and the feet and hands are broadly webbed. All the Trionycidae live in fresh water, the genus *Trionyx* being found throughout the tropics. The young are very active ashore, walking and running about. Adults, on the other hand, hardly ever leave the water except to sun themselves on the banks.

The Trionycidae feed entirely on live animals—crustaceans, molluscs, fishes, etc.

A close relative of the Trionycidae is found in New Guinea. It is the plateless turtle (*Carettochelys insculpta*), which has a complete bony skeleton but no horny covering. This provides a link between the two soft-shelled turtles (Trionycidae) and the others.

The Emydidae (freshwater tortoises)

The Emydidae or freshwater tortoises have the greatest number of genera and species—25 genera and 76 species—and are distributed mainly in the northern hemisphere. Their carapaces are oval and their back plates are only slightly convex. Although described as aquatic, they are really amphibian, for they do not hesitate to come ashore and walk about.

The genus *Clemmys* has several species distributed over North America, but only one representative in Europe.

There are two species of cistudes (*Emys*): the pond turtle of Europe (*Emys orbicularis*) and that of North America (*Emys blandingi*), found in the Great Lakes region. Both prey on live animals but, in captivity, will accept chopped meat and spleen pulp.

The European pond turtle mates in water. In June it lays from 4 to 16 eggs. Incubation lasts from 3 to 4 months. At a year old, the young weigh about $\frac{1}{5}$ of an ounce, at 2 years from $\frac{1}{2}$ to $\frac{2}{3}$ of an ounce, at 3 years from $\frac{3}{4}$ to 1 ounce, at 4 years from $1\frac{1}{5}$ to $1\frac{1}{4}$ ounces and at 6 years from 2 to $3\frac{1}{2}$ ounces. One pond turtle was kept in captivity by one family for nearly 100 years. Another lived for 120 years in the Botanical Gardens at Montpellier. Pond turtles reach maturity at the age of 12 to 13 years, but females do not begin to lay until they are over 15 years old. They hibernate in the bottom mud or on the banks of pools or swamps.

In general habits, the Emydidae resemble pond turtles. They mate in spring, shortly after emerging from hibernation, and lay in June/July. With her hind legs, the female digs a hole from three to four inches in depth, expanding it at the bottom into a flat nest for her eggs. In this she lays four or five eggs. She then fills in the hole with earth but does not cover the eggs. The young turtles hatch in September/October, but if there is an early cold spell this is delayed until the following spring. Normally, the young hibernate in the nesting hollow.

North American box turtles are mainly terrestrial. Some species, like the eastern box turtle (*Terrapene carolina*) have brightly coloured carapaces. The edges of the plastron are hinged and, when the hinge closes, the animal can literally box itself in. Hence its name.

The red-eared terrapin (*Pseudemys scripta*) is an emydid which is common in fresh water in the centre of the United States. Its diet is half-flesh, half-vegetable. Each individual has its territory, to which it persistently returns. *Phot. Aldo Margiocco*

The diamond-back terrapin (*Malaclemys centrata*) derives its popular name from the appearance of its plates which look as though they had been chiselled into many facets. Males of this species are under 7 inches in length; females under 5½ inches. It is found in brackish water in the southeastern United States. Its flesh is highly esteemed by gourmets and it was such a common species in the 18th century that slaves were fed on it. Before 1920 it had become very rare and correspondingly expensive to buy for food—about 90 dollars a dozen. Artificial rearing, combined with a fall in demand, brought the price down to 30 dollars a dozen in 1920. *Malaclemys* grow slowly, reaching about 4½ inches at the age of 5 years. After mating, the female stores spermatozoa in her genital tracts, and these remain active for at least 3 years, fertilizing the eggs she lays over the period.

The Testudinae

The Testudinae live to a great age and it has been claimed that a *Testudo graeca*, kept in captivity in England, lived for 220 years; but the documents on which this claim is based have been judged to be false. In 1766, the French naturalist Marion de Fresne introduced *Testudo gigantes* into Mauritius It was captured by the English in 1810 and died accidentally in 1818, by which time it was blind. If these facts are correct, this specimen lived for more than 152 years—a record for a land animal.

In Testudinae the carapace is markedly convex. The feet, which are massive, are covered with small scales. The only prominent projections are the claws in the feet. As a result, when the feet and head are withdrawn into the shell, the animal becomes a single compact unit without protuberances. All the Testudinae are vegetarian. The group is not found in Australia.

The giant tortoises of the Galapagos (*Testudo elephantopus*), like those of the Seychelles and of Aldabara, are threatened with extinction. They have long been intensively hunted by whalers, as well as by the native, for their edible flesh. Native predation was subsistence hunting and made little impact, but the real threats came from outside.

Testudo hermanni and *Testudo graeca* are found in southern Europe. Although mainly vegetarians, they also eat slugs and earth-worms. They hibernate in cavities which they hollow out in the ground.

The Chelonidae (true sea turtles)

These turtles reach a great size. They are strictly marine species, and come ashore only to lay their eggs. Their limbs

The European pond tortoise (*Emys orbicularis*) lives in ponds and at the muddy edges of rivers. It is carnivorous and will eat almost anything that moves. Its geographical distribution covers middle and southern Europe, southwest Asia, north Africa. *Phot. M. C. Noailles*

The Greek land tortoise, *Testudo hermanni*, although mainly vegetarian also feeds on live prey. It is seen here ingesting an earth worm. *Phot. Jean Vasserot*

The eastern box turtle *Terrapene carolina*, ventral view. *Phot. J. Vasserot*

have become oars, well adapted for swimming. Sea turtles are found almost exclusively in warm or temperate seas.

In the breeding season, the turtles come ashore and lay their eggs on sandy beaches. As soon as they emerge from the eggs, the young turtles move to the sea and never go in the wrong direction. It is not known what guides them, but they never take a landward course. This field is wide open to research.

The loggerhead (*Caretta caretta*) has a very large head. It feeds on fish and other marine organisms. Present-day specimens rarely exceed 286 pounds in weight.

The closely related green turtle (*Chelonia mydas*) is found mostly in the same tropical habitats, but is sometimes recorded much further north. It feeds on algae. Its flesh and eggs are edible and highly prized as food. The beaches on which it lays its eggs are well known, so it is highly vulnerable to egg collectors and, in fact, it has become rare as a result of this kind of predation. In Indo-Malaysia the collection of eggs is controlled by law, which may help to restore the balance. This species often exceeds 440 pounds in weight.

The hawksbill turtle

The hawksbill turtle is smaller than the loggerhead and green turtles, reaching a maximum of 34 inches in length and weighing about 310 pounds. This is the species that provides the well-known tortoiseshell, once so widely used in

commerce. Tortoiseshell was then in great demand, but it has now been largely replaced by plastics which can be made to simulate it very closely. The turtles were caught when they came ashore to lay their eggs. In India, Ceylon and the West Indies, they were, at one time, under heavy pressure. Their flesh is edible. Claims have been made that it is toxic, but this is highly improbable.

The carapace was stripped from the turtles by plunging them into boiling water. Thereafter, by the action of heat, which renders it plastic, the shell could be moulded into almost any shape. When cooled, it retained the shape into which it had been moulded. It was then polished. One fully grown turtle can provide up to 10 pounds of tortoiseshell.

Pleuredira

The pleuredire turtles are found mainly in the southern hemisphere. The Pelomedusidae are the most important of these, the most widely distributed species being *Pelomedusa rufa* which ranges from southern Africa to the southern Sahara. They are found in swamps. In South America, these turtles are represented by the genus *Podocnemis*. *Podocnemis expansa* is abundant in the Amazon basins, breeding on the islands of these large rivers. The eggs are edible and are harvested

405

annually by the local Indians, who obtain an oil from them. They also eat the turtle's flesh. A hundred years ago the English explorer Bates estimated that the number of eggs harvested annually in the Amazon region was 48 million. As a result of this heavy toll of eggs, the numbers of *Podecnemis expansa* were greatly reduced. Another species (*P. madagascariensis*) is native to Madagascar.

The Chelidae, or snake-necked turtles, have flattened carapaces, small heads and long, flexible serpentine necks. They live in swamps, where they lie up waiting for prey.

One of the strangest of all turtles is the matamata (*Chelys fimbriata*). Its carapace, which is about 16 inches in length, bristles with cones which are in fact projections of its vertebral plates. The skin of the neck is loose and wrinkled, with a pronounced frill. It has a wide mouth, but is weak jawed, the mandibles being no more than a pair of slim bones. When waiting for prey, the matamata settles down with its mouth wide open. Fish and crustaceans drift into its mouth and are swallowed without chewing. It has been suggested that prey is attracted by the movement of the frill in the current. The matamata is found in swamps and slow-moving rivers of South America. A few genera of Chelidae are found in Australia, examples being the snake-necked turtles (*Emydura : Chelodina*).

Luth—biggest of the turtles

The luth or leathery turtle (*Dermochelys coriacea*) is unique, differing widely from all the others. It has a heart-shaped carapace, with the tip pointing backwards. The carapace looks

The matamata (*Chelys fimbriata*) is a predator with a huge mouth, which swallows any prey passing within its reach. Its carapace may reach 16 inches in length. *Phot. Aldo Margiocco*

like leather and is, in fact, a tough tissue connecting the small polygonal plates into a mosaic. There are seven keels on the carapace, running from front to back. The limbs have become transformed into powerful swimming paddles. The front paddles are extremely long and, in young animals, stretch right to the rear end of the carapace. The luth is the only turtle whose spine is not fused to its carapace.

The hawksbill turtle (*Eretmochelys imbricata*) is a marine species which lives in almost all the tropical and temperate seas. It is hunted for its shell, which plastic materials have not yet totally replaced. *Phot. Aldo Margiocco*

The Iberian land tortoise (*Testudo graeca*), badly named, because it is by no means confined to Greece, inhabits southeast and southwest Europe. It is famous for its longevity. *Phot. Aldo Margiocco*

The leathery turtle or luth (*Dermochelys coriacea*), the giant of the chelonians, after having laid, makes its way back to the sea. *Phot. Jane Burton—Photo Researchers*

The luth comes ashore only to lay its eggs. In Ceylon certain beaches are always used, so the species is easy to locate year after year. The female digs holes in the sand and, in each of such 'nests', she lays about 80 eggs. One female caught on the coast of Senegal was found to contain 620 eggs. The fore-paddles of the newly born luth are remarkable for their great length. Another feature of the young luth is that the tip of its head, the paddles and the back of the plastron are covered with scales.

Luths are found in all the tropical seas, and have been recorded in the Mediterranean. In 1558, Rondelet captured one at Frontignan on the French Mediterranean coast.

The luth reaches about 8 feet in length and weighs from 880 to 1212 pounds. It is the largest living species. Although it is thought to travel great distances, its migrations—if it does migrate—have yet to be studied. Its main food appears to be jellyfishes.

The lepidosaurs

If we look at the reptiles' family tree, we shall see that three groups (Rhynchocephalia, lizards and snakes) derive from the eosuchians. These groups bear the name lepidosaurs (saurians: reptiles with scales).

The eosuchians have two temporal cavities, foreshadowing the true lizards. From them evolved two branches—the Rhynchocephalia and the Squamata. The most important of their fossils is *Youngina*, found in the upper Permian in South Africa. This fossil had two temporal cavities and these, with various other features, heralded the lizards.

The order Rhynchocephalia

This order is now represented by a single species, the tuatara (*Sphenodon punctatus*), now found only on islets in Cook Strait in New Zealand. In the Mesozoic era, the Rhynchocephalia were quite important in the world of reptiles. They appeared in the Triassic, when they produced a number of fairly diversified types that never reached any great size. They were all lizard-like, but differed from the true lizards in having two pairs of temporal cavities.

The tuatara is robust and lizard-like, measuring about 14 inches from the tip of its snout to its vent. The male is larger than the female. In tuatara the pineal eye is functional. The anterior and posterior surfaces of the vertebrae are concave. The wall of the abdomen has a special skeleton—the abdominal sternum—made up of 24 to 26 V-shaped bones formed by the sub-cutaneous tissue. The male has no copulatory organ. Tuatara is oviparous. The female digs a hole in which she lays her eggs. Development lasts for more than a year and may stop altogether for a period during the southern winter.

Tuataras inhabit the vegetation zone around islands. They either dig their own nests or take over those of the petrels that breed there. This association favours the hatterias which feed on the numerous insects attracted by the birds' excrement.

The order Squamata: lizards (saurians)

At present, because they have certain common characteristics, it is usual to group lizards and snakes in the same super-order: the Squamata. The skull in the two orders appears to have undergone a similar evolution from a common ancestor, the bones fringing the lower temporal cavity degenerating and disappearing. The ancestry of lizards goes back to the eosuchians, which means there is a wide gap between them and crocodiles which are derived from the archosuchians.

The lizard, with four legs and a tail, is the most common form, though there are species that appear snake-like in that they have no limbs or only vestigial limbs; this loss is accompanied by a lengthening of the body, which becomes cylindrical. The slow-worm is a typical example.

The lizard skin is covered with epidermal scales which may or may not be lined with thin dermal body plates. The anterior surface of the vertebra is concave (in geckos both surfaces are concave). The skull roof is pierced by a hole corresponding to the pineal eye which, in many species, is deep.

Spontaneous self-fracture of the tail, known as autotomy, is a feature of many saurians—geckos, lizards, slow-worms and hatteria. Self-fracture occurs when the tail is seized by an enemy, but sometimes as a result of stress or fear. Self-fracture is entirely spontaneous; the lizard has no control over it. It occurs because the structure of the tail is designed to make it possible. Pinching of the tail, or pressure on it, sets off a reflex contraction of the muscles. The contraction acts on the weak partition between the masses of muscle and the middle of a vertebra. This device is repeated along the length of the tail, vertebra by vertebra. A little in front of each break-point, the tail artery has a circular muscle (sphincter) which contracts at the moment of autotomy to prevent haemorrhage.

The tail regenerates the amputated part, but not in its original form, and the points of cleavage are lacking in the new part, so there can be no repeat of self-fracture.

Autotomy is often an effective defence because it allows the lizard to escape, leaving the attacker with part of its tail. Geckos, lizards and iguanas with regenerated tails are common enough in nature.

Geckos:
nocturnal lizards with adhesive feet

These lizards are cosmopolitan, but are especially plentiful in the dry, warm regions of the world. They possess a number of archaic characters, such as persistence of the notochord between the biconcave vertebrae, and laterally inserted teeth.

Geckos (Geckonidae), of which there are about seventy genera, have short fleshy tongues, notched in front and partly protractile. The larynx has vocal cords and is, therefore, capable of producing sounds. The name gecko is of onomatopoeic origin.

Geckos are extraordinarily agile climbers, with very flattened bodies. Their widespread toes are broad and fleshy, with folds on the inner surfaces that enable them to adhere to surfaces as smooth as a sheet of glass or a plaster ceiling. The surface cells of these fleshy folds form microscopic hooks which enable the gecko to cling to the tiniest foothold. When the gecko takes hold, it lowers the tips of its toes and the small hooks turn downwards to grip. When the lizard wishes to free its foot, it raises the tips of its toes to break this hold. On smooth surfaces, the fleshy pads appear to act as suckers. The arrangement of the fleshy folds varies from one gecko genus to another. Adhesive feet are one of the outstanding characteristics of these lizards.

Most geckos are active at night and their eyes are adapted for seeing in poor light. The retina contains only rods and the contracted pupil is no more than a tiny vertical slit. In a few species, the edges of the pupil are lobed and, when the iris contracts, the slit becomes four very small circular orifices. This results in the formation of four images that are super-

The gecko (*Tarentola mauritanica*) enters houses in the Mediterranean region, from Egypt and Syria to the Canary Islands, for the purpose of eating nocturnal insects attracted by the light of lamps. Notice its narrow lobate pupil as well as the reptilian position of the right foreleg

Opposite right, the ventral surface of the gecko's left foot, pressed against a pane of glass to which it adheres. The total length of the animal is no more than 6 inches
Phot. Aldo Margiocco and J. Six.

This *Phelsuma* is a diurnal gecko from Madagascar; it is a beautiful green colour. *Phot. Jean-Jacques Petter*

imposed on the retina. Geckos that are active by day—
Phelsuma of Madagascar is an example—have a circular
pupil. They are brightly coloured, while the colour of the
nocturnal species is dull.

Except for a few New Zealand species, geckos are oviparous. They are not great egg layers. Two eggs are usual,
but some species lay only one.

In *Ptychozoon*, or the flying gecko, the head, body and
limbs have skin flaps that act as parachutes when the lizard
is gliding or leaping from one tree-top to another. Autotomy
is the rule in geckos but there is extraordinary variation in
the tail from species to species. In the simplest case, it is
flattened and considerably broadened. *Uroplatus*, from
Madagascar, the limbs and body of which are edged with
projecting scales, has a racket-shaped tail. *Phyllurus platurus*,
from Australia, has a broad flat tail, ragged at the edges and
ending in an unmodified stump. The strangest species is
perhaps the turnip-tailed gecko of South America, *Theca-
dactylus rapicaudatus*, which has a swollen tail resembling a
turnip. In *Nephrurus*, or the Australian gecko, the tail is very
short and, in some, is reduced to a large knob, as in *N.
asper*. The tail of the Australian geckos, *Oedura, Gymno-
dactylus milii*, and of those from the deserts of southeastern
Asia, are packed with fat which is used as a food reserve
during hibernation.

In many countries, geckos are believed to be poisonous
and, in some places, are greatly feared. In fact, they are
completely harmless and there is no foundation whatever
for believing otherwise.

Iguanas:
all American, with rare exceptions

Iguanas, which are mainly American, constitute a very
important group of lizards. Outside America they occur only
in Madagascar (*Oplurus* and *Chalorodon*), and in the Fiji
Islands and the Friendly Islands (*Brachylophus*). They are the
New World representatives of the Old World Varanidae.

All iguanas have well developed limbs, mobile eyelids
and fairly long tails. They are oviparous, except for the
mountain species, *Sceloporus* and *Liolaemus*, which incubate
their eggs in the oviduct. Skull structure is often the only
difference between certain species. The lateral teeth are often
tricuspid or surmounted by denticles.

Tree-dwelling iguanas have transversely flattened bodies,
and strong feet with powerful claws.

The common iguana, *Iguana iguana*, is a beautiful creature,
up to six feet in length, with a tail almost as long as its head
and body combined. It is strictly vegetarian and haunts
forests near rivers. Its flesh and eggs are highly esteemed

The basilisk (*Basiliscus basiliscus*) from Central America lives in forests close to water. *Phot. Aldo Margiocco*

This flat-tailed gecko (*Uroplatus*) has sides and limbs fringed with strong close-set scales. *Photo. Jean-Jacques Petter*

items of food. These iguanas are found in the Greater Antilles and in Central and South America.

In iguanas of the genera *Phenacosaurus* and *Xiphocercus* the tail is prehensile.

In tropical America there are several very special species of iguana, those of the Galapagos Islands being of unusual interest. The marine iguana, *Amblyrhynchus cristatus*, lives on the seashore and feeds almost entirely on seaweed. It is a good swimmer, resorting to the water quickly when alarmed.

The land iguana, *Conolophus pallidus*, is found in the interior of these islands. It is a plant eater and is especially fond of cactus, the spines of which, in this case, provide no protection.

Brachylophus, of the Fiji Islands, is almost three feet long. It is arboreal and vegetarian. This species is in great danger, for it is reckoned that it will become extinct in the near future if not actively protected. On Madagascar and the neighbouring islands there are two small iguanas about a foot in length. *Chalorodon*, which has smooth scales, lives in trees: *Oplurus*, which has strong scales streamlined round its tail, is a ground dweller.

Basilisks—biped runners

The basilisks (*Basiliscus*) of Central and South America are large species, about 2½ feet long. They live in trees beside the banks of streams. They run on their hind legs in upright position and, notably, they can cross streams without sinking in the water and possibly use their tails when doing so. The Panamanians call this lizard 'the Jesus Christ beast' because it can walk on water.

Anoles ('American chameleons')

The anoles, wrongly called American chameleons, are a large arboreal genus. In these lizards, all the toes have long claws, as well as being fitted with adhesive pads like those of geckos. Size varies between 4½ and 7 inches, the biggest being *Anolis equestris* from Cuba, which can reach a total length of 15 inches. There are many species, especially in the West Indies, where fifty have been described between Cuba and the Windward Islands.

Anoles have the ability to change colour remarkably, and one species, *Anolis carolinensis*, has been closely studied in this respect. It has been observed that its colour varies according to the surrounding temperature and the light intensity. If it is subjected to a temperature of 50° F it becomes brown; at a temperature of 70° F it changes to green, but only if it is kept in darkness or very poor light. In bright light, it remains brown. If the temperature is increased to 86° F, the lizard turns a bright greenish-grey and remains like that whatever the state of the light. These colour variations are dependent on two hormones, one secreted by the intermediary lobe of the hypophysis, the other by the suprarenal glands (adrenalin). The first hormone disperses pigment in the chromatophores, which results in a darkening of the outer skin. The second concentrates them, resulting in lightening of the skin. There are no nerve filaments in the chromatophores, so they are not influenced directly by the central nervous system.

Anolis carolinensis has achieved a notable degree of social organization. Territorial boundaries are clearly defined and there is a hierarchical system among males, the position of each in the hierarchy being determined by aggressive displays or fighting. When two males meet, they flatten themselves, inflate their throats, become paler in colour and circle each other. Aggressive display is often sufficient to scare off an opponent. If this fails, a fight ensues. The lizards then seize each other by the jaws and shake vigorously until one of them falls from the tree.

Phrynosomes: ant-eating horned toads

These toads are found in arid and semi-desert regions of the southwest of the United States, but bear a striking resemblance to the Australian moloch—another example of convergence that has long intrigued naturalists. Both species are ant-eaters. The Australian molochs, Agamidae, inhabit regions where the climatic conditions resemble closely those of the American semi-desert areas where the Iguanidae are found. Both families burrow into the surface layer of the sand, leaving only their heads showing so that, although almost completely hidden, they can still see.

The grey zones of the phrynosomes' skin can change colour. Against a light background the animal becomes lighter in colour and, against a dark background, it becomes darker. The phrynosomes are unique among vertebrates in bleeding slightly when frightened. The significance of this bleeding has still not been explained.

Agamas

The agamas are a well defined group, characterized mainly by the peculiarities of their skeleton. There are more than 300 species in the Old World tropics, with the exception of Madagascar. Only species of particular interest, either because of structure or habits, will be discussed here.

Tree agamas have transversely flattened bodies. These include *Calotes*, the Bornean gonyocephalus (*Gonyocephalus liogaster*) and *Cophotis*, which has a prehensile tail. The flying dragons (*Draco*) of eastern India and southeast Asia, are arboreal.

Close-up of head of female common iguana (*Iguana iguana*). This species is hunted for its flesh and its eggs, especially at breeding time. The females dig holes in which to lay their eggs. *Phot. C. M. Hladik*

The common iguana (*Iguana iguana*) walking on ground strewn with bamboo branches and leaves. *Phot. C. M. Hladik*

Terrestrial species include numerous runners like the Australian frilled lizard, *Chlamydosaurus kingi*, which runs upright with its body bent forward. The genus *Phrynocephalus*, e.g. *Ph. nejdensis*—the Arabian toad-headed lizard, is found in the sub-desert regions of southwestern Asia. It is a swift runner and uses its long claws to dig into the sand.

The true agamas (*Agama*), which range from India to eastern Europe and over most of Africa, are not specialized in any way. They include both runners and tree-dwellers.

The East Indian water lizard (*Hydrosaurus amboinensis*) of New Guinea and the Molucca archipelago, is the only aquatic species. The body of this beautiful lizard is slightly flattened transversely and it has a vertically flattened dorsal crest of erect scales. It inhabits forests near water, and is a strong swimmer. It is the giant of the group, being over three feet in length. Little or nothing is known about its habits.

Emotions make calotes change colour

One of the striking features of the Agamidae is their ability to change colour under certain conditions. Males of *Calotes versicolor*, an Indian species, go through a series of ritual manoeuvres when two of them meet. Each inflates his throat, which has a dewlap (fold of loose skin), and manoeuvres towards the other, displaying his crest. Then they raise and lower their heads before biting. A single bite is usually enough to bring the fight to an end. As a general rule, these lizards are brown or olive-grey in colour, with dark brown spots. During a fight the antagonists change colour quickly, becoming lighter or darker as they move about. At the end of the fight the winner turns red, where the loser remains brown or greyish, thus resembling a female. When a male meets a female, he behaves as though in the presence of a rival, changing colour to yellowish or fleshy pink with a black spot on each side of his dewlap. Male and female *Calotes* hold separate territories which they defend against all others. The holder of the territory threatens intruders by inflating its throat and changing colour.

Other Agamidae change colour under the influence of stress, e.g. when defending food or territory, or during fighting or mating. The Australian bearded lizard, *Amphibolurus barbatus*, is an example. The beard of this species consists of a covering of long pointed scales arranged in longitudinal rows on the throat and the sides of the neck. When threatened, it opens its mouth and inflates its throat so that the beard spreads out fan-like, with the points of the scales erect. When the lizard is not aroused or frightened its beard is dark olive brown; when it is upset it turns bright yellow with orange stripes.

The Australian dragon, *Chlamydosaurus kingi*, behaves in similar fashion. It has a membrane or dewlap extending backwards for 2 to 2½ inches from the throat and the sides of the neck. At rest, this dewlap is folded close to the body. The contraction of the muscles attached to the tongue bones (hyoid) raises the membrane into a collar. The spread can be 6 inches in a dragon that is only 7 inches long. As the dragon spreads its collar, it opens its mouth, an action giving it an extremely ferocious and frightening appearance.

The African agama, *Agama atricollis*, is a tree-dweller, and is usually brown in colour with zones of silvery grey, sepia, bluish-green and yellow. When confronted by an enemy it raises its head and opens its mouth widely, displaying the bright orange yellow inside. This is a defensive manoeuvre that relies on the sudden appearance of a bright colour to surprise or halt an aggressor.

The agama of the sands: Uromastix and molochs

Some agamids have heavy bodies flattened slightly vertically. They live in burrows and bury themselves in the sand. The spiny-tailed lizard, *Uromastix*, of this group lives in burrows, blocking the entrances with its tail which has whorls of spiny scales. *Uromastix* inhabits arid zones from northern Africa to northern India.

The molochs (*Moloch horridus*) inhabit sandy zones in the Australian deserts. They are six or seven inches in length, yellow and brown in colour and bristle all over with large conical spines. Their slowness of movement belies a lightening tongue, so that they can catch ants easily. A moloch will eat between 1000 and 5000 ants at a single meal. Molochs change colour according to what can best be described as their emotional state.

The Australian moloch (*Moloch horridus*) lives superficially buried in the sand in dry regions of West Australia. This agamid, quite harmless despite its appearance, feeds only on ants and termites. Maximum length 8 inches. *Phot. Z. F. A.*

Marine iguana from the Galapagos (*Amblyrhynchus cristatus*). *Phot. A. Brosset*

Chameleons: telescopic eyes, changing coat and dart-like tongue

The chameleon is highly specialized in its arboreal life. It catches insects by flicking out its tongue which is sticky with saliva. Almost everything about the chameleon is highly specialized, and all its specializations are co-related. The head and body is vertically flattened. A tiny pineal orifice persists between the parietal bones. The tail is long in almost all genera, and prehensile in some. The feet and hands are like pincers, with claw-like jaws for gripping branches. The axis of the pincers is transverse in relation to the large axis of the limb—two digits on one side and three on the other.

The eyes are unique among vertebrates. The eyelids are fused but have a narrow vertical slit. The eyeballs protrude so prominently that they appear to be out of their sockets. They can be moved at will in any direction round their point of attachment, directed by muscles directly inserted on them and on the inner surface of the sockets. They can even look independently, one to the front, the other to the rear. The retina is highly developed, and chameleons have marvellous vision with several photoreceptor cells connected to a single ganglionic (nerve) cell.

The tongue of the chameleon resembles a long fleshy string which, at its free end, swells into a club. It is highly contractile and housed in a sheath situated on the floor of the mouth and stretching far into the visceral cavity. Because of its powerful muscles, it can be extended and retracted in a fraction of a second. Under the throat, at the junction of the larynx and the wind-pipe, there is a membraneous pouch which the chameleon can inflate at will—thus quickly changing its appearance. The lungs connect to visceral sacs which the chameleon, by swallowing air, can again inflate at will.

Chameleons feed exclusively upon insects. The tongue, coated with the sticky saliva, is pointed like a javelin and strikes unerringly at its prey. The eyes, at this moment, converge, giving the chameleon precise three-dimensional vision.

All the chameleon's movements are so slow, restrained

The bearded lizard (*Amphibolurus barbatus*) is an agamid remarkable for its coloured dewlap which is like a beard when inflated. This reptile lives in Australia. *Phot. John Markham*

and silent that insects are not scared away by its presence. It can lie in ambush for hours, perfectly motionless, exploring its surroundings with its telescopic eyes.

Because of their ability to change colour chameleons are masters of camouflage—whether it is to match the background or in response to emotional stress. The pigment cells of the skin have highly contractile extensions into which flow varying amounts of coloured granules (pigments). These pigments are: white (particles of guanine), yellow (carotenes dissolved in a fatty liquid), black (melanin) or red. A chromatophore contains only one pigment and receives a nerve filament from the autonomous nervous system. Up until now, special nerves causing expansion of the chromatophores and the dispersion of the pigment grains have not been found, but some biologists consider that they exist. All the colour variations in chameleons seem attributable to a nervous control mechanism without the intervention of any hormone (compare with *Anolis* above).

It is known that several species of chameleon can turn blue from time to time, but this colour may not be due to any pigment. It could be caused by refraction of light by particles of extremely small dimensions—of the order of a few thousandths of a micron.

Chameleons are Old World lizards but are not found in Australia. They are most numerous and varied in Madagascar.

Some chameleons are found in the under-storey of the large forests of Madagascar and Africa. They are brown, with darker transverse bands, and have short tails curled like a comma. They look like dead leaves with their tails as petioles.

The terrestrial iguana of the Galapagos Islands (*Conolophus pallidus*) has become rare; it is found only on the small island of Barrington. This species is of a red shade very similar to that of the ground on the island. It feeds on plants and especially on cactus, the spikes presenting no difficulty. *Phot. A. Brosset*

Two agamids (*Agama agama*) from tropical Africa, startled, abandon their support and dive into space. There are about fifty known species of agamids spread over a vast territory extending from southeast Europe to central India, but their true homeland is Africa. Australia is rich in endemic Agamidae (*Amphibolorus*, *Chlamydosaurus*, *Moloch*, etc.). Without special adaptation, agamids represent the average type of lizard. *Phot. J. Six*

There are two genera like this: the stump-tailed chameleon, *Brookesia*, of Madagascar, and *Rhampholeon* from equatorial Africa. Lizards of the African genera often walk among the leaf litter on the ground.

Chameleons are oviparous, except for a few species living in mountainous country.

Skinks: from quadruped to apod

These lizards have many anatomical characteristics peculiar to themselves. The orifice of Jacobson's organ, concerned with smell, is separated from the internal nostrils (choanae) by a bony protuberance. The tongue is scaly or folded obliquely. They have a lemellated penis. In this group, there is a notable tendency towards reduction of the limbs which, in some genera, are missing altogether.

This is a large family, the largest of the saurians, with more than 600 species dissributed throughout the world. They are least numerous in America. Some skinks retain the appearance of typical lizards. Others have become snake-like.

Skinks of the typical lizard type include *Leiolopisma* of North and Central America, and *Eumeces* from North America· which live among rocks. Both are oviparous and lay their eggs under stones or fallen trees.

The true skinks (*Scincus*) have become adapted to a half terrestrial, half subterranean life, and are known as sand-fish. They have thick squat bodies and short powerful

The spiny-tailed lizard (*Uromastix*) is the agamid of the sub-desert arid zones of North Africa. Its diet is herbivorous. *Phot. J. L. S. Dubois*

claw-like feet with which they can dig quickly into loose sand. They are found in the sub-desert zones of northern Africa and Asia, as far as Pakistan.

In several genera there is a tendency towards lengthening of the body, which becomes cylindrical and snake-like, while the limbs are reduced in size and the snout becomes wedge-shaped. A good example of this tendency is the cylindrical skink, seps (*Chalcides lineatus*), from the western Mediterranean. Although this skink can use its small feet in the ordinary way, it dispenses with them when it wants to move at speed, and glides along like a snake. It manages this by retracting its feet into special body recesses in much the same way as an aircraft retracts its under-carriage. This species feeds on insects and small molluscs, and is oviparous.

The legless blind skinks (*Typhlosaurus*), which burrow in the soil for insect larvae and earthworms, inhabit southern Africa. The *Acontias* from Madagascar and the coasts of southern Africa are also legless. The legless genus, *Ablepharus*, is found in Australia, Asia Minor and eastern Europe. Its eyelids are fused and transparent.

The *Tiliqua* of Australia are of medium size. They are remarkable in that they are mainly vegetarian and viviparous. The female incubates the young inside her body, nourishing them through an anatomical structure similar to the mammalian placenta. In aggressive or defensive display, *Tiliqua* opens its mouth wide, showing a cobalt-blue tongue.

The true lizards

Under this heading are grouped two large families, the Lacertidae and the Teiidae. They are typical lizards, and only their habits are of special interest.

The Lacertidae inhabit temperate regions of the Old World, and are adapted to withstanding cold. The viviparous lizard, *Lacerta vivipara*, inhabits mountain regions from Scandinavia to the Arctic Circle; it has been found at up to 5600 feet in the Massif Central, up to 8700 feet in the Pyrenees and up to 9800 feet in the Alps. As mentioned earlier (p. 396), it incubates its eggs in the oviduct and lays them just before the young are due to emerge.

The genus *Lacerta* is represented in Europe by several species: the wall lizard, *Lacerta muralis*, the jewelled lizard *Lacerta lepida* (the biggest and most handsome species reaching almost 2½ feet in length), the green lizard, *Lacerta viridis*, and the sand lizard, *Lacerta agilis*.

The *Acanthodactylus* from the deserts of Africa and south eastern Asia are remarkable runners which can be seen moving over the burning sand in broad daylight.

The Teiidae are New World lizards which resemble the Lacertidae in general appearance, differing from them only in certain anatomical details. They inhabit savannas and steppes.

The Caiman lizards are the biggest of all, about three feet in length. They are amphibious in habits, and have broad transversely flattened tails with a double scaly crest like that of the Caimans or alligators. They have flat crowned teeth well suited to crushing the molluscs on which they feed. They are found in the northern areas of South America.

The tegu, *Tupinambis nigropunctatus*, of Brazil and Colombia frequents human habitations. It is notable for preying upon domestic fowls and stealing eggs. Because of this it is much hunted, but it is difficult to capture and still remains numerous. Like certain birds, tegus often lay their eggs in the arboreal nests of termites.

The rough teiids (*Echinosaura*) are true lizards which inhabit rain forests from Panama to Colombia. They are cryptically coloured and look like dry branches. When touched these lizards freeze immediately and become rigid to look like a branch. This phenomenon, common in insects is known as an immobilization reflex.

Monitors

The Varanidae have narrow elongated snouts, long clearly-defined necks and long extensible forked tongues. They are Old World lizards, found also in Australia. Their size varies from eight inches (Australian monitor, *Varanus brevicaudatus*) to nearly twelve feet (Komodo dragon, *Varanus Komodoensis*). Some are arboreal, others exclusively ground-dwellers, and

The very spectacular mode of capturing prey used by chameleons is well illustrated by these photographs; the common chameleon (*Chamaeleo chamaeleo*) can be seen taking hold of an insect and bringing it with its tongue into its mouth. *Phot. J. M. Baufle*

Chamaeleo dilepis dilepis is a medium-sized chameleon, common over much of Africa. Its distribution zone extends from the Cameroons, north and eastwards, to Somaliland, and south to the Transvaal. It is characterized mainly by its highly developed mobile occipital lobes. *Phot. J. F. and M. Terrasse*

a few amphibious. They are carnivorous and oviparous. They have powerful claws, so are able to dig deep burrows. All are similar in general appearance, and all, except the Australian species, are of large size.

Heloderms (venomous lizards)

These compactly built saurians are nowadays classified close to the monitors. Although their lateral teeth have grooved poison ducts, these are not connected to the poison glands. There are two known species: the Gila monster, *Heloderma suspectum* from southeastern United States, and the beaded lizard, *H. horridum*, from western Mexico. They are the only poisonous lizards. Their poison glands, situated on the outer surface of the lower jaw, are of the salivary type, and pour their secretions through five or six ducts, draining into grooved teeth. Heloderms are powerful biters, and inoculate their potent poison in the act of biting. A dose of 1/6 of an ounce of this poison is believed to be enough to kill a man. The poison acts on the heart and respiratory system, and

The Algerian ocellated skink *(Eumeces schneiderei algeriensis)* inhabits North Africa. It is the most common skink; its still sturdy limbs enable it to move quite quickly. *Phot. J. L. S. Dubois*

417

The seps, or cylindrical skink (*Chalcides chalcides*), inhabits the periphery of the western Mediterranean. *Chalcides* are natives of North Africa; one species occurs in Italy, two others are found in the Iberian Peninsula. The short and ineffective legs are, in fact, functional. When rapid movement is necessary, however, seps wriggles like a snake, with its legs folded along its body. *Phot. Aldo Margiocco*

Below
The short-tailed spiny skink (*Egernia depressa*) lives in the southern provinces of Australia. Length 6 inches. *Phot. Aldo Margiocco*

internal haemorrhage may occur, but deaths are very rare. Heloderms are not aggressive.

Anguimorphs

The tongue of the members of this group is a highly specialized structure, being divided by a transverse groove into a forked non-elastic tip that can be withdrawn into the posterior part, which acts as a sheath.

The Anguidae include several legless genera as well as genera with normal feet, such as *Diploglossus* of Central America. Between the two extremes, there are other forms with limbs more or less reduced in size. The Anguidae are mainly American, but the blindworm or slow-worm, *Anguis fragilis*, is widely distributed in Eurasia.

In spite of its snake-like appearance, the slow-worm can be recognized at once as a saurian by its mobile eyelids, as well as by the uniformity of its dorsal and ventral scales—characteristics never found in snakes. The tail, not readily apparent as it looks more like a tapering part of the body, fractures easily: hence the name 'glass snake' sometimes applied to the slow-worm in parts of Europe. The species is found in damp meadows and on the edges of woods. It likes to burrow in the ground litter, and very often lies up in an abandoned rodent's nest. The skin, at the time of casting, does not come away in one piece, but in strips. Incubation lasts about three months, and the species is ovoviviparous. The young, numbering from six to 24, break free of the the foetal membranes at the moment of birth. Slow-worms feed on snails, earthworms and insects.

The alligator lizard, *Gerrhonotus*, of North America, is a normal saurian, but *Ophiodes* of South America is as snake-like the slow-worm although it has vestigial hind legs. *Ophisaurus* (Borneo, Asia, North America and the borders of eastern Europe) are large slow-worms, some of them legless, others with vestigial limbs. They lie up in underground galleries which they dig for themselves.

The burrowing lizard, *Trogonophis wiegmanni (above)*, is a north African amphisbaena, typical of the family Trogonophidae, confined to the Old World. *Phot. E. Sochurek*

Amphisbaenas

Modern research has revealed so many archaic anatomical features in these lizards that they have now been classified apart from other lizards and reptiles. Their skull structure suggests that, at some time in their evolution, they diverged from the stock that produced lizards and snakes.

The amphisbaenas are snake-like and limbless, except the genus *Bipes* which has retained its two forefeet. They have no visible ears, vestigial eyes that can nearly be seen, and a single lung on the left side. They are burrowing creatures, and so are not often seen.

Amphisbaenas are very similar in general appearance. The biggest is the African genus *Monopeltis*, which reaches a length of 26 inches. The head and tail are both very short, and look so alike that it is difficult to tell one end of the animal from the other—hence the name two-headed snakes sometimes applied to them. They can move forwards or backwards in their burrows in much the same way as earthworms, and are known as 'worm lizards' in North America. On the ground they move by undulations of the body on the vertical plane, i.e. like caterpillars.

Amphisbaenas are found almost exclusively in the tropics. All of them live underground and are mainly insectivorous. They are specialist predators on ants and termites, and enter their underground nests to prey upon them.

Snakes (ophidians)

Snakes are limbless reptiles with very long cylindrical bodies, fused transparent eyelids, and ears without drums or tympanic cavities. They have rectractile forked tongues and transverse cloacal slits. The ventral surface is covered by a single row of broad scales.

Little is known about the origin of snakes, since no fossil remains have so far been discovered to link them with lizards, so we are reduced to theorizing about their ancestors.

The fossils of the oldest snakes date from the lower Cretaceous period (Neocomian of Herzegovina) and, in general, closely resemble the snakes of the present day. Large sea snakes, twenty to thirty feet in length, resembling the present-day boas, are known from early Tertiary (Eocene) deposits: but these shed no light on the origin of the ophidians.

Modern research and comparative anatomy have tended to show that the gap between snakes and lizards is wider than was once thought. Probably both derived from common or closely related ancestors, but it is most unlikely that snakes are derived from lizards.

Are snakes the product of regressive evolution?

Snakes are highly specialized animals deserving special consideration. It is tempting to speak of regressive evolution for, in some ways, the total loss of limbs can be considered regression: but on closer examination, they are found to have a highly complex structure in compensation. Instead of walking on four limbs, they move by undulating the muscles of the body and finding a purchase on the ground with their ventral scales. This method of locomotion is well suited

The sand lizard *Lacerta agilis* catching a large fly; this one is tame and eats insects out of its keeper's hand. The sand lizard lives in central Europe and most of France, but becomes rare in the Midi. *Phot. J. Six*

Flat lizards (*Platysaurus*) belong to the Cordylidae family, characterized by rings of spiny scales on the tail. Flat lizards live in the South of Africa. *Phot. E. Sochurek*

to their cylindrical shape, as well as to the structure and distribution of their ribs. The flexibility of the snake's backbone, which enables it to coil up like a spring, is also suited to its style of hunting and locomotion. Without any serious modifications, the snake is equally well adapted to live on land, underground, in the trees or in the water.

Biological regression almost always implies the loss of preexisting organs, not their remodelling, and certainly not new developments.

The head of a snake is a museum of inventions and adaptations to its special way of life. The unique structure of its skull enables the snake to open its mouth so wide that the upper and lower jaw are almost on the vertical plane. Nothing in the exterior appearance of the snake suggests this ability, but the fact that it can do so enables it easily to swallow prey out of all proportion to its size. This ability depends on three factors: the extreme looseness of the articulations, the elasticity of the membranes of the mouth, throat and gullet, and the highly specialized muscle arrangements.

The internal anatomy of the snake is in keeping with its long narrow cylindrical shape—the posterior position of the heart, the drawn-out carotids and jugulars, the lengthening of the single lung and of the windpipe.

So the snake is not a monstrous animal; it is well shaped, balanced in all its parts, and well adapted to its mode of life. When one looks at the poisonous species, one finds that they have at their disposal a highly developed and potent weapon: the poisoned arrow. The snake is the body of the arrow; its

The Nile monitor (*Varanus niloticus*) is widely distributed in Africa and has amphibious habits; it swims perfectly, runs swiftly and digs its burrow in river-banks. It feeds on fish and other vertebrates. This individual is over five feet long. The Nile monitor is an amazing diver; it can remain submerged for more than an hour without coming up for air; but nothing is known about how it escapes asphyxiation. *Phot. A. R. Devez—Biological Mission to Gabon*

The Gila monster (*Heloderma suspectum*) can be recognized immediately by the four or five yellow or red rings with black median band around the tail. The largest known individual measured two feet in length. *Phot. Aldo Margiocco*

The desert monitor (*Varanus griseus*) inhabits desert or sub-desert zones from the Western Sahara to Pakistan. *Phot. J. L. S. Dubois*

poison fangs are the offensive tip. The venom, distilled in a specialized salivary gland, attacks the central nervous system of vertebrate prey.

Snakes, like amphibians, have no temperature control mechanism, and so sink into a state of torpor when the environment becomes too cold or too hot. It is not difficult to understand how snakes have managed to survive where the massive dinosaurs which once dominated the earth and the titanic plesiosaurs, which dominated the oceans, have disappeared without leaving a single survivor. It cannot, therefore, be argued that the snakes are the failures or decadents of evolution.

The poison apparatus

Snakes have numerous salivary glands, one of which secretes the venom. This gland is present in most snakes, but it is not always fully developed and the potency of the venom varies

The glass-snake or scheltopusik, *Ophisaurus apodus*, is a large slow-worm which inhabits Asia Minor and the Balkans; this legless lizard some-times reaches nearly 4 feet in length. To its diet of insects it adds voles, lizards and other small vertebrates. *Phot. Aldo Margiocco*

The slow-worm or common glass-snake *(Anguis fragilis)*, lives in damp meadows; its retreat is an abandoned vole's burrow, or a gallery dug by it. It feeds mainly on insects and small snails. The mother incubates her eggs in her oviduct. The membrane of the shell is very thin; the young is born surrounded by this membrane, which it sheds immediately on reaching the exterior. Maximum size: female 20 inches; male 18 inches. The tail autotomizes easily. *Phot. Jean Vasserot*

The tegu (*Tupinambis teguixin*) is a strong South American lizard which attacks small birds, especially domestic chickens, and is fond of eggs. Length 3 feet or more. *Phot. John Markham*

from species to species. It is the parotid gland, situated behind the eye, above the upper lip and extending well back, that secretes the venom.

Above, Agamodon anguliceps is an amphisbaena which lives in East Africa; it is related to *Trogonophis,* which reaches North Africa. *Opposite,* its front end, with the wedge-shaped head suitable for burrowing in loose soil. *Phot. Aldo Margiocco*

Thelotornis kirtlandi is an African colubrid remarkable for its very elongate and apparently swollen head. Its eyes are large and have horizontal pupils. *Phot. E. Sochurek*

This gland is lacking in several of the colubrid snakes, e.g. *Coluber esculapii* in Europe, *Boaedon* and *Dasypeltis* in Africa. It is missing even in those species that have some fangs noticeably bigger than others. The upper labial gland, or true salivary gland, is situated along the upper gum in front of the parotid. It has several drainage ducts, while the venomous or parotid gland has only one. For a long time, snakes were classified on the basis of the relationship between the parotid duct and the teeth. Distinctions were then made between the Aglyphs, the Opisthoglyphs, the Proteroglyphs and the Solenoglyphs. These distinctions, some of which are described below, have now been abandoned as a system of classification.

In the Aglyphs, none of the teeth is connected with the poison gland. These are the most numerous snakes, and include all the western European species except one. In snakes with a parotid gland, the poison flows into the mouth, where it mixes with the saliva, but the prey has to be thoroughly chewed and torn before the poison can act. These snakes are harmless to man.

In the Opisthoglyphs the poison fang is at the back of the mouth, and fixed to the upper maxillary bone. It is surrounded by a sheath which is part of the gum. The poison duct leads into the upper part of this sheath at the base of the tooth, which has a shallow groove. The venom and the saliva do not mix. The gland is emptied of its poison by the pressure of the temporal muscle. Because the poison fang is situated at the back of the mouth, these snakes cannot inoculate poison into a victim. For this reason the Opisthoglyphs are not regarded as dangerous snakes. In Europe, the Montpellier snake (*Malpolon monspessulanus*) is the main representative of this group. Aglyphs and Opisthoglyphs are harmless or not very dangerous biting snakes.

The poison fangs of the Proteroglyphs are carried on the upper maxillary bones. These functional fangs can be replaced by others situated immediately behind them. There are from five to ten replacements, the smallest being the least mature.

Poison fangs have a more or less deep groove running through them and, in some species, the edges of the groove almost close to form a duct. The fangs are housed in a mucous sheath, which is erected at the time of biting.

Biting is perhaps not the correct word in this case, striking being perhaps more apt.

The Proteroglyph, when striking a victim, opens its mouth with the two fangs aimed towards the front. The snake suddenly relaxes the anterior part of its body. When the fangs pierce the victim's body, the venom is automatically inoculated, supplied by the glands which are subjected to powerful muscular contractions at this time.

The poison fangs of the Solenoglyphs, which are much more developed than the other teeth, are situated very far forward. They are supplied with a duct which opens out on top near the opening of the poison duct and, at the bottom, on the concave side, a short distance from the free end. These fangs can, therefore, be compared to a curved needle fitted to a syringe. The duct of the parotid gland is long, and opens on to the base of the poison fang.

The Solenoglyph, when it is about to bite, opens its mouth wide and lowers its short upper maxillaries which rotate from the horizontal to the near vertical. The fangs follow the same rotation, almost 90°. In the act of striking, the snake thrusts its whole body forward, becoming, in fact, a living arrow.

Proteroglyphs and Solenoglyphs swallow their victims only after the venom has acted and they have become paralysed. Swallowing is a difficult process, and the time taken depends on the size of the prey.

Venoms and their effects

Snake venoms are liquid, clear-coloured or citrine when they leave the fangs. They are a complex mixture of substances, each one of which plays its part in the process of poisoning. Some, like the coagulins, are enzymes, which clot blood and cause necrosis of the tissues into which they are injected. Others are mainly toxins, the two main types being: *neurotoxins*, which attack the central nervous system, especially the ganglia of the pneumogastric nerve. This results in paralysis of the heart and the breathing muscles; and *haemotoxins*, which destroy the red corpuscles and damage the inner walls of the blood vessels, causing serious haemorrhages.

The venom of the Proteroglyphs (Elapidae) causes smarting and slight swelling at the point of inoculation, and gives rise to numerous symptoms: shivering and sweating; dry throat, paralysis of the tongue and of the pharynx; dizziness; prostration; loosening of the sphincters; irregular breathing; suffocation; interference with the heart rhythm and failure of the heart muscles.

The poison of the Solenoglyphs (vipers and rattlesnakes) produces severe local pain and livid, hot swelling. The victim sweats profusely and suffers from dizziness, and blood pressure falls. This is followed by cardiac and pulmonary failure. A patient who has survived poisoning by these snakes suffers for some time afterwards the necrotic action of the cytotoxins, which can cause gangrene.

The best cure for snake-bite is an anti-venom serum, which is derived from horses. The venom is injected into the horse in stronger and stronger dozes. The horse produces antibodies which neutralize the poisons. The globules of the plasma are then separated and used as anti-venom serum. Nowadays, the serum is purified by removing its proteins, which can produce painful and sometimes serious allergies in man.

The first treatment must be potent. Two injections are usually made in equal doses, one under the skin round about and above the bite, and one into a muscle or under the skin of the abdomen. The use of cardiotonics is always recommended. In very serious cases artificial respiration is necessary, mouth to mouth.

Each genus, even each species of snake, has its own special kind of venom. It is, therefore, necessary to be quite sure of the identity of the snake that has bitten one. New sera (polyvalent) are now being manufactured, which are effective against the poisons of the different genera; for instance, a *Bitis-Naja* serum is now being commercially produced in tropical Africa.

The main groups of snakes

The typhlopoid or blind snakes

This cylindrical snake, which is small or medium in size, has a blunt head and a very short tail. Its skull, unlike that of other snakes, is solid, strongly formed and well articulated. The face is elongated into a kind of ploughshare well suited for burrowing. The whole skeleton is rich in unusual features. In the Leptotyphlopidae, the pelvis is well developed with recognizable femora that may even project slightly. In the the Typhlopidae there are only two cartilaginous rudiments

of the pelvis; the mouth is small and situated on the ventral surface. The lower jaws have no teeth, and the eyes, which are tiny, are hardly visible under the skin. The body is uniformly covered with small overlapping cycloid scales. These snakes are oviparous.

These snakes live in the soil, into which they burrow with their wedge-shaped snouts. They feed mainly on ants and

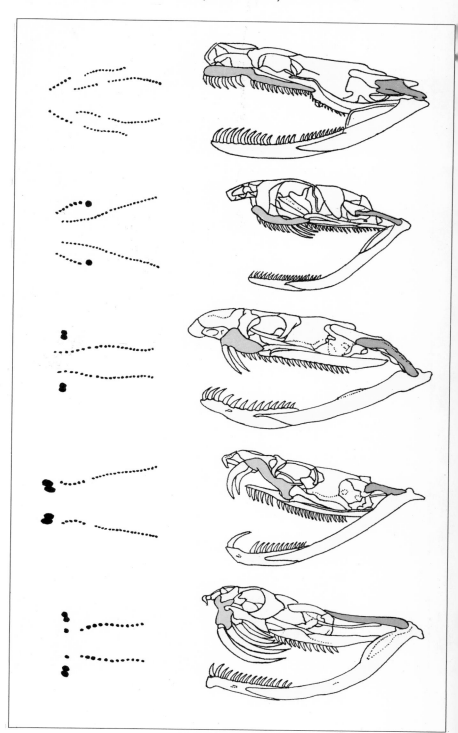

Skulls of snakes with the marks of their teeth after biting. *Starting from the top:* a snake without poisonous teeth (Aglyph), an Opisthoglyph snake (*Dispholidus typus*), a Proteroglyph elapine cobra (*Naja melanoleuca*), another elapine, with slightly swinging maxillary (*Dendroaspis* sp.), and a viperid (Solenoglyph), *Bitis lachesis*, with maxillary swinging 90° at the moment of biting. *After A. Bouillon*

The egg-eating snakes (here *Dasypeltis scaber*) are Aglyphs adapted for finding and eating birds' eggs. Their mouths and necks are amazingly extensible as is shown in the photographs. The vertebrae of the neck (6 or 8) send out ventrally sharp apophyses, which taken together form a kind of saw; they are pointed and break the shell of the egg. When the shell is broken, its contents pass into the stomach. The membranes of the egg and the debris of the shell are then vomited up by the snake. which consequently has very reduced teeth. The species of *Dasypeltis* all live in tropical Africa. *A*, the snake swallows an egg; *B*, end of swallowing; *C*, the egg has been broken by the vertebral processes, and its contents flow into the stomach. *Phot. J. and M. Fiévet*

termites. They are found only in the tropics, but there are numerous species (200 in the single genus *Typhlops*).

Judged by their skeletons, the Typhlopidae are an archaic group. The evidence suggests that shortly after the appearance of the snake type, the Typhlopidae followed along the path of a very strict double specialization: spending their whole lives underground, like moles, and feeding exclusively on termites. As always, this over-specialization stopped their evolution (one can compare their case with that of the *Orycteropas*).

The Colubridae

This immense family, with about 300 genera and more than 2500 species, is more numerous than all the others put together, and it is still not possible to identify all the evolutionary lines with certainty.

The Colubridae have elongated upper maxillaries. These are horizontal and incapable of moving or being raised perpendicularly to other points of the skull roof. In most species, the teeth are all of the same size, with none specialized as fangs; but, in some, the fluted back teeth do function as such (Opisthoglyphs).

The largest snakes in this family belong to the genus *Zaocys* of Burma and Malaysia. The longest specimens reach a length of thirteen feet, and they are, after the Boidae, the biggest of the non-poisonous snakes.

The European Colubridae are not highly specialized. *Elaphe longissima*, for example, which is often called the Aesculapian snake, is very agile and able to climb trees to rob birds' nests. It feeds on small vertebrates, especially mammals. Exceptionally, it may reach a length of six feet. This species mates in May and early June, and lays from five to eight eggs at the end of June or the beginning of July, in a hole in the ground or under a manure heap. Hatching takes place in September. The newly born young measure about eight inches in length, and at the age of a year, they reach a length of fourteen inches. This snake inhabits most of southern Europe.

The ladder snake (*Elaphe scalaris*) is brown with two black bands along its back joined at intervals by transverse bars. It is aggressive and very voracious, and can swallow prey out of all proportion to its size. For example, a snake measuring less than $4\frac{1}{2}$ feet is able to swallow such things as young rabbits and rats. This species is found in the coastal region of the western Mediterranean. Other *Elaphe* are found in the United States.

The genus *Natrix* is found in the northern hemisphere. Two species are found in western Europe—the grass snake (*Natrix natrix*) and the viperine snake (*Natrix viperinus*). The females are much bigger than the males (maximum lengths: male, $3\frac{1}{2}$ feet; female, $5\frac{3}{4}$ feet). The grass snake normally lives near water and in damp places, where it swims with ease and feeds readily on fish and frogs: but it can also thrive in dry areas and is sometimes found in such places. The viperine snake, which derives its name from its resemblance to the aspic viper, is not fond of water and prefers dry places. It is replaced in central Europe by another species, *Natrix tesselata*, the checkered water snake.

The common water snake of the United States, *Natrix sipedon*, is similar in habits to *N. natrix*. Smooth snakes (*Coronella*) are small species, rarely exceeding 23 inches in length. The southern smooth snake (*Coronella girondica*) is very common in southwest France and throughout the western Mediterranean basin.

The green whip snake (*Coluber viridiflavus*) is the most handsome species in western Europe. An inhabitant of dry areas, it feeds on a variety of prey, but is especially fond of lizards. In France, it reaches a length of over $3\frac{1}{2}$ feet, but in southeast Europe some specimens grow to almost 8 feet.

The Montpellier snake (*Malpolon monspessulana*) is an Opisthoglyph, and has already been mentioned. Specimens have been measured from 7 feet $9\frac{1}{2}$ inches to 8 feet $2\frac{1}{2}$ inches, which makes it the biggest snake in Europe. The preferred habitat of this species is arid scrub land, where it feeds on small mammals, birds, lizards and, sometimes, smaller snakes. Although it is venomous, it has only rarely been involved with man—its poison fangs are situated too far back to inoculate venom without first chewing the prey. In the Mediterranean basin, it is found mainly in olive groves. Eastwards, it is distributed as far as Iran.

The *Achalinus*, from Indochina and Japan, feed entirely on earthworms.

The hog-nosed snake, *Heterodon*, from eastern North America, has a broad upturned snout like that of a pig. It uses its hog nose for burrowing. When confronting an enemy, this snake inflates the forward part of its body which becomes twice as thick as normal, and displays its flattened head and neck, so that it looks like a cobra. The bright colours of the skin between its scales produce a beautiful checkered effect. In this posture, the snake hisses loudly by expelling air from its lung. This posture may be called bluff, but, when the hog-nosed snake is seriously threatened, it adopts different tactics. It goes into apparent convulsions, then 'plays dead', lying on its back and putting out its tongue.

The Boidae (boas) and Pythonidae (pythons)

The constrictor snakes are confined to the families of the Boidae and Pythonidae, which are closely related anatomically. Some of the Boidae are ovoviviparous and others oviparous, whereas the Pythonidae are all oviparous. Constrictors have two little claws, one on each side of the cloaca, the claws being articulated with three internal processes. Two of these are connected with the vestigial hind limbs, and the other with the pelvis.

Boas and pythons usually strike their prey with the mouth open, gripping it with their powerful teeth. At the same time, and at great speed, they coil their bodies round the fore part of the victim, exerting a powerful pressure that stops breathing and heart action. The prey therefore dies of asphyxiation.

The biggest species in this group is the anaconda (*Eunectes murinus*), which is found in South America—Amazonia, the Orinoco basin and the Guianas. Some specimens reach a length of 27 feet. The anaconda is ovoviviparous, and gives birth to a large number of young, which measure about $2\frac{1}{2}$ feet in length. This giant snake frequents the banks of tree-lined rivers and catches prey coming to drink.

The boa constrictor (*Constrictor constrictor*), another South American species, is also found along the banks of rivers.

The best way of immobilizing a viper (here an asp, *Vipera aspis*) and rendering it harmless: *A*, by applying a cleft stick immediately behind the head; *B*, by catching it between the thumb and the index finger; *C*, the asp, held between the two fingers behind the head, opens its mouth. The upper maxillary has swung through 90°, the fang hangs out of its mucous sheath; a tiny drop of poison spurts from the duct of the poison-gland. *Phot. A. Margiocco*

The garden tree boa, *Boa hortulana*, and Cook's tree boa, *Boa cooki*, climb trees, using the so-called 'accordion' technique. They begin by coiling the front of the body round the trunk, and then raise the rear end of the body and coil it round the tree. Then they relax the anterior part of the body. By repeating this manoeuvre, they are able to climb trees.

Another boa, *Bolveria*, is now found only on Round Island, off Mauritius. The snakes on the main island were exterminated by wild pigs.

Sand boas (*Eryx*) are distributed from north Africa to central Asia. They are burrowing snakes which hunt in the sand.

The pythons of Africa occupy the same ecological niche as boas in America. There are two species. The African python (*Python sebae*) is a very large snake, probably longer than the anaconda, and one specimen, measuring 33 feet in length, has been recorded. This python is found from the southern Sahara to South Africa, and is as much at home in the savannas as it is in forest, but it is always found near watercourses or swamps.

The royal or ball python (*Python regius*), which is about 10 feet long, is found in west Africa. *Python molurus* is found in India and Sumatra. The amethyst python (*Liasis amethystinus*), found in Australia, the Moluccas, New Guinea and the Bismark Islands, rarely exceed 15 feet in length, but a specimen has been recorded at $27\frac{1}{2}$ feet.

The burrowing python of Africa (*Calabria reinhardti*) measures up to $3\frac{1}{2}$ feet in length. Its head and tail are the same colour, as a result of which it is sometimes known locally as the two-headed snake.

The dark green snake, *Coluber viridiflavus*, coiled up around eggs which it has just laid under a stone on the bare ground. This beautiful snake, found all over the South of Europe, is terrestrial. It feeds mainly on lizards, snakes and small rodents (field mice, voles, etc.), and sometimes frogs. *Phot. Aldo Margiocco*

The grass or ringed snake, *Natrix natrix*, is one of the commonest snakes in Europe. It has a predilection for damp places. Its length reaches $6\frac{1}{2}$ feet in exceptional cases. In winter, it withdraws into crevices, piles of straw or manure and stays there from November to March. In captivity, it is docile and does not try to bite. *Phot. J. Six*

The Montpellier snake (*Malpolon monspessulanus*) is the only European Opisthoglyph which is in any way dangerous. *Below*, an individual bearing under its head two enormous ticks full of eggs and engorged with blood. *Phot. J. L. S. Dubois*

The Elapidae: cobras, najas and coral snakes

These snakes are closely related to the colubrids. All of them have short upper maxillaries, carrying grooved poison fangs. Their poison is highly toxic, and they are considered the most dangerous of all snakes. There are more than 180 species in this family, all of them found in tropical countries.

The king cobra (*Ophiophagus hannah*) is the biggest of all the poisonous snakes, growing to nearly twenty feet in

The emerald boa (*Boa canina*), coiled round a branch, is an arboreal species whose favourite prey is lizards or birds. Its tail, which is extremely prehensile, gives it the solid support which enables it to strike quickly with one movement. It lives in South America. *Phot. J. Six*

length. It is often aggressive, especially near its nest which is a hollow in the ground lined with leaves and twigs. It is the only snake in this family that nests on the ground. The nest is divided into two compartments. The lower one, which is filled with leaves, is the one in which the eggs are laid. In the upper one, the female mounts guard, a duty which the male sometimes takes over.

Like the king cobra, the Indian cobra (*Naja naja*) can raise the sides of its collar so that its neck becomes broadened and flattened into the great hood. The snake rears up vertically with the rear end of its body coiled round itself.

The African najas (*Naja hemachatus*) do not have a hood like the Indian species. They spit their venom; hence the name spitting cobra. When attacking an enemy, they can spit their venom a great distance, aiming it at the face and eyes. The poison is ejected by powerful contractions of the muscles surrounding the poison gland. The venom causes great irritation to the eye, producing a strong burning sensation, and, if the eye is not washed promptly, the injury can be permanent.

The eastern coral snake (*Maticora* or *Doliophis*) has a yellow skin tending to red, and striped with yellow or blue lines on a brown or black background. Three Indian and Indo–Malaysian species have been identified. Their poison glands are located at the back of the head within the anterior third of the body. These snakes are not at all aggressive, and it is most unusual for them to bite man.

The true coral snakes (*Micrurus*) are widely distributed from Mexico to north Argentina. The biggest species (*Micrurus spixi*) reaches a length of five feet. The bodies of

The boa constrictor (*Boa constrictor*) coiled round a branch. This American boa is found from Mexico to Paraguay as well as the North of Argentina. *Phot. Aldo Margiocco*

427

The sand boas (here *Eryx jaculus*), are Boidae, within which they form a sub-family (Erycinae). The sand boa does not exceed 3¼ feet in length; its tail is very short. It lives buried in the sand. *Eryx jaculus* lives in Greece, in the Ionian Islands, Asia Minor, and the steppes of central Asia. *Phot. E. Sochurek*

Indian charmer of cobras (*Naja naja*). Most if not all of the snakes used by these entertainers have their poison fangs carefully removed. Notice the black spots, like eyes, on the dorsal surface of the snake's hood. *Phot. Aldo Margiocco*

Micrurus fulvius is the true coral snake, which has a vast geographical distribution. It is found from the North of Mexico to Paraguay and the North of the Argentine. It may be as long as 2½ feet. Its black, yellow and red rings are in threes, the black median ring being separated from the others by two yellow rings; each triad is in its turn separated from the following one by a red ring. The genus *Micrurus*, entirely tropical American, includes about 40 species, all poisonous. *Phot. F. Petter-Jacana*

these snakes are ringed alternately in black, red and yellow, in groups of three. The arrangement of the rings varies in all forty species.

There are 25 genera and 70 species of Elapidae in Australia, where conditions are highly favourable, especially in the humid southeast. Most of the Australian species are small and not notably poisonous, but a few are very dangerous to man. Among these are the taipan (*Oxyuranus scutellatus*), the tiger snake (*Notechis scutatus*), the death adder (*Acanthophis antarcticus*), the Australian copperhead (*Denisonia superba*) and the Australian brown snake (*Demansia textilis*).

The poison from the gland of a single tiger snake is enough to kill 118 sheep. The poison from a viper gland is enough to kill 84 sheep; that from an Indian cobra can kill 31 sheep; that from the Australian copperhead can kill eight sheep; and that from one Russell's viper, two sheep.

The taipan (length eight feet: record twelve feet) is considered to be the most dangerous species. Its glands contain enough dry poison to kill 200 men. Before the use of anti-venom, there were only two known cases of human beings surviving a bite from this snake.

Denisonia superba is a truly viviparous species. It has an organ which functions like the mammalian placenta, linking the mother and embryo closely.

In addition to the najas, discussed above, Africa has several other species of Elapidae, notable among them being the mambas (*Dendroaspis*) which have a fearful reputation. They are powerful, active and aggressive snakes whose poison fangs reach a great size.

The green mamba (*Dendroaspis viridis*) is a tree climber, while the black mamba (*D. jamesoni*) is a forest species, often found on the edge of swamps. The poison of both species is extremely toxic.

The Hydrophinae (sea snakes)

These snakes, which are of moderate size, spend most of their lives in the sea. Their bodies, and more especially their

This African python (*Python sebae*) after strangling an antelope by constriction is now going to swallow it. *Phot. Aldo Margiocco*

The Indian cobra (*Naja naja*), sometimes called the hooded cobra, broadening the front part of its body by raising its ribs and in an erect attitude of intimidation. Each year, several thousand Indians die from its bites. *Phot. Aldo Margiocco*

The green mamba (*Dendroapsis viridis* or *Dendroapsis angusticeps*), a beautiful arboreal snake of the family Elapidae, lives in secondary forests and plantations. It feeds on birds and arboreal lizards, and its virulent poison makes it one of the most feared snakes. Mambas are found throughout tropical Africa. *Phot. Müller-Roebild*

A true sea serpent (*Laticauda laticauda*) in its natural environment, on the coasts of New Caledonia. The photograph shows a couple, the male being ringed, and the female having a uniform livery. *Under-sea photo by Théodor*

tails, are flattened transversely. When they dive, a valve closes their nostrils. They swim by undulating movements, very often in the vertical position. In some species, the scales do not overlap, but are simply pieced together like a mosaic.

Sea snakes feed on fish and bite man only accidentally. They are all viviparous. Fifteen genera and fifty species have so far been described.

In one respect· the geographical distribution of the Hydrophinae is unusual: none is found in the Atlantic Ocean. One species *Pelamis platurus*, is found from the west coast of North America to the other extremity of the Indo–Pacific area—on the coast of Madagascar. This species, which is abundant along the coast, is often seen in groups around flotsam—coconuts, wooden planks and the like.

Laticauda septemfasciata from the Philippines is the biggest sea snake, measuring over six feet in length and three inches in diameter. Its flesh, when roasted and smoked, is highly esteemed in Japan.

In *Hydrophis* (about thirty species), the ventral plates are so greatly reduced in size that they are hardly broader than the lateral scales. The head is small and the neck slender, but the rest of the body is broad and thick. It has been suggested that this shape, similar to that of the plesiosaur which hunted the Jurassic seas, indicates a mechanical adaptation for hunting underwater prey. The swollen body, it is thought, may set up a resistance to the forward thrust, thus ensuring greater accuracy when the snake strikes its prey.

Although they spend most of their lives in the sea, sea snakes do come ashore from time to time. The yellow-bellied sea snake, *Pelamis platurus*, is the only species that leads an entirely oceanic existence, never visiting land. It is widely distributed.

Two sea snakes have reverted to a freshwater habitat: *Hydrophis semperi*, which is found in the small crater-lake Taal, south of Luzon in the Philippines, and *Enhydrina schistosa*, which has gone back to the Great Lake of the Khmer (Cambodia).

The Viperidae (vipers) and Crotalinae (rattlesnakes)

These are nowadays grouped in one family corresponding to the former sub-order Solenoglyphs—snakes with hollow poison fangs. The retina, which contains cone cells mixed with rod cells, enables the snakes to see by day and night.

Old World vipers

Atractaspes or mole-vipers—twelve species in all—are found from the southern Sahara to South Africa, with one species in Sinai. All of them are burrowers; hence their name. None of them is aggressive and, so far as is known, their venom has caused no human casualties. The vipers (genera *Vipera, Atheris, Cerastes, Vitis, Echis, Azemiops*) have several features in common. They have a triangular head, flattened towards the rear, and two large poison glands. The top of the head is usually covered with small scales and not with broad plates, as in colubrid snakes. The tail is very short and thin.

Vipers lie and wait for their prey, bite it, wait until it is dead, and then swallow it.

The true vipers, of which the common adder is one, belong to the genus *Vipera*. The asp (*Vipera aspis*), which measures up to 2½ feet in length, is found in Western Europe, except in Spain, on plains and in mountains. In the Alps, it has been

In the adder (*Vipera berus*), *on the right*, there is only one row of scales between the eye and the upper lip, whereas there are two in the asp (*Vipera aspis*), *on the left*. The tip of the snout is slightly more turned up in the asp than in the adder. *Phot. Aldo Margiocco*

The asp (*Vipera aspis*) has very variable colouring: reddish or greyish, sometimes very dark, verging on black. *Phot. J. Six*

A female adder (*Vipera berus*) and its brood. *Phot. Hosking*

recorded up to 7900 feet. It prefers dry ground where it can sun itself, but dislikes extremes of heat or cold. Sometimes it is found on the edge of damp areas, and it has been recorded entering water. As soon as the weather turns cold it hibernates, either underground, under stones, or in a hollow tree. On fine winter days it may leave its hibernaculum for a short period to bask in the sunshine. It is not unusual for asps to hibernate in groups. Hence the expression 'nests of vipers'.

The asps emerge from hibernation in spring and mate in the period April–May. The young, numbering from four to eighteen, measure about eight inches in length, and are born in August–September.

The European viper or adder (*Vipera berus*), which measures up to 2½ feet in length, has a much wider range than the asp. It is found over a great area of mid-Asia up the River Amur, and in Central, Western and Northern Europe. It has been recorded as far north as the 67th degree of latitude. It is common in England and very common in certain parts of Scotland. The adder is active by day and by night, but it has been said that its main hunting period is at dusk. It likes cool regions, and dislikes extremes of heat or cold. The adder is notable for territorial battles between rival males. Such battles, misunderstood, were once described as nuptial dances. Like the asp, the adder regularly hibernates in groups, sometimes large groups. The breeding season is April–May, and the young are born in August–September. Females are larger and less contrastingly marked than males.

Orsini's viper (*Vipera ursinii*) is smaller than the asp or the adder. Its poison has little or no effect on man. It is found from Asia Minor to the western Alps and in Italy.

Two other species are found in southern Europe. The sand viper (*Vipera ammodytes*), which is about three feet in length and has a turned up snout, is found in Austria, the Tyrol, Venetia, the Balkans and Transylvania. Lataste's viper (*Vipera latastei*) is found in Spain and the north west corner of North Africa.

The horned vipers (*Cerastes cornutus* and *Cerastes cerastes*) are desert and semi-desert species found in North Africa, Egypt and Arabia. Their lateral scales have keels which push aside

the sand when the viper wriggles transversely. As a result, the snake can sink beneath the surface of the sand without any appreciable forward movement.

The *Bitis* are the most characteristic African vipers. *Bitis peringueyi*, the dwarf viper, is small and occurs as far south as South Africa. The puff adder (*Bitis arientans*), about five feet in length, is found on savanna, from the Southern Sahara to South Africa. The Gabon viper (*Bitis gabonica*), which reaches a length of six feet, is found in the forests of West Africa. The rhinoceros-viper (*Bitis nasicornis*) is also a forest species.

The *Bitis* are heavy, thick-set snakes, with short, slim tails. They move about slowly and appear sluggish but, when attacking a prey, their strike is direct and almost too swift for the eye to follow. Although not aggressive, *Bitis* are highly dangerous when surprised or trampled upon. Their colours blend with their background, so they are not easy to see, and they will lie until trampled. Their bite is dangerous, not only because of its toxicity, but also because of the large amount of poison injected.

The Gabon viper weighs up to nine pounds, which was the weight of the first specimen captured in Gabon. In this specimen, the intestine contained a poison fang over an inch long. A replacement fang had already appeared in the upper jaw.

Puff adders produce big families, and have been known to lay sixty eggs. The eggs hatch immediately after expulsion.

The African tree vipers belong to the genus *Atheris* and are found in dense woodland and large forests. Their tails, which are longer than those of other vipers, are prehensile and used during climbing. Tree vipers are green, of varying shades, that harmonise with the surrounding foliage. It has been claimed that their poison is one of the most deadly.

Night vipers (*Causus*) are active during the night. Their poison glands are disproportionately long and large. In snakes only 16 inches long, the poison glands vary between 2¾ and 4 inches in length. Despite their great size, however, these glands secrete only small quantities of poison. It has been said that night vipers spit like cobras, and the position of the gland (inside the anterior temporal muscle) certainly makes this possible. But night vipers are considered to be fairly harmless. When alarmed, they expand the neck, then, with a sudden movement, shoot straight forward. They are supposed to be oviparous and sit on their eggs, but this has never been established.

Rattlesnakes

It may be said that rattlesnakes are the vipers of the New World—fully equipped with sensory organs and facial pits between eye and nostril. The presence of these organs strengthens the validity of the idea that vipers and rattlesnakes had a common ancestry, although they evolved independently at an early stage.

Although rattlesnakes are thought of as exclusively American, some are found in Asia. They have colonized all the usual habitats—the ground, the trees and the water—but none has gone underground like the mole-vipers.

Each facial pit is a deep depression divided by a membrane into two compartments, one internal, the other external. The external chamber opens directly to the outside. The internal one opens by means of a duct leading to the internal angle of the eye. The membrane, which is supplied with numerous nerve endings from the trigeminal nerve, is highly sensitive to variations in temperature. It can register a rise, or fall, amounting at most to 3 thousandths of a degree centigrade. A rattlesnake that has been deprived of sight and smell can still pinpoint a mouse, by the heat that it radiates, at a distance of over six feet, relying solely on its facial pits to do so.

The puff adder (*Bitis arietans*) is the species of the genus *Bitis* which has the widest geographical distribution: from North Africa (edge of the Sahara) to the Cape of Good Hope. Average size from 3 to 4 feet: specimens of over 4½ feet have been captured. *Phot. J. L. S. Dubois*

The Crotalinae evolved in America—the rattlesnakes in North America and the fer-de-lance in South America. A few species have reached Asia.

Rattlesnakes belong to the genera *Crotalus* and *Sistrurus*. As the name suggests, they can rattle their tails. The sound is produced by the crotalon, or crepitaculum, which is made up of articulated horny rings, the last of which is shaped like a cone. Muscular contractions set up tremors in the horny rings which produce the well-known sound as they knock against each other. Hence the snake's name. The rings are, in fact, interlocking bonnets. Each is derived from a part of skin which remained attached to the body at the time of sloughing. If the rings are less numerous than the sloughings, the reason is that some of them fall off when the snake is casting its old coat.

Nobody knows whether the sound made by the crotalon has any practical value. Many arguments have been put forward, none of them satisfactory. Some naturalists have subscribed to the idea that the rattle is a warning sound to divert heavy mammals that might tread on the snake and crush it.

Rattlesnakes are found as far north as Canada, the home of *Crotalus viridis*. A few species inhabit Mexico. One, the South American rattlesnake (*Crotalis durissus = terrificus*), is found as far south as Uruguay and the northern Argentine. All rattlesnakes are fond of dry rocky places. On the prairies of North America, they feed mainly on rodents. They are not big snakes, the biggest (*Crotalus atrex*) rarely exceeding five feet in length. The bite of all is extremely dangerous.

The sidewinder (*Crotalus cerastes*) is a medium-sized species, no more than two feet in length. It lives mostly beneath a layer of sand, with only the top of its snout showing. Its name derives from its peculiar method of progression.

The moccasin snakes (*Agkistrodon* or *Ancistrodon*) have a wide distribution, being found in North America, Central America, Asia, Malaysia and southeastern Europe (from the Volga to Turkestan and southern Siberia). The water moccasin (*Agkistrodon piscivorus*) of the southeastern United States, is found near swamps, rice-fields, lakes and rivers. It climbs riverside trees from which it drops into the water when alarmed. It feeds on a wide variety of aquatic prey.

The fer-de-lance (*Bothrops*) is the species that most closely resembles a viper. It derives its name from the triangular shape of its head which is narrow in front and broad behind. It is an extremely poisonous snake. *Bothrops lanceolatus*, from Martinique, is no more than a local race of *Bothrops atrox* whose range extends from southern Mexico to the northern part of South America. Several species are found in Brazil. *Bothrops ammodytoides*, which has a turned-up snout, is found as far south as the Argentine.

Several species of fer-de-lance (*Trimeresurus*) are found in Asia. They closely resemble the *Bothrops*. They are found mainly in tropical regions. Some species live entirely on the ground; others live in trees, and have a prehensile tail.

The order Crocodilia

The skull of the crocodile has two temporal cavities. The square bone is immovable. The secondary bony palate is complete. In the upper jaw the teeth are located in the maxillary bones; on the lower jaw, on the dental bones. Crocodiles have two sacral vertebrae, articulated with the pelvis. The wall of the abdomen has 'ribs' formed by connective tissue, and not joined to the vertebral column and the scales contain thick bony growths. The heart has four cavities. The snout is elongated, and some teeth remain visible when the mouth is closed. The tail has three scaly crests, two in the forward part and one towards the rear. The opening of the cloaca is longitudinal. Crocodiles are able to float on the surface of the water with only their nostrils and eyes showing, and they can remain thus, completely motionless, for hours at a time.

The true crocodiles

When the crocodile closes its mouth, the fourth tooth of the mandible remains visible, housed in a cut-away part of the

Skulls of crocodilians. *A, Crocodylus americanus; B, Alligator mississippiensis. Phot. Aldo Margiocco*

upper lip. The fifth upper tooth is the strongest. Upper and lower teeth interlock when the mouth is closed.

The genus *Crocodylus* is found throughout the tropics. The best known species, and the one most widely distributed in Africa, is the Nile crocodile (*Crocodylus niloticus*) which usually reaches about thirteen feet in length, although specimens over seventeen feet long have been killed. Not so very long ago, the Nile crocodile was common throughout tropical Africa, but heavy slaughter has reduced its numbers, and it has been exterminated in many areas.

The Nile crocodile is found in large rivers and swamps, and even in estuaries. It readily comes ashore, where it will lie motionless for long periods, basking in the sun. The female makes a nest for her eggs, and mounts guard over them from time to time. Behaviour varies from place to place. In some areas the crocodile will attack man; in others it does not. In the latter regions, children can bathe quite close to crocodiles without running any risk. It is probable that the man-eaters are old animals that have graduated to killing man after

The Ganges gavial (*Gavialis gangeticus*) is distinguished from all the other crocodiles by the length and narrowness of its snout. It feeds mainly on fish, and does not attack man; bracelets and necklaces sometimes found in its stomach come from human corpses thrown into the Ganges after funeral ceremonies. *Phot. Aldo Margiocco*

A Mississippi alligator sleeping on the surface. The projecting nostrils and the eyes emerge, whereas the rest of the body is almost entirely under water. Rigid, like a piece of wood, the reptile waits for a prey deceived by its immobility to pass within its reach; with one blow of its vast fang-studded mouth, it will snap it up, then drown it. *Phot. M. Terrasse*

learning to prey on dogs and other domestic animals coming to drink.

The marine crocodile (*Crocodylus porosus*) of India, which measures up to 22 feet in length, is a formidable man-eater. It is found in India, Malaysia, Australia and Polynesia. This species swims readily in the sea and will travel from one island to another. One crocodile made a monitored journey of over 600 miles, starting from the Cocos Islands, in the Indian Ocean.

Besides the Nile crocodile, Africa has three other species—the slender-nosed crocodile (*Crocodylus cataphractus*), the West African dwarf crocodile (*Osteolaemus tetraspis*) and *Osteolaemus*, a relatively small species, found in central and western Africa. The dwarf crocodile has a broad snout and its nostrils are separated by cartilage. Its abdominal scales have very thick bony plates.

The false gavial (*Tomistoma schlegeli*) is found in Indo-Malaysia. It has a long narrow snout, resembling that of the gavial. In north Australia there is a native species (*Crocodylus johnstoni*).

The alligators

Alligators and crocodiles look very much alike. In alligators, however, the fourth tooth of the mandible is not visible when the mouth is shut. It fits into a lateral groove on the upper maxillary, and is the strongest tooth. When the mouth is shut, the lower teeth fit inside the upper rows instead of interlocking, as in crocodiles.

There are two main genera under this heading: the genus *Cayman* and the genus *Alligator*. The first, found only in tropical and equatorial America, resembles the crocodile in general habits. The second is found in North America and in China. The Chinese species is *Alligator sinensis*, and is found in the lower reaches of the Yangtse-Kiang. The North American species is *Alligator mississipiensis*, which may reach a length of over twenty feet.

Alligators live on river banks and in swamps, where they space themselves out by territorial behaviour. Territorial males will not tolerate the presence of other males. Their roaring appears to do two things: it warns off other males and attracts females. Alligators do not feed entirely on vertebrates; they also eat crustaceans and insects in large quantities.

The gavial

The gavial of the Ganges (*Gavialis gangeticus*) has a very long, narrow snout—five times longer than its width at the base. It reaches a length of 23 feet. It is a fish eater, found in the larger rivers of India and Burma.

Nile crocodiles (*Crocodylus niloticus*) threatening at the river's edge
Phot. Naud-Africa Photo by Klemm—Atlas-Photo

Birds

Young whooper swan (*Cygnus cygnus*) taking off. *Phot. Jean Philippe Varin-Jacana*

Structure and anatomy

The most remarkable of all the features of a bird's body are its feathers: a bird depends on its feathers for its powers of flight. Some reptiles and mammals are adapted to flight, but in their case, the bones of the hand became very long as they evolved, and skin stretched out between the bones to act as wings. Birds evolved differently and reduced their hand bones, growing feathers from the rigid stump that remained to form wings. Feathers are highly specialized structures: light but strong and flexible yet stiff.

Structure of the feather: lightness, flexibility and thermal insulation

A feather is made of protein and is produced at a papilla—a projection in the epidermis or outer layer of skin. When it is fully grown, it is composed entirely of keratin (a tough protein containing sulphur) with a large number of dead cells filled with air. The feather is therefore extremely light, as well as being one of the most complicated epidermal products in the whole of the animal world.

At the centre of a feather is a rigid shaft called the quill. The lower part, which is generally short, is called the calamus and sticks into the skin. The upper part, called the rachis, bears a set of barbs on each side. The barbs mesh together to produce a vane or vexillum. The barbs themselves each bear a set of tiny barbules that hold the barbs together. The side of each barb facing the base of the feather has smooth barbules with turned-in trailing ends. On the other side, the barbules have hooked ends. The hooked barbules on one barb hook on to the trailing barbules of the barb next to it, thus meshing the barbs together to form a vane. The barbs are hooked powerfully together, for they must not part and allow air to pass through them when the bird is in flight.

The complexity of a bird's feathers goes further, in response to its requirements. The wing feathers must not become separated from each other in flight, and the whole wing must maintain a smooth surface if it is to give the lift and aerodynamic control that the bird requires. To keep the feathers in contact, there are further hooks that hold them together. In certain aquatic birds, such as grebes (*Podiceps*) and small auks (*Alca*), cohesion of the plumage in contact with water is essential to make the bird's outer covering completely waterproof. In this case, the barbules are very long and are twisted in spirals for part of their length, helping them to adhere to each other more completely. But other birds may have com-

Left, in the cassowary, exceptionally, the hypoptile is as important as the vexillum. The hypoptile is not found in all birds. *Right*, feather from a pheasant's body bearing on the ventral part a second vestigial vexillum, the downy hypoptile. *Phot. Lauros—Atlas-Photo*

pletely different requirements for their feathers. Owls, for example, are birds of prey that need to swoop down on their victims in complete silence, in order to take their prey by surprise. In their case, the barbules are fine and flexible, enabling the feathers to bend with the flow of air and reducing any noise as the owl swoops, without impairing the bird's ability to fly.

All body feathers also possess a patch of down around the lower part of the quill, below the vane. The barbs of down feathers have hookless barbules and therefore do not adhere to each other. This lower downy part of the feathers is not visible, except in chicks. Only the upper vanes can be seen. They define the contours of the bird and vaned feathers are therefore called contour feathers. Beneath the outer surface of the body is a layer of down around the lower parts of the quills: this layer of down is used to trap air, which helps to insulate the body and keep it warm.

The goldfinch (*Carduelis carduelis*) shows in its plumage two basic categories of pigment melanins (black coloration—eumelanins; brownish—phaemelanins) and carotenoids (yellow coloration provided by lutein from the liver; red, obtained by oxidation of lutein, probably at the level of the feather papillae). *Phot. Visage Albert-Jacana.*

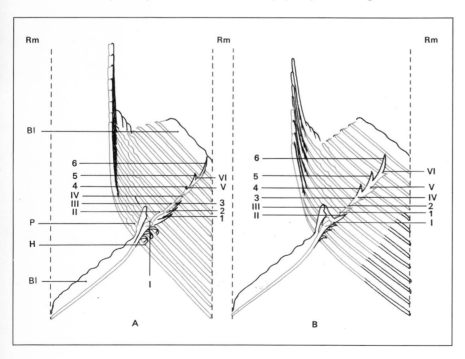

Diagram showing the normal arrangement of the barbs. The hooklets (hamules) of the distal barbules slide along the smooth proximal barbules and engage on their flanges. Dorsal surface *A*, at rest; *B*, extended position with hooks in action; *Bl*, base of distal barbule; *H*, hooklet or hamule; *P*, flange of proximal barbule; *Rm*, barb or ramus; I to VI dorsal processes; 1 to 6 ventral hooklets of the distal barbules. *After Sick*

Coloration

Most birds have coloured feathers. If a feather is white on both sides, then it does not possess any pigment. However, colour is not only due to pigments. Interference of light waves at the surface of the feather may produce a sheen of iridescent colour.

The pigments known to be present in feathers are melanins, carotenoids, porphyrins and perhaps flavins. All are deposited in the feathers when they are formed. No subsequent addition of pigments is possible, but the pigments already present may undergo alteration. For example, some ducks have feathers which contain iron and sometimes take on a red-brown coloration. It is possible that this could be the result of oxidation. Melanins, which are produced by the break-up of proteins, are the most common pigments in feathers. (They also occur in human hair, and are mainly responsible for our hair colours.) Melanins produce a range of colours that varies from black (large amounts of eumelanins), through pure grey (small amounts of eumelanins), grey-brown, brown, and red-brown to yellowish shades (produced by various amounts of phaemelanins).

Pure red and yellow, orange and violet are due to the presence of carotenoids. These pigments are formed from the breakdown of food. A yellow carotenoid pigment called lutein accumulates in the liver and may then be transformed into other carotenoid pigments. Volker has made a study of carotenoid pigmentation in birds, and has discovered that a bird, starting from lutein, can synthesize red carotenoids such as astaxanthin or rhodoxanthin. The synthesis seems to take place at the feather's papilla in species that display red and yellow in their plumage.

A single feather may contain two kinds of pigments. One may mask the other, or the two basic colours may combine to produce a different colour. Some green colours are caused by the joint presence of melanins and carotenoids.

Some colours are produced, not by pigments, but by the structure of the feathers. Blues are often produced in this way, and so are all sheens of colour. The colour is produced by interference of light waves caused as light is reflected from the feathers. The feathers have a very intricate and minute pattern of grooves or a similar surface structure. As light leaves the feathers, some colours are removed because the light waves of these colours interfere with each other and cancel each other out. We see the colours that remain in the light. These colours are not necessarily the same as those of the pigments in the feathers. The wing feathers of a jay contain uniform amounts of melanin. Nevertheless they appear black on the undersides but exhibit pure blue and blue-white bars on the upper surface. A difference of surface structure between the two sides produces this effect. However, in some cases the pigment in the feather may influence the colour. Yellow carotenoids in the feather and a structure surface producing blue by interference may combine to give green. Similarly, feathers containing rhodoxanthin (a red pigment) may appear red, blue or violet depending on the surface structure. The surface structure of the feathers may also affect a bird's appearance in other ways. In certain birds, including pelicans, terns and petrels, some black-pigmented feathers in the wings may in fact have a silvery appearance. The silver gleam is caused by light reflected from very long, fine, non-pigmented fibres in the feathers. After some time as the feathers become worn, these fibres break away and the feathers assume a progressively darker shade.

The red-brown colour of the underparts of the adult lammergeier is caused by a deposit of iron oxide. The feathers are basically white and remain so in a few rare individuals. In most, they quickly become red-brown as the birds grow.

Distribution of feathers

The papillae from which the feathers grow are arranged over a bird's body in a definite number of rows. There are usually two main rows on the lower parts, and they are particularly broad and extensive in aquatic birds. One or two main rows cover the upper parts, frequently arranged in a complicated manner. The head is usually entirely covered with feathers, though some birds have bare heads, notably the vultures.

Most birds need their tails for balance. The tail also acts as a rudder in some species and steers them in flight. In woodpeckers, the tail supports the bird as it clings to tree trunks. The tail is made up of a small number—from ten to sixteen in most birds and usually twelve—of long, stiff feathers. These tail feathers, called rectrices, are arranged in a closely-packed row. They are surrounded, above and below, by the upper and under tail coverts, or tectrices.

The arrangement of feathers in the wings is, except in flightless birds, very complicated. The flight feathers, which are called remiges, must be long and stiff. The feathers that are attached to the finger bones are known as the primary feathers. There are between nine and twelve in each wing, and in most cases there are ten. The primary feathers drive the bird through the air, and so they are the largest remiges. They get longer towards the end of the wing, except for the very last primary, which is often short. At the very end are three to five

been counted on a wren, whereas a barbet (*Pogoniulus chrysoconus*) of the same size had 2200. A larger bird, the African laughing dove (*Streptopelia senegalensis*) had 4200 feathers, little more than the tiny white-eye (*Zosterops pallidus*). A mallard duck has about 11,000 feathers, and the most ever counted was more than 25,000 for a whistling swan (*Cygnus columbianus*).

The number of feathers also varies from season to season, especially in birds of cold or temperate regions that are subjected to widely differing temperatures between summer and winter. The feather count of a North American sparrow varies over the year by as much as $11\frac{1}{2}$ per cent. In species of cold regions, such as the ptarmigan, the winter feathers are broader and longer than the summer feathers, thus protecting the bird from loss of body heat in winter.

Moulting

It usually takes from ten to twenty days for a feather to grow completely. In the case of tail and wing feathers, complete growth may take from thirty to fifty days, and sometimes as much as ninety days. Once grown, the feathers last only until the next moult. A bird may replace all its plumage when it moults, or it may undergo a partial moult. Moulting is triggered off by thyroid activity.

When a feather is moulted, the papilla loosens around the

Three views of a pied flycatcher (*Ficedula hypoleuca*) in flight. About 5½ inches. *Phot. J.-P. Varin-Jacana*

small feathers attached to the thumb bone. These small feathers, called the alula, help to control flight at slow speeds.

The remiges attached to the arm bones are called the secondary feathers. They make up the half of the wing nearest the body, and are less stiff and shorter than the primaries. There are from nine to more than forty secondaries, depending on the family in which a bird is classified. The secondary feathers act to lift the bird in flight.

All flight feathers are covered at the base, both above and below, with several rows of small feathers, or coverts. The coverts overlap each other and give the leading edge of the wing a smooth, rounded surface so that air will flow smoothly over it. Fine hooks in the coverts anchor them firmly together so that the airflow is not disturbed in flight.

The number of feathers

The total number of feathers that a bird possesses depends very much on which family it belongs to. As few as 1100 have

quill and a new feather of the same shape and appearance begins to grow. In some birds, including penguins, the new feather pushes the old feather out of the way as it grows, and the old feather may remain stuck to the tip of the new feather for some time. From this, it may seem that the activation of the papilla and the growth of the new feather simply cause the old feather to drop out. But the phenomenon is not this simple, for cases have been recorded of patches of feathers dropping out instantaneously when a bird is severely frightened.

Moulting occurs at regular intervals in the life of a bird. Many species moult once every year, usually after breeding or, more rarely, just before breeding. But a large number of birds moult twice a year. They undergo a full moult after breeding and, more rarely before breeding, a partial moult involving only certain areas of the plumage. This partial moult does not usually extend to the larger tail and wing feathers. Some birds have two complete moults every year, and the ptarmigan has three—one full moult and two partial ones. One of the partial moults results in the change to a completely white plumage that gives the bird protection among the winter snows.

The extent of a moult also varies according to the age and

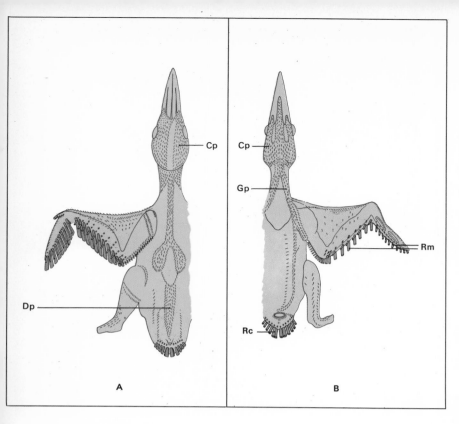

Arrangement of the feathers in a woodpecker (*Dryocopus pileatus*). *A*, dorsal; *B*, ventral. An orderly group of feathers constitutes a pteryla. *Cp*, cephalic pteryla; *Dp*, dorsal pteryla; *Gp*, gastric pteryla. *Rm*, remiges or primaries; *Rc*, rectrices or tail feathers. *After Burt*

sex of the bird. In their first year, the young usually moult less completely than do the adults, and the females moult less fully than the males.

Many birds change their appearance

During its life, a bird periodically replaces its plumage. Its appearance as a chick is very different from its adult appearance. Nidifugous birds (birds that leave the nest soon after hatching) are covered with down feathers when they are born. Down feathers are soft and fluffy, for their barbs do not hook together to produce stiff vanes. The downy covering is very important in these chicks, for they must be able to survive away from the nest as soon as they are born. Ducks and fowls are nidifugous birds. Birds that remain in the nest for some time after hatching are called nidicolous birds. Since they are protected by their parents, feathers are not immediately essential. Many passerine (perching) birds have just a few tufts of down at first, and cormorants and pelicans are born naked, soon growing a downy covering. In woodpecker chicks, down is completely lacking but these young birds are well protected as their nests are built inside holes in trees. The downy plumage of chicks is called neoptile plumage, as opposed to the teleoptile plumage that will grow later and eventually mark them as being of a particular species.

The first teleoptile plumage is usually different from those to come. The feathers are softer than the adult feathers and of a different length and shape. Often, the colours are so different that the young and adult birds may appear to be of different species. This juvenile plumage is worn for from two weeks up to a year. After a full or partial moult, the large flight and tail feathers appear, though not always in full. This plumage may then be worn for a year until the first of the annual moults

occurs. But many birds—including ducks, gulls, waders and many passerines—have two moults a year. The two plumages produced may be very different, as an ornate covering may be grown for the breeding season and a less attractive one for the rest of the year.

In the far north, the willow grouse and ptarmigan undergo a remarkable change of plumage over the year. Breeding is not the stimulus here, but the change in season. The summer and autumn plumage consists of patches of white and brown, concealing these ground-living birds among the patches of snow on the ground. A late autumn moult produces a totally white covering and prepares the birds for winter, when snow completely covers the ground. The white plumage cuts down heat losses by radiation, and also camouflages the birds against their white surroundings and lessens their chances of being seen by predators. As soon as summer arrives and the snow begins to melt, a less complete moult occurs and patches of brown appear in the white plumage. In this way, the birds maintain their camouflage all the year round. There is more brown in the summer plumage, when the snow almost disappears, than in the autumn plumage, when snow begins to fall again. The red grouse of the British Isles, a sub-species of the willow grouse, lives in areas where snow does not usually blanket the ground in winter. It therefore remains a red-brown all the year round.

Long-eared owl fledglings in the nest, covered with neoptile down. *Atlas-Photo—Phot. Merlet*

Polymorphism and dimorphism

The birds of many species exhibit an individual change of plumage over the year. In other species, individuals may have plumages that do not change but are permanently different from each other. Differences in appearance such as this are known as dimorphism or, if there are more than two such differences in a species, polymorphism.

The most frequent example of dimorphism in birds is sexual dimorphism—that is, the female wears a plumage that is clearly different from the male's plumage. Often, the sizes of the two birds are a little different as well. In fowls, most

The golden pheasant (*Chrysolophus pictus*) lives in northwestern China. It is easily reared in captivity. It provides a very good example of sexual dimorphism: *left*, the superbly coloured male; *right*, the female without ornamental feathers and with very dull livery. *Phot. Visage Albert*

passerines, waterfowl, flamingos and shearwaters, the female is smaller than the male. But in some hawks and eagles, the female is the larger bird. In many birds, including humming-birds, ducks and fowls, the plumage of the male is far more colourful than that of the female. However, the opposite is the case in phalaropes, in which the male performs most of the duties that females undertake in other species.

Sexual dimorphism may be of purely genetic origin, as in the house sparrow. Alternatively, the changes may be induced by hormones. In fowls and ducks, it has been shown that castration, which prevents the production of sex hormones, causes a neutral coloration to occur.

In some species, differences in plumage occur in individuals of the same sex and age. This dimorphism is of a genetic kind. Montagu's harrier (*Circus pygargus*) exhibits sexual dimor-phism—the males are grey and the females brown—but there are also some birds that are black. The black-eared wheatear (*Oenanthe hispanica*) is another example. Some males have a black throat and some a light-coloured one.

Evolution of plumage during a bird's lifetime

In the course of its life, a bird dons a variety of plumages. It eventually assumes a plumage that enables it to live in a particular way as an adult bird. The adult plumage is usually acquired at the same time as sexual maturity. In passerine birds, this occurs at the age of one year; in other birds, such as gulls and large birds of prey, maturity comes after several

flock of very young white pelicans (*Pelecanus onocrotalus*) startled by the photographer. These young birds, laden with fat, may weigh more than adults. They have the downy neoptile plumage of the fledgling. *Atlas-Photo—Dragesco*

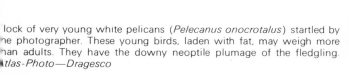

Below, the feathers of the lanner falcon (*Falco biarmicus*). *C*, cere; *R*, rump; *Br*, bastard wing remiges (alula); *Rh*, remiges of the hand; *Pr*, primary remiges; *Sr*, secondary remiges; *S*, scapulars; *T*, coverts or tectrices; *Ta*, breech feathers which cover part of the tarsus and the tibia.

Above, the wild duck or mallard (*Anas platyrhynchos*) presents sexual polymorphism which is expressed by differences in the coloration of the plumage. In this flock, photographed at the edge of a pond, in the foreground on the left, two males; on the right, two females. *Photo Burnand—Atlas-Photo*

years of life. In late-maturing birds, the plumage gradually changes each year with every moult until the adult form is achieved. Only adult birds possess fully-developed ornamental feathers. Where there is sexual dimorphism, these feathers are worn only by the active sex, which is almost always the male.

The uropygial gland

The uropygial or preen gland is situated at the back of the rump. It produces an oily secretion that a bird uses in cleaning and in fact consists of a pair of glands. In some birds, each has its own duct that secretes the oil, and in others, the two ducts are joined together. The bird uses its beak to take oil from the gland and spreads it over its feathers, usually after bathing and before preening. Long-necked water-birds, such as grebes, rub their heads over the preen gland to obtain the oil. The preen gland is not present in all birds. It is lacking in many pigeons and parrots, and in cassowaries, rheas and ostriches.

There has been much argument over the function of the oil. It has been thought that the secretion helps to keep the plumage airtight and waterproof; and it has been suggested that it produces vitamin D in sunlight, helping to prevent rickets

(Hou's theory). Experiments have not always confirmed these theories, and the evidence from the birds themselves is contradictory. The dipper, the most aquatic of passerine birds, has a very large preen gland, suggesting that oil waterproofs its feathers; but the cormorant, which is also a very active water-bird, does not have one at all. Rutschke has maintained that the oil serves to keep keratin (the material of which feathers are made) pliant, and therefore simply facilitates the feathers' normal functions of retaining air near the skin and repelling water.

The Skeleton

The skeleton of a bird is more highly specialized than that of any other vertebrate animal. Adaptation to swift and powerful flight is the reason for such specialization. Compared with a human skeleton, the bird's skeleton has a shortened trunk, and some of the bones of the backbone are fused together to give great rigidity. In front of the trunk, there is a very large sternum or breastbone, which is shaped like a deep keel in flying birds. The flight muscles are firmly anchored to the sides of the keel. The sternum extends as far as the shoulder girdle, which consists of the wishbone (fused collarbones), coracoids and shoulder blades, which are much reduced compared with man. In strong fliers, the girdle is well developed and may give extra anchorage for the flight muscles. In some birds, including fowls, pigeons and owls, the wishbone is very small and has no function. Normally the muscle attached to the wishbone draws the upper arm forward, and in these birds this action is powered by a muscle attached to

the coracoid and sternum instead. The bones of the shoulder girdle and the breastbone are solidly bound to give the front and upper part of the trunk great rigidity. In some cases, the tip of the wishbone may be fused to the end of the sternum to increase strength.

Because the rib cage is so rigid, the bird can maintain its body in a fixed position during flight, thus providing stable fulcra (points of balance) for the movements of the wing bones. These bones are highly modified compared with other vertebrates. The humerus (upper arm bone) and ulna (one of the two forearm bones) are usually long and robust. The radius (other forearm bone) is less strong. The structure of the hand is completely different. In prehistoric birds such as *Archaeopteryx*, there are three digits capable of free movement and they each possess a claw. In almost all present-day birds, such wing claws are absent. The metacarpals (bones of the palm of the hand) are fused into a single bone, reducing the possible actions of the digits to slight backwards and forwards movements. Finally, the three digits are much reduced. The thumb or first digit has only a single bone or phalanx, the second digit two phalanges and the third one, which is almost vestigial. In flightless land birds, the reduction of the digits is greater still and some bones may be lacking. In ostriches and other ratite birds, the sternum is flat and has no keel, for the wing muscles are weak and do not require a large anchor. Penguins, although flightless, use their wings for swimming and so the wing bones are equal in number and as broad and robust as those of flying birds.

The rear limbs, although definitely specialized, do not display such unusual development as the forelimbs. Each leg is composed of a femur (thigh bone), a tibio-tarsus resulting from the fusion of the tibia (shin bone) with part of the tarsus (ankle), a vestigial fibula (other shin bone), a tarso-metarsus formed by the fusion of part of the tarsus and the metatarsus

In birds, the legs are modified in accordance with the mode of life. For instance, in waders, they are thin and very long, as is shown by this African jabiru stork, (*Ephippiorhynchus senegalensis*) on the left. In climbers, the legs are short with, in some, two digits in front and two to the rear. The middle-spotted woodpecker (*Dendrocopus medius*), in the middle, is admirably adapted for climbing along tree-trunks because of its hooked nails. The tail, which is stiff, gives the body purchase. The legs of running biards are high and the number of digits often reduced to three functional ones. The ostrich has only two digits turned towards the front. *Right,* female ostrich with its young. *Phot. J. F. and M. Terrasse — Merlet—Atlas-Photo—J. Fiévet*

Partial anatomy of the domestic hen. *B*, brain; *C*, crop; *Cl*, cloaca; *Cr*, crest; *Gi*, gizzard; *H*, heart; *Hu*, humerus; *I*, intestine; *L*, liver; *Oe*, oesophagus; *Ov*, oviduct starting to the left of the ovary; *Pr*, proventriculus or glandular stomach; *Py*, pygostyle or ploughshare bone; *R*, radius; *Re*, rectum; *S*, spleen; *Sp*, sacrum and pelvis (fused); *Tm*, tarso-metatarsus; *Tr*, trachea; *Tt*, tibio-tarsus; *U*, uropygial gland; *W*, wattle. I to IV toes.

Young pheasants still under their mother's care. *Phot. Merlet—Atlas-Photo*

(foot bones), and generally four toes, usually arranged three in front and one behind. The hallux (rear toe) is vestigial or even absent in many running birds, waders and swimming birds, such as seagulls, geese, swans and ducks. However, in perching birds, the rear toe is well developed. All the toes have claws, and the inner front one has three phalanges, the middle one four and the outer one five. Except in owls, the toes have scales, and so do much of the tarsus and sometimes, as in waders, the lower part of the tibia. The leg muscles are very powerful. The tendons act automatically to close the toes when the leg is bent. This action enables a bird to grip a perch without using any effort, so that it can sleep on its perch.

Many birds that use their feet for swimming have webs (thin membranes) between the toes. The webs join the three front toes in most swimmers, and the four toes in pelicans, cormorants, anhingas (darters), gannets and tropical birds. Grebes, coots and phalaropes have lobes around their toes instead of webs. Moorhens have no such membranes, although they swim well.

In parrots and woodpeckers, the toes are arranged with two in front and two behind. The toe that is normally the outer toe goes behind the leg beside the hallux. This arrangement gives these birds a good grip on tree trunks, although birds such as nuthatches, which have one strong toe to the rear, also climb well. In some owls, the outer toe is to the rear and in others, to the front. Swifts have all four toes in front to help them cling to surfaces.

The skeleton is completed by a round skull without any visible sutures, and a long (sometimes very long) and flexible neck.

Lightening the skeleton

One of the most striking characters of the skeleton of a bird is its lightness for such a strong structure. The bones are light because they are hollow (known as pneumaticity), though the larger bones are strengthened by a framework of internal struts. In the animal kingdom, only birds possess a skeleton of this kind, although crocodiles and elephants show vestiges of it in the cranium. But it seems that the bones of some dinosaurs and especially of the flying reptiles, the pterosaurs, were hollow. It therefore appears that hollow bones develop along with the ability to fly. Hollow bones certainly lighten the skeleton, but there are other physiological advantages, for they also aid in regulating the bird's internal temperature.

In most species, a large number of bones, including the cranium, backbone, sternum, and limb bones, are hollow. Some birds have fewer hollow bones, but this does not mean that they are less capable of flight. The ratite birds, which are flightless, exhibit a large number of hollow bones, whereas shearwaters, which soar well, do not. Eagles and hornbills, which are heavy flying birds, display few hollow bones, but so do swifts, which are among the best fliers. Cormorants, which dive, understandably also possess few hollow bones, but neither do seagulls, which are not divers. Terns dive by falling from a great height into the water, and have few hollow bones, but gannets, which dive in the same way, have a large number. The only generalization that can be made is that small birds tend to possess fewer hollow bones than large birds.

The African eagle owl (*Bubo bubo ascalaphus*) of the desert regions of North Africa is a great eater of rodents. Like all owls and diurnal birds of prey, it casts out through its beak balls of undigested parts and deposits them in pre-selected places. *Phot. J. L. S. Dubois*

The lungs

The breathing apparatus of a bird does not consist only of its lungs, which are situated dorsally, but also of air sacs. These are small reservoirs of air that connect with the lungs and also with the hollow, pneumatic bones. There are nine air sacs in all, distributed in the thorax from the front of the lungs to the inside of the abdominal cavity. This arrangement enables a bird to make the best possible use of oxygen, and also to breathe powerfully.

Powerful breathing is essential if the bird is to maintain a constant internal temperature. The violent muscular action during flight produces large amounts of heat. In man, excess heat is lost by evaporation of sweat from the skin—evaporation takes up large amounts of heat. But a bird has no sweat glands, and the plumage is an insulating cover that does not allow much heat to pass in or out of the body. Cooling therefore depends completely on respiratory ventilation. The excess heat warms up air inside the bird, and when this air is breathed out the heat is lost. In hot weather, birds half open their beaks and then considerably quicken their breathing (and heartbeat) to keep cool. In the sparrow, a rise of 36° F increases the rate of respiration from 46 to 510 per minute!

Like hollow bones, the presence of air sacs in a bird's body also has the effect of lightening it.

The internal temperature is variable

The ability to maintain an internal temperature is not present immediately a bird begins its life; it is acquired only some time after hatching. During its first few days of life, the young bird must be protected by its parents from changes of temperature in its surroundings. This period lasts from two to twelve days, according to the species. It is a week in the case of young pheasants, and also in the American sparrow.

When the internal temperature does stabilize, it settles at a value between 97° F and 113° F, depending on the species. This is a high temperature, and would indicate fever in a human being. But, unlike humans, the internal temperature of a healthy bird does not always remain at exactly the same value. The temperature changes somewhat during the course of a day, and there is often an appreciable difference between the internal temperature during the daytime and that at night. Diurnal birds (active during daylight) undergo a lowering of body temperature in the middle of the night, whereas nocturnal birds (active by night) decrease their internal temperature in the middle of the day. For example, the kiwi which is a nocturnal bird, has a temperature of from 100.8° F to 103.8° F at night, and from 97.5° F to 98.9° F during the day. The times when the internal temperature is lowered correspond, of course, to the times when a bird is normally asleep.

Flying involves great effort of the muscles, and greatly increases the temperature because of the heat that is produced. Metabolism increases its rate as well to give the bird sufficient energy to fly. But a lower internal temperature leads to a decreased metabolism and a lessening of activity. The lowering of the surrounding temperature at night induces in some hummingbirds and swifts a state of torpor in which the internal temperature falls considerably, rendering the bird incapable of movement. When day returns and the external temperature increases, the bird's internal temperature also rises and it wakes up. A similar effect takes place over a much longer period in the case of the poor-will, a nightjar of the western United States. When winter comes, the poor-will's internal temperature falls as low as 64° F to 66° F. At this tempera-

ture, it is capable of little movement and it spends the winter in a state of hibernation. No other bird is known to hibernate.

Some other birds exhibit a wide range of internal temperature, enabling them to take advantage of adverse conditions. The sparrow's internal temperature may vary from 73° F up to 116.1° F without any ill effects being apparent. Chicks of the common swift (*Apus apus*) suffer a drop of 50° F if they get no food. This is an advantage, for metabolism decreases and the bird can survive longer without food than if its temperature remained unchanged. In fact, it can live for more than a week without being fed.

The cooling and heating systems of birds are therefore well developed to enable them to survive in a wide variety of conditions. They are made up of the breathing apparatus and the circulatory system which, although less advanced than that of mammals and nearer to that of reptiles, is nevertheless the most efficient of all animals. This is because the bird has a comparatively large heart and blood circulates very rapidly through the body. In the smallest birds, such as hummingbirds, the production and use of energy is comparatively at its largest and the heart is also relatively at its greatest.

The digestive system

The salivary glands, when they are well developed as in woodpeckers, edible-nest swiftlets and swifts, function mainly to produce a sticky mucous liquid. The saliva does not play a great part in digestion. Instead, woodpeckers make use of it by catching insects with their sticky tongues, and the swifts use it to glue together nest material. The swiftlets' edible nests consist of hardened saliva. They are gathered and made into birds'-nest soup.

The oesophagus or gullet is unusual in that it is often capable of being widened. In some birds, such as cormorants

The kiwi or apteryx, a wingless New Zealand bird, of which there are three species in existence. The nostrils are situated at the end of the beak. Hunting for prey is carried out with the help of olfactory receptors. *Phot. Ron Garnison*

and divers, it serves as a temporary storing place for food when the stomach is full. In many finches and fowls, the widening forms a pouch known as the crop.

The stomach is divided into two parts. The first part, the proventriculus, partially digests the food and then passes it into the second stomach, called the gizzard. Here, the food may be ground up by muscular action. This is important in

salt water, the nasal glands. The nasal glands, which often extend beneath the eyes, eliminate surplus salt from the system. The extra salt comes from salt water taken in while swallowing marine fish and other sea creatures. The nasal glands are ten times more active than the kidneys in eliminating salt, and they provide an excellent example of adaptation to life in a salty environment.

On the beak of this giant albatros (*Diomedea exulans*) the openings of the nostrils are prolonged into a tube, and through them is excreted saline liquid produced by the nasal glands. (The nasal glands excrete more salt than the kidneys.) *Phot. Benoit Tollu —Jacana*

the digestion of hard food particles, such as grain. In omnivorous birds such as seagulls, the gizzard is capable of crushing the shells of crabs and mussels.

In several birds of prey and some perching birds such as crows and starlings, matter that is not digested in the stomach is formed into pellets there and then ejected from the beak. Examination of these pellets often helps to show the kind of food that a bird eats.

Pigeons that are raising young develop a cheese-like substance known as pigeon milk in their crops. The 'milk' forms from the lining of the crop. It is rich in proteins and vitamins, and makes a good food for the chicks. A similar liquid is used to nourish young emperor penguins, and the chicks of flamingos and some shearwaters. Like the milk of mammals, it is sufficient to nourish the chicks in their first few days.

The excretory system

The excretory system comprises the kidneys, which are of ample size, and, as an accessory in some sea birds (pelicans, cormorants, albatrosses and penguins) and birds living near

Sense organs

Sight is by far the best developed of a bird's senses. Examination of the structure of the eyes shows that birds have far more acute vision than man, and are more easily able to distinguish distant objects. Birds that have eyes at the sides of the head have monocular or flat vision on each side. They can see almost all round, and have only to move their heads slightly to make a complete view of their surroundings. In front, where the two fields of vision overlap, some binocular vision or vision in depth is obtained. Owls, which have their eyes at the front of their heads, possess good depth vision. But their side vision and back vision is severely restricted, although they can turn their heads easily.

Most birds have good vision in dim light. Nocturnal hunters such as owls and nightjars possess night vision to a very high degree, but they also have good day vision.

Hearing is good in birds, and particularly acute in owls, which hunt at night and may sense their prey by the sound it makes. Very loud noises are often a source of discomfort to birds; hens shake their heads if a loud noise disturbs them. The oilbird or guacharo (*Steatornis caripensis*) has the same extraordinary sense of hearing as the bat. It lives in caves in South America, and finds its way through the darkness by emitting high-pitched clicks and sensing the distance of the walls of the cave from the time that the echo takes to return. Cave swiftlets (*Collocalia brevirostris*) also use this echo location system when flying about in the dark caves of Sri Lanka where they live.

Smell does not seem to play a very great part in the lives of most birds, just as it does not in man (though it is most important to other mammals). However, in some species the olfactory lobe of the brain is well developed, indicating that the sense of smell is acute. The kiwi, which possesses nostrils at the tip of its beak, hunts at night by smell. Some American vultures seem to be able to locate carrion by smell, and the tube-nosed birds seem to be attracted by the smell of fish.

Taste is certainly among the bird's senses, although it seems to be less well developed than in mammals.

Touch is well developed, not only on the skin but also on the tongue. Several birds—woodpeckers, ducks and birds that live on honey, nectar and similar foods—use their tongues to seize food. The beaks of wading birds, such as curlews, woodcocks and sandpipers, are well endowed with a sense of touch, so that the birds can easily locate and seize their prey, which lie buried in mud or soil.

Reproductive organs

The reproductive organs are internal, both in the male and female. In most species, the ducts that lead from the testes or the ovaries open into the cloaca, as do the passages from the

excretory and digestive systems. In the male, the testes are situated at the front part of the kidneys, beside the suprarenal glands. They vary greatly in size according to the species and also the breeding cycle. A penis is present only in ratite birds, tinamous, swans, geese, ducks and guans, with a vestige in bustards, flamingos, storks and herons.

The female normally has only one ovary on the left side. Two ovaries occur in most birds of prey, though only the left one is functional. In the ovary, the microscopic ova (egg cells) increase in size and form yolks. Each ovum in turn then passes into the oviduct, where it is fertilized. As it progresses down the oviduct, it develops into an egg. Albumen and shell membrane are added and, when the ovum reaches the uterus, it is surrounded by a calciferous shell. This chalky shell gives protection to the embryo. Its shape may vary from spherical (as in owls), pear-shaped (plovers and kingfishers), almost cylindrical (sandgrouse) to ovoid (most other birds).

Where the male has no penis, copulation is performed by simple contact of the two cloacae. It is usually rapid and takes only a few seconds. The first egg is laid shortly after mating, and mating may continue until all the eggs are laid. However, it has been shown in the case of a hen pheasant that a single copulation is sufficient to fertilize all the eggs laid during the month-long laying period.

Flight

The feature most often associated with birds is the ability to fly. Flight enables the fastest birds to move more swiftly than any other animal, and allows them to travel considerable distances.

There are two main kinds of flight: gliding or soaring flight, in which the wings do not beat, and flapping flight, in which they do. Gliding flight expends much less energy than flapping flight because the wings hardly move. But only birds with long wings can soar, taking advantage of ascending air currents, for short wings do not provide enough lift. However, not all long-winged birds habitually indulge in gliding. Gliding is observed in diurnal birds of prey, swifts (swallows to a lesser degree), flamingos, storks, herons, gulls, frigate birds, gannets and pelicans; albatrosses, shearwaters and petrels can soar particularly well. In some gliding birds, such as albatrosses, one of the muscles that holds the wing open is partially ossified, thus improving rigidity of the wing.

The long wing of a gliding bird may be either narrow or broad. The longest and narrowest wings are those of the albatrosses, followed by the petrels and frigate birds. The leading edge and tip of the wing are very important in giving lift. A long, sharp-tipped wing is therefore very good for soaring flight, and birds with such wings can glide extremely well, utilizing even very slight upcurrents of air, for example, those rising off waves.

But how are large broad-winged birds, such as buzzards, eagles, vultures and storks, able to soar so effortlessly? Their wings are comparatively shorter than those of the oceanic soarers, and they are heavy birds. Although the wings lack a pointed tip, the arrangement and shape of the longest primary feathers aid lift instead. These feathers, of which there are from three to six depending on the species, taper sharply for a

Eugenes fulgens. This humming-bird lives in the mountains of Central America and is found as far north as Arizona. It is photographed here hovering. *Phot. B. Brower-Hall*

much as half their length. The vanes are very rigid, and when the wing is extended, the feathers are separated from each other. In flight, the primaries are able to pivot independently of each other, so that each feather can act as a miniature wing.

In gliding birds the alula, or bastard wing, consists of a few short primary feathers attached to the thumb bone. The feathers stick out in front of the wing. The alula plays a definite role in enabling birds to hover, and it is also important at slow speeds, as when a bird is about to land. The tail has a balancing role in gliding flight, and may also act to produce ascent or descent, like the wing flaps in an aircraft.

Gliding flight is not completely effortless, but it is certainly economical of energy. Instead of beating its wings to gain height, a soaring bird can ride on an ascending current of air, such as is found at a cliff face or in a thermal (a bubble of warm rising air). It circles in the current, gradually climbing, until sufficient height is gained. Then it may descend at a slight angle, picking up speed until another rising air current is found. All this can be done without once beating the wings. Oceanic soarers such as albatrosses glide up and down just above the waves, taking advantage of different wind speeds near the surface of the sea. This kind of gliding, called dynamic soaring, can be kept up for days as long as a wind blows.

Flapping flight is used by practically all birds that have not lost the ability to fly, for birds that glide can also fly by beating their wings. Powerful muscles attached to the breastbone and upper arm bone, via the shoulder girdle, raise and lower the wings. As the wing is lowered, the primaries close and push the air down and back, the reaction thrusting the bird up and forward. After this downstroke, the wing is raised and the primaries part to allow the air through. Then another downstroke commences and so on. Beating the wings in this way enables the bird to fly wherever it wants to go; it does not have

Scissor-bills or skimmers are pantropical; Africa has its species (*Rhynchops flavirostris*), America and Asia have theirs. Quite closely related to terns, the scissor-bill ploughs the surface of the water with its beak, whose upper jaw is shorter than the lower one, and catches the small organisms on which it feeds. This colony was photographed on the banks of the Nile, in Uganda, and shows all the phases of flapping flight. *Phot. J. F. & M. Terrasse*

Couple of griffon vultures (*Gyps fulvus*) on nuptial display flight, gliding in ascending air currents. *Phot. M. Terrasse*

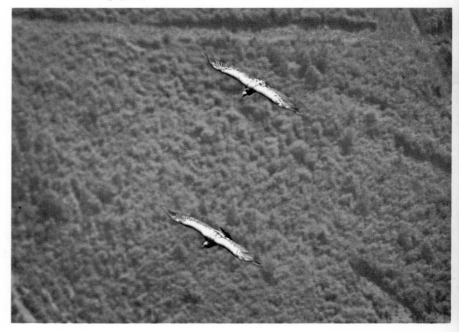

to seek a rising air current as does the soaring bird. And although flapping flight requires a great deal of effort, some birds can keep it up for days and cover thousands of miles.

Some wheatears (*Oenanthe oenanthe*), for example, migrate from Greenland across the Atlantic Ocean to Senegal. As they cannot glide, they must cross the ocean by flapping flight. One race of the Pacific golden plover migrates non-stop across the Pacific from Alaska to Hawaii. The amount of energy needed to make such flights is considerable, and it has been observed that birds about to make long migrations put on a lot of weight before they start, the fat being a reserve of energy.

Take-off is usually a particularly energetic action for a bird. The wings have to beat faster and are more spread than in normal flight. Normally, take-off is helped by movements of the legs; the bird jumps into the air, or makes a run across water to get up speed for take-off. However, some birds can take-off without using their legs. Swifts, which have very

Black-winged stilt (*Himantopus himantopus*) just after taking wing and settling down to cruising flight. It is both a first-class long-distance flier and a skilful fisher. Perched on its high legs, it scratches about in shallow swamps for worms, insect larvae, shellfish and other organisms. *Phot. J. F. Terrasse*

The pink-backed pelican (*Pelecanus rufescens*) from the Nile basin, in spite of its heavy and awkward bearing, is an efficient flier. Its long wings propel it at great speed and enable it to carry out flights of considerable duration. *Phot. J. F. and M. Terrasse*

African marabou (*Leptoptilos crumeniferus*). In landing, the wings act as a brake and the legs are extended. *Phot. J. F. & M. Terrasse, Jean Philippe Varin—Jacana*

weak legs, can rise straight into the air by beating their wings.

Landing requires a reduction in speed, and the bird brakes by spreading its wings and tail to increase air resistance. Slight flapping at the last moment enables the bird to land precisely on target, the legs being thrust out as far as possible so as to make a gentle touch-down.

Flying actions vary greatly from one bird to another. Some birds, such as hummingbirds, beat their wings very quickly whereas others, such as vultures, flap slowly. Some birds alternate flapping flight with gliding flight as in swifts, or, in some woodpeckers, with dives in which the wings are folded against the body.

Apart from its rapid wingbeats, the flight of hummingbirds is unusual in another way. The inner part of the wing containing the secondary feathers is so short that the wing is composed almost solely of primaries. The wingbeats are so quick, about 50 per second on average, that the hummingbird can choose either to fly forward very fast, hover motionless or even, uniquely among birds, fly backwards. The kestrel (*Falco tinnunculus*) is one of the few other birds that can hover, using a special and peculiar wing action to keep itself aloft.

Even the slowest birds can move quickly compared with other animals. Small birds that fly laboriously can travel up

to 20 miles in an hour; jays, which have an ungainly flight, exceed 25 miles per hour, and swallows reach a speed of about 40 mph in normal flight. Waders, such as lapwings, plovers, sandpipers and curlews achieve some 50 mph. Mallards are even faster and, at sea, scoters and cormorants exceed 60 mph. These figures indicate normal 'cruising' speeds. Speeds are reduced if the bird is hunting on the wing and swerving, as swallows do, or stalking prey. But they increase sharply if the bird is fleeing from danger or pursuing prey. Breath-taking accelerations to very high speeds may occur. The peregrine falcon (*Falco peregrinus*) was once ascribed a diving speed of 185 mph, but instruments have since measured it at 82 mph. The fastest recorded flight is that of the spine-tailed swift (*Chaetura caudacuta*), which has been measured at 106 mph.

Swimming and diving

Several birds, such as diving petrels and dippers, can swim under water by using their wings like oars. Penguins are the most adept of birds at underwater swimming, their fin-shaped wings being so adapted for this purpose that they cannot fly.

In most diving birds, however, the wings are not used to drive the bird along under the water. At the most, they are raised slightly to act as rudders and steer the bird as it swims. The feet provide the motive power instead, the toes being webbed in most cases to propel the bird both on and under the water. Mute swans also get some power from the wind when they are swimming, for they may raise their wings to act as sails and bear them along over the water.

Some birds dive by plunging into the water from the air. Gannets and pelicans do this, entering the water head first with a great splash. Ospreys dive with their sharp talons extended to snatch a fish from the water. Grebes, divers, diving ducks, cormorants and anhingas dive from the surface of the water. These birds rock their bodies and lower their heads and necks and then, with a violent kick of the legs, vanish beneath the water. In grebes, these actions take place so quickly that they appear to be instantaneous.

Walking

Almost all birds can walk. The legs of birds such as grebes and divers are placed so far back towards the rear of the body that they cannot raise the front part of the body with ease. They therefore have trouble in walking. Penguins have legs that are also placed far back, but because they keep their bodies upright they can walk quite well. They do so with a waddling gait and cannot walk very fast. In fact, if they need a sudden burst of speed, penguins flop down on their bellies and push themselves over the snow and ice by 'rowing' with their flippers. The action is rather like a man on skis propelling himself over level ground with his ski sticks.

Long-toed birds, such as larks and wagtails, can walk very well, sometimes at great speed. The best walkers are the waders and bustards, which have a much reduced or vestigial hind toe, and the ratite birds such as the ostrich. Being flightless, the ratites must be able to run fast to escape their predators. The ostriches are particularly fleet-footed birds, possessing only two toes on each foot to make for speed. In this

King penguin (*Aptenodytes patagonica*) about to dive. Penguins are the best adapted birds to underwater swimming; their wings, which are unsuitable for flying, serve as paddles. The enemies of penguins are found in the sea, especially the sea-leopard, which explains why penguins examine the water before diving. *Phot. J. Six*

respect, they are like fast-running mammals such as antelopes, which have hooves of a similar shape. This is an example of convergent evolution—the evolution of similar features in unrelated animals so that they all are adapted to the same environment. The loss or reduction of the hind toe gives speed, but it deprives the bird of the grip that is required to seize a branch when perching or roosting. Herons and storks are good walkers, but they also have a long hind toe and so can roost without difficulty. Rails have such long toes that they are able to walk on floating vegetation without sinking into the water. The jacana is even able to walk on water-lilies. The long toes spread the weight of the bird.

Arboreal (tree-living) birds have to be adept at climbing and roosting, and so they may experience some difficulty in

Swifts (*Apus apus*), good long-distance fliers as well as excellent gliders, do not roost because their feet are too short; their toes, arranged all at the front, have strong hooked nails, enabling the birds to hang on to a rock. *Phot. Brosselin—Jacana*

walking on the ground. Although they may move from one branch to another with great agility, on the ground they may only be able to hop along. Woodpeckers are remarkably well adapted for climbing trees. They have strong toes with tough, hooked claws that give them a good purchase on the trunk, and the tail is made up of very stiff feathers so that it can be braced against the tree to provide a support. The wood-creepers (Dendrocolaptidae) of tropical America and the tree-creepers (Certhiidae) of the northern hemisphere climb in the same way as the woodpeckers.

Useful though they may be, stiff tails are not essential for climbing trees. Nuthatches and parrots are both good climbers, but get no help from their tails when climbing. Hooked toes provide the necessary grip. Parrots, which are reckoned to be among the best climbers, also help themselves to climb by using their beaks to get a good grip.

Swifts have four toes that all point forward. The claws are curved, enabling the birds to cling well to vertical surfaces, even of brick or stone. Having no hind toe, they cannot walk or roost well but this matters little for swifts as they spend most of their time in the air and seem to be able to sleep on the wing.

Origins and evolution

The evidence of the origin and evolution of birds that comes to us from fossils is scanty compared with that unearthed for the other vertebrates. The reason is that bird bones are fragile and the outline of the feathers is very rarely preserved. The history of birds must be inferred from the few good fossils that have been found.

However, it appears reasonably certain that birds, like mammals, evolved from reptiles and probably from a group of flesh-eating reptiles of the Triassic period called pseudo-suchians. Birds have since developed less than mammals from an anatomical point of view, except in the evolution of the bones and feathers that enable them to fly.

The moa, *Dinornis ingens*, from *Extinct Birds*, by W. Rothschild, *Photographic library of the French National Museum of Natural History*

A link between reptiles and birds

The first known bird was *Archaeopteryx*. It lived about 150 million years ago and, being recently evolved from reptiles, had many reptilian characters. Its jaws had teeth, it had a long tail, and there were three claws jutting from the front of each wing. The hand bones had not developed to a degree that made *Archaeopteryx* a good flier. However, most important, it had feathers and so was definitely a bird. Three fossils of *Archaeopteryx* are known, all from Bavaria in Germany. These birds lived in marshy regions. They could probably glide rather than undertake sustained flight.

Present-day orders

It is probable that the Cretaceous period of 136 million years ago, saw the emergence of some of the orders of present-day birds. This period ended 64 million years ago, and shortly before this date the first waterfowl, flamingos and birds of the pelican order appeared. We also know of two extinct orders of aquatic birds from the Cretaceous period—the Hesperornithi-formes, which were diver-like birds with jaws still equipped with teeth and atrophied forelimbs reduced to a single

humerus; and the Ichthyornithiformes, which comprised at least seven species of gull-like birds with skeletons like those of present-day birds and of undoubted good flying ability. *Ichthyornis* was thought for some time to have possessed teeth, but the jaw bearing them turned out to belong to a reptile!

The beginning of the next period, the Tertiary, sees the emergence of the main orders of birds that now exist. By this time, the basic evolution of birds had taken place. The new animals were ready to conquer the air and take the place vacated by the disappearance of the flying reptiles during the Tertiary. From the Eocene epoch onwards (about 50 million years ago), the orders had begun to get as specialized as they are today. Even the penguins had ceased to fly and become completely adapted to an aquatic environment. The basic anatomy of these birds suggests that their nearest relatives are the albatrosses and allied birds, which are among the best fliers in the world. The penguins use their arms, not for flying, but for swimming and rowing themselves over the snow. The two groups therefore evolved from common ancestors in totally opposite directions in response to widely differing habitats. The split was apparently established at the beginning of the Tertiary period.

From the Miocene epoch up to the Pleistocene epoch (from 26 million to about 2 million years ago), we find more and more birds closely related to present-day birds. Birds that lived at the beginning of the Quaternary period (about 2 million years ago) can, in many cases, be related to species that are alive today.

Throughout geological time, many species have come and gone as primitive birds were replaced by more developed birds. Inevitably, many of the species that disappeared were highly specialized, such as the Odontornithes, gigantic birds with serrated beaks but no teeth.

Several lines soon disappeared

In North America and Europe, remains from the Eocene epoch indicate the existence then of enormous birds that had lost the ability to fly and had become runners like the ostrich. They

Facsimile of an engraving by Van Neck, made in the island of Mauritius in 1658. A dodo is represented top left (no. 2). These birds 'called by us nauseous birds have a round rump covered with two or three frizzy feathers, lack wings, but instead of the latter have three or four small black feathers. *After H. E. Strickland and A. G. Melville (The Dodo and its Kindred)*

are called *Gastornis* and *Diatryma*. The latter had affinities with the cranes. With its hatchet-like beak, it must have been a formidable bird. Nevertheless, these giant birds rapidly disappeared, probably because the competition of mammals for food was too fierce for them. But in South America, where such mammals did not appear until later, similar birds with enormous beaks lived on into the Miocene. One such bird has been found in the Pleistocene strata in Florida.

Some giant birds survived until historic times. In Madagascar, there was the *Aepyornis* or elephant bird, and in New Zealand, the moas (*Dinornis*). In such remote islands, large predators were absent and great flightless birds could survive—until man arrived and rapidly stamped them out. Even today, the large running birds, the ratites, find survival difficult in the company of man. For example, the ostrich has almost been annihilated in Asia.

Man has exterminated many species

The increase in human population and the increasing efficiency of hunting weapons have brought about the extermination of many species in historic times. Flightless birds were the first to succumb, for they were comparatively defenceless. In addition to the moas and *Aepyornis* mentioned above, the dodo (now a symbol of extinction) and two related birds disappeared in the 17th and 18th centuries after Europeans colonized their islands in the Indian Ocean. In the 19th century, it was the turn of the great auk (*Alca impennis*), a flightless bird of the North Atlantic. But flying birds have also died out at the hands of man. Some of these were birds with small populations, often concentrated on islands, especially the West Indies, Hawaii and New Zealand. A few extinct birds, however, once roamed the earth in great numbers. During the last hundred years, two such birds have died out in North America, both victims of greedy, thoughtless hunters. They were the passenger pigeon (*Ectopistes migratorius*) and the Carolina parakeet (*Conuropsis carolinensis*). It is possible that changes in the environment, indirectly man-made, may have sealed the fate of the Carolina parakeet, but man is certainly directly culpable in the case of the passenger pigeon, which was slaughtered in hundreds of millions during the second half of the 19th century.

Many birds are today on the danger list. They include the California condor (*Gymnogyps californianus*) and the crested ibis (*Ciconia boyciana* or *Nipponia nippon*) of Japan, both of which are reduced to some 40 or 50 birds. Hunting is not only to blame, for man's depradations may be indirect. The introduction of predatory animals, and sometimes parasites, upsets the balance of nature where these animals were previously unknown, as is often the case on islands. Rats carried by ships have colonized many islands, preying on the local birds, which are unable to defend themselves against such an unexpected adversary. Cats, introduced by settlers to catch rats, have gone wild and become formidable predators. The same is true of mongooses introduced to control snakes. In the Galapagos Islands, where several rare and interesting birds are at risk, wardens are systematically hunting down the wild descendants of former domestic animals in an effort to save endangered wildlife.

The action of hunters and of predators introduced by man is usually on a local scale, but birds may also be threatened by man's actions on a wider scale. Alteration of the land, particularly the clearing of forests for cultivation or grazing, endangers the animals living there. Forest birds disappear as their habitat is destroyed. Draining marshland threatens the existence of waders and other birds adapted to such an environment. Often, the birds find no alternative home and cannot long survive in the new environment that man creates for himself.

Bird sounds

Most birds produce a sound of some kind. Even the mute swan can make a hiss. The truly mute birds are the kiwi, the American vultures and the storks. All other birds emit vocal sounds produced by the syrinx. This is a special organ situ-

Some snakes are great destroyers of birds. This photographic sequence represents the capture on its nest of a striped bunting (*Emberiza striolata*) by a mailed snake (*Malpolon moilensis*), Opisthoglypha. Phot. J. L. S. Dubois

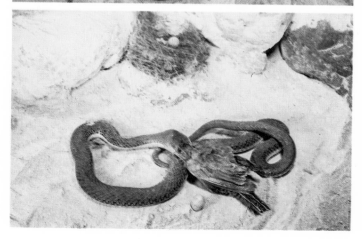

ated at the forking of the two bronchi (the tubes that lead from the lungs to the windpipe). It is made up of vibrating membranes. By varying the air pressure on the syrinx and using the muscles associated with it, the pitch and volume of the sound can be varied. In some geese and ducks, there is a pouch on the side of the syrinx at the base of the trachea (windpipe). It is found only in the males. Some birds have special adaptations of the windpipe to enable them to make special sounds. The whooping swan (*Cygnus cygnus*) and the trumpeter swan (*Cygnus buccinator*) produce bugle-like calls, as can the cranes. The windpipe of these birds is very long and twisted into several loops—rather like the coiled pipes of a trumpet or French horn—that may penetrate into the breastbone. The convolutions of the windpipe give the birds extraordinarily loud voices. Their calls can be heard several miles away and, in flight, help to keep a flock together. A bird of paradise, *Phonygammus keraudrenii*, has a similarly convoluted windpipe. The syrinx is surrounded by the clavicular sac, an air sac which is indispensable for the production of sounds.

A bird's voice is one of its principal means of communicating with other birds of the same species. A bird produces two main kinds of sounds: calls and songs. Calls are short simple bursts of sounds, whereas songs are longer and more complex. Calls are usually stereotyped and are the simplest of utterances. Each species has a set of calls that will each provoke a reaction of a particular kind in another member of the same species, while birds of other species will usually remain unaffected. However, a call may produce a reaction in another species

that is closely related to the calling species or is associated with it in everyday life. The meanings of calls are simple—they indicate that the calling bird is in pain or distress, raise alarms when the bird is threatened, menace a predator or rival, or summon other birds. Chicks make instinctive calls when they are hungry. Being simple and direct, the calls are immediately understood. Some hunters are able to imitate bird calls, and make birds leave their hiding places and scatter in alarm. Birds will certainly react to recorded calls as if they were real ones.

Some birds, such as owls, have a wide repertoire of calls, whereas other birds have very few. Birds that spend their lives concealed among bushes or reeds often have strong voices. The calls help the birds to locate each other and, being well hidden, they have no fear that a loud noise will expose them to danger from predators.

Not all birds sing. The ability is best developed in songbirds, passerines, and owls. A song consists of a certain group of notes emitted over a set period of time to form an identifiable phrase. The notes may vary in pitch, rather as the notes of a tune do, and the rhythm is similarly fixed. The song may be repeated over and over again as the bird sings. It is instinctive in its fundamental characteristics, though a young bird may have to perfect its song by listening to the song of other birds of its species. The instinct to sing is present right from birth, even when the bird is a chick and as yet incapable of singing. Only when a bird grows up is it able to produce its song, and then it must usually wait until it has reached maturity. In many species, it is only the male that sings, but there are species in which the female sings as well, sometimes in a different way. Some pairs of birds even sing duets, one phrase answering another.

Singing often appears to be a sign that the bird is feeling joyful. It is particularly evident in sunshine. Certain species sing only for a short period of the year. Tits, for instance, sing only at mating time, accompanying their song with a fluttering of the body. Some other birds sing all the year round, though their song may intensify during the breeding season and cease during the moult, when the bird is at great risk and will not want to attract predators. In the breeding season, a bird sings mainly before mating. The song may act as an advertisement to inform likely mates of the presence of the singer, and it may also act directly to attract a mate. Often, it has also another meaning to rivals, warning them that the singer possesses a certain territory from which the rivals are totally excluded. But a bird may also sing outside its territory, so that it does not provoke reactions from birds neighbouring its territory. When rearing young, birds may sing for hours at night from outside their territories.

Some species can perfect a song more than others, although it may take several years for them to achieve perfection. A good number of birds can imitate sounds that they hear. These may be the songs of other birds, animal calls, or even human voices. Among the best mimics are the lyrebird of Australia, the mockingbirds of America, shrikes, starlings, and, of course, parrots.

Musical transcription of birds' songs. *A*, green woodpecker; *B*, yellowhammer; *C*, chaffinch; *D*, robin; *E*, nightingale.

Non-vocal sounds

Some birds produce meaningful sounds by other means than using their voices. Snipe make special display flights during the breeding season in which the tail feathers produce a bleating noise. The feathers are specially modified and held out in the bird's slip-stream. An African honeyguide, *Melichneutes robustus*, produces a siren-like noise in the same way, and lapwings produce a muffled noise. Manakins make a buzzing noise as they fly, and bustards and some ducks produce a whistling noise due to the configuration of their primary feathers. African larks (*Mirafra*) and fan-tailed warblers (*Cisticola*) can produce dry clapping sounds with their wings.

But the most remarkable non-vocal sounds are those of woodpeckers. At breeding times, and occasionally at other times, several species select a dead branch and strike it sharply and repeatedly with their beaks. A loud, resonant drumming noise is produced that can be heard some distance away. The sound varies in its characteristics from one species to another. Woodpeckers have no true song, and the drumming serves as a replacement for demarcating territory and attracting a mate. Drumming is so important to the bird that it will choose a pole or even a drainpipe if a branch is not handy. Some species, such as the great spotted and lesser spotted woodpeckers and the grey-headed woodpecker drum frequently, whereas the green woodpecker does so only exceptionally.

Breeding

Birds are oviparous—that is, the young hatch from eggs incubated outside the body of the mother. In most species, the chick then requires a high degree of protection from its parents until it is ready to fend for itself. The behaviour of birds during the breeding season must above all provide for the incubation of the eggs and protection of the young.

The age of maturity varies between species

Passerines are usually mature at one year old. However, in captivity, the ability to breed sometimes appears much earlier. Some Bengalese finches (*Lonchura striata*), a species raised in captivity over the past two centuries, become adults at the age of three months, and sometimes a little earlier. A female that hatched on 18 June laid eggs that hatched on 24 September. The rufous-collared sparrow (*Zonotrichia capensis*) can breed from the age of five months. Fowls may also exhibit such precocity, though normally it takes a year before they are ready to breed. Grey partridges reared in New Zealand began to breed at five or six months, and Japanese quails matured in a rearing experiment at ninety days. Woodpeckers, swifts and pigeons take a year to become adult. But many birds take a long time to reach maturity. Crows, widowbirds, many waders, small gulls, geese, male golden pheasants and Lady Amherst's pheasants begin to breed at two years; large sea-gulls, cormorants and storks at three years or more; the Manx shearwater (*Puffinus puffinus*) usually at five years, but sometimes three; the slender-billed shearwater (*P. tenuirostris*) at six years; and the large birds of prey at between four and eight years.

The breeding cycle

The onset of the breeding season and a bird's behaviour during the season are triggered by changes in the hormones secreted inside the body and also by changes in the bird's environment.

When environmental conditions change little throughout the year and both food and nesting material are equally abundant at any time, as happens in the hot, rainy tropics,

White storks (*Ciconia ciconia*) mating on a tree-top. In this countryside of 'marismas' of the delta of the Guadalquivir river, egrets, herons and spoonbills also nest. *Phot. J. M. Baufle*

Gulls are birds with a very shrill cry. This couple of swallow-tailed gulls (*Creagrus furcatus*), near their young, utter loud screaming noises which have a definite meaning. *Phot. A. Brosset*

Skuas resemble gulls, but they are unable to catch their prey under water; they are natives of the Arctic and Antarctic regions. Shown here are a couple of MacCormick's skuas (*Catharacta maccormicki*) from Adelie Land strutting about. These birds have predatory habits; they kill and eat the fledglings of penguins and petrels. *Phot. Suinot—Jacana*

The swallow-tailed gull (*Creagrus furcatus*) is a native of the Galapagos Islands. It has strange habits; this species flies by night. It lays a single egg on the bare ground strewn with pebbles and fish-bones. *Phot. A. Brosset*

Male kori bustard (*Ardeotis kori*) in a nuptial display attitude. East Africa. *Phot. J. and M. Fiévet*

then behaviour is entirely governed by the endocrine glands. An activity cycle regulated by the pituitary gland is set up, producing regular development and regression of the genital organs.

The rufous-collared sparrow (*Zonotrichia capensis*) lives in the equatorial Andes, where conditions are constant the year round. The bird could breed at any time, but in fact it goes through two four-month periods of breeding activity each year and two periods of two months when it is sexually inactive. Similarly the sooty tern (*Sterna fuscata*), a tropical oceanic bird, has been observed on Ascension Island to breed during ten of the year's thirteen lunar months. Such breeding behaviour must be related to an endocrine cycle.

However, these are rare cases, and in most birds it appears that the endocrine cycle is itself influenced by external factors, chiefly by the abundance of food and the ease with which it can be obtained. In turn, this normally depends on the cycle of the seasons. Consequently, the breeding season of birds is usually related to the season of the year, and in temperate climates birds breed mostly in spring or at the beginning of summer. This is of course the time when food is most abundant.

In most birds therefore, the endocrine cycle is linked to the cycle of the seasons. It is sensitive to such seasonal factors as the duration of daylight and the amount of rainfall. As the length of daylight increases during the spring, a time comes when it triggers off the secretion of sex hormones from the ovaries and testes and the bird becomes sexually active.

This can be tested in artificial conditions. An immature drake suddenly subjected to artificial light for fifteen hours a day shows an increase in the size of the testes and, after a

fortnight in such conditions, produces normal sperms. The female duck also displays such sexual sensitivity to light, though to a lesser degree. Such an increase in the hours of daylight has a stimulating effect on many birds.

But not all species behave in this way. In some, longer hours of daylight have an inhibiting effect on breeding behaviour. Proof of this can be found in the birds living in the Kerguelen Islands, which lie in the Indian Ocean 1500 miles to the north of Antarctica. Being so far south, the length of day varies considerably over the year. Even so, there is no month, even during the winter when the days are very short, in which some birds do not mate, nest or sit on their eggs. Each species has its particular photoperiodicity, or physiological reaction to the length of day. The reaction stems from the hypothalamus, a part of the brain that controls primitive physical behaviour. Light stimulates the retina of the eyes, from which a signal passes to the hypothalamus. This in turn controls the pituitary gland, which secretes hormones that activate the ovaries and testes.

If birds from a temperate region north of the equator are transported to a region an equal distance south of the equator, or vice-versa, then they adapt their breeding behaviour to follow the seasons, which take place six months earlier or later. The adaptation may be rapid or it may take years, sometimes generations. For example, some populations of the sooty tern (*Sterna fuscata*) that live north and south of the equator both follow annual breeding cycles, but these are at different times of the year.

Birds that live in or near deserts have to cope with very hard conditions. Breeding is dependent upon the arrival of rain, for then what little vegetation there is will briefly flourish and provide extra food for the young. The zebra finch (*Taeniopygia castanotis*), a small Australian finch, becomes sexually active a little before the rains come, probably sensing the change in air pressure that occurs. Accelerated breeding then takes place in the bird's arid habitat. The male continues to rear the young already there, while the female builds a new nest and the young begin courting displays. In this way, the young can breed in time for the rains, even though they may not have finished their juvenile moult. This is a good example of a species making immediate use of a rare period that is favourable to breeding.

Finally, the breeding seasons of birds are timed so that the birth of the young coincides with the maximum availability of food. When the period between the laying of the eggs and the final departure of the young is long, laying must take place very early, often in rigorous climatic conditions. The lammergeier (*Gypaetus barbartus*) has to lay its eggs in the middle of the winter, when it may be freezing cold, for the young will not be ready to leave until the end of the following summer. The emperor penguin (*Aptenodytes forsteri*) of the Antarctic does likewise. To keep the egg alive during the savage winter, the parent holds the egg on its feet above the snow and ice and lowers a fold of warm fur over it. The chick is born when conditions are at their mildest, though it may still be freezing, and its rearing will not be complete even by the beginning of the following winter.

Falcons provide another example of the breeding season being linked to the availability of food. Peregrine falcons (*Falco peregrinus*) prey on other birds, and therefore breed in the spring when birds are plentiful. But Eleonora's falcon (*F. eleonorae*) lives on Mediterranean islands, which do not have large resident bird populations, and mainly depends for food on capturing migrating birds in transit. In the region inhabited by these falcons, which is from the Canary Islands to the eastern Mediterranean, there are two main times for the passage of migratory birds. These are from the end of February to the end of April, when the birds are flying north to breed, and from the end of August to October, when they are flying south with the young for the winter. The second passage provides more prey for the falcons, and they therefore lay in July and early August, so that the chicks are born in September and October to coincide with the migration of the prey.

The wandering albatross (*Diomedea exulans*), whose young grow very slowly, breeds only once every two years. However, if anything happens to the egg or to the very young chick, they can breed again the following year. At the other end of the breeding scale, a large number of species raise several broods every year. The climatic conditions determine the number of broods in this case. The same species may raise two or even three broods per year in temperate regions, but only one in cold climates (whether towards the poles or at high altitudes). Even if there is normally only one brood per year, as in birds of prey, gulls and plovers of the genus *Charadrius*, the birds will breed again to replace a brood that is destroyed.

In tropical climates, birds breed either during the dry season or the rainy season, according to their food needs. Birds of prey usually breed during the dry season and insect-eating birds during the rainy season.

When climatic conditions are totally unfavourable, breed-ing is held up for as long as they last. In birds that live in or near deserts, and in birds of the Arctic, some species do not breed at all in years when living conditions are so hard that any young could not survive.

Birds form pairs shortly before breeding

Most mature birds spend the greater part of the year on their own and only form pairs before breeding. Some birds come together only a few days before mating, but others pair up months in advance. Migrating birds may form pairs before they begin their journey to the breeding grounds. Usually, the pair breaks up after the breeding season and the birds go their separate ways. However, some birds, including swans, geese,

Nuptial display of rockhopper penguins (*Eudyptes crestatus*). *Phot. Michel Robert—Jacana*

ravens and probably large eagles, pair for life. On the other hand, when there are several broods a year, partners may change between one brood and another.

Birds are mostly monogamous and mate with only one partner before laying. However, polygamy exists in some species. In domestic fowls, rheas, peacocks and European wrens, about half the males live polygamously. Occasional cases have been reported in other species, but they are due mostly to a local imbalance in the numbers of each sex. Polyandry has been observed in species in which the female plays an active role in breeding, searching for a mate and threatening rival hens. Polyandrous birds include painted snipe, tinamous and hemipodes.

Polygamy and polyandry occur simultaneously in some birds that live communally such as anis and penguins, and in some brood parasites, such as the cuckoo (*Cuculus canorus*). Male and female territories overlap, making multiple mating virtually inevitable. There are also several species, including hummingbirds and birds of paradise, in which the partners come together briefly to mate and then part, the female being left to bring up the young alone.

At the start of the breeding season one sex becomes active and the other passive. Competition arises between the active birds for mates of the passive sex. The birds intimidate their rivals, using calls, songs, threatening postures and in many species, actual fights. The birds that win are free to pair with the passive birds. Usually the males are active and the females passive. However, in tinamous, hemipodes, phalaropes and painted snipe, the females are active and the males passive.

Courting displays

One of the most essential acts in pairing is the courting display. This is distinct from the intimidation display, and is designed primarily to attract a partner and pave the way for mating and make repeated mating possible. It is usually carried out by the active sex, but in species in which there is no sexual dimorphism, it is indulged in by both sexes. A courting display consists of a repertoire of successive postures of the body, often carried out to display special areas of plumage and sometimes involving extraordinary poses. Vocal sounds, both calls and songs, may also be part of the courting display. Many fowls, especially peacocks and pheasants, are particularly well-known for their displays, for they involve the parading of very beautiful plumage. Also spectacular are the displays of hummingbirds, lyrebirds, birds of paradise, cocks of the rock, manakins and ruffs. Displays by grebes and albatrosses, in which the partners take up postures facing each other, are also remarkable.

Ruffs, manakins and other species with loose, short-lived or non-existent pair bonds, have special parade grounds called leks on which the males gather to display in front of the waiting females. They strut and posture, endeavouring to attract a female and, at the same time, prevent a rival stealing a march on them. Group displays have also been observed in house sparrows, some hummingbirds (*Phaethornis*), and cranes, which leap and jump about in crazy dances, both sexes taking part.

Courtship behaviour is frequently accompanied by symbolic gestures in which one bird offers another a piece of food or nesting material. The arctic tern may offer its partner a fish; if the fish is accepted, the pair bond is established. Often a twig or a blade of grass is offered, not for building an actual nest, but purely as a gesture of affection. In the Antarctic, where there is no vegetation, adelie penguins offer a pebble instead.

Bower birds are perching birds closely related to the birds of paradise. Although their plumage is rather dull, they have the most elaborate of courtship displays. Their displays are elegant pageants of postures, calls, dances and symbolic gestures, all performed in a special construction called a bower. The bower is made of twigs in such shapes as a little hut or a walled avenue, and it is decorated with flowers, leaves and stones or any colourful (often blue) objects that the bower bird can find. One species even daubs its bower with a paint made by chewing up grass, fruit, or even charcoal. As the males perform their antics in their bowers, the females gather to watch. The bower, which may be of very elaborate construction, is not a nest and is only for display. There is a relationship between the magnificence of the bower and the quality of the plumage, for the dullest-coloured species are the best builders. The bower is maintained by its builder for months on end, and it may even be restored and used again the following year.

Courtship display has a double effect on the birds involved. It is both psychological and physiological, inducing a desire to mate as well as the physical changes necessary for mating. Display hastens the development of the sexual organs, and in some cases, it must induce egg-laying. When both sexes are mutually involved in the display, they both undergo sexual arousal. When only one displays, it is the passive bird that is excited by the display. In either case, the aim is to achieve coition. This is very brief, usually lasting only a few seconds. The male bestrides the female, usually on the ground or on a branch. Swans, geese and ducks copulate on the water, sometimes on the nest. In swifts, mating is believed to take place on the wing. Very rapid repetition of mating—some ten to

Two attitudes of the male ruff (*Philomachus pugnax*), in the course of its nuptial display. *Phot. Bel-Vienne—Jacana*

twenty times at intervals of seconds only—occurs in sparrows, but such a performance is perhaps done only for show.

Nest-building

Once a couple has paired off, the choice of a suitable site for the nest is the next move.

The first requirement for a nest site is security. While they are incubating their eggs, most birds are forced to leave the nest to feed, leaving the eggs exposed. A good shelter is therefore needed and it will also help to keep the eggs warm. The most primitive nest builders choose a cavity, such as a hole in a tree or some rock or even in the ground. Some birds make the hole themselves, woodpeckers drilling into a tree trunk, and bee-eaters, puffins and petrels burrowing in the ground or a cliff-face. Other birds are content with natural shelters—the space beneath the overhang of a rock, or a crevice in a rock-face.

Birds which nest in holes do not line the bottom of the cavity, and the egg or eggs are laid on the bare surface. Petrels, puffins, bee-eaters, kingfishers and owls are among these birds. Fragments of wood are found in the cavities of wood-peckers and parrots, but these probably fall into the hole when it is drilled and do not constitute a true lining.

Many birds lay eggs on the bare ground. They include all the ratite birds except the kiwi, guillemots, penguins, giant petrels, plovers, sandpipers, terns and nightjars. Other species first scratch out a little earth to make a hollow, and then put down a layer of twigs, feathers or small pebbles. A more advanced stage in sheltering the eggs is reached by birds that build a true nest on the ground. These birds include gulls, gannets, cormorants, pelicans, larks and pipits, and the nest may be made of twigs, grass, seaweed etc. As these species know how to build a nest, some of them, such as cormorants and the red-footed booby (*Sula sula*) occasionally nest in trees. One of the most unusual of the primitive nest builders that use trees is the fairy tern (*Gygis alba*), which lays its single egg in a small hollow of a branch without in fact building a nest of any kind. The tern then perches over the egg to incubate it.

Ground-nesting birds usually place their nests in a small hollow scraped in the soil to gain a little shelter. Some desert larks place their nest in a hollow at the base of a tuft of grass, and then build a little wall of pebbles around the hollow for protection. On ground liable to flooding, where waders tend to nest, material is added to the nest to raise it.

Albatrosses usually build nests of soil, moss and grass, and flamingos use dried mud. However, should the ground be rocky, sandy or in any other way unsuitable for nest building, these birds forego the task. Albatrosses content themselves with a rim of sand around the eggs, and flamingos nest on a few scattered twigs.

Water birds often have simple nesting habits. Divers usually make do with a patch of mosses or other plants lining a hollow by the shore. Grebes build large floating heaps of aquatic vegetation. The eggs are incubated in moist conditions and, although white when laid, they soon turn brown. Coots make nests consisting of heaps of rushes or reeds placed on a little mound of earth amid some bent reeds. The giant coot (*Fulica gigantea*) of the Andes builds a heap of stones in the water and makes its nest on top.

Nests built above the ground have to be of a more complex construction than the simple nests of most ground-nesting birds. They must be weather-proof and, when placed among branches, must be solidly anchored to their support. The larger nests, such as those of storks, are imposing structures. Material is added year after year until the nest reaches huge dimensions. The hammerhead (*Scopus umbretta*), a stork of Arabia and Africa, builds a vast dome-shaped chamber some ten feet across, with a small opening in one side. Such a nest is out of all proportion to the size of the bird itself, which is a mere twenty inches long.

Pigeons and turtle doves build nests of loosely-woven twigs, but they are always placed low in a tree so as to escape the force of strong winds. Most diurnal birds of prey make solid,

Nest of skylark *(Alauda arvensis)* built under the shelter of beetroot leaves. *Phot. J. Markham*

Seagulls usually build very simple nests of grass, twigs and vegetable debris, such as this one by the lava gull, *Larus fuliginosus*, on the Island of Santa Cruz (Galapagos). *Phot. A. Brosset*

Young of the greater flamingo (*Phoenicopterus ruber roseus*) on its nest of dried mud which measures about 12 inches in height by about 2 feet in diameter. Next to it are its parents, or other members of the colony (Camargue). *Phot. Jean Philippe Varin—Jacana*

Young coots (*Fulica atra*) in their nest of rushes and dry reeds. *Phot. Michel Brosselin*

Falcons lay on the bare ground, or else in the nest of another species. Shown here are kestrel's eggs (*Falco tinnunculus*). *Phot. Dubois*

imposing nests. The osprey, for example, builds with sticks as much as five feet long! Some other daytime hunters, such as harriers, are ground nesters. Old World vultures usually nest in trees, except for the griffon vulture, which makes a rudimentary nest among rocks, on cliff faces or in caves. The lammergeier, and its near relative the Egyptian vulture, build their nests in similar places, but the nests are spacious constructions lined with wool.

Falcons do not build their own nests but take over the nest of some other bird, such as a crow or buzzard. If one cannot be found, they simply lay their eggs on the ground.

The best constructed nests are those of the passerines, and also the hummingbirds and their close relatives the swifts. These are among the most highly evolved of birds, and their nesting abilities reflect this.

All modes of nest construction are found in the passerines. Some, such as the bullfinch (*Pyrrhula pyrrhula*) and warblers, build simple cups of roots and twigs, lining the inside with fine plant fibres or animal hair. The chaffinch (*Fringilla coelebs*) makes a deep cup with compact walls. Redstarts (*Phoenicurus phoenicurus*) line their nests with feathers, and rooks use wool. Some nests are masterpieces of intricate construction, taking weeks to build. The long-tailed tit (*Aegithalos caudatus*) builds a spherical nest with a side opening. The nest takes at least a thousand feathers and is disguised with a covering of lichen. The penduline tit (*Remiz pendulinus*) and several weaver birds (*Ploceus*) build globe-shaped nests suspended from branches. The birds enter the nests through a long funnel-like entrance hanging from one side or below the nest. Several icterids, such as caciques and American orioles, construct deep pouches that hang from branches, the entrance being at the side or top. The tailor birds (*Orthotomus*) take large leaves and stitch them together with plant fibres, using their beaks as needles. The nest is then built in the deep cup formed by the leaves. Hummingbirds build delicate little cups plentifully lined with moss.

Materials other than plants are often used to make some of the more unusual and interesting nests. Swallows, ovenbirds (*Furnarius*) and the apostle bird (*Struthidea*) of Australia build cup-shaped or spherical nests of mud, sometimes reinforced with grass or twigs. Old World nuthatches nest in a cavity in a tree, but plaster mud around the entrance to reduce its size. In hornbills, this method of improving safety is taken to extremes, for the female is imprisoned in the nesting hole with only her beak poking through a tiny hole in the plastered-up entrance. The male brings food, and the female takes advantage of its shelter to moult.

Swifts, especially the cave swiftlets (*Collocalia*), use their saliva to bind their nest materials together. This secretion is more abundant at nesting time and two cave swiftlets (*C. vestita* and *C. francica*) are able to make their nests entirely of saliva. The saliva hardens as it dries and is fashioned into cups that adhere to the walls and roofs of the caves. The nests are gathered by knocking them down with sticks and they are then cooked to make bird's-nest soup. The best-quality soup comes from nests made of pure saliva. Nests containing materials such as feathers and plant fibres are also gathered, and then processed to remove these impurities.

The scissor-tailed swifts (*Panyptila*) stick together plant materials to form a long stocking-shaped nest and suspend it from trees or rock faces. The entrance is at the bottom, making it virtually impossible for predators to enter the nest. The eggs are laid on a shelf high up inside.

Fantail warblers are small insectivorous passerines with an immense distribution area. Their pouch-shaped nests are fixed to grass or plants, as indicated by the photograph above of the golden-headed fantail warbler, *Cisticola exilis*, of Australia, which resembles the European species, *Cisticola juncidis*. Phot. John Warham

Communal nest-building

Some species of birds that live in colonies build their nests so close to each other that they form a single group of nests. The buffalo weavers (*Bubalornis*) build loose structures of heaped sticks each containing as many as ten nests. This communal nest-building is taken to its greatest development in the social weaver (*Philetairus socius*) of southern Africa. A colony of these birds builds its own vast nesting house in a tree. The structure looks like a grass hut suspended among the branches, and may measure as much as ten feet high and fifteen feet across. Inside are as many as 300 separate nesting chambers, each having its own entrance at the base of the structure. Over all the nests is a thatched roof.

Another kind of communal nesting occurs in the anis, which are American members of the cuckoo family. Often, a colony of anis will build only one nest and then all the females lay their eggs in this nest. They are not parasitic, like Old World cuckoos, and raise the young themselves. One anis nest was found to contain 25 eggs, but the usual number is about half as many.

Either or both sexes may build the nest

The task of nest-building may fall to either or both of the sexes, depending on the species. In cases where no lasting pair bond is formed during the breeding season, as in the fowls, hummingbirds and birds of paradise, it is the female who chooses the

Below, little tern (*Sterna albifrons*), on its eggs. This small tern nests as readily on sea beaches as on the banks of rivers or lakes. *Phot. John Markham*

Above, colony of common guillemots (*Uria aalge*) and, on the ledges of the cliff, of kittiwakes (*Rissa tridactyla*). These pelagic gulls live in the open sea, and nest on rugged cliffs in the Arctic and north temperate zone; after breeding, they think nothing of crossing the Atlantic in both directions. *Phot. Hosking*

nesting site and builds the nest. In birds where the active sex is the female, as in tinamous and phalaropes, nest-building is usually left to the male. In migratory species in which the male usually arrives first at the breeding grounds, it is often the male who chooses a nesting site or sites. The female then arrives and visits the sites, choosing to stay if she wishes. In the case of the wren, the male builds the nest (or nests, when he is polygamous).

The egg

The shell of an egg has a particular colour and often a pattern that usually identifies it as belonging to a certain species. However, several birds lay pure-white eggs that are difficult to tell apart. These birds are the albatrosses and their allies,

462

woodpeckers, bee-eaters, parrots, owls, and other birds that nest in holes or under shelters. Pigeons, swifts, and humming-birds also lay white eggs. In other families of birds, the egg is almost always coloured, even if only slightly tinted (as in the ivory-tinted ostrich egg) or lightly spotted with a white back-ground. The eggs otherwise have a background of blue, green, reddish brown, olive or near black, as in some tinamous. This colour is either uniform all over the egg, or speckled with brown, russet red, lilac or black spots, in a pattern that varies from one species to another. All these colours, whether back-ground colours or spots, are produced by pigments derived from natural pigments known as porphyrins and from decomposed haemoglobin.

The size of the egg also varies according to the species. For one particular family, the fewer eggs there are in a clutch, the bigger the individual eggs tend to be. Although large birds have big eggs—the largest egg is laid by the biggest bird, the ostrich—the bigger the bird, the smaller the egg is in proportion to the bird.

The number of eggs in the clutch

Some birds lay only one egg in each breeding season. They include the albatrosses, shearwaters and petrels, some pigeons, most Old World vultures, the birds of the auk family, the king and emperor penguins, some terns and gulls, a few gannets, and flamingos. Most pigeons, eagles, nightjars, humming-birds, the lammergeier and the Egyptian vulture lay two eggs, occasionally three. Three or four is the most usual number in sandpipers, the woodcock and plovers. The largest numbers of eggs per clutch are laid by the passerines, such as tits, and the fowls, such as the partridge.

Some birds lay a set number of eggs each season, whereas others, such as woodpeckers, ducks and sparrows, will lay more than the usual number if eggs are removed or destroyed as they are laid. By taking away eggs from a laying hen, the bird continued to lay until she had produced fifty eggs! Such an event is very unlikely to occur in nature—usually the whole clutch of eggs is destroyed by a predator. If this happens, most species lay a second clutch and, if further destruction occurs, a third or even a fourth clutch may be possible. However, the replacement clutches usually have fewer eggs than the first clutch. Not all birds have this replacing ability; large penguins, albatrosses, shearwaters and petrels, and large birds of prey do not lay again if their eggs are destroyed. Either the time of laying is so critical or the young take so long to raise that it is too late to lay again. Later broods stand less chance of survival than earlier broods because food availability diminishes and climatic conditions worsen later in the year. In temperate climates, the later broods of swifts and swallows have difficulty in surviving and are often abandoned by their parents.

Some birds, mainly passerines and pigeons, normally rear several broods a year and these are not replacement clutches. Others, such as the barn owl, do so only when there is an abundance of food. The breeding rate of a species is a measure of the bird's vulnerability; where food is plentiful, parents can raise a large brood. The fertility of the red-necked raven (*Corvus ruficollis*) of North Africa provides proof of this. In desert regions, this bird lays two or three eggs, exceptionally four, in a clutch. In more favourable regions, five eggs may be produced but in years of famine, scarcely a single chick is raised.

Many small tropical birds lay only a few eggs—usually two or three. However, they may have several successive broods in a year and in this way raise the number of young needed to maintain the numbers of the species, for mortality is very high among the young of small birds. Young passerines individually

Colony of common cormorants (*Phalacrocorax carbo*) at breeding time. *Phot. Dragesco—Atlas Photo*

The baya weaver (*Ploceus philippinus*), very closely related to the European sparrow, weaves strips of palm leaves into nests, like long hanging pouches with an opening at their lower end. *Phot. Aldo Margiocco*

have a low chance of survival. Only ten to fourteen per cent of the eggs laid eventually produce adult birds, and normal life span is short in any case—only a year or two. In less vulnerable birds, such as albatrosses and shearwaters, the life span is much greater, as it is in oystercatchers, which are well able to defend themselves against predators. In such cases, a bird may live as long as twenty years. Even so, mortality among the young is still high. It has been estimated at 95

per cent for young terns during their first year. But once the first few dangerous months are past, the life span does express the degree of vulnerability of the species, although man through hunting and interference with the bird's environment may upset this relationship.

When there are several eggs in a clutch, they are laid at intervals of a day in the case of passerines, especially small birds, and ducks. Ravens lay at two-day intervals, New World vultures every five days, and lammergeiers at three- or four-day intervals. Laying very often takes place in late morning, though pigeons prefer the early afternoon and pheasants the evening.

Two examples of eggs. *Left,* eggs of the European bee-eater (*Merops apiaster*); they are white like those of most birds nesting in holes. (Bee-eaters nest in galleries dug in sandy banks.) *Right,* three eggs of the spur-winged plover (*Hoplopterus armatus*), homochromous with the stony ground on which they are laid. *Phot. J.-P. Varin—Jacana*

Waved albatross (*Diomedea irrorata*) with its young. The whole world population breeds on Hood island (Galapagos). *Phot. A. Brosset*

Incubation

An embryo needs warmth to grow and develop to the point at which it is ready to be born. In mammals, the embryo remains inside the mother's body and receives the necessary heat from her. In birds, the embryo is inside the egg and the egg must therefore be incubated to enable the embryo to grow. The mother or both parents incubate the egg; very rarely is it the task of the male alone. The necessary heat is usually provided by the body heat of the parent as it sits on the eggs. In most birds, apart from gannets and cormorants, a remarkable change occurs in the plumage that comes into contact with the egg. At breeding time, some down feathers fall out, leaving bare patches of skin on the underside. These patches are called brood patches, and they fit around the eggs as the bird sits on them. An increased flow of blood to the abdominal region makes the skin of the brood patches very warm, and this heat is transferred direct from the skin to the eggs. If the brood patches

volcanic ground. Others build mounds of vegetation and sand or soil, and bury their eggs in the mounds. The vegetation produces heat as it rots and incubates the eggs. The mallee fowl (*Leipoa ocellata*) is the most specialized of the mound builders, for it can precisely control the temperature of the eggs by removing or adding material to the mound. The bird seems to be able to test the temperature with its tongue. The female lays a variable but often high number of eggs each a few days apart. The young therefore hatch at similar intervals. The chicks, which are highly independent, struggle to the top of the mound and are able to fly from the first day.

Staggered hatching, as happens with the mallee fowl, also occurs in birds that begin to incubate the eggs as soon as one is laid. But others do not commence incubation until all the eggs of a clutch have been laid, and these eggs therefore hatch simultaneously.

Duration of incubation and temperature of nest

Small passerine birds, woodpeckers and cuckoos have a very short incubation period, lasting ten to fifteen days at the most. Pigeons sit on their eggs for fifteen days, hens about 21 days, and ducks and geese some 28 days. Eagles and related large birds take from 45 to 47 days. Shearwaters incubate for nearly sixty days and large albatrosses and the kiwi as long as eighty days. The incubation period may be prolonged by some ten per cent in bad weather.

The presence or absence of the parent naturally influences nest temperature. An enclosed wren's nest was recorded at 92.1° F with the parent bird and 91.2° F without. The average

Nest of pheasant (*Phasianus colchicus*). *Phot. John Markham*

did not form and there were feathers between the skin and eggs, then the warming of the eggs would be much less effective because feathers act to insulate the body. The formation of brood patches occurs in the parent that incubates the eggs, or in both parents if incubation duties are shared.

During incubation, the parent periodically turns over the eggs with its beak. Usually, it has also to leave the eggs on occasions, either to feed or to hand over incubation to its mate. However, incubation of the eggs is continuous in some species. The female hornbill is imprisoned inside the nesting hole and cannot leave the eggs. In other cases, as with some tropical bee-eaters, the nesting hole reaches such a high temperature during the day that the air is sufficiently warm to incubate the eggs without the parent sitting on them.

King and emperor penguins experience conditions at the other extreme and must continually protect their eggs from the bitterly cold air by holding the egg on their feet and lowering a fold of warm fur over the egg. In such conditions, the compulsion to incubate must be very strong if the egg is to survive. In fact, it is so strong in these penguins that, when one parent is transferring the egg to the other, other penguins without eggs will fight to try and steal it. Although this compulsion to brood normally aids the egg, here it acts against it for the egg is sometimes broken in the quarrel that ensues, or it may roll away and not be recovered.

The megapodes or mound builders, birds of the fowl family found from the Nicobar Islands west of Malaysia to the Philippines and in New Guinea and Australia, do not use body heat to incubate their eggs. Instead they bury them in the ground. In some species, the heat of the sun on the soil is sufficient to incubate the eggs or else the eggs are buried in hot

A rockhopper penguin *(Eudyptes crestatus)* on its nest. The rockhoppers are penguins which live indifferently in temperate climate zones (New Zealand in the case of the species shown here) and in cold climates (Antarctic islands etc.). They are recognized by the long plumes on the sides of their head. During their frolics at sea, they jump out of the water like porpoises, hence the name hoppers which is sometimes given to them. *Phot. John Warham*

The gentoo penguin *(Pygoscelis papua)* with its chick on its nest. *Phot. Benoit Tollu*

nest temperature for many species is 93° F. The number of eggs in the nest also affects their temperature, because the eggs at the centre of a large clutch will vary less in temperature than those at the edge.

The developing embryo may also contribute to its own warmth. In birds that hatch in a well-developed state, the

Stages in the hatching of the eider duck *(Somateria mollissima)*. *Phot. Jean-Philippe Varin—Jacana*

temperature of the eggs rises during incubation as the young bird grows inside the egg. For instance, penguin eggs take 42 days to incubate. Their temperature has been measured at 68° F to 77° F during the first two days, rising to 100° F towards the fifteenth day and staying at this level. In ducks and geese, which line their nests with layers of down to protect the eggs, the eggs may occasionally be left towards the end of the incubation period as they will remain sufficiently warm without the parent brooding them. In the stiff-tailed ducks *(Oxyura)*, the parents virtually stop brooding altogether as hatching time approaches.

Hatching

As the incubation period ends, the embryo prepares for hatching. The neck muscles increase in strength to aid the head movements needed for leaving the egg. This extra strength is lost soon after hatching, when it is no longer required. Early on in the embryo's life—from the sixth or seventh day in domestic chickens—a hard tip forms on the upper mandible of the beak and often on the lower mandible too. This tip, formed of an extra deposit of keratin, rubs away at the inside of the shell and eventually causes it to break. The tip may decrease in size or disappear shortly before hatching, as in some megapodes (which, however, have a very hard beak instead). Otherwise, it disappears after hatching, usually within a week. This hatching aid seems to be a feature that birds have inherited from reptiles, for young reptiles also possess one.

When a bird hatches from its egg, it may already be able to move about and even, in the case of the megapodes, fend for

itself. Alternatively, it may be born naked and blind in what is virtually a larval state. In between these two extremes come other states in which the chick's eyes are open, and there are either sparse tufts of down or a complete down plumage. The first kind of birds can leave the nest immediately after hatching, and are therefore called nidifugous. The others must remain in the nest and need close attention from their parents, who keep them warm and find them food. Such birds that stay in the nest are called nidicolous. This stage need not last long; flamingo chicks can leave the nest only three or four days after hatching.

Species that produce nidifugous young appear to be more primitive or less highly evolved than other birds. The brain is less well developed, even though the birds are physically so advanced at birth. The most intelligent birds, the passerines and the parrots, are nidicolous—the chicks are born naked and blind, or nearly so.

Although physical development is not far advanced in nidicolous chicks at birth, they soon make up for lost time and grow extremely quickly. Large eagles gain 30 times their birth weight in two months, and cuckoos put on weight by 50 times in less than a month! Their metabolism operates immediately at high gear, unlike nidifugous birds, which are much slower growing.

Rearing and education

Even nidifugous birds, apart from the megapodes, need their parents immediately after hatching. The chicks must be shielded from changes in temperature, because during the first few days they are unable to maintain a constant body temperature. In fact, they are rather like cold-blooded animals. A small passerine such as a newly-hatched wren will remain in this state for three days and then, over the following two days, become more and more warm-blooded. But, before this happens, the parent must protect its offspring from both heat and cold. To keep out the cold, it sits over the young or buries them in its plumage. To shade them from the sun, it may make a screen by spreading its wings.

Feeding the young makes considerable demands on the parents. Even those with nidifugous young must lead them to a feeding place and perhaps show them how to seize and swallow food. Hens allowed to run loose with their chicks will seize a grain of corn, an insect or a small worm and offer it to their young. The feeding ground may be too far from the nest for the chicks to make their way unaided, as with ducks that nest in holes or high up in trees. In this case, the parent must carry the chick either in its beak or in its feet, as in the Cracidae (the curassows, guans and chachalacas) or the young may deliberately fall from the nest to the ground.

Nidicolous chicks are, of course, fed in the nest. They react instinctively when food arrives, raising their heads and opening their beaks wide. Even chicks born blind and deaf will do this, sensing the arrival of the parent by the way the nest shakes as it alights. The parent sees the gaping mouth, often coloured a bright red or yellow and sometimes decorated with spots of colour. Its instinctive reaction to such a sight is to drop food into it.

Feeding methods vary a great deal. In some species, the parent disgorges food to feed its young. Heron chicks feed by seizing the parent's beak in their own; some other chicks, such

Nest of a nightingale (*Luscinia megarhynchos*), made from a pile of dried leaves and stalks, hidden in a thicket. *Phot. John Markham*

Black redstart (*Phoenicurus ochruros*), holding out at the end of its beak food intended for its nidicolous young, which are incapable of feeding themselves. *Phot. Visage Albert*

Day-old chicks of the slender-billed gull, (*Larus genei*). *Phot. J. L. S. Dubois*

as black vultures (*Necrosyrtes monachus*), American vultures and gannets, poke their beaks inside the parent's bill to get food. In other birds of prey, the food may be carried to the nest in the talons or the bill and then cut up into small pieces, each morsel being given to the young with the bill. Later, when the chicks grow bigger, the prey is simply laid in the nest or disgorged on the edge of the nest, and the young seize it unaided.

The frequency with which the parent brings food to its young varies according to the nature of the food, the way in which it is brought, and the bird's way of life. Birds that store food (either animal or vegetable) in their crops or other internal storage organs feed their chicks daily, though the meals may be few in number. Young vultures, lammergeiers and albatrosses get only one meal a day, if that. Birds of prey (either diurnal or nocturnal) that carry food to their young can only provide meals at long, irregular intervals depending on the success of their hunt. On the other hand, young insect-eating birds are usually assured of a constant food supply. The parents feed their chicks frequently, making as many as 25 food-gathering trips every hour. However, each

meal will be very small as the parent can hold only a few insects or worms at a time, and sometimes only one. The frequency of the meals varies with the time of day. In the case of the blue tit (*Parus caeruleus*), feeding is most frenzied in the morning, 72 trips being made per hour. The parent pauses towards noon and resumes again, though at a reduced rate, in the evening. The task is arduous for parents with a large brood. The great tit (*Parus major*) may have to provide as many as 400 meals a day!

When both parents incubate the eggs, they also co-operate as a rule in feeding the young. If the female alone sits on the eggs, unless she has been abandoned by the male (as in hummingbirds), she may or may not be fed by him. But, either way, the male will still take part in rearing the young, either by bringing food to the nest or by distributing it among the young. The male Montagu's harrier (*Circus pygargus*) is the only male bird that feeds a brood unaided.

Young pigeons are raised from their first days of life on pigeon milk—a cheesy substance that is rich in vitamins. It is secreted from the lining of both of the parent pigeons' crops. Young emperor penguins receive a similar substance that is produced in the oesophagus of the male parent, and the chicks of some albatrosses, shearwaters and petrels feed on a kind of stomach oil disgorged by the parents. Very young

European blackbird (*Turdus merula*) feeding its young. *Phot. Visage Albert—Jacana*

Griffon vulture (*Gyps fulvus*) and its chick. This vulture, found in Europe, Asia and Africa, nests in the Pyrenees in small cononies. *Phot. M. Terrasse*

flamingos are nourished on a red liquid containing blood. This is very rich in carotenoid pigments and has a food value similar to that of the milk of mammals.

However, such food is unusual. Normally, the food brought to the young is much the same as that eaten by the parents. Some grain eaters, such as sparrows, feed their young on insects, especially grubs or caterpillars, as this kind of food is richer in protein than grain.

Nest hygiene and safety

The parents of young birds must ensure that the young are defended from disease as well as predators, although hygiene is important only in the case of nest and hole dwellers. The nest or hole must be kept clean and free from droppings that would otherwise begin to fill it and create a health hazard.

Many chicks instinctively keep the nest clean. They back up to the edge of the nest and raise their vents to expel their faeces with sufficient force to make it fall clear of the nest. Young herons and cormorants do this. In perching birds, the faeces are produced in a gelatinous sac secreted around the faeces at the cloaca; the parents seize the sac and either swallow it or carry it away from the nest. At the end of the nesting period, they may not be able to cope with the quantities produced and the edge of the nest becomes covered with droppings. Birds that nest in holes take the same hygiene precautions. There are, however, some exceptions; pigeons, some sparrows and weavers, gannets and ground-nesting cormorants do not worry about cleanliness. The vast and valuable deposits of guano of Chile and elsewhere are produced by cormorants and gannets.

Wherever it is, the brood is always in some danger of attack

from predators. Even those birds which nest in holes are not spared. Martens enter holes in trees and destroy broods of owls and woodpeckers. Squirrels, jays, magpies, crows and snakes are responsible for pillaging many nests, taking both eggs and young birds; some birds of prey, mammals such as foxes and reptiles are also culprits. With few exceptions, birds are not able to erect very good defences against predators. Large owls and skuas make direct and violent attacks on any creature that approaches the nest, striking out with their beaks and claws. Terns dive on their predators. These aggressive birds can successfully defend their young, but most birds are too small

European greenfinch (*Carduelis chloris*) disgorging into the beak of its young the food stored in its crop. *Phot. Visage Albert*

469

of a winged or four-legged predator. Chicks react to an alarm call by freezing stock-still. Nidifugous chicks, out and about, lie on the ground with their necks extended. Their plumage camouflages them against the ground and they become very hard to spot. Even adult birds act in this way, especially when the predator is a keen-eyed bird of prey.

The chick's dependence on its parents varies between species

Nidifugous chicks rapidly become independent of their parents and can look after themselves. Even so, goslings and cygnets (young geese and swans) and some other young birds stay with their parents and make up small families. The families normally remain as separate units, and come together only at migration time.

The young of penguins and flamingos are raised in large nursery groups or rookeries, receiving care and food from the adults around them even after they leave the nest. In some birds, only the parent feeds its young, but in others, the young may be fed by any adult.

Nidicolous birds remain in the nest until they can fly, or at least until they can flutter about for a short time. They are said to be fledging as they grow their flight feathers. Some birds, such as young herons, leave their nests before they are fledged and climb about among the branches of their trees. Others, either deliberately or by accident, fall from the nest and survive. Young penguins and guillemots fall into the sea before their wings are fully developed. But many birds remain in the nest for a very long time, so that they are capable of sustained flight as soon as they leave. These birds include swifts, which may set off on a long migration almost immediately after fledging. All the procellarian birds, from the great albatrosses to the small storm petrel (*Hydrobates pelagicus*), can fly extremely well as soon as they leave the nest. But they remain in the nest for a long time—at least two months and as long as nine months in the larger albatrosses. During this time, they not only fledge but build up reserves of fat, sometimes growing bigger than their parents. The parents finally abandon their young, which may then spend a few days fasting and surviving on their fat reserves while preparing to take flight.

Accentor or hedge-sparrow *(Prunella modularis)* removing from its nest the faecal sac expelled by a chick. *Phot. A. Margiocco*

Parasitism

A remarkable trait among the breeding of birds is the parasitic behaviour of the cuckoos in the Old World and the cowbirds in the New. The parents do not raise their own young, but lay their eggs in other birds' nests and saddle the other birds with the incubation of their eggs and the rearing of their young. This behaviour is called brood parasitism.

The first stages of brood parasitism are found in some ducks (*Anas, Netta, Fuligula*), which not infrequently lay in each others' nests. A study of a population of the redhead (*Aythya americana*) in the United States showed that a high proportion of the females were parasites while others were semi-parasitic. The parasites were completely incapable of nesting, and laid in neighbouring nests; as many as 87 eggs were found in one nest! The black-headed duck (*Heteronetta atricapilla*) of South America is always parasitic, laying in the nest of other ducks, coscoroba swans, coots and other water birds.

Brood parasitism is developed to its highest degree in the cowbirds of the New World, and the cuckoos, honeyguides and some weavers of the Old World. In the cowbirds, parasitic

and weak to mount an effective counter-attack. Social birds band together to harass a predator that comes near the flock, organizing themselves by alarm calls. Solitary birds have little chance of saving their brood from a direct attack.

Some birds that nest on or near the ground have a special tactic to prevent any ground-living creature (such as a dog or man) from intruding on their nests. The parents draw the attention of the intruder by feigning an injury, and lead them away from the nest. They may limp along the ground, one wing spread as if it is broken, or they are hurt and unable to move. When the intruder has been led far enough from the nest, the parent simply abandons its act and flies quickly away. This behaviour has been observed in partridges, grouse, plovers, larks, some warblers and some finches. There is no doubt that this injury feigning is successful and helps to conserve these species.

Apart from such special defence tactics, birds nearly always utter a special alarm call to warn their young or neighbouring birds of the presence of danger, which usually takes the shape

behaviour varies in extent. At one end of the scale is the brown-headed cowbird of North America, which lays its eggs in almost any other nest it can find. The parent bird keeps an eye on the building of other nests, and then lays in one as soon as an egg appears in it, destroying or carrying off some of the other eggs but never all of them. The foster parent then rears its own and the parasite's young, although the young parasites may be so greedy that its own chicks may well die for lack of attention. The screaming cowbird of South America, on the other hand, lays only in the nests of one other species—the bay-winged cowbird, which is not a parasite.

Among the weavers, the widowbirds of Africa have developed brood parasitism to an interesting degree. Apart from one species that is parasitic on various hosts, these widowbirds are all parasites of waxbills (a member of a subfamily of the weavers to which the house sparrow belongs). There is a high degree of imitation, the widowbird's eggs and the mouth markings of its young closely resembling those of the host waxbills. Certain species only are chosen as hosts, sometimes only one particular species.

It appears that all the honeyguides are parasites, making up the only family of birds that is totally parasitic. Their hosts are mainly woodpeckers or barbets (i.e. closely related families), but bee-eaters, hoopoes, and starlings are often chosen, and occasionally other species, including even swallows. The intruding chick destroys the host's brood, either by pushing them out of the nest or by pecking them to death with its beak. The other nestlings stand no chance of survival, for the young honeyguide's beak is equipped with a sharp hook at its tip. Its work done, the hook drops off after a week.

The cuckoos are famed for their parasitic behaviour, but not all cuckoos indulge in it. No American cuckoos are parasitic, and neither are some cuckoos of Africa and the East. The common cuckoo (*Cuculus canorus*) is the most frequently studied. As a rule, it lays only one egg per nest. The female cuckoo keeps an eye on one or more particular species of birds and waits for them to lay. As soon as the host bird has laid, the cuckoo either lays directly in the nest (an action that may take as little as five seconds); or it lays its egg on the ground and carries it to the nest in its beak. Often it takes out one or more of the host's eggs. Usually, the host accepts the egg and sits on it along with its own eggs. The young cuckoo often hatches

before the other birds, its incubation taking $12\frac{1}{4}$ days whereas most host birds require at least 13 or 14 days for incubation. About ten hours after birth, the young cuckoo exhibits a strange reflex action. As it comes into contact with the other eggs or chicks, it struggles violently and tries to heave them onto its back. When it has succeeded, it raises its wing bones and backs to the edge of the nest, where it tips its load over the side. It may seem that the strangest thing about this business is the reaction of the parents, who seem to see nothing of the drama. Even if one of their young should be caught on the side of the nest, they will allow it to starve. However, this is not

Threatening attitude of a strong eagle owl chick (*Bubo bubo*). National park of Grand-Paradis (Italy). *Phot. Aldo Margiocco*

callous behaviour on the part of the parents; it just shows how fixed and instinctive their life patterns are.

The young cuckoo loses this reflex action by the fifth day of life; if it is not then alone in the nest, it puts up with the host's chicks. However, as it needs much more food than they do, it takes more than its share and they starve to death.

Female cuckoos normally lay in the nests of the species in which they were themselves reared. There are therefore races of cuckoos raised only by reed warblers, or only by hedge sparrows, or only by redstarts, and so on. In these races, a remarkable adaptation to this breeding pattern exists: the parasite's egg is very like that of the host. It is the same shape and colour and just a little bigger, though very small for a bird of the cuckoo's size. There are other races of cuckoos that may lay their eggs among host eggs of a clearly different appearance. In such cases, the host in question is either one used only occasionally, or else it is one of recent origin and the egg colouring has not had sufficient time to change in imitation of the host's eggs. This is confirmed by differences in egg

Linnet (*Carduelis cannabina*) feeding its young among the vines. When the breeding season is over, this species forms large flocks. The male is a tuneful singer. *Phot. Merlet—Atlas-Photo*

Young cuckoo fed by an accentor *(Prunella modularis)*. Phot. John Markham

Young cuckoo pushing out the egg of its host, a reed warbler *(Acrocephalus scirpaceus)*. Phot. Bel-Vienne—Jacana

Young cuckoo, already well feathered and having expelled the eggs and young of its host, being fed by the latter (reed warbler) *(Acrocephalus scirpaceus)*. Phot. Bel-Vienne—Jacana

adaptation between Europe and Asia. In Europe, cuckoo eggs and host eggs are quite often different in appearance, whereas in Asia they are similar. In Japan, for example, several species of cuckoos live side by side and each one confines itself to a specific host with similar eggs. The explanation for this difference is that the stocking of birds in Europe took place after the last ice age—that is, comparatively recently. Such recent climatic changes have not taken place over most of Asia, giving the birds time to evolve more specific parasitic behaviour.

Parasitic behaviour varies somewhat in other species of cuckoos. Young cuckoos of the genera *Clamator* and *Eudynamis* do not throw out the host eggs or chicks from the nest and live several to a nest. These birds, and also *Chrysococcyx*, *Surniculus* and *Cacomantis*, are much more specialized in their choice of host than is the common cuckoo. In some species, especially *Chrysococcyx*, the adult parasite comes back to the host nest and takes charge of its young when it is ready to leave.

Biology and habits

Every bird is adapted to its particular environment in several different ways. The kind of food to be found there will shape its beak, for example, and often its feet as well. The extent or lack of cover will give it a certain behaviour and coloration to enable it to avoid predators. Breeding is another important factor, for the environment must contain suitable nesting sites. Birds are highly adaptable creatures overall, and have colonized almost every part of the globe, from lush tropical forests through grasslands to the polar wastes, and from the surface of the oceans to the summits of high mountains. The only places where birds are not found are at the poles themselves and the tops of the very highest mountains, where it is too cold to provide them with food, and of course deep underwater. Birds are classed generally by the kind of food they eat, and their preference for food may restrict them to a particular environment. Indeed, to maintain a constant environment, many birds have to migrate.

Omnivorous birds

Omnivorous birds, as their name suggests, can eat a wide variety of food and so are adapted to many environments. They include the raven *(Corvus corax)*, which is as much at home on sea cliffs as in mountains, in forest as in grassland, and even in desert or semi-desert surroundings. It is also remarkably resistant to differences in climate, being found from Greenland to the edge of the Sahara. Even in the Sahara, it is replaced by another bird so similar that many ornithologists consider it to be the same species.

Seagulls are also well-known omnivorous birds. They eat small vertebrates, insects, worms and molluscs as well as seeds. Their lack of any particular preference for food enables them to scavenge almost anywhere, and many will come inland if necessary. However, at the coast, they never go so far out to sea as to lose sight of land. The exception to this rule is the kittiwake *(Rissa)*, which ranges over the North Atlantic and North Pacific oceans, usually following the fishing fleets.

Opposite page, colony of herring gulls *(Larus argentatus)*, adults and young. Phot. Weiss-Rapho

Insect- and seed-eaters

Birds which have a particular diet have remarkable adaptations that enable them to find and digest their food. Insect-eaters are not usually distinguished by very special anatomical features. However, those which catch insects on the wing, such as swifts (*Apus*), swallows (*Hirundo*), flycatchers (*Muscicapa*) and night jars (*Caprimulgus*), have wide, gaping mouths fringed with stiff bristles to help capture their prey. They can fly with remarkable speed and manoeuvrability. Since their feet are not needed for walking, they are reduced and of use only for roosting and clinging to surfaces. On the other hand, birds such as wagtails that find insects on the ground are rapid walkers. Worm-eaters, such as European blackbirds and thrushes, also take small molluscs and berries, and so they can walk or hop easily over the ground as well as perch in woods and thickets. However, in birds that live in trees and bushes, the feet vary according to whether they feed among the leaves or on the ground. In the first case, the feet are strong and enable the bird to cling to a branch or twig in all positions—tits (*Parus*) and sedge warblers (*Acrocephalus*) are good examples. Ground feeders have high tarsi, so that they can move quickly through the undergrowth in search of insects. They include thrushes, the blue throat (*Luscinia svecica*), and pittas (*Pitta*) in the Old World, and antpittas (*Grallaria*) in the New World.

Seed-eaters, such as sparrows and finches, possess small but strong beaks. The shape and strength of the beak varies according to the kinds of seeds eaten. A greenfinch can open large hard seeds, such as sunflower seeds, and so has a stout bill. A linnet has a light bill and therefore eats small seeds such as millet seeds. It has to eat far more seeds than a greenfinch does to get the same amount of food, but it takes a linnet so long to crack open large seeds that it cannot get enough to eat by tackling them. Some seed-eaters have amazingly powerful beaks. Cockatoos can crack nuts so hard that a man would need a hammer or axe to split them open.

In addition to a strong beak, many seed-eaters, including parrots, finches and tanagers, also have a few small stones in their gizzards. The stones act like mill-stones and help to grind up the seeds before they are digested.

Birds of prey

Carnivorous birds possess either a powerful bill, able to seize or strike the prey, or sharp talons that have the same functions. The talons are also used in flight to deal slashing blows to the prey before it is seized. The bill, hooked and sharp though it is, is normally used for only tearing the prey apart after it is killed. Small victims may be gripped in the talons and carried off to the bird's lair. Diurnal birds of prey, which hunt by day, usually dismember their victims, swallowing them mouthful by mouthful. However, owls, which are nocturnal hunters, have broad gullets and can swallow them whole. After the flesh is digested, indigestible matter such as skin and bone is

473

The common tree-creeper (*Certhia familiaris*) of Europe, Asia and North America is found in the east of France and in forests in mountainous regions. On the plains, its place is taken by a very closely related species. Exclusively insectivorous, it is therefore very useful to agriculture. *Phot. John Markham*

Right, rollers (*Coracias caudata*) have a variegated plumage in which blues predominate; insects are their favourite food. *Phot. Jean Roche*

The European bee-eater (*Merops apiaster*) of Europe, Asia and Africa. Bee-eaters are insectivorous birds which readily capture wasps and bees. Endowed with brilliant colours, they nest in holes in the ground or in banks. *Phot. J. M. Baufle*

regurgitated in a pellet. Pellets are also brought up by herons, seagulls, shrikes and crows. They provide ornithologists with valuable information on the diets of these birds.

Carrion-eaters

Birds that feed only on dead animals have sharp, powerful beaks for dismembering the remains, but the feet, needed only for walking, do not possess clutching talons and sharp claws. Such carrion-eaters include vultures and marabou storks. Fast flight is not necessary to obtain carrion, and so vultures fly slowly, peering intently down in search of a corpse. Several birds feed both on carrion and on living prey, and these birds are capable of fast flight like other birds of prey. If they capture their victims on the wing, then they must be able to fly with tremendous acceleration and great manoeuvrability. Birds that find their prey on the ground fly less swiftly. The lammergeier feeds on carrion and also captures small animals. It has some unusual feeding habits, such as dropping bones from the air to break them open so that it can get at the marrow inside, or rushing at large animals in an attempt, sometimes successful, to drive them over a precipice and kill them.

Fish-eaters

Birds that live on fish or other aquatic animals, such as crustaceans, water insects and frogs, have very special adaptations to enable them to feed. They may be good swimmers and have

webbed feet, like cormorants, darters (anhingas), penguins, puffins, divers and mergansers. Grebes are also good swimmers: their feet are not webbed but have broad lobes along the toes that open out as the bird propels itself through the water. All these birds catch their food by diving for it from the surface. Their bills are strong, straight and pointed (as in darters, divers and grebes), hooked (cormorants), or even hooked and serrated (mergansers). Penguins, which feed on fish and crustaceans, do not have webbed feet, but they can swim powerfully underwater by using their wings as fins. Auks, which fill the same role in the north as penguins do in the south, can also swim well underwater with their wings.

In addition to these birds that capture their food by hunting underwater, there are birds that seize their victims by diving from the air. They do not have webbed feet, because the speed of the dive thrusts them beneath the surface. These birds have

Golden eagle (*Aquila chrysaetos*) cutting up the carcass of a fox. Photograph taken in the Alps. *Phot. Visage Albert—Jacana*

strong beaks, for they must be quick and effective in seizing a catch. They include terns, gannets, one species of pelican and kingfishers. The gannets dive from a great height and cause a tremendous splash. Kingfishers dart down from an overhanging branch, and quickly fly up again from the water with their prey, as do the terns. Gannets and pelicans, good at swimming on the surface, remain on the water long enough to swallow their catch.

One kind of behaviour that at first seems to be odd is displayed by some Caspian terns (*Hydroprogne tschegrava*), royal terns (*Sterna maxima*), and especially their cousins the skimmers (*Rynchops*). These birds fly low over the water with their bills opened so that the lower mandible cuts through the surface. As soon as this mandible touches a fish or shrimp, the upper mandible snaps down to grab it. The lower one is longer than the upper, especially adapting the skimmer to this unusual method of fishing. The skimmer prefers to hunt by dusk or at night, having slit-like pupils like those of a cat to ensure sensitive vision.

Some birds of prey feed on fish that they catch by diving. They do not enter the water head-first to capture a fish with their beaks, but swoop down with talons extended to grab their victim. They may only partially immerse themselves. This fishing technique is used by ospreys, sea eagles and some other diurnal birds of prey, and among the owls, by *Ketupa* and *Scotopelia* in Asia and Africa. The talons of these fish-eating birds of prey are adapted slightly: beneath the toes are prominent 'spikelets' with which the bird gains a firm grip on the slippery scales of their catch.

Herons also fish. The heron's beak is strong, long and pointed and its legs are very long, enabling the bird to wade in shallow water or stand there motionless in wait. When a fish passes within reach, the long, curved neck suddenly darts down towards it.

Some pelicans and cormorants fish in flocks, positioning themselves in a circle around a place where they suspect that fish are swimming. Then the birds drive the fish into shallow water, the cormorants circling round and round and the

475

pelicans flapping their wings in a great commotion, and seize them at or near the surface.

Worm-eaters

Woodcock, snipe, sandpipers, curlews and several other birds dig up worms and other soft-bodied invertebrates in soft damp ground, or find them underwater or under leaves or stones. These birds can walk easily and quickly. Most have long legs so that they can stand in shallow water or on flooded ground. Many live on the sea shore or on the banks of estuaries where the tide floods over the feeding ground regularly. Their beaks are long—sometimes very long—so that they can dig well down into the ground. The beaks are also very sensitive to touch, enabling the birds to identify and seize their prey without seeing it. Plovers and lapwings, which eat the same kind of food, have short beaks and must therefore feed on the surface of the ground.

The flamingo has an unusual way of feeding. It stands in shallow water, swinging its head from side to side with the bill immersed upside-down in the water. The bill is in fact closed, but there are rows of comb-like platelets between the mandibles. The bird sucks and pumps water or mud through the bill, and microscopic animals and plants are trapped in the platelets. Swans, geese and ducks can also strain food from water in a similar way.

Nectar-eaters

Some birds are able to collect nectar. They have long tube-like or brush-tipped tongues that reach into the flowers. Nectar-eaters include the hummingbirds, which are able to hover above a flower and divest it of its nectar with ease. Hummingbirds are found only in the New World; their Old World counterparts are the sunbirds. Other nectar-eaters include the honeyeaters and flowerpeckers (*Dicaeum*) of eastern Australia,

Puffin (*Fratercula arctica*), or sea-parrot, with its beak full of small fish which it has just caught. Plankton, small cephalopods and fish make up the menu of this strange northern bird. *Phot. Bel-Vienne—Jacana*

Vultures are foremost among the eaters of carrion. Battle of lappet-faced vultures (*Torgos tracheliotus*) for the remains of a corpse. *Phot. J. and M. Fiévet—Vasselet-Jacana*

the African sugarbirds (*Promerops*), white-eyes (*Zosterops*) of the Old World tropics, American honeycreepers (*Cyanerpes*) and Hawaiian honeycreepers (Drepanididae), and lories, which are bright-coloured parrots from Australasia. Lories and honeyeaters are important in the pollination of many Australian trees and shrubs.

Apart from the hummingbirds, most nectar-eaters sit beside a flower and reach down among the petals or peck through them to reach the nectar inside. Few birds feed exclusively on nectar, and many nectar-eaters supplement their diets with insects or fruit.

A bird's day

The daily activities of birds vary greatly from one species to another, depending on the ways in which they are adapted to their various environments. The behaviour of any single bird, however, will not change much from day to day, for it always faces the same tasks—the need to find food, to be comfortable, to find a safe place to shelter, and to work with others if it is a social bird. Behaviour will change from season to season, as food availability varies or migration takes place, and a bird's activities undergo a drastic change during the breeding season.

The duration of the search for food varies from species to species. Birds that feed on insects, worms and nectar must look for food almost ceaselessly whereas seed-eaters can often afford to take a rest. Birds that eat fish, flesh or carrion will gorge themselves after making a catch, kill or find, and then often fast for days on end. When replete, these birds rest and hardly move, unless they have to find food for a mate on the nest or for their young.

In the course of a day, a bird may fly an astonishing distance, covering many miles without becoming fatigued as mammals do. A tit, on the lookout for grubs and insects, has to fly some 50 to 60 miles a day flitting to and fro among a patch of woodland or park just to ensure a meagre supply of food for its

Long-legged buzzard (*Buteo rufinus*) dismembering a pigeon. *Phot. Brosset—Jacana*

The wood kingfisher (*below*) in the same family (Alcedinidae) as kingfishers; it lives not near water, but in forests, feeding on reptiles, insects, and small vertebrates. Its beak is remarkably strong. This photograph shows the giant Australian laughing kookaburra (*Dacelo gigas*). Its call sounds like mocking laughter. *Photo. Researchers—Brownlie*

European kingfisher returning to its nest with a fish. *Phot. Hosking*

young. In tracing out their arabesques in the sky, swifts can fly a total of some 600 miles between sunrise and sunset. The grey gull (*Larus modestus*), which nests in the deserts of Chile, thinks nothing of flying 60 miles to the sea coast for a meal, and it makes this journey every day. Some Manx shearwaters (*Puffinus puffinus*) ringed on the island of Skokholm off the coast of Wales were found to fly more than 300 miles to the Bay of Biscay in search of food during the breeding season.

In deserts, the need to find water may force seed-eating species to cover considerable distances. The sandgrouse (*Pterocles*) does so, but seed-eating passerines such as the trumpeter bullfinch (*Bucanetes githagineus*) live only near springs and wells.

Activities relating to comfort comprise, among others, the need to keep clean and maintain the plumage in good condition. Many birds bath in water, dew, or snow. Not only aquatic birds do so, but also many passerines. Birds of prey take dust baths, and so too do some passerines and even birds that also bath in water. A strange cleaning method using ants

Opposite page, herons (Ardeidae) eat fish, frogs, worms, molluscs and even small mammals. This species is a night heron (*Nycticorax nycticorax*), a mainly nocturnal species, on the fishing grounds. *Phot. J. L. S. Dubois*
Below, Sarus crane (*Grus antigona*) fishing. This beautiful crane is found in the South of Asia. A closely related species inhabits Australia (*G. rubicunda*). Here it is searching the water for fish, molluscs and worms with the end of its long beak. *Atlas-Photo—de Klemm*

The little hermit hummingbird (*Phaetornis longuemareus*), found in Mexico and Brazil, lives in the shadow of tall brushwood or at the edge of the primitive forest. It visits flowers to collect its food, tiny insects or nectar, by plunging its beak into the corollas or by piercing them at their base. *Phot. B. Brower Hall*

Sunbirds, charming little birds of the family Nectariniidae, which feed on the nectar of flowers, are particularly abundant in tropical Africa.
Phot. J. F. and M. Terrasse

has been observed in more than 200 species of birds. The bird finds a group of ants, or attacks an anthill to stir up some ants. It then lies over the ants with its wings spread out. The ants swarm over the feathers, killing parasites and squirting out formic acid, which acts as an insecticide. Some birds, especially small species, apply ants to their plumage instead of lying over them. The ants are picked up one by one in the bill and placed among the feathers, especially the undersides of the wings and tail. Immediately after anting, the bird takes a bath in water. In some species, small beetles are used instead of ants.

Bathing cleans the plumage, but the bird's toilet has not yet finished. After the bath, the bird gives itself a good shake to dry the feathers and then runs its large wing feathers, and often the tail feathers too, one by one through its beak. This action zips up any ragged vanes and enables the bird to examine its most important feathers individually and thoroughly. Cormorants and darters dry out their plumage by roosting with their wings held wide open.

With the feathers clean and dry, the bird now begins to preen itself. It dips its beak in the oil secreted by the preen gland (see page 442), and spreads the oil over its feathers. The plumage of the head and neck, which is out of reach of the beak, is oiled by rubbing these parts directly on the preen gland. The oil serves to keep the keratin supple and helps to keep the plumage waterproof and air tight.

Grooming, by scratching with the claws, shaking the feathers and stretching the wings, usually takes place on waking. It is also done at intervals during the day.

After waking, birds may utter a series of calls or some snatches of song, depending on the species and on the time of year. Their toilet performed, most birds then set out in search of food. A break is nearly always taken about the middle of the day and then the quest is resumed in the afternoon, normally going on until the early evening. Pigeons break off early, finding their way back to their sleeping quarters long before sunset. Woodpeckers finish searching for food around sunset, but falcons and sparrowhawks carry on until it is almost completely dark.

Some birds spend the night together in groups. Starlings do so, and so too do migrating swallows, which often sleep in enormous formations among reeds. The group usually consists of birds of the same species, but sometimes birds of related species sleep together. Wood pigeons and doves often roost for the night in certain trees in woods and parks. In the morning, one can sometimes see them setting off in different directions to their various feeding grounds. A bird must find a quiet sheltered place in which to sleep. Many small insect-eaters and seed-eaters will retire to a thick bush. Woodpeckers choose a hole in a tree. Treecreepers sleep hanging vertically between projecting pieces of bark on a tree trunk and, in winter, they often sleep huddled together in groups to keep warm. The same desire to keep out the cold once led some migrating spinetailed swifts (*Chaetura vauxi*) to swarm together along the

480

Male green woodpecker (*Picus viridis*) emerging from its nest hole with wood shavings in its beak. *Atlas-Photo—Merlet*

trunk of a tamarisk in an extraordinary cluster. The mass of birds measured four feet long and a foot broad, and was as many as three birds thick!

Many birds take up a territory for breeding, tolerating no other birds of their species except for their mates. When the offspring are old enough, they are driven from the territory to begin their own lives. Many birds also adopt a certain territory for wintering. A territory may in fact be no more than a certain amount of space around the bird, wherever it happens to be. But it is often a fixed piece of ground, either centred around the nest or existing as a personal feeding place for the bird. The territory may be very restricted, being limited, for example, to the nest itself and its immediate vicinity. This is often the case with birds that nest communally.

With solitary birds, the territory that is selected and subsequently defended against all intruders is often extensive, comprising the nest and an area large enough to provide an adequate food supply. The area must be large enough to support the parents and young during the breeding season.

The defence of the territory is usually the responsibility of the male, but often the female also takes part. It is directed against other birds of the same species, though rarely against those of closely related species. If such birds are present, there is competition both for food and nesting sites. Defence of the territory is of course also directed against predators. It is not unusual at breeding time for passerines, especially ravens (*Corvus corax*) and hooded crows (*C. corone cornix*), to attack birds of prey that are much stronger than themselves. Predatory mammals such as foxes and snakes may be violently attacked by ground-nesting birds such as skuas, gulls and terns, and also by tree-dwelling birds. Some owls will attack in-

Most birds are careful about their toilet and, in hot weather, bathe each day. Here, a redstart (*Phoenicurus phoenicurus*) is seen taking a bath at the edge of a stream. *Atlas-Photo—Merlet*

Eleonora's falcon (*Falco eleonorae*) attacking a montpellier snake (*Malpolon monspessulanus*) *Phot. J. L. S. Dubois*

truders on their territories. Intimidating postures of the body or vocal menaces are usually sufficient to 'repel boarders'. Singing is indulged in to proclaim ownership of a territory and to warn off all intruders, as well as to attract a mate. Birds often sing loudly at the boundaries of their territories—presumably in order continually to define the positions of the boundaries. Repeated calls from the territory may also be defensive in purpose. If such intimidation fails, then the territory owner, particularly if it is an aggressive bird, may resort to actual combat. Usually, however, intimidation is sufficient to prevent intrusion.

There is no doubt that the dividing up of land into territories is of great survival value to the species involved. The food supplies in a given area are not overstretched if the birds space themselves out in this way. The value is obvious where the territories are situated around the nests, but some birds defend territories that are far from the nest and not used for food. However, these territories are used as display grounds by the males and it is there that the males and females come together for mating. Even though their union may be very short-lived and the birds soon part and disperse, the brief existence of their territories is essential to the propagation of these species. Birds that breed in this way include the ruff (*Philomachus pugnax*), the red grouse, the capercaillie (*Tetrao urogallus*), the black grouse (*Lyrurus tetrix*), the prairie chicken (*Tympanuchus cupido*), the sharp-tailed hazel grouse (*Pediocetes phasianellus*), the manakins (*Manacus*), some birds of paradise and hummingbirds (*Phaetornis*), and the cock of the rock (*Rupicola rupicola*). It ensures that the birds come together at the most suitable time of year, rather than leaving meetings to chance.

Social life

The first days of life of almost all birds are spent as members of a family. But the family ties are temporary, for the young bird will sooner or later leave its parents. If social life is to continue, as it does among many birds, then other ties must take the place of the family ties. In fact, many birds find it to their advantage to live among others of their kind. They experience social ties binding them to a group of birds throughout their lives. Other birds lead solitary lives for most of the year, but organize themselves in social ways for breeding and migration; for example, birds such as ruffs gather at their display grounds prior to mating. At migration time, solitary birds such as bitterns and orioles may be seen travelling together in loosely-knit groups. Other birds are social outside the breeding season, and in birds that nest in isolation, flocks may form at other times. This is the case with larks, cranes, geese, thrushes and partridges. This social behaviour ceases shortly before breeding, when couples pair off and keep to themselves.

Sometimes social ties are not directed towards birds of the same species, but towards other species, especially when both species feed in the same way. Outside the breeding season, it is possible to see parties of birds on the move in search of insects or a particular fruit. In temperate regions, it is common to see mixed groups of different species of tits, for example. In tropical countries, parties of more varied species may assemble. In Central and South America, these parties readily follow armies of ants; the birds do not attack the ants themselves but eat the insects that flee from the marauders. These groups may

Spoonbills (*Platalea leucorodia*) nest in a group on the same trees. Each one defends its nest very vigorously. *Phot. J. M. Baufle*

Many water birds have social habits. In some species of terns, in a colony, the female lays only if the society falls below a certain number of individuals. Here, a society of sooty terns which, having been startled, has just taken off. *Phot. J. F. Terrasse*

be made up of birds that come to spend the winter in the tropics as well as of indigenous birds.

In a society of birds, a heirarchy is set up between its various members. This is most apparent in small groups and difficult to assess in large flocks.

Instinct

Instinct guides a bird through its life, ruling its every action at a basic level. Among the many examples of instinctive behaviour, take for example the begging of nidicolous chicks for food. This behaviour—stretching their necks up and opening their mouths—takes place in response to a definite stimulus, such as a slight tremor of the nest or a darkening at the entrance hole in the case of a nest built inside a tree hole or burrow. The stimuli are, of course, produced by the arrival of the parent with food. The parent also acts instinctively in feeding the young, finding that the gaping mouths produce an irresistible urge to drop food into them. Another example of an instinctive action is the way in which some birds freeze stock-still when in danger. At such times, the correct action must be performed immediately and instinct comes to the rescue, for there is no time to think. Instinctive behaviour for dealing with danger exists right from birth. It may be very specific, for birds will react in alarm when shown a silhouette of a bird of prey (long wings and a short neck) but not a silhouette of a harmless bird such as a goose (short wings and a long neck).

Acquired behaviour and learning

Although instinct gives a bird a basic set of instructions for life, many aspects of its behaviour must be refined by learning. Some birds can learn quickly and adapt their behaviour to suit changing circumstances. Others cannot, and are usually less successful because they are less adaptable. But many birds will adjust their behaviour, for example, in situations of danger, in relationships with other birds both of their own species and other species, and in breeding. The various actions may be modified by the individual bird as it gets older. This is not necessarily intelligent behaviour, but simply the conditioning of existing actions by experience.

Birds will sometimes make do with a diet alien to them if their usual food supply diminishes. In order to find new food, they may perform a new and unexpected action. Thus tits and lesser spotted woodpeckers have learned to remove or peck through the foil tops of milk bottles; it has been possible to observe this perhaps chance discovery evolve into a habit.

The most remarkable kind of acquired behaviour in any animal is the choice and use of tools, and birds provide several examples of tool using. Although it might seem a most intelligent thing to do, tool using in birds appears to be completely instinctive. Several species use the ground as a tool, dropping bones or shells from the air to open them and get at the food inside. Lammergeiers drop large bones and tortoise, Australian gulls (*Gabianus pacificus*) drop hard-shelled molluscs, and songthrushes (*Turdus philomelus*) break open snails in this way. The

483

Egyptian vulture (*Neophron percnopterus*) breaks open eggs by dropping them, but if the egg is too large to pick up, as is an ostrich egg, it will pick up stones instead and drop them on the egg to shatter the shell.

A more complex case of tool using has been observed in the woodpecker finch (*Cactospiza pallida*) of the Galapagos Islands. Like a woodpecker, it feeds on insects and grubs to be found among the bark of trees. However, it lacks the woodpecker's long tongue and so cannot rake out insects from crevices in the bark. Instead it takes a cactus spine or thin twig in its beak, and probes in the holes in the bark to flush out its prey. Another extraordinary example of the use of a tool by a bird is provided by three species of bowerbirds (*Chlamydera* and especially *Ptilonorhynchus violaceus*). These birds take up a twig as a brush, and daub the walls of their bowers with a paint made of saliva

Congregation of mainly Ardeiform birds around a water point: jabiru (*Ephippiorhynchus senegalensis*), woolly-necked stork (*Dissoura episcopus*), wood ibis (*Ibis ibis*), egret (*Egretta* sp. pl.) marabou (*Leptoptilos crumeniferus*), pelican (*Pelecanus*). *Phot. Vasselet—Jacana*

and natural pigments. Young bowerbirds are not shown this behaviour by their parents and so it cannot be learned. It must be completely hereditary.

Imprinting

In some species, the new-born chicks will follow the first living thing or moving object that they see and attach themselves to it as if it were their mother. Of course, in most cases it is the mother. The phenomenon is called imprinting, and it is so

strong that chicks can be imprinted on human beings or even models if the mother is absent. It takes place only in the first few hours after birth, and so is a totally instinctive action. Imprinting has been observed in turkeys, chickens, pheasants, quails and ducks. These birds are nidifugous, and imprinting helps to keep the well-developed young with their parents when they need their assistance.

Migration

Migration, particularly of birds, is a natural phenomenon that has long attracted man's attention and exercised his curiosity. Why do small birds such as swifts and swallows and large birds such as geese and storks undertake such spectacular journeys every year? Where do they go, and how do they manage to find their way? These are questions that demand answers from science, but migration is so complex that the answers are still incomplete.

Before examining bird migration in detail, we must remember that birds are not the only animals that migrate. Arthropods such as crustaceans, locusts and butterflies, several mammals (especially bats), and many fish carry out regular migrations, sometimes of remarkable distances. But migration is much more a feature of bird life than the life of other kinds of animals, for great numbers of birds migrate and they may cover world-wide distances. The reason of course is that birds can travel great distances with comparative ease, and so many choose to migrate rather than adapt to the varying climatic conditions of one particular place.

Even so, birds may have to pass through regions of varying conditions while migrating and they may have to fly at high altitudes, where it is cold. But birds are able to resist both great heat and great cold, being well insulated against temperature changes and having a circulatory and breathing system that enables them to maintain an optimum internal temperature in unfavourable external conditions. They also have the ability to adapt very rapidly to differences of altitude. And although a migration is a vast journey, it must not be forgotten that a bird covers a good many miles in the course of a normal day—searching for food, building a nest, feeding its young and flying in formation with the other birds of a flock. When the time comes for migration, the extra effort required is usually little more than that demanded by the bird's normal daily activities.

Birds may not be able to feed very much during the journey, however, and so they acquire a considerable layer of fat before setting off. This acts as a reserve of energy for the migration, especially for the crossing of inhospitable regions such as deserts. The weights of young passerine birds have been recorded in Nigeria, and they are always higher in the spring than in the autumn, when they have crossed the Sahara on returning from their breeding grounds. On the other hand, some long-distance migrants on their arrival in the extreme north of America during spring show no loss of weight. They lose weight some ten days after their arrival, but this is as a result of their breeding activities.

Causes of migration

The reason for migration is the fact that many birds cannot live all the year round in the place in which they were born and in which they breed. They are forced to leave when conditions become inhospitable, and return later when they improve. The most important factor controlling migration is the food supply: temperature comes second to this, because birds are well adapted to resist changes in temperature, although some species are more sensitive to cold than others. For example, the ortolan (*Emberiza hortulana*) is more sensitive to cold than the yellowhammer (*E. citrinella*). From this it follows that the former is a long-distance migrant, whereas the latter travels only short distances.

The main physical cause of migration then is lack of food; for instance, birds that nest in the tundra, which is covered with ice and snow during winter, must obviously leave at the end of summer, for they could not possibly survive the winter. Ducks must leave when it gets so cold that the water in which they find their food freezes over. Insect-eaters must also leave as winter approaches and their prey vanishes. The migration dates of white storks (*Ciconia ciconia*) in various regions perfectly illustrate how dependent migration is upon the food supply. In continental Europe, the storks arrive in February, March or April (depending on the mildness of the climate) and depart in mid-August. In warmer Spain, they appear sooner—at the end of January or February—but leave sooner—between 20 July and 10 August. In Morocco, they depart at about the same time as the storks in Spain but they arrive as early as December. The storks' arrival gets progressively earlier the farther south they go, for the necessary temperature to provide their food supply occurs earlier. But because it is hotter farther south, drought also occurs earlier in the year, and so the birds must leave earlier too as their food supply diminishes.

Not all members of a particular species migrate. Some populations may be migratory and others sedentary. The magpie (*Pica pica*) is a migrant in one part of Russia where the winter is savage; elsewhere in Europe, where it is milder, magpies are sedentary birds. Thrushes, blackbirds and finches are usually sedentary in the warmer parts of Europe and migratory in the colder parts. However, there may be appreciable variations within a given population. For example, some British song thrushes and lapwings (*Vanellus vanellus*) remain in Britain all the year round whereas others migrate to Spain and Morocco.

Apart from birds that breed in the far north, which are driven to migrate as snow and ice arrive, long-distance migrants take wing some time before their food supply runs out and usually depart when the weather is still favourable. Somehow, the birds have a warning system that tells them it is time to migrate, even though external conditions have not changed very much. There has been some research into the internal or external stimuli that actuate migration.

The demands of migration require that the bird be in good physical condition. Its annual cycle of physiological changes is therefore important. In the course of a year, the bird breeds, changes its plumage once or twice, and makes journeys of varying scope, depending on the species. These journeys are called migrations if they take place over long distances. The factor that governs these various functions is the endocrine cycle. The development of the sexual organs prior to breeding depends on the production of gonadatrophic hormones by the pituitary gland. Moulting depends on thyroid activity, which

Flight of herring-gulls (*Larus argentatus*) in the neighbourhood of the colony. *Phot. Brosselin—Jacana*

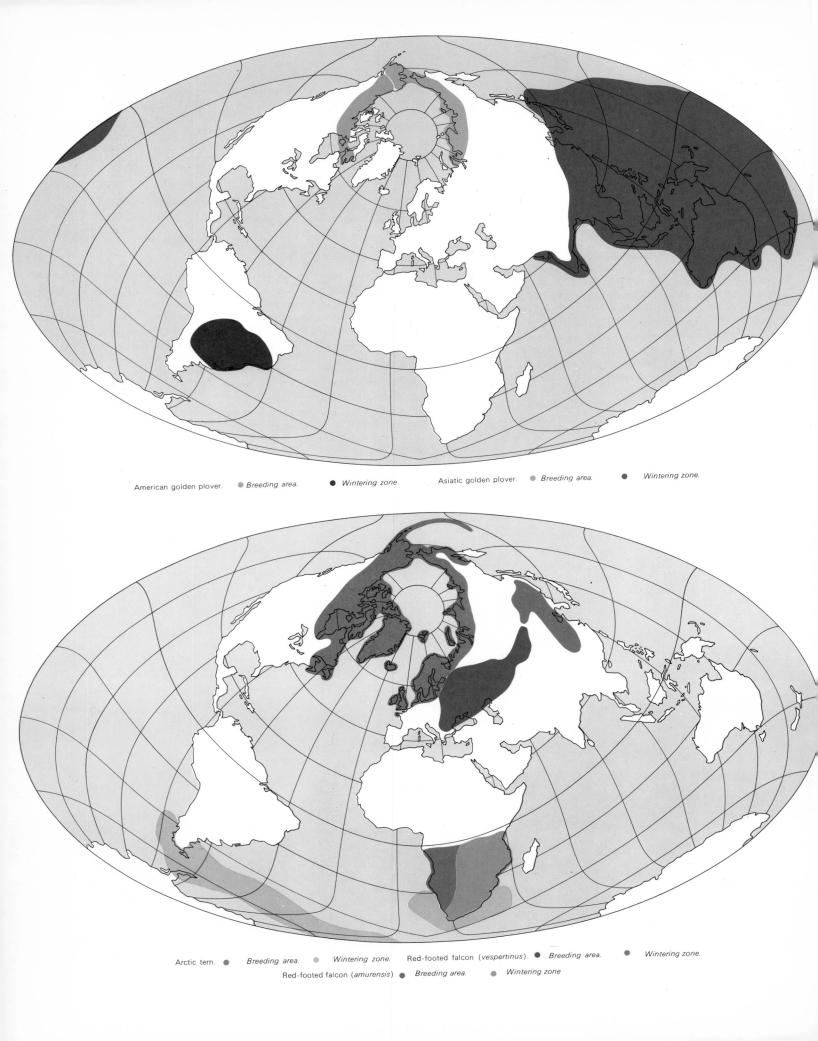

American golden plover. ● *Breeding area.* ● *Wintering zone.*   Asiatic golden plover. ● *Breeding area.* ● *Wintering zone.*

Arctic tern. ● *Breeding area.* ● *Wintering zone.*   Red-footed falcon (*vespertinus*). ● *Breeding area.* ● *Wintering zone.*

Red-footed falcon (*amurensis*). ● *Breeding area.* ● *Wintering zone*

is controlled by the thyrotrophic hormone made in the pituitary gland. Proclactin, another pituitary hormone, inhibits moulting, whereas progesterone, a female sex hormone produced by the ovary, promotes moulting. A bird cannot migrate when it is breeding, for the young must have become independent (or nearly so in the case of terns) to be able to take part in the migration. Usually the migrant moults before its journey, although some migrants moult afterwards. As moulting uses up valuable reserves of fat which are needed for migration, it is unusual for birds to migrate when they are actually changing their plumage.

After breeding, the sexual organs become inactive until the next breeding season. The change in metabolism that results causes deposits of fat to be formed. Even if they are immediately used up, they quickly form again. These deposits of fat must be present before the bird can migrate. Then certain stimuli become capable of triggering off the urge to migrate, and these stimuli appear to vary from species to species.

As it is obvious that the whole sexual cycle and metabolism of a bird are under the general control of the pituitary gland, attempts have been made to determine which stimuli can act directly on the gland. It has been found that the pituitary passes through phases of receptivity and non-receptivity to certain stimuli, including a daily increase in hours of daylight. This increase, which is readily noticeable in the Northern Hemisphere from January to February, could therefore play a decisive role in sparking off the spring migration of species that live to the north of the tropic of cancer. But species that winter around the equator, between the Tropic of Cancer or Tropic of Capricorn, experience no appreciable variation in the hours of daylight from one time of the year to the next, and yet the spring migration to the breeding grounds takes place at the necessary time. External factors cannot operate in such cases, and we must look for internal changes. There must be an internal rhythm in the activity of the pituitary gland.

The migration behaviour of the various subspecies of yellow wagtails (*Motacilla flava*) provides evidence of such an internal rhythm. The European populations of these birds winter in tropical Africa. Because of the differences in the pattern of the head plumage in these subspecies, it has been easy to trace their migration movements, and ornithologists have found that they do not return to their countries of origin at the same time.

The black-headed subspecies (*M.f. feldegg*) sets off first and

rhythm operating at a differing pace depending on the latitude of origin of each subspecies. The biological rhythm of the yellow wagtail comprises a pre-nuptial moult carried out in winter before migration, then a building-up of fat reserves and finally, but only in the course of migration, the development of the sexual organs. It is possible that the stimulus for sexual development is external, being triggered off by changes in hours of daylight, for it occurs only when the birds have reached the Mediterranean region and are well towards the temperate zone.

Similar differences in internal rhythm can be observed in birds of related species. The common swift (*Apus apus*) and pallid swift (*A. pallidus*) both nest in the Mediterranean region, but the pallid swift arrives sooner and leaves much later than the common swift, and it usually rears two broods whereas the common swift raises one. Such breeding behaviour indicates a great difference in internal rhythm, which is confirmed by the early departure of the common swift. This swift leaves when the food supply obviously is still adequate, for the pallid swift can remain.

More is known about the stimuli that determine the departure date of the autumn migration. Here external factors, such as a decrease in temperature and a shortening in the hours of daylight may operate, but the internal rhythm seems to be dominant, even if it is influenced by external factors.

Ringing and birdwatching

In Europe and North America there are now many centres for ringing and observing birds. Birdwatchers can provide valuable information on the numbers and directions of migrating flocks during the day, and radar observations complete their work by night. Ringing makes it possible to find out the routes that migrating birds follow, the location of their winter quarters and breeding grounds, the duration and speed of the migration flights, and whether birds use the same wintering and breeding places every year. Ringing may also tell us the average lifespans of different birds.

Ringing stations also operate in Asia (mainly Japan and India), South Africa, Australia and New Zealand. The

Flight of brent geese (*Branta bernicla*) on the western coasts of France *Phot. Brosselin—Jacana*

nests in southeast Europe. It is followed by the blue-headed (*flava*) and kirghiz steppes (*lutea*) subspecies from western Europe and southeast Russia respectively. Finally, the grey-headed (*thunbergi*) subspecies sets off for the far north, leaving two months later than the first wagtails. A similar movement occurs in Asia for the Asiatic subspecies. Being members of the same species, the birds have basically the same internal rhythm. External conditions in the wintering grounds are the same, and so migration must be triggered by an internal

percentage of ringed birds subsequently recovered varies greatly from species to species. The fraction is relatively high in the case of ducks, reaching almost twenty per cent. But only about one per cent of small insect-eating passerines that have been ringed are ever found again.

Birds are ringed in the nest or when they pass near ringing stations, which are mostly situated along migration routes. The job is done by trained experts, though subsequent recovery may depend on amateur birdwatchers.

Ringing a European kingfisher (*Alcedo atthis*). *Atlas-Photo—Dragesco*

Types of migration

A fair number of birds migrate alone and not in flocks. They include hummingbirds; passerines such as orioles (*Oriolus oriolus*), nightingales and warblers; cuckoos; birds of prey such as the osprey (*Pandion haliaetus*) and short-toed eagle (*Circaetus gallicus*), and marine robbers such as skuas. But in certain solitary birds such as bitterns, birdwatchers in some places have observed a tendency for them to gather in small groups for migration. Willow warblers, pipits and some other species travel in small and sometimes loose groups, so that the individual birds may be seen arriving one after the other. Goldfinches, linnets (*Acanthis cannabina*), yellow wagtails and turtle doves travel in much larger groups. Some gulls and terns travel in families, or in groups of families. The parents migrate with their young, which can fly well, but occasionally have to be fed by their elders. Honey buzzards (*Pernis apivorus*) migrate in many small, compact groups, each comprising a few dozen individuals. On the other hand, some species, such as starlings and pigeons, migrate in vast flocks that may contain hundreds or even thousands of birds. Among the most spectacular migration flights ever seen were those of the passenger pigeon (*Ectopistes migratorius*), which used to darken the skies of North America as flocks of millions passed overhead. Audubon writes of flocks stretching for 2 miles in length and $\frac{1}{4}$ of a mile in width! In spite of its enormous numbers, the passenger pigeon is today extinct, having been slaughtered out of existence.

It is not rare to see different species accompanying each other on migration. This applies to many ducks, waders, finches, crows, birds of prey, terns and gulls. Clearly, birds flying together must have similar flight patterns, but it is unlikely that such communal journeying takes place on any permanent basis.

Migrating birds fly at a more or less constant pace, without the bursts of speed or periods of slow flight that occur in their everyday life. Migrating swifts keep up a steady 60 miles an hour, geese manage 50 mph, and roller swallows and crows maintain some 40 mph. Ducks can do up to 50 to 55 mph, scoters (*Melanitta*) going even faster. On the other hand, small passerines such as tits and willow warblers (*Phylloscopus*) scarcely exceed 20 mph.

Wind is a very important factor in migration, for a strong wind can impede flight. Direction is not as important as strength. When the wind is of light or average force, birds migrate irrespective of wind direction. However, some species prefer a head wind on their autumn migration and small passerines undertake their spring migrations with the aid of a following wind. A strong head wind seriously interferes with flying and a strong following wind stops migration. Wind can also force migrating birds off course, especially if they are flying over the sea and the wind is strong and sustained. This often explains the appearance of 'accidental' species—birds that are seen in a region only on rare occasions. Strong winds may even carry migrating birds across the Atlantic Ocean, usually from America to Europe, although there is a well-

White-rumped swift (*Apus affinis*) and pallid swift (*Apus pallidus*), from the South of the Mediterranean, hanging on to a rock. *Phot. J. L. S. Dubois*

known case of a flock of lapwings being blown in the other direction. Small passerines are sometimes able to cross the ocean, though they may alight on ships and not fly all the way.

Other meteorological conditions besides wind may affect migration. Heavy rain can delay migration, and a rainy front may even cause migrating birds to turn back. Thick fog confuses the birds' sense of direction, and birds lost in fog at sea may tire and drown.

Flying height varies with climatic conditions and the nature of the terrain below. When the weather is fine and the wind is light or moderate, many migrants can be seen flying low over sea or land. Finches migrating along the coast of Holland fly at some 650 feet, but a following wind will force them up a thousand feet higher. Some species fly higher than others. On crossings of the Sahara, swallows are attracted to desert convoys in search for food. House martens and swifts, however, are not seen by the convoys and must therefore fly much higher than swallows.

Mountain ranges are not necessarily obstacles to migration, though birds tend to use passes in crossing them. Altitude does

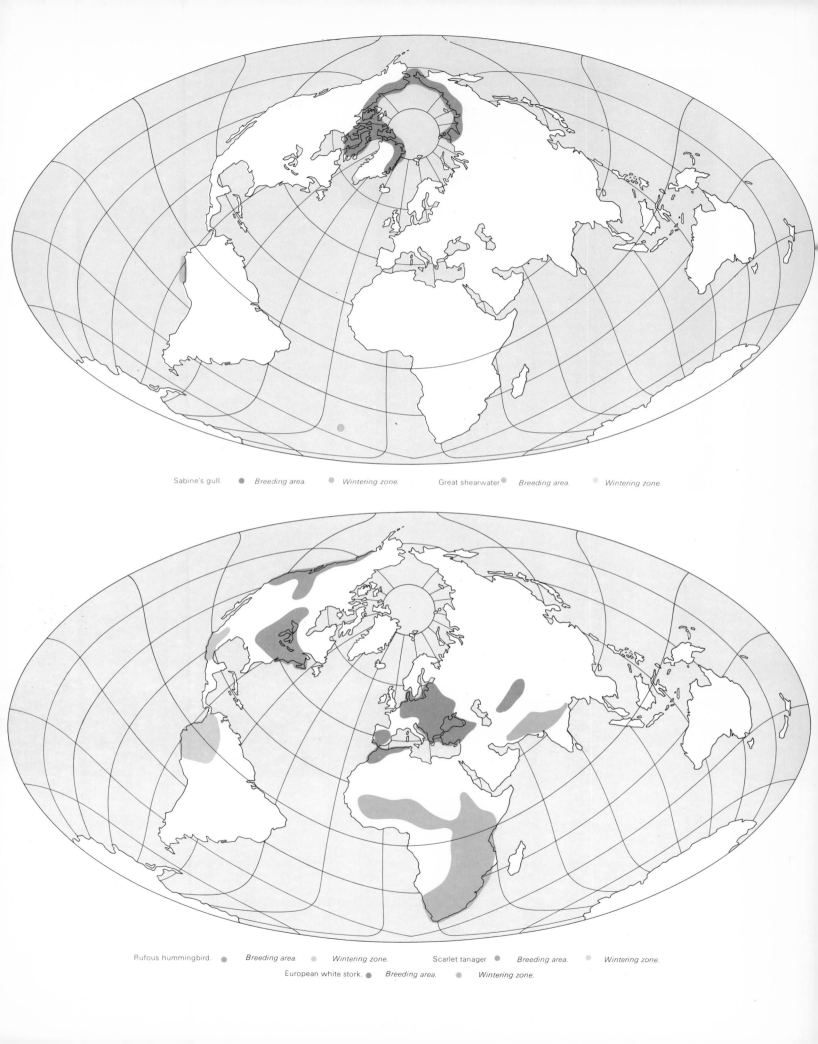

Sabine's gull.   ● *Breeding area.*   ● *Wintering zone.*   Great shearwater. ● *Breeding area.*   ● *Wintering zone.*

Rufous hummingbird.   ● *Breeding area.*   ● *Wintering zone.*   Scarlet tanager ● *Breeding area.*   ● *Wintering zone.*

European white stork. ● *Breeding area.*   ● *Wintering zone.*

not seem to have very much effect, for teal, geese and terns regularly cross ranges as high as the Himalayas. The main danger presented by such high mountains is the likelihood of bad weather such as snow storms and thick cloud. Birds are able to cope with considerable differences in temperature and atmospheric pressure, and some birds have been observed around the summits of the highest mountains. Alpine choughs (*Pyrrhocorax graculus*) have been observed at 26,900 feet on Mount Everest. Even above flat, low-lying ground or the sea, birds have been recorded at immense heights. Radar observations have detected nocturnal passerine migrants at over 20,000 feet. But such heights are not common. Most passerines fly below 5000 feet, a few rising to 14,000 feet. Above the Rhineland in Germany, flying heights of 2500 to 8000 feet have been reported for wood pigeons, 2000 to 6500 feet for cranes, and 2000 to 7500 feet for rooks. In Britain, waders, especially lapwings, migrate at 3000 to 6000 feet, maintaining this height over the sea at night. A case is known of a flock of 200 wood pigeons crossing southern Greece at 13,000 feet. Flying height therefore seems to vary a great deal and depend on local conditions.

The sea is not usually an obstacle to migration. Bad weather is dangerous at sea, so birds mainly cross water in good weather, when they are in fact likely to encounter fewer difficulties than migrating over land. Along the coast of the Landes in southwest France, larks have been observed to fly over the sea rather than above the sand dunes on the shore. Similarly, regular flights by large flocks of turtle doves and ring ouzels over the island of Yeu in the Bay of Biscay show that these birds prefer a sea crossing to a detour—however slight—via the nearby continental coastline. Although a sea crossing may be extremely tiring, some species regularly migrate several thousand

moorhens and rails. Although oases and wells may provide occasional resting places, birds try to cross the Sahara as quickly as possible and speed up their flight accordingly. However, it is odd to note that some birds do not always cross the desert in a north-south direction, which is the shortest route, but may fly to the north-east or south-west.

In some species migration is carried out by day and in others by night. Diurnal birds of prey, orioles, swallows, larks, finches and buntings, wagtails, bee-eaters and storks migrate by day. Thrushes, warblers, flycatchers and shrikes travel at night. Ducks, geese and waders are more likely to migrate during the night, but cranes show no preference either way. Swifts (*Apus* and *Chaetura*) migrate by day, but in some cases, the flight may continue overnight.

Birds that migrate at night set off shortly after sunset and their flight continues, apparently, until daylight. Then they stop, spending the day resting and finding food. Birds that travel by day do so mainly in the morning.

During migration, birds may halt for one or two days or perhaps even longer. These halts probably come after long stretches of sustained flight, and they are made in places that are particularly rich in food. Sometimes unfavourable weather dictates that a stop be made. This is very likely to occur when the bird is returning to its breeding grounds, cold regions holding up progress.

It has been noted that the arrival of certain species in Europe roughly follows a particular isotherm (a line joining places of the same temperature). The swallow (*Hirundo rustica*) and the willow warbler (*Phylloscopus trochilus*) move into Europe at the same time as the 48° F isotherm does. But these birds stop or even turn back if they encounter regions below this temperature.

Left, black-tailed godwits (*Limosa limosa*). Godwits migrate in large groups. *Right,* flight of European starlings (*Sturnus vulgaris*) wintering in Algeria. *Phot. Brosselin-Fornairon—Jacana*

miles across oceans. Only if they encounter storms en route do large numbers of birds perish. However, a few species avoid sea crossings as much as possible; the white stork is an example, for the European populations mostly travel south via the Bosporus or the Straits of Gibraltar.

Desert crossings constitute another hazard for migrating birds, especially over large tracts of desert such as the Sahara. Even so, many migrants fly over this desert twice a year, especially small passerines and aquatic birds such as ducks,

How far do migrating birds fly in a day? Obviously this depends on the speed they can maintain, which in turn is related to climatic conditions and the nature of the terrain. Diurnal migrants probably travel more slowly than nocturnal ones, for birds flying by night must experience some difficulty in making a landfall in the dark and so press on with their journeys. However, birds are believed to cover from 125 to 375 miles for each period of 24 hours. When halts are taken into consideration, the daily average is lower, often much so.

A yellow wagtail ringed in Poland and recovered 26 days later in Italy had covered an average of only 28 miles a day. But birds recovered only a few days after ringing show higher averages—60 miles a day for 10 days and 240 miles a day over 4 days in the case of the garden warbler (*Sylvia borin*), 50 miles a day over 3 days for the sedge warbler (*Acrocephalus schoenobaenus*), and nearly 70 miles a day for periods of 9 and 15 days for the wheatear. One of the most remarkable migration flights ever recorded was that of a knot (*Calidris canutus*) which had covered more than 3000 miles in 8 days—an average speed of nearly 400 miles a day!

The return to the breeding grounds takes place more quickly than the second migration of the year. But a complete population of a given species does not migrate at the same time and individual differences in migration speed occur in birds of different sex and age. In species where one sex (usually the male) takes no part in rearing the young, the migration of the males takes place separately and earlier than the females' journeys. In many ducks, the males set off first, often to carry out a 'moulting migration'. This kind of migration is found mostly in ducks. They lose all their flight feathers at once, and then are unable to fly for some time. During this enforced halt for moulting, the ducks hide among water plants on ponds and lakes in favourable regions, such as the Volga delta or the high plateau of Tibet. With the exception of the shelduck (*Tadorna tadorna*), males and females arrive at the moulting grounds at different times. Shelducks arrive together at little bays, such as those of Heligoland, to moult. Both parents are concerned with rearing the young.

Apart from these moulting migrations, it is not unusual for individuals of different sex and age to travel at different times. In chaffinches (*Fringilla coelebs*), the adult males are more

from the summer-autumn journey. In many species that occupy fixed territories for breeding, the males migrate first and select the territory. They then await the females, which arrive, on average, a fortnight later.

But such behaviour in which birds of different sexes migrate separately, is not the rule. For example, in some geese such as the snow goose (*Anser caerulescens*), family ties are maintained during the journey from the breeding grounds and do not fade on the wintering grounds. Families of the brent goose (*Branta bernicla*) remain together for only part of the migration. In some species, pairing may take place on the wintering grounds so that the return to the breeding grounds is made by couples rather than by individual birds. Pairing may also take place during pauses in the migration flight.

There are individual variations; for example, white storks, among others, are more likely to return to their nesting places alone rather than in couples.

Migration of young birds

In some species, especially herons, the young have only just fledged when they make considerable journeys. These journeys may take place in any direction, but are quite often to colder regions, i.e. towards the north in Europe and North America. In starlings (*Sturnus vulgaris*), the young gather in flocks in the summer and travel to places far from the breeding grounds. It seems that these special migrations by the young are not like normal migrations, but are merely a very pronounced manifestation of their tendency to disperse from the nest as soon as they leave it.

Left, white-fronted geese (*Anser albifrons*). White-fronted geese from Greenland and Iceland undertake southerly transatlantic flights to winter in the British Isles and France. *Right,* common wild ducks (*Anas platyrhynchos*) taking off. *Atlas-Photo —Morel; Jacana —Brosselin*

sedentary than the females; the females leave the breeding grounds first, sometimes preceded by the young, and some of the adult males follow but the majority stay put. Many other species act in the same way. But the opposite also happens: in the red-backed shrike (*Lanurius colluric*), the adults set off first and the young follow one by one. The fact is that there are no fixed laws regulating migration behaviour. Frequently local or annual variations are reported.

The spring migration may be quite different in character

Returning to the wintering grounds

By ringing, it has been found that many migrants show remarkable fidelity to their wintering grounds. Year after year they return to the same place, not only to the same country or region but often to the very same locality. Such fidelity is also found in the way many birds return to the same nesting site every year. But however much a bird may endeavour to reach the same destination, it may be led astray and deviate from its route for several reasons. Unfavourable meteorological conditions, especially strong winds, will make birds drift off-course. For example, in Britain birdwatchers have observed Scandinavian birds that should have migrated to the south or southeast but have been driven to the west by strong winds.

Among sociable birds such as ducks and herons, some owls that travel in groups, and storks, remarkable cases occur of birds flying off-course. A stork that usually wintered in Tunisia was once found in Israel. It seems that this bird had met up with some storks that wintered towards the east, and had gone along with them. Some British ducks, thought to be non-migratory, were once found in Finland. A night heron (*Nycticorax nycticorax*) from Spain was found two years later in Bulgaria, having been led there by eastern migrants like the stork already mentioned. A little bittern (*Ixobrychus minutus*) ringed in France was recovered the following spring in southern Russia. A short-eared owl (*Asio flammeus*), also of French origin, was recovered after five years in the Astrakhan district of Russia. Even individuals of species that are used to travelling singly may sometimes get completely lost and end up far away from their country of origin.

Navigation . . .

The ability of birds to navigate with such precision has been the subject of much research. A mistake was made at first in attempting to understand this ability by carrying out experiments with carrier pigeons. This particular bird, although it can navigate well over long distances, is in fact not a migratory bird and is normally a sedentary species. It is therefore not adapted physiologically to migration, and any conclusions drawn from its homing behaviour will not necessarily also apply to migrating birds.

We know from observations that a migrating bird selects a particular direction when it sets out to migrate to its winter quarters, and that this direction is not always in a straight line towards its destination, though it gets there eventually. The process is repeated when the bird returns to its country of origin.

How is a bird able to orientate itself in this way? It may seem that the bird possesses a special sense that enables it to get its bearings as infallibly as if it were guided by a compass. The existence of such a sense has not, however, been proved. It was once thought that the migrating bird is sensitive to the Earth's magnetism just as a compass is, but no indisputable proof of this theory has been found. Experiments concerned with direction finding often have unsettling effects on their subjects, and any results obtained with individual captive birds which are upset in this way do not prove anything.

In understanding migration, it is necessary to distinguish between two kinds of navigation. The first is simple navigation over short distances, depending on visual memory of the features of the terrain below. On setting out, the bird will fly up to a certain height and flutter around, looking out for landmarks before choosing its direction. The second kind of navigation is over long distances (sometimes of many thousands of miles), in which the correct direction is decided very rapidly and subsequently maintained over a long period often in unfamiliar surroundings.

Experiments by Kramer, Saver and Mathews have demonstrated that migrating birds possess the ability to take their bearings from the direction of the sun and, at night, from the stars. But, to make use of the sun or stars as direction indicators, the exact time of day or night must also be known so as to compensate for the rotation of the Earth. Ships and aircraft

have highly accurate chronometers, but birds too have a kind of clock, for it seems that they are able to judge time from the height of the sun above the horizon, which is at a maximum at noon. The stars change their pattern in the sky as the constellations circle around the celestial poles (the pole star in the northern hemisphere), and some birds can detect such changes in star pattern and derive the time from them. Experiments involving a special cage with an artificial sun that can be raised or lowered have demonstrated that birds react to the height of the sun. From this height, the bird seems to calculate the time that has passed since sunrise. Birds ready to migrate will orientate themselves in a certain direction in the cage, but if the height of the artificial sun is suddenly altered, the direction of orientation will also change abruptly.

The navigation of long-distance migrants such as European warblers, which fly as far as South Africa, can be explained in this way, provided that they experience clear weather during their flight. It is also believed that penguins find their way about the ocean and the featureless ice-cap in the same way. Cloudy weather and especially fog are known to disorientate migrants and cause penguins to swim or wander aimlessly. It makes migration so difficult that such weather conditions sometimes halt migrations.

The positions of the sun and stars in the sky are not necessarily the only factors governing navigation. Wind direction may also help a bird to find its bearings, although variations in wind direction are liable to lead the bird astray. It was probably an ability to sense the direction of the prevailing wind as well as the relative positions of the sun and stars that enabled some Manx shearwaters (*Puffinus puffinus*) taken from Skokholm in Wales and released at various points in Europe to find their way unerringly back to Skokholm very quickly. One bird was in fact taken to Boston in the United States, over 3000 miles away, and it was back at Skokholm only 12½ days after being released! To achieve such a speed, it must have flown on a precise and undeviating course across the Atlantic Ocean.

Experiments by Merkel and Wiltschko in 1965 carried out on European robins that were about to migrate tended to show that these birds continually flew off in the same direction, even when placed in a room or cage with no view of the outside. However, when the birds were placed in a special chamber made entirely of steel, they lost all sense of direction. The chamber was then subjected to an artificial magnetic field and the birds began to fly in different directions to their direction of migration. This experiment seems to show that the birds may respond to the Earth's magnetic field, though much work remains to be done to elucidate this.

Research on migration in general appears to show that the orientation of the bird is instinctive in the first place, but experience enables the bird to rectify its course more easily if it should drift off-route or take the wrong direction. One of the first experiments to test this conclusion was made by Schüz with white storks. These storks migrate south from central Europe by two main routes. One route goes west to the Straits of Gibraltar and other goes east to the Bosporus, for these birds do not like to cross water. A group of young storks raised by east-bound parents, and therefore about to make their first journey to the east, were taken to the departure point of some west-bound storks. They were released after the west-bound storks had gone, so that the young storks would not be influenced by any others. Schüz observed that more than 80 per cent of them made for the east, showing that the environment had little to do with migration and that the behaviour was mainly hereditary. However, on all occasions when the young birds flew with their elders, they were guided by the more experienced birds.

To these experiments on white storks must be added later

European starling (*Sturnus vulgaris*) feeding its young. *Phot. John Markham*

experiments made from 1948 to 1957 on starlings and finches. Starlings that breed in the lands around the Baltic Sea winter in Belgium, the British Isles and northwest France. Some also winter in Holland, though the majority of starlings seen there appear to be passing through. About 11,000 of these birds ringed, and captured were taken by aircraft to Basle, Zurich or Geneva in Switzerland and then released. Only 354 were later recovered, but this number of recoveries was sufficient to reveal some basic facts about migrating.

Normally, the birds that pass through Holland fly on in a westerly direction (from west-northwest to west-southwest). The young birds released in Switzerland maintained this direction, and therefore wintered in southern France and northern Spain. But the adult birds, who had made the wintering migration at least once before, rectified their orientation and were recovered in the Rhineland of Germany, in Holland and in northwest France and in Britain. Orientation is therefore instinctive in the first year of life, but the memory of previous journeys comes into play for older birds.

When young and adult birds were released together, the same results, curiously enough, were obtained. Although starlings are birds that travel in large flocks, there was a very marked difference between recoveries of young birds and recoveries of adults. The adults were found from the west to the northwest of the releasing site and the young from the west to the southwest. At first sight, therefore, it seems that instinct is so strong in the young that they cannot be diverted from their course by the older, more experienced birds. However, it does not follow that adult influence is never effective.

... is it instinctive or acquired?

A remarkable result of these experiments on young starlings was that the winter quarters subsequently chosen by the young birds that went off-course in their first year were the same as those reached in the first year, i.e. southern France and northern Spain, even though they returned to their places of origin, the Baltic lands, for breeding. The memory of the first winter quarters was stronger than the instinctive urge to fly to the west, for the winter quarters now lay to the south. Similar experiments with finches produced too few recoveries to come to any firm conclusions; however, the few recoveries that did occur tended to confirm those obtained from starlings. The experiments did show that young starlings migrate in the same direction as that followed by the population of which they are a part, and that they return in the following years to the winter quarters of their first year; if the adult birds go astray, they are able to re-orientate themselves to find their usual winter quarters.

Many experiments have been carried out to find out how migrating birds react to imposed deviations from their routes, and they generally indicate that a bird which has already experienced migration is capable of swiftly correcting its direction of travel to compensate for the deviation and will reach its intended destination. If an experiment is repeated with the same bird, it recovers more quickly than it did the

This Japanese brown shrike, which closely resembles the red-backed shrike, migrates to winter in the south of China, Indochina, Malaysia, and the Sunda Islands. *Phot. John Markham*

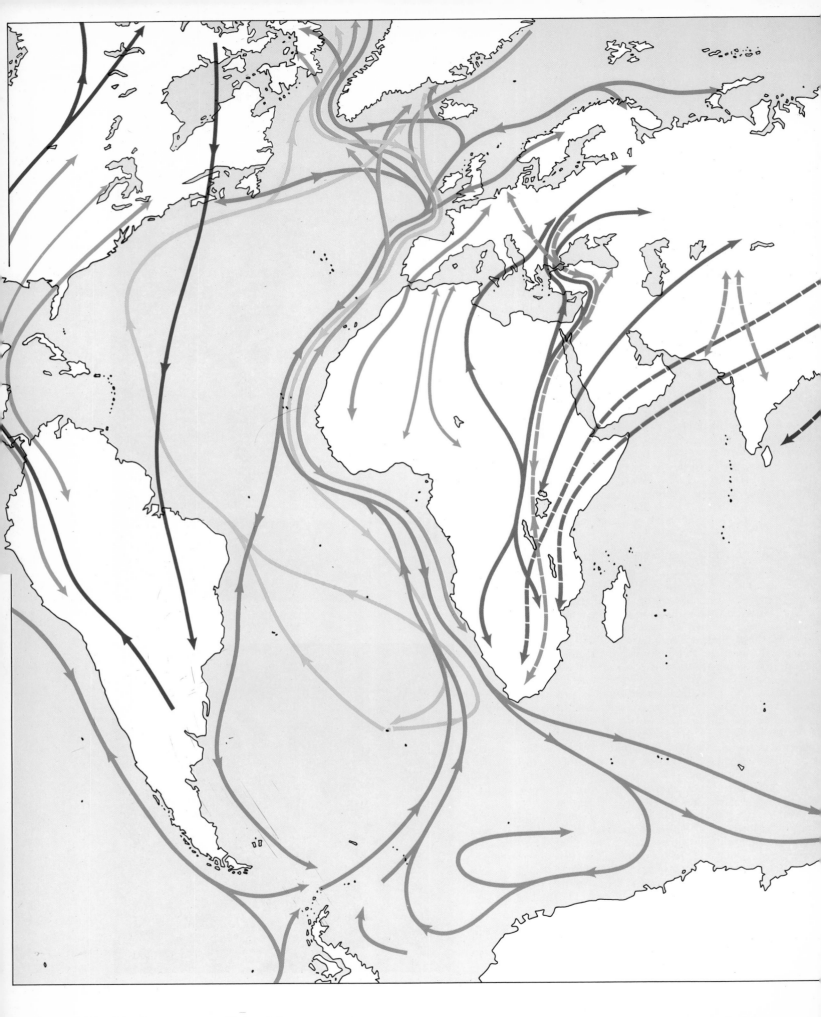

Routes of the long-distance migratory birds.

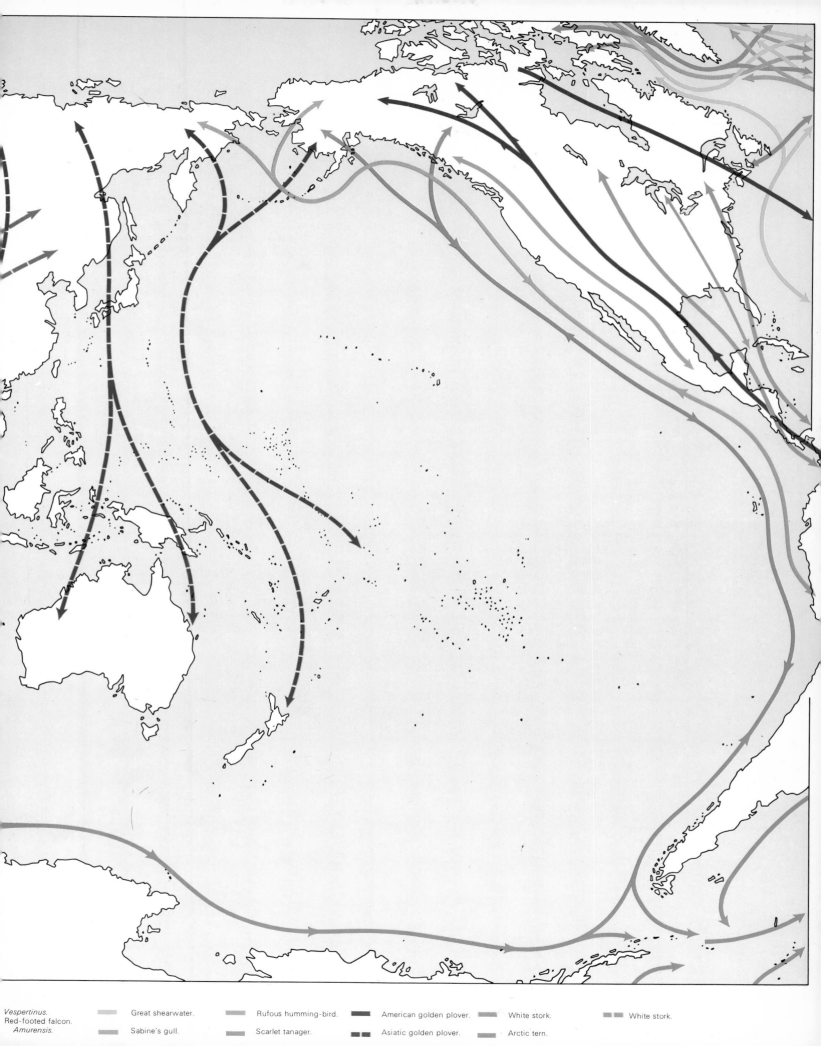

Vespertinus.
Red-footed falcon.
Amurensis.

Great shearwater.

Sabine's gull.

Rufous humming-bird.

Scarlet tanager.

American golden plover.

Asiatic golden plover.

White stork.

Arctic tern.

White stork.

previous time, probably because it remembers how to deal with the problem.

In general, the normal direction followed by a bird population seems to be clearly preferred to any other direction and, in most cases, young birds will migrate in this direction and disregard any misleading influences that the adults might bring to bear. Is such a preference instinctive? One would tend to think so, although this conclusion is not as yet incontrovertible.

It is certain however, that birds are physically highly sensitive towards migration. The approach of migration induces physiological changes that produce a certain 'excitement' in the bird. Fresh research on the physiology of migration is obviously desirable to investigate the hereditary and instinctive character of flight orientation.

Origins of migration

Migration appears to be primarily concerned with the maintenance of desirable living conditions. Its origins must be sought in the history of each species and even in the histories of the various populations within each species.

At the present time, migration in tropical and subtropical regions is usually not very extensive. As soon as the bird finds some food, it tends to stop. But the migration of birds in cold and temperate regions may be vast, involving journeys of many thousands of miles, often to other continents and sometimes to the other side of the world. How did such habits evolve?

There is every reason to believe that migration occurred in prehistoric time, probably as soon as birds themselves evolved. We cannot actually prove this of course, but the most recent glacial periods provide some evidence of early migration in the northern hemisphere.

Because of their great extent, glaciations have strongly influenced the climate of this hemisphere. Where snow and ice covered the land, no birds could survive. Even at the edges of the ice-cap, only a few species well adapted to the cold could live. There is an existing example of this in the distribution of birds in Greenland. Species that lived in regions that underwent glaciation were either annihilated as the snow and ice advanced, or they retreated before it and managed to survive in a region farther south, for example the Mediterranean lands. When the glaciers subsequently retreated, they left behind them great tracts of empty land open for recolonization. Birds came back to the northern lands, establishing themselves as far as the fringes of the Arctic Ocean. But the winter conditions of the lands were still too harsh to support most bird life, and the birds were forced to migrate during the cold season and return when conditions every year became more favourable. These annual migrations were short versions of the longer-term movements dictated by the advance and retreat of the glaciers.

This explanation fully accounts for the behaviour of European migrants such as starlings, thrushes and blackbirds, which winter in the mild climate of the Mediterranean. But there are also many birds that breed in the far north and migrate to tropical regions, frequently reaching beyond the equator to southern Africa, South America and Oceania. The history of these species may help to explain the problems posed by their migrations. It seems probable that many species driven to the Mediterranean by glaciation must, at that time, have migrated farther south in winter, soon reaching the equator and flying on beyond. When the

glaciers retreated and they established themselves in the far north, they retained their old wintering grounds even though they had farther to travel to reach them. This behaviour recalls that of the young starlings forcibly displaced and taking up new winter quarters as a result.

The retaining of the wintering grounds meant that the migration journey was considerably lengthened, and the old breeding grounds were crossed during the journey to and from them. A number of Palaearctic species (birds of Europe, north Africa and most of Asia) which nested as far as the east tip of eastern Siberia have crossed to the New World and become established in Alaska. They are the yellow wagtail (*Moticilla flava*), arctic warbler (*Phylloscopus borealis*) and wheatear (*Oenanthe oenanthe*). The crossing occurred a long time ago, and the New World populations have since evolved separately from their Asiatic neighbours and have developed a slightly different appearance. However, these birds have retained their Asiatic winter quarters and cross the Bering Sea in the course of their migrations. An American thrush has done the same thing in the opposite direction, becoming established in Siberia for breeding but still wintering in America.

The red-backed shrike (*Lanius collurio*) and the lesser grey shrike (*L. minor*) now breed from western France east to Iran and Turkestan (extending to northwest Spain and southern Britain at one end and Mongolia at the other in the case of *L. collurio*). The wintering zone of both these species is in southern and southeast Africa, and both use the eastern Mediterranean route to get there. This route is fairly direct for the nearer Asiatic populations, but a detour for the European populations. It is therefore probable that the colonization of Europe, and of the most easterly fringes of the breeding grounds, occurred after these migration habits had become established, and that the birds spread out from the Near East to colonize these regions.

Migration and climate

It has been observed that an improvement in the winter climate of a region induces the migratory birds there to migrate less far or even to remain in winter. Over the past

The ringed plover (*Charadrius hiaticula*) of Europe and Asia is one of the numerous migratory birds on the coasts of Europe. *Phot. Jean Philippe Varin—Jacana*

century in Finland the winters have become increasingly mild and birdwatchers have noticed that hooded crows (*Corvus corone cornix*) now migrate much less far in winter. Indeed, some do not now migrate at all. Although these birds used to be common winter visitors to France, sometimes travelling as far as the Pyrenees, by 1930 they had more or less ceased to fly beyond central France and they are now hardly seen there at all.

Fieldfares *(Turdus pilaris)* are normally migratory, and at the present time they are extending their breeding grounds to western Europe. A small group has even flown to the south of Greenland and bred there; but this thriving population is not migratory as it is probably averse to crossing the sea.

North America was colonized by European starlings from 1890 onwards. At first, there was a small sedentary local population in New York state, but with the rapid increase in numbers that ensued, the breeding area enlarged and migration developed in a part of the population. Now starlings from Quebec, Ontario and New York state winter as far afield as Ohio, some 600 miles from their breeding grounds.

It should be noted that within a given species, the populations inhabiting a region with a favourable climate are only slightly or not at all migratory, whereas populations situated in unfavourable areas are compelled to migrate some distance. For example, yellow wagtails are migratory throughout Europe but not in Egypt. Many birds that are migratory on the continent of Europe are sedentary in the less extreme climate of the British Isles.

It has also been observed that the farther north a population of birds nests, the farther south it migrates. Within a given species occupying a wide range of latitude, populations winter further and further to the south according to the degree northwards that they nest in summer. In Europe and Asia, the ringed plover (*Charadrius hiaticula*) is sedentary in the British Isles only; the populations in north Germany and Denmark winter in France and the Iberian peninsula; those in Scandinavia winter from Spain to Guinea; finally the most northern populations, in Lapland, northern Russia and Siberia, migrate all the way to Africa (including southern Africa), Arabia and India. In North America, the fox sparrow (*Passerella iliaca*) provides a similar example. It nests from the Aleutian Islands to Washington state, and whereas the most southerly populations are almost sedentary, the northernmost ones migrate farthest south to California. In between these two extremes, the populations winter farther south the more northerly they nest.

The influence of migration on distribution and physiology

It sometimes happens, for one reason or another, that birds remain in their winter quarters and breed there instead of returning to their breeding grounds. At the present time, a few pairs of white storks and European bee-eaters (*Merops apiaster*) are breeding in southern Africa. The former may come to be the nucleus of a southern population of white storks. It is probable that the pintail ducks (*Anas acuta*) of the Kerguelen Islands and the Crozet Islands in the Indian Ocean originated in this way. Over the ages, similar establishments of species must have taken place here and there.

The natural colonization of America by birds from the Old World provides a remarkable example of a small migrating group of birds causing a major change in the distribution of a species. The cattle egret or buff-backed heron (*Ardeola ibis*), which is widely distributed throughout Africa, was observed for the first time in America in French Guiana between 1877

and 1882, and then in Guyana (then British Guiana) in 1911 and 1912. It became common in Surinam from 1926 onwards, and today is found in South America as far south as Bolivia, in the Greater Antilles, in Florida, and it has been observed breeding in Texas as well as on the east coast of the United States. It is now approaching the New York area. In the United States, this species has kept is migratory habits.

Migration may also affect the size and shape of a bird as well as its distribution. In many animals, Bergman's law

The cattle egret or buff-backed heron (*Ardeola ibis*), of African origin, has crossed the Atlantic and become established in America, from the North of the United States to Bolivia. *Phot. Philippe Summ—Jacana*

operates. This law states that an animal is bigger the farther from the equator (north or south) that it lives. The reason is that large animals lose relatively less heat from their bodies than small animals. Migrating birds however do not obey the law. Migrants that nest in the far north and winter far to the south are in general smaller than birds of populations that occupy more temperate regions and either migrate shorter distances or are sedentary. Examples of this influence of migration on size are provided by ringed plovers (*Charadrius hiaticula*), redshanks (*Tringa totanus*) and European buzzards (*Buteo buteo*).

Wing shape may also be affected by migration. Within a given family of birds, the migratory species have narrower and longer wings than the sedentary species. Orioles, warblers and thrushes, to cite only three well-known kinds, provide characteristic cases of this effect. The reason is obvious, for birds with narrow, long wings have powers of flight superior to those with short, broad wings.

Birds and the balance of nature

By their feeding habits, which involve the consumption of all kinds of living things, both plant and animal, birds contribute

A male kestrel (*Falco tinnunculus*) dismembering a rodent for its chicks. *Atlas-Photo—Merlet*

Right, red-legged partridge (*Alectoris rufa*). This partridge from western Europe is replaced in north Africa by a closely related species, and in Asia, eastern Europe and the Alps by the Greek partridge and chuckar partridge. *Phot. Atlas-Photo—Merlet*

Lammergeier (*Gypaetus barbatus*) and its young. The lammergeier, one of the largest birds of prey, builds an enormous nest. It lays in the middle of winter, but incubation and rearing in the nest last a long time, and the young bird does not fly away until summer. The lammergeier is fond of tortoises and of bones, and it also eats carrion. *Phot. Michel Terrasse*

appreciably to the balance of nature in the various natural environments. Birds help keep the numbers of insects down to reasonable proportions, and thus prevent them from inflicting great damage on plant life. If there is a sudden population explosion in one particular species, which could threaten the delicate ecological balance of a habitat, then birds help to restore the balance by turning their attention away from their usual food towards that species. If there is a plague of voles, for example, magpies, crows and both diurnal and nocturnal birds of prey will feed on them in preference to their usual prey, voles being at such a time the most plentiful source of food and the easiest to obtain. The reverse can happen when men deliberately or accidentally, destroy such birds as birds of prey, for pests such as mice and rats may proliferate as a consequence.

Many birds unknowingly carry seeds and pollen about with them and are responsible for the continuation and spreading of a great deal of plant life. Some birds store nuts and cannot find them again, thus giving rise to new trees. Seeds pass through the bodies of birds as they eat fruits, and it seems that they subsequently germinate better as a result.

Birds and the human economy

Domestic fowl and birds of prey

Domestic birds such as chickens are kept as a source of food, both for their meat and eggs, and a number of wild species

are hunted both for food and for sport. These game birds include tinamous; many fowls including pheasants, partridges, guinea fowl and grouse; several waterfowl such as geese and ducks; snipe, woodcock and lapwings; and pigeons. On a local scale, other less edible birds are hunted for food, and seabird eggs are sometimes taken here and there. Lapwing eggs have a reputation among gastronomes, and small birds are netted in some places to make pâté, though conservation laws have banned such hunting in several countries. Other parts of the bird have some use, for feathers are collected for making bedding and also for ornamental purposes.

Birds may also have a less direct effect on the human economy. They are important for their crucial role in maintaining the balance of nature, and the destruction or proliferation of bird populations will inevitably upset this balance. The present balance of nature mostly operates to man's advantage, so overall birds are best left alone. Some birds especially birds of prey, have been blamed for killing domestic birds and game birds. A ravaging bird of prey will probably kill chickens much as a marauding fox does, but it is unlikely to affect game bird populations for only weak and sickly game birds are normally taken. In fact, in the long term, their actions may help to improve the stock of game birds in a district. And, as noted above, destroying birds of prey may lead to the proliferation of pests, for other birds are not their only food.

Several species of birds are considered to be harmful because they make inroads on agricultural crops. Starlings take grapes, olives and rice; sparrows destroy cereals; European blackbirds and thrushes steal raspberries and cherries. These are only a few examples of crop damage, which in some cases can be very serious. The red-billed quelea (*Quelea quelea*) devastates cereal crops in Africa. It breeds so prolifically that even using such measures as flame throwers against the birds has little effect.

Birds may also occasionally be a nuisance to man. Pigeons and starlings soil city squares and buildings, and birds are a hazard to aircraft landing and taking off from airports. Some fishermen blame fish-eating birds for robbing lakes of their stock (although it has been observed on some African lakes that a reduction in the number of birds does not improve the fishing). Also, the role of birds in keeping down pests may easily be overexaggerated; rodents are kept more in check by lack of food and epidemics than by birds; and insects fall victim much more to each other than to birds.

But the few disadvantages of having birds around us, even counting the few bird pests such as the red-billed quelea, are amply compensated by their value to us as food and by their indispensable role in maintaining the harmonious balance of nature. For the last reason alone, birds must be effectively protected.

The hunting of birds and the taking of their eggs should be forbidden everywhere, except where measures need to be taken against pests. Fortunately, there are now stringent conservation laws in many countries to protect rare and endangered species. But common birds are in need of protection too, and the fate of the passenger pigeon should remind us that we can never afford to be complacent. In practice, it often proves difficult to get conservation laws through the machinery of government. Fearful of offending them, some governments are reluctant to act against their interests of hunters. This is particularly so in Italy, where netting takes an annual toll of some 150 million wild birds. This does not necessarily affect only the offending country, for many of the victims will be passing migrants unwittingly running the gauntlet.

Classification

Birds make up the class of the animal kingdom called Aves. This class is divided into 27 orders of equal status, even though some of them contain only one species of bird and one—the passerines—contains more than half of all bird species. The classification is made on an anatomical basis. The passerines are so similar anatomically that they are grouped together in one order. The ostrich, on the other hand, is so unlike other birds in structure that it occupies an order by itself. Within an order, there are one or more families of anatomically related birds. Each family consists of a certain number of species—from one to several hundred.

Similar species are grouped together in genera, and the names of the genus and species together are sufficient to distinguish one bird from another. All together, there are some 8600 species of birds. The rules for classification are not so rigid that a bird may not be reclassified if desired, and a new species may be created if it seems sufficiently distinct from all other birds. For these reasons, it is impossible to give an exact total for the complete number of bird species, or even of families.

Order Struthioniformes (Ostriches)

This order contains only one family (Struthionidae), comprising one genus and one species: the ostrich. It is the largest living bird at the present time, and is flightless. However, ostriches are fleet of foot and escape danger by running. Polygamous, they live in flocks on the grasslands of Africa.

Order Apterygiformes (Kiwis)

This order contains the kiwi family (Apterygidae), which comprises three species of these flightless birds of New Zealand. The moas, which became extinct some 600 years ago, are also classified in this order.

Order Casuariiformes (Cassowaries and emus)

This order comprises two families: the three species of cassowaries (Casuariidae) and the emu (Dromaiidae), all flightless birds of Australasia. Cassowaries live in forests whereas the emu inhabits the plains.

The red-billed quelea (*Quelea quelea*), whose colonies may number millions of individuals, cause great damage to cereals; flame-throwers are sometimes used to destroy their nests. *Atlas-Photo—Dragesco*

Order Rheiformes (Rheas)

One family of two species of rheas (Rheidae) makes up this order. The rheas are the New World counterparts of the ostrich, being large flightless birds of South American grasslands.

Order Tinamiformes (Tinamous)

This order comprises the family of tinamous (Tinamidae), of which there are some fifty species. They are game girds of Central and South America, ground-living though capable

Ostrich, *Struthio camelus*, Phot. Fiévet

Rheas or nandus, *Rhea americana*. Phot. Margiocco

of flight. They are similar in living habits to pheasants and partridges, being both polygamous and polyandrous. The male incubates the eggs and rears the young, which are nidifugous.

All the preceding orders were once grouped together in one super-order, indicating that they are probably all of common origin. This idea has now been abandoned because the features linking the birds are too variable. The ratites (ostriches, kiwis, cassowaries and emus, and rheas) may have a common distant ancestor, but the tinamous are among the most recently evolved of birds.

Order Sphenisciformes (Penguins)

This order comprises a single family of the eighteen species of penguins (Spheniscidae). These birds are totally adapted to an aquatic life, their wings being used for swimming and not for flight. Their feathers act more like scales and are rigidly fixed all over the body. Penguins can fast and can withstand very low temperatures. They stand upright and waddle as they walk. The largest species, the emperor penguin and the king penguin incubate their single egg on their feet and not in a nest.

Penguins feed on fish, crustaceans, worms and molluscs, and live in large colonies called rookeries in the Antarctic region, and also along the coasts of South Africa; southern Australia, Tasmania and New Zealand; and South America as far north as the Galapagos Islands.

Penguins are an ancient order of birds which evolved long ago from flying ancestors, as their keel-shaped breast-bone indicates. Although they look superficially very different, they have anatomical affinities with the albatrosses and other procellarians. They are thought to be distant cousins of the

Cassowary, *Casuarius*, Phot. Margiocco

Black-necked grebe, *Podiceps nigricollis. Phot. Fatras*

Adélie penguins, *Pygoscelis adeliae. Phot. Helly*

procellarians that have followed a completely different line of evolution.

Order Gaviiformes (Divers or loons)

This order is made up of the single family of divers or loons, comprising five species (Gaviidae). They are large aquatic birds found throughout the Arctic region. They drag themselves clumsily about on land, for their webbed feet are placed well back on the body, but they are capable of sustained flight.

Order Podicipediformes (Grebes)

The single family of grebes (Podicipedidae) makes up this order. Grebes are found throughout the world. They lead an aquatic life, the toes being lobed and not webbed. The grebes build floating nests of water plants. They dive often and quickly, and their flight is flapping and rapid. Grebes have remarkable courtship dances.

Order Procellariiformes (Albatrosses, shearwaters and petrels)

This order comprises four families: the albatrosses (Diomedeidae), shearwaters (Procellariidae), storm petrels (Hydrobatidae) and diving petrels (Pelecanoididae). All are marine birds with pelagic habits, coming to land (mainly islands) only for breeding. The procellarians are among the best fliers of all birds, and some species can also swim and even dive. They lay a single egg, the incubation and rearing of the young lasting a very long time (nearly a year for incubation and fledging in the case of the wandering albatross).

Order Pelicaniformes (Pelicans and allies)

These birds have all four toes webbed. There are six families—the gannets and boobies (Sulidae), cormorants (Phalacrocoracidae), darters (Anhingidae), pelicans (Pelecanidae), frigate birds (Fregatidae) and tropic birds (Phaethonitidae).

They are mostly large or very large birds and, apart from the anhingas, mostly marine. They breed in colonies. Some species are economically important for the guano they produce. These are, in Peru, the Bougainville cormorant, the Peruvian booby and the brown pelican. This order includes only fish-eating birds, though the frigate birds live mainly by robbing other sea birds.

Order Ciconiiformes (Herons, storks and flamingos)

Some of the birds in this world-wide order are large and others are of medium size. The largest family (Ardeidae) contains the herons and bitterns, as well as the egrets and night herons. The next biggest (Threskiornithidae) contains the ibises and spoonbills. Then comes the stork family (Ciconidae). The flamingo family (Phoenicopteridae) comprises four species of flamingos, and there are three single-species families. These are the boat-billed heron (Cochlearidae), showbill or whale-headed stork (Balaenicipitidae) and hammerhead (Scopidae).

These long-legged birds usually live near water, many of them wading in the water and finding their food there. The herons and bitterns have S-shaped necks (often concealed beneath plumage), and they hold their necks in this position when flying. Storks fly slowly with the neck outstretched. Ibises and spoonbills can be recognized by their bills: in ibises, it is thin and curves downwards, whereas spoonbills have straight, flat paddle-like bills. The long sinuous neck

Kiwi, *Apteryx australis.*
Phot. Garnison, San Diego Zoo

Black-throated diver,
Gavia arctica. Phot. Hosking

Frigates, *Fregata. Phot. Brosset—Jacana*   Gannets or solan geese (*Morus bassanus*).   Fulmar, *Fulmarus glacialis.*   Albatross from the Galapago

and pink-white plumage of the flamingo make it unmistakable. The other three orders comprise thick-billed birds.

Order Anseriformes (Geese and ducks)

Swans, geese and the many kinds of ducks, such as scoters teal, eiders, mergansers and tree ducks make up one large family (Anatidae) in this order. All are of medium or large size and web-footed, and most lead an aquatic life. They are inclined to be sociable outside the breeding season, and are distributed throughout the world, including the Arctic. They are economically important almost everywhere, whether as game or for their eggs or feathers (eiderdown). Also included in this order is the family of three screamers (Anhimidae), large birds of South American forests and rivers. Screamers are armed with sharp spurs on each wing.

Order Falconiformes (Eagles, hawks and vultures)

This order of birds is often called the birds of prey, although they are all daylight hunters, the nocturnal owls being in another order. There are five families. The largest (Accipitridae) comprises the vultures of the Old World, which live on carrion, and the eagles and hawks, which hunt live prey. This last group includes buzzards, kites, and harriers as well as birds called eagles and hawks. The New World vultures are in another family (Cathartidae) together with the condors, and are carrion-eaters. The falcons make up a large family (Falconidae) containing such birds as merlins and kestrels. They have long pointed wings, as opposed to the broad wings of eagles and hawks. There are also two single-species families: the ground-living secretary bird of Africa (Sagittariidae), and the fish-eating osprey (Pandionidae).

Order Galliformes (Game birds)

Included in this order are the best of the game birds. They live mainly on the ground, where they eat seeds or insects, and although capable of flight, they do not often fly. The largest family is made up of the fowls (Phasianidae), which includes such prized game birds as partridges and pheasants as well as the Indian jungle fowl, from which all domestic chickens are descended. The peacock is another well-known fowl. The grouse comprise another family (Tetraonidae) of important game birds, and the guinea fowl of Africa (Numididae) and turkeys of America (Meleagrididae) makes up two families also containing well-known domestic species. The tree-nesting curassows of tropical America (Gacidae) are also members of this order. Two unusual families complete the list. These are the megapodes of Australasia (Megapodidae), and southeast Asia which bury their eggs in warm soil or rotting vegetation; and the strange hoatzin of South America (Opisthocomidae), whose young bear wing claws with which they crawl among branches.

Order Gruiformes (Cranes and allies)

These are long-necked birds, though as in the herons, the neck may be concealed beneath plumage. Most are also long-legged, but there is considerable variation in appearance from the tall elegant cranes to the squat moorhens. The largest family (Rallidae) comprises the world-wide rails, moorhens and coots, which are mostly reed-living birds and weak fliers. They have slim bodies to enable them to move easily among the reeds. The bustards (Otididae) are the next largest family; they are ground-living runners of Old World grasslands that rarely fly (which may be explained by the fact that they are among the world's heaviest flying birds).

Anhinga, *Anhinga rufa.*
Phot. Varin—Jacana

Black-headed heron, *Ardea melanocephala. Phot. Roche.*

American flamingo, *Phœnicopterus ruber.*
Phot. Zūber-Rapho

Young goshawk, *Accipiter gentilis. Phot. Varin-Jacana.*

Vultures. *Phot. A. Margiocco.*

Black swan, *Cygnus atratus. Phot. J. Pierre*

The family of cranes (Gruidae) comprises several species noted for their elegance as well as their crazy dances. They live in all continents except South America, but some are in danger of extinction. Other families include the odd flightless mesites (Mesitornithidae) of Madagascar—odd because they have wings that look as if they should function; the little button quails (Turnicidae) of Old World grasslands; the limpkin (Aramidae) of tropical America; its neighbours, the trumpeters (Psophidae) and the seriamas (Cariamidae), both long-legged, short-billed birds; the tropical finfoots (Heliornithidae), which can dive like grebes and have similar lobed toes; the sun bittern (Eurypygidae), a solitary wader of tropical America; and the kagu (Rhynochetidae), a nocturnal crested bird from New Caledonia which is only just able to fly.

Order Charadriiformes (Waders, auks and gulls)

The birds of this world-wide order are mostly waders or birds that live along sea coasts. The largest family of the waders comprises the sandpipers and snipe (Scolopacidae): its members are very varied and include the curlew, woodcock and the ruff. The male ruff displays colourful patches of plumage to entice a mate, the colour varying from one bird to the next. The plovers (Charadiidae) are plump, short-billed birds, of which the best known is probably the lapwing or peewit. Among birds of this order found more often at coasts are the oyster-catchers (Haematopodidae), which force open shellfish with their strong, blunt bills; and the avocets and stilts (Recurvirostridae), elegant waders with long bills that are up-curved (avocets) or straight (stilts). The phalaropes (Phalaropodidae) are an unusual family because the males initiate courtship, incubate the eggs and

rear the young. All the females have to do is lay the eggs. The jacanas (Jacanidae) make up another strange family, for their toes are so long that they can safely cross lakes by walking on floating leaves such as water-lily leaves. Five more families complete this section of the order.

In the north, auks (Alcidae) are the counterparts of the penguins in the south, even though they can fly well, for they dive and swim underwater so well. This family includes razorbills, guillemots and puffins. They nest in colonies, often of vast size, on cliff ledges or in burrows in ground near the sea. The gulls and terns (Laridae) make up the largest family of the order. They can be told apart with ease, for terns are smaller and more slender than gulls and have thin, sharp bills whereas gulls have long, stout, slightly hooked bills. They are common shore birds. Related families include the skuas or jaegers (Stercorariidae), strong-flying robbers of the cold oceans, and the sheathbills (Chionididae), pure white birds of the Antarctic. The skimmers (Rynchopidae) make up a small family that fish by 'ploughing' the water with their open bills.

Order Columbiformes (Pigeons and sandgrouse)

This order comprises over 300 species of land birds that are physically similar to birds of the preceding order. Almost all of them belong to the world-wide pigeon family (Columbidae), which includes all the birds known as doves. The millions of domestic pigeons are all descended from the wild rock dove of the Old World. The sandgrouse (Pteroclidae) of the warm regions of the Old World make up the only other existing family. The dodo and related solitaires comprise another family which has now been extinct for over two centuries. The dodo was flightless.

King rail, *Rallus elegans. Phot. Terrasse*

Sunbittern *Eurypyga helias. Atlas-Photo—Schultz*

Domestic fowl (*Gallus*). *Atlas-Photo—Dautreppe*

Snipe, *Gallinago gallinago*.
Phot. Fatras-Jacana

Pallas' sand-grouse, *Syrrhaptes paradoxus*. Phot. Margiocco

Kittiwake, *Rissa tridactyla*. Phot. Brosselin-Jacana

Order Psittaciformes (Parrots)

There is only one family (Psittacidae), comprising more than 300 species of parrots, parakeets, cockatoos, lories and macaws. These are tropical birds, mostly of forests. They have heavy, strong bills and raucous voices, and can often imitate the sounds around them. The feet have two toes in front and two behind, and the plumage is often gaudily coloured.

Order Cuculiformes (Cuckoos and turacos)

The birds of this order are like the parrots in that they have the same kind of feet, but their bills are very different. There are two families, of which the cuckoo family (Cuculidae) is much the larger. It includes the anis, the coucals and the roadrunner, as well as the many birds known as cuckoos. They are found in hot and temperate regions throughout the World, though almost all the parasitic cuckoos occur in the Old World. The other family (Musophagidae) contains the turacos or plantain-eaters, long-tailed crested birds of Africa. They live mostly in deep forests, and are coloured bright greens, reds and blues.

Order Strigiformes (Owls)

The birds of this order are found throughout the world, except Antarctica. Their eyes face forward to give binocular vision, and they have highly mobile necks to compensate for the restricted field of view. The feathers are flexible, enabling owls to fly silently. Most of the species are nocturnal and the sense of hearing is well developed. All owls are birds of prey, eating small mammals, birds and (in certain cases) fish, as well as insects on occasions. Prey is swallowed whole, and indigestible matter is ejected from the beak in the form of pellets. Owls do not build nests, but lay their eggs on the ground, in holes in trees or in old nests. There are two families. The barn owls (Tytonidae) have heart-shaped faces and hunt mainly by sound. The typical owls (Strigidae), of which there are far more species, are round-faced and have huge eyes.

Order Caprimulgiformes (Night jars)

These birds are aerial insect-eaters of tropical and temperate regions. They fly by night or at dusk, and have mouths that open wide to catch their prey. There are five families. The largest comprises the night jars (Caprimulgidae), which occur around the world. The frogmouths (Podargidae) of Australasia and southeast Asia have large flat bills, and take small vertebrates as well as insects. In a separate family (Aegothelidae) are the owlet frogmouths of Australasia, which are like small, long-tailed owls. The fourth family (Nyctibiidae) contains the protoos of tropical America, which are camouflaged to resemble broken branches. Lastly comes the oilbird (Steatornithidae) in a family by itself; it dwells in caves in South America, findings its way in the darkness by the bat's method of echo sounding.

Order Apodiformes (Swifts and hummingbirds)

These two apparently unlike groups of birds are linked in one order because they are both excellent fliers and have short legs and weak feet. The hummingbirds (Trochilidae) make up the largest family. They have colonized virtually all but the cold regions of the New World. They have amazing

Touraco, *Tauraco persa*. Phot. Brosset-Devez

Long-eared owl, *Asio otus*.
Atlas-Photo—Vienne

Egyptian nightjar, *Caprimulgus aegyptius*. Phot. Du...

powers of flight, being able to hover and even fly backwards. The second family (Apodidae) comprises the world-wide swifts, which are the most aerial of all birds and the fastest fliers, and swiftlets, some of which are cave dwellers and have edible nests. In a third family (Hemiprochidae) are the crested swifts, which are not such good fliers as swifts, but can perch whereas swifts cling to surfaces.

Order Trogoniformes (Trogons)

The single family (Troginidae) that makes up this order contains the brightly-coloured trogons of tropical forests. The quetzal is their finest representative and, with its magnificent train of green tail feathers, one of the most striking of all birds.

Order Coliiformes (Colies)

This order also has only one family: the colies of tropical Africa (Coliidae). They are also called mousebirds from the way they run about among the foliage.

Order Coraciiformes (Kingfishers, hornbills and allies)

Several families of birds that differ widely in appearance are grouped together in this order. The largest family (Alcedinidae) comprises the kingfishers and kookaburras. They live mostly in hot regions, feeding on fish, insects and small vertebrates. Many are brightly coloured and while some live near water, others are birds of forests and grasslands. The todies (Todidae) are small birds of the West Indies, which

catch insects in a sudden darting flight like that of king-fishers. Another family (Momotidae) contains the motmots, long-tailed birds of tropical American forests.

The colourful bee-eaters (Meropidae) also come within this order. They take other insects besides bees, and live in warm regions of the Old World. Similarly distributed are the rollers (Coraciidae), which are known for the acrobatics they perform in flight. They eat reptiles and small vertebrates as well as insects. In a family by itself, comes the hoopoe (Urupidae). It has a large crest and a long curved bill and feeds on the ground, taking insects and worms. Hoopoes nest in holes, but never clean out their nests. They live in the Old World. In another family are the wood hoopoes (Phoenicu-lidae), found only in Africa. They are similar to the hoopoe, but have no crest and are rarely found on the ground.

The final family of this order comprises the hornbills (Bucerotidae). The huge bill often has a protuberance on top. These birds live in the Old World tropics. They are very specialized hole nesters, for the female is sealed up inside a tree cavity while she incubates the eggs. A small hole is left for her beak to protrude, so that the male may feed her. In this protected position, she also undergoes a moult.

Order Piciformes (Woodpeckers, barbets and toucans)

These birds live in trees, having two toes pointing forwards and two backwards. The largest family contains the wood-peckers (Picidae), of which there are more than 200 species. Their strong front toes and sharp claws enable them to grip a tree trunk firmly, and they also support themselves by bracing their stiff tails against the trunk. They bore holes in

Middle spotted woodpecker, *Dendrocopus medius.*
Atlas-Photo—Merlet

European bee-eater, *Merops apiaster. Phot. Baufle*

Great spotted woodpecker. *Dendrocopus major. Phot. Visage*

the bark to get insects and to excavate holes for nesting. Woodpeckers live throughout the world. Barbets (Capitonidae) make up another family. They live in tropical forests of the Old World, and have thick solid beaks. The honeyguides (Indicatoridae) of tropical Africa and Asia can feed on beeswax. They are known to attract the attention of animals or even men to help them open bees' nests and get the honeycomb. The jacamars (Galbulidae) are brightly-coloured insect-eaters of tropical American forests. They have long, thin bills. Similarly distributed are the puffbirds (Bucconidae), but they have stouter, shorter bills. The last family comprises the toucans (Ramphastidae), known for their great gaudy beaks. They are also forest birds of the American tropics, and they use their beaks to push through the thick foliage and reach fruit.

Order Passeriformes (Perching birds)

The passerines or perching birds are among the most highly evolved orders of birds. One characteristic of advanced evolution is that the young are completely helpless at birth, being naked or nearly so. Another is intelligence, for such passerine families as crows and tits exhibit the greatest degree of intelligence to be found in birds. The passerines have colonized all terrestrial environments, both continents and islands, except for Antarctica. The order contains more than 5000 species of birds—more than all the other orders put together. All these birds have one feature in common that links them in one order—they all possess feet with four unwebbed toes, three in front and one behind. All toes are well-developed, enabling all the members of the order to perch easily. The passerines emerged recently, and the differences between the various families are not always well defined. For this reason, ornithologists disagree about the precise number and content of passerine families, though most consider that they are nearly 60 families in all.

The broadbills (Eurylaimidae) are large-headed birds of old world tropical forests. Their front toes are partly joined together. Similar, but inhabiting the New World tropics, are the wood-creepers (Dendrocolaptidae). The ovenbirds (Furnariidae) get their strange name because some of them build nests of mud that are shaped like ovens, although others nest in burrows. The antbirds (Formicariidae) also live in the forests of Central and South America. They get their name from the way in which they feed on ants, or follow columns of ants and take the insects disturbed by the invaders. The small family of antpipits or gnatcatchers (Conopophagidae) are birds of the forest floor found in the New World tropics.

The tapaculos (Rhinocryptidae) are a family of ground-living small birds with unusual raised tails. They live in the plains and forests of Central and South America. Extending farther north into the southern United States are the cotingas (Cotingidae), solitary birds of striking appearance. One of the best-known cotingas is the cock-of-the-rock, whose vast crest often covers its beak. The manakins (Pipridae) are brightly coloured little birds of South American forests. The males perform extraordinary courting dances. Related to cotingas and manakins are the tyrant flycatchers (Tyrannidae); they live in the open spaces throughout the New World except in the very coldest parts. They are mostly dull in colour, but can raise a striking crest of head feathers. The plant-cutters (Phytotomidae) make up a small family of finch-like birds of the Andes, and the aptly-named sharpbill (Oxyruncidae) of New World tropics occupies a family of its own.

Barbet. *Phot. Visage Albert*

Toucan. *Atlas-Photo—Schultz*

dow pipit. *Phot. Visage-Jacana*   Ravens, *Corvus corax. Phot. Dubois*   Skylark, *Alauda arvensis. Phot. J. Markham*

The pittas (Pittidae) are plump little birds of Old World tropical forests. They are brightly coloured, though their striking patterns are not conspicuous in the dim light of the forests. The New Zealand wrens (Acanthisittidae) make up a tiny family of antipodean insect-eaters. Relegated to Madagascar are the asitys or false sunbirds (Philepittidae), probably survivors of some ancient line of birds that died out elsewhere. Just as untypical but much better-known are the two lyrebirds of Australia (Menuridae). The male raises a magnificent lacy fan of tail feathers in courtship. The fan is lyre-shaped with two long feathers forming the frame and a group of filmy central plumes making the strings of the lyre. Lyrebirds are also remarkable mimics. Related to them are the scrub birds of Australia (Atrichornithidae). The resemblance is internal, for scrub birds look like large wrens with long tails.

Next in the long list of passerine families come the larks (Alaudidae), a large family of ground-nesting birds. All are Old World birds with the sole exception of the horned lark, which is found throughout the northern hemisphere. The swallows (Hirundinidae) are found around the world except in cold regions. They are excellent fliers and spend most of their time aloft, being weak perchers. Included with the swallows are the various martins. The cuckoo shrikes (Campephagidae) are neither cuckoos nor shrikes, being smallish sociable insect-eaters of Old World tropics. They get their name because they do resemble the other birds in appearance. They are also known as minivets. The drongos (Dicruridae) are a family of insect-eaters of the same distribution as the cuckoo shrikes. They have stout, arched bills.

The orioles (Oriolidae) make up the next passerine family. These birds are often called true orioles or Old World orioles, for the American orioles are in another family—the icterids. The orioles are generally yellow and black in colour. Most are tropical birds, though the golden oriole breeds in Europe. The crow family (Corvidae) is one of the best-known passerine families, for some of these intelligent birds are often to be seen near human habitation. They are omnivorous and aggressive birds, qualities that ensure them success, especially when allied to intelligence. The family is large, and included in it are rooks, ravens, magpies, choughs, jackdaws, nutcrackers and jays. The family is almost world-wide in distribution, though concentrated in the northern hemisphere.

Found only in the forests of New Zealand are the wattle-birds (Callaeidae), which include the huia. Male and female huias have such different beaks that they were once thought to be different species. The mudnest builders (Grallinidae) are aptly-named birds of Australia, and also found in this continent are the song shrikes (Cracticidae), noisy birds that impale their prey on thorns as true shrikes do. These birds are also called bellmagpies or Australian butcherbirds. Next come two more Australian families that are among the most interesting of all birds—the bowerbirds (Ptilornorhynchidae) and birds of paradise (Paradisaeidae). The bowerbirds are famed for their bowers, elaborate constructions built as part of the courtship displays. The male birds of paradise rely on extravagant ornamentation to court the females, often possessing long trailing plumes. They are perhaps the most beautiful of all birds, receiving their name because their feathers are so magnificent that people long ago thought they could have come only from paradise.

The next family of birds could hardly be more different than the preceding one. The tits and chickadees (Paridae) are active little birds found throughout the northern hemisphere,

Green grackle, *Ailuroedus crassirostris. Phot. Warham*

Brown shrike, *Lanius cristatus. Phot. Markham*

Wren, *Troglodytes troglodytes. Phot. Markham*

Blue and white flycatcher, *Cyanoptila cyanomelana.*
Phot. Markham

Cardinal, *Richmondena cardinalis.*
Phot. Visage Albert

Japanese nightingale, *Leiothrix lutea.*
Phot. Visage Albert

but south of the equator only in Africa. The great tit and blue tit are much in evidence around homes and gardens in Europe and Asia, as is the black-capped chickadee in North America. These birds are primarily insect-eaters, but they easily change to seeds when insects are scarce, particularly in winter. Several species make bag-shaped nests, some of which are suspended from branches. Treecreepers (Certhiidae) are also insect-eaters, but confine themselves to tree trunks. They work around a trunk, propping themselves up with their stiff tails and poking their long, curved beaks into the bark. They occur in the northern hemisphere. In a separate family are some Australian treecreepers (Climacteridae), birds similar to those of the preceding family but having shorter beaks and tails less adapted to tree climbing. The nuthatches (Sittidae) are also tree-living birds, and may be immediately recognized from the way they cling to trunks with their heads towards the ground. They too seek insects in the bark but, like the tits, can turn to seeds when times are hard. They are found everywhere except New Zealand and South America.

Next comes the large family of bulbuls (Pycnonotidae), rather dull-coloured songbirds of Africa and southern Asia. They eat mostly fruit, and all possess an unusual patch of hair-like feathers on the napes of their necks. Closely related to the bulbuls and of similar habits and distribution are the leafbirds (Irenidae). The main difference is that the leafbirds are more brightly coloured.

The four dippers (Cinclidae) make up a small and unusual family of passerine birds. These birds are well adapted to an aquatic existence, being found in cool rivers and streams in most parts of the world. Being perching birds, their feet are not webbed but dippers swim well underwater by using their wings. They feed mainly on water insects, and often nest behind waterfalls. Such an aquatic life is very unusual for a perching bird, and dippers have a preen gland ten times the size of that in any other passerine to help keep their plumage watertight.

The wrens (Troglodytidae) are among the smallest of passerine birds. They live near the ground, and can be recognized by the way they hold their tails upright. They are almost entirely inhabitants of the New World, only one species being also found in the Old World. Closely related to the wrens, although larger, are the mockingbirds (Mimidae). These birds, which get their name from their remarkable powers of mimicry, are confined to the New World. The family includes the catbird, which is often seen living around American homes.

Next comes the largest family in the classification of birds—the flycatchers, babblers, thrushes and warblers (Muscicapidae). Altogether, more than 1000 different species are grouped in this family. Although superficially different, they all possess ten primary wing feathers in each wing.

They are also all insect-eaters, and almost all of the Old World. There are differences between the various members, but they are not sufficiently well defined to break the family up into several separate smaller families. The flycatchers have broad, flat bills ringed with bristles to help catch insects in flight. They vary greatly in appearance, some being dull and others brightly coloured. The paradise flycatchers look particularly elegant with their long tail plumes. These Old World flycatchers are completely different from the tyrant flycatchers of the New World. The babblers get their name because they are noisy birds, chattering through the undergrowth in small flocks. The group is extremely varied in appearance, the most unusual

Jerdon's green bulbul. *Chloropsis jerdonii.*
Phot. Visage-Jacana

Blue-throat, *Luscinia svecica.*
Phot. Varin-Jacana

Zebra finch, *Toeniopyga castanotis.*

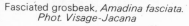

Fasciated grosbeak, *Amadina fasciata.*
Phot. Visage-Jacana

Painted bunting. *Passerina ciris. Photos Visage Albert*

being the bald crows or bare-headed rock fowl of West Africa, named for the patches of bare skin over their heads.

The thrushes include the world's best-known songbirds—particularly the songthrush and nightingale. These members of this vast family are also to be found in the Americas, one of the best-known New World thrushes being the American robin. This bird is larger than the European robin and its underside is completely red, whereas the European robin has a red breast and is white beneath the wings. Other thrushes include the European blackbird (but not the American blackbird, which is an icterid), the various American blue-birds, the European redstart (but not American redstarts, which are wood warblers), the ring ouzel and fieldfare of Europe, and the wheatears and chats of the Old World, as well as the many birds with the word 'thrush' in their names, such as mistle thrush, wren thrush and rock thrush. The warblers of this family are inhabitants of the Old World only. (The American warblers belong to the family of wood warblers.) They are dull-coloured birds of forests and grass-lands. They include the tailorbird, which fashions a nest by sewing leaves together: the chiffchaff; the kinglets, including the goldcrest; and the gnatcatchers; as well as the many Old World birds called warblers. The name is a good one, for they are melodious singers.

The next family comprises the accentors (Prunellidae), Eurasian birds that look rather like sparrows. The wagtails and pipits (Motacillidae) are more distinctive, being slender birds that run along the ground. They are birds of open country, and are found throughout the world. The waxwings and palmchats (Bombycillidae) are fruit-eaters of the northern hemisphere. They live in nomadic flocks, wandering wherever food is to be found. The wood swallows (Artamidae) are small serial insect-eaters of Australia and southeast

Asia. For passerines, they are remarkably efficient fliers.

The vanga shrikes (Vangidae) are confined to Madagascar; they are of similar appearance but not as predatory as the true shrikes (Laniidae). These latter birds make up their own family, found in all continents except South America and Australasia. Shrikes are insect-eaters, but also attack small reptiles and rodents and even birds, impaling their prey on sharp thorns to store it. This habit gives them their common names of butcherbirds. The starlings (Sturnidae) make up a large passerine family. They are to be found in the Old World, mainly in tropical regions. They are sociable birds and many are good mimics, the mynahs being among the best 'talking' birds. Many are strikingly patterned, the glossy black common starling being adorned with white spangles in its fresh autumn plumage. It has the distinction of being the most common wild bird, with a world population of about a thousand million.

The honey-eaters (Meliphagidae) make up a large family of nectar-eaters and insect-eaters of Australasia and Oceania. They are good songbirds, the tui being the best singing bird of New Zealand. Also included in this family are the Cape sugarbirds of South Africa. The brilliantly-coloured sun-birds (Nectariniidae) are the Old World counterparts of the hummingbirds, being also nectar-feeders, although they perch on flowers to feed rather than hover before them as hummingbirds do. The flowerpeckers (Dicaeidae) of south-east Asia and Australia are tiny birds that make up another nectar-eating family. The white-eyes (Zosteropidae), too, live on nectar and inhabit the same regions as well as Africa. Less colourful than the other nectar-eaters, they are green-yellow with a white ring around the eyes.

Next some several families of small New World birds. The vireos (Vireonidae) are greenish, tree-living birds, that feed

Bullfinches, *Pyrrhula pyrrhula.*
Phot. Visage-Jacana

Blue tit, *Parus caeruleus.*
Phot. Visage-Jacana

White-eye, *Zosterops palebrosa. Phot. Visage-Jacana*

Dominican widowbirds,
Vidua macroura.
Phot. Visage-Jacana

Giant widowbird. *Phot. Visage-Jacana*   Magpie, *Pica pica.* Atlas-Photo—Merlet   Jay, *Garrulus glandarius. Bel-Vienne-Jaca*

mainly on insects. The Hawaiian honeycreepers (Drepanididae) are an unusual group of nectar-eaters, each having a different kind of beak according to the kinds of flowers or insects they feed from. Being highly-specialized island species, several are in danger of extinction. The wood warblers (Parulidae) are the American warblers, an unfortunate name for they do not sing well. The wood warblers are mainly insect-eaters, but turn to seeds in winter. They are usually coloured yellow. The icterids or American orioles (Icteridae) make up another family of New World passerines. They are mostly yellow and black in colour, and include several well-known American birds, such as the Baltimore oriole, American blackbird, meadowlark and bobolink. Many of these birds are long-distance migrants. Also included among the icterids are the parasitic cowbirds.

The next family (Emberizidae) is the second largest in the passerine order, containing more than 500 species of tanagers, sugarbirds, cardinals and buntings. These are small birds. The tanagers are mainly birds of the New World tropics, and mostly have very bright colours. They are insect and fruit-eaters. Grouped together with them in this family are some nectar-eaters of the New World tropics known as honeycreepers or sugarbirds; these birds are different from the Hawaiian honeycreepers and the Cape sugarbirds. The cardinals are seed-eaters of the New World. The common names of these birds, and of the remaining birds in this family and in the other families not yet mentioned, are very confusing. The names finch, sparrow, bunting and grosbeak are used indiscriminately and have no significance in classification. Thus, the cardinals are often called cardinal finches, the best-known being the bright red cardinal, and the cardinal group also contains the beautiful blue grosbeak and painted bunting. The birds first referred to above as buntings are Old World seed-eaters and include many birds actually called buntings as well as the yellowhammer and snow finch.

The family of birds called finches (Fringillidae) comprises seed-eaters of all parts of the world that make open cup nests. They include the Galapagos finches or Darwin's finches, of which the tool-using woodpecker finch is an example; the chaffinch, bullfinch; goldfinch; greenfinch; linnet; pine grosbeak; redpoll; and the crossbills; as well as many birds that Americans call sparrows.

The weaver finches (Estrildidae) are seed-eaters of the Old World tropics that make untidy nests. Colourful little birds, many of which are popular as cage birds, they include the zebra finch, gouldian finch, avadavat and waxbill.

Lastly in the great order of passerines comes the family of weaverbirds (Plociedae), of Europe, Asia and Africa. The common house sparrow is the best-known member. Many weavers are colonial nesters, the social weavers building vast communal nesting structures that may fill a whole tree. This family also includes the destructive red-billed quelea and the strange parasitic widowbirds.

Golden oriole, *Oriolus oriolus. Phot. Hosking*

Yellow-headed rockfowl,
Picathartes gymnocephalus.
Phot. Markham

Ox-peckers, *Buphagus africanus.* Atlas-Photo—Vasselet

(Opposite) Broad-billed roller, *Eurystomus orientalis. Phot. Warha*

Mammals

Mammals are the most highly developed of all animals—the pinnacle of animal evolution. Their success began within a very short time of their appearance, and those which avoided excessive adaptation succeeded most quickly. Mammals owe much of their success to their breaking the shackles of innate habits, and their ability to adapt their behaviour to changing circumstances. They were helped in all these things because of the constancy of their internal environment.

The class of mammals includes species considered to be the most highly evolved in the animal kingdom and to top the pyramid of animal evolution, but to consider biological evolution as a simple pyramid with the most highly evolved occupying the tip is not quite exact. A mountain range with several peaks provides a more faithful illustration of the process.

Although the three present-day sub-classes of mammals differ profoundly from each other in many ways, they still form a homogeneous whole. They are all derived from ancient reptiles, and many skeletons have been found to confirm this. The transition took place very slowly, and there were many intermediate stages, some of which are well understood and authenticated.

Mammals have two unique characteristics: they have body hair and mammary glands—*Mammae*. It is from these glands that the class derives its name.

Young mammals, without exception, are fed on milk produced by the breakdown of cells in the mother's mammary glands. These glands are symmetrically arranged on the underside of the body. The young mammal is under the care of the mother, or the parents, at least until it is weaned.

The mammalian skull has certain characteristic features. Its vault is continuous and there is no trace whatever of a pineal eye. The temporal region opens out so that the mandibular muscles are firmly anchored on it. In front, the bones form an arch known as the zygomatic arch. The proportions of the skull have kept pace with the brain, whose volume is much greater than in reptiles. The first vertebra, known as the atlas, is articulated to the skull by two occipital condyles (rounded protrusions at the base of the skull). The mandible consists of a single bone. Mammals have two successive sets of teeth, and the teeth can be divided into categories—incisors, canines and molars.

The limbs are parallel with the body and not perpendicular to it, as in the case of reptiles. The trunk of the body is divided into two compartments by a muscular partition known as the diaphragm, which plays an important role in breathing. The front compartment, known as the thoracic cage, contains the heart and lungs. The rear compartment contains the stomach, intestine and the urinary and genital systems.

The mammalian heart is divided into four chambers and, in all normal mammals, there is no mixing of venous and arterial blood. The skin, whose growth is continuous, produces a layer of dead cells, rich in sulphurous proteins (*keratin*).

The embryo mammal—except in some oviparous monotremes—develops in a special compartment known as the uterus, and is totally enveloped in an amnion.

Grant's zebras (*Hippotigris burchelli bohmi*) have become very numerous in the reserves of East Africa where they form vast herds and are unafraid of tourist photographers. *Phot. de Klemm—Atlas-Photo*

The young korrigum or topi (*Damaliscus korrigum*) kneels down to suck its mother, assuming an imploring attitude which is very characteristic. The korrigum lives in a wide territory which includes Nigeria, Gambia and Chad. *Phot. Jean-Philippe Varin—Jacana*

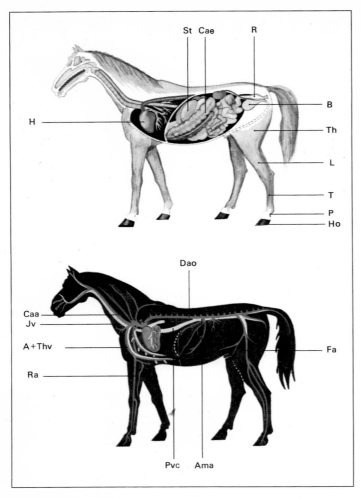

Diagram of the anatomy of the horse. *Above*, main viscera. *B*, urinary bladder; *Cae*, intestinal caecum; *H*, heart; *Ho*, hoof; *L*, leg; *P*, pastern; *R*, rectum; *St*, stomach; *T*, tarsus; *Th*, thigh. *Below*, circulatory system. *A+Thv*, external thoracic artery and vein; *Ama*, anterior mesenteric artery; *Caa*, carotid artery; *Dao*, dorsal aorta; *Fa*, femoral artery; *Jv*, jugular vein; *Pvc*, posterior vena cava; *Ra*, radial artery.

The enormous mammae of whales open into a common groove situated in front of the vulva. The teat scarcely protrudes. *Phot. docteur Soulaire*

Some features of the mammal's anatomy

The skin and its appendages

The skin of mammals is more than a protective covering: it excretes, it records messages from outside, and it is through it that hairs and mammary glands are formed. It is the skin that protects mammals from variations in temperature and humidity as well as from mechanical, chemical and microbe attacks. The skin is thick, sometimes thick enough to form a cutaneous shield or pachyderm. It is lubricated on the surface by a fatty secretion and a coating of hair, and is lined with a sheet of fat known as the adipose layer. The network of blood vessels supplying the skin contributes to the general heat regulation of the body.

The skin eliminates waste matter in the form of sweat, and builds up reserves with the help of the adipose layer. It picks up information through the nerve endings contained in touch corpuscles which act as receptors; it sends out chemical messages by way of certain glands; and it contributes to the feeding of the young by means of the milk glands.

Structure of the skin

Skin is complex, formed by the association of two heterogeneous tissues. The outer, or epidermis, is stratified and superficially cornified, and is of ectodermic origin (epithelium). The other is the dermis, a connective tissue rich in blood vessels and touch corpuscles, and is of mesodermic origin.

The epidermis is made up of several layers of cells which are renewed by proliferation from the bottom or Malpighian layer. The cells from this bottom layer push through the layers above them and are eliminated on the surface. By the time they reach the surface, they are merely fatty particles, flattened and degenerated. They are eliminated continuously and individually, a process known as desquamation. With a few exceptions, there is no moulting of the skin in mammals, as there is in reptiles and amphibians. But there is moulting of hair.

The outer cornified layer of the skin becomes thicker in zones subject to friction, where they form calluses. Such calluses can be seen on the buttocks of monkeys and on the elbow, wrist, knee and breast of camels. On the hand and foot, there are pads or cushions that act as buffers when in contact with the ground or branches of trees. The hand and foot pads are known as palmar, plantar and digital. In the case of ungulates, the pads become cushions. Cushions are skin rich in fat and elastic fibres, covered with a thick but flexible cornified layer.

The dermis unites the epidermis with the underlying bones and muscles. It is made up of connective tissue, loose where it adjoins the epidermis, and, at this level, rich in blood vessels. It is thicker than the epidermis, streaked with smooth muscle fibres (the hair-raising muscles) and straited ones (skin muscles). The deep zone of the dermis, known as the hypodermis, is fatty. This is the adipose layer which serves both as a reserve of food and as an insulator. Not surprisingly, therefore, it is thickest in the marine mammals—whales, seals and sealions—insulating them against the lowest temperatures.

Colour of mammals derives mainly from the coat, but the skin itself may be coloured by the presence in the dermis and epidermis of cells with black pigment—the melanophores.

The appendages of the skin are of two types: cutaneous glands that are hidden in depth and others that are visible.

Glands

Skin glands—sweat, sebaceous and mammary—are located in the dermis, with ducts passing through the epidermis. Sweat glands are simple and contained in a coiled tube. Their sweat helps in the elimination of waste products and in the regulation of body heat. Although usually distributed throughout the skin, sweat glands may be localized in certain parts of the body, as in rodents. They may be rudimentary, as in carnivores, or absent altogether, as in whales and sirenians.

The sebaceous glands are closely associated with hair, and secrete a fatty substance called sebum. There are other associated glands situated, according to the mammalian group, in different parts of the body. These are the carpal and tarsal glands, post-cornual (situated immediately behind

hippopotamus. The milk-carrying ducts converge in the centre of the mamma, or teat. If they open separately out-outwards, the teat is of the nipple type, as in man. If they all open into a common cavity, the teat is a dug, as in the cow. The flow of milk is stimulated by the suction of the lips of the young mammal.

In some mammals, however, the young is unable to suck the mother: examples being the young marsupial born in a precocious larval state, and the young whale which has no lips at all. In male animals, the mamma is rudimentary or absent. In monotremes, there are no mammae in the true sense of the word, the mammary glands being distributed over two flat areas and debouching at the base of the long hairs, along which the milk flows.

Derivatives

In mammals, skin derivatives are mainly produced by the epidermis—examples are hair, claws, nails, hooves, spines, scales, and certain horns. Derivatives of purely dermal origin are rarer, for example the shields and carapace of armadillos. Finally, there are derivatives of mixed dermo-epidermal origin, for example the horns of cattle and giraffes, and the antlers of deer.

Left, the sow, in common with the females of some insectivores, has the most teats and young. The number of piglets in a single litter may be as many as 12. *Phot. J. Six*
Right, the sea elephant (*Mirounga leonina*) breeds on land. The young grows very rapidly and swims well from the age of three months.

At the end of the Antarctic summer, it is capable of accompanying its parents in their long migration across the ocean. Rapid growth is made possible by the richness of the mother's milk in fat and protein. To enable the young to suck, the mother lies completely on her side. *Phot. Tollu—Jacana*

the horns), facial, scapular, dorsal, ano-genital, caudal, and others. The secretions of these glands often have a strong smell (for example, the musk glands of polecats and dogs) which plays an important part in social life, in the demarcation of territories, individual recognition, or sexual advertisement. Sebaceous glands are particularly numerous in ruminants and carnivores.

The milk, or mammary glands, are grouped in mammae, aligned in parallel fashion on each side of the medio-ventral line. The number of mammae varies from one pair, as in man and other primates, to eleven pairs, as in certain insectivores. The mammae may be axillary, as in pangolins; pectoral, as in monkeys and man; pectore-abdominal, as in the cat and dog; or inguinal, as in the cow, the horse and the

Hair is as characteristic of mammals as feathers are of birds. All mammals have hair, even those that appear to be smooth-skinned, like elephants and pigs. Whales, which seem totally naked, have hair during their development period in the uterus. This pre-natal hair is lost shortly before birth, a phenomenon probably associated with the animal's marine life. The skin of whales is extremely thin compared with that of land mammals, the epidermis being no more than $\frac{1}{5}$ to $\frac{1}{4}$ of an inch thick. With one exception, *Delphinapterus*, the skin of whales cannot, therefore, be made into leather. On the other hand, the underlying adipose tissue is extremely thick.

Hair grows from a bulb at the base of an invagination of the dermis. The cells of this bulb give rise to the shaft of the hair and to the sheaths that surround it. Each hair has a

Stoat or ermine (*Mustela erminea*) in winter and summer coat. *Phot. Visage Albert-Jacana*

sebaceous gland and a smooth muscle that can cause it to erect.

Hair grows only for a time; then the bulb degenerates. The shaft becomes progressively keratinized towards the root and, finally, the hair falls out. But the hair is quickly replaced by another emerging from a new bulb. The shaft of the hair is pigmented, and this pigmentation determines the colour of the coat, which varies from species to species and is an aid to recognition.

Hair may fall continually, or the fall may be periodic, when it is known as a moult. In some species, there is a seasonal renewal of the whole coat, as in the case of the Arctic hare and the stoat, both of which turn white in winter. But the mammal moult is a mere replacement of hair, not a change of skin, as in the case of amphibians and reptiles.

Only the pinnipeds have any kind of cutaneous moult, which means that the falling hair takes with it a piece of skin. The moult in pinnipeds may be periodic, and takes place once a year in the sea-elephant. Young pinnipeds usually have a moult early in life, within a few weeks of their birth, before they make their first journey to the sea. In grey seals, such animals are known as moulters.

Hair varies in texture from one species to another and, in some, has become modified out of recognition. Under-fur, which is short and pliant, is an insulator. Guard hairs and manes, on the other hand, are long, stiff and separated. The spines of the porcupine and the hedgehog are modified guard hairs. Finally, there are vibrissae, like the whiskers of cats and otters, which contain networks of nerves and are highly sensitive tactile organs. Sometimes such sensitive hairs are found on the hand or foot.

Claws, nails and hooves are horny formations, but are really modified hairs. A claw is formed by modification of the epidermic layer on the last phalange. This matrix, situated at the base of the claw, gives rise to two cornified layers, one on top of the other, the blade on top, the sole underneath. The nail is a variant of the claw, but has only one cornified layer. Claws and nails, unlike the hooves or ungulates, are never used as supporting surfaces.

A hoof is a highly modified and very complex claw. The blade forms the forward wall of the hoof, the sole forms the base, and the pad of skin that fits into the cut-away portion at the rear forms the frog.

The horns of mammals are of various types. Rhinoceros horn is agglutinated hair and purely epidermal. The horns of cattle are epidermal sheaths, covering a dermal bony axis. This axis is the core of the horn and is fused to the frontal bone of the skull. Such horns are permanent, except in the case of the pronghorn antelope (*Antilocapra americana*) which sheds the horny covering each year. Giraffe horns are of the same type, although there is no horny covering, except in the okapi, in which it is rudimentary and liable to be shed.

Giraffes, according to species, have one or two pairs of horns plus a protuberance in the middle. These horns have no horny covering; instead, they are sheathed in velvet. Thus, the horns of giraffes represent an intermediate type between the horns of oxen and the antlers of deer.

The antlers of deer, in fact, are dermal bones, with no horny covering. They are sheathed in velvety skin only during their growth. They grow from two extensions of the frontal bone, known as pedicles. Pedicles are permanent; the antlers are cast and regrown each year.

In most deer, including the European red deer, antlers are a secondary sexual characteristic. With one exception, the reindeer or caribou, only male deer grow antlers. Antlers are shed each year and new growth begins immediately.

During their growth, antlers are covered in velvet. When the antlers have attained their full growth, the velvet is starved of blood. Then it dries and rubs off, leaving the bone bare.

Antlers, which hunters call the head, consist of paired branching growths from two main trunks called beams. The first antlers appear when the young male is about a year old. Over the years, the antlers grow and produce more and more points, and it has been said that an animal's age can be calculated by the number of points. But this is not always so, as antler growth varies with quantity and quality of food. When the animal grows older, the number of points becomes reduced again, and the stag is said to be going back. Thus the antlers of a very old stag can look like those of a very young one. A Royal red deer stag is a stag with twelve points: it has brow, bay, tray tines, and three-point top on each beam.

The scales of the pangolin, like those on the tails of some rodents, are of epidermic origin. In armadillos, the scales cover bony plates of dermic origin.

The digestive system

The mammalian digestive system is the most complicated in the animal kingdom. Mastication is made possible by the way in which the upper jaw is articulated with the cranium. Mammals have cheek bones which are not found, or are imperfectly developed, in other vertebrates. The lips are mobile, so that the young is able to suckle its mother. In animals with a trunk, the upper lip forms part of it.

In mammals, the mouth is lined with a mucous membrane similar in structure to that of the skin. This mucous membrane has two layers, the surface one being stratified and partly cornified epithelium. In man, the superficial epithelium is not very cornified, but there are cornified papillae on the tongues of carnivores. In the case of the duckbilled platypus there are powerful lamellae.

Just as the mammalian skin produces hair, claws and horn, the mucous lining of the mouth also gives rise to derivatives—baleen and teeth. Baleen, of course, is found only in whalebone whales. It is produced entirely by the epithelium and consists of triangular, horny fringed blades that filter sea water and trap the plankton on which these animals feed.

Teeth, on the other hand, derive from the epithelium and the dermis. They are so important that a description of them will be found under a separate heading. The salivary glands, producing the saliva involved in digestion, are numerous and varied types—parotid, sub-maxillary and sublingual. In animals like pangolins and ant-eaters, which feed exclusively on ants and termites, the parotid and sub-maxillary glands are rudimentary.

The tongue is an organ of complex origin. Rooted in the mucous membrane, it is itself muscular, and contains numerous sensory receptor corpuscles which are the organs of taste. The muscles of the tongue, which give it its mobility, are attached to the hyoid bone, and there are 21 such muscles in the human tongue. In the case of pangolins and ant-eaters, the tongue is extremely long and worm-like, adapted for probing into termite heaps. The termites are caught on the sticky saliva which covers the whole tongue. A tongue of such great length requires special adaptations of the body to house

Young nine-banded armadillo (*Dasypus novemcinctus*). This species has a very extensive geographical distribution, from the north of the Argentine to the south of the United States. Maximum length, not including tail, 27 inches. Weight up to 15 pounds. This insectivore has a predilection for ants. *Phot. C. M. Hladik*

it when it is withdrawn. In fact, in the case of the termite eaters, the tongue is attached on the xyphoid appendage of the sternum which, in pangolins, covers the abdominal cavity almost to the pelvis.

The human alimentary canal is the most generalized in mammals, and consists of the oesophagus, the stomach and the intestines.

The oesophagus, or gullet, is a simple tube that conveys food from the mouth to the stomach. It passes through the diaphragm into the abdominal cavity but plays no part in digestion as such, being little more than a connecting tube. The wall of the gullet has an epithelium underlaid by a thin layer of connective tissue and a thin sheet of muscle. The

1. Coke's hartebeest (*Alcephalus cokei*) is a powerful East African antelope (Kenya, Kilimanjaro, Tanzania); it is about 4 feet at the withers. Its inward horns are curved. *Phot. Armelle Kerneis—Jacana*
2. Thomson's gazelle (*Gazella thomsoni*), one of the most graceful East African antelopes, has a strong pair of ringed horns, slightly curved and rising vertically from the forehead. *Phot. Armelle Kerneis—Jacana*

3. The European roe-deer (*Capreolus capreolus*) is characterized by its three-pointed antlers without basal tines. Still found from Europe to Siberia and as far afield as China. *Phot. Visage Albert—Jacana*
4. The chamois (*Rupicapra rupicapra*), regardless of its sex, has a pair of frontal horns hooked at the tip and turned backward. *Phot. Merlet—Atlas-Photo*

whole is supported by encircling connective tissue and muscle fibres, and is rich in blood vessels.

The stomach is like a pocket, and may be simple or compartmented. But even the simple stomach, as found in man, pigs and horses, shows local variations in structure. The glands are not all the same, being different in different areas of the stomach, and playing different roles in digestion.

The ruminant stomach—that found in cattle and deer—is four-chambered. The compartments are the rumen or paunch, the reticulum, the manyplies or omasum, and the abdomasum. The paunch is far the largest compartment. The first three compartments—rumen, reticulum and many-plies—are similar in structure to the oesophagus, being lined with a squamous epithelium. The abdomasum alone is richly

Upper jaw of a rorqual with its baleen; the edge of the cheek has been removed to make the latter visible. The horny filaments fringing the baleen form the filter which retains crustaceans and small planktonic organisms. *Phot. docteur Soulaire*

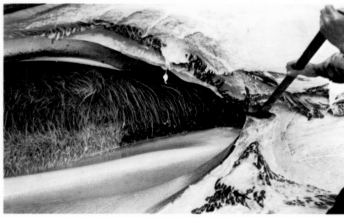

supplied with glands secreting gastric juices containing digestive enzymes. In camels, the walls of the paunch are lined with cells which, presumably, act as water reservoirs.

Unlike other mammals, ruminants do not chew their food before ingesting it. They tear the herbage and swallow it as they graze. All this food goes into the paunch, where it is mixed with saliva and worked upon by bacteria that cause it to ferment into a cud. Once the grazing animal has eaten its fill, it lies down to 'ruminate'—i.e. to chew the cud.

Chewing the cud is a process that can be easily observed. The resting cow chews and swallows. Then there is a spasm and a cud of grass, soaked in saliva and paunch juices, can be seen as a ripple in the skin of the neck as it passes up the gullet into the mouth. The cow swallows it again, and it passes straight into the reticulum. From there it passes into the other

compartments to undergo the normal processes of digestion. As soon as it is passed down, another cud of grass comes into the mouth, and so the process of chewing and swallowing goes on until the paunch is emptied.

Although the four-chambered stomach is characteristic of ruminants, they are not the only mammals with such compartments. In animals as diverse as sloths and whales, the stomach has three or four lobes and, in some whales (Zyphidae, or beaked whales), there are probably not less than fourteen.

In ant-eaters and termite-eaters, the stomach has a thick lining of keratin to protect it from the formic acid in the prey. In addition, the terminal region of the stomach is powerfully muscled. In pangolins, it is equipped with horny protuberances like teeth which act as grinders whose function is to crush insects that have been swallowed whole.

The passage from the stomach to the intestine is a sphincter known as the pylorus. The intestine is highly differentiated into the small intestine, the caecum, and the large intestine, the last being subdivided into colon and rectum. The small intestine plays a very important part in digestion, being lined with cells that secrete digestive and absorbent enzymes. The small intestine ends at the caecum and, in some mammals (man, apes and rodents), this gives rise to a vermiform appendix. A special valve, the ileo-caecal, prevents any reflux of food. In the large caecum of hares, rodents and horses, the passage of food is very slow. Bacterial flora set up fermentation in the cellulose of the food mass, producing, as a result, various fatty acids of high nutritional value. Here, too, vitamins are produced by the gut flora.

The large intestine plays a much less notable part in digestion. Its forward part, known as the colon, is more or less coiled, and varies greatly in length from one species to another, according to diet. In all mammals, except the monotremes, the rectum opens through a special orifice, the anus, whose opening and closing are controlled by a circular muscle—the anal sphincter. In monotremes, the rectum opens into a cloaca similar to that of reptiles.

The teeth

Diversified and complex teeth

In lower vertebrates, the teeth are simple and similar in shape, if not always in size. There are exceptions, of course, fish being obvious ones. Other exceptions are reptiles with poison fangs.

Mammals, on the other hand, have diversified teeth, classified from front to back, in each half jaw, as incisors and canines, pre-molars and molars. This diversification can be traced in the reptilian ancestors of mammals (Ictidosaurs) which had incisors, canines and post-canines.

Teeth vary according to diet and their number and structure are characteristic in the different orders of mammals. Consequently, teeth play an important part in the study of mammal fossils.

The upper incisors are implanted in the pre-maxillary bone. The upper canines, pre-molars and molars are implanted in the maxillary bone. All the teeth of the lower jaw are implanted in a single bone: the dentary (mandible). The incisors are sharp and have only one root (two in *Galeopithecus*). Their crowns may be conical, as in bats and insectivores. They may be like the teeth of a comb, as in the lower incisors of lemurs. They may be spatulate, as in cattle, monkeys and man, or multi-lobed, as in the dog.

Incisor teeth are elaborately specialized. In the vampire bat, the upper incisors are large, sharp and powerful. In conjunction with the canines, they bite a triangle of skin out of the prey while the bat is sucking its blood. The tusks of the elephant and the single tusk of the male narwhal (*Monodon monoceros*) are merely hypertrophied upper incisors and are continuous growth teeth. This is explained by the fact that they are not subject to wear, like the incisors of ruminants or rodents. When they appear, they are covered with a thin layer of enamel, but this quickly disappears, leaving the ivory bare.

In each half-jaw, the mammal has a single canine with only one root. *Galeopithecus* and the Talpidae are rare exceptions. The canine crown is conical. The development of canine teeth varies according to the diet of the species, and often according to sex, being bigger in males than in females. Canines are usually absent in herbivores, and reach their maximum development in carnivores, when they are known as fangs. In the horses, they appear only in males, are poorly developed and separated from the cheek teeth by an empty space, the disastema. In some groups, the upper canines are hypertrophied into tusks. In others, like the male chevrotain, the male musk deer, and the walrus, they point downwards. In the walrus, as in the elephant, the enamel soon wears off to leave the ivory bare. In male pigs, like the babiroussa and the warthog, the canines are curved upwards and, progressively with age, backwards.

The lower canines sometimes take on the appearance of tusks, curving upwards and backwards, like the upper canines of babiroussa. In the hippopotamus, they may reach a length of over three feet and weigh up to seven pounds. Like incisor-tusks, all these canine tusks are continuous growth

Pangolins (here, the Indian pangolin, *Manis crassicaudata*) are distinguished from all other mammals by their scaly covering. *Phot. A. Margiocco*

teeth, not used for chewing, and therefore escaping wear.

The pre-molar teeth vary widely in structure, and, in some cases, may be shaped like canines or molars.

But the outstanding mammalian teeth are the molars. They are grinding teeth used for crushing food. Their grinding surfaces are rugged, and vary according to the diet of the animal. They have from two to five roots. They have blunt tubercles and sharp cusps which, before they begin to wear by use, are separated by ridges and joined together by crests.

This complexity of the cheek teeth is peculiar to mammals, although it was foreshadowed in some mammalian reptiles of the Mesozoic Era (Tritylodonts). But the primitive mammalian design itself first appeared in certain mammals of the

Hippopotamus yawning and showing its teeth. *Phot. J. and M. Fiévet*

tubercles, and is found in omnivorous species, like monkeys, man and pigs, whose mandibles are highly mobile. This is a typical grinding molar.

(2) the secodont type has three sharp triangular cusps. It is typical of carnivores, and is associated with vertical movements of the mandible.

These two types are limited growth teeth, with a low crown and a long root.

(3) and (4) the selenodont and lophodont types are confined to herbivores whose mandibular movements are horizontal. Their cusps are joined by crests which are vertical to the direction of movement: crescent-shaped and front to rear for transverse movement (selenodont type of ruminants): transverse for front to rear movement (lophodont type of rodents and proboscidians) with parallel crests. In the tapir and the rhinoceros, the molars are crenellated and a variant of the first.

In fossil horses of the Tertiary period, the lophodont state arose progressively from the bunodont form (*Eohippus*) which represents the primitive type of mammalian molar. All these types are prolonged growth, or continuous growth, teeth, and have a high crown (hypsodont) and a short root that is never closed. Wear of the crown produces a flat surface showing a 'wear table', on which the hardest enamel can be clearly seen on the eroded areas of cement and dentine. Wear alone limits the length of continuous growth teeth.

In some mammals the teeth are all similar (homodont). In this category are dolphins, porpoises and sperm whales (toothed-whales), the sloth and the armadillo.

Gaping mouth of a sperm-whale brought to land and laid on its left side. Notice the narrowness of the mandible, armed with two parallel rows of enormous conical teeth which are solely prehensile. When the sperm-whale shuts its mouth, they fit into the cavities intended for them in the upper jaw. About 40 in number, they weigh about 1 pound apiece and are about 8 inches long. The mouth opens ventrally and as far back as the level of the eyes. *Phot. docteur Soulaire*

Engagement of the upper and lower teeth

The upper and lower teeth of mammals form two facing arcs, and, when the upper and lower come together, they effectively close the mouth. If upper and lower teeth meet tip to tip, there is occlusion by opposition or super-imposition (incisors of rodents). If the points of the upper and lower teeth overlap and interlock, occlusion is cuneiform (dolphins). Finally, occlusion is imbedding or shearing if cusps and grooves of one tooth fit exactly into the other.

In apes and man, overlapping results in an upper molar occluding with each of two consecutive lower molars.

Various types of occlusion may be found in the mouth of

Jurassic period. Various theories, usually referred to as trituberculate and multituberculate, have been tested to explain the evolution from simple to compound teeth.

Molars may be classified into four main types, according to the shape of their crowns:

(1) the parabunodont type is made up of several rounded

Three redoubtable felines, all belonging to the same genus *Panthera*. *Left*, the tiger (*Panthera tigris*), *right* the leopard (*Panthera pardus*), *in the middle* the black panther, a melanic mutation of the leopard, all roaring and showing their formidable teeth. Their sharp canines are much longer than their other teeth and act as prehensile fangs rather than for tearing flesh. *Phot. Parbst-Ifot—Rapho*

one animal. In carnivores, there are two teeth in each half-jaw that play a predominant role in locking the jaws—the canines or fangs in front and the carnassials (fourth upper pre-molar and the first lower molar). The dog is a good example of an average carnivore, in which the functional importance of the fangs and the carnassials is in balance. But in cats and hyenas the fangs are preponderant, and all the cheek teeth are sharp. On the other hand, the carnassials are preponderant in mammals like bears and sea otters which have a more omnivorous diet. Their molars are of the parabunodont type.

Number of teeth

The number of teeth varies from one group of mammals to another, but is fixed for any genus. The dental formula is one that gives the number of teeth per half-jaw in each category. The top figure represents the upper jaw and the bottom figure the lower. As a rule, the number of teeth does not exceed 44, corresponding to the primitive dental formula:

$$I\frac{3}{3};\ C\frac{1}{1}-Pm\frac{4}{4};\ M\frac{3}{3}$$

More often than not, however, this number is reduced (see table opposite) and a few rare species have no teeth at all (anodontia). The toothless ones are the ant-eaters and pangolins which prey upon ants and termites, and whalebone whales and rorquals which, in place of teeth, have baleen plates for filtering plankton. In adult monotremes, the teeth are replaced by horny plates.

But there is a paradox here. We have seen that certain animals that feed on insects, fish and plankton have no teeth. Yet in others of the same groups (Cetacea, Xenarthra), there is a spectacular increase in the number of teeth—100 in porpoises, 200 in the dolphin or toothed whales, and between 70 and 100 in the armadillo from the Mato Grosso. These teeth, however, are prehensile, not masticatory.

Formation and structure of teeth

The teeth are produced from the epidermis and the dermis. The dental lamina, which penetrates the dermis deeply, gives off buds that become teeth. The body becomes constricted into a cone of cells—enamel. Within this organ, the dental papilla develops and pushes upwards, producing dentine. Hardening of the tooth crown increases as the result of progressive deposits of enamel and dentine. The pulp cavity containing connective tissue and nerves is contained within the dentine. The enamel organ is destroyed when the tooth erupts, but secondary dentine may be deposited in the pulp cavity throughout the life of the teeth. In mammals, as in crocodiles, the tooth is set in a bone socket and attached by a periodontal membrane. The cement, which isolates the root from the bone, and which, in continuous growth teeth, overflows on to the crown, is a bony tissue.

Successive dentition—mode of replacement

Mammals develop, at most, two successive sets of teeth—the milk or baby teeth and the permanent teeth. In this, they differ from all other vertebrates with multiple dentition—for example fish, which can replace a tooth a hundred times, or reptiles which can do so up to twenty-five times. Many mammals, however, have only a single dentition, either because the milk teeth abort, as in pinnipeds and sloths, or

Dental formulae of some large groups of mammals (variable figures)

	Number of Teeth	Incisors	Canines	Pre-molars	Molars
Marsupials					
Opossums	50	I $\frac{5}{4}$	C $\frac{1}{1}$	Pm $\frac{3}{3}$	M $\frac{4}{4}$
Kangaroos	34	I $\frac{3}{1}$	C $\frac{1}{0}$	Pm $\frac{2}{2}$	M $\frac{4}{4}$
Carnivores					
Mongooses, civet cats	40	I $\frac{3}{3}$	C $\frac{1}{1}$	Pm $\frac{4}{4}$	M $\frac{2}{2}$
Cats	30	I $\frac{3}{3}$	C $\frac{1}{1}$	Pm $\frac{3}{2}$	M $\frac{1}{1}$
Seals, sea-lions	34–36	I $\frac{3}{2-3}$	C $\frac{1}{1}$	Pm $\frac{4}{4}$	M $\frac{1}{1}$
Artiodactyls					
Hippopotamus	36	I $\frac{2}{2}$	C $\frac{1}{1}$	Pm $\frac{3}{3}$	M $\frac{3}{3}$
Pig, wild boar	44	I $\frac{3}{3}$	C $\frac{1}{1}$	Pm $\frac{4}{4}$	M $\frac{3}{3}$
Oxen, deer, giraffes	34–36	I $\frac{0}{3}$	C $\frac{1-0}{1}$	Pm $\frac{3}{3}$	M $\frac{3}{3}$
Proboscidians					
Elephants	28–32	I $\frac{2}{0}$	C $\frac{0}{0}$	Pm $\frac{3-4}{3-4}$	M $\frac{3}{3}$
Perissodactyls					
Horses, tapirs	36–42	I $\frac{3}{3}$	C $\frac{1-0}{1-0}$	Pm $\frac{4-3}{3}$	M $\frac{3}{3}$
Hyracoidea					
Damans	34	I $\frac{1}{2}$	C $\frac{0}{0}$	Pm $\frac{4}{4}$	M $\frac{3}{3}$
Tubulidentae					
Aardvark	20	I $\frac{0}{0}$	C $\frac{0}{0}$	Pm 1	M $\frac{5}{5}$
Xenarthra (Edentata)					
Armadillo	44–46	I $\frac{0}{5-6}$	C $\frac{0}{1}$	Pm $\frac{7}{7}$	M $\frac{1}{1}$
Sloth	9–10	I $\frac{0}{0}$	C $\frac{1}{1}$	Pm $+$	M $\frac{4}{4}$
Ant-eaters *Pholidota* **Pangolins**	0				
Lagomorpha					
Hare	28	I $\frac{2}{1}$	C $\frac{0}{0}$	Pm $\frac{3}{2}$	M $\frac{3}{3}$
Rodents	24–16	I $\frac{1}{1}$	C $\frac{0}{0}$	Pm $\frac{2-0}{2-0}$	M $\frac{3}{3}$
Insectivores	44–28	I $\frac{3-2}{3-2}$	C $\frac{1}{1}$	Pm $\frac{4-1}{4-1}$	M $\frac{3}{3}$
Chiroptera	38–20	I $\frac{2-1}{3-2}$	C $\frac{1}{1}$	Pm $\frac{3-1}{3-2}$	M $\frac{3-1}{3-1}$
Primates					
Lemurians	36–26	I $\frac{2}{2}$	C $\frac{1}{1-0}$	Pm $\frac{3-2}{3-2}$	M $\frac{3}{3}$
Platyrhines	36–34	I $\frac{2}{2}$	C $\frac{1}{1}$	Pm $\frac{3}{3}$	M $\frac{3-2}{3-2}$
Catarhines	32	I $\frac{2}{2}$	C $\frac{1}{1}$	Pm $\frac{2}{2}$	M $\frac{3}{3}$
Man	32	I $\frac{2}{2}$	C $\frac{1}{1}$	Pm $\frac{2}{2}$	M $\frac{3}{3}$

because the permanent teeth remain in the germ state, as in toothed whales, dolphins, porpoises, sperm whales, armadillos and elephants. The third molar in man, known as the wisdom tooth, is a permanent tooth with retarded development which sometimes remains included in the bone.

Mammalian teeth are replaced vertically, the germ of each permanent tooth forming under the milk tooth and taking its

East Africa, from Somaliland to Tanzania, includes in its fauna the strange mole rats (*Tachyoryctes*, here *T. splendens*), remarkable for the great development of their incisors. Their eyes are small and their paws very strong. They live in burrows and dig galleries in the grassy savannas. *Phot. J. Burton—Photo-Researchers*

place when it falls out. In the case of the elephant, however, the teeth are replaced one at a time, the six cheek teeth of the permanent dentition succeeding each other from back to front.

Habits and classification of mammals

Mammals are the latest arrival on the stage of animal evolution, their oldest fossilized remains dating back to about 180 million years ago. The earliest mammals were derived from the reptilian stock of the Theropsida.

The first mammals were small and relatively unspecialized, and remained almost unchanged for about 120 million years. Then, in the Eocene, about 60 million years ago, the great leap forward took place, with a great multiplication and diversification of mammalian types, and the beginning of colonization. The number of mammal species alive today is about 6000, divided into 19 orders and more than 160 families.

Being highly adaptable and warm-blooded, with temperature control, they can stand great variations in climatic conditions, and so have succeeded in colonizing almost every environment. Their evolutionary dynamism has resulted in a multiplicity of forms and types, showing great variation in structure and habits. Despite tremendous superficial differences, they are really all alike. From the small shrew to the flying bat and the 130 ton whale, they are structurally the same. Their profound similarities outweigh their superficial differences.

Their common features distinguish them from all other vertebrates, and proclaim their common origin. All have a four-chambered heart and pulmonary breathing. They grow hair. They are all warm-blooded, with a stable temperature controlled by the nervous system, in most species at between 35 and 40 degrees centigrade. Finally, they all feed their young on milk secreted by the mammary glands.

The nineteen orders of present-day mammals are very unequal in terms of the number of species in each. In rodents and bats, there are a thousand species or more, whereas there are only four species of monotremes, two of Dermoptera and, in the Tubulidentata, only one.

The class of mammals is divided into three sub-classes. The most primitive are the monotremes, which lay eggs and incubate them, like birds. Then there are the marsupials, whose young are born in an immature state and complete their development in an external pouch or marsupium. Finally, there are the placental mammals, whose young develop in the uterus, linked to their mother by means of a temporary organ, the placenta or after-birth. After the young mammal is born, the placenta is shed.

The sub-class Monotremata

A milk-producer with a bird's beak
Reptile-like mammals

In form and biology, the monotremes are the mammals most like their reptilian ancestors. Their skeleton is relatively primitive, and they have a single ventral orifice. Their internal temperature is lower than that of any other mammal, but the most important difference between them and others in their class is that they are oviparous, like birds and reptiles. Monotremes are confined to Australia, Tasmania and New

Guinea. There are two types: the platypus (*Ornithorhynchus*) and the spiny ant-eaters (*Echidna*).

The duckbill platypus

The duckbill platypus (*Ornithorhynchus anatinus*) is about the size of a rabbit, and weighs about 4 pounds. It has the bill of a duck (from which it derives its name), the flattened tail of a beaver, and can swim like an otter. Its eyes are on the sides of its head and have the triple reptilian eyelid, and it has short legs and webbed feet, with strongly clawed toes. The thick body-fur is brown, with a silvery sheen.

The platypus is found in Australia and Tasmania, where it frequents river banks overgrown with vegetation. It is as much at home in mountain rivers as it is in the swamps of the tropical zone. It is completely at home in the water, and spends several hours each day, round the clock, diving in the mud for the worms, insects and molluscs on which it preys. It can remain submerged for long periods.

The platypus lives singly or in pairs. It is a burrowing animal, living mainly on river banks. The entrance to its sleeping burrow is under water. The nesting burrow, excavated by the female, is long and winding, and has an entrance slightly above water level. At the end of this burrow, she makes her nest of leaves and other moist vegetation. The nest has to be moist because the eggs cannot stand dry conditions.

The female platypus seals off the burrow entrance with plugs of mud, isolating herself while she incubates her two or three eggs which are oval in shape and up to $\frac{3}{4}$ of an inch in length. They adhere to each other. The incubation period is about ten days, but the young animals remain a long time in the nest, perhaps for as long as eighteen weeks. They feed on their mother's milk, but do not suckle in the usual way. When feeding her young, the female lies on her back. The milk trickles from the numerous small pores in the mammary area, soaking her fur, which is then licked or sucked by the young. At this time, the young animals have ten milk teeth, but they lose these when they reach maturity and grow little horny plates instead.

The platypus is one of the very few poisonous mammals. The males have a horny spur on the heel, with poison glands. The poison is powerful enough to kill small mammals, like rabbits, and can cause great pain in man.

The spiny ant-eater (echidna)

The spiny ant-eaters are found in Australia, Tasmania and New Guinea. They resemble the European hedgehog, and are immediately recognizable because of the array of spines protruding from their thick fur. Two genera are known: the straight-beaked spiny ant-eaters, *Tachyglossus*, with two species (*T. aculeatus*, which is widely distributed in South Australia, and *T. setosus* from Tasmania) and the curved-beaked spiny ant-eater, *Zaglossus*. All of them have a tapering snout, like a beak; hence the name. They have small mouths and long worm-like tongues. Instead of teeth, the echidnas have warts on the palate that act as food grinders.

The straight-beaked ant-eater, also known as the five-toed spiny ant-eater, is an inhabitant of rocky areas. It is active by day, and the peak of its activity is reached after noon. When hunting, it crawls here and there, sniffing around stones and turning them over in search of prey. Along with its food, it swallows a lot of gravel, the whole mass being crushed in the

The duckbill (*Ornithorhynchus [Platypus] anatinus*) in an unusual attitude. The male reaches nearly 2 feet in length, with a tail of about 6 inches. The muzzle, like a duck's bill, is very well adapted to seeking out small animals living in mud. *Phot. A. Margiocco*

stomach which has powerful walls like the gizzard of birds. Its main prey is insects and termites which are located by smell. The ant-eater tears open an ant-hill and gathers the disturbed ants on its sticky tongue. Caught thus, they are like flies on a fly-paper, and are ground to pulp by the horny warts on the palate.

The echidnas are immensely strong and not easily handled, even with leather gloves, which give little protection against the spines. Like the hedgehog, the echidnas can coil into a defensive ball, thus presenting enemies with a hedgehog defence.

The echidna is able to fast for long periods. Because of its unstable body temperature, it quickly becomes torpid in cold weather, becoming active again only during the months when the weather is sufficiently warm.

During the breeding season, which is in July and August, the female ant-eater develops a pouch on her abdomen and in this she lays her eggs, which are the size of hazel nuts. She will lay up to three eggs, all of which are sticky and adhere to the hairs inside the pouch. After hatching, the young remain in the pouch until their spines harden. The newly born ant-eater is a very tiny animal, but it grows quickly, reaching a length of three inches or more in a matter of six weeks.

The curved-beaked or three-toed spiny ant-eater (*Zaglossus bruynii*) is found in New Guinea and in the island of Salwati. It, too, is an inhabitant of rocky areas. This is a much bigger species than the previous one, differing from it not only in size but by its extremely strong and longer feet which give it much greater agility and freedom of movement. Although it is covered with spines when young, the curved-beaked species loses them with age, so that the skin of old animals becomes almost bare.

The sub-class Marsupialia

Most of the marsupials in the world are found in Australia. They are more highly evolved than monotremes, differing from them in anatomy and physiology, and by the fact that they are viviparous. Young marsupials are born long before they are fully developed. From then on, they continue their development in a marsupial pouch which is a sort of external uterus, giving them shelter and protection.

Present-day marsupials form two distinct groups which have been separated for a very long time. One group is found in Australia, the other in South America.

Australian marsupials

These are the original mammalian fauna of the Australian Continent. Before the arrival of man on the Continent, the isolation of Australia made colonizing by other wildlife species from outside difficult and rare. Hence the small number of placental mammals on the Continent before then.

Absence of competition enabled the marsupials to develop a wide variety of forms able to colonize an equally wide variety of environments. As a result, there are marsupials that closely resemble many of the higher mammals, like rats, squirrels, rabbits, jerboas, ferrets, moles and wolves. The resemblances are so striking that, for a time, it was widely believed that the marsupials were the ancestors of all other mammals. But this is not so. It is one more example of convergent evolution, like the swift and swallow. Comparative study of the Australian marsupials, especially of their convergence with placental mammals from other continents, may lead to a better understanding of how animal species become differentiated.

Most of the marsupials are, unfortunately, threatened with extinction. The early threats came from man; later they came from species introduced by him—placental animals like rats, rabbits, foxes, dingoes, sheep and cattle, all or most of which compete in one way or another with the native marsupials.

The Dasyuridae: Carnivorous and insectivorous marsupials

In the Dasyuridae there is great variation in size and appearance, the biggest species being carnivores and the smallest insectivores. All are nocturnal in habits.

In the Phascogalinae there are several remarkable genera. The brush-tailed pouched mice (*Phascogale*) are rather like squirrels, and they are extremely voracious. They inhabit trees, and are very common.

The long-legged jumping marsupial mice (*Antechinomys*) are a remarkable example of convergent evolution, in this case with jerboas. Because of their long tails and long hind legs, they look like rodents. The narrow-footed marsupial

mice (*Sminthopsis*) are more mouse-like and feed on insects and smaller rodents.

Jerboa-like mice (*Antechinus*), of which there are twelve species, are found over most of Australia. They might almost be described as omnivorous, being partly carnivorous, partly insectivorous and, to a lesser extent, vegetarian. All twelve species live in holes in trees and tree stumps or under rocks.

The flat-skulled marsupial mice (*Planigale*) resemble *Antechinus*, differing from them by their markedly flattened heads. *Planigale subtillissima* is probably the smallest known marsupial. It is found in Western Australia, and measures about 1¾ inches from the tip of its muzzle to the root of its tail. It feeds on insects.

Crest-tailed pouched mice (*Dasycercus*) are related to *Antechinus*, but are distinguished by the erect crest of hairs on the tip of their tails. They have no marsupium, merely a fold of skin covering the mammae.

The marsupial cat and the Tasmanian devil

This sub-family includes the marsupial cats and the Tasmanian devil (*Sarcophilus*) which, in general appearance, resembles the badger.

Native cats are partly arboreal and are still quite common. Some of them have spotted coats. They are all active hunters, preying upon rodents and birds. There are several genera.

Dasyurus viverrinus is the common native cat, also known as the dasyure cat. It preys on mice, rats and small rabbits, and is an important species in the ecological equilibrium. *D. geoffroy* is threatened with extinction. *Satanellus hellacatus* is the smallest of the Dasyures. *D. maculatus*, known as the spot-tailed native cat or tiger, is the largest of the native cats, reaching 26 inches in length, including its tail. It is found in Eastern Australia.

The Tasmanian devil (*Sarcophilus harrisii*), formerly found in Australia, is now confined to Tasmania. It is a burrowing carnivore, with powerful teeth, and able to kill prey bigger than itself. The first farmers to settle in Tasmania hunted the Tasmanian devil because of its predation on poultry and lambs. They persecuted it so ruthlessly that it has been

The Australian echidna (*Tachyglossus aculeatus*) feeds exclusively on insects which stick to the saliva moistening its very protractile tongue. Ants are among its favourite food. *Phot. Aldo Margiocco*

almost wiped out. In spite of its savage character and forbidding appearance, the Tasmanian devil can be tamed.

The marsupial wolf (thylacine)

The thylacine or marsupial wolf (*Thylacinus cynocephalus*) formerly inhabited South Australia, but is now found only in Tasmania, where it is extremely rare, if not extinct. It is protected by law, but protection may have come too late. Hillary, the conquerer of Everest, who organized an expedition to Tasmania, did not see a single Tasmanian wolf.

The marsupial wolf is also known as the tiger and the Tasmanian hyena. In physique and general habits, it is like the wolf. It is a large animal, measuring 5 feet in over-all length, of which 20 inches is tail. It is the most powerful of the carnivorous marsupials, preying upon all kinds of Australian birds and mammals, but it is not dangerous to man. It can snort like a kangaroo, a sound that has been likened to the barking of a dog. The bitch thylacine usually has a family of four, which the mother brings up in her marsupial pouch before depositing them in a nest. This extraordinary animal was systematically destroyed by the first colonists because of its predation on sheep. It was formerly abundant in Australia and New Guinea. If it exists at all, it will be in the most inaccessible parts of Tasmania.

The marsupial ant-eater (numbat)

These insectivorous marsupials, which are about the size of a large rat, have long snouts and bushy tails. They have from 50 to 52 small and practically useless teeth. Prey is restricted to ants and termites, which are swallowed whole. Like the true ant-eaters, the marsupials have long, worm-like, sticky tongues, used for licking up termites.

Numbats (*Myrmecobius*) have no marsupial pouch. They are found in areas of acacias and eucalyptus trees. They are quite defenceless, easily killed by cats and dogs, and seem fated to become extinct in the near future.

The marsupial mole

There are two species of marsupial mole, both of which are now extremely rare. Their habitat is sandy desert. They can literally dive into the sand, then emerge without making any real kind of tunnel, swimming through the ground as though it were a liquid rather than solid earth. Both are voracious predators. This family, the Notoryctidae, provides yet another extraordinary example of convergent evolution in marsupials and placental mammals. In general appearance, the notoryctes show a close resemblance to the African golden mole (*Carysochloris*) which is a true mole.

The bandicoot

Bandicoots (Peramelidae), of which there are 20 species, are about the size of a brown rat. The muzzle is long and pointed; the fore-limbs shorter than the hind limbs. The tail varies in length from species to species and is more or less bushy, but never prehensile.

Bandicoots have numerous incisor teeth, like those of the preceding families—teeth designed for eating flesh or insects. Their limb structure shows characters associated with herbivorous marsupials. The second and third toes are fused, and there is a muscle arrangement that makes it possible for the animal to move both toes as one.

Bandicoots are notable in having a placenta similar to that of placental mammals, but, in spite of this, the young are born in the usual marsupial premature state.

The family, Peramelidae, is made up of seven genera.

The long-nosed bandicoot (*Perameles*) is a sprightly, graceful creature and practically omnivorous, eating insects, worms and other prey, as well as seeds, roots and tubers. This species is still numerous in some parts of Australia.

The rabbit bandicoot (*Macrotis*) is notable for the beauty of its silvery, bluish-grey fur. It has ears like a rabbit; hence the name. The molars are flattened. Rabbit bandicoots feed on

The thylacine, or Tasmanian wolf (*Thylacinus cynocephalus*), is a species which is on the point of extinction and is now confined to wild and inaccessible places in Tasmania. It has the outward appearance and habits of a wolf living in a den among rocks. This photograph is taken from a mounted specimen. So far as is known, the living thylacine has not been photographed in its natural environment. *Phot. Aldo Margiocco*

insects and mice, and dig burrows in which they sleep during the day.

In the pig-footed bandicoot (*Chaeropus ecaudatus*) the feet are highly modified. The first and fifth toes have disappeared, while the fourth is no more than a horny tubercle. The second and third toes are strong, resembling the hooves of cattle. This explains the animal's popular name. The limbs, as a whole, are frail in construction. Pig-footed bandicoots are small—about eight inches from tip of nose to root of tail. Their diet is said to be mainly insects. They build nests of branches in which they hide during the day. Although the females have eight teats, they never have more than two young in the marsupial pouch.

Four or five genera of Peramelidae, most of them closely related to the *Perameles* of Australia, are found in New Guinea, the Bismarck archipelago and various other islands.

The Phalangeridae

This family is noted for its number of species and for its wide distribution. There is also great variation in size and habits between one species and another.

Opossums are tree-dwellers, feeding on insects, flowers and leaves. Their long tails are adapted for movement in the branches, whether they are prehensile or used as balancing-poles or rudders. The nails are long and curved, except the one on the thumb which is opposable to the other digits. All except *Trichosurus* are active at dusk, or later. The marsupial pouch opens forward, and there are from two to six mammae.

The honey mouse (honey opossum)

The honey mouse (*Tarsipes spenserae*), which is about 3 inches in length, excluding its tail, has a pointed trunk-like muzzle which it uses for probing into flowers to suck their nectar. The extended lips form a tube adapted for sucking nectar and pollen. The tongue is similar to that of nectar-sipping birds, being long and covered with long papillae that form a tuft at the tip. This brush acts as a whisk, and nectar and pollen adhere to it. The teeth are much reduced in number and size.

The honey mouse lives in the old nests of birds or in grass nests which it constructs itself. It is unique in being the most highly specialized marsupial and the only nectar-sucking mammal. Its main enemy is the cat.

Phalangers

The Phalangeridae are widely distributed in the Celebes, Australia and Tasmania. There are about 30 species, differing greatly in size and habits. The best known are the phalangers.

Phalangers, or cuscuses, have prehensile tails. They have woolly coats, variable in colour, but usually spotted with brown, white and russet-red in males. They live in trees, and feed mainly on leaves, although they are occasional carnivores. They are nocturnal in habits, but their presence can be detected by the strong scent of musk they leave on the air. Males are apparently territorial. Females breed once a year, giving birth to a single young one which spends many weeks in the marsupial pouch, bathed in a sticky secretion which presumably insulates it against desiccation.

The Australian opossum (*Trichosurus*) closely resembles the American species. It is fox-like, with a bushy tail, pointed muzzle and long ears. Common in Australia and Tasmania, it is a fruit eater and a vegetarian, and completely harmless. It has always been hunted for its beautiful fur, and was formerly heavily exploited. Its former abundance can be judged from the fact that four million pelts were sold on the London and New York markets in 1906. Despite this heavy predation by man, it is not yet threatened with extinction, but is certainly in need of effective protection. Its great adaptability has perhaps helped to save it. It is widely distributed in Australia, and is not unduly upset by the presence of man, whose dwellings it will readily invade and settle in.

The phalanger of the genus *Dactylopsils* has white fur longitudinally striped with black. It preys upon grubs and insects which it obtains by splitting rotten tree stumps with its incisor teeth. The fourth toe of the fore-feet, which is long and slender, is used to extract prey from holes and chinks in the wood. An identical modification of the toe is found in the aye-aye—a lemur from Madagascar, which also specializes in extracting grubs from decayed wood.

The dormice-phalangers, or mouse-opossums, are small mouse-like animals. They are found in forested areas and build spherical nests in the branches or under the bark of trees. They are nocturnal, and eat a wide variety of food—insects, fruit, seeds and leaves. Like the dormouse, they are hibernators, living through the winter on the fat reserves stored in their tails.

Flying phalangers are divided into several genera, ranging from the tiny *Acrobates*, which is the size of a mouse, to the great gliding opossum (*Schoinobates*) which is about the size of a rabbit. In all of them the front and hind legs are joined by a membrane which, unlike the membrane of bats, is covered with fur. This membrane acts as a parachute and enables them to glide from one tree to another, an ability they share with the African and Asiatic flying squirrels which they resemble in appearance and habits. Flights of 100 yards and more have been recorded.

The koala

The well-known koala—a living teddybear—is in a class by itself, generally regarded by zoologists as a sub-family of the Phalangeridae, i.e. an isolated family that may or may not include wombats.

The koala (*Phasolarctos cinereus*) is highly adapted for life in the trees, and has often been compared with the tailless lorises. Its marsupial pouch opens backwards, whereas in the phalangers it opens forward. It has cheek-pouches, in which it can store leaves to be eaten later. In fact, there are more reasons for classifying the koala as a separate family than there are for retaining it in the Phalangeridae.

No animal looks more like a bear cub except a bear cub. The koala has a heavy body, thick snout and rudimentary tail. It lives in the trees, and is slow-moving and peaceful. It feeds entirely on the leaves of twelve species of eucalyptus, the leaves of all other species being poisonous to it.

During the day, the koala sleeps on the top of a eucalyptus tree. At dusk, it comes out to feed on the tenderest shoots in the topmost branches. The female gives birth to a single young which is about an inch long at birth and spends three months in the marsupial pouch. After that, it spends several months clinging to its mother's back. From the time it is weaned until it begins to eat eucalyptus leaves, the young koala is fed on a kind of pap of semi-digested leaves evacuated by the mother. Breeding is slow, only one young being produced by the female every two years.

Once extremely common in eastern Australia, the koala was decimated by hunting as well as by epidemic disease: 600,000 were killed in 1927. At present, there are only a few colonies in New South Wales, and they are protected by law.

This very attractive animal is easy to tame, but its specialized diet makes it difficult to keep in captivity outside its native country. The exception is London where eucalyptus trees were planted before the koalas were installed. The capture and export of koalas is now prohibited by the Australian authorities.

Ventral surface of a phalanger suckling its young. The tiny immature young one is seen extracted from the marsupium, with the filiform teat which extends into its mouth and, beyond, into the oesophagus. *Phot. P. Pfeffer*

The great kangaroos (*Macropus* and *Megaleia*) live in the grassy zones or the tree-dotted savannas (scrub) in Australia. Their size may be considerable: a red kangaroo (*Magaleia rufa*) can reach 8½ feet from the tip of its muzzle to the end of its tail and weighs about 175 pounds. *Phot. J. Six*

The koala (*Phascolarctos cinereus*) would have disappeared from Australia if strict protective measures had not rescued it in the nick of time. This gentle, oddly-shaped marsupial, is a tree-dweller, which climbs well with the help of its clawed digits. The big toe is opposable to the other digits and functions like that of the primates. It only eats the leaves of species of eucalyptus which do not contain a volatile hydrocyanic compound whose accumulation is fatal to the animal. The young grows slowly; it remains for eight months in its mother's pouch. *Phot. Bruno Barbey—Magnum*

The Wombatidae and the Macropodidae

The Wombatidae (genera *Wombatus*, *Lasiorhinus* and *Wombatula*) have the same dentition as kangaroos and phalangers, but they are very different from both in appearance and general habits. They are as big as a dog and look like rodents, with bulky body and short, strong limbs. The incisor teeth keep growing, as in rodents. Wombats are found in mountain areas, where they dig extensive burrows. Their diet consists of plants. Wombats are not prolific breeders and are now rare in many parts of Australia where they were formerly common.

The kangaroos are the most remarkable representatives of the Macropodidae. A large number of species, differing widely in appearance and habits, are included in this family. Some are no bigger than rats, while others, such as the great grey kangaroo, are as tall as a man when they are sitting down. In this family, the marsupial pouch is well developed, and opens forward. The short fore-limbs have five digits. The hind limbs, which can be very long, usually have no first digit.

The biology of many species is not well-known. One of the most remarkable is the musk-rat kangaroo (*Hypsiprymnodon*) which, like the true musk-rat, is found in swampy areas, and gives off a strong body odour. Rat kangaroos (*Bettongis* and *Potorous*) occupy the same ecological niche in Australia as rodents do in Europe. They resemble shrews and rats. They are found in a wide variety of habitats and feed on insects, plants and a variety of waste matter.

The name kangaroo is commonly used to describe marsupials that fall into three categories: tree kangaroos, wallabies and true kangaroos.

There are six species of tree kangaroos (*Dendrogalus*), found in the forests of Queensland and New Guinea. All of them are small and have long prehensile tails. Despite their name, these kangaroos spend a great deal of time on the ground, feeding mainly on plants and fruit, but occasionally on worms. Although agile in trees, they are not specially adapted for climbing. They are usually found in groups of one male and several females.

There are about ten genera of wallabies. The best known are the *Lagorchestes* or hare wallabies which resemble hares in appearance and general habits. Like hares, they are remarkable for their speed and endurance. They spend the day in hiding, often in a tussock of grass, and come out at night to feed—another characteristic of the true hares.

True wallabies (*Wallabis* or *Protemnodon*) are medium-sized kangaroos found in Australia, Tasmania and New Guinea.

Rock wallabies (*Petrogale*) are common in the scarped or semi-desert regions of Australia. They are social animals, not easily seen when at rest because their colour matches their surroundings. Because of their sure-footedness, they have been called the Australian mountain goats.

The true kangaroos (*Macropus*) occupy, in Australia, the ecological niche occupied by antelopes in other parts of the world. There are three species, the largest of them reaching a length of ten feet, including tail.

Kangaroos live on the great Australian plains, living in small clans of six to a dozen individuals grouped under a dominant male or clan chief. They lie up during the day and come out at night to graze on grass and leaves.

When grazing, kangaroos move forward in short leaps like rabbits. When startled and put on foot, they display their fantastic jumping powers, going away in 30 feet bounds. Some individuals have been recorded bounding nearly 38

The Tasmanian wombat (*Wombatus ursinus*) is the smallest of the genus (about 2 feet in length); the colour of its fur is very variable, ranging from light grey, in the mountains, to dark brown on the plains. It lives in deep burrows and feeds on plants—grass, roots, bark, mushrooms, etc. Its incisors are suitable for gnawing. *Phot. Brownlie—Photo-Researchers*

feet, but no kangaroo is able to maintain this pace for long, and any kangaroo under severe pressure soon collapses, exhausted. When attacked by dogs or dingoes, the kangaroo defends itself vigorously. An extremely powerful animal, it is capable of inflicting severe wounds with the claw of the fourth toe on its hind limbs. When left alone or not ill-treated, most kangaroos are usually timid and harmless.

Winter is the main breeding season. Uterine development lasts about 40 days, and the young are no more than an inch long at birth. Considering the size of the mother, the young kangaroo holds the record as the smallest newly-born mammal. The young immediately makes its way to the marsupial pouch, guided there by a saliva trail, which the mother licks along her abdomen. The young kangaroo does not leave the marsupial pouch at all before the age of six months, and abandons it completely only when it is a year old.

The kangaroo population has been greatly reduced over the past century. The animals have been hunted for their fur and driven from the best pastures because they compete with sheep and cattle. Like other marsupials, they have been unable to stand up to the increasing pressure of man and his domestic stock. The farmer sees the kangaroo as a direct competitor for grazing, but recent research has shown that this is not always so. The kangaroo's last hope rests with the Australian authorities who are now making a serious effort to study and save their native marsupials and ensure the survival of those that remain.

Great kangaroos (*Macropus* sp.) grazing. *Phot. Bruno Barbey—Magnum*

American marsupials

Unlike the marsupials of Australia, the American species form only a tiny part of the native wildlife. Exposed for millions of years to competition with the higher mammals, they have adapted to environments in which they can maintain themselves successfully. The two families of American marsupials are quite different from those that exist in Australia. Separated since remote times, the marsupials of the two continents have developed independently of each other.

American opossums

The representatives of this family have a double uterus, a long muzzle and a long prehensile tail which is partly bare. A marsupial pouch is present in some genera but absent in others. The Didelphidae are native Americans and abundant in the tropical zone, where about 40 species are known. The best known is the opossum *Didelphis marsupialia*, widely distributed as far north as the northern United States. It is about the size of a cat, with a grey coat of thick down and long, stiff guard hairs. It is nocturnal in habits and, although omnivorous, prefers a flesh diet. It is often found living close to man, when it raids chicken coops or rummages in garbage heaps. It is a prolific breeder, but, although litters up to

eighteen are common, not more than a dozen can be reared because there are not enough teats to go round. When the young are strong enough to leave the mother's breast they will climb on to her back and coil their tails round hers. The female will move about, carrying her young in this fashion.

'Playing possum' or 'acting dead' is a well-known habit—a reaction to the presence of an enemy. The opossum lies quite still and appears to be dead. It is well-known that opossums survive serious injuries.

Other Didelphidae are *Philander,* the woolly opossum, which is about ten inches long, excluding its tail: *Monodelphis,* which is a small forest-dwelling species: and *Marmosa,* a small species, found in sub-tropical areas. *Marmosa* are extremely active in the trees, where they hunt insects. They have thick tails in which fat accumulates, and this is probably used as a reserve during periods of food shortages. They have been known to enter houses.

The most curious South American marsupials are probably the yapoks (*Chironectes*). They are small, otter-like animals that feed on crustaceans and other fresh-water creatures. They make burrows with entrances below water level. It is not known how the young, which remain anchored to the mother's teats, breathe when she dives in search of food.

The Caenolestidae

The marsupials of this group are found only in South America, in the Andean region, from Colombia to the island of Chiloe. In structure and dentition, they are typical insectivores. They are tree-dwellers and feed on live prey. They are the sole present-day survivors of a family which, in the Tertiary, was strongly represented in South America.

The order Carnivora

Carnivores are flesh-eating land mammals, found throughout the world in a variety of sizes, and noted for the fact that their feet end in free digits equipped with claws. Their teeth are designed for cutting flesh. They are mostly powerful animals with a highly developed nervous system, making for fast and accurate reflexes. Their intelligence is well developed. The young are born in a helpless state, and spend a long time with the parent or parents. Their subsequent behaviour depends, to a great extent, on this apprenticeship.

The carnivores are divided into two super-families, the Canoidae, which includes wolves, bears, racoons and weasels; and the Feloidae, which includes genets, hyenas and cats.

The Canoidae

The Canidae

This is the dog family and includes the wolf, the fox and the jackal.

The wolf and its social complex

The wolf (*Canis lupus*), the central character of so many legends and the villain of folklore, was once widely distributed in the northern hemisphere. It is still quite common in the remoter areas of northern and eastern Europe, and even in parts of southern Europe. It has disappeared from western Europe, having been systematically killed off. Present-day reports of wolves in these areas are based on the sighting of feral wolf-dogs. In any case, there are few parts of western Europe where the animal could find the vast undisturbed areas of forest that suit it.

The timber wolf of North America, also known as the lobo, is a sub-species. Wolves breed in the spring, when the bitch gives birth to a litter of three to a dozen puppies. The dog wolf is a good father, and plays an active part in rearing the family. Dog and bitch regurgitate food for the cubs. When the cubs are three or four months old, they begin to follow the mother, and are taught to hunt. This is the family pack or unit. From then until they are fully grown, the cubs are known as wolflings. By then, they have the strength and endurance for which the wolf is notable and cannot be run down in straight pursuit. Specialist wolf hunters consider it almost impossible to bring an adult wolf to bay.

Wolves are social animals and, in each pack, there is a hierarchical system. Their communications system is well developed, and is based on a variety of calls, the best known of which is the wolf howl. Wolves do not appear to defend a particular territory, and several bitches may litter in a restricted area.

The winter wolf pack is made up of families that have joined together. Although such packs appear to be wanderers, there is some evidence from North America that they work a definite circuit, returning to their former breeding area. The winter pack can be a threat to domestic stock, but there is no evidence of wild non-rabid wolves attacking man, except in self-defence. In folklore, famished wolves devoured people, but this has never been established as a fact.

Although wolves sometimes attack and eat dogs, they are members of the same family, and the wolf/dog hybrid is fertile. Like the dog, the wolf can become rabid.

The fox

While the wolf lost the battle with man over most of its range, the fox has adapted itself, withstanding all the pressures man has brought to bear and all the upheavals he has caused. The fox remains a common animal in Europe, where neither trapping nor hunting have succeeded in reducing its numbers.

Foxes can live literally anywhere, on mountains, in forests, marshes, by the sea-shore, and even in towns. In many parts, they have become increasingly urbanized.

Although they usually hunt at night, foxes can often be seen on foot by day, especially where they are not under severe pressure from man. Where they are much persecuted, they lie up by day and hunt by night in cover.

The prey range is wide, from insects and earthworms up to deer fawns. In forest areas, the fox feeds largely on the field vole. It will track a rabbit or hare in the same way as a hound. If it has a staple diet at all, that staple is certainly small rodents. Foxes in the Highlands of Scotland have been shown to eat about 2 000 voles a year. Some fruit is eaten in autumn.

Despite its reputation, the fox is probably more of an asset

European fox (*Canis vulpes*) emerging from its den. *Phot. Aldo Margiocco*

than a liability to the farmer. Not so many foxes carry off hens nowadays, because most poultry are in battery cages, or kept intensively. A great deal has been learned about the fox's food by the examination of its droppings which it deposits ritually in certain places. Their commonest content is rodent hair. Hen-killers are usually vixens with a family on their hands.

Although foxes are burrowing animals, they sleep as much above ground as below, except in the breeding season, when the vixen lies up with her cubs. Sometimes the vixen digs a new burrow; sometimes she uses an established one; and sometimes she will move into a badger sett. Badgers will tolerate a fox so long as she does not settle in a part of the sett they are using themselves. There can be two to nine cubs in a litter; they grow quickly and can breed by the time they are one year old.

Despite its reputation for cunning—and it is a cunning animal—the fox appears to be less intelligent than, say, the badger or the otter. Fox cubs reared in captivity mostly remain timid and seldom settle down in the way that badger cubs do.

In Eurasia, there are other foxes, desert species and Arctic species, among them the fennec (*Fennecus zerda*) and the Arctic fox (*Alopex lagopus*).

The fennec is a very small fox with huge ears, found in the sandy desert areas of the Sahara and Arabia. It appears to lead a social life, and feeds on insects and rodents. Little research has been done on the fennec in the wild state, but it is often kept in captivity.

The Arctic fox, noted for its magnificent fur, is found within the Arctic Circle. There is much individual colour variation, animals being sometimes white, sometimes blue-grey. Arctic foxes feed mainly on lemmings and the migratory birds that nest along the shores in millions. In winter, they become much more vegetarian, feeding largely on lichens which they uncover by scratching away the snow.

The jackal—a carrion-eater

Jackals (*Canis*, sub-genus *Thos*: *Canis aureus*, *C. adustus*, *C. mesomelas*), of which there are several species, are found on dry steppe-lands of Eurasia. They inhabit a wide variety of environments and are not readily upset by the presence of man. In fact, they are his camp followers and, in Africa, can be heard howling at night near villages or encampments. Adaptable and cunning, and able to conceal itself in the scantiest cover, the jackal more than holds its own wherever it is found.

Despite being so well-known, its ecology has been little studied, but it is probably more wolf-life than fox-like. During the day, it lies up in thickets, coming out at night to hunt or scavenge. Although a true carnivore, taking any kind of prey it can catch and hold (including lambs), it is outstandingly a scavenger, feeding on the bodies of cattle, reptiles and fish. It also eats a considerable amount of fruit. In some Arab countries, where the dead are buried just below ground level, the graves are covered with heavy stones to prevent jackals from unearthing the corpses.

There are about ten other species of wild dog. The red dog of Asia (*Cuon alpinus*) was made famous by Kipling. The wild dog of Africa (*Lycaon pictus*) is a large animal with a dappled coat and prominent ears. It is also known as the Cape hunting dog. Both species hunt in packs, like wolves. They have tremendous stamina and persistence, and are able to attack and kill animals very much bigger than themselves. Much research has recently been done on the African wild dog which has changed the popular image of this animal completely.

The lycaon (*Lycaon pictus*) is a wild African dog living on the savannas. Like many members of the Canidae, it hunts in a pack and brings its victims to bay. *Phot. J. and M. Fiévet*

South America has a variety of wild dogs. *Dusicyon*, which is fox-like, is found in open country from Patagonia to the Equator; *Cerdocyon*, a close relative of the *Dusicyon*, is found in the forests of Guiana and Amazonia; *Lycalopex* lives on the savannas of southern and central Brazil and the deserts and northeastern Peru; *Chrysocyon*, the long-legged, maned wolf, is found in Paraguay, northern Argentina and southern Brazil. The last is easily recognized by its awkward gait and its long ears; *Speothos* from Amazonia has a short muzzle and short legs.

The grey fox (*Urocyon*) is found in North America and the northern areas of South America, where it inhabits arid areas. It climbs trees to reach nesting birds, but does not dig burrows.

The bears

The bear family is represented in Eurasia and America, but is not nowadays found in Africa.

The brown bear (*Ursus arctos*) is found over a large part of Europe, Asia and North America. Although the brown bears of Europe, Asia and America all belong to the same species, they show great variations in size, and are often given separate names. This is not surprising when one considers that the small brown bear from the Mediterranean area rarely exceeds 450 pounds in weight, while the large brown bear of North America, especially those from Kodiak, may reach a weight of more than 1550 pounds. From South to North, the bear increases in size and weight, and is a typical example of the so-called Bergmann's Law, which is that, in any given species, the most northerly representatives are the biggest, and the most southerly representative the smallest. This is as true of weasels, foxes and wolves as it is of bears.

The brown bear is omnivorous. An occasional predator, it lives mainly on dead animals, insects, honey, a variety of fruits and even grass and growing crops. In the autumn it lays on fat, and in winter it retires into a cave, where it lies asleep, or half asleep, until spring. But it does not hibernate in the true sense. It lives on its fat.

The brown bear is found in Europe, Asia and North America. It is a polymorphic species of variable size, ranging from the small Spanish bears to the giants of Alaska. *Atlas-Photo—Lauros*

The she-bear usually gives birth to two cubs which are no bigger than rats at birth, and quite helpless. The cubs remain with their mother until the following autumn. Although highly intelligent and easily trained, the brown bear remains an unpredictable animal, often sullen, and sometimes dangerous. In many countries it is protected, and in such areas it is more than holding its own. It is not in danger anywhere, except perhaps in France, where the remaining population—100 or so in the Central Pyrenees—is strictly protected.

The polar bear (*Thalarctos maritimus*) is the most northerly species, its range being within the Arctic Circle. It spends most of its time on the pack-ice or ice-floes, and preys mainly on seals. During the past century, it has been cut to pieces by irresponsible hunting, and it is on the danger list, if not immediately threatened with extinction.

The Procyonidae

This family is made up of several remarkable species, found in Asia and America. Two of them, the giant and lesser pandas, are found in the foothills of the Himalayas.

The giant panda (*Ailuropoda melanoleuca*), discovered at the end of last century by the Rev. Père David, is found in China, and looks like a black and white bear. It feeds on bamboo shoots. An extremely rare species, it is much sought after by zoos, but attempts to breed the species in captivity have, so far, failed.

The lesser panda (*Ailurus fulgens*) is about the size of a fox. It is an elegant creature with a beautiful coat. Being easily tamed, it is in great demand as a pet.

The kinkajou (*Potos flavus*) is a marine species that looks as though it were part monkey, part bear cub and part cat. It is a small, agile carnivore, with a long prehensile tail, and is an

The polar bear (*Thalarctos martimus*) is, along with the Arctic fox (*Alopex lagopus*), the most northerly of mammals. A fish eater, it can live on ice-floes. It does not hibernate, even in the depths of the polar winter. Sometimes, it lets itself be carried on drifting icebergs. *Phot. World Wildlife Fund.*

The giant panda (*Ailuropoda melanoleuca*), with its plantigrade manner of walking and its shaggy coat resembles a bear, but it belongs to a quite different family, the Procyonidae of which the racoon is the prototype. The giant panda feeds exclusively on bamboo. It is rare and confined to the mountains of western Szechwan and Kansu. *Phot. R. Michaud-Rapho*

accomplished climber. A tree dweller, active at night, it feeds mainly on fruit, supplemented by insects and birds' eggs. Kinkajous settle down well in captivity, but are experts at escaping, a flair they share with the *Bassariscus*—an allied species distinguishable by its black and white ringed tail.

The coati (*Nasua*) is mainly a South American species, but its range extends into the southern areas of North America. About 36 inches in length, including its tail, it has a long head with a turned-up nose. It is a skilful climber and a good runner. When climbing or running, it carries its tail up straight. The coati feeds on fruit, insects, slugs, snails, small birds' eggs and small mammals. It is highly intelligent and easily tamed.

The best known species in this family is undoubtedly the racoon (*Procyon lotor*). The most notable habit of this species is that of washing all its food before eating it. So far, no-one has been able to explain the significance of the habit. The racoon will wash crayfish and fish newly taken from the water. The captive racoon will even try to wash sugar cubes, with the result that the cubes dissolve in its paws. Intelligent and highly adaptable in the way of habitat and food, racoons were well equipped to colonize the whole of America, and this they have done. They have been imported into Europe and are beginning to live wild there, especially in Germany.

The Mustelidae

This is a large family represented by many species in Europe, Asia and North America. Most of the present-day European carnivores belong to this group, many of whose species are renowned for their magnificent winter fur.

The pine marten (*Martes martes*) is a forest weasel, widely distributed, but local in mountainous and forest areas of Western Europe. It is shy and nocturnal and a specialist predator on squirrels. It will eat anything it can catch and hold, but also feeds largely on insects and their larvae, and, to a certain extent, on wild berries. The stone marten (*Martes*

foins) is found in flat, cultivated areas. The two species can be distinguished by the colour of the throad. In the stone marten the throat is white; in the pine marten, it is orange-yellow. Stone martens are often found in haylofts and barns, and families have been observed in the centre of Paris. A marten seen in a farm building or a street will almost certainly be a stone marten.

The polecat (*Mustela putorius*), common in Western Europe, is shy and nocturnal, and not often seen except perhaps in car headlamps at night. In size, it comes between the marten and the stoat. Its outer fur is dark brown, through which the yellowish underfur shows clearly. The underparts are black. Polecats have a pervading distinguishing smell which some people find unpleasant. They feed mainly on rodents, but also eat frogs, insects and fruit. The ferret (*Mustela furo*) is a domesticated polecat.

The European mink (*Mustela lutreola*) is closely related to the polecat, but occupies a different ecological niche, being as much a water-weasel as a land-weasel. It is now almost extinct in France. The American mink (*Mustela vison*) is reared commercially on a large scale for its valuable fur. The American form differs only slightly from the European.

The stoat or ermine (*Mustela erminea*) and the weasel (*Mustela nivalis*) are the small carnivores most likely to be seen in the European countryside because they are active by day as well as night. The stoat is about twice the size of the weasel and turns white or partially white in winter. The stoat's tail is long, bushy and tipped with black; the weasel's is short and smooth with no black tip. Both are territorial, the males holding an area within which the female lives and breeds. Stoat and weasel may occupy the same ground at the same time, especially in areas where voles are abundant. Although both can kill prey much bigger than themselves, their normal food consists of voles and field mice. Stoats breed once a year; weasels twice. The systematic destruction of these animals cannot be justified on ecological or economic grounds.

There are several other species of weasels and martens in Asia and America. The sable (*Martes hibellina*), noted for its magnificent fur, inhabits Russia and Siberia. The yellow-throated marten of India (*Martes flavigula*) is one of the most handsome members of the family.

Skunks (*Mephitis, Spilogale, Conepatus*) are small American species. All the weasels have anal glands, but these are highly developed in the skunk which has two such glands, one on each side of the tail. By muscular contraction, the skunk is able to squirt out the contents of these glands for a distance of several yards. Before defending itself in this way, the skunk strikes a warning posture with its tail erect. In a similar situation, *Spilogale putorius* even walks on its fore-paws with the rear part of its body vertically erect.

In Central and South America, there are several other genera of Mustelidae. *Galera barbara,* which is of great size, ranges from southern Mexico to Paraguay. It is a fruit-eater and a carnivore. The grison (*Galictis*) ranges from Mexico to the Argentine.

The wolverine or glutton (*Gulo gulo*) is bear-like or badger-like, and weighs up to 44 pounds, thus competing with the badger for the title of the biggest weasel. This is a circum-polar species. Weighing as much as 100 dog-weasels, it is a weasel in every way, tremendously tough and powerful. All Arctic animals, including the bear and the wolf, treat it with caution and respect. It will attack the biggest prey, including elk and reindeer, dropping on to their backs from the high branches of a tree. Unlike most weasels, the wolverine is highly intelligent and cunning, and perhaps the best equipped mammal in the whole Arctic region.

Finally, there is the tayra (*Tayra barbara*) from South

America—a widely distributed large, marten-like species. According to locality, its fur varies in colour from dark yellow to almost black. Almost nothing is known about the life of the tayra in the wild state, which is true of most South American mammals. It is thought, however, to be very suitable for domestication.

There are six species of badger in Asia and North America, and one in Europe. The European badger (*Meles meles*) is still widely distributed, although its numbers have been drastically reduced in some areas over the past 25 years, mainly by gassing. In general appearance, the badger resembles a small bear. Its face is white with black stripes, and this black and white pattern is conspicuous at all times, even at night. It is probably a warning pattern.

The badger is crepuscular and nocturnal. It is a compulsive burrower and a badger sett becomes, over the years, like a series of small quarries. The sleeping nests, in which the badgers stay in daytime, are lined with hay. They are sociable animals, and as many as nine may be seen emerging from the same sett at night. This is a truly omnivorous animal. It will eat anything it can catch and hold, but preys mainly on small vertebrates, worms and snails. It also eats roots, maize, cereals, fruit and even grass. It can be a nuisance in vineyards because it scatters grapes all over the place while it is nibbling at the clusters. On the whole, however, it can be described as neutral from the point of

A forest species, the European pine marten (*Martes martes*) is found mainly in mountainous regions. It often deposits its young in old nests of birds of prey, and hunts squirrels in the trees. *Phot. Lundin-Ostman*

also eats shell-fish and crabs. It rarely takes fish. It hunts and sleeps in the sea, lying on its back, coiled up amongst the seaweed. Here it rears its single offspring. When feeding, it lies on its back, breaking shells on its stomach, often with the help of a stone. It is, therefore, one of the rare examples of a vertebrate, other than man, capable of using a tool. This species has been almost completely exterminated by fur-hunters.

Grisons (*Grison*) are terrestrial Mustelidae which occupy in South America the ecological niche of polecats and zorils in the Old World. They live in burrows and give off a fetid smell. *Phot. A. R. Devez-Lauros—Atlas-Photo*

view of man, and its systematic destruction is unjustified.

As in many other members of the family, there is delayed implantation in the badger. Although mating takes place in the spring, true development of the embryo does not begin until the end of the year. The young are born in the period February/March. Badgers are said to hibernate in the most northerly regions. They most certainly do not do so in Western Europe, although they become less active in winter, when they draw on their stores of accumulated fat.

Otters have colonized almost all the continents. At least ten species are known, of which the least typical is the gigantic Brazilian otter (*Pteronura brasiliensis*) which reaches a length of eight feet, and closely resembles a seal.

The sea-otter (*Enhydra lutris*) is found along the North American Pacific coasts. It measures 5 feet in length and weighs up to 88 pounds. It feeds mostly on sea urchins, but

The racoon (*Procyon lotor*) is a carnivore with considerable intelligence; easily tamed, it can be trained to behave in a sophisticated manner. It has a mania for washing its food, even when it is of aquatic origin (live crayfish, for instance), before eating it. *Phot. Visage Albert—Jacana*

The European otter (*Lutra lutra*) is in decline over a great part of its range. This is not due entirely to being over-hunted. River pollution is also a factor, but there are probably others.

The otter is shy and wary, but it is also playful and, where not disturbed, can be seen by day. It is a predator on fish which it catches by diving under stones and roots, although

The badger (*Meles meles*), the largest European mustelid, has a very varied but mainly vegetarian diet. The fertilized egg, after a short period of segmentation, remains inert for several weeks in the uterus, or matrix: it resumes development only after this lapse of time (this is the phenomenon of delayed implantation of the egg, which exists also in the roe-deer). *Atlas-Photo—Merlet*

it will hunt them in mid-stream as well. It is a skilful swimmer and diver. Eels are an important prey item, but crustaceans, amphibians, birds and mammals are also taken. Analysis of the otter's droppings reveals this. The droppings are called spraints and are deposited in prominent places, where they are easily collected by the zoologist for examination.

During the day, the otter lies up in a rudimentary burrow, almost invariably below an old tree stump. The lower entrance to this burrow is under water; the upper entrance, used for ventilation, is hidden among the roots. When alarmed, the otter dives silently into the water, normally escaping without being seen.

European otters are said to be nomadic, and they do travel a great deal, but they are settled when the bitch has her cubs, which may be in any month of the year. It may well be that travelling otters eventually return to their starting point, as wolves do. Certainly, the same routes are followed by succeeding generations of otters, which use the same boulders and the same crossing places. Otters are, therefore, easily trapped.

The otter is probably the most rewarding wild mammal pet. It becomes extremely attached to its owner whom it follows everywhere. It can be trained to catch fish, an ability that is exploited in some eastern countries.

The large Brazilian otter (*Pteronura brasiliensis*), up to nearly 10 feet in length, is an agile and powerful swimmer. It moves about in the water like a seal and with the same ease; its broadly webbed feet, its powerful laterally flattened tail, and the undulations of its amazingly supple body make it a first-rate swimmer: It is seen here floating like a log and being carried along by the current. *Phot. A. R. Devez; Lauros Atlas-Photo*

These three young polecats (*Mustela putorius*), still under their mother's care, enjoy this frog which she has brought them and on which they are cutting their teeth. Batrachians are the favourite food of polecats, which are always on the lookout for frogs, which they eat in large quantities (the easiest way to catch them is to bait a trap with dried frog). *Phot. Aldo Margiocco*

The Feloidae:
from the tomcat to the
greatest beast of prey

The second great division of the order of carnivores is the Feloidae, the most distinctive types being the genets (Viverridae), hyenas (Hyaenidae) and cats (Felidae).

The Viverridae

The Viverridae are small, long-bodied carnivores, found mainly in the tropics of the Old World. A few species are found in the southern parts of the temperate zone.

Genets are essentially an African group, although the common genet (*Genetta genetta*) is found in southern Europe up to the Loire. Although rare in many places, it is sometimes locally abundant. It is a shy animal, living in secluded areas of woodland, moors or copses, and it is a rare thing to come across one in its lair. Thus, it exists where its presence is often unsuspected. Even woodcutters and hunters pass it by without ever seeing it.

Little is known about the habits of genets in the wild. All are nocturnal, lying up during the day in burrows or holes in trees, and therefore difficult to study. They come out at night to hunt birds and ground rodents. They are commonest in Equatorial Africa, where it is not unusual to meet half a dozen or more in the course of a night walk through the forest. Genets settle down very well in captivity. The Romans

The wolverine or glutton (*Gulo gulo*) is noted for its strength, disproportionate to its size which is that of an average dog. Arctic regions. *Sven Iillsater*

The ratel (*Mellivora capensis*) is a powerful and aggressive African carnivore. Its coat, light on top, dark underneath, is perhaps a warning livery, intended to inform a possible adversary and to dissuade it in advance. *Phot. J. P. Varin—Jacana*

The European otter (*Lutra lutra*), in intimidating attitude. *Phot. Aldo Margiocco*

A mongoose (*Herpestes mangosta*), the Rikki-tikki-tavi of 'The Jungle Book' in a fight to the death with a fair sized cobra. *Phot. A. Margiocco*

domesticated them and kept them in their houses to catch mice.

The African palm civets (*Nandinia*) and the Asian palm civets (*Paradoxurus*) are closely related to genets. They are found throughout the tropics. Although they are carnivores, they feed mainly on plants and fruits. They live in trees.

Mongooses are found in tropical regions of the Old World, but one species, the ichneumon (*Herpestes ichneumon*) ranges as far north as Andalusia. The Indian mongoose (*Herpestes qriseus*), was imported into the West Indies to kill snakes. The mongooses multiplied and the snakes were eventually destroyed, but it was then the trouble began, for the snake-killers became poultry killers and, therefore, a great pest.

Ecologically, the mongooses are a very dynamic group, and have produced a type for every kind of environment. Thus, there are species highly adapted to savanna, forest, swamp and mountains. Combined with this wide adaptability, there is great diversification of size, which varies from that of a large weasel, the dwarf mongoose (*Helogale*) to that of a medium-sized dog, the *Bdeogale* (southern, eastern and western Africa).

Mongooses prey upon insects, rodents and crustaceans which they often hunt during daylight. They are well-known as killers of snakes, even the most venemous, which they attack fearlessly. This is all the more remarkable as the animals are not immune to snake venom. But the mongoose's reflexes are swift; it knows how to kill snakes, and it knows how to kill them without being bitten. In a confrontation with a cobra, the mongoose makes a rattling sound. Almost immediately the cobra coils itself up. When it unwinds itself to strike, the mongoose jumps backwards. Then, before the extended snake can resume its defensive position, the mongoose rushes in and crushes its head between its teeth.

The mongoose settles down readily in captivity and tames easily, and has long been used as a vermin killer.

Civets (*Civettictis civetta*) of Asia and Africa are another numerous group, the largest species of which reach the size of an average dog. They are heavy animals—the Indian civet reaches up to 26 pounds in weight—with coarse fur that forms a mane on their back. They are exploited for their anal secretions, which have a musk odour, and are used in the manufacture of the most expensive perfumes. The animals are farmed in Asia for their secretions, as mink are farmed for their fur. In its unrefined state, the anal secretion has a fetid odour.

In Madagascar, there are several genera, *Galidia*, *Fossa* and *Cryptoprocta*, but next to nothing is known about their biology.

The Hyaenidae—carrion-eaters

There are four species in this family: the striped hyena, found in North Africa, Arabia and South East Asia; the spotted hyena of tropical Africa; and the brown hyena and aardwolf in South Africa.

The aardwolf (*Proteles cristatus*) is insectivorous. The three other species are mainly carrion-eaters, although they hunt much more than was once thought, and are considerable predators in their own right. They are strong-jawed, with extremely powerful molars designed for crushing even the biggest bones. Bones are a main food item.

The spotted hyena (*Crocuta crocuta*) follows the big beasts of prey, like lions, always ready to devour what they leave. It has a keen sense of smell, and is said to be quite intelligent. This species tames easily, but is not usually kept as a pet.

The common genet (*Genetta genetta*) lives in the south of Europe. It hunts rodents, and is extremely agile. *Phot. Fatras—Jacana*

The two-spotted palm civet (*Nandinia binotata*), which lives in the African equatorial forest belt, climbs with agility in trees, whose fruit it eats. Its diet is only to a slight degree carnivorous. Size of a large stone-marten. *Phot. A. R. Devez—Biological Mission to Gabon*

The spotted hyena (*Crocuta crocuta*), in spite of its brutal habits, is a good mother, as this photograph indicates. This carnivore, found in Africa south of the 14th parallel, feeds on sick or defenceless animals. Height at withers, about 2½ feet. Total length, including tail, about 5 feet. *Africa Photo—Myers*

because of its smell and its call which sounds like laughter. The hyena plays an important part in the ecology of the African plains. In some areas, their dried brains are used as an ingredient of supposedly infallible love potions.

The striped hyena (*Hyaena hyaena*) is on the verge of extinction throughout its range, particularly in North Africa, where only a few survive in the most remote areas.

The brown hyena (*Hyaena brunnea*), whose habits are similar, is found in South and South East Africa.

The Felidae (cats)

Cats are the outstanding carnivores—the hunters par excellence—the best designed of all for capturing and killing live prey. They are intelligent, alert and powerfully muscled. They have strong retractile claws for holding prey, and long canines for biting deep and holding on.

The family varies greatly in size, from the smallest domestic cat, which hunts small rodents, to the gigantic Siberian tiger, biggest of them all, which is able to kill the biggest herbivores. But all of them are built on the same lines, and there is very little difference in the behaviour pattern. Apart from size, there is no significant difference in the physical make-up of the alley cat and the tiger, and hardly any difference in their hunting style.

The domestic cat (*Felis domesticus*) belongs to the genus *Felis*. In the same genus is the wildcat (*Felis sylvestris*) which everybody knows by reputation, but which hardly anybody ever sees. Most cats described as wild are merely feral domestic cats. The true wildcat is distinguished by its greater size, longer legs and ringed, blunt tail which is always black at the tip.

The wildcat is a forest species, although it can exist in areas where the trees have been felled, as in many parts of the Scottish Highlands. The Scottish Highlands are, in fact, the only part of Great Britain where the species is still found. It manages to keep its numbers up in forested mountain areas and is certainly less rare than is often believed. It is nocturnal and elusive, lying up by day among rocks, or in trees, or sometimes even in a disused eagle's eyrie. So it is not often seen on foot. Its food consists mainly of rodents. Untamable unless taken before its eyes open, it has the reputation of a spitting, ill-natured fury. But in fact, it is no different from any other cat. When threatened or brought to bay, it becomes a tiger.

There are numerous species of wildcats in the tropics of America and in the Old World. Many of these, and especially the South American species, remain comparatively unknown, and it is difficult, in the present state of knowledge, even to guess at their numbers. It is difficult even to classify species because there is such a wide variety of forms (polymorphism) from one region to another. In addition, the relative rareness of certain species and their extreme shyness makes it difficult to collect a sufficient number of specimens to make systematic study possible.

The ocelot (*Felis pardalis*) is a magnificent South American cat, more frequently seen in zoological gardens than in the wild state. Many are kept privately as pets. This is an extremely polymorphous species and it is almost impossible to find two that are exactly alike. It is about 4½ feet in overall length—bigger than the wildcat and smaller than the panther. As in the case of most cats, little is known about its biology. Judging by the number of pelts exhibited for sale in South American markets, it must still be common in many

Grey meerkats or suricates (*Suricata suricata*), which are the mongooses of South Africa, live in fairly numerous societies. They dig burrows. Their diet largely consists of insects. Suricates often sit up on their hind legs as in this photograph. They are the size of a large wild rabbit. *Phot. Tierbilder-Okapia-A.L.I.*

regions. But it is doubtful if it can withstand for much longer the incessant hunting to which it is subjected.

The puma (*Felis concolor*), also known as pampas lion, ranges from Argentina to southern Canada. The North American form is the biggest and is the one known as the cougar or mountain lion. Young pumas have spotted coats. The adult coat is rusty-brown or silvery-grey. Despite its size, a mature puma will always yield ground to a man with a dog.

Lynxes are remarkable among cats because of their stub tails and prominent ear tufts. They are found mainly in the temperate and cold regions of the Old World and North America. One species, the caracal (*Felis caracal*) is found in Africa and India. The northern lynx (*Felis lynx*) is still found in central and northern Europe. There is a smaller southern form (*Lynx pardellus*) in the Spanish Pyrenees.

The genus *Panthera* includes all the well-known big cats, the lion, the tiger and the leopard or panther.

The big cats: the lion

The lion (*Panthera leo*) survived in Europe into historic times. Herodotus records that lions attacked camels in Xenophon's baggage train in the Peloponnese. There were lions in Palestine and the Middle East in Biblical times. It is only a little more than a century since they disappeared from Algeria and Morocco, and they are still locally common on savannas south of the Sahara.

The lions of Asia have been reduced to a remnant of about 250 in the Forest of Gir, in northwest India. The Asian lion is smaller than the African race, and not so heavily maned. It is possible that there are more lions in circuses and zoos at the present time than there are existing in the wild state. The lion thrives and breeds freely in captivity but, when deprived of its liberty, it rarely achieves the size of its free-born kind.

Lions are social carnivores, living in parties known as prides, each pride being made up of a dominant lion, lionesses and cubs. They prey mainly on the ungulates of the plains—zebras, wildebeeste and such like—so in east Africa they are most numerous on savannas or in forests with well spaced trees. The lions of the Gir Forest of India feed largely on stray cattle.

Group hunting is the rule, with several lions stalking, then stampeding the prey towards others lying in ambush. Although the male is dominant, it is usually the lionesses that do the killing. The hierarchical system is very obvious at feeding time. The adult male eats first, then the lionesses, then the cubs. If the prey is large, there is enough left for the cubs; if it is small, they go without. As a result of this strict hierarchical system, there is often high mortality among lion cubs. This system helps to ensure that a balance is held between the lion population and the species on which they prey.

Under normal conditions, lions show little fear of man, but are rarely dangerous. The few that become man-eaters are almost invariably aged animals, or animals wounded by hunters, so that they are unable to hunt their normal prey.

The tiger

The tiger (*Panthera tigris*) is confined entirely to Asia, where it is widely distributed, it's range extending as far as the Caucasus and Siberia. There is considerable variation in size from one part of its range to another, Manchurian tigers being the biggest. Manchurian and Siberian tigers do not have the bold black and orange striping characteristic of other races; their fur is thick and pale. Tigers are still fairly numerous in India—their population has been estimated at about 4000—as well as in southeast Asia.

Structurally, there is little to choose between these big cats, and they will inter-breed in captivity. With their skins off, the bodies are indistinguishable. The two, however, differ greatly in their habits and ecology.

The tiger is an animal of the jungle and lives a solitary life except for a brief period during the mating season. It preys mainly on wild ungulates, and does not often kill cattle. From time to time, individual tigers become man-eaters, for the same reasons as the lion. Ordinarily, the human presence upsets the tiger, and it will desert a forest where it is too often disturbed or molested.

Tigers are wary animals and difficult to see against their jungle background when they are standing still. They avoid great heat, and show a distinct preference for cool places. Unlike most of the cats, they are very fond of bathing. These, and other habits, suggest that the tiger may originally have been confined to more northerly areas, and that it moved into tropical areas in comparatively recent times.

The leopard (panther)

Unlike the lion and the tiger, the leopard or panther (*Panthera pardus*) is not highly specialized ecologically, in the sense that it adapts well to the most diversified habitats—savanna, equatorial forest and mountains. It has a wide prey

Angora or Persian cats result from mutations with thick soft fur. *Phot. Buzzini*

Domestic Siamese cat. Some regard it as a native of Thailand, but others consider it to be merely a mutation of the Indian cat, descended from the sub-species *Felis libyca ornata*. Lauros—Atlas-Photo

The caracal (*Felis caracal*) is a superb animal with the cat's lithe bearing, but high on its legs (18 inches at the withers); it is by nature sly and difficult to observe, found from tropical Africa to India. The caracal belongs to the African sub-species *Nubica. Phot. A. Margiocco*

range that includes domestic animals like dogs and cats. Because of its adaptability, it is able to survive in close proximity to man, and in places from which lions and tigers have long since disappeared. This great adaptability explains its wide distribution, which covers most of Africa, Asia and the Indonesian Islands.

The so-called black panther is no more than a black leopard—the result of melanism. Melanism is common in leopards from southeast Asia, and black kittens can appear in any litter. An adult leopard weighs between 130 and 180 pounds, depending on age and sex.

In tropical America, the leopard's niche is filled by the jaguar (*Panthera onca*) which is a slightly bigger animal with a particularly handsome coat. The spots on the back and flanks become rings with dark spots inside. Like other big cats, the jaguar (known locally as the tiger) has immense strength. It is able to kill a cow and drag it several hundred yards into the forest. It has been recorded as flattening a four-strand barbed wire fence while doing so. After it has eaten, the jaguar hides the remains of its prey in some forest thicket. It is generally found close to rivers and streams, and is said to be a predator on fish. Folklore, indeed, suggests that it uses its tail-tip as a bait.

The cheetah—the dog-like cat

The cheetah (*Acinonyx jubatus*) is a cat apart, differing from all others in having non-retractile claws. It is long-legged and slender—greyhound-like, in fact—and is built for running. It is, in fact, the fastest of all land mammals, and

Lions (*Panthera leo*), which used to be hunted by the Assyrian kings, have now almost disappeared from the whole of the continent of Asia except for a small population in northwest India, which is rigorously preserved. *Phot. Aldo Margiocco*

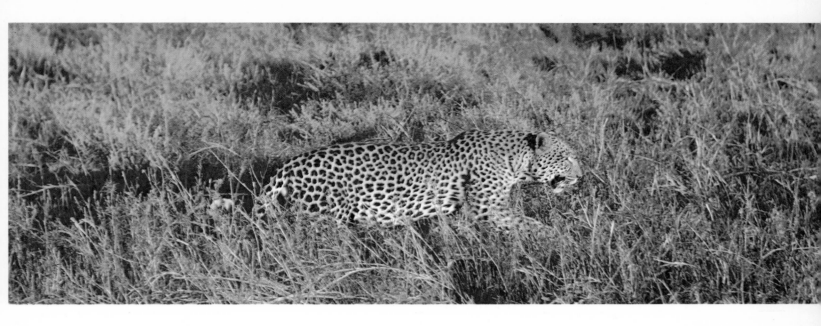

(*Above*)
On the savanna, in the dry season, the spotted coat of the leopard (*Panthera pardus*) blends with the bleached grass. East Africa. *Phot. J. and M. Fiévet*

has been timed at top speeds of 65–70 miles per hour. But it cannot keep up such a speed for long.

The cheetah is found on the savannas and semi-deserts of Africa. In southwest Asia it is now very rare, if not extinct. It tames easily—tame cheetahs are not uncommon—and, not so long ago, Indian maharajahs kept packs of them for hunting antelopes, especially black bucks.

The cheetah (*Acinonyx jubatus*), a felid with the appearance of a dog, is not wholly confined to the African steppes. The one shown here lived in the grassy tree-dotted zones of northwest India. *Phot. A. Margiocco*

(*Left*)
The Bengal tiger (*Panthera tigris*) seen in the jungle of northwest India. *Phot. A. Margiocco*

The order Pinnipedia Sealions (eared seals), walruses and seals

Pinnipeds—the word means fin-footed, which distinguishes them from the fissipeds or split-footed land carnivores—were once classed in the order of carnivores as a sub-order, but are now usually classified in a separate order, as above.

While other carnivores, even those that spend some time in the water, are land mammals, the pinnipeds are strictly marine, coming ashore only to breed. They spend most of their lives in the sea, feeding on fish, crustaceans and, occasionally, other vertebrates. Such a highly specialized life requires special adaptation in a mammal, and the pinnipeds are perfectly designed for it. They have streamlined bodies, well adapted for swimming and diving. On their snouts, they have highly sensitive hairs (vibrissae) which are tactile organs. The nostrils, placed at the tip of the nose, close automatically when the animals dive.

It has been established that a seal can dive to a depth of

Weddell's seal (*Leptonychotes weddelli*), an admirable swimmer, haunts the southern seas, from Patagonia to the Kerguelen Islands and as far as the Antarctic ice-cap. *Phot. J. Six*

nearly 58 fathoms, an ability explained by its highly specialized physiology. During a dive, the heart beats fall from 100 to about 10 per minute. The brain and the heart are supplied by well oxygenated blood while other parts of the body are starved of it for the time being. When it surfaces, it replaces this oxygen deficit. These adjustments are not under the animal's control.

Although pinnipeds, under the skins, are built like any other carnivores, or other mammals for that matter, the limbs are highly modified externally into flippers. But the mode of propulsion is not the same in eared seals and true seals. The eared seals use their fore-flippers as oars; seals, on

the other hand, use mainly their hind flippers. Thus, the true seals swim more like fish, their hind flippers controlled by the very powerful muscles of the dorsal region. On land, the sealion walks with the help of its four flippers, whereas the seal drags itself on its stomach, assisted only by its fore-flippers.

Pinnipeds are found in all the seas of the world except the Indian Ocean, and their greatest concentrations are in the Polar seas, perhaps because these waters are so rich in plankton and fish. True seals are found mainly in the Arctic, whereas the eared seals are found mostly in the Antarctic.

Like other carnivores, pinnipeds show a high degree of intelligence. In zoos and circuses, they are highly popular because of their playful disposition and their ability to perform great balancing feats. In the wild state, they show little fear of man. This, combined with the high commercial value of their skin and fat, has resulted in the slaughter of whole populations, and the survival of some species is seriously threatened.

The Otaridae (eared seals)

This family is made up of two groups—sealions and fur seals.

Sealions are distinguished by their smooth coats, which have no under-fur. The best known species is the Californian sealion (*Zalophus californianus*) which is the one most often seen in captivity, in zoos and circuses. It is extremely agile, with a great sense of balance, and is often trained as a juggler.

The adult male is a massive animal, weighing over 400 pounds; females, as in most pinnipeds, are slimmer, smaller and lighter in weight. This sealion is found on the north-eastern coasts of the Pacific, but there are considerable populations on the shores of the Galapagos. Like other animals inhabiting these islands, the Galapagos sealions show no fear of man. This trait make them easy to study in the wild state.

The sealion society is a hierarchical one, the females being organised in harems, each dominated by a mature bull. Harems usually number between five and twenty animals, adult cows with their young. The master bull, known as a pasha, constantly patrols the perimeter of his territory, barking most of the time. Any rival bull invading the territory is immediately attacked. In the Galapagos man is treated as an intruder by the bulls; females, on the other hand, pay no attention to him.

Outside the occupied territories, other groups assemble. These groups are composed of bachelor males, not yet strong enough to challenge the pashas, and elderly retired bulls bearing the signs of age and the scars of combat.

Fur seals can be distinguished from sealions at a glance. Their coat has a thick under-fur and is extremely valuable.

The Northern fur-seal (*Callorhinus ursinus*) is the one with the most highly prized fur. It is a migratory species. From October to April it is found along the eastern and western coasts of the Pacific. Some time in mid April, the males begin their migration northwards; the females follow them much later, in June/July. The sexes join up on the shores of the Pribilof Islands on the Bering Sea. By the time the females arrive, the males have established their territories, which they defend against all rivals.

Powerful bulls may hold harems of up to 80 females. Soon after their arrival, the cows give birth to a single pup, ashore. Four days later, they are mated by the bulls. Gestation lasts for a year. In October, the breeding season over, the fur-seals return to the sea and migrate southwards.

Californian sealions (*Zalophus californianus*) form colonies on the islands off the west coast of America. This photograph, taken on the coast of Barrington Island (Galapagos archipelago), shows a group of females and young playing in the sea. *Phot. A. Brosset*

This seal was once so heavily hunted that it was on the verge of extinction; 800,000 were killed in one year on Unalaska Island alone, and by 1900 the world population was down to 130,000. International agreement has saved it, and the population is now estimated at 1½ million. The species is now in such a strong position that controlled hunting is permitted by the signatories to the agreement that saved it. The cull is mainly of young males. The skin of adults, torn and scarred by many fights, has little value.

The walrus (*Odobenus rosmarus*), which weighs about a ton, is another Arctic species. In general, it resembles a sealion more closely than a seal. Its long, down-pointing tusks, which are its outstanding feature, are really lengthened upper incisors which keep on growing like the gnawing teeth of rodents. They are not really weapons, although the males sometimes use them for fighting each other. Their real use is for scraping shell-fish from the sea bottom. The Greek name for them means 'walking teeth', but they are not used for walking.

Not much is known about the walrus's habits. It is an off-shore species, keeping close to the coast and to the edges of the ice-floes. Unlike other pinnipeds, it appears to be

Californian sealion (*Zalophus californianus*) walking on a beach in the Galapagos Islands. *Phot. A. Brosset*

A male walrus, seen close-up and in profile. Notice the special sensory hairs (vibrissae) on the upper lip, and the absence of a coat. The reason is that this one is moulting, but the adult walrus has in any case only very sparse fur. Protection against the cold is ensured by the layer of subcutaneous fat. *Phot. by courtesy of the Canadian National Film Office*

The sea leopard (*Hydrurga leptonyx*) is widely distributed in the southern seas, from the Antarctic ice-cap to southern Australia. It is an aggressive species with very powerful teeth and it feeds on the young of other seals as well as penguins. *Phot. John Warham*

monogamous. The female has a single offspring every two or three years. In most pinnipeds the lactation period is short; in walruses it is said to last for two years.

The Phocidae

These are the true or earless seals, and there are many species, most of them found in the north Polar regions. But several, including the sea elephants, have colonized the Antarctic, and one species, the monk seal, is found in the Mediterranean.

Arctic seals include the bearded seal (*Erignathus barbatus*), the grey seal (*Halichoerus grypus*) and the common seal, also known as the harbour seal (*Phoca vitulina*).

Grey and common seals breed in northern Europe, including the British Isles, and on the Atlantic and Pacific coasts of Canada. The common seal is a small species, the males being under six feet in length. It has a spotted coat with variable markings. This species feeds on fish and crustaceans, and mates at sea.

The members of the sub-family Lobodontinae are Antarctic species: the crab-eating seal (*Lobodon carcinophagus*), and

Weddell's seal (*Loptonychotes weddelli*), both found in the Kerguelen Islands; and the leopard seal (*Hydrurga leptonyx*). The leopard seal is a formidable predator which feeds on young seals and penguins.

The sub-family Monachinae is represented by the monk seal (*Monachus monachus*) which, although now rare, still exists on the rocky coasts of the Mediterranean and northwest Africa. It is a large seal, sedentary in habits, and feeds mainly on cephalopods.

Seals of the sub-family Cystophorinae are distinguished by the structure of the nose, which, in the male, is like a bladder when inflated. The best known species is the sea elephant (*Mirounga leonina*), found mainly in the Antarctic. The sea elephant is the biggest of the pinnipeds, adult males reaching 21 feet in length and weighing up to and over 3 tons. During the Antarctic summer, the sea elephant frequents islands, including the Kerguelen Islands, where it breeds. The cows have a single pup, and mate shortly after it is born.

Shedding of the coat follows quickly on the breeding season. Males and females then form separate groups. In the month of March, they move seawards, but details of their migrations are not known. Sea elephants are thought to feed mainly on cephalopods.

The hooded seal (*Cystophera cristata*) is found in the northern seas (Greenland, Newfoundland, etc.). It can inflate its nasal cavity by closing its nostrils. It feeds on cephalopods and fish.

Walruses (*Odobenus rosmarus*) have an anatomy similar to that of sea-lions and seals. The individual seen here head-on is a female; its sex can be recognized from the divergence of its tusks (canine teeth); the other is its male. Walruses are exclusively Arctic. Maximum length about 15 feet; maximum weight, 1 ton. *Phot. by courtesy of the Canadian National Film Office*

Above, this female sea elephant (*Mirounga leonina*) has just given birth on a beach in the Kerguelen Islands. Its young, covered with long hairs, shows its long umbilical cord still attached to the placenta, which seems to be incompletely expelled. Skuas (*Catharacta skua lonnbergi*), which have arrived, will devour the placenta after having cut the umbilical cord. *Phot. Benoît Tollu—Jacana*

The order Cetacea
Whales and dolphins

The order Cetacea comprises about a hundred species, all highly specialized for life in the sea. They have fish-like streamlined bodies, and their forelimbs have become modified into flippers. The rear limbs are completely atrophied and invisible externally. The body tapers to a powerful tail with horizontal flukes, used for propulsion, as in fish.

Cetaceans are divided into two groups: the toothed whales (Odontoceti), of which the best known type is the sperm

Tursiops are highly intelligent animals. The structure of the brain bears witness to considerable powers of association, and the areas of the cerebral hemispheres connected with hearing are the most extensive. These dolphins live in groups and communicate with each other by very varied sounds. Shown here is a bottle-nosed dolphin, an inmate of an aquarium in Florida, jumping vertically to take hold of a titbit attached to a bell. *Phot. Tierbilder—Okapia*

whale; and the whalebone or baleen whales (Mystacoceti), in which the teeth are replaced by whalebone plates (lamellae). These plates filter out the plankton on which the whales feed.

Animals in this group reach an enormous size—up to 100 feet in length and a weight of nearly 120 tons. The blue whale is the biggest animal that has ever existed. The evolution of species of such gigantic size is only conceivable in terms of an aquatic habitat: on land, such animals would be

crushed by their own weight. Some of the cetaceans are, however, relatively small, not exceeding 5 feet in length and a weight of 65 pounds.

It is generally accepted that cetaceans have evolved from land mammals that returned to the water. No animals are more, or better, adapted to a pelagic life. Many aspects of their biology remain to be investigated, for example, how they are able to stay under water for periods of up to 2 hours without breathing, and to survive at depths of more than 160 fathoms.

Several species are migratory, breeding in tropical oceans, then moving to the Arctic or Antarctic to feed. The study of captive dolphins shows that cetaceans are able to navigate by echolocation, like bats. In spite of their fish-like appearance, cetaceans are typical mammals in behaviour and level of intelligence.

The Odontoceti (toothed whales)

These are the toothed whales. The number of teeth varies from 2 in Cuvier's whale to 260 in the dolphin. There is great diversity of types within this group.

The Platanistidae (freshwater dolphins)

The Platanistidae are a very special family, in that they have a rudimentary neck and are able to live in fresh or brackish water.

The Gangetic dolphin (*Platanista gangetica*) and the Amazon dolphin (*Inia geoffroyensis*) from South America are found in rivers. They travel upstream until they are halted by some natural barrier. They are small whales with long beak-like snouts which they use for burrowing in the mud, where they catch the fish and crustaceans that are their prey.

The La Plata dolphin (*Stenodelphis blainvillei*) is even smaller, measuring about five feet in length. This species is found at the mouth of the River Plate, hence its name; it is also found in other rivers of Brazil.

The Delphinidae (dolphins)

The dolphin family, with about 72 species, is the most numerous in the order Cetacea. Length varies from 4 to 14 feet, and weight from 50 to 500 pounds, but some species are much bigger and heavier, the biggest being the killer whale which may reach 30 feet in length and weigh 1500 pounds.

The common dolphin (*Delphinus delphis*) is found in all tropical and temperate seas. It is gregarious, and may be seen in groups of up to 100, roving the sea in search of the herrings and sardines which are their main prey. They can move at high speed, probably 25 knots. They are notable for their habit of following ships or, rather, travelling in front of the bows. They are lithe, powerful and frolicsome, and leap frequently out of the water.

The bottle-nosed dolphin (*Tursiops*) is distinguished from the common dolphin by its short, well defined snout or beak, as well as by its greater size—up to twelve feet. This is a common species in the Atlantic. It has a wide prey range, including sharks, shrimps, rays and cuttlefish. Bottle-nosed dolphins settle well in captivity, and are good subjects for behaviour studies.

Dolphins of the genus *Cephalorhynchus* are small and have an ill-defined beak. They have pied skins, the black and white areas being variable in size. There are four species, all found in southern seas. They feed on jellyfish and shrimps, but little is known of their habits.

The *Sotalia* include several species found in the firths and estuaries of rivers flowing into the warm seas of America, Africa and Asia. They are generally known as 'river dolphins' because of their habit of ascending rivers. They measure from three to six feet in length, and have well developed beaks equipped with strong teeth. They move about in small schools, and are notable for their well synchronized manoeuvres. They feed on fish and shrimps. One species, from Cameroon, is said to be entirely vegetarian. It is said that many native people believe that the *Sotalia* retrieve the bodies of people who have been accidentally drowned and bring them ashore. For this reason, they look upon them as friends and refuse to kill them.

The black fish or pilot whale (*Globicephala*) is a much bigger species, ranging up to 28 feet in length. It has a bulbous head, no beak, and long narrow flippers. The number of species of pilot whales has not yet been scientifically agreed, but the general opinion is that there are at least three. They occur in all the oceans outside the Polar regions. Highly gregarious, they travel in schools up to two or three hundred strong, led by an old bull. In one way they resemble sheep, the school following the leader wherever he goes. In fact, if a few frightened individuals rush shorewards and beach themselves, all the others are likely to follow, so that the whole school becomes stranded.

Pilot whales are migratory, travelling from warm seas to cold, and then back, according to the time of year. Their food consists mainly of cuttlefish. They are late maturers, the breeding age being six years for females and thirteen years for males, which are polygamous. Their life span is believed to be about 50 years. Pilot whales are actively hunted by whalers, mainly for their oil.

There are perhaps another ten species of dolphin, none of which has been closely studied. The most remarkable of these is the killer whale or grampus (*Orcinus orca*) which is the largest of all, and the only really ferocious species. Old males reach a length of thirty feet. Colour is black and white, with a white spot behind and above the eye. The killer whale is easily identified because of its large dorsal fin and the eye-spot.

A school of killer whales may sometimes be seen from the deck of a liner, a sight that cannot fail to delight the layman or the naturalist. A big liner makes a safe observation post. Small fishing boats do not. In fact, killer whales sometimes attack small boats, probably in mistake for seals or smaller whales. If the occupant of such a boat is thrown into the sea, he is in some danger of being swallowed.

The killer whale's voracity knows no bounds. No fewer than fourteen dolphins and fourteen seals have been found in stomach of one animal which was mortally wounded when it was in the process of swallowing its fourteenth seal. Sea-birds or seals resting on ice-floes are not safe from attack, for the killer will dive, rise under the floe at great speed and break it up. The seals and birds are attacked when they fall into the water. The killer has been known to smash up floes more than three feet thick.

Ordinarily, these whales hunt in packs of three to fifty. They do not hesitate to attack species much bigger than

Porpoise jumping out of the water photographed from the deck of a ship it was escorting. *Phot. docteur Soulaire*

themselves, even the biggest and most harmless whales. They kill the biggest whales by tearing great lumps out of their bodies.

The Phocaenidae (porpoises)

Porpoises are the best known of all cetaceans, and the ones most commonly seen by the shore-based observer because they often come close to land, from which they can be easily observed, surfacing four times a minute to breathe.

The common porpoise (*Phocaena phocaena*) measures from 5 to 6 feet in length and averages about 110 pounds in weight. It travels in schools, and is often found in river estuaries; but, unlike the dolphin, it does not follow ships. Its food consists of fish, cephalopods and crustaceans. Porpoise flesh is, itself, edible. Because it damages fishing nets, the porpoise is not popular with fishermen. It is still common along coasts of Western Europe.

The Delphinapteridae

The beluga or white whale (*Delphinapterus leucas*) is of medium size, measuring about fifteen feet in length. It is found in Arctic and sub-Arctic seas. As its name suggests, its skin is whitish. White whales live in small schools and hunt fish, cuttlefish and crustaceans. Their skin provides leather of exceptional quality.

The narwhal (*Monodon monoceros*) is the second species in the group. Of medium size—maximum length about sixteen feet—it is also an inhabitant of the Arctic seas. The male narwhal can be distinguished at a glance from all other cetaceans because of his single spiralled tusk, which may reach a length of eight feet. This tusk, which is a modified incisor tooth, grows horizontally forward from the left side of the jaw. It has been suggested that it is used for breaking the ice, but this is not so. It is, however, sometimes used in fighting, and this is confirmed by the fact that it seldom remains undamaged. Whatever its real function—if it has one at all—the narwhal's tusk lent colour to the legend of the unicorn. In the Middle Ages there was a brisk trade in narwhal tusks because of the therapeutic qualities claimed for them by the doctors of the time.

The Physeteridae (sperm whales)

The large sperm whale (*Physeter catodon*) is both interesting and important, not only because of its great size but also because of its specialized biology and economic importance. It is still much hunted by whalers.

An adult sperm whale bull may reach a length of 60 feet and weigh over 100 tons. It has an enormous box-like head, the forward cavity of which is filled, in adults, with a colourless oil known as spermaceti, the biological significance of which is not understood. There are no upper teeth, but the lower jaw has a large number of narrow, strong teeth. The immense non-symmetrical head of the sperm whale is unique among mammals.

Although sperm whales occur in the oceans of both hemispheres, they are found mainly in the deepest areas of warm seas. They are sociable animals, schools of between 20 and 100 females and young being led by an old male. They are probably migratory, moving in spring towards more temperate latitudes. They swim with their heads out of the water at a speed of 12 to 15 knots. Their food, which consists mainly of cephalopods, is often taken at great depths —160 fathoms or more. The duration of a dive varies from 20 to 75 minutes.

Sperm whales attack and kill giant squids, some of them unknown to science outside the sperm whale's stomach. There are records of men who, having fallen into the sea, have been swallowed and digested by sperm whales.

This whale is still heavily hunted. The spermaceti in its skull yields up to five tons of oil which is superior to the oil of any other whale. Blubber and flesh are commercially exploited. Finally, the sperm whale produces in its intestine a substance known as ambergris, which was once widely used therapeutically, and is still very much in demand as a fixative for perfumes. Why the whale should produce ambergris in its intestine is still debated. The largest mass of ambergris recorded in a sperm whale weighed 992 pounds.

The pygmy sperm whale (*Kogia breviceps*) rarely exceeds thirteen feet in length. It is cosmopolitan, and is of no great commercial value.

The Ziphiidae

The beaked whale is closely related to the sperm whale. It has an elongated head, tapering into a beak-like snout. This family has several genera, including *Hyperoodon* and *Berardius*, whose size varies from 15 to 40 feet. All are fast swimmers and said to be the best divers of the whole order. The bottlenosed whale (*Hyperoodon rostratus*), formerly intensively hunted, is now uncommon in the North Atlantic.

The Mystacoceti (baleen whales)

In this group, the teeth of the embryo are replaced by baleen plates in the adult. The Mystacoceti include not only the biggest whales, but the biggest animals ever known.

The grey whale

The Californian grey whale (*Eschrichtius gibbosus*) is an Arctic species, measuring up to 53 feet in length. Brought to the verge of extinction in the 19th century, it has been protected since 1938, and is now increasing in numbers. It is a migrant, wintering on the coasts of Mexico and California. The grey whale is an off-shore species, often found in shallow water.

The Balenopteridae

Size in this group ranges from 30 feet in the pikewhale or rorqual (*Balaenoptera acutorostrata*) to 100 feet in the blue whale (*Balaenoptera musculus*) which can reach a weight of 120 tons. Rorquals have a small pointed head. On their throat and chest they have from 50 to 70 longitudinal grooves, and they have a triangular dorsal fin situated near the tail. They are fast swimmers, and the common rorqual (*Balaenoptera physalus*) has been recorded travelling at 30 knots. These whales have blow-holes from which they spout when they surface to breathe. The shape of the spout is characteristic, and whalers are able to identify any species at a distance.

Rorquals travel alone, in pairs or in large schools. They

are long-distance migrants. In winter, they are found between the warm and temperate zones, where they breed. Cows of the large species breed at two-year intervals, giving birth to a single calf about 20 feet long. The calf suckles its mother, whose milk is extremely rich in fat, and grows rapidly, reaching a length of 53 feet at the age of seven months. Puberty is reached about the age of two years.

The whales fast during their stay of several months in temperate seas. In summer, they migrate to the Arctic and the Antarctic in search of food which consists mainly of planktonic crustaceans, especially a shrimp known as krill (*Euphausia superba*). In the Antarctic, krill is found in dense masses over immense areas. The whale simply swims through the masses with its mouth open, engulfing krill. Water is expelled from the mouth by special muscles, while the baleen plates filter out the plankton which is then swallowed. It has been recorded that the contents of one blue whale's stomach contained five million krill, weighing almost two tons.

For several centuries, whales have been intensively hunted for their fat, oil, flesh, baleen and bones which were used, and

legislation has not been very successful and is a faith more than a fact. The terrible thing is that there is no longer any need to exploit whales at all.

The Megaptera

The humpback whale (*Magaptera boops*) differs from the rorqual in having a short squat body, conical head and large fins. It measures up to 53 feet in length and up to 45 tons in weight. The humpbacks are long-distance migrants, summering in the Polar seas and wintering in the tropics. They prey mainly upon crustaceans, but also take fish and, sometimes, sea-birds. This species is dwindling at an alarming rate because it is still ruthlessly hunted.

The Balenidae (true whales)

This family has three genera, the best known of which is the

Mouth of a rorqual in the process of being cut up in a Norwegian whale factory. In the open mouth, the baleen can be seen. Notice that this is a dorsal view of the animal. The animal shown here is the common rorqual or fin whale, *Balaenoptera physalus*. Its flesh is edible. After the carcass has been dismembered, the meat will be stored in refrigerators. *Phot. docteur Soulaire*

still are used, in industry, agriculture, and for food. Commercial hunting, which might sometimes be more aptly described as wholesale slaughter, has resulted in many species being decimated or brought to the verge of extinction. There is now some international control of hunting, aimed at striking a balance between the annual harvest and the breeding capacity of the various species of whales. But

right whale (*Balaena mysticetus*), which averages from fifty to seventy feet long. It has an enormous head, about a third of the body length, a hooked profile and an immense mouth with long blackish baleen plates. It is almost black in colour, but the front part of its lower jaw is white and it has a white eye-ring. It is an Arctic species, now extremely rare because of uncontrolled hunting. It feeds on plankton and shrimps.

D   A   B

SPERM-WHALE HUNTING

Hunting the sperm-whale by harpoon as it is carried out on the coasts of the island of Madeira, breeding zone of this species. *A*, a sperm-whale has just revealed its presence by its spout (breath emerging from its blow-hole); *B*, the boat has approached the sperm-whale, and the harpooner gets ready to go into action. *C*, the harpoon finds its mark in the whale's body. *D*, the sperm-whale dives vertically, its tail sticking 10–12 feet out of the water (note its shape and horizontal position in relation to the body's plane of symmetry); *E*, the wounded animal surfaces (the tip of its enormous snout can be seen); *F*, the animal, after having drawn breath, and dragging the harpoon cable, dives but not vertically; from another boat, a whaler fires a second harpoon at it. *Phot. docteur Soulaire*

E   F

The order Perissodactyla

Present-day members of this order are medium to large-sized mammals, more or less adapted for running on hard ground. They have one thing in common: the axis of the limbs passes through the third toe, and this supports the animal's entire weight.

This is a declining order. Their range has shrunk and there are fewer species than there were in the last geological period. Wild horses and asses, as well as rhinoceroses, have a much more restricted distribution, and present-day populations of surviving types are much fewer than formerly.

The Equidae
horses, asses and zebras

In this group—horses, asses and zebras—the third toe is the only one that has persisted in the course of evolution. The fossil record shows the stages of regression of the other toes right up to the one-toed limb of the present-day horse.

Przewalski's horse (*Equus caballus przewalskii*) is the only surviving wild species. It, too, was thought to be extinct, but there are still a few surviving on the steppes of central Asia. Przewalski's horse stands about four feet tall at the withers, and is short and stocky. It has a rigid vertical mane that distinguishes it from the domestic horse.

The coat is reddish-brown on the back, yellowish on the belly. A fully grown adult weighs about 770 pounds. Unfortunately, the wild Przewalski crosses readily with the Mongolian pony, and it is possible that, before long, it will cease to exist as a pure breed, even in the wild state.

The ancestry of the modern horse appears to have been the tarpan which was common in Europe and Asia in prehistoric times. A few are still preserved in Poland. Tarpans were the favourite game of primitive man, who also domesticated them. Prehistoric horses may also have con-

The Indian tapir (*Tapirus indicus*) is now found only in certain parts of India, Malaysia and Borneo. Although leading a hidden life in swamps it falls easy prey to carnivores and is shot by sportsmen. *Phot. A. Margiocco*

tributed to the creation of present-day domestic stock which certainly derived from two or perhaps three wild ancestors.

Wild horses roam the plains in herds, led by a dominant stallion, and the leader will fight furiously with any rival to maintain his domination over the mares. Breeding is seasonal, foals being born in April and May, after eleven months' gestation.

Wild horses are alert animals, always on guard, and are swift runners. After man, the wolf is their main predator, but it is man who has been mainly responsible for their near extinction. In America there are great herds of feral horses, but all of these are the descendants of domestic horses introduced by the conquistadores, some of which escaped. American wild horses are known as mustangs from the Spanish word *mestiño*.

Zebras (*Dolichohippus*, *Hippotigris*) inhabit the eastern, central and southern plains of Africa. Although, in the main, they are plains animals, some also live in mountains. They are distinctive horses, with black and white stripes, the stripes varying in number and arrangement according to species. Zebras live in herds of a dozen or so, and often mix with herds of wildebeeste and antelopes. They can run fast, reaching a speed of 35 miles per hour. The lion is their main wild predator. The predator responsible for their decimation is man. It was man who wiped out the quagga (*Hippotigris quagga quagga*) and has reduced several other forms to the status of rarities.

Being immune to the diseases and parasites of horses, zebras were obvious candidates for domestication, and many efforts have been made to do this. Zebras have also been crossed with other species, but all these efforts failed because of the zebra's temperament and intractable disposition.

Asses are natives of the semi-desert areas of Asia and Africa, where they inhabit arid areas of scant vegetation and prickly scrub. Several wild forms are found in northern India and Persia. Others are found in the mountains south of the Sahara, but these are probably the descendants of escaped domestic stock, and not of pure wild origin.

The Nubian wild ass (*Asinus africanus*) is still found in small herds in the Sahara (especially Mouïdir, Tibesti, etc.). But it may be that these are domestic animals which have reverted to a wild state. *Phot. J. Six*

In northwest India, wild asses or onagers (*Hemionus onager*) are distributed over great areas, through which they move according to the vegetation cycles. Usually, they live in small herds of different sexes, but periodically they occur in great congregations. The breeding season is at the end of summer. When a mare comes in season, she separates from the herd and spends two or three days alone with the stallion. These wild asses are very shy, although they are easily tamed when young. When adult, they are stubborn and cannot be tamed. Although the donkey is looked upon as a slow plodding animal, the wild ass can reach a speed of thirty miles per hour.

Products of their harsh semi-desert environment, asses are justly famed for their frugality and endurance. They can eat the harshest vegetation rejected by other herbivores, and can survive without water for long periods. Domesticated, they have become invaluable beasts of burden in areas where the inhabitants are too poor to keep horses. An obvious step to improve this was crossing the ass with the horse. A jackass crossed with a horse mare produces a mule, an animal of great stamina and sure-footedness, widely used in mountanous areas. A cross between a she-ass and a horse stallion produces a hinny, a much less useful animal, and one not commonly bred. Both mule and hinny are sterile. The gestation period in asses is about nine months, and the life span between 25 and thirty years.

The Tapiridae (tapirs)

Four species of tapir still exist: *Tapirus indicus* of tropical Asia, and three in central and South America—*Tapirella bairdi*, *Tapirus terrestris,* with its several sub-species, and *Tapirus pinchaque* from the high plateaux of the Andes. The fact that these unique animals are found in tropical regions of Asia and America is a strong argument in favour of the theory that, in recent geological times, the two continents were joined.

The tapir is a thick-bodied animal, noted for its long muzzle which resembles a short trunk. The Asiatic or Malayan tapir is a striking animal, with black limbs, shoulders, head and neck, the rest of the body being white. The young of all species are brilliantly marked with yellow stripes and spots on a dark background. The adult coat appears at the age of six to eight months. Adult weight is between 440 and 660 pounds.

Although they occur in a variety of habitats, tapirs are essentially animals of hill forests and are most likely to be found near hill streams. They are skilful swimmers and wallow like wild deer or wild boars. They are entirely vegetarian, eating a wide variety of plants. Their principal predators are tigers and jaguars. In some areas, they have been saved as a result of human superstition. Some American Indians, for example, protected the tapir for religious reasons, and in Burma, killing is taboo.

The Rhinocerotidae (rhinoceroses)

There are five species of rhinoceros still in existence—three in Asia and two in Africa. They were much more widely distributed during the Pliocene, when they ranged over a large part of the Old World, including western Europe, the home of the prehistoric woolly rhinoceros.

Present-day rhinoceroses are confined to the tropics, where they are all threatened with extinction. The great one-horned rhinoceros (*Rhinoceros unicornis*), the largest species, is found in Nepal and northwestern India. This species may reach a height of 6½ feet at the shoulder and weigh 4 tons. The folds of its skin look like armour plating.

The Chinese attribute aphrodisiac properties to rhinoceros horn, but the notion is totally unfounded. They also prize its blood and urine, which they use in medicine. However useful or useless these things may be, the result is that the species has been massacred and the population is now down to about 600 animals.

The one-horned or Javan rhinoceros (*Rhinoceros sondaicus*) is similar, but smaller. Formerly widely distributed, it is now reduced to about 25 animals, maintained on a reserve on the Island of Java.

The third species is the Asiatic two-horned rhinoceros (*Didermocerus sumatrensis*) which is smaller still, and exceedingly rare. It is estimated that there are fewer than two hundred left, scattered through the jungles of Burma, Malaya and the Sunda Islands.

The rhinoceroses of Asia confine themselves to swamps and wet forests. They bathe and wallow daily. In the morning and evening, they come out to eat grass, reeds and stalks. They

Male Indian rhinoceros (*Rhinoceros unicornis*), at the edge of a swamp. *Phot. A. Margiocco*

lead solitary lives outside the breeding season. Their eyesight is poor, but their hearing and sense of smell are acute. Rhinoceroses are slow breeders, which is a factor in their decline. Females of the one-horned species give birth to a single offspring after a gestation period of nineteen months, and there is a space of several years between each pregnancy.

In Africa, the future of the rhinoceros is a little more promising.

The black rhinoceros (*Diceros bicornis*) is widely distributed in east and south Africa and is abundant in places where it is protected; for example, in Kenya.

The range of the white rhinoceros is more restricted, and it is found mainly in Zululand and the eastern Congo. It, too, was slaughtered in the past, but it is now increasing in areas where it is effectively protected.

The habitat of the black rhinoceros in Africa is thorn savanna plentifully supplied with water holes, because this rhinoceros drinks a great deal. It is a browser rather than a grazer, feeding on the leaves and stalks of bushes. Because of its unpredictability, the black rhinoceros can be dangerous, although it usually runs off when alarmed. There are times when it charges without warning, usually in response to an unaccustomed scent or sound. Then it will charge into men, vehicles or encampments that get in its way. Outside the breeding season, it is a solitary animal. It is territorial, and marks its boundary with heaps of dung and with scent which it rubs off on to stems and tree trunks.

The white rhinoceros (*Ceratotherium simum*) weighs up

This female Indian rhinoceros (*Rhinoceros unicornis*) and her offspring have been wallowing in a pool and have emerged from it covered by a layer of whitish mud. *Phot. A. Margiocco*

to four tons. It is paler in colour than the black rhinoceros, but not white. The name 'white' is probably a corruption of the Afrikaans word *weit*, meaning wide, a reference to its broad mouth. Its colour is the colour of the dried mud in which it wallows at any convenient time. This species is much more sociable and less aggressive than the black. It is a grazing animal rather than a browser. Its continued survival depends on effective protection.

The great Indian rhinoceros has a short, broad head and a single horn. Formerly found over India, it is now very rare. It is estimated that there are still 300 of them in Nepal and another 350 on reservations in Assam.

The order Artiodactyla

This order comprises medium to large sized mammals whose limbs end in an even number of toes: hence the name even-toed ungulates. The axis of the limb passes between the third and fourth toes instead of through the middle of the third toe, as in horses.

There are 9 present-day families in the order and 82 genera. With the exception of Australia, there are representatives in all parts of the world. The group includes oxen, camels, goats and sheep—the species most valuable to man as domesticated animals. In the order there is great diversification of size and appearance. The ungainly hippopotamus weighs about 4 tons, whereas some antelopes hardly reach the weight of a hare.

Most of the animals in this order are ruminants: that is, they chew the cud. The biological interest of this phenomenon is twofold. It enables the animal to limit the time spent grazing—a time fraught with danger from predators—and aids the digestion of cellulose.

The Suiformes (pigs, hippopotamuses)

The pig group, which includes the hippopotamus, differs from other families in the order in many ways. There is a great deal of difference, for example, between a pig and a camel. But the main difference is that the animals of this group are non-ruminants.

The domestic pig is descended from the wild boar, and the differences between the modern pig and its wild relative are the result of selective breeding by man. But the two still belong to the same species and inter-breed freely wherever possible. In Asia, the wild and the domestic pig are so alike that it is sometimes difficult to tell them apart.

The wild boar (*Sus scrofa*) is found in Europe, Asia and Africa, and is still common in places where it is not over-hunted by man. Highly adaptable in the matter of habitat, it is found in forests, swamps and rocky areas right up to the fringe of the Sahara desert. Because of its wide distribution in a variety of habitats, various races have evolved, differing from each other in build, size and density of coat. The smallest races are found in the Mediterranean area of north Africa, whereas those of Asia and northern Europe may reach a weight of 440 pounds.

Wild boars feed on roots, bulbs, leaves, fruit, snails, reptiles and rodents. They root about in the ground litter with their snout and tusks to uproot plants and uncover soil animals. They have poor eyesight, but their senses of smell and hearing are excellent. They are gregarious animals, the family group comprising boar, females and young ones of various ages. Old boars are often solitary, but they are sometimes accompanied by younger males.

Man is the main enemy of the wild boar in Europe, and the pigs will change ground, moving from one forest to another, if human pressure becomes too great. They also undertake true migrations which may be caused either by human pressure or failure of the local food supply.

During the day, the pigs lie up in thick undergrowth, usually near a wallowing place. They come out at night to feed, and are mainly nocturnal in habits. Although they are destructive in agricultural regions, especially in fields of potatoes or cereals, they can be an asset in forest. They are much hunted throughout their range and can be highly dangerous to man and dogs when brought to bay. They are able to survive severe wounds.

The gestation period in the wild boar is just under four months. Litter size varies from two to twelve young which are striped during the early months. They grow rapidly and are sexually mature at the age of a year and a half.

Africa has three species of wild pig: the warthog (*Phacochoerus aethiopicus*), which is found mainly on savannas; the giant forest hog (*Hylochoerus meinertzhageni*); and the African bushpig or red river hog (*Potamochoerus porcus*), which are found in forested areas.

The giant forest hog is a large animal, weighing up to 550 pounds. It is now rare. The bush pig, on the other hand, is common in the forests of Equatorial Africa, where it is intensively hunted and is the natives' main source of animal protein.

Among the wild pigs found in the tropical forests of Asia are the pygmy hogs (*Sus salvanius*) which stand only eleven inches tall at the shoulder. There have been no sightings of this small pig during the last few years, and it may be extinct. The babiroussa (*Babirussa babirussa*) is found in Celebes and the neighbouring islands.

In tropical America, peccaries (*Dicotyles*) take the place of the wild boars. Although they resemble the European wild boar in many ways, they are also very different. One such difference is the dorsal gland whose secretions have a musky odour. Peccaries vary in weight from 35 to 66 pounds. They live in large herds and are usually quite harmless where not

Couple of black rhinoceroses (*Diceros bicornis*). East African savanna. *Phot. J. and M. Fiévet*

A wild sow (*Sus scrofa*) with its young. Forest of Laon. *Phot. Lauros—Atlas-Photo*

The warthog (*Phacochoerus aethiopicus*) is the most widespread member of the pig family in Africa. It lives on savannas and in forests, seeking out damp and swampy places in which to wallow. *Phot. J. Roche*

disturbed, but they can be dangerous when hunted or wounded. Then the entire herd will counter-attack with great determination, and the hunter has often to climb into a tree to escape. Before attacking, the peccaries gnash their canine teeth in warning.

There are two species of hippopotamus, both African. The common hippopotamus (*Hippopotamus amphibiusi*) inhabits the rivers of tropical and equatorial Africa: the pygmy hippopotamus (*Choeropsis liberiensis*) is found only in marshy forests of Liberia.

The adult common hippopotamus can reach a length of fifteen feet, and weigh between four and five tons, which makes it the largest land mammal after the elephant. It is an amphibious animal, found along river courses. It spends the day in deep water, either totally or partially submerged. It can walk along the river bottom, surfacing periodically to breathe, with only its eyes, ears and nostrils showing above the surface. When it dives, its ears close automatically. Hippopotamuses feed at night, following well defined paths to their grazing grounds. Over the years, these paths become like sunken roads.

The hippopotamus marks its territory with heaps of dung. Small groups are the rule, but old males often lead a solitary life. During the mating season, the males fight fiercely, using their lower canines, which may reach a length of 23 inches and weigh seven pounds. The gestation period is 230 days. The female gives birth to a single young which is born in the water and swims before it can walk. It suckles its mother in the water and climbs on to her back to avoid attack by crocodiles.

In many regions, the hippopotamus has become rare because of hunting. On the other hand, where they have been protected, they have become locally numerous, so that culling has had to be undertaken. This shows that a species can be over-protected as well as over-exploited.

As things are at the moment, the survival of the large hippopotamus gives no cause for concern. The survival of the pygmy hippopotamus is less assured. This miniature species,

which, when adult, weighs barely 440 pounds, is now rare. It is an inhabitant of wet forests, solitary and difficult to observe. Little is known about its habits, except that it is not so amphibious as its large relative.

The Camelidae: camels and llamas

The bactrian or two-humped camel (*Camelus bactrianus*) survives in the wild state only in small numbers, and only in the Gobi Desert of Mongolia. The dromedary, or one-humped camel (*Camelus dromedarius*), now survives only as a domesticated animal. It is also known as the Arabian camel, and probably originated there. It is now found mainly in Arabia and the Sahara.

Camels are highly adapted to life in the desert. The broad round pads on their feet enable them to walk on burning sand and on rocky terrain. They can close their nostrils to protect the nasal cavities from hard particles of sand during a sand-storm. Tongue, mouth and teeth are adapted for grasping and crushing the toughest desert plants. Finally, there is the hump, or two humps, as the case may be. The hump contains fat which can produce water by body chemistry. It has been shown that 66 pounds of fat can release 70 pints of water.

Without the camel, with its frugal diet, resistance to thirst and general stamina, life would be impossible for man in many parts of the desert where neither horses nor oxen can survive. A strong pack camel can carry 600 pounds and travel over twenty miles in a day. The camel also provides milk, meat and wool. The female gives birth to a single

This domestic pig from Assam is very like the wild boar. But its origin is perhaps not the same as that of our domestic pig; it may be descended either from *Sus vittatus* or *Sus cristatus*, two Asiatic wild boars. *Phot. A. Margiocco*

This pygmy hippopotamus from Liberia (*Choeropsis liberiensis*) sprawled out in a zoo on the edge of a pool in which it has been swimming, shows very well the structure of its hands and feet: 4 digits or 4 toes, ending in poorly developed claws (unguligrade animals). *Phot. Jean Philippe Varin—Jacana*

offspring after a gestation period of thirteen or fourteen months. The young camel is not mature until it is five years old. Breeding takes place every second year.

According to palaentologists, camels evolved on the continent of America, from which they migrated to the deserts of the Old World. Llamas, on the other hand—the common llama (*Lama glama*), the guanaco (*Lama huanacus*), alpacas and vicunas—remained in their country of origin: the Andean regions of South America.

When the Spaniards arrived in America, the llamas and alpacas no longer existed in the wild state: all were domesti-

The dromedary (*Camelus dromedarius*), unknown in the wild state, was apparently a native of Asia in bygone times. But, in North Africa and in the Sahara, into which some naturalists believe it was introduced, it was used by the Carthaginians and the Romans, who frequently represented it in drawings. *Phot. Bel-Vienne—Jacana*

cated animals. The Indians used the llama as the bedouin uses the camel—as a pack animal and a source of meat and wool. Every part of the animal is used by man, even its excrement, which is used as a fuel in the high Andes where wood is unobtainable.

The alpaca is also reared entirely for its wool, which is unsurpassed in quality by that of any other animal.

The only American species still found in a wild state is the vicuna (*Lama vicugna*) which lives at high altitudes in the pampas and on the plateaux of the Andes. Vicunas live in small herds of females and young, led by a male. They are extremely graceful animals, and can run fast over long distances. Their main food is grass. Like llamas and camels, they have a habit of spitting when upset or angry.

The Tragulidae: chevrotains

There are six species of chevrotain in Asia and one in Africa. All are small deer-like ruminants. The upper canines of the males develop into sharp pointed tusks. The Asiatic species are very small, their weight varying between four and nine pounds. All of them have striped and spotted coats. Shy and easily frightened, they hide by day in grass and thickets, sometimes even in hollow trees.

The African water chevrotain (*Hyemoschus aquaticus*) is larger, weighing about 22 pounds, and is found on the banks of rivers in equatorial forests. It is solitary and nocturnal, and one of the most difficult of all animals to observe. Although it feeds mainly on fallen fruit, it occasionally takes

Hippopotamuses (*Hippopotamus amphibiusi*) are found nowadays only in Africa; in the lower Pleistocene, they lived also in Europe. The remains of their ancestors, the hexaprotodons, who roamed from North Africa and the Mediterranean to Java, are found in lower Pliocene deposits to the beginning of the Quaternary. *Atlas-Photo—de Klemm*

fish and meat. When disturbed, it takes refuge in the water, into which it dives without hesitation.

The Cervidae: elk and reindeer

The distribution of the Cervidae is world-wide, except for Australia, and Africa outside Algeria and Tunisia. In America and Eurasia, they are found in a wide variety of habitats—forests, tundra, plains, scrub, marshes and mountains. There are about fifty species in the family.

The feature that sets the cervidae apart is their antlers, which are shed annually. Growth begins immediately afterwards, and is controlled by a sex hormone. Except in the case of the reindeer, only males grow antlers. During the growing period, the antlers are covered in a furry skin called velvet, which dries up and is rubbed off when the antlers are fully grown. The velvet dries up when the blood supply is cut off. Now the antlers are clean and ready for the rutting season. In castrated deer, the antlers normally become permanent.

The fallow deer (*Dama dama*) is native to the Mediterranean region and Asia Minor, but has been introduced to many parts of Europe, and to North America. In Britain, it exists in the wild state in Scotland and England. The fallow buck has palmate antlers. There are two varieties of fallow, the spotted type (menil) and the dark variety. Pure white fallow deer are the result of human selection.

The European red deer (*Cervus elaphus*) is widely distributed in Europe. It is also found in some parts of North Africa and Asia. In many parts of Europe, it is still a common animal, highly prized as a game species. In the Scottish Highlands, there are about 180,000 red deer, from which an annual crop of about 30,000 is taken. This keeps the herds stable. There is no doubt that the red deer's continued survival depends on such controlled hunting. Where hunting is indiscriminate, the species can be exterminated.

Red deer are woodland animals, but they are adaptable, and, in Scotland, have managed to survive for more than a century in mountain areas barren of trees. They are active mainly at dusk and dawn. Browsers and grazers, they feed on leaves, stalks, bark, grass, mushrooms and lichens. Grass is not very important to red deer living in large forests. In other parts, grasses, heather and such like are their principal food.

. The red deer society is a matriarchy, the sexes living in separate herds for most of the year. The rut is in autumn, when the stags collect harems. Then they can be heard roaring. Most of their time is spent driving off intruding stags. Eventually, the master stag retires and the hind group is split up among lesser males. Red deer hinds breed annually, and one calf is the rule. The calves are spotted at birth, but the spots begin to fade in autumn. Hinds breed as yearlings and may have their first calf at two years old. Life span is about fifteen years.

In America and Asia, there are a number of closely related species. The largest of these is the North American wapiti (*Cervus canadensis*) and the sambar (*Rusa unicolor unicolor*) of India. The sambar weighs about 770 pounds, whereas a first-class Highland deer stag will weigh no more than 300 pounds.

The muntjac or barking deer (*Muntiacus*) is a small

European red deer stag (*Cervus elaphus*) with its antlers at the height of their development; it is a magnificent 20 pointer. Its upper tines are bifurcated. *Phot. Bel-Vienne—Jacana*

South American fauna is deficient in large herbivorous mammals; the swamp deer (*Blastocerus dichotomus*) is (along with the llamas) the largest of them all. It lives in sparsely wooded preferably marshy zones, in Brazil, the Guianas, Paraguay, Uruguay, and the Argentinian Gran Chaco. Height at the withers, about 3½ feet. *Phot. A. R. Devez—Lauros-Atlas-Photo*

Asiatic species, weighing about 33 pounds. There are a few small species in South America, about which little is known. These include the Andean deer (*Hippocamelus*), found in Peru, Chile and Patagonia; the pudus (*Pudu*, Chilean Andes); the brocket (*Mazama*, from Central America to Brazil); the pampas deer (*Ozotoceros bezoarticus*); and the swamp deer (*Blastocerus dichotomus*) which is the biggest South American species.

The roe deer (*Capreolus capreolus*) is widely distributed in the temperate regions of Eurasia. It is a woodland species, and territorial. The bucks hold a territory from which they exclude all rivals. As a result, roe deer are usually seen singly or in pairs, although winter groups are common enough. The roe deer rut is in the period July/August, but because of

Herd of fallow-deer stags in a park, where they are living in a semi-domesticated state. *Phot. J. F. Terrasse*

This American moose (*Alces alces*), a male, has its antlers incompletely developed and covered with velvet. *Phot. Simon-Ostman*

delayed implantation until the end of the year, the fawns are not born until the end of May or early June. This is the only species of deer in which there is delayed implantation. Twins are normal: some does have a single fawn. Triplets are periodically recorded.

This deer is mainly a browsing animal, feeding on young shoots and leaves, but it also eats grass and a variety of wild plants. Although it can be destructive in young forests, it is no problem in mature woods. As a game animal, it is highly esteemed in many parts of Europe, while, in Britain, it was, until recently, looked upon as vermin. It is a graceful animal and highly attractive, but tame bucks can be dangerous, and should not be kept as pets.

The elk (*Alces alces*) of the Old World is the moose of the New World. It inhabits swampy northern forests. In Europe, it is found in Norway, Sweden and Russia, and it ranges as far eastwards as Siberia. It is the largest of the deer family—a mature bull standing six feet tall at the withers and weighing 1200 pounds or more. The moose of America is heavier, on average, than the elk of Europe. Moose can be distinguished from all other species of deer by their big elongated heads, their wide-cleft nostrils and their fleshy overhanging upper lips. The antlers are palmate and, in adult bulls, may reach a length of 6 feet and weigh up to 44 pounds. Moose feed on the shoots of trees and bushes, but also spend a lot of time in the water, feeding on aquatic plants. When feeding thus, the animal will sometimes completely submerge itself. Because of uncontrolled hunting, the moose had become rare by the end of the 19th century. Protection has led to an increase in its numbers, especially in Canada.

The reindeer (*Tarandus rangifer*) is the only species in which both sexes grow antlers. It is confined to the most northerly regions of the Old and New Worlds. In the Old World, the species is known as reindeer; in North America as caribou. Reindeer were domesticated early in human history and are still the main domestic stock of the Lapps of northern Europe. The wild reindeer are the caribou of North America.

The hooves of the reindeer are broad and flat, adapted for

Wild Indian buffaloes (*Bubalus bubalus*), north India. *Phot. Aldo Margiocco*

walking on soft snow. There is great variation in coat colour, as there is in the shape of the antlers. Weight varies but, in the best adults, may be as much as 660 pounds.

Reindeer are gregarious and form immense herds at certain periods of the year. In autumn, the herds migrate from the tundra southwards into wooded regions, where they spend the winter. Their main food in the barren lands is a lichen known as reindeer moss, which they uncover by scraping away the snow.

The flesh, skin, bones and milk of reindeer are used by the Lapps and, without the reindeer, it is doubtful if man could have colonized and populated the most northerly regions.

The Bovidae

All the species in the family Bovidae have hollow horns, which at once distinguishes them from deer whose antlers are made of bone. Whereas deer cast and re-grow their antlers each year, the horns of this family are permanent.

This is an important family, including, as it does, oxen, sheep and goats, so many of which have been domesticated and are so important to man. There are about 500 species, most of them quite large in size.

Classification of wild oxen is not very easy, partly because of the existence of geographical races and partly as a result of cross-breeding between domestic animals and their wild ancestors. Most wild oxen are of Asiatic origin.

The Indian buffalo (*Bubalus bubalus*), which is quite different from the African species, is seen mainly as a domestic animal throughout its range—from Italy to the Philippines. As a wild animal, it still exists in India, Nepal, Assam and Borneo, but there is some doubt even about these. Some of them could be the descendants of escaped domestic stock. This buffalo weighs over 1700 pounds. It is a thick-set animal, black and grey in colour, with powerful horns, flattened and crescent-shaped, spanning up to six feet. It is often called the water buffalo because of its habit of standing in pools and lakes with only its muzzle showing above the surface. Although quiet and docile with people it knows, it is always liable to attack a stranger. Buffalo milk is of good quality and is, in fact, the only kind sold commercially in places like Bombay.

The gaur (*Bibos frontalis gaurus*) is found on wooded hill-sides in India and Burma. It is a well-built animal, usually considered the most handsome of cattle beasts. The bull may reach a height of seven feet at the shoulder and weigh over a ton.

The banteng (*Bibos banteng*) and the kouprey (*Bibos sauveli*) are two Asiatic species, closely related to the gaur. The kouprey was not known to science before 1936, when it was discovered in Indo-China. The problem of its classification has still to be resolved, but it does seem to be a genuine species. Whether it will continue to survive in a part of the world so long ravaged by war remains to be seen.

The Indian zebu (*Bos indicus*), ancestor of all the Indian cattle breeds, exists today only in the domestic state, and is still widely crossed with other breeds. The gayal (*Bibos frontalis frontalis*) is probably a domesticated form of the gaur, and does not exist in the wild state. It is found in Assam and Burma. The yak (*Poephagus grunniens*) is a native of the Himalayas and Tibet, where it ranges up to 20,000 feet. It is a powerful animal, standing six feet tall and measuring fourteen feet in length. Its hair is long and soft and curly on the forehead, like the bison's. On the back and sides of the body, the hair forms a long mane, reaching almost to the ground. The yak has exceptional stamina, and can climb like a goat. Although it still exists in the wild state, it has been domesticated for centuries by the Tibetans who use it as a beast of burden and as a source of milk and meat.

The origin of the domestic ox (*Bos taurus*) still remains obscure. Its main ancestor was probably the wild auroch (*Bos primigenius*) which became extinct in the 17th century. By careful selection and cross-breeding, man has developed the auroch into all the well-known breeds, each developed for a specific purpose, for example, work, milk or meat production.

Many breed types, differing in colour, shape and productivity, have been established by farmers. Man controls the breeding programme; he also controls the feeding programme. Such manipulation has left little room for cattle to display their innate pattern of behaviour, but this can be seen in animals that have reverted to the wild state, as in some Pacific islands. A one-year study in the Galapagos has suggested that cattle living wild quickly rediscover their ancestral social structure and habits.

The Cape buffalo (*S. caffer*) is the only species of the genus *Syncerus*, and is found all over Africa, south of the Sahara. Two distinct races have evolved—the large black savanna buffalo and the small red, forest race.

Buffaloes are usually found near water where there is ample grazing near at hand. They also require cover in which

The gayal (*Bibos frontalis*) is a domestic ox of which the gaur is the wild form. Found in India, Burma and the Malay archipelago, its horns have an oval section; it has a very broad forehead; a hump on the back and white legs. Specimen from Jaldapara (India). *Phot. A. Margiocco*

they can hide or ruminate. Being fond of bathing and wallowing, they like swamps and the back-waters of slow-moving rivers.

African buffaloes are gregarious, living in herds of a dozen or so, but gatherings of 100 and more are not rare. Because of its great size and strength, the adult male buffalo fears nothing, and is considered to be the most dangerous African game animal. Lions take a certain number of calves.

A buffalo, surprised and put on foot, is liable to charge without warning, and a wounded animal can be extremely aggressive. It will hide up in tall grass, allow a man to approach closely, then run him down. A few big game hunters are killed every year by African buffaloes, which are responsible for more human deaths than lions and elephants.

There are two species of bison: the American (*Bison bison*) and the European (*Bison bonasus*).

Before the arrival of the European settlers, immense herds of bison roamed the American prairies, and their population, at one time, was probably in the region of 50 million. The herds were systematically massacred by European settlers, animals being killed sometimes for no more than their tongue and hide. Bisons were also killed off in the war against the Indians who depended largely on buffalo meat for survival.

The American bison (*Bison bison*) no longer has at its disposal vast stretches of prairie-land. It survives only because of the protection it enjoys in a few nature reserves. This male shows to perfection the power of the front part of its body. *Phot. S. A. Thompson*

Whereas the Indians had never over-hunted the bison, the white settlers brought it to the verge of extinction within a few decades. According to Walker, the herds had been reduced to a little over 500 animals by 1899. Since then the Bison has been protected and, although it is still numbered only in hundreds, its future seems safe.

The European bison has had a similar, if not quite so spectacular, history. The last herds came close to extinction during the recent wars. Selections from semi-domesticated animals were used in an attempt to re-stock areas of Poland, Sweden and the U.S.S.R. The number of truly wild European bison is presently reckoned at about 400.

The musk ox (*Ovibos moschatus*) is found in the tundra of North Canada and Greenland, and in some islands of the Canadian Arctic. During the last ice age, it ranged over Europe, Asia and North America. Fossil remains show that it ranged as far south in Europe as the Pyrenees, and in America to the Gulf of Mexico.

The antelope

These are the handsome members of the family, most of them built for running at high speed, and the majority of them African.

The bush-buck (*Tragelaphus scriptus*) is found in large herds on the savannas of central and west Africa. Only the males have horns, 8 to 12 inches long, with a single spiral.

The giant kudu (*Strepsiceros strepsiceros*) is one of the biggest of the family, standing 3 feet tall at the withers and weighing 650 pounds.

The bongo (*Boccercus euryceros*) lives in the jungles of equatorial Africa. In this species, both sexes have horns, which are lyre-shaped with white or yellow tips. Extremely handsome, and difficult to stalk, the bongo is, beyond question, the greatest trophy sought after by big game hunters.

The giant eland (*Taurotragus derbianus*) is the biggest of all antelopes, and may reach a weight of over 1900 pounds. It is found in central and southern Africa, on plains or on grassy hills with bushes and scattered trees. Because of the excellent quality of its flesh and skin, the eland has suffered from over-hunting. However, it tames easily, and attempts are now being made to domesticate it. Results so far are encouraging, and there seems no reason why African stock breeders should not succeed in establishing profitable herds.

The cape eland (*Taurotragus oryx*) is found on savannas from Kenya to Angola, and in some parts of South Africa.

The nilgai (*Boselaphus tragocamelus*) is the biggest of the Indian antelopes, standing about 4 feet tall at the shoulder and weighing about 440 pounds. As a wild animal, it is still plentiful in western India and eastern Bengal, usually in dry jungle areas. It is also found in arable districts, however, where it sometimes grazes standing crops.

Although still hunted in some parts, the nilgai enjoys special protection, especially in a region like Gujerat, where protection is carried to the extreme. Here, the nilgai shows no fear of man. Because of its resemblance to the cow, the natives look upon it as a sacred animal and leave it alone. Its wild predators are the tiger and the leopard.

The duiker

Duikers are small antelopes with a slim head, a hair tuft on the nape and straight or slightly curved horns. All of them come from Africa, where they are very common in equatorial forests. Active in the early morning and evening, they feed mainly on fallen fruit. They are hunted for their flesh which makes up a large part of the local meat ration. Hunters sometimes use nets; at other times they 'call' them within rifle range, in the way that Canadian hunters 'call' the

Fight between two male impalas (*Aepyceros melampus*). This very beautiful antelope lives in small herds in the tree-dotted (as shown here) or grassy savanna. *Phot. J. F. and M. Terrasse*

The nilghai (*Boselaphus tragocamelus*) is one of the two Asiatic tragelaphines. Large in size—nearly 4½ feet at the withers—with short horns implanted above the eye-sockets, it lives in the Indian plains *Phot. Aldo Margiocco*

Arabian oryx (*Oryx leucoryx*), found in Arabia and Iraq, has been decimated by the local sheiks who hunt them from jeeps and fire at them with machine-guns.

The addax (*Addax nasomaculatus*) of the Sahara is a species perfectly adapted ecologically to life in the desert. It feeds on the driest herbage, and can go for long periods without drinking, extracting water from its food by body metabolism. It has a whitish-grey coat that blends with its environment. It is a strong, clumsy antelope, with horns twisted in the shape of a lyre. Being easy to kill, and much hunted, it is threatened with extinction.

In the family Alcelaphinae are the topis (*Damaliscus*), hartebeests (*Alcelaphus*), the white-tailed gnu (*Connochaetes gnu*) and the brindle gnu (*Connochaetes taurinus*). The white-tailed gnu is no longer found in a wild state, being now confined to reserves in South Africa or in zoos.

The antelopes in this group are of medium to large size, and taller at the withers than at the rump, which means their backs slope down to the rear. They have elongated heads and ringed horns that grow outwards, then turn up and inwards. Gnus or wildebeeste are bull-like in front, but have the mane and tail of a horse. Wildebeeste are still plentiful on grassy plains and savannas, and are a main prey of the lion.

The Antilopinae are the gazelles, of which there are fifteen species, found in arid regions of Africa and Asia. All of them are lightweights of elegant form, and designed for speed.

The gerenuk or giraffe-gazelle (*Litocranius walleri*) of east Africa has long legs and a long neck, so that it is able to nibble the leaves of high acacia branches. Having the same sort of diet as the giraffe, it has evolved the same kind of body structure.

The dorcas gazelle (*Gazella dorcas*), which is found north of the Sahara, is probably the best known species. This graceful creature roams on the high plateaux in herds of five to ten, feeding on artemisia and steppe-grass. Unfortunately, it has disappeared from many places because the herds have been decimated along the whole northern fringe of the Sahara.

moose. Calling duikers also attracts the great apes, panthers and eagles.

The blue duiker (*Philantombs*), wrongly called a gazelle by the colonials, has a very short tail. The yellow-backed duiker (*Cephalophus sylvicultor*) is the largest species, and weighs about 130 pounds. The bush duiker (*Sylvicapra*) is a small species, found mainly on the Alpine plateaux of mountains. The kobs (*Kobus* and others) are confined to swampy areas. Sable and roan antelopes (*Hippotragus*) are both large species with ringed back-curving horns.

In east Africa there are four species of *Oryx* found from the Sudan southwards, in semi-desert areas. They have been exterminated in many parts by uncontrolled hunting. The

The banded duiker (*Cephalophus zebra*) lives in the forests of East Africa. *Phot. Lauros—Atlas-Photo*

The blue duiker (*Philantomba monticola*) is a forest-dwelling antelope. Height at the withers, 1 foot. Notice the arched slit, unconnected with the ocular region, which corresponds with the maxillary gland. Inside the slit are many glands of the sebaceous and sudoriparous (sweat) type.

Lelwel hartebeest (*Alcelaphus lelwel*) are superb large antelopes (about 4 feet at the withers) which populate the grassy savannas of much of Africa. Five species are distributed over the continent from north to south. *Phot. J. and M. Fiévet*

Hunter's hartebeest (*Damaliscus hunteri*) is one of the rarest antelopes in East Africa (Jubaland). Height at the withers, 4 feet. To right and left of the hartebeests can be seen Grant's gazelles (*Gazella granti*). *Phot. Jean Roche*

This herd of brindled gnus or wildebeeste (*Connochaetes taurinus*) is escorted by spotted hyenas waiting for the females to give birth, when they will eat the discarded placentas. Wildebeeste are often confused with white-tailed gnus, now almost exterminated. *Phot. J. and M. Fiévet*

Gazelles have almost disappeared from this fringe in the last fifteen years, their destruction due almost entirely to motorized poaching. This type of hunting is not a matter of sport, but a matter of slaughtering for meat, the flesh of the dorcas gazelle being of excellent quality. It is not easily kept in captivity, and cannot put up with dampness in any degree.

The black-buck or Indian antelope (*Antilope cervicapra*) is found on open plateaux in western India, but not close to

mouflon species because there are many races, varying widely in build and in the shape of their horns. It is reasonable to assume that the mouflons, ranging from Corsica to the eastern Himalayas (*Ovis ammon*), constitute one species, and that those found in eastern Siberia and North America (*Ovis canadensis*) form another. Nevertheless, they may be no more than geographical races of the same species.

Mouflons live on rough, rocky ground, mainly in flocks composed of males or females. Each flock occupies a clearly defined territory. Mature rams join the female flocks at rutting time, in the autumn, then retire to join the male flocks again. The gestation period is from 150 to 180 days, and the ewe may give birth to one, two or three lambs. Wild mouflons feed mainly by browsing.

On the Island of Corsica, there is a natural wild population of mouflons which survives only because part of their range has been turned into a nature reserve. Before that, their numbers were decimated by poaching and forest fires. The mouflon has been successfully introduced into other mountainous parts of Europe.

The dorcas gazelle (*Gazella dorcas*) is one of the finest species in the Sahara, in which it is widely distributed. Hunted down and shot at with machine guns by motorized 'sportsmen', it is disappearing at an alarming rate. *Phot. Aldo Margiocco*

The Caprinae (goats)

Under this heading come the wild and domestic goats. Separating the sheep from the goats is not always as easy as it sounds. In goats, both sexes have horns with a pyriform base. In most species, the animals have a beard. Billy-goats have malodorous glands under the tail. There are also certain skeletal differences. Goats are essentially mountain animals.

Wild goats are natives of Eurasia. The wild goat of the Caucasus (*Capra aegagrus hircus*) was probably the main ancestor of the domestic goat, but several types may have been involved. The markhor (*Capra falconeri*) was probably the ancestor of oriental goats. This species has large corkscrew horns, and is found in the western Himalayas. The bharal or blue sheep (*Pseudois nahoor*) is found further east, from Kashmir to China. The tahr (*Hemitragus*) ranges from

the Himalayas. It is widely agreed that the black-buck is the most handsome member of this zoological group, most of which are attractive animals. The black-buck stands about three feet tall at the shoulder and is, therefore, smaller than a fallow deer. The male's coat is black on the upper part and white on the belly and round the eyes. The female is fawn and white. The horns have three spirals and measure up to twenty inches long. Females rarely grow horns. The black-buck is a fiery, aggressive animal, and retains these characteristics in captivity. Despite intensive hunting, the species appears to be holding its own. This is the species the maharajas used to hunt with tame cheetahs.

The Ovinae (sheep)

This is the family of the sheep and their wild ancestors, the mouflons. Experts disagree about the exact number of

The giraffe-gazelle or gerenuk (*Lithorcranius walleri*), of East Africa (Somaliland, Kilimanjaro) leaping about in the savanna during the rainy season. *Phot. Jean Roche*

Arabia to India, but its distribution is for the most part intermittent.

It is remarkable that Africa, so rich in antelopes, has no sheep and only one goat, called paradoxically the barbary sheep (*Ammotragus lervia*). It is found in the mountains of North Africa. It differs from goats in having no beard, and in the absence of smell in the males in the breeding season, but it has a long mane hanging from its throat and breast. It is found only in the most desolate rocky zones of the Sahara mountain ranges. It is hunted for its flesh wherever it makes contact with man, so has become rare in the vicinity of inhabited regions.

There are two species of ibex in Western Europe: the Pyrenean ibex (*Capra aegagrus pyrenaica*) and the Alpine ibex (*Capra aegagrus ibex*). Ibexes are found as far east as the Caucasus. In many parts of Europe, the Alpine ibex was decimated or exterminated by irresponsible hunting. It is now protected in reservations on the French-Italian border, where its numbers are increasing.

The Rupicaprinae

The animals in this group are intermediate between goats and antelopes. All of them are mountain dwellers.

The goral (*Naemorhaedus goral*), the serow (*Naemorhaedus caudatus*) and the takin (*Budorcas*) are found in the Himalayas. The Rocky Mountain goat (*Oreamnos americanus*) is American: a remarkable animal with a pure white coat and resembling a true goat. Lastly, there is the chamois (*Rupicapra rupicapra*) of the Pyrenees and the Alps, which is probably the best known of all. Chamois are beautiful animals, combining strength with grace. They have small horns which hook outward at the tip. Their weight varies between 55 and 80 pounds. The Pyrenean race is smaller than the Alpine. During the summer, the chamois move up above the forest line on to the Alpine grasslands. In winter,

The black-buck (*Antilope cervicapra*) lives in India. *Phot. Aldo Margiocco*

they come down into the forests where they feed on young shoots, mosses and lichens.

Chamois herds are made up of females and kids; adult

The short-tailed goral (*Naemorhaedus goral*) is a small wild goat which lives in the Himalayas. Its tail is only 3 inches long. Its biology is almost unknown. *Phot. Aldo Margiocco*

Among the many races of domestic sheep (*Ovis ammon*) there are some, mostly natives of southern central Asia, which accumulate fat in their tails, which become heavy and thick. *Phot. J. Six*

males are solitary outside the breeding season, which is in autumn. In April or May, the female gives birth to one or two kids. The chamois has always been a highly esteemed game animal, not only because it provides sport, but because of the high quality of its venison. Its extinction was threatened by uncontrolled hunting, but large reserves have now been set up where it can live and breed in peace.

The Giraffidae
(giraffes and okapi)

Giraffes (*Giraffa*) and the okapi (*okapia johnstoni*) are the only members of this group. Both are found in tropical Africa. There is no need to describe the giraffe except to point out that some males stand over nineteen feet tall and weigh close on two tons.

The giraffe is widely distributed over a large part of Africa, south of the Sahara, in open forest or on plains with plenty of acacia trees. Its long neck enables it to reach the highest leafage of the vegetation on which it feeds. In fact, its diet is made up almost exclusively of acacia stems and leaves. When drinking, the giraffe has to spread its long front legs wide apart so that its muzzle can reach the water.

Giraffes live in herds of twelve or so. They are always on the alert. The length of their neck gives them a wide field of view, which is an additional advantage because sight appears to be their best developed sense. When alarmed, giraffes go off at a gallop, which is not their everyday gait. Normally they amble, which means that the legs on the same side of the body move forward together. Their main enemy is the lion. Because of their slow breeding rate—one calf every two or three years—the giraffe population cannot stand high annual casualties, and over-hunting by man is the reason for their rarity in many places. Wild predators make no significant impact on giraffe numbers.

Unlike the giraffe, the okapi lives in the equatorial forests. It was unknown before 1900, when it was first discovered in the Congo forests, causing a sensation among zoologists.

The okapi stands five feet tall at the withers. The body hair is bright reddish-brown; the hair on the legs is black with white horizontal stripes. It does not have the long neck or the long legs of the giraffe. When feeding, it plucks grass and leaves with its tongue. Because of its shy behaviour and its inaccessibility, not much is known about the okapi's biology. It can be seen, however, in zoological gardens, and has been bred in captivity.

In order to drink the giraffe has to lower the front part of its body. To make this possible, it spreads its front legs wide apart; it is only in this position that its mouth can reach the water. *Phot. Dragesco—Atlas-Photo*

Animals in nature reserves are so used to man's presence that the photographer can, at any time, approach them without scaring them. This pair of giraffes provides the proof. *Phot. J. and M. Fiévet—Jacana*

The order Tubulidentata (aardvarks)

There is only one present-day species in this order, the aardvark or ground hog (*Orycteropus afer*), which is found in most parts of Africa, south of the Sahara and the Sudan. It is commonest in savannas with trees, but it is also found in equatorial forests.

The aardvark is a large animal—up to 180 pounds—and, in many ways, is pig-like. Once classified with the ant-eaters, it is now agreed by zoologists that it is a primitive even-toed ungulate. Its body is bulky, and its elongated head ends in a long, tubular snout. It has long, narrow, mobile ears. Its limbs are short and powerful, and it has strong nails for burrowing. The skin, which is extremely thick and tough, is thinly covered with stiff hairs.

Aardvarks are nocturnal, sleeping by day in nests at the end of large burrows which they dig for themselves. They eat only termites and ants which they lick up with their long tongues after breaking open their nests. They also attack the close-packed columns of these insects when they are moving about in the undergrowth. Their most highly developed senses are smell and hearing.

The flesh of the aardvark, although tough, is highly esteemed as a delicacy by the local population. As a result, they have been actively hunted, and their numbers have decreased greatly. For its size, the aardvark is a tremendously powerful animal, like the great ant-eater and the giant pangolin, which also eat ants and termites. It takes several strong men to capture an aardvark in the wild, and, in captivity, it can smash the strongest cages. When it can be confined, it thrives on a mixture of boiled rice and hard-boiled eggs and chopped meat.

The order Proboscidea (elephants)

The only animals in this order are the elephants. During the Pleistocene, elephants had a world-wide distribution. Palaeontologists have identified six families, five of which are extinct. Some of the extinct species have been recovered intact in the permanent ice of Siberia. Prehistoric cave-dwellers carved elephants out of ivory and painted or engraved recognizable pictures of them on the walls of their caves.

Two genera of elephants still exist: the Asian elephant and the African elephant. All the Asian elephants belong to the species *Elephas indicus*.

African elephants vary from one part of the continent to another, and whether there are three species or only one is still disputed by zoologists. Some experts consider that there are three: the large savanna elephant, the forest elephant and the pygmy elephant. Others consider that all these forms are merely local races of the same species (*Loxodonta africans*). Probably they all belong to a single species, despite the distinctive types. Where the ranges of the equatorial elephants and the savanna elephants overlap, the two interbreed.

The status of the pygmy elephant is also doubtful because captured specimens have been known to grow on to normal size in captivity. In this way, elephants resemble red deer, whose size varies with habitat and feeding. Nevertheless, the pygmy elephant, as a species, is still widely believed in, despite the lack of proof.

The Asian elephant reaches a height of 10 feet and a weight of 5 tons. It has smaller ears than the African species, and this is the most notable difference between them. In addition, the Asian elephant has 4 toes on its hind limbs instead of only 3, 10 pairs of ribs instead of 12, and 33 vertebrae on its tail instead of 26. It is found in India, Burma, Thailand, Malaysia, Sumatra and Ceylon.

Asiatic elephants are forest animals, living in small herds of about twenty, made up of females and calves, led by a mature bull. The herd is usually led by an old female. From time to time, several herds join up to form bigger bands on a temporary basis. Elephants rest during the day and are active in the early morning and evening. They eat a wide variety of food: grass, shoots, leaves and fruit.

There is no special breeding season, and the young may be born in any month of the year. The gestation period is about 630 days, and the calf, at birth, weighs about 300 pounds. It is dependent on its mother for several years. Sexual maturity is reached between the ages of 8 and 12 years, and the potential life span is about 80 years.

Asian elephants are among the most intelligent of animals. They are easily domesticated and, when well treated, work well. Throughout their range, they are used as draught animals, carrying heavy burdens or extracting timber from swamps and forests in which tractors cannot operate. This is the species most frequently seen in circuses and zoos.

The African elephant is a much bigger species, adult males reaching a height of 13 feet at the shoulder and weighing $7\frac{1}{2}$ tons. The tusks of the African also reach much greater dimensions, the record tusk being 11 feet 6 inches long and 258 pounds in weight. The African species is found in a great variety of habitats, including forest and wooded savanna. It is a frequent visitor to swampy areas, where it drinks and wallows in the mud. Wallowing probably protects the skin against parasites. African elephants require about 440 pounds of vegetable matter per day.

Although African elephants are sociable animals, living in herds of varying size, old bulls are usually solitary. Within the social unit, there is a kind of mutual aid system, the wounded being cared for by members of the group, while several females may look after a single calf. African elephants are not much used for work, although they are as intelligent and as easily tamed as the Asian species. The notion that they are wild and intractable is discredited by the fact that Hannibal used African elephants when he crossed the Alps to meet the Roman legions. In the Congo, the Belgians have carried out various domestication experiments since the beginning of the present century. Probably the difference between the two is that the Indian elephant has been domesticated for a long time, whereas the taming of the African is a first-time venture.

The African elephant has always been hunted for its ivory. Massacred by ivory hunters, it is now rare in many parts of Africa. Wherever it is protected, it has increased in numbers; so much so that, in some reserves, culling programmes have had to be carried out to reduce the local population. It seems

The Asian elephant (*Elephas indicus*) has become very rare in its wild state. It is not as tall as the African elephant and is generally less than 11 feet in length. *Phot. Le Tellier—Jacana*

The elephant's tusks are the two upper incisors (lateral incisors I_2) enormously hypertrophied and endowed with continuous growth (the record is held by the African elephant). The tusks of the males are larger than those of the females. Shown here is a large savanna-dwelling male elephant covered with red dust of laterite soil. *Phot. Jean-Philippe Varin —Jacana*

that its future is secure. The African elephant is the biggest living land mammal.

The order Hyracoidea

The animals of this order—variously known as rock badgers, hyraxes, damans, dassies and conies—are the smallest hooved animals, and are no bigger than rabbits. In some ways, they resemble the odd-toed ungulates. In other ways, they are similar to elephants, so they have always been of great interest to zoologists. Being rodent-like in many respects, they were once classified as such. Anatomically, however, they have affinities with elephants and even-toed ungulates although, even today, there is no great certainty about where they really belong. They are found in Africa, Syria, Israel, Sinai and southeast Arabia, and there are three genera.

The tree daman or tree dassie (*Dendrohyrax dorsalis*) is found in the jungles of tropical Africa. During the day, it lies up in hollow trees or among tangled foliage or creepers,

The rock dassie or hyrax (*Procavia* sp.), lives in the south of the Sahara and in southern Africa, in isolated and rocky places, in which it forms small societies. Each individual seems to have a burrow of its own. Size of a very large rabbit. *Phot. J. and M. Fiévet*

The tree dassie (*Dendrohyrax dorsalis*) is found throughout the East African forest zone and also in the tree savannas of this region. Its activity is nocturnal; at night it launches its sonorous appeals which reach a crescendo and end in sobs. *Phot. Michel Boulard*

coming out at night to feed on fruits and leaves. It is an excellent tree-climber.

At night, the tree dassie advertises its presence by its loud cries which can be heard above all the other sounds of the equatorial forest, and which never fail to astonish those who hear them for the first time. Most species of this group have up to six young; the tree dassie usually has two. Apart from this, very little is known about its biology.

The grey hyrax (*Heterohyrax*) is found in East Africa, South Africa, Syria and a few other parts of the near east. This is a mountain species, found in rocky regions, where colonies can sometimes be numbered in hundreds. The grey hyrax closely resembles a large guinea-pig. It is active by day, has excellent eyesight, and is always alert. Its main enemies are eagles, carnivores, pythons and, occasionally, man. Roots, shoots and grasshoppers are its main food.

Rock damans, also known as rock hyraxes or conies (*Procavia*) are widely distributed in rocky areas of Africa south of the Sahara. They are bigger than grey hyraxes, some individuals reaching a weight of 45 pounds. This species also lives in colonies and is active by day and night. It is a vegetarian, feeding on a variety of grasses, leaves and bark. Strong and agile, this species defends itself vigorously against attack.

The order Sirenia (sea cows)

The dugong and the manatees

The sirenians or sea cows reminded the old-time sailors of mermaids; hence the name of the order. Although they resemble whales, they are plant-eaters, and evolved from plant-eaters. They have no hind limbs, and the fore limbs have developed into paddles. The tail fin is horizontally flattened, rounded in the manatees, notched in the dugong. Sirenians were very common during the Miocene and the Pliocene. Today, the order is represented by three manatees and one dugong.

Steller's sea cow (*Rhytina gigas*) was exterminated in the 18th century, surviving for only 27 years after its first discovery in 1741, when several thousands of them existed. By 1768, all of them had been killed by Russian hunters. Steller's sea cow measured up to 30 feet in length and up to 4 tons in weight.

The dugong (*Dugong dugong*) is a marine species, distributed from the Red Sea to Australia. Adults measure about 10 feet in length and weigh up to 440 pounds. The name 'sea cow' is also applied to this species because they graze the sea bottom like cattle, eating seaweed and other plants.

The female dugong gives birth to a single offspring which she nurses attentively. Old-time sailors brought back stories about having seen mermaids suckling their young, just like human beings, and there is no doubt that the stories were based on encounters with dugongs, which have two pectoral mammae. The story was that the dugong sat upright on the waves with her young at her breast: which may or may not be true. It is increasingly believed that she suckles her young under water in a horizontal position. Too little is known, however, for anyone to be dogmatic on the subject.

Dugong meat is not very palatable, but the animals are killed for their oil and skin. A number of tribes also kill them for medicinal use. It is said that even their tears are collected because they bring good luck. One thing is certain: continuing slaughter, for whatever reason, has reduced the dugong to a rarity in many areas.

Three species, or sub-species, of manatees (*Trichechus*) are recognized. Two of these (*T. manatus manatus* and *T. manatus latirostris*) are found along the east coast of America from Texas to the Amazon. The third (*T. inunguis*) is found on the the coasts of West Africa and in the Chad Basin.

Manatees frequent coastal bays and inlets, but they also ascend large rivers. They are bigger than dugongs, measuring up to close on 15 feet in length and weighing up to 1500 pounds. They are entirely vegetarian, their diet being mainly seaweed, which they uproot with their strong protractile upper lip. Manatees live in small, tightly-knit social units. They are entirely aquatic, and totally incapable of movements on land. Like the dugong, they are still over-hunted, and their numbers are steadily decreasing.

The order Edentata

There are three families in this order—American ant-eaters, sloths and armadillos. Superficially, there is nothing to suggest that they belong to the same order, but palaeontologists have discovered remains of extinct species that provide the links between the present-day forms. There seems little doubt that the order stems from a single root. South America was the evolutionary centre, and that is where all the present-day species are found.

The Myrmecophagidae

Ant-eaters

The great ant-eater (*Myrmecophaga tridactyla*) ranges from Honduras to the Argentine. It is a big animal, 6½ feet or more in length, with powerful claws used for tearing open the nests of the ants and termites on which it feeds exclusively. It has a long, thin snout and a long, worm-like tongue with a coating of sticky saliva. With this it captures its prey.

Ant-eaters are solitary animals, hunting by day in regions where they are not disturbed, but nocturnal when they are under pressure. Almost all their activity is devoted to finding food, which they need in large quantities. The female has a single young which she carries on her back until it is well enough grown to follow her around.

The tamandua (*Tamandua tetradactyla*) is also widely distributed in South America. It is smaller than the great ant-eater, and arboreal in habits.

The third species is the pygmy ant-eater (*Cyclopes didactylus*) which is about the size of a large rat. Not much is known about it, except that it is arboreal and nocturnal, and feeds on termites which it catches with its long, saliva-coated tongue.

Sloths

Sloths derive their name from their slow, unhurried movements. There are seven species found in the tropical forests of southern and Central America. They have small round heads and very long arms, ending in powerful curved claws with which they grip branches when they are hanging upside-down. The toes cannot be moved independently. The body temperatures of sloths varies from 75 degrees to 95 degrees fahrenheit, which means it varies with the temperature of the surroundings. Its imperfect heat regulation mechanism may explain why it is found only in tropical areas.

The three-toed sloth or aye (*Bradypus*) ranges from Honduras to the southern Argentine. The name 'aye' is descriptive of its distinctive call. The coat is green and, therefore, provides camouflage, but the green is not due to pigment. It is caused by algae that grow and live in the hollow or grooved hairs. The hair has another peculiarity, adapted to the sloth's upside-down way of life. It sleeps upside-down and feeds upside-down on young leaves, shoots and buds. Its hair grows from the abdomen to the back, and not the other way round, as in other mammals. The hair on its legs grows in the same way. In other words, the upside-down sloth has reversed hair for shedding rain.

The two-toed sloth (*Choloepus*) is not so widely distributed, being found from Venezuela to Brazil. It is a larger species, weighing up to twenty pounds, but its general behaviour is similar. It eats, sleeps and gives birth upside-down. In the trees, it moves about slowly. On the ground, it can barely crawl. Despite its slow movements, however, this sloth can defend itself vigorously with its fore claws. It is amazingly strong and can survive severe wounding. Unlike the three-toed species, the two-toed sloth settles down readily in captivity and sometimes breeds.

In the Panamanian forest, a tamandua or lesser ant-eater (*Tamandua tridactyla*) looks for ants (this is a species which lives in clay nests). The dart-like tongue on which insects are caught can be seen. *Phot. C. M. Hladik*

The Dasypodidae (armadillos)

There are about ten genera and twenty species of armadillo, found mainly on savannas and pampas from the southern United States to the Argentine. They are armour-plated on the head and body, the plates being formed of small bony discs with a horny covering. The plates and the horn are skin derivatives. When threatened, the armadillo rolls itself into a tight ball, thus protecting its vulnerable under-parts. The only other animal with the ability to roll itself into a ball is the hedgehog.

There is great variation in size from one species to another. The giant armadillo (*Priodontes giganteus*) weighs about 130 pounds. It is found in the east of South America, usually near water. It has powerful claws, is an active burrower, and feeds on termites, insects, small vertebrates and carrion.

At the other end of the scale, armadillos of the genera *Chlamydophorus* and *Burmeisteria* are no bigger than rats. They

The great ant-eater (*Myrmecophaga tridactyla= M. jubata*), which is found from Central America to the north of the Argentine, lives mainly in forests, rich in termites and in ants, on which it feeds; large individuals may exceed 6½ feet in length, including the tail. *Phot. A. R. Devez-Lauros—Atlas-Photo*

are armoured only along the dorsal region. These pygmy armadillos do not curl up into a ball; when threatened, they lie flat on the ground, presenting their back-armour to the enemy. They are strong burrowers and, in emergency, dig themselves in until only their back-armour is exposed.

The nine-banded armadillo (*Dasypus novemoinctus*) ranges over a large part of the American continent. It is of medium size, varying from nine to twenty pounds in weight.

Armadillos are burrowing animals, and live underground. Outside the breeding season, males and females occupy separate burrows; during the mating season, they are gregarious. In many ways, their behaviour resembles that of the hedgehog. They hunt at night, poking into holes and crevices and turning over stones and dry leaves in their search for earthworms, other soil animals, and the small vertebrates on which they prey. They are noisy when active, and their activities are not affected by the mere presence of human beings. Like hedgehogs, they are easily tamed, but few of them are able to adapt to life in a zoo.

The order Pholidota

There is only one present-day genus in this order, that of the pangolins or scaly ant-eaters. There are seven species, found in tropical Africa and Asia.

At one time, pangolins were classified with the Edentata because they so closely resemble each other in so many ways. Then it was discovered that, despite the resemblances between the Edentata of America and the pangolins of the Old World, they had no common origin. The similarities can be explained by the fact that they have adapted to the same kind of life—another example of convergent evolution in unrelated groups.

Bizarre is probably the best word to describe pangolins. The body is covered entirely with horny scales, so the animal has been likened to a giant pine-cone. The head is small and elongated, and the fore-limbs are armed with powerful claws. The tail is long and muscular, and completely covered in the same horny scales as the body.

The pangolin feeds on termites and ants which it catches on its sticky, worm-like tongue. The long-tailed pangolin (*Manis longicaudata*), which is arboreal, hunts its prey in the trees. The great ground pangolin, which lives on the ground, is a burrowing animal. Its powerful claws, used for burrowing, are also used for breaking into termite mounds. Arboreal species have prehensile tails which are used when the animals are moving about the branches.

Pangolins, with the exception of the long-tailed species, are nocturnal animals. They spend the day either in holes in trees or in burrows. Once thought of as solitary animals, modern research suggests that there is some sort of social structure governing the relationship between the individuals in a population.

The female pangolin gives birth to a single young which she usually carries astride the base of her tail.

The great ground pangolin (*Manis gigantes*) is noted for its prodigious strength. It can escape from the strongest cages, twisting iron bars and tearing concrete apart with its powerful fore-claws.

Pangolins protect themselves by curling up tightly and emitting an anal secretion with an unpleasant smell. They are not very intelligent, and do not adapt well to captivity. Their flesh is highly esteemed by some Africans.

The sloth, or ai (*Bradypus cuculliger*), lives in the forest zone which extends from the Guianas to Bolivia. It has roughly the same habits as the three-toed sloth (*Bradypus tridactylus*). Normally, the young sloth, pressed against its mother's belly, puts its arms on her shoulders and grips her with its legs at waist level. Here, the young one, already weaned, shows its climbing ability, watched by its mother. Weight of the mother: 8¾ pounds. *Phot. A. R. Devez-Lauros—Atlas-Photo*

A Malaysian pangolin (*Manis javanica*) climbing along a tree-trunk on the lookout for arboreal termites. Malaysian forest. *Phot. I. Polunin*

The order Lagomorpha

Hares and rabbits

Hares and rabbits were once classified as rodents. Now they have been placed in a separate order, the Lagomorphs. There is no doubt that this revision was sound as there are profound anatomical and physical differences between the two orders, backed up by the study of fossil forms which indicate that they did not have a common origin. Whatever resemblance there is between rabbits and some rodents is again an example of convergent evolution due to a similar mode of life.

Anatomically, hares and rabbits differ from each other only in minor details; but biologically, they differ greatly. Young rabbits are born blind, naked and helpless, in a warm underground nest prepared by the doe. Young hares, on the other hand, are born above ground, completely furred, with their eyes open, and able to move about almost at once.

The European rabbit usually lives in burrows, although many animals are out-liers at certain seasons. The brown hare never burrows, but the mountain hare will use holes and other hiding places under cover. When the biology of hares and rabbits is considered on a world scale all intermediate stages between the two kinds of behaviour can be observed. Although hares and rabbits are closely related, they do not inter-breed, and the so-called 'Belgian hare', supposed to be a hybrid between the two species, is a myth.

Although some species of hare have been closely studied in recent years, very little is known about hare relationships throughout their wide range. For example, experts are still arguing about the number of species found in the Old World. Some of them believe there are dozens of species, while others, notably Francis Petter, have cut this number to fewer than six. He suggests that the European brown hare (*Lepus europaeus*) occurs as far afield as Natal in Africa, and even in India and Asia, in a number of local forms, varying in size and colour, but all of them belonging to the same species.

Brown hares are shy, solitary animals, mainly nocturnal in habits. During the day, they lie up in a 'form' or seat, which is usually in a tussock of grass. On its ground the hare has several such forms, which it uses in turn according to wind and weather. At night, the hare becomes active, feeding on grass, plants, tender stalks and bark, according to the area in which it lives. Some hares lie up in woodland; others move into such cover only during severe winter weather. When put on foot by man or dogs, the hare runs off, relying on its great speed to escape. A strong hare may reach a speed of fifty miles per hour in short bursts.

The brown hare may or may not be territorial; certainly the same animals can be seen on the same ground day after day. Young animals wander, and it may well be that hares persistently hunted become unsettled.

Mating time is spring and, in March, hares traditionally 'go mad'; the sexes gather in certain places and pair off. Such meeting places are used year after year, and hares seem to know where they are. The gestation period is six weeks. The doe gives birth to two or three young which she leaves alone for long spells in their separate forms, returning periodically to suckle them. Two or three litters a year are the rule, and there is no peak breeding season. Superfoetation, mentioned by Pliny, has been established as a fact. This means that the doe hare can become pregnant again several days before she gives birth to a litter.

Brown hares have many enemies. They are preyed upon by all the carnivores, and by golden eagles. Man, however, is the main predator in temperate regions, but the hare remains numerous where it is not too heavily hunted.

The Arctic hare, also known as the mountain hare, is found in the Alps and in more northerly areas, including the Highlands of Scotland. The species derives its name from its coat, which is greyish-brown in summer and white in winter. It is smaller than the brown hare and, in many ways, resembles the rabbit—for example, it uses burrows. In summer, it will lie under rocks or peat overhangs or in other holes. In winter, it will lie under snow.

The European rabbit (*Oryctolagus cuniculus*), from which all domestic rabbits have been derived, seems to have originated in the western Mediterranean. Introduced by man into other countries, it has since colonized several continents. It has proved to be highly adaptable, but it cannot stand extreme heat or cold. Wild rabbits vary in weight between two and three pounds. On average, they are smaller than most of the domestic varieties. The North African race is the smallest of all.

Rabbits are notable burrowers, warrens being mostly in banks on the edge of woods or streams. The burrow systems link up, so that colonies can become large. It is not unusual to find foxes, badgers and rabbits using the same burrow system, but living in different parts of it. The doe rabbit digs a special burrow for her nest, sometimes within the warren, sometimes away from it. The main food is grass and a variety of plants, roots and stalks. Seeds and the bark of trees are taken in severe winters.

Hares and rabbits practise refection, which means that food is passed twice through the gut. Soft pellets are passed during the night, which are eaten as they leave the anus. The normal hard droppings, which are the result of the second digestion, are passed by day. Refection seems to be indispensable for the development and normal health of lagomorphs. It is now thought that the soft droppings contain certain vitamins produced by bacteria in the caecum.

The wild rabbit breeds from January to July. Mating is preceded by a special ceremonial in which the rabbits chase and lick each other and the bucks spray streams of urine on to the backs of does. The doe rabbit may remain in season for a month or more. Ovulation is stimulated by actual mating.

The gestation period is 30 to 32 days. Shortly before she is due to give birth to her young, the doe rabbit digs a special burrow, two or three feet long, at the end of which she makes a nest with hay mixed with wool which she plucks from her body. Litter size varies from three to nine. During the day, the doe rabbit stays away from the nest; at night, she makes several visits to suckle the young. Each time she leaves she seals the burrow, but the earth with which she seals it sometimes becomes mixed with wool from the nest, thus betraying the site. The doe may have up to six litters in a year.

Before myxomatosis reduced rabbits to a fraction of their former numbers, they were shot by sportsmen all over Europe. Myxomatosis was a serious blow to shooting interests; on the other hand, it was a boon to farmers and foresters whose harvests and seedlings often suffered severe damage from rabbits.

Following myxomatosis, many attempts were made to introduce the American cottontail (*Sylvilagus*) into Europe. The dangers of such attempts are self-evident and are usually a mistake. This is especially true of the cottontail which, like the European rabbit, can become a major farming pest. In addition, it is extremely prolific and immune to myxomatosis. It has not the food value of the European species, and its

The wild rabbit, *Oryctolagus cuniculus*, a boon to sportsmen, but frowned on by foresters and farmers, has had its populations decimated by myxomatosis. *Atlas—Merlet*

sporting qualities are considered to be almost nil. All responsible people consider that its introduction to the continent of Europe would be a grave mistake.

The Ochotonidae (pikas)

The last lagomorphs are the pikas (*Ochotona*) which are charming little animals, found in the mountains of temperate Asia and North America. They are about the size of guinea-pigs and resemble big-eared field-voles. They are found mainly among rocks, where they live in colonies. People travelling in the Himalayas above the tree line, where animal life is relatively scarce, are always likely to come upon pikas because of their habit of climbing on to rocks to watch intruders. Pikas do not hibernate; instead, they lay in stocks of hay for winter use. They make hay as the farmer does, spreading it out in the sun to dry, and storing it only when it has been completely made. Pikas refect like rabbits and hares.

The European mountain hare presents two phases in the coloration of its coat; grey in summer, white in winter. The camouflage of the animal, which lives among the rocks in summer and on the snow in winter, is thus continually ensured. *Phot. Bille*

The order Rodentia

Rodents are by far the commonest animals in the world. The order has 352 genera and 2300 species. New species are always being described and, doubtless, there are many tropical species still awaiting discovery.

The great adaptability of rodents is reflected in their world-wide distribution; they are found everywhere except the Antarctic. Even the South Sea Islands have been colonized by rats and mice. Every habitat, underground, aquatic, or forests, has been colonized by some species specially adapted for burrowing, running, jumping, climbing, gliding or swimming, depending on the ecological niche it occupies.

Despite this diversity of behaviour, rodents are all built on much the same lines. They are mostly small or medium sized animals. The harvest mouse (*Micromys*) of the Old World weighs about a third of an ounce. The biggest rodent of all is the cabybara (*Hydrochoerus hydrochoeris*) which can weigh up to a hundredweight.

The teeth of all rodents are very much alike, the main difference being in the grinding surface of the molars which varies widely. All have four large incisors, two in the upper jaw and two in the lower. The lower incisors are continuous growth teeth, which the animal keeps worn by gnawing. There are no canines or pre-molars, so, in all rodents, there is a wide interval between the incisors and the back teeth (molars). This allows the incisors free play. They cut and chop the food which then passes easily to the molars, which crush it. The molars are either tubercled or crested; some of them are low, others high.

Rodents have made a considerable impact on human ecology and pathology. Many of them cause great destruction which is not compensated for by any use that can be made of them, as food animals or experimental animals. Rats and voles can cause immense damage, and it is well-known that the brown rat is a reservoir for some of the most dangerous human diseases. It is an unfortunate fact that man, who has succeeded in exterminating so many harmless species, has never really been able to come to grips with rats and mice, whose fertility has enabled them to survive the most costly and repeated campaigns to destroy them. Many people are certain that 'clean' cities, like London and Paris, contain more rats than people.

It is impossible to deal here with all the rodents: there are too many of them. Many of them inhabit tropical regions and little, if anything, is known about their biology. We shall, therefore, select certain types from among the most remarkable and the most closely studied.

The Sciuridae (squirrels)

Although poorly represented in Europe, there are several hundred species in other parts of the world. Most of the squirrels are arboreal species, but there are several species of ground squirrels. Marmots and ground squirrels are burrowers, and live underground. The so-called flying squirrels include many species adapted to gliding flight. They are found in the forests of Asia, northern Europe and North America. The gliding squirrels, like all the so-called 'flying' mammals, are nocturnal in habit, while the tree squirrels and marmots are active by day.

The red squirrel (*Sciurus vulgaris*) is common in Europe, and is familiar to everyone, even those who have never seen one alive and free. It is red-furred and has a bushy tail. Lively and agile, and expert climbers, red squirrels spend a great part of their lives in trees, running along branches or leaping from one to another with the greatest of ease.

The red squirrel builds its nest or drey in a tree fork, often at a great height from the ground. As a rule, each animal has three or four dreys, built of fibre, twigs and moss. In one of these, the female has her young. The drey has no entrance or exit hole; the squirrel breaks in and breaks out at each visit. Some squirrels make their homes in hollow trees or in rock clefts, and some even use rabbit burrows.

Although squirrels rise at daybreak and are active mainly. in the morning, they can also be seen on and off during the day, each squirrel operating within well defined limits. The diet, which is extremely varied, includes walnuts, hazel-nuts, beech-nuts, acorns, pine-cones and bark. Mushrooms are another favourite item, and the squirrel eats species that are poisonous to man. Some squirrels will take the eggs and young of small birds. Surplus food is hidden in the ground, but the squirrels seem to forget most of their hiding places. It is quite likely that food unearthed afterwards is found by accident. Squirrels in Western Europe have litters of three or four young in spring.

The giant forest squirrel (*Protoxerus stangeri*) is a fairly common tree-dweller in the African forest belt (West Africa, Kenya, Uganda). 8 to 12 inches, excluding tail. *Phot. A. R. Devez—Biological Mission to Gabon*

The common red squirrel (*Sciurus vulgaris*) is a graceful creature of conifer woods. It is found throughout Europe, and even approaches the Arctic Circle; it is found also in northern Siberia. *Phot. Aldo Margiocco*

The red squirrel settles down well in captivity, but is always liable to bite. If caged, it will keep on trying to gnaw its way out.

Although it has become rare in many areas, there are still plenty of red squirrels in the big coniferous forests of the north. The real niche of this squirrel is, in fact, coniferous forest.

Many tropical squirrels are brightly and contrastingly coloured—light or dark striping on the fur, which varies in shade from grey to red, and even green.

Notable among the ground squirrels is the Barbary ground squirrel (*Atlantoxerus getulus*) of North Africa. It is mainly terrestrial, and lives among rocks. Active by day, it is fond of basking in the sun, so it is often seen by travellers using the trails across the Atlas foothills. Barbary squirrels are gregarious. Like other members of the squirrel tribe, they utter piercing cries at the approach of danger, thus warning other members of the group.

Within this family, there is great variation in size. The giant squirrels (*Ratufa*) of India reach over three feet in length, and are as big-bodied as cats. They are shy animals, not often seen when hiding in high tree tops. On the other hand, they attract attention by their loud alarm calls, thus making it possible to view them from a distance. The smallest species is the pygmy squirrel (*Myoscurius pumilio*) from equitorial Africa. It is really tiny, with a body hardly thicker than a pencil and a tail no longer than a match. The pygmy is active among the creepers that form part of the undergrowth of the dark African forest. It is difficult to imagine that this tiny creature is a close relative of the giant squirrels of India.

Marmots, ground squirrels and prairie dogs

Although they spend a great part of their lives underground, and never leave the ground, marmots are related to squirrels. They are large, heavily built rodents, with short ears and large prominent eyes. There are about fifteen species, most of them confined to mountainous areas in the cold and temperate regions of the Northern Hemisphere.

The Alpine marmot (*Marmota marmota*) grows to two feet in length and weighs between eleven and thirteen pounds. Originally confined to the rocky slopes of the Alps, between 4900 and 9800 feet, it is now also found in the Pyrenees, having been introduced there by man. Alpine marmots live in colonies of about a dozen. They spend most of the day searching for plants, roots and seeds. Young animals spend much of their time at play. Any marmot that sights an approaching enemy, whether it is man, carnivore or eagle, gives a warning whistle that alerts the colony and sends them running to the shelter of their burrows.

The burrows are permanent quarters. The marmots sleep in them during the night and hibernate in them during the long winter—up to eight months—in the most northerly regions. During this winter sleep, the marmots exist on their fat reserves, and have lost about a quarter of their body weight when they wake up.

Marmots are hunted for their flesh and fur. One way of catching them is by digging them out during their winter sleep. The young are easily tamed, and settle down readily in captivity. Marmots are still plentiful and, at present, there is no threat to their survival.

Ground squirrels (*Citellus*), numbering about 144 species

and sub-species, are distributed over most of the temperate zone of the Northern Hemisphere. They are much smaller than marmots, but their behaviour is similar. As a rule, they are spotted or striped. All are well adapted to an underground life.

In the most northerly part of their range, ground squirrels hibernate, while those in arid regions aestivate during the hottest season. In other words, some species sleep when conditions are too cold: others do so when conditions become too hot. It has been shown that lack of water, combined with the drying-up of vegetation, stimulates aestivation in the ground squirrels of the desert. They become active again in winter when the vegetation revives with the rains. These examples illustrate a fact that is becoming increasingly clear: hibernation is not a simple response to cold conditions. It is under the control of the animal's nervous system, and the stimulation that determines the state may vary according to conditions of time and place.

Prairie-dogs (*Cynomys ludovicianus*), once widely distributed and abundant on the plains of North America, are closely related to ground squirrels and marmots. Despite their name, they are not dogs: they are heavily built squirrels which live in communities, sometimes several thousand strong. Hence the term 'prairie-dog towns'.

In the prairie-dog town, there is a fairly complex hierarchical system. The defence of the group's territorial boundaries is undertaken by dominant males. Prairie-dogs have a considerable vocabulary and a well-developed communications system, a different call being used in any given situation. For example, danger approaching from the air is signalled by an alarm call different from that used to warn of an enemy on the ground. When alerted, the prairie-dogs take shelter in their deep burrows which can be identified from a distance by the mound of loose earth beside them. These hillocks are carefully looked after by the prairie-dogs, and are used as look-out posts.

Prairie-dogs were formerly a dominant species in the fauna of the grass plains of America. At one time, their numbers were estimated at 800 million in the state of Texas. American stock-breeders quickly changed this, exterminating them over vast areas because they competed with cattle for the grass. Nowadays, prairie-dog populations are confined to a few pockets.

Flying squirrels

Europeans are not generally familiar with flying squirrels, although they form a large group, with numerous species in northern Europe, America and in the forests of Asia. In flying squirrels, there is a membranous skin fold along the sides of the body between the fore and hind limbs, and this, when open, enables the animals to glide from tree to tree. But this is simple gliding, not true flight, as in bats.

There is great variety in size, Asian species reaching a length of over three feet, while other forms are no bigger than dormice.

It has often been argued that flying mammals are all active at night to avoid competition with birds, most of which are active by day. Although this explanation is plausible in the case of bats, it is extremely doubtful if it is valid for flying squirrels.

The development of lateral membranes, which make gliding flight possible for several classes of arboreal animals, has given rise to an ingenious explanation. According to this

The Canadian beaver (*Castor canadensis*) is very closely related to the European one, of which there are still a few populations in the valleys of the Rhône and of its tributaries. Beavers show morphological and ethological adaptations to aquatic life. *Phot. Simon Ostman*

theory, gliding flight evolved in species inhabiting swampy flooded forests, where passage from one tree to another was possible only by swimming or flying. Selection, in those forms not adapted for swimming, led to an adaptation towards gliding flight. Weight is lent to this theory by the fact that an early stage of such behaviour is apparent in non-flying arboreal species. When the European red squirrel jumps, it spreads out its limbs and tail as much as possible, thus forming itself into a kind of parachute. In Africa, scaly-tailed squirrels have been observed at twilight gliding over flooded river banks, passing from islet to islet, and taking short-cuts across bends. No land mammal could have manoeuvred with comparable ease in such an environment. All these things considered, one has no hesitation in subscribing to the hypothesis that the ancestors of the flying squirrels were the squirrels of the primeval flooded forest.

Beavers

Beavers are found in Europe and North America—*Castor fiber* in Europe; *Castor canadensis* in America. The adult measures over three feet in length and weighs about 66 pounds.

In prehistoric times, beavers were distributed over the greater part of the Northern Hemisphere; since then their range has been considerably reduced. In France, for example, they were once common in many regions, and the Bièvre, a river flowing into the Seine at Paris, takes its name from the word *biber*, which is Celtic for beaver. Nowadays only a few remain, in the Rhône Valley and some of its tributaries. In Northern Europe and Canada, there are thriving colonies. Wholesale destruction by fur trappers once brought it to the verge of extinction, but it has been saved by modern protective measures, and its future seems assured.

The beaver is a robust, square-built animal with a broad head and a longitudinally flattened, spade-like tail. The root of the tail is covered with hair; the remainder is covered with skin-like scales. Beavers measure from 31 inches to 40 inches in length, the tail being under 12 inches. It was once thought that the beavers of the Old World and the New were distinct species; it is now considered that they are merely geographical races of the same species. Beaver populations in the U.S.S.R. have been boosted by animals imported from Canada.

Although there are behavioural differences between the North American and European beavers, they are basically alike. Both are colonial species, the colonies being made up of animals living close to each other. Colonies are always established on rivers or lakes, the beavers living in lodges which they build of branches solidified with mud.

A beaver lodge is a solid structure, built on a foundation of an old tree trunk or a raised part of the stream bed. The beavers dam the river or stream, so that the entrance to the lodge remains under water, a habit more characteristic of the American than of the European species. Dam walls have been recorded over 600 yards long and several yards high.

In Canadian beavers, the urge to build is so strong that they will do so even when it is not necessary.

The marmot (*Marmota marmota*) is a large Alpine rodent which lives in colonies on stony screes and feeds on plants; it hibernates in deep burrows. Its chief enemy is the golden eagle. *Phot. Bille*

Scaly-tailed squirrels

Scaly-tailed squirrels (*Anomalurus* and *Anomalurops*) replace flying squirrels in Africa, occupying the same ecological niche. Despite their resemblance to flying squirrels, and the fact that they have a membrane that enables them to glide, they are not true squirrels, and there are profound anatomical differences between them. The similarity of the two types is another example of convergent evolution—unrelated species coming to resemble each other because of their similar way of life.

The nine species of scaly-tailed squirrel are found in the tropical forests of Central and West Africa. The largest are the size of a cat; the smallest the size of a mouse. On the under-side of their tails they have scales which act as suction discs when they press their bodies against a vertical tree trunk—a favourite position. These squirrels live in hollow trees and are usually found in large colonies.

The scaly-tailed squirrel, when travelling from tree to tree, climbs to the topmost branches of one, launches itself into space and glides in the direction of the other. When it alights, it climbs to the trunk, using its belly-scales. Gliding in this way, the scaly-tailed squirrel can cover its whole territory without ever descending to the ground.

The Cricetidae

This family is made up of American rats and mice, hamsters, lemmings and voles, of which there are a hundred genera and several hundred species.

The animals of this group have a world-wide distribution, with the exception of a few Australian and Malaysian Islands. All are small or medium-sized rodents and most of them are ground dwellers, vegetarian and prolific. Some have become pests.

Rodents of this group are well represented in America, where they have become diversified into a number of distinct forms, able to exploit ecological niches like those occupied in Europe by brown rats and mice, which are not found in America. Because they occupy similar ecological niches, they have come to resemble the Old World rats to which they are not zoologically related. An example of this is the white-footed mouse (*Peromyscus*) which, in America, occupies the niche of the European field mouse. Similarly, the rice rat (*Oryzomys*) occupies the niche of the European brown rat. Similarity of habit has resulted in convergent evolution and certain Cricetidae, *Peromyscus* and *Oryzomys*, closely resemble field mice and brown rats which belong to another family entirely.

Most of the Cricetidae rodents are very ordinary, and little is yet known, even by experts, about their biology. What is known is that they occupy a great variety of habitats—underground, in trees, in the water—indicating that the American rodents have exploited the total natural environment as ably as the Europeans.

Hamsters

Hamsters (*Cricetus*), numbering about ten species, are found in temperate regions of the Old World from northeast France to Siberia. The best known species are the common hamster (*Cricetus cricetus*) and the golden hamster (*Mesocricetus auratus*). The common hamster is about the size of a guinea-pig. It has a three-coloured coat, pale yellow ochre above, black underneath, with a transverse white spot on the breast. It is a burrowing animal, ranging from Belgium and Alsace in the west to Lake Baikal in the east, and as far as the Black Sea and the Caspian. A steppe-dweller, it is also found on arable land wherever the top soil (loess) is deep enough to allow it to dig burrows. Hamster

burrows are of two types: the summer one, which is short and shallow, and the winter one, which is deeper and more complex.

In its winter burrow the hamster stores up enormous quantities of food—up to 190 pounds of corn and potatoes. Right alongside this store-house, it has a compartment for its nest and another one for its droppings.

Hamsters are territorial and defend their territory vigorously. The females have two litters a year, each numbering from four to eighteen young. Hamsters sleep for long periods in the winter and wake up frequently to eat the food they have stored.

The golden hamster, native to Asia Minor, has become known throughout the world in recent years as a laboratory animal and household pet. All golden hamsters are descended from a few individuals brought from Syria in 1930. They are smaller, more attractively coloured and less aggressive than the common hamster, and are now kept as pets all over the world. There was no such thing as a golden hamster in Europe before 1930.

Lemmings

Lemmings, which are thick-furred animals resembling large voles, inhabit the Arctic and sub-Arctic tundra, and are universally known because of their migrations which constitute one of the most astonishing phenomena in the animal world. In times of plenty their populations increase spectacularly; when the food supply fails, they either emigrate or die. Scandinavian lemmings emigrate. Alaskan lemmings die where they are.

The Scandinavian lemming has caught the popular imagination, but the facts about it should be put straight. Like other voles, it fluctuates on a four-year cycle of abundance and scarcity. The population rises to a peak; then there is a crash. When Scandinavian lemmings reach their peak, they emigrate in force, and these migrations are now a part of folklore, but it should be borne in mind that the emigration of the lemming is an exodus from a devastated range in

The common hamster (*Cricetus cricetus*) occurs from Belgium to Lake Baikal. It lives in burrows in which it accumulates substantial stores of food, chiefly grain, for winter use. *Phot. Brosset-Caubère*

search of new pastures and not a race to the sea to commit suicide. Almost all that has been written about their behaviour is true—that they invade towns and villages, swarm in fields, fall over cliffs and drown in rivers and in the sea—but the movement is not a rush to suicide. The sea was never their destination nor death by drowning their aim. Not all the lemmings move out, however; some remain, otherwise there would be no lemmings in the future.

Whatever the reason for lemming migration, it is not entirely due to failure of food supply. Stress is a factor. Many animals show profound alterations of the liver and certain glands. They sink into a kind of coma and go into convulsions and die. One thing is certain: none of the immigrants returns to its starting place. Various explanations have been given for this exodus—sun-spots, climatic conditions, chemical composition of food—but no satisfactory explanation has yet been given for peak and crash.

Voles

There are many species of vole in the temperate regions of the Northern Hemisphere. The bank vole (*Clethrionomys glareolus*) is a woodland species, also found on slopes with plenty of ground cover, and is easily identified by its long tail, its mouse-like profile and its reddish fur. The tail, which is dark above and pale below, is more than half the body length, and this is a characteristic feature. It is more agile and less nocturnal than the field vole, which is blunt-nosed, with a tail less than half its body length. Bank voles are not often found on cultivated ground. They prefer bramble thickets, overgrown banks, old tree stumps, rocks and screes.

The short-tailed vole or field vole (*Microtus agrestis*) and the common vole (*Microtus arvalis*) are agricultural pests in some parts of the world, e.g. France. Elsewhere, the field vole can be a problem on grasslands or in forests.

Short-tailed voles are found mainly on grassland and in young forests where the grass is tall. In such areas, they build up rapidly, and their numbers fluctuate on a four-year cycle of abundance and scarcity, the population reaching a peak, then crashing to a low level by mass deaths. This vole certainly benefits from environmental modifications caused by man—as in modern agriculture and forestry—when he creates monocultures. In habitats with more varied plant and animal life, population cycles do not take place. Practically every predator that can hunt voles hunts them, and obviously the killing of such predators as buzzards, stoats and weasels is a great mistake.

Short-tailed voles and common voles are distinguished from rats and mice by their thicker bodies, short tails and their small eyes. The ears are almost hidden in the fur. Their fur is usually grey or reddish grey, lighter on top, and they are about 4 inches long. They live in burrows and are mainly nocturnal, but are often active by day. Both eat abundance of grass and other herbage, the common vole consuming at least 1½ times its own body weight in green food each day. Both are extremely prolific, the females mating for the first time at the age of 3 weeks. Gestation lasts 21 days, and mating follows immediately on the birth of a litter. Litter size varies from 4 to 8, the young being weaned at the age of 10 to 12 days. Very few voles survive through a second winter.

The alpine vole (*Microtus nivalis*), which is more local in its distribution, is found in southern Europe. It is a fairly large species with a greyish coat. Although its name suggests that it is a mountain species, it is found mainly among rocks, especially on sunny slopes, and often at low altitudes.

The northern pine-vole (*Pitymys subterraneus*), the com-

Periodical eruptions in the numbers of Scandinavian lemmings (*Lemmus lemmus*), lead to the so-called migrations which have been famous since the Middle Ages. In his *History of the Northern Peoples* (1555), Olaüs Magnus explains that lemmings fall from the clouds on stormy days! *Phot. Holmasen-Ostman*

monest species in its group, is found in damp places, in gardens and meadows, where it moves about among the ground cover and under low vegetation. It is distinguished from the others by its small size, greyish-brown fur and minute eyes.

The water vole (*Arvicola terrestris*), often confused with the brown rat, is a large vole adapted to life in the water. They live in burrows which are dug in the banks of streams and rivers. They are territorial animals, each pair holding about 200 yards of a stretch of stream, and a considerable area on both banks. They are good swimmers and divers. Exclusively vegetarian, they eat a variety of water plants and lay up stocks of such fodder to last them through the winter. The females produce two litters a year, which may number anything from two to five young. Water voles are relatively unimportant species so far as man is concerned, but they suffer a great deal through being mistaken for brown rats.

The musk rat (*Ondatra zibethica*) is very much like the water vole in appearance and in its ecology. It is readily

A. The Iberian root vole (*Pitymys duodecimcostatus*), intermediate between the field vole and the northern root vole. B. The bank vole (*Clethrionomys glareolus*), common in woods. C. The northern root vole (*Pitymys subterraneus*). D. The yellow-necked mouse (*Apodemus* *flavicollis*), a woodland mouse of Europe and Asia. E. The alpine vole (*Microtus nivalis*). F. The short-tailed vole (*Microtus agrestis*), a destroyer of crops. *Phot. Caubère-Brosset*

distinguished from the water vole by its much greater size—it weighs between 26 ounces and 4 pounds—and its scaly, vertically flattened tail. It was introduced into Europe from its native North America to be farmed for its fur and, as so often happens in such cases, some animals escaped and bred successfully. Since then, the descendants have colonized many parts of Europe.

Sometimes musk rats live in burrows which they dig in river banks; at other times, they copy the beaver and make lodges of piled-up plants. On their territory, they keep the water channels clear of vegetation and other obstacles to allow themselves freedom of movement. They feed mainly on aquatic plants but, in farming areas, they will raid fields of growing crops. They also occasionally kill shrimps and fish.

Tunnelling by musk rats in places where they have settled in numbers sometimes results in the collapse of river banks, and for this reason its introduction into Europe was a mistake. Introduction of exotic species usually results in one of two things: the incomers either quickly die out because they cannot find a niche, or they succeed spectacularly and multiply, especially where there is no competition. In the latter case, their numbers quickly get out of control, and this is exactly what happened with the musk rat.

The coypu (*Mytocastor coypus*), known to the fur trade as nutria, was also introduced into Europe, where it has settled in many areas, including Britain. It is a much bigger animal than the musk rat, with a porcupine-like face and prominent yellow incisor teeth. Adults weigh from nine to eleven pounds.

Rats and mice

This family, the most numerous in the class of mammals, has about 100 genera and something like 1000 species. All were natives of the Old World, but man introduced them to the American continent and elsewhere where they found conditions exactly to their liking. They are now the most widely distributed mammalian group, and it seems unarguable that the total number of rats and mice in the world is much greater than the number of human beings.

Most species of rat are found in tropical forests, and not very much is known about their ecology or biology. As a generic type, they show great uniformity of size and shape, with the result that very few species are significantly different from domestic rats and mice. A better knowledge of their biology might, however, discover substantial differences in behaviour.

The harvest-mouse (*Micromys minutus*) and the wood-mouse (*Apodemus sylvaticus*) are European species, both of them country mice. The first is a tiny attractive mammal, with a bright red coat; it is about two inches in length, and weighs less than a third of an ounce. It lives mainly in long grass, climbing the tall stalks as a squirrel climbs trees, and it has been described as 'adapted to arboreal life in long grass'. But it is not confined to grass. It is also found among sedges along river banks and in fields of young grain.

The harvest-mouse builds her nest of woven grass high on the stalks of cereals, grass or sedges. The nest has an entrance at the side. Breeding nests are often lined with thistledown and, in these, the female rears her litter of eight or nine young. Outwith the breeding season, the harvest-mouse lives in burrows and shelters under stacks of straw or hay. In summer, its diet is mainly insectivorous. Harvest-mice are in decline over most of their range, a decline almost certainly associated with modern farming methods.

The wood-mouse or field mouse is, on the other hand, widely distributed and is abundant everywhere in the countryside of western Europe, including the British Isles. It is a common animal in woods and cultivated areas, and its population is usually stable, unlike that of the short-tailed vole. Although a true outdoor species, the wood-mouse sometimes enters houses. It also inhabits old walls and straw stacks.

Wood-mice are attractive rodents, with long trumpet ears,

large dark eyes with the shine of the night-hunter, and a tail at least as long as the head and body put together. The fur is reddish-grey on the back, yellowish on the flanks and white underneath.

The wood-mouse is strictly nocturnal; even bright moonlight inhibits it. During the day it lies up in its burrow, sometimes in a bird's nest or a hole in a tree. It is an excellent jumper and climber. Although it is mainly vegetarian, feeding on seeds, roots and berries, it eats snails, gnawing through the shell as it gnaws through a hazel-nut. It lays in stores of food for the winter. Females breed several times a year, and litter size varies from five to nine young.

In some localities wood-mice can be destructive, especially in gardens. They are preyed upon by weasels, stoats, polecats, owls and other predators which kill them in large numbers, an ecological relationship that results in stability.

Unlike the mice of the fields, the brown rat and the black rat are commensals of man, which means that they live at his expense and do nothing for him in return. Both species originated in the Far East, the black reaching Europe towards the end of the Middle Ages. Brown rats arrived on the scene much later. They were reported in Paris in 1753, in Norway in 1726 and in Spain in 1800. Carried in ships, they reached England in 1728, and the United States of America in 1775. Brown rats reached Britain from Norway; hence their other name of Norway rat.

The brown rat (*Rattus norvegicus*) is distinguished from the black rat (*Rattus rattus*) by its heavier build and its relatively shorter tail and ears. The two occupy different ecological niches and differ considerably in habits, so they seldom come into direct competition. The black rat, sometimes known as the ship rat, likes dry places, e.g. buildings, and is mainly found in such places near docks. It also climbs trees, and was probably a tree rat originally.

The brown rat, on the other hand, prefers to live at ground level at farms, in buildings, in sewers and along canal banks. It is very common in large towns—in fact, it is common everywhere—but wild populations can be observed in river banks and such places, especially in summer. This rat swims and dives with the greatest of ease and is frequently confused with the water vole, whose burrows it sometimes takes over.

In brown rats, a strict hierarchical structure has been noticed. This order applies throughout the social structure, regulating access to food and priority in mating, according to the rank of the individuals. Each couple defends its territory vigorously. If food is plentiful, the young stay with their parents, thus forming large family groups in which the hierarchical system breaks down. Marking experiments have shown that brown rats are, on the whole, sedentary.

Brown rats will eat practically anything, which helps to explain their world-wide success. Apart from waste matter, they eat a wide variety of stored foodstuffs, causing considerable commercial loss. In addition to this kind of destruction, they constitute a danger to health because they form a reservoir of many dangerous diseases, including bubonic plague, typhus and rabies, and it has been calculated that, during the past 1000 years, they have caused more deaths than all the wars and revolutions put together.

Ironically, it turns out that man, who has so stupidly destroyed so many harmless species, seems incapable of wiping out or controlling the resourceful brown rat, despite all the methods he has used or tried. It would be even more

The long-tailed field mouse (*Apodemus sylvaticus*) is a charming little rodent very common on wooded sites in Western Europe. In winter, it does not hesitate to enter houses, in which it is often mistaken for the house-mouse. *Phot. Aldo Margiocco*

The brown or sewer rat (*Rattus norvegicus*) is an aggressive animal whose bite is dangerous because of the germs it inoculates. As it needs large quantities of water, it does not stray far from sources of supply. *Phot. J. Six*

The house mouse (*Mus musculus*) is a species associated with man which is found in almost all the warm or temperate countries on the globe. *Phot. J. L. S. Dubois*

The pacarana (*Dinomys branickii*) is part of the legion of large rodents characteristic of South American fauna. It lives in the equatorial or sub-equatorial zones. Little is known of its habits. Weight: 9 to 22 pounds. *Phot. A. R. Devez-Lauros—Atlas Photo*

ironic if all his efforts—ruthless hunting, uncontrolled use of pesticides and tampering with the natural environment—resulted in rats taking over the world at his expense. Man, it seems, is being defeated by his worst and most destructive enemy—the brown rat.

The house mouse (*Mus musculus*), a small rodent, has also managed to colonize most of the world, surviving all threats by its fertility, and has become a pest and a danger to public health. Apart from its smaller size, it is similar to the brown rat in every other way, living an almost identical social and family life.

A field species in its native Asia—it still is—the house mouse elsewhere has become a commensal of man. Being so small, it finds no difficulty in entering houses, inside which it builds its nests in a variety of places. So long as it can find plenty of food, it may be satisfied with no more than a few square yards of territory. House mice consume all sorts of foodstuffs, even eating materials normally considered inedible, such as glue and soap. They waste more than they eat, and soil their whole territory with their odorous secretions, droppings and urine.

In his war against mice, man has, through the ages, used traps and poison; in addition, he has called on the services of other species—carnivores like genets, mongooses and cats: cats above all. In certain parts of Africa and Asia, some species of snakes are tolerated inside houses because they are predators on mice. Predation, however, is usually a balanced thing: all the cats in the world have never succeeded in reducing the world's mice.

The success of the house mouse is certainly connected with

its high fertility. The young mouse is adult at the age of 35 days and can then breed. The gestation period is short—from 18 to 21 days—and the usual family is from 4 to 7 young. Litters succeed each other rapidly, more rapidly in the absence of any check by predators.

The Gliridae: dormice

There are three species of dormouse in Western Europe: the common or hazel dormouse (*Muscardinus avellanarius*), the garden dormouse (*Eliomys quercinus*) and the edible dormouse (*Glis glis*).

The common dormouse is an attractive mouse with a bushy squirrel tail. This, combined with its richly coloured coat (reddish-orange on the back, white on the throat, breast and feet) makes it easily identified. It is a woodland species, frequenting low ground vegetation among shrubs and brushwood. In summer, it builds its globular nest of bark, leaves and moss under low branches. In this nest, the female gives birth to a litter of two to nine young. This dormouse feeds on berries, seeds, buds, insects and, occasionally, birds' eggs. After the breeding season, the dormouse builds another kind of nest at ground level, hidden under piled-up leaves or under a tree or bush. This is the hibernating nest in which it sleeps from October to April.

The garden dormouse is common and widespread in Western Europe. It has a reddish-grey coat with a black band round the eyes, and a black and white tail tuft. It is about the size of a small rat. It frequents woods and gardens, and is sometimes found among rocks, or even in lofts, which it sometimes invades when it is ready to hibernate.

Nocturnal in habits, the garden dormouse is active in trees, bushes and on walls where it finds most of its food—fruit, seeds, beech-nuts, a variety of invertebrates and even small rodents and birds. Its nest is not usually high above ground, and almost invariably it takes over a squirrel's drey or the old nest of blackbird or magpie, which it lines with moss and in which it sometimes stores a substantial stock of acorns. The rule seems to be one litter per year, averaging four young, born in June or July. The garden dormouse is aggressive and difficult to tame.

The edible or fat dormouse (*Glis glis*) is easily recognized by its greater size and its silvery-grey coat. This species is easily tamed, and the Romans used to breed it in captivity for the table. It is common in hilly and mountainous regions, building its nest in holes in trees or among rocks or in birds' nests. Like the garden dormouse, it feeds on both vegetable and animal matter.

The young are born in June, numbering from two to nine in a litter. In Autumn, *Glis glis* puts on a tremendous amount of fat—hence its other name—which it uses up slowly during its six months hibernation.

The Dipodidae

Jerboas live in dry steppes and deserts

Jerboas are jumping rodents, found in arid and desert regions of the Old World, and are very common in some parts of the Sahara. With their weak, short fore limbs, long hind legs and long tails, they look more like tiny kangaroos than anything else. They are nocturnal and solitary, lying up by day in

Dollman's tree mouse, *Prionomys batesi* is a curious African forest rodent, presenting arboreal adaptations (prehensile feet) and adapted to an insectivorous diet. Its favourite food is believed to be ants. *Phot. F. Petter*

The hazel dormouse (*Muscardinus avellanarius*) is the smallest but surely the most graceful dormouse of the European fauna. An eater of fruit, seeds and buds, it haunts woods, usually being found among the undergrowth. Maximum weight: 1 ounce. *Phot. A. Fatras—Jacana*

Edible dormouse (*Glis glis*) in state of torpor during the winter. *Phot. Aldo Margiocco*

burrows which are not easily seen because the animal seals the entrance behind it. At night they come out in search of food, which consists mainly of seeds and dry grass. Jerboas never drink water. They produce it from their food by body chemistry. Despite its small size, the jerboa can leap six feet. Its long tail is used as a prop and balancing pole. Life span is not known, but jerboas have survived for five years in captivity.

Porcupines

The Old World porcupines—about twenty species—are ground dwellers: the American species belong to a different unrelated family, and are all tree dwellers.

The best known Old World species (*Hystrix cristata*) is found in north Africa and southern Europe. It is a large animal, weighing up to sixty pounds, with an array of sharp quills on its back and tail which are effective defensive and offensive weapons. The quills are ringed with black and white. At the approach of any enemy, the porcupine stamps its feet and rattles its quills. If this warning is disregarded, the porcupine attacks backwards at high speed, stabbing at the enemy with the sharp quills of its tail and rump. Any quills that make contact with the enemy become automatically embedded, like the sting of a honey bee, and remain in the enemy's skin. This method of attack helps to explain the legend that the porcupine can shoot its quills at an enemy. In fact, European porcupines have been known to release quills in this way by muscular contraction.

Porcupines spend the day under rocks and in natural cavities, coming out at night to feed on roots and tubers. Although vegetarian, there is no doubt that captive animals will gnaw at bones and, in equatorial forests, the tusks of dead elephants are destroyed by porcupines gnawing at them.

The tree porcupines of North America eat bark, and Canadian porcupines have been known to strip completely all the trees in an area.

The Caviidae: guinea-pigs, laboratory animals

The guinea-pig (*Cavis porcellus*) is the best known animal in this group. It was imported into Europe, where it has been bred in a great variety of colours, is popular as a domestic pet, and is used widely in medical research.

The Indians of the Andes rear guinea-pigs for food as Europeans rear rabbits. In South America, wild guinea-pigs inhabit rocky regions, the forest fringe, savannas and swamps. They are burrowing animals and nocturnal in habits. Their fur is rough in texture and uniformly greenish-grey in colour. Unlike domestic guinea-pigs, which are slow and quiet, the wild animals are lively and quick-moving. Captive guinea-pigs breed throughout the year, the females giving birth to three or four young after a gestation period of two months. The young are able to breed at the age of two months. Life span is about eight years.

Right
The crested porcupine (*Hystrix cristata senegalensis*) in defensive attitude. Height at shoulder level: 10 to 20 inches. *Phot. J. Six*

The jerboa (*Jaculus orientalis*) lives in oases and steppe desert zones. Its diet is half-vegetarian, half-insectivorous. *Phot. Aldo Margiocco*

(*Right*) the brush-tailed porcupine, *Atherurus africanus* is widespread in tropical and equatorial Africa. Maximum size: 16 inches excluding tail. *Phot. Devez— M.B.G.*

Capybaras: the largest rodents

The capybara (*Hydrochoerus hydrochoeris*), found in the humid forests of South America, is the largest rodent in existence. It resembles a gigantic guinea-pig and can weigh up to 110 pounds. Capybaras are social animals, and are found along the banks of rivers. They are good swimmers and divers, and, when hunting or alarmed, hide in floating vegetation. Their main predators are the jaguar on land, and the alligator in swamps and rivers.

The order Insectivora

In this order, there are eight families with about three hundred species, all small or very small, with longish muzzles. All have five toes on each limb. Dentition is primitive and the coat, which is smooth and compact, usually consists of one kind of hair, sometimes modified into spines, as in the hedgehog.

Insectivores are mainly terrestrial, but a few are semi-aquatic. Most are either nocturnal or crepuscular in habits. As the name suggests, most are insect eaters; in other species, the prey range is wide and varied. Almost all are incapable of burrowing, so they lie up during the day in burrows made by other animals, in rock clefts or under piles of vegetable debris or brushwood.

In view of what is known of vertebrate evolution, it is clear that many present-day insectivores are primitive types, closely resembling the earliest mammals. Primitive insecti-

vores are believed to have been the fore-runners of many present-day orders of mammals, including the primates to which man belongs. The link between them may be represented by the Tupaiidae which shows a number of intermediate characteristics.

The Solenodontidae: an extremely rare family

The solenodonts, of which there are only two species, found in the West Indies, are now extremely rare, and may be extinct over much of their former range. The two present-day species appear to be the last of a group that is on the way out because they have reached the end of the evolutionary line.

The giant African water shrew or otter shrew (*Potamogale velox*) lives in the forest zones of West Africa. It is abundant in the Cameroons and in Gabon. Its body is like that of an otter: the tail, which is very slender and strong, is laterally flattened. The otter shrew is amphibious, but it does not stray far from the banks of streams or marshland. It is an excellent swimmer and feeds on varied prey: small fish, crustaceans, the larvae of insects. Length, including tail: 20 inches. *Phot. A. R. Devez—Biological Mission to Gabon*

They are isolated on the islands of Cuba and Haiti, where their populations are rapidly declining, and are probably doomed to early extinction.

Solenodonts resemble giant shrews. During the day, they hide in holes in the ground or in trees, coming out at night to hunt. They probe around with their muzzles in the ground litter in much the same way as hedgehogs and shrews, taking live prey and a variety of vegetable matter. Compared with most of the insectivores, they have a low breeding rate: only one or two young to a litter. Another factor in their decline is predation by imported carnivores, such as dogs, cats and mongooses.

The Tenrecidae (tenrecs and potamogales)

Tenrecs and potamogales are found in Madagascar, where they occupy the niche held by hedgehogs, moles and shrews in Europe. This is a numerous family, with ten genera and about 30 species. When the Tenrecidae became established in Madagascar, probably in the Cretaceous (late Mesozoic era), absence of competition probably favoured their occupation of vacant ecological niches. This would explain why there are so many species of this family in Madagascar.

Many members of the family resemble hedgehogs, having spines on their bodies. The tail-less tenrec (*Tenrec ecaudatus*) is common throughout Madagascar and the neighbouring islands, which it probably colonized by way of ships. Like the hedgehog, it is active at night, hiding during the day in a burrow or in a hole in a tree. It feeds on insects, worms and roots.

Having an imperfect heat regulation system, tenrecs become torpid during the dry season. The most remarkable feature of their biology—of which little is known—is their extreme fertility, the females giving birth to 25 young in a single litter. A case of 35 young in a litter has been reported. The number of young reared is usually 15, and there is little doubt that this high fertility is a big factor in their survival and success.

The hedgehog tenrec of Madagascar (*Setifer setosus*) is a special type. Its body is protected by white-tipped spines that point in all directions. Like the European hedgehog, it rolls itself into a ball when alarmed or attacked. It is common in dry forests, but not much is known about its habits. It seems to be mainly insectivorous and may not hibernate.

The streaked tenrecs (*Hemicentetes*) are small animals. Mixed with their fur, they have long sharp spines, black with reddish or white spots and stripes.

The genera *Dasogale* and *Echinops* each include species that closely resemble the European hedgehog. Practically nothing is known about the first, and its biology had not been studied. The second is a small version of the hedgehog tenrec, differing from it in the number of its teeth—32 instead of 36. It is believed to hibernate.

Rice tenrecs (*Oryzorictes*) are like moles. They have velvety fur, conical muzzles, short fore limbs with powerful claws, and are well adapted for burrowing and living like moles. The genera has three species widely distributed in Madagascar, all of them scarce and difficult to observe. They appear to spend most of their time in their burrows and are probably nocturnal in their habits. They are thought to prey on a variety of invertebrates.

The long-tailed tenrecs (*Microgale*) are shrew-like, and weigh about a third of an ounce. There are about twenty species. *Microgale* lives in forests, moving about under the cover of thick vegetation. It is active by day and by night, and from what little is known about its behaviour, its biology is similar to that of the common shrew.

The web-footed tenrec (*Limnogale*) is adapted to life in the water, having webbed hind feet and a thick vertically flattened tail which acts as a swimming web and a rudder. *L. mergulus* is about the size of a rat. A rare species, it is found in the east of Madagascar. It feeds on tubers and aquatic plants, but is sometimes caught in fish traps which it enters to eat the bait.

The giant African water shrew or otter shrew (*Potamogale*), although classified with the Tenrecidae, differs from them in certain anatomical details. It is widely distributed in Africa, and is one of the largest insectivores, measuring about two feet in length, including its tail.

It is highly specialized for its aquatic life, resembling a small otter. Its flattened muzzle is equipped with strong whiskers. Its nostrils close automatically when it dives. The body is streamlined, with a powerfully muscled tail, cylindrical at the base and flattened laterally towards its tip. The otter shrew has no webs on its feet, a lack compensated for by its tail which acts both as a swimming web and a rudder—an adaptation also found in the closely related *Micropotamogale* of West Africa.

The otter shrew is an expert swimmer, able to stay under water for several minutes at a time. It makes its burrows on the banks of streams and backwaters, and there it sleeps by day. At night it hunts a variety of aquatic prey—fish, crabs, etc. It hunts in bursts of intense activity, interrupted by periods of rest. In its hunting, it may be helped by its sense of touch. It is solitary outside the breeding season. Seasonal variations in food supply may drive it to undertake short migrations. It is frequently caught in fish traps and nets.

The Chrysochloridae (golden moles)

Golden moles are found in Africa, south of the equator, and there are about twenty species. Because they are highly adapted to an underground life, golden moles resemble true moles in general appearance, another case of convergent evolution as the result of an identical way of life, and not to any real relationship. Anatomically, golden moles form a separate group in the order, and are more closely related to tenrecs than anything else.

Golden moles are small and squat-bodied with a conical muzzle and a vestigial tail. The eyes are tiny or covered by skin, the ears being hidden in thick, glossy fur which has a metallic sheen. The front feet have four toes. The middle one is prolonged into an enormous claw adapted for burrowing.

Very little is known about their biology. Some genera, like *Eremitalpa* and *Cryptochloris*, are confined to areas of sand-dunes or sandy soil. Others, like *Amblysomus* and *Chrysospalax* are found in forests and cultivated areas, including gardens.

They live in burrows which vary in structure and complexity according to the nature of the soil. Quite often golden moles use tunnels made by rodents.

Like true moles *Chrysochloris* puts up heaps of loose earth above its tunnels, but nothing resembling the so-called fortress of the male. During the night, and in rainy weather, they move about above ground, but it is likely that they also use underground galleries when hunting. They prey mainly upon invertebrates, especially worms, but also eat lizards. In a deep burrow the female gives birth to a litter of two young—a low breeding rate for an insectivore. The female *Chrysochloris* suckles her young until they are almost as big as herself.

The Erinaceidae (hedgehogs and allied genera)

This family includes the true hedgehogs, the gymnures and moon rats. Hedgehogs are found in many parts of the Old World, but gymnures are confined to southeast Asia.

The Malayan gymnure (*Echinosorex*) is the largest of the family and also the largest living insectivore, reaching a length of 29 inches, including tail, and weighing about 3¼ pounds. The pygmy gymnure (*Hylomys suillus*), on the other hand, is no bigger than a small rat. Superficially, gymnures are not very like hedgehogs; they have no quills, and more closely resemble rodents. They are found in humid tropical forests, where they spend the day in rock clefts or old tree trunks, coming out at night to prey upon small vertebrates and invertebrates. *Echinosorex* probably leads a semi-aquatic life. Gymnures have a pair of anal glands with a strong-smelling secretion.

Hedgehogs are divided into five genera, all very similar in

The capybara or carpyncho (*Hydrochoerus hydrochoeris*), is the giant of South American rodents. Some individuals reach a length of 4 feet and a weight of 110 pounds. The capybara has a well-built body with short legs and no tail. It lives on the banks of streams, and in swamps, in societies of between 10 and 20 individuals. It is an excellent swimmer. The capybara is found in most parts of South America. *Phot. A. R. Devez—Lauros*

Golden moles (*Chrysochloris*) occupy quite a distinctive place among insectivores. Their shape, like an artillery shell, and their short fore-limbs set low down on their sides with each paw equipped with two powerful claws, bear witness to their close adaptation to underground life. They live in southern Africa, on the western side. The genus *Chrysochloris* is found as far north as Cameroun. They are difficult to find, and their habits are unknown. *Phot. Michel Boulard*

appearance. The main difference between the species is in the structure of the skull. *Paraechinus* and *Hemiechinus*, which have big ears, are found in the deserts and arid regions of Africa and Asia. The genus *Erinaceus*, which includes the European hedgehog (*E. europaeus*) is widely distributed in all the temperate regions of the Old World.

The European hedgehog is found mainly in areas of cultivation with plenty of hedgerows, copses and woodland, but it is also found in town gardens. Crepuscular and nocturnal in habits, hedgehogs spend the day curled up under dry leaves, under tree roots or in rabbit burrows, and come out at dusk to feed. They hunt on and off during the night, probing here and there in grass tussocks and in the ground litter, and eating practically anything they come across. They will kill anything they can catch and hold. Their prey range is wide, and includes insects, earthworms, snails, voles, frogs, lizards, roots and fruit. Sometimes hedgehogs raid birds' nests, taking eggs and chicks; they also eat carrion. When hunting, they use mainly their sense of smell.

When alarmed or threatened, the hedgehog rolls itself into a tight ball, presenting an array of quills to the enemy. In this position its stomach and feet are protected. The spines are brought erect by muscles in the skin. This hedgehog-defence is effective against most, but not all, of the hedgehog's enemies. Some dogs, notably terriers, can open hedgehogs. Badgers kill them, tearing them apart with their powerful bear-like claws. Foxes have been known to urinate on hedgehogs to make them uncurl, and it is a fact that a

In late autumn, the hedgehog builds a nest of leaves or dry grass, usually under a bush, in a burrow or under tree roots. This is its hibernaculum, where it will spend the winter. The duration of this winter sleep may be as much as six months in northern Europe. In the British Isles, it lasts for five or six months. In the warmer South, it is possible that the hedgehog may not hibernate at all.

Female hedgehogs have two litters a year: one at the beginning of summer and one in early autumn. Gestation varies from 34 to 39 days, and litter size from 3 to 5. The young, at birth are covered with soft white spines which harden as they grow, the permanent quills pushing through between the 36th and 40th day. The young are independent of their mother at the age of 40 days.

There is another species of European hedgehog—the North African hedgehog (*Aethechinus algirus*) which is found along the Mediterranean coast.

The Soricidae (shrews and crociduras)

Shrews are distributed over most of the world except the Arctic and South America. Voracious and highly adaptable, they are important animals in ecosystems at ground level.

The largest species are no bigger than a rat, while those of the genus *Suncus* include the smallest known mammals. One

hedgehog dropped in water uncurls immediately. Eagle owls kill and eat hedgehogs, but there is no doubt that, at the present day, their main predator is the motor car. Innumerable hedgehogs are killed on roads.

Hedgehogs are able to kill snakes, but the behaviour of individual animals varies greatly, and some hedgehogs either refuse to attack a snake or run away from it. The hedgehog is not immune to the venom of the adder, although it is considered to be about 40 times more resistant to it than the guinea-pig. In a confrontation between hedgehog and adder, the snake usually bites at the quills, thus damaging itself and doing the hedgehog no harm. But if the adder manages to bite the hedgehog on the nose, there is a different result. It is reliably recorded that hedgehogs thus bitten die within 24 hours.

of the tiniest, the pygmy white-toothed shrew, found mainly in the south and west of Europe, weighs about one fourteenth of an ounce. A still smaller species has just been discovered in Gabon.

Shrews have long flexible trunk-like snouts, small eyes and ears that are usually visible. They have five toes on each foot, and an obvious tail, variable in length. The coat is smooth, soft and thick. Many species have musk glands that give off an unpleasant smell. As in the solenedonts, the salivary glands of some shrews secrete a poison capable of killing mammals as big as themselves.

The red-toothed shrews have red or reddish-brown spots on the crown of their teeth. The common red-toothed shrew (*Sorex araneus*) is a common species in Europe, found in a variety of environments, but especially where there is plenty of ground cover, such as dry leaves. There is no peak period of activity. The shrew hunts round the clock, and has to do so because of its highly active metabolism (850 respirations and 800 heart beats a minute). Such an expenditure of energy requires an abundant and continuous food supply. It has been established that the shrew can eat at least its own weight in 24 hours. If compelled to fast for more than six hours, the animal quickly dies.

Unlike hedgehogs, shrews do not hibernate. They are as active throughout the year as they are round the clock. The hunting shrew moves in short, nervous spurts, turning over stones and poking among dry leaves with its flexible snout to uncover the small invertebrates on which it feeds. It locates their prey at short range, perhaps by smell and touch, perhaps by sonar. It has recently been discovered that, like bats and dolphins, shrews emit ultrasonic pulses, but the use they make of sonar is not yet understood. Anyone observing the hunting common shrew gets the impression that it finds food by falling over it.

Whereas *Sorex* is found in temperate regions of the northern hemisphere, *Crocidura* is found in the tropical and temperate regions of the Old World. This family has, by far, the largest number of species (about 200) and new ones are still being discovered, especially in Africa.

In Western Europe, the most widespread species is the white-toothed shrew (*Crocidura russula*), which is easily distinguished from the red-toothed shrew by the white tips of its teeth. It is common almost everywhere, but especially

Shrews (here the common European white-toothed shrew *Crocidura russula*) which do not occur in the New World, feed on insects and earthworms. *Phot. Aldo Margiocco*

The desert hedgehog (*Para echnius deserti*) unrolling. *Phot. Dubois*

near houses, where it takes advantage of hiding places created by man—old walls, stables, straw stacks, wood piles and such like. All the species in this group are small, voracious, bold and aggressive. They hunt live prey, mainly invertebrates, but they also kill small rodents which they attack ferociously and without fear. They also take carrion.

Although the white-toothed shrew can dig burrows, it usually occupies those already made by field-mice or voles. In such a burrow it builds its nest of grass and moss, and here the female gives birth to her family of one to ten young, after a gestation period of about 28 days. There are probably two or three litters a year.

This species is noted for the habit of caravanning. As soon

as the young are old enough to walk, they follow their mother in single file, holding on to each other's tails. This is the well-known caravan. The young hang on to each other and their mother, whatever the obstacles in their path. If the mother is lifted from the ground, the whole chain is lifted with her. The young shrews behave in this manner until they

are three weeks old. At the age of two or three months, they are mature. Under natural conditions, their life span is about a year, but they have survived in captivity for four years.

The water shrew (*Neomys fodiens*) is an Old World species, and one of the red-tooths in Western Europe. It inhabits the banks of clear streams where it hunts alevins, small crustaceans, larvae, fresh-water shrimps and young frogs. This is the biggest European shrew, easily identified by its size and its thick, velvety black and brown coat. On its feet and along the underside of its tail it has stiff hairs that form swimming webs. Although it can be seen by day, it is active mostly at night. It prefers clear water streams; the water shrew can sometimes be found thriving in ditches far from water.

There are many other genera and species of shrews throughout the world, but not much is known about their habits because they have been studied by only a handful of experts. They are particularly numerous in tropical regions. In the African forest belt, eleven different species were once captured in the same place. Wherever they are found, shrews plan an important part in the stability of ecosystems. If they are incapable of making any significant impact on the number of vertebrates on which they prey, they certainly live in equilibrium with them, and that is what balance really means.

The Macroscelidae (elephant shrews)

Elephant shrews are found up and down the length of Africa, mainly in regions of semi-desert, and about eighteen species have been described. As the name indicates, this shrew is easily recognizable by the fact that its muzzle has become elongated into a small, flexible, mobile trunk, with nostrils at the tip. The general shape of the body is rat-like, but the hind limbs, which are disproportionately long, are designed for jumping.

Elephant shrews hunt mainly by day, but are also active at night, and their skulls have been found in the pellets of owls which are, of course, night hunters. Areas of rock and scree are the favourite habitat of these shrews. They catch their prey by probing with their sensitive, flexible snouts into cracks and holes in the rocks. Although they are classified as insectivores, they have a wide prey range, and have even been caught in traps baited with carrots and bananas.

In its breeding and anatomy, this shrew has special interest for zoologists. When the female comes into breeding condition, the ovary sheds up to 80 ovules, but only one or two of these mature to develop into young shrews. So far, no-one has been able to explain this tremendous wastage of ovary material. This shrew also presents problems of evolution. The study of its anatomy reveals that it represents a stage between relatively unevolved insectivores and the *Tupaia*, the latter being itself a link between insectivores and primates, the order to which man belongs.

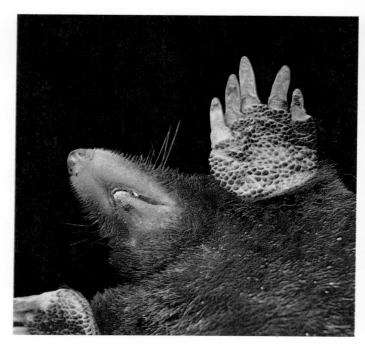

The Macroscelidae, or elephant shrews, are African. *Elephantulus rozeti* is the only species living in North Africa. *Phot. J. L. S. Dubois*

The Talpidae (moles)

The last family in this order is the family of the moles. The true moles (*Talpa*) are well-known animals, found in temperate regions of the Old World and common throughout Europe. Different forms inhabit Asia and North America.

The European mole (*Talpa europaea*) is perfectly adapted for its underground life, being designed for digging and burrowing. It has a wedge-shaped head, highly sensitive snout, vestigial eyes, a cylindrical body and shovel-like fore feet with powerful claws. Its fur is thick, velvety, supple and glossy, and cannot be ruffled the 'wrong' way. Moles spend the greater part of their lives underground. Their burrows are a complex system of galleries, the earth from which is deposited above ground in the form of the well-known heaps.

The so-called 'fortress' is a large heap, containing a nest

made of leaves and grass, which the mole uses for sleeping in. This heap has its own galleries and bolt-runs, but the fortress is not designed to any regular plan. Sometimes the female mole has her young in a fortress nest; more usually, the nest is well below ground, with no heap directly above it.

Apart from the tunnels it drives when hunting near the surface, the mole uses a network of permanent galleries for getting from one place to another. This type of tunnel is usually deep and runs alongside or under obstacles, such as drains, walls, hedgerows and pathways. It is in these runs that mole-catchers set their traps.

Earthworms are the mole's main prey, but it eats other types of soil-animals, and its stomach usually contains a small amount of vegetable matter. When worms are plentiful, the mole disables them by biting them on the back. Thus immobilized, they are stored for future use, sometimes in considerable masses. The mole requires a lot of food. The hunting mole locates its prey, in the first instance, by ground vibrations, then by its sense of smell at close range, perhaps a radius of $2\frac{1}{2}$ inches.

The female mole has intersexual features. The ovary has two parts, one completely normal, the other composed of cellular connective tissue, considered to be a testis arrested in its development. The normal ovary functions normally.

Moles breed once a year. The gestation period varies from 28 to 42 days, and the young, numbering from two to seven, are born in May and early June. They leave the nest five weeks later. They are sexually mature at the age of a year.

Moles can be a nuisance, not because of any damage they do themselves, but because of the heaps of earth they put up in gardens, on pastures, on golf courses and the like. In the mole's favour, it has been argued that it helps to aerate and drain the soil, as well as destroying many insect larvae harmful to crops.

Desmana, from southwest Europe and central and western Asia, are very different from moles, although they belong to the same family.

The Pyrenean desman (*Galemys pyrenaicus*), found only in the Pyrenees, is an aquatic species, about the size of a rat. It has webbed feet and a web of stiff hairs on its long tail that acts as a rudder. Its soft, thick, glossy fur is completely waterproof. The whiskers on its trunk-like muzzle are

The mole (*Talpa europaea*) has short arms set so far forward that they seem to emerge from the neck. The broadened hands, equipped with claws and set low on the sides, act as shovels. *Phot. J. Six and Aldo Margiocco*

probably tactile organs used to locate under-water prey. It hunts at night, preying mainly upon aquatic insects, crustaceans and alevins, and sleeps by day in holes in river banks.

It should be remembered that other unrelated species are similarly adapted for gliding flight; flying squirrels and scaly-tailed squirrels, which are rodents; and the phalanger, which is a marsupial.

The order Dermoptera

The flying lemurs are strange animals, not at all easy to classify. They belong to the genus *Cynocephalus* (formerly *Galeopithecus*), and whether there are one or two species depends on the point of view of the individual taxonomist. Any resemblance between them and the true lemurs appears to be a matter of convergent evolution, and not because they are in any way related. Placing them among the bats is absolutely out of the question because the anatomy of the two orders is completely different. It is now thought that the Dermoptera derived from very ancient primitive insectivores, from which bats and man probably also derived.

There are two species, both found in southeast Asia and the Sonda Isles. In both, the head resembles that of a lemur. The fur of the body, which is usually spotted, covers the whole surface of the flying membranes. These are well developed, extending from the base of the neck to the tips of the limbs and the tail. With the membranes fully extended, the lemur, despite its weight (about 4 pounds), is able to glide for distances up to 150 yards.

During the day, the flying lemur lies up in holes in trees or hangs from a branch by its hands and feet, with head and tail pressed against the breast and abdomen. This sleeping position is characteristic of bats. Resting thus, the lemur is difficult to see because its spotted fur matches the background of lichens and creepers.

At nightfall the flying lemur becomes active, climbing among the branches or gliding from tree to tree. It feeds on fruit, buds, leaves and flowers. When it wants to get from one tree to another, the lemur climbs to the topmost branches, launches into space, extends its membranes and glides.

The order Chiroptera (bats)

Bats are nocturnal animals, all very much alike, despite great differences in size, and the only mammals with the power of true flight. This ability derives from their highly specialized structure. The greatly elongated fingers of the hand are joined together by a membrane which extends along the fore-arm and the body to the feet, and, in some species, even to the tip of the tail. The bat's arms have, therefore, become true wings.

Like the flying lemurs and flying squirrels, present-day bats are derived from gliding arboreal insectivores. The development of true flapping flight meant that bats could compete with birds. As most birds are active by day, it is thought that bats, as a result, evolved towards nocturnal habits.

Everybody now knows that bats navigate by echolocation. In flight, they send out continuous ultrasonic waves which bounce back, warning of any obstacle ahead, including prey.

Although bats inhabit temperate areas of the world, the greatest numbers and the greatest variety of species are found in the tropics. Many are insectivores, but others are fruit-eaters, nectar-sippers, flesh-eaters, fishers and even blood-suckers. But however much they may vary in size and food habits, they have one thing in common—a low breeding rate. One young per female is the rule, but the life span may exceed twenty years.

Bats are mainly gregarious, and may be found in small or large groups, in caves, rock clefts, holes in trees or under the roofs of houses. Most species live a settled life; some American species are migratory. Bats in temperate regions hibernate.

Next to rodents, the order of bats has the largest number of species among mammals, about 1000 having been described. The order has been divided into two sub-orders: Megachiroptera and Microchiroptera. Although the biggest bats are found in the sub-order Megachiroptera, the name is hardly accurate because a number of small species, smaller even than the majority of the Microchiroptera, come within this sub-order.

The sub-order Megachiroptera

Fruit-eating bats are found in the tropical zone of the Old World.

The true rousette bats (*Rousettus*), of which there are thirteen species, are common in all the hot regions of Africa and Asia. They are highly gregarious, roosting in caves and in the darkest parts of old monuments. At night, they disperse over the countryside, in forests and gardens, in search of food.

Flying foxes (*Pteropus*), about 51 species, are found in the tropics from India to Australia, as well as in Madagascar. They are the giants among bats—the Malayan kalongs having a wing span of five feet. During the day the flying foxes hang in trees in noisy groups. Colonies up to 100,000 strong can be seen in Australia, hanging in the branches like large fruit. These bats use their wings to protect themselves against the monsoon, and to fan themselves when the sun becomes too hot.

At nightfall the flying foxes leave their roosts and disperse over the countryside in search of food, trailing in long lines against the red tropical sky, like migrating wild geese. Their flight is not in the least like that of European bats. They beat their wings slowly and combine flying with gliding, their silhouettes being more buzzard-like than bat-like. Each night they fly considerable distances to find the right fruit on which they feed.

Australian flying foxes migrate seasonally, their movements being dictated by the blossoming of eucalyptus trees, whose flowers are their favourite food. They can be very destructive locally and, in some areas, attempts have been made from time to time to exterminate them. Such attempts have been mostly unsuccessful. In other countries, these bats are hunted for food. They settle down well in captivity and show a fair degree of intelligence.

The hammer-headed bat (*Hypsignathus monstrosus*) is the biggest African species, with a wing span of over three feet. The male has an enormous horse-like head. This species frequents the banks of streams and rivers. During the night they congregate in branches above the water and strike up their vocal orchestra. Their call—a very powerful repetitive 'kurn'—never fails to arrest the attention of anyone new to the Congolese forest belt. The significance of this chorus has not been studied, but it is not unlikely that the calls are uttered by males to stimulate the females.

The Macroglossinae, an oriental sub-family of long-tongued fruit bats, feed on the nectar and pollen of flowers. These bats have long thin noses. Their tongues are as long as their bodies, and covered with brush-like papillae—a perfect design for collecting pollen from flowers with deep corollas. During these night visits, the bats pollinate the flowers in the same way as bees by day. In fact, they do what humming-birds and bees do by day, but they do more. They pollinate the flowers of certain tropical trees which blossom only at night, and which are entirely dependent on these bats for pollination.

The sub-order Microchiroptera

The majority of bats, including all species found in temperate regions, belong to this sub-order.

The Rhinolophoidae

The horse-shoe bats (Rhinolophoidae) make up a super-family of about 200 species, found in temperate and tropical regions of the Old World.

The European Rhinolophoidae all belong to the genus *Rhinolophus*. Three species are confined to southern Europe. Two others, the greater and lesser horse-shoe bats are more generally distributed. These bats have a horse-shoe shaped nose-leaf from which they derive their name. Horse-shoe bats spend the winter in cellars, caves and pot-holes, hanging upside-down from the roof, with their wings folded round their bodies. In this way they sleep from October to March.

Some bats inhabit ruins and lofts. Mating takes place in autumn, but fertilization is delayed until the spring, when the female ovulates. The eggs are then fertilized by the sperm which she has stored in her body all winter. During pregnancy, and while they are rearing their young, the females congregate in large groups from which males are excluded. This segregation of the sexes, total in some species and not practised at all by others, has not yet been satisfactorily explained. The flight of the horse-shoe bat is slow and fluid. They hunt mainly among foliage, finding their prey by echolocation. Insects are their only source of food.

The Indian false vampire (*Megaderma lyra*), a large Asiatic species, preys upon mice, frogs, fledgling birds, alevins and sometimes other bats. It hunts around tree-trunks, cliffs and walls, locating its prey by sonar specially adapted for pin-pointing prey at rest against a solid background. When the bat catches a frog it carries it off to its den before eating it. Oddly enough, it eats only the head and trunk. Mice are skinned before being eaten, while fledglings taken from nests are neatly plucked. In India, the false vampires are frequently observed in underground temples. In fact, such places are favourite haunts.

The Phyllostomatidae

The bats in this group probably derive from primitive horse-shoe bats. They inhabit the American continent and include species that differ markedly from all others.

The fish-eating bat (*Noctilio leporinus*) is widely distributed in South America. As its name indicates, this is a fishing bat, preying upon fish and crustaceans which it catches with its clawed feet in the same way as a bird of prey uses its talons. As this bat finds its prey entirely by echolocation, and its ultrasonic pulses are almost totally thrown off by the surface of the water, scientists were for a long time unable to explain how it could locate fish swimming under the surface. Recent research has shown that the bat can detect only fish skimming the surface of the water or in the act of causing ripples.

The American leaf-nosed bats, in many of which the nose-leaf is actually shaped like a lance-head, include species that exploit a great variety of food sources. Besides the insectivorous species, there are fruit-eaters which are very common in tropical America; pollen-eaters, such as the long-tongued

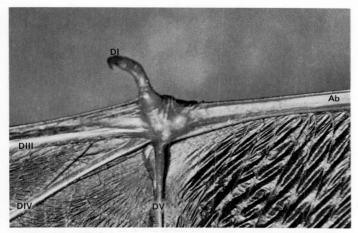

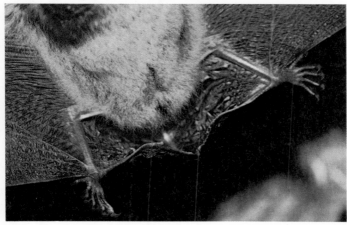

When cattle are bitten night after night, they become weak from loss of blood and, in this way, vampires can cause heavy losses to South American stock farmers. Even more serious is the part played by vampires in spreading rabies. It now seems certain that vampire populations in South America are a reservoir of this disease. The bats themselves are immune, but they carry the virus in their salivary glands and introduce it to the victim when they bite (in much the same way as the malarial mosquito spreads malaria).

In Venezuela, it is claimed that vampires have been responsible for the death of millions of cattle. Human casualties are common in Trinidad and Brazil. It has been claimed that mammals can contract rabies merely by close contact with a vampire and without actually being bitten.

The Emballonuridae

In this super-family are the mouse-tailed bats (*Rhinopoma*) and the tomb bats (*Taphozous*), which are confined mainly to the east, in mausoleums, tombs and old monuments. They are the animals responsible for the distinctive smell associated with Indian temples and some parts of the Egyptian pyramids.

The mouse-tailed bats have long snouts and free-moving long, thin tails which they wave about at the approach of an intruder. In summer, they become so fat that they are unable to fly. They spend the winter under cover, resting and sleeping, but without falling into the true torpor of hiberna-

Above, fragment of the upper region of the wing of the mouse-eared bat (*Myotis myotis*). The thumb (*DI*) is free from the membrane of the wing and forms a hook which the bat uses to haul itself along when walking quadruped fashion. *DIII* to *DV* are used as tensors for the wing. *Below,* hindquarters of the mouse-eared bat: hind legs and tail are connected to the alar membrane; the feet, by means of which the animal hangs upside-down, are free. *Fa,* forearm. *Phot. Chaumeton-Jacana*

bats; and carnivores, like the tropical American false vampire bat (*Vampyrum spectrum*) which is the biggest of the Microchiroptera. Then there is the fringe-lipped bat (*Trachops*) which preys upon geckos. And above all, there is the true vampire (Desmodinae) which feeds on the blood of warmblooded vertebrates.

True vampires (*Desmodus* and *Diphylla*) are mainly cave dwellers. Although they are no bigger than a small rat, they are aggressive and powerful, agile and intelligent, and extremely adaptable concerning habitat. As a result of all these qualities, the vampire has survived all efforts to wipe it out in areas where it has become a serious problem.

Vampires fly out at night in search of sleeping mammals and birds. When the vampire finds a victim, it alights silently and cuts a deep slit in the sleeper's skin with its razor-sharp incisors. The wound is painless. The vampire then puts its mouth to the slit and sips the blood, which continues to flow for a time afterwards because the bat's saliva contains an anticoagulant. It has been established that a vampire can fill up with its own weight of blood in a single operation. Almost invariably, the vampire attacks a hairless part of the victim's body: the teats of a cow, the back of the ears of horses, the cloaca of birds, and the nose and toes of humans.

Flying foxes have a frugivorous diet. Some reach a span of nearly 5 feet. They do not use echo-location and find their way about with the help of sight and sense of smell. *Phot. Zuber-Rapho*

Colony of flying foxes (*Pteropus* sp.). Many can be seen hanging on to branches, whilst one, with its wings fully extended, takes off. *India. Phot. Aldo Margiocco*

tion. The mouse-tailed bat is a semi-desert species, notable for its periodic weight increase, a phenomenon also characteristic of the camel and certain rodents.

The Vespertilionidae

Most European bats belong to this super-family which has the largest number of species.

Woolly bats (*Kerivoula*) are tropical species, found in the forests of Africa and Asia. They are tiny and delicate, notable for their powerful butterfly flight. The painted bat (*Kerivoula picta*) is perhaps the most highly coloured of all mammals. Its coat and part of its membrane are bright orange-red. During the day it hides under heaps of dried leaves. Another species (*Kerivoula lanosa*) sleeps in birds' nests.

It has just been discovered that another species (*Kerivoula harrisoni*), recently discovered in Gabon, spends the day in spiders' webs.

Long-fingered bats (*Miniopterus*) are more familiar to European naturalists, and one species, *Miniopterus schreibersi*, is found from France to north Japan, and from the Solomon Islands to south Natal.

Long-fingered bats are found mainly in forested hill country. They are cave dwellers and gregarious. As many as 100,000 long-fingered bats have been found in one cave in India. They are noisy and, when flying, can be heard long before they appear in view. There are about 100 species of vespertilians. Apart from the Polar regions, their distribution is world-wide.

The mouse-eared bat (*Myotis myotis*) is probably the best known of the genus. It is a fairly large species, with a wing span of up to sixteen inches. It is often found in association with man, summering in places like belfries and hibernating in cellars, where it wedges itself into chinks in the stonework. But by far the greatest numbers are cave dwellers. Like the greater horse-shoe bat, this one segregates by sex in spring, the females associating in nurseries from which males are excluded. Females and young are very often found in close-packed congregations, in places like vaults, where the warm, still air ensures satisfactory heat regulation for the colony.

The other small European *Myotis* are not so well-known as the mouse-eared bat. Some of them, like Bechstein's bat (*Myotis bechsteini*) which roosts in holes in trees in summer, appear to be quite rare. Daubenton's bat (*Myotis daubentoni*), often known as the water bat, hunts over water, and is the one most frequently caught on the fisherman's fly. It has recently been discovered that Daubenton's bat 'angles' for fish. Cappaccini's bat (*Myotis cappaccinii*) is a Mediterranean species. The marsh vespertilian crosses France's northern frontier at only a few places. Geoffrey's bat (*Myotis emarginatus*) is almost always found in association with greater horse-shoes, taking over their winter and summer roosting places.

The long-eared bat (*Plecotus auritus*) can be recognized at once because of its ears which are almost as long as its head

Horse-shoe bat (*Rhinolophus ferrum equinum*) hanging by a foot and enfolded by its wings. *Phot. Aldo Margiocco*

Greater horse-shoe bat (*Rhinolophus ferrum equinum*), front view, showing the leaf-like expansions of its nose. *Phot. Aldo Margiocco*

and body put together. When at rest, the bat folds its ears under its wings; when it is alerted, it unfolds them and they curve up like a ram's horns. This species sleeps in buildings and trees during the summer. Preying mainly on moths and butterflies, it also takes beetles and a variety of other insects. It hibernates alone in rock fissures or in hollow trees or houses.

The pipistrelle is the best known of all bats, and the one most often seen. Most of the small bats seen flying at twilight or in the late evening near towns and villages are pipistrelles. There are about 100 species distributed throughout the world. The least pipistrelle (*Pipistrellus musiculus*) from equatorial Africa is the smallest bat, and perhaps the world's smallest mammal, its maximum weight being only 1/16 of an ounce. The Old World noctule (*Nyctalus noctula*) ranges quite far north in Europe. It is a large species with a wing span up to fourteen inches, and hunts in swift effortless flight. It has often been likened to a falcon. It is found mostly in wooded and forest areas, and is known for its habit of roosting in woodpecker's holes in the trunks of large trees.

The barbastelle (*Barbastella barbastellus*), which is a common species in Europe, can be recognized almost at once by its near-black fur. It sometimes roosts in colonies numbering several thousand. The serotine bat (*Eptesicus serotinus*) is a large species, common and widely distributed, which can often be seen hunting in small groups above parks and public gardens at twilight.

The hairy-tailed bats (*Lasiurus*) of America are members of the same family, and all of them are regular migrants, summering in northern areas and wintering in the warmer south. Some species range as far north as Canada, where they roost in trees among the foliage. During migration, they are often found flying across the sea or roosting on small islands. In summer, the sexes live apart in different areas, the males in the northeastern region of North America, the females in the northwestern region, where they give birth to their young.

603

The lesser horse-shoe bat (*Rhinolophus hipposideros*), hanging by its feet, scared and shrieking. *Phot. J. Six*

Bechstein's bat (*Myotis bechsteini*), a very rare species in Europe, lives in hollow tree-trunks in summer and hibernates in crevices in underground caves. *Phot. Varin—Jacana*

The Molossidae (mastiffs and free-tailed bats)

The members of this family are almost all tropical species. Only one, Cestoni's mastiff (*Tadarida taeniotis*), is found in Europe, mainly in the Mediterranean area, although it has been recorded in France. It is the biggest of all European bats, easily identified because of its folded snout, its visor-shaped ears and its fleshy tail, 2/3 of which projects beyond the interfemoral membrane.

Bats of this group seem incapable of sustained hibernation, and this probably explains why they are uncommon in areas where the winters are cold. On the other hand, they are extremely abundant in tropical Africa, Asia and America. The *Tadarida brasiliensis* of Texas forms the biggest colonies in the world of bats and, indeed, in the world of mammals, some colonies numbering up to twenty millions. When they emerge at twilight, they darken the sky, and their vast numbers, viewed from a distance, have been likened to the smoke from a volcano. In South America and in equatorial Africa, large numbers of free-tailed bats often assemble in the roof-timbers and the eaves of houses. As a result, many houses become uninhabitable because of the foul smell of the bats and their almost incessant noisy chorus.

The order Primates

The Tupaiidae (tree-shrews)

The Tupaiidae or tree-shrews (*Tupaia*), of which there are about fifteen species and many sub-species, all native to southeast Asia, resemble squirrels in general appearance. The group has special interest for zoologists.

Their anatomy clearly shows that they are related to insectivores and primates, but experts have never been able to agree about their exact classification, some placing them in one order and some in the other. The tree-shrews are a living link between the two orders, which suggests that primates, including man, have evolved from primitive insectivores.

The tupaias are commonly referred to nowadays as semi-apes. They are forest dwellers, solitary and nocturnal, as

The grey gentle lemur (*Hapalemur griseus*) a very rare primate of the Malagasy humid forest region, photographed in the wild. *Ph. Petter*

much at home in trees as they are on the ground. They are diligent when searching for food, probing into holes and fissures, and eating almost anything that they can: insects, small vertebrates, fruit, corn and leaves. They appear to have no fixed breeding season. The gestation period is about fifty days, and the two young are weaned about the age of forty days. Tree-shrews do well in captivity and are easily tamed.

The feather-tailed tree shrew (*Ptilocercus*) differs in many ways from other members of the family. It resembles the garden dormouse, and the tip of its tail has a plumed tuft. These shrews are believed to be nocturnal and arboreal. They are found in the Malayan archipelago, but are rare, and not much is known about them.

The Lemuroidae

These primitive primates have bold, striking features: a hairy face; fingers and toes with claws or nails; eye-sockets which communicate broadly with the temporal cavity; well developed olfactory senses; and a diffuse placenta. They are nocturnal and arboreal, and feed on fruit and insects.

The Lemuridae

In this family there are thirteen species and twenty-four sub-species, not very well differentiated. They are natives of Madagascar and the Comoro Islands. Mostly forest species, they vary from the size of a rat to the size of a medium-sized dog. All are in danger of extinction, mainly as the result of deforestation which destroys their habitat. A great responsibility rests on Madagascar to save these animals, which are among the most interesting of the world's fauna.

The Lemurinae

The gentle-lemurs (*Hapalemur*) are all medium-sized. They are woodland animals, all of them nocturnal in habits. They live on a mixed diet of insects, bamboo shoots and reeds. Although some superstitious natives show great fear of them, they are all harmless.

The weasel lemur (*Lepilemur*), which has a fox-like face, is notable for having no upper incisors, or poorly developed ones. The common or true lemur (*Lemur*) is a larger species. It, too, has a long muzzle like a fox. All the lemurs in this family have long tails and thick, glossy coats which vary in colour from species to species, and sometimes between the sexes in the same species. The ring-tailed lemur (*Lemur catta*), which has black and white rings on its tail, is an inhabitant of rocky areas, while the acoumba lemur (*Lemur macaco*) is arboreal and confined to forests. Lemurs are crepuscular in habits. They are also social, moving about in troops of five or six and making a great deal of noise. They feed mainly on insects and fruit.

The gestation period is four or five months; single births are usual, but twins have been recorded from time to time. Most births take place between March and June, suggesting a fixed breeding season. These lemurs have been known to survive in captivity for twenty-five years.

The Cheirogaleinae

The fat-tailed dwarf lemurs (*Cheirogaleus*) are small, nocturnal forest-dwellers. During the day, they lie up in nests which they build in the branches, or against the trunks, of trees. When food is plentiful they lay on fat which is stored in their tails—hence the name. During the dry season, which they spend in a state of semi-torpor, they draw on this store of fat.

Mouse lemurs (*Microcebus*) are rat-sized. They are distributed over most of Madagascar, adapting themselves to a wide variety of habitats, including plantations. Because of this adaptability, they have kept up their numbers and are still quite common locally, so they are not under the same threat as most other species. They spend the day lying up in their nests, which they build in holes in trees, and come out at night to hunt for insects among the branches. Insects are their main food. This species breeds twice a year, litter size varying from one to three young.

Fork-marked lemurs (*Phaner furcifer*) have a black stripe running from each eye to the nape of the neck, where they join up and continue as a dorsal band. This lemur is a forest-dweller, inhabiting northern Madagascar.

The Indridae (avahi, sikafa, and indris)

The members of this family are the avahi, sikafa and indris. Avahis are small animals, typically with long tails and woolly coats. Because of their flattened muzzles, they are ape-like in appearance. During the day, they lie up in holes in trees, coming out only at night to feed on leaves, buds and the bark of trees.

Sikafas (*Propithecus*) are found in the tropical forests of Madagascar. There are two species, both large lemurs with long tails and thick, contrastingly coloured fur. Sikafas are active by day, when they move about in groups of six to ten, feeding on flowers, leaves and bark. They are extremely agile animals, travelling from tree to tree in tremendous leaps. They are difficult to keep alive in captivity, and there are few people fortunate enough to have seen them, alive and free, in their native forests.

The indris (*Indri indri*) is found in the forests of eastern and central Madagascar. It is the biggest of the lemurs, standing about three feet tall. Its face is dog-like and hairless. The indris lives in trees, usually in family parties, and rarely sets foot on the ground, but when it does, it leaps about in an

The acoumba lemur (*Lemur macaco*) has diurnal habits. It lives in bands in the open forests of western Madagascar, and shows a distinctly territorial behaviour. *Phot. J. J. Petter*

upright posture. Indrises are diurnal. Family parties make a great deal of noise at daybreak and twilight. Although they are mainly leaf-eaters, they also take a variety of fruits and some insects.

The Daubentoniidae (aye-ayes)

The aye-aye (*Daubentonia madagascariensis*) also comes from Madagascar. It is about the size of a large cat, with a bushy squirrel tail, big ears and teeth like a rodent; at one time it was looked upon as some kind of squirrel. It has large round eyes, indicating that it is a nocturnal animal. Its fingers, especially the third one, are long and thin, and used for probing into holes in trees in search of insects. The aye-aye feeds largely on the pith of bamboo and sugar-cane, gnawing into the hard stalks with its incisors. At the same time, it catches any insects hiding within the stalk. It has sharp ears, and appears to listen for the movement of larvae inside the stalks. Occasionally it will tap the bark with its middle finger, as a woodpecker does with its bill.

The Lorisidae

Not all the members of the Lorisidae family come from Madagascar: a few special forms are found in tropical Africa and Asia. The family includes lorises, pottos and bush babies.

Lorises come from Asia, and there are two closely related genera—the slow loris (*Nycticebus*) and the slender loris (*Loris tardigradus*).

The slenderloris, which is found in the south of India and in Sri Lanka, is nocturnal and arboreal, remarkable for its long, slender limbs, and for its cautious tread on branches and twigs. This loris does well in captivity. It prefers insects to all other food, and there is a record of one in India that lived for more than a year on a diet of nothing but cockroaches. In many parts of India the eyes of the slender loris are considered to have magical powers, notably as a cure for disease of the eyes and in the preparation of love potions.

The slow loris is distributed from Assam to the Philippines. It is a more heavily built animal than the slender loris, but its biology appears to be similar. There are two species.

Pottos are found in the African forest belt. The golden potto (*Arctocebus calabarensis*) is small and slenderly built, with a stub tail and a yellow-brown coat with a golden sheen. Little was known about the golden pottos until the Biological Mission in Gabon carried out a systematic field study. They are arboreal, solitary and nocturnal, and feed mainly on insects, especially caterpillars, which they locate by their sense of smell and seize in both hands after a slow and stealthy approach.

Bosman's potto (*Perodictitus potto*) is similar to the golden potto in general appearance and way of life, and is found in the same regions. It is strictly nocturnal, spending the day-time in holes in trees or hanging by its four limbs under a branch, with its head resting between its arms. The diet consists largely of fruit, and individuals have been known to

The aye-aye (*Daubentonia*) is a native of Madagascar, where it lives in the forest belt of the eastern and northeastern region. Strictly arboreal, it nests in the forks of large branches. Its food consists of insects and fruit. *Phot. Jacques Stevens*

The weasel lemur (*Lepilemur mustelinus*) is widely distributed in the Malagasy forest zone. Leading a solitary existence, it sleeps by day, rolled up into a ball in a hole in a tree. *Phot. J. Petter*

The lesser mouse lemur (*Microcebus murinus*), a tiny nocturnal lemur, lives in the forests of the east and west of Madagascar. Its diet is mainly insectivorous. *Phot. F. Petter*

thrive for months on bananas. A potto captured as an adult can be a dangerous animal, capable of inflicting harmful bites.

There are five species of bush babies (*Galago*), all found in tropical Africa. They are graceful little animals, varying from the size of a dormouse to that of a squirrel. They are arboreal, gregarious and nocturnal, spending the day in communal nests built in branches or in holes in trees. Needle-clawed galagos (*Galago elegantulus*) merely huddle together among thick foliage, like a bee swarm. When the group breaks up, the individuals keep in touch with each other by almost continuous contact calls. They feed mainly on insects and small invertebrates which they catch with their hands, but they also take some fruit. When startled, galagos are capable of considerable leaps.

They mark their territory with urine which they take up in their hands. Females usually give birth to a single young, but occasionally to two or three. The family stays with the mother for several months. Galagos settle down well in captivity and are very popular.

The tarsiers

The tarsiers of southeast Asia are primitive primates about the size of a small rat. They are nocturnal animals with enormous eyes, well adapted for seeing at night. They feed on insects, lizards, young birds and eggs, but also eat some fruit. Tarsiers have fingers like a tree frog, move like frogs, and can leap in the branches for distances of up to six feet.

Tarsiers were once widely distributed in Europe and America, where their fossils are common. The group is closely related to the insectivores which were the ancestors of the primates, so tarsiers are an important link in the chain of evolution between the lemuroids and higher primates, including man.

The golden potto (*Arctocebus calabarensis*) in a sleeping position. Usually it rests in a tree fork. *Phot. M. Boulard*

Allen's bush baby (*Galago alleni*) is found quite frequently in the Cameroons and Gabon. Secondary forest with shrubs suits it particularly well. Entirely nocturnal habits. Total length 16 to 18 inches. *Photo. R. Pujol*

The slow loris (*Nycticebus coucang*) is the Asiatic equivalent of the African potto. Their habits are very similar. It is found from Assam to the Philippine Islands. *Phot. J. Burton—Researchers*

The slender loris (*Loris tardigradus*) is found in Ceylon and southern India. In spite of its need for heat, it can live at mountain altitudes of 6000 feet. Its favourite environment is the rain-forest. It becomes active during the night. Its diet is based on insects, with, as extras, young birds and small lizards. *Phot. Aldo Margiocco*

The platyrrhines
(New World monkeys)

The monkeys from tropical America are a very distinctive group. They are arboreal and mostly small in size with round heads and no muzzle, as such. The nostrils are set wide apart and directed sideways, so the animals in this group are often referred to as the broad-nosed monkeys. In most species, the tail is very long and, in some, it is prehensile. There are about sixty species.

The douroucoulis or night monkey (*Aotus*) is the only nocturnal species. It is medium sized, adults weighing about two pounds.

The night monkey has thick fur which completely hides its ears. The face is naked with a black fringe, like the facial disc of an owl. During the day, the night monkey sleeps in hollow trees or among thick foliage. At night, it comes out to search for fruit, insects, small birds and small mammals. These monkeys have well developed vocal sacs, and have a wide vocal range.

The titi (*Callicebus*) is widely distributed in South America, and there are about nine species or races. The body fur is reddish-brown in colour, but the forearms, hind legs and tail are black. Like the douroucoulis, they have powerful voices which carry over long distances. Titis in captivity display considerable intelligence.

Uakaris (*Cacojao*) are natives of the Amazon jungles. There are three species, all of medium size, remarkable for their short tails. The skin of the head and face is scarlet, which deepens in colour when the monkey has been frightened or disturbed. Uakaris live in small groups in the highest trees. They are now uncommon and rarely seen even in zoos.

The saki (*Pithecia*) is the least monkey-like of monkeys. It has the face of an old man, canine teeth like a cat, and a bird-like voice. The saki also has a bushy tail like a fox. The hair on the head and shoulders is long and rough; in the monk saki, it resembles a hood.

Sakis can move through the trees at high speed. They are omnivorous and have been observed catching sleeping bats which they skin before eating.

Howler monkeys (*Alouatta*) are the largest American species, about the size of a medium-sized dog and weighing up to twenty pounds. There are about six species, found in the forests of tropical America.

These monkeys derive their name from their powerful voices. Usually only the biggest male howls, but if a whole troop gives voice it can be heard two or three miles away.

Howlers live in troops of twenty to forty, and each group holds a territory which it defends against other groups. The troop is made up usually of three males, eight females and their young. There is no single leader, all three males sharing the task, and the whole troop lives in harmony.

There is no particular breeding season. The female in breeding condition can be distinguished by the way she sticks out and pulls in her tongue. This is her way of courting the male who responds by using his tongue in the same way.

Howler monkeys feed on leaves and tree shoots, and are entirely vegetarian, but they eat a great variety of plants and are, therefore, difficult to keep in captivity.

Capuchins (*Cebus*) are probably the best known American

The bald uakari monkey (*Cacajao calvus*) belongs to the fauna of the upper Amazon. It reaches the height of oddity with its bare skull and its pink face, which turns purple when it is excited. Short tail, non-prehensile, about 19 inches long excluding the tail. *Phot. C. M. Hladik*

A howler monkey (*Alouatta palliata*) eating *Cecropia* leaves, head down, hanging by its feet; the prehensile tail has coiled round a small branch. Forest on the banks of the Panama Canal. Male: 15 pounds; female: less than 13 pounds. Head and trunk of males: about 2 feet—the females are smaller. *Phot. Hladik*

A white-throated capuchin (*Cebus capucinus*) on a branch, in a relaxed attitude. Every 2 hours, it ceases all activity for 5 or 6 minutes. Forest on the banks of Panama Canal. *Phot. C. M. Hladik*

Geoffroy's spider monkey (*Ateles geoffroyi*) is on the verge of extinction, due to intensive hunting. Its flesh is regarded as a delicacy. This individual belongs to a colony introduced into the small island of Barro Colorado (Panama Canal). *Phot. C. M. Hladik*

monkeys. There are about a dozen species, all of them adaptable, so they do well in captivity and even make good household pets. All are of medium size, varying between four and nine pounds in weight. They are easily recognizable by their coat of stiff bristly hairs· which resembles the cowl of a Franciscan monk, hence the name.

The capuchins are mostly greyish-brown in colour with semi-prehensile tails. In the wild state, they live in troops, led by a powerful male whose rule is absolute. As leader, he claims the best sleeping places and the choicest titbits. These monkeys are omnivorous, feeding on fruit, leaves, small birds, insects, larvae and spiders, and they will use simple tools, such as a heavy stone, to crack a nut.

The female capuchin gives birth to a single offspring after a gestation period of six months. The male shares the task of bringing up the young which he will carry about on occasion.

Squirrel monkeys (*Saimiri*), of which there are two species, are small and brilliantly coloured. Fully grown animals measure twelve inches in length plus twenty inches of tail. The short fur varies in colour from yellowish-green to orange. Squirrel monkeys are active by day, when they move about in bands up to a hundred strong. They can move with the greatest of ease in the highest and thinnest branches, and they show a great interest in people. Even in the wild state they will approach man closely. As a result of this friendly disposition, they are often kept in captivity, but they have a

A young spider monkey (*Ateles geoffroyi*) sucking royal palm shoots. After having chewed them, it spits them out. The adults weigh up to 15 pounds; the thumb is lacking (whence the scientific name *Ateles*, which in Greek means imperfect); head and trunk: about 2 feet. *Phot. C. M. Hladik*

great need for social life, and do not survive long without company.

The spider monkey (*Ateles*) has very long arms and a long prehensile tail which it uses as a fifth limb. There are about fifteen species, ranging from Mexico to Brazil. Spider monkeys are the best adapted to all South American monkeys for life in the trees, but on the ground they move about awkwardly. They are fruit-eaters, and not notably territorial, their movements being determined by the availability of fruit. Even when gathering food, the spider monkey uses its tail tip as a hand, taking up fruit with it, and using it as a touch organ.

Tamarins (*Saguinus*) are found in Amazonia, bounded to the west by the Andes and to the east by the Atlantic Ocean. They live in the forests and, in the mountains, are still encountered at an altitude of over 3000 feet. Tree-tops are their favourite haunt. They are diurnal and their diet consists mainly of fruit and insects. *Phot. C. M. Hladik*

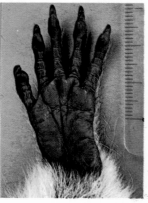

Surface of the palm of a tamarin's left hand, showing the characteristic designs (dermatoglyphics) formed by the folds of the skin.

Woolly monkeys (*Lagothrix*) weigh up to thirteen pounds, and have thick woolly fur and prehensile tails. They live in troops and move about by day, and are not as noisy and demonstrative as most monkeys. They thrive in captivity if well looked after, and, if taken young, become docile and affectionate.

Marmosets (Hapalidae) are the smallest known monkeys and are found in South America, in the Amazonian region. They are squirrel size, resemble squirrels and move very much like squirrels. They have clawed fingers and toes, and are sometimes known as clawed monkeys. The smallest of all the family and the smallest of all monkeys is the pygmy marmoset (*Cebuelle pygmaea*) which reaches a maximum weight of $2\frac{1}{2}$ ounces.

The black-tailed marmoset (*Callithrix argentata*) has a white silky coat and a contrasting ringed tail. The most common species is the white ear-tufted marmoset (*Callithrix jacchus*), which has a grey coat and black ear tufts.

Marmosets move about in troops during the day, searching for food in trees and bushes. Like other American species, their diet is varied, consisting not only of plants and fruit, but also of insects, spiders and small birds. They are quarrelsome, arguing unceasingly among themselves and baring their sharp teeth. At dusk, the troop settles down, each animal seeking a hollow tree to sleep in.

The gestation period is 150 days, and the female may give birth to a single young, twins or triplets. Life span is about 15 years.

The golden marmoset or lion marmoset (*Leonideus*) measures about fourteen inches in length plus fourteen inches of tail. This species has fine, shimmering golden-yellow fur which glows bright gold in the sunshine. It derives its name from the grey mane of hair on its head, neck and shoulders.

Tamarins (*Sanguinus*) are closely related to the marmosets, and there are about twenty species, widely distributed in tropical America. They live in small groups and are active by day. In general habits, they closely resemble marmosets. The animals of this group are the ones most commonly kept in captivity. Each species has its diagnostic features—contrasting coat colour, hairiness of the face and skull, presence or absence of moustache and hair tufts of varying shape and colour.

The catarrhines (Old World monkeys)

Old World monkeys have their nostrils set close together and a thin nasal partition. Although all are basically tree dwellers, they are at home on the ground where they use all four limbs for walking. They can stand upright and walk on two legs: but, as bipeds, they are not in the same class as man, who stands at the peak of this pyramid of evolution.

Macaques

Macaques were once found in Europe. Nowadays, the only species found there is the Barbary ape, familiar on the cliffs of Gibraltar and in southern Spain. All the other species are Asiatic, some of them ranging high into the mountains of Tibet.

All the species in this group are strong, vigorous animals,

as much at home on the ground as in the trees. They inhabit rocky areas as well as forests. Being highly adaptable, with no specialized food requirements, they have managed to maintain thriving populations throughout their range. Although they have been little studied in the wild state, they are well known in captivity.

The rhesus monkey or Indian macaque (*Macaca mulatta*) is much used in medical research, and was the first monkey sent into space in a rocket.

All macaques become destructive and aggressive as adults.

Mangabeys

There are six species of mangabey (*Cercocebus*), all found in equatorial Africa. This monkey is slenderly built, with a long, rough coat which in some species becomes a mantle, and in others becomes fur crests or tufts. The tail, which is at least as long as the body, is carried upright with the tip curled backwards. Mangabeys live in small troops high in the trees, often in association with guenons. They feed on fruit, leaves and shoots.

Baboons and mandrills

Baboons are tall monkeys, the biggest of the family, all of them well adapted for living on the ground. There are three genera.

The yellow baboon (*Papio cynocephalus*), found in all the rocky and arid areas of tropical Africa, lives in large troops, up to a hundred strong. These troops are not one large unit but an aggregation of small harems, each consisting of a male and several females with their young.

Baboons, although largely vegetarian, also eat insects, scorpions and small vertebrates which they capture by overturning stones. At times they attack domestic stock such as sheep. Their main enemy is the leopard, but even this powerful cat stands little chance against a group of old males. Another and greater enemy is man but, although baboons appreciate the danger represented by the approach of a man with a gun, they sometimes attack human beings and are formidable opponents.

The sacred or Arabian baboon (*Papio hamadryas*), found in Ethiopia, Somaliland and Southern Arabia, has no fear of man and will sometimes drink alongside people. The ancient Egyptians considered it sacred and sculpted giant sphinxes with baboon heads. These sculptures always faced east because the ancients believed that the baboons could make the sun rise by uttering their cries before dawn.

Mandrills (*Mandrillus*) are closely related to baboons. They are among the largest species. Dog-faced, with large powerful teeth, adult males have massive heads, apparently too big for their bodies. They weigh about 120 pounds.

The mandrill is noted for its vivid colourings, an unusual characteristic in mammals. It has a red nose, blue wrinkled cheeks and orange whiskers. Drills (*Mandrillus leucophaeus*), which are also found in the equatorial forest belt, have shorter muzzles and are less vividly coloured.

Drills and mandrills live in large troops and spend most of their lives on the ground, where they find most of their food. Nevertheless, they are as agile in the trees as most of the arboreal monkeys.

Guenons or Cercopitheci

Guenons are small to medium-sized monkeys, found mainly in Africa, although a few species are found in Arabia. There are about a dozen species, the best known being the Diana monkey (*C. diana*), the greater white-nosed monkey (*C. nictitans*), the moustached monkey (*C. cephus*) and the green monkey or vervet monkey (*C. aethiops*). All of them are medium-sized, with long tails which they use as balancing

The bonnet macaque (*Macaca radiata*) is widely distributed in India. Photographed in the state of Mysore. *Phot. Aldo Margiocco*

poles when they are moving among the high branches. Colour varies from greenish-grey to white, black or near-red. Some species have vividly contrasting spots or stripes on their face, a good example being Brazza's monkey (*Cercopithocus neglectus*) which has a prominent white beard and whiskers.

Guenons feed during the day. They are entirely vegetarian, feeding on plants, tree shoots and fruit. They travel in troops, numbering from twenty to forty, and such troops may be made up of several species. In Gabon, for example, it is not

The rhesus macaque (*Macaca mulatta*) lives in bands over most of India. In many regions, it enjoys total protection. It has a fondness for temples, especially those dedicated to the monkey-god Hanuman, in which it is fed by pilgrims. Here, a few individuals are eating on the elaborately ornamented cornice of a temple. *Phot. Aldo Margiocco*

The moustached monkey (*Cercopithecus cephus*) is one of the strangest monkeys in the African forest. Its many-coloured face gives it a clown-like appearance, whilst a black border on the upper lip produces a moustache effect and emphasizes the wideness of the mouth. The moustached monkey lives in the rain-forest of Gabon and Zaire (between the river Sanaga, the Congo and the Ubangi). It has a predilection for the fruit of the oil-palm. *Phot. A. R. Devez—Biological Mission to Gabon*

unusual to find troops of moustached and greater white-nosed monkeys living together, often with some mangabeys mixed through them. In such groups, the adults occupy the middle of the group area, with the young animals distributed round the boundaries. When alarmed, guenons will leap from the tree tops into the undergrowth fifty or sixty feet below, clutching at branches on the way down to break their fall.

In some parts of Africa, man is a considerable predator on guenons whose flesh forms the staple meat diet of many tribes, although it is fibrous and tasteless to the European palate. As a result, guenons have been almost exterminated in many heavily populated parts of Africa. Young guenons show great affection towards the people who look after them, but are unsuitable for domestication because of their destructive and dirty habits. Adults can be aggressive.

The talapoin monkey (*Miopithecus talapoin*), which is closely related to the guenons, is a small species, found in central and west Africa, where it is found in large bands near streams. It is an accomplished diver and swimmer. Talapoins are respected for their supposed magical powers and are not molested. As a result, they are common around villages, where they pillage crops and the supplies of manioc which the womenfolk steep in the rivers.

The red hussar monkey (*Erythrocebus patas*) differs from the others in being a ground dweller and inhabiting the wooded savannas of northern and central Africa instead of forests.

The common langur (*Presbytis entellus*), is the sacred monkey of India; its bands are much in evidence around villages and temples. It is found as far as Nepal in the north and Sri Lanka in the south. Photograph taken at Jaipur. *Phot. Aldo Margiocco*

Two young *Cercopithecus*: *left*, greater white-nosed (*Cercopithecus nictitans*) and *right*, Brazza's monkey (*C. neglectus*) fight over an apple. Societies of the former are far from closed and willingly mix with those of other species which exploit the same ecological niche as themselves. *Phot. A. R. Dèvez—Biological Mission to Gabon*

The vervet (*Cercopithecus pygerythrus*) is a monkey of the tree-planted savannas and forest-galleries, mainly in East Africa. It forms fairly populous bands and is not averse to operating at ground level. *Phot. J. F. and M. Terrasse*

Males of this species reach a weight of 55 pounds. The fur is red. These hussars are long-legged and can run at great speed when alarmed or molested.

Langurs and colobus monkeys

Langurs (*Presbytis*) and colobus monkeys (*Colobus*) are highly adapted for living in trees. Langurs are widely distributed in tropical Asia, from sea-level up to 13,000 feet in the Himalayas. They are slenderly built, handsome monkeys whose fur varies in colour from white to black with intermediate shades of grey. They live in troops in the trees, where they feed for the most part on leaves, flowers and fruit. In India, they are looked upon as sacred because of their supposed association with the mythological monkey god Hanuman. As a result of this protection, they are common

and can often be seen in their large troops. In India, where so many people go hungry, forty million monkeys freely pillage crops without the least sign of hostility from the human population.

A closely related species, the douc langur (*Pygathrix nemaeus*), is found in the forests of Indo-China. This is a vividly coloured species, with contrasting fur of red, yellow, black and white. Snub-nosed monkeys (*Rhinopithecus*) are found in southern China. Tibetan snub-nosed monkeys can live at altitudes up to 9000 feet. Their thick fur, up to a foot in length, protects them against the cold up to such altitudes. The proboscis monkey (*Nasalis larvatus*) of Borneo has a long, banana-like nose, and is probably the oddest looking of all monkeys. In adult males, the nose is about three inches long. These large monkeys live in mangrove-swamps and on the banks of rivers. They are accomplished swimmers and divers. The main food is palm leaves.

The colobus monkeys (*Colobus*) of Africa are tree-dwellers, with black and white fur which forms a mane along the back. The long tail ends in a tuft, the body is thin and the thumb is absent or vestigial. Colobus monkeys are leaf-eaters and hardly ever leave the treetops. Because of their handsome fur, they are still much hunted and have become rare or extinct in many areas. Natives and Europeans alike exploited this monkey and thousands used to be killed every year.

The last large group of Old World primates is the Anthropoidae which includes the species most closely related to man—gibbons, orang-outangs, gorillas and chimpanzees.

The Hylobatidae (gibbons)

Gibbons are found in southeast Asia, and there are seven species including the siamang (*Symphalangus*) which inhabits the Malay Archipelago. Gibbons differ from other anthropoids in being smaller, having callouses on their buttocks, and above all by the great length of their arms. They travel through the treetops with remarkable agility, using their long arms to swing from branch to branch, often for distances of several yards. Their arms are, indeed, their means of locomotion. On the ground, they are the only monkeys that walk upright. They move about with short steps, with their arms raised above their heads, or fully stretched for balancing. They can make considerable leaps, but are unable to swim.

Social structure in this species is based on the family, each band being made up of an adult male and female, with young of various ages. Each band holds a territory, which it defends against intruders, advertising possession by loud shrieks that can be heard several miles away. Unlike other anthropoids, gibbons do not build a nest or den. Puberty is reached at the age of eight or ten years. Gestation lasts from 200 to 212 days, and a single young is the rule. Intelligent and good-tempered, the gibbon is quite easily tamed, and some gibbons have lived for more than 23 years in captivity.

Young black and white colobus (*Colobus polykomos*) from Gabon. *Phot. A. Devez—Biological Mission to Gabon*

Female gibbon (*Hylobates*) carrying out acrobatics with its offspring which, hanging on to its mother, stretches out its right arm to take hold of a branch. Notice the very minimal role played by the thumb in gripping the branch and the very effective use of the feet—although the animal relies mainly on its arms—in balance. *Phot. A. R. Devez—Lauros*

Gibbons (*Hylobates*), the most skilful animals there are at using their arms, carry out amazing acrobatic feats. *Right,* a gibbon progressing rapidly along a branch by its arms (brachiation); *left,* a gibbon swings to give itself impetus for jumping. *Phot. A. R. Devez*

The orang-outang

The orang-outang (*Pongo pygmaeus*) is found in Borneo and Sumatra. It shares with the gorilla and the chimpanzee the distinction of being the most 'human' of monkeys, and its Malayan name, in fact, means 'old man of the woods'. The mature animal looks like a caricature of a very old man. Orangs are highly intelligent, and have a wide vocal range. Formerly common, this species has become rare, and in some places is threatened with extinction.

The male orang-outang stands up to five feet tall; females measure about a foot shorter. Mature males weigh up to

The gorilla

The gorilla (*Gorilla gorilla*) is the biggest of the primates, adult males reaching a weight of up to 660 pounds, and a height of six feet or more. There are two well differentiated sub-species: the lowland or coast gorilla (*Gorilla gorilla gorilla*) and the mountain gorilla (*Gorilla gorilla beringei*) which is found in a restricted area of the eastern Congo and western Uganda (Albert Park).

A fully-grown male gorilla, with his heavy, powerful body, and muscular arms spanning up to ten feet, is a truly formidable looking animal. But the reputation foisted on it by

Young orang-outang (*Pongo pygmaeus*) progressing on floor of the forest. Its face is not yet broadened as in the adult. *Borneo. Phot. W. W. F.*

two hundred and twenty pounds, but most are much lighter than that. Orangs have long, rust-red hair, sparse on the breast and belly. Their arms are exceptionally long, reaching almost to the ground even in the erect posture. Mature males have bluish-red cheek pouches and a pronounced throat pouch like a goitre.

Orang-outangs move about in the trees in a slow, deliberate manner: on the ground they travel on all fours. In the trees they build sleeping nests of branches and creepers, in which they spend the night. They also use broad leaves as umbrellas during rain. They are entirely vegetarian.

The orang-outang is the least sociable of monkeys. The usual group is a female with one or two young; the males, except at mating time, live alone. As in other anthropoids, sexual maturity is late, and adult size is not reached until the age of ten or twelve years. Little is known about the biology of this species. In captivity, it shows a keen intelligence, but its introvert nature makes it a less suitable subject for research than the chimpanzee.

early explorers is not deserved; it is more ferocious in appearance than in fact and, with rare exceptions, does not molest man without provocation. When accidents occur they are usually serious. Gorillas prefer to keep out of man's way. It is a matter of record that, in the Gabon forest, many travellers have had the experience of arriving unexpectedly in the midst of a gorilla band, then watching the animals run away with every sign of fear. Nevertheless, where Africans still hunt the gorilla for food, the hunter is in danger if he wounds one instead of killing it, and he may be scalped or have a limb torn off before the animal dies.

Like the chimpanzee the gorilla is a forest dweller, and the two can be seen on the same ground. The gorilla can be distinguished from the chimpanzee by its greater size, heavier build, black face, short broad hands, and its small ears which are identical in shape with the human ear. The coat, which is black in young animals, often develops a silvery bloom in adults.

Gorillas live almost entirely on the ground, and it now

seems clear that only some young males and females climb trees in search of fruit, which they throw down to older animals. Adult males, because of their great weight, are not good at climbing trees. All gorillas love sunshine, and a whole troop will sometimes gather in a clearing to bask in it. At night the troop sleeps on the ground, each member making a nest of branches and foliage to insulate it against the damp earth. It has been said that females and young will sometimes build their nests in trees, but in the forest of Gabon all the nests so far examined have been on the ground.

A gorilla troop may number from five to forty; usually the number is under twenty. The troop is always led by an old male with a silvery back, but he tolerates other males among his followers, so long as they show him due respect and accept his dominance. There is hardly ever any fighting; even territorial defence is not based on fighting.

The gorilla is a vegetarian, a large part of its diet being shoots and juicy stalks. The animals move daily through part of their territory, travelling perhaps three miles in search of food. Movement is largely dictated by the weather.

The gestation period is nine months, and the single young weighs about four pounds at birth. The young animal grows slowly, and is not adult until the age of ten to fifteen years. Young gorillas in captivity are engaging animals, but need as much care and attention as a human baby. When fully grown they can be dangerous because of their tremendous strength, which can be unleashed at any moment by blind instinct.

The chimpanzee

The chimpanzee (*Pan troglodytes*) is usually considered the closest of all to man in structure, appearance and intelligence. Like the gorilla it is an inhabitant of the African tropical forest belt; but it is much more widely distributed, and is still common in areas where human pressure is not too great.

Although smaller than the gorilla, the chimpanzee is a big

These three young chimpanzees from Gabon (*Pan troglodytes*), deprived of their mother, are inseparable. They spend their time eating and playing. In young monkeys, play activity is the predominant factor in their behaviour. *Phot. A. R. Devez—M.G.B.*

primate, the adult male standing five and a half feet tall and weighing up to one hundred and seventy-five pounds. Females are smaller and lighter. The chimpanzee's hair is black, the face, hands and feet flesh-coloured. In older animals the face becomes covered with freckles which may join together to form large black spots. In some races the face, hands and feet are naturally black.

Chimpanzees are mainly arboreal, but can be seen frequently on the ground. In the wild state they live in troops of between four and fifteen, led by an old, strong male, who allows young, strong males within the troop. The leading male is never a tyrant, and life within the troop is peaceful. Males will even pick dirt and dandruff from each other's coats. They do not fight over females, but the leader can reprimand and punish any adult member of the troop who breaks the rules of chimpanzee behaviour. The young are allowed to do as they please.

general rule: twins are rare. The life span is about forty years.

Although they are extremely wary in the wild state, chimpanzees taken young are easily reared and tamed. Some observers claim that they are less amiable and attractive than young gorillas. Their lack of docility becomes more pronounced with age.

Man

The genus *Homo*, the human race, is made up today of only one species: *Homo sapiens*. Anthropologists usually divide the species into three races: europoid, mongoloid and negroid.

Man is the only animal who walks upright. His big toe cannot be opposed to any other toe in the way that his

Male gorilla (*Gorilla gorilla*). A formidable brute whose weight is sometimes well in excess of 400 pounds. Its muscles are so powerful that a maddened wounded animal is capable of breaking a gun-barrel into pieces. *Phot. Zalewski-Rapho*

The chimpanzee (*Pan troglodytes*) has 4 geographical sub-species. The white-faced (sometimes speckled with black) Tschego chimpanzee lives in central Africa and the forest belt of Zaire, Gabon and Cameroun. *Phot. A. R. Devez —Biological Mission to Gabon*

During the day the troops move about feeding, mainly on vegetable matter but also on animal matter. At night they sleep in makeshift nests built in the trees. They appear to use these nests only for one night, probably because they become infested with ants and are rendered uninhabitable.

After man, the chimpanzee is certainly the most intelligent land mammal, although the degree of intelligence varies considerably from one individual to another. Besides having great powers of mimicry, the chimpanzee is capable of expressing simple emotions, of the same order as in man. It has been shown that individuals have become capable of recognizing at least thirty-two different sounds.

Sexual maturity is reached at the age of eight years, but growth continues up to the age of twelve. Females come into breeding condition at intervals of thirty-five days, the peak being marked by swelling of the genitals. One young is the

thumb and fingers can. He has a remarkably developed brain, besides a psychic make-up that gives him pre-eminence among living things.

Because he can create his own micro-environment in the way of clothing and houses, and because of his ability to build transport to take him from one end of the earth to another, he has managed to colonize most of the planet. The development of language, then of writing, combined with education, have enabled him to establish cultural traditions, all of them developed and widened by succeeding generations. Modern science has played a major role in man's recent development, opening up still wider horizons, and giving him a frightening power over all other life on earth.

A black-faced chimpanzee (*Pan troglodytes schweinfurthii*) from central and eastern Africa. *Phot. J. and M. Fiévet*

Glossary

abomasum, the fourth compartment of the ruminant stomach.

aboral, the side away from the mouth in echinoderms.

acontia, stinging threads arising from the MESENTERIES of the intestinal cavity of some sea anemones (*Actinia*) which may be discharged through the mouth or special pores when the animal is stimulated.

actinula, a larval stage in colonial hydroids (e.g. *Tubularia*) like the polyp with tentacles, developing within the gonotheca.

adductor muscle, a muscle which draws the two parts together as in bivalve molluscs and in barnacles; a muscle which draws a limb towards the body axis.

adipose tissue, connective tissue composed of large cells containing fat droplets.

aestivation, a state of greatly reduced activity undergone by some animals (amphibians, fishes) in response to drought and heat.

aglyph, harmless snake of the Colubridae having no fangs.

allantois, a sac-like highly vascularized outgrowth of the hind gut of embryos of reptiles, birds and mammals which becomes the chief organ for absorbing oxygen and nutrients. In reptiles and birds it partly surrounds the yolk-sac but in mammals it fuses with the CHORION to form part of the placenta.

alternation of generations, alternate development of two types of individual (sexual and asexual) in the life cycle of an organism.

amino acids, organic compounds containing amino (NH_2) and carboxyl (COOH) groups—the constituents of proteins. Synthesized by autotrophic organisms and derived by digestion of proteins in food of HETEROTROPHIC organisms. About twenty amino acids are known.

amnion, the inner foetal membrane of reptiles, birds and mammals forming a fluid-filled sac or 'private pool' surrounding the developing embryo.

amoebocyte, cells capable of amoeboid behaviour.

amphitoky, production of males and females by parthenogenesis.

anadromous fish, fish which migrate up river to spawn (e.g. salmonids).

anaerobic respiration, respiration in the absence of free oxygen.

antennae, jointed feelers on the head of most arthropods. Called antennules in most crustaceans.

antibody, a substance produced in an organism as a protection against the actions and toxins of parasites or other foreign bodies.

antigen, any substance which stimulates the production of an antibody.

aposematic, having a warning coloration (e.g. yellow of wasps) or a repulsive scent (e.g. skunk).

arborvirus, virus disease transmitted from arthropod to man.

Aristotle's lantern, a complex five-sided masticatory organ of sea urchins.

arrhenotoky, production of males by parthenogenesis.

auricularia, planktonic larva of sea cucumbers (holothurians).

autotomy, self-amputation of a part of the body (usually part of a limb or tail) when an animal is attacked, as in worms, arthropods and lizards.

autotroph, an organism capable of metabolizing inorganic materials.

autozooid, a polyp capable of independent existence.

Batesian mimicry, the protective resemblance of a harmless animal to a poisonous one.

bathypelagic, inhabiting the deep sea.

Bergmann's law, based on the assumption that small animals have a larger surface area-to-volume ratio than large animals and therefore lose heat more rapidly; consequently animals in cold climates tend to be larger.

bilateral symmetry, having two sides identical about an axis.

binary fission, reproduction by cell division into two equal parts (e.g. *Amoeba*).

bipinnaria, the planktonic larva of starfishes (Asteroidea).

blastozooid, zooid arising by budding from the parent organism (e.g. coelenterates and tunicates).

blepharoplast, a small structure of unknown function near the base of the flagellum in some protozoans.

buccal, of the mouth.

byssus, threads secreted by mussels and some other bivalve molluscs as a means of attachment to solid objects.

carapace, chitinous or bony shield covering the whole or part of the back of some animals (e.g. crabs and turtles).

carbohydrates, compounds of carbon, hydrogen, and oxygen constituting sugars and starches.

carotenoids, pigments in some plant and animal tissues including carotenes, xanthophylls and other fat-soluble pigments.

cellulose, a carbohydrate forming the main part of plant cell walls; also found in the testes of tunicates.

cerebral ganglia, the large supra-oesophageal ganglia of invertebrates.

chelicerae, first pair of chelate or sharp-pointed appendages in front of the mouth in arachnids.

chitin, a nitrogenous carbohydrate derivative forming the cuticle of insects and other arthropods.

chloragogens, yellow cells associated with the alimentary canal of earthworms and their allies which absorb nitrogenous waste matter from fluid of the COELOM.

chlorophyll, the green colouring matter of plants and some animals.

chloroplasts, minute granules or plastids containing chlorophyll.

chorion, the outer foetal membrane of reptiles, birds and mammals.

chromatophores, pigment cells in the skin of amphibians, reptiles (especially chameleons) and some invertebrates whose rapid change of shape and size causes the animal to change colour. Such changes are controlled by pituitary hormones and the sympathetic nervous system.

chromosomes, small elongate bodies in the nucleus containing hereditary information. Normally occurring in homologous pairs, the members of a pair derive one from each parent (see MEIOSIS and MITOSIS).

cilia, thread-like outgrowths from a cell generally shorter and more numerous than FLAGELLA. Their continuous rhythmic beating drives fluids past the cell. In some ciliated protozoans the whole organism may move by these means.

cirrus (pl. *cirri*), the thoracic appendages of barnacles; filaments or appendages surrounding the mouths of some marine worms; the jointed aboral filaments of crinoids or the locomotory filaments of some ciliates.

cloaca, the common chamber into which the intestine, genital and excretory canals open.

cnidoblast, stinging cell of the coelenterates containing the NEMATOCYST.

coelom, the body cavity of animals higher than coelenterates.

commensal, an organism living with another whose food it shares, both species usually benefiting from the association.

compound eyes, the eyes of insects and some crustacea which consist of many visual sub-units or ommatidia.

conjugation, the temporary fusion or union of two gametes or unicellular organisms.

contractile vacuole, a small spherical vesicle found in the cytoplasm of many protozoans and having excretory and hydrostatic functions.

convergent evolution, the development of similar characters in widely different organisms brought about by similar function (e.g. caecilians and burrowing snakes, ichthyosaurs and dolphins, South African golden mole and Australian marsupial mole).

cormidium, complex aggregation of various types of polyps in a siphonophore.

corpora allata, paired ovoid whitish endocrine glands behind the cephalic ganglion in insects and their larvae which secrete hormones regulating metamorphosis and ecdysis.

cosmoid scale, found in lungfishes and the coelacanth, having an outer layer of cosmin (similar to dentine), a middle layer of spongy bone and an underlayer of closely-packed layers of bone.

crystalline style, proteid gelantinous rod with an amylolytic enzyme, found in the stomachs of certain bivalve molluscs.

ctenidium, feather or comb-like gill of molluscs.

cuticle, horny (keratinized) non-cellular layer secreted by the epidermis of many invertebrates.

Cuvier's organ, organs of defence in sea cucumbers (holothurians); consist of numerous sticky glandular tubes opening into the cloaca. These are shot out when the animal is attacked.

cysticercus, the larva or bladder-worm stage of a tapeworm.

cytoplasm, the protoplasm of the cell body as distinct from the nucleus.

cytotoxin, cell-poisoning substance in the venom of certain snakes.

cytozooid, trophozoite of sporozoa living in a host's cell.

dactylozooid, a stinging polyp for catching prey and passing it on to other polyps for digestion.

dermis, the innermost layer of the vertebrate skin containing connective tissue, collagen fibres, blood and lymph vessels and sensory nerves. Provides the tensile strength of skin and may contain scales or bony plates.

diapause, a spontaneous suspension of development particularly in insects, arachnids and rotifers, accompanied by greatly decreased metabolism. Hibernation or aestivation when correlated with seasons.

dimorphism, existing in two forms, e.g. male and female individuals.

diploblastic, organism in which the body wall consists of two layers—ectoderm and endoderm with a gelatinous mesogloea between them (e.g. coelenterates).

diploid, having the full number (double set) of chromosomes. Body cells are normally diploid and gametes HAPLOID.

DNA, deoxyribonucleic acid, the stable nucleic acid component of kinetoplasts, chromosomes, and bacteria. Consists structurally of two spirals (the double helix), chains of sugar molecules and phosphate groups transversely linked by pairs of bases (thymine, cytosine, adenine and guanine). It is the inherited material of all living things.

echinopluteus, planktonic larva of a sea urchin (Echinoidea).

echolocation, the location of objects by means of echos. Bats and some other animals emit supersonic sounds whose echos are received by the ear and other sensory receptors. The direction and time lag enables objects to be located with great accuracy.

ectoderm, the outer layer tissue in animal embryos giving rise to skin and nervous tissue; also the outer layer of coelenterates.

ectoparasite, an organism living parasitically on the outside of another organism.

ectoplasm, the outer layer of cytoplasm, usually differing in structure from the endoplasm being more clear and in a semi-solid state. Plays an important part in cell division and amoeboid movement.

elytron (pl. *elytra*), the hardened case-like forewing of certain insects (beetles and bugs) and shield-like plates on the dorsal surface of some polychaetes.

endocrine glands, glands which produce hormones.

endoderm, the inner layer of tissue in embryos giving rise to the lining of the alimentary canal, its glands as well as the respiratory organs.

endogenous cycle, part of the reproductive cycle of a parasite taking place within itself (i.e. spore formation).

endoparasite, an organism living parasitically within another organism.

endophytic, living within the tissues of plants (e.g. gall-forming, leaf-mining and stem-boring insect larvae).

endoplasm, cytoplasm internal to the ectoplasm (plasma membrane). Contains many granules and is a more fluid state.

endoplasmic reticulum (*ergastoplasm*), a complex network of paired membranes forming fluid-like vesicles extending throughout the cytoplasm of most cells and probably forming an internal circulatory system.

enzmes, proteins secreted by cells of an organism which act as biological catalysts speeding up the rate of reactions.

ephippium, the winter-egg case formed from the carapace of certain crustaceans (water fleas); also the pituitary fossa in the base of the vertebrate skull.

ephyra, the small free-swimming stage of jellyfishes produced by STROBILATION.

epidermis, the outer layer of skin cells. Contains the sweat glands and hair follicles in mammals: the outermost layer of cells being dead or horny (keratinized) in land vertebrates; invertebrates have an epidermis one cell-layer thick and may secrete a cuticle.

epithelium, cells forming a thin covering layer protecting the body, lining the alimentary canal and the secretary ducts of glands.

emuelanin, black melanin (pigment).

exoskeleton, an outer rigid body covering secreted by the skin with joints against which locomotory muscles exert their force.

fertilization, union of male and female gametes to form a zygote.

flagellum (pl. *flagella*), a thread-like process found in the cells of many protozoans, sponges and male gametes, which by controlled undulations can propel an organism or drive food particles to its oral region.

foramen of Panizza, small opening connecting the two systematic aortae where they arch across one another (e.g. in crocodiles).

gamete, a haploid sex cell egg or sperm.

gametocyte, the parent cell of a gamete.

gametogenesis, the formation of gametes.

gamont, the stage in the life cycle of a protozoan which gives rise to gametes.

gestation, the period during which a developing embryo is within the uterus of the parent.

gill raker, a series of cartilaginous or bony spines on the inner margin of the gill arches in many fishes which acts as a strainer of food particles.

gills, respiratory organs by which aquatic animals obtain dissolved oxygen from water. Fundamentally, gills are highly vascularized outgrowths of the body wall. Many invertebrates as well as larval amphibians have external gills. Some crustaceans and insect larvae have gills at the base of their legs and sometimes enclosed in a branchial chamber. Most fishes have internal gills within gill slits.

gizzard, a muscular part of the alimentary canal specialized for grinding food. Gizzards are present in birds and many invertebrates, including worms.

glochidium, the larva of a bivalve mollusc (swan mussel) having a hooked bivalve shell and filament for attachment to a fish.

glycogen, a carbohydrate storage product sometimes known as 'animal starch'. It is mobilized as glucose, an essential substance in respiration and energy production.

gnathopods, crustacean limbs in oral region modified for shedding food.

Golgi apparatus, a compact arrangement of cytoplasmic tubules of LIPOPROTEINS in which proteins are processed.

gonadrotrophic hormones, hormone secreted by the anterior lobe of the pituitary body stimulating the development of the gonads.

gonopodium, modified anal fin which acts as an inserting organ in certain male fishes. A gonopod is also a clasper or modified appendage in insects and myriapods.

gonotheca, chitinous cup surrounding the reproductive polyps in thecate hydroids.

guanine, nitrogenous compound found in the excretory products of animals: one of the four bases combined with sugar and phosphate groups in DNA and RNA molecules.

haemoglobin, red iron-containing respiratory pigment occurring in the red blood cells of vertebrates and in the blood of earthworms, the muscles of some nematodes and a few insects.

haploid, having a single set of un-paired chromosomes in each nucleus—as in gametes, some sporozoa and the somatic nuclei of parthenogenetically-produced males.

hectocotylus, one of the arms of a male cephalopod modified for transferring spermatophores.

hepatopancreas, a liver-like organ opening into the alimentary canal and combining the functions of digestion and absorption in molluscs and arthropods.

hermaphrodite, an organism with both male and female reproductive organs.

heterocercal, tail in which vertebral column ends in the upper lobe which is generally longer than the lower lobe.

heterotrophic, applied to all animals (as well as fungi, bacteria and a few plants) which require organic food substances from which to obtain their nourishment.

homocercal, tail having equal or sub-equal lobes and axis ending at middle of base.

hormones, organic substances secreted by endocrine gland cells into the blood. They are necessary for the normal functioning of the body.

hydatid cyst, a watery sac formed by a CYSTICERCUS larva of certain tapeworms (*Echinococcus*) in sheep and man. It may contain up to a gallon of fluid and its walls bear a large number of larval heads, each of which if swallowed by a dog may develop into a tapeworm.

hyperparasite, an organism which lives parasitically on or in another parasite.

hypophysis, the pituitary body (an endocrine gland) beneath the floor of the brain of vertebrates. Secretes a number of hormones which control the activity of the ovaries, thyroid, uterus, mammary glands; and colour change of skin in fishes, amphibians and reptiles.

hypoptile, an aftershaft or accessory plume in close connection with the base of a feather.

ink sac, a pear-shaped organ in the wall of the mantle cavity of squids (e.g. *Sepia*) secreting a black substance, ink or sepia which is ejected as a means of defence.

inquiline, animal living in the home of another and thereby getting a share of food and shelter, e.g. insect and other arthropod 'hangers-on' in ants' and termites' nests.

Jacobson's organ, a blind tube (diverticulum) of the olfactory organ (especially in snakes and skinks) often developing into an epithelium-lined sac opening into the mouth.

keratin, a hard, water-resistant protein forming the basis of scales, feathers, horn and hair in vertebrates.

labium, the lower lip of insects formed by the fusion of the second maxillae.

lateral line system, a system of sense organs occurring in aquatic verte-brates (agnathans, fishes and amphibians), in pores and canals arranged in a line down each side of the body and forming a pattern on the head. Detects vibrations and changes in water pressure.

lipoproteins, proteins combined with fatty compounds.

lophophore, a horse-shoe shaped organ supporting the tentacles in polyzoans and brachiopods.

lutein, the yellow pigment of the *corpus luteum* and of egg-yolk.

lymph, a colourless fluid drained by vessels from intercellular spaces in vertebrates.

macronucleus, the larger of the nuclei occurring in some protozoans, especially ciliates. It appears to regulate normal meta-bolic functions and disintegrates just before cell division.

madreporite, a perforated plate on the aboral surface through which sea water enters the water vascular system of an echinoderm.

Malpighian tubules, tubular ex-cretory glands opening into the anterior part of the hind gut in insects, arachnids and myriapods.

mandible, the lower jaw of verte-brates; one of a pair of laterally-moving horny jaws anterior to the maxillae in arthropods; any strong horny jaws in other invertebrates.

mantle, the fold of skin in molluscs covering the whole or part of the body. The outer surface secretes the shell.

manubrium, the elongated tubular mouth of jellyfishes: the anterior segment of the sternum of mammals.

manyplies, the third part (or omasum) of the stomach of a ruminant.

marginal vesicles, name applied to the marginal statocysts of a medusa or jellyfish.

marrow, yellow or red pulp-like tissue in the cylindrical cavities of large bones. Is the centre of produc-tion of red blood corpuscles and some white ones.

marsupium, the pouch by which marsupials are characterized and in which the young develop and are transported.

masseter muscle, principal muscle which raises the lower jaw and assists in chewing.

mastax, the muscular toothed pharynx of the rotifer.

matrix, the intercellular substance in which cells are embedded, as in cartilage and bone where solid or as in connective tissue where fibrous. It is liquid in blood.

maxilla, one of a pair of large bones of the upper jaw of verte-brates bearing molar and premolar teeth: one of a pair of laterally-moving mouthparts behind the mandibles in most arthropods. (In crustaceans there may be a first, maxillules, and a second pair of maxillae. In insects the second pair are fused to form the labium or lower lip.)

maxillipede, one of three pairs of appendages posterior to maxillae in arthropods and acting as accessory mouthparts.

medusa, the free-swimming sexual generation in coelenterates—usually a disc or ball-shaped jelly-fish with marginal tentacles and a centrally-placed mouth under-neath.

megalopa, the final larval stage of a crab resembling the adult but with abdomen extended backwards.

meiosis, the process of cell division in which the number of chromo-somes is halved, as in the produc-tion of gametes.

merozoite, minute cells formed by multiple asexual fission in some protozoans.

mesentary, the peritoneum or double membrane of vertebrates in which the viscera are slung from the dorsal body wall: also the vertical partitions in the body cavity of a sea anemone.

mesogloea, layer of jelly-like material between the ectoderm

(outer layer) and the endoderm (inner layer) in coelenterates. May be thin and contain the inner prolongations of cells from both layers or it may be bulky containing cells as in the jellyfishes.

metabolism, the sum total of all chemical reaction carried out in a living organism.

metamorphosis, rapid transforma-tion from larval to adult form. Often involves the breaking down of tissues as from chrysalis to butter-fly or amphibian tadpole to adult.

metazoea, a larval stage in some Crustacea between zoaea and megalopa.

micron, one thousandth of a milli-metre or a micromillimetre.

micronucleus, the smaller of two nuclei covering in some form protozoans especially ciliates. It appears to be concerned with cell division.

micro-organism, microscopically small organism, e.g. unicellular plant, animal or bacterium.

mimetism or *mimicry*, protective resemblance of one species to another. See BATESIAN MIMICRY; MULLERIAN MIMICRY.

miracidium, first larval stage in the life cycle of parasitic flatworms (trematodes).

mitochondria, minute rod-shaped organelles consisting of protein and lipoid material. Occur in the cytoplasm of most cells and are concerned in the production of respiratory enzymes.

mitosis, the normal process of cell division in which the diploid chromosome number is main-tained.

monoxenus, parasite inhabiting only one host.

mucous membrane, an epithelium which secretes mucus, e.g. lining of alimentary canal and urino-genital ducts.

Müllerian mimicry, a form of mimicry in insects in which two harmful or distasteful species resemble each other and so derive benefit from would-be predators.

mutation, genetic change resulting from modification of DNA.

myonemes, contractile fibrils in the cytoplasm of some protozoans.

myrmecomophy, imitation of ants by other insects and arachnids for protection from predators.

myrmecophiles, miscellaneous in-vertebrates (chiefly arthropods) which inhabit ants' nests either as guests fed and tended by their hosts or as scavengers.

nasal salt glands, organs secreting concentrated salt solution. Found in many sea birds.

nauplius, the early larval stage of many crustaceans. Oval, un-segmented, with three pairs of appendages.

nematocyst, the active poison sac containing the stinging thread of the cnidoblast cell of coelenterates.

neoptile, the downy plumage of chicks.

neoteny, temporary or permanent retention of larval structures. See PAEDOGENESIS.

nephridia, the excretory organs of many invertebrates.

neuromotor centre, a coordinating centre for locomotive organelles (cilia and flagella) in some protozoans.

neurones, nerve cells or the fine prolongations of the nerve cell-body.

neurosecretory cells, nerve cells secreting chemical substances at their endings.

notochord, a semi-rigid internal supporting rod of large vacuolated cells lying along and beneath the central nervous system and the alimentary canal. Characteristic of the chordates.

nucleus, a large body within a

cell containing the chromosomes and essential for the life of most cells (except red blood corpuscles).

ocellus, a simple light receptor occurring in many invertebrates.

oesophagus, part of the alimentary canal between the pharynx and the stomach.

omasum, see MANYPLIES.

ommatidium, (pl. *ommatidia*) in-dependent photoreceptor unit in the compound eyes of insects and some crustaceans.

oocyst, cyst formed round two conjugating gametes in sporozoans.

operculum, cover of gill-slits of fishes and amphibians; an exo-skeletal plate in some gastropod molluscs and tube-dwelling poly-chaetes used to close the mouth of the shell or tube.

ophiopluteus, the free-swimming planktonic larva of some brittle stars (echinoderms).

opisthoglyph, rear-fanged, rela-tively harmless poisonous snakes.

organelle, a persistent structure with specialized function forming part of a cell (e.g. mitochondria, flagellum, Golgi apparatus) and is analogous to an organ in an organism.

osmeterium, a forked protrusible organ borne on the first thoracic segment of some butterfly larvae, emitting a strong disagreeable odour.

otolith, the 'earstone' of bony fishes: also the chalky articles suspended in the statocysts of certain inverte-brates.

ovariole, egg tube in an insect's ovary.

oviparous, reproducing by laying eggs.

ovoviviparous, producing eggs which hatch within the mother's body before they are laid.

paedogenesis, becoming sexually mature while retaining larval characters (e.g. the axolotl and some dipterous insect larvae).

paramylon, starch-like substance found as platelets or granules of reserve food in certain flagellates and algae.

parapodium, paired lateral projec-tion of the body wall of polychaete worms bearing chaetae (bristles) and arranged segmentally as organs of locomotion. In some molluscs, lateral extensions of the foot.

parasitism, symbiotic relationship beneficial to one species (parasite) and harmful to the other (host).

parenchyma, large-celled connec-tive tissue packing spaces between the organs in acoelomate animals such as flatworms (Turbellaria).

parotid glands, salivary glands of amphibians, reptiles and mam-mals. In some toads and snakes, may secrete toxins.

parthenogenesis, the development of an unfertilized ovum into a new individual.

pedicellariae, minute pincer-like organs embedded in the skin of starfishes and sea urchins. Function appears to be to protect the animal from ectoparasites.

pelagic, inhabiting open water (salt or fresh) in contrast to the bottom fauna.

periostracum, the outermost horny layer of the shell of a mollusc or brachiopod.

perisarc, the horny tubular cover-ing of some colonial coelenterates.

phaeomelanin, brown melanin (pig-ment).

phagocyte, white blood corpuscle able to engulf bacteria and other foreign bodies in an amoeboid manner.

phagocytosis, the engulfing and digestion of cells by phagocytes.

pharynx, that part of the alimentary canal between mouth and oesophagus.

phonotaxy, response to specific sound stimuli.

photogenic organs, light-producing organs of glow worms, fireflies (beetles) and other insects.

photophore, a luminous organ of certain abyssal squids, crustaceans and fishes.

photosynthesis, synthesis by green plants of organic compounds from water and carbon dioxide, using energy absorbed by chlorophyll from sunlight.

phytoplankton, plant plankton.

pilidium, the ciliated free swim-ming larva of some ribbon worms (nemerteans).

pituitary gland, see HYPOPHYSIS.

placoid scales, skin denticles of cartilaginous fishes.

plankton, animal and plant life, mostly microscopic, which floats or drifts near the surface of fresh or salt water expanses.

planula, the flat ciliated free-swimming larva of a coelenterate. Consists of ectoderm and solid core of endoderm.

plastron, ventral bony plate of chelonians (turtles and tortoises); sternum of arachnids; layer of gas bubbles retained by hairs on the abdomen of aquatic insects.

pluteus, free-swimming planktonic echinoderm larva with long ciliated 'arms'.

pneumatophore, the float of siphono-phores, e.g. Portuguese man-of-war.

Polian vesicles, small, stalked sacs attached to the water-vascular ring in many echinoderms.

polyembryony, the production of two or more individuals from a single egg by division of the embryo at an early stage. Widespread in the animal kingdom, reaches spec-tacular proportions in the parasitic hymenoptera where thousands of embryos may develop from a single egg.

polymorphism, occurrence of different forms of individuals of the same species (e.g. various types of polyps in a coelenterate colony; the castes of termites, ants).

polyp, individual or member of a colonial group of animals, especi-ally coelenterates and polyzoans; often characterized by having tentacles and mouth at its anterior end. In some colonies there is division of labour, with polyps specialized for feeding, reproduc-tion and defence.

polyploidy, possession of more than two sets of chromosomes.

progenesis, maturation of the gametes before bodily growth is completed.

progesterone, female sex hormone produced by the *corpus luteum*. Responsible for the implantation of the embryo and the formation of the placenta and inhibiting ovulation during pregnancy.

proglottid, a segment of a tapeworm formed by strobilation from the head or scolex.

proteins, complex nitrogenous com-pounds whose molecules consist of numerous amino-acid molecules linked together. The basic con-stituents of living matter and a necessary constituent in the diet of animals.

proteroglyph, front-fanged ex-tremely poisonous snakes, having the anterior fangs grooved or with poison ducts.

prothetely, development of pupal or imaginal characters in insect larva.

protoplasm, the living material of a cell.

pupiparous, laying young in pu-pal state as in some parasitic in-sects.

quill, the calamus or barrel of a feather: the hollow spine of a porcupine.

rachis, the shaft of a feather.

radial symmetry, arrangement of similar parts round a median vertical axis, as in jellyfishes and echinoderms.

radula, short broad membranous strip with longitudinal rows of chitinous teeth on the floor of the mouth of gastropods and cephalopod molluscs.

rectrices, the stiff tail feathers of a bird used in steering.

remiges, the stiff major flight feathers (or primaries) in a bird's wing.

respiration, gaseous interchange between an organism and its environment. In cells, the oxidation of organic substances to form carbon dioxide, water and the release of energy.

respiratory tree, organs of sea cucumbers, consisting of complex branched tubes leading from the cloaca to various parts of the body; enable dissolved oxygen to pass into the body fluid.

reticulo-endothelial system, phagocytic cells in blood, bone, spleen, liver and lymph freeing those tissues from foreign particles as well as producing antibodies.

reticulum, second chamber in the stomach of a ruminant.

retina, internal layer of sensitive cells and nerve fibres lining the eye.

ribosomes, minute granules composed mainly of ribonucleic acid on nuclear membrane and the endoplasmic reticulum. Protein synthesis takes place on them.

rumen, first stomach or paunch of a ruminant in which food is partly digested, before being regurgitated into the mouth for 'cud-chewing'.

salivary glands, glands secreting saliva into the mouth. In many vertebrates this fluid contains ptyaline—an enzyme which hydrolyses starch. In poisonous snakes the glands are modified as poison sacs, and in blood-sucking insects and leeches the saliva has anticoagulant properties.

saprophyte, growing on decayed organic matter. Also, a plant which lives on decaying organic matter.

scapular, a shoulder feather.

schizont, cell of a sporozoan which by multiple fission (schizogony) gives rise to numerous small cells or schizozoites.

scissiparity, reproduction by fission.

sclerotin, a tough water-resistant nitrogenous substance found with chitin in the cuticle of insects and other arthropods.

scolex, head-like part of a tapeworm, provided with suckers or hooks or both as means of attachment to the host's intestine.

sebaceous gland, skin gland of mammals secreting a fatty substance (sebum) usually located in a hair follicle.

secondary sexual characters, characters shown by male or female individual resulting from the effects of the sex hormones (e.g. antlers of stags; facial hair and deep voice in man; differences in size, shape and colour in many animals).

septum, a partition separating two cavities or tissue masses, e.g. in the pearly nautilus, segmented worms, jellyfishes and corals, and the mammalian heart and nose.

siphon, paired extensions of the mantle of molluscs forming a single or double tube for the intake and expulsion of water. In cephalopods the tube is ventral and jet-like expulsion of water propels the animal backwards. In tunicates the oral and atrial openings by which water enters and leaves the basket walls of the pharynx.

siphonozooid, small polyp without tentacles whose function is to drive water through colonies in certain Alcyonaria.

siphuncle, a median calcareous tube connecting the chambers of septate cephalopod shells with the body and through which gases are secreted.

smooth muscle, plain unstriated involuntary muscle found in walls of alimentary canal, blood vessels and other organs.

solenia, endodermal canals linking polyps in coelenterate colony and giving rise to new polyps.

spermatophore, a mucilaginous sperm mass produced by some animals (e.g. newts, molluscs, arthropods and other invertebrates) and transferred to the receptive parts of the female.

sphincter, a ring of smooth muscle surrounding the opening of a tubular organ which by contraction closes the lumen, e.g. cardiac and pyloric sphincters of stomach, and anal sphincter.

spinnerets, small tubular appendages from which silk threads are exuded by spiders and some insects. In spiders these are at the apex of the abdomen. In caterpillars silk is produced by modified salivary glands and there is a median spinneret at the base of the labium.

sporocyst, the protective envelope containing numerous spores resulting from multiple fission of parent cell (Sporozoa): the encysted embryo stage of a trematode after entry into an intermediate host.

sporozoite, small mobile individuals produced by fission of a zygote (sporont) in the sporozoa.

statocyst, a fluid-filled sensory vesicle which functions in perception of position of body.

sternum, the breastbone of vertebrates to which the ribs are attached: also the cuticle on the ventral side of each segment in crustaceans and insects.

stigma, an eye-spot in some protozoans; an external opening (spiracle) in arthropods; an opening in the branchial basket of tunicates.

stolon, horizontal tubular branch from which new individuals arise at intervals by budding (e.g. polyzoans and colonial coelenterates). Also, bud-forming ventral outgrowth of tunicates.

stone canal, an 'S'-shaped duct leading from the madreporite to the perioral ring of the water vascular system in echinoderms.

striated muscle, voluntary or skeletal muscles with transverse striations, e.g. long muscles of vertebrate's body.

stridulation, chirping or scraping sound produced by insects by rubbing one hard part of the body against the other.

strobilation, reproduction by body-segmentation into zooids (ephyrae) or proglottids (tapeworms).

subimago, the dull-winged stage before the imago in the development of mayflies (Ephemeroptera).

sweat gland, skin gland of mammals secreting dilute salty solution which cools the skin on evaporation.

swim bladder, gas-filled sac of bony fishes, lying dorsally to the alimentary canal to which it may be connected. Regulates buoyancy and in some fishes (including lungfishes) has developed a respiratory function.

swimmerets, small biramous appendages on the abdomen of Crustacea—also called pleopods.

symbiosis, close partnership of two organisms for mutual benefit.

syncytium, cytoplasmic mass enclosed in a membrane and containing many nuclei not separated by cell membranes (e.g. Myxosporidia).

syrinx, vocal organ of birds at the base of the trachea.

tadpoles, larvae of frogs and toads; also the larva of certain tunicates.

tarsus, the heel bones of tetrapod vertebrates; also the jointed extension of an insect's leg distal to the tibia.

tectrices, small feathers covering the tail feathers.

teleoptile, true plumage feathers giving character to species.

theca, protective sheath of an organism, e.g. in hydroids and corals.

theletoky, parthenogenesis in which females only are produced.

thyroid, a highly vascular endocrine gland on the front and sides of the larynx. Secretes thyroxin, a hormone concerned in control of basal metabolism.

Tiedemann's bodies, small glands of unknown function on the water vascular ring in starfishes.

timbal, sound-producing organ of cicadas.

trachea, windpipe of vertebrates or respiratory tubule of insects and some arthropods.

trichocyst, sensitive structures, of uncertain function, in the ectoplasm of some ciliated protozoa. Consists of minute cavities from which a long thread can be ejected as a response to stimulation.

triploblastic, with three primary embryonic cell layers (ectoderm, mesoderm and endoderm). Applies to all animals except protozoans, sponges and coelenterates.

triungulin, minute six-legged parasitic larva of some insects, e.g. Strepsiptera and Cantharidae (oil beetles).

trochophore larva, free-swimming planktonic larva of many marine annelids and molluscs.

trophozoite, adult stage of a sporozoan.

tympanum, the ear drum. A cavity in the middle ear in land vertebrates or in the tympanic membrane.

uropygial gland, 'preen gland' on a bird's rump secreting oil used by bird to make its feathers waterproof.

veliger larva, second stage larva of some molluscs, bearing a tiny shell and a ciliated membrane which acts as locomotor and food-collecting organ.

vexillum, the vane or web of a feather consisting of barbs and barbules hooked together.

vibrissae, stiff sensitive hairs or whiskers on the face of animals.

vitellarium, yolk-gland of flatworms, leeches and rotifers: the nutritive part of an ovariole.

viviparous, bringing forth young alive.

water vascular system, unique development of the coelom in echinoderms. Consists of a ring vessel around mouth, communicating externally by the stone canal and madreporite, and giving off radial canals containing fluid. This is supplied through lateral branches to the tube feet which when used for locomotion are distended by contraction of swellings (ampullae) at their base.

Weberian ossicles, chain of small bones or ossicles connecting the swim bladder with the ear. Forms a sensitive hearing organ or hydrophone in certain freshwater fishes (the ostariophysans).

zoaea, planktonic early larva of crabs and other crustaceans, in which abdomen is well developed but thorax has only a few pairs of appendages.

zooid, individual polyp in colonial coelenterates and polyzoans. See also gastrozooids, dactylozooids, gonozooids.

zooxanthellae, yellow or brown cells of symbiotic unicellular algae living in various animals.

zygote, a fertilized ovum: cell formed by the union of male and female gametes.

Index